Fodor's

NEW ENGLAND

29th Edition

Fodor's Travel Publications   New York, Toronto, London, Sydney, Auckland

www.fodors.com

Be a Fodor's Correspondent

Your opinion matters. It matters to us. It matters to your fellow Fodor's travelers, too. And we'd like to hear it. In fact, we need to hear it.

When you share your experiences and opinions, you become an active member of the Fodor's community. That means we'll not only use your feedback to make our books better, but we'll publish your names and comments whenever possible. Throughout our guides, look for "Word of Mouth," excerpts of your unvarnished feedback.

Here's how you can help improve Fodor's for all of us.

Tell us when we're right. We rely on local writers to give you an insider's perspective. But our writers and staff editors—who are the best in the business—depend on you. Your positive feedback is a vote to renew our recommendations for the next edition.

Tell us when we're wrong. We're proud that we update most of our guides every year. But we're not perfect. Things change. Hotels cut services. Museums change hours. Charming cafés lose charm. If our writer didn't quite capture the essence of a place, tell us how you'd do it differently. If any of our descriptions are inaccurate or inadequate, we'll incorporate your changes in the next edition and will correct factual errors at fodors.com immediately.

Tell us what to include. You probably have had fantastic travel experiences that aren't yet in Fodor's. Why not share them with a community of like-minded travelers? Maybe you chanced upon a beach or bistro or B&B that you don't want to keep to yourself. Tell us why we should include it. And share your discoveries and experiences with everyone directly at fodors.com. Your input may lead us to add a new listing or highlight a place we cover with a "Highly Recommended" star or with our highest rating, "Fodor's Choice."

Give us your opinion instantly at our feedback center at www.fodors.com/feedback. You may also e-mail editors@fodors.com with the subject line "New England Editor." Or send your nominations, comments, and complaints by mail to New England Editor, Fodor's, 1745 Broadway, New York, NY 10019.

You and travelers like you are the heart of the Fodor's community. Make our community richer by sharing your experiences. Be a Fodor's correspondent.

Happy traveling!

Tim Jarrell, Publisher

FODOR'S NEW ENGLAND

Editors: Debbie Harmsen and Cate Starmer

Editorial Contributors: Joanna Cantor, Carolyn Galgano, Josh McIlvain
Writers: Neva Allen, Stephen Allen, John Blodgett, Andrew Collins, Bethany Cassin Beckerlegge, Sascha de Gersdorff, Amanda Knorr, Susan MacCallum-Whitcomb, Michael Nalepa, Brigid Sweeney, Linh Tran, Mary Ruoff, Laura V. Scheel, George Semler, Sarah Stebbins, and Michael de Zayas

Production Editor: Jennifer DePrima
Maps & Illustrations: Mark Stroud and David Lindroth, *cartographers;* Bob Blake, Rebecca Baer, *map editors;* William Wu, *information graphics*
Design: Fabrizio La Rocca, *creative director;* Guido Caroti, Siobhan O'Hare, *art directors;* Tina Malaney, Chie Ushio, Ann McBride, Jessica Walsh, *designers;* Melanie Marin, *senior picture editor*
Cover Photo: (Androscoggin River, New Hampshire): Stephen Gorman/Aurora Photos
Production Manager: Amanda Bullock

SPECIAL SALES

This book is available at special discounts for bulk purchases for sales promotions or premiums. Special editions, including personalized covers, excerpts of existing books, and corporate imprints, can be created in large quantities for special needs. For more information, write to Special Markets/Premium Sales, 1745 Broadway, MD 6-2, New York, New York 10019, or e-mail specialmarkets@randomhouse.com.

AN IMPORTANT TIP & AN INVITATION

Although all prices, opening times, and other details in this book are based on information supplied to us at press time, changes occur all the time in the travel world, and Fodor's cannot accept responsibility for facts that become outdated or for inadvertent errors or omissions. So **always confirm information when it matters,** especially if you're making a detour to visit a specific place. Your experiences—positive and negative— matter to us. If we have missed or misstated something, **please write to us.** We follow up on all suggestions. Contact the New England editor at editors@fodors.com or c/o Fodor's at 1745 Broadway, New York, NY 10019.

PRINTED IN CHINA

10 9 8 7 6 5 4 3 2

CONTENTS

Fodor's Features

MAPS

ABOUT
THIS BOOK

Our Ratings

Sometimes you find terrific travel experiences and sometimes they just find you. But usually the burden is on you to select the right combination of experiences. That's where our ratings come in.

As travelers we've all discovered places whose worthiness is obvious. And sometimes a place is so wonderful that superlatives don't do it justice: you just have to see for yourself. These sights, properties, and experiences get our highest rating, **Fodor's Choice**, indicated by orange stars throughout this book.

Black stars highlight sights and properties we deem **Highly Recommended,** places that our writers, editors, and readers praise again and again for consistency and excellence.

By default, there's another category: any place we include in this book is by definition worth your time, unless we say otherwise. And we will.

Disagree with any of our choices? Care to nominate a place or suggest that we rate one more highly? Visit our feedback center at www.fodors.com/feedback.

Budget Well

Hotel and restaurant price categories from ¢ to $$$$ are defined in the opening pages of each chapter. For attractions, we always give standard adult admission fees; reductions are usually available for children, students, and senior citizens. Want to pay with plastic? **AE, D, DC, MC, V** following restaurant and hotel listings indicate if American Express, Discover, Diners Club, MasterCard, and Visa are accepted.

Restaurants

Unless we state otherwise, restaurants are open for lunch and dinner daily. We mention dress only when there's a specific requirement and reservations only when they're essential or not accepted—it's always best to book ahead.

Hotels

Hotels have private bath, phone, TV, and air-conditioning and operate on the European Plan (a.k.a. EP, meaning without meals), unless we specify that they use the Continental Plan (CP, with a continental breakfast), Breakfast Plan (BP, with a full breakfast), or Modified American Plan (MAP, with breakfast and dinner), Full American Plan (FAP, with all means), or are all-inclusive (AI, with all meals and most activities). We always list facilities but not whether you'll be charged an extra fee to use them, so when pricing accommodations, find out what's included.

Listings
★ Fodor's Choice
★ Highly recommended
✉ Physical address
✦ Directions or Map coordinates
✉ Mailing address
☎ Telephone
🖷 Fax
⊕ On the Web
✉ E-mail
💷 Admission fee
☉ Open/closed times
Ⓜ Metro stations
▭ Credit cards

Hotels & Restaurants
🏨 Hotel
🛏 Number of rooms
♨ Facilities
🍴 Meal plans
✗ Restaurant
♨ Reservations
👗 Dress code
🚭 Smoking
🍷 BYOB

Outdoors
🏌 Golf
🏕 Camping

Other
♣ Family-friendly
⇨ See also
✉ Branch address
☞ Take note

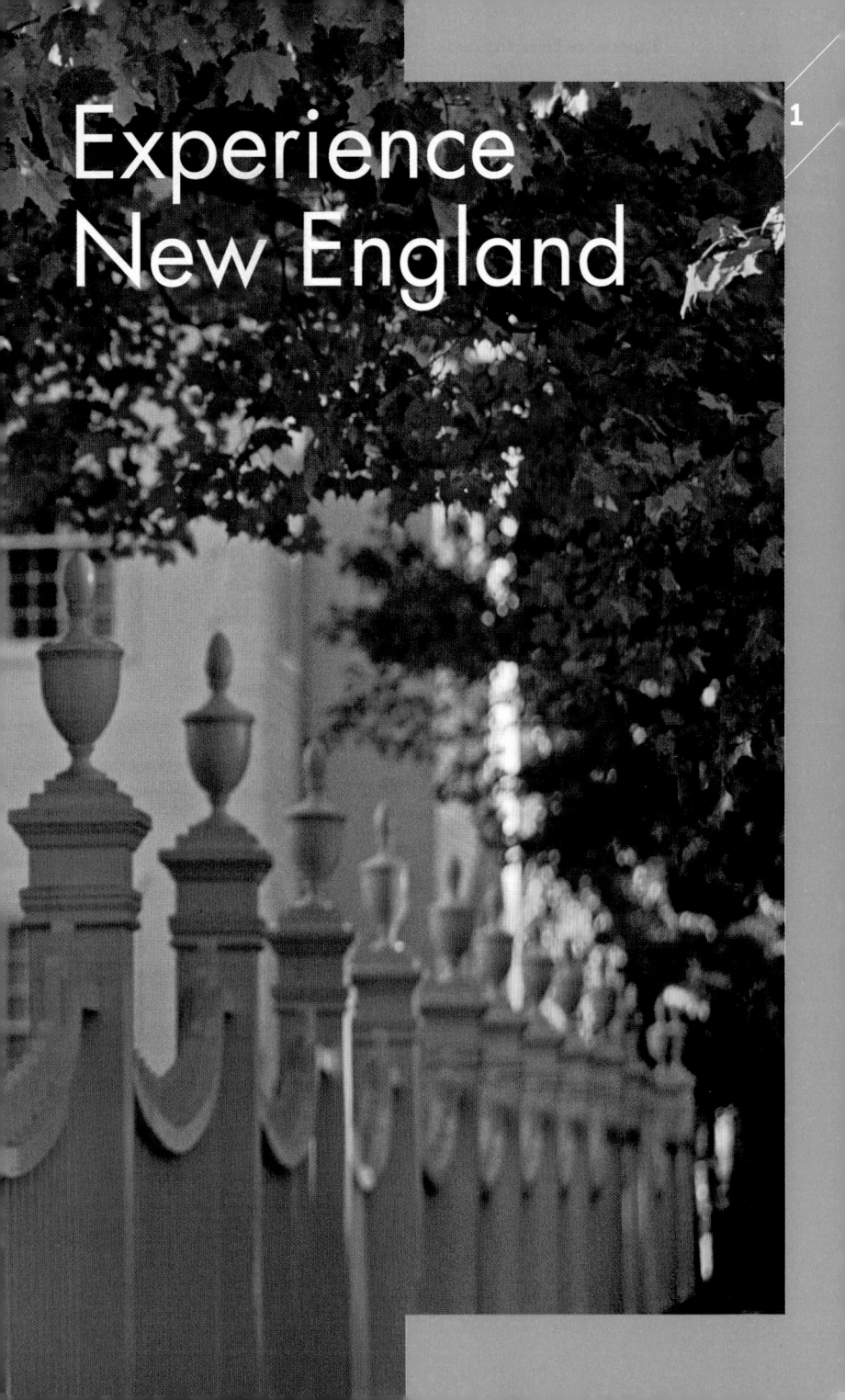

Experience
New England

WHAT'S WHERE

The following numbers refer to chapters.

2 Boston. Massachusetts's capital city is also New England's hub. Boston's many universities make it a cosmopolitan town, but there are also blue-collar roots in the distinct neighborhoods. This is the cradle of American democracy, a place where soaring skyscrapers cast shadows on Colonial graveyards.

3 Cape Cod, Nantucket, and Martha's Vineyard. Great beaches, delicious seafood, and artisan-filled shopping districts fill scenic Cape Cod, chic Martha's Vineyard, and cozy Nantucket.

4 The Berkshires and Western Massachusetts. The mountainous Berkshires lives up to the storybook image of rural New England; it also has a thriving arts community. Farther east, the Pioneer Valley is home to a string of historic settlements.

5 Connecticut. The densely populated southwest region contrasts with the sparsely populated Quiet Corner, known for antiquing. Small shoreline villages and casinos line the southeastern coast. The Connecticut River Valley and Litchfield Hills have grand old inns, rolling farmlands, and plenty of state parks.

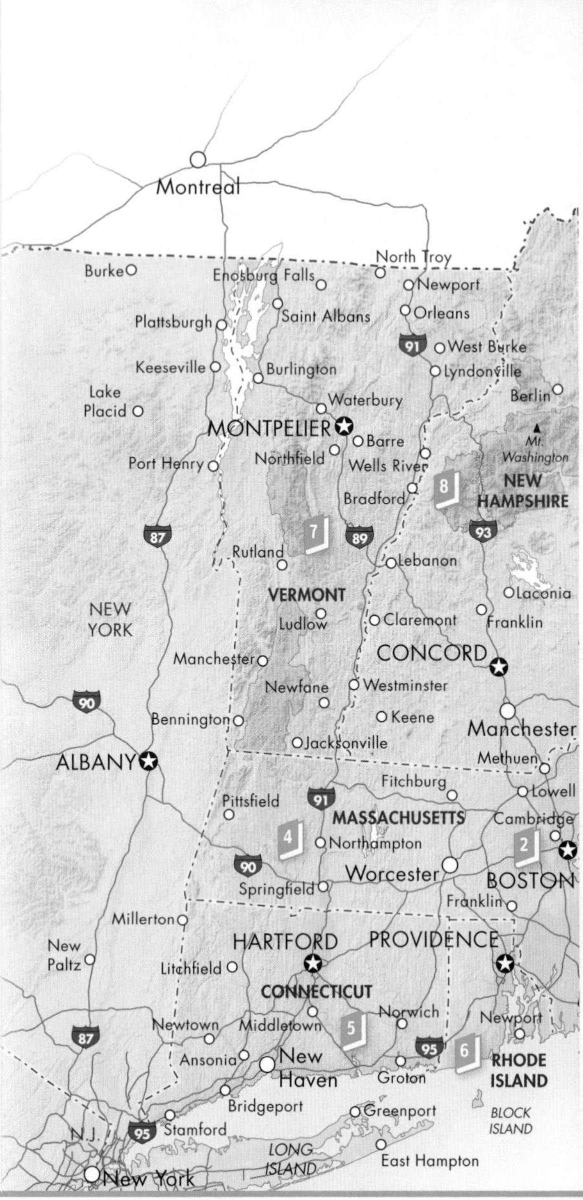

Montreal

Burke

Enosburg Falls

North Troy

Newport

Plattsburgh

Saint Albans

Orleans

Keeseville

Burlington

91

West Burke

Lyndonville

Lake Placid

Waterbury

Berlin

MONTPELIER

Barre

Port Henry

Northfield

Wells River

Mt. Washington

Bradford

8

NEW HAMPSHIRE

87

7

89

93

Rutland

Lebanon

NEW YORK

VERMONT

Ludlow

Claremont

Laconia

Franklin

Manchester

CONCORD

90

Newfane

Westminster

Bennington

Keene

Jacksonville

Manchester

ALBANY

Methuen

Pittsfield

Fitchburg

Lowell

91

MASSACHUSETTS

Cambridge

4

Northampton

2

90

Springfield

Worcester

BOSTON

Franklin

Millerton

New Paltz

HARTFORD

PROVIDENCE

Litchfield

CONNECTICUT

Norwich

Newport

Newtown

Middletown

5

95

6

Ansonia

New Haven

Groton

RHODE ISLAND

Bridgeport

Greenport

BLOCK ISLAND

N.J.

95

Stamford

LONG ISLAND

East Hampton

New York

6 Rhode Island. The smallest state is home to great sailing and glitzy mansions in Newport. In South County are sparsely populated beaches and rolling farmland; scenic Block Island is just a short ferry ride away.

7 Vermont. Vermont has farms, freshly starched New England towns, quiet back roads, and bustling ski resorts. With Montréal only an hour from the border, the Canadian influence is strong here.

8 New Hampshire. Portsmouth is the star of the independent state's 18-mi coastline. The Lakes Region are a popular summertime escape; the White Mountains dramatic vistas attract photographers and adventurous hikers farther north.

9 Inland Maine. The largest New England state's rugged interior, including the Western Lakes and vast North Woods regions, attract skiers, hikers, campers, anglers, and other outdoors enthusiasts.

10 The Maine Coast. Classic townscapes, rocky shorelines punctuated by sandy beaches, and picturesque downtowns draw vacationing New Englanders to Maine like a magnet. Acadia National Park is where majestic mountains meet the coast; Bar Harbor is the park's gateway town.

Houlton

Baxter
State Park

Mt.
Katahdin

95

9

MAINE

Old Town

Skowhegan
Bangor

Waterville

Ellsworth

Belfast

Bar Harbor

AUGUSTA

Gardiner
Mt. DESERT
ISLAND

Auburn
Rockland
Acadia
National Park

Lewiston

95
Bath
10

Portland
Gulf of Maine

South Portland
Casco
Bay

Rochester
Biddeford

Somersworth
Dover

Portsmouth

Atlantic Ocean

Newburyport

CAPE ANN

Gloucester

Massachusetts Bay

CAPE COD

Plymouth
Provincetown

Cape Cod
National Seashore

Cape Cod Bay

New
Bedford
3
Hyannis

Oak Bluffs
NANTUCKET

MARTHA'S
VINEYARD
Nantucket

0   50 mi

0   50 km

EXPERIENCE NEW ENGLAND PLANNER

Average Temperatures

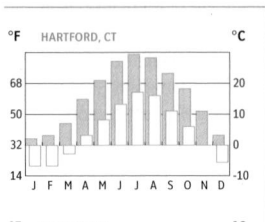

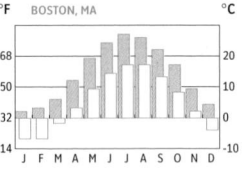

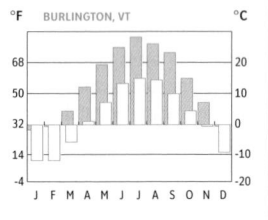

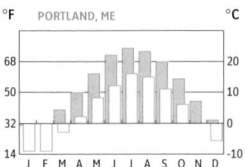

When to Go

All six New England states are year-round destinations, with winter popular with skiers, summer a draw for families and beach lovers, and fall a delight to those who love the bursts of autumnal color. Spring can also be a great time, with sugar shacks transforming maple sap into all sorts of tasty things. ■TIP→ You'll probably want to avoid rural areas during mud season (April) and black-fly season (mid-May to mid-June).

Memorial Day signals migration to the beaches and the mountains, and summer begins in earnest on July 4. Those who want to drive to Cape Cod in July or August beware: on Friday and Sunday weekenders clog the overburdened U.S. 6. The same applies to the Maine Coast and its feeder roads, Interstate 95 and U.S. 1.

In the fall, a rainbow of reds, oranges, yellows, purples, and other vibrant hues emerges. The first scarlet and gold colors appear in mid-September in northern areas; "peak" color occurs at different times from year to year. Generally, it's best to visit the northern reaches in late September and early October and move south as October progresses.

CLIMATE

In winter, coastal New England is cold and damp; inland temperatures may be lower, but generally drier conditions make them easier to bear. Snowfall is heaviest in the interior mountains and can range up to several hundred inches per year in northern Maine, New Hampshire, and Vermont. Spring is often windy and rainy; in many years winter appears to segue almost immediately into summer. Coastal areas can be quite humid in summer, while inland, particularly at higher elevations, there's a prevalence of cool summer nights. Autumn temperatures can be mild even into October. The charts to the left show the average daily maximum and minimum temperatures.

Getting Here and Around

⇨ *For more information, see Travel Smart New England.*

Air Travel: The main gateway to New England is Boston's Logan International Airport (BOS). Other New England airports include Bradley International Airport (BDL, 12 mi north of Hartford), T. F. Green Airport (PVD, just outside Providence), Manchester Boston Regional Airport (MHT, in New Hampshire about an hour from Boston), Portland International Jetport (PWM, in Maine), and Burlington International Airport (BTV, in Vermont).

Car Travel: New England is best explored by car. Areas in the interior are largely without heavy traffic and congestion, and parking is consistently easy to find. Coastal New England is considerably more congested, and parking can be hard to find or expensive in Boston, Providence, and many smaller resort towns along the coast. Still, a car is typically the best way to get around even on the coast (though once you arrive you may want to explore on foot, on a bike, or by local transit and cabs). In New England's interior, public transportation options are more limited and a car is almost necessary.

Train Travel: Amtrak offers frequent daily service to several New England destinations, including Boston; Portland, Maine; coastal New Hampshire; several points in Vermont; and Pittsfield, Springfield, Worcester, and Framingham, Massachusetts. The Massachusetts Bay Transportation Authority (MBTA) connects Boston with outlying areas.

Travel Times from Boston to:	By Air	By Car	By Bus	By Train
Acadia National Park (ME)	1 hour	5 hours	not applicable	not applicable
Burlington, VT	no direct flight	3½ hours	4½–5 hours	8¾ hours
Hartford, CT	no direct flight	1¾ hours	2–2¾ hours	4½–5¼ hours
New York, NY	¾–1 hour	4 hours	4½–7 hours	3½–4¼ hours
Portland, ME	no direct flight	2 hours	2¼ hours	2½ hours
Providence, RI	no direct flight	1 hour	1 hour	½–¾ hour
Provincetown, MA	½ hour	2¼ hours	3–3½ hours	not applicable

Visitor Information

Each New England state provides a helpful free information kit, including a guidebook, map, and listings of attractions and events. All include listings and advertisements for lodging and dining establishments. Each state also has an official Web site with material on sights and lodgings; most of these sites have a calendar of events and other special features.

Contacts Greater Boston Convention & Visitors Bureau (📞 888/733–2678 ⊕ www.bostonusa.com).

Connecticut Commission on Culture & Tourism (📞 888/288–4748 ⊕ www.ctbound.org).

Maine Office of Tourism (📞 888/624–6345 ⊕ www.visitmaine.com).

Massachusetts Office of Travel and Tourism (📞 800/227–6277 or 617/973–8500 ⊕ www.massvacation.com).

State of New Hampshire Division of Travel and Tourism Development (📞 800/386–4664 or 603/271–2665 ⊕ www.visitnh.gov).

Rhode Island Tourism Division (📞 800/556–2484 ⊕ www.visitrhodeisland.com).

Vermont Department of Tourism and Marketing (📞 802/828–3237, 800/837–6668 brochures ⊕ www.vermontvacation.com).

NEW ENGLAND TODAY

The People

The idea of the self-reliant, thrifty, and often stoic New England Yankee has taken on almost mythic proportions in American folklore, but in some parts of New England—especially in rural Maine, New Hampshire, and Vermont—there still is some truth to this image, which shouldn't come as a surprise. You need to be independent if you farm an isolated field, live in the middle of a vast forest, or work a fishing boat miles off the coast. Like any part of the country, there are stark differences between urban New Englanders and those you encounter outside the cities. Both, though, are usually fiercely proud of the region, its rugged beauty, and its contributions to the nation. New Englanders also tend to be well educated.

In terms of ethnicity, Vermont, Maine, and New Hampshire are the nation's whitest states. African American and Asian populations are increasing, especially in Massachusetts and Connecticut. In northern Maine, there is a heavy French influence from nearby Québec.

The Politics

Though they're often portrayed as a bunch of loony liberals, the political views of New Englanders are actually more complex. The region's representation in both the United States Senate and the House of Representatives is heavily Democratic, even in those states that elect a Republican governor. Voters in New Hampshire, which now hosts the nation's first primary each presidential election season, tend to lean conservative but with a distinctly libertarian slant, as do residents in many rural portions of New England.

During the civil rights era in the 1960s, racial tension in Boston was high, with people clashing in the streets over public school segregation. In 2006, however, Massachusetts residents elected Deval Patrick as governor, the second black governor ever to be elected in the United States. Four of the five states that allow same-sex marriage are in New England (Massachusetts, Vermont, New Hampshire, and Connecticut).

The Economy

Long gone are the days since New England's shoe and textile industries sailed overseas, when many a mill town suffered blows to employment and self-image. In recent years, the unemployment rate has fallen below the national average (though Rhode Island has one of the highest in the country at 13%). In Maine, the lobster-fishing industry, a main component of that state's economy, is in crisis. As lobster is viewed as an expensive delicacy, demand has decreased dramatically in tough times. Between 2005 and 2009 lobster prices dropped nearly two dollars a pound, putting a financial squeeze on the industry as fuel costs have risen.

Exports are a major part of the modern New England economy, consisting heavily of computer and other electronics, chemicals, and specialized machinery. The Boston area is home to a thriving biotech industry, currently growing by leaps and bounds. The service industries also are strong, especially in the insurance and financial sectors. Some towns are known for a particular export: Groton, Connecticut, and Bath, Maine, both have naval shipyards supplying the military with high-technology fighting ships; Springfield, Massachusetts, is a gun-manufacturing center; and Barre, Vermont, quarries granite. Assorted foods produced include maple syrup, blueberries, cranberries, lobster, and other seafood.

Sports

Professional sports are a huge draw in New England. Though Massachusetts is home to the region's major-league teams—Boston Red Sox baseball, Boston Bruins hockey, New England Patriots football, and Boston Celtics basketball—fans from the other five states follow them as if they were the home team. Red Sox fans in particular are fanatical, and their legions have grown since the BoSox won the World Championships in 2004 and 2007 (after an 86-season drought).

In a similar fashion, the Patriots, perennial lackluster performers, have won an unprecedented three Super Bowls since the start of the 21st century. The team's 2007 regular season was "perfect," in that they won all 16 games; going into the Super Bowl their record was 18–0, but in one of the greatest upsets of all time, the New York Giants beat them with a touchdown in the final moments. The Bruins and Celtics both have successful and storied pasts, with the Celtics enjoying an exceptional season in 2007–8, capturing their 17th title (an NBA record).

The Language

As people move around, the local accents have begun to blend, creating more of a general New England accent. (In fact, in some urban areas, you may not hear any accent.) Linguistic differences, however, are still evident in some places, especially close to the coast.

Boston's distinct accent is similar in tone to that of New York City's Bronx and is noted by the dropping of the R in certain places, as in the pronunciation of the famous sports arena "the Gahden." Bostonians also lengthen their vowels, so chowder sounds like "chowdah." Town names in Massachusetts are often spoken very differently than they are spelled; Gloucester, for example, becomes "Glawstuh" and Holyoke becomes "Hoy-yoke." Bostonians also rush their speech, so "Hi, how are you?" is "hihawaya?" and "Did You Eat?" sounds like "Jeet?"

Connecticut, Maine, and Rhode Island also have a Boston-like accent with nuanced differences. Rhode Islanders drop their R's at the end of words and use an "aw" sound for the O or A in words like "coffee" or "talk" but an "ah" sound for the short O's in words like "Providence" and "mom." To hear some before your trip, tune in to Fox's *Family Guy*. Set in the fictional town of Quahog, Rhode Island, the TV show features characters who speak in pure, perfect Rhode Islandese. In Connecticut and New Hampshire the accent is not nearly as strong, but it comes out in certain words, like how locals pronounce their capital "Cahn-cuhd."

Meanwhile, true Mainers drop or soften their R's—making their favorite dish "lobstah"; they also often accentuate the vowel, so a one-word syllable can be pronounced like two, meaning "here" may become "hee-yuh."

A few New England words and phrases:

- **The Cape**—short for Cape Cod
- **Chowdah**—always New England–style, *never* Manhattan-style
- **Gravy**—tomato sauce
- **Grinda**—a submarine sandwich
- **The Hub**—Boston
- **Jimmies**—ice-cream sprinkles
- **Regular coffee**—not black, but with cream and sugar
- **Wicked**—"very," added as a modifier (e.g., wicked awesome, wicked good)

QUINTESSENTIAL NEW ENGLAND

Fall Foliage

It's impossible to discuss New England without mentioning that time of year when the region's deciduous (leaf-shedding) trees—maples, oaks, birches, and beeches—explode in reds, yellows, oranges, and other rich hues. Autumn is the most colorful season in New England, but it can be finicky, defined as much by the weather as it is by the species of trees; a single rainstorm can strip trees of their grandeur. What happens in one area of the region doesn't necessarily happen in another, and if you have the time you can follow the colors from one area to the next. You'll be competing with thousands of other like-minded leaf peepers, so be sure to book lodging early. Your preparedness will pay off the first time you drive down a winding country road aflame in the bright sun of a New England autumn day.

The Coast

The coast of New England is both workplace and playground. From the 17th century, boatbuilders sprung up in one town after another to support the shipping and fishing trades. Today, the boatyards are far fewer than in historical times, but shipping and especially fishing remain important to the economy on the coast and beyond. It's not all work and no play—some of the classic wooden sailboats now serve cruise-goers, and some fishermen have traded in their lobster boats for whale-watching vessels. The coast's lighthouses are another New England staple; more than 60 of these beacons of light line Maine's jagged coast like sentinels along the shore. In Massachusetts, Cape Cod is a beachcombers' paradise, and the relatively chilly waters of the North Atlantic don't scare away swimmers come summertime.

New Englanders are a varied group joined by a shared past and a singular pride in their roots. It's therefore no surprise that New England spans a spectrum of activities and locales, yet offers visitors and residents alike distinct experiences that still can perfectly define the region.

Food, Glorious Food

Maine lobster. Vermont Grade A maple syrup. Portuguese sausage from Cape Cod. Blueberries from Maine. Fine food prepared under the influence of every region of Italy in Boston's North End (there's plenty of Italian to go around Atwells Avenue in Providence's Federal Hill, too). This is just a sampling to whet your appetite. New England dining is truly a feast for the gastronomist, and it runs the gamut from the simply prepared to the most artistic of presentations: from blueberry pie just like grandma used to make to molecular gastronomy in some Boston restaurants. Local ingredients and sustainable methods are common in foodie-focused cities and also Vermont. Chefs who grew up here sometimes leave to learn their trade, only to return and enrich the dining scene, but the region is attracting newcomers as well.

Artisans

New England's independent artisans have built a thriving cottage industry. Some of the finest potters spin their wheels on the coast, and one-off, often whimsical jewelry is wrought in silver, pewter, and other metals. Modern furniture makers take classic simple New England designs, including those of the Shakers and Quakers, and refine them for buyers the world over who are willing to pay thousands for craftsmanship that has withstood the test of time. The varied landscapes of Vermont and New Hampshire, with their respective Green and White Mountains; Massachusetts, with its Berkshire Mountains, Pioneer Valley, and historic coast; Connecticut, with its southern shore; and Rhode Island, with its oceanfront cliffs, have patiently sat for thousands of painters, whose canvases are sold in small shops and local museums.

NEW ENGLAND TOP ATTRACTIONS

Acadia National Park

(A) Hosting more than 2 million visitors annually, this wonder of the Maine Coast was the first national park established east of the Mississippi River. It is regularly one of the most visited in the United States. In the warmer months, take a drive around Mount Desert Island's 20-mi Park Loop Road to acquaint yourself with the area and indulge in spectacular views of the mountains and the sea. Head to the top of Cadillac Mountain for amazing 360-degree views (especially popular at sunrise) or bike the scenic 45-mi carriage-road system, inspecting each of the 17 stone bridges along the way. Go on a park ranger–led boat trip in search of local wildlife such as porpoises, seals, and seabirds or cruise to the fjordlike bay of Somes Sound, where steep rocky cliffs jut out of the sea. Adorable Bar Harbor is the park's gateway town.

Appalachian Trail

(B) The 2,160-mi Appalachian Trail, running from Springer Mountain, Georgia, to Katahdin, Maine, cuts through five of New England's six states: Connecticut, Massachusetts, New Hampshire, Vermont, and Maine. Though the trail is best known as a weeks-long endurance test for expert hikers, many short stretches can be walked in a few hours. "AT" terrain in Maine and New Hampshire can be quite challenging; the trail is a bit more manageable in southern New England. If you're a complete novice, you can also drive to many of the trail heads—if only to say you've set foot on the most famous walk in the country.

Baxter State Park

(C) Over the span of 32 years, from 1930 to 1962, former Maine governor Percival Baxter began buying and donating parcels of land, with the goal of creating a natural park in the wilds of northern Maine.

The result is Baxter State Park: more than 200,000 acres containing numerous lakes and streams, plus Mt. Katahdin, Maine's tallest peak and the northern terminus of the Appalachian Trail. Offering frequent sightings of moose, white-tailed deer, and black bear, and attracting only 60,000 visitors a year, Baxter State Park provides a wilderness experience not found elsewhere in New England.

Boston

(D) New England's largest and most cosmopolitan city is the region's hub for modern commerce, education, and culture, and the early history of the United States is never far from view. Orient yourself with a 360-degree view from the Prudential Skywalk Observation Deck before you hit the ground exploring. The 50-acre Boston Common is the oldest public park in the nation; across the street is the Public Garden, where a ride on a Swan Boat has been a popular pastime and a harbinger of spring since 1877. Two lanterns hung from the Old North Church kicked off the Revolutionary War and made Paul Revere a legend; the Freedom Trail is a 2.5-mi trail that winds past 16 of the city's most historic landmarks. Be sure to include a visit to the Museum of Fine Arts, containing more than 450,000 works of art from almost every corner of the world, including Egyptian mummies and Asian scrolls.

Cape Cod National Seashore

(E) Comprising 40 mi of sandy beaches and 44,000 acres of a landscape that has been the muse of countless painters and photographers, the Cape Cod National Seashore is the best of what New England has to offer, the perfect place for explorers and strollers looking for an untouched stretch of coastline. An exhaustive amount of programs—from guided bird walks to surf rescue demonstrations to snorkeling

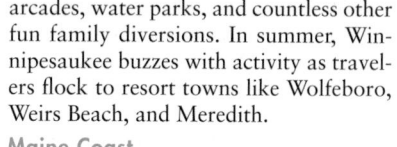

in Wellfleet's kettle ponds—take place year-round; most are free.

Green Mountains

(F) Vermont takes its nickname (the Green Mountain State) and its actual name (*verts monts* is "green mountains" in French) from this 250-mi-long mountain range that forms the spine of the state. Part of the Appalachian Mountains, the Green Mountains are a wild paradise filled with rugged hiking trails (most notably the Long Trail and the Appalachian Trail), unspoiled forests, quaint towns, and some of the East Coast's best ski resorts. About 400,000 acres are protected in Green Mountain National Forest.

Lake Winnipesaukee

(G) As fun to fish as it is to pronounce, the largest (and longest) lake in New Hampshire is home to three species of trout, small- and largemouth bass, bluegill, and more. The 72-square-mi lake also contains more than 250 islands, beaches, arcades, water parks, and countless other fun family diversions. In summer, Winnipesaukee buzzes with activity as travelers flock to resort towns like Wolfeboro, Weirs Beach, and Meredith.

Maine Coast

(H) Counting all its nooks, crannies, and crags, Maine's coast would stretch for thousands of miles if you could pull it straight. The Southern Coast is the most visited section, stretching north from Kittery to just outside Portland, but don't let that stop you from heading farther "Down East" (Maine-speak for "up the coast"). Despite the cold North Atlantic waters, beachgoers enjoy miles of sandy— or, more frequently, rocky—beaches, with sweeping views of lighthouses, forested islands, and the wide-open sea.

Mt. Washington

(I) New England's highest mountain, this New Hampshire peak has been scaled by many a car (as the bumper stickers will

attest). You can also take a cog railway to the top or, if you're an intrepid hiker, navigate a maze of trails. The weather station here recorded a wind gust of 231 MPH in April 1934—the highest wind speed ever recorded at a surface station. Bundle up if you make the trek—the average temperature at the summit is below freezing.

Mystic

(J) Home to two great museums—the Mystic Aquarium and Institute for Exploration and Mystic Seaport (the world's largest maritime museum)—this Connecticut seaside town is one of the state's biggest draws. When you finish touring the town's two impressive institutions, peruse the boutiques and galleries downtown.

Newport

(K) Rhode Island's treasure trove preserved Colonial buildings and Gilded Age mansions like no other city in the country. Here you'll find more than 200 pre-Revolutionary structures and scores of jaw-dropping, ridiculously over-the-top castles from the late 19th century. Newport is also a picturesque seaside town and one of the world's great sailing capitals.

Portland Head Light

(L) One of the most-photographed lighthouses in the nation, the historic Portland Head Light was commissioned by George Washington and completed in 1791 for the whopping sum of $2,250. It welcomes nearly a million visitors a year and features an informative museum in the Victorian-style innkeeper's cottage. The towering white stone lighthouse stands over the keeper's house, a white home with a red roof. Besides a harbor view, its park has walking paths, picnic facilities, and wide, grassy expanses perfect for flying a kite in the gusty ocean winds. The lighthouse is in Fort Williams Park, about 2 mi from the town center of Cape Elizabeth, at the southwest entrance of Portland harbor.

TOP EXPERIENCES

Peep a Leaf

Tourist season in most of New England is concentrated in the late spring and summer, but a resurgence happens in September and October, especially in the northern states, when leaf peepers from all corners descend by the car- and busload to see the leaves turn red, yellow, orange, and all shades in between. Foliage season can be fragile and unpredictable—temperature, winds, latitude, and rain all influence when the leaves turn and how long they remain on the trees—but that makes the season even more precious. Don't discount the beauty of fallen leaves; watch them glisten in fall rains or float in the winds of approaching winter.

Comb a Beach

Whether sandy or rocky, New England beaches can be filled with flotsam and jetsam. Anything from crab traps unmoored by heavy waves to colored sea glass worn smooth by the water to lost watches, jewelry, and the like can appear at your feet. Also common are shells of sea urchins, clams, and other bivalves that gulls have dropped from to crack open and eat the tender insides. During certain times of the year sand dollars of all sizes and colors are plentiful—you may even find one still whole.

Take Yourself Out to a Ballgame

Boston Red Sox fans are best known for being two things: unwaveringly fanatical and vehemently opposed to all things New York Yankees (pity the family with members in both camps). Fenway Park is the oldest stadium in the major leagues and one of the few left to use a hand-operated scoreboard. Though the cheapest seats and farthest from the field, the bleachers are quite popular with the faithful, who gather to drink beer in plastic cups and watch as batters attempt to clear the 37-foot-tall left-field wall known as the Green Monster. Seat 21 of Section 42, Row 37 in the right bleachers is painted red in honor of the longest measurable home run ever hit at Fenway, Ted Williams's legendary 502-foot blast on June 9, 1946.

Hit the Slopes

Though the mountain snow in New England is not as legendary as the powder out West (and, in fact, can be downright unpleasant when packed snow becomes crusty ice), skiing is quite popular here. Vermont has several ski areas, with Killington being the largest resort in the Northeast: its 200 trails span seven mountains. New Hampshire's White Mountains and Massachusetts's Berkshires also cater to snow-sport lovers, while Sunday River and Sugarloaf in Maine are perennial favorites with advanced intermediate and expert skiers. Beginners (and lift-ticket bargain hunters) can choose from a number of small but fun hills throughout northern New England.

Eat a Maine Lobster

Maine lobsters are world-renowned, and lobstermen and fish markets all along the coast will pack a live lobster in seaweed for overnight shipment to almost anywhere nationwide. These delectable crustaceans are available throughout New England, but without a doubt the best place to eat them is near the waters of origin. Lobster meat is sweet, especially the claws, and most agree that simple preparation is the best way to go: steamed and eaten with drawn butter or pulled into chunks and placed in a hot dog bun with a leaf of lettuce and the barest amount of mayonnaise—the famous New England lobster roll. Don't forget to save room for

New England's other culinary treasure: *chowdah*. No two clam chowders taste the same, but they're all delicious.

Rise and Shine at a B&B

New England's distinct architecture, much of it originating in the 18th and 19th centuries, has resulted in beautiful buildings of all shapes and sizes, many of which have been restored as bed-and-breakfasts. These inns typify the cozy, down-home, and historic feel of New England, and are an ideal lodging choice. This is especially true when the weather is cold, and the warm ambience of many of these inns more than justifies the slightly higher prices you'll pay here versus a hotel or motel.

Watch a Whale

The deep, cold waters of the North Atlantic serve as feeding grounds and migration routes for a variety of whales, including the fin, humpback, the occasional blue, and endangered right whales. Cape Cod and Maine's Southern Coast and Mid-Coast regions are the best places to hop aboard a whale-watching boat to motor 10 mi or more off the coast, but whale-watching boats also depart from Boston's harbor. Some boat captains go so far as to guarantee at least a single sighting. The tours head to the whale feeding grounds about 20 mi offshore, where the majestic animals are so numerous, some tours may offer a money back guarantee if you don't see one.

Fair Thee Well

New Englanders love their fairs and festivals. Maine-iacs celebrate the moose, clam, lobster, and blueberry, and a fair highlights organic farmers and their products. Maple sugar and maple syrup are feted in Vermont, while "live free or die" New Hampshire honors American independence. Newport, Rhode Island, hosts two highly regarded music festivals, one folk and one jazz. Many rural communities throughout New England hold agricultural fairs in late August and September.

Find the Perfect Souvenir

Artists and craftspeople abound in New England, meaning that finding the perfect souvenir of your vacation will be an enjoyable hunt. Whether you choose a watercolor of a picturesque fishing village, a riotously colorful piece of hand-painted pottery, or a handcrafted piece of jewelry, you'll be supporting the local economy while taking a little piece of the region home with you.

Get Up Close and Personal with Nature

New England might be known for its flashy foliage in the fall and spectacular slopes in the winter, but the outdoors in the spring and summer delights all the senses as well. You can breathe in the ocean air as you drive along the Maine Coast or amble on Newport's 3½-mi Cliff Walk. Alternatively, enjoy the fragrance of the mountains and forests in the Berkshires, Vermont's Green Mountains, and New Hampshire's White Mountains while hiking along the Appalachian Trail. You may observe such animals as moose and bear. Close to the ocean there are numerous chances to see birds, seals, dolphins, and whales.

Savor Sweet Stuff

Summer vacations in New England go hand in hand with sweet treats; it's difficult to visit without sampling homemade fudge at an old-fashioned candy store, buying an ice cream for your sweetie, or bringing home some saltwater taffy to share with the folks back at the ranch. Be sure

to try a Maine specialty—the whoopie pie. Made from two chocolate circles of cake with vanilla cream filling in between, it's a delectable Maine tradition. If you are visiting Maine when the tiny but succulent wild blueberry is in season, take every opportunity to savor this flavorful fruit, whether in pie, muffin, or pancake form, and you'll understand its legendary culinary status. In Vermont, go on a factory tour at Ben & Jerry's and have a delicious cone afterward. The Green Mountain state's favorite sons by no means have the market cornered on ice cream goodness; you'll find excellent frozen treats in every corner of the region (Cape Cod is an especially blessed area). In Boston, head to the Italian North End for legendary cannoli. You can even have dessert for breakfast when you top your pancakes with Vermont's legendary maple syrup.

Check Out Lighthouses

Maine's long and jagged coastline is home to more than 60 lighthouses, perched high on rocky ledges or on the tips of wayward islands. Though modern technology in navigation has made many of the lights obsolete, lighthouse enthusiasts and preservation groups restore and maintain many of them and often make them accessible to the public. Some of the state's more famous lights include Portland Head Light, commissioned by President George Washington in 1790 and immortalized in one of Edward Hopper's paintings; Two Lights, a few miles down the coast in Cape Elizabeth; and West Quoddy Head, on the easternmost tip of land in the United States. Some lighthouses are privately owned and others accessible only by boat, but plenty are within easy reach and open to the public, some with museums and tours. At Rocklands Maine Lighthouse Museum visitors can view a collection of Fresnel lenses and Coast Guard artifacts.

Sail the Coast

The coastline of northern New England is a sailor's paradise, complete with hidden coves, windswept islands, and picture-perfect harbors where you can pick up a mooring for the night. With nearly 3,500 mi of undulating, rocky shoreline, you could spend a lifetime of summers sailing the waters off the Maine Coast and never see it all. If you're not one of the lucky few with a sailboat to call your own, there are many companies that offer sailboat charters, whether for day trips or weeklong excursions. It might sound like an expensive getaway, but as meals and drinks are usually included, an overnight sailing charter might not cost any more than a seaside hotel room, plus you have the advantage of an experienced captain to provide history and insight along the voyage.

Get the First Sight of First Light

At 1,530 feet, Cadillac Mountain, in Maine's Acadia National Park, is the highest mountain on the New England coast—so what better place to view the sunrise? Drive the winding and narrow 3.5-mi road to the summit before dawn (not accessible when the Loop Road is closed in the winter), and you could be the first person in the United States to see the summer sun's rays. (Note that this depends on the time of year; sometimes the first sunrise is at West Quoddy Head Lighthouse in Lubec, Maine).

FLAVORS OF NEW ENGLAND

The locavore movement has finally hit New England. New farms, greenmarkets, and gourmet food shops are sprouting up everyday and chefs are exploring more seasonably-based, farm-to-table options.

New England's Natural Bounty

With the long stretches of fertile farmland and the Atlantic Ocean, the region has many natural food sources.

Fruit: Blueberries, strawberries, raspberries, and blackberries grow wild (and on farms) all over the northeast in summertime. Concord grapes started growing in the namesake Massachusetts village way back in 1849. Autumn brings sugar pumpkins and an array of regional apple varieties. Cranberries are cultivated on marshy bogs, mostly in Massachusetts.

Vegetables: Local farmers grow many different kinds of vegetables (and veggie-like fruits). Big, colorful piles of sweet corn, squash, zucchini, tomatoes, peppers, cucumbers, eggplant, gourds, potatoes, beets, asparagus, peas, beans, mushrooms, and rhubarb appear at farm stands and markets throughout summer and fall.

Dairy: Milk and cream from the region's dairy farms are used in chowders, bisques, and cream-based sauces; in cheeses, like the famous Vermont cheddars; and in ice cream and yogurt.

Seafood: There is a sizeable fishing industry in the northeast. People here consume cod, haddock, halibut, scrod, bass, and trout, as well as shellfish, such as lobster, steamers, quahogs, scallops, mussels, and oysters.

By Land or By Sea

New England cuisine has always had a somewhat austere, no-frills reputation (like the people), and that simplicity is still present today.

Thanksgiving Dinner: The most traditional Yankee food has got to be from our national day of feasting: roasted turkey, cranberry sauce, mashed potatoes, gravy, bread-based stuffing, baked winter squash, and boiled turnips with apple or pumpkin pie, and Indian pudding for dessert.

Boiled Dinner: Perhaps the second most well-known dinner in New England is the one that's traditionally served on St. Patrick's Day: hunks of corned beef and cabbage simmered in a pot with potatoes, carrots, turnips, onions, and broth.

Coastal Cuisine: Look for fish dishes, steamed lobster, lobster bisque, and lobster rolls; chowders; crab cakes; baskets of fried clams, shrimp, and scallops; steamers; oysters; or clam bakes/boils.

Sweets: Blueberry pancakes with maple syrup, muffins, pumpkin bread, or fried cornmeal johnnycakes for breakfast. For dessert: apples baked into pies, crisps, and brown betties or pressed into cider. Berry pies and strawberry shortcake are also popular. Mainers love whoopie pies, which are cake-like chocolate sandwiches stuffed with frosting. Vermonters are big on maple sugar candy, while Rhode Islanders like to sip their frappes, or "cabinets." And everybody loves ice cream.

Spices: The flavors of New England cuisine were historically derived from the fresh and unadorned ingredients used to create it; however, certain spices, such as black pepper, basil, oregano, bay leaf, cloves, cinnamon, cardamom, and nutmeg, are often used in New England dishes.

Beantown: Let's not forget about Boston baked beans slow-cooked with salt pork and molasses!

IF YOU LIKE

The Beach

Long, wide beaches edge the New England coast from southern Maine to southern Connecticut, with dozens dotting the shores of Cape Cod, Martha's Vineyard, and Nantucket. The waters are at their warmest in August, though they're cold even at the height of summer along much of Maine. Inland, small lake beaches abound, most notably in New Hampshire and Vermont. Though most hit these sandy getaways in summer, beaches can even be enjoyable in winter (for a stroll, not swim), as you'll likely have the shore to yourself.

Many of the beaches have lifeguards on duty in season; some have picnic facilities, restrooms, changing facilities, and concession stands. Depending on the locale, you may need a parking sticker to use the lot.

Block Island, Rhode Island. Twelve miles off Rhode Island's coast, this 11-square-mi island has 12 mi of shoreline, 365 freshwater ponds, and plenty of hiking trails. Due to its rolling green hills, some liken the island to Ireland. Preserved homes and inns lend it a Victorian charm. Most visitors arrive via ferry from Port Judith, a one-hour trip, but if you're strapped for time (and not for cash), you can hop a plane at the airport in Westerly for a 20-minute flight.

Cape Cod National Seashore, Massachusetts. With more than 150 beaches—roughly 40 mi worth—Cape Cod has enough to keep any beachcomber happy and sandy year-round. They range from the tourist-packed sand in Dennis to the almost untouched stretches of coast protected by the Cape Cod National Seashore. Favorite activities include swimming, bicycling,

and even off-road ("oversand") travel (permit required).

Gloucester Beaches, Massachusetts. Along the North Shore, Gloucester is also the oldest seaport in the nation. Its trio of beaches—Good Harbor Beach, Long Beach, and Wingaersheek Beach—cools those coming north of Boston for some sun and sand. For a peek at a lighthouse, head to Wingaersheek. For excellent sunbathing, Long Beach is your best bet. For crowds, showers, and a snack bar, head to the large Good Harbor. All three have dunes.

Hampton Beach State Park, New Hampshire. The Granite State's ocean shore is short, but this state park along historic Route 1 takes full advantage of the space it has. In addition to swimming and fishing, there are campsites with full hookups for RVs and an amphitheater with a band shell for fair-weather concerts.

Old Orchard Beach, Maine. Think Coney Island on a smaller scale. A ghost town in the off-season, the main drag fills with cruising cars and amblers of all ages come summer. There's a white sand beach to be sure (lapped by cold North Atlantic waters), but many come to ride the Pirate Ship at Palace Playland, drop quarters at the arcade, and browse the multitude of trinket-and-T-shirt shops. For a meal, grab a slice of pizza and an order of french fries doused with white vinegar.

Reid State Park, Maine. Just east of Sheepscot Bay on Georgetown Island, oceanside Reid State Park, with its large dunes, is a beach bum's wonderland. The water is cold much of the year, but it's a beautiful and quiet place to spend some solitary time looking for sand dollars or climbing the rocks at low tide, exploring tidal

pools. Great views can be had from the park's rocky Griffith Head.

Bicycling

Biking on a road through New England's countryside is an idyllic way to spend a day. Many ski resorts allow mountain bikes in summer.

Acadia National Park, Maine. At the heart of this popular park is the 45-mi network of historic carriage roads covered in crushed rock that bicyclists share only with equestrians and hikers. Sturdier riders can ascend the road to the top of Cadillac Mountain, but take caution: heavy traffic in the high season can make this a dangerous proposition. Biking in Maine is also scenic in and around Kennebunkport, Camden, Deer Isle, and the Schoodic Peninsula.

Cape Cod, Massachusetts. Cape Cod has miles of bike trails, some paralleling the national seashore, most on level terrain. On either side of the Cape Cod Canal is an easy 7-mi straight trail with views of the canal traffic. Extending 28 mi from South Dennis to Wellfleet, the Cape Cod Rail Trail is a converted railbed that is now a paved, mostly flat bike path passing through a handful of the Cape's scenic towns, offering plenty of opportunity to take side trips.

Killington Resort, Vermont. Following the lead of many ski resorts in the western United States, Killington allows fat-tire riders on many of its ski trails long after the snow has melted. Stunt riders can enjoy the jumps and bumps of the mountain bike park.

All Along the Coast. U.S. 1, Maine. The major road that travels along the Maine Coast is only a narrow two-lane highway for most of its route, but it is still one of the country's most historic highways. As a result, it's very popular in spring, summer, and fall with serious long-distance bike riders. Bicyclists should ride carefully and look out for motorists who may be trying to catch a glimpse of the sea.

Boston, Massachusetts. Commuters, students, and hard-core cyclists alike buzz along the streets and bike paths of New England's largest city. For a scenic ride, the 17-mi-long Dr. Paul Dudley White Bike Path can't be beat. It hugs the Charles River, with great views of practicing crew teams, the spires of Harvard University, and the Boston skyline. Or, for a bit of history with your ride, hop on the Minuteman Bikeway, which runs from the Alewife T stop (on the Red Line, in North Cambridge) to Lexington. From here, you can cycle to Concord, following the path the minutemen traveled on the first day of the American Revolution.

Boating

Along many of New England's larger lakes, sailboats, rowboats, canoes, kayaks, and outboards are available for rent at local marinas. Sailboats are available for rent at a number of seacoast locations, but you may be required to prove your seaworthiness. Lessons are frequently available.

Newport and Block Island, Rhode Island. Narragansett Bay, Newport Harbor, and Block Island Sound are among the premier sailing areas in the world. (Newport hosted the America's Cup, yachting's most prestigious race, from 1930 to 1983.) Numerous outfitters provide public and private sailing tours, sailing lessons, and boat rentals.

Allagash Wilderness Waterway, Maine. This scenic and remote waterway—92 mi of lakes, ponds, rivers, and streams—is part of the 740-mi Northern Forest Canoe

Trail, which floats through New York, Vermont, Québec, and New Hampshire as well as Maine.

Lake Champlain, Vermont. Called by some the Sixth Great Lake, 435-square-mi Lake Champlain is bordered by Vermont's Green Mountains to the east and the Adirondacks of New York to the west. Burlington, Vermont, is the largest lakeside city and a good bet for renting a boat—be it canoe, kayak, rowboat, skiff, or motorboat. Attractions include numerous islands and deep-blue water that's often brushed by pleasant New England breezes.

Mystic, Connecticut. The world's largest maritime museum, Mystic Seaport, is also a good place to get out on the water. A wide variety of sailing programs are available here—including lessons on a 61-foot schooner—as is instruction on power boating. If you're eager to test your skills against other sailors, there's also a weekly race series.

Food

Seafood is king throughout New England. Clams are a favorite, fried, steamed, or in New England–style chowder, which is made with milk or cream (unlike the tomato-based Manhattan version, the very existence of which many locals will deny) and big, meaty quahogs. Lobster classics include plain boiled lobster—a staple at "in the rough" picnic-bench-and-paper-plate spots along the Maine Coast—and lobster rolls, a lobster meat and mayo or melted butter preparation served in a toasted hot dog bun. The leading fin fish is scrod—young cod or haddock—best sampled baked, broiled, or fried fish-and-chips style.

Inland, specialties run to the familiar dishes of old-fashioned Sunday-dinner America—pot roast, roast turkey, baked ham, hefty stacks of pancakes (with local maple syrup, of course), and apple pie. One regional favorite is Indian pudding, a long-boiled cornmeal-and-molasses concoction that's delicious with vanilla ice cream. Speaking of ice cream, New England has many home-grown varieties, from Ben & Jerry's in Vermont to Emack & Bolio's out of Boston.

Gilbert's Chowderhouse and Becky's Diner, Portland, Maine. The town's waterfront Commercial Street is bookended by these two typical Maine diners. The former has one of the state's finest lobster rolls and homemade clam cakes; the latter opens for breakfast at 4 AM to feed the fishermen before they head out to sea. Order a slice of fresh pie or buy one whole to take with you.

North End, Boston, Massachusetts. Ethnic Italians put this corner of Boston on the map, and the area is known for its Italian restaurants and bakeries. Known as "Little Italy," the North End contains almost 90 restaurants; you'll find everything from hole-in-the-wall pizza joints to elegant eateries serving regional cuisine from every corner of the boot. No trip here is complete without a post-dinner cannoli from Mike's Pastry.

Thin-Crust Pizza, New Haven, Connecticut. The iconic New Haven–style pizza, a decidedly thin-crust pie, can be found at several pizzerias in the Yale-infused town. Frank Pepe Pizzeria Napoletana has been around since 1925, while two blocks away is Sally's Apizza, established in 1938. If you prefer a newcomer, try BAR, a nightclub-cum-microbrewery popular with the college crowd. At any of the above, ask for fresh mootz (mozzarella in East Coast speak).

Federal Hill and the Waterfront, Providence, Rhode Island. The Ocean State may be a small one, but its capital's food reputation is big, thanks to its status as the home of Johnson & Wales, an upper-echelon culinary academy. Some of its graduates open restaurants in town, drawing discriminating diners from near and far. Savor Italian food along Providence's Atwells Avenue in the Federal Hill neighborhood or nosh with the posh at upscale river-view establishments in downtown Providence.

Golf

Golf caught on early in New England. The region has an ample supply of public and semiprivate courses, many of which are part of distinctive resorts or even ski areas. One dilemma facing golfers is keeping their eye on the ball instead of the scenery. The views are marvelous at Balsams Wilderness grand resort in Dixville Notch, New Hampshire, and the nearby course at the splendid old Mount Washington Hotel in Bretton Woods. During prime season, make sure you reserve ahead for tee times, particularly near urban areas and at resorts.

The Gleneagles Golf Course at the Equinox, Vermont. One of the stateliest lodging resorts in all of New England, the Equinox opened in 1769 and has hosted the likes of Teddy Roosevelt and Mary Todd Lincoln. The golf course is par-71 and 6,423 yards, and is especially alluring in the fall when the trees that line the fairways explode in color. After golf, go to the 13,000-square-foot spa for some pampering. The resort is ringed by mountain splendor.

Newton Commonwealth Golf Course, Massachusetts. Minutes from downtown Boston, this municipal golf course is open to the public seven days a week. Even with 18 holes it isn't a long course, but it can't be beat for a quick break from sightseeing in Beantown.

Samoset Resort on the Ocean, Maine. Few things match playing 18 holes on a championship course that's bordered by the North Atlantic. In Rockport, Maine, along Penobscot Bay, Samoset Resort's course is open from May through October. Book a room at the luxurious hotel here to make it a complete golf vacation.

Hiking

Probably the most famous trails in the region are the 255-mi Long Trail, which runs north–south through the center of Vermont, and the Maine-to-Georgia Appalachian Trail, which runs through New England on both private and public land. The Appalachian Mountain Club (AMC) maintains a system of staffed huts in New Hampshire's Presidential Range, with bunk space and meals available by reservation. State parks throughout the region afford good hiking.

Mt. Washington, New Hampshire. The cog railroad and the auto road to the summit are popular routes up New England's highest mountain, but for those with stamina and legs of steel it's one heck of a hike. There are a handful of trails to the top, the most popular beginning at Pinkham Notch Visitor Center. Be sure to dress in layers and have some warm clothing for the frequent winds toward the peak.

The Long Trail, Vermont. Following the main ridge of the Green Mountains from one end of Vermont to the other, this is the nation's oldest long-distance trail. In fact, some say it was the inspiration for the Appalachian Trail. Hardy hikers make a go of its 270-mi length, but day hikers can drop in and out at many places along the way.

HISTORY YOU CAN SEE

History lies thick on the ground in New England—from Pilgrims to pirates, witches to whalers, the American Revolution to the Industrial Revolution.

Pilgrim's Progress

The story of the Pilgrims comes alive when you visit New England. From Provincetown (where the *Mayflower* actually first landed) to Plymouth and throughout Cape Cod, these early New England settlers left an indelible mark on the region. Their contemporaries, the Puritans, founded the city of Boston. Both groups, seeking religious freedom, planted the seeds for the founding of the United States.

What to See:

In Plymouth (south of Boston) you can visit **Plimoth Plantation,** *Mayflower II,* the **National Monument to the Forefathers,** and, of course, **Plymouth Rock** itself *(⇨ Sidetrips from Boston in Chapter 2).* On Cape Cod, visit **First Encounter Beach** in Eastham and the **Pilgrim Monument** in Provincetown *(⇨ Cape Cod in Chapter 3).*

Talkin' 'Bout a Revolution

New England is the cradle of democracy. Home to many of the patriots who launched the American Revolution and the war's first battles, here you can see real evidence of the events you read about in history class. From battlefields to the Boston Tea Party ship, New England (and especially Massachusetts) is filled with touchstones of our national story.

What to See:

In Boston, walk the **Freedom Trail** *(⇨ Boston in Chapter 2)* or just be on the lookout for markers and plaques as you walk around downtown—you can literally trip over history wherever you step. Outside the city, **Lexington** and **Concord** *(⇨ The North Shore and South of Boston in Chapter 2)* are easy visits for a quick primer on the start of the American Revolution.

Sea to Shining Sea

New England has a proud (and long) maritime history. From the *Mayflower* to boatbuilders in Maine who still produce wooden ships, you'll feel New England's seafaring traditions anywhere on the coast here. Many museums tell the story of the region's contributions to shipbuilding, nautical exploration, and whaling. And although the latter is no longer a pillar of the local economy, today you can go visit Earth's largest mammals on whale-watching expeditions that leave from many points along the New England coast.

What to See:

Arguably the nation's most famous ship, the **USS *Constitution,*** is docked in Charlestown, Massachusetts, just outside of Boston *(⇨ Exploring Boston in Chapter 2).* The **Maine Maritime Museum** in Bath, Maine, is the last remaining intact shipyard in the United States to have built large wooden sailing vessels *(⇨ Portland and Environs in Chapter 10).* But the granddaddy of New England maritime experiences is undoubtedly **Mystic Seaport,** where almost 500 vessels are preserved *(⇨ New Haven to Mystic in Chapter 5).*

Frozen in Time

New England preserves its past like no other region of the United States. In addition to countless museums, historic sites, refurbished homes, and historical markers, the area has several wonderfully preserved villages, each trying to capture a specific moment in time.

A mile-long stretch of Main Street in Deerfield, Massachusetts, contains a remarkably well-preserved portion of an 18th-century village. Historic Deerfield contains 13 homes built between 1730

and 1850, all maintained as interpretive museums. Together, they house more than 25,000 artifacts harking back to a quintessential New England town.

One of the country's finest re-creations of a Colonial-era village, Old Sturbridge Village emulates an early-19th-century New England town, with more than 40 historic buildings moved here from other communities. Staff interpreters, clad in period costumes, do the sort of activities that villagers did back in the day: farmers plow, blacksmiths pound, and bakers bake. Though you might think it a static, if re-enactive, slice of quintessential New England life, the village represents a period of transition brought about by the growing significance of commerce and manufacturing, improvements in agriculture and transportation, and various social changes.

Near Lake Champlain, the Shelburne Museum spans 39 exhibition halls—many of which are restored 18th- and 19th-century buildings relocated here from locales throughout New England and New York. The sheer size and breadth of the museum's collections are dizzying. On display are more than 150,000 artifacts and works of art, as well as period structures that include a one-room schoolhouse, a lighthouse, a covered bridge, and even the 220-foot steamboat *Ticonderoga*, which once sailed Lake Champlain and is the last side-wheel steamboat of its kind. Landscaping recalls a classic New England village and features more than 400 lilac trees and various gardens.

What to See:

Effortlessly travel back in time by visiting **Historic Deerfield** (⇨ *The Pioneer Valley in Chapter 4*), **Old Sturbridge Village** (⇨ *The Pioneer Valley in Chapter 4*), and

Shelburne (⇨ *Northern Vermont in Chapter 7*).

Writing the Story of America

The list of New England writers who have shaped American culture is long indeed. Massachusetts alone has produced great poets in every generation: Anne Bradstreet, Phillis Wheatley, Emily Dickinson, Henry Wadsworth Longfellow, William Cullen Bryant, e. e. cummings, Robert Lowell, Elizabeth Bishop, Sylvia Plath, and Anne Sexton. Bay State writers include Louisa May Alcott, author of the enduring classic *Little Women*; Nathaniel Hawthorne, who re-created the Salem of his Puritan ancestors in *The Scarlet Letter*; Herman Melville, who wrote *Moby-Dick* in a house at the foot of Mt. Greylock; Eugene O'Neill, whose early plays were produced at a makeshift theater in Provincetown on Cape Cod; Lowell native Jack Kerouac, author of *On the Road*; and John Cheever, chronicler of suburban angst. Mark Twain, arguably the most famous American author of all, lived in Connecticut for much of his writing career (in Hartford and later Redding).

What to See:

Many homes of famous New England writers are preserved. An especially rich stop is **Concord, Massachusetts**, where you can see the homes of Alcott, Ralph Waldo Emerson, Henry David Thoreau, and Hawthorne (as well as Thoreau's Walden Pond). You can visit their graves (as well as those of other authors) in the Author's Ridge section of the town's **Sleepy Hollow Cemetery** (⇨ *Sidetrips from Boston in Chapter 2*). Another favorite stop is the **Mark Twain House** in Hartford, Connecticut (⇨ *Hartford and the Connecticut River Valley in Chapter 5*).

NEW ENGLAND WITH KIDS

Children's Museum, Boston. Make bubbles, climb through a maze, and while away some hours in "Adventure Zone" at this fun museum just for tykes in downtown Boston. A special play area for those under three lets them run around in a safe environment. Festivals happen throughout the year. (⇨ *Chapter 2.*)

Hampton Beach, New Hampshire. This seaside diversion draws families to its almost Coney Island–like fun. Along the boardwalk, kids enjoy arcade games, parasailing, live music, and an annual children's festival. They can even learn how saltwater taffy is made. (⇨ *Chapter 8.*)

Magic Wings Butterfly Conservatory & Gardens, Deerfield, Massachusetts. Almost 4,000 free-flying native and tropical butterflies are the star attraction here, contained within an 8,000-square-foot glassed enclosure that keeps the temperature upward of 80 degrees year-round. Relax around the Japanese koi pond on one of numerous benches and watch the kids chase the colorful creatures as they flit about. Or walk outside to the Iron Butterfly Outdoor Gardens, where flowers attract even more butterflies. (⇨ *Chapter 4.*)

Mystic Aquarium and Institute for Exploration, Mystic, Connecticut. This aquarium and research institute is one of only four North American facilities to feature stellar sea lions, and New England's only beluga whale calls the aquarium home. Kids can touch a cownose ray, and you'll also see African penguins, harbor seals, graceful sea horses, Pacific octopuses, and sand tiger sharks. Nearby Mystic Seaport is another great attraction for kids and families. (⇨ *Chapter 5.*)

Montshire Museum of Science, Norwich, Vermont. This interactive museum uses more than 60 hands-on exhibits to explore nature and technology. The building sits amid 110 acres of woodlands and nature trails. Live animals are on-site as well. (⇨ *Chapter 7.*)

Massachusetts Audubon Wellfleet Bay Wildlife Sanctuary, South Wellfleet, Massachusetts. With its numerous programs and its beautiful salt-marsh surroundings, this is a favorite migration stop for Cape vacationers year-round. Five miles of nature trails weave throughout the sanctuary's 1,100 acres of marsh, beach, and woods. If you're careful and quiet, you might be able to get close to seals basking in the sun or birds such as the great blue heron. Naturalists are on hand for guided walks and lectures. (⇨ *Chapter 3.*)

Plimoth Plantation, Plymouth, Massachusetts. Want to know what life was like in Colonial America? A visit to this living-history museum is like stepping into a time machine and zooming back to the year 1627. Curators are dressed in period costume and act like early-17th-century Pilgrims. (⇨ *Chapter 2.*)

Shelburne Farms, Shelburne, Vermont. This working dairy farm is also an educational and cultural resource center. Visitors can watch artisans make the farm's famous cheddar cheese from the milk of more than 100 purebred and registered Brown Swiss cows, and a children's farmyard and walking trails round out the experience. (⇨ *Chapter 7.*)

Southworth Planetarium, Portland, Maine. This University of Southern Maine facility offers classes such as night sky mythology and introductory astronomy. The 30-foot dome houses a star theater complete with lasers, digital sounds, and a star projector that displays more than 5,000 heavenly bodies. (⇨ *Chapter 10.*)

GREAT ITINERARIES

NEW ENGLAND HIGHLIGHTS

In a nation where distances can often be daunting, New England packs its top attractions into a remarkably compact area. Understanding Yankeedom might take a lifetime—but it's possible to get a good appreciation for the six-state region in a 2- to 2½-week drive. The following itinerary assumes you're beginning your trip in Hartford, Connecticut (which is about three hours northeast of New York City).

Hartford

1 day. The Mark Twain House resembles a Mississippi steamboat beached in a Victorian neighborhood (adjacent to it is the Harriet Beecher Stowe House museum). Downtown, you can visit Connecticut's ornate State Capitol and the Wadsworth Atheneum, which houses fine Impressionist and Hudson River School paintings. (⇨ *Hartford and the Connecticut River Valley in Chapter 5.*)

Lower Connecticut River Valley and Block Island Sound

1 or 2 days. Here centuries-old towns such as Essex and Chester coexist with a well-preserved natural environment. In Rhode Island, sandy beaches dot the coast in Watch Hill, Charlestown, and Narragansett. (⇨ *Hartford and the Connecticut River Valley in Chapter 5, South County in Chapter 6.*)

Newport

1 day. Despite its Colonial downtown and seaside parks, to most people Newport means mansions—the most opulent, cost-be-damned enclave of private homes ever built in the United States. Turn-of-the-20th-century "cottages" such as the Breakers and Marble House are beyond

duplication today. (⇨ *Newport County in Chapter 6.*)

Providence

1 day. Rhode Island's capital holds treasures like Benefit Street, with its Federal-era homes, and the Museum of Art at the Rhode Island School of Design. Be sure to savor a knockout Italian meal on Federal Hill and visit Waterplace Park. (⇨ *Providence in Chapter 6.*)

Cape Cod

2 or 3 days. Meander along Massachusetts's beach-lined arm-shaped peninsula and explore Cape Cod National Seashore. Fun Provincetown, at the Cape's tip, is Bohemian, gay, and touristy, a Portuguese fishing village built on a Colonial foundation. In season, you can also whale-watch here. (⇨ *Cape Cod in Chapter 3.*)

Plymouth

1 day. "America's hometown" is where 102 weary settlers landed in 1620. You can climb aboard the replica *Mayflower II*, then spend time at Plimoth Plantation, staffed by costumed "Pilgrims." (⇨ *The North Shore and South of Boston in Chapter 2.*)

Boston

2 or 3 days. In Boston, famous buildings such as Faneuil Hall are not merely civic landmarks but national icons. From the Boston Common, the 2.5-mi Freedom Trail links treasures of American liberty such as the USS *Constitution* ("Old Ironsides") and the Old North Church (of "one if by land, two if by sea" fame). Be sure to walk the gaslit streets of Beacon Hill, too. On your second day, explore the massive Museum of Fine Arts and the grand boulevards and shops of Back Bay. Another day, visit colorful Cambridge, Harvard University, and its museums. (⇨ *Boston, Chapter 2.*)

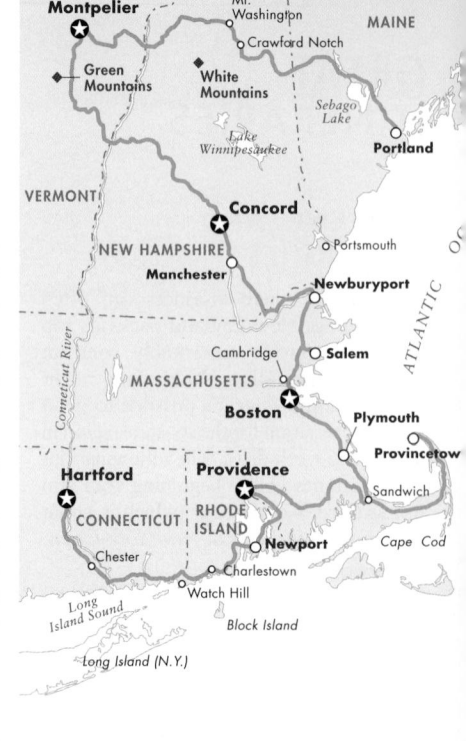

Salem and Newburyport

1 or 2 days. In Salem, many sites, including the Peabody Essex Museum, recall the dark days of the 1690s witch hysteria and the fortunes amassed in the China trade. Newburyport's Colonial and Federal-style homes testify to Yankee enterprise on the seas. (⇨ *The North Shore in Chapter 2.*)

Manchester and Concord

1 day. Manchester, New Hampshire's largest city, holds the Amoskeag Mills, a reminder of New England's industrial past. Smaller Concord is the state capital. Near the State House is the fine Museum of New Hampshire History, housing one of the locally built stagecoaches that carried Concord's name throughout the West. (⇨ *The Monadnocks and Merrimack Valley in Chapter 8.*)

Green Mountains and Montpelier

1 or 2 days. Route 100 travels through the heart of the Green Mountains, whose rounded peaks assert a modest grandeur. Vermont's vest-pocket capital, Montpelier, has the gold-dome Vermont State House and the quirky Vermont Museum. (⇨ *Central Vermont and Northern Vermont in Chapter 7.*)

White Mountains

1 day. U.S. 302 threads through New Hampshire's White Mountains, passing beneath brooding Mt. Washington and through Crawford Notch. In Bretton Woods, the Mt. Washington Cog Railway still chugs to the summit, and the Mount Washington Hotel recalls the glory days of White Mountain resorts. (⇨ *The White Mountains in Chapter 8.*)

Portland

1 day. Maine's maritime capital shows off its restored waterfront at the Old Port. Nearby, two lighthouses on Cape Elizabeth, Two Lights and Portland Head, still stand vigil. (⇨ *Portland to Waldoboro in Chapter 10.*)

THE SEACOAST

Every New England state except Vermont borders on saltwater. For history buffs, vivid links to the days when the sea was the region's lifeblood abound; for watersports enthusiasts, the sea guarantees fun. A journey along the coast also brings the promise of fresh seafood, incomparable sunrises, and a quality of light that has entranced artists from Winslow Homer to Edward Hopper.

Southeastern Connecticut and Newport

1 to 3 days. Begin in New London, home of the U.S. Coast Guard Academy, and stop at Groton to tour the *Nautilus* at the Submarine Force Museum. In Mystic, the days of wooden ships and whaling adventures live on at Mystic Seaport. In Rhode

Island, savor the Victorian resort of Watch Hill and the Block Island Sound beaches. See the extravagant summer mansions in Newport. (⇨ *Chapter 6.*)

Massachusetts's South Shore and Cape Cod

2 to 4 days. New Bedford was once a major whaling center; exhibits at the New Bedford Whaling Museum capture this vanished world. Cape Cod can be nearly all things to all visitors, with quiet Colonial villages and lively resorts, gentle bayside wavelets, and crashing surf. In Plymouth, visit the *Mayflower II* and Plimoth Plantation, the re-created Pilgrim village. (⇨ *Chapters 2 and 3.*)

Boston and the North Shore

2 days. To savor Boston's centuries-old ties to the sea, take a half-day stroll by Faneuil Hall and Quincy Market or a boat tour of the harbor (you can even head out on a whale-watching tour from here). In Salem, the Peabody Essex Museum and the Salem Maritime National Historic Site chronicle the country's early shipping fortunes. Spend a day exploring more of the North Shore, including the old fishing port of Gloucester and Rockport, one possible place to buy that seascape painted in oils. Newburyport, with its Federal-style shipowners' homes, is home to the Parker River National Wildlife Refuge, beloved by birders and beach walkers. (⇨ *Chapter 2.*)

New Hampshire and Southern Maine

1 or 2 days. New Hampshire fronts the Atlantic for a scant 18 mi, but its coastal landmarks range from honky-tonk Hampton Beach to quiet Odiorne Point State Park in Rye and pretty Portsmouth, where the cream of pre-Revolutionary society built Georgian- and Federal-style mansions—visit a few at Strawbery Banke

Museum and elsewhere. Between here and Portland, Maine's largest city, lie oceanside resorts such as Kennebunkport. Near Portland is Cape Elizabeth, with its Portland Head and Two Lights lighthouses. (⇨ *Chapter 8 and Chapter 10.*)

Down East

2 or 3 days. Beyond Portland ranges the ragged, island-strewn coast of Down East Maine. Some highlights are the retail outlets of Freeport, home of L. L. Bean; Brunswick, with the museums of Bowdoin College; and Bath, with the Maine Maritime Museum. Perhaps you'll think about cruising on one of the majestic schooners that sail out of Rockland. In Camden and Castine, exquisite inns occupy homes built from inland Maine's gold, timber. On your second day, visit the spectacular rocky coast of Acadia National Park, near the resort town of Bar Harbor. (⇨ *Chapter 10.*)

A CELEBRATION

Picture this: one scarlet maple offset by the stark white spire of a country church, a whole hillside of brilliant foliage foregrounded by a vintage barn or perhaps a covered bridge that straddles a cobalt river. Such iconic scenes have launched a thousand postcards and turned New England into the ultimate fall destination for leaf peepers.

OF COLOR

By Susan
MacCallum-Whitcomb

Mother Nature, of course, puts on an annual autumn performance elsewhere, but this one is a showstopper. Like the landscape, the mix of deciduous (leaf-shedding) trees is remarkably varied here and creates a broader than usual palette. New England's abundant evergreens lend contrast, making the display even more vivid. Every September and October, leaf peepers arrive to cruise along country lanes, join outdoor adventures, or simply stroll on town greens.

Did you know the brilliant shades actually lurk in the leaves all year long? Leaves contain three pigments. The green chlorophyll, so dominant in summer that it obscures the red anthocyanins and orangey-yellow carotenoids, decreases in fall and reveals a crayon box of color.

Above, Vermont's Green Mountains are multicolored in the fall (and often white in winter).

PREDICTING THE PEAK

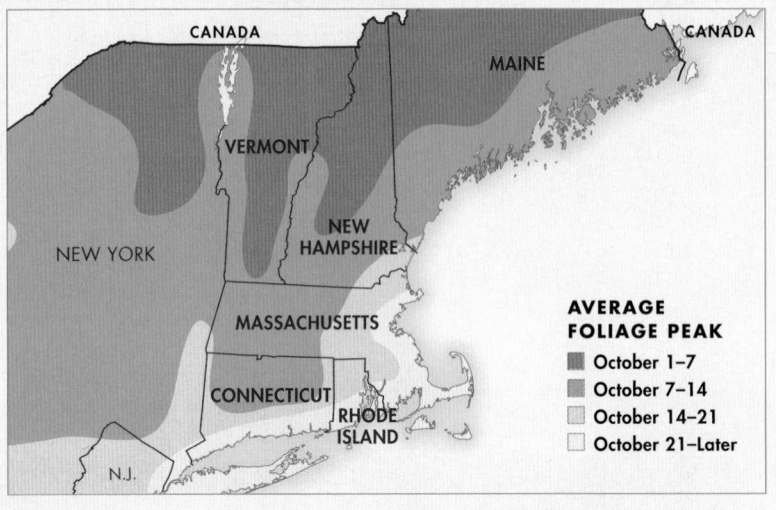

AVERAGE FOLIAGE PEAK
- October 1–7
- October 7–14
- October 14–21
- October 21–Later

LOCATION

Pinning down precisely when colors will appear remains an inexact science, although location plays a major role. Typically, the transformation begins in the highest and northernmost parts of New England in mid-September, then moves steadily into lower altitudes and southern sectors throughout October.

For trip planning, think in terms of regions rather than states. In Maine (a huge state that runs north–south) leaf color can peak anytime from the fourth week of September to the third week of October, depending on the locale.

WEATHER

Early September weather is another deciding factor. From the foliage aficionado's perspective, the ideal scenario is calm, temperate days capped by nights that are cool but still above freezing. If the weather is too warm, it delays the onset of the season. If it's too dry or windy, they shrivel up or blow off.

COLOR CHECK RESOURCES

Curious about current conditions? In season, each state maintains a dedicated Web site reporting on foliage conditions. Weather Channel has peak viewing maps and Foliage Network uses a network of spotters to chart changes.

- **Connecticut:** ☎ 800/282-6863 ⊕ www.ct.gov/dep
- **Foliage Network:** ⊕ www.foliagenetwork.com
- **Maine:** ☎ 888/624-6345 ⊕ www.mainefoliage.com
- **Massachusetts:** ☎ 800/632-8038 ⊕ www.massvacation.com
- **New Hampshire:** ☎ 800/258-3608 ⊕ www.visitnh.gov
- **Rhode Island:** ☎ 800/556-2484 ⊕ www.visitri.com
- **Vermont:** ☎ 800/837-6668 ⊕ www.foliage-vermont.com
- **Weather Channel:** ⊕ www.weather.com

TOP TREES FOR COLOR

A AMERICAN BEECH. This tree's smooth, steel-gray trunk is crowned with gold, copper, and bronze-tinted leaves in autumn, giving it a metallic sheen. Though the elliptical leaves sometimes hang on all winter, its "fruit" goes fast because beechnuts are a popular snack for birds, squirrels, and even bears.

B NORTHERN RED OAK. The upside of oaks is that they retain their fall shading until late in the season—the downside is that, for most species, that color is a boring brown. Happily, the northern red isn't like other members of the oak family. Its elongated, flame-shaped leaves turn fiery crimson and incandescent orange.

C QUAKING ASPEN. Eyes and ears both prove useful when identifying this aspen. Look for small, ovate leaves that usually become almost flaxen. Or listen for the leaves' quake: a sound, audible in even a gentle breeze, which the U.S. Forest Service likens to that made by "thousands of fluttering butterfly wings."

D SUGAR MAPLE. The leaf of the largest North American maple species is so lovely that Canada put it on its national flag. Each generally has five multipointed lobes—plus enough anthocyanin to produce a deep red color. The tree itself produces plentiful sap and is the cornerstone of New England's syrup industry.

E WHITE ASH. This tall tree typically grows to between 65 to 100 feet. Baseball enthusiasts admire the wood (which is used to craft bats); while foliage fans admire the compound leaves, each consisting of five to nine slightly serrated, tapering leaflets. They range in hue from burgundy and purple to amber.

F WHITE BIRCH. A papery, light, bright bark makes this slender hardwood easily recognizable. Centuries ago, Native Americans used birch wood to make everything from canoes to medicinal teas. Today's photographers know the bark also makes great pictures since it provides a sharp contrast to the tree's vibrant yellow leaves.

FANTASTIC FALL ITINERARY

The Berkshires

Fall is the perfect time to visit New England—country roads wind through dense forests exploding into reds, oranges, yellows, and purples. For inspiration, here is an itinerary for the truly ambitious that links the most stunning foliage areas; choose a section to explore more closely. Like autumn itself, this route works its way south from northern Vermont into Connecticut, with one or two days in each area.

VERMONT

NORTHWEST VERMONT

In Burlington, the elms will be turning colors on the University of Vermont campus. You can ride the ferry across Lake Champlain for great views of Vermont's Green Mountains and New York's Adirondacks. After visiting the resort town of Stowe, detour off Route 100 beneath the cliffs of Smugglers' Notch. The north country's palette unfolds in Newport, where the blue waters of Lake Memphremagog reflect the foliage. (⇨ *Northern Vermont in Chapter 7.*)

NORTHEAST KINGDOM

After a side trip along Lake Willoughby, explore St. Johnsbury, where the Fairbanks Museum and St. Johnsbury Athenaeum reveal Victorian tastes in art and natural-history collecting. In Peacham, stock up for a picnic at the Peacham Store. (⇨ *Northern Vermont in Chapter 7.*)

NEW HAMPSHIRE

WHITE MOUNTAINS AND LAKES REGION

In New Hampshire, Interstate 93 narrows as it winds through craggy Franconia Notch. Get off the interstate for the sinuous Kancamagus Highway portion of Route 112 that passes through the mountains to Conway. In Center Harbor, in the Lakes Region, you can ride the *MS Mount Washington* for views of the Lake Winnipesaukee shoreline, or ascend to Moultonborough's Castle in the Clouds for a falcon's-eye look at the colors. (⇨ *The White Mountains and Lakes Region in Chapter 8.*)

MT. MONADNOCK

In Concord, stop at the Museum of New Hampshire History and the State House. Several trails climb Mt. Monadnock, near Jaffrey Center, and colorful vistas extend as far as Boston. (⇨ *The Monadnocks and Merrimack Valley in Chapter 8.*)

⇨ For local drives perfect for an afternoon, also see our Fall Foliage Drive Spotlights in Chapters 4 (Western Massachusetts), 5 (Connecticut), 6 (Rhode Island), 7 (Vermont), 8 (New Hampshire), and 9 (Inland Maine).

THE MOOSE IS LOOSE!

Take "Moose Crossing" signs seriously because things won't end well if you hit an animal that stands six feet tall and weighs 1,200 pounds. Some 40,000 reside in northern New England. To search out these ungainly creatures in the wild, consider an orgaznized moose safari in northern New Hampshire or Maine.

MASSACHUSETTS

THE MOHAWK TRAIL

In Shelburne Falls, Massachusetts, the Bridge of Flowers displays the last of autumn's blossoms. Follow the Mohawk Trail section of Route 2 as it ascends into the Berkshire Hills—and stop to take in the view at the hairpin turn just east of North Adams (or drive up Mt. Greylock, the tallest peak in New England, for more stunning vistas). In Williamstown, the Sterling and Francine Clark Art Institute houses a collection of impressionist works. (⇨ *The Pioneer Valley and the Berkshires in Chapter 4.*)

THE BERKSHIRES

The scenery around Lenox, Stockbridge, and Great Barrington has long attracted the talented and the wealthy. Near U.S. 7, you can visit the homes of novelist Edith Wharton (the Mount, in Lenox), sculptor Daniel Chester French (Chesterwood, in Stockbridge), and diplomat Joseph Choate (Naumkeag, in Stockbridge). (⇨ *The Berkshires in Chapter 4.*)

CONNECTICUT

THE LITCHFIELD HILLS

This area of Connecticut combines the feel of upcountry New England with exclusive urban polish. The wooded shores of Lake Waramaug are home to country inns and wineries in pretty towns. Litchfield has a perfect village green—an idealized New England town center. (⇨ *The Litchfield Hills in Chapter 5.*)

(Map of New England showing Canada, Vermont, New Hampshire, Maine, New York, Massachusetts, Connecticut, and Rhode Island, with labeled locations including: Lake Memphremagog, Newport, 50/91, Lake Champlain, Smugglers' Notch, 100, 108, 5, St. Johnsbury, Lake Willoughby, MAINE, Burlington, 2, Stowe, Kancamagus Hwy., 112, 100, Peacham, 93, Franconia Notch, Conway, Green Mountains, White Mountain, 25, 16, Center Harbor, Moultonborough, 104, VERMONT, Lake Winnipesaukee, Connecticut River, 132, NEW YORK, 202, Concord, NEW HAMPSHIRE, Mt. Monadnock, Williamstown, Jaffrey Center, North Adams, Shelburne Falls, 2, 7, Lenox, Stockbridge, Mohawk Trail, Great Barrington, MASSACHUSETTS, CONNECTICUT, RHODE ISLAND, Litchfield Hills, 202, New Preston)

FOLIAGE PHOTO HINT

Don't just snap the big panoramic views. Look for single, brilliantly colored trees with interesting elements nearby, like a weathered gray stone wall or a freshly painted white church. These images are often more evocative than big blobs of color or panoramic shots.

LEAF PEEPER PLANNER

Hot-air balloons and ski-lift rides give a different perspective on fall's color.

Enjoying fall doesn't necessarily require a multistate road trip. If you are short on time (or energy), a simple autumnal stroll might be just the ticket: many state parks even offer free short ranger-led rambles.

HIKE AND BIKE ON A TOUR

You can sign on for foliage-focused hiking holidays with **Country Walkers** (☎ 800/464-9255 ⊕ www.countrywalkers.com) and **Boundless Journeys** (☎ 800/941-8010 ⊕ www.boundlessjourneys.com); or cycling ones with **Bike Vermont** (☎ 800/257-2226 ⊕ www.bikevt.com) and **VBT Bicycling Vacations** (☎ 800/245-3868, ⊕ www.vbt.com). Individual state tourism boards list similar operators elsewhere.

SOAR ABOVE THE CROWDS

New Hampshire's **Cannon Mountain** (☎ 603/823-8800 ⊕ www.cannonmt.com) is only one of several New England ski resorts that provides gondola or aerial tram rides during foliage season. Area hot-air balloon operators, like the **Balloon School of Massachusetts** (☎ 413/245-7013 ⊕ www.balloonschoolmassachusetts.com), help you take it in from the top.

ROOM AT THE INN?

Accommodations fill quickly in autumn. Vermont's top lodgings sell out months in advance for the first two weeks in October. So book early and expect a two-night minimum stay requirement. If you can't find a quaint inn, try basing yourself at a B&B or off-season ski resort. Also, be prepared for some sticker shock; if you can travel midweek, you'll often save quite a bit.

RIDE THE RAILS OR THE CURRENT

Board the **Essex Steam Train** for a ride through the Connecticut countryside (☎ 800/377-3987 ⊕ www.essexsteamtrain.com) or float through northern Rhode Island on the **Blackstone Valley Explorer** riverboat (☎ 401/724-2200 ⊕ www.rivertourblackstone.com).

Boston

WORD OF MOUTH

"For us, the Freedom Trail was a don't miss."

—volcanogirl

"You should definitely walk through the Boston Common and Public Garden—and make sure to check out the Make Way for Ducklings statue, which is near the corner of Beacon and Charles Streets."

—ats16

WELCOME TO BOSTON

TOP REASONS TO GO

★ **Freedom's Ring:** Walk through America's early history on the 2½-mi Freedom Trail that snakes through town.

★ **Ivy-Draped Campus:** Hang in Harvard Square like a collegiate or hit the university's museums: the Sackler (ancient art), the Botanical Museum, the Peabody (archeology), and the Natural History Museum.

★ **Posh Purchases:** Strap on some stilettos and join the quest for fashionable finds on Newbury Street, Boston's answer to Manhattan's 5th Avenue.

★ **Sacred Ground:** Root for (or boo) the Red Sox at baseball's most hallowed shrine, Fenway Park.

★ **Painted Glory:** Check out the beautiful Isabella Stewart Gardner Museum or stop by the Museum of Fine Arts, and view works by French masters Edouard Manet, Camille Passarro, and Pierre-Auguste Renoir, and American painters Mary Cassatt, John Singer Sargent, and Edward Hopper.

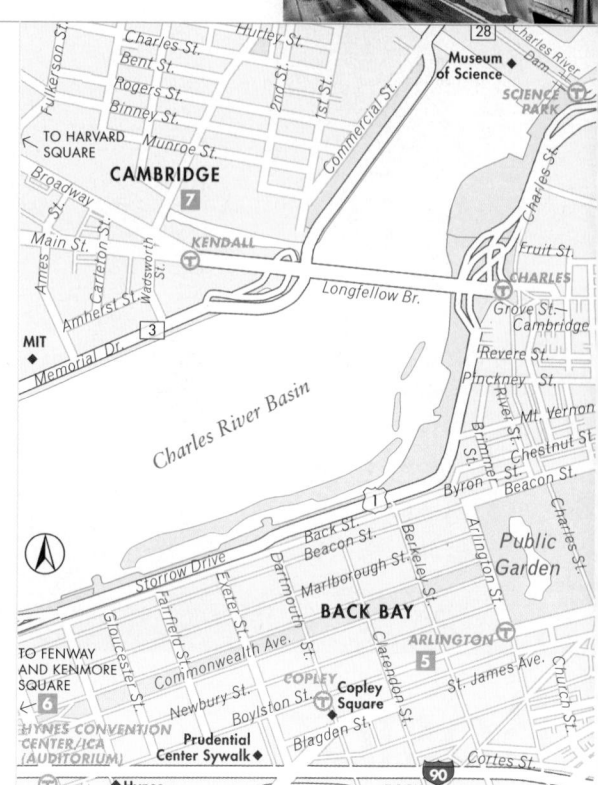

1 Beacon Hill, Boston Common, and the Old West End. The Brahmins' old stomping ground has many landmarks (Boston Common and the State House among them). The Old West End has the Museum of Science and TD Garden.

2 Government Center and the North End. The sterile Government Center area is home to lovely Faneuil Hall and the trio of restored buildings that share its name. The small North End is full of history and a strong Italian influence.

3 Charlestown. Charlestown's Freedom Trail sights can't be missed—literally. The Bunker Hill Monument is a towering tribute to a pivotal 1775 battle; the USS *Constitution*, a towering tangle of masts and rigging, highlights the neighborhood's naval heritage.

GETTING ORIENTED

With such a complex identity, it's no surprise that Boston, despite its relatively small size, offers visitors a diverse set of experiences. History buffs—and just about everyone else—will spend a day or more following the thick red line of the Freedom Trail and tracing Revolutionary history through town. Shopaholics can join the quest for fashionable finds on Newbury Street, while sports fiends gravitate toward Fenway Park for a tour (or if very lucky a game) of the beloved Boston Red Sox's home. The Museum of Fine Art's expansive catalog of French Impressionists and American painters, the Isabella Stewart Gardner Museum's palazzo of painting masters, and the Institute of Contemporary Art's modern works satisfy any artistic taste.

4 Downtown. This section of central Boston encompasses the Financial District and Downtown Crossing (a retail zone); as well as Chinatown, the Theater District, and portions of the Freedom Trail and HarborWalk.

5 The Back Bay. Back Bay's chichi shops, upscale restaurants, and deluxe lodgings sit alongside attractions like the Public Garden and Public Library.

6 The Fenway. Sox fans, art lovers, and college students all frequent the Fens. Fenway Park, the Museum of Fine Arts, the Isabella Stewart Gardner Museum are here.

7 Cambridge. A separate city across the Charles River, Cambridge has long been a haven for intellectuals. Along with Harvard and MIT, you'll find bookstores, cafés, and funky boutiques.

BOSTON PLANNER

Arriving By Air

Boston's major airport, Logan International (BOS), is across the harbor from Downtown, about 2 mi outside the city center, and can be reached by taxi, water taxi, or bus/subway via MBTA's Silver or Blue line). Logan has four passenger terminals, identified by letters A, B, C, and E. A free airport shuttle runs between the terminals and airport hotels. Some airlines use different terminals for international and domestic flights; most international flights arrive at Terminal E. A visitor center in Terminal C offers tourist information. T.F. Green Airport, in Providence, Rhode Island, and the Manchester Boston Regional Airport in Manchester, New Hampshire, are both about an hour from Boston.

Airport Information Logan International Airport (Boston) (⊠ I-90 east to Ted Williams Tunnel ☎ 800/235–6426 ⊕ www.massport.com/ logan Ⓣ Airport). **Manchester Boston Regional Airport** (⊠ Off I-293/Rte. 101, Exit 2, Manchester, NH ☎ 603/624–6556 ⊕ www.flymanchester. com). **T.F. Green Airport** (⊠ Off I-95, Exit 13, Providence, RI ☎ 888/268-7222 or 401/737-8222 ⊕ www. pvdairport.com).

Getting Around

"America's Walking City," with all its historic nooks and scenic crannies, is best explored on foot. But when hoofing it around town seems too arduous, there are alternatives.

Car Travel. In a place where roads often evolved from cow paths, driving is no simple task. A surfeit of one-way streets and inconsistent signage add to the confusion. Street parking is hard to come by as much of it is resident permit only. Your own car is helpful if you're taking side trips, but for exploring the city it will only be a burden. Also, Bostonians give terrible directions since few of them actually drive.

Cabs are available 24/7. Rides within the city cost $2.60 for the first 1/7 mi and 40¢ for each 1/7 mi thereafter (tolls, where applicable, are extra).

Public Transit. The "T," as the Massachusetts Bay Transportation Authority's subway system is nicknamed, is the cornerstone of an efficient, far-reaching public transit network that also includes aboveground trains, buses, and ferries. Its five color-coded lines will put you within a block of almost anywhere you want to go. Subways operate from about 5:30 AM to 12:30 PM, as do buses, which crisscross the city and reach into suburbia.

A standard adult subway fare is $1.70 with a Charlie-Card or $2 with a ticket or cash. For buses it's $1.25 with a CharlieCard or $1.50 with a ticket or cash (more if you are using an Inner or Outer Express bus). Commuter rail and ferry fares vary by route; yet all options charge seniors and students reduced prices, and kids under 12 ride free with a paying adult. Contact the MBTA (☎ 617/222-3200 or 800/392-6100 ⊕ www.mbta. com) for schedules, routes, and rates.

2

Visitor Information

Contact the city and state tourism offices for details about seasonal events, discount passes, trip planning, and attraction information. The National Park Service has a Boston office for Boston's historic sites that provides maps and directions. The Welcome Center and Boston Common Visitor Information Center offer general information. The Cambridge Tourism Office's information booth is in Harvard Square, near the main entrance to the Harvard T stop.

Contacts Boston Common Visitor Information Center (⊠ *148 Tremont St. where Freedom Trail begins, Downtown* ☎ *888/733–2678* ⊕ *www.thefreedomtrail.org*). **Boston National Historical Park Visitor Center** (⊠ *15 State St., Downtown* ☎ *617/242–5642* ⊕ *www.nps.gov/bost*). **Cambridge Tourism Office** (⊠ *4 Brattle St., Harvard Sq., Cambridge* ☎ *800/862–5678 or 617/441–2884* ⊕ *www.cambridge-usa.org*). **Greater Boston Convention and Visitors Bureau** (⊠ *2 Copley Pl., Suite 105, Back Bay* ☎ *888/733–2678 or 617/536–4100* ⊕ *www.bostonusa.com*). **Massachusetts Office of Travel and Tourism** (☎ *800/227–6277 or 617/973–8500* ⊕ *www.massvacation.com*).

Online Resources

Boston.com, home of the *Boston Globe* online, has news and feature articles, ample travel information, and links to towns throughout Massachusetts. The site for Boston's arts and entertainment weekly, the *Boston Phoenix* has nightlife, movie, restaurant, and arts listings. The Bostonian Society answers some frequently asked questions about Beantown history on their Web site. The iBoston page has wonderful photographs of architecturally and historically important buildings. *Bostonist, The Improper Bostonian,* and *Wicked-Local* provide a more relaxed (and irreverent) take on Boston news and information.

All About Boston Boston.com (⊕ *www.boston.com*). **Boston Phoenix** (⊕ *www.bostonphoenix.com*). **Bostonian Society** (⊕ *bostonhistory.org*). **Bostonist** (⊕ *www.bostonist.com*). **iBoston** (⊕ *www.iboston.org*). **The Improper Bostonian** (⊕ *www.improper.com*). **Wicked Local** (⊕ *www.wickedlocal.com*).

Safety Transportation Security Administration (*TSA* ⊕ *www.tsa.gov*).

When to Go

Summer brings reliable sunshine, sailboats to Boston Harbor, concerts to the Esplanade, and café tables to assorted sidewalks. If you're dreaming of a classic shore vacation, summer is prime.

Weather-wise, late spring and fall are the optimal times to visit Boston. Aside from mild temperatures, the former offers blooming gardens throughout the city and the latter sees the surrounding countryside ablaze with brilliantly colored foliage. At both times expect crowds.

Autumn attracts hordes of leaf-peepers, and more than 250,000 of students flood into the area each September; then pull out in May and June. Hotels and restaurants fill up quickly on move-in, move-out, and graduation weekends.

Winters are cold and windy.

Planning Your Time

If you have a couple of days, hit Boston's highlights—Beacon Hill, the Freedom Trail and the Public Garden—the first day, and then check out the Museum of Fine Arts or the Isabella Stewart Gardner Museum the morning of the second day. Reserve day two's afternoon for an excursion to Harvard or shopping on Newbury Street.

FENWAY PARK

For baseball fans of any age a trip to Fenway Park is a religious pilgrimage to see the home of former baseball greats such as Ted Williams and Carl Yastrzemski. The Boston Red Sox have played here since 1912. The oldest Major League ballpark is one of the last of its kind, a place where the scoreboard is hand operated and fans endure uncomfortable seats.

(above) Take yourself out to a ballgame at legendary Fenway Park. (lower right) Iconic sox mark the park walls. (upper right) Flags adorn the epicenter of Red Sox Nation.

For much of the ballpark's history Babe Ruth's specter loomed large. The team won five titles by 1918 but endured an 86-year title drought after trading away the Sultan of Swat. It wasn't enough to lose; the team vexed generations of loyal fans with colossal late-season collapses and post-season bungles. The Sox "reversed the curse" in 2004, defeating the rival Yanks in the American League Championship Series after being down 3–0 in the series (an unheard of comeback in baseball) and sweeping the St. Louis Cardinals in the World Series. The Red Sox won it all again in 2007, completely exorcising the curse.

FUN FACT

A lone red seat in the right-field bleachers marks the spot where Ted Williams's 502-foot shot—the longest measurable home run hit inside Fenway Park—landed on June 9, 1946.

THE SPORTS GUY

For an in-depth view of the psyche of a die-hard Red Sox fan read Bill Simmons' book *Now I Can Die in Peace.*

THE NATION

The Red Sox have the most rabid fans in baseball. Knowledge-able and dedicated, they follow the team with religiouslike intensity. Red Sox Nation has grown in recent years, much to the chagrin of "die-hards." You may hear the term "pink hat" used to derisively tag someone who is a bandwagon fan (i.e., anyone who didn't suffer with the rest of the Nation during the title drought).

THE MONSTER

Fenway's most dominant feature is the 37-foot-high "Green Monster," the wall the looms over left field. It's just over 300 feet from home plate and in the field of play, so deep fly balls that would have been outs in other parks sometimes become home runs. The Monster also stops line drives that would have been over the walls of other stadiums, but runners can often leg these hits out into doubles (since balls are difficult to field after they ricochet off the wall).

THE MUSIC

Fans sing "Take Me Out to the Ballgame" during the 7th-inning stretch in every ballpark … but at Fenway, they also sing Neil Diamond's "Sweet Caroline" in the middle of the 8th. If the Sox win, the Standell's "Dirty Water" blasts over the loudspeakers at the end of the game.

THE CURSE

In 1920 the Red Sox traded pitcher Babe Ruth to the Yankees, where he became a home-run-hitting baseball legend. Some fans—most famously *Boston Globe* columnist Dan Shaugh-nessy, who wrote a book called *The Curse of the Bambino*—blamed this move for the team's 86-year title drought, but others will claim that "The Curse" was just a media-driven storyline used to explain the team's past woes. Still fans who watched a ground ball roll between Bill Buckner's legs in the 1986 World Series or saw Aaron Boone's winning home run in the 2003 American League Division Series swear the curse was real.

VISIT THE NATION

Not lucky enough to nab tickets ahead of time? Try your luck at Gate E two hours before the game, when a handful of tickets are sold. There's a one-ticket limit, so everyone in your party must be in line. If that doesn't yield results, you can still experience the Nation. Head down to the park and hang out on Yawkey Way, which bor-ders the stadium. On game days it's closed to cars and filled with vendors, creating a street-fair atmo-sphere. Duck into a nearby sports bar and enjoy the game with other fans who weren't fortunate enough to secure seats. A favorite is the **Cask'n Flagon,** at Brookline Avenue and Lansdowne Street, across the street from Fenway. The closest you can get to Fenway without buying a ticket is the **Bleacher Bar** (✉ *82A Lansdowne St.*), which actually has a huge window in the center field wall overlooking the field. If you want to see a game from this unique vantage point, get here early— it starts filling up a few hours before game time.

Updated by Bethany Cassin Beckerlegge

There's history and culture around every bend in Boston—skyscrapers nestle next to historic hotels, while modern marketplaces line the antique cobblestone streets. But to Bostonians, living in a city that blends yesterday and today is just another day in their beloved Beantown.

It's difficult to fit Boston into a stereotype because of the city's many layers. The deepest is the historical one, the place where musket-bearing revolutionaries vowed to hang together or hang separately. The next tier, a dense spread of Brahmin fortune and fortitude, might be labeled the Hub. It was this elite caste of Boston society, descended from wealthy English Protestants who first settled the state, that funded and patronized the city's universities and cultural institutions, gaining Boston the label "the Athens of America" and felt only pride in the slogan "Banned in Boston." Over that layer lies Beantown, home to the Red Sox faithful and the raucous Bruins fans who crowded the old Boston "*Gah*-den"; this is the city whose ethnic loyalties account for its many distinct neighborhoods. Crowning these layers are the students who converge on the area's universities and colleges every fall.

EXPLORING BOSTON

BEACON HILL AND BOSTON COMMON

Past and present home of the old-money elite, contender for the "Most Beautiful" award among the city's neighborhoods, and hallowed address for many literary lights, Beacon Hill is Boston at its most Bostonian. The redbrick elegance of its narrow streets sends you back to the 19th century just as surely as if you had stumbled into a time machine. But Beacon Hill residents would never make the social faux pas of being out of date. The neighborhood is home to hip boutiques and trendy restaurants. Beacon Hill is bounded by Cambridge Street on the north, Beacon Street on the south, the Charles River Esplanade on the west, and Bowdoin Street on the east.

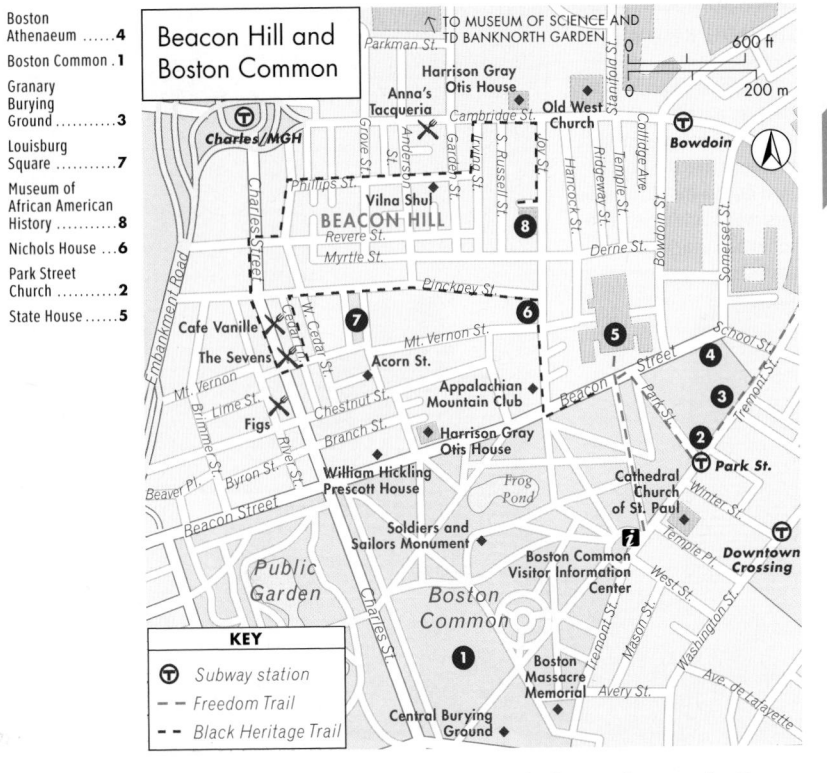

Numbers in the margin correspond with the numbers on the Beacon Hill and Boston Common map.

1 Boston Common. Nothing is more central to Boston than the Common, the oldest public park in the United States. Boston Common started as 50 acres where the freemen of Boston could graze their cattle. (Cows were banned in 1830.) Dating from 1634, it's as old as the city around it. The Common is home to such landmarks as the **Boston Massacre Memorial,** the **Frog Pond,** and the **Robert Gould Shaw 54th Regiment Memorial.** The **Central Burying Ground** (⊠ *Boylston St., near Tremont St., Beacon Hill* **T** *Park St.*) is the final resting place of Tories and Patriots alike, as well as many British casualties of the Battle of Bunker Hill. The Burying Ground is open daily 9–5. ⊠ *Bounded by Beacon, Charles, Tremont, and Park Sts., Beacon Hill* **T** *Park St.*

3 Granary Burying Ground. If you found a resting place here at the Old Granary, as it's called, chances are your headstone would have been elaborately ornamented with skeletons and winged skulls. Your neighbors would have been impressive, too: among them Samuel Adams, John Hancock, Paul Revere, and Benjamin Franklin's parents. ⊠ *Entrance on Tremont St., Beacon Hill* ☉ *Daily 9–5* **T** *Park St.*

7 Louisburg Square. One of Beacon Hill's most charming corners, Louisburg Square (proper Bostonians pronounce the "s") was an 1840s model for

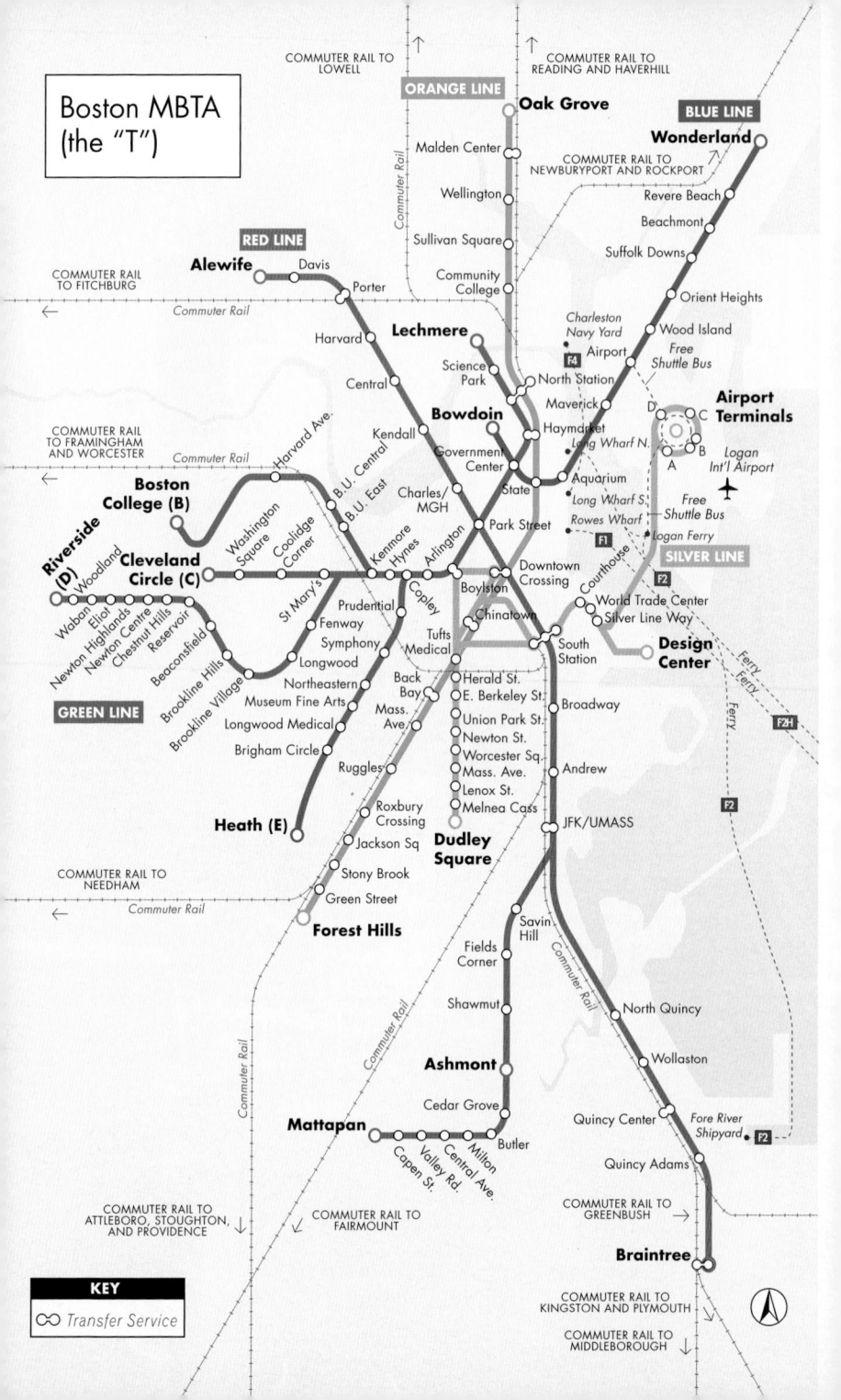

town-house development that was never repeated on the Hill because of space restrictions. Today, the grassy square, enclosed by a wrought-iron fence, belongs collectively to the owners of the houses facing it. The statue at the north end of the green is of Columbus, the one at the south end of Aristides the Just; both were donated in 1850 by a Greek merchant who lived on the square. The houses, most of which are now divided into apartments and condominiums, have seen their share of famous tenants, including author and critic William Dean Howells at Nos. 4 and 16, and the Alcotts at No. 10 (Louisa May not only lived but died here, on the day of her father's funeral). In 1852 the singer Jenny Lind was married in the parlor of No. 20. Louisburg Square is also the home of Massachusetts Senator John Kerry. ⊠ *Between Mt. Vernon and Pickney Sts., Beacon Hill* Ⓣ *Park St.*

> **DID YOU KNOW?**
>
> Beacon Hill's north slope played a key part in African American history. A community of free blacks lived here in the 1800s; many worshipped at the African Meeting House, established in 1805 and still standing. It came to be known as the "Black Faneuil Hall" for the fervent antislavery activism that started within its walls.

❽ **Museum of African American History.** Ever since runaway slave Crispus Attucks became one of the famous victims of the Boston Massacre of 1770, the African American community of Boston has played an important part in the city's history. Throughout the 19th century, abolition was the cause célèbre for Boston's intellectual elite, and during that time, blacks came to thrive in neighborhoods throughout the city. The Museum of African American History was established in 1964 to promote this history. The organization includes a trio of historic sites: the Abiel Smith School, the first public school in the nation built specifically for black children; the African Meeting House, where in 1832 the New England Anti-Slavery Society was formed under William Lloyd Garrison; and the African Meeting House on the island of Nantucket, off the coast of Cape Cod. Park Service personnel lead tours of the Black Heritage Trail, starting from the Shaw Memorial. The museum also has lectures, children's storytelling, and concerts focusing on black composers. ⊠ *46 Joy St., Beacon Hill* ☎ *617/725–0022* ⊕ *www.afroammuseum.org* ☞ *Free, $5 suggested donation* ⊙ *Mon.–Sat. 10–4* Ⓣ *Charles/MGH.*

Fodor's Choice
★

❹ **Boston Athenaeum.** The Athenaeum was founded in 1807 from the seeds sown by the Anthology Club (headed by Ralph Waldo Emerson's father) and moved to its present imposing quarters—modeled after Palladio's Palazzo da Porta Festa in Vicenza, Italy—in 1849. The first floor is open to the public and houses an art gallery with rotating exhibits, marble busts, porcelain vases, paintings, and books. Among the Athenaeum's holdings are most of George Washington's private library and the King's Chapel Library, sent from England by William III in 1698. An online catalog contains records for more than 600,000 volumes. Only 1,049 proprietary shares exist for membership in this cathedral of scholarship, and most have been passed down for generations; its holdings are available to qualified scholars, and yearly memberships are open to all by application. The Athenaeum extends into 14 Beacon Street. ⊠ *10½*

Beacon St., Beacon Hill ☎ *617/227–0270* ⊕ *www.bostonathenaeum. org* ⊠ *Free* ☉ *Mon. and Wed. 9–8, Tues., Thurs., and Fri. 9–5:30, Sat. 9–4 (excluding summer). Tours Tues. and Thurs. at 3* Ⓣ *Park St.*

❻ **Nichols House.** The only Mt. Vernon Street home open to the public, the Nichols House was built in 1804 and is attributed to Charles Bulfinch. It became the lifelong home of Rose Standish Nichols (1872–1960), Beacon Hill eccentric, philanthropist, peace advocate, and one of the first female landscape designers. Nichols made arrangements in her will for the house to become a museum, and knowledgeable volunteers from the neighborhood have been playing host since then. ⊠ *55 Mt. Vernon St., Beacon Hill* ☎ *617/227–6993* ⊕ *www.nicholshousemuseum.org* ⊠ *$7* ☉ *Apr.–Oct., Tues.–Sat. 11–4; Nov.–Mar., Thurs.–Sat. 11–4. First tour at 11, tours on ½ hr thereafter; last tour starts at 4* Ⓣ *Park St.*

❷ **Park Street Church.** On July 4, 1831, at the corner of Tremont and Park streets, Samuel Smith's hymn "America" was first sung inside this Congregationalist church, which was designed by Peter Banner and erected in 1809–10. The country's oldest musical organization, the Handel & Haydn Society, was founded here in 1815; in 1829 William Lloyd Garrison began his public campaign for the abolition of slavery here. The distinguished steeple is considered by many to be the most beautiful in New England. ⊠ *1 Park St., Beacon Hill* ☎ *617/523–3383* ⊕ *www. parkstreet.org* ☉ *Tours mid-June–Aug., Tues.–Fri. 9–4, Sat. 9–3. Sun. services at 8:30, 11, 4, and 6* Ⓣ *Park St.*

QUICK BITES

While window-shopping on Charles Street, stop in at the **Panificio Bakery** (⊠ **144 Charles St., Beacon Hill** ☎ **617/227–4340**), a cozy hangout and old-fashioned Italian café. Soups and pizzas are made on the premises; or you can satisfy your sweet tooth with a raspberry turnover and a cappuccino.

❺ **State House.** On July 4, 1795, the surviving fathers of the Revolution were on hand to enshrine the ideals of their new Commonwealth in a graceful seat of government designed by Charles Bulfinch. Governor Samuel Adams and Paul Revere laid the cornerstone; Revere would later roll the copper sheathing for the dome.

Bulfinch's neoclassical design is poised between Georgian and Federal; its finest features are the Corinthian columns of the portico, the graceful pediment and window arches, and the vast yet visually weightless golden dome (gilded in 1874 and again in 1997). During World War II the dome was painted gray so that it would not reflect moonlight during blackouts. It's capped with a pinecone, a symbol of the importance of pinewood, which was integral to the construction of Boston's early houses and churches—as well as the State House.

Inside are Doric Hall, with its statuary and portraits; the Hall of Flags, which displays the battle flags from the wars in which Massachusetts regiments have participated; the Great Hall, an open space used for state functions that houses 351 flags from the cities and towns of Massachusetts; the governor's office; and the chambers of the House and Senate. ⊠ *Beacon St. between Hancock and Bowdoin Sts., Beacon Hill* ☎ *617/727–3676* ⊕ *www.state.ma.us/sec/trs/trsidx.htm* ⊠ *Free* ☉ *Weekdays 9–5. Tours 10–4; call ahead to schedule* Ⓣ *Park St.*

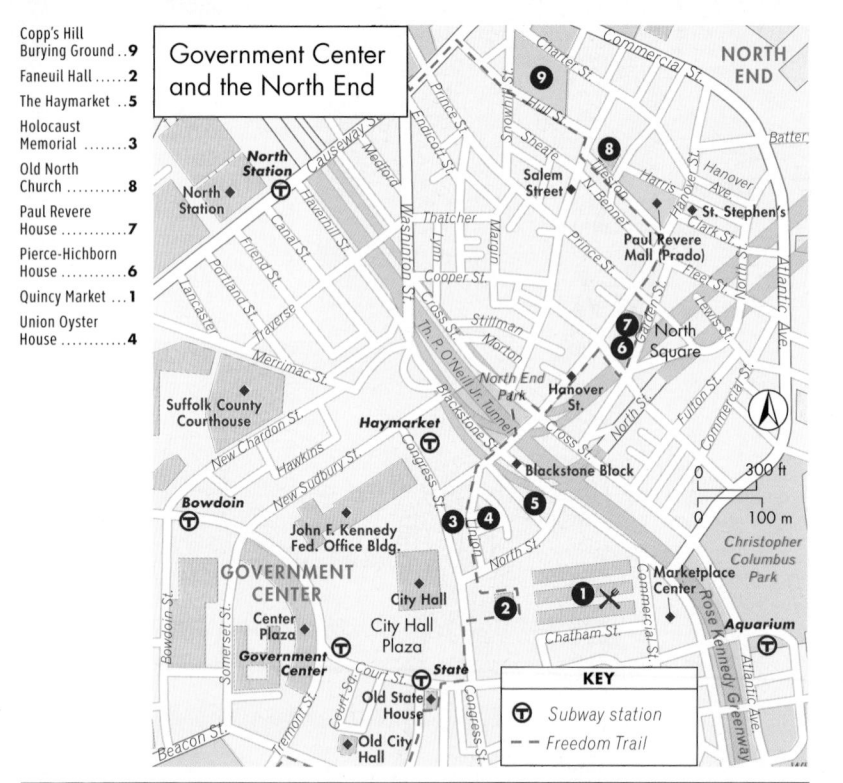

THE OLD WEST END

A few decades ago, this district—separated from Beacon Hill by Cambridge Street—resembled a typical medieval city: thoroughfares that twisted and turned, maddening one-way lanes, and streets that were a veritable hive of people. Today, little remains of the *old* Old West End except for a few brick tenements and a handful of monuments, including the first house built for Harrison Gray Otis. The biggest surviving structures with any real history are two public institutions, Massachusetts General Hospital and the former Suffolk County Jail, which dates from 1849. The onetime prison is now part of the luxurious, and wryly named, Liberty Hotel. Here you'll also find TD Banknorth Garden, the home away from home for loyal Bruins and Celtics fans. In addition, the innovative Museum of Science is one of the neighborhood's more modern attractions. The newest addition to the skyline here is the Leonard P. Zakim Bunker Hill Bridge, which spans the Charles River just across from the TD Banknorth Garden.

Museum of Science. With 15-foot lightning bolts in the Theater of Electricity and a 20-foot-long *Tyrannosaurus rex* model, this is the place to ignite a child's scientific curiosity. More than 550 displays cover astronomy, astrophysics, anthropology, progress in medicine, computers, the organic and inorganic earth sciences, and more. The museum houses

Fodor'sChoice
★

the **Charles Hayden Planetarium** (☎ 617/723–2500), which produces exciting programs on astronomical discoveries, and the **Mugar Omni Theater** (☎ 617/723–2500), a five-story dome screen. ✉ *Science Park at the Charles River Dam, Old West End* ☎ *617/723–2500* ⊕ *www.mos. org* ✍ *$19* ☉ *July 5–Labor Day, Sat.–Thurs. 9–7, Fri. 9–9; after Labor Day–July 4, Sat.–Thurs. 9–5, Fri. 9–9* Ⓣ *Science Park.*

↻ **TD Garden.** Diehards still moan about the loss of the old Boston Garden, where the legendary Bill Russell, Larry Bird, and Bobby Orr played, a much more intimate venue than this mammoth facility, which opened in 1995. But now the home of the Celtics (basketball) and Bruins (hockey) is once again known as the good old "Gah-den." The new Garden, with its air-conditioning, comfier seats, improved food, a 1,200-vehicle parking garage, and nearly double the number of bathrooms, has won grudging acceptance. The fifth and sixth levels of the TD Garden house the **Sports Museum of New England** (✉ *Use west premium seating entrance* ☎ *617/624–1234* ⊕ *www.sportsmuseum.org*), where displays of memorabilia and photographs showcase local sports history and legends. Take a tour of locker and interview rooms (off-season only), and test your sports knowledge with interactive games. The museum is open daily 11–5, with admission allowed only on the hour. Last entrance is at 3 PM on most days, 2 PM on game days; admission is $6. ✉ *Causeway St. at Canal St., Old West End* ☎ *617/624–1000* ⊕ *www. tdbanknorthgarden.com* Ⓣ *North Station.*

GOVERNMENT CENTER

This is a section of town Bostonians love to hate. Not only does Government Center house what they can't fight—City Hall—but it also contains some of the bleakest architecture since the advent of poured concrete. But though the stark, treeless plain surrounding City Hall has been roundly jeered, the expanse is enlivened by feisty political rallies, free summer concerts, and the occasional festival.

Numbers in the margin correspond to numbers on the Government Center and North End map.

②
★ **Faneuil Hall.** The single building facing Congress Street is the real Faneuil Hall, though locals often give that name to all five buildings in this shopping complex. Bostonians pronounce it *Fan*-yoo'uhl or *Fan*-yuhl. Like other Boston landmarks, Faneuil Hall has evolved over many years. It was erected in 1742, the gift of wealthy merchant Peter Faneuil, who wanted the hall to serve as a place for town meetings and a public market. It burned in 1761 and was immediately reconstructed according to the original plan of its designer, the Scottish portrait painter John Smibert (who lies in the Granary Burying Ground). In 1763 the political leader James Otis dedicated the rebuilt hall to the cause of liberty.

In 1772 Samuel Adams stood here and first suggested that Massachusetts and the other colonies organize a Committee of Correspondence to maintain semiclandestine lines of communication in the face of hardening British repression. In later years the hall again lived up to Otis's dedication when the abolitionists Wendell Phillips and Charles Sumner pleaded for support from its podium. The tradition continues to this day: in presidential-election years the hall is the site of debates between contenders in the Massachusetts primary.

Inside Faneuil Hall are dozens of paintings of famous Americans, including the mural *Webster's Reply to Hayne,* Gilbert Stuart's portrait of Washington at Dorchester Heights. Park rangers give informational talks about the history and importance of Faneuil Hall on the hour and half-hour. The rangers are a good resource, as interpretive plaques are few. ⊠ *Faneuil Hall Sq., Government Center* ☎ *617/ 523–1300* ⊕ *www.cityofboston. gov/freedomtrail/faneuilhall.asp* ⊡ *Free* ☉ *Great Hall daily 9–5; informational talks every ½ hr. Shops Mon.–Sat. 10* AM*–9* PM*, Sun. noon–6* PM Ⓣ *Government Center, Aquarium, State.*

> ### THE STORY BEHIND THE GRASSHOPPER
>
> Why is the gold-plated weather vane atop Faneuil Hall's cupola in the shape of a grasshopper? One apocryphal story has it that Sir Thomas Gresham—founder of London's Royal Exchange—was discovered in a field in 1519 as a babe by children chasing grasshoppers. He later placed a gilded metal version of the insect over the Exchange to commemorate his salvation. Years later Peter Faneuil admired the critter (a symbol of good luck) and had a model of it mounted over Faneuil Hall. The 8-pound, 52-inch-long grasshopper is the only unmodified part of the original structure.

❸ **Holocaust Memorial.** At night its six 50-foot-high glass-and-steel towers

Fodor'sChoice glow like ghosts. During the day the monument seems at odds with the

★ 18th-century streetscape of Blackstone Square behind it. Shoehorned into the north end of Union Park, the Holocaust Memorial is the work of Stanley Saitowitz. Recollections by Holocaust survivors are set into the glass-and-granite walls; the upper levels of the towers are etched with 6 million numbers in random sequence, symbolizing the Jewish victims of the Nazi horror. Manufactured steam from grates in the granite base makes for a particularly haunting scene after dark. ⊠ *Union St. near Hanover St., Government Center.*

❶ **Quincy Market.** Not everyone likes Quincy Market, also known as Faneuil Hall Marketplace; some people prefer grit to polish, and disdain the shiny cafés and boutiques. But there's no denying that it has brought tremendous vitality to a once-tired corner of Boston.

The market consists of three block-long annexes: **Quincy Market, North Market,** and **South Market,** each 535 feet long and across a plaza from Faneuil Hall. The structures were designed in 1826 by Alexander Parris as part of a public-works project instituted by Boston's second mayor, Josiah Quincy, to alleviate the cramped conditions of Faneuil Hall and clean up the refuse that collected in Town Dock, the pond behind it. The central structure, made of granite, with a Doric colonnade at either end and topped by a classical dome and rotunda, has kept its traditional market-stall layout, but the stalls now purvey international and specialty foods: sushi, frozen yogurt, bagels, calzones, sausage-on-a-stick, Chinese noodles, barbecue, and baklava, plus all the boutique chocolate-chip cookies your heart desires. This is perhaps Boston's best locale for grazing.

NEW ENGLAND AQUARIUM

✉ *Central Wharf between Central and Milk Sts., Downtown* ☎ *617/973–5200* ⊕ *www.neaq.org* 🗐 *$20.95, IMAX $9.95, entrance plus IMAX $26.95* ⊙ *July–early Sept., Sun.–Thurs. 9–6, Fri. and Sat. 9–7; early Sept.–June, weekdays 9–5, weekends 9–6* Ⓣ *Aquarium, State.*

TIPS

■ If you plan to see an IMAX show as well as check out the aquarium, buy a combo ticket; you'll save $3.95 for the adult ticket.

■ Also, buy the combo ticket if you'd like to do the whale watch and the aquarium; you'll save $7.95 over purchasing them separately.

■ Save yourself the torture of waiting in long weekend lines, and purchase your tickets ahead of time online at www.neaq.org. You can skip ahead of the crowd and pick up your tickets at the will call window, or print them out at home.

■ Want to make your day at the aquarium really special for the kids? Call ahead to for a reservation to play with the seals! For $45, kids 9 and up can go behind the scenes and help feed and entertain the seals. Call Central Reservations at 617/973–5206 for more information.

This aquarium challenges you to imagine life under and around the sea. Seals bark outside the West Wing, its glass-and-steel exterior constructed to mimic fish scales. Inside the main facility you can see penguins, sea otters, sharks, and other exotic sea creatures—more than 2,000 species in all.

HIGHLIGHTS

In the semi-enclosed outdoor space of the **New Balance Foundation Marine Mammal Center** visitors enjoy the antics of northern fur seals while gazing at a stunning view of Boston Harbor.

One of the aquarium's exhibits, **"Amazing Jellies,"** features thousands of jellyfish, many of which were grown in the museum's labs.

Some of the aquarium's 2,000 sea creatures make their home in the aquarium's four-story, 200,000-gallon **ocean-reef tank,** one of the largest of its kind in the world. Ramps winding around the tank lead to the top level and allow you to view the inhabitants from many vantage points. Don't miss the five-times-a-day feedings; each lasts nearly an hour and takes divers 24 feet into the tank.

From outside the glassed-off **Aquarium Medical Center** you can watch veterinarians treat sick animals—here's where you can see an eel in a "hospital bed." At the **"Edge of the Sea"** exhibit children can pick up starfish and other creatures, while **"The Curious George Discovery Corner"** is a fun spot for younger kids. Whale-watch cruises leave from the aquarium's dock from April to October, and cost $35.95. Across the plaza is the aquarium's **Education Center;** it, too, has changing exhibits. The 6½-story-high **IMAX** theater takes you on virtual journeys from the bottom of the sea to the depths of outer space with its 3-D films.

Along the arcades on either side of the Central Market are vendors selling sweatshirts, photographs of Boston, and arts and crafts—some schlocky, some not—along with a couple of patioed bars and restaurants. The North and South markets house a mixture of chain stores and specialty boutiques. Quintessential Boston remains here only in Durgin Park, opened in 1826 and known for its plain interior, brassy waitresses, and large portions of traditional New England fare.

At Christmastime trees along the cobblestone walks are strung sparkling lights. In summer up to 50,000 people a day come to the market; the outdoor cafés are an excellent spot to watch the hordes. The walkways draw street performers, and crowds ring around magicians and musicians. ☒ *Bordered by Clinton, Commercial, and Chatham Sts., Government Center* ☎ *617/523–1300* ⊕ *www.faneuilhallmarketplace. com* ☉ *Mon.–Sat. 10–9, Sun. noon–6. Restaurants and bars generally open daily 11* AM*–2* AM; *food stalls open earlier* Ⓣ *Government Center, Aquarium, State.*

❹ **Union Oyster House.** Billed as the oldest restaurant in continuous service in the United States, the Union Oyster House first opened its doors as the Atwood & Bacon Oyster House in 1826. With its scallop, clam, and lobster dishes—as well as the de rigueur oyster—the menu hasn't changed much since ye olde days. ☒ *41 Union St., Government Center* ☎ *617/227–2750* ⊕ *www.unionoysterhouse.com* ☉ *Sun.–Thurs. 11–9:30, Fri. and Sat. 11–10; bar open until midnight* Ⓣ *Haymarket.*

❺ **The Haymarket.** Loud, self-promoting vendors pack this exuberant maze of a marketplace at Marshall and Blackstone streets on Friday and Saturday from 7 AM until mid-afternoon (all vendors will likely be gone by 5). Pushcart vendors hawk fruits and vegetables against a backdrop of fish, meat, and cheese shops. The accumulation of debris left every evening has been celebrated in a whimsical 1976 public-arts project—Mags Harries's *Asaroton,* a Greek word meaning "unswept floors"—consisting of bronze fruit peels and other detritus smashed into pavement. At Creek Square, near the Haymarket, is the **Boston Stone.** Set into the brick wall of the gift shop of the same name, this was a marker long used as milepost zero in measuring distances from Boston. ☒ *Marshall and Blackstone Sts., Government Center* Ⓣ *Government Center* ☉ *Fri. and Sat. 7* AM*–mid-afternoon.*

THE NORTH END

The warren of small streets on the northeast side of Government Center is the North End, Boston's Little Italy. In the 17th century the North End *was* Boston, as much of the rest of the peninsula was still under water or had yet to be cleared. Here the town grew rich for a century and a half before the birth of American independence. The quarter's dwindling ethnic character lingers along Salem or Hanover Street where you can still hear people speaking with Abruzzese accents.

Numbers in the margin correspond with numbers on the Government Center and the North End map.

❾ Copp's Hill Burying Ground. An ancient and melancholy air hovers like a fine mist over this colonial-era burial ground. The North End graveyard incorporates four cemeteries established between 1660 and 1819. Near the Charter Street gate is the tomb of the Mather family, the dynasty of church divines (Cotton and Increase were the most famous sons) who held sway in Boston during the heyday of the old theocracy. Also buried here is Robert Newman, who crept into the steeple of the Old North Church to hang the lanterns warning of the British attack the night of Paul Revere's ride. Look for the tombstone of Captain Daniel Malcolm; it's pockmarked with musket-ball fire from British soldiers, who used the stones for target practice. Across the street at 44 Hull is the **narrowest house in Boston**—it's a mere 10 feet across. ⊠ *Intersection of Hull and Snowhill Sts., North End* ⊗ *Daily 9–5* Ⓣ *North Station.*

Hanover Street. This is the North End's main thoroughfare, along with the smaller and narrower Salem Street. Hanover's business center is thick with restaurants, pastry shops, and Italian cafés; on weekends Italian immigrants who have moved to the suburbs return to share an espresso with old friends and maybe catch a soccer game on TV.

❽ Old North Church. Standing at one end of the **Paul Revere Mall** is a church famous not only for being the oldest one in Boston (built in 1723) but for housing the two lanterns that glimmered from its steeple on the night of April 18, 1775. This is Christ, or Old North, Church, where Paul Revere and the young sexton Robert Newman managed to signal the departure by water of the British regulars to Lexington and Concord. Try to visit when changes are rung on the bells, after the 11 AM Sunday service. On the Sunday closest to April 18, descendants of the patriots reenact the raising of the lanterns in the church belfry during a special evening service. ⊠ *193 Salem St., North End* 🖀 *617/523–6676* ⊕ *www. oldnorth.com* ⊗ *Jan. and Feb., Tues.–Sun. 10–4; Mar.–May, daily 9–5; June–Oct., daily 9–6; Nov. and Dec., daily 10–5. Sun. services at 9 and 11 AM* Ⓣ *Haymarket, North Station.*

❼ Paul Revere House. It's an interesting coincidence that the oldest house standing in downtown Boston was also once the home of Paul Revere, patriot activist and silversmith, as many homes of famous Bostonians have burned or been demolished over the years. The Revere house could easily have become one of them back when it was just another makeshift tenement in the heyday of European immigration. It was saved from oblivion in 1902 and restored to an approximation of its original 17th-century appearance. Revere owned it from 1770 until 1800, although he lived there for only 10 years and rented it out for the next two decades. Pre-1900 photographs show it as a shabby warren of storefronts and apartments. The clapboard sheathing is a replacement, but 90% of the framework is original; note the Elizabethan-style overhang and leaded windowpanes. A few Revere furnishings are on display here, including his silverwork—much more of which is displayed at the Museum of Fine Arts. ⊠ *19 North Sq., North End* 🖀 *617/523–2338* ⊕ *www. paulreverehouse.org* 🖅 *$3.50, $5.50 with Pierce-Hichborn House* ⊗ *Jan.–Mar., Tues.–Sun. 9:30–4:15; Nov. and Dec. and 1st 2 wks of Apr., daily 9:30–4:15; mid-Apr.–Oct., daily 9:30–5:15* Ⓣ *Haymarket, Aquarium, Government Center.*

Fodor's Choice
★

6 Pierce-Hichborn House. One of the city's oldest brick buildings, this structure, just to the left of the Paul Revere House, was once owned by Nathaniel Hichborn, a boatbuilder and Revere's cousin. Built circa 1711 for a window maker named Moses Pierce, the Pierce-Hichborn House is an excellent example of early Georgian architecture. The home's symmetrical style was a radical change from the wood-frame Tudor buildings, such as the Revere House, then common. Its four rooms providing a peek into typical middle-class life with with modest 18th-century furnishings.

> ### A STICKY SUBJECT
>
> Boston has had its share of grim historic events, from massacres to stranglers, but on the sheer weirdness scale, nothing beats the Great Molasses Flood. In 1919 a steel container of molasses exploded on the Boston Harbor waterfront, killing 21 people and 20 horses. More than 2.3 million gallons of goo oozed onto unsuspecting citizenry. Some say you can still smell molasses on the waterfront during steamy weather.

✉ *29 North Sq., North End* ☎ *617/523–2338* 💲 *$2, $5.50 with Paul Revere House* ☼ *Guided tours only; call to schedule* Ⓣ *Haymarket, Aquarium, Government Center.*

CHARLESTOWN

Boston started here. Charlestown was a thriving settlement a year before colonials headed across the Charles River at William Blaxton's invitation to found the city proper. Today the district's attractions include two of the most visible—and vertical—monuments in Boston: the Bunker Hill Monument, which commemorates the grisly battle that became a symbol of patriotic resistance against the British, and the USS *Constitution,* whose masts continue to tower over the waterfront where she was built more than 200 years ago.

Fodor'sChoice
★
Bunker Hill Monument. Three misunderstandings surround this famous monument. First, the Battle of Bunker Hill was actually fought on Breed's Hill, which is where the monument sits today. (The real Bunker Hill is about ½ mi to the north of the monument.) Bunker was the original planned locale for the battle, and for that reason its name stuck. Second, although the battle is generally considered a colonial success, the Americans lost. It was a Pyrrhic victory for the British Redcoats, who sacrificed nearly half of their 2,200 men; American casualties numbered 400–600. And third: the famous war cry "Don't fire until you see the whites of their eyes" may never have been uttered by American Colonel William Prescott or General Israel Putnam, but if either one did shout it, he was quoting an old Prussian command made necessary by the notorious inaccuracy of the musket. No matter. The Americans did employ a deadly delayed-action strategy on June 17, 1775, and conclusively proved themselves worthy fighters.

In 1823 the committee formed to construct a monument on the site of the battle chose the form of an Egyptian obelisk. Architect Solomon Willard designed a 221-foot-tall granite obelisk, a tremendous feat of engineering for its day. The Marquis de Lafayette laid the cornerstone of

BOSTON FOR KIDS

■ **Children's Museum.** Founded in 1913, this was among the first children's museums to focus on hands-on learning. Kids take the lead here, where learning about science and cultural diversity is one big game in which exhibits come out of their cases and into the hands of young ones. (⇨ *Downtown.*)

■ **Museum of Science.** Your youngsters can be shocked in the Theater of Electricity (housed in a two-story, 2.5 million–volt Van de Graaf generator), step back in time with a life-size Tyrannosaurus rex, and learn Newton's laws of physics while playing on a seesaw. Other attractions include a 3-D and Omni cinema (the latter with a five-story screen), planetarium and laser shows, and live presentations that might feature animals, optical illusions, or lightning. (⇨ *Old West End.*)

■ **New England Aquarium.** The little ones will find discover all kinds of sea life, sea lion shows, and a 24-foot deep, 200,000-gallon ocean reef tank filled with sharks, sea turtles, and the scary moray eel. The see-through tank permits a view not unlike that enjoyed by divers. An activity center provides a quieter place for storytelling, puppet shows, and hands-on projects. (⇨ *Downtown.*)

the monument in 1825, but because of a nagging lack of funds, it wasn't dedicated until 1843. The monument's zenith is reached by a flight of 294 steps. There's no elevator, but the views from the observatory are worth the the arduous climb. A statue of Colonel Prescott stands guard at the base. In the Bunker Hill Museum across the street, artifacts and exhibits tell the story of the battle, while a detailed diorama shows the action in miniature. ☎ *617/242–5641* ⊕ *www.nps.gov/bost/ historyculture/bhm.htm* ✉ *Free* ☉ *Museum daily 9–5, monument daily 9–4:30* Ⓣ *Community College.*

Ⓒ **USS Constitution.** Better known as "Old Ironsides," the USS *Constitution* rides proudly at anchor in her berth at the Charlestown Navy Yard. The oldest commissioned ship in the U.S. fleet is a battlewagon of the old school, of the days of "wooden ships and iron men"—when she and her crew of 200 succeeded at the perilous task of asserting the sovereignty of an improbable new nation. Every July 4 and on certain other occasions she's towed out for a turnabout in Boston Harbor, the very place her keel was laid in 1797.

Fodor's Choice
★

The nickname "Old Ironsides" was acquired during the War of 1812, when shots from the British warship *Guerrière* appeared to bounce off her hull. Talk of scrapping the ship began as early as 1830, but she was saved by a public campaign sparked by Oliver Wendell Holmes's poem "Old Ironsides." After a major restoration in the 1990s, only about 8%–10% of her original wood remains in place, including the keel. ✉ *Charlestown Navy Yard, 55 Constitution Rd., Charlestown* ☎ *617/242–7511* ⊕ *www.history.navy.mil/USSconstitution/index.html* ✉ *Free* ☉ *Apr. 1–Oct., Tues.–Sun. 10–6; Nov.–Mar. 31, Thurs.–Sun. 10–4; last tour at 3:30* Ⓣ *North Station.*

Continued on page 73

FOLLOW THE REDBRICK ROAD

BOSTON'S FREEDOM TRAIL

by Mike Nalepa

Paul Revere

Paul Revere's ride

Benjamin Franklin

Samuel Adams

John Hancock

The Freedom Trail is more than a collection of historic sites related to the American Revolution or a suggested itinerary connecting Boston's unique neighborhoods. It's a chance to walk in the footsteps of our forefathers—literally, by following a crimson path on public sidewalks—and pay tribute to the figures all school kids know, like Paul Revere, John Hancock, and Ben Franklin. In history-proud Boston, past and present intersect before your eyes not as a re-creation but as living history accessible to all.

Boston played a key role in the dramatic events leading up to the American Revolution. Many of the founding fathers called the city home, and many of the initial meetings and actions that sparked the fight against the British took place here. In one day, you can visit Faneuil Hall—the "Cradle of Liberty"—where outraged colonial radicals met to oppose British authority; the site of the incendiary Boston Massacre; and the Old North Church, where lanterns hung to signal Paul Revere on his thrilling midnight ride. Colonists may have originally landed in Jamestown and Plymouth, but if you really want to see where America began, come to Boston.

Boston Common, Founder's Statue

⊕ www.nps.gov/bost
⊕ www.thefreedomtrail.org

☎ 617/242–5642

📷 Admission to the Freedom Trail itself is free. Several museum sites charge for admission. However, most attractions are free monuments, parks, and landmarks.

The 1729 Old South Meeting House, where many protesters gathered during the American Revolution.

PLANNING YOUR TRAIL TRIP

THE ROUTE

The 2½-mi Freedom Trail begins at Boston Common, winds through Downtown, Government Center, and the North End, and ends in Charlestown at the USS *Constitution*. The entire Freedom Trail is marked by a red line on the sidewalk; it's made of paint or brick at various points on the Trail. *For more information on Freedom Trail sites, see listings in Exploring.*

GETTING HERE AND BACK

The route starts near the Park Street T stop. When you've completed the Freedom Trail, head for the nearby Charlestown water shuttle, which goes directly to the downtown area. For schedules and maps, visit ⊕ *www.mbta.com.*

TIMING

If you're stopping at a few (or all) of the 16 sites, it takes a full day to complete the route comfortably. ■ TIP→ If you have children in tow, you may want to split the trail into two or more days.

VISITOR CENTERS

There are Freedom Trail information centers in Boston Common (Tremont Street), at 15 State Street (near the Old State House), and at the Charlestown Navy Yard Visitor Center (in Building 5).

TOURS

The National Park Service's free 90-minute Freedom Trail walking tours begin at the Boston National Historical Park Visitor Center at 15 State Street and cover sites from the Old South Meeting House to the Old North Church. Check online for times; it's a good idea to show up at least 30 minutes early, as the popular tours are limited to 30 people.

Half-hour tours of the USS *Constitution* are offered Tuesday through Sunday. Note that visitors to the ship must go through security screening.

FUEL UP

The trail winds through the heart of Downtown Boston, so finding a quick bite or a nice sit-down meal isn't difficult. Quincy Market, near Faneuil Hall, is packed with cafés and eateries. Another good lunch choice is one of the North End's wonderful Italian restaurants.

WHAT'S NEARBY

For a short break from revolutionary history, be sure to check out the major attractions nearby, including the Boston Public Garden, New England Aquarium, and Union Oyster House.

Above: In front of the Old State House a cobblestone circle marks the site of the Boston Massacre.

TOP SIGHTS

Benjamin Franklin Statue

Boston Common

The Granary Burial Grounds

Faneuil Hall

Park Street Church

Old North Church

Bunker Hill Monument

2

IN FOCUS FOLLOW THE REDBRICK ROAD: BOSTON'S FREEDOM TRAIL

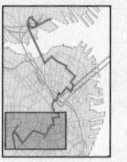

BOSTON COMMON TO FANEUIL HALL

Old State House

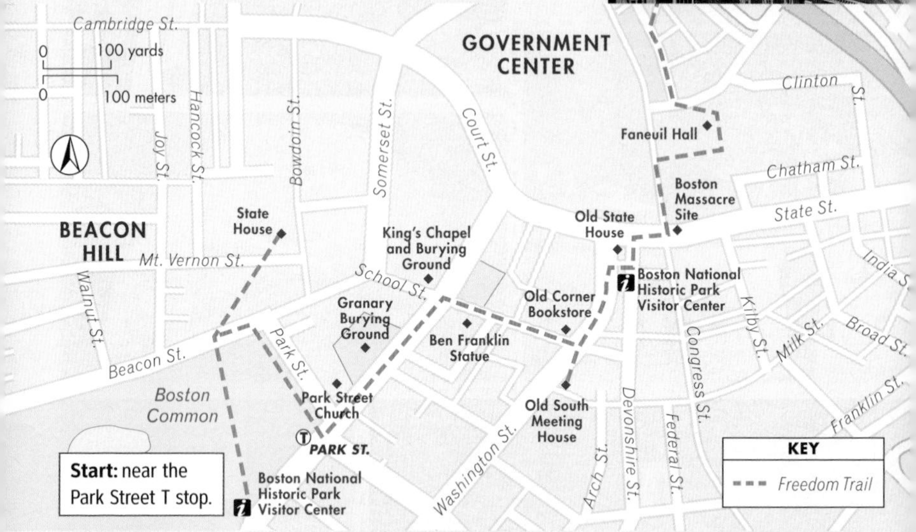

[MAP]

Cambridge St.

0 — 100 yards
0 — 100 meters

Hancock St.
Joy St.
Bowdoin St.
Somerset St.
Court St.

GOVERNMENT CENTER

Clinton St.

Faneuil Hall ■

Boston Massacre Site

Chatham St.

State St.

BEACON HILL
Mt. Vernon St.

State House ■

King's Chapel and Burying Ground

Old State House ■

Boston National Historic Park Visitor Center 🛈

India St.

Kilby St.

Broad St.

Walnut St.

School St.

Old Corner Bookstore

Granary Burying Ground

Ben Franklin Statue

Congress St.

Franklin St.

Milk St.

Beacon St.

Park St.

Park Street Church

Ⓣ **PARK ST.**

Old South Meeting House

Devonshire St.

Federal St.

Arch St.

Boston Common

Washington St.

Start: near the Park Street T stop.

Boston National Historic Park Visitor Center 🛈

KEY
--- *Freedom Trail*

Many of the Freedom Trail sites between Boston Common and the North End are close together. Walking this 1-mile segment of the trail makes for a pleasant morning.

THE ROUTE

Begin at ★ **Boston Common**, then head for the **State House**, Boston's finest example of Federal architecture. Several blocks away is the **Park Street Church**, whose 217-foot steeple is considered to be the most beautiful in New England. The church was actually founded in 1809, and it played a key role in the movement to abolish slavery.

Reposing in the church's shadows is the ★ **Granary Burying Ground**, final resting place of Samuel Adams, John Hancock, and Paul Revere. A short stroll to Downtown brings you to **King's Chapel**, founded in 1686 by King James II for the Church of England.

Follow the trail past the **Benjamin Franklin statue** to the **Old Corner Bookstore** site, where Hawthorne, Emerson, and Longfellow were published. Nearby is the **Old South Meeting House**, where arguments in 1773 led to the Boston Tea Party. Overlooking the site of the Boston Massacre is the city's oldest public building, the **Old State House**, a Georgian beauty.

In 1770 the Boston Massacre occurred directly in front of here—look for the commemorative stone circle.

Cross the plaza to ★ **Faneuil Hall** and explore where Samuel Adams railed against "taxation without representation." ■TIP→ A good mid-trail break is the shops and eateries of Faneuil Hall Marketplace, which includes Quincy Market.

[PHOTO: Old Corner Book Store Site]

★ = Fodor's Choice   ★ = Highly Recommended   🕓 = Family Friendly

NORTH END
TO CHARLESTOWN

USS *Constitution*

Freedom Trail sites between Faneuil Hall and Charlestown are more spread out along 1½ miles. The sites here, though more difficult to reach, are certainly worth the walk.

THE ROUTE

When you depart Faneuil Hall, follow the red stripe to the North End, Boston's Little Italy.

The ♥ **Paul Revere House** takes you back 200 years—here are the hero's own saddlebags, a toddy warmer, and a pine cradle made from a molasses cask. It's also air-conditioned in the summer, so try to stop here in mid-afternoon to escape the heat. Next to the Paul Revere House is one of the city's oldest brick buildings, the **Pierce-Hichborn House**.

Next, peek inside a place guaranteed to trigger a wave of patriotism: the ★ **Old North Church** of "One if by land, two if by sea" fame. Then head toward **Copp's**

Paul Revere House

Bunker Hill Monument

Water Shuttle Dock

1st Ave.

USS Constitution

1

🛈 Boston National Historic Park Visitor Center

CHARLESTOWN

End: In Charlestown head for the nearby water shuttle, which takes you downtown

Charlestown Bridge

0   100 yards
0   100 meters

NORTH END

Commercial St.

Copp's Hill Burying Ground

Hull St.   Charter St.

Tileston St.

Salem St.   Old North Church

Prince St.

Tilumour   Margin St.   Endicott St.

Pierce-Hichborn House   Paul Revere House

Hanover St.   Richmond St.

North St.

Hill Burying Ground, where you can view graves from the late 17th century through the early 19th century. Afterward, cross the bridge over the Charles and check out that revered icon, the ♥ **USS Constitution,** "Old Ironsides." It's open until 6 PM (4 PM November through March), and you'll need about an hour for a visit, so plan accordingly.

The perfect ending to the trail? A walk to the top of the ♥ **Bunker Hill Monument** for the incomparable vistas. The hill was the site of one of the first battles of the Revolutionary War. Though the colonial rebels actually lost, they inflicted large casualties on the better-trained British, proving themselves against the empire.

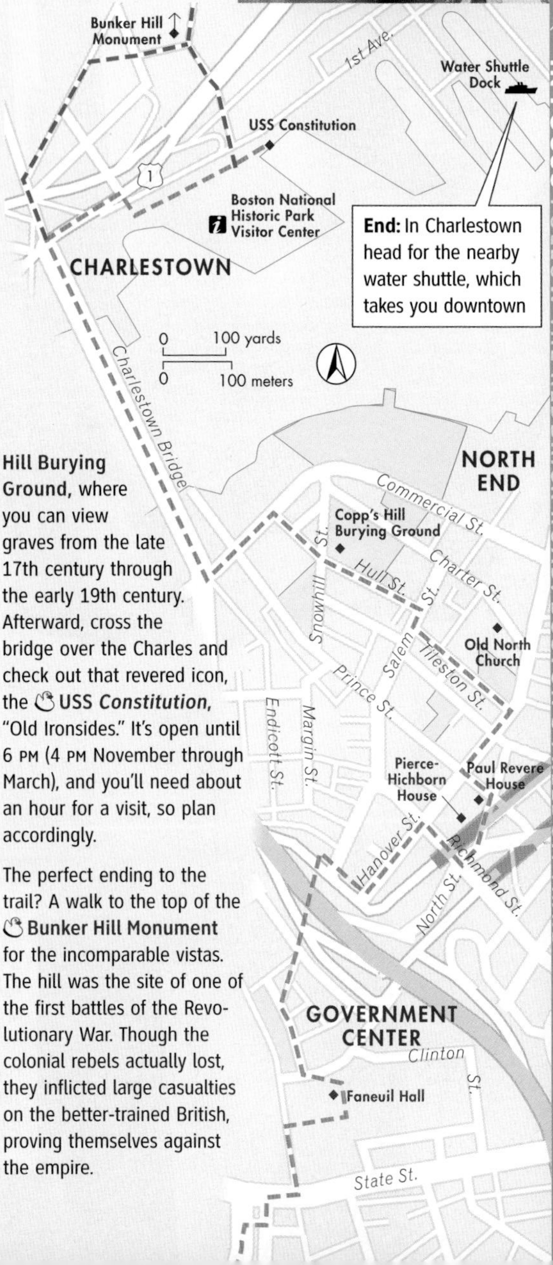

GOVERNMENT CENTER

Clinton St.

♦ Faneuil Hall

State St.

DID YOU KNOW?

If the Freedom Trail leaves you eager to see more Revolutionary War sites, drive about 30 minutes to Lexington and Concord, where the "shot heard 'round the world" launched the first battles in 1775.

DOWNTOWN

Boston's commercial and financial districts—the area commonly called Downtown—are in a maze of streets that seem to have been laid out with little logic; they are village lanes now lined with modern 40-story office towers. Just as the Great Fire of 1872 swept the old Financial District clear, the Downtown construction in more-recent times has obliterated many of the buildings where 19th-century Boston businessmen sat in front of their rolltop desks. Yet historic sites remain tucked among the skyscrapers; a number of them have been linked together to make up a fascinating section of the Freedom Trail.

The area is bordered by State Street on the north and by South Station and Chinatown on the south. Tremont Street and the Common form the west boundary, and the harbor wharves the eastern edge. Locals navigate the tangle of thoroughfares in between, but few of them manage to give intelligible directions, so carry a map.

Numbers in the margin correspond to numbers on the Downtown Boston map.

6 Children's Museum. Most children have so much fun here that they don't realize they're learning something. Creative hands-on exhibits demonstrate scientific laws, cultural diversity, and problem solving. After completing a massive 23,000-square-foot expansion in 2007, the museum has updated a lot of its old exhibitions and added new ones. Some of the most popular stops are also the simplest, like the bubble-making machinery and the two-story climbing maze. At the Japanese House you're invited to take off your shoes and step inside a two-story silk merchant's home from Kyoto. The "Boston Black" exhibit stimulates dialogue about ethnicity and community while children play in a Cape Verdean restaurant and the "African Queen Beauty Salon." There's also a full schedule of special exhibits, festivals, and performances. ⊠ *300 Congress St., Downtown* ☎ *617/426–6500* ⊕ *www.bostonkids.org* ✉ *$12, Fri. 5–9 $1* ⊙ *Sat.–Thurs. 10–5, Fri. 10–9* Ⓣ *South Station.*

5 Institute of Contemporary Art. Housed in a cantilevered edifice that juts out over the Boston waterfront, the ICA moved to this site in 2006 and the museum is becoming one of Boston's most exciting attractions. Since its foundation in 1936, the institute has cultivated a cutting-edge status: it's played host to works by Edvard Munch, Egon Schiele, and Oskar Kokoschka. Andy Warhol, Robert Rauschenberg, and Roy Lichtenstein mounted pivotal exhibitions here early in their careers. Now the ICA is building a major permanent collection for the first time ry, while continuing to showcase innovative paintings, videos, installations, and multimedia shows. The performing arts get their due in the museum's new theater, and the Water Café features cuisine from Wolfgang Puck. ⊠ *100 Northern Ave., South Boston* ☎ *617/478–3100* ⊕ *www. icaboston.org* ✉ *$15, free Thurs. 5–9, free for families last Sat. of every month* ⊙ *Tues. and Wed. 10–5, Thurs. and Fri. 10–9, weekends 10–5. Tours on select weekends at 2 and select Thurs. at 6* Ⓣ *Courthouse.*

7 Boston Tea Party Ships & Museum. After a lengthy renovation, the museum is, as of this writing, scheduled to reopen in the summer of 2010 (though the opening date has been extended more than once). The *Beaver II,*

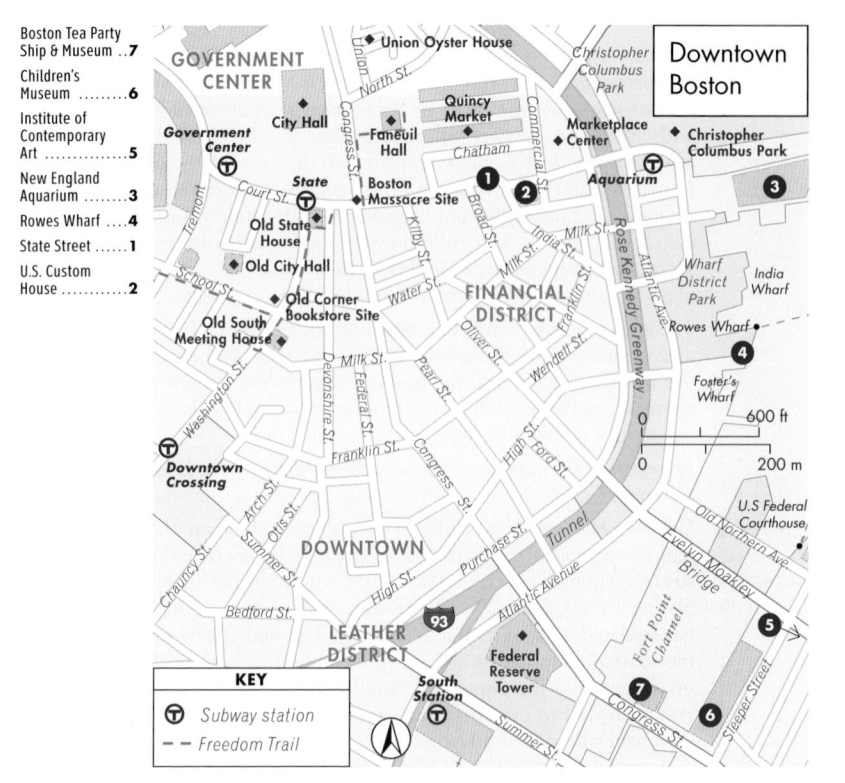

a reproduction of one of the ships forcibly boarded and unloaded the night Boston Harbor became a teapot, is supposed to return to the Fort Point Channel at the Congress Street Bridge and be joined by two tall ships, the *Dartmouth* and the *Eleanor*. Visitors are promised a chance to explore the ships and museum exhibits, meet reenactors, or drink a cup of tea in a new Tea Room. ✉ *Fort Point Channel at Congress St. Bridge, Downtown* ⊕ *www.bostonteapartyship.com* ☉ *Check Web site for updated information* Ⓣ *South Station.*

❹ **Rowes Wharf.** Take a Beacon Hill redbrick town house, blow it up to the *n*th power, and you get this 15-story Skidmore, Owings & Merrill extravaganza from 1987. From under the complex's gateway six-story arch, you can get great views of Boston Harbor and the yachts docked at the marina. Water shuttles pull up here from Logan Airport—the most intriguing way to enter the city. Enjoy a windswept stroll along the HarborWalk waterfront promenade at dusk for an unforgettable sunset. ✉ *Atlantic Ave. south of India Wharf* Ⓣ *Aquarium.*

❶ **State Street.** During the 19th century State Street was headquarters for banks, brokerages, and insurance firms; although these businesses have spread throughout the Downtown District, "State Street" still connotes much the same thing as "Wall Street" does in New York. The early commercial hegemony of State Street was symbolized by Long Wharf,

2

built in 1710 and extending some 1,700 feet into the harbor. If today's Long Wharf doesn't appear to be that long, it's not because it has been shortened but because the land has crept out toward its end. State Street once met the water at the base of the Custom House; landfill operations were pursued relentlessly through the years.

② **U.S. Custom House.** This 1847 structure resembles a Greek Revival temple that appears to have sprouted a tower. It's just that. This is the work of architects Ammi Young and Isaiah Rogers—at least, the bottom part is. The tower was added in 1915, at which time the Custom House became Boston's tallest building. It remains one of the most visible and best loved structures in the city's skyline. To appreciate the grafting job, go inside and look at the domed rotunda. The outer surface of that dome was once the roof of the building, but now the dome is embedded in the base of the tower.

The federal government moved out of the Custom House in 1987 and sold it to the city of Boston, which, in turn, sold it to the Marriott Corporation, which has converted the building into hotel space and luxury time-share units. You can now sip a cocktail in the hotel's Counting Room Lounge, or visit the 26th-floor observation deck. The magnificent Rotunda Room sports maritime prints and antique artifacts, courtesy of the Peabody Essex Museum in Salem. ⊠ *3 McKinley Sq., Downtown* ☎ *617/310–6300* Ⓣ *State, Aquarium.*

THE BACK BAY

In the folklore of American neighborhoods, the Back Bay stands as a symbol of propriety and high social standing. Before the 1850s it really was a bay, a tidal flat that formed the south bank of a distended Charles River. The filling in of land along the isthmus that joined Boston to the mainland (the Neck) began in 1850, and resulted in the creation of the South End. To the north a narrow causeway called the Mill Dam (later Beacon Street) was built in 1814 to separate the Back Bay from the Charles. By the late 1800s Bostonians had filled in the shallows to as far as the marshland known as the Fenway, and the original 783-acre peninsula had been expanded by about 450 acres. Thus the waters of Back Bay became the neighborhood of Back Bay.

Heavily influenced by the then-recent rebuilding of Paris according to the plans of Baron Georges-Eugène Haussmann, the Back Bay planners created thoroughfares that resemble Parisian boulevards. Almost immediately, fashionable families began to decamp from Beacon Hill and South End and establish themselves in the Back Bay's brick and brownstone row houses. By 1900 the streets between the Public Garden and Massachusetts Avenue had become the smartest, most desirable neighborhood in all of Boston.

Today the area retains its posh spirit, but mansions are no longer the main draw. Locals and tourists flock to the commercial streets of Boylston and Newbury to shop at boutiques, galleries, and the usual mall stores. Many of the bars and restaurants have patio seating and bay windows. The Boston Public Library, Symphony Hall, and numer-

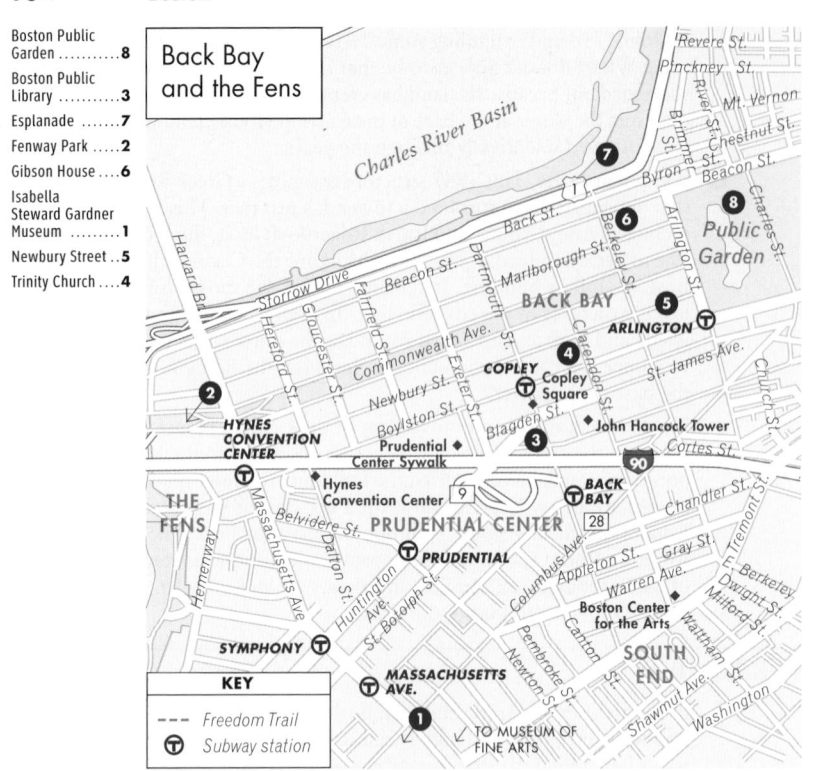

Back Bay
and the Fens

KEY

- - - *Freedom Trail*

Ⓣ *Subway station*

ous churches ensure that high culture is not lost amid the frenzy of consumerism.

Numbers in the margin correspond to numbers on the Back Bay and the Fens map.

8 **Boston Public Garden.** Although the Boston Public Garden is often lumped together with Boston Common, the two are separate entities with a distinct boundary between them at Charles Street. The Common has been public land since Boston was founded in 1630, whereas the Public Garden belongs to a newer Boston, occupying what had been salt marshes on the edge of the Common. By 1837 the tract was covered with an abundance of ornamental plantings donated by private citizens. The area was defined in 1856 by the building of Arlington Street, and in 1860 the architect George Meacham was commissioned to plan the park.

The central feature of the Public Garden is its irregularly shaped pond, intended to appear, from any vantage point along its banks, much larger than its nearly 4 acres. The pond has been famous since 1877 for its foot-pedal-powered (by a captain) **Swan Boats** (☎ 617/522–1966 ⊕ *www. swanboats.com* ✉ *Swan Boats $2.75* ⊙ *Swan Boats mid-Apr.–June 20, daily 10–4; June 21–Labor Day, daily 10–5; day after Labor Day–mid-Sept., weekdays noon–4, weekends 10–4).* The pond is favored by

Fodor'sChoice
★

TAKE A TOUR

Boston Movie Tours (☎ 866/668–4345 ⊕ www.bostonmovietours.net) takes you to Boston's television and movie hot spots like the South Boston of *The Departed*, the *Ally McBeal* building, the tavern from *Good Will Hunting*, the *Cheers* bar, and Fenway Park, home of the Red Sox and location for movies like *Field of Dreams* and *Fever Pitch*. Guides share filming secrets and trivia from movies like *Legally Blonde* and *Mystic River*

along with the best celeb spots in town. The "theater-on-wheels" bus tour takes 2–3 hours, depending on traffic ($37).

Boston Women's Heritage Trail (☎ 617/364–2449 ⊕ www.bwht. org) has nine self-guided walks that highlight remarkable women who played an integral role in shaping the history of Boston and the nation as patriots, intellectuals, abolitionists, suffragists, artists, and writers.

ducks and swans, and for the modest price of a few boat rides you can amuse children for an hour or more. Near the Swan Boat dock is what has been described as the world's smallest suspension bridge, designed in 1867 to cross the pond at its narrowest point.

The Public Garden is America's oldest botanical garden, and has the finest formal plantings in central Boston. The beds along the main walkways are replanted for spring and summer. The tulips during the first two weeks of May are especially colorful, and there's a sampling of native and European tree species. ⊠ *Bounded by Arlington, Boylston, Charles, and Beacon Sts., Back Bay.*

❸ ★ Boston Public Library. This handsome temple to literature and a valuable research library was opened in 1895, and it confirmed the status of architects McKim, Mead & White as apostles of the Renaissance Revival style. Philip Johnson's 1972 addition emulates the mass and proportion of the original, though not its extraordinary detail; this skylighted annex houses the library's circulating collections. The corridor leading from the annex opens onto the Renaissance-style **courtyard**—a copy of the one in Rome's Palazzo della Cancelleria—around which the original library is built. You can bring books or lunch into the courtyard, which is open all the hours the library is open. Beyond the courtyard is the main entrance hall of the 1895 building, with its immense stone lions by Louis St. Gaudens, vaulted ceiling, and marble staircase. The corridor at the top of the stairs leads to **Bates Hall,** one of Boston's most sumptuous interior spaces. This is the main reference reading room, 218 feet long with a barrel-arch ceiling 50 feet high. ⊠ *700 Boylston St., at Copley Sq., Back Bay* ☎ *617/536–5400* ⊕ *www. bpl.org* ☉ *Mon.–Thurs. 9–9, Fri. and Sat. 9–5; Oct.–May, also Sun. 1–5. Free guided art and architecture tours Mon. at 2:30, Tues. and Thurs. at 6, Fri. and Sat. at 11, Sun. (Oct.–May) at 2* Ⓣ *Copley.*

QUICK BITES

Take a lunch break at **The Courtyard** (⊠ *700 Boylston St., at Copley Sq., Back Bay* ☎ *617/859–2251*) or the **MapRoom Café**, adjoining restaurants in the Boston Public Library. The café serves breakfast and lunch in the 1895 map room, and the main restaurant is open for lunch and afternoon

Shoppers take a break at a Newbury Street café.

tea. Enter through the Dartmouth entrance and turn right; the restaurants are at the end of the corridor. The Courtyard is open weekdays 11:30–4, and the MapRoom Café is open Monday–Saturday 9–5.

4 **Trinity Church.** In his 1877 masterpiece, architect Henry Hobson Richardson brought his Romanesque Revival style to maturity; all the aesthetic elements for which he was famous come together magnificently—bold polychromatic masonry, careful arrangement of masses, sumptuously carved interior woodwork—in this crowning centerpiece of Copley Square. Richardson engaged some of the best artists of his day—John LaFarge, William Morris, and Edward Burne-Jones among them—to execute the paintings and stained glass. LaFarge's intricate paintings and ornamented ceilings received a much-needed overhaul during the extensive renovations that wrapped up in 2005. Along the north side of the church, note the Augustus Saint-Gaudens statue of Phillips Brooks—the most charismatic rector in New England, who almost single-handedly got Trinity built and furnished. For a nice respite, try to catch one of the Friday organ concerts beginning at 12:15. ■ TIP→ The 11:15 Sunday service is followed by a free guided tour. ✉ *206 Clarendon St., Back Bay* ☎ *617/536–0944* ⊕ *www.trinityboston.org* ✉ *Church free, guided and self-guided tours $6* ⊙ *Mon.–Sat. 9–5, Sun. 1–5; services Sun. at 7:45, 9, and 11:15* AM *and 6* PM*; Tues. and Thurs. at 6* PM*; Wed. at 12:10* PM*. Tours take place several times daily; call to confirm times* Ⓣ *Copley.*

7 **Esplanade.** Near the corner of Beacon and Arlington streets, the Arthur Fiedler Footbridge crosses Storrow Drive to the Esplanade and the **Hatch Memorial Shell.** The free concerts here in summer include the Boston Pops' televised Fourth of July performance.

6 Gibson House. Through the foresight of an eccentric bon vivant, this house provides an authentic glimpse into daily life in Boston's Victorian era. One of the first Back Bay residences (1859), the Gibson House is relatively modest in comparison with some of the grand mansions built during the decades that followed; yet its furnishings, from its circa-1790 Willard clock to the raised and gilded wallpaper to the multipiece faux-bamboo bedroom set, seem sumptuous to modern eyes. Unlike other Back Bay houses, the Gibson family home has been preserved with all its Victorian fixtures and furniture intact. ■TIP➜ Though the sign out front instructs visitors not to ring the bell until the stroke of the hour, you will have better luck catching the tour if you arrive a few minutes early and ring forcefully. ✉ *137 Beacon St., Back Bay* ☎ *617/267–6338* ⊕ *www. thegibsonhouse.org* 🔖 *$7* ⊘ *Tours Wed.–Sun. at 1, 2, and 3 and by appointment* Ⓣ *Arlington.*

> **FRUGAL FUN**
>
> Take a cue from locals and sign up for one of the Boston Park Rangers' programs. Top picks include a visit to the city stables to meet the Mounties and their horses, regularly scheduled readings of Robert McCloskey's *Make Way for Ducklings* in Boston's Public Garden, and city scavenger hunts geared for families. Contact **Boston Parks and Recreation** (☎ *617/635–7487* ⊕ *www.cityofboston.gov/parks/ parkrangers*).

5 Newbury Street. Eight-block-long Newbury Street has been compared to New York's 5th Avenue, and certainly this is the city's poshest shopping area, with branches of Chanel, Brooks Brothers, Armani, Burberry, and other top names in fashion. But here the pricey boutiques are more intimate than grand, and people live above the trendy restaurants and hair salons. Toward the Mass Ave. end cafés proliferate and the stores get funkier, ending with Newbury Comics, Urban Outfitters, and Best Buy. Ⓣ *Hynes, Copley.*

THE FENWAY

The marshland known as the Back Bay Fens gave this section of Boston its name, but two quirky institutions give it its character: Fenway Park, home of Boston's beloved Red Sox, and the Isabella Stewart Gardner Museum, the legacy of a high-living Brahmin who attended a concert at Symphony Hall in 1912 wearing a headband that read, OH, YOU RED SOX. Not far from the Gardner is another major cultural magnet: the Museum of Fine Arts. Kenmore Square, a favorite haunt for Boston University students, adds a bit of funky flavor to the mix.

Numbers in the margin correspond to numbers on the Back Bay and the Fens map.

2 Fenway Park. For 86 years, the Boston Red Sox suffered a World Series dry spell, bad luck that fans attributed to the "Curse of the Bambino," which struck the team in 1920 when they sold Babe Ruth (the "Bambino") to the New York Yankees. All that changed in 2004, when a maverick squad broke the curse in a thrilling seven-game series against the team's nemesis in the Series semifinals. This win against the Yankees

Fodor's Choice
★

MUSEUM OF FINE ARTS

✉ *465 Huntington Ave.,*
The Fenway ☎ *617/267–9300*
🌐 *www.mfa.org* 💲 *$17;*
by donation Wed. 4–9:45
🕐 *Sat.–Tues. 10–4:45, Wed.–*
Fri. 10–9:45. 1-hr tours daily;
call for scheduled times
Ⓣ *Museum.*

TIPS

■ From October to April, tea is served 2:30–4 in the second-floor Upper Rotunda. Take a much-needed break from the art viewing and enjoy.

■ The year-round cocktail party "MFA Fridays," from 5:30 to 9:30—held weekly in summer and monthly at other times—has become quite the social event. Stop by to admire the art in a festive atmosphere.

■ Be aware that the museum will require you to check any bag larger than 11"x15", even if it's your purse. Save that oversized "it" bag for another day and bring along only the essentials.

■ With such extensive collections, you could easily spend a whole afternoon perusing the galleries, but if you only have an hour, head to the second floor and take in the Monets.

Count on staying a while if you have any hope of seeing what's here. Eclecticism and thoroughness, often an incompatible pair, have coexisted agreeably at the MFA since its earliest days. From Renaissance and baroque masters to impressionist marvels to African masks to sublime samples of Native American pottery and contemporary crafts, the collections are happily shorn of both cultural snobbery and shortsighted trendiness.

HIGHLIGHTS

The MFA's collection of approximately 450,000 objects was built from a core of paintings and sculpture from the Boston Athenaeum, historical portraits from the city of Boston, and donations by area universities. The MFA has more than 60 works by John Singleton Copley; major paintings by Winslow Homer, John Singer Sargent, Fitz Hugh Lane, and Edward Hopper; and a wealth of American works ranging from native New England folk art and colonial portraiture to New York abstract expressionism of the 1950s and 1960s. Also of particular note are the **John Singer Sargent paintings** adorning the Rotunda. They were specially commissioned for the museum in 1921, and make for a dazzling first impression on visitors coming through the Huntington Street entrance.

American decorative arts are also liberally represented, particularly those of New England in the years before the Civil War. Native son Paul Revere, much more than a sounder of alarms, is amply represented as well, with superb silver teapots, sauceboats, and other tableware.

The museum also owns one of the world's most extensive collections of **Asian art** under one roof. Its Japanese art collection is the finest outside Japan, and Chinese porcelains of the Tang Dynasty are especially well represented. The Egyptian rooms display statuary, furniture, and exquisite gold jewelry; a special funerary-arts gallery exhibits coffins, mummies, and burial treasures.

French impressionists abound, and are perhaps more comprehensively displayed here than at any other New World museum aside from the Art Institute of Chicago; many of the 38 Monets (the largest collection of his work outside France) vibrate with color. There are canvases by Renoir, Pissarro, Manet, and the American painters Mary Cassatt and Childe Hassam.

Three important galleries explore the **art of Africa, Oceania, and the Ancient Americas,** expanding the MFA's emphasis on civilizations outside the Western tradition. The museum also has strong collections of textiles, costumes, and prints dating from the 15th century, including many works by Dürer and Goya, and its collection of antique musical instruments is among the finest in the world.

Fifteen second-floor galleries contain the MFA's European painting and sculpture collection, dating from the 11th century to the 20th. Among the standouts are Donatello's marble relief *The Madonna of the Clouds* and J. M. W. Turner's powerful work *The Slave Ship*. Most striking, however, is the William I. Koch Gallery, a former tapestry room whose 40-foot-high marble walls are now hung, nearly floor to ceiling, with 53 dramatic Renaissance and baroque paintings by El Greco, Claude Lorraine, Poussin, Rubens, Tintoretto, Titian, Van Dyck, Velázquez, Veronese, and other masters.

The **West Wing,** an airy, well-lighted space, is used primarily to mount special exhibitions, temporary shows drawn from the museum's holdings, and lively contemporary-art and photography exhibits. It also has the Bravo Restaurant, a cafeteria, and a café serving light snacks.

EXPANDING THE ARTS

Founded in 1870, the MFA first resided on the upper floors of the Boston Athenaeum, then in a Gothic structure on the site where the Copley Plaza Hotel now stands. As the museum was beginning to outgrow that space, the Fenway area was becoming fashionable, and in 1909 the move was made to Guy Lowell's somewhat severe Beaux Arts building, to which the West Wing, designed by I. M. Pei, was added in 1981. The move helped cap the half-century of expansion of the Back Bay area.

In 2005 the museum broke ground on a massive construction project that the trustees hope will keep it in America's cultural vanguard for the next 100 years. In its first phase, a new **East Wing** will be built to house the Art of the Americas collection, expanding the current gallery space by 50%. Other aspects of the 133-year-old building's enormous face-lift will include a new glass-enclosed courtyard, the reopening of the Fenway entrance, and a "crystal spine" to run the full length of the museum. The new American Wing is expected to open in November 2010; the museum will remain open during construction.

was followed by a four-game sweep of St. Louis in the World Series. Boston, and its citizens' ingrained sense of pessimism, hasn't been the same since. The repeat World Series win in 2007 has just cemented Bostonians' sense that the universe is finally working correctly. *See the Fenway Park spotlight at the beginning of this chapter for more information.* ☒ *4 Yawkey Way, between Van Ness and Lansdowne Sts., The Fenway* ☎ *877/733–7699 box office; 617/226–6666 tours* ⊕ *www. redsox.com* ☒ *Tours $12* ☉ *Tours Mon.–Sat. 9–4, Sun. 9–3; on game days, last tour is 3 hrs before game time* Ⓣ *Kenmore.*

Fodor's Choice
★

❶ Isabella Stewart Gardner Museum. A spirited young society woman, Isabella Stewart had come in 1860 from New York to marry John Lowell Gardner, one of Boston's leading citizens. Through her flamboyance and energetic acquisition of art, "Mrs. Jack" promptly set about becoming the most un-Bostonian of the Proper Bostonians. When it came time finally to settle down with the old master paintings and Medici treasures she and her husband had acquired in Europe—with *her* money (she was heir to the Stewart mining fortune)—she decided to build the Venetian palazzo of her dreams in an isolated corner of Boston's newest neighborhood. She built her palace to center on a spacious inner courtyard and on New Year's Day 1903 she threw open the entrance to Fenway Court (to use the museum's original name).

When Gardner died, the terms of her will stipulated that the building remain exactly as she left it—paintings, furniture, everything, down to the smallest object in a hall cabinet, and that is as it has remained. Today, it's probably America's most idiosyncratic treasure house.

Gardner's palazzo contains a trove of amazing paintings—including Titian's *Europa*, Giotto's *Presentation of Christ in the Temple*, Piero della Francesca's *Hercules*, and John Singer Sargent's *El Jaleo*. Spanish leather panels, Renaissance hooded fireplaces, and Gothic tapestries accent salons; eight balconies adorn the majestic Venetian courtyard. There's a Raphael Room, a Spanish Cloister, a Gothic Room, a Chinese Loggia, and a magnificent Tapestry Room for concerts, where Gardner entertained Henry James and Edith Wharton.

Though the museum is packed with Mrs. Jack's collection, there are some conspicuously bare spots on the walls. On March 18, 1990, the Gardner was the target of one of the world's most sensational art heists. Thieves disguised as police officers stole 12 works of art with an estimated value of $200–$300 million. Vermeer's *The Concert* was taken, along with works by Rembrandt, Manet, and Degas. To date, none of the art has been recovered, despite a $5 million reward. ■**TIP➔ If you've visited the MFA in the past two days, there's a $2 discount to the admission fee. The museum waives entrance fees to anyone named Isabella.** ☒ *280 The Fenway, The Fenway* ☎ *617/566–1401; 617/566–1088 café* ⊕ *www.gardnermuseum.org* ☒ *$12* ☉ *Museum Tues.–Sun. 11–5, open some holidays; café Tues.–Fri. 11:30–4, weekends 11–4. Weekend concerts at 1:30* Ⓣ *Museum.*

EXPLORING CAMBRIDGE

Updated
by Michael
Nalepa

Across the Charles River is the überliberal academic enclave of Cambridge. The city is punctuated at one end by the funky tech-noids of MIT and at the other by the grand academic fortress that is Harvard University. Civic life connects the two camps into an urban stew of 100,000 residents who represent nearly every nationality in the world, work at every kind of job from tenured professor to taxi driver, and are passionate about living on this side of the river.

The Charles River is the Cantabrigians' backyard, and there's virtually no place in Cambridge more than a 10-minute walk from its banks. Strolling, running, or biking here is one of the great pleasures of Cambridge, and views include graceful bridges, the distant Boston skyline, crew teams rowing through the calm water, and the elegant spires of Harvard soaring into the sky.

No visit to Cambridge is complete without an afternoon in Harvard Square. It's home to every variation of the human condition; Nobel laureates, homeless buskers, trust-fund babies, and working-class Joes mill around the same piece of real estate. Walk down Brattle Street past Henry Wadsworth Longfellow's house. Farther along Massachusetts Avenue is Central Square, an ethnic melting pot of people and restaurants. Ten minutes more brings you to MIT, with its eclectic architecture from postwar pedestrian to Frank Gehry's futuristic fantasyland. In addition to providing a stellar view, the Mass Ave. Bridge, spanning the Charles from Cambridge to Boston, is also notorious in MIT lore for its Smoot measurements.

Numbers in the margin correspond to numbers on the Harvard Square map.

⑤ Arthur M. Sackler Museum. The artistic treasures of the ancient Greeks, Egyptians, and Romans are the major draw here. Make a beeline for the Ancient and Asian art galleries, the permanent installations on the fourth floor, which include Chinese bronzes, Buddhist sculptures, Greek friezes, and Roman marbles. Currently, the Sackler is the only one of the University's art museums open to the public. The Busch-Reisinger and Fogg museums closed in 2008. At present, visitors to the Sackler can enjoy a sampling of works culled from both. In 2013 the combined collections of all three museums will be represented under one roof under the umbrella name Harvard Art Museum. ⊠ *485 Broadway* ☎ *617/495–9400* ⊕ *www.artmuseums.harvard.edu/collection/sackler* ⛟ *$9* ⊗ *Mon.–Sat. 10–5, Sun. 1–5* ⓣ *Harvard.*

④ Harvard Museum of Natural History. Many museums promise something for every member of the family; the vast Harvard Museum complex actually delivers. Swiss naturalist Louis Agassiz, who founded the zoology museum, envisioned a museum that would bring under one roof the study of all kinds of life: plants, animals, and humankind. The result is three distinct museums, all accessible for one admission fee.

Fodor's Choice
★

The **Museum of Comparative Zoology** traces the evolution of animals and humans. You can't miss the 42-foot-long skeleton of the underwater *Kronosaurus*. Dinosaur fossils and a zoo of stuffed exotic animals

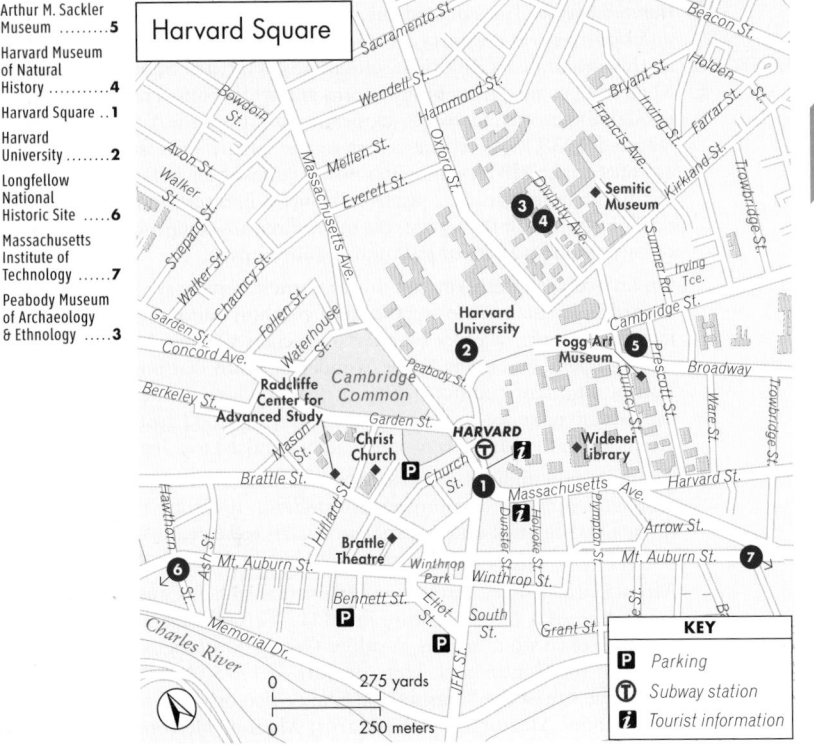

can occupy young minds for hours. The museum is old-fashioned. You can almost feel the brush of the whiskers of the ardent explorers and the naturalists who combed the world for these treasures.

■ TIP➜ Check the Web site for children's events.

Oversize garnets and crystals sparkle at the **Mineralogical and Geological Museum,** founded in 1784. The museum also contains an extensive collection of meteorites.

Perhaps the most famous exhibits of the museum complex are the glass flowers in the **Harvard University Herbaria (Botanical Museum),** created as teaching tools that would never wither and die. This unique collection holds 3,000 models of 847 plant species. Each one is a masterpiece, meticulously created in glass by a father and son in Dresden, Germany, who worked continuously from 1887 to 1936. Even more amazing than the colorful flower petals are the delicate roots of some plants. ✉ *26 Oxford St.* ☎ *617/495–3045* ⊕ *www.hmnh.harvard.edu* 💲 *$9, includes admission to Peabody Museum of Archaeology & Ethnology; free for Massachusetts residents Sun. 9–noon year-round and Wed. 3–5 Sept.–May* ☺ *Daily 9–5* Ⓣ *Harvard.*

① **Harvard Square.** Tides of students, tourists, political-cause proponents,
Ⓒ and bizarre street creatures are all part of the nonstop pedestrian flow
Fodor'sChoice at this celebrated Cambridge crossroads. Harvard Square is where
★ Mass Ave., coming from Boston, turns and widens into a triangle broad
enough to accommodate a brick peninsula (above the T station). The
restored 1928 kiosk in the center of the square once served as the
entrance to the MBTA station (it's now a fantastic newsstand). Harvard
Yard, with its lecture halls, residential houses, libraries, and museums, is
one long border of the square; the other three are comprised of clusters
of banks and a variety of restaurants and shops.

On an average afternoon you'll hear earnest conversations in dozens
of foreign languages; see every kind of youthful uniform from Goth to
impeccable prep; wander by street musicians playing Andean flutes,
singing opera, and doing Stevie Wonder or Edith Piaf imitations; and
lean in on a tense outdoor game of pickup chess, while you slurp a
cappuccino or an ice-cream cone (the two major food groups here). An
afternoon in the square is people-watching raised to a high art.

The historic buildings are also worth noting. Even if you're only a
visitor (as opposed to a prospective student), it's still a thrill to walk
though the big brick-and-wrought-iron gates to Harvard Yard, past the
residence halls and statues, on up to Widener Library.

Across Garden Street, through an ornamental arch, is **Cambridge Common,** decreed a public pasture in 1631. It's said that under a large
tree that once stood in this meadow George Washington took command of the Continental Army on July 3, 1775. A stone memorial
marks the site of the "Washington Elm." Also on the Common is the
Irish Famine Memorial by Derry artist Maurice Herron, unveiled in
1997 to coincide with the 150th anniversary of "Black '47," the dead-
liest year of the potato famine. At the center of the Common a large
memorial commemorates the Union soldiers and sailors who lost their
lives in the Civil War. On the far side of the Common (on Waterhouse
St. between Garden St. and Massachusetts Ave.) is a fantastic park.
⊕ *www.harvardsquare.com* Ⓣ *Harvard.*

**QUICK
BITES**

The **Broadway Gourmet** (✉ *468 Broadway* ☎ *617/547–2334*) is just around
the corner from Harvard Yard. Besides the excellent fresh produce, there's
a selection of sandwiches and prepared meals; choose one to be heated up
and then grab a seat for a quick, delicious (if pricey) bite.

② **Harvard University.** The tree-studded, shady, and redbrick expanse of
★ Harvard Yard—the very center of Harvard University—has weathered
the footsteps of Harvard students for more than 300 years. In 1636
the Great and General Court of the Massachusetts Bay Colony voted
to establish the colony's first college, and a year later chose Cambridge
as the site. Named in 1639 for John Harvard, a young Charlestown
clergyman who died in 1638 and left the college his entire library and
half his estate, Harvard remained the only college in the New World
until 1693.

Although the college dates from the 17th century, the oldest buildings
in Harvard Yard are from the 18th century. Together the buildings

chronicle American architecture from the colonial era to the present. **Holden Chapel,** completed in 1744, is a Georgian gem. The graceful **University Hall** was designed in 1815 by Charles Bulfinch. **Sever Hall,** completed in 1880 and designed by Henry Hobson Richardson, represents the Romanesque revival that was followed by the neoclassical (note the pillared facade of Widener Library) and the neo-Georgian, represented by the sumptuous brick houses along the Charles River. **Memorial Church,** a graceful steepled edifice of modified Colonial Revival design, was dedicated in 1932. Just north of the Yard is **Memorial Hall,** completed in 1878 as a memorial to Harvard men who died in the Union cause; it's High Victorian both inside and out. It also contains the 1,166-seat Sanders Theatre, which serves as the university's largest lecture hall, site of year-round concerts by students and professionals, and the venue for the festive Christmas Revels.

Many of Harvard's cultural and scholarly facilities are important sights in themselves, including the **Harvard Museum of Natural History,** the **Peabody Museum of Archaeology & Ethnology,** and the **Widener Library.** Of the three much-loved art museums (the Fogg, the Busch-Reisinger, and the Arthur M. Sackler), only the latter remains. The two former are currently closed for extensive renovations and will reopen in 2013 as the Harvard Art Museum (which will also include the Sackler Museum). Most campus buildings, other than museums and concert halls, are off-limits to the general public.

Harvard University Events & Information Center (⌧ *Holyoke Center, 1350 Massachusetts Ave.* ☎ *617/495–1573* ⊕ *www.harvard.edu*), run by students, includes a small library, a video-viewing area, computer terminals, and an exhibit space. It also distributes maps of the university area and has free student-led tours of Harvard Yard. The tour doesn't include visits to museums, and it doesn't take you into campus buildings, but it provides a fine orientation. The information center is open year-round (except during spring recess and other semester breaks), Monday through Saturday 9–5. Tours are offered September–May, Monday–Friday at 10 and 2 and Saturday at 2 (except during university breaks). From the end of June through August, guides offer four tours Monday–Saturday at 10, 11:15, 2, and 3:15. ⌧ *Bounded by Massachusetts Ave. and Mt. Auburn, Holyoke, and Dunster Sts.* ☎ *617/495–1573 for Harvard directory assistance* ⊕ *www.harvard.edu* Ⓣ *Harvard.*

❸ **Peabody Museum of Archaeology & Ethnology.** With one of the world's outstanding anthropological collections, the Peabody focuses on Native American and Central and South American cultures; there are also interesting displays on Africa. The Hall of the North American Indian is particularly outstanding, with art, textiles, and models of traditional dwellings from across the continent. The Mesoamerican room juxtaposes ancient relief carvings and weavings with contemporary works from the Maya and other peoples. ⌧ *11 Divinity Ave.* ☎ *617/496–1027* ⊕ *www.peabody.harvard.edu* 🎟 *$9, includes admission to Harvard Museum of Natural History, accessible through the museum; free for Massachusetts residents only Sun. 9–noon year-round and Wed. 3–5 Sept.–May* ⊙ *Daily 9–5* Ⓣ *Harvard.*

CLOSE UP

Old School

Cambridge dates from 1630, when the Puritan leader John Winthrop chose this meadowland as the site of a carefully planned village he named Newtowne. The Massachusetts Bay Colony chose Newtowne as the site for the country's first college in 1636. Two years later, John Harvard bequeathed half his estate and his private library to the fledgling school, and the college was named in his honor. The town elders changed the name to Cambridge, emulating the university in England where most of the Puritan leaders had been educated.

When Cambridge was incorporated as a city in 1846, the boundaries were drawn to include the university area (today's Harvard Square and Tory Row), and the industrial communities of Cambridgeport and East Cambridge. By 1900 the population of the working-class communities, made up of Irish, Polish, Italian, Portuguese, and French Canadian residents, dwarfed the Harvard end of town. Today's city is much more a multiethnic urban community than an academic village. Nearly any kind of ethnic food or music can be found in Cambridge— the local high school educates students who speak more than 40 different languages at home.

When MIT, originally Boston Tech, moved to Cambridge in 1916, it was the first educational institution that aimed to be more than a trade school, training engineers but also grounding them in the humanities and liberal arts. Many of MIT's postwar graduates remained in the area, and went on to form hundreds of technology-based firms engaged in camera manufacturing, electronics, and space research. By the 1990s manufacturing had moved to the burbs, and software developers, venture capitalists, and robotics and biotech companies claimed the former industrial spaces. This area around Kendall Square is now nicknamed "Intelligence Alley."

 Longfellow National Historic Site. Henry Wadsworth Longfellow, the poet whose stirring tales of the Village Blacksmith, Evangeline, Hiawatha, and Paul Revere's midnight ride thrilled 19th-century America, once lived in this elegant mansion. If there's one historic house to visit in Cambridge, this is it. The house was built in 1759 by John Vassall Jr., and is one of several original Tory Row homes on Brattle Street; George Washington lived here during the Siege of Boston from July 1775 to April 1776. Longfellow first boarded here in 1837, and later received the house as a gift from his father-in-law on his marriage to Frances Appleton, who burned to death here in an accident in 1861. For 45 years Longfellow wrote his famous verses here and filled the house with the exuberant spirit of his literary circle, which included Ralph Waldo Emerson, Nathaniel Hawthorne, and Charles Sumner, an abolitionist senator. Longfellow died in 1882; but the splendor of the house remains—from the Longfellow family furniture to the wallpaper to the books on the shelves (many the poet's own)—all preserved for future generations by the National Park Service. ■ TIP→ Longfellow Park, across the street, is the place to stand to take photos of the house. The park was created to preserve the view immortalized in the poet's "To the River Charles."

✉ *105 Brattle St.* ☎ *617/876–4491*
⊕ *www.nps.gov/long* ✉ *$3* ☉ *Check
Web site for seasonal tour schedules*
Ⓣ *Harvard.*

❼ Massachusetts Institute of Technology.
Celebrated for both its brains and
its cerebral sense of humor, this
once-tidy engineering school at right
angles to the Charles River is growing like a sprawling adolescent, consuming old industrial buildings and
city blocks with every passing year.
MIT mints graduates that are the

sharp blades on the edge of the information revolution. It's perennially
in the top five of *U.S. News and World Report*'s college rankings.

Architecture is important at MIT. The **Kresge Auditorium,** designed by
Eero Saarinen, with a curving roof and unusual thrust, rests on three,
instead of four, points. The nondenominational **MIT Chapel,** a circular Saarinen design, is lighted primarily by a roof oculus that focuses
natural light on the altar and by reflections from the water in a small
surrounding moat; it's topped by an aluminum sculpture by Theodore
Roszak. The serpentine **Baker House,** now a dormitory, was designed
in 1947 by the Finnish architect Alvar Aalto in such a way as to provide every room with a view of the Charles River. Sculptures by Henry
Moore and other notable artists dot the campus.

The East Campus, which has grown around the university's original
neoclassical buildings of 1916, also has outstanding modern architecture and sculpture, including the stark high-rise **Green Building** by
I. M. Pei, housing the Earth Science Center. Just outside is Alexander
Calder's giant stabile (a stationary mobile) *The Big Sail.* Another Pei
work on the East Campus is the **Wiesner Building,** designed in 1985,
which houses the **List Visual Arts Center.** Architect Frank Gehry made
his mark on the campus with the cockeyed, improbable **Ray & Maria
Stata Center,** a complex of buildings on Vassar Street. The center houses
computer, artificial intelligence, and information systems laboratories,
and is reputedly as confusing to navigate on the inside as it is to follow
on the outside. East Campus's **Great Dome,** which looms over neoclassical Killian Court, has often been the target of student "hacks," and
has at various times supported a telephone booth with a ringing phone,
a life-size statue of a cow, and a campus police cruiser. Nearby, the
domed **Rogers Building** has earned unusual notoriety as the center of
a series of hallways and tunnels dubbed "the infinite corridor." Twice
each winter the sun's path lines up perfectly with the corridor's axis.
The phenomenon is known as "MIT-henge."

MIT maintains an information center in the Rogers Building, and offers
free tours of the campus weekdays at 11 and 3. Check the holiday
schedule, as the tours are often suspended during school holidays. General hours for the information center are weekdays 9–5. ✉ *77 Massachusetts Ave.* ☎ *617/253–1000* ⊕ *web.mit.edu* Ⓣ *Kendall/MIT.*

NIGHTLIFE AND THE ARTS

NIGHTLIFE

BARS

Updated by
Linh Tran

The Black Rose is decorated with family crests, pictures of Ireland, and portraits of Samuel Beckett, Lady Gregory, and James Joyce—just like a Dublin pub. Its Faneuil Hall location draws as many tourists as locals, but nightly shows by traditional Irish and contemporary performers make it worth braving the crowds. ⊠ *160 State St., Faneuil Hall* ☎ *617/742–2286* ⊕ *www.irishconnection.com/blackrose.html* Ⓣ *Aquarium, State.*

Boston Beer Works is a "naked brewery," with all the works exposed—the tanks, pipes, and gleaming stainless-steel and copper kettles used in producing beer. Seasonal brews, in addition to 16 microbrews on tap, draw students, young adults, and tourists to the original location (its sibling is by the TD Garden). It's too crowded and noisy for intimate chats, and good luck getting in when there's a home game. ⊠ *61 Brookline Ave., The Fens* ☎ *617/536–2337* ⊕ *beerworks.net* Ⓣ *Kenmore.*

Cheers, formerly known as the Bull & Finch Pub, was dismantled in England, shipped to Boston, and reassembled here. Though it was the inspiration for the TV series *Cheers*, it doesn't look anything like the bar in the show. Addressing that complaint, however, a branch in Faneuil Hall that opened in 2001 is an exact reproduction of the TV set. ⊠ *Hampshire House, 84 Beacon St., Beacon Hill* ☎ *617/227–9605* ⊕ *www.cheersboston.com* Ⓣ *Park St., Charles/MGH.*

Fodor'sChoice
★

Saint, despite its name, draws patrons who are anything but. The spacious underground lounge consists of two rooms. An airy main space is decorated in blue and silver, with long couches to lounge on over appetizers while making eyes across the room. A more devilish "bordello room" is all plush red velvet and tasseled light fixtures, and offers private alcoves for intimate conversations. ⊠ *90 Exeter St., Back Bay* ☎ *617/236–1134* ⊕ *www.saintnitery.com* Ⓣ *Copley.*

Sonsie keeps the stereo volume at a manageable level. The bar crowd, which spills through the French doors onto a sidewalk café in warm weather, is full of young, trendy, cosmopolitan types, and professionals—and on some nights, local sports celebrities. ⊠ *327 Newbury St., Back Bay* ☎ *617/351–2500* ⊕ *www.sonsieboston.com* Ⓣ *Hynes.*

> **THE REAL CHEERS**
>
> TV's *Cheers* may have ended in 1993, but that doesn't stop die-hard fans from paying their respects at the "real" Cheers bar on Beacon Street (or its second location in Faneuil Hall). Although the inspiration for the TV show doesn't quite look like its fictional double, the same atmosphere of good spirits persists. You can find your own kind of notoriety here by devouring the double-decker "Giant Norm burger" and adding your name to the Hall of Fame.

HOMETOWN BREW

A fun way to get to know a town is to acquaint oneself with its hometown drinks. And there are few beverages as closely affiliated with their town of origin as Samuel Adams beer is to Boston.

It was in 1984 when Samuel Adams founder, Jim Koch, unhappy with the low quality of industrially produced beers at the time, decided to try his hand at the family business and introduce a new way of brewing and selling beer based on traditional methods and high-quality ingredients. He decided to name his new beer after another man who had revolutionary ideas—early Bostonian Samuel Adams. (Interestingly enough, generations of Adams's family had produced the malt used for beer.)

You can tour the **Boston Beer Company**'s Jamaica Plain facility (⊠ *30 Germania St., 02130* ☎ *617/368–5080* ⏱ *Mon.–Thurs. 10–3; Fri. 10–5:30; Sat. 10–3*), where research and development into new products are conducted (the bulk of Samuel Adams production is done elsewhere). The entertaining hour-long tour is free, and, naturally, includes a tasting. You will get to smell and taste the various elements of brewing: hops, malt, and barley; get a good look at the flavoring process, and hear about and perhaps even see new beers in development. On fair-weather weekends, there can be a wait, so arrive early to avoid standing around. Tours run continuously throughout the day.

COMEDY CLUBS

Comedy Connection, which has been voted the best comedy club in the country by *USA Today*, has a mix of local and nationally known acts seven nights a week, with two shows Friday and Saturday. The cover is $15–$29. ⊠ *246 Tremont St., in the Wilbur Theatre* ☎ *617/931–2000* ⊕ *www.comedyconnectionboston.com* Ⓣ *Boylston.*

★ **ImprovAsylum** features comedians who weave audience suggestions into seven weekly shows blending topical sketches with improv in shows such as "Lost in Boston" and "New Kids on the Blog." Tickets are $20; students can get a two-for-one deal for $10 apiece. ⊠ *216 Hanover St., North End* ☎ *617/263–6887* ⊕ *www.improvasylum.com* Ⓣ *Haymarket, North Station.*

DANCE CLUBS

Gypsy Bar calls to mind the decadence of a dark European castle, with its rich red velvet and crystal chandeliers. Rows of video screens broadcast the Fashion Network, adding a sexier, more modern touch. Thirtysomething revelers and European students snack on lime-and-ginger-marinated tiger shrimp and sip "See You in Church" martinis (vodka with fresh marmalade) while the trendy dance floor throbs to Top 40 and house music. ⊠ *116 Boylston St., Theater District* ☎ *617/482–7799* ⊕ *www.gypsybarboston.com* Ⓣ *Boylston.*

★ **The Roxy** has a spacious interior that resembles an early-20th-century ballroom, but this club is hardly sedate. It throws theme nights such as "Sexy Fridays," as well as Chippendales male reviews and Latin dance parties. Watch for occasional rock concerts with bands such as the

The first club in the U.S. to host U2, Paradise Rock Club has offered big names in an intimate venue since 1977.

Killers. ✉ *279 Tremont St., Theater District* ☎ *617/338–7699* ⊕ *www.roxyboston.com* Ⓣ *Boylston.*

BLUES AND R&B CLUBS

★ **The Cantab Lounge/Third Rail** hums every night with live Motown, rhythm and blues, folk, or bluegrass. The Third Rail bar, downstairs, holds poetry slams, open-mike readings, and bohemia nights. ✉ *738 Massachusetts Ave., Cambridge* ☎ *617/354–2685* ⊕ *www.cantab-lounge.com* ▭ *No credit cards* Ⓣ *Central.*

JAZZ CLUBS

Regattabar hosts some of the top names in jazz, including Sonny Rollins and Herbie Hancock. Tickets are $15–$35. Even when there's no entertainment, the large, low-ceiling club is a pleasant (if expensive) place for a drink. ✉ *Charles Hotel, 1 Bennett St., Cambridge* ☎ *617/661–5000 or 617/395–7757* ⊕ *www.regattabarjazz.com* Ⓣ *Harvard.*

★ **Ryles Jazz Club** uses soft lights, mirrors, and greenery to set the mood for first-rate jazz. The first-floor stage is one of the best places for new music and musicians. Upstairs is a dance hall staging regular tango, salsa, and merengue nights, often with lessons before the dancing starts. Ryles also has a Sunday jazz brunch (call for reservations). It's open nightly, with a cover charge. ✉ *212 Hampshire St., Cambridge* ☎ *617/876–9330* ⊕ *www.ryles.com* Ⓣ *Bus 69, 83, or 91.*

ROCK CLUBS

★ **The Middle East Restaurant & Nightclub** manages to be both a Middle Eastern restaurant and one of the area's most eclectic rock clubs, with three rooms showcasing live local and national acts. Local phenoms the Mighty Mighty Bosstones got their start here. There's also belly dancing, folk, jazz, and even the occasional country-tinged rock band. ✉ *472–480 Massachusetts Ave., Cambridge* ☎ *617/497–0576 or 617/864–3278* ⊕ *www.mideastclub.com* T *Central.*

Fodor'sChoice   **Paradise Rock Club** is a small place known for hosting big-name talent ★ like U2, Coldplay, and local stars such as the Dresden Dolls. Two tiers of booths provide good sight lines anywhere in the club, as well as some intimate and out-of-the-way corners, and four bars quench the crowd's thirst. The 18-plus crowd varies with the shows. The newer Paradise Lounge, next door, is a more intimate space to experience local, often acoustic songsters, as well as literary readings and other artistic events. It serves dinner. ✉ *967–969 Commonwealth Ave., Allston ✛ Near Boston University* ☎ *617/562–8800* ⊕ *www.thedise.com* T *Pleasant St.*

THE ARTS

BALLET

★ **Boston Ballet,** the city's premier dance company, performs at the Citi Performing Arts Center from October through May. In addition to a repertory of classical and high-spirited modern works, it presents an elaborate *Nutcracker* during the holidays at the restored downtown Opera House. ✉ *19 Clarendon St., South End* ☎ *617/695–6950* ⊕ *www.bostonballet.org* T *Back Bay.*

José Mateo's Ballet Theatre is a troupe building an exciting, contemporary repertory under Cuban-born José Mateo, the resident artistic director-choreographer. The troupe's performances include an original *Nutcracker,* and take place October through April at the **Sanctuary Theatre,** a beautifully converted former church at Mass Ave. and Harvard Street in Harvard Square. ✉ *400 Harvard St., Cambridge* ☎ *617/354–7467* ⊕ *www.ballettheatre.org* T *Harvard.*

FILM

Brattle Theatre shows classic movies, new foreign and independent films, themed series, and directors' cuts. Tickets sell out every year for its acclaimed Bogart festival, scheduled around Harvard's exam period; the Bugs Bunny Film Festival in February; and *Trailer Treats,* an annual fund-raiser featuring an hour or two of classic and modern movie previews in July. It also has holiday screenings such as *It's a Wonderful Life* at Christmas. ✉ *40 Brattle St., Harvard Sq., Cambridge* ☎ *617/876–6837* ⊕ *www.brattlefilm.org* T *Harvard.*

Harvard Film Archive screens works from its vast collection of classics and foreign films that are not usually shown at commercial cinemas. The theater was created for student and faculty use, but the general public may attend regular screenings for $9 per person. ✉ *Carpenter Center for the Visual Arts, 24 Quincy St., Cambridge* ☎ *617/495–4700* ⊕ *hcl.harvard.edu/hfa/* T *Harvard.*

MUSIC

Bank of America Pavilion gathers up to 5,000 people on the city's waterfront for summertime concerts. National pop, folk, and country acts play the tentlike pavilion from about mid-June to mid-September.

✉ *290 Northern Ave., South Boston* ☎ *617/728–1600* ⊕ *www.bankofamericapavilion.com* Ⓣ *South Station.*

Berklee Performance Center, associated with Berklee College of Music, is best known for its jazz programs, but it's also host to folk performers such as Joan Baez and pop and rock stars such as Andrew Bird, Aimee Mann, and Henry Rollins. ✉ *136 Massachusetts Ave., Back Bay* ☎ *617/747–2261 box office; 617/747–8890 recorded info* ⊕ *www.berkleebpc.com* Ⓣ *Hynes.*

The Boston Opera House hosts plays, musicals, and traveling Broadway shows, but also has booked diverse performers such as David Copperfield, B.B. King, and Pat Metheny. ✉ *539 Washington St., Downtown* ☎ *617/259–3400* ⊕ *www.bostonoperahouse.com* Ⓣ *Boylston, Chinatown, Downtown Crossing, Park Street.*

CONCERTS

★ **Hatch Memorial Shell,** on the bank of the Charles River, is a wonderful acoustic shell where the Boston Pops perform their famous free summer concerts (including their Fourth of July show). Local radio stations also put on music shows and festivals here April through October. ✉ *Off Storrow Dr. at embankment, Beacon Hill* ☎ *617/626–4970* ⊕ *www.mass.gov/dcr/hatch_events.htm* Ⓣ *Charles/MGH, Arlington.*

★ **New England Conservatory's Jordan Hall,** one of the world's acoustic treasures, is ideal for chamber music yet large enough to accommodate a full orchestra. The Boston Philharmonic and the Boston Baroque ensemble often perform at the relatively intimate 1,000-seat hall. ✉ *30 Gainsborough St., Back Bay* ☎ *617/585–1260 box office* ⊕ *concerts.newenglandconservatory.edu* Ⓣ *Symphony.*

Fodor's Choice
★ **Symphony Hall,** one of the world's best acoustical settings is home to the Boston Symphony Orchestra (BSO) and the Boston Pops. The BSO is led by James Levine, who's known for commissioning special works by contemporary composers, as well as for presenting innovative programs such as his two-year Beethoven/Schoenberg series. The Pops concerts, led by conductor Keith Lockhart, take place in May and June and around the winter holidays. The hall is also used by visiting orchestras, chamber groups, soloists, and local performers. Rehearsals are sometimes open to the public. ✉ *301 Massachusetts Ave., Back Bay* ☎ *617/266–1492* ⊕ *www.bostonsymphonyhall.org* Ⓣ *Symphony.*

OPERA

Boston Lyric Opera stages four full productions each season at Citi Performing Arts Center, which usually include one 20th-century work. Recent highlights have included Bizet's *Carmen* and Mozart's *The Magic Flute.* ☎ *617/542–4912; 617/542–6772 audience services office* ⊕ *www.blo.org* Ⓣ *Boylston.*

THEATER

The Huntington Theatre Company, Boston's largest resident theater company, performs a high-quality mix of 20th-century plays, new works, and classics under the leadership of artistic director Nicholas Martin, and commissions artists to create original dramas. The Huntington performs at the Boston University Theatre and at the Calderwood

Candlepin Bowling

Back in 1880 Justin White adjusted the size of his pins at his Worcester, Massachussetts, bowling hall, giving birth to candlepin bowling, a highly popular pint-sized version of ten-pin bowling. Now played almost exclusively in northern New England and in the Canadian Maritime Provinces, candlepin bowling is a game of power and accuracy.

Paradoxically, candlepin bowling is both much easier and far more difficult than regular bowling. The balls are significantly smaller, weighing less than 3 pounds. There are no finger holes, and players of all ages and abilities can whip the ball down the alley. But because both the ball and the pins are lighter, it is far more difficult to bowl strikes and spares. Players are allowed three throws per frame, and bowlers may hit fallen pins (called wood) to knock down other pins. There has never been a perfect "300" score. The top score is 245.

Good players score around 100 to 110, and novice players should be content with a score of 90.

A handful of alleys are in and around Boston, and many of them maintain their own quirky charm and history. Needham's **Bowlaway** (⊠ 16 Chestnut St., Needham ☎ 781/444–9614), one of the area's oldest bowling alleys, has eight cramped lanes in a tucked-away facility down a flight of stairs. Fans say Bowlaway is like bowling in your own basement. **Boston Bowl** (⊠ 820 Morrissey Blvd., Dorchester ☎ 617/825–3800) attracts a more adult crowd, and is open 24 hours a day. It has both ten-pin and candlestick bowling as well as pool tables. **Sacco's Bowl Haven** (⊠ 45 Day St., Somerville ☎ 617/776–0552) is proud that its '50s decor "makes bowling the way it was, the way it is." Run by the fourth generation of the Sacco family, the alley is decorated with old newspaper clippings and has few modern frills.

Theatre Pavilion in the South End. ⊠ Boston University Theatre, 264 Huntington Ave., Back Bay ☎ 617/266–0800 box office ⊕ www.huntingtontheatre.org Ⓣ Symphony ⊠ Calderwood Theatre Pavilion, Boston Center for the Arts, 527 Tremont St., South End ☎ 617/426–5000 ⊕ www.bcaonline.org Ⓣ Back Bay/South End, Copley.

★ **American Repertory Theater** stages experimental, classic, and contemporary plays, often with unusual lighting, stage design, or multimedia effects. With new director Diane Paulus bringing in immersive theatre performances, like The Donkey Show and Sleep No More (where audience and actors interact), the A.R.T. is selling out shows at its multiple venues. Its home at the Loeb Drama Center has two theaters; the smaller also holds productions by the Harvard-Radcliffe Drama Club. A modern theater space down the street, called the Zero Arrow Theatre, has a more flexible stage design. ⊠ 64 Brattle St., Harvard Sq., Cambridge ☎ 617/547–8300 ⊕ www.amrep.org Ⓣ Harvard.

★ **Boston Center for the Arts** houses more than a dozen quirky, low-budget troupes in six performance areas, including the 300-seat Stanford Calderwood Pavilion, two black-box theaters, and the massive Cyclorama, built to hold a 360-degree mural of the Battle of Gettysburg (the painting is now in a building at the battlefield). The experimental Pilgrim Theater, multiracial Company One, gay/lesbian Theatre Offensive, Irish-American Súgan Theatre troupe, and contemporary SpeakEasy Stage Company perform here year-round. ⊠ *539 Tremont St., South End* ☎ *617/426–5000* ⊕ *www.bcaonline.org* Ⓣ *Back Bay/South End, Copley.*

SPORTS AND THE OUTDOORS

Updated by Michael Nalepa

Everything you've heard about the zeal of Boston fans is true; you cheer, and you pray, and you root some more. "Red Sox Nation" witnessed a miracle in 2004, with the reverse of the curse and the team's first World Series victory since 1918.

Then in 2007 they proved it wasn't just a fluke with another Series win. In 2008 the Celtics ended their 18-year NBA championship drought with a victory over longtime rivals the LA Lakers. And three-time champions the New England Patriots are still a force to be reckoned with.

Bostonians' fervor for sports is equally evident in their leisure-time activities. Harsh winters keep locals wrapped up for months, only to emerge at the earliest sign of oncoming spring. Once the mercury tops freezing and the snows begin to melt, Boston's extensive parks, paths, woods, and waterways teem with sun worshippers and athletes.

NATURAL PARKS AND BEACHES

Fodor'sChoice
★

Comprising 34 islands and peninsulas, the **Boston Harbor Islands National Park Area** is a somewhat hidden gem for nature lovers and history buffs, with miles of lightly traveled trails and shoreline and several little-visited historic sites to explore. The focal point of the national park is 39-acre Georges Island, where you'll find the partially restored pre–Civil War Fort Warren that once held Confederate prisoners. Other islands worth visiting include Peddocks Island, which holds the remains of Fort Andrews, and Lovells Island, a popular destination for campers. Lovells, Peddocks, Grape, and Bumpkin islands allow camping with a permit from late June through Labor Day. There are swimming areas at the four camping-friendly islands, but only Lovells has lifeguards. Pets and alcohol are not allowed on the Harbor Islands. The **National Park Service** (☎ *617/223–8666* ⊕ *www.bostonislands.com*) is a good source for information about camping, transportation, and the like. To reach the islands, take the **Harbor Express** (☎ *617/222–6999* ⊕ *www.harborexpress.com*) from Long Wharf (Downtown) or the Hingham Shipyard to Georges Island or Spectacle Island. High-speed catamarans run daily from May through mid-October and cost $14. Other islands can be reached by the free interisland water shuttles that depart from Georges Island.

Runners, bikers, and in-line skaters crowd the **Charles River Reservation** (⊕ *www.mass.gov/dcr/parks/charlesRiver*) at the Esplanade along Storrow Drive, the Memorial Drive Embankment in Cambridge, or any of the smaller and less-busy parks farther upriver. Here you can cheer a crew race, rent a canoe or a kayak, or simply sit on the grass, observing packs of hard-jogging university athletes, in-line skaters, moms with strollers, dreamily entwined couples, and intense academics talking to themselves as they sort out their intellectual—or perhaps personal—dilemmas.

The six large public parks known as Boston's **Emerald Necklace** stretch
Fodor's Choice   5 mi from the Back Bay Fens through Franklin Park, in Dorchester; it
★   also includes Arnold Arboretum, Jamaica Pond, Olmstead Park, and The Riverway. Frederick Law Olmsted's design heightened the beauty of the Emerald Necklace, which remains a well-groomed urban masterpiece. Locals make good use of its open spaces and its pathways and bridges connecting rivers and ponds. The **Emerald Necklace Conservancy** (☎ *617/522–2700* ⊕ *www.emeraldnecklace.org*) maintains a regular calendar of nature walks and other events in the parks. Rangers with the **Boston Parks & Recreation Department** (✉ *1010 Massachusetts Ave.* ☎ *617/635–4505* ⊕ *www.cityofboston.gov/parks/parkrangers*) lead tours highlighting the area's historic sites and surprising ecological diversity. The sumptuously landscaped **Arnold Arboretum** (✉ *125 Arborway, Jamaica Plain* ☎ *617/524–1718* ⊕ *www.arboretum.harvard.edu* Ⓣ *Forest Hills*) is open all year to joggers and in-line skaters. Volunteer docents give free walking tours in spring, summer, and fall.

PARTICIPANT SPORTS

BICYCLING

★   It's common to see suited-up doctors, lawyers, and businessmen commuting on two wheels through Downtown; unfortunately, bike lanes are few and far between. Boston's dedicated bike paths are well used, as much by joggers and in-line skaters as by bicyclists. The **Dr. Paul Dudley White Bike Path**, about 17 mi long, follows both banks of the Charles River as it winds from Watertown Square to the Museum of Science. The **Pierre Lallement Bike Path** winds 4 mi through the South End and Roxbury, from Copley Place to Franklin Park. The tranquil **Minuteman Bikeway** courses 11 mi from the Alewife Red Line T station in Cambridge through Arlington, Lexington, and Bedford. The trail, on the bed of an old rail line, cuts through a few busy intersections—be particularly careful in Arlington Center.

For other path locations, consult the **Department of Conservation & Recreation** (*DCR* ⊕ *www.mass.gov/dcr*) Web site.

The **Massachusetts Bicycle Coalition** (*MassBike* ✉ *171 Milk St., Suite 33, Downtown* ☎ *617/542–2453* ⊕ *www.massbike.org*), an advocacy group for area cyclists, has information on organized rides and sells good bike maps of Boston and the state. Thanks to MassBike, the MBTA now allows bicycles on subway and commuter-rail trains during nonpeak hours. **Community Bicycle Supply** (✉ *496 Tremont St., at E. Berkeley St., South End* ☎ *617/542–8623* ⊕ *www.communitybicycle.com*) rents cycles from April through October, at rates of $25 for 24 hours. **Back Bay Bicycles** (✉ *362 Commonwealth Ave., Back Bay* ☎ *617/247–2336* ⊕ *www.backbaybicycles.com*) has city cruiser bike rentals for $35 per day, road bikes for $55 per day, and full-suspension mountain bikes for $100 per day (weekly rates are also available). Staff members also lead group mountain-bike rides on nearby trails.

Many of the local University teams row on the Charles River.

BOATING

Except when frozen over, the waterways coursing through the city serve as a playground for boaters of all stripes. All types of pleasure craft, with the exception of inflatables, are allowed from the Charles River and Inner Harbor to North Washington Street on the waters of Boston Harbor, Dorchester inner and outer bays, and the Neponset River from the Granite Avenue Bridge to Dorchester Bay.

Sailboats can be rented from one of the many boathouses or docks along the Charles. Downtown, public landings and float docks are available at the **Christopher Columbus Waterfront Park** (⊠ *Commercial St., Boston Harbor, North End* ☎ *617/635–4505*) with a permit from the Boston harbormaster. Along the Charles, **boat drop sites** are at **Clarendon Street** (⊠ *Back Bay*), the **Hatch Shell** (⊠ *Embankment Rd., Back Bay*), **Pinckney Street Landing** (⊠ *Back Bay*), **Brooks Street** (⊠ *Nonantum Rd., Brighton*), **Richard T. Artesani Playground** (⊠ *Off Soldiers Field Rd., Brighton*), **Charles River Dam, Museum of Science** (⊠ *Cambridge*), and **Watertown Square** (⊠ *Charles River Rd., Watertown*).

The **Charles River Watershed Association** (☎ *781/788–0007* ⊕ *www. charlesriver.org*) publishes boating information on its Web site.

SPECTATOR SPORTS

See the Fenway Park spotlight at the beginning of this chapter.

BASKETBALL

★ The **Boston Celtics** (⊠ *TD Garden, Old West End* ☎ *617/624–1000; 617/931–2222 Ticketmaster* ⊕ *www.celtics.com*), one of the most storied franchises in the National Basketball Association, have won the

CLOSE UP

The Boston Marathon

Though it missed being the first U.S. marathon by one year (the first, in 1896, went from Stamford, Connecticut, to New York City), the Boston Marathon is arguably the nation's most prestigious. Why? It's the only marathon for which runners have to qualify; it's the world's oldest continuously run marathon; it's been run on the same course since it began. Spectators have returned to the same spot for generations, bringing their lawn chairs and barbecues.

Held every Patriots' Day (the third Monday in April), the marathon passes through Hopkinton, Ashland, Framingham, Natick, Wellesley, Newton, Brookline, and Boston; only the last few miles are run in the city proper. The first marathon was organized by members of the Boston Athletic Association (BAA), who in 1896 had attended the first modern Olympic games in Athens. When they saw that the Olympics ended with a marathon, they decided the same would be a fitting end to their own Spring Sports Festival.

The first race was run on April 19, 1897, when Olympian Tom Burke drew a line in the dirt in Ashland and began a 24.5-mi dash (increased to its current 26.2 mi in 1924) to Boston with 15 men. For most of its history, the race concluded on Exeter Street outside the BAA's clubhouse. In 1965 the finish was moved to the front of the Prudential Center, and in 1986 it was moved to its current location, Copley Square. The race's guardian spirit is the indefatigable John A. Kelley, who ran his first marathon shortly after Warren G. Harding was sworn in as president. Kelley won twice—in 1935 and 1945—took the second-place spot seven times, and

continued to run well into his 80s, finishing 58 Boston Marathons in all. Until his retirement in 1992, his arrival at the finish signaled the official end of the race. A double statue of an older Kelley greeting his younger self stands at the route's most strenuous incline—dubbed "Heartbreak Hill"—on Commonwealth Avenue in Newton.

Women weren't allowed to race until 1972, but in 1966 Roberta Gibb slipped into the throngs under a hooded sweatshirt; she was the first known female participant. In 1967 cameras captured BAA organizer Jock Semple screaming, "Get out of my race," as he tried to rip off the number of Kathrine Switzer, who had registered as K. Switzer. But the marathon's most infamous moment was when 26-year-old Rosie Ruiz came out of nowhere to be the first woman to cross the finish line in the 1980 race. Ruiz apparently started running less than 1 mi from the end of the course, and her title was stripped eight days later.

WORD OF MOUTH

Traveler's at Fodors.com have enjoyed the race, both as spectators and runners:

"The town was hopping!...we set up curbside on a blanket near mile 24, with books and snacks till runners started arriving. Saw all the elite runners, Lance Armstrong, and it was a blast." —ilana25841

"I don't remember much of mile 24–25 other than pain. The last mile we round the corner and on the home stretch I see the big blue finish line... Shortly I feel better and celebrate with a cheeseburger, fries, and two Sam Adams beers. Life is sweet; I love Boston." —Queenie

NBA championship a record 17 times since 1957. The last title came in 2008, after a solid defeat of longtime rivals the LA Lakers ended an 18-year championship dry spell. Basketball season runs from late October to April, and play-offs last until mid-June.

FOOTBALL

New England Patriots' (⊠ *Gillette Stadium, Rte. 1, off I–95 Exit 9, Foxborough* ☎ *617/931–2222 Ticketmaster* ⊕ *www.patriots.com*) football dynasty started with their come-from-behind victory against the St. Louis Rams in the 2002 Super Bowl. Coach Bill Belichick and heart-throb quarterback Tom Brady then brought the team two more championship rings in 2004 and 2005, and Patriots fans are now as zealous as their baseball counterparts. Exhibition games begin in August, and the season runs through the playoffs in January. The Gillette Stadium is in Foxborough, 30 mi southwest of Boston.

HOCKEY

The **Boston Bruins** (⊠ *TD Garden, 100 Legends Way, Old West End* ☎ *617/624–1900; 617/931–2222 Ticketmaster* ⊕ *www.bostonbruins. com*) are on the ice from September until April, frequently on Thursday and Saturday evenings. Play-offs last through early June.

Boston College, Boston University, Harvard, and Northeastern teams face off every February in the **Beanpot Hockey Tournament** (☎ *617/624– 1900* ⊕ *www.beanpothockey.com*) at the TD Garden. The colleges in this fiercely contested tournament traditionally yield some of the finest squads in the country.

RUNNING

Fodor'sChoice
★

Every Patriots' Day (the third Monday in April), fans gather along the Hopkinton-to-Boston route of the **Boston Marathon** (⇨ *Close-Up box in this chapter*) to cheer on more than 25,000 runners from all over the world. The race ends near Copley Square in the Back Bay. For information, call the **Boston Athletic Association** (☎ *617/236–1652* ⊕ *www. bostonmarathon.org*).

SHOPPING

Updated by
Amanda Knorr

Boston's shops are generally open Monday through Saturday from 10 or 11 until 6 or 7 and Sunday noon to 5. Many stay open until 8 PM one night a week, usually Thursday. Malls are open Monday through Saturday from 9 or 10 until 8 or 9 and Sunday noon to 6.

MAJOR SHOPPING DISTRICTS

Boston's shops and department stores are concentrated in the area bounded by Quincy Market, the Back Bay, and Downtown. There are plenty of bargains in the Downtown Crossing area. The South End's gentrification creates its own kind of consumerist milieus, from housewares shops to avant-garde art galleries. In Cambridge you can find lots of shopping around Harvard and Central squares, with independent boutiques migrating west along Massachusetts Avenue (or Mass Ave., as almost everyone else calls it) toward Porter Square and beyond.

BOSTON

Charles Street is crammed beginning to end with top-notch antiques stores such as Judith Dowling Asian Art, Eugene Galleries, and Devonia, as well as a handful of independently owned fashion boutiques whose prices reflect their high Beacon Hill rents. River Street, parallel to Charles Street, is also an excellent source for antiques. Both are easy walks from the Charles Street T stop on the Red Line.

Copley Place (⊠ *100 Huntington Ave., Back Bay* ☎ *617/369–5000* T *Copley*), an indoor shopping mall in the Back Bay, includes such high-end shops as Christian Dior, Louis Vuitton, and Gucci, anchored by the pricey but dependable Neiman Marcus and the flashy, overpriced Barneys.

Downtown Crossing (⊠ *Washington St. from Amory St. to about Milk St., Downtown* T *Downtown Crossing, Park St.*) is a pedestrian mall with a Macy's, H&M, and TJ Maxx. Millennium Place, a 1.8-million-square-foot complex with a Ritz-Carlton Hotel, condos, a massive sports club, a 19-screen Loews Cineplex, and the new W Hotel, turned this once seedy hangout into a happening spot.

Faneuil Hall Marketplace (⊠ *Bounded by Congress St., Atlantic Ave., the Waterfront, and Government Center, Downtown* ☎ *617/523–1300* T *Government Center*) is a huge complex that's also hugely popular, even though most of its independent shops have given way to Banana Republic, Crate & Barrel, and other chains. The place has one of the area's great à la carte casual dining experiences (Quincy Market), and carnival-like trappings: pushcarts sell everything from silver jewelry to Peruvian sweaters, and buskers perform crowd-pleasing feats such as break dancing.

★ **Newbury Street** (T *Arlington, Copley, Hynes*) is Boston's version of New York's 5th Avenue. The entire street is a shoppers' paradise, from high-end names such as Brooks Brothers to tiny specialty boutiques such as Diptyque. Upscale clothing stores, up-to-the-minute art galleries, and dazzling jewelers line the street near the Public Garden. As you head toward Mass Ave., Newbury gets funkier and the cacophony builds, with skateboarders zipping through traffic and garbage-pail drummers burning licks outside the hip boutiques. The big-name stores run from Arlington Street to the Prudential Center.

South End (T *Back Bay/South End*) merchants are benefiting from the ongoing gentrification that has brought high real-estate prices and trendy restaurants to the area. Explore the chic home-furnishings and gift shops that line Tremont Street, starting at Berkeley Street. The MBTA's Silver Line bus runs through the South End.

CAMBRIDGE

Central Square (⊠ *East of Harvard Sq.* T *Central*) has an eclectic mix of furniture stores, used-record shops, ethnic restaurants, and small, hip performance venues.

Harvard Square (T *Harvard*) takes up just a few blocks but holds more than 150 stores selling clothes, books, records, furnishings, and specialty items.

The **Galleria** (⊠ *57 JFK St.* ⊤ *Harvard*) has various boutiques and a few decent, independently owned restaurants. A handful of chains and independent boutiques are clustered in **Brattle Square** (⊠ *Behind Harvard Sq.* ⊤ *Harvard*).

Porter Square (⊠ *West on Mass Ave. from Harvard Sq.* ⊤ *Porter*) has distinctive clothing stores, as well as crafts shops, coffee shops, natural-food stores, restaurants, and bars with live music.

DEPARTMENT STORES

★ **Barneys New York.** The hoopla generated by this store's arrival was surprising in a city where everything new is viewed with trepidation. But clearly Boston's denizens have embraced the lofty, two-story space because it's filled with cutting-edge lines like Comme des Garçons and Nina Ricci, as well as a few bargains in the second-level Co-op section. ⊠ *100 Huntington Ave., Back Bay* ☎ *617/385–3300* ⊤ *Copley*.

Lord & Taylor. This is a reliable, if somewhat overstuffed with merchandise, stop for classic clothing by such designers as Anne Klein and Ralph Lauren, along with accessories, cosmetics, and jewelry. ⊠ *760 Boylston St., Back Bay* ☎ *617/262–6000* ⊤ *Prudential Center*.

Macy's. Three floors offer men's and women's clothing and shoes, housewares, and cosmetics. Although top designers are part of the mix, Macy's doesn't feel exclusive; instead, it's a popular source for family basics. ⊠ *450 Washington St., Downtown* ☎ *617/357–3000* ⊤ *Downtown Crossing*.

Neiman Marcus. The flashy Texas-based retailer known to many as "Needless Markup" has three levels of swank designers and a jaw-dropping shoe section, as well as cosmetics and housewares. ⊠ *5 Copley Pl., Back Bay* ☎ *617/536–3660* ⊤ *Back Bay/South End*.

Saks Fifth Avenue. The clothing and accessories at Saks run from the traditional to the flamboyant. It's a pricey but excellent place to find high-quality merchandise, including shoes and cosmetics. ⊠ *Prudential Center, 1 Ring Rd., Back Bay* ☎ *617/262–8500* ⊤ *Prudential Center*.

SPECIALTY STORES

ANTIQUES

Newbury Street and the South End have some excellent (and expensive) antiques stores, but Charles Street—one of the city's oldest streets—is the place to go for a concentrated selection.

Autrefois Antiques. Come here to find French country and Italian 18th-, 19th-, and 20th-century furniture, mirrors, and lighting. ⊠ *130 Harvard St., Brookline* ☎ *617/566–0113* ⊤ *Coolidge Corner*.

Boston Antique Co-op. This flea market–style collection of dealers occupies two floors, containing everything from vintage photos and paintings to porcelain, silver, bronzes, and furniture. ⊠ *119 Charles St., Beacon Hill* ☎ *617/227–9810 or 617/227–9811* ⊤ *Charles/MGH*.

Cambridge Antique Market. Off the beaten track this may be, but it has a selection bordering on overwhelming: five floors of goods ranging

The Harvard Coop has peddled books to university students since 1882.

from 19th-century furniture to vintage clothing, much of it reasonably priced. There are two parking lots next to the building. ⊠ *201 Monsignor O'Brien Hwy., Cambridge* ☎ *617/868–9655* Ⓣ *Lechmere.*

BOOKS

☺ **Barefoot Books.** Don't come looking for the same old kids' books; Barefoot is full of beautifully illustrated, creatively told reading for kids of all ages. These are the books that kids remember and keep as adults. ⊠ *1771 Massachusetts Ave., Cambridge* ☎ *617/349–1610* Ⓣ *Porter.*

Fodor's Choice ★

Brattle Bookshop. The late George Gloss built this into Boston's best used- and rare-book shop. Today his son Kenneth fields queries from passionate book lovers. If the book you want is out of print, Brattle has it or can probably find it. ⊠ *9 West St., Downtown* ☎ *617/542–0210 or 800/447–9595* Ⓣ *Downtown Crossing.*

Fodor's Choice ★

Harvard Book Store. The intellectual community is well served here, with a slew of new titles upstairs and used and remaindered books downstairs. The collection's diversity has made the store a favored destination for academics. ⊠ *1256 Massachusetts Ave., Cambridge* ☎ *617/661–1515* Ⓣ *Harvard.*

Trident Booksellers & Café. Browse through an eclectic collection of books, tapes, and magazines; then settle in with a snack. It's open until midnight daily, making it a favorite with students. ⊠ *338 Newbury St., Back Bay* ☎ *617/267–8688* Ⓣ *Hynes.*

2

CLOTHING AND SHOES

★ **Alan Bilzerian.** Satisfying the Euro crowd, this store sells luxe men's and women's clothing by such fashion darlings as Yohji Yamamoto and Ann Demeulemeester. ⊠ *34 Newbury St., Back Bay* ☎ *617/536–1001* Ⓣ *Arlington.*

Anne Fontaine. You can never have too many white shirts—especially if they're designed by this Parisienne. The simple, sophisticated designs are mostly executed in cotton and priced around $160. ⊠ *318 Boylston St., Back Bay* ☎ *617/423–0366* Ⓣ *Arlington, Boylston.*

Betsy Jenney. Ms. Jenney herself is likely to wait on you in this small, personal store, where the well-made, comfortable lines are for women who cannot walk into a fitted size-4 suit—in other words, most of the female population. The designers found here, such as Philippe Adec, Teenflo, and Nicole Miller, are fashionable yet forgiving. ⊠ *114 Newbury St., Back Bay* ☎ *617/536–2610* Ⓣ *Copley.*

Daniela Corte. Local designer Corte cuts women's clothes that flatter from her sunny Back Bay studio. Look for gorgeous suiting, flirty halter dresses, and formal frocks that can be bought off the rack or custom tailored. ⊠ *91 Newbury St., Back Bay* ☎ *617/262–2100* Ⓣ *Copley.*

Grettaluxe. Drop by Copley's sassy little boutique and pick up the latest "it" pieces—from velour hoodies by Juicy Couture to the must-have Stella McCartney design *du moment.* ⊠ *Westin Hotel, 10 Huntington Ave., Back Bay* ☎ *617/266–6166* Ⓣ *Copley.*

Fodor'sChoice **Louis Boston.** Impeccably tailored designs, subtly updated classics, and
★ the latest Italian styles highlight a wide selection of imported clothing and accessories. ■ TIP➔ The store plans to move to the Fort Point Channel area in Spring of 2010. Check with the company for its new location. ⊠ *234 Berkeley St., Back Bay* ☎ *617/262–6100* Ⓣ *Arlington.*

GIFTS

Buckaroo's Mercantile. It's Howdy Doody time at Buckaroo's—a great destination for the kitsch inclined. Find pink poodle skirts, lunch-box clocks, Barbie lamps, *Front Page Detective* posters, and everything Elvis. ⊠ *5 Brookline St., Cambridge* ☎ *617/492–4792* Ⓣ *Central.*

★ **Diptyque.** The venerable Paris house has its flagship U.S. store on Newbury Street. The hand-poured candles, room sprays, and gender-neutral eau de toilettes are expensive, but each is like a little work of art—and just entering the calmly inviting store is like having a mini–aromatherapy session. ⊠ *123 Newbury St., Back Bay* ☎ *617/351–2430* Ⓣ *Copley.*

The Flat of the Hill. There's nothing flat about this fun collection of seasonal items, toiletries, toys, pillows, and whatever else catches the fancy of the shop's young owner. Her passion for pets is evident—pick up a Fetch & Glow ball and your dog will never again have to wait until daytime to play in the park. ⊠ *60 Charles St., Beacon Hill* ☎ *617/619–9977* Ⓣ *Charles/MGH.*

★ **Fresh.** You won't know whether to wash with these soaps or nibble on them. The shea butter–rich bars come in such scents as clove-hazelnut and orange-cranberry. ⊠ *121 Newbury St., Back Bay* ☎ *617/421–1212* Ⓣ *Copley.*

WHERE TO EAT

Updated
by Brigid
Sweeney

In a city synonymous with tradition, Boston chefs have spent recent years rewriting culinary history. The stuffy, wood-paneled formality is gone; the endless renditions of chowdah, lobster, and cod have retired. A crop of young chefs have ascended, opening small, upscale neighborhood spots that use New England ingredients to delicious effect.

Traditional eats can still be found (Durgin-Park remains as the best place to get baked beans), but many diners now gravitate toward innovative food in understated environs. Whether you're looking for casual French, down-home Southern cooking, some of the best sushi in the country, or Vietnamese banh mi sandwiches, Boston restaurants are ready to deliver. The fish and shellfish brought in from nearby shores continue to inform the regional cuisine: expect to see several seafood options on local menus, but don't expect them to be boiled or dumped into the lobster stew that JFK loved. Instead, you might be offered swordfish with salsa verde, cornmeal-crusted scallops, or lobster cassoulet with black truffles.

In many ways, though, Boston remains solidly skeptical of trends. If you close your eyes in the North End, Boston's Little Italy, you can easily imagine you're in Rome circa 1955. And over in the university culture of Cambridge, places like East Coast Grill and Oleana espoused the locovore and slow-food movements before they became buzzwords.

WHAT IT COSTS IN BOSTON				
	¢	$	$$	$$$	$$$$
AT DINNER	under $10	$10–$17	$18–$24	$25–$35	over $35

Price per person for a median main course or equivalent combination of smaller dishes.

Use the coordinate (✛ B2) at the end of each listing to locate a site on the Where to Eat and Stay in Boston map.

BACK BAY AND SOUTH END

$–$$
SEAFOOD
★

✕**B&G Oysters, Ltd.** Chef Barbara Lynch (of No. 9 Park, the Butcher Shop, and Sportello fame) has made yet another fabulous mark on Boston with a style-conscious seafood restaurant that updates New England's traditional bounty with flair. Designed to imitate the inside of an oyster shell, the bar glows with silvery, candlelit tiles and a sophisticated crowd. They're in for the lobster roll, no doubt—an expensive proposition at $25, but worth every cent for its decadent chunks of crustacean in a perfectly textured dressing. If you're sans reservation, the line for a seat can be epic. ✉ *550 Tremont St., South End* ☎ *617/423–0550* ⊕ *www.bandgoysters.com* ⊟ *AE, D, MC, V* Ⓣ *Back Bay/South End* ✛ *E6.*

$$$$
FRENCH
Fodor's Choice
★

✕**Clio.** Years ago, when Ken Oringer opened his snazzy leopard skin–lined hot spot in the tasteful boutique Eliot Hotel, the hordes were fighting over reservations. Things have quieted down since then, but the food hasn't. Foie gras, Maine lobster, and Kobe sirloin share menu space with

BEST BETS FOR BOSTON DINING

2

Fodor's Choice★

East Coast Grill and Raw Bar, p. 115
L'Espalier, p. 110
Oleana, p. 116
Radius, p. 114
Toro, p. 112

By Price

$

Barking Crab Restaurant, p. 113
Tanjore, p. 116

$$

B&G Oysters Ltd., p. 106
Eastern Standard, p. 107
Oleana, p. 116
Pomodoro, p. 115

$$$

Chez Henri, p. 115
Grill 23 & Bar, p. 107
Neptune Oyster, p. 115
Radius, p. 114
Sel de la Terre, p. 114
Toro, p. 112

$$$$

Clio, p. 106
L'Espalier, p. 110
Pigalle, p. 110

By Cuisine

AMERICAN

Eastern Standard, p. 107
East Coast Grill and Raw Bar, p. 115

ITALIAN

Pomodoro, p. 115

SEAFOOD

B&G Oysters Ltd., p. 106
Barking Crab Restaurant, p. 113
Legal Seafood, p. 111

By Experience

FAMILY FRIENDLY

Bartley's Burger Cottage, p. 111
Charley's Saloon, p. 111
Full Moon, p. 116
Sweet Cupcakes, p. 111

HISTORIC INTEREST

Durgin-Park Market Dining Room, p. 114
Union Oyster House, p. 114

---

fail-safe crispy chicken and Scottish salmon. A magnet for romantics and foodies alike, Clio continues to serve some of the city's most decadent and well-crafted meals. ⊠ *Eliot Hotel, 370 Commonwealth Ave., Back Bay* ☎ *617/536–7200* ⊕ *www.cliorestaurant.com* ⌕ *Reservations essential* ⊟ *AE, D, MC, V* ☉ *No lunch* Ⓣ *Hynes* ✛ *B5.*

$$ ✕ **Eastern Standard Kitchen and Drinks.** A vivid red awning beckons patrons
AMERICAN to this spacious brasserie-style restaurant. The bar area and red ban-
Fodor's Choice quettes are filled most nights with Boston's power players (members of
★ the Red Sox management are known to stop in), thirtysomethings, and students all noshing on raw-bar specialties and such comfort dishes as ricotta cavatelli, rib eye, and burgers. The cocktail list is one of the best in town, filled with old classics and new concoctions. A covered, heated patio offers alfresco dining much of the year. ⊠ *528 Commonwealth Ave., Kenmore Sq.* ☎ *617/532–9100* ⊕ *www.easternstandardboston. com* ⊟ *AE, D, DC, MC, V* Ⓣ *Kenmore* ✛ *A5.*

$$$ ✕ **Grill 23 & Bar.** Pinstriped suits, dark paneling, Persian rugs, and wait-
STEAK ers in white jackets give this steak house a posh demeanor. The food is anything but predictable, with dishes such as prime steak tartar with a

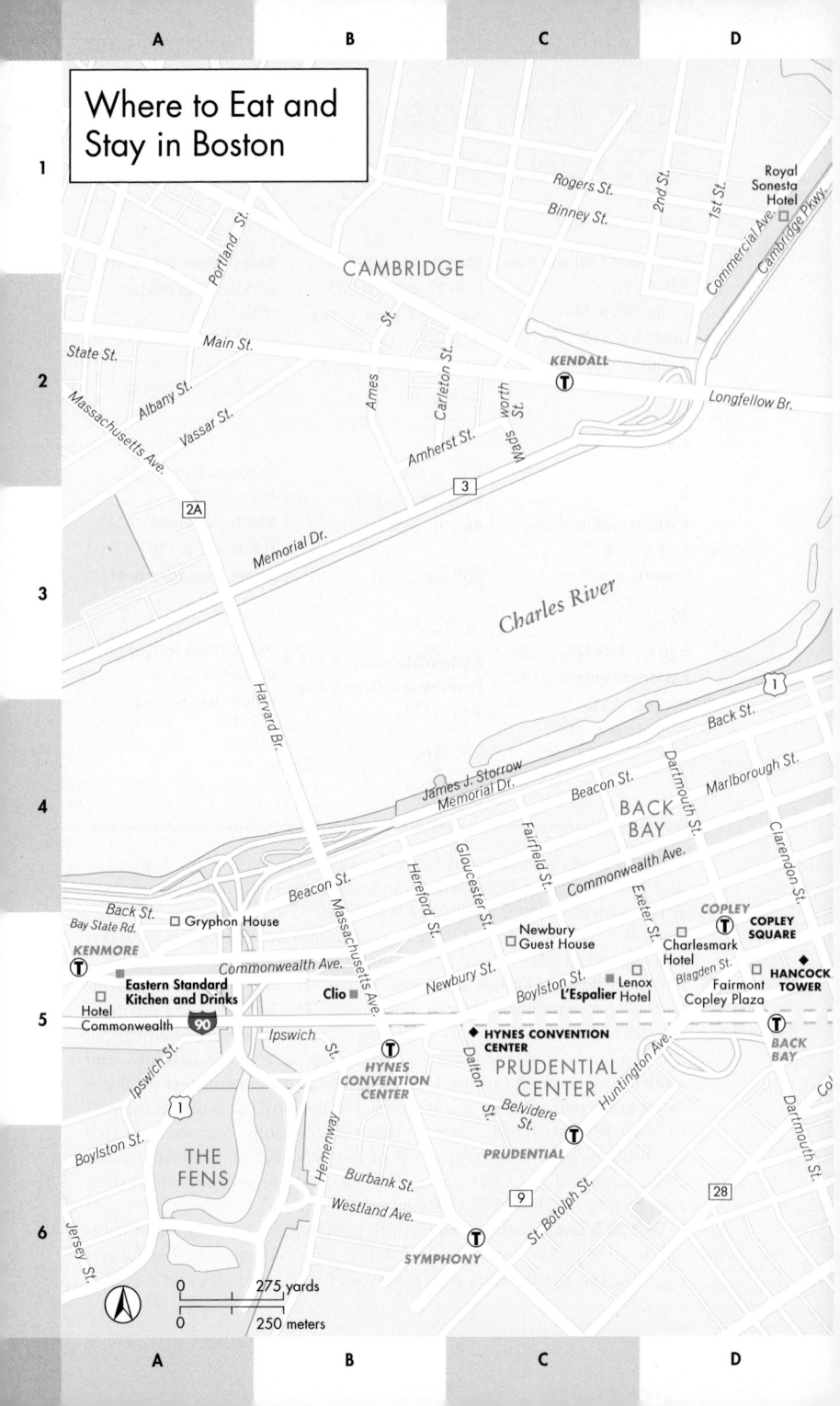

Where to Eat and Stay in Boston

CAMBRIDGE

Rogers St.
Binney St.

Royal Sonesta Hotel

KENDALL ⊤

Longfellow Br.

State St.
Albany St.
Vassar St.
Main St.
Massachusetts Ave.
Portland St.
Ames St.
Carleton St.
Wadsworth St.
Amherst St.

2A

3

Memorial Dr.

Charles River

1

Back St.

Harvard Br.

James J. Storrow Memorial Dr.

Beacon St.
Dartmouth St.
Marlborough St.

BACK BAY

Back St.
Bay State Rd.
Gryphon House

KENMORE ⊤

Eastern Standard Kitchen and Drinks

Hotel Commonwealth

90

Ipswich

Beacon St.
Commonwealth Ave.
Hereford St.
Gloucester St.
Fairfield St.
Exeter St.
Clarendon St.

COPLEY

COPLEY SQUARE

Newbury Guest House
Charlesmark Hotel
HANCOCK TOWER

Clio

Newbury St.
Boylston St.
L'Espalier
Lenox Hotel
Blagden St.
Fairmont Copley Plaza

⊤ BACK BAY

HYNES CONVENTION CENTER

⊤ HYNES CONVENTION CENTER

Dalton St.

PRUDENTIAL CENTER

Huntington Ave.

Dartmouth St.

Ipswich St.

1

Boylston St.

THE FENS

Hemenway

Belvidere St.

⊤ PRUDENTIAL

Burbank St.
Westland Ave.

9

St. Botolph St.

28

⊤ SYMPHONY

Jersey St.

0   275 yards
0   250 meters

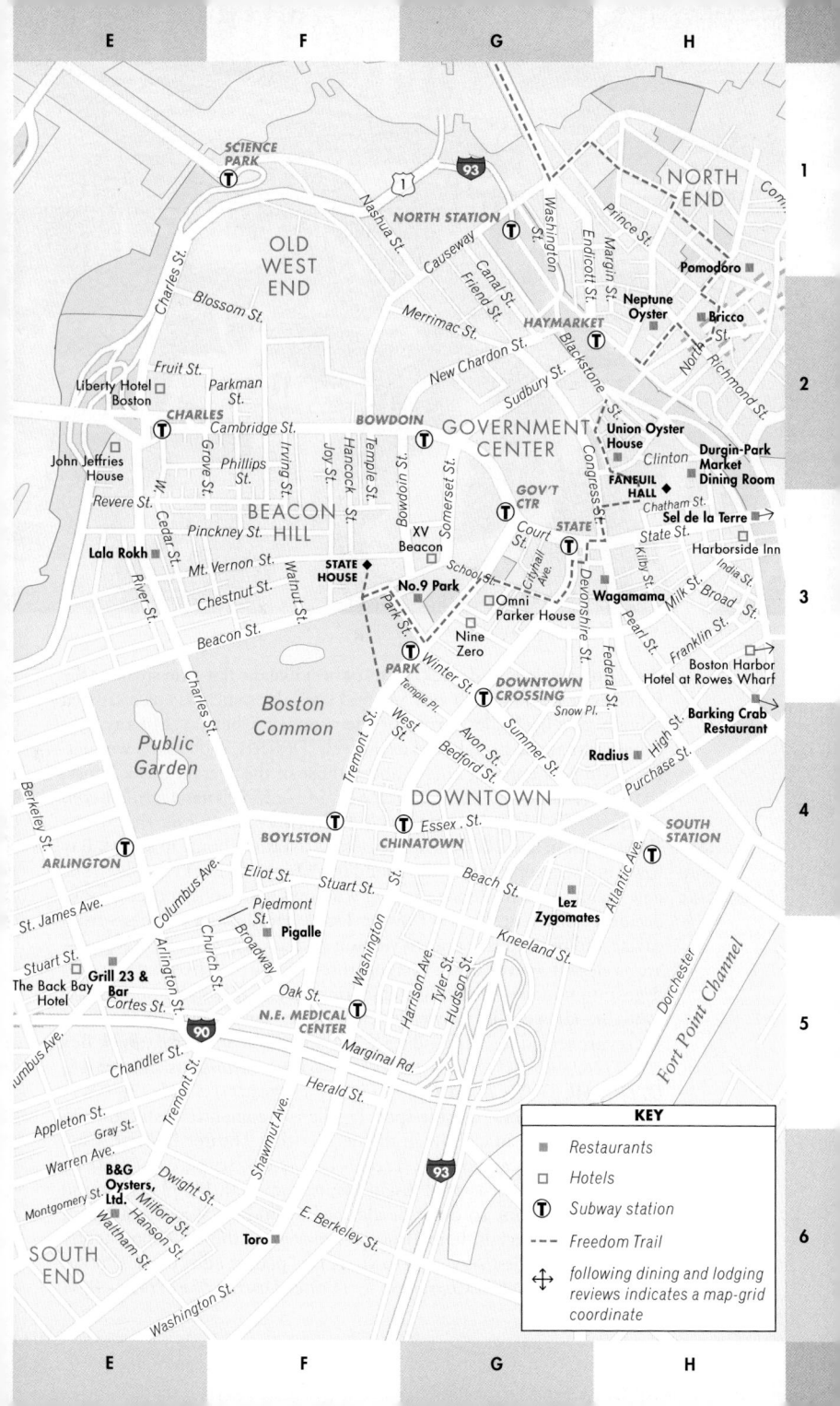

The bustling dining room at Eastern Standard Kitchen and Drinks.

shallot marmalade and weekly cuts of beef like the flat-iron steak or the Berkeley, a 16-ounce rib eye. Seafood specialties such as spice-crusted salmon give beef sales a run for their money. Chef Jay Murray uses prime, all-natural Brandt beef exclusively. Desserts, such as the wonderful warm pear cobbler, are far above those of the average steak house. ⊠ *161 Berkeley St., Back Bay* ☎ *617/542–2255* ⊕ *www.grill23.com* ⊟ *AE, D, DC, MC, V* ⊗ *No lunch* Ⓣ *Back Bay/South End* ⊹ *E5.*

$$$$ ╳ **L'Espalier.** In late 2008 L'Espalier left its longtime home in a Back Bay
FRENCH town house, reopening in the Mandarin Oriental Hotel complex. The
Fodor's Choice new locale, with its floor-to-ceiling windows and modern decor, looks
★ decidedly different. But chef-owner Frank McClelland's dishes—from caviar and roasted foie gras to venison with escargots de Bourgogne—are as elegant as ever. In the evening, three-course prix-fixe and seasonal degustation menus tempt discriminating diners. À la carte options are available for weekday power lunches; finger sandwiches and sublime sweets are served for weekend tea. ⊠ *774 Boylston St., 2nd fl., Back Bay* ☎ *617/262–3023* ⊕ *www.lespalier.com* ⇗ *Reservations essential* ⊟ *AE, D, DC, MC, V* ⊗ *Closed Sun. No lunch weekends* Ⓣ *Copley* ⊹ *C5.*

$$$$ ╳ **Pigalle.** A quaint, 20-table spot, Pigalle is a romantic destination to
FRENCH hit before taking in a show in the neighboring Theater District. Chef
★ Marc Orfaly spices up basic French fare (steak frites, cassoulet) by throwing in the occasional Asian-inspired special. He plays around with global flavors, so don't be alarmed to find spicy Szechuan pork on the nightly specials. For a delicious, cozy meal, this spot consistently has some of the best service in town. A jazz pianist adds musical notes Friday evenings. ⊠ *75 Charles St. S, Theater District* ☎ *617/423–4944*

CLOSE UP

Kid-Friendly Restaurants

Though it's unusual to see children in Boston's most elite restaurants, eating out with youngsters does not have to mean culinary exile. Here are some particularly family-friendly options.

Charley's Saloon. Saloons may be no place for kids, but this is no real saloon. Charley's doles out American classics (cheeseburgers, steaks, and apple pies) in a fun retro setting. Kids can color and people-watch. ⊠ *284 Newbury St., Back Bay* ☎ *617/266–3000.*

Full Moon. Kids will delight in the play kitchen and dollhouse, and parents can cheer that they get to tuck into lovelies such as grilled salmon with sautéed spinach. Meanwhile there's plenty of macaroni and cheese or quesadillas for the young ones. ⊠ *344 Huron Ave., Cambridge* ☎ *617/354–6699.*

Joe's American Bar & Grille. So what if the restaurant looks as if it has been decorated by a raving mob at a July 4 parade? Next to an oversize burger and a slice of apple pie, the red-white-and-blue overload is kind of fun. The clam chowder is almost always a hit with all generations. ⊠ *279 Dartmouth St., Back Bay* ☎ *617/536–4200.*

Kingfish Hall. Parents can dig into the fresh raw bar and junior can sup on clam chowder while watching the grill in the open kitchen. ⊠ *188 Faneuil Hall Market Pl., South Market Bldg.* ☎ *617/523–8860.*

Legal Sea Foods. Smack between Faneuil Hall and the New England Aquarium, Legal is a great break after a long day on your feet. The children's meals, extra rolls, and playful menus

don't hurt matters either. ⊠ *255 State St., Waterfront* ☎ *617/227–3115.*

Mr. Bartley's Burger Cottage. Maybe it's the frappés (thick milk shakes), silly cartoons all over the walls, or just the fun, high-energy vibe. Whatever it is, Bartley's is a hit with kids. ⊠ *1246 Massachusetts Ave., Cambridge* ☎ *617/354–6559.*

P. F. Chang's China Bistro. Straightforward, Americanized, and inexpensive Chinese food makes the rounds in this theatrically decorated spot. Kids love the lemon chicken and the fake Imperial sculptures and screens; parents love the prices and the accommodating staff. ⊠ *8 Park Plaza, Back Bay* ☎ *617/573–0821.*

Pizzeria Regina. This North End favorite offers kid-pleasing thin-crust slices that just might be the best pie in town. ⊠ *11 Thatcher Ct., North End* ☎ *617/227–0765.*

Sweet Cupcakes. This old-fashioned, pink-and-brown Back Bay shop, serving cupcakes topped with buttercream frosting is an 8-year-old girl's dream; frazzled parents can get a much-needed sugar jolt from the cappuccino and dark chocolate cake flavors. There's also a second, Harvard Square outpost. ⊠ *49 Massachusetts Ave., Back Bay* ☎ *617/247–2253* ⊠ *Zero Brattle St., Harvard Square* ☎ *617/547–2253.*

Zaftigs. Fill up on huge plates of deli fixings such as matzo-ball soup, first-rate knishes, and heaping plates of grilled chicken, thick-cut onion rings, and three-cheese macaroni. ⊠ *335 Harvard St., Brookline* ☎ *617/975–0075.*

2

A smoked salmon amuse bouche served at L'Espalier.

🕭 *Reservations essential* ⊕ *www.pigalleboston.com* ▭ *AE, D, DC, MC, V* ☺ *Closed Mon. No lunch* Ⓣ *Boylston* ✛ *F5.*

$$–$$$
SPANISH
Fodor's Choice
★

✕ **Toro.** The buzz from chef Ken Oringer's tapas joint still hasn't quieted down—for good reason. Small plates of garlic shrimp and crusty bread smothered in tomato paste are hefty enough to make a meal out of many, or share the regular or vegetarian paella with a group. An all-Spanish wine list complements the plates. Crowds have been known to wait it out for more than an hour. ⊠ *1704 Washington St., South End* ☎ *617/536–4300* ⊕ *www.toro-restaurant.com* 🕭 *Reservations not accepted* ▭ *AE, MC, V* Ⓣ *Massachusetts Ave.* ✛ *F6.*

BEACON HILL

$
MIDDLE EASTERN

✕ **Lala Rokh.** Persian miniatures and medieval maps cover the walls of this beautifully detailed fantasy of food and art. The focus is on the Azerbaijanian corner of what is now northwest Iran, including exotically flavored specialties and dishes such as familiar (and superb here) eggplant puree, pilaf, kebabs, *fesanjoon* (the classic pomegranate-walnut sauce), and lamb stews. The staff obviously enjoys explaining the menu, and the wine list is well selected for foods that often defy wine matches. ⊠ *97 Mt. Vernon St., Beacon Hill* ☎ *617/720–5511* ⊕ *www.lalarokh.com* ▭ *AE, DC, MC, V* ☺ *No lunch weekends* Ⓣ *Charles/MGH* ✛ *E3.*

$$$$
CONTINENTAL
★

✕ **No. 9 Park.** Chef Barbara Lynch's stellar cuisine draws plenty of well-deserved attention from its place in the shadow of the State House's golden dome. Settle into the plush but unpretentious dining room and indulge in pumpkin risotto with rare lamb or the memorably rich prune-

CLOSE UP

Refueling

If you're on the go, you might want to try a local chain restaurant where you can stop for a quick bite or get some takeout. The places listed below are fairly priced, committed to quality, and use decent, fresh ingredients.

B.Good. This chainlet's avocado- and salsa-topped veggie burgers, baked sweet-potato fries, and sesame-ginger chicken salad are redefining fast food in Boston.

Bertucci's. Thin-crust pizzas fly fast from the brick ovens here, along with pastas and a decent tiramisu.

BoLoCo. For quick, cheap, healthful, and high-quality wraps and burritos, this is easily the city's most

dependable (and also locally based) chain. BoLoCo's menu also includes smoothies and breakfast options, and its hours are some of the longest in this notoriously early-to-bed city.

Finagle A Bagel. Find fresh, doughy bagels in flavors from jalapeño cheddar to triple chocolate, plus sandwiches and salads. Service is swift and efficient.

UBurger. Better-than-average burgers with toppings that lean toward the gourmet (sautéed mushrooms, blue cheese) and a great chocolate frappe (Boston-ese for milkshake) make this spot the East Coast's answer to California's much-loved In-n-Out.

stuffed gnocchi drizzled with bits of foie gras. The wine list bobs and weaves into new territory, but is always well chosen, and the savvy bartenders are of the classic ilk, so you'll find plenty of classics and very few cloying, dessertlike sips here. ⊠ *9 Park St., Beacon Hill* 🕿 *617/742–9991* ⊕ *www.no9park.com* ⊟ *AE, D, DC, MC, V* Ⓣ *Park St.* ✢ *G3.*

DOWNTOWN

$–$$
SEAFOOD

✕ **Barking Crab Restaurant.** It is a seaside clam shack plunk in the middle of Boston, with a stunning view of the downtown skyscrapers. An outdoor lobster tent in summer, in winter it retreats indoors to a warmhearted version of a waterfront dive, with chestnuts roasting on a woodstove. Look for the classic New England clambake—chowder, lobster, steamed clams, corn on the cob—or the spicier crab boil. ⊠ *88 Sleeper St., Northern Ave. Bridge, Waterfront* 🕿 *617/426–2722* ⊕ *www. barkingcrab.com* ⊟ *AE, DC, MC, V* Ⓣ *South Station* ✢ *H4.*

$$–$$$
FRENCH

✕ **Les Zygomates.** *Les zygomates* is the French expression for the muscles on the human face that make you smile—and this combination wine bar–bistro lives up to its name, with quintessential French bistro fare that is simple (made with a number of New England sourced ingredients) and simply delicious. The lunch and dinner prix-fixe menus match the ever-changing wine list, with all wines served by the 2-ounce taste, 6-ounce glass, or bottle. An oyster bar has recently been added, and there is live jazz six nights a week. ⊠ *129 South St., Downtown* 🕿 *617/542–5108* ⊕ *www.winebar.com* ⌦ *Reservations essential* ⊟ *AE, D, DC, MC, V* ◷ *Closed Sun. No lunch Sat.* Ⓣ *South Station* ✢ *G4.*

$$$–$$$$ ✕ **Radius.** Acclaimed chef Michael Schlow's notable contemporary
FRENCH   French cooking lures scores of designer- and suit-clad diners to the
Fodor'sChoice   Financial District. The decor and menu are minimalist at first glance,
★   but closer inspection reveals equal shares of luxury, complexity, and
whimsy. Explore such choices as roasted beet salad, a selection of
ceviches, buttery Scottish salmon, or huckleberry-and-goat-cheese
cheesecake for dessert. At the bar they serve a phenomenal (and award-
winning) burger. Either way, it's a meal made for special occasions
and business dinners alike. ⊠ *8 High St., Downtown* ☏ *617/426–1234*
⊕ *www.radiusrestaurant.com* ⌲ *Reservations essential* ▭ *AE, DC, MC,
V* ☾ *Closed Sun. No lunch Sat.* Ⓣ *South Station* ✛ *H4.*

$$$ ✕ **Sel de la Terre.** Sitting between the waterfront and what used to be the
FRENCH   Central Artery, this is a hot spot to hit before the theater, after sight-
seeing, or for a simple lunch Downtown. The rustic, country-French
menu features items like steak frites with red wine–shallot reduction.
Stop by the *boulangerie* (bread shop) to take home fresh, homemade
loaves, which are some of the best in the city. ⊠ *255 State St., Waterfront* ☏ *617/720–1300* ⊕ *www.seldelaterre.com* ⌲ *Reservations essential* ▭ *AE, D, DC, MC, V* Ⓣ *Aquarium* ✛ *H3.*

GOVERNMENT CENTER/FANEUIL HALL

$$ ✕ **Durgin-Park Market Dining Room.** You should be hungry enough to
AMERICAN   cope with enormous portions, yet not so hungry you can't tolerate a
long wait (or sharing a table with others). Durgin-Park was serving its
same hearty New England fare (Indian pudding, baked beans, corned
beef and cabbage, and a prime rib that hangs over the edge of the plate)
back when Faneuil Hall was a working market instead of a tourist
attraction. The service is as brusque as it was when fishmongers and
boat captains dined here. ⊠ *340 Faneuil Hall Market Pl., North Market
Bldg.* ☏ *617/227–2038* ⊕ *www.arkrestaurant.com/durgin_park* ▭ *AE,
D, DC, MC, V* Ⓣ *Government Center* ✛ *H2.*

$$–$$$ ✕ **Union Oyster House.** Established in 1826, this is Boston's oldest con-
SEAFOOD   tinuing restaurant, and almost every tourist considers it a must-see. If
you like, you can have what Daniel Webster had—oysters on the half
shell at the ground-floor raw bar, which is the oldest part of the restau-
rant and still the best. The rooms at the top of the narrow staircase are
dark and have low ceilings—very Ye Olde New England—and plenty
of nonrestaurant history. The small tables and chairs (as well as the
endless lines and kitschy nostalgia) are as much a part of the charm as
the simple and decent (albeit pricey) food. One cautionary note: locals
hardly ever eat here. There is valet parking after 5:30 PM Monday
through Saturday. ⊠ *41 Union St., Government Center* ☏ *617/227–
2750* ⊕ *www.unionoysterhouse.com* ▭ *AE, D, DC, MC, V* Ⓣ *Hay-
market* ✛ *H2.*

NORTH END

$$$ ✕ **Bricco.** A sophisticated but unpretentious enclave of nouveau Italian,
ITALIAN   Bricco has carved out quite a following. And no wonder: the hand-made
pastas alone are argument for a reservation. Simple but well-balanced

2

main courses such as roast chicken marinated in seven spices and a brimming *brodetto* (fish stew) with half a lobster and a pile of seafood may linger in your memory. You're likely to want to linger in the warm room, too, gazing through the floor-to-ceiling windows while sipping a glass of Sangiovese from the all-Italian wine list. ✉ *241 Hanover St., North End* ☎ *617/248–6800* ⊕ *www.bricco.com* ⌕ *Reservations essential* ▭ *AE, D, MC, V* ☾ *No lunch* ⊤ *Haymarket* ⊹ *H2.*

$$–$$$
SEAFOOD

⚔ **Neptune Oyster.** This tiny oyster bar, the first of its kind in the neighborhood, has only 20 chairs, but the long marble bar has extra seating for about 20 more patrons and mirrors hang over the bar with handwritten menus. From there, watch the oyster shuckers deftly unhinge handfuls of bivalves. The *plateau di frutti di mare* is a tower of oysters and other raw-bar items piled over ice that you can order from the slip of paper they pass out listing each day's crustacean options. The lobster roll, hot or cold, overflows with meat. Service is prompt even when it gets busy. Go early to avoid a long wait. ✉ *63 Salem St., North End* ☎ *617/742–3474* ⊕ *www.neptuneoyster.com* ⌕ *Reservations not accepted* ▭ *AE, DC, MC, V* ⊤ *Haymarket* ⊹ *H2.*

$$
ITALIAN

⚔ **Pomodoro.** This teeny trattoria—just eight tables—is worth the wait. It serves excellent country Italian favorites such as rigatoni with white beans and arugula, and a sweet veal scaloppini with balsamic glaze, light-but-filling *zuppa di pesce*. The best choice could well be the clam-and-tomato stew with herbed flat bread, accompanied by a bottle of Vernaccia. Pomodoro doesn't serve dessert, but the cafés on Hanover Street have great espresso and pastries. ✉ *319 Hanover St., North End* ☎ *617/367–4348* ⊕ *www.pomodoroboston.com* ⌕ *Reservations essential* ▭ *No credit cards* ☾ *No lunch weekdays* ⊤ *Haymarket* ⊹ *H1.*

CAMBRIDGE

Use the coordinate (⊹ B2) at the end of each listing to locate a site on the Where to Eat and Stay in Cambridge map.

$$–$$$
ECLECTIC
★

⚔ **Chez Henri.** French with a Cuban twist—odd bedfellows, but it works for this sexy, confident restaurant. The dinner menu gets serious, with cassoulet with braised lamb and white beans, tuna au poivre, and sinfully sweet double-decker chocolate cake. At the cozy bar you can sample spiced fries, clam fritters, and the best grilled three-pork Cuban sandwich in Boston. The place fills quickly with Cantabrigian locals—an interesting mix of students, professors, and sundry intelligentsia. ✉ *1 Shepard St., Cambridge* ☎ *617/354–8980* ⊕ *www.chezhenri.com* ▭ *AE, DC, MC, V* ☾ *No lunch* ⊤ *Harvard* ⊹ *A1.*

$$
AMERICAN
Fodor's Choice
★

⚔ **East Coast Grill and Raw Bar.** Owner-chef-author Chris Schlesinger built his national reputation on grilled foods and red-hot condiments. The Jamaican jerk, North Carolina pulled pork, and habañero-laced "pasta from Hell" are still here, but this restaurant has made an extraordinary play to establish itself in the front ranks of fish restaurants. Spices and condiments are more restrained, and Schlesinger has compiled a wine list bold and flavorful enough to match the highly spiced food. The dining space is completely informal. A killer brunch (complete with a do-it-yourself Bloody Mary bar) is served on Sunday. ✉ *1271 Cambridge*

St., Cambridge ☎ *617/491–6568* ⊕ *www.eastcoastgrill.com* ▭ *AE, D, MC, V* ⊗ *No lunch* Ⓣ *Central* ✛ *A4.*

$–$$ ✕ **Full Moon.** Here's a happy reminder that dinner with children doesn't
AMERICAN have to mean hamburgers. Choices include child pleasers like home-
ⓒ made mac and cheese as well as grown-up entrées that include grilled
sirloin with blue-cheese butter. Youngsters can spread out with plenty
of designated play space and juice-filled sippy cups while adults weigh
the substantial menu and a well-paired wine list. ⊠ *344 Huron Ave.,
Cambridge* ☎ *617/354–6699* ⊕ *www.fullmoonrestaurant.com* ⚱ *Reservations not accepted* ▭ *MC, V* Ⓣ *Harvard* ✛ *B1.*

$$–$$$ ✕ **Oleana.** Chef-owner Ana Sortun is one of the city's culinary trea-
MEDITERRANEAN sures—and so is Oleana. Flavors from all over the Eastern Mediterra-
Fodor's Choice nean sing loud and clear, in the hot, crispy fried mussels starter and in
★ the smoky eggplant puree beside tamarind-glazed beef. Lamb is infused
with Turkish spices, while the rabbit is accented by Moroccan-spiced
almonds. In warm weather dine in the back patio—a homey garden that
hits the perfect note of casual refinement. ⊠ *134 Hampshire St., Cambridge* ☎ *617/661–0505* ⊕ *www.oleanarestaurant.com* ⚱ *Reservations
essential* ▭ *AE, MC, V* ⊗ *No lunch* Ⓣ *Central* ✛ *B5.*

$ ✕ **Tanjore.** The menu at this fully regional restaurant reaches from Sindh
INDIAN to Bengal, with some strength in the western provincial foods (Gujarat,
★ Bombay) and their interesting sweet-hot flavors. The *Baigan Bhurta* is
a platter of grilled, mashed eggplant; the rice dishes, chais, and breads
are all excellent, and the lunchtime buffet is usually a quick in-and-out
affair. The spicing starts mild, so don't be afraid to order "medium."
⊠ *18 Eliot St., Cambridge* ☎ *617/868–1900* ⊕ *www.tanjoreharvardsq.
com* ▭ *AE, D, MC, V* Ⓣ *Harvard* ✛ *1C.*

WHERE TO STAY

Updated by
Sascha de
Gersdorff

About five years ago Boston finally got wise to modernization, and a
rush of new construction took the local hotel scene by storm. Sleek,
boutique accommodations began inviting guests to Cambridge and
Downtown, areas once relegated to alumni and business traveler sets.
Plus, it seems that nearly every hotel in town just got a facelift. From
spruced up decor (goodbye, grandma's bedspread; hello, puffy white
duvets) to hopping restaurant-bars to new spas and fitness centers, Boston's lodgings are feeling the competitive heat and acting accordingly.
You don't just get a room anymore—you get an experience.

Of course, as in any industry, the recession hit new and old properties
hard. While business is picking up, many lodgings have slashed their
rates—and introduced stellar weekend deals—so don't be afraid to aim
four-star if you think you can only afford three. If you're more of a
"I just need a bed and a bathroom type," there are better affordable
options than ever, thanks to a host of made-over B&Bs in the South
End, Harvard Square, and Beacon Hill.

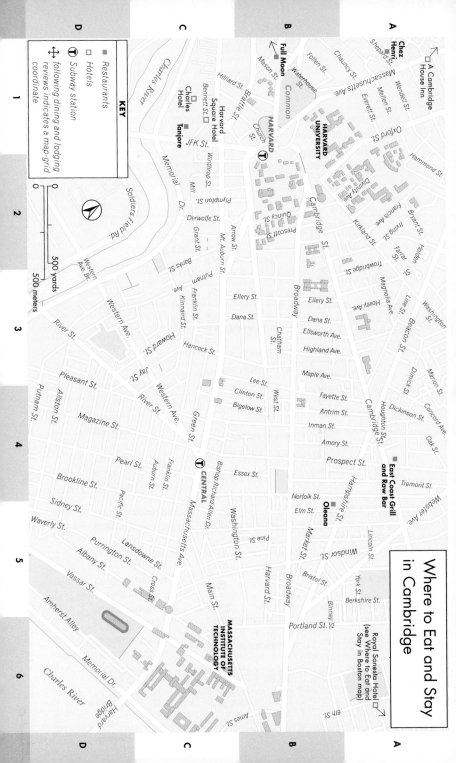

Where to Eat and Stay in Cambridge

KEY

- ■ Restaurants
- □ Hotels
- Ⓣ Subway station

✛ following dining and lodging reviews indicates a map-grid coordinate

500 yards
500 meters

A Cambridge House Inn □
Chez Henri ■
Full Moon ■
Charles Hotel □
Harvard Square Hotel □
Tanjore ■

HARVARD UNIVERSITY
Ⓣ HARVARD
Ⓣ CENTRAL

MASSACHUSETTS INSTITUTE OF TECHNOLOGY

East Coast Grill and Raw Bar ■
Oleana ■

Royal Sonesta Hotel □
(see Where to Eat and Stay in Boston map)

Charles River
Soldiers Field Rd.
Memorial Dr.
Western Ave. Br.
Harvard Bridge
Charles River

Follen St.
Chauncy St.
Massachusetts Ave.
Wendell St.
Mellen St.
Everett St.
Shepard St.
Oxford St.
Hammond St.
Waterhouse St.
Mason St.
Common
Dunster Ave.
Dimity Ave.
Hilliard St.
Brattle St.
Church St.
Francis Ave.
Irving St.
Bryant St.
Holden St.
Kirkland St.
Farrar St.
Bennett St.
JFK St.
Winthrop St.
Cambridge St.
Quincy St.
Prescott St.
Magnolia Ave.
Washington St.
Plympton St.
Arrow St.
Trowbridge St.
Hovey Ave.
Lime St.
Beacon St.
Derwolfe St.
Mt. Auburn St.
Broadway
Ellery St.
Dana St.
Ellsworth Ave.
Highland Ave.
Marion St.
Dimick St.
Concord Ave.
Grant St.
Banks St.
Putnam Ave.
Kinnaird St.
Franklin St.
Ellery St.
Dana St.
Chatham St.
Maple Ave.
Cambridge St.
Houghton St.
Dickinson St.
Oak St.
River St.
Western Ave.
Howard St.
Jay St.
Hancock St.
Lee St.
Clinton St.
Bigelow St.
West St.
Fayette St.
Antrim St.
Inman St.
Amory St.
Prospect St.
Tremont St.
Webster Ave.
Pleasant St.
Allston St.
Putnam St.
Magazine St.
River St.
Western Ave.
Green St.
Bishop Richard Allen Dr.
Essex St.
Washington St.
Norfolk St.
Elm St.
Hampshire St.
Lincoln St.
Pearl St.
Auburn St.
Franklin St.
Pacific St.
Massachusetts Ave.
Market St.
Windsor St.
York St.
Brookline St.
Sidney St.
Waverly St.
Lansdowne St.
Cross St.
Main St.
Harvard St.
Broadway
Bristol St.
Berkshire St.
Binney St.
Portland St.
6th St.
Purrington St.
Albany St.
Vassar St.
Amherst Alley
Memorial Dr.
Ames St.

A
B
C
D

1
2
3
4
5
6

BEST BETS FOR BOSTON LODGING

Fodor's Choice ★

Boston Harbor Hotel at Rowes Wharf, p. 124

Charles Hotel, p. 126

Charlesmark Hotel, p. 120

Fairmont Copley Plaza, p. 120

Gryphon House, p. 125

Hotel Commonwealth, p. 126

Liberty Hotel Boston, p. 122

Nine Zero, p. 124

By Price

$

Charlesmark Hotel, p. 120

John Jeffries House, p. 121

$$

Gryphon House, p. 125

$$$

Charles Hotel, p. 126

Fairmont Copley Plaza, p. 120

Hotel Commonwealth, p. 126

Liberty Hotel Boston, p. 122

$$$$

Boston Harbor Hotel at Rowes Wharf, p. 124

Nine Zero, p. 124

XV Beacon, p. 122

By Experience

BEST HOTEL BAR

Charles Hotel, p. 126

Hotel Commonwealth, p. 126

Liberty Hotel, p. 122

BEST FOR KIDS

Charles Hotel, p. 126

Fairmont Copley Plaza, p. 120

Omni Parker House, p. 125

BEST LOCATION

Charles Hotel, p. 126

Nine Zero, p. 124

BEST FOR ROMANCE

Charles Hotel, p. 126

Fairmont Copley Plaza, p. 120

XV Beacon, p. 122

BEST VIEWS

Liberty Hotel, p. 122

BEST HIP HOTELS

Charlesmark Hotel, p. 120

Nine Zero, p. 124

BEST PET HOTELS

Charles Hotel, p. 126

Fairmont Copley Plaza, p. 120

Nine Zero, p. 124

XV Beacon, p. 122

BEST GRANDES DAMES

Boston Harbor Hotel at Rowes Wharf, p. 124

Fairmont Copley Plaza, p. 120

Omni Parker House, p. 125

BEST DESIGN

Liberty Hotel, p. 122

WHAT IT COSTS

	¢	$	$$	$$$	$$$$
FOR TWO PEOPLE	under $100	$100–$199	$200–$299	$300–$400	over $400

Prices are for two people in a standard double room in high season, excluding 14.45% tax and service charges.

WHERE SHOULD I STAY?

	Neighborhood Vibe	Pros	Cons
Beacon Hill and Boston Common	Old brick and stone buildings host luxe boutique hotels and B&Bs on the hill or along busy, preppy Charles Street; some skyscraper lodging right on Boston Common.	Safe, quaint area with lamp-lit streets; chain-free upscale shopping and dining; outdoor fun abounds in the park; good T access.	Street parking is extremely hard to come by; not budget friendly; very close to noisy hospital; hills can be very steep.
Downtown	The city's financial center hums with activity and busy hotels during the week; new boutique lodging is moving in to compete with the big-box chains.	Excellent area for business travelers; frequent low weekend rates; good T and bus access; walking distance to Theater District and some museums.	All but dead at night; expensive garage parking during the day; Downtown Crossing is mobbed at lunchtime and on weekends; poorly marked streets.
The Back Bay	High-priced hotels in the city's poshest neighborhood, home to excellent shops, restaurants, bars, spas, and salons. Commonwealth Avenue is lined with historic mansions.	Easy, central location; safe, beautiful area to walk around at night; ample T access; excellent people-watching.	Rooms, shopping, and eating can be ridiculously expensive; Newbury Street is overcrowded with tourists on weekends.
The South End	Small, funky lodgings in a very hip and happening (and gay-friendly) area packed with awesome independent restaurants and shops.	The city's best dining scene; easy T and bus access; myriad parks; walking distance from the Back Bay and Downtown; safe along the main avenues at night.	Some bordering blocks turn seedy after dusk; difficult street parking (and few garages); only a handful of hotel options.
The Fenway and Kenmore Square	A sampling of large and small hotels and inns, plus two hostels; the area is a mix of students, young professionals, and die-hard Sox fans	Close to Fenway Park (home of the Red Sox); up-and-coming dining scene; less expensive than most 'hoods; very accessible by T.	Impossible street parking on game days (and pricey garages); expect big crowds for concert and sporting events; some bars are loud and tacky.
Boston Outskirts	Mostly mid-size chain hotels in student neighborhoods full of coffee shops, convenience stores, and rowdy college bars; except for sweet inns in lovely Brookline.	Serviceable airport lodging near Logan; cheap rates on rooms in Brighton, Allston, and parts of Brookline; easier driving than downtown.	No overnight street parking in Brookline; far from Boston center and museums, shopping, and the river; some areas get dicey at night; T rides into the city proper can take an hour.
Cambridge	A mix of grand and small hotels pepper the hip, multi-university neighborhood; expect loads of young freethinkers and efficient (if laid-back) service.	Hallowed academia; verdant squares; good low- and high-cost eating and lodging; excellent neighborhood restaurants; very few chain anythings.	Spotty T access; less of a city feel; a few areas can be very quiet and slightly dodgy at night; lots of one-way streets make driving difficult.

Use the coordinate (✥ B2) at the end of each listing to locate a site on the Where to Eat and Stay in Boston map.

BACK BAY

$$$–$$$$ 🖼 **The Back Bay Hotel.** "Great staff." "Great bar." "Great vibe." See a pattern yet? Travelers rave about the renamed Jurys Boston, one of the few hotels in the city where you can nip into the bar for a beverage and actually chat with a friendly local or two. Part of the Doyle Collection, a Dublin-based chain, the Back Bay Hotel may remind you more of Iceland than Ireland; its fire-and-ice decor, from the bed of icy glass shards in the lobby's igloo-like gas fireplace to the puffs of steam coming from the main staircase's waterfall, is eye-catching. The hotel gets the small touches right, such as free bottled water in the guest-room fridges, toasty down comforters, and heated towel racks. Readers praise the pub grub at on-site Cuff's Bar, a great place for a post-work cocktail. **Pros:** lively bar; laptop safes; Korres toiletries; friendly staff. **Cons:** very small gym; the bar scene can get loud. ⊠ *350 Stuart St., Back Bay* ☎ *617/266–7200* ⊕ *www.doylecollection.com* ⬌ *222 rooms, 3 suites* ⌂ *In-room: refrigerator, DVD (some), Wi-Fi. In-hotel: restaurant, room service, bar, laundry service, concierge, public Wi-Fi, parking (fee)* ⊟ *AE, D, DC, MC, V* ⍟ *EP* Ⓣ *Back Bay* ✥ *E5.*

$–$$ 🖼 **Charlesmark Hotel.** Hipsters and romantics who'd rather spend their
Fodor's Choice   cash on a great meal than a hotel bill have put this skinny little place
★   on the map. Formally just another Boylston Street office building, the 40-room spot has rooms that go for as low at $119, an almost unheard of price for Back Bay lodging. The funky, eclectic design is just zany enough, and attracts guests who want to relax on the outdoor patio and check out passersby—or the Boston Marathon (the hotel sits on the finish line). Smallish guest rooms have contemporary custom-made oak furnishings, plus surround-sound stereo and free wireless Internet. You can order Thai food in the cocktail lounge, but would be better off walking to one of some 40 nearby restaurants. The Charlesmark doubles as a gallery, displaying the work of local artists along its winding brick corridors. **Pros:** fantastic price for the location; free Wi-Fi. **Cons:** heating system is noisy; rooms at the front of the house can be noisy. ⊠ *655 Boylston St., Back Bay* ☎ *617/247–1212* ⊕ *www. thecharlesmarkhotel.com* ⬌ *40 rooms* ⌂ *In-room: DVD, Wi-Fi. In-hotel: bar, laundry service, concierge, public Wi-Fi* ⊟ *AE, D, DC, MC, V* ⍟ *CP* Ⓣ *Copley* ✥ *D5.*

$$$–$$$$ 🖼 **Fairmont Copley Plaza.** Too much of a good thing is just fine by the
☾   Fairmont's loyal clientele. Past guests, including one Judy Garland, felt
Fodor's Choice   at home in the decadent, unabashedly romantic hotel. Present guests
★   feel much the same way, thanks to the meticulous preservation of the 1912 stallwart. Those who *really* love pampering should book the Fairmont Gold floor (worth the extra cost, readers say), an ultradeluxe club level offering a dedicated staff, free breakfast and tea-time snacks, and a library. Shopping fanatics adore the close proximity to Newbury Street, the Prudential Center, and Copley Place. The hotel's venerable Oak Room restaurant is worth a meal; the equally stately—and tryst-worthy—Oak Bar has live music and one of the longest martini menus

2

in town. **Pros:** very elegant; famous cozy bar; if you drive a hybrid, you can park for free. **Cons:** tiny bathrooms with scratchy towels; charge for Internet access; small fitness center. ⊠ *138 St. James Ave., Back Bay* ☎ *617/267–5300 or 800/441–1414* 🖷 *617/375–9648* ⊕ *www.fairmont. com/copleyplaza* ⟿ *366 rooms, 17 suites* ♿ *In-room: safe, refrigerator, DVD (some), Wi-Fi (fee). In-hotel: restaurant, room service, bar, gym, laundry service, concierge, public Wi-Fi, parking (fee), pets allowed* ▭ *AE, D, DC, MC, V* ⎸⊙⎸ *EP* Ⓣ *Copley, Back Bay/South End* ✛ *D5.*

$$$–$$$$ ⚏ **Lenox Hotel.** A good alternative to chain-owned, big-box Back Bay
♻ hotels, the family-owned Lenox nearly sparkles after a $30 million makeover. Its biggest news is the brand new restaurant City Table, already enjoying local foodie buzz. Top-notch service continues to please a well-groomed clientele. A T stop is right across the street, making the hotel a good launching pad for exploring the city sans car. Readers appreciate the Lenox's sweet, small touches, like cookies and bottled water at turndown service, and give kudos to the friendly staff. Standard guest rooms have custom-made furnishings, marble baths, and flat-screen TVs (suites have mirror TVs in their bathrooms). Of the 24 more spacious corner rooms, 12 come with working fireplaces. **Pros:** free Wi-Fi; fantastic Copley Square location; historic/architectural charm. **Cons:** bathrooms are small; costly parking. ⊠ *61 Exeter St., Back Bay* ☎ *617/536–5300 or 800/225–7676* ⊕ *www.lenoxhotel.com* ⟿ *187 rooms, 27 suites* ♿ *In-room: DVD (upon request), Wi-Fi. In-hotel: 3 restaurants, room service, bars, gym, children's programs; laundry service, concierge, public Wi-Fi, parking (fee); some pets allowed* ▭ *AE, D, DC, MC, V* ⎸⊙⎸ *EP* Ⓣ *Copley* ✛ *D5.*

$–$$ ⚏ **Newbury Guest House.** Shopping enthusiasts have designated this elegant brownstone the "center of the universe." On Boston's most fashionable shopping street, the 1882 row house looks the part, with natural pine flooring, Victorian furnishings, and prints from the Museum of Fine Arts. A recent re-do prettied-up the lobby, but some complain that guest rooms look worn. On the plus side, guests can order room service from the tiny French bistro, La Voile, downstairs. Some rooms have bay windows; others have decorative fireplaces. Room 209 is the prettiest. Limited parking is available. **Pros:** cozy; homey; great location. **Cons:** dated rooms; small bathrooms; street noise. ⊠ *261 Newbury St., Back Bay* ☎ *617/670–6100 or 800/437–7668* ⊕ *www. newburyguesthouse.com* ⟿ *32 rooms* ♿ *In-room: Wi-Fi. In-hotel: no elevator, concierge, public Wi-Fi, parking (fee)* ▭ *AE, D, DC, MC, V* ⎸⊙⎸ *BP* Ⓣ *Hynes, Copley* ✛ *C5.*

BEACON HILL

$ ⚏ **John Jeffries House.** If there's one thing all Bostonians can agree on, it's that driving in the city should be avoided at all costs. So savvy travelers should find lodging near the T, Boston's metro system. Right next to the Charles/MGH stop, the John Jeffries isn't only accessible, it's affordable—a veritable home run in this city. The turn-of-the-20th-century building, across from Massachusetts General Hospital, was once a housing facility for nurses. Now it's a four-story inn with a Federal-style double parlor that serves afternoon tea or coffee. Rooms are full of handsome upholstered pieces; nearly all have kitchenettes. Triple-glazed windows block noise from the busy Charles Circle, and many rooms have river views. Nearby Charles Street is home to lovely cafés, specialty stores, and antiques shops. **Pros:** great Beacon Hill location; free Wi-Fi; good value. **Cons:** the busy (and noisy) hospital across the street; no spa or gym facilities. ⊠ *14 David G. Mugar Way, Beacon Hill* ☎ *617/367–1866* ⊕ *www.johnjeffrieshouse.com* ⤴ *23 rooms, 23 suites* ⌂ *In-room: kitchen (some), DVD (some), Wi-Fi. In-hotel: public Wi-Fi, parking (fee)* ▭ *AE, D, DC, MC, V* ¶⊙¶ *CP* ⊤ *Charles/MGH* ✛ *E2.*

$$$–$$$$
Fodor's Choice
★
🔲 **Liberty Hotel Boston.** When it opened in late 2007, the buzz around the Liberty was deafening, and after a few months the hotel felt more like a nightclub than a tourist's retreat. A few years later, the hype has thankfully died down. Yes, scenesters still hit the reborn Charles Street Jail's cheekily named bar and restaurant, Alibi and Clink, and its outstanding Italian-Mediterranean restaurant, Scampo, but the focus is more or less on guests. Rooms are either in the original granite building or an adjacent 16-story modern tower; both sets carry a jailhouse chic aesthetic, albeit one with luxe linens, Wi-Fi, and views of the Charles River. Some Fodorites complain that quarters in the old section reverberate with noise from Alibi well into the night, but others know that the lively environs are part of the experience. All parties agree that few places in town can rival the hotel's soaring lobby—ringed by several layers of revamped metal catwalks—for a glass of bubbly on plush leather couches. **Pros:** Scampo's mouth-watering house-made mozzarella bar; bustling nightlife; proximity to the river and Beacon Hill. **Cons:** loud in-house nightlife; long waits at bars and restaurants. ⊠ *215 Charles St., Beacon Hill* ☎ *617/224–4000 or 860/507–5245* ⊕ *www.libertyhotel. com* ⤴ *298 rooms* ⌂ *In-room: safe, refrigerator (some), Wi-Fi (fee). In-hotel: 2 restaurants, room service, bars, gym, bicycles, laundry service, concierge, public Wi-Fi, parking (fee), some pets allowed* ▭ *AE, D, DC, MC, V* ¶⊙¶ *EP* ⊤ *Charles* ✛ *E2.*

$$$$
🔲 **XV Beacon.** Though its 1903 Beaux Arts exterior remains the same—a study in understated class and elegance—one of the city's first small luxury hotels just got an internal facelift. The much-needed renovation ushered in new carpeting, paint, and 42-inch TVs in all guest rooms, as well as a completely revamped fitness center. The tiny lobby is all black mahogany with bold splashes of red, brightened with recessed lighting and abstract art. The refreshed rooms are done up in soothing, gender-neutral shades of espresso, taupe, and cream, and each has a gas fireplace and surround-sound stereo. ■TIP➜ **If your stay coincides with the July 4 Harborfest celebration, make your way to the hotel's roof deck (open from Memorial Day through Labor Day) for unparalleled fireworks viewing.** **Pros:** in-room massages; chef Jamie Mammano's steak house, Mooo; pet grooming service. **Cons:** some rooms are small; mattresses are average; can be very expensive on weekends during peak months (May, June, September, October). ⊠ *15 Beacon St., Beacon Hill* ☎ *617/670–1500 or 877/982–3226* ⊕ *www.xvbeacon.com* ⤴ *58 rooms, 2 suites* ⌂ *In-room: safe, refrigerator, Wi-Fi (free). In-hotel: restaurant, room service, bar, gym, laundry service, concierge, public Wi-Fi, parking (fee), some pets allowed* ▭ *AE, D, DC, MC, V* ¶⊙¶ *EP* ⊤ *Government Center, Park St.* ✛ *G3.*

Charlesmark Hotel

Fairmont Copley Plaza

Boston Harbor Hotel at Rowes Wharf

Liberty Hotel Boston

Charles Hotel

Hotel Commonwealth

DOWNTOWN

$$$$ **Boston Harbor Hotel at Rowes Wharf.** Boston has plenty of iconic land-
Fodor'sChoice marks—the "salt and pepper" bridge, Fenway Park, the Public Garden
★ ducklings. But none are as synonymous with über-hospitality as the
Boston Harbor Hotel's 80-foot-tall outdoor archway and rotunda. The
splurge-worthiness continues inside, thanks to smaller marble arches,
framed antique maps, and an ample placement of fresh flowers. Marble
bathrooms, custom-made desks, Frette linens, and flat-panel TVs give
the guestrooms a leg up on other city lodgings. Amenities abound—
there are even complimentary daily shoe shines. The hotel's older, well-
heeled clientele has been coming here for ages, and the city and Boston
harbor views just get better. The excellent on-site restaurant, Meritage,
offers a unique menu that pairs small plates with appropriate vintages,
all under light fixtures that mimic a starry sky. Eat up and work it off
later—the health club will lend you athletic gear if you forget yours.
Pros: Sea Grille restaurant; easy walk to Faneuil Hall; water shuttle to
Logan Airport. **Cons:** pricey; the spa gets booked up early; less convenient to the Back Bay and South End. ⊠ *70 Rowes Wharf, Down-
town/Waterfront* ☎ *617/439–7000 or 800/752–7077* ⊕ *www.bhh.com*
🖙 *204 rooms, 26 suites* ⚐ *In-room: safe, refrigerator, Wi-Fi. In-hotel:
2 restaurants, room service, bar, pool, gym, spa, laundry service, concierge, public Wi-Fi, airport shuttle, parking (fee), some pets allowed*
⊟ *AE, D, DC, MC, V* ⦿| *EP* Ⓣ *Aquarium, South Station* ✛ *H3.*

$$–$$$ **Harborside Inn.** Not quite as hip as its sister property the Charlesmark,
the Harborside nonetheless carries a certain charm. And by charm, we
mean rates considerably lower than most Waterfront hotels. That's
welcome to budget-conscious travelers who parade through the modern
marine-minimalist lobby and rooms decorated with shipwreck prints,
exposed brick walls, hardwood floors, and Federal-style furnishings.
Many of the snug, variously shaped rooms (no two are alike) have windows overlooking the small, open lobby, which extends eight stories up
to the roof. Amenities include flat-screen TVs and complimentary Wi-Fi;
Faneuil Hall, Quincy Market, and the North End are all short walks
away. A new, high-end restaurant-lounge with seating for 100 is set to
open off the lobby in the fall of 2010. ■ TIP➔ **For a great view, request
a room overlooking the city; for a quieter stay, book a room that faces the
interior atrium. Pros:** free Wi-Fi; rare value for the location; close to
Quincy Market and the New England Aquarium; nearby water taxi.
Cons: neighboring nightclubs can be noisy; the area might be too touristy for some. ⊠ *185 State St., Downtown/Waterfront* ☎ *617/723–7500
or 888/723–7565* ⊕ *www.harborsideinnboston.com* 🖙 *98 rooms, 2
suites* ⚐ *In-room: safe (some), refrigerator (some), DVD, Wi-Fi. In-
hotel: laundry service, concierge, public Wi-Fi* ⊟ *AE, D, DC, MC, V*
⦿| *EP* Ⓣ *Aquarium* ✛ *H3.*

$$$$ **Nine Zero.** Nine Zero knows that hotel rooms get a little lonely. That's
Fodor'sChoice why the Downtown spot instated its "guppy love" program; yes, that's
★ right, you get a pet fish on loan. Feeling tight? Turn on the TV and tune
into the in-house yoga channel. (Forgot your mat? They'll lend you
that, too.) It's touches like these that set this Kimpton property apart
from other up-and-coming boutique hotels. Style-wise, the place is all

smooth lines with sudden bursts of vibrant color. Request corner rooms (ending in 05) for the best city and river views. Then, partake of the hotel's personal-shopper-for-hire program and dress to join the young, hip crowds at in-house modern steak house KO Prime, run by celeb chef Ken Oringer. **Pros:** pet-friendly; kid-friendly; lobby wine-tasting every evening (from 5 to 6); Mario Russo bath products. **Cons:** smallish rooms; high parking fees. ⊠ *90 Tremont St., Downtown* ☎ *617/772–5800 or 866/646–3937* ⊕ *www.ninezero.com* ⤳ *185 rooms, 5 suites* ⚒ *In-room: safe, refrigerator, Internet (fee). In-hotel: restaurant, room service, bar, gym, children's programs, laundry service, concierge, public Wi-Fi, parking (fee), pets allowed* ⊟ *AE, D, DC, MC, V* ⊺⊙⊺ *EP* Ⓣ *Park St., Government Center* ✛ *G3.*

$$$$ 🛏 **Omni Parker House.** In 2008 America's oldest continuously operat-
☾ ing hotel got a $30 million makeover, so you can still steep yourself in Boston history . . . while watching a flat-screen TV. As at many city lodgings, the guestrooms are a tad small, but here they're nicely turned out with cherry-wood furniture, red-and-gold Roman shades, ivory wall coverings, and cushy mattress covers. The lobby and restaurants were also invigorated with new decor and menu items. Longtimers, rest easy: the Omni's famous Boston Cream Pie is still on hand (even for breakfast); but now you can work it off in a new in-house gym. If any hotel really says "Boston," it's this one, where JFK proposed to Jackie, and Charles Dickens gave his first reading of "A Christmas Carol." In fact, you may well see a Dickens impersonator in the lobby, since history tours always include the Parker House on their routes. **Pros:** very historic; near Downtown Crossing on the Freedom Trail. **Cons:** small rooms, some quite dark; thin-walled rooms can be noisy. ⊠ *60 School St, Downtown* ☎ *617/227–8600 or 800/843–6664* ⊕ *www. omniparkerhouse.com* ⤳ *551 rooms, 21 suites* ⚒ *In-room: safe, Internet. In-hotel: 2 restaurants, room service, bars, gym, children's program, laundry service, concierge, public Wi-Fi, parking (fee), some pets allowed* ⊟ *AE, DC, MC, V* ⊺⊙⊺ *BP* Ⓣ *Government Center, Park St.* ✛ *G3.*

KENMORE SQUARE

$–$$ 🛏 **Gryphon House.** The suites in this four-story 19th-century brown-
Fodor's Choice stone are thematically decorated: one evokes rustic Italy; another is
★ inspired by neo-Gothic art. Among the many amenities—including gas fireplaces, wet bars, DVD and CD players—the enormous bathrooms with oversize tubs and separate showers are the most appealing. Even the staircase is extraordinary: a wallpaper mural, *El Dorado,* wraps along the walls. Trompe-l'oeil paintings and murals by local artist Michael Ernest Kirk decorate the common spaces. **Pros:** awesome value; free Wi-Fi; gas fireplaces in all rooms; helpful staff. **Cons:** closed from Christmas to New Year's Eve; may be too fussy for some; no elevator. ⊠ *9 Bay State Rd., Kenmore Sq.* ☎ *617/375–9003 or 877/375–9003* ⊕ *www.innboston.com* ⤳ *8 suites* ⚒ *In-room: kitchen (some), refrigerator, DVD, Wi-Fi. In-hotel: no elevator, laundry facilities, public Wi-Fi, parking (fee)* ⊟ *AE, D, MC, V* ⊺⊙⊺ *CP* Ⓣ *Kenmore* ✛ *A5.*

$$$-$$$$ 🖼 **Hotel Commonwealth.** Rumor has it that Bono and the Boss have
      ☪   walked the hallways of the Hotel Commonwealth. Luxury and service
Fodor's Choice   without pretense makes the hip spot a solid choice. Rich color schemes
      ★   enhance the elegant lodgings, and king- or queen-size beds are piled
with down pillows and Italian linens. All rooms have marble baths,
floor-to-ceiling windows, separate work areas, and flat-screen TVs.
The accommodating staff and chauffeur are added bonuses. Sadly, the
hotel's much-acclaimed seafood restaurant, Great Bay, closed last year.
But in-house Eastern Standard is alive and well, and serves some of the
best old-school cocktails in the city. **Pros:** free Wi-Fi; down bedding; per-
fect locale for Red Sox fans; happening bar scene. **Cons:** area is mobbed
during Sox games; small gym. ⊠ *500 Commonwealth Ave., Kenmore
Sq.* ☎ *617/933–5000 or 866/784–4000* ⊕ *www.hotelcommonwealth.
com* ⤵ *149 rooms, 1 suite △ In-room: safe, refrigerator, DVD, Wi-Fi.
In-hotel: restaurant, room service, bar, gym, children's programs, laun-
dry service, concierge, public Wi-Fi, parking (fee), some pets allowed.*
⊟ *AE, D, DC, MC, V* ⧫ *EP* ⊤ *Kenmore* ✛ *A5.*

CAMBRIDGE

*Use the coordinate (✛ B2) at the end of each listing to locate a site on
the Where to Eat and Stay in Cambridge map.*

$-$$ 🖼 **A Cambridge House Inn.** Last year, this sweet Cambridge spot bought
and renovated the adjacent building, adding 18 rooms and a new
look to its Victorian aesthetic. Now guests can choose between old-
school B&B charm and modernized hospitality. The original property,
a restored 1892 National Register of Historic Places house, has richly
carved cherry paneling, a grand fireplace, elegant antiques, and polished
wood floors overlaid with Oriental rugs. Its antique-filled guest rooms
come with fabric-covered walls, four-poster canopy beds, and the standard New England doily decor. Rooms in the new part are decidedly less
frilly, and outfitted with single-color paints and furnishings. Harvard
Square isn't terribly close, but public transportation is nearby. **Pros:**
cozy fireplace lounges; free parking and Wi-Fi. **Cons:** not for modern-
ists; very quiet area; no elevators. ⊠ *2218 Massachusetts Ave., Cambridge* ☎ *617/491–6300 or 800/232–9989* ⊕ *www.acambridgehouse.
com* ⤵ *33 rooms △ In-room: Wi-Fi. In-hotel: public Wi-Fi, concierge,
parking (no fee)* ⊟ *AE, MC, V* ⧫ *CP* ⊤ *Davis Sq.* ✛ *A1.*

$$$-$$$$ 🖼 **Charles Hotel.** Used to be that the Charles was *the* place to stay in
      ☪   Boston. Other luxury hotels now provide some healthy competition,
Fodor's Choice   but this Harvard Square staple is standing strong. A 2009 lobby and
      ★   public space renovation refreshed the lower floors with Le Corbusier
furniture, sketches by JFK himself, and work by various local artists.
Gracious service and top-notch room amenities like terrycloth robes,
handmade quilts, and LCD mirror-TVs also keep the hotel in high
demand. Relax in the lobby library, chock-full of titles, some auto-
graphed by authors who happen to be frequent guests. Sign up for an
art tour of the property or pick up a self-guided map of Cambridge.
For a partial river or skyline view, ask for something above the seventh
floor. In-house restaurants Rialto and Henrietta's Table are excellent;

the latter especially for weekend brunch. ■TIP➔ **For the best rate, call the hotel directly. Pros:** free Wi-Fi; free domestic calls; kid-friendly; on-site jazz club and hip Noir bar; outdoor skating rink in winter. **Cons:** luxury comes at a price. ⊠ *1 Bennett St., Cambridge* 🕾 *617/864–1200 or 800/882–1818* ⊕ *www.charleshotel.com* ⇗ *294 rooms, 45 suites* ⚘ *In-room: safe, refrigerator, DVD, wetbar, Wi-Fi. In-hotel: 2 restaurants, room service, bars, pool, laundry service, concierge, children's programs, public Wi-Fi, parking (fee), some pets allowed* ⊟ *AE, DC, MC, V* Ⓣ *Harvard* ✥ *C1.*

$$–$$$ ▦ **Harvard Square Hotel.** Don't feel like shelling out a week's salary to stay at the venerable Charles? Check in to the next-door Harvard Square Hotel, where you'll get the location and convenience for half the cost. The lodging is basic, some say nondescript, but it's just steps from the square's shops, eateries, and bars. Rooms are simple but clean, with refrigerators and Internet access. Thankfully, the bathrooms—always a sore point here—have been modernized, and in-room flat-screen TVs were added as well. The desk clerks are particularly helpful, assisting with everything from sending faxes to securing dinner reservations. **Pros:** awesome location; some windows open for fresh air. **Cons:** unexciting decor; Wi-Fi and parking cost extra. ⊠ *110 Mt. Auburn St., Cambridge/Harvard Square* 🕾 *617/864–5200 or 800/458–5886* ⊕ *www. harvardsquarehotel.com* ⇗ *73 rooms* ⚘ *In-room: refrigerator, Wi-Fi (fee). In-hotel: laundry service, concierge, public Wi-Fi, parking (fee)* ⊟ *AE, D, DC, MC, V* ⍟ *EP* Ⓣ *Harvard* ✥ *C1.*

$$$–$$$$ ▦ **Royal Sonesta Hotel.** Right next to the Charles River, the Sonesta has one of the best sunset views in Boston. Diners at in-house Italian restaurant, dante, can sip a glass of prosecco while watching dusk fall on the boats sailing by. Inside, modern art lines the hotel's hallways, and the staff of this just-renovated Cambridge riverfront property is professional and friendly. Also great: the indoor-outdoor pool. Guest rooms are done in neutral earth tones, with modern amenities such as flat-screen TVs, gaming consoles, Wi-Fi, and CD clock radios. Note to parents: kids 12 and under eat and stay for free if you book via the hotel's Web site. **Pros:** free Wi-Fi; nice pool; certified green hotel. **Cons:** a bit sterile; a far walk from the Back Bay and South End. ⊠ *40 Edwin Land Blvd., off Memorial Dr., Cambridge* 🕾 *617/806–4200 or 800/766–3782* ⊕ *www. sonesta.com/boston* ⇗ *379 rooms, 21 suites* ⚘ *In-room: safe, refrigerator, Wi-Fi. In-hotel: 2 restaurants, room service, bars, pool, gym, spa, bicycles, laundry service, concierge, public Internet, public Wi-Fi, parking (fee)* ⊟ *AE, D, DC, MC, V* ⍟ *EP* Ⓣ *Lechmere* ✥ *A6.*

SIDE TRIPS FROM BOSTON

LEXINGTON

16 mi northwest of Boston.

Discontent with the British, American colonials burst into action in Lexington in April 1775. On April 18, patriot leader Paul Revere alerted the town that British soldiers were approaching. The next day, as the

British advance troops arrived in Lexington on their march toward Concord, the Minutemen were waiting to confront the Redcoats in what became the first skirmish of the Revolutionary War.

These first military encounters of the American Revolution are very much a part of present-day Lexington, a modern suburban town that sprawls out from the historic sites

TAKE A TOUR

Liberty Ride (☎ 781/862–0500 Ext. 702 ⊕ www.libertyride.us 🎫 $25) offers guided trolley tours that visit many of the historic sites in Lexington and Concord. Tickets are good for 24 hours and allow on-off privileges.

near its center. Although the downtown area is generally lively, with ice-cream and coffee shops, boutiques, and a great little movie theater, the town becomes especially animated each Patriots' Day (April 19 but celebrated on the third Monday in April), when costume-clad groups re-create the Minutemen's battle maneuvers and Paul Revere rides again.

To learn more about the city and the 1775 clash, stop by the **Lexington Visitor Center.**

GETTING HERE AND AROUND

Massachusetts Bay Transportation Authority (MBTA) operates bus service in the greater Boston area and serves Lexington.

ESSENTIALS

Bus Contacts MBTA (☎ 617/222–3200 or 800/392–6100 ⊕ www.mbta.com).

Pharmacy Walgreens (✉ 60 Bedford St. ☎ 781/863–1111).

Visitor Information Lexington Visitor Center (✉ 1875 Massachusetts Ave. ☎ 781/862–2480 ⊕ www.lexingtonchamber.org ⊘ Apr.–Nov., daily 9–5; Dec.–Mar., daily 10–4).

EXPLORING

Battle Green. It was on this two-acre triangle of land, on April 19, 1775, that the first confrontation between British soldiers, who were marching from Boston toward Concord, and the colonial militia known as the Minutemen took place. The Minutemen—so called because they were able to prepare themselves at a moment's notice—were led by Captain John Parker, whose role in the American Revolution is commemorated in Henry Hudson Kitson's renowned 1900 *Minuteman* statue. Facing downtown Lexington at the tip of Battle Green, the statue's in a traffic island, and therefore makes for a difficult photo op.

Buckman Tavern. While waiting for the arrival of the British on the morning of April 19, 1775, the Minutemen gathered at this 1690 tavern. A half-hour tour takes in the tavern's seven rooms, which have been restored to the way they looked in the 1770s. Among the items on display is an old front door with a hole made by a British musket ball. ✉ 1 Bedford St. ☎ 781/862–1703 ⊕ www.lexingtonhistory.org 🎫 $5; $10 combination ticket includes Hancock-Clarke House and Munroe Tavern ⊘ Apr.–Oct., daily 10–4.

Hancock-Clarke House. On April 18, 1775, Paul Revere came here to warn patriots John Hancock and Sam Adams, who were staying at the

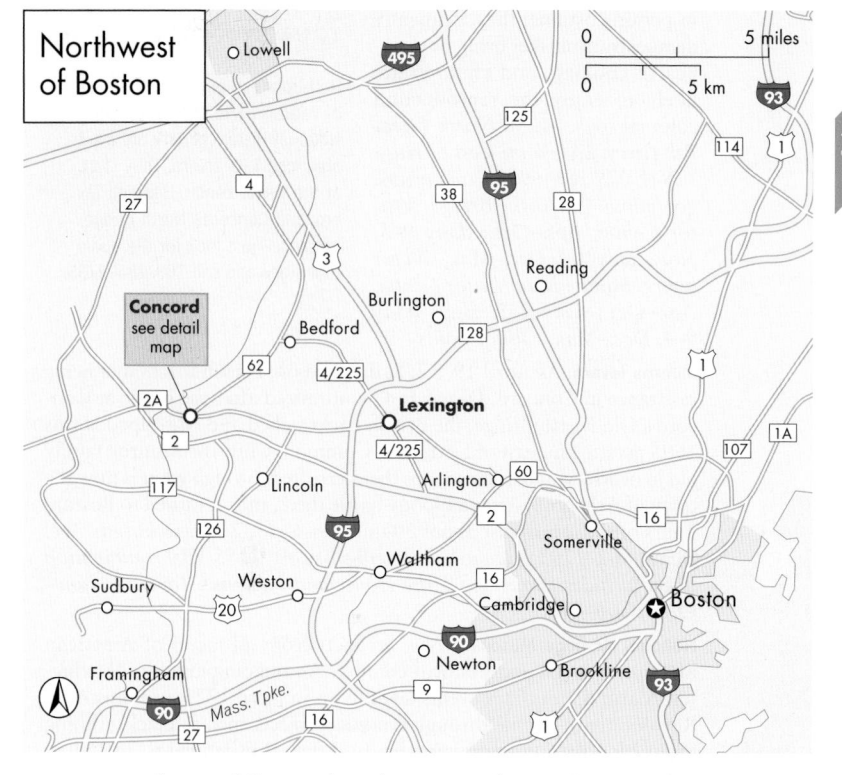

Northwest of Boston

house while attending the Provincial Congress in nearby Concord, of the advance of British troops. Hancock and Adams, on whose heads the British king had put a price, fled to avoid capture. The house, a parsonage built in 1698, is a 10-minute walk from Lexington Common. Inside are the pistols of the British major John Pitcairn, as well as period furnishings and portraits. ⊠ *36 Hancock St.* ☎ *781/862–1703* ⊕ *www. lexingtonhistory.org* ⊒ *$5; $10 combination ticket includes Buckman Tavern and Munroe Tavern* ⊗ *Apr.–mid-June, weekends; mid-June– Oct., daily 11–2.*

☺ **Minute Man National Historical Park.** West of Lexington's center stretches
★ this 1,000-acre, three-parcel park that also extends into nearby Lincoln and Concord (⇨ *Concord, Exploring*). Begin your park visit at Lexington's **Minute Man Visitor Center** to see its free multimedia presentation, "The Road to Revolution," a captivating introduction to the events of April 1775. Then, continuing along Highway 2A toward Concord, you pass the point where Revere's midnight ride ended with his capture by the British; it's marked with a boulder and plaque, as well as an enclosure where rangers sometimes give educational presentations. You can also visit the 1732 **Hartwell Tavern** (open mid-April through late May, weekends 9:30–5:30, and late May through late October, daily 9:30–5:30), a restored drover's (driver's) tavern staffed by park employees

in period costume; they frequently demonstrate musket firing or open-hearth cooking, and children are likely to enjoy the reproduction colonial toys. ⊠ *250 North Great Rd. (Hwy. 2A), ¼ mi west of Hwy. 128* 🕾 *978/369–6993* ⊕ *www.nps.gov/mima* ⊙ *North Bridge Visitor Center, Apr.–Oct., daily 9–5; Nov., daily 9–4; Dec.–Mar., call for hours. Minute Man Visitor Center, Apr.–Oct., daily 9–5; Nov., daily 9–4; Dec.–Mar., call for hours*

TOUR BY PHONE

Half-hour cell-phone audio tours of various parts of Minute Man National Historical Park are available for $5.99 apiece. They start at the visitor center, Hartwell Tavern, and Concord's North Bridge entrance—just look for the audio tour signs and call 703/286–2755.

Munroe Tavern. As April 19, 1775, dragged on, British forces met fierce resistance in Concord. Dazed and demoralized after the battle at Concord's Old North Bridge, the British backtracked and regrouped at this 1695 tavern 1 mi east of Lexington Common, while the Munroe family hid in nearby woods. The troops then retreated through what is now the town of Arlington. After a bloody battle there, they returned to Boston. Tours of the tavern last about 30 minutes. ⊠ *1332 Massachusetts Ave.* 🕾 *781/862–1703* ⊕ *www.lexingtonhistory.org* 🖾 *$5; $10 combination ticket includes Hancock-Clarke House and Buckman Tavern* ⊙ *June–Oct., noon–4* PM.

National Heritage Museum. View artifacts from all facets of American life, put in social and political context. An ongoing exhibit, "Lexington Alarm'd," outlines events leading up to April 1775 and illustrates Revolutionary-era life through everyday objects such as blacksmithing tools, bloodletting paraphernalia, and dental instruments, including a "tooth key" used to extract teeth. ⊠ *33 Marrett Rd., Hwy. 2A at Massachusetts Ave.* 🕾 *781/861–6559* ⊕ *www.monh.org* 🖾 *Donations accepted* ⊙ *Tues.–Sat. 10–4:30, Sun. noon–4:30. Closed Mon.*

CONCORD

About 10 mi west of Lexington, 21 mi northwest of Boston.

The Concord of today is a modern suburb with a busy center filled with arty shops, places to eat, and old bookstores. Autumn lovers, take note: Concord is a great place to start a fall foliage tour. From Boston, head west along Route 2 to Concord, and then continue on to find harvest stands and apple-picking around Harvard and Stow.

GETTING HERE AND AROUND

The MBTA runs buses to Concord. On the MBTA Commuter Rail Concord is a 40-minute ride on the Fitchburg Line, which departs from Boston's North Station.

ESSENTIALS

Bus and Train Contact MBTA (🕾 *617/222–3200* ⊕ *www.mbta.com*).

Hospital Emerson Hospital (⊠ *133 Old Rd., off Rte. 2, Concord* 🕾 *978/369–1400*).

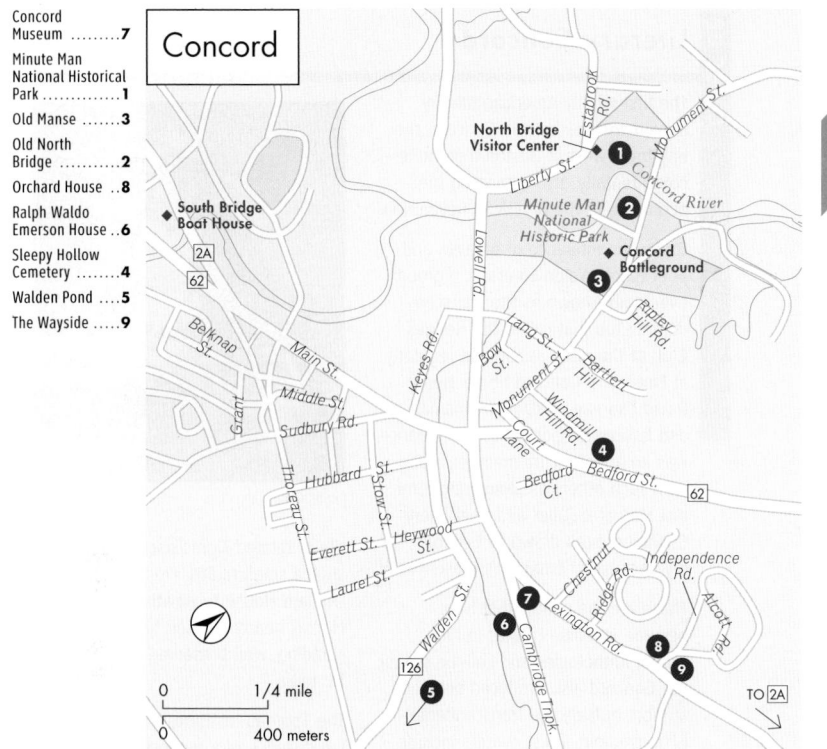

Visitor Information **Concord Visitor Center** (✉ *58 Main St.* ☎ *978/369–3120* ⊕ *www.concordchamberofcommerce.org*).

EXPLORING

❼ Concord Museum. The original contents of Emerson's private study, as well as the world's largest collection of Thoreau artifacts, reside in this 1930 Colonial Revival building just east of the town center. The museum provides a good overview of the town's history, from its original American Indian settlement to the present. Highlights include American Indian artifacts, furnishings from Thoreau's Walden Pond cabin (there's a replica of the cabin itself on the museum's lawn), and one of the two lanterns hung at Boston's Old North Church to signal that the British were coming by sea. ✉ *200 Lexington Rd., entrance on Cambridge Tpke.* ☎ *978/369–9763* ⊕ *www.concordmuseum.org* 🖾 *$10* ☉ *Jan.–Mar., Mon.–Sat. 11–4, Sun. 1–4; Apr.–Dec, Mon.–Sat. 9–5, Sun. noon–5; June–Aug., daily 9–5.*

❶ Minute Man National Historical Park. Along Highway 2A is a three-parcel park with 1,000 acres. The park contains many of the sites important to Concord's role in the Revolution, including Old North Bridge, as well as two visitor centers, one each in Concord and Lexington (⇨ *Lexington, Essentials*). Although the initial Revolutionary War sorties were in Lexington, word of the American losses spread rapidly

Literary Concord

The first wholly American literary movement was born in Concord, the tiny town west of Boston that, quite coincidentally, also witnessed the beginning of the American Revolution.

Under the influence of essayist and poet Ralph Waldo Emerson, a group eventually known as the Transcendental Club (but called the Hedges Club at the time) assembled regularly in Emerson's Concord home. Henry David Thoreau, a fellow townsman and famous proponent of self-reliance, was an integral club member, along with such others as pioneering feminist Margaret Fuller and poet Ellery Channing, both drawn to Concord simply because of Emerson's presence.

These are the names that have become indelible bylines in high school anthologies and college syllabi, but Concord also produced beloved authors outside the Transcendentalist movement. These writers include Louisa May Alcott of *Little Women* fame and children's book author Harriet Lothrop, pseudonymously known as Margaret Sydney. Even Nathaniel Hawthorne, whose various temporary homes around Massachusetts constitute a literary trail all their own, resided in Concord during the early and later portions of his career.

The cumulative inkwells of these authors have bestowed upon Concord a literary legacy unique in the United States, both for its influence on literature in general and for the quan-

Louisa May Alcott

tity of related sights packed within such a small radius. From Alcott's Orchard House to Hawthorne's Old Manse, nearly all their houses remain standing, well preserved and open for tours.

The Thoreau Institute, within walking distance of a reconstruction of Thoreau's famous cabin in the woods at Walden Pond, is a repository of his papers and original editions. Emerson's study sits in the Concord Museum, across the street from his house. Even their final resting places are here, on Authors Ridge in Sleepy Hollow Cemetery, a few short blocks from the town common. **Concord Bike Tours** (☎ 978/697–1897 ⊕ *www.concordbiketours.com*) will guide you through the sites on two wheels, usually April through November (weather permitting).

to surrounding towns: when the British marched into Concord, more than 400 Minutemen were waiting. The park's **North Bridge Visitor Center** (✉ *174 Liberty St.* ☎ *978/369–6993*) is open from April through October, daily 9–5, and November, daily 9–4 (call for winter hours). ✉ *Bounded by Monument St., Liberty St., and Lowell Rd.* ⊕ *www.nps.gov/mima* ☉ *Grounds daily dawn–dusk.*

3 Old Manse. The Reverend William Emerson, grandfather of Ralph Waldo Emerson, watched rebels and redcoats battle from behind his home, which was within sight of the Old North Bridge. The house, built in 1770, was occupied continuously by the Emerson family for almost two centuries, except for the 3½-years when Nathaniel Hawthorne rented it. Furnishings date from the late 18th century. Tours run throughout the day and last 45 minutes, with a new tour starting within 15 minutes of when the first person signs up. ⊠ *269 Monument St.* ☎ *978/369–3909* ⊕ *www. thetrustees.org/places-to-visit/greater-boston/old-manse.html* ▨ *$8* ⊙ *Mid-Apr.–Oct., Mon.–Fri. 10–5, Sun. noon–5; Nov.–Mar. weekends noon–5 (weather permitting).*

> **TEA ON THE GO**
>
> Fancy a scone or a spot of tea while you're at the North Bridge? Well, you're in luck. **Gay Grace Teas** (☎ *508/650–5797* ⊕ *www. gaygraceteas.com*) operates a mobile tea room that's often parked outside the visitor center. Check the Web site to confirm that it'll be there when you are.

2 Old North Bridge. A half-mile from Concord center, at this bridge the Concord Minutemen turned the tables on the British on the morning of April 19, 1775. The Americans didn't fire first, but when two of their own fell dead from a Redcoat volley, Major John Buttrick of Concord roared, "Fire, fellow soldiers, for God's sake, fire." The Minutemen released volley after volley, and the Redcoats fled. Daniel Chester French's famous statue *The Minuteman* (1875) honors the country's first freedom fighters. Inscribed at the foot of the statue are words Ralph Waldo Emerson wrote in 1837 describing the confrontation: BY THE RUDE BRIDGE THAT ARCHED THE FLOOD / THEIR FLAG TO APRIL'S BREEZE UNFURLED / HERE ONCE THE EMBATTLED FARMERS STOOD / AND FIRED THE SHOT HEARD ROUND THE WORLD. The lovely wooded surroundings give a sense of what the landscape was like in more rural times.

6 Ralph Waldo Emerson House. The 19th-century essayist and poet Ralph Waldo Emerson lived briefly in the Old Manse in 1834–35, then moved to this home, where he lived until his death in 1882. Here he wrote the *Essays*. Except for artifacts from Emerson's study, now at the nearby Concord Museum, the Emerson House furnishings have been preserved as the writer left them, down to his hat resting on the newel post. You must join one of the half-hour-long tours to see the interior. ⊠ *28 Cambridge Tpke., at Lexington Rd.* ☎ *978/369–2236* ⊕ *www.rwe.org/ emersonhouse* ▨ *$8* ⊙ *Mid-Apr.–mid-Oct., Thurs.–Sat. 10–4:30, Sun. 1–4:30; call for tour schedule.*

8 Orchard House. The dark brown exterior of Louisa May Alcott's family home sharply contrasts with the light, wit, and energy so much in evidence inside. Named for the apple orchard that once surrounded it, Orchard House was the Alcott family home from 1857 to 1877. Here Louisa wrote *Little Women,* based on her life with her three sisters; and her father, Bronson, founded his school of philosophy—the building remains behind the house. Because Orchard House had just one owner after the Alcotts left, and because it became a museum in 1911, many of the original furnishings remain, including the semicircular

Retrace Henry David Thoreau's steps at Walden Pond.

shelf-desk where Louisa wrote *Little Women*. ⊠ *399 Lexington Rd.* ☎ *978/369–4118* ⊕ *www.louisamayalcott.org* ✉ *$9, tours free* ⊙ *Apr.– Oct., Mon.–Sat. 10–4:30, Sun. 1–4:30; Nov.–Dec. and Jan. 16–Mar., weekdays 11–3, Sat. 10–4:30, Sun. 1–4:30. Half-hr tours begin every 30 mins Apr.–Oct.; call for off-season schedule.*

④ Sleepy Hollow Cemetery. In the Author's Ridge section of this cemetery are the graves of American literary greats Louisa May Alcott, Ralph Waldo Emerson, Henry David Thoreau, and Nathaniel Hawthorne. ⊠ *Bedford St. (Hwy. 62)* ☎ *978/318–3233* ⊙ *Daily dawn–dusk.*

⑤ Walden Pond. For lovers of early American literature, a trip to Concord isn't complete without a pilgrimage to Henry David Thoreau's most famous residence. Here, in 1845, at age 28, Thoreau moved into a one-room cabin—built for $28.12—on the shore of this 100-foot-deep kettle hole formed by the retreat of an ancient glacier. Living alone for the next two years, Thoreau discovered the benefits of solitude and the beauties of nature. The essays in *Walden*, published in 1854, are a mixture of philosophy, nature writing, and proto-ecology. The site of the first cabin is staked out in stone. A full-size, authentically furnished replica of the cabin stands about ½ mi from the original site, near the Walden Pond State Reservation parking lot. Now, as in Thoreau's time, the pond is a delightful summertime spot for swimming, fishing, and rowing, and there's hiking in the nearby woods. To get to Walden Pond State Reservation from the center of Concord—a trip of only 1½ mi—take Concord's Main Street a block west from Monument Square, turn left onto Walden Street, and head for the intersection of Highways 2 and 126. Cross over Highway 2 onto Highway 126, heading south for ½ mi.

Fodor's Choice
★

✉ *915 Walden St. (Hwy. 126)* ☎ *978/369–3254* ⊕ *www.mass.gov/dcr/ parks/walden* 🏷 *Free, parking $5* ☼ *Daily from 8* AM *until about ½ hr before sunset, weather permitting.*

❾ The Wayside. Nathaniel Hawthorne lived at the Old Manse in 1842–45, working on stories and sketches; he then moved to Salem (where he wrote *The Scarlet Letter*) and later to Lenox (*The House of the Seven Gables*). In 1852 he returned to Concord, bought this rambling structure called The Wayside, and lived here until his death in 1864. The subsequent owner, Margaret Sidney, wrote the children's book *Five Little Peppers and How They Grew* (1881). Before Hawthorne moved in, the Alcotts lived here, from 1845 to 1848. An exhibit center, in the former barn, provides information about the Wayside authors and links them to major events in American history. Hawthorne's tower-study, with his stand-up writing desk, is substantially as he left it. ✉ *455 Lexington Rd.* ☎ *978/318–7863* ⊕ *www.nps.gov/archive/mima/wayside* 🏷 *$5* ☼ *Open by guided tour only, May–Oct.; call for reservations.*

SPORTS AND THE OUTDOORS

BOATING   You can paddle along the Sudbury and Concord rivers to the North Bridge section of the Minute Man National Historical Park if you rent a canoe or kayak at the **South Bridge Boat House**. You can even paddle all the way to Sudbury or up to Billerica. ✉ *496 Main St.* ☎ *978/369–9438* ⊕ *www.canoeconcord.com* 🏷 *Canoes $13.50/hour weekdays, $15.50/ hour weekends; kayaks $15/hour single, $17/hour double* ☼ *Apr.–mid-June 10–5, mid-June–Nov., weekdays 10–one hour before dusk, weekends and holidays 9–one hour before dusk.*

WHERE TO EAT

$ ✕ **Main Streets Cafe**. Cyclists, families, and sightseers pack into this brick
AMERICAN   building, which was used to store munitions during the Revolutionary War.
★   Breakfast offerings include a quiche and breakfast sandwich of the day. At lunch, the grilled panini are excellent; they also serve flatbread pizza and pub fare. At night heartier offerings dominate the menu, including baked lobster mac and cheese, scallop and shrimp risotto, and a Yankee pot roast dinner. There's a full bar, and in summer the small alley outside leads to a counter that serves ice cream. ✉ *42 Main St.* ☎ *978/369–9948* ⊕ *www.mainstreetsmarketandcafe.com* ▭ *AE, D, MC, V.*

$$–$$$ ✕ **Walden Grille**. Chowders, salads, and sandwiches are typical fare
AMERICAN   at this old brick firehouse-turned-dining room. Start with the Philly spring rolls or crispy fried oysters. Sandwiches include run-of-the-mill burgers and BLTs, plus more creative options like the chicken curry roll-up. Entrées run the gamut from vegetarian cannelloni to grilled tuna with wasabi ginger cream. ✉ *24 Walden St.* ☎ *978/371–2233* ⊕ *www. waldengrille.com* ▭ *AE, D, MC, V.*

THE NORTH SHORE

The slice of Massachusetts's Atlantic Coast known as the North Shore extends past Boston to the Cape Ann region just shy of the New Hampshire border. In addition to miles of woods and beaches, the North Shore's highlights include Marblehead, a classic New England sea town;

Salem, which thrives on a history of witches, writers, and maritime trades; Gloucester, the oldest seaport in America; Rockport, rich with crafts shops and artists' studios; and Newburyport, with its redbrick center and clapboard mansions, and a handful of typical New England towns in between. Bustling during the short summer season and breathtaking during the autumn foliage, the North Shore is calmer (and colder) between November and June. Many restaurants, inns, and attractions operate on reduced hours during the off-season.

MARBLEHEAD

17 mi north of Boston.

Marblehead, with its narrow and winding streets, beautifully preserved clapboard homes, sea captains' mansions, and harbor, looks much as it must have when it was founded in 1629 by fishermen from Cornwall and the Channel Islands. One of New England's premier sailing capitals, Marblehead attracts boats from along the Eastern seaboard each July during Race Week—first held in 1889. Parking in town can be difficult; lots at the end of Front Street or on State Street by the Landing restaurant are the best options.

ESSENTIALS

Visitor Information Marblehead Chamber of Commerce Information Booth (⊠ *62 Pleasant St.* ☎ *781/631–2868* ⊕ *www.visitmarblehead.com*).

EXPLORING

Abbott Hall. The town's Victorian-era municipal building, built in 1876, displays Archibald Willard's painting *The Spirit of '76*. Many visitors, familiar since childhood with this image of the three Revolutionary veterans with fife, drum, and flag, are surprised to find the original in an otherwise unassuming town hall. Also on-site is a small naval museum exploring Marblehead's maritime past. ⊠ *188 Washington St.* ☎ *781/631–0000* 🖙 *Free* ☉ *Call for hrs.*

Fort Sewall. Marblehead's magnificent views of the harbor, the Misery Islands, and the Atlantic are best enjoyed from this fort built in 1644 atop the rocky cliffs of the harbor. Used as a defense against the French in 1742 as well as during the War of 1812, Fort Sewall is today open to the public as community parkland. Barracks and underground quarters can still be seen, and Revolutionary War reenactments by members of the modern-day Glover's Marblehead Regiment are staged at the fort annually. ⊠ *End of Front St.* ⊕ *www.essexheritage.org/sites/fort_sewall. shtml* 🖙 *Free* ☉ *Daily, sunrise to sunset.*

WHERE TO EAT AND STAY

$$

SEAFOOD

✕ **The Landing**. Decorated in nautical blues and whites, this pleasant restaurant sits right on Marblehead harbor, with a deck that's nearly in the water. The menu mixes classic New England fare (clam chowder, lobster, broiled scrod) with more contemporary dishes like the Asian stir-fry basket. Brunch is served on Sunday. The pub area has a lighter menu and local feel. ⊠ *81 Front St.* ☎ *781/639–1266* ▭ *AE, D, DC, MC, V* ⊕ *www.thelandingrestaurant.com.*

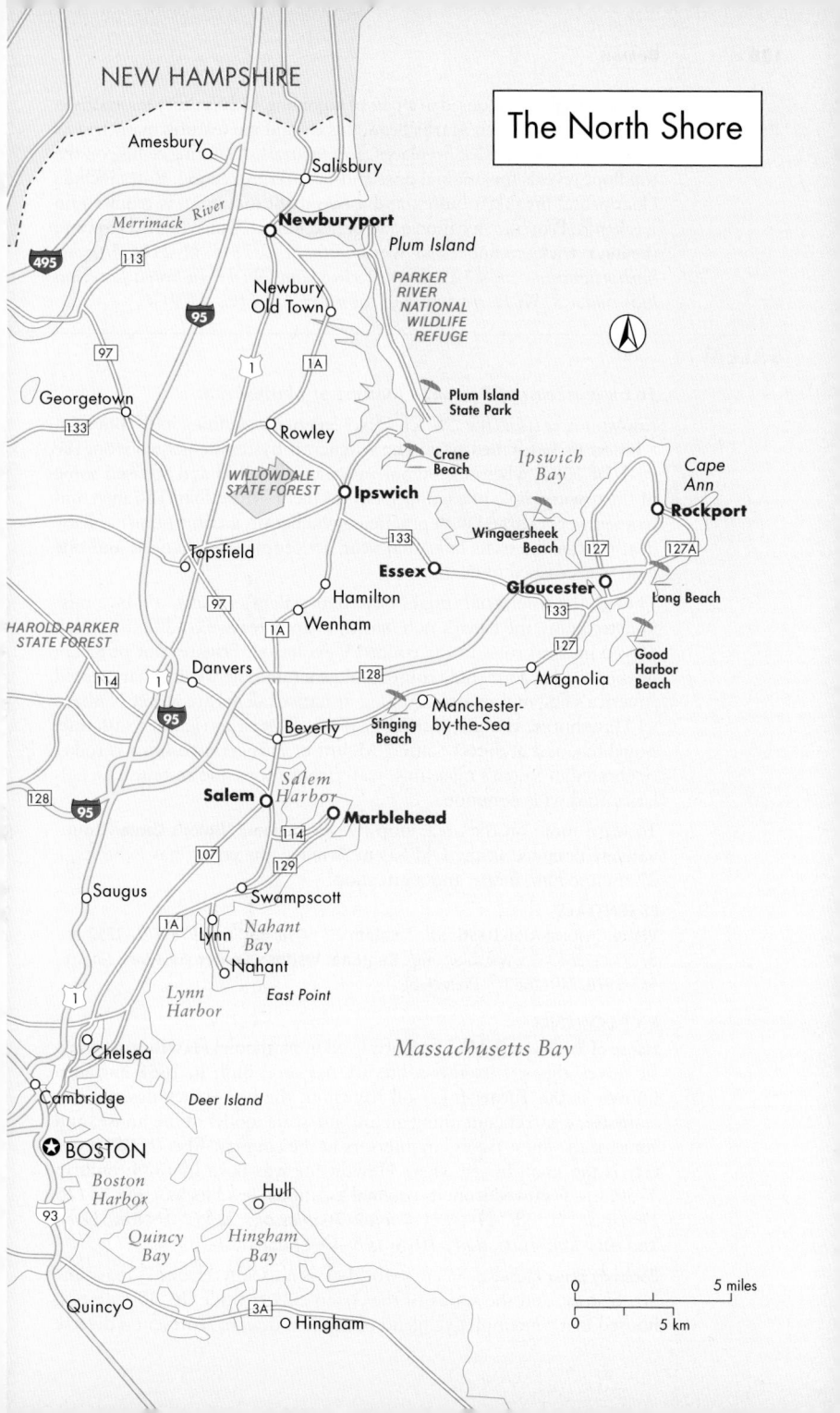

$$$ 🖼 **Harbor Light Inn.** Housed in a pair of adjoining 18th-century mansions in

Fodor's Choice the heart of Old Town Marblehead, this elegant inn features many rooms

★ with canopy beds, brick fireplaces, and Jacuzzis. A soaring ceiling on the top floor reveals the original post-and-beam construction. Rates include Continental breakfast buffet, and a two-night minimum is required on weekends. **Pros:** nice location amid period homes. **Cons:** limited parking; the inn is tricky to find. ☒ *58 Washington St.* ☎ *781/631–2186* ⊕ *www. harborlightinn.com* ⇥ *21 rooms* ☖ *In-room: Wi-Fi. In-hotel: pool, no kids under 8, Wi-Fi, no-smoking rooms* ⊟ *AE, MC, V* ⦿ *CP.*

SALEM

16 mi northeast of Boston, 4 mi west of Marblehead.

Known for years as the "Witch City," Salem is redefining itself. But first, a bit on its bewitched past. The witchcraft hysteria emerged from the trials of 1692, when several Salem-area girls fell ill and accused some of the townspeople of casting spells on them. More than 150 men and women were charged with practicing witchcraft, a crime punishable by death. After the trials later that year, 19 people were hanged and one man was crushed to death.

Though the witch trials might have built Salem's infamy, it'd be a mistake to ignore the town's rich maritime and creative traditions, which played integral roles in the country's evolution. Frigates out of Salem opened the Far East trade routes and generated the wealth that created America's first millionaires. Among its native talents are writer Nathaniel Hawthorne, the intellectual Peabody Sisters, navigator Nathaniel Bowditch, and architect Samuel McIntire. This creative spirit is today celebrated in Salem's museums, waterfront shops and restaurants, galleries, and wide common.

To learn more on the area, stop by the **Regional Visitor's Center.** Innovatively designed in the Old Salem Armory, the center has exhibits, a 27-minute film, maps, and a gift shop.

ESSENTIALS

Visitor Information Destination Salem (☒ *54 Turner St.* ☎ *978/741–3252 or 877/725–3662* ⊕ *www.salem.org*). **Regional Visitor's Center** (☒ *2 New Liberty St.* ☎ *978/740–1660* ⊗ *Daily 9–5*).

EXPLORING

House of the Seven Gables. Immortalized in Nathaniel Hawthorne's classic novel, this site itself is a literary treasure. Built in 1668 and also known as the Turner-Ingersoll Mansion, the house includes a secret staircase, a garret containing an antique scale model of the house, and some of the finest Georgian interiors in the country. Also on the property is the small house where Hawthorne was born in 1804; built in 1750, it was moved from its original location a few blocks away. ☒ *115 Derby St.* ☎ *978/744–0991* ⊕ *www.7gables.org* ⧉ *$12* ⊗ *Nov., Dec., and mid-Jan.–June, daily 10–5; July–Oct., daily 10–7.*

Peabody Essex Museum. Salem's world-class museum celebrates maritime art, history, and the spoils of the Asian export trade. Its 30 galleries, housed in a contemplative blend of modern design, represent a diverse range of styles; ranging from American decorative and seamen's art to idea studios and photography. ⊠ *East India Sq.* ☎ *978/745–9500 or 866/745–1876* ⊕ *www.pem.org* 🖃 *$15* ⊙ *Tues.–Sun. 10–5.*

Salem Maritime National Historic Site. Near Derby Wharf, this 9¼-acre site focuses on Salem's heritage as a major seaport with a thriving overseas trade. It includes an orientation center with an 18-minute film; the 1762 home of Elias Derby, America's first millionaire; the 1819 Customs House, made famous in Nathaniel Hawthorne's *The Scarlet Letter*; and a replica of the *Friendship*, a 171-foot, three-masted 1797 merchant vessel. There's also an active lighthouse dating from 1871, as well as the nation's last surviving 18th-century wharves. The West India Goods Store, across the street, is still a working 19th-century store, with glass jars of spices, teas, and coffees. ⊠ *193 Derby St.* ☎ *978/740–1650* ⊕ *www.nps.gov/ sama* 🖃 *Site free, tours $5* ⊙ *Hours vary; check Web site or call ahead.*

Salem Witch Museum. An informative, if hokey, introduction to the 1692 witchcraft hysteria, this museum's short walk-through exhibit, "Witches: Evolving Perceptions," describes witch hunts through the years. ⊠ *Washington Sq. N* ☎ *978/744–1692* ⊕ *www.salemwitchmuseum.com* 🖃 *$8* ⊙ *Sept.–June, daily 10–5; July–Aug., daily 10–7.*

Salem Witch Trials Memorial. Dedicated by Nobel Laureate Elie Wiesel in 1992, this melancholy space—an antidote to the relentless marketing of the merry-witches motif—honors those who died because they refused to confess that they were witches. A stone wall is studded with 20 stone benches, each inscribed with a victim's name, and sits next to Salem's oldest burying ground. ⊠ *Off Liberty St. near Charter St.*

ARTS AND ENTERTAINMENT

THEATER **Cry Innocent: The People versus Bridget Bishop.** This show, the longest continuously running play north of Boston, transports audience members to Bridget Bishop's trial of 1692. After hearing historical testimonies, the audience cross-examines the witnesses and must then decide the verdict. Actors respond in character revealing much about the Puritan frame of mind. ⊠ *Old Town Hall, 32 Derby Sq.* ☎ *978/867–4767* ⊕ *www. gordon.edu/historyalive* 🖃 *$9* ⊙ *June–Oct., showtimes vary.*

WHERE TO EAT AND STAY

$$
SEAFOOD
Fodor's Choice
★

✕ **The Lyceum Bar & Grill.** The restaurant takes advantage of its historic building, where Alexander Graham Bell made the first long-distance phone call. The "local ingredients, global flavors" philosophy is seen best in the panko-crusted fish-and-chips, oysters, and lobster crepe. Jazz is played most weekends. ⊠ *43 Church St.* ☎ *978/745–7665* ⊕ *www. lyceumsalem.com* ☰ *AE, D, MC, V* ⊙ *No dinner Sun. (brunch only).*

$$–$$$ 🛏 **The Hawthorne Hotel.** Elegantly restored, this full-service landmark hotel celebrates the town's most famous writer. The historic hotel and tavern is within walking distance from the town common, all museums, and the waterfront. Across the street is Nathaniel's statue and a fine gift shop named after his wife Sophia (Peabody) in the couple's former home. **Pros:** lobby is historic and lovely; parking behind hotel; easy walk to all the town's features. **Cons:** many rooms are small; management sometimes too busy to give personal attention. ⊠ *18 Washington Sq. W*

The First Witch Trial

It was in Danvers, not Salem, that the first witch trial was held, originating with the family of Samuel Parris, a minister who moved to the area in 1680 from Barbados, bringing with him two slaves, including one named Tituba. In 1691 Samuel's daughter, Betty, and niece, Abigail, began having "fits." Tituba, who had told Betty and Abigail stories of magic and witchcraft from her homeland, baked a "witch cake" to identify the witches who were harming the girls. The girls in turn accused Tituba of witchcraft. After three days of "questioning," which included beatings from Samuel and a promise from him to free her if she cooperated, Tituba confessed to meeting the devil (in the form of a black hog or dog). She also claimed there were other witches in the village, confirming the girls' accusations against Sarah Good and Sarah Osborne, but she refused to name any others. Tituba's trial prompted the frenzy that led to the deaths of 20 accused "witches."

☎ 978/744–4080 ⊕ *www.hawthornehotel.com* ⇢ *93 rooms* ♿ *In-room: Wi-Fi. In-hotel: Wi-Fi, no-smoking rooms* ⊟ *AE, D, MC, V.*

GLOUCESTER

37 mi northeast of Boston, 8 mi northeast of Manchester-by-the-Sea.

On Gloucester's fine seaside promenade is a famous statue of a man steering a ship's wheel, his eyes searching the horizon. The statue, which honors those "who go down to the sea in ships" was commissioned by the town citizens in celebration of Gloucester's 300th anniversary in 1923. The oldest seaport in the nation (with some of the North Shore's best beaches) is still a major fishing port. Sebastian Junger's 1997 book *A Perfect Storm* was an account of the fate of the *Andrea Gail*, a Gloucester fishing boat caught in "the storm of the century" in October 1991.

ESSENTIALS

Visitor Information **Cape Ann Chamber of Commerce** (⊠ *33 Commercial St., Gloucester* ☎ *978/283–1601* ⊕ *www.capeannvacations.com*).

EXPLORING

Hammond Castle Museum. Inventor John Hays Hammond Jr. built this structure in 1926 to resemble a "medieval" stone castle. Hammond is credited with more than 500 patents, including inventions associated with the organ that bears his name. The museum contains medieval-style furnishings and paintings, and the Great Hall houses an impressive 8,200-pipe organ. From the castle you can see Norman's Woe Rock, made famous by Longfellow in his poem "The Wreck of the Hesperus." ⊠ *80 Hesperus Ave., south side of Gloucester off Rte. 127* ☎ *978/283–2080 or 978/283–7673* ⊕ *www.hammondcastle.org* 🎫 *$9* ⊗ *May–early June, weekends and mid-June–Oct., daily. Call for hrs.*

Rocky Neck. The town's creative side thrives in this neighborhood, the first-settled artists' colony in the United States. Its alumni include Winslow Homer, Maurice Prendergast, Jane Peter, and Cecilia Beaux. ⊠ *Rocky*

Neck Ave. ⊕ *www.rockyneckartcolony.org* ☎ *978/282–0917* ⊙ *Galleries 10–10, May 15–Oct. 15th. Call or check the Web site for winter hours.*

The Cape Ann Historical Association. Downtown in the Captain Elias Davis 1804 house, this museum and gallery reflects the town's commitment to artists, and has the world's largest collection by maritime luminist Fitz Henry (Hugh) Lane. There's also an excellent exhibit on Gloucester's maritime history. ⊠ *27 Pleasant St.* ☎ *978/283–0455* ⊕ *www. capeannmuseum.org* ☜ *$8* ⊙ *Tues.–Sat. 10–5, Sun. 1–4.*

SPORTS AND THE OUTDOORS

BEACHES   Gloucester has the best beaches on the North Shore. From Memorial Day through mid-September parking costs $20 on weekdays and $25 on weekends, when the lots often fill by 10 AM. **Good Harbor Beach** (⊠ *Signposted from Rte. 127A*) is a huge, sandy, dune-backed beach, with showers and a snack bar, and a rocky islet just offshore. For excellent sunbathing, visit **Long Beach** (⊠ *Off Rte. 127A on Gloucester-Rockport town line*). **Wingaersheek Beach** (⊠ *Exit 13 off Rte. 128*) is a well-protected cove of white sand and dunes, with the white Annisquam lighthouse in the bay.

BOATING   Consider a sail along the harbor and coast aboard the 65-foot schooner **Thomas E. Lannon** (⊠ *63 Rear Rogers St., Seven Seas Wharf* ☎ *978/281–6634* ⊕ *www.schooner.org*) crafted in Essex in 1996 and modeled after the great boats built a century before. From mid-May through mid-October there are several two-hour sails, including trips that let you enjoy the sunset or participate in a lobster bake. Tickets are $37.50.

WHERE TO EAT AND STAY

$$ ✕ **Franklin Cape Ann.** This contemporary nightspot offers bistro-style
AMERICAN   chicken, roast cod, and steak frites, perfect for the late-night crowd (it's open until midnight). Live jazz is on tap most Tuesday evenings. Look for the signature martini glass over the door. ⊠ *118 Main St.* ☎ *978/283–7888* ▭ *AE, D, MC, V* ⊙ *No lunch.*

$–$$ ✕ **Passports.** With an eclectic lunch and dinner menu—hence the name—
SEAFOOD   Passports is a bright and airy café with French, Spanish, and Thai dishes, as well as (of course) lobster sandwiches. The fried calamari and house haddock are favorites here, and there's always local art hanging on the walls for patrons to buy. Occasionally there are wine tastings. ⊠ *110 Main St.* ☎ *978/281–3680* ▭ *AE, D, MC, V.*

$$ ⌂ **Cape Ann's Marina Resort.** This year-round hotel and spa less than a mile from Gloucester comes alive in summer. A whale-watch boat and deep-sea fishing excursions are available from the premises. The rooms all have balconies and water views. The Gull restaurant is closed November to mid-April. **Pros:** guests get a free river cruise during summer. **Cons:** "Resort" is a misnomer, as the hotel is surrounded by parking lots, with no walking path to or from town. ⊠ *75 Essex Ave.* ☎ *978/283–2116 or 800/626–7660* ⊕ *www.capeannmarina.com* ⇆ *31 rooms* △ *In-room: kitchen (some). In-hotel: restaurant, Wi-Fi, pool, no-smoking rooms* ▭ *AE, D, DC, MC, V.*

$$ ⌂ **Cape Ann Motor Inn.** On the sands of Long Beach, this three-story, shingled motel has no-frills rooms except for the balconies and ocean views. Half of them have well-furnished kitchenettes. The Honeymoon

Kids enjoy the white sands of Wingaersheek Beach in Gloucester.

Suite is pricier but has a full kitchen, fireplace, whirlpool bath, king-size bed, and private balcony. **Pros:** exceptional view from every room; kids under 5 stay free. **Cons:** summer season can be loud. ⊠ *33 Rockport Rd.* ☎ *978/281–2900 or 800/464–8439* ⊕ *www.capeannmotorinn.com* ⤳ *30 rooms, 1 suite* ⌂ *In-room: no a/c, kitchen (some). In-hotel: some pets allowed, no-smoking rooms* ▭ *AE, D, MC, V* ¦◯¦ *CP.*

ROCKPORT

41 mi northeast of Boston, 4 mi northeast of Gloucester on Rte. 127.

Rockport, at the very tip of Cape Ann, derives its name from local granite formations. Many Boston-area structures are made of stone cut from its long-gone quarries. Today the town is a tourist center with a well-marked, centralized downtown that is easy to navigate on foot. Walk past shops and colorful clapboard houses to the end of Bearskin Neck for an impressive view of the Atlantic Ocean and the old, weather-beaten lobster shack known as "Motif No. 1" because of its popularity as a subject for amateur painters and photographers.

ESSENTIALS

Visitor Information Rockport Chamber of Commerce (⊠ 33 Commercial St., Gloucester ☎ 978/546–6575 ⊕ www.rockportusa.com).

WHERE TO EAT AND STAY

$–$$ ✕ **Brackett's Ocean View.** A big bay window in this quiet, homey restaurant
SEAFOOD   provides an excellent view across Sandy Bay. The menu includes chowders, fish cakes, and other seafood dishes. ⊠ *25 Main St.* ☎ *978/546–2797* ▭ *AE, D, DC, MC, V* ⊙ *Closed Mon.–Tues. and Nov.–mid-Apr.*

$$ ✕ **The Greenery Restaurant and Café.** This spot is one of Rockport's only
AMERICAN restaurants open year-round. In-season, the second floor opens to
accommodate the boom of tourists. Stop in for a sandwich or pastry
from the bakery or dine in the back room surrounded by bay windows
overlooking the harbor. Breakfast is served daily until 4 PM. ⊠ *15 Dock
Sq.* ☎ *978/546–9593* ◬ *Reservations not accepted* ▭ *AE, MC, V.*

$$ ▦ **Addison Choate Inn and Periwinkle Cottage.** Just a minute's walk from
★ both the center of Rockport and the train station, this 1851 inn sits in a
prime location. The sizable and beautifully decorated rooms have their
share of antiques and local seascape paintings, as well as pine floors and
large bathrooms; the Captain's Room contains a canopy bed, handmade
quilts, and Oriental rugs. In the third-floor suite huge windows look out
over the rooftops to the sea. Two spacious stable-house apartments have
skylights, cathedral ceilings, and exposed wood beams. Rates include
afternoon tea. **Pros:** proximity to the ocean, shopping, and train station.
Cons: only one bedroom on the first floor. ⊠ *49 Broadway* ☎ *978/546–
7543 or 800/245–7543* ⊕ *www.addisonchoateinn.com* ⬎ *6 rooms, 2
apartments* ♿ *In-room: no TV, Wi-Fi. In-hotel: restaurant, no-smoking
rooms* ▭ *MC, V* ☉ *Closed Jan.–Mar.* ⦿*CP.*

$ ▦ **Sally Webster Inn.** This inn was named for a member of Hannah Jump-
Fodor'sChoice er's "Hatchet Gang," teetotalers who smashed up the town's liquor
★ stores in 1856 and turned Rockport into the dry town it remains today.
Sally lived in this house for much of her life, and the poshly decorated
guest rooms are named for members of her family. Caleb's Room is a
romantic retreat with a four-poster bed and floral quilts, and William's
Room has a crisply nautical theme. Other rooms have wide-board pine
floors, nonworking brick fireplaces, rocking chairs, and four-poster,
brass, or canopy beds. **Pros:** homey atmosphere in an excellent location
with attentive staff. **Cons:** only two rooms have fireplaces. ⊠ *34 Mt.
Pleasant St.* ☎ *978/546–9251 or 877/546–9251* ⊕ *www.sallywebster.
com* ⬎ *8 rooms* ♿ *In-room: no TV. In-hotel: Internet terminal, no-
smoking rooms* ▭ *MC, V* ☉ *Closed Jan.* ⦿*CP.*

ESSEX

35 mi northeast of Boston, 12 mi west of Rockport.

The small seafaring town of Essex, once an important shipbuilding
center, is surrounded by salt marshes and is filled with antiques stores
and seafood restaurants.

GETTING HERE AND AROUND

Head west out of Cape Ann on Rte. 128, turning north on Rte. 133.

EXPLORING

☺ **Essex Shipbuilding Museum.** At what is still an active shipyard, this
museum traces the evolution of the American schooner, which was
first created in Essex. The museum sometimes offers shipbuilding demonstrations. One-hour tours take in the museum's many buildings and
boats, especially the *Evelina M. Goulart*—one of only seven remaining Essex-built schooners. ⊠ *66 Main St. (Rte. 133)* ☎ *978/768–7541*
⊕ *www.essexshipbuildingmuseum.org* ⊟ *$7* ☉ *June–Oct., Wed.–Sun.
10–5; Nov.–May, Sat. and Sun. 10–5.*

WHERE TO EAT

$$ ✕ **Woodman's of Essex**. According to local legend, this is where Law-
SEAFOOD   rence "Chubby" Woodman invented the first fried clam back in 1916.
Fodor'sChoice   Today this sprawling wooden shack with indoor booths and outdoor
★   picnic tables is *the* place for seafood in the rough. Besides fried clams,
you can tuck into clam chowder, lobster rolls, or the popular "down-
river" lobster combo. ⊠ *121 Main St. (Rte. 133)* ☎ *978/768–2559 or
800/649–1773* ⊕ *www.woodmans.com* ⊟ *AE, MC, V.*

IPSWICH

30 mi north of Boston, 6 mi northwest of Essex.

Quiet little Ipswich, settled in 1633 and famous for its clams, is said to
have more 17th-century houses standing and occupied than any other
place in America; more than 40 were built before 1725. Information
and a booklet with a suggested walking tour are available at the **Ipswich
Visitor Information Center.**

ESSENTIALS

Visitor Information Ipswich Visitor Information Center (⊠ *36 S. Main St.,*
☎ *978/356-8540* ⊕ *www.ipswichma.com*).

EXPLORING

Great House at Castle Hill. This 59-room Stuart-style mansion, built in
1927 for Richard Crane—of the Crane plumbing company—and his
family, is part of the Crane Estate, a stretch of more than 2,100 acres
along the Essex and Ipswich rivers, encompassing Castle Hill, Crane
Beach, and the Crane Wildlife Refuge. Although the original furnish-
ings were sold at auction, the mansion has been elaborately refurnished
in period style; photographs in most of the rooms show their original
appearance. The Great House is open for one-hour tours and also hosts
concerts and other events. ⊠ *Argilla Rd.* ☎ *978/356–4351* ⊕ *www.
thetrustees.org* ◪ *$5 to $8 per car weekends, Monday holidays, and
Memorial Day to Labor Day; $5 per car at other times; 50% discount
after 3 PM. Tours $10* ⊙ *Memorial Day–Oct., Wed.–Sat.; call for hrs.*

SPORTS AND THE OUTDOORS

★   **Crane Beach**, one of New England's most beautiful beaches, is a sandy,
4-mi-long stretch backed by dunes and a nature trail. Public park-
ing is available, but on a nice summer weekend it's usually full before
lunch. There are lifeguards and changing rooms. Check ahead before
visiting mid-July to early August, when greenhead flies terrorize sun-
bathers. ■TIP→ **The Ipswich Essex Explorer bus runs between the Ipswich
train station and Crane Beach Saturday, Sunday, and holidays from June to
September; the $5 pass includes round trip bus fare and beach admission.
Contact the Ipswich Visitor Information Center for information.** ⊠ *Argilla
Rd.* ☎ *978/356–4354* ⊕ *www.thetrustees.org* ◪ *$2 on foot; additional
charges apply if you arrive by automobile. Check the Web site for
details. Parking $15 weekdays, $22 weekends mid-May–early Sept.;
$7 early Sept.–mid-May* ⊙ *Daily 8–sunset.*

HIKING   The Massachusetts Audubon Society's **Ipswich River Wildlife Sanctuary** has
trails through marshland hills, where there are remains of early colonial

settlements as well as abundant wildlife. Enjoy bridges, man-made rock structures, and other surprises on the Rockery Trail. ⊠ *87 Perkins Row, southwest of Ipswich, 1 mi off Rte. 97, Topsfield* ☎ *978/887–9264* ⊕ *www. massaudubon.org* ⊠ *$4* ⊘ *Office May–Oct., Tues.–Sun. 9–5; Nov.–Apr., Tues.–Fri. 9–4, Sat.–Sun. 10–4. Trails Tues.–Sun. dawn–dusk.*

WHERE TO EAT

¢–$
SEAFOOD
Fodor's Choice
★

✕ **Clam Box.** Shaped like a giant fried clam box, this small roadside stand is the best place to sample Ipswich's famous bivalves. Since 1938 locals and tourists have been lining up for clams, oysters, scallops, and onion rings. ⊠ *246 High St. (Rte. 1A)* ☎ *978/356–9707* ⊕ *www.ipswichma. com/clambox* ⊘ *Reservations not accepted* ⊟ *No credit cards* ⊘ *Closed mid-Dec.–Feb.*

$$–$$$
SEAFOOD

✕ **Stone Soup Café.** This cheery café provides consistently good food. Excellent breakfasts include omelets, French toast, and assorted pancakes; lunch features chowders, pot roast, or delicious Cuban sandwiches. Dinner can include lobster bisque, porcini ravioli, or whatever contemporary fare the chef is inspired to cook from the day's farm-stand finds. ⊠ *141 High St., off Rte. 1A* ☎ *978/356–4222* ⊟ *No credit cards* ⊘ *No dinner Mon.–Wed., breakfast but no lunch Sun.*

NEWBURYPORT

38 mi north of Boston, 12 mi north of Ipswich on Rte. 1A.

Newburyport's High Street is lined with some of the finest examples of Federal-period (roughly, 1790–1810) mansions in New England. The city was once a leading port and shipbuilding center; the houses were built for prosperous sea captains. Although Newburyport's maritime significance ended with the decline of the clipper ships, the town was revived in the 1970s. Today the town has shops, restaurants, galleries, and a waterfront park and boardwalk. Newburyport is walker-friendly, with well-marked restrooms and free parking all day down by the water.

A stroll through the **Waterfront Park and Promenade** offers a view of the harbor as well as the fishing and pleasure boats that moor here. A causeway leads from Newburyport to a narrow piece of land known as Plum Island, which harbors a summer colony at one end.

EXPLORING

Custom House Maritime Museum. Built in 1835 in Greek Revival style, this museum contains exhibits on maritime history, ship models, tools, and paintings. ⊠ *25 Water St.* ☎ *978/462–8681* ⊕ *www.customhouse-maritimemuseum.org* ⊠ *$7* ⊘ *Tues.–Sat. 10–4, Sun. noon–4.*

SPORTS AND THE OUTDOORS

Parker River National Wildlife Refuge. On Plum Island, this 4,662-acre refuge of salt marsh, freshwater marsh, beaches, and dunes is one of the few natural barrier beach–dune–salt marsh complexes left on the Northeast coast. Here you can bird-watch, fish, swim, and pick plums and cranberries. The refuge is a popular place in summer, especially on weekends; cars begin to line up at the gate before 7 AM. There's no restriction on the number of people using the beach, but only a limited number of cars are let in; no pets are allowed in the refuge. ⊠ *6 Plum*

Island Tpk. ☎ *978/465–5753* ⊕ *www.fws.gov/northeast/parkerriver* ✉ *$5 per car, bicycles and walk-ins $2* ☉ *Daily dawn–dusk. Beach usually closed during nesting season in spring and early summer.*

Fodor's Choice **Salisbury Beach State Reservation.** Relax at the long sandy beach, or play ★ at the amusement area and nearby arcades. From Newburyport center, follow Bridge Road north, take a right on Beach Road, and follow it until you reach State Reservation Road. ✉ *Rte. 1A, 5 mi northeast of Newburyport, Salisbury* ☎ *978/462–4481* ⊕ *www.mass.gov/dcr/parks/ northeast/salb.htm* ✉ *Beach free, parking $7.*

SHOPPING

Todd Farm Flea Market. A New England tradition since 1971, the Todd Farm Flea Market features up to 240 vendors from all over New England and New York. It's open every Sunday from mid-April through late November, though its busiest months are May, September, and October. Merchandise varies from antique furniture, clocks, jewelry, recordings, and tools to fishing rods, golf accessories, honey products, cedar fencing, vintage toys, and seasonal plants and flowers. ✉ *303 Main St. Rowley, off of Route 1A* ☎ *978/948–3300* ⊕ *www.toddfarm. com* ☉ *Apr.–Nov., Sun. 5 AM–3 PM.*

WHERE TO EAT AND STAY

$$–$$$ ✕ **Glenn's Restaurant & Cool Bar.** A block from the waterfront parking lot,
SEAFOOD Glenn's offers creative combinations from around the world, with the occasional New England twist. The ever-changing menu might include sesame-crusted yellowfin tuna or house-smoked baby-back ribs. There's live jazz or blues on Sunday. ✉ *44 Merrimac St.* ☎ *978/465–3811* ✉ *AE, D, DC, MC, V* ☉ *Closed Mon. No lunch.*

$$ 🏨 **Clark Currier Inn.** Once the home of the 19th-century sea captain
★ Thomas March Clark, this 1803 Federal mansion has been beautifully restored. Guest rooms are spacious and furnished with antiques. Rates include Continental breakfast and afternoon tea. **Pros:** close to shopping and the oceanfront; perfect for couples looking for quiet. **Cons:** perhaps too quiet for some. ✉ *45 Green St.* ☎ *978/465–8363* ⊕ *www. clarkcurrierinn.com* 🛏 *8 rooms* ♿ *In-room: no TV (some). In-hotel: no kids under 10, no-smoking rooms* ✉ *AE, D, MC, V* ⊧ *CP.*

SOUTH OF BOSTON

People from all over the world travel south of Boston to visit Plymouth for a glimpse into the country's earliest beginnings. The two main stops are the Plimoth Plantation, which re-creates the everyday life of the Pilgrims; and the *Mayflower II*, which gives you an idea of how frightening the journey across the Atlantic must have been. As you may guess, November in Plymouth brings special events focused on Thanksgiving. Farther south, New Bedford recalls the world of whaling.

EN ROUTE While driving from Boston to Plymouth, stop at **Quincy,** where the **Adams National Historic Park** (✉ *Carriage house, 135 Adams St.; visitor center and bookstore, 1250 Hancock St.* ☎ *617/770–1175* ⊕ *www.nps. gov/adam* ✉ *$5* ☉ *Tours 9:15–3:15 daily mid-Apr.–mid-Nov.*) contains the birthplaces, homes, and graves of John Adams and his son John

Quincy Adams. Guided and trolley tours of the property and family church are available.

PLYMOUTH

40 mi south of Boston.

On December 26, 1620, 102 weary men, women, and children disembarked from the *Mayflower* to found the first permanent European settlement north of Virginia. Today Plymouth is characterized by narrow streets, clapboard mansions, shops, antiques stores, and a scenic waterfront. To mark Thanksgiving, the town holds a parade, historic-house tours, and other activities. Historic statues dot the town, including depictions of William Bradford, Pilgrim leader and governor of Plymouth Colony for more than 30 years, on Water Street; a Pilgrim maiden in Brewster Gardens; and Massasoit, the Wampanoag chief who helped the Pilgrims survive, on Carver Street.

ESSENTIALS

Hospital Jordan Hospital (⊠ *275 Sandwich St.* ☎ *508/746–2000*).

Pharmacy CVS (⊠ *8 Pilgrim Hill Rd., off Rte. 44* ☎ *508/747–1465*).

Visitor Information Plymouth Visitor Information Center (⊠ *170 Water St., at Hwy. 44* ☎ *508/747–7533 or 800/872–1620* ⊕ *www.visit-plymouth.com*).

EXPLORING

★ **Mayflower II.** This seaworthy replica of the 1620 *Mayflower* was built in England through research and a bit of guesswork, then sailed across the Atlantic in 1957. As you explore the interior and exterior of the ship, sailors in modern dress answer your questions about both the reproduction and the original ship, while costumed guides provide a 17th-century perspective. Plymouth Rock is nearby. ⊠ *State Pier* ☎ *508/746–1622* ⊕ *www.plimoth.org/features/mayflower-2* ☞ *$10, $28 with admission to Plimoth Plantation* ☉ *Late Mar.–Nov., daily 9–5.*

Fodor's Choice ★ **Plimoth Plantation.** Over the entrance to this popular attraction is the caution: YOU ARE NOW ENTERING 1627. Believe it. Against the backdrop of the Atlantic Ocean, and just 3 mi south of downtown Plymouth, this Pilgrim village has been carefully re-created, from the thatch roofs, cramped quarters, and open fireplaces to the long-horned livestock. Throw away your preconception of white collars and funny hats; through ongoing research, the Plimoth staff has developed a portrait of the Pilgrims that's more complex than the dour folk in school textbooks. Listen to the accents of the "residents," who never break out of character. You might see them plucking ducks, cooking rabbit stew, or tending gardens. Feel free to engage them in conversation about their life, but expect only curious looks if you ask about anything that happened after 1627. "Thanksgiving: Memory, Myth & Meaning," an exhibit in the visitor center, offers a fresh perspective on the 1621 harvest celebration that is now known as "the first Thanksgiving." ⊠ *137 Warren Ave. (Hwy. 3A)* ☎ *508/746–1622* ⊕ *www.plimoth.org* ☞ *$24, $28 with Mayflower II* ☉ *Late Mar.–Nov., daily 9–5.*

DID YOU KNOW?

Plimoth Plantation is about more than Pilgrims. It also honors Native Americans at Wampanoag Site. Visit a traditional house, learn about family life, and chat with Wampanoag people. Note that presenters are not in character as at the plantation site.

2

★ **Plymouth Rock.** This landmark rock, just a few dozen yards from the *Mayflower II*, is popularly believed to have been the Pilgrims' stepping-stone when they left the ship. Given the stone's unimpressive appearance—it's little more than a boulder—and dubious authenticity (as explained on a nearby plaque), the grand canopy overhead seems a trifle ostentatious.

Sparrow House. Built in 1640, this is Plymouth's oldest structure. It is among several historic houses in town that are open for visits. You can peek into a pair of rooms furnished in the spartan style of the Pilgrims' era. The contemporary crafts gallery also on the premises seems somewhat incongruous, but the works on view are of high quality. ⊠ *42 Summer St.* ☎ *508/747–1240* ⊕ *www.sparrowhouse.com* ⬚ *House $2, gallery free* ☉ *Open daily 10–5.*

WHERE TO EAT AND STAY

$$ ✕ **Blue-eyed Crab Grille & Raw Bar.** Grab a seat on the outside deck over-
SEAFOOD looking the water at this friendly, somewhat funky (plastic fish dangling from the ceiling), fresh-fish shack. If the local Island Creek raw oysters are on the menu, go for them! Otherwise start with thick crab bisque full of floating crabmeat or the steamed mussels. Dinner entrées include seafood stew with chorizo and sweet potatoes and the classic fish-and-chips. Locals come for the brunch specials, too, like grilled shrimp and poached eggs over red-pepper grits, the lobster omelet, and banana-ginger pancakes. ⊠ *170 Water St.* ☎ *508/747–6776* ⊕ *www.blueeyedcrab.com* ⊟ *D, MC, V.*

$ ⬚ **Best Western Cold Spring.** Walk to the waterfront and downtown Plymouth from this clean, family-friendly, two-story motel. Rooms, some with balconies and ocean views, are minimalist, with white walls, dark carpeted floors, and contemporary furniture. **Pros:** half-mile from Plymouth Rock and *Mayflower II*; some of the best wallet-pleasing rates in the area; friendly owners. **Cons:** basic rooms without much character. ⊠ *188 Court St.* ☎ *508/746–2222 or 800/678–8667* ⊕ *www.bestwesternmassachusetts.com* ⬚ *56 rooms* ⚒ *In-room: Internet. In-hotel: pool, laundry facilities, Internet terminal, parking (free), no-smoking rooms* ⊟ *AE, D, DC, MC, V.*

$$ ⬚ **John Carver Inn & Spa.** This three-story colonial-style redbrick building is steps from Plymouth's main attractions. Lavish public rooms have period furnishings. The guest rooms include six "environmentally sensitive" options with filtered air and water and four-poster beds; others are a bit drab (time for refurbishing!). The suites have fireplaces and whirlpool baths. There's also an indoor pool with a *Mayflower* ship model and a waterslide. **Pros:** waterfront setting. **Cons:** pool is often overcrowded; some rooms need updating. ⊠ *25 Summer St.* ☎ *508/746–7100 or 800/274–1620* ⊕ *www.johncarverinn.com* ⬚ *74 rooms, 6 suites* ⚒ *In-room: Wi-Fi. In-hotel: restaurant, bar, pool, gym, spa, laundry facilities, parking (free), no-smoking rooms* ⊟ *AE, D, DC, MC, V.*

NEW BEDFORD

45 mi southwest of Plymouth, 50 mi south of Boston.

In 1652 colonists from Plymouth settled in the area that now includes the city of New Bedford. The city has a long maritime tradition, beginning as a shipbuilding center and small whaling port in the late 1700s. By the mid-1800s it had developed into a center of North American whaling. Today New Bedford has the largest fishing fleet on the East Coast. Although much of the town is industrial, the restored historic district near the water is a delight. It was here that Herman Melville set his masterpiece, *Moby-Dick,* a novel about whaling.

ESSENTIALS

Hospital St. Luke's Hospital (⊠ *101 Page St.* ☎ *508/997–1515*).

Visitor Information New Bedford Office of Tourism (⊠ *Waterfront Visitor Center, Pier 3* ☎ *508/979–1745 or 800/508–5353* ⊕ *www.ci.new-bedford.ma.us*).

EXPLORING

New Bedford Whaling Museum. Established in 1903, this is the world's largest museum of its kind. A highlight is the skeleton of a 66-foot blue whale, one of only three on view anywhere. An interactive exhibit lets you listen to the underwater sounds of whales, dolphins, and other sea life—plus the sounds of a thunderstorm and a whale-watching boat—as a whale might hear them. You can also see the collection of scrimshaw, visit exhibits on regional history, and climb aboard an 89-foot, half-scale model of the 1826 whaling ship *Lagoda*—the world's largest ship model. A small chapel across the street from the museum is the one described in *Moby-Dick.* ⊠ *18 Johnny Cake Hill* ☎ *508/997–0046* ⊕ *www.whalingmuseum.org* ☞ *$10* ⊗ *Mon.–Sat. 9–4, Sun. noon–4.*

New Bedford Whaling National Historical Park. The city's whaling tradition is commemorated at this park that takes up 13 blocks of the waterfront historic district. The park visitor center, housed in an 1853 Greek Revival building, provides maps and information about whaling-related sites. Free walking tours of the park leave from the visitor center at 10:30, 12:30, and 2:30 in July and August. ⊠ *33 William St.* ☎ *508/996–4095* ⊕ *www.nps.gov/nebe* ☞ *Free* ⊗ *Daily 9–5.*

WHERE TO EAT

$$
PORTUGUESE
✕**Antonio's.** Expect the a long wait and a loud dining room, but it's worth the hassle to sample the traditional fare of New Bedford's large Portuguese population at this friendly, unadorned restaurant. Dishes include hearty portions of pork and shellfish stew, *bacalau* (salt cod), and grilled sardines, often on plates piled high with crispy fried potatoes and rice. ⊠ *267 Coggeshall St., near intersection of I–195 and Hwy. 18* ☎ *508/990–3636* ▤ *No credit cards.*

$$
SEAFOOD
✕**Davy's Locker.** A huge seafood menu is the main draw at this spot overlooking Buzzards Bay. Choose from more than a dozen shrimp preparations, or a choice of healthful entrées—dishes prepared with olive oil, vegetables, garlic, and herbs. For landlubbers, chicken, steak, ribs, and the like are also available. ⊠ *1480 E. Rodney French Blvd.* ☎ *508/992–7359* ▤ *AE, D, DC, MC, V.*

Cape Cod, Martha's Vineyard, and Nantucket

WORD OF MOUTH

"For truly wonderful beaches, Cape Cod is hard to beat. There are ocean beaches for surfing, quiet bay beaches, and warm water beaches along the southern side. Some of the nicer towns include Chatham, Wellfleet and Dennis."

—zootsi

WELCOME TO CAPE COD, MARTHA'S VINEYARD, AND NANTUCKET

TOP REASONS TO GO

★ **Follow the Light:** Lighthouses rise along Cape Cod's coast like architectural exclamation marks. Some are active, others decommissioned; many are open for tours. Each has its own personality.

★ **Explore on Two Wheels:** The Cape Cod Rail Trail is the definitive bike route, with 25 mi of relatively flat terrain. Several parks also maintain impressive trails. Martha's Vineyard and Nantucket have dedicated bike paths.

★ **Say "Anchors Aweigh":** Area tour operators offer everything from sunset schooner cruises to charter fishing expeditions. Mid-April through October, whale-watching adventures are popular.

★ **Get to the Art of the Matter:** The Cape was a prominent art colony in the 19th century, and today has a high concentration of galleries. The Provincetown Art Association and Museum and the Cape Cod Museum of Art both focus on artists with a Cape connection.

1 Cape Cod. Typically divided into regions—the Upper, Mid, Lower, and Outer—Cape Cod is a place of many moods. The Upper Cape (closest to the bridges) has Cape Cod's oldest towns, plus fine beaches and fascinating little museums. The Mid Cape has sophisticated Colonial-era hamlets but also motels and miniature golf courses. In the midst of it all sits Hyannis, the Cape's unofficial capital. The Lower Cape has casual clam shacks, lovely lighthouses, funky art galleries, and stellar natural attractions. The narrow "forearm" of the Outer Cape is famous for sand dunes, crashing surf, and scrubby pines. Frenetic and fun-loving Provincetown is a leading gay getaway.

2 Martha's Vineyard. The Vineyard lies 5 mi off the Cape's southwest tip. The Down-Island towns are the most popular and most populated, but much of what makes this island special is found in its rural Up-Island reaches where dirt roads lead past crystalline ponds, cranberry bogs, and conservation lands.

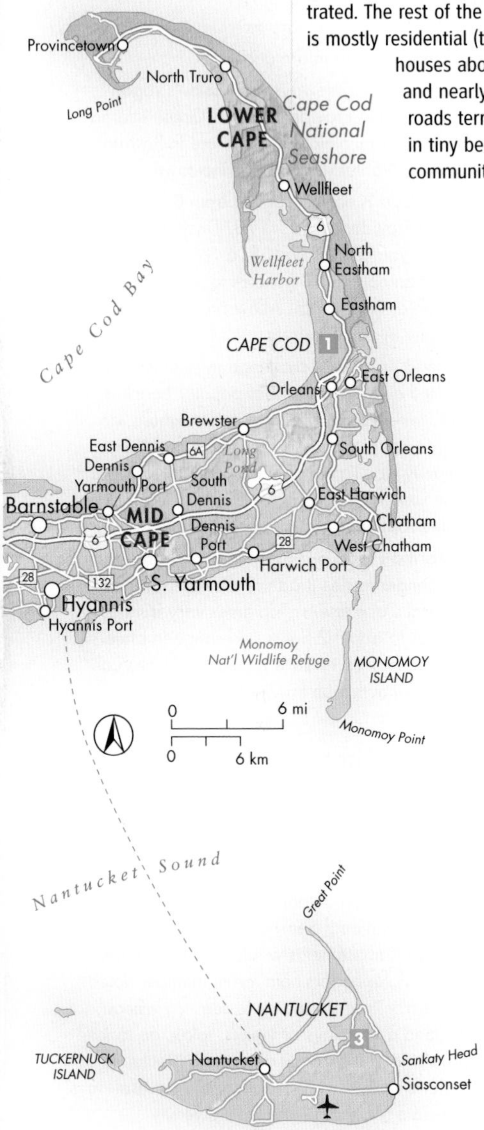

3 Nantucket. Nantucket, or "Far Away Island" in the Wampanoag tongue, is some 25 mi south of Hyannis. Ferries dock in pretty Nantucket Town, where tourism services are concentrated. The rest of the island is mostly residential (trophy houses abound), and nearly all roads terminate in tiny beach communities.

GETTING ORIENTED

Henry David Thoreau, who famously traveled the sparsely populated mid-19th-century Cape Cod, likened the peninsula to "a bare and bended arm." Indeed—looking at a map the outline is obvious, and many people hold their own arm aloft and point to various places from shoulder to fist when asked for directions. There are three main roads that travel, more or less, the entire Cape: U.S. Highway 6, Route 28, and Route 6A, a designated historic road also called the Old King's Highway. Most visitors stick to these main byways, though the back roads can save time and aggravation in summer. The Cape is surrounded by water, though it's not a true island. Several bodies of water define the peninsula's land and seascapes: Just off the mainland to the southeast are the gentler, warmer waters of Buzzards Bay, Vineyard Sound, and Nantucket Sound. Cape Cod Bay extends north to the tip of Provincetown, where it meets the Atlantic Ocean.

Provincetown

North Truro

Long Point

LOWER CAPE

Cape Cod National Seashore

Wellfleet

Cape Cod Bay

Wellfleet Harbor

North Eastham

Eastham

CAPE COD 1

Orleans — East Orleans

Brewster

East Dennis

Dennis

Yarmouth Port

Long Pond

South Dennis

South Orleans

Barnstable

MID CAPE

Dennis Port

6

East Harwich

Chatham

West Chatham

Harwich Port

28

S. Yarmouth

132

Hyannis

Hyannis Port

Monomoy Nat'l Wildlife Refuge

MONOMOY ISLAND

Monomoy Point

0   6 mi

0   6 km

Nantucket Sound

Great Point

NANTUCKET

TUCKERNUCK ISLAND

Nantucket

3

Sankaty Head

Siasconset

CAPE COD, MARTHA'S VINEYARD, AND NANTUCKET PLANNER

When to Go

The Cape and islands teem with activity during high season: roughly late June to Labor Day. If you're dreaming of a classic shore vacation, this is prime time.

However, with the dream come daunting crowds and high costs. Fall has begun to rival summer in popularity, at least on weekends through late October, when the weather is temperate and the scenery remarkable. Many restaurants, shops, and hotels remain open in winter, too, making the area desirable even during the coldest months. The region enjoys fairly moderate weather most of the year, with highs typically in the upper 70s and 80s in summer, and in the upper 30s and lower 40s in winter. Snow and rain are not uncommon during the cooler months, and it can be windy any time.

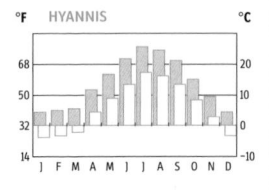

Getting Here and Around

See specific towns for more information.

Air Travel: The major air gateways are Boston's Logan International Airport and Providence's T. F. Green International Airport. Smaller municipal airports are in Barnstable, Martha's Vineyard, Nantucket, and Provincetown.

Car Travel: Cape Cod is easily reached from Boston via Route 3 and from Providence via I-195. Once you cross Cape Cod Canal, you can follow U.S. 6. Without any traffic, it takes about an hour to 90 minutes to reach the Canal from either Boston or Providence. Allow an extra 30 to 60 minutes' travel time in peak periods.

Parking, in general, is a great challenge in summer, especially in congested downtowns and at popular beaches. If you can walk, bike, carpool, or cab it somewhere, do so. But unless you are planning to focus your attention on a single community, you'll probably need a car. Taking a vehicle onto the island ferries is expensive and requires reservations (another option is renting upon arrival).

Ferry Travel: Martha's Vineyard and Nantucket are easily reached by passenger ferries (traditional and high-speed boats) from several Cape towns. Trip times vary from as little as 45 minutes to about 2 hours and range in price from about $8 one-way up to $33. In season, ferries connect Boston and Plymouth with Provincetown.

Planning Your Time

The region can be enjoyed for a few days or a few weeks, depending on the nature of your trip. As the towns are all quite distinct on Cape Cod, it's best to cater your trip based on your interests: an outdoors enthusiast would want to head to the National Seashore region; those who prefer shopping and amusements would do better in the Mid-Cape area. As one Fodors.com forum member noted, the Cape is generally "not something to see . . . instead, people go to spend a few days or weeks, relax, go to the beach . . . that sort of thing." A full-day trip to Nantucket to wander the historic downtown is manageable; several days is best to appreciate Martha's Vineyard's diversity.

About the Restaurants

Cape Cod kitchens have long been closely associated with seafood—the waters off the Cape and the Islands yield a bounty of lobsters, clams, scallops, and myriad fish that make their way onto local menus. In addition to the region's strong Portuguese influence, globally inspired and contemporary fare commonly flavor restaurant offerings. Also gaining in popularity is the use of locally—and often organically—raised produce, meat, and dairy.

Note that ordering an expensive lobster dinner may push your meal into a higher price category than this guide's price range shows for the restaurant.

You can indulge in fresh local seafood and clambakes at seat-yourself shanties for a lower price than at their fine-dining counterparts. Often, the tackier the decor (plastic fish on the walls), the better the seafood. These laid-back local haunts usually operate a fish market on the premises and are in every town on the Cape.

About the Hotels

Dozens of heritage buildings now welcome overnight guests, so you can bed down in a former sea captain's home or a converted church. Scores of rental homes and condominiums are available for long-term stays. Several large resorts encompass numerous amenities—swimming, golf, restaurants, children's programs—all on one property, but often lack the intimate charm and serenity of the smaller establishments. Large chain hotels exist in very small numbers in the region; the vast majority of lodging properties are locally owned. You'll want to make reservations for inns well in advance during peak summer periods. Smoking is prohibited in all Massachusetts hotels. For more information on the state-park camping areas on Cape Cod contact the Massachusetts Department of Conservation and Recreation (☎ 617/626–1250 ⊕ www.mass.gov/dcr/forparks.htm).

WHAT IT COSTS

	¢	$	$$	$$$	$$$$
Restaurants	under $8	$8–$14	$15–$24	$25–$32	over $32
Hotels	under $75	$75–$150	$151–$225	$226–$325	over $325

For restaurants, prices are per person, for a main course at dinner. For hotels, prices are for two people in a standard double room in high season, excluding 12.45% tax and service charges.

Outdoor Activities

Beaches: The beaches on Nantucket Sound and those fronting Cape Cod Bay have both gentler and warmer waters for swimming. Ocean beaches on the Cape's eastern flank are colder and have serious surf. Beaches not restricted to residents charge parking fees; lots can fill up by 10 AM in summer.

Boating: Sea kayaking is popular within the region's calmer harbors and bays; many outfitters offer rental gear as well as instruction and guided tours. All manner of boats are available for rental; otherwise there are plenty of touring captains eager to take you out on the water.

Fishing: Charter boats and party boats fish in season for striped bass, bluefish, and tuna. Year-round there's bottom fishing for flounder, fluke, cod, and pollack. Surf casters line up along the ocean beaches for blues and stripers, while others try their luck in the ponds.

Whale-Watching: One of the true thrills of the Cape is spotting massive and gentle whales swimming and playing in and around the feeding grounds at Stellwagen Bank. Several operators head out to sea daily from mid-April to late October.

Bird-Watching: The Cape and Islands have nesting and resting grounds for hundreds of avian species. The region is also part of the North Atlantic Flyway for waterfowl and shorebirds—peak migration times are May and late July.

CAPE COD NATIONAL SEASHORE

John F. Kennedy certainly knew a good thing when he saw it. During his presidency, Kennedy marked off a magnificent 40-mi swath of the Massachusetts coast, protecting it for future generations. Today the Cape Cod National Seashore remains the Cape's signature site.

Encompassing over 44,000 acres of coastline from Chatham to Provincetown, the park is truly a national treasure. Without protection, such expansive beauty would surely have been lost to rampant overdevelopment long ago. Within its borders are extraordinary ocean beaches, dramatic dunes, ancient swamps, salt marshes, and wetlands; pitch-pine and scrub-oak forest; much wildlife; and a number of historic structures open for touring.

There's no question that the National Seashore's beaches are the main attractions for sunbathers, swimmers, and surfers. It's not at all uncommon for the parking lots to fill up by 11 AM on hot sunny days. Arrive early to find your spot on the sand, or venture out on some of the less traveled trails to find solitude in the high season.

BEST TIME TO GO

Swimming is best in summer; the park becomes sublime in the fall with golden salt-marsh grasses and ruby-red cranberry bogs. Winter and early spring nearly guarantee you'll have the place to yourself.

CONTACT INFORMATION

✉ Doane Rd. off U.S. 6 ☎ 508/255–3421 ⊕ www.nps.gov/caco 🎫 Free ⊗ Daily 9–4:30, hrs extended slightly in summer.

BEST WAYS TO EXPLORE

TAKE A WALK

Walking the marked trails, beaches, and wooded fire roads is an excellent way to truly experience the diverse natural splendor within the park. There are 11 self-guided trails that begin at various points, leading through shaded swamps, alongside marshes, and through meadows, forest, and dunes. Most of the terrain is flat and sometimes sandy.

RIDE A BIKE

Three well-maintained bicycle trails run through parts of the park. In Eastham, the short Nauset Trail heads from the Salt Pond Visitor Center through the woods and out to Coast Guard Beach. Truro's Head off the Meadow Trail edges a large salt meadow, an ideal place for birding. The most physically demanding—and most dramatic—of the park's bike trails is the Province Lands Trail, more than 7 mi of steep hills and hairpin curves through forest and sand dunes. Mountain bikers can make their own trails on the miles of fire roads.

SEE THE SIGHTS

Several historic homes and sites are open for touring; there are also a few notable overlooks easily accessible by car. Climb the steep steps of lighthouses in Eastham and Truro or see rescue reenactments at the Old Harbor Life-Saving Station in Provincetown. Scenic overlooks include Eastham's exquisite Fort Hill area; Wellfleet's Marconi Station Site, where the first transatlantic wireless message was sent in 1903; Truro's Pilgrim Heights; and Provincetown's scenic 2-mi Race Point Road.

TOUR WITH A RANGER

From mid-April through Thanksgiving there is a full schedule of mostly free ranger-guided activities. Combining history, folklore, science, and nature, rangers take visitors right to the source, whether for a full-moon hike in the dunes, a campfire on the beach, a paddling trip, or a photography workshop.

SHIFTING SANDS

Forged by massive moving glaciers more than 20,000 years ago, Cape Cod's landscape is still in perpetual motion, continually shaped by the powerful forces of sand, wind, and water. The Cape's land is slowly giving way to rising ocean levels and erosion, losing an average of nearly 4 feet of outer beach per year. Many a home or structure has succumbed to the unrelenting ocean over the years; some—like Truro's Highland Light and Eastham's Nauset Light—have been moved to safety. Eventually Cape Cod will likely be lost to the sea, though not for thousands of years.

You'll see many signs on beaches and trails asking walkers to keep off the dunes. Take heed, for much of the fragile landscape of the outer Cape is held together by its dune formations and the vegetation that grows within them.

Updated by Laura V. Scheel

Even if you haven't visited Cape Cod and islands, you can likely—and accurately—imagine "sand dunes and salty air, quaint little villages here and there." As the 1950s Patti Page song promises, "you're sure to fall in love with old Cape Cod."

Cape Codders are fiercely protective of the environment. Despite some occasionally rampant development, planners have been careful to preserve nature and encourage responsible, eco-conscious building. Nearly 30% of the Cape's 412 square mi is protected from development, and another 35% has not yet been developed (on Nantucket and Martha's Vineyard, the percentages of protected land are far higher). Opportunities for sports and recreation abound, as the region is rife with biking and hiking trails, serene beaches, and waterways for boating and fishing. One somewhat controversial potential development has been a large-scale "wind farm" in Nantucket Sound, comprising some 130 turbines, each about 260 feet tall and several miles offshore.

The area is also rich in history. Many don't realize that the Pilgrims landed here first: in November 1620, the lost and travel-weary sailors dropped anchor in what is now Provincetown Harbor and spent five weeks here, scouring the area for food and possible settlement. Were it not for the aid of the resident Native Americans, the strangers would have barely survived. Even so, they set sail again for fairer lands, ending up across Cape Cod Bay in Plymouth.

Virtually every period style of residential American architecture is well represented on Cape Cod, including—of course—that seminal form named for the region, the Cape-style house. These low, one-and-a-half-story domiciles with clapboard or shingle (more traditionally the latter in these parts) siding and gable roofs have been a fixture throughout Cape Cod since the late 17th century. You'll also find grand Georgian and Federal mansions from the Colonial era, as well as handsome Greek Revival, Italianate, and Second Empire houses that date to Victorian times. Many of the most prominent residences were built for ship captains and sea merchants. In recent decades, the region has seen an influx of angular, glassy, contemporary homes, many with soaring windows and skylights and massive wraparound porches that take advantage of their enviable sea views.

CAPE COD

Continually shaped by ocean currents, this windswept land of sandy beaches and dunes has compelling natural beauty. Everyone comes for the seaside, yet the crimson cranberry bogs, forests of birch and beech, freshwater ponds, and marshlands that grace the interior are just as splendid. Local history is fascinating; whale-watching provides an exhilarating experience of the natural world; cycling trails lace the landscape; shops purvey everything from antiques to pure kitsch; and you can dine on simple fresh seafood, creative contemporary cuisine, or most anything in between.

Separated from the Massachusetts mainland by the 17.5-mi Cape Cod canal—at 480 feet, the world's widest sea-level canal—and linked to it by two heavily trafficked bridges, the Cape is likened in shape to an outstretched arm bent at the elbow, its Provincetown fist turned back toward the mainland.

Each of the Cape's 15 towns is broken up into villages, which is where things can get complicated. The town of Barnstable, for example, consists of Barnstable, West Barnstable, Cotuit, Marston Mills, Osterville, Centerville, and Hyannis. The terms Upper Cape and Lower Cape can also be confusing. Upper Cape—think upper arm, as in the shape of the Cape—refers to the towns of Bourne, Falmouth, Mashpee, and Sandwich. Mid Cape includes Barnstable, Yarmouth, and Dennis. Brewster, Harwich, Chatham, Orleans, Eastham, Wellfleet, Truro, and Provincetown make up the Lower Cape.

ESSENTIALS

Visitor Information Cape Cod Chamber of Commerce (⊠ *Rtes. 6 and 132, Hyannis* ☎ *508/362–3225 or 888/332–2732* ⊕ *www.capecodchamber.org*).

SANDWICH

★ *3 mi east of Sagamore Bridge, 11 mi west of Barnstable.*

The oldest town on Cape Cod, Sandwich was established in 1637 by some of the Plymouth Pilgrims and incorporated on March 6, 1638. Today, it is a well-preserved, quintessential New England village with a white-columned town hall and streets lined with 18th- and 19th-century houses.

ESSENTIALS

Visitor Information Sandwich Chamber of Commerce (⊠ *4 Water St., Box 744* ☎ *508/833–9755* ⊕ *www.sandwichchamber.com*).

EXPLORING

Sandwich Glass Museum. From 1825 to 1888, the main industry in Sandwich was the production of vividly colored glass, made in the Boston and Sandwich Glass Company's factory. This museum contains relics of the town's early history and displays of shimmering blown and

pressed glass. The extensive, ornate gift shop sells handsome reproductions, including some made by local and national artisans. The museum also sponsors walking tours of the town offered July through October. ⊠ *129 Main St.* ☎ *508/888–0251* ⊕ *www.sandwichglassmuseum.org* ☞ *$5* ⊗ *Apr.–Dec., daily 9:30–5; Feb. and Mar., Wed.–Sun. 9:30–4. Closed Jan.*

Heritage Museums and Gardens. On 100 beautifully landscaped acres overlooking the upper end of Shawme Pond, this complex includes gardens and a café as well as an impressive array of museum buildings with specialty collections ranging from cars to toys. A highlight is the Shaker Round Barn, which showcases classic and historic cars as well as art exhibitions. The art museum has an extensive Currier & Ives collection, antique toys, and a working 1912 Coney Island–style carousel that both adults and little ones can ride as often as they like. Paths crisscross the grounds, which include gardens planted with daylilies, hostas, heather, herbs, and fruit trees. From mid-June to early September, the gardens play host to organized croquet games and instruction. ⊠ *67 Grove St.* ☎ *508/888–3300* ⊕ *www.heritagemuseumsandgardens.org* ☞ *$12* ⊗ *Apr.–Oct., daily 10–5; Nov.–Mar., call for very limited hrs.*

Fodor's Choice ★

SHOPPING

Fodor's Choice ★

Titcomb's Bookshop (⊠ *432 Rte. 6A, East Sandwich* ☎ *508/888–2331* ⊕ *www.titcombsbookshop.com*) stocks used, rare, and new books, including a large collection of Cape and nautical titles and Americana, as well as an extensive selection of children's books.

NIGHTLIFE

British Beer Company (⊠ *46 Rte. 6A* ☎ *508/833–9590* ⊕ *www.britishbeer.com*) is styled after a traditional English "public house" with an eclectic menu that includes fish, ribs, and pasty pies. In summer, a variety of bands play Thursday through Saturday nights.

WHERE TO EAT AND STAY

$-$$
ECLECTIC
★

✕ **Aqua Grille.** At this smart-casual and reasonably priced bistro by the marina, you can choose from Cape basics (clam chowder, fried seafood, boiled lobsters) and creative contemporary fare, such as nut-crusted halibut with an orange beurre blanc. The excellent lobster salad comprises a hearty serving of greens, tomatoes, avocado, baby green beans, and big, meaty chunks of lobster. ⊠ *14 Gallo Rd.* ☎ *508/888–8889* ⊕ *www.aquagrille.com* ☰ *AE, DC, MC, V* ⊗ *Closed Mon.–Wed. Nov.–mid-Apr.*

$$-$$$
Fodor's Choice
★

▥ **Belfry Inn & Bistro.** This delightful one-of-a-kind inn comprises a former church built in 1902, an ornate wood-frame Victorian, and an 1830 Federal-style house clustered on a main campus. Room themes in each building nod to their respective histories—the Painted Lady's charmingly appointed rooms, for example, are named after former inhabitants. The luxurious rooms in the Abbey, named for the six days of creation, have whirlpool tubs and gas fireplaces and are set along a corridor overlooking the restaurant below. The Bistro ($$–$$$) serves dazzling, globally inspired dishes, such as black grouper roasted with tamarind-yogurt sauce, and next door, in the Victorian building, you can dine on home-style American favorites at the Painted Lady Cafe

CLOSE UP

Brigham's Ice Cream

Ice cream is a timeworn tradition in New England. All summer long, people make pilgrimages to local ice cream shops for cups and cones filled with their favorite flavors. Yet, up here in the northeast, ice cream is very much a year-round treat. In fact, **Brigham's**, one of New England's best-loved premium ice cream makers, has been pleasing the palates of Boston area ice cream devotees for over 95 years, and Brigham's sells most of its ice cream during November and December—typically the slowest months for ice cream sales nationwide. But everyone who hails from the Boston area knows why—that's pie season. And, simply put, Brigham's Vanilla is what you plop on top of any fresh-out-of-the-oven apple pie.

Edward L. Brigham began producing his ice cream in 1914. Ten years later, in 1924, he was serving up his homemade ice cream and candies at a place in Newton Highlands that he called "The Little Shop." Within five years, the huge success of his "little" shop enabled him to start opening up Brigham's restaurants and ice cream shops (⊕ *www.brighamsrestaurants. com*) all over Massachusetts.

While Brigham's makes more than 20 regular and specialty flavors, its Vanilla is the one with the cult following. Massachusetts purists wouldn't even think of substituting Brigham's Vanilla on their pies, in their hot fudge sundaes, or alongside their slices of birthday cake. The full 15 percent butterfat ice cream made with Madagascar vanilla and Vermont cream consistently ranks as the top-selling ice cream in the Boston area—it's also the number-one frozen food served in all of New England, according to Brigham's. As for the award-winning recipe, it remains top secret and safely locked in a vault. Lucky for us, the ice cream is widely available at Brigham's restaurants, and by the quart at supermarkets around New England.

—Jen Laskey

($–$$). **Pros:** great in-town location; some rooms have whirlpool tubs and fireplaces; massages available. **Cons:** some rooms don't have TVs; some rooms accessed only by steep stairs. ⊠ *8 Jarves St.* ☎ *Box 2211, Sandwich, MA 02563* ☎ *508/888–8550 or 800/844–4542* ☎ *508/888– 3922* ⊕ *www.belfryinn.com* ⇆ *22 rooms* ♿ *In-room: no TV (some), Wi-Fi. In-hotel: 2 restaurants, bar* ⊟ *AE, D, DC, MC, V* ⎮⊙⎮ *BP.*

FALMOUTH

15 mi south of Bourne Bridge, 20 mi South of Sandwich.

Falmouth, the Cape's second-largest town, was settled in 1660. Much of Falmouth today is suburban, with a mix of old and new developments and a large year-round population. Many residents commute to other towns on the Cape, to southeastern Massachusetts, and even to Boston. The town has a quaint village center, with a typically old New England village green and a shop-lined Main Street. South of town center, Falmouth faces Nantucket Sound and has several often-crowded beaches popular with families. To the east, the Falmouth Heights neighborhood mixes inns, B&Bs, and private homes, nestled close together on

residential streets leading to the sea. Bustling Grand Avenue, the main drag in Falmouth Heights, hugs the shore and the beach.

The village of Woods Hole, part of Falmouth, is home to several major scientific institutions, and is a departure point for ferries to Martha's Vineyard.

GETTING HERE AND AROUND

Heading from the Bourne Bridge toward Falmouth, County Road and Route 28A are prettier alternatives to Route 28, and Sippewisset Road meanders near Buzzards Bay between West Falmouth and Woods Hole.

If you're coming from Falmouth to Woods Hole, either ride your bicycle down the straight and flat Shining Sea Trail or take the Cape Cod Regional Transit Authority's WHOOSH trolley. In summer, the basically one-street village overflows with thousands of visiting scientists, students, and tourists heading to the islands. Parking, limited to a relatively small number of metered spots on the street, can be nearly impossible.

ESSENTIALS

Transportation Contacts **Cape Cod Regional Transit Authority** (☎ 800/352–7155 ⊕ www.capecodtransit.org).

Visitor Information **Falmouth Chamber of Commerce** (✉ 20 Academy La., Falmouth ☎ 508/548–8500 or 800/526–8532 ⊕ www.falmouthchamber.com).

EXPLORING

Marine Biological Laboratory–Woods Hole Oceanographic Institution Library. Scientific forces join at this library, one of the best collections of biological, ecological, and oceanographic literature in the world. The library has access to more than 200 computer databases and subscribes to more than 5,000 scientific journals in 40 languages, with complete collections of most. The Rare Books Collection and Special Collections contain photographs, monographs, and prints, as well as journal collections that date from 1665. ✉ 7 *Marine Biological Laboratory St., off Water St., Woods Hole* ☎ 508/289–7002 ⊕ *www.mbl.edu* ⬚ *Free* ☽ *Weekdays 8–5.*

Nobska Light. From its base, this impressive lighthouse has spectacular views of the nearby Elizabeth Islands and of Martha's Vineyard, across Vineyard Sound. (✉ *Church St., Woods Hole* ⊕ *www.lighthouse. cc/nobska* ⬚ *Free* ☽ *See Web site for tour times*).

☾ **Waquoit Bay National Estuarine Research Reserve**. Encompassing 2,500 acres of estuary and barrier beach around the bay, this reserve is a good birding site. **South Cape Beach** is part of the reserve; you can lie out on the sand or join one of the interpretive walks. **Flat Pond Trail** runs through several different habitats, including fresh- and saltwater marshes. ✉ *149 Rte. 28, 3 mi west of Mashpee rotary, Waquoit* ☎ *508/457–0495* ⊕ *www.waquoitbayreserve.org* ⬚ *Free* ☽ *Exhibit center late June–early Sept., Mon.–Sat. 10–4; late May–late June, weekdays 10–4.*

☾ **Woods Hole Science Aquarium**. Twenty tanks of regional fish and shellfish are on display in several rooms of this compact aquarium that is cramped but crammed with stuff to see. Magnifying glasses, a dissecting scope, and mini-squeegees hanging from the frosty tanks (a favorite

Fodor's Choice
★

tool for kids) help you examine marine life. Several hands-on pools hold banded lobsters, crabs, snails, starfish, and other creatures. The top attraction is two harbor seals, on view in the outdoor pool near the entrance in summer; you can watch their feedings weekdays at 11 and 4. ⊠ *166 Water St., at Albatross St., Woods Hole* ☎ *508/495–2267; 508/495–2001 recorded information* ⊕ *aquarium.nefsc.noaa.gov* ◎ *Free* ◷ *June–Aug., Tues.–Sat. 11–4; Sept.–May, Mon.–Fri. 11–4.*

SPORTS AND THE OUTDOORS

★ **Old Silver Beach** (⊠ *Off Quaker Rd., North Falmouth*) is a long, beautiful crescent of soft white sand bordered by the Sea Crest Resort at one end. It's especially good for small children because a sandbar keeps it shallow at the southern end and creates tidal pools full of crabs and minnows. The beach has lifeguards, restrooms, showers, and a snack bar. There's a $20 fee for parking in summer.

BIKING The **Shining Sea Trail** is an easy 3½-mi route between Locust Street, Falmouth, and the Woods Hole ferry parking lot. It follows the coast, providing views of Vineyard Sound and dipping into oak and pine woods; a detour onto Church Street takes you to Nobska Light.

FISHING Freshwater ponds are good for perch, pickerel, trout, and more; you can obtain the required license and rental gear at tackle shops, such as **Eastman's Sport & Tackle** (⊠ *783 Main St. [Rte. 28], Falmouth* ☎ *508/548–6900* ⊕ *www.eastmanstackle.com*).

SHOPPING

★ **Bean & Cod** (⊠ *140 Main St. (Rte. 28), Falmouth Center* ☎ *508/548–8840 or 800/558–8840*), a specialty food shop, sells cheeses, breads, and picnic fixings, along with pastas, coffees, teas, and unusual condiments. The store also packs and ships gift baskets.

NIGHTLIFE AND THE ARTS

Nimrod Inn (⊠ *100 Dillingham Ave., Falmouth Center* ☎ *508/540–4132* ⊕ *www.thenimrod.com*) presents jazz and contemporary music at least six nights a week year-round. It's also a great spot for late-night dining.

WHERE TO EAT AND STAY

$$–$$$ ✕ **La Cucina Sul Mare.** Northern Italian and Mediterranean cooking is the
ITALIAN specialty at this classy, popular place. The staff is friendly and the setting
Fodor's Choice is both intimate and festive, if a bit crowded. Calamari, warm green
★ salad with goat cheese and cranberries, a classic lemon chicken sautéed with shallots and capers, and a variety of specials—including plenty of local fresh fish—adorn the menu. The *zuppa de pesce,* a medley of seafood sautéed in olive oil and garlic and finished in a white wine herb-and-tomato broth, is a specialty. ⊠ *237 Main St. (Rte. 28), Falmouth Center* ☎ *508/548–5600* ⊕ *www.lacucinadelmare.com* ⊘ *Reservations not accepted* ⊟ *AE, D, MC, V.*

$$–$$$ ☷ **Mostly Hall B&B.** With its deep, landscaped yard and wrought-iron
★ fence, this elegant inn with a wraparound porch resembles a private estate. The imposing 1849 Italianate house has an upscale European style with painted wall murals in several bedrooms; the Tuscany Room's walls suggest an intimate Mediterranean garden. Three of the rooms are more traditionally decorated, with Colonial antiques; all have canopy beds. **Pros:** walk to town center; ample, parklike grounds; grand home

Continued on page 172

A WHALE OF A TALE

by Steve Larese

WHALING IN NEW ENGLAND TIMELINE

mid-1600s	America enters whaling industry
1690	Nantucket enters whaling industry
1820	*Essex* ship sunk by sperm whale
1840s	American whaling peaked
1851	*Moby-Dick* published
1927	The last U.S. whaler sails from New Bedford
1970s	Cape Cod whale-watching trips begin
1986	Ban on whaling by the International Whaling Commission
1992	Stellwagen Bank National Marine Sanctuary established

Cameras have replaced harpoons in the waters north of Cape Cod. While you can learn about New England's whaling history and perhaps see whales in the distance from shore, a whale-watching excursion is the best way to connect with these magnificent creatures—who may be just as curious about you as you are about them.

Once relentlessly hunted around the world by New Englanders, whales today are celebrated as intelligent, friendly, and curious creatures. Whales are still important to the region's economy and culture, but now in the form of ecotourism. Easily accessible from several ports in Massachusetts, the 842-square-mi Stellwagen Bank National Marine Sanctuary attracts finback, humpback, minke, and right whales who feed and frolic here twice a year during their migration. The same conditions that made the Stellwagen Bank area of the mouth of Massachusetts Bay a good hunting ground make it a good viewing area. Temperature, currents, and nutrients combine to produce plankton, krill, and fish to feed marine mammals.

(opposite) Whaling museum custodian and a sperm whale jaw in the 1930s. (top) Hunted to near extinction, humpbacks today number about 80,000, and are found in oceans worldwide.

ON LAND: MARINE AND MARITIME MUSEUMS

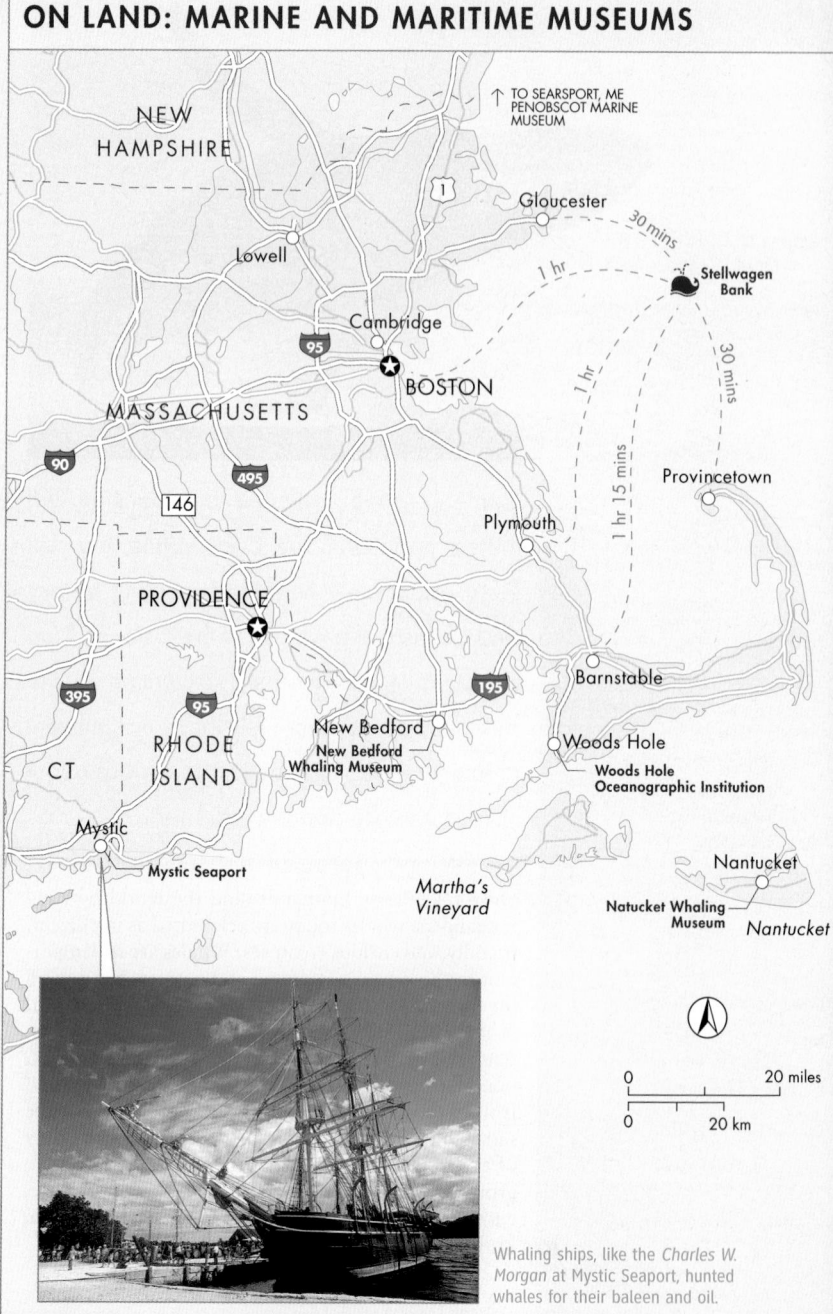

NEW HAMPSHIRE

↑ TO SEARSPORT, ME
PENOBSCOT MARINE
MUSEUM

1

Gloucester

30 mins

Lowell

1 hr

Stellwagen
Bank

Cambridge

MASSACHUSETTS

BOSTON

1 hr

30 mins

90

495

Provincetown

146

1 hr 15 mins

Plymouth

PROVIDENCE

395

95

195

Barnstable

CT

RHODE
ISLAND

New Bedford

Woods Hole

New Bedford
Whaling Museum

Woods Hole
Oceanographic Institution

Mystic

Nantucket

Mystic Seaport

Natucket Whaling
Museum

Martha's
Vineyard

Nantucket

0   20 miles

0   20 km

Whaling ships, like the *Charles W.
Morgan* at Mystic Seaport, hunted
whales for their baleen and oil.

3

Even landlubbers can learn about whales and whaling at these top New England institutions.

Nantucket Whaling Museum. This former whale-processing center and candle factory was converted into a museum in 1929. See art made by sailors, including masterful scrimshaw—intricate nautical scenes carved into whale bone or teeth and filled in with ink (⊠ *Nantucket, Massachusetts* ⊕ *www.nha.org*).

★ **New Bedford Whaling Museum.** More than 200,000 artifacts are collected here, from ships' logbooks to harpoons. A must-see is the 89-foot, half-scale model of the 1826 whaling ship *Lagoda* (⊠ *New Bedford, Massachusetts* ⊕ *www.whalingmuseum.org*).

Woods Hole Oceanographic Institution. The Ocean Science Exhibit Center at this famous Cape Cod research facility highlights deep-sea exploration. An interactive exhibit examines the importance of sound to cetaceans, or marine mammals (⊠ *Woods Hole, Massachusetts* ⊕ *www.whoi. edu*).

Nantucket Whaling Museum

★ **Mystic Seaport.** Actors portray life in a 19th-century seafaring village at this 37-acre living-history museum. Don't miss the 1841 *Charles W. Morgan*, the world's only surviving wooden whaling ship (⊠ *Mystic, Connecticut* ⊕ *www. mysticseaport.org*).

Penobscot Marine Museum. Maine's seafaring history and mostly shore-whaling industry is detailed inside seven historic buildings (⊠ *Searsport, Maine* ⊕ *www.penobscotbayhistory.org*).

New Bedford Whaling Museum

THE GREAT WHITE WHALE

Herman Melville based his 1851 classic *Moby-Dick: or, The Whale* on the true story of the *Essex*, which was sunk in 1821 by huge whale; an albino sperm whale called Mocha Dick; and his time aboard the whaling ship *Acushnet*.

Mystic Seaport

★ = **Fodor's** Choice

AT SEA: WHALE-WATCHING TOURS

COMMON NORTH ATLANTIC SPECIES

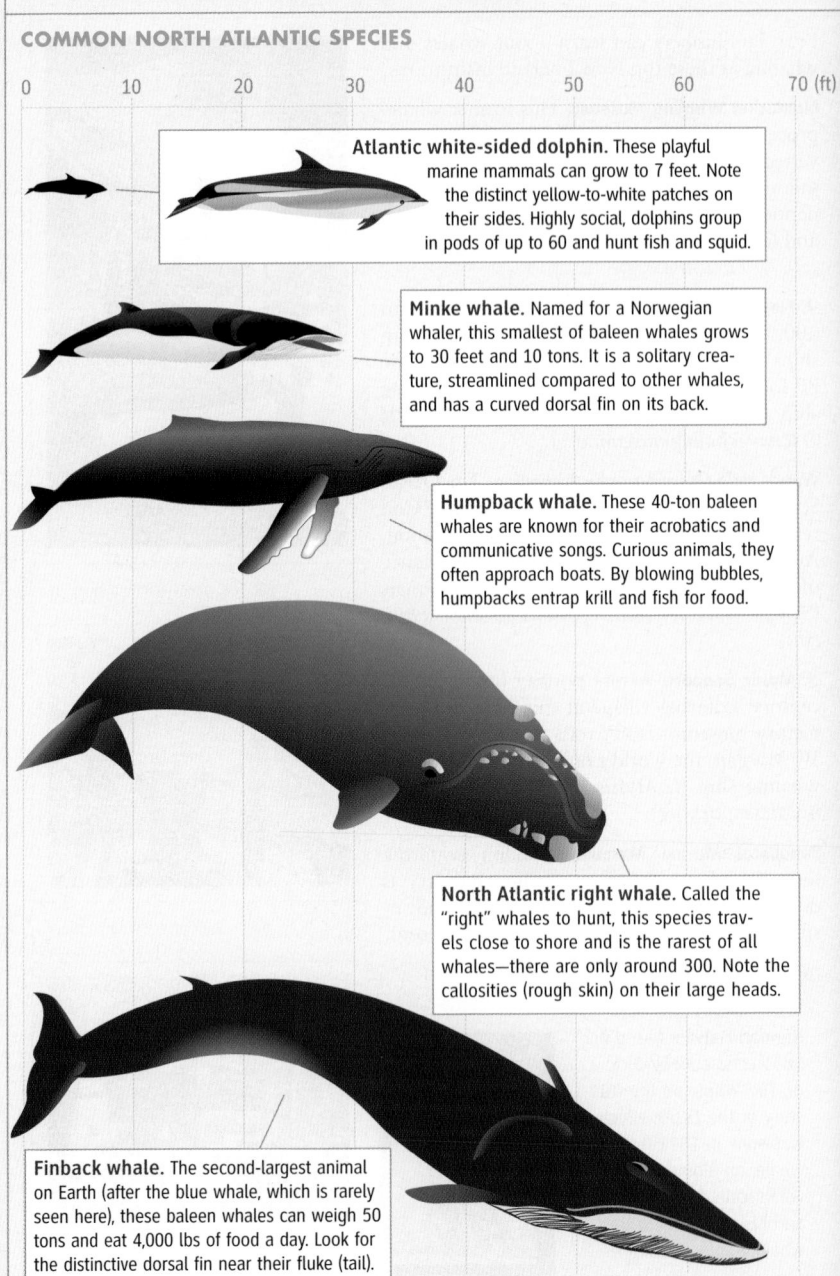

0   10   20   30   40   50   60   70 (ft)

Atlantic white-sided dolphin. These playful marine mammals can grow to 7 feet. Note the distinct yellow-to-white patches on their sides. Highly social, dolphins group in pods of up to 60 and hunt fish and squid.

Minke whale. Named for a Norwegian whaler, this smallest of baleen whales grows to 30 feet and 10 tons. It is a solitary creature, streamlined compared to other whales, and has a curved dorsal fin on its back.

Humpback whale. These 40-ton baleen whales are known for their acrobatics and communicative songs. Curious animals, they often approach boats. By blowing bubbles, humpbacks entrap krill and fish for food.

North Atlantic right whale. Called the "right" whales to hunt, this species travels close to shore and is the rarest of all whales—there are only around 300. Note the callosities (rough skin) on their large heads.

Finback whale. The second-largest animal on Earth (after the blue whale, which is rarely seen here), these baleen whales can weigh 50 tons and eat 4,000 lbs of food a day. Look for the distinctive dorsal fin near their fluke (tail).

3

SEAWORTHY TRIP TIPS

When to Go: Tours operate April through October; May through September are the most active months in the Stellwagen Bank area.

Ports of Departure: Boats leave from Barnstable and Provincetown on Cape Cod, and Plymouth, Boston, and Gloucester, cutting across the Cape Cod bay to the Stellwagen area. Book tours at least a day ahead. Hyannis Whale Watcher in Barnstable, the Dolphin Fleet, Alpha Whale Watch and Captain John's Whale Watch in Provincetown, and the New England Aquarium, Beantown Whale Watch and Boston Harbor Cruises in Boston are just a few of your options. *For more specifics, see the Cape Cod and Boston sections.*

Cost: Around $40. Check company Web sites for coupons.

What to Expect: All companies abide by guidelines so as not to harass whales. Tours last 3 to 4 hours and almost always encounter whales; if not, vouchers are often given for another tour. Passengers are encouraged to watch the horizon for water spouts, which indicate a surfaced whale clearing its blowhole to breathe air. Upon spotting an animal, the boat slows and approaches the whale to a safe distance; often, whales will approach an idling boat and even swim underneath it.

What to Bring: Plastic bags protect binoculars and cameras from damp spray. Most boats have a concession stand, but pack bottled water and snacks. ■TIP→ Kids (and adults) will appreciate games or other items to pass the time in between whale sightings.

What to Wear: Wear rubber-soled footwear for slick decks. A waterproof outer layer and layers of clothing will help in

Hyannis Whale Watcher Cruises, Cape Cod Bay

varied conditions, as will sunscreen, sunglasses, and a hat that can be secured. Most boats have cabins where you can warm up and get out of the wind.

Comforting Advice: Small seat cushions like those used at sporting events may be appreciated. Consider taking motion-sickness medication before setting out. Ginger candy and acupressure wristbands can also help. If you feel queasy, get some fresh air and focus your eyes on a stable feature on the shore or horizon.

Photo Hints: Use a fast shutter speed, or sport mode, to avoid blurry photographs. Most whales will be a distance from the boat; have a telephoto lens ready. To avoid shutter delay on your point-and-shoot camera, lock the focus at infinity so you don't miss that breaching whale shot.

DID YOU KNOW?

Most boats have a naturalist aboard to discuss the whales and their environment. Many companies contribute to population studies by reporting the individual whales they spot. Whale tails, called flukes, are distinct and used like fingerprints for identification.

in the Victorian tradition. **Cons:** rooms accessed via steep stairs; bathrooms are a bit small; the bathroom for one room (discounted) is down a set of stairs. ⊠ *27 Main St. (Rte. 28), Falmouth Center* ☎ *508/548–3786* 🖷 *508/548–5778* ⊕ *www.mostlyhall.com* ⤴ *6 rooms, 5 with bath* ⚬ *In-room: DVD, Wi-Fi. In-hotel: no kids under 18* ☰ *AE, D, MC, V* ⎟◎⎟ *BP.*

HYANNIS

23 mi east of the Bourne Bridge, 21 mi northeast of Falmouth.

Perhaps best known for its association with the Kennedy clan, the Hyannis area was also a vacation site for President Ulysses S. Grant in 1874 and later for President Grover Cleveland. A bustling year-round hub of activity, Hyannis has the Cape's largest concentration of businesses, shops, malls, hotels and motels, restaurants, and entertainment venues.

GETTING HERE AND AROUND

There's plenty of public parking around town, on both sides of Main Street as well as in several public parking lots. The island ferry companies have designated parking lots (daily fee is $15 in summer season) with free shuttles to the docks. Hyannis is the Cape's transit hub and is served by a number of bus routes.

ESSENTIALS

Transportation Contacts **Barnstable Municipal Airport** (HYA) (☎ *508/775–2020* ⊕ *www.town.barnstable.ma.us).* **Hyannis Transportation Center** (⊠ *215 Iyanough Rd., Hyannis* ☎ *508/775–8504* ⊕ *www.capecodtransit.org).*

Visitor Information **Hyannis Chamber of Commerce** (⊠ *397 Main St.* ☎ *508/775–2201 or 877/492–6647* ⊕ *www.hyannis.com).*

EXPLORING

John F. Kennedy Hyannis Museum. In Main Street's Old Town Hall, this museum explores JFK's Cape years (1934–63). Downstairs, visit the **Cape Cod Baseball League Hall of Fame and Museum** (⊕ *www.capecodbaseball.org/*), dedicated to the area's thriving and beloved summer league. The baseball museum shares hours with the JFK museum; a joint ticket ($8) allows admission to both museums. ⊠ *397 Main St.* ☎ *508/790–3077* ⊕ *www.jfkhyannismuseum.org* ⊠ *$5* ◷ *Memorial Day–Oct., Mon.–Sat. 9–5, Sun. noon–5; Nov.–early Dec. and mid-Feb.–mid-Apr., Thurs.–Sat. 10–4, Sun. noon–4. Closed Jan.*

OFF THE BEATEN PATH

Cape Cod Potato Chips Factory. There's a standing invitation on the back of the bag: come for a free tour of the factory and get free samples of the crunchy all-natural chips hand-cooked in kettles in small batches. ⊠ *Independence Dr. to 100 Breed's Hill Rd., off Rte. 132* ☎ *508/775–3358* ⊕ *www.capecodchips.com* ◷ *Weekdays 9–5.*

SPORTS AND THE OUTDOORS

BEACH **Kalmus Park Beach,** at the south end of Ocean Street, is a wide, sandy beach with an area set aside for windsurfers and a sheltered area that's good for kids. It has a snack bar, restrooms, showers, and lifeguards.

NIGHTLIFE AND THE ARTS

In 1950 actress Gertrude Lawrence and her husband, producer-manager Richard Aldrich, opened the **Cape Cod Melody Tent** (⊠ *21 W. Main St., at West End rotary, Hyannis* ☎ *508/775–5630; 800/347–0808 for tickets* ⊕ *www.melodytent.com*) to showcase Broadway musicals. Today it's the Cape's top venue for pop concerts and comedy shows.

★ **Harry's Blues Bar** (⊠ *700 Main St., Hyannis* ☎ *508/778–4188* ⊕ *www. harrysbluesbar.com*) is hopping nearly every night year-round, drawing blues lovers of all ages.

3

WHERE TO EAT

¢–$$
BRAZILIAN
Fodor'sChoice
★

✕ **Brazilian Grill.** The Cape has a large Brazilian population, and you can find many of these residents, plus plenty of satisfied visitors, at this loud and jovial all-you-can-eat *churrascaria* (Brazilian barbecue). Waiters circulate through the dining room offering more than a dozen grilled meats—beef, pork, chicken, sausage, even quail—on long swordlike skewers. You can help yourself to a buffet of salads and side dishes, including *farofa* (a couscouslike dish), plantains, rice, and beans. For dessert, try the homemade flan. Dine on the redbrick patio in warm weather. ⊠ *680 Main St., West End* ☎ *508/771–0109* ⊕ *www. braziliangrill-capecod.net* ▭ *AE, D, DC, MC, V.*

$$–$$$
SEAFOOD
Fodor'sChoice
★

✕ **Naked Oyster.** The big draw at this dapper restaurant with dark-wood-paneled walls and soft lighting is the extensive list of weekly specials, which truly show off the kitchen's talents. You'll always find several raw and "dressed" oyster dishes (such as barbecue oysters on the half shell with blue cheese, caramelized onions, and bacon) plus a nice range of salads and appetizers. Among the main dishes, consider the superb haddock and lobster in a champagne beurre blanc, or the out-of-this-world oyster stew. ⊠ *20 Independence Dr., off Rte. 132* ☎ *508/778–6500* ⊕ *www.nakedoyster.com* ▭ *AE, D, DC, MC, V* ◷ *No lunch weekends.*

WHERE TO STAY

$$$

▦ **Anchor-In.** Most rooms at this lovely, small-scale hotel on the north end of Hyannis Harbor have harbor views and private balconies overlooking the water. Its simple street-side appearance belies its spacious accommodations and extensive grounds. Rooms are up-to-date with down comforters, terry robes, triple sheets, king-size beds, and flat-screen televisions. Some rooms have refrigerators, and the larger deluxe and executive rooms have wraparound porches. Lisa and Skip Simpson deliver the warm, personal service of a small B&B. The expanded Continental breakfast is a real treat, served in the Lewis Bay Library with its extraordinary views. **Pros:** easy walk to downtown activity, island ferry terminals, and several waterfront restaurants; great harbor views from many rooms. **Cons:** second-floor rooms accessed via stairways; in busy part of town. ⊠ *1 South St., Hyannis Harbor* ☎ *508/775–0357* ⊕ *www.anchorin.com* ⇥ *42 rooms* ⌂ *In-room: refrigerator (some), DVD (some), Wi-Fi. In-hotel: pool* ▭ *AE, D, MC, V* ⌾ *CP.*

$$
★

▦ **Breakwaters.** These privately owned, weathered gray-shingle cottages rent by the week in summer (or nightly in spring and fall). Cottages are divided into one-, two-, and three-bedroom units and offer all the comforts of home. Each unit has one or two full baths; a kitchen with

CLOSE UP

Clam Shacks and Clamming Excursion

Cape Codders have been clamming for generations, and their iconic mollusks are a celebrated part of the culture here.

Commercial shellfishing on the Cape is one of America's oldest industries, and locals aren't the only ones clamoring for shellfishing licenses these days. Some of the Cape's more "clambitious" visitors also want to get in on the hunt for these scrumptious fruits of the sea. But it's not as easy as just hitting the shore with your rake and basket. Shellfishing is regulated by the state, and each town has its own regulations regarding license costs, clam size and quantity, and the areas and days shellfishing is permitted. If you're ready to try recreational clamming, put on your clamdiggers, grab your rake and basket, and head to the local town hall to get your license and any other necessary information. You can also take a class, like the ones offered by **Barnstable's Association for Recreational Shellfishing** (⊕ www.shellfishing.org) and **Eastham's Salt Pond Visitor Center** (⊕ www.easthamchamber.com/activities.cfm), or check in with the local shellfish warden to find out about any organized clamming excursions.

We all know that the best thing about clams is not wading around and looking for them in the wet sand; it's eating them! Classic clam shacks are known for their bountiful baskets of crispy fried clams, which, according to Cape Codders, should always be ordered "whole"—that is, with the bellies. Fried clams are never the only item on the menu. Typical fare also includes clam chowder, lobster rolls, fried fish, scallops, shrimp, coleslaw, fries, potato salad, and other non-seafood items. The quintessential

experience usually involves ordering at one window, picking up at another, and eating at a picnic table—hopefully one with a beach or harbor view! Check out a few of our favorites:

A Cape Cod institution, the **Clam Shack** (⊠ 227 Clinton Ave., Falmouth ☎ 508/540-7758) serves up fried clams and other shack fare with a picturesque harbor view.

Mac's Seafood (⊠ 265 Commercial St., Wellfleet ☎ 508/349-0404 ⊕ www.macsseafood.com) boasts typical clam shack vittles and more—sushi, burritos, vegetarian options, and grilled fish. Get it to go and eat on the beach, or visit their nearby sit-down restaurant: Mac's Shack.

When it comes to fried fare, **Arnold's Lobster and Clam Bar** (⊠ 3580 State Highway [Rte. 6], Eastham ☎ 508/255-2575 ⊕ www.arnoldsrestaurant.com) is known for its heaping portions and reasonable prices. It also serves fresh-shucked oysters, raw bar clams, steamed lobsters, and clam chowder.

At **The Bite** (⊠ 29 Basin Rd, Menemsha, Martha's Vineyard ☎ 508/645-9239 ⊕ www.thebitemenemsha.com) try the fried clams, the local flounder and chips, or the quahog chowder with a side of coleslaw made with the owners' grandmother's secret recipe.

Sayle's Seafood (⊠ 99 Washington St., Nantucket ☎ 508/228-4599 ⊕ www.saylesseafood.com), a fish market that specializes in Nantucket fruits of the sea, doubles as a take-out restaurant with a wide variety of fresh clam, lobster, and seafood dishes made to order.

—Jen Laskey

microwave, coffeemaker, refrigerator, toaster, and stove; TV and phone (local calls are free); and a deck or patio with a grill and picnic table. An in-ground heated pool is less than 200 feet from the lifeguarded town beach on Nantucket Sound. **Pros:** excellent waterfront location; ideal for families and groups traveling together. **Cons:** hard to reserve unless you're staying for a week; not the place for a quiet, private getaway (unless it's spring or fall); payment only by cash or checks. ⊠ *432 Sea St., Box 118* 🕾 *508/775–6831* ⊕ *www.thebreakwaters.com* ⇲ *19 cottages* ⚲ *In-room: no a/c, kitchen. In-hotel: pool, beachfront, Wi-Fi hotspot* ⊟ *No credit cards* ⊘ *Closed mid-Oct.–Apr.*

BARNSTABLE

4 mi north of Hyannis

With nearly 50,000 year-round residents, Barnstable is the largest town on the Cape. It's also the second oldest (founded in 1639). You can get a feeling for its age in Barnstable Village, on and near Main Street (Route 6A), a lovely area of large old homes.

SPORTS AND THE OUTDOORS

BEACHES   Hovering above Barnstable Harbor and the 4,000-acre **Great Salt Marsh, Sandy Neck Beach** stretches some 6 mi across a peninsula that ends at **Sandy Neck Light.** The beach is one of the Cape's most beautiful—dunes, sand, and sea spread endlessly east, west, and north. The lighthouse, standing a few feet from the eroding shoreline at the tip of the neck, has been out of commission since 1952. The main beach at Sandy Neck has lifeguards, a snack bar, restrooms, and showers. There is a $15 daily parking fee from Memorial Day through Labor Day. ⊠ *Sandy Neck Rd., West Barnstable* 🕾 *508/362–8300* ⊘ *Daily 8 AM– 9 PM, but staffed only until 5 PM.*

WHERE TO STAY

$$ 🏠 **Beechwood Inn.** Debbie and Ken Traugot's yellow-and-pale-green 1853 ★   Queen Anne house has gingerbread trim and a wide porch with wicker furniture and a glider swing. Although the parlor is pure mahogany-and-red-velvet Victorian, guest rooms have antiques in lighter Victorian styles; several have fireplaces, and one has a bay view. Bathrooms have pedestal sinks and antique lighting fixtures. Breakfast is served in the dining room, which has a pressed-tin ceiling, a fireplace, and lace-covered tables. **Pros:** exquisite lodging in historic Victorian; spacious rooms; choose from seven different beaches within a 5-mi radius. **Cons:** most rooms accessed via narrow, curved stairs. ⊠ *2839 Main St. (Rte. 6A), Barnstable* 🕾 *508/362–6618 or 800/609–6618* ⊕ *www. beechwoodinn.com* ⇲ *6 rooms* ⚲ *In-room: no phone, refrigerator, Wi-Fi. In-hotel: bicycles, no kids under 12* ⊟ *AE, D, MC, V* ⦿| *BP.*

$$–$$$ 🏠 **Honeysuckle Hill.** Innkeepers Freddy and Ruth Riley provide plenty of
Fodor's Choice   little touches: a guest fridge stocked with beverages (including wine and ★   beer), beach chairs with umbrellas, and an always-full cookie jar. The airy, country-style guest rooms in this 1810 Queen Anne–style cottage have lots of white wicker, featherbeds, checked curtains, and pastel-painted floors. **Pros:** gracious and generous innkeepers; lush gardens on the grounds; tasteful, large rooms; very short drive to Sandy Neck

Beach. **Cons:** not an in-town location; must drive to most area attractions. ⊠ *591 Main St. (Rte. 6A), West Barnstable* ☎ *508/362–8418 or 866/444–5522* ⊕ *www.honeysucklehill.com* ⤴ *4 rooms, 1 suite* ⚭ *In-room: no phone, Wi-Fi. In-hotel: bicycles, no kids under 12* ☐ *AE, MC, V* ⊠*BP.*

YARMOUTH

Yarmouth Port is 3 mi east of Barnstable Village, West Yarmouth is 2 mi east of Hyannis

Once known as Mattacheese, or "the planting lands," Yarmouth was settled in 1639 by farmers from the Plymouth Bay Colony. By then the Cape had begun a thriving maritime industry, and men turned to the sea to make their fortunes. Many impressive sea captains' houses—some now B&Bs and museums—still line enchanting Route 6A and nearby side streets, and Yarmouth Port has some real old-time stores in town. West Yarmouth has a very different atmosphere, stretched on busy commercial Route 28 south of Yarmouth Port.

ESSENTIALS

Visitor Information Yarmouth Chamber of Commerce (⊠ *424 Rte. 28, West Yarmouth* ☎ *508/778–1008 or 800/732–1008* ⊕ *www.yarmouthcapecod. com* ⊠ *Information centerU.S. 6 heading east between exits 6 and 7* ☎ *508/362–9796).*

EXPLORING

☺ ★ **Bass Hole Boardwalk.** One of Yarmouth Port's most beautiful areas is Bass Hole, which stretches from Homer's Dock Road to the salt marsh. The boardwalk extends over a marshy creek; amid salt marshes, vegetated wetlands, and upland woods meander the 2½-mi **Callery-Darling nature trails.** Gray's Beach is a little crescent of sand with calm waters. ⊠ *Trail entrance on Center St. near Gray's Beach parking lot.*

☺ **Edward Gorey House Museum.** Eccentric illustrations and offbeat humor defined the late acclaimed artist (1925–2000) whose former home is now the site of regularly changing exhibitions. The downstairs rooms include drawings of his oddball characters and reveal the mysterious psyche of the sometimes dark but always playful illustrator. ⊠ *8 Strawberry La., Yarmouth Port* ☎ *508/362–3909* ⊕ *www.edwardgoreyhouse. org* ⊠*$5* ⊙ *Mid-Apr.–July and early Oct.–late Dec., Thurs.–Sat. 11–4, Sun. noon–4; July–early Oct., Wed.–Sat. 11–4, Sun. noon–4; call to confirm off-season hours; closed Jan.–mid-Apr.*

QUICK BITES

Jerry's Seafood and Dairy Freeze (⊠ *654 Main St. [Rte. 28], West Yarmouth* ☎ *508/775–9752),* open year-round, serves fried clams and onion rings, along with thick frappes (milk shakes), frozen yogurt, and soft-serve ice cream at good prices.

SHOPPING

Peach Tree Designs (⊠ *173 Rte. 6A, Yarmouth Port* ☎ *508/362–8317* ⊕ *www.peachtreedesigns.com)* carries home furnishings and decorative accessories, some from local craftspeople and all beautifully made.

WHERE TO EAT AND STAY

$$ ✕ **Inaho.** Yuji Watanabe, chef-owner of the Cape's best Japanese restau-
JAPANESE rant, makes early-morning journeys to Boston's fish markets to shop for
Fodor'sChoice the freshest local catch. His selection of sushi and sashimi is vast and
★ artful, and vegetable and seafood tempura come out of the kitchen fluffy
and light. If you're a teriyaki lover, you can't do any better than the
chicken's beautiful blend of sweet and sour. Can't decide what to order
Try the Omakase Kaiseki dinner: for $100 and up per person, the chef
designs a varied and generous tasting menu (advance notice is neces-
sary). The serene and simple Japanese garden out back has a traditional
koi pond. ⊠ *157 Main St. (Rte. 6A), Yarmouth Port* ☎ *508/362–5522*
⊕ *www.inahocapecod.com* ⊟ *MC, V* ⊘ *Closed Sun.*

$–$$$ ☷ **Bayside Resort.** A bit more upscale than most of the properties along
★ Route 28, the Bayside overlooks pristine salt marshes and, beyond
them, Lewis Bay. Although it's not right on the water, it has a small
beach and a large outdoor pool with a café (there's also an indoor pool).
Rooms have contemporary light-wood furnishings, and several have
whirlpool tubs. **Pros:** ideal for families with children (organized kids'
programs available for ages 12 and under); close to attractions of busy
Route 28; reasonable rates; some water views; lots of specialized package deals. **Cons:** beach is more like a sandy tanning area; no swimming;
not for those seeking quiet and intimate surroundings. ⊠ *225 Main St.
(Rte. 28), West Yarmouth* ☎ *508/775–5669 or 800/243–1114* ⊕ *www.
baysideresort.com* ⇱ *128 rooms* ⚭ *In-room: refrigerator, Wi-Fi. In-
hotel: bar, pools, gym, beachfront, children's programs (ages 1–12)*
⊟ *AE, D, MC, V* ⦿ *CP.*

$$–$$$ ☷ **Liberty Hill Inn.** Smartly but traditionally furnished common areas are
Fodor'sChoice a major draw to this dignified 1825 Greek Revival house. Guest rooms
★ are filled with a mix of old-world romantic charm and modern amenities; each is uniquely decorated, and some have whirlpool tubs and fireplaces for those chilly evenings. If you're traveling with children under
five, make advance arrangements with the innkeepers. **Pros:** elegant,
historic, and tasteful surroundings; beautiful grounds; romantic and
intimate setting. **Cons:** some rooms accessed only via steep stairs; some
bathrooms have only small shower stalls; not a waterfront location.
⊠ *77 Main St. (Rte. 6A), Yarmouth Port* ☎ *508/362–3976 or 800/821–
3977* ⊕ *www.libertyhillinn.com* ⇱ *8 rooms, 1 suite* ⚭ *In-room: Wi-Fi.
In-hotel: Wi-Fi hotspot* ⊟ *AE, D, MC, V* ⦿ *BP.*

DENNIS

*Dennis Village is 4 mi east of Yarmouth Port, West Dennis is 1 mi east
of South Yarmouth.*

The backstreets of Dennis Village still retain the Colonial charm of its
seafaring days. The town, which was incorporated in 1793, was named
for the Reverend Josiah Dennis. There were 379 sea captains living here
when fishing, salt making, and shipbuilding were the main industries,
and the elegant houses they constructed—now museums and B&Bs—
still line the streets.

ESSENTIALS

Visitor Information Dennis Chamber of Commerce (✉ *238 Swan River Rd., West Dennis* ☎ *508/398–3568* ⊕ *www.dennischamber.com*).

EXPLORING

Cape Cod Museum of Art. The permanent collection of more than 850 works by Cape-associated artists includes important pieces such as a portrait of a fisherman's wife by Charles Hawthorne, the father of the Provincetown art colony. The museum also hosts interesting temporary exhibitions, film festivals, lectures, art classes, and trips. The outdoor sculpture garden displays an eclectic collection; it's a pleasant place for a short stroll. Admission is by donation on Thursday. ✉ *60 Hope La., on grounds of Cape Playhouse, off Rte. 6A, Dennis Village* ☎ *508/385–4477* ⊕ *www.ccmoa.org* 🖃 *$8* ⊙ *Late May–mid-Oct., Mon.–Wed., Fri., and Sat. 10–5, Thurs. 10–8, Sun. noon–5; mid-Oct–late May, Tues.–Sat. 10–5, Sun. noon–5.*

SPORTS AND THE OUTDOORS

BEACHES Parking at all Dennis beaches is $15 a day in season for nonresidents. A beautiful crescent of white sand backed by low dunes, **Corporation Beach** (✉ *Corporation Rd., Dennis Village*) has lifeguards, showers, restrooms, and a food stand.

NIGHTLIFE AND THE ARTS

THEATER The **Cape Playhouse** (✉ *820 Main St. [Rte. 6A]), Dennis Village* ☎ *508/385–3911 or 877/385–3911* ⊕ *www.capeplayhouse.com*), an 1838 former Unitarian meetinghouse, is the oldest professional summer theater in the country. On the grounds of the Cape Playhouse is the artsy **Cape Cinema** (☎ *508/385–2503* ⊕ *www.capecinema.com*), which shows foreign and first-run films throughout the summer.

NIGHTLIFE **Harvest Gallery Wine Bar** (✉ *776 Main St., Dennis Village* ☎ *508/385–2444* ⊕ *www.harvestgallerywinebar.com*) is right at home in the neighborhood of so many cultural offerings. Enjoy eclectic artwork and live music with an extensive wine list, a good variety of hors d'oeuvres, salads, and desserts. Closed Tuesdays.

WHERE TO EAT AND STAY

$–$$
SEAFOOD ✕ **Captain Frosty's.** A great stop after the beach, this is where locals go to get their fried seafood. This modest joint has a regular menu that includes ice cream, a small specials board, and a counter where you order your meal. There's seating inside as well as outside on a shady brick patio. The staff is young and hardworking, pumping out fresh-fried clams and fish-and-chips on paper plates. All frying is done in 100% canola oil, and rice pilaf is offered as a substitute for fries. ✉ *219 Main St. (Rte. 6A), Dennis* ☎ *508/385–8548* ⊕ *captainfrosty. com* 🖃 *Reservations not accepted* ▭ *MC, V* ⊙ *Closed mid-Oct.–Mar.*

$$–$$$
AMERICAN
Fodor's Choice
★ ✕ **Red Pheasant.** In Dennis Village, this is one of the Cape's best cozy country restaurants, with a consistently good kitchen where creative American food is prepared with elaborate sauces and herb combinations. For instance, organic chicken is served with an intense preserved-lemon-and-fresh-thyme sauce, and exquisitely grilled veal chops come with a dense red-wine-and-portobello-mushroom sauce. In fall, look for the specialty game dishes, including buffalo, venison, and quail. Try

Learn more about the Cape's marshlands, forests, and ponds at the local Museum of Natural History.

to reserve a table in the more intimate Garden Room. The expansive wine list is excellent, or try one of the many elaborate martini offerings. Those with little ones in tow may want to go elsewhere for dinner; this is not the place for a family meal. ⊠ *905 Main St. (Rte. 6A), Box 486, Dennis, MA02638* ☏ *508/385–2133* ⊕ *www.redpheasantinn.com* ⌂ *Reservations essential* ▭ *AE, D, MC, V* ⊘ *No lunch.*

$–$$
Fodor's Choice
★

🏠 **Isaiah Hall B&B Inn.** Lilacs and pink roses trail along the white-picket fence outside this 1857 Greek Revival farmhouse on a quiet residential road near the bay. Innkeepers Jerry and Judy Neal set the scene for a romantic getaway with guest rooms that have country antiques and floral-print wallpapers. In the attached carriage house, some rooms have small balconies overlooking a wooded lawn with lush gardens, grape arbors, and berry bushes. **Pros:** beautiful grounds in very quiet, historic setting; not far from area beaches and attractions. **Cons:** many rooms accessed via very steep steps; some rooms are on the small side. ⊠ *152 Whig St., Box 1007* ☏ *508/385–9928 or 800/736–0160* ⊕ *www. isaiahhallinn.com* ⤴ *10 rooms, 2 suites* ⌂ *In-room: DVD, Wi-Fi. In-hotel: Wi-Fi hotspot* ▭ *AE, D, MC, V* ⊙| *BP.*

BREWSTER

7 mi northeast of Dennis, 20 mi east of Sandwich.

Brewster's location on Cape Cod Bay makes it a perfect place to learn about the region's ecology. The Cape Cod Museum of Natural History is here, and the area is rich in conservation lands, state parks, forests, freshwater ponds, and brackish marshes. When the tide is low in Cape Cod

Bay, you can stroll the beaches and explore tidal pools up to 2 mi from the shore on the Brewster flats.

ESSENTIALS

Visitor Information Brewster Chamber of Commerce (✉ *2198 Main St. [Rte. 6A], at the Town Hall* ☎ *508/896–3500* ⊕ *www.brewstercapecod.org*).

EXPLORING

☾ **Cape Cod Museum of Natural History.**
Fodor'sChoice For nature enthusiasts, a visit to
★ this museum is a must; it's just a short drive west from the heart of Brewster along Route 6A. The spacious museum and pristine grounds include guided field walks, a shop, a natural-history library, lectures, classes, and nature and marine exhibits such as a sea-life room with live specimens. Walking trails wind through 80 acres of forest, marshland, and ponds, all rich in birds and other wildlife. The museum also has guided canoe and kayak trips from May through September and several cruises that explore Cape waterways. ✉ *869 Main St. (Rte. 6A), West Brewster* ☎ *508/896–3867; 800/479–3867 in Massachusetts* ⊕ *www.ccmnh.org* ☜ *$8* ☉ *Oct.–Dec., Apr., and May, Wed.–Sun. 11–3; Feb. and Mar., Tues.–Sun., 11–3; June–Sept., daily 9:30–4. Closed Jan.*

SPORTS AND THE OUTDOORS

☾ **Nickerson State Park.** The 1,961 acres of this park were once part of a vast estate belonging to Roland C. Nickerson, son of Samuel Nickerson, a Chatham native who became a multimillionaire and founded of the First National Bank of Chicago. Today the land—acres of oak, pitch pine, hemlock, and spruce forest speckled with seven freshwater ponds—is open to the public for recreation. You can swim in the ponds, canoe, sail, kayak, bike along 8 mi of paved trails (including part of the Cape Cod Rail Trail), picnic, and cross-country ski in winter. Both tent and RV camping are extremely popular here, and nature programs are offered in season. ✉ *3488 Rte. 6A, East Brewster* ☎ *508/896–3491* ⊕ *www.mass.gov/dcr* ☜ *Free* ☉ *Daily dawn–dusk.*

WATER **Jack's Boat Rentals** (✉ *Flax Pond, Nickerson State Park, Rte. 6A, East*
SPORTS *Brewster* ☎ *508/896–8556* ⊕ *www.jacksboatrental.com*) rents canoes, kayaks, Seacycles, Sunfish, pedal boats, and sailboards and offers guided kayak tours.

SHOPPING

★ **Brewster Book Store** (✉ *2648 Main St. [Rte. 6A], East Brewster* ☎ *508/896–6543 or 800/823–6543* ⊕ *www.brewsterbookstore.com*) prides itself on being special. It's filled to the rafters with all manner of books by local and international authors and has extensive sections of fiction and kids' books. Built in 1852 as a church, **Brewster Store** (✉ *1935 Main St. [Rte.*

BIKE THE RAIL TRAIL

The Cape's premier bike path, the **Cape Cod Rail Trail** (⊕ *www.mass.gov/dcr*), follows the paved right-of-way of the old Penn Central Railroad. About 25 mi long, the easy-to-moderate trail passes salt marshes, cranberry bogs, and ponds.

The trail starts at the parking lot off Route 134 south of U.S. 6, near Theophilus Smith Road in South Dennis, and it ends at the post office in South Wellfleet. Access points in Brewster are Long Pond Road, Underpass Road, and Nickerson State Park.

3

6A], at Rte. 124 ☎ 508/896–3744 ⊕ *www.brewsterstore.com*), a local landmark, is a typical New England general store with such essentials as the daily papers, penny candy, and benches out front for conversation. Open May through September, the **Satucket Farm Stand** (✉ *76 Harwich Rd. [Rte. 124], off Rte. 6A* ☎ *508/896–5540* ⊕ *www.satucketfarm.com*) is a real old-fashioned farm stand and bakery. Most produce is grown on the premises, and you can fill your basket with home-baked scones and breads, fruit pies, produce, herbs, and flowers.

WHERE TO EAT AND STAY

$$$$
FRENCH
Fodor's Choice
★

✕ **Chillingsworth**. One of the crown jewels of Cape restaurants, Chillingsworth combines formal presentation with an excellent French menu and a diverse wine cellar to create a memorable dining experience. Superrich risotto, roast lobster, and grilled Angus sirloin are favorites. Dinner in the main dining rooms is prix fixe and includes seven courses—appetizer, soup, salad, sorbet, entrée, "amusements," and dessert, plus coffee or tea. Less expensive à la carte options for lunch, dinner, and Sunday brunch are served in the more casual, patio-style Bistro. There are also a few guest rooms here for overnighting. ✉ *2449 Main St. (Rte. 6A), East Brewster, Brewster* ☎ *508/896–3640* ⊕ *www.chillingsworth.com* ▭ *AE, DC, MC, V* ⊙ *Closed Thanksgiving–mid-May.*

$–$$
Fodor's Choice
★

▦ **Old Sea Pines Inn**. With its white-columned portico and wraparound veranda overlooking a broad lawn, Old Sea Pines, which housed a young ladies' boarding school in the early 1900s, resembles a vintage summer estate. Climb the sweeping staircase to guest rooms decorated with reproduction wallpaper, antiques, and framed old photographs. Children under eight years are allowed only in the family suites. The inn also holds a Sunday-night Broadway musical dinner revue from mid-June through mid-September. **Pros:** not far from town center; beautiful grounds; reasonable rates in historic setting. **Cons:** some rooms have shared baths; many rooms accessed via steep stairway on upper floors. ✉ *2553 Main St. (Rte. 6A)* ⊡ *Box 1070, Brewster 02631* ☎ *508/896–6114* ⊕ *www.oldseapinesinn.com* ↪ *24 rooms, 19 with bath, 5 suites* ♨ *In-room: no phone, no TV (some), Wi-Fi. In-hotel: restaurant* ▭ *AE, D, MC, V* ⊙ *Closed Jan.–Mar.* ⦿ *BP.*

HARWICH

6 mi south of Brewster, 5 mi east of Dennis.

The Cape's famous cranberry industry took off in Harwich in 1844, when Alvin Cahoon was its principal grower. Today you'll still find working cranberry bogs throughout Harwich. Three naturally sheltered harbors on Nantucket Sound make the town, like its English namesake, popular with boaters. You'll find dozens of elegant sailboats and elaborate yachts in Harwich's harbors, plus plenty of charter-fishing boats. Each year in August the town pays celebratory homage to its large boating population with a grand regatta, Sails Around the Cape.

ESSENTIALS

Visitor Information Harwich Chamber of Commerce (☎ *508/430–1165 or 800/442–7942* ⊕ *www.harwichcc.com Seasonal visitor center*✉ *One Schoolhouse Rd. and Rte. 28, Harwich Port*).

WHERE TO STAY

$$$–$$$$ ⊞ **Winstead Inn and Beach Resort.** Comprising two distinct properties,
★ the Winstead Inn and Beach Resort offers a two-for-one Cape Cod
experience. Harking back to an earlier era, the airy, attractive Beach
Resort sits on a private beach overlooking Nantucket Sound. You can
gaze at the sweep of coast and surrounding grasslands while enjoying a
generous Continental breakfast on the deck and wraparound porches.
At the other end of the spectrum, the Winstead Inn sits along a quiet
street on the edge of downtown. Greenery surrounds this Gothic Vic-
torian house, and many of the rooms have a view of the outdoor pool.
Guests at either property can use all the amenities and facilities. **Pros:**
Beach Resort sits right on the sand of private beach, and most rooms
have water views; pool privileges at sister property; spacious, elegant
rooms. **Cons:** many rooms up steep stairs; expensive. ⊠ *114 Parallel St.*
⊠ *4 Braddock La., Harwich Port* ☎ *508/432–4444 or 800/870–4405*
⊕ *www.winsteadinn.com* ⤴ *18 rooms, 4 suites* ♿ *In-room: Wi-Fi. In-
hotel: pool* ⊟ *AE, MC, V* ⦺⦿⦾ *CP.*

CHATHAM

5 mi east of Harwich

At the bent elbow of the Cape, with water nearly surrounding it,
Chatham has all the charm of a quietly posh seaside resort, with plenty
of shops but none of the crass commercialism that plagues some other
towns on the Cape. The town has gray-shingle houses with tidy awnings
and cheerful flower gardens, an attractive Main Street with crafts and
antiques stores alongside dapper cafés, and a five-and-dime. Although it
can get crowded in high season—and even on weekends during shoulder
seasons—Chatham remains a true New England village.

ESSENTIALS

Visitor Information Chatham Chamber of Commerce (☎ *508/945–5199 or
800/715–5567* ⊕ *www.chathaminfo.com*).

EXPLORING

★ **Atwood House Museum.** Built by sea captain Joseph C. Atwood in 1752
and occupied by his descendants until it was sold to the Chatham His-
torical Society in 1926, the museum has a gambrel roof, variable-width
floor planks, fireplaces, an old kitchen with a wide hearth and a beehive
oven, and some antique dolls and toys. In a remodeled freight shed are
stunning and provocative murals (1932–45) by Alice Stallknecht Wight
portraying religious scenes in Chatham settings. ⊠ *347 Stage Harbor
Rd., West Chatham* ☎ *508/945–2493* ⊕ *www.chathamhistoricalsociety.
org* ⌑ *$5* ☉ *Mid–late June and Sept.–mid-Oct., Tues.–Sat. 1–4 (opens
at 10 AM on rainy days); July and Aug., Tues.–Sat. 10–4.*

★ **Chatham Light.** The famous view of the harbor, the offshore sandbars,
and the ocean beyond from this lighthouse justifies the crowds that
gather to share it. The U.S. Coast Guard auxiliary offers free tours April
through October on most Wednesdays. ⊠ *Main St. near Bridge St., West
Chatham* ☎ *508/430–0628* ⊕ *www.lighthouse.cc/chatham.*

SPORTS AND THE OUTDOORS

Fodor's Choice
★
Monomoy National Wildlife Refuge. This 2,500-acre preserve includes the Monomoy Islands, a fragile 9-mi-long barrier-beach area south of Chatham. A haven for bird-watchers, the island is an important stop along the North Atlantic Flyway for migratory waterfowl and shorebirds—peak migration times are May and late July. The only structure on the islands is the **South Monomoy Lighthouse,** built in 1849. The refuge headquarters has a visitor center and bookstore, open daily 8 to 4. ⊠ *Off Morris Island Rd., Morris Island* ☎ *508/945–0594* ⊕ *www. fws.gov/northeast/monomoy/.*

SHOPPING

★ **Chatham Jam and Jelly Shop** (⊠ *10 Vineyard Ave., at Rte. 28, West Chatham* ☎ *508/945–3052 or 877/526–7467* ⊕ *chathamjamandjellyshop.com*) sells delicious concoctions like rose-petal jelly, apple-lavender chutney, and beach-plum jam, as well as all the old standbys. **Yankee Ingenuity** (⊠ *525 Main St., Chatham Center* ☎ *508/945–1288* ⊕ *www. yankee-ingenuity.com*) stocks unique jewelry and lamps and a wide assortment of unusual, beautiful trinkets at reasonable—especially for Chatham—prices.

NIGHTLIFE AND THE ARTS

Chatham Squire (⊠ *487 Main St., Chatham Center* ☎ *508/945–0945* ⊕ *www.thesquire.com*), with four bars, including a raw bar, is a rollicking hangout, drawing a young crowd to the bar side and a mixed crowd of locals to the restaurant.

WHERE TO EAT AND STAY

$–$$$
SEAFOOD
★
✕ **Impudent Oyster.** A cozy, festive locals' tavern with an unfailingly cheerful staff and superb but reasonably priced seafood, this always-packed restaurant sits inside a dapper house just off Main Street. It's a great place for a romantic meal or for dinner with friends or kids, and the menu offers light burgers and sandwiches as well as more substantial fare. Mussels with white-wine sauce is a consistent favorite. The dining room is split-level, with a bar in back on the lower level. There's not a ton of seating, so reserve early on weekends. ⊠ *15 Chatham Bars Ave., Chatham Center* ☎ *508/945–3545* ▤ *AE, MC, V.*

$$$–$$$$
★
▥ **Queen Anne Inn.** Built in 1840 as a wedding present for the daughter of a famous clipper-ship captain, the Queen Anne first opened as an inn in 1874. Some of the large guest rooms have working fireplaces, balconies, and hot tubs. Run by locally renowned chef Toby Hill, the Eldredge Room ($$$–$$$$; closed Jan.–Apr., no lunch) turns out sublime regional American fare, including an updated fish-and-chips with truffle-crusted flounder, frites, truffle tartar sauce, and a malt vinaigrette. **Pros:** spacious and thoughtfully decorated rooms in historic setting; well-suited for relaxing with hot tubs and fireplaces. **Cons:** it's a generous walk to the town center; rooms accessed via steep stairs. ⊠ *70 Queen Anne Rd.* ☎ *508/945–0394 or 800/545–4667* ⊕ *www. queenanneinn.com* ⊅ *33 rooms* ♿ *In-room: Wi-Fi. In-hotel: restaurant, bar, tennis courts, pool, gym, spa* ▤ *AE, D, MC, V* ⊗ *Closed Jan.–Mar.* ⅼ◉ⅼ *CP.*

ORLEANS

8 mi north of Chatham, 35 mi east of Sagamore Bridge.

Orleans has a long heritage in fishing and seafaring, and many beautifully preserved homes remain from the Colonial era in the small village of East Orleans, home of the town's Historical Society and Museum. In other areas of town, such as down by Rock Harbor, more modestly grand homes stand near the water's edge.

GETTING HERE AND AROUND

A bus connecting Hyannis and Orleans serves the Lower Cape region. Year-round transport on the Flex service goes from Harwich to Provincetown, serving the towns of Brewster, Orleans, Eastham, Wellfleet, and Truro along the way.

ESSENTIALS

Visitor Information Orleans Chamber of Commerce (☎ *508/255–1386 or 800/865–1386* ⊕ *www.capecod-orleans.com*).

EXPLORING

Rock Harbor. A walk along Rock Harbor Road, a winding street lined with gray-shingle Cape houses, white-picket fences, and neat gardens, leads to this bay-side harbor, site of a skirmish in the War of 1812 in which the Orleans militia kept a British warship from docking.

SPORTS AND THE OUTDOORS

BEACHES The town-managed **Nauset Beach** (⊠ *Beach Rd., Nauset Heights* ☎ *508/ 240–3780*) —not to be confused with Nauset Light Beach on the National Seashore—is a 10-mi sweep of sandy ocean beach with low dunes and large waves good for bodysurfing or board surfing. The beach has lifeguards, restrooms, showers, and a food concession. **Skaket Beach** (⊠ *Skaket Beach Rd., Namskaket* ☎ *508/240–3775*) on Cape Cod Bay is a sandy stretch with calm, warm water good for children, plus restrooms, lifeguards, and a snack bar. There is a daily parking fee of $15 from mid-June to Labor Day for both beaches.

BOATING AND **Arey's Pond Boat Yard** (⊠ *43 Arey's La., off Rte. 28, South Orleans* ☎ *508/*
FISHING *255–0994* ⊕ *www.areyspondboatyard.com*) has a sailing school with individual and group lessons. Many of Orleans's freshwater ponds offer good fishing for perch, pickerel, trout, and more. The required fishing license, along with rental gear, is available at the **Goose Hummock Shop** (⊠ *15 Rte. 6A* ☎ *508/255–0455* ⊕ *www.goose.com*).

WHERE TO EAT AND STAY

$$$ ✕ **Abba.** Abba serves inspired pan-Mediterranean cuisine in an elegant
MEDITERRANEAN and intimate setting. Chef and co-owner Erez Pinhas skillfully combines
★ Middle Eastern, Asian, and southern European flavors in such dishes as herb-crusted rack of venison with shiitake risotto and asparagus in a port sauce and grilled tuna with vegetable nori roll tempura in a balsamic miso and mustard sauce. Cushy pillows on the banquettes and soft candlelight flickering from Moroccan glass votives add a touch of opulence. Reservations suggested. ⊠ *89 Old Colony Way, at West Rd.* ☎ *508/255–8144* ⊕ *www.abbarestaurant.com* ⌂ *Reservations essential* ▭ *AE, D, MC, V* ☺ *No lunch.*

$$$-$$$$ 🔲 **A Little Inn on Pleasant Bay.** This gorgeously decorated inn occupies
Fodor's Choice   a 1798 building set on a bluff beside a cranberry bog, across Route
★   28 from its namesake bay. The main house has four rooms, and two
adjoining nearby buildings contain another five rooms. Many of the
accommodations look clear out to the bay, and others face the lush
gardens. The Mercury room has French doors leading out to a private
garden patio, and the spacious Wianno room is warmed by a fireplace
and has a lovely sitting area; all bathrooms are roomy and modern. The
breakfast buffet is more substantial than many full breakfasts, and you
can enjoy it while sitting on the pretty patio, admiring Pleasant Bay in
the distance. Walk across the street to a small private beach with its
own dock. **Pros:** peaceful, pastoral setting with great water views; abun-
dant breakfast buffet; spacious, well-appointed rooms. **Cons:** not an
in-town location; must drive a distance to either Orleans or Chatham.
⊠ *654 S. Orleans Rd., Box 190, South Orleans* ☎ *508/255–0780 or
888/332–3351* ⊕ *www.alittleinnonpleasantbay.com* 🛏 *9 rooms* ♿ *In-
room: no phone, no TV. In-hotel: Wi-Fi, no kids under 10* ⊟ *AE, MC,
V* ﺍ◯ﺍ *CP* ☉ *Closed Nov.–Apr.*

EASTHAM

3 mi north of Orleans, 6 mi south of Wellfleet.

Often overlooked on the speedy drive up toward Provincetown on U.S.
6, Eastham is a town full of hidden treasures. Unlike other towns on
the Cape, it has no official town center or Main Street; the highway
bisects it, and the town touches both Cape Cod Bay and the Atlantic.
Amid the gas stations, convenience stores, restaurants, and large motel
complexes, Eastham's wealth of natural beauty takes a little exploring
to find.

ESSENTIALS

Visitor Information Eastham Chamber of Commerce (☎ *508/240–7211*
⊕ *www.easthamchamber.com*).

EXPLORING

☾ **Cape Cod National Seashore.** *See the highlighted listing at the start of*
Fodor's Choice   *this chapter.*
★

SPORTS AND THE OUTDOORS

Fodor's Choice   **Nauset Light Beach** (⊠ *Off Ocean View Dr.*), adjacent to Coast Guard
★   Beach, continues the National Seashore landscape of long, sandy beach
backed by tall dunes and grass. It has showers and lifeguards in summer,
but as with other National Seashore beaches, there's no food conces-
sion. Nauset charges $15 daily per car; a $45 season pass admits you
here and to the other five National Seashore swimming beaches.

WHERE TO EAT AND STAY

¢–$ ✕ **The Friendly Fisherman.** Not just another roadside lobster shack with
SEAFOOD   buoys and nets for decoration, this place is serious about its fresh sea-
food. It's both a great place to pick up ingredients to cook at home—
there's a fish and produce market on-site—and a good bet for dining out
on such favorites as fish-and-chips, fried scallops, and lobster. The mar-
ket also sells homemade pies, breads, soups, stews, and pasta. ⊠ *4580*

U.S. 6, North Eastham ☎ *508/255–6770 or 508/255–3009* ▤ *AE, MC,*
V ⊘ *Closed Nov.–Apr.*

$$$–$$$$
Fodor's Choice
★

▦ **Whalewalk Inn & Spa.** This 1830 whaling master's home is on 3 land-
scaped acres. Rooms in the main inn have four-poster twin, double, or
queen beds; floral fabrics; and antique or reproduction furniture. Suites
with fully equipped kitchens are in the converted barn and guesthouse.
The property also has an opulent state-of-the-art spa, complete with
a small resistance pool and fitness center. Breakfast is served in the
cheerful sunroom or on the garden patio. **Pros:** beautiful grounds; ele-
gantly appointed rooms with added benefit of decadent spa treatments.
Cons: no water views or beachfront; not an in-town location. ✉ *220*
Bridge Rd., Eastham ☎ *508/255–0617 or 800/440–1281* ⊕ *www.*
whalewalkinn.com ⋥ *11 rooms, 5 suites* ⚲ *In-room: kitchen (some),*
refrigerator (some), DVD (some), Wi-Fi. In-hotel: pool, gym, spa ▤ *AE,*
D, MC, V ⦿ *BP.*

WELLFLEET AND SOUTH WELLFLEET

6 mi north of Eastham, 13 mi southeast of Provincetown.

Still famous for its world-renowned and succulent namesake oysters,
Wellfleet is today a tranquil community; many artists and writers call it
home. Less than 2 mi wide, it's one of the most attractively developed
Cape resort towns, with a number of fine restaurants, historic houses,
art galleries, and a good old Main Street in the village proper.

ESSENTIALS

Visitor Information Wellfleet Chamber of Commerce (☎ *508/349–2510*
⊕ *www.wellfleetchamber.com*).

EXPLORING

★ **Marconi Station.** On the Atlantic side of the Cape's forearm, Marconi
Station is the site of the first transatlantic wireless station erected on the
U.S. mainland. Italian radio and wireless-telegraphy pioneer Guglielmo
Marconi sent the first American wireless message from here to Europe—
"most cordial greetings and good wishes," from President Theodore
Roosevelt to King Edward VII of England—on January 18, 1903. Off
the parking lot, a 1½-mi trail and boardwalk lead through the **Atlantic
White Cedar Swamp,** one of the most beautiful trails on the seashore.
✉ *Marconi Site Rd., South Wellfleet* ☎ *508/349–3785* ⊕ *www.nps.gov/*
caco ⊡ *Free* ⊘ *Daily 8–4:30.*

SPORTS AND THE OUTDOORS

♲ **Massachusetts Audubon Wellfleet Bay Wildlife Sanctuary.** A trip to the Outer
Fodor's Choice Cape isn't complete without a visit to this 1,100-acre haven for more
★ than 250 species of birds attracted by the varied habitats found here.
The jewel of the Massachusetts Audubon Society, the sanctuary is a
superb place for walking, birding, and watching the sun set over the salt
marsh and bay. The **Esther Underwood Johnson Nature Center** contains
two 700-gallon aquariums that offer an up-close look at marine life
common to the Cape's tidal flats and marshlands. Other rotating exhib-
its illustrate different facets of the area's ecology and natural history.
✉ *291 U.S. 6, South Wellfleet* ☎ *508/349–2615* ⊕ *www.wellfleetbay.*

Artists and birders flock to the Wellfleet Bay Wildlife Sanctuary, protected by the Massachusetts Audubon Society.

org ✉ *$5* ◷ *Trails daily 8AM–dusk; nature center late May–mid-Oct., daily 8:30–5; mid-Oct.–late May, Tues.–Sun. 8:30–5.*

BEACHES **Cahoon Hollow Beach** (✉ *Ocean View Dr.*) has lifeguards, restrooms, and a restaurant and music club on the sand. This beach tends to attract younger and slightly rowdier crowds; it's a big Sunday-afternoon party place. **White Crest Beach** (✉ *Ocean View Dr.*) is a prime surfer hangout, where the dudes often spend more time waiting for waves than actually riding them. Both beaches are open to the public for a daily parking fee of $15; lots fill up quickly on hot and sunny summer days.

BOATING **Jack's Boat Rental** (✉ *Gull Pond Rd., off U.S. 6* ☎ *508/349–9808 or 508/349–7553* ⊕ *www.jacksboatrental.com*) also has a location at U.S. 6 and Cahoon Hollow Road. Canoes, kayaks, Sunfish, pedal boats, surfboards, Boogie boards, and sailboards are available for rent.

NIGHTLIFE AND THE ARTS

The drive-in movie is alive and well on Cape Cod at the **Wellfleet Drive-In Theater** (✉ *51 U.S. 6, South Wellfleet* ☎ *508/349–7176* ⊕ *www.wellfleetcinemas.com*), which is right by the Eastham town line. Films start at dusk nightly in season. It's also the site of a very popular weekend flea market, held from mid-April through October.

WHERE TO EAT AND STAY

$–$$$ ✕ **Finely JP's.** Chef John Pontius consistently turns out wonderful, afford-
AMERICAN able food full of the best Mediterranean and local influences and ingre-
★ dients at his beloved restaurant along U.S. 6. The Wellfleet paella and the roast duck with cranberry-orange sauce draw rave reviews and a steady handful of locals, but Pontius is not afraid to cook down-home

barbecue pork ribs either. Appetizers are especially good, among them oysters *Bienville* (baked in a white wine–cream sauce topped with Parmesan cheese and bread crumbs) and jerk-spiced duck salad with raspberry vinaigrette. Off-season hours vary, so call ahead—and be sure not to confuse this place with PJ's, down the road. ⊠ *554 U.S. 6, South Wellfleet* ☎ *508/349–7500* ⚠ *Reservations not accepted* ⊟ *D, MC, V* ☽ *Closed some nights during off-season. No lunch.*

$$
Fodor's Choice
★

Stone Lion Inn. The Stone Lion Inn, a gracious mansard-roof Victorian, sits just outside the town center and is a short walk from both the harbor and the village. Rooms have queen beds, ceiling fans to encourage breezes, hardwood floors, and a mix of antiques and contemporary pieces that balances the house's 19th-century heritage with today's decorating sensibilities. **Pros:** short walk from harbor and shopping; stylish yet unpretentious decor; friendly and helpful owners. **Cons:** no phone or TV in most rooms; need a car to get to ocean; not appropriate for younger kids. ⊠ *130 Commercial St., Wellfleet Center* ☎ *508/349–9565* ⊕ *www.stonelioncapecod.com* ⤳ *4 rooms, 1 apartment, 1 cottage* ⚐ *In-room: no phone (some), kitchen (some), refrigerator, no TV (some), Wi-Fi. In-hotel: no kids under 5* ⊟ *MC, V* ⦿|*BP.*

EN ROUTE

Edward Hopper summered in **Truro** from 1930 to 1967, finding the Cape light ideal for his austere brand of realism. One of the largest towns on the Cape in terms of land area—almost 43 square mi—it's also the smallest in population, with about 1,400 year-round residents. Truro is also the Cape's narrowest town, and from a high perch you can see the Atlantic Ocean on one side and Cape Cod Bay on the other. Its **Highland Light,** also called Cape Cod Light, is the Cape's oldest lighthouse and truly a breathtaking sight. Tours ($4) of the lighthouse are given daily from mid-May to October.

PROVINCETOWN

★ *9 mi northwest of Wellfleet, 62 mi from Sagamore Bridge.*

Many people know that the Pilgrims stopped here at the curved tip of Cape Cod before proceeding to Plymouth. Historical records suggest that an earlier visitor was Thorvald, brother of Viking Leif Erikson, who came ashore here in AD 1004 to repair the keel of his boat and consequently named the area Kjalarness, or Cape of the Keel. Bartholomew Gosnold came to Provincetown in 1602 and named the area Cape Cod after the abundant codfish he found in the local waters.

Incorporated as a town in 1727, Provincetown was for many decades a bustling seaport, with fishing and whaling as its major industries. In the late 19th century, groups of Portuguese fishermen and whalers began to settle here, lending their expertise and culture to an already cosmopolitan town. Fishing is still an important source of income for many Provincetown locals, but now the town ranks among the world's leading whale-watching—rather than whale-hunting—outposts.

Artists began coming here in the late 1890s to take advantage of the unusual Cape Cod light—in fact, Provincetown is the nation's oldest continuous art colony. By 1916, with five art schools flourishing here, painters' easels were nearly as common as shells on the beach.

This bohemian community, along with the availability of inexpensive summer lodgings, attracted young rebels and writers as well, including John Reed (*Ten Days That Shook the World*) and Mary Heaton Vorse (*Footnote to Folly*), who in 1915 began the Cape's first significant theater group, the Provincetown Players. The young, then unknown Eugene O'Neill joined them in 1916, when his *Bound East for Cardiff* premiered in a tiny wharf-side East End fish house.

America's original gay resort, Provincetown today is as appealing to artists as it is to gay and lesbian—as well as straight—tourists. The awareness brought by the AIDS crisis and, most recently, Massachusetts's legalization of same-sex marriage has turned the town into the most visibly gay vacation community in America.

GETTING HERE AND AROUND

AIR TRAVEL Year-round flight service by Cape Air connects Provincetown with Boston's Logan Airport.

CAR TRAVEL The busiest travel time is early morning—especially on rainy days—when it seems that everyone on Cape Cod is determined to make it to Provincetown. Traffic is heaviest around Wellfleet and it can be slow going. Driving the 3 mi of Provincetown's main downtown thoroughfare, Commercial Street, in season could take forever. Parking is not one of Provincetown's better amenities, so bike and foot are the best ways to explore the downtown area.

FERRY TRAVEL Bay State Cruise Company offers standard and high-speed ferry service between Commonwealth Pier in Boston and MacMillan Wharf in Provincetown. High-speed service runs a few times daily from mid-May through September ($72 round-trip); the ride takes 90 minutes. Standard service runs weekends from late June through early September ($33 round-trip); the ride takes three hours. Boston Harbor Cruises runs a fast ferry from Long Wharf in Boston mid-May to mid-October for $79 round-trip. From the State Pier in Plymouth, Capt. John Boats operates a 90-minute ferry daily from late June to Labor Day ($40 round-trip).

SHUTTLE TRAVEL The Shuttle, run by the Cape Cod Regional Transit Authority, provides a seasonal (mid-June–mid-September) route from Truro, heading into town, with trips to Herring Cove Beach, Race Point Beach, and the Provincetown Airport. Bikes are accommodated.

ESSENTIALS

Transportation Contacts Bay State Cruise Company (☎ *617/748–1428 or 877/783–3779* ⊕ *www.baystatecruisecompany.com*). **Boston Harbor Cruises** (☎ *617/227–4321 or 877/733–9425* ⊕ *www.bostonharborcruises.com*). **Cape Air** (☎ *800/352–0714 or 508/771–6944* ⊕ *www.flycapeair.com*). **Cape Cod Regional Transit Authority** (☎ *800/352–7155* ⊕ *www.capecodtransit. org*). **Capt. John Boats** (☎ *508/747–2400 or 800/225–4000* ⊕ *www. provincetownferry.com*).

Visitor Information Provincetown Chamber of Commerce (☎ *508/487–3424* ⊕ *www.ptownchamber.com*). **Provincetown Business Guild (gay and lesbian)** ✉ *3 Freeman St., Downtown Center* ☎ *508/487–2313 or 800/637–8696* ⊕ *www. ptown.org*).

EXPLORING

★ **Commercial Street**. Take a casual stroll by the many architectural styles (Greek Revival, Victorian, Second Empire, and Gothic, to name a few) used in the design of the impressive houses for wealthy sea captains and merchants. The Provincetown Historical Society puts out a series of walking-tour pamphlets available for about $1 each at many shops in town. The center of town is where the crowds and most of the touristy shops are. The East End is mostly residential, with an increasing number of nationally renowned galleries; the similarly quiet West End has a number of small inns with neat lawns and elaborate gardens.

QUICK BITES

The local bars close at 1 AM, at which point the pizza joint/coffee stand Spiritus (⊠ *190 Commercial St., Downtown Center* ☎ *508/487–2808* ⊕ *www.spirituspizza.com* ⊙ *Closed Nov.–Apr.*) becomes the town's epicenter. It's the ultimate place to see and be seen, slice in hand and witty banter at the ready. In the morning, the same counter serves restorative coffee and croissants as well as Häagen-Dazs ice cream.

★ **Pilgrim Monument**. The first thing you'll see in Provincetown is this grandiose edifice, which seems somewhat out of proportion to the rest of the low-rise town. The monument commemorates the Pilgrims' first landing in the New World and their signing of the Mayflower Compact (the first Colonial-American rules of self-governance) before they set off from Provincetown Harbor to explore the mainland. Climb the 116 steps and 60 short ramps of the 252-foot-high tower for a panoramic view—dunes on one side, harbor on the other, and the entire bay side of Cape Cod beyond. At the tower's base is a museum of Lower Cape and Provincetown history, with exhibits on whaling, shipwrecks, and scrimshaw. ⊠ *1 High Pole Hill Rd., Downtown Center* ☎ *508/487–1310* ⊕ *www.pilgrim-monument.org* 🎫 *$7* ⊙ *Early Apr.–June, Sept., and Oct., daily 9–5; July and Aug., daily 9–7; Nov., weekends 9–5; Closed Dec.–Mar.*

SPORTS AND THE OUTDOORS

BEACHES
Fodor's Choice
★

Race Point Beach (⊠ *Race Point Rd., east of U.S. 6*), one of the Cape Cod National Seashore beaches in Provincetown, has a wide swath of sand stretching far off into the distance around the point and Coast Guard station. Because of its position facing north, the beach gets sun all day long. Parking costs $15 per day.

Fodor's Choice
★

Art's Dune Tours (⊠ *4 Standish St., Downtown Center* ☎ *508/487–1950* ⊕ *www.artsdunetours.com*) has been taking eager passengers into the dunes of Province Lands since 1946. Bumpy but controlled rides transport you through sometimes surreal sandy vistas peppered with beach grass and along a shoreline patrolled by seagulls and sandpipers. Regular tours start at $25.

WHALE-
WATCHING

Dolphin Fleet (⊠ *Ticket office: Chamber of Commerce building at MacMillan Wharf, Downtown Center* ☎ *508/240–3636 or 800/826–9300* ⊕ *www.whalewatch.com* 🎫 *$39* ⊙ *Tours mid-Apr.–Oct.*). Tours are accompanied by scientists from the Center for Coastal Studies in Provincetown, who provide commentary while collecting data on the whales they've been monitoring for years. They know many of them by name and will tell you about their habits and histories.

Provincetown is still bustling after dark, especially the late night food scene and gay nightlife.

NIGHTLIFE

Atlantic House (⊠ *4 Masonic Pl., Downtown Center* ☎ *508/487–3821* ⊕ *www.ahouse.com*) is the grandfather of the gay nightlife scene.

WHERE TO EAT

$$–$$$
AMERICAN
Fodor's Choice
★

✕ **Devon's.** This unassuming tiny white cottage—with a dining room that seats just 42 lucky patrons—serves up some of the best food in town, judging by the continual crowds that wait for seats. Specialties from the oft-changing menu include pan-seared halibut with caramelized orange glaze, black rice, and sautéed beet greens and free-range seared duck with a Syrah reduction, red-onion marmalade, and couscous primavera. Be sure to save some room for knockout dessert selections like blackberry mousse over ginger-lemon polenta cake with wild-berry coulis. It's also a good spot for breakfast. ⊠ *401½ Commercial St. Downtown Center* ☎ *508/487–4773* ⊕ *www.devons.org* ⌦ *Reservations essential* ▭ *MC, V* ☉ *Closed Wed. and Nov.–Apr. No lunch.*

$$
SEAFOOD

✕ **Lobster Pot.** Provincetown's Lobster Pot is fit to do battle with all the lobster shanties anywhere (and everywhere) else on the Cape—it's often jammed with tourists, but the crowds reflect the generally high quality. The hardworking kitchen turns out classic New England cooking: lobsters, generous and filling seafood platters, and some of the best chowder around. Try the seafood Pico with a half lobster, shrimp, littlenecks, mussels, calamari, and fish over pasta with tomatoes, rose wine, onions, and garlic. ⊠ *321 Commercial St., Downtown Center* ☎ *508/487–0842* ⊕ *www.ptownlobsterpot.com* ⌦ *Reservations not accepted* ▭ *AE, D, DC, MC, V* ☉ *Closed Jan.*

$$-$$$
AMERICAN
Fodor'sChoice
★

✕**The Mews.** This perennial favorite with magnificent harbor views focuses on seafood and grilled meats with a cross-cultural flair. Sit upstairs at the café and choose from a lighter bistro menu or the regular fine-dining fare. Some popular entrées include roasted vegetable and polenta lasagna with a tomato-olive sauce and Shaking Beef, a Vietnamese-inspired dish with beef tenderloin sautéed with scallions and red onions and a lime–black pepper sauce. The view of the bay from the bar is nearly perfect, and the gentle lighting makes this a romantic spot to have a drink. The vodka bar has more than 275 varieties. ⊠ *429 Commercial St., East End* ☎ *508/487–1500* ⊕ *www.mews.com* ⊟ *AE, D, DC, MC, V* ☺ *No lunch.*

WHERE TO STAY

$$$-$$$$
Fodor'sChoice
★

⊞ **Brass Key.** One of the Cape's most luxurious small resorts, this meticulously kept year-round getaway comprises a beautifully restored main house—originally a sea captain's home built in 1828—and several other carefully groomed buildings and cottages. Rooms mix antiques with such modern amenities as Bose stereos and DVD players (loaner laptops and iPod docks are also available). Deluxe rooms come with gas fireplaces and whirlpool baths or French doors opening onto wrought-iron balconies. A widow's-walk sundeck has a panoramic view of Cape Cod Bay. **Pros:** ultra-posh rooms; beautiful and secluded grounds; pool on-site. **Cons:** among the highest rates in town; rooms close to Bradford Street can get a bit of noise; significant minimum-stay requirements in summer. ⊠ *67 Bradford St., Downtown Center* ☎ *508/487–9005 or 800/842–9858* ⊕ *www.brasskey.com* ⤴*42 rooms* ⌂ *In-room: safe, refrigerator, DVD, Wi-Fi. In-hotel: pool, spa, no kids under 16* ⊟ *AE, D, MC, V* ⧖*CP.*

$$

⊞ **Snug Cottage.** Noted for its extensive flower gardens and enviable perch atop one of the larger bluffs in town, this convivial Arts and Crafts–style inn dates to 1825 and is decked in smashing English country antiques and fabrics. The oversize accommodations have distinctly British names (Victoria Suite, Royal Scott); most are full suites with sitting areas, and many have wood-burning fireplaces and private outdoor entrances. The Churchill Suite has 10 big windows overlooking the flowers and bushes outside, and the York Suite has a partial view of Cape Cod Bay. **Pros:** steps from East End dining and shopping; stunning grounds and gardens; most units are extremely spacious. **Cons:** rooms close to Bradford Street can get some noise; a bit of a walk from West End businesses; top suites don't come cheaply. ⊠ *178 Bradford St., east of Downtown Center* ☎ *508/487–1616 or 800/432–2334* ⊕ *www. snugcottage.com* ⤴*3 rooms, 5 suites* ⌂ *In-room: kitchen (some), DVD, Wi-Fi* ⊟ *AE, D, MC, V* ⧖*BP.*

MARTHA'S VINEYARD

Far less developed than Cape Cod—thanks to a few local conservation organizations—yet more cosmopolitan than neighboring Nantucket, Martha's Vineyard is an island with a double life. From Memorial Day through Labor Day the quieter (some might say real) Vineyard quickens into a vibrant, star-studded place.

The busy main port, Vineyard Haven, welcomes day-trippers fresh off ferries and private yachts to browse in its array of shops. Oak Bluffs, where pizza and ice-cream emporiums reign supreme, has the air of a Victorian boardwalk. Edgartown is flooded with seekers of chic who wander tiny streets that hold boutiques, stately whaling captains' homes, and charming inns.

Summer regulars have included a host of celebrities over the years, among them Carly Simon, Ted Danson, Spike Lee, and Diane Sawyer. If you're planning to stay overnight on a summer weekend, be sure to make reservations well in advance; spring is not too early. Things stay busy on September and October weekends, a favorite time for weddings, but begin to slow down soon after. In many ways the Vineyard's off-season persona is even more appealing than its summer self, with more time to linger over pastoral and ocean vistas, free from the throngs of cars, bicycles, and mopeds.

Except for Oak Bluffs and Edgartown, the Vineyard is "dry," but many restaurants allow you to bring your own beer or wine.

ESSENTIALS
Visitor Information Martha's Vineyard Chamber of Commerce (⊠ *24 Beach Rd., Vineyard Haven* ☎ *508/693–0085 or 800/505–4815* ⊕ *www.mvy.com*).

VINEYARD HAVEN (TISBURY)

7 mi southeast of Woods Hole, 3½ mi west of Oak Bluffs, 8 mi northwest of Edgartown.

Most people call this town Vineyard Haven because of the name of the port where ferries arrive, but its official name is Tisbury. Not as high-toned as Edgartown or as honky-tonk as Oak Bluffs, Vineyard Haven blends the past and the present with a touch of the bohemian. Visitors step off the ferry right into the bustle of the harbor, a block from the shops and restaurants of Main Street.

GETTING HERE AND AROUND
It can be handy to have a car to see all of Martha's Vineyard and travel freely. Instead of bringing one over on the ferry in summer it's sometimes easier and more economical to rent a car once you're on the island for the days you plan on exploring. The Martha's Vineyard Transit Authority (VTA) provides regular service to all six towns on the island. The buses can accommodate a limited number of bicycles and the island has an excellent network of well-maintained bike trails. The VTA also has free in-town shuttle-bus routes in Edgartown and Vineyard Haven.

AIR TRAVEL Cape Air has regular, year-round flight service to the island from Hyannis, Boston, and Providence's T. F. Green Airport. From New York's LaGuardia Airport, Philadelphia, and Washington, D.C., U.S. Airways Express provides seasonal service.

FERRY TRAVEL The Steamship Authority runs the only car ferries to Martha's Vineyard, which make the 45-minute trip from Woods Hole on Cape Cod to Vineyard Haven year-round and to Oak Bluffs from late May through mid-October ($7.50 for passenger fare; $3 for bicycles; $42.50–$65

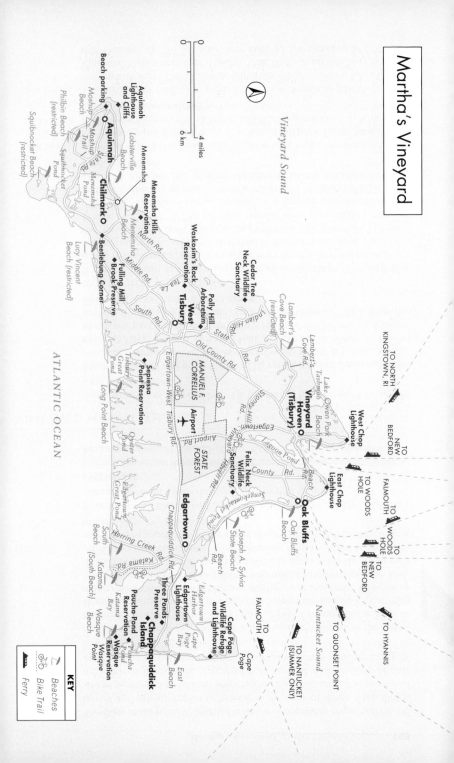

Martha's Vineyard

KEY
- Beaches
- Bike Trail
- Ferry

Vineyard Sound

ATLANTIC OCEAN

Nantucket Sound

Aquinnah Lighthouse and Cliffs
Beach parking
Moshup Beach
Aquinnah
Philbin Beach (restricted)
Squibnocket Beach (restricted)
Squibnocket Pond
Moshup Trail
Lobsterville Beach
State Rd.
Menemsha Pond
Menemsha
Menemsha Beach
Chilmark
Lucy Vincent Beach (restricted)
Beetlebung Corner
Menemsha Hills Reservation
North Rd.
Middle Rd.
Fulling Mill Brook Preserve
Waskosim's Rock Reservation
Cedar Tree Neck Wildlife Sanctuary
Polly Hill Arboretum
Tea La.
South Rd.
West Tisbury
Great Pond
Long Point Beach
Sepiessa Point Reservation
Tisbury Great Pond
Oyster Pond
STATE FOREST
Airport
Airport Rd.
Edgartown-West Tisbury Rd.
MANUEL F. CORRELLUS
Indian Hill Rd.
Old County Rd.
State Rd.
Lambert's Cove Beach (restricted)
Lambert's Cove Rd.
Tashmoo Beach
Lake Tashmoo
Vineyard Haven (Tisbury)
West Chop Lighthouse
East Chop Lighthouse
Lagoon Pond
Sengekontacket Pond
Felix Neck Wildlife Sanctuary
Edgartown-Vineyard Haven Rd.
Stoney Hill Rd.
County Rd.
Beach Rd.
Oak Bluffs
Oak Bluffs Beach
Joseph A. Sylvia State Beach
Edgartown
Edgartown Great Pond
Chappaquiddick Rd.
Herring Creek Rd.
Katama Rd.
South Beach
Three Ponds Preserve
Katama Beach (South Beach)
Wasque Beach
Wasque Point
Wasque Reservation
Poucha Pond Reservation
Poucha Pond
Chappaquiddick Island
Edgartown Lighthouse
Cape Poge Wildlife Refuge and Lighthouse
Cape Poge
East Beach
Katama Bay
Cape Poge Bay
Edgartown Harbor

TO NORTH KINGSTOWN, RI
TO NEW BEDFORD
TO WOODS HOLE
TO FALMOUTH
TO WOODS HOLE
TO WOODS HOLE
TO NEW BEDFORD
TO FALMOUTH
TO QUONSET POINT
TO HYANNIS
TO NANTUCKET (SUMMER ONLY)

0   6 km
0   4 miles

for a car). In summer and on autumn weekends, you must have a reservation if you want to bring your car; passenger reservations are never necessary.

The Island Queen makes the 35-minute trip from Falmouth Harbor to Oak Bluffs from late May through early October. Credit cards are not accepted for payment ($18 round-trip). The Vineyard Fast Ferry offers high-speed passenger service to Martha's Vineyard from North Kingstown, Rhode Island—a half-hour south of Providence and a half-hour northwest of Newport. The ride takes 90 minutes, making this a great option for those flying in to T. F. Green Airport, just south of Providence. Service is from late May through early October and costs $51 one-way or $74 round-trip.

Hy-Line offers both high-speed and conventional ferry service to Martha's Vineyard from Hyannis. The regular ferries offer a 95-minute run ($21.50) from Hyannis to Oak Bluffs early May to late October. The 55-minute high-speed ferry ($36) runs from late May through late November. Call to reserve a parking space in high season.

The New England Fast Ferry Company makes the hour-long trip by high-speed catamaran ($35) from New Bedford to Oak Bluffs and Vineyard Haven from mid-May to mid-October several times daily.

ESSENTIALS

Transportation Contacts Hy-Line (☎ *800/492–8082* ⊕ *www.hy-linecruises. com*). **Island Queen** (☎ *508/548–4800* ⊕ *www.islandqueen.com*). **Martha's Vineyard Airport** (MVY) (☎ *508/693–7022* ⊕ *www.mvyairport.com*). **Martha's Vineyard Transit Authority** (VTA ☎ *508/693–9940* ⊕ *www.vineyardtransit.com*). **New England Fast Ferry** (☎ *866/683–3779* ⊕ *www.nefastferry.com*). **Steamship Authority** (☎ *508/477–8600* ⊕ *www.steamshipauthority.com*). **Vineyard Fast Ferry** (☎ *401/295–4040* ⊕ *www.vineyardfastferry.com*).

SPORTS AND THE OUTDOORS

BEACHES **Lake Tashmoo Town Beach** (⊠ *End of Herring Creek Rd.*) provides swimmers with access to the warm, relatively shallow, brackish lake—or cooler, gentler Vineyard Sound. **Owen Park Beach** (⊠ *Off Main St.*), a small, sandy harbor beach, is just steps away from the ferry terminal in Vineyard Haven, making it a great spot to catch some last rays before heading home. **Tisbury Town Beach** (⊠ *End of Owen Little Way, off Main St.*) is a public beach next to the Vineyard Haven Yacht Club.

SHOPPING

Fodor's Choice ★ **Rainy Day** (⊠ *66 Main St.* ☎ *508/693–1830* ⊕ *www.rainydaymv.com*) carries gifts and amusements that are perfect for one of the island's gloomy rainy days. You'll find toys, crafts, cards, soaps, and more.

WHERE TO EAT AND STAY

$$$–$$$$

AMERICAN

✕ **Black Dog Tavern.** This island landmark, which is more popular with tourists than locals, lies just steps from the ferry terminal in Vineyard Haven. In July and August, the wait for breakfast (with an expansive omelet assortment) can be as much as an hour from 8 AM on. Why? Partly because the ambience inside—roaring fireplace, dark-wood walls, and a grand view of the water—makes everyone feel so at home. The menu is heavy on local fish, chowders, and chops. ⊠ *20 Beach St.*

Ext. ☎ *508/693–9223* ⊕ *www.theblackdog.com* ♨ *Reservations not accepted* ⊟ *AE, D, MC, V* ⑂ *BYOB.*

$$$–$$$$ 🏠 **Crocker House Inn.** This 1924 farmhouse-style inn is tucked into a
    ★   quiet lane off Main Street, minutes from the ferries and Owen Park
Beach. The rooms are decorated casually with understated flair—pastel-
painted walls, softly upholstered wingback chairs, and white-wicker
nightstands. No. 6, with a small porch and a private entrance, has the
best view of the harbor. **Pros:** great owners; short walk from town; easy-
going vibe. **Cons:** you pay a premium for this location; decor is more
casual than posh; books up quickly in summer. ⊠ *12 Crocker Ave.,
Box 1658* ☎ *508/693–1151 or 800/772–0206* ⊕ *www.crockerhouseinn.
com* ↰ *8 rooms* ⚘ *In-room: DVD, Wi-Fi. In-hotel: no kids under 12*
⊟ *MC, V* ⑂ *BP.*

OAK BLUFFS

3½ mi east of Vineyard Haven.

Circuit Avenue is the bustling center of the Oak Bluffs action, with
most of the town's shops, bars, and restaurants. Colorful gingerbread-
trimmed guesthouses and food and souvenir joints enliven Oak Bluffs
Harbor, once the setting for several grand hotels (the 1879 Wesley Hotel
on Lake Avenue is the last remaining one). This small town is more
high-spirited than haute, more fun than refined.

EXPLORING

East Chop Lighthouse. In 1876 this lighthouse was built out of cast iron to
replace an 1828 tower (used as part of a semaphore system of visual sig-
naling between the island and Boston) that burned down. The 40-foot
structure stands high atop a 79-foot bluff with spectacular views of
Nantucket Sound. ⊠ *E. Chop Dr.* ☎ *508/627–4441* ≦ *$3* ☉ *Late June–
mid-Sept., Sun. 1 hr before sunset–1 hr after sunset.*

☾ **Flying Horses Carousel.** This is the nation's oldest continuously operating
carousel and a National Historic Landmark. Handcrafted in 1876 (the
horses have real horsehair and glass eyes), the ride gives children a taste
of entertainment from a TV-free era. ⊠ *Oak Bluffs Ave.* ☎ *508/693–
9481* ≦ *Rides $1.50 each, book of 8 tickets $10* ☉ *Easter–late May,
weekends 10–5; late May–early Sept., daily 10–10; early Sept.–mid-Oct.,
weekdays 11–4:30, weekends 10–5; closed mid-Oct.–Easter.*

SPORTS AND THE OUTDOORS

BEACH **Joseph A. Sylvia State Beach** (⊠ *Between Oak Bluffs and Edgartown, off
Beach Rd.*) is a 2-mi-long sandy beach with a view of Cape Cod across
Nantucket Sound. Food vendors and calm, warm waters make this a
popular spot for families.

FISHING **Dick's Bait & Tackle** (⊠ *108 New York Ave.* ☎ *508/693–7669*) sells acces-
sories and bait and keeps a current copy of the fishing regulations.

GOLF **Farm Neck Golf Club** (⊠ *1 Farm Neck Way, off County Rd.* ☎ *508/693–
3057*), a semiprivate club on marsh-rimmed Sengekontacket Pond, has
a driving range and 18 holes in a championship layout. Reservations
are required 48 hours in advance.

NIGHTLIFE

The island's only family brewpub, **Offshore Ale** (⊠ *30 Kennebec Ave.* ☎ *508/693–2626* ⊕ *www.offshoreale.com*) hosts live Latin, folk, and blues year-round and serves its own beer and ales and a terrific pub menu. Cozy up to the fireplace with a pint on cool nights.

WHERE TO EAT AND STAY

$–$$
MEXICAN
★
✕ **Sharky's Cantina.** This small storefront restaurant serves tasty Mexican and Southwestern fare and great drinks, and you may wait awhile to get a table. But once you're in, savor spicy tortilla soup, lobster quesadillas, steak burritos, chicken mole, and skirt steak with chimichurri sauce. There's an extensive margarita list (they're strong here), and for dessert try apple-pie empanadas drizzled with caramel sauce. ⊠ *31 Circuit Ave.* ☎ *508/693–7501* ⊕ *www.sharkyscantina.com* ⌦ *Reservations not accepted* ⊟ *AE, MC, V.*

$$$$
AMERICAN
Fodor's Choice
★
✕ **Sweet Life Café.** Housed in a charming Victorian house, this island favorite's warm tones, low lighting, and handsome antique furniture will make you feel like you've entered someone's home, but the cooking is more sophisticated than home-style. Dishes on the menu are prepared in inventive ways; for example, duck breast is roasted with a lavender-rosemary-honey glaze, and the gazpacho is a white version with steamed clams, sliced red grapes, and smoked-paprika oil. ⊠ *63 Circuit Ave., at far end of town* ⊕ *www.sweetlifemv.com* ☎ *508/696–0200* ⌦ *Reservations essential* ⊟ *AE, D, MC, V* ☉ *Closed Jan.–Mar.*

$$–$$$
⌂ **Pequot Hotel.** The bustle of downtown Oak Bluffs is a pleasant five-minute walk past Carpenter Gothic houses from this casual cedar-shingle inn on a tree-lined street. The furniture is quirky but comfortable, and the old wing has more character. In the main section of the building, the first floor has a wide porch with rocking chairs—perfect for enjoying coffee or tea with the cookies that are set out in the afternoon—and a small breakfast room. Rooms vary in size and bedding arrangement, so be sure to specify your sleeping needs. The hotel is one block from the beaches that line Oak Bluffs–Edgartown Road. **Pros:** steps from shops and dining; reasonable rates; charmingly offbeat. **Cons:** dated decor; no room phones; some rooms are small. ⊠ *19 Pequot Ave.,* ☎ *508/693–5087 or 800/947–8704* ☐ *508/696–9413* ⊕ *www.pequothotel.com* ⌲ *31 rooms, 1 3-bedroom apartment* ⌂ *In-room: no phone, refrigerator (some), no TV (some). In-hotel: Wi-Fi* ⊟ *AE, D, MC, V* ☉ *Closed mid-Oct.–Apr.* ⎢⎜⎥ *CP.*

EDGARTOWN

6 mi southeast of Oak Bluffs.

Once a well-to-do whaling center, Edgartown remains the Vineyard's toniest town and has preserved parts of its elegant past. Sea captains' houses from the 18th and 19th centuries, with well-manicured gardens and lawns, line the streets.

SPORTS AND THE OUTDOORS

Felix Neck Wildlife Sanctuary. This 350-acre Massachusetts Audubon Society preserve 3 mi outside Edgartown toward Oak Bluffs and Vineyard Haven has 4 mi of hiking trails traversing marshland, fields, woods, seashore, and ponds. ✉ *Felix Neck Dr., off Edgartown–Vineyard Haven Rd.* 🕾 *508/627–4850* 🌁 *$4* ⊘ *Center May–Sept., Mon.–Sat. 9–4, Sun. 10–3; Oct.–Apr., weekdays 9–4, Sat. 10–2, closed Sun. Trails daily dawn to dusk.*

TAKE A TOUR

Liz Villard's **Vineyard History Tours** (🕾 *508/627–8619* ⊕ *www. mvpreservation.org/tours.html*) leads walking tours of Edgartown's "history, architecture, ghosts, and gossip," including a stop at the Vincent House. Tours run from April through December; call for times. Liz and her guides also lead similar tours of Oak Bluffs and Vineyard Haven. Walks last a little more than an hour.

OFF THE BEATEN PATH

A sparsely populated area with many nature preserves, where you can fish, **Chappaquiddick Island**, 1 mi southeast of Edgartown, makes for a pleasant day trip or bike ride on a sunny day. The "island" is actually connected to the Vineyard by a long sand spit that begins in South Beach in Katama. It's a spectacular 2¾-mi walk, or you can take the ferry, which departs about every five minutes. On the island's Mytoi preserve, a boardwalk runs through part of the grounds, where you're apt to see box turtles and hear the sounds of songbirds. Elsewhere you can fish, sunbathe, or even dip into the surf—use caution, as the currents are strong.

SHOPPING

David Le Breton, the owner of **Edgartown Books** (✉ *44 Main St.* 🕾 *508/ 627–8463* ⊕ *www.edgartownbooks.net*), is a true bibliophile. He carries a large selection of current and island-related titles and will be happy to make a summer reading recommendation. The **Old Sculpin Gallery** (✉ *58 Dock St.* 🕾 *508/627–4881* ⊕ *www.oldsculpingallery.org*) is the Martha's Vineyard Art Association's headquarters.

NIGHTLIFE

The **Atria Bar** (✉ *137 Main St.* 🕾 *508/627–5850* ⊕ *www.atriamv.com*) is off the beaten path, but it's a quiet, comfortable place to escape the summer crowds. **Outerland** (✉ *Martha's Vineyard Airport, 17 Airport Rd.* 🕾 *508/693–1137* ⊕ *www.outerlandmv.com*) books big-name acts such as Medeski, Martin and Wood, Ben Lee, Kate Taylor, and the Derek Trucks Band.

QUICK BITES

If you need a pick-me-up, pop into **Espresso Love** (✉ *17 Church St.* 🕾 *508/627–9211*) for a cappuccino and a homemade raspberry scone or blueberry muffin. If you prefer something cold, the staff also makes fruit smoothies. It's a great place for an inventive and hearty sandwich or a casual dinner; beer and wine are served also. At **Morning Glory Farm** (✉ *100 Meshacket Rd.* 🕾 *508/627–9003* ⊕ *www.morninggloryfarmstand. com*), fresh farm greens in the salads and vegetables in the soups; homemade pies, cookies, and cakes; and a picnic table and grass to enjoy them on make this an ideal place for a simple country lunch.

WHERE TO EAT AND STAY

$$$–$$$$ ✕ **Alchemy Bistro and Bar.** According to the menu, the definition of
FRENCH   "*alchemy*" is "a magic power having as its asserted aim the discovery
of a panacea and the preparation of the elixir of longevity"—lofty goals
for a French-style bistro. This high-class version has elegant gray wain-
scoting, classic paper-covered white tablecloths, old wooden floors, and
an opening cut into the ceiling to reveal the second-floor tables. The
only things missing are the patina of age, experience, cigarette smoke,
and French working folk's prices, but you can expect quality and imagi-
nation. One example is the fried cornmeal-dusted soft-shell crab with
lemon risotto, sweet peas, and artichokes. The alcohol list, long and
complete, includes cognac, grappa, and beer. On balmy evenings, the
half-dozen tables on the candlelit brick patio are highly coveted. ⊠ *71
Main St.* ☎ *508/627–9999* ⊕ *www.alchemymv.com* ⊟ *AE, MC, V.*

$$$$ ⬚ **Charlotte Inn.** From the moment you walk up to the dark-wood Scot-
Fodor'sChoice   tish barrister's check-in desk at this regal 1864 inn, you'll be surrounded
★   by the trappings and customs of a bygone era. The elegant atmosphere
that pervades the property extends to the inn's swank restaurant, The
Catch ($$$$). **Pros:** over-the-top lavish; quiet yet convenient location;
beautifully landscaped. **Cons:** can feel overly formal; intimidating if you
don't adore museum-quality antiques; no Internet access in the build-
ing. ⊠ *27 S. Summer St.* ☎ *508/627–4151 or 800/735–2478* ⊕ *www.
relaischateaux.com* ⇗ *21 rooms, 2 suites* ⚐ *In-room: DVD (some),
Wi-Fi, In-hotel: restaurant, no kids under 14* ⊟ *AE, MC, V* ⏴⎸ *CP.*

WEST TISBURY

8 mi west of Edgartown, 6½ mi south of Vineyard Haven.

West Tisbury retains its rural appeal and maintains its agricultural tradi-
tion at several active horse and produce farms. The town center looks
very much like a small New England village, complete with a white-
steepled church.

SHOPPING

Step back in time with a visit to **Alley's General Store** (⊠ *299 State Rd.*
☎ *508/693–0088*), the heart of town since 1858. Alley's sells a truly
general variety of goods: everything from hammers to housewares and
dill pickles to sweet muffins as well as great things you find only in a
country store. There's even a post office inside. Behind the parking lot,
Garcia's at Back Alley's serves tasty sandwiches and pastries to go.

SPORTS AND THE OUTDOORS

★   **Sepiessa Point Reservation.** A paradise for bird-watchers, this reservation
consists of 164 acres on splendid Tisbury Great Pond, with expan-
sive pond and ocean views, walking trails around coves and saltwater
marshes, bird-watching, horse trails, swimming, and a boat launch.
⊠ *New La., which becomes Tiah's Cove Rd., off W. Tisbury Rd.* ☎ *508/
627–7141* ⊠ *Free* ☉ *Daily sunrise–sunset.*

Sacred to the Wampanoag Tribe, the red-hued Aquinnah Cliffs are a popular attraction on Martha's Vineyard.

CHILMARK

5½ mi southwest of West Tisbury.

Chilmark is a rural village where ocean-view roads, rustic woodlands, and sparse crowds have drawn chic summer visitors and resulted in stratospheric real-estate prices. Laced with rough roads and winding stone fences that once separated fields and pastures, Chilmark reminds people of what the Vineyard was like in an earlier time, before the developers came.

SHOPPING

★ **Chilmark Chocolates** (⊠ *19 State Rd.* ☎ *508/645–3013*) sells superior chocolates and what might just be the world's finest butter crunch, which you can sometimes watch being made in the back room.

AQUINNAH

6½ mi west of Menemsha, 10 mi southwest of West Tisbury, 17 mi southwest of Vineyard Haven.

Aquinnah, called Gay Head until the town voted to change its name in 1997, is an official Native American township. The Wampanoag tribe is the guardian of the 420 acres that constitute the Aquinnah Native American Reservation. Aquinnah (pronounced a-*kwih*-nah) is Wampanoag for "land under the hill." You can get a good view of Menemsha and Nashaquitsa ponds, the woods, and the ocean beyond from Quitsa Pond Lookout on State Road. The town is best known for the red-hued Aquinnah Cliffs.

EXPLORING

Fodor's Choice
★

Aquinnah Cliffs. These spectacular cliffs, a National Historic Landmark, are part of the Wampanoag reservation land. The dramatically striated walls of red clay are the island's major attraction, as evidenced by the tour bus–filled parking lot. Native American crafts and food shops line the short approach to the overlook, from which you can see the Elizabeth Islands to the northeast across Vineyard Sound and Nomans Land Island—part wildlife preserve, part military bombing-practice site—3 mi off the Vineyard's southern coast. The brick **Aquinnah Lighthouse** (⊠ *Lighthouse Rd.* ☎ *508/645–2211* 💲 *$5* ☺ *Summer, Fri.—Sun. at sunset, weather permitting*) is stationed precariously atop the rapidly eroding cliffs. ⊠ *State Rd.*

NANTUCKET

At the height of its prosperity in the early 19th century, the little island of Nantucket was the foremost whaling port in the world. Its harbor bustled with whaling ships and merchant vessels; chandleries, cooperages, and other shops crowded the wharves. Burly ship hands loaded barrels of whale oil onto wagons, which they wheeled along cobblestone streets to refineries and candle factories. Sea breezes carried the smoke and smells of booming industry through town as its inhabitants eagerly took care of business. Shipowners and sea captains built elegant mansions, which today remain remarkably unchanged, thanks to a very strict building code initiated in the 1950s. The entire town of Nantucket is now an official National Historic District encompassing more than 800 pre-1850 structures within 1 square mi.

Day-trippers usually take in the architecture and historical sites, dine at one of the many delightful restaurants, and browse in the pricey boutiques, most of which stay open from mid-April through December. Signature items include Nantucket lightship baskets, originally crafted by sailors whiling away a long watch; artisans who continue the tradition now command prices of $700 and up, and the antiques are exponentially more expensive.

NANTUCKET TOWN

30 mi southeast of Hyannis, 107 mi southeast of Boston.

Nantucket Town has one of the country's finest historical districts, with beautiful 18th- and 19th-century architecture and a museum of whaling history.

GETTING HERE AND AROUND

Arriving by ferry puts you in the center of town. There is little need for a car here to explore; ample public transportation and smoothly paved bike paths can take you to the further reaches with ease. The Nantucket Regional Transit Authority (NRTA) runs shuttle buses from in town to most areas of the island. Service is generally available from late May to mid-October.

Each beach on Nantucket has a unique approach—sometimes getting there is half the fun.

AIR TRAVEL Year-round flight service to Nantucket from Boston and Hyannis is provided by Cape Air, Island Airlines, and Nantucket Airlines. U.S. Airways Express offers seasonal service to the island from Washington, D.C., Philadelphia, and New York's LaGuardia; from Newark Airport in New Jersey, Continental Express provides a seasonal route to the island.

FERRY TRAVEL Hy-Line's high-end, high-speed Grey Lady ferries run between Hyannis and Nantucket year-round in an hour ($39). Hy-Line's slower ferry makes the roughly two-hour trip from Hyannis between early May and late October. The MV *Great Point* offers a first-class section ($28) with a private lounge and a bar or a standard fare ($21.50).

The Steamship Authority runs car-and-passenger ferries from Hyannis year-round, a 2¼-hour trip ($16.50 for passenger fare; $130–$190 for a car). There's also high-speed passenger ferry service, which takes only an hour, from late March through late December ($32.50).

In season, the passenger-only (some bikes allowed) ferry from Harwich Port to Nantucket is a less hectic alternative to the Hyannis crowd. The Freedom Cruise Line runs express high-speed 75-minute ferries between late May and early October ($39).

ESSENTIALS

Transportation Contacts Freedom Cruise Line (☎ 508/432–8999 ⊕ www. nantucketislandferry.com). **Hy-Line** (☎ 800/492–8082 ⊕ www.hy-linecruises. com). **Nantucket Airport** (ACK) (☎ 508/325–5300 ⊕ www.nantucketairport. com). **Nantucket Regional Transit Authority (NRTA)** (✉ 3 E. Chestnut St. ☎ 508/228–7025 ⊕ www.shuttlenantucket.com) **Steamship Authority** (☎ 508/477–8600 ⊕ www.steamshipauthority.com).

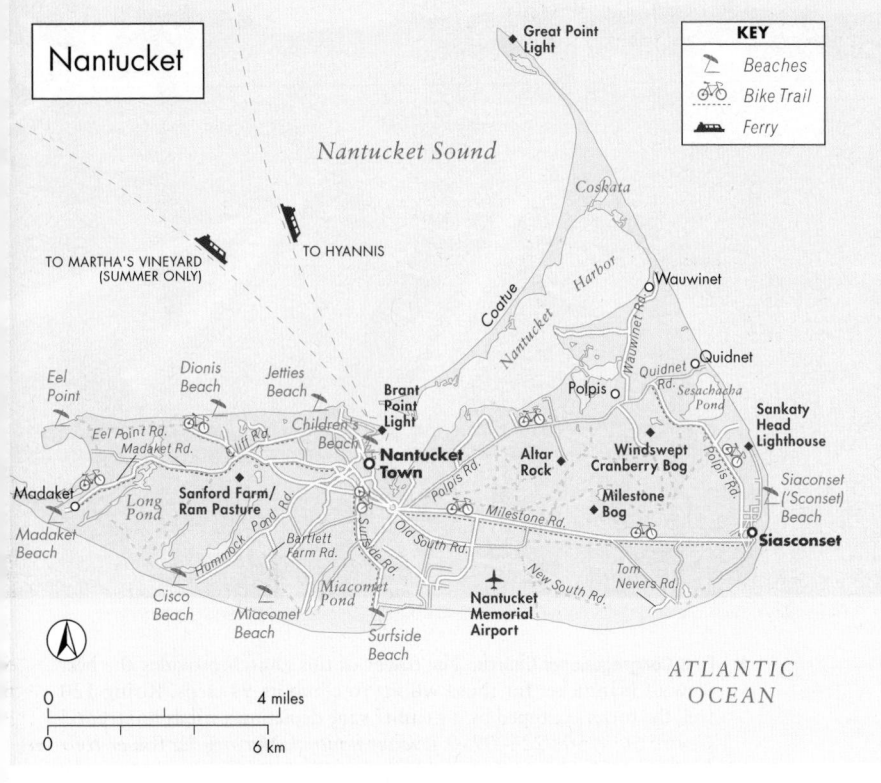

Nantucket

KEY

- Beaches
- Bike Trail
- Ferry

Nantucket Sound

Great Point Light

TO MARTHA'S VINEYARD (SUMMER ONLY)

TO HYANNIS

Coskata

Coatue

Nantucket

Harbor

Wauwinet

Wauwinet Rd.

Quidnet

Quidnet

Polpis

Sesachacha Pond

Sankaty Head Lighthouse

Eel Point

Dionis Beach

Jetties Beach

Brant Point Light

Children's Beach

Nantucket Town

Altar Rock

Windswept Cranberry Bog

Polpis Rd.

Siasconset ('Sconset) Beach

Eel Point Rd.
Madaket Rd.

Cliff Rd.

Madaket

Sanford Farm/ Ram Pasture

Long Pond

Hummock Pond Rd.

Polpis Rd.

Milestone Bog

Siasconset

Madaket Beach

Bartlett Farm Rd.

Milestone Rd.

Old South Rd.

Surfside Rd.

Cisco Beach

Miacomet Pond

Miacomet Beach

Surfside Beach

Nantucket Memorial Airport

New South Rd.

Tom Nevers Rd.

ATLANTIC OCEAN

0 ___ 4 miles

0 ___ 6 km

Visitor Information **Nantucket Island Chamber of Commerce** (✉ *Zero Main St., 2nd floor* ☎ *508/228–1700* ⊕ *www.nantucketchamber.org*). **Nantucket Visitor Services and Information Bureau** (✉ *25 Federal St.* ☎ *508/228–0925* ⊕ *www.nantucket-ma.gov/Pages/NantucketMA_Visitor/index*).

EXPLORING

Fodor'sChoice ★ **Nantucket Historical Association (NHA)** (✉ *15 Broad St.* ☎ *508/228–1894* ⊕ *www.nha.org*). An assortment of venerable properties in town, including the gloriously expanded Whaling Museum, are maintained by the NHA. An $18 pass gets you into all of the association's sites.

African Meeting House. When the island abolished slavery in 1773, Nantucket became a destination for free blacks and escaping slaves. The African Meeting House was built in the 1820s as a schoolhouse, and it functioned as such until 1846, when the island's schools were integrated. A complete restoration has returned the site to its authentic 1880s appearance. ✉ *29 York St.* ☎ *508/228–9833* ⊕ *www.afroammuseum. org* ⊡ *Free* ⊗ *June–Oct., weekdays 11–3, Sat. 11–1, Sun. 1–3.*

Brant Point Light. This 26-foot-tall, white-painted beauty has views of the harbor and town. The point was once the site of the second-oldest lighthouse in the country (1746); the present, much-photographed light was built in 1902. ✉ *End of Easton St., across footbridge.*

When farmers flood cranberry fields during harvest season, the ripe crimson fruit floats to the surface.

★ **First Congregational Church.** The tower of this church provides the best view of Nantucket for those willing to climb its 94 steps. Rising 120 feet, the tower is capped by a weather vane depicting a whale hunt. ⊠ *62 Centre St.* ☎ *508/228–0950* ⊕ *www.nantucketfcc.org* ✉ *Tower tour $2.50* ⊙ *Mid-June–mid-Oct., Mon.–Sat. 10–4; Daffodil and Memorial Day weekends, Fri. and Sat.; services Sun. 10 AM.*

Fodor's Choice
★

☾ **Whaling Museum.** Immersing you in Nantucket's whaling past with exhibits that include a fully rigged whaleboat and a skeleton of a 46-foot sperm whale, the Whaling Museum—a complex that includes a restored 1846 spermaceti candle factory—is a must-see. Items on view in the handsome galleries include harpoons and other whale-hunting implements, portraits of whaling captains and their wives, a large collection of sailors' crafts, and the original 16-foot-high 1850 lens from Sankaty Head Lighthouse. ⊠ *13–15 Broad St.* ☎ *508/228–1894* ✉ *$15 or $18 NHA Combination Pass* ⊙ *May–Oct., daily 10–5; Nov. and Dec., Thurs.–Mon. 11–4; Jan.–Apr. call for hours.*

SPORTS AND THE OUTDOORS

BEACH
☾
★

A short bike- or shuttle- ride from town, **Jetties Beach** (⊠ *Bathing Beach Rd., 1½ mi from Straight Wharf*) is popular with families because of its calm surf, lifeguards, bathhouse, restrooms, and snack bar.

BOATING **Nantucket Community Sailing** (⊠ *4 Winter St.* ☎ *508/228–6600* ⊕ *www. nantucketcommunitysailing.org*) rents Sunfish sailboats, sailboards, and kayaks from Jetties Beach, mid-June to Labor Day. Sailing instructional programs are offered for all ages.

SHOPPING

ARTWORK The **Artists' Association of Nantucket** (⊠ *19 Washington St.* ☎ *508/228–0294* ⊕ *www.nantucketarts.org*), housed in the Joyce & Seward Johnson Gallery, is the best place to get an overview of the work being done on the island; many members have galleries of their own. **Nantucket Looms** (⊠ *16 Federal St.* ☎ *508/228–1908* ⊕ *www.nantucketlooms.com*) stocks luscious woven-on-the-premises textiles and chunky Susan Lister Locke jewelry, among other adornments for self and home.

TAKE A TOUR

Sixth-generation Nantucketer Gail Johnson of **Gail's Tours** (☎ *508/257-6557* ⊕ *www.nantucket.net/tours/gails*) narrates a lively 1½-hour van tour of the island's highlights: moors, cranberry bogs, and lighthouses, in addition to Nantucket Town.

NIGHTLIFE AND THE ARTS

The **Chicken Box** (⊠ *14 Dave St., off Lower Orange St.* ☎ *508/228–9717* ⊕ *www.thechickenbox.com*) rocks! Live music plays six nights a week in season and on weekends throughout the year. The **Muse** (⊠ *44 Surfside Rd.* ☎ *508/228–6873* ⊕ *www.228-muse.com*) is *the* place to catch big-name acts year-round.

WHERE TO EAT AND STAY

$-$$ ✕ **Fog Island Café.** Cherished year-round for its exceptional breakfasts,
AMERICAN Fog Island is just as fine a spot for lunch—and on weekends in season,
ⓒ a charitably priced dinner. The chef-owners Mark and Anne Dawson—both Culinary Institute of America grads—seem determined to provide the best possible value to transients and natives alike. Consider starting the day with pesto scrambled eggs and ending it with sesame-crusted tuna with Thai noodles. ⊠ *7 S. Water St.* ☎ *508/228–1818* ⊕ *www.fogisland.com* ═ *MC, V.*

$$$$ 🏨 **Nantucket Whaler.** Let's not mince words: the rooms and suites carved
★ out of this 1850 Greek Revival house are gorgeous. Each suite has a private entrance and a kitchen. The spacious bedrooms are lavished with flowers, well-chosen antiques, and fine linens, including plush robes. **Pros:** pretty rooms with designer style; details not overlooked; romantic. **Cons:** no real reception area; lacks a common room; the usual in-town noise. ⊠ *8 N. Water St., Box 1337* ☎ *508/228–6597 or 888/808–6597* 🖷 *508/228–6291* ⊕ *www.nantucketwhaler.com* ⤴ *4 rooms, 6 suites* ⌂ *In-room: no phone, refrigerator, DVD, Wi-Fi. In-hotel: no kids under 11* ═ *AE, MC, V* ⊗ *Closed Jan. and Feb.*

$$$-$$$$ 🏨 **Union Street Inn.** With experience in both the hotel business and high-
Fodor'sChoice end retail display, husband and wife team Ken and Deborah With-
★ row give guests the best of both worlds. This 1770 house, a stone's throw from the bustle of Main Street, has been respectfully yet lavishly restored. Guests are treated to Frette linens, plump duvets, and lush robes, as well as a full gourmet breakfast served on the tree-shaded garden patio. Some rooms have a wood-burning fireplace. **Pros:** pampering by pros; romantic. **Cons:** no nearby beach; some small rooms. ⊠ *7 Union St.* ☎ *508/228–9222 or 888/517–0707* ⊕ *www.unioninn.com* ⤴ *12 rooms* ⌂ *In-room: Wi-Fi. In-hotel: no kids under 12* ═ *AE, MC, V* ⊘| *BP.*

SIASCONSET

★ *7 mi east of Nantucket Town.*

First a fishing outpost and then an artist's colony (Broadway actors favored it in the late 19th century), Siasconset—or 'Sconset, in the local vernacular—is a charming cluster of rose-covered cottages linked by driveways of crushed clamshells; at the edges of town, the former fishing shacks give way to magnificent sea-view mansions. The small town center consists of a market, post office, café, lunchroom, and a combination liquor store–lending library.

EXPLORING

Altar Rock. Altar Rock Road, a dirt track about 3 mi west of the Milestone Road Rotary on Polpis Road, leads to the island's highest point. The spectacular view includes open moor and bog land—technically called lowland heath—which is very rare in the United States. The entire area is laced with paths leading in every direction.

SPORTS AND THE OUTDOORS

BIKING   The 6½-mi **'Sconset Bike Path** starts at the rotary east of Nantucket Town and parallels Milestone Road, ending in 'Sconset. It is mostly level, with some gentle hills.

WHERE TO EAT AND STAY

$$$$ ✕ **Topper's.** The Wauwinet—a lavishly restored 19th-century inn on
ECLECTIC   Nantucket's northeastern shore—is where islanders and visitors alike
★   go to experience utmost luxury. You can order right from the menu or opt for the three-course prix fixe ($87); there's also the four-course clambake dinner offered for $49. David Daniel's cuisine delivers a menu of intentional "simplicity"—if that's how you would describe a "surf and turf" of butter-basted lobster in a carrot-yuzu (a Japanese citrus fruit) broth with foie-gras-and-Kobe-beef dim sum. ⊠ *120 Wauwinet Rd., Wauwinet* ☎ *508/228–8768* ⊕ *www.wauwinet.com* ⚱ *Reservations essential* ⊟ *AE, D, DC, MC, V* ⊘ *Closed mid-Oct.–Apr.*

$$$$ ⊡ **Wauwinet.** This resplendently updated 1850 resort straddles a "haulo-
Fodor's Choice   ver" poised between ocean and bay—which means beaches on both
★   sides. Head out by complimentary van or launch to partake of utmost pampering. Of course, it's tempting just to stay put, what with the cushy country-chic rooms (lavished with Pratesi linens) and a splendid restaurant, Topper's. **Pros:** solicitous staff; dual beaches; peaceful setting; town shuttle. **Cons:** distance from town; tiny rooms on the third floor. ⊠ *120 Wauwinet Rd., Wauwinet* ⊕ *Box 2580, Nantucket 02584* ☎ *508/228–0145 or 800/426–8718* 🖷 *508/228–7135* ⊕ *www.wauwinet.com* ⇩ *25 rooms, 5 cottages* ⚙ *In-room: safe, DVD, Wi-Fi. In-hotel: restaurant, room service, bar, tennis courts, spa, beachfront, bicycles, no kids under 12* ⊟ *AE, DC, MC, V* ⊘ *Closed mid-Oct.–Apr.* ⎮⚬⎮ *BP.*

The Berkshires and Western Massachusetts

WELCOME TO WESTERN MASSACHUSETTS AND THE BERKSHIRES

TOP REASONS TO GO

★ **The Countryside:** Rolling hills, dense stands of forest, open pastures, even a few mountains.

★ **Early American History:** Visit preserved villages, homes, and inns where memories of Colonial history and personalities are kept alive.

★ **Summer Festivals:** Watch-renowned dance companies perform against the Berkshire mountains backdrop at Jacob's Pillow or have the Boston Symphony Orchestra accompany your lawn picnic at Tanglewood in Lenox.

★ **Under-the-Radar Museums:** Western Massachusetts has an eclectic collection of institutions, from the Eric Carle Museum of Picture Book Art to the Basketball Hall of Fame.

★ **College Towns:** The Pioneer Valley is home to some lovely academic centers: Amherst (University of Massachusetts, Amherst College, and Hampshire College), Northampton (Smith College), and South Hadley (Mount Holyoke College).

1 **The Berkshires.** The "hills" you'll see here are actually part of the same range that contains Vermont's Green Mountains. And though it's only a few hours from Boston or New York City, a trip to the Berkshires is an escape from all things urban. This is a place of ski resorts and winding forest drives, leaf-peeping and gallery browsing. There are extreme sports and extreme spas. If you're looking for a place to recharge your batteries and your soul, you'll be hard-pressed to find a better option in the Northeast.

2 **Sturbridge and the Pioneer Valley.** Often overshadowed by Boston to the East and the Berkshires to the West, the Pioneer Valley is filled with historic settlements and college towns, natural treasures, and unique museums. Old Sturbridge Village, a recreated an early-19th-century village with restored historic buildings, reenactments, and activities, is the premier attraction here. The main city, Springfield, is home to the Naismith Memorial Basketball Hall of Fame, but most of the area is quite rural—this is where the idyllic New England countryside you've imagined comes to life.

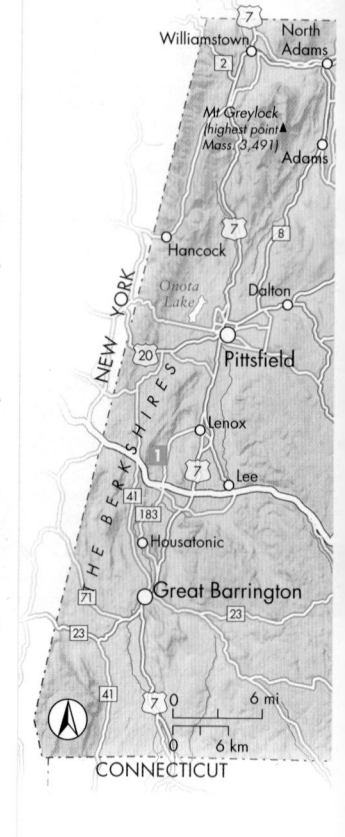

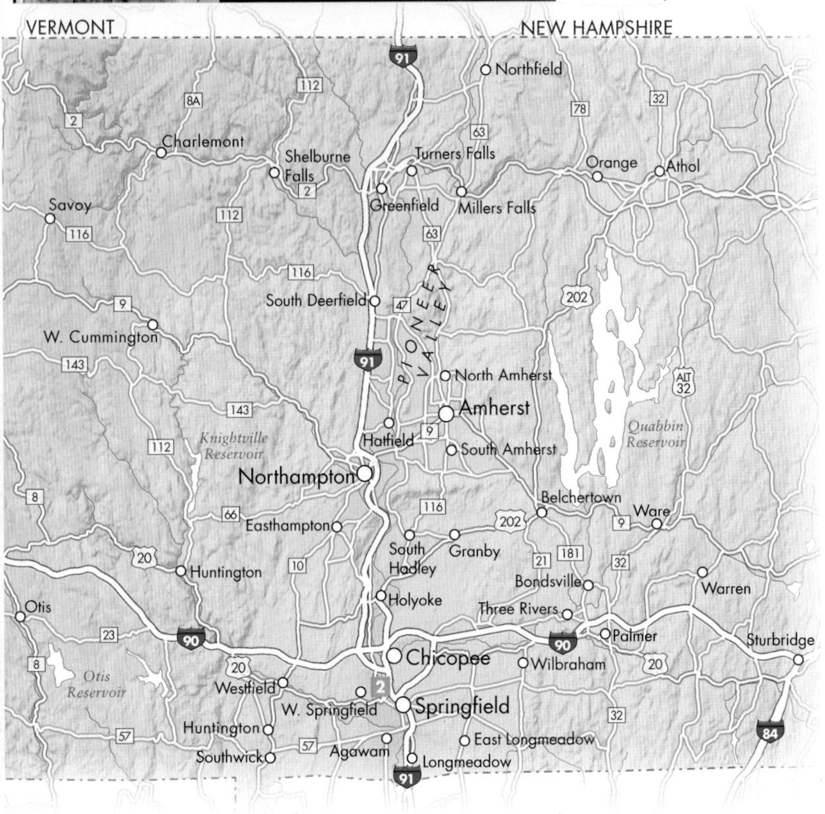

VERMONT

NEW HAMPSHIRE

4

GETTING ORIENTED

Interstate 90 (the Massachusetts Turnpike) leads west from Boston to the Berkshires. The main north–south road within the Berkshires is U.S. 7. Highway 2 runs from the northern Berkshires to

Greenfield at the head of the Pioneer Valley and continues across Massachusetts into Boston. The scenic section of Highway 2 known as the Mohawk Trail runs from Williamstown to Orange. Interstate 91 runs north–south in the Pioneer Valley in western Massachusetts.

WESTERN MASSACHUSETTS AND THE BERKSHIRES PLANNER

When to Go

The dazzling foliage and cool temperatures make fall the best time to visit western Massachusetts, but the Berkshires and the Pioneer Valley are increasingly a year-round destination. Visit in spring, and witness the burst of color that signals winter's end. Summer is a time of festivals, adventure sports, and outdoor concerts.

Many towns save their best for winter—inns open their doors to carolers and shops serve eggnog. The off-season is the perfect time to try cross-country skiing or spend a night by the fire, tucked under a quilt, catching up on books by Nathaniel Hawthorne or Henry David Thoreau.

Getting Here and Around

Bradley International Airport in Windsor Locks, Connecticut, 18 mi south of Springfield on Interstate 91, serves the Pioneer Valley and the Berkshires.

Most travelers arrive at Boston's Logan International Airport, the state's major airline hub. From Boston, you can reach most parts of the Pioneer Valley in less than two hours by car, and the Berkshires are about three hours' drive from Bean Town.

Other airport alternatives include Manchester Boston Regional Airport in New Hampshire, 50 mi northwest of Boston, and T. F. Green International Airport in Providence, Rhode Island, 59 mi south of Boston.

By Train and Transit: The Northeast Corridor and high-speed Acela services of Amtrak link Boston with the principal cities between it and Washington, D.C. Amtrak's Lake Shore Limited, which stops at Springfield and Pittsfield in the Berkshires, carries passengers from Chicago to Boston. For destinations north and west of Boston, trains depart from Boston's North Station.

Train Information Amtrak (☎ *800/872–7245* ⊕ *www.amtrak.com*).

Visitor Information

Massachusetts Office of Travel & Tourism (✉ *10 Park Plaza, Suite 4510, Boston* ☎ *617/973–8500; 800/447–6277 brochures* ⊕ *www.massvacation.com*).

About the Restaurants

At country inns in the Berkshires and the Pioneer Valley you find creative contemporary fare as well as traditional New England dinners strongly reminiscent of old England: double-cut pork chops, rack of lamb, game, Boston baked beans, Indian pudding, and the dubiously glorified "New England boiled dinner" (meat and vegetables slow-boiled). Even though the area is landlocked, it's still possible to get great seafood.

Love your international foods? You won't be disappointed in Western Massachusetts. The area may be the polar opposite of urban areas like Boston, but that doesn't mean you won't find global cuisine like Polish, Thai, and South American.

About the Hotels

The signature accommodation outside Boston is the country inn; in the Berkshires, where magnificent mansions have been converted into lodgings, the inns reach a very grand scale indeed. Less extravagant and less expensive are bed-and-breakfast establishments, many of them in private homes. Make reservations for inns well in advance during peak periods (summer through winter in the Berkshires). Smoking is banned in all Massachusetts hotels.

Campers can pitch their tents amid acres of pine forest dotted with rivers and lakes or in the shadows of the rolling Berkshire Hills. The camping season in Massachusetts generally runs from Memorial Day to Columbus Day. For more about camping, contact the Massachusetts Department of Conservation and Recreation (☎ *617/626–1250* ⊕ *www. mass.gov/dcr/forparks.htm*).

Outdoor Activities

If you want to reconnect with nature, this is the place. You will be hard pressed to find a skyscraper or a Starbucks. A hiking trail? No problem. A gurgling stream or quiet forest? A dime a dozen. Western Massachusetts is the polar opposite of its eastern side. When you've had enough of Boston's excitement, head here for peace.

Boating: With numerous lakes, rivers, and ponds throughout western Massachusetts, the region is rife with opportunities for sailing, canoeing, kayaking, rafting, and boating. For more information, contact **Mass Outdoors** (☎ *617/626–1600* ⊕ *www.sport.state.ma.us*).

Fishing: For information about fishing and licenses, call the **Massachusetts Division of Fisheries & Wildlife** (☎ *617/626–1600* ⊕ *www. mass.gov*).

WHAT IT COSTS

	¢	$	$$	$$$	$$$$
Restaurants	under $8	$8–$14	$15–$24	$25–$32	over $32
Hotels		under $75	$75–$150	$151–$225	$226–$325	over $325

For restaurants, prices are per person, for a main course at dinner. For hotels, prices are for two people in a standard double room in high season, excluding 12.45% tax and service charges.

MASSACHUSETTS FALL FOLIAGE DRIVE

When fall foliage season arrives, the Berkshires are the place to appreciate this autumnal grandeur. Winding roads lined with the drama of trees ablaze pass alongside meadows, pasture, farmland, mountains, rivers, and lakes. Although this complete scenic loop is only about 35 mi, you could easily spend the day making your way leisurely along the circuit.

BEST TIME TO GO

Peak season for leaf viewing in the Berkshires generally happens in mid-October. Trees growing near waterways—and they are plentiful in the area—tend to have more vibrant colors that peak a bit sooner than those elsewhere. The state regularly updates fall foliage information by phone and online (☎ 800/632–8038 ⊕ *www.massvacation. com*).

Begin in North Adams, a city transformed by art, and spend some time at the Massachusetts Museum of Contemporary Art (MASS MoCA). Just west of downtown off Route 2, the Notch Road leads into the **Mt. Greylock State Reservation**, ambling upward to the summit. At 3,491 feet, it's the state's highest point and affords expansive views of the countryside. Hike any of the many trails throughout the park, picnic at the peak, or stay for a meal at the rustic **Bascom Lodge**—you could spend several hours here. Continue your descent on the Notch Road to Rockwell Road to exit the park and join Route 7 South.

Follow Route 7 South into the small town center of Lanesborough, where you'll turn left onto Summer Street. Horse farms and wide-open pastures make up the landscape, with distant mountain peaks hovering grandly in the background. If you want to pick your own apples, take a 1½-mi detour off Summer St. and stop at **Lakeview Orchard.**

Summer Street continues to tiny Berkshire Village, where you'll pick up Route 8 heading back toward North Adams. Running parallel to Route 8 from Lanesborough to Adams, is the paved **Ashuwillticook Rail Trail** for biking and walking. Right in the midst of two mountain ranges, the trail abuts wetlands, woods, the Hoosic River, and the Cheshire Reservoir. In Cheshire, **Whitney's Farm Market** is busy on fall weekends with pony rides, pumpkin picking, a corn maze, and hayrides; plus baked goods like the pumpkin whoopie pie.

Continuing on Route 8, you'll start to leave farm country as you make your way back to North Adams. Once a part of its much larger neighbor, the town of Adams still has active mills and the **Susan B. Anthony Birthplace Museum** opened in 2010. The 1817 Federal home of her birth has been fully restored.

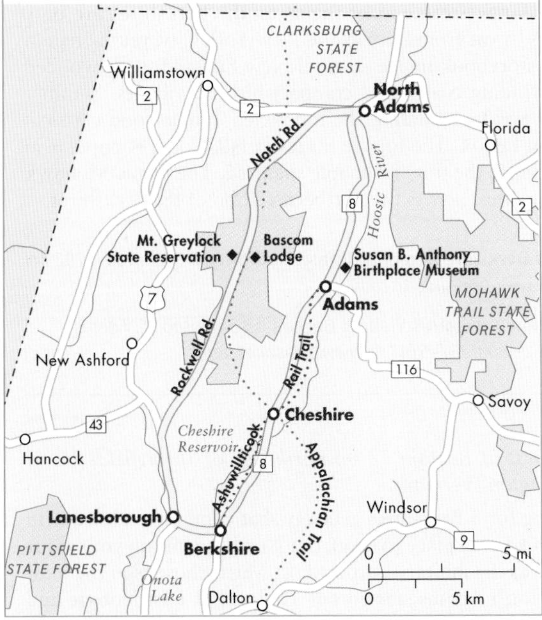

NEED A BREAK?

At **Lakeview Orchard** (✉ 94 Old Cheshire Rd., Lanesboro ☎ 413/448–6009 ⊕ www.lakevieworchard. com ⊗ Open Tues.–Sun., early July through Halloween) pick your own bushel of apples and sample freshly pressed hot cider.

Passing through the Hoosic River Valley, walkers and cyclists enjoy the paved **11-mi Ashuwillticook Rail Trail** (⊕ www.mass.gov/dcr/ parks/western/asrt.htm).

Berkshire Outfitters (✉ 169 Grove St., Adams ☎ 413/743–5900 ⊕ www. berkshireoutfitters.com ⊗ Mon.–Sat. 10–5, Sun. 11–4) has bicycle, kayak, snowshoe, and cross-country ski rentals.

Whitney's Farm (✉ 1775 South State Rd. [Rte. 8], Cheshire ☎ 413/442–4749 ⊕ www.whitneysfarm.com ⊗ Daily, hours vary) has a large market with produce, bakery items, and flowers.

Susan B. Anthony Birthplace Museum (✉ 67 East Rd., ☎ 413/ 743–7121 ⊕ www. susanbanthonybirthplace. com ⌦ $8 ⊗ Thurs.–Mon. 11–4, Memorial Day to Columbus Day) celebrates the extraordinary life and legacy of Susan B. Anthony and her family.

4

Map:

CLARKSBURG STATE FOREST

Williamstown ② ②

North Adams

Natch Rd.

8

Florida

Hoosic River

2

Mt. Greylock State Reservation ◆ ◆ Bascom Lodge

Susan B. Anthony Birthplace Museum ◆

Adams

MOHAWK TRAIL STATE FOREST

⑦

Rockwell Rd.

Rail Trail

New Ashford

116

Savoy

43

Cheshire Reservoir

Cheshire

Ashuwillticook

Appalachian Trail

8

Hancock

Windsor

9

Lanesborough ○

Berkshire

PITTSFIELD STATE FOREST

Onota Lake

Dalton

0   5 mi

0   5 km

Updated by Michael Nalepa

Rolling terrain defines the landscape of Western Massachusetts. The Pioneer Valley, which runs north-to-south through the heart of the Bay State, is home to elite institutions like Amherst, Williams, and Smith. Farther west, the Berkshires are even more rural, relaxed, and hilly. The area is also a bastion of arts and culture: countless craftspeople, small museums, and artisans call the Berkshires home.

THE BERKSHIRES

Occupying the far western end of the state, the Berkshires are only about 2½ hours by car from Boston and New York City, yet the region lives up to the storybook image of rural New England, with wooded hills, narrow winding roads, and compact historic villages. Summer brings cultural events, including the renowned Tanglewood classical music festival in Lenox. The foliage blazes in fall, skiing is popular in winter, and spring is the time for maple sugaring. The scenic Mohawk Trail runs east to west across the northern section of the Berkshires.

ESSENTIALS

Bus Information Berkshire Regional Transit Authority (📞 413/499–2782 or 800/292–2782 ⊕ www.berkshirerta.com).

Visitor Information Berkshires Visitors Bureau (✉ 3 Hoosac St., Adams 📞 413/743–4500 or 800/237–5747 ⊕ www.berkshires.org).

NORTH ADAMS

130 mi northwest of Boston; 73 mi northwest of Springfield; 20 mi south of Bennington, Vermont.

If you're looking for a Berkshires getaway that combines culture with outdoor fun (and a cool place to stay), put North Adams on your short list. Established as the military outpost Fort Massachusetts in the mid-18th century, North Adams started out as a part of East Hoosac and then became part of Adams before incorporating as its own city in the late 19th century. By then its economy had become dependent upon its textile industry. After North Adams became a strong producer of electrical and radio parts, its fortunes waned following World War II.

In the recent past, however, the city has staged an impressive comeback as a center of contemporary art. In addition to the Massachusetts Museum of Contemporary Arts (Mass MoCA), North Adams has mills and factory buildings that have been converted to artists' studios and residences. (The town's Downstreet Art boasts 33 galleries in a four-block area.) The Porches Inn, a row of eye-catching multihued Victorians, has added an additional helping of hip to downtown. In addition, the 11-mi Ashuwillticook Rail Trail is easily accessible in nearby Adams, as is Mount Greylock State Reservation, if you explore it by foot via one of the local trailheads.

EXPLORING

At 13 acres, the **Massachusetts Museum of Contemporary Arts** (⊠ *87 Marshall St.* ☎ *413/664–4111* ⊕ *www.massmoca.org* ☜ *$15* ⊙ *July and Aug., daily 10–6; Sept.–June, Wed.–Mon. 11–5*) is the nation's largest center for contemporary performing and visual arts. The huge 19th-century complex of 27 buildings once housed the now-defunct Sprague Electric Co. Six of the factory buildings have been transformed into more than 250,000 square feet of galleries, studios, performance venues, cafés, and shops. Its size enables the museum to display monumentally scaled works such as Robert Rauschenberg's ¼ *Mile or 2 Furlong Piece*. Exhibits and performances include everything from art shows and concerts to dance and film presentations.

Fodor's Choice ★

North Adams Museum of History & Science. North Adams's best kept secret, this museum has more than 25 permanent exhibits on three floors of a building that was once part of a railroad yard. A store sells local historical society publications. ⊠ *Western Gateway Heritage State Park, Bldg. 5A, State St.* ☎ *413/664–4700* ☜ *Free* ⊙ *Nov.–Apr., Sat. 10–4, Sun. 1–4; May–Oct., Thurs.–Sat. 10–4, Sun. 1–4.*

Western Gateway Heritage State Park. This park occupies the old Boston & Maine Railroad yard. The visitor center houses exhibits that trace the impact of train travel on the region. A 30-minute documentary provides a look at the intense labor that went into the construction of the nearby Hoosac Tunnel. ⊠ *115 State St.* ☎ *413/663–6312* ☜ *Free* ⊙ *Visitor center daily 10–5.*

QUICK BITES

A North Adams institution since 1917, **Jack's Hot Dog Stand** is where locals go for a frank. This hole-in-the-wall also serves burgers and fries. It's cash only and there is minimal seating (⊠ *12 Eagle St.* ☎ *413/664–9006* ⊕ *www.jackshotdogstand.com*).

SPORTS AND THE OUTDOORS

★ The city's 48-acre is **Natural Bridge State Park** (⊠ *Hwy. 8* ☎ *413/663–6392* ⊕ *www.mass.gov/dcr*) was named for the 30-foot span that crosses Hudson Brook. The marble arch at park's center rises in what was a marble quarry from the early 1880s to the mid-1900s. There are picnic sites, hiking trails, and well-maintained restrooms. In winter the park is popular for cross-country skiing.

KAYAKING If you're itching to explore the Cheshire (Hoosic) lakes by kayak, Ashuwillticook Rail Trail by bike, or Mt. Greylock's summit on snowshoes, visit **Berkshire Outfitters** (⌧ *Hwy. 8, Adams* ☎ *413/743–5900* ⊕ *www.berkshireoutfitters.com*). Just 300 yards from the Rail Trail, this shop rents bicycles, kayaks, canoes, Nordic skis, and snowshoes, and has a very knowledgeable staff.

THE ARTS

Down Street Art (⊕ *www.downstreetart.org*) is a public art project with 33 member art galleries in downtown North Adams. (The city has more contemporary art spaces than any town in the Berkshires.)

WHERE TO EAT

$$–$$$ ✕ **Gramercy Bistro.** Occupying what was once a downtown diner, this
AMERICAN casual, upbeat eatery has developed a loyal following. The intimate
★ space, with a wood-beam ceiling and walls lined with black-and-white photos of the town, serves an eclectic menu, ranging from sautéed sweetbreads to an irresistible paella. Chef-owner Alexander Smith relies on organic meats and locally grown produce when possible, adding serious zip with sauces made from wasabi and fire-roasted poblano peppers. Come by on weekends for the memorable brunch. ⌧ *26 Marshall St.* ☎ *413/663–5300* ⊕ *www.gramercybistro.com* ▭ *AE, MC, V* ☾ *Closed Tues. No lunch.*

WHERE TO STAY

$$–$$$ ⬚ **Porches Inn.** These once-dilapidated mill-workers' houses dating from
Fodor's Choice the 1890s were refurbished to become one of New England's quirkiest
★ hotels. They now strike a perfect balance between high-tech and historic—rooms have a mix of retro 1940s and '50s lamps and bungalow-style furnishings along with stunning bathrooms with slate floors, hot tubs, and mirrors fashioned out of old window frames. Some two-room suites have loft sleeping areas reached by spiral staircases. Suites have pull-out sofas and can sleep up to six. **Pros:** outdoor heated pool and hot tub (hot tub is open all year); large guest rooms; walk to town. **Cons:** small breakfast room. ⌧ *231 River St.* ☎ *413/664–0400* ⊕ *www.porches.com* ⇆ *47 rooms, 12 suites* ⌂ *In-room: a/c, kitchen (some), Wi-Fi. In-hotel: bar, pool, laundry service* ▭ *AE, DC, MC, V* ⎟◯⎥ *CP.*

$–$$ ⬚ **Topia Inn.** Park your shoes and your toiletries at the door. This Adams
★ property, which opened in 2007 just off the Ashuwillticook Rail Trail, is the greenest inn in the Berkshires. Innkeepers Nana Simopoulous and Caryn Heilman transformed a derelict downtown Colonial into an LEED-rated marvel, with a solar hot-water system, soybean oil heating, and natural clay walls. Beds and linens are organic cotton, and the innkeepers provide nontoxic toiletries. Rooms are decorated by the innkeepers' artsy pals; themes include Morocco and Retro 1960s. A fun quirk: some rooms have spa tubs with colored lights (chromatherapy, it's called), so you can have a little light show as you bathe. **Pros:** organic toiletries in guest rooms; organic breakfast; steam showers and spa tubs. **Cons:** next door to a bar; some of the room designs aren't that well-executed; neighborhood is dreary. ⌧ *10 Pleasant St., Adams*

Winslow Homer's *West Point, Prout's Neck* is just one of the notable paintings at Williamstown's Clark Art Institute.

☎ *413/743–9605* ⊕ *www.topiainn.com* ➦ *10 rooms* ⚭ *In-room: a/c, DVD, Wi-Fi. In-hotel: Wi-Fi hotspot* ☰ *AE, D, MC, V* ⦿ *BP.*

WILLIAMSTOWN

5 mi west of North Adams.

When Colonel Ephraim Williams left money to found a free school in what was then known as West Hoosac, he stipulated that the town's name be changed to Williamstown. Williams College opened in 1793, and even today life in this placid town revolves around it. Graceful campus buildings like the Gothic cathedral, built in 1904, line Main Street. Along Spring Street are a handful of upscale shops and lively eateries.

EXPLORING

Fodor's Choice **Clark Art Institute.** One of the nation's notable small art museums, the
★ Clark Art Institute has more than 30 paintings by Pierre-Auguste Renoir (among them *Mademoiselle Fleury in Algerian Costume*) as well as canvases by Monet and Camille Pissarro. *The Little Dancer,* an important sculpture by Degas, is another exceptional work. Other items include English silver, European and American photography from the 1840s through the 1910s, and 17th and 18th century Flemish and Dutch masterworks. ⊠ *225 South St.* ☎ *413/458–2303* ⊕ *www.clarkart.edu* 🎟 *July–Oct. $12.50, Nov.–May free* ☉ *Sept.–June, Tues.–Sun. 10–5; July and Aug., daily 10–5.*

☾ **Williams College Museum of Art.** The collections at this fine museum focus
Fodor's Choice on American and 20th-century art. One of the country's best college art
★ museums, the WCMA's 12,000 objects also span a range of eras and

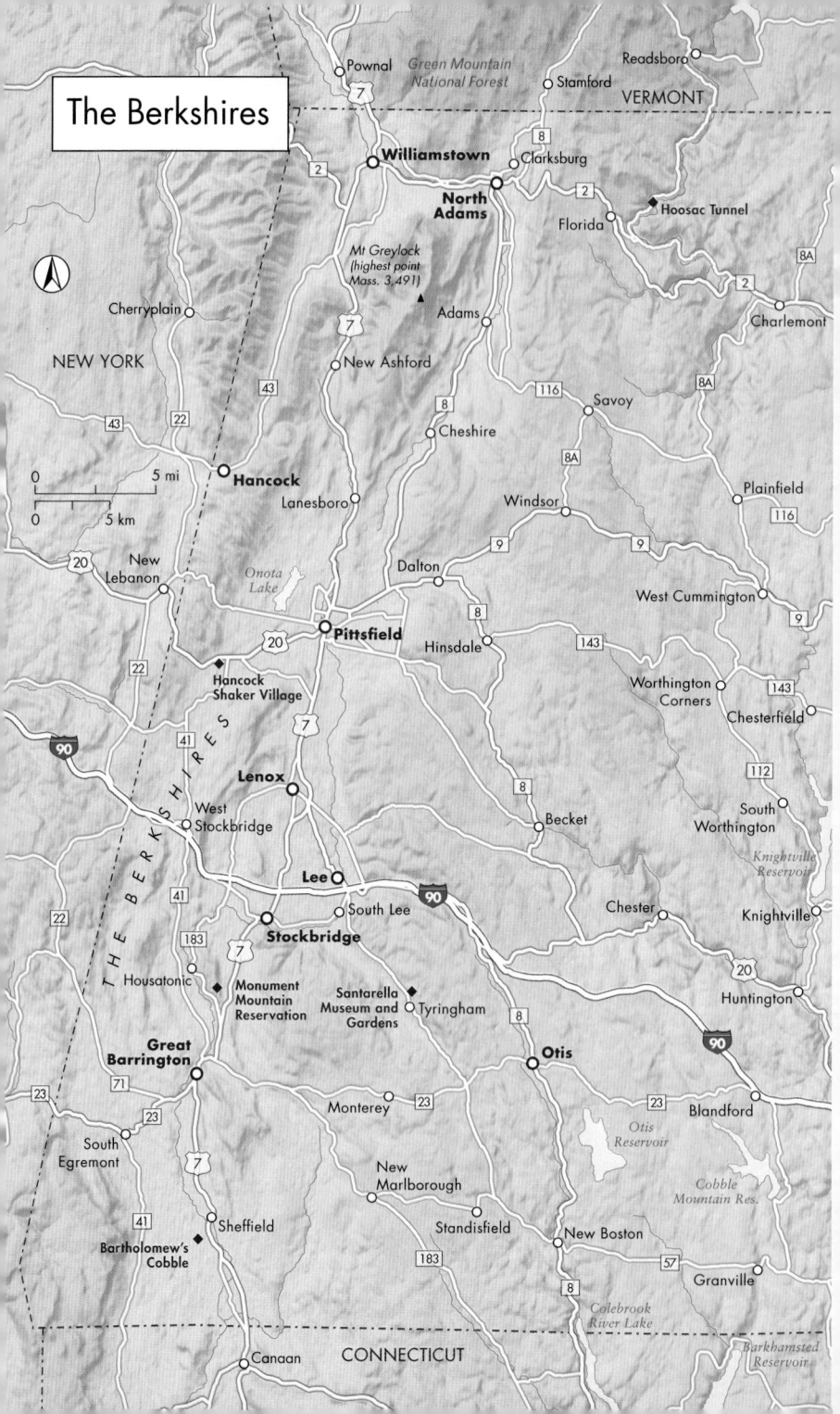

cultures. The original octagonal structure facing Main Street was built as a library in 1846. ⊠ *15 Lawrence Hall Dr.* ☎ *413/597–2429* ⊕ *www. wcma.org* ⊡ *Free* ☾ *Tues.–Sat. 10–5, Sun. 1–5.*

SPORTS AND THE OUTDOORS

The centerpiece of the 10,327-acre **Mt. Greylock State Reservation** (⊠ *Rockwell Rd., Lanesboro* ☎ *413/499–4262 or 413/499–4263*) is Mt. Greylock (3,491 feet), the highest point in Massachusetts. The reservation, south of Williamstown, has facilities for cycling, fishing, horseback riding, camping, and snowmobiling. Many treks—including a portion of the Appalachian Trail—start from the parking lot at the summit, an 8-mi drive from the mountain's base. The Bascom Lodge (⊕ *www. bascomlodge.net*) and Veterans War Memorial are at the peak.

SHOPPING

Spring Street is downtown Williamstown's main drag. At **Library Antiques** (⊠ *70 Spring St.* ☎ *413/458–3436* ⊕ *www.libraryantiques.com*) are an array of prints, folk art, jewelry, antiquarian books, and distinctive gifts. Some people consider tiny **Toonerville Trolley** (⊠ *131 Water St.* ☎ *413/458–5229*) the best music store in the world. Toonerville carries hard-to-find jazz, rock, and classical recordings. Jam-packed with every imaginable toy and game, **Where'd You Get That?** (⊠ *100 Spring St.* ☎ *413/458–2206* ⊕ *www.wygt.com*) also benefits from the enthusiasm of owners Ken and Michele Gietz.

THE ARTS

Fodor's Choice ★ At the Adams Memorial Theatre, the **Williamstown Theatre Festival** (⊠ *1000 Main St.* ☎ *413/597–3400 or 413/597–3399* ⊕ *www.wtfestival.org*) is summer's hottest ticket. From June through August, the long-running production presents well-known theatrical works with famous performers on the Main Stage and contemporary works on the Nikos Stage.

WHERE TO EAT

$–$$
AMERICAN
Fodor's Choice ★

✕ **'6 House Pub.** Set in an old cow barn at the 1896 House Inn, this dark, wood-paneled pub has loads of character and a mounted mascot, Harold the Hereford, who doesn't seem to mind that at least half the patrons are downing burgers. Not a meat eater? Not a problem. Chef Matt Schilling's extensive menu includes several "supper salads" (including a grilled plum salad with Granny Smith apples, Gorgonzola, and glazed walnuts over mixed greens), veggie three-bean chili, and sweet-potato fries. The restaurant also sells a bazillion lobster rolls, as well it should; this toothsome roll is all lobster meat, sans fillers, on a buttery grilled roll. ⊠ *910 Cold Spring Rd. (U.S. 7)* ☎ *413/458–1896* ⊕ *www.1896house.com* ▭ *AE, D, MC, V.*

$$–$$$
ECLECTIC
Fodor's Choice ★

✕ **Mezze Bistro & Bar.** This is, without a doubt, Williamstown's hot spot. On summer evenings it's not uncommon to find yourself rubbing elbows with stars from the Williamstown Theatre Festival. The interior mixes urban chic with hardwood floors and exposed-brick walls. The spectacular menu is always in flux, but don't be surprised to encounter sashimi with watercress alongside filet mignon with roasted root vegetables. ⊠ *16 Water St.* ☎ *413/458–0123* ⊕ *www.mezzeinc.com* ⌂ *Reservations essential* ▭ *AE, D, MC, V* ☾ *No lunch.*

WHERE TO STAY

$$–$$$ ★ **Guest House at Field Farm.** Built in 1948, this guesthouse contains a fine collection of art on loan from Williams College. The former owners, who gave part of their own art collection to the college, donated the 296-acre property to the Trustees of Reservations, which runs it as a B&B. The guest rooms have expansive views of the grounds. Three rooms have private decks; two have working tile fireplaces. The East Room has the best views of Mt. Greylock, while the Gallery Room has the best art. You can prepare your own simple meals in the pantry. The grounds, open to the public, have 4 mi of hiking trails. **Pros:** great views of the Berkshires; luxury (Frette) robes and towels plus high-thread-count linens. **Cons:** no TV in rooms. ✉ *554 Sloan Rd.* ☎ *413/458–3135* ⊕ *www.guesthouseatfieldfarm.org* ↪ *5 rooms* ⚘ *In-room: a/c, no TV, Wi-Fi. In-hotel: pool, no kids under 12* ⊟ *D, MC, V* ⦿ *BP.*

$$$–$$$$ ★ **Orchards Hotel.** Although it's near Highway 2 and surrounded by parking lots, this thoroughly proper hostelry compensates with a courtyard filled with fruit trees and a pond stocked with koi. English antiques furnish most of the spacious accommodations. The inner rooms, which look onto the courtyard, are best for summer stays. The outer rooms have less distinguished views, but their fireplaces add appeal for winter visits. Bedtime is a delicious affair—the beds are comfy, the linens are great, and the staff leaves chocolate-chip cookies at turndown. **Pros:** good beds; flat-screen TVs; good alternative to B&Bs and chain hotels. **Cons:** no coffeemakers in rooms; some guests complain of service lapses; minor signs of wear and tear. ✉ *222 Adams Rd.* ☎ *413/458–9611 or 800/225–1517* ⊕ *www.orchardshotel.com* ↪ *49 rooms* ⚘ *In-room: a/c, refrigerator (some). In-hotel: restaurant, bar, pool, gym, Internet terminal* ⊟ *AE, DC, MC, V.*

$ ★ **River Bend Farm.** Listed on the National Register of Historic Places, this 1770 Georgian Colonial is not on a river, nor is it a farm, but this rustic inn is a great place to discover simpler times, before TV and Internet and (alas) private bathrooms! The guest rooms are sprinkled with antique pieces—chamber pots, washstands, wing chairs, and spinning wheels. Some bedrooms have wide-plank walls, curtains of unbleached muslin, and four-poster beds or rope beds. A gracious library awaits you downstairs. **Pros:** good breakfast; friendly innkeepers. **Cons:** set on a busy road with train sounds at night; guests share one shower. ✉ *643 Simonds Rd.* ☎ *413/458–3121* ⊕ *www.riverbendfarmbb.com* ↪ *4 rooms without bath* ⚘ *In-room: no phone, no a/c, no TV* ⊟ *No credit cards* ⊙ *Closed Nov.–Mar.* ⦿ *CP.*

HANCOCK

15 mi south of Williamstown.

Tiny Hancock, the village closest to the Jiminy Peak ski resort, comes into its own in winter. It's also a great base for outdoors enthusiasts year-round, with biking, hiking, and other options in summer.

EXPLORING

🕐 **Ioka Valley Farm.** Established in the 1930s, this 600-acre farm is one of the best-known pick-your-own farms in the Berkshires. You can pick berries all summer, then apples and pumpkins in fall. In winter you can cut your own Christmas tree. Other activities include hayrides, pedal tractors for kids, and a petting zoo with pigs, sheep, goats, and calves. ✉ *Hwy. 43* ☎ *413/738–5915* ⏰ *Hrs seasonal, please call ahead.*

SPORTS AND THE OUTDOORS

SKI AREA **Jiminy Peak** (✉ *Corey Rd.* ☎ *413/738–5500 or 888/454–6469* ⊕ *www. jiminypeak.com*) is the only full-service ski and snowboard resort in the Berkshires and the largest in southern New England, with a vertical of 1,150 feet, 44 trails, and 9 lifts. It's mostly a cruising mountain—trails are groomed daily, and only on some are small moguls left to build up along the side of the slope. The steepest black-diamond runs are on the upper head walls; longer, outer runs make for good intermediate terrain. There's skiing nightly, and snowmaking covers 93% of the skiable terrain. Jiminy also has three terrain parks and a mountain coaster (weekends and holidays only), a two-person cart shoots down the mountain at speeds of up to 25 mph.

WHERE TO STAY

$$–$$$ 🏨 **Country Inn at Jiminy Peak.** Massive stone fireplaces in its lobby and lounge lend this hotel a ski-lodge atmosphere. The condo-style suites— privately owned but put into a rental pool—accommodate up to four people and have kitchenettes separated from living areas by bars with high stools. The roomiest units are on the second and third floors; the suites at the rear of the building overlook the slopes. Ski packages are available. **Pros:** John Harvard's Restaurant is on-site; bathrooms are nice; rooms have eat-in kitchenettes. **Cons:** hallways are a bit dark; burgundy and green color scheme is dated. ✉ *Corey Rd.* ☎ *413/738–5500 or 800/882–8859* ⊕ *www.jiminypeak.com* 🛏 *105 suites* ⚒ *In-room: a/c, kitchen. In-hotel: 2 restaurants, bar, tennis courts, pool, gym, Wi-Fi hotspot* ▭ *AE, D, DC, MC, V.*

PITTSFIELD

21 mi south of Williamstown, 11 mi southeast of Hancock.

Pittsfield is a workaday city without the quaint, rural demeanor of the comparatively small Colonial towns that surround it. There's a positive buzz in Pittsfield these days, though. Symbols of resurgence include the gorgeous Colonial Theatre, which was restored in 2007 and hosts 250 nights of performances per year, and a spate of new shops and eateries along North Street. City-sponsored art walks and a major renovation of the venerable Berkshire Museum are more evidence of Pittsfield's comeback.

EXPLORING

🕐 **Berkshire Museum.** Opened in 1903, this museum displays varied and sometimes curious collections relating to history, the natural world, and art, imcluding a collection of Hudson River School paintings, including works by Frederic Church and Albert Bierstadt. In 2008, the museum unveiled its first new gallery in more than 100 years: the Feigenbaum

HOLISTIC HIDEAWAYS

Kripalu

Choose from among more than 40 fitness classes per day, plus lifestyle management workshops and private consultations with wellness experts in the field of medicine, nutrition, behavior, and physiology. You can change your life in three days (truly), while trying new fitness techniques, eating great food (even chocolate sauce, craftily made from white grape juice and cocoa), and enjoying the Berkshires countryside on hikes and paddling excursions.

Kripalu Center (☎ 866/200–5203 ⊕ www.kripalu.org) is a health and yoga retreat in Stockbridge. Kripalu means grace, and there is even a hatha yoga method named after the institution.

The Berkshires have become known for holistic retreats that send you home with the ultimate souvenir: a new-and-improved you, with a refreshed spirit, revitalized body, and healthier habits. Here are three places you might like to try.

The Berkshires' outpost of **Canyon Ranch** (☎ 800/742–9000 ⊕ www.canyonranch.com) in Lenox couldn't be more elegantly old-fashioned; the famous spa is set in Bellefontaine Mansion, a 1897 replica of Le Petit Trianon in Versailles. Looks can be deceiving, though. This holistic spa is home to a state-of-the-art, 100,000-square-foot fitness center, with the latest classes and the best equipment—perfect for gym junkies.

The Option Institute (☎ 800/714–2779 ⊕ www.option.org) in Sheffield is all about learning to make emotional choices that enhance your life experience. Founded in 1983 by author Barry Neil Kaufman (*Happiness Is a Choice*) and Samahria Lyte Kaufman, the Option Institute is based on the premise that emotions like misery, fear, anger, and distress are optional, not inevitable. Personal growth workshops are designed to help participants develop tools that will improve the quality of their relationships, leading to a happier life. "Energizing" and "empowering" are words used by happy fans to describe their experience. Participants stay in rustic guesthouses and eat veggie meals served family-style.

Hall of Innovation. This multimedia, interactive exhibit includes historical artifacts, works of art, and video about Berkshire innovators such as Crane & Co., the company that produces the paper for U.S. currency, and Douglas Trumbull, who created special effects for films including *2001: A Space Odyssey* and *Star Wars*. At 10 feet high and 26 feet long, "Wally" the Stegosaurus highlights the Dinosaurs and Paleontology gallery. At the Dino Dig, kids and adults can dig together for replicas of dinosaur bones.

Many of New England's back roads are lined with historic split-rail fences or stone walls.

An ancient civilization gallery displays Roman and Greek jewelry and an ancient Egyptian mummy. ✉ *39 South St.* ☎ *413/443–7171* ⊕ *www. berkshiremuseum.org* ✉ *$10* ☼ *Mon.–Sat. 10–5, Sun. noon–5.*

Fodor's Choice
★
Hancock Shaker Village. The third Shaker community in America, Hancock was founded in the 1790s. At its peak in the 1840s, the village had almost 300 inhabitants, who made their living farming, selling seeds and herbs, making medicines, and producing crafts. The religious community officially closed in 1960, its 170-year life span a small miracle considering its population's vows of celibacy (they took in orphans to maintain their constituency). Many examples of Shaker ingenuity are visible at Hancock today: the **Round Stone Barn** and the **Laundry and Machine Shop** are two of the most interesting buildings. Also on site are a farm (with a wonderful barn), some period gardens, a museum shop with reproduction Shaker furniture, a picnic area, and a café. ✉ *U.S. 20, 6 mi west of Pittsfield* ☎ *413/443–0188 or 800/817–1137* ⊕ *www. hancockshakervillage.org* ✉ *$16.50, $12.50 in winter* ☼ *Late May–late Oct., daily 10–5 for self-guided tours; late Oct.–late May, guided tours at 1 on weekdays and noon and 2 on weekends.*

SPORTS AND THE OUTDOORS

SKI AREA The **Bousquet Ski Area** (✉ *101 Dan Fox Dr., off U.S. 7 near Pittsfield Airport* ☎ *413/442–8316; 413/442–2436 snow conditions* ⊕ *www. bousquets.com*) is an economical, no-nonsense place to ski. The inexpensive lift tickets are the same price every day, and there's night skiing every night except Sunday. You can go snow tubing for just $18 for the day when conditions allow.

With a 750-foot vertical drop, Bousquet has 21 trails, but only if you count every change in steepness and every merging slope. Still, you will find some good beginner and intermediate runs, with a few steeper pitches. There are two double chairlifts, three surface lifts, and a small snowboard park. Ski instruction classes are given twice daily on weekends and holidays for children ages 5 and up.

Play Bousquet uses three drop funnels to pour kids out into a large activity pool and enough twists and turns and chute-to-chutes to scare the pants off many parents. There's also a minigolf course, 32-foot climbing wall, go-karts, alpine carts, and a scenic chairlift.

THE ARTS

For the serious music lover, **South Mountain Concerts** (⊠ *U.S. 7 and 202 mi south of Pittsfield center* ☎ *413/442–2106*) is one of the country's most distinguished centers for chamber-music events. On the wooded slope of South Mountain, the 500-seat auditorium presents concerts every Sunday in September at 3.

WHERE TO EAT

$–$$

STEAKHOUSE

✕ **Dakota.** Moose and elk heads watch over diners, and the motto is "Steak, seafood, and smiles" at this large and popular chain restaurant decorated like a hunting lodge. Meals cooked on the mesquite grill include steaks and salmon, shrimp, and trout; the 32-item salad bar has many organic foods. A hearty Sunday brunch buffet includes Belgian pancakes, omelets, ham, lox and bagels, fruit, salads, and rich desserts. ⊠ *1035 South St.* ☎ *413/499–7900* ▭ *AE, D, DC, MC, V* ⊗ *No lunch Mon.–Sat.*

LENOX

10 mi south of Pittsfield, 130 mi west of Boston.

The famed Tanglewood music festival has been a fixture in upscale Lenox for decades, and it's a part of the reason the town remains fiercely popular in summer. Booking a room here or in any of the nearby communities can set you back dearly when music or theatrical events are in town. Many of the town's most impressive homes are downtown; others you can only see by setting off on the curving, tortuous back roads that traverse the region. In the center of the village, a few blocks of shabby-chic Colonial buildings contain shops and eateries.

ESSENTIALS

Visitor Information Lenox Chamber of Commerce (⊠ *5 Walker St.* ☎ *413/637–3646* ⊕ *www.lenox.org*)

EXPLORING

Ⓒ **Berkshires Scenic Railway Museum.** In a restored 1903 railroad station in central Lenox, this museum displays antique rail equipment, vintage exhibits, and a large working model railway. It's the starting point for the diesel-hauled **Berkshire Scenic Railway,** a 1½-hour narrated round-trip train ride between Lenox and Stockbridge. There's also a 45-minute trip to Lee. ⊠ *10 Willow Creek Rd.* ☎ *413/637–2210* ⊕ *www. berkshirescenicrailroad.org* ⊠ *Museum free, Lenox–Stockbridge train*

$15, Lenox–Lee train $9 ⊙ *May–Oct., weekends (see Web site for current schedule).*

Frelinghuysen Morris House & Studio. This modernist property on a 46-acre site exhibits the works of American abstract artists Suzy Frelinghuysen and George L.K. Morris as well as contemporaries including Pablo Picasso, Georges Braque, and Juan Gris. A 57-minute documentary on Frelinghuysen and Morris plays on a continuous loop in the classroom. ⊠ *92 Hawthorne St.* ☎ *413/637–0166* ⊕ *www.frelinghuysen.org* ✉ *$12* ⊙ *May–late June, guided tours by appointment; late June–Labor Day, Thurs.–Sun. 10–3; early Sept.–Columbus Day, Thurs.–Sat. 10–3; early Oct.–late Oct., guided tours by appointment.*

Fodor's Choice **The Mount.** This mansion built in 1902 with myriad classical influences
★ was the summer home of novelist Edith Wharton. The 42-room house and 3 acres of formal gardens were designed by Wharton, who is considered by many to have set the standard for 20th-century interior decoration. In designing the Mount, she followed the principles set forth in her book *The Decoration of Houses* (1897), creating a calm and well-ordered home. Nearly $15 million has been spent to date on an extensive, ongoing restoration project. ⊠ *2 Plunkett St.* ☎ *413/551–5104 or 888/637–1902* ⊕ *www.edithwharton.org* ✉ *$16* ⊙ *May–Oct., daily 10–5; Nov.–Dec. 20, weekends 10–4.*

Ventfort Hall Mansion and Gilded Age Museum. Built in 1893, Ventfort Hall was the summer "cottage" of Sarah Morgan, the sister of financier J.P. Morgan. Lively, information-packed tours offer a peek into the lifestyles of Lenox's super-rich "cottage class." Inside is a museum that explores the role of Lenox and the Berkshires as the era's definitive mountain retreat. ⊠ *104 Walker St.* ☎ *413/637–3206* ⊕ *www.gildedage. org* ✉ *$12* ⊙ *Daily 10–3, call for tour times.*

SPORTS AND THE OUTDOORS

HIKING Part of the Massachusetts Audubon Society's system, the **Pleasant Valley Wildlife Sanctuary** (⊠ *472 W. Mountain Rd.* ☎ *413/637–0320* ⊕ *www. massaudubon.org* ✉ *$4*) abounds with beaver ponds, meadows, hardwood forests, and woodlands. Its 1,400 acres and 7 mi of trails offer excellent bird- and beaver-watching. Hiking trails are open for cross-country skiing and snowshoeing in winter. Town-owned **Kennedy Park** (⊠ *Main St.*) offers hiking and cross-country skiing on old carriage roads, plus nearly 15 mi of trails within a hardwood forest.

HORSEBACK Travel along the shaded trails of Kennedy Park and Lenox Mountain
RIDING and enjoy breathtaking views of Berkshire County when you book an hour, half-day, or overnight ride at **Berkshire Horseback Adventures** (⊠ *293 Main St.* ☎ *413/637–9090* ⊕ *www.berkshirehorseback.net*).

SHOPPING

★ One of the foremost crafts centers in New England, **Hoadley Gallery** (⊠ *21 Church St.* ☎ *413/637–2814* ⊕ *www.hoadleygallery.com*), shows and sells American arts and crafts with a strong focus on pottery, jewelry, and textiles. **R.W. Wise** (⊠ *81 Church St.* ☎ *413/637–1589* ⊕ *www. rwwise.com*) produces high-quality jewelry designed on site and sells estate and antique pieces.

Lawn tickets are a great way to experience the Boston Symphony Orchestra at Tanglewood—don't forget your blanket and picnic.

THE ARTS

Fodor's Choice ★ **Tanglewood** (✉ *297 West St., off Hwy. 183* ☎ *617/266–1492 or 888/ 266–1492* ⊕ *www.tanglewood.org*), the 200-acre summer home of the Boston Symphony Orchestra (BSO), attracts thousands every year to concerts by world-famous performers from mid-June to Labor Day. The 5,000-seat main shed hosts larger concerts; the Seiji Ozawa Hall (named for the former BSO conductor) seats around 1,200 and is used for recitals, chamber music, and more intimate performances by summer program students and soloists. One of the most rewarding ways to experience Tanglewood is to purchase lawn tickets, arrive early with blankets or lawn chairs, and have a picnic. Except for the occasional celebrity concert, lawn tickets remain below $20, and concerts can be clearly heard from just about any spot. Inside the shed, tickets vary in price, with most of the good seats costing between $38 and $100.

Shakespeare & Company (✉ *70 Kemble St.* ☎ *413/637–1199; 413/637– 3353 tickets* ⊕ *www.shakespeare.org*) performs the works of William Shakespeare and Edith Wharton from late May through October at the 466-seat Founders' Theatre and the 99-seat Spring Lawn Theatre.

WHERE TO EAT

$$–$$$
FRENCH

✗ **Bistro Zinc.** Crisp lemon-yellow walls, warm tile floors, and tall windows are bright and inviting in this stellar French bistro, which feels like a country house in Provence. The kitchen turns out expertly prepared and refreshingly simple classics like steak frites, grilled lamb chops, and mussels marinières (with white wine and garlic). The long, zinc-topped wood bar, always full and determinedly sophisticated, is the best Lenox can offer for nightlife. ✉ *56 Church St.* ☎ *413/637–8800* ⊕ *www.bistrozinc.com* ☐ *AE, MC, V.*

$$–$$$ ✕ **Café Lucia.** *Bistecca alla fiorentina* (porterhouse steak grilled with olive
ITALIAN   oil, garlic, and rosemary) and ravioli *basilico e pomodoro* (with fresh
tomatoes, garlic, and basil) are among the dishes that change seasonally
at this northern Italian restaurant. Weekend reservations are essential
during the Tanglewood music festival. ✉ *80 Church St.* ☎ *413/637–
2640* ⊕ *www.cafelucialenox.com* ☐ *AE, D, MC, V* ☻ *Closed Mon.
July–Oct., Sun. and Mon. Nov.–June. No lunch.*

¢   ✕ **Chocolate Springs Café.** Escape into chocolate bliss here, where even the
BAKERY   aroma is intoxicating. This award-winning chocolatier offers wedges
Fodor's Choice   of decadent cakes, store-made ice cream and sorbets, and a dazzling
★   array of chocolates, including green-tea bonbons, chocolate-covered
pretzels, and even chocolate-dipped prunes. You can eat at one of a
handful of tables, but don't expect so much as a salad or a wrap—it's
all chocolate, all the time. ✉ *Aspinwell Shops 55 Pittsfield/Lenox Rd.*
☎ *413/637–9820* ⊕ *www.chocolatesprings.com* ☐ *AE, D, MC, V.*

$$–$$$ ✕ **Church Street Café.** More laid-back than its nearby competitors, Church
CAFE   Street Café serves an intriguing array of globally inspired dishes. From
the baked onion-and-Saint-André-cheese tart to the vegetarian mous-
saka and the New Mexican home-style tortilla stuffed with barbecued
brisket, the dishes served are an international culinary treat that change
seasonally. In warm weather you can dine on a shaded outdoor deck.
✉ *65 Church St.* ☎ *413/637–2745* ⊕ *www.churchstreetcafe.biz* ☐ *MC,
V* ☻ *Closed Sun. and Mon. mid-Oct.–May.*

WHERE TO STAY

$$–$$$ ☷ **Brook Farm Inn.** This 1870s Victorian inn and its gardens are tucked
away in a beautiful wooded glen a short distance from Tanglewood.
The innkeepers are music and literature aficionados and often have
light opera, jazz, or Broadway tunes playing in the fireplace-lighted
library. On some Saturdays, mostly in winter, poetry readings enhance
afternoon tea. Rooms have antiques, pastel color schemes, and, in many
cases, four-poster beds. Even the smallest units, with their eaved ceilings
and cozy configurations, are very romantic. **Pros:** attentive innkeepers;
delicious breakfast; afternoon tea with scones. **Cons:** thin towels; no
TV. ✉ *15 Hawthorne St.* ☎ *413/637–3013 or 800/285–7638* ⊕ *www.
brookfarm.com* ⇆ *12 rooms, 1 suite* ⌂ *In-room: no TV, Wi-Fi. In-hotel:
pool, no kids under 15* ☐ *MC, V* ⦿I *BP.*

$$$–$$$$ ☷ **Devonfield Inn.** This grand, yellow-and-cream Federal house sits atop
Fodor's Choice   a birch-shaded hillside, dotted with a few quaint outbuildings and 32
★   acres of rolling meadows. The nine guest rooms have Colonial-style fur-
nishings—many have Oriental rugs, lace-canopy four-poster beds, and
working fireplaces. A separate, contemporary cottage with a pitched
cathedral ceiling has its own kitchen and private deck. A gracious pool
and cottage unit sit behind the house. Expect such toothsome fare as
vanilla-cinnamon crème brûlée or orange yogurt pancakes at breakfast,
and details such as chocolates and spring water in each room. There
is a video library and a butler's pantry with cookies, popcorn, and
beverages. **Pros:** charming innkeepers; good breakfasts; nice pool and
lawn. **Cons:** not for families with young kids. ✉ *85 Stockbridge Rd.,*

4

Lee ☎ *413/243–3298 or 800/664–0880* ⊕ *www.devonfield.com* 📶 *6 rooms, 3 suites, 1 cottage* ⚒ *In-room: a/c, DVD, Wi-Fi. In-hotel: tennis court, pool, bicycles, Wi-Fi, no kids under 12 (in summer)* 🟰 *AE, D, MC, V* 🍴 *BP.*

$$–$$$$

Fodor's Choice

★

🏨 **Gateways Inn.** The 1912 summer cottage of Harley Proctor (as in Proctor and Gamble) has experienced some ups and downs during its tenure as a country inn, but under innkeepers Fabrizio and Rosemary Chiariello, it looks better than ever. Rooms come in a variety of configurations and styles, most with working fireplaces, detailed moldings, and plush carpeting. Some guest rooms and bathrooms have been recently upgraded; ask if one of these is available when you make your reservation. The on-site restaurant, La Terrazza, offers late-night dining in summer. **Pros:** great location in the heart of Lenox; concierge service can arrange activities for you, including in-room massage. **Cons:** public areas have a faded glory feel; lots of stairs. ✉ *51 Walker St.* ☎ *413/637–2532* ⊕ *www.gatewaysinn.com* 📶 *11 rooms, 1 suite* ⚒ *In-room: a/c, DVD (some), Internet. In-hotel: restaurant, bar* 🟰 *AE, MC, V* 🍴 *BP.*

$–$$

★

🏨 **Yankee Inn.** Custom-crafted Amish canopy beds, gas fireplaces, and high-end fabrics decorate the top rooms at this immaculately kept, two-story motor inn, one of several modern hotels and motels along U.S. 7. The more economical units contain attractive, if nondescript, country-style furnishings. If you can, avoid the wings of the motel and stay in the main building for a nicer, less motel-y experience. **Pros:** convenient location to attractions; good value. **Cons:** closer to Pittsfield than Lenox; some rooms smell musty; dreary pool area. ✉ *461 Pittsfield-Lenox Rd. off U.S. 7 and 20* ☎ *413/499–3700 or 800/835–2364* ⊕ *www.yankeeinn.com* 📶 *96 rooms* ⚒ *In-room: a/c, refrigerator, Internet. In-hotel: pool, gym, Wi-Fi hotspot* 🟰 *AE, D, MC, V* 🍴 *CP.*

OTIS

20 mi southeast of Lenox.

A more rustic alternative to Stockbridge and Lenox, Otis, with a ski area and 20 lakes and ponds, supplies plenty of what made the Berkshires desirable in the first place—the great outdoors. Dining and lodgings options are slim; you can stay in Lee or Great Barrington or head southwest to Old Marlborough and stay at the Old Inn on the Green, where you can sample chef Peter Platt's swoon-worthy cuisine. Nearby Becket hosts the outstanding Jacob's Pillow Dance Festival in summer.

EXPLORING

Deer Run Maples. This is one of several sugarhouses where you can spend the morning tasting freshly tapped maple syrup that's been drizzled onto a dish of snow. Sugaring season varies with the weather; it can be anytime between late February and early April. Call before coming to confirm opening hours. ✉ *135 Ed Jones Rd.* ☎ *413/269–7588* ✉ *Free* ☉ *Late Feb.–early Apr., hrs vary.*

SPORTS AND THE OUTDOORS

SKI AREA   The least expensive ski area in New England, **Otis Ridge** has long been a haven for beginners and families, but experts will find slopes here, too. The remote location is quite stunning, the buildings historic. Six downhill trails are serviced by a pair of lifts, with 100% snowmaking coverage and night skiing Tuesday through Sunday. ⊠ *Hwy. 23* ☎ *413/269–4444* ⊕ *www.otisridge.com.*

THE ARTS

Fodor's Choice ★ For nine weeks each summer, the tiny town of Becket, 8 mi north of Otis, becomes a hub of the dance world during the **Jacob's Pillow Dance Festival** (⊠ *358 George Carter Rd., at U.S. 20 Becket* ☎ *413/327–1234* ⊕ *www.jacobspillow.org*), which showcases world-renowned performers of ballet, modern, and international dance. Before the main events, works in progress and even some of the final productions are staged outdoors, often free of charge.

STOCKBRIDGE

4

20 mi northwest of Otis, 7 mi south of Lenox.

Stockbridge is the quintessence of small-town New England charm, untainted by large-scale development. It is also the blueprint for small-town America as represented on the covers of the *Saturday Evening Post* by painter Norman Rockwell (the official state artist of Massachusetts). From 1953 until his death in 1978, Rockwell lived in Stockbridge and painted the simple charm of its buildings and residents. James Taylor sang about the town in his hit "Sweet Baby James," as did balladeer Arlo Guthrie in his famous Thanksgiving anthem "Alice's Restaurant," in which he tells what ensued when he tossed some garbage out the back of his Volkswagen bus down a Stockbridge hillside.

Indeed, Stockbridge is the stuff of legend. Travelers have been checking into the Red Lion Inn on Main Street since the 18th century, and Stockbridge is only slightly altered in appearance since that time. In 18th- and 19th-century buildings surrounding the inn are a handful of engaging shops and eateries. The rest of Stockbridge is best appreciated via a country drive or bike ride over its hilly, narrow lanes.

ESSENTIALS

Visitor Information Stockbridge Chamber of Commerce (⊠ *Elm St.* ☎ *413/298–5200 or 866/626–5327* ⊕ *www.stockbridgechamber.org*).

EXPLORING

Berkshire Botanical Gardens. This 15-acre garden contains perennial, rose, daylily, and herb gardens of exotic and native plantings—some 2,500 varieties in all—plus greenhouses, ponds, and nature trails. ⊠ *Hwys. 102 and 183, 2 mi east of downtown* ☎ *413/298–3926* ⊕ *www.berkshirebotanical.org* ⊠ *$10* ⊗ *May–Columbus Day, daily 10–5.*

Fodor's Choice ★ **Chesterwood.** For 33 years, this was the summer home of the sculptor Daniel Chester French (1850–1931), who created *The Minuteman* in Concord and the Lincoln Memorial's famous seated statue of the president in Washington, D.C. Tours are given of the house, which is maintained in the style of the 1920s, and of the studio, where you can view the casts and models French used to create the Lincoln Memorial. The beautifully landscaped 122-acre grounds also make for an enchanting stroll. ⊠ *4 Williamsville Rd., off Hwy. 183* ☎ *413/298–3579* ⊕ *www.chesterwood.org* ⊠ *$15* ⊗ *May–Oct., daily 10–5.*

Norman Rockwell: Illustrating America

CLOSE UP

I was showing the America I knew and observed to others who might not have noticed. My fundamental purpose is to interpret the typical American. I am a story teller.

—Norman Rockwell

If you've ever seen old copies of the *Saturday Evening Post*, no doubt you're familiar with American artist Norman Rockwell. He created 321 covers for the well-regarded magazine, and the *Post* always sold more copies when one of Rockwell's drawings was on the front page. The accomplished artist also illustrated Boy Scouts of America calendars, Christmas cards, children's books, and even a few stamps for the U.S. Postal Service—in 1994, a stamp bearing his image came out in his honor. His illustrations tended to fit the theme of Americana, family, or patriotism.

Born in New York City in 1894, the talented designer had a knack for art early on but strengthened his talent with instruction at the National Academy of Design and the Art Students League. He was only 22 when he sold his first cover to the *Post*. He was married three times and had three sons by his second wife. He died in 1978 in Stockbridge, Massachusetts, where he had lived since 1953.

Norman Rockwell 1920 magazine cover.

Famous works include his *Triple Self-Portrait* and the *Four Freedoms* illustrations done during World War II. They represent freedom of speech, freedom to worship, freedom from want, and freedom from fear. In a poetic twist, in 1977, President Gerald R. Ford bestowed on Rockwell the Presidential Medal of Freedom, the highest civilian honor a U.S. citizen can be given. Ford praised Rockwell for his "vivid and affectionate portraits of our country."

—Debbie Harmsen

★ **Naumkeag.** This Berkshire cottage once owned by Joseph Choate, a successful New York lawyer and an ambassador to Great Britain during President William McKinley's administration provides a glimpse into the gracious living of the gilded era of the Berkshires. The 26-room gabled mansion, designed by Stanford White in 1886, sits atop Prospect Hill. Its many original furnishings and art span three centuries; the collection of Chinese porcelain is also noteworthy. The meticulously kept 8 acres of formal gardens designed by Fletcher Steele are worth the visit. ✉ *5 Prospect Hill Rd.* ☎ *413/298–3239* ⊕ *www.thetrustees.org* 🎫 *$12* ☺ *Memorial Day–Columbus Day, daily 10–5.*

Stockbridge's churches are just some of the charming buildings on Main Street.

Norman Rockwell Museum. This charming museum traces the career of one of America's most beloved illustrators, beginning with his first *Saturday Evening Post* cover in 1916. In addition to housing its collection of 570 Rockwell illustrations, the museum also mounts exhibits by other artists. Rockwell's studio was moved to the museum grounds and is complete in every detail. Stroll the 36-acre site, picnic on the grounds, or relax at the outdoor café (open from Memorial Day to Columbus Day). A child's version of the audio tour ($5 adults/$4 children) with a scavenger-hunt theme makes this museum more fun for kids. There's also a kid's creativity room with storybooks and art materials. ⊠ *Hwy. 183, 2 mi from Stockbridge* ☎ *413/298–4100* ⊕ *www.nrm.org* ✉ *$15* ⊙ *May–Oct., daily 10–5; Nov.–Apr., weekdays 10–4, weekends 10–5.*

SHOPPING

The dynamic **Holsten Galleries** (⊠ *3 Elm St.* ☎ *413/298–3044* ⊕ *www. holstengalleries.com*) shows the wares of top glass sculptors, including Dale Chihuly and Lino Tagliapietra.

THE ARTS

Since 1929, the **Berkshire Theatre Festival** (⊠ *6 Main St.* ☎ *413/298–5536; 413/298–5576 box office* ⊕ *www.berkshiretheatre.org*) has presented plays nightly in summer. The four plays performed each summer on the Main Stage tend to be better-known vehicles with established actors. The Unicorn, a smaller theater, mounts experimental and new works.

WHERE TO EAT AND STAY

$$–$$$ ✕ **Once Upon a Table.** The atmosphere is casual yet vaguely romantic at
ECLECTIC this little restaurant-in-the-mews off Stockbridge's Main Street. The Continental and contemporary American cuisine includes seasonal

The Red Lion Inn is a classic New England lodging experience: romantic, intimate, and historic.

dishes, with appetizers such as potpie of escargots and entrées that include seared crab cakes with horseradish-cream sauce as well as rack of lamb with garlic mashed potatoes. At lunch try the Caesar salad or the Reuben sandwich. ⊠ *36 Main St.* ☎ *413/298–3870* ⊕ *www. onceuponatablebistro.com* ⌁ *Reservations essential* ☰ *AE, MC, V.*

$$–$$$
FRENCH
Fodor's Choice
★

✕ **Rouge.** In West Stockbridge, 5 mi northwest of Stockbridge, this little house with gray-green shingles, an illuminated small red sign, and simple and comfortable interior is reminiscent of a restaurant in the French countryside. Owner-chef William Merelle is indeed from Provence, where he met his American wife (and co-owner), Maggie, formerly a wine merchant. Try the steak au poivre with watercress, pommes frites, and cognac sauce or the lemon-crusted free-range chicken. ⊠ *3 Center St., West Stockbridge* ☎ *413/232–4111* ⊕ *www.rougerestaurant.com* ☰ *AE, D, MC, V* ☉ *Closed Mon. and Tues. No lunch.*

$$–$$$
Fodor's Choice
★

▥ **Inn at Stockbridge.** Antiques and feather comforters are among the accents in the rooms of this 1906 Georgian Revival inn run by the attentive Alice and Len Schiller. The two serve breakfast in their elegant dining room, and every evening they provide wine and cheese. Each of the rooms in the adjacent "cottage" building has a decorative theme such as Kashmir, St. Andrews, or Provence; the junior suites in the barn building have Berkshire themes. The airy rooms have CD players and in some cases gas fireplaces, flat-screen TVs, and whirlpool tubs. **Pros:** beautiful grounds; good breakfast. **Cons:** noise from MA turnpike (most noticeable in suites); not within walking distance to town. ⊠ *30 East St.* ☎ *413/298–3337 or 888/466–7865* ⊕ *www.stockbridgeinn.com* ⇖ *8 rooms, 8 suites* ⌂ *In-room: a/c, DVD (some). In-hotel: pool, gym, Internet terminal, no kids under 12* ☰ *AE, D, MC, V* ⊖|*BP.*

CLOSE UP

Massachusetts Farms

Living like a locavore (someone who consumes only locally grown food) is easy in the Berkshires and western Massachusetts. The area's many farms, farm stands, and farmers' markets make everything from produce, dairy, and meat to maple syrup, flowers, and Christmas trees.

FARM STANDS

A great place to find farm stands is south of Routes 7 and 8. More than 30 run along or just off these routes

Boardman Farm (✉ 64 Hewins St., Sheffield ☎ 413/229–8554) offers fresh vegetables and is open all day, every day, on an honor system from mid-July through Thanksgiving.

Whitney's Farm (✉ 1775 S. State Rd. [Rte. 8], Cheshire ☎ 413/442–4749 ⊕ www.whitneysfarm.com ☉ Mon.–Sat. 8–7, Sun. 9–6) sells fresh produce, plants and flowers, herbs, baked goods, and dairy products.

Sidehill Farm (✉ 137 Beldingville Rd., Ashfield ☎ 413/625–0011 ⊕ www.sidehillfarm.net), a little farther east (closer to Route 2 and Interstate 91), has vegetables, plus yogurt (year-round) and raw milk (April through Nov.) from grass-fed cows

YOU-PICK FARMS

Farms where you pick your own produce are very popular in Massachusetts. pend a morning or afternoon wandering these fields and orchards for fresh fruits and veggies right off vine and branch.

Taft Farms (✉ Route 183 and Division St., Great Barrington ☎ 413/528–1515 ⊕ www.taftfarms.com) has strawberries from mid-June through early July, raspberries from early July through mid-October (calling ahead

is recommended), and pumpkins from September through October. Picking hours are daily 9–6.

Green River Farms (✉ 2480 Green River Rd., Williamstown ☎ 413/458–2470 ⊕ www.greenriverfarms.com) is flush with blueberries and strawberries from mid-June through early July, and apples and pumpkins from September through October. It's open Tues.–Sat. 10–6, Sunday 11–5.

Blueberry Hill Farm (✉ 100 East St., Mount Washington ☎ 413/528–1479 ⊕ www.austinfarm.com) offers blueberries for the picking from late July through August. Operating hours are Thursday through Monday 9–5. Bring your own container for berries, and they'll be priced at $2 per pound.

Howden Farm (✉ 303 Rannopo Rd., Sheffield ☎ 413/229–8481 ⊕ www.howdenfarm.com) has raspberries for picking from mid-August through mid-October, 11–5 daily; and pumpkin picking from late September through October, weekends only, 11–5.

Ioka Valley Farm (✉ 3475 Route 43, Hancock ☎ 413/738–5915 ⊕ www.iokavalleyfarm.com) has strawberries from mid-June to early July—picking times vary, so call ahead—and pumpkins and Indian corn from mid-September through October on weekends only, 10–5:30.

FOR MORE INFORMATION

To learn more about Berkshire farms, food producers, farm-to-table restaurants, workshops, and other events, check out **Berkshire Grown** (☎ 413/528–0041 ⊕ www.berkshiregrown.org) or the **Northeast Organic Farming Association** (☎ 978/355–2853 ⊕ www.nofamass.org).

—Jen Laskey

4

$$–$$$$ 🛏 **Red Lion Inn**. An inn since 1773, the Red Lion has hosted presidents,
Fodor's Choice vice presidents, senators, and other celebrities. It consists of a large
★ main building and eight annexes, each of which is different (one is a
converted fire station). If you like historic buildings filled with antiques,
request a room in the main building: many of these units are small,
and the furnishings are a tad worn in places, but this is the authentic
inn. If you want more space and more modern furnishings, request a
room in one of the annex buildings. **Pros:** inviting lobby with fireplace;
quaintly romantic. **Cons:** overpriced dining room; puny fitness center.
⊠ *30 Main St.* ☎ *413/298–5545 or 413/298–1690* ⊕ *www.redlioninn.*
com ⊅ *82 rooms, 71 with bath, 26 suites* ⟳ *In-room: a/c, DVD (some),*
Wi-Fi. In-hotel: 3 restaurants, bars, pool, gym, Internet terminal ⊟ *AE,*
D, DC, MC, V ﾁⓄﾁ *CP.*

GREAT BARRINGTON

7 mi southwest of Stockbridge; 13 mi north of Canaan, Connecticut.

The largest town in South County became, in 1781, the first place in the
United States to free a slave under due process of law and was also the
birthplace, in 1868, of W. E. B. DuBois, the civil rights leader, author,
and educator. The many ex–New Yorkers who live in Great Barrington
expect great food and service, and the restaurants here deliver complex,
delicious fare. The town is also a favorite of antique hunters, as are the
nearby villages of South Egremont and Sheffield.

ESSENTIALS

Visitor Information Southern Berkshire Chamber of Commerce (⊠ *362*
Main St. 413/528–1510 or 800/269–4825 ⊕ *www.southernberkshires.com*).

SPORTS AND THE OUTDOORS

Bartholomew's Cobble. This natural rock garden beside the Housatonic
River (the Native American name means "river beyond the mountains")
is filled with trees, ferns, wildflowers, and 5 mi of hiking trails. The
277-acre site has a visitor center and museum. ⊠ *Weatogue Rd., U.S.*
7A, Sheffield ☎ *413/229–8600* ⊕ *www.thetrustees.org* ⊠ *$5* ⓸ *Daily*
dawn–dusk.

HIKING A 90-mi swath of the Appalachian Trail cuts through the Berkshires.
You'll also find hundreds of miles of trails elsewhere throughout the
area's forests and parks. On Highway 23, about 4 mi east of where U.S.
7 and Highway 23 intersect, is a sign for the **Appalachian Trail** (⊕ *www.*
nps.gov/appa) and a parking lot. Enter the trail for a moderately strenu-
ous 45-minute hike. At the top of the trail is Ice Gulch, a gorge so deep
and cold that there is often ice in it even in summer. Follow the Ice
Gulch ridge to the shelter and a large flat rock from which you can see
a wide panorama of the valley.

For great views with minimal effort, hike **Monument Mountain** (☎ *413/*
298–3239 ⊕ *www.thetrustees.org*), famous as a spot for literary inspira-
tion. Nathaniel Hawthorne and Herman Melville trekked it on August
5, 1850, and sought shelter in a cave when a thunderstorm hit. In the
cave, they discussed ideas that would become part of a novel called
Moby-Dick. While poet William Cullen Bryant stayed in the area, he

penned a lyrical poem, "Monument Mountain," about a lovesick Mohican maiden who jumped to her death from the cliffs. Feel like hiking? An easy 2.5-mi loop is reachable via a parking lot off U.S. 7, 4 mi north of Great Barrington.

SKI AREAS   With a 1,000-foot vertical drop, 100% snowmaking capacity, and even grades, **Catamount Ski Area** (⊠ *Hwy. 23, South Egremont* ☎ *413/528–1262; 800/342–1840 snow conditions* ⊕ *www.catamountski.com*) is ideal for family skiing. It has the most varied terrain in the Berkshires. There are 28 trails, served by seven lifts, plus a snowboard area called Megaplex Terrain Park, which is separated from the downhill area and has its own lift and a 400-foot half-pipe. The Sidewinder, an intermediate cruising trail, is more than 1 mi from top to bottom. There's also lighted nighttime boarding and skiing.

Ski Butternut (⊠ *380 State Rd. [Hwy. 23]* ☎ *413/528–2000 Ext. 112; 413/528–4433 ski school; 800/438–7669 snow conditions* ⊕ *www.skibutternut.com*) has good base facilities, pleasant skiing, 100% snowmaking capabilities, and the longest quad lift in the Berkshires. Two top-to-bottom terrain parks are for snowboarders, and Butternut Basin has 6 mi of groomed cross-country trails. There are five lanes of snow tubing. For downhill skiing, only a steep chute or two interrupt the mellow terrain on 22 mostly intermediate trails. Eight lifts keep skier traffic spread out. Ski and snowboard lessons are available. In summer Butternut usually hosts a crafts show and children's activities.

SHOPPING

ANTIQUES   The Great Barrington area, including the small towns of Sheffield and South Egremont, has the Berkshires' greatest concentration of antiques stores. Some shops are open sporadically, and many are closed on Tuesday. At the **Great Barrington Antiques Center** (⊠ *964 S. Main St., U.S. 7* ☎ *413/644–8848* ⊕ *www.greatbarringtonantiquescenter.com*) 50 dealers crowd onto one floor, selling Oriental rugs, furniture, and smaller decorative pieces. At the **Country Dining Room** (⊠ *178 Main St., U.S. 7* ☎ *413/528–5050* ⊕ *www.countrydiningroomantiq.com*) you can find elegant antique furniture, glass, and china. **Elise Abrams Antiques** (⊠ *11 Stockbridge Rd., U.S. 7* ☎ *413/528–3201* ⊕ *www.eliseabrams.com*) sells fine antique china, glassware, and furniture.

FOOD AND   **Bizalion** (⊠ *684 Main St.* ☎ *413/644–9988* ⊕ *www.bizalionsfinefood.*
COOKWARE   *blogspot.com*), a French specialty food shop and café, has imported cheeses, 10 different olive oils, cured meats, and brick-oven-baked baguettes and pastries.

THE ARTS

Catch a classic movie or a performance by, perhaps, Suzanne Vega or the Berkshire Bach Society at the **Mahaiwe Performing Arts Center** (⊠ *14 Castle St.* ☎ *413/528–0100* ⊕ *www.mahaiwe.org*). This stunning 1905 theater offers a year-round schedule of live music, dance, and film.

WHERE TO EAT AND STAY

$–$$ ✕ **Baba Louie's Sourdough Pizza Co.** How good is the pizza at Baba Louie's?
PIZZA   So good that crowds spill into the sidewalk waiting for a table at 2 PM in the off season. Could be the wonderful chewy-crunchy crusts made of organic wheat and spelt berries (in case you need to feel virtuous about

eating pizza). Could be the inspired toppings, like wilted spinach, figs, prosciutto, and Parmesan (on the Dolce Vita) or roasted sweet potatoes and parsnips, shaved fennel, caramelized onions, and fresh mozzarella with a hint of balsamic vinegar (on the Isabella Pizzarella). The wait for the table is so worth it. ⊠ *286 Main St.* ☎ *413/528–8100* ⊕ *www. babalouiessourdoughpizzacompany.com* ▭ *AE, MC, V.*

$$–$$$ ✕ **Castle Steet Café.** Chef-owner Michael Ballon wins raves for his simple-
CAFÉ but-elegant cuisine and masterful hand with fresh local produce. Local
★ artwork, hardwood floors, and sleek furnishings create an understated interior—a perfect backdrop for sautéed sea scallops with wild ramps and garlic sauce, local shad roe with bacon and onion, and warm duck salad with cashews and Asian slaw. Other things to love about Castle Street Café: The fabulous wine list, the bread basket (featuring a warm potato-onion loaf from Berkshire Mountain Bakery), and nightly jazz at the Celestial Bar (no cover charge). ⊠ *10 Castle St.* ☎ *413/528–5244* ⊕ *www.castlestreetcafe.com* ▭ *AE, MC, V* ⊘ *Closed Tues.*

$–$$$ ⌂ **Egremont Inn.** The public rooms in this 1780 stagecoach inn are enor-mous, and each has a fireplace. Bedrooms are on the small side but have four-poster beds (some have claw-foot baths) and unpretentious furnishings. On weekends in July and August you can book only two-night packages, which include breakfast daily and one dinner during your stay. **Pros:** good food in on-site restaurant. **Cons:** small, rustic bathrooms; some signs of age. ⊠ *10 Old Sheffield Rd., South Egremont* ☎ *413/528–2111 or 800/859–1780* ⊕ *www.egremontinn.com* ⇡ *22 rooms, 1 suite* ⌂ *In-room: a/c, no phone, no TV. In-hotel: restaurant, bar, tennis court, pool* ▭ *AE, D, MC, V* ⊚ *CP, MAP.*

STURBRIDGE AND THE PIONEER VALLEY

A string of historic settlements lines the majestic Connecticut River, the wide and winding waterway that runs through western Massachusetts. The bustling city of Springfield, known for its family-friendly attractions and museums, along with a cluster of college towns and quaint, rural villages is part of the Pioneer Valley, which formed the western frontier of New England from the early 1600s until the late 1900s.

Educational pioneers came to this region and created a wealth of major colleges including Mount Holyoke (the first college in the country for women), Amherst, Smith, Hampshire, and the University of Massa-chusetts. Northampton and Amherst serve as the valley's cultural hubs today; both have become increasingly desirable places to live, drawing former city dwellers who relish the ample natural scenery, sophisticated cultural venues, and lively dining and shopping.

SPRINGFIELD

90 mi west of Boston; 30 mi north of Hartford, Connecticut.

Springfield, easily accessed from Interstates 90 and 91, is the busy hub of the Pioneer Valley. Known as the birthplace of basketball (the game was devised by local gym instructor James Naismith in 1891 as a last-

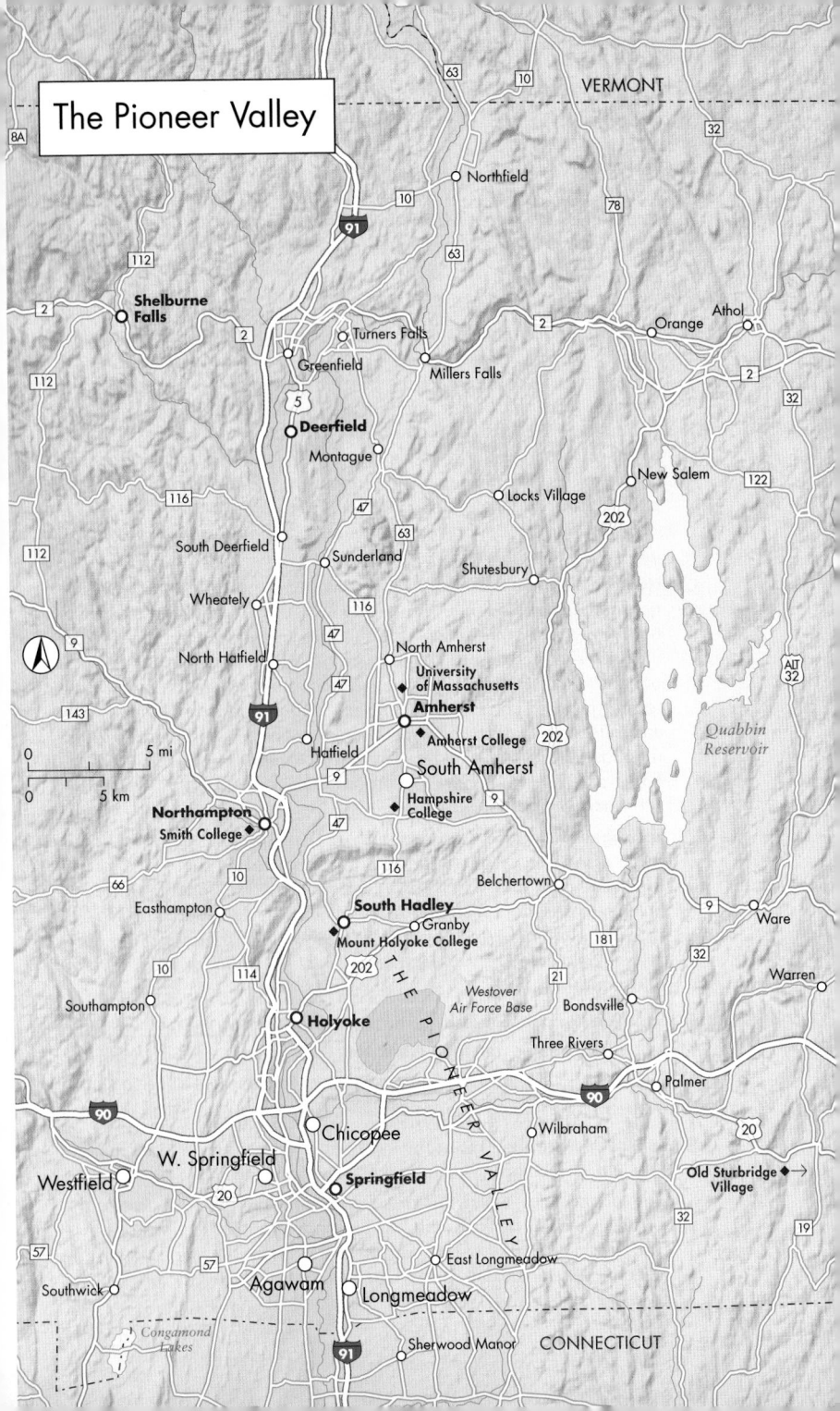

The Pioneer Valley

VERMONT

8A

112
2 **Shelburne Falls**

91

2

Turners Falls

Greenfield

63

10

Northfield

78

32

Orange

Athol

2

32

5

112

116

Deerfield

Montague

Millers Falls

Locks Village

New Salem

122

202

South Deerfield

Sunderland

63

Shutesbury

112

47

116

Wheately

47

North Hatfield

North Amherst

University of Massachusetts

9

143

91

Hatfield

9

Amherst

♦ Amherst College

202

South Amherst

Quabbin Reservoir

ALT 32

0   5 mi
0   5 km

Northampton
Smith College ♦

47

♦ **Hampshire College**

9

66

10

116

Belchertown

9

Ware

Easthampton

South Hadley
♦ Granby
Mount Holyoke College ♦

181

32

Warren

10

114

Southampton

202

T H E   P I O N E E R

Westover Air Force Base

21

Bondsville

32

Holyoke

Three Rivers

90

Palmer

20

90

Westfield

W. Springfield

♦ Chicopee

Wilbraham

Old Sturbridge ♦ →
Village

32

19

20

57

57

Southwick

Congamond Lakes

Agawam

Springfield

Longmeadow

East Longmeadow

V A L L E Y

91

Sherwood Manor

CONNECTICUT

minute attempt to keep a group of unruly teenagers occupied in winter), the city has a cluster of fine museums and family attractions.

ESSENTIALS

Visitor Information Greater Springfield Convention & Visitors Bureau (⌧ *1441 Main St.* ☎ *413/787–1548 or 800/723–1548* ⊕ *www.valleyvisitor.com*). **Sturbridge Area Tourist Association** (⌧ *380 Main St.* ☎ *888/788–7274 or 800/628–8379* ⊕ *www.sturbridge.org*).

EXPLORING

Forest Park. At this leafy, 735-acre retreat hiking paths wind through the trees, paddleboats navigate Porter Lake, and hungry ducks float on a small pond. The zoo, where Theodore Geisel—better known as Dr. Seuss—found inspiration for his children's books, is home to nearly 200 animals, from black bears and bobcats to emus, lemurs, and wallabies. It's manageable in size, and spotting animals in the exhibits is fairly easy, which makes this an especially good stop for families with small children. Another plus: you can purchase small bags of food from the gift shop and feed many of the animals. ⌧ *302 Sumner Ave.* ☎ *413/733–2251* ⊕ *www.forestparkzoo.org* ⌧ *Zoo $6* ⊙ *Zoo Apr.–Columbus Day, daily 10–5; Columbus Day–Nov., weekends 10–3:30.*

Fodor's Choice
★

Naismith Memorial Basketball Hall of Fame. Along the banks of the Connecticut River, this 80,000-square-foot facility is dedicated to Springfield's own Dr. James Naismith, who invented the game in 1891. It includes a soaring domed arena where you can practice jumpers, dozens of high-tech interactive exhibits, and video footage and interviews with former players. The Honors Rings pay tribute to the hall's nearly 300 enshrinees. It's easy to find—just look for the 15-story spire with an illuminated basketball on top. ⌧ *1000 W. Columbus Ave.* ☎ *413/781–6500 or 877/446–6752* ⊕ *www.hoophall.com* ⌧ *$17* ⊙ *Weekdays 10–4, weekends 10–5.*

Six Flags New England. Containing more than 160 rides and shows, this mega attraction, 4 mi southwest of Springfield, is the region's largest theme park and water park. Rides include the Superman Ride of Steel, which is more than 20 stories tall and has a top speed of 77 MPH. ⌧ *1623 Main St., Agawam* ☎ *413/786–9300* ⊕ *www.sixflags.com/newengland* ⌧ *$41.99* ⊙ *Hrs vary. Check Web site or call for more information.*

QUICK BITES

Springfield's South End is the home of a lively Little Italy with some excellent restaurants, as well as La Fiorentina Pastry Shop (⌧ *883 Main St.* ☎ *413/732–3151* ⊕ *www.lafiorentinapastry.com*), which has been doling out heavenly pastries, butter cookies, and coffees since the 1940s.

Springfield Museums. One of the most ambitious cultural venues in New England, this complex includes five impressive facilities:

The **Connecticut Valley Historical Museum**, the most modest of the group, presents changing exhibits drawn from its collections of furniture, silver, industrial objects, autos, and firearms; its main draw is the in-depth genealogical library, where folks from all over the world come to research their family trees.

The must-see **George Walter Vincent Smith Art Museum** houses a fascinating private art collection that includes 19th-century American paintings by Frederic Church and Albert Bierstadt. A Japanese antiquities room is filled with armor, textiles, and porcelain, as well as carved jade and rock-crystal snuff bottles.

The **Museum of Fine Arts** has paintings by Paul Gauguin, Claude Monet, Pierre-Auguste Renoir, Edgar Degas, Winslow Homer, and J. Alden Weir, as well as 18th-century American paintings and contemporary works by Georgia O'Keeffe, Frank Stella, and George Bellows. Rotating exhibits are open throughout the year.

The **Springfield Science Museum** has an Exploration Center of touchable displays, the oldest operating planetarium in the United States, an extensive collection of stuffed and mounted animals, dinosaur exhibits, and the African Hall, through which you can take an interactive tour of that continent's flora and fauna.

The **Museum of Springfield History** opened in fall of 2009 and tells the story of the town's manufacturing heritage. (Springfield was home to the former Indian Motorcycle Company, and the museum has a rich collection of Indian bikes and memorabilia.) Also on the grounds is the **Dr. Seuss National Memorial Sculpture Garden,** an installation of five bronze statues depicting scenes from Theodore Geisel's famously whimsical children's books. Born in Springfield in 1904, Geisel was inspired by the animals at Forest Park Zoo, where his father served as director. The statues include a 4-foot Lorax, a 10-foot Yertle the Turtle, and a towering book inscribed with the entire text of *Oh the Places You'll Go!*

⊠ *220 State St., at Chestnut St.* ☎ *413/263–6800* ⊕ *www. springfieldmuseums.org* ⊠ *$10 for all museums* ☉ *Springfield Science Museum Tues.–Sat. 10–5, Sun 11–5. Museum of Fine Arts, George Walter Vincent Art Museum, and Connecticut Valley Historical Museum Tues.– Sun. 11–4. Outdoor Dr. Seuss Sculpture Garden daily dawn–dusk.*

**OFF THE
BEATEN
PATH**

Fodor's Choice ★ **Old Sturbridge Village** (⊠ *1 Old Sturbridge Village Rd.* ☎ *508/347–3362 or 800/733–1830* ⊕ *www.osv.org* ⊠ *$20* ☉ *Mid-Apr.–late Oct., daily 9:30–4; late Oct.–mid-Apr., Tues.–Sun. 9:30–4*), modeled on an early-19th-century New England town, is a re-creation of a Colonial-era village with more than 40 historic buildings that were moved here from other towns. Some of the homes are filled with canopy beds and elaborate furnishings; in the simpler, single-story cottages, interpreters wearing period costumes demonstrate home-based crafts like spinning, weaving, and shoe making. There are several industrial buildings, including a working sawmill. On the informative boat ride along the Quinebaug River, you can learn about river life in 19th-century New England and catch a glimpse of ducks, geese, turtles, and other local wildlife. Nearby is the tiny town of Brimfield, home to one of the country's largest antiques fairs, held several times a year.

WHERE TO EAT

$–$$

CREOLE

✕ **Big Mamou.** If you're cravin' Creole, you can't miss this casual joint, with seriously good, uncomplicated Louisiana cuisine. Owner/chef Wayne Booker stands behind the kitchen counter, and his hometown

Costumed historians are part of the 19th-century Old Sturbridge Village.

recipes, like Louisiana Lenny's sausage and chicken ya-ya (chicken breast wrapped around andouille sausage with Creole spices), shrimp-and-sausage jambalaya, barbecue pulled pork, and Bayou meatloaf. Added bonus: You can bring your own bottle. ⊠ *63 Liberty St.* ☎ *413/732–1011* ⊕ *www.chefwaynes-bigmamou.com* ⊟ *MC, V* ⊗ *Closed Sun.*

$$–$$$
ECLECTIC
Fodor'sChoice
★
✕ **Cedar Street.** Arguably the finest, most creative place to dine in Sturbridge and beyond, this intimate eatery, housed in a modest but charming Victorian house, is a showcase for culinary creations. The menu changes frequently, but you can expect starters like crab Napoleon topped with cucumber ceviche or sweet-potato ravioli. Entrées include signature dishes like the cedar plank salmon and the rich bouillabaisse brimming with shrimp, scallops, tuna, clams, and more. ⊠ *12 Cedar St., Sturbridge* ☎ *508/347–5800* ⊕ *www.cedarstreeetrestaurant.com* ⊟ *AE, MC, V* ⊗ *No lunch.*

¢–$
VIETNAMESE
★
✕ **Pho Saigon.** This ethnic eatery, which is small, tastefully understated, and a little out of the way, serves up some of the best authentic Vietnamese cuisine in the city at wallet-pleasing prices. Enjoy full-of-flavor, made-from-scratch soups, the shrimp cakes with shredded yam, and the vermicelli dishes. There are lots of rice dishes and vegetarian options, as well as house specialties like the sizzling catfish filets and the Vietnamese Happy Pancake, a rice batter crepe stuffed with shrimp and chicken. ⊠ *398 Dickinson St.* ☎ *413/781–4488* ⊟ *MC, V* ⊗ *Closed Wed.*

WHERE TO STAY

$
★
🏠 **Naomi's Inn.** This elegantly restored house in a residential neighborhood has six individually decorated suites, all with lush comfort and artistic flair. The Louis XIV suite has two large rooms, 19th-century

armoires, a down-filled sofa, and custom-tiled bath. The French Provincial suite has a custom-made iron king-sized bed, tiled bath, and an adjoining room with two twin beds that is perfect for families. The bright and airy kitchen is a pleasant place to gather, and a group of area restaurants will deliver food, which the owner is happy to serve on china plates. **Pros:** elegantly designed; deluxe linens and baths; warm and knowledgeable hosts. **Cons:** near the hospital, so you may hear sirens. ✉ *20 Springfield St.* ☎ *413/433–6019 or 888/762–6647* ⊕ *www. naomisinn.net* ⇱ *6 suites* ⚬ *In-room: a/c, refrigerator (some), Wi-Fi. In-hotel: laundry facilities, Wi-Fi hotspot, parking (free)* ═ *AE, D, DC, MC, V* ⊙ *BP.*

$–$$

Fodor'sChoice

★

4

🏠 **Publick House Historic Inn.** Step back in time at this rambling 1771 inn. Rooms are Colonial in design, with wide plank floors, period antiques and reproductions, and canopy beds. The public areas, including several dining rooms and a tavern, have original woodwork and fireplaces. The inn, with 60 surrounding acres, sits on the picturesque Town Green. It also owns and maintains the neighboring Chamberlain House, consisting of six larger suites (all need serious updating), and the Country Motor Lodge, with spacious, no-frills motel-style rooms. **Pros:** Colonial ambience and architecture; historical significance; log fires and candlelight throughout. **Cons:** rattling pipes; thin walls; small bathrooms. ✉ *227 Main St. (Hwy. 131), Sturbridge* ☎ *508/347–3313 or 800/782–5425* ⊕ *www.publickhouse.com* ⇱ *14 rooms, 3 suites in main inn* ⚬ *In-room: a/c, Wi-Fi. In-hotel: 4 restaurants, bar, Wi-Fi hotspot, Internet terminal, parking (free)* ═ *AE, D, DC, MC, V.*

SOUTH HADLEY

12 north of Springfield.

Nestled in the heart of Pioneer Valley, this small, quiet college town, with a cluster of Main Street cafés and stores, is surrounded by rolling hills and farmlands. It's best known for the Mount Holyoke College Art Museum, one of the finest in the region.

EXPLORING

Mount Holyoke College. Founded in 1837, Mount Holyoke was the first women's college in the United States. Among its alumnae are poet Emily Dickinson and playwright Wendy Wasserstein. The handsome wooded campus, encompassing two lakes and lovely walking or riding trails, was landscaped by Frederick Law Olmsted. ✉ *50 College St.* ☎ *413/538–2000* ⊕ *www.mtholyoke.edu.*

Mount Holyoke College Art Museum. This museum contains some 11,000 works, including Asian, European, and American paintings and sculpture. ✉ *Lower Lake Rd.* ☎ *413/538–2245* ⊕ *www.mtholyoke.edu* 🎟 *Free* ☉ *Tues.–Fri. 11–5, weekends 1–5.*

SHOPPING

In addition to stocking 50,000 new and used titles, the **Odyssey Bookshop** (✉ *9 College St.* ☎ *413/534–7307* ⊕ *www.odysseybks.com*) has readings and book signings by locally and nationally known authors.

WHERE TO EAT

$$–$$$ ✕ **Food 101 Bar and Bistro.** There's nothing basic about this popular, oh-
ECLECTIC so-calm, candle-lighted eatery across from the Mount Holyoke campus.
Fodor'sChoice Dishes are complicated but mostly successful, like the best-selling risotto
★ with sautéed green squash and basil oil; the upscale *pommes frites*
(french fries) with spicy ketchup and wasabi mayonnaise; and the pan-
seared sea scallops with cauliflower risotto, crab and mâche salad, and
warm curry oil. This spot is a magnet for foodies, yuppies, and college
students on their parents' tab. ✉ *19 College St.* ☎ *413/535–3101* ▭ *AE,
DC, MC, V* ☉ *Closed Mon. No lunch*.

NORTHAMPTON

10 mi northeast of South Hadley.

The cultural center of western Massachusetts is without a doubt the
city of Northampton (nicknamed "Noho"), whose vibrant downtown
is packed with interesting eateries, lively clubs, and offbeat boutiques.
The city attracts artsy types, academics, activists, lesbians and gays, and
just about anyone else seeking the culture and sophistication of a big
metropolis but the friendliness and easy pace of a small town.

ESSENTIALS

Visitor Information Greater Northampton Chamber of Commerce (✉ *99 Pleasant St.* ☎ *413/584–1900 or 800/238–6869* ⊕ *www.northamptonuncommon.com*).

EXPLORING

Forbes Library. The Coolidge Room at this library contains a collection
of President Calvin Coolidge's papers and memorabilia. Northampton
was the 30th president's Massachusetts home. He practiced law here
and served as mayor from 1910 to 1911. ✉ *20 West St.* ☎ *413/587–
1011* ⊕ *www.forbeslibrary.org*.

▌QUICK
│ BITES

On the lower level of Thorne's Marketplace, **Herrell's Ice Cream** (✉ *8
Old South St.* ☎ *413/586–9700* ⊕ *www.herrells.com*) is famous for its
chocolate pudding, vanilla malt, and cinnamon flavors, as well as delicious
homemade hot fudge.

Historic Northampton Museum and Education Center. Three houses here
are open for tours: Parsons House (1730), Shepherd House (1798),
and Damon House (1813). Together, they hold some 50,000 historical
artifacts, including photographs, manuscripts dating back to the 17th
century, fine furniture, ceramics, glass, and costumes. Exhibits in the
main building chronicle the history of Northampton with documents,
photos, and collectibles. ✉ *46 Bridge St.* ☎ *413/584–6011* ⊕ *www.
historic-northampton.org* ▭ *$3* ☉ *Mon.–Sat. 10–5, Sun. noon–5.*

Smith College. The nation's largest liberal arts college for women opened
its doors in 1875 (thanks to heiress Sophia Smith). Renowned for its
School of Social Work, Smith has a long list of distinguished alumnae, among them activist Gloria Steinem, chef Julia Child, and writer
Margaret Mitchell. One of the most serene campuses in New England,
Smith is also a leading center of political and cultural activity. Two sites
on Smith's campus, the Lyman Plant House and the Botanic Garden of

Smith College, should be visited. The **Lyman Plant House** (📠 *413/585–2740* ⊕ *www.smith.edu*) is home to more than 2,500 species of plants. The flourishing **Botanic Garden of Smith College** covers the entirety of Smith's 150-acre campus.

The **Smith College Museum of Art** (✉ *Brown Fine Arts Center, Elm St.* 📠 *413/585–2760* ⊕ *www.smith.edu/artmuseum* 🎟 *$5* ⊗ *Tues.–Sat. 10–4, Sun. noon–4*) includes a floor of skylighted galleries, an enclosed courtyard for performances and receptions, and a high-tech art-history library. Highlights of the permanent collection include European masterworks by Paul Cézanne, Degas, Auguste Rodin, and Georges Seurat, and works by woman artists like Mary Cassatt and Alice Neel.

William Cullen Bryant Homestead. About 20 mi northwest of Northampton, in the scenic hills west of the Pioneer Valley, is the country estate of the 19th-century poet and author William Cullen Bryant. Inside the Dutch Colonial mansion built in 1783 are furnishings and collectibles from Bryant's life, work, and travels. Outside, the 465-acre grounds overlooking the Westfield River Valley are a great venue for bird-watching, cross-country skiing, snowshoeing, fishing, hiking, and picnics. ✉ *207 Bryant Rd., Cummington* 📠 *413/634–2244* ⊕ *www. thetrustees.org* 🎟 *Grounds free, house open by guided tours only, $5* ⊗ *House late June–Columbus Day, weekends and Mon. holidays 1–5; Grounds daily sunrise–sunset.*

SPORTS AND THE OUTDOORS

The **Norwottuck Rail Trail**, part of the Connecticut River Greenway State Park, is a paved 10-mi path that links Northampton with Belchertown by way of Amherst. Great for biking, rollerblading, jogging, and cross-country skiing, it runs along the old Boston & Maine Railroad route. ✉ *Entry points include Hwy. 9 in Northampton at the junction of Damon Rd. (near Coolidge Bridge) and Hwy. 9 in Hadley at the junction of River Dr. (Hwy. 47 N)* 📠 *413/586–8706 Ext. 12.*

NIGHTLIFE AND THE ARTS

The spacious **Diva's** (✉ *492 Pleasant St.* 📠 *413/586–8161* ⊕ *www. divasofnoho.com*) serves the region's sizable lesbian and gay community with great music that draws people to the cavernous dance floor. The reliable **Fitzwilly's** (✉ *23 Main St.* 📠 *413/584–8666* ⊕ *www.fitzwillys. com*) draws a friendly mix of locals and tourists for drinks and tasty pub fare. The dimly lighted and somewhat dive-y **Hugo's** (✉ *315 Pleasant St.* 📠 *413/534–9800*) has cheap beer, affordable pool, a rocking jukebox, and all the local color you'll ever want to see.

WHERE TO EAT

$–$$ ✕ **Mulino's Trattoria.** In sleek quarters (which also contain the upstairs ITALIAN Bishop's Lounge), this modern trattoria carefully prepares Sicilian-inspired, home-style Italian food. You'll rarely taste a better carbonara sauce this side of the Atlantic, but don't overlook the smoked salmon in a lemon-caper-shallot sauce tossed with fettuccine or the melt-in-your-mouth grilled veal porterhouse. Portions are huge, and the wine list is extensive. Parents like to take their college kids here for a special night out. ✉ *41 Strong Ave.* 📠 *413/586–8900* ⊕ *www.mulinosrestaurant.com* 🍴 *AE, D, DC, MC, V* ⊗ *No lunch.*

$-$$
AMERICAN
✕ **Northampton Brewery.** In a rambling building in Brewster Court, this noisy and often-packed pub and microbrewery has extensive outdoor seating on a deck. The kitchen serves an array of sandwiches and tasty comfort food, including black-bean dip, chicken-and-shrimp jambalaya, and the blackened blue burger (with blue cheese and caramelized onions). ⊠ *13 Old South St.* ☎ *413/584–9903* ⊕ *www.northamptonbrewery.com* ⊟ *AE, D, DC, MC, V.*

$$
ITALIAN
Fodor'sChoice
★
✕ **Spoleto.** A Noho mainstay since the 1980s, Spoleto, in the heart of downtown, offers a something-for-everyone menu: basic beef, chicken, seafood, and pasta dishes served with a dash of creative flair and flavor. The beef carpaccio and angel-hair crab cakes are first-rate. You'll find typical spaghetti and meatball and chicken Parmesan dishes alongside the more adventurous pork saltimbocca. The Gorgonzola bread is a nice side dish. Join the locals for the excellent Sunday brunch (11–2:30). ⊠ *50 Main St.* ☎ *413/586–6313* ⊕ *www.spoletorestaurants.com* ⊟ *AE, DC, MC, V* ☺ *No lunch.*

AMHERST

★   *8 mi northeast of Northampton.*

One of the most visited spots in all of New England, Amherst is known for its scores of world-renowned authors, poets, and artists. The above-average intelligence quotient of its population is no accident, as Amherst is home to a trio of colleges—Amherst, Hampshire, and the University of Massachusetts. The high concentration of college-age humanity bolsters Amherst's downtown area, which includes a wide range of art galleries, music stores, and clothing boutiques.

ESSENTIALS

Visitor Information Amherst Area Chamber of Commerce (⊠ 409 Main St. 413/253–0700 ⊕ www.amherstarea.com).

EXPLORING

Emily Dickinson Museum. The famed Amherst poet lived here her entire life (1830–86) in this brick Federal-style home. Admission is by guided tour only, and the highlight is getting to stand in the sunlit bedroom where the poet wrote many of her works. The museum is outfitted with period accoutrements, including original wall hangings and lace curtains. To say that the tour guides are knowledgeable in Dickinson's story would be a massive understatement. Next door is **The Evergreens** (⊠ *214 Main St.* ☎ *413/253–5272*), an imposing Italianate Victorian mansion in which Emily's brother Austin and his family resided for more than 50 years. Unlike the Dickinson homestead, which has few of the family's original possessions, the Evergreens is packed with Austin's family's heirlooms. ⊠ *280 Main St.* ☎ *413/542–8161* ⊕ *www. emilydickinsonmuseum.org* ▣ *Guided tours $3–$8* ☺ *Mar.–May and Sept.–mid-Dec., Wed.–Sun. 11–4; June–Aug., Wed.–Sun. 10–5.*

QUICK BITES

Newspapers and books are strewn about the tables at the **Black Sheep** (⊠ **79 Main St.** ☎ **413/253–3442** ⊕ **www.blacksheepdeli.com**), a funky downtown café specializing in coffees and creative sandwiches, salads, and soups. It's a great place to pick up on the college vibe; free Wi-Fi, too.

Eric Carle Museum of Picture Book Art. If you have kids in tow—or if you
FodorsChoice just love children's books art—"The Carle" is a must-see. This light-
★ filled museum celebrates and preserves not only the works of renowned
children's book author Eric Carle (who penned *The Very Hungry Caterpillar*), but also Maurice Sendak, Lucy Cousins, Petra Mathers, Tomie
DePaola, and Leo and Diane Dillon. Puppet shows, lectures, author
events, and storytelling are part of the museum's ongoing calendar of
events. Children are invited to create their own works of art in the
museum's studio or read a few classics (or discover new authors) in the
library. ⊠ *125 W. Bay Rd.* ☎ *413/658–1100* ⊕ *www.picturebookart.
org* ⊠ *$7* ☉ *Tues.–Fri. 10–4, Sat. 10–5, Sun. noon–5.*

★ **National Yiddish Book Center.** Founded in 1980 by Aaron Lansky, a student on a mission to rescue Yiddish books from basements and dump-
sters, this nonprofit organization has become a major force in the effort
to preserve the Yiddish language and Jewish culture. On the campus of
Hampshire College, the center is housed in a thatch-roof building that
resembles a cluster of houses in a traditional Eastern European *shtetl,*
or village. Inside, a contemporary space contains more than 1.5 million
books, a fireside reading area, a kosher dining room, and a visitor center
with changing exhibits. The work here is performed out in the open:
hundreds of books pour in daily, everything from family keepsakes
to rare manuscripts. ⊠ *1021 West St. (Hwy. 116)* ☎ *413/256–4900*
⊕ *www.yiddishbookcenter.org* ⊠ *Free* ☉ *Weekdays 10–4, Sun. 11–4.*

SHOPPING

An institution in the Pioneer Valley, the **Atkins Farms Country Market**
(⊠ *Hwy. 116, South Amherst* ☎ *413/253–9528* ⊕ *www.atkinsfarms.
com*) is surrounded by apple orchards and gorgeous views of the Holyoke Ridge. Hayrides are offered in fall, and children's events happen
throughout the year. Inside, you'll find a bakery and deli; the market
sells produce, baked goods, and specialty foods.

NIGHTLIFE AND THE ARTS

Amherst Brewing Company (⊠ *24 N. Pleasant St.* ☎ *413/253–4400*
⊕ *www.amherstbrewing.com*) (aka "the ABC") has a decent-size dance
floor, lounge, game room, and a vast selection of beers brewed on the
premises. The **Harp** (⊠ *163 Sunderland Rd.* ☎ *413/548–6900* ⊕ *www.
theharp.net*) is a small but cozy Irish tavern with live music on Thursday and Saturday nights.

WHERE TO EAT AND STAY

$–$$ ✕ **Bub's Bar-B-Q.** This rib joint, open for more than three decades, is one
SOUTHERN of the best in the state. Maybe it's the tangy, homemade sauce; maybe
★ it's the sides, like wilted collard greens, orange-glazed sweet potatoes,
black-eyed corn, and spicy ranch beans; likely, it's the heaping platters
of fall-off-the-bone ribs and pulled pork. ⊠ *676 Amherst Rd. (Hwy.
116), north of Amherst town line, Sunderland* ☎ *413/548–9630* ⊕ *www.
bubsbbq.com* ▭ *MC, V* ☉ *Closed Mon. No lunch on weekdays.*

¢–$$ ✕ **Judie's.** Since 1977, academic types have crowded around small tables
AMERICAN on the glassed-in porch, ordering traditional dishes like grilled chicken
FodorsChoice topped with lobster ravioli, steak and potatoes, seafood gumbo, and
★ probably the best bowl of French onion soup the town has to offer.

Your best bet? Try the more creative popover specials in flavors like gumbo and shrimp scampi. The atmosphere is hip and artsy; a painting covers each tabletop. ✉ *51 N. Pleasant St.* ☎ *413/253–3491* ⊕ *www.judiesrestaurant.com* ▭ *AE, D, MC, V.*

$$ 🏠 **Allen House Victorian & Amherst Inns.** A rare find, these late-19th-century inns a block apart from each other have been gloriously restored in accordance with the aesthetics of the Victorian era. Busy, colorful wall coverings reach to the high ceilings. Antiques include a burled-walnut headboard and dresser set, carved golden-oak beds, and wicker steamship chairs. Lace curtains and hand stenciling grace the rooms, which have supremely comfortable beds with goose-down comforters. **Pros:** lots of charm and elegance; great linens; free parking. **Cons:** rooms chock-full of ornate furnishings may be a bit much for some; tiny baths. ✉ *599 Main St. and 257 Main St.* ☎ *413/253–5000* ⊕ *www.allenhouse.com* 🛏 *14 rooms* 🖢 *In-room: a/c, no TV, Wi-Fi. In-hotel: Wi-Fi hotspot, parking (free)* ▭ *AE, MC, V* 🍽 *BP.*

DEERFIELD

10 mi northwest of Amherst.

In Deerfield, a horse pulling a carriage clip-clops past perfectly maintained 18th-century homes, neighbors tip their hats to strangers, kids play ball in fields by the river, and the bell of the impossibly beautiful brick church peals from a white steeple. This is the perfect New England village, though not without a past darkened by tragedy. Its original Native American inhabitants, the Pocumtucks, were all but wiped out by deadly epidemics and a war with the Mohawks. English pioneers eagerly settled into this frontier outpost in the 1660s and 1670s, but two bloody massacres at the hands of the Native Americans and the French caused the village to be abandoned until 1707, when construction began on the buildings that remain today.

EXPLORING

Fodor's Choice ★ **Historic Deerfield.** Although it has a turbulent past, this village now basks in a genteel aura. With 52 buildings on 93 acres, Historic Deerfield provides a vivid glimpse into 18th- and 19th-century America. Along the tree-lined main street are 13 museum houses, built between 1720 and 1850; two are open to the public on self-guided tours, and the remainder can be seen by guided tours that begin on the hour. At the **Wells-Thorn House,** various rooms depict life as it changed from 1725 to 1850. The adjacent **Frary House** has arts and crafts from the 1700s on display; the attached Barnard Tavern was the main meeting place for Deerfield's villagers. Also of note is the **Hinsdale and Anna Williams House,** the stately home for an affluent early New England couple. Purchased a ticket that lets you visit all the houses at the **Flynt Center of Early New England Life** (✉ *37-D Old Main St.*), which contains two galleries of silver and pewter as well as needlework and clothing dating back to the 1600s. lan at least one full day at Historic Deerfield. ✉ *Old Main St.* ☎ *413/775–7214* ⊕ *www.historic-deerfield.org* 🎟 *$12* ⊗ *Apr.–Nov., daily 9:30–4:30; Dec.–Mar., house museums open by appointment only, Flynt Center open weekends 9:30–4:30.*

Historic Deerfield is one of many places in the region to experience America's past through living history.

QUICK
BITES

A short drive from Historic Deerfield, **Richardson's Candy Kitchen** (✉ *500 Greenfield Rd.* ☎ *413/772-0443* ⊕ *www.richardsonscandy.com*) makes and sells luscious cream-filled truffles as well as other handmade chocolates and confections.

☺
Fodor's Choice
★

Magic Wings Butterfly Conservatory & Gardens. This lush place has a glass conservatory filled with more than 4,000 fluttering butterflies, as well as an extensive three-season outdoor garden filled with plants that attract local species. Observe the butterfly nursery, where newborns first take flight. An extensive garden shop sells butterfly-friendly plants; there are also Sunday-afternoon children's programs and events, a snack bar, and gift shop. ✉ *281 Greenfield Rd., South Deerfield* ☎ *413/665-2805* ⊕ *www.magicwings.net* ☑ *$12* ⊙ *Labor Day–Memorial Day, daily 9–5; Memorial Day–Labor Day, daily 9–6.*

WHERE TO EAT AND STAY

$$$$
AMERICAN
Fodor's Choice
★

✕ **Chandler's.** Inside Yankee Candle Village, devoted to candle making and selling, is also to one of the area's best restaurants. Though it's quite large, the restaurant retains a very intimate feel; the staff could not be more attentive. Start out with an asparagus, chive, and goat cheese tart or seared scallops with avocado and lime gastrique (a thick reduction sauce), then enjoy entrées like grilled organic salmon with lemon-marinated vegetables and grilled lamb rib chop with smoky lentils and gremolata (a condiment of chopped parsley, garlic, and lemon zest). Even though this is fine dining, Chandler's also has an excellent kids' menu. ✉ *25 Deerfield Rd., South Deerfield* ☎ *413/665-1277* ⊕ *www. yankeecandle.com* ⊟ *AE, DC, MC, V.*

$$$ Deerfield Inn. Period wallpaper, wide pine flooring, and fireplaces deco-
Fodor'sChoice   rate this historic 1884 inn and tavern. Rooms are snug and handsomely
★   appointed with both period antiques and reproductions; some rooms
have four-poster or canopy beds. Check out the cozy Colonial tavern,
with leather booths and candlelight. **Pros:** authentic Colonial details
and architecture; tiny on-site tavern oozes atmosphere; set in historic
Deerfield Village, surrounded by museum houses. **Cons:** bathrooms are
basic and tiny; sounds travel through halls (and into rooms). ⊠ *81 Old
Main St.* ☎ *413/774–5587 or 800/926–3865* ⊕ *www.deerfieldinn.com*
⇘ *23 rooms* ⚲ *In-room: a/c, DVD, Wi-Fi. In-hotel: 2 restaurants, bar,
Wi-Fi hotspot, parking (free)* ═ *AE, MC, V* ⦿ *BP.*

$ Sunnyside Farm Bed & Breakfast. Homey atmosphere, reasonable prices,
and a quiet, out-of-the-way location make this countryside B&B a favor-
ite with older couples and outdoor lovers. Maple antiques and family
heirlooms decorate this circa-1800 Victorian farmhouse's country-style
rooms, all of which are hung with fine-art reproductions and have views
across the fields. A full country breakfast is served family-style in the
dining room. The 50-acre farm is about 8 mi south of Deerfield, conve-
nient to cross-country skiing, mountain biking, and hiking. **Pros:** quiet
and serene; wallet-pleasing prices. **Cons:** you're miles from anywhere;
shared baths. ⊠ *21 River Rd., Whately* ☎ *413/665–3113* ⇘ *5 rooms
without bath* ⚲ *In-room: a/c. In-hotel: restaurant, pool, parking (free),
no kids under 10* ═ *No credit cards* ⦿ *BP.*

SHELBURNE FALLS

18 mi northwest of Deerfield.

A tour of New England's fall foliage wouldn't be complete without a
trek across the famed Mohawk Trail, a 63-mi section of Highway 2 that
runs past picturesque Shelburne Falls. The community, separated from
neighboring Buckland by the Deerfield River, is filled with little art gal-
leries and surrounded by orchards, farm stands, and sugar houses.

EXPLORING

★   **Bridge of Flowers.** From May to October, an arched, 400-foot trolley
bridge is transformed into this promenade bursting with color. ⊠ *Water
St.* ☎ *413/625–2544.*

SPORTS AND THE OUTDOORS

RAFTING   White-water rafting in the Class II–III rapids of the Deerfield River is a
popular summer activity. From April to October, **Zoar Outdoor** (⊠ *7 Main
St., off Hwy. 2, Charlemont* ☎ *800/532–7483* ⊕ *www.zoaroutdoor.
com*) conducts daylong rafting trips along 10 mi of challenging rapids,
as well as floats along gentler sections of the river.

Connecticut

WORD OF MOUTH

"For maritime history, go to Mystic Seaport—there also is a very good aquarium in Mystic. For art museums, [visit the] Atheneum in Hartford, any of the Yale art museums in New Haven, or the Museum of American Art in New Britain."

—emalloy

WELCOME TO CONNECTICUT

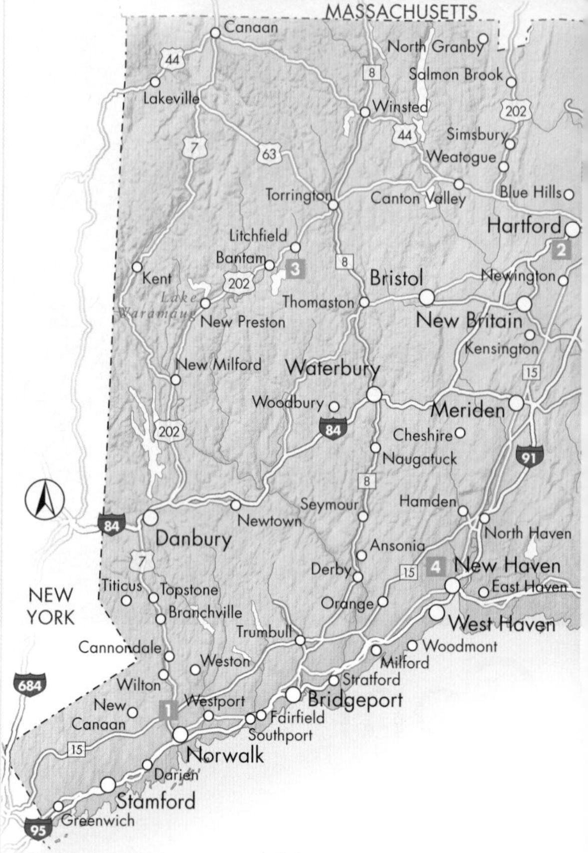

TOP REASONS TO GO

★ **Country Driving:** Follow the rolling, twisting roads of Litchfield County, such as U.S. 7, U.S. 44, and Route 63, through the charmed villages of Kent, Salisbury, and Litchfield.

★ **Maritime History:** The village of Mystic is packed with interesting nautical attractions related to Connecticut's rich seafaring history.

★ **Urban Exploring:** Anchored by Yale University, downtown New Haven now (finally) buzzes with hip restaurants, smart boutiques, and acclaimed theaters.

★ **Literary Giants:** In the same historic Hartford neighborhood, you can explore the homes—and legacies—of Mark Twain and Harriett Beecher Stowe.

★ **Antique Hunting:** You'll find numerous fine shops, galleries, and auction houses specializing in antiques all over the state. Two stand-out towns: Woodbury and Putnam.

1 Southwestern Connecticut. Enjoy a mix of moneyed bedroom communities and small, dynamic cities, with miles of gorgeous Long Island Sound shoreline. Shop Greenwich Avenue's boutiques, catch a show at the Westport Playhouse, and end with a nightcap in Norwalk's lively SoNo neighborhood.

2 Hartford and the Connecticut River Valley. Get your arts-and-culture fix in Hartford with a visit to the historic Old State House, the new Connecticut Science Center, or the Wadsworth Atheneum. Drive south through the Connecticut River valley for a scenic, small-town New England experience.

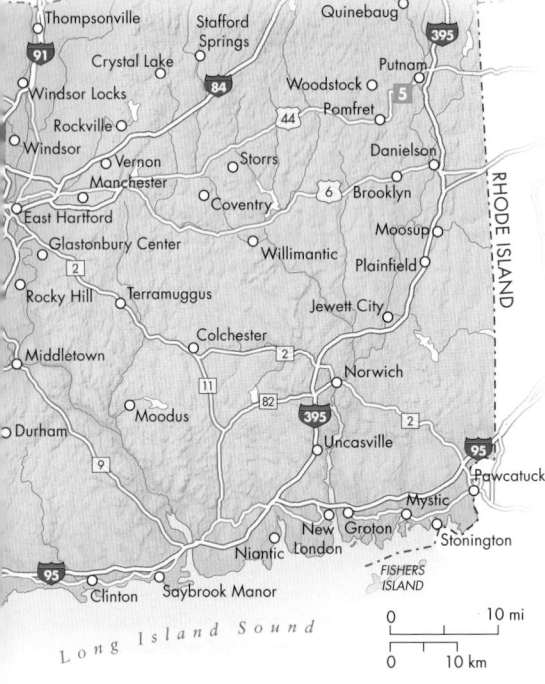

Thompsonville · Stafford Springs · Quinebaug · 395 · Putnam · Crystal Lake · Woodstock · 5 · Windsor Locks · 84 · Pomfret · 44 · Rockville · Danielson · Windsor · Storrs · Vernon · Manchester · Brooklyn · 6 · East Hartford · Coventry · Moosup · Glastonbury Center · Willimantic · Plainfield · Rocky Hill · Terramuggus · Jewett City · Colchester · Middletown · 2 · Norwich · 11 · 82 · Durham · Moodus · 395 · 2 · 9 · Uncasville · 95 · Pawcatuck · Mystic · New London · Groton · Stonington · 95 · Niantic · Clinton · Saybrook Manor · FISHERS ISLAND · RHODE ISLAND

Long Island Sound

0 — 10 mi
0 — 10 km

GETTING ORIENTED

Connecticut's coastline runs east–west, from the towns of Stonington and Mystic at the Rhode Island border, down to Greenwich in the southwest corner of the state. Head north from the Greenwich vicinity to the hills of Litchfield County in the northwest, bordered by New York and Massachusetts. In the center of the state, you'll find the capital, Hartford: travel south from here to tour the small towns of the Connecticut River valley. Northeast of Hartford is the less-traveled Quiet Corner, whose rural towns abut Massachusetts and Rhode Island.

5

3 The Litchfield Hills. Litchfield County's pastoral countryside is the perfect setting for an autumn weekend: nestle into a romantic country inn, leaf-peep around Lake Waramaug, and hunt for undiscovered treasures in the antique shops of Woodbury.

4 New Haven to Mystic. Wander through Yale's campus or visit the dinosaurs at the Peabody Museum of Natural History before dining at a chic New Haven eatery.

Head east along the coastline for unspoiled seaside towns or roll the dice and head inland to the casinos at Foxwoods or Mohegan Sun.

5 The Quiet Corner. The scenic drive along Route 169 through Brooklyn toward Woodstock affords glimpses of authentic Colonial homes, rolling hills, and bucolic views. Try the local wines at Sharpe Hill Vineyard in Pomfret and or go antiquing in downtown Putnam.

CONNECTICUT PLANNER

When to Go

Connecticut is lovely year-round, but fall and spring are particularly appealing times to visit. A fall drive along the state's back roads or the Merritt Parkway (a National Scenic Byway) is a memorable experience. Leaves of yellow, orange, and red color the fall landscape, but the state blooms in springtime, too—town greens are painted with daffodils and tulips, and blooming trees punctuate the rich green countryside. Summer, of course, is prime time for most attractions; travelers have the most options then but also plenty of company, especially along the shore.

Visitor Information

Connecticut Commission on Culture & Tourism (✉ *1 Financial Plaza, 755 Main St., Hartford* ☎ *860/256-2800 or 888/288-4748* ⊕ *www.ctvisit.com*).

Getting Here and Around

Car Travel: The interstates are the quickest routes between many points in Connecticut, but they can be busy and ugly. From New York City head north on Interstate 95, which hugs the Connecticut shoreline into Rhode Island, or, to reach the Litchfield Hills and Hartford, head north on Interstate 684, then east on Interstate 84. From central New England, go south on Interstate 91, which bisects Interstate 84 in Hartford and Interstate 95 in New Haven. From Boston take Interstate 95 south through Providence or take the Massachusetts Turnpike west to Interstate 84. Interstate 395 runs north–south from southeastern Connecticut to Massachusetts.

Often faster because of less traffic, the historic Merritt Parkway (Route 15) winds between Greenwich and Middletown; U.S. 7 and Route 8, extending between Interstate 95 and the Litchfield Hills; Route 9, which heads south from Hartford through the Connecticut River valley to Old Saybrook; and scenic Route 169, which meanders through the Quiet Corner.

Air Travel: People visiting Connecticut from afar can fly into New York City, Boston, or Providence or smaller airports in or near Hartford and New Haven. **Bradley International Airport** (✉ *11 Schoephoester Rd., Windsor Locks* ☎ *860/292-2000* ⊕ *www.bradleyairport.com*), north of Hartford, is served by most major airlines and has direct flights from most major cities. **Tweed/New Haven Airport** (✉ *155 Burr St., New Haven* ☎ *203/466-8833* ⊕ *www.flytweed.com*) has several flights per day on US Airways to Philadelphia.

Train Travel: Amtrak (☎ *800/872-7245* ⊕ *www.amtrak.com*) runs from New York to Boston, stopping in Stamford, Bridgeport, and New Haven before heading north through Hartford and several other towns or east to Old Saybrook and Mystic. **Metro-North Railroad** (☎ *212/532-4900 or 800/638-7646* ⊕ *www.mta.info*) trains from New York stop locally between Greenwich and New Haven, and a few head inland to New Canaan, Danbury, and Waterbury.

About the Restaurants

Call it the fennel factor or the arugula influx: southern New England has witnessed a gastronomic revolution. Preparation and ingredients reflect the culinary trends of nearby Manhattan and Boston; indeed, the quality and diversity of Connecticut restaurants now rival those of such sophisticated metropolitan areas. Although traditional favorites remain—such as New England clam chowder, buttery lobster rolls, Yankee pot roast, and fish-and-chips—Grand Marnier is now favored on ice cream over hot fudge sauce; sliced duck is wrapped in phyllo and served with a ginger-plum sauce (the orange glaze decidedly absent); and everything from lavender to fresh figs is used to season and complement dishes. Dining is increasingly international: you'll find Indian, Vietnamese, Thai, Malaysian, South American, and Japanese restaurants—even Spanish tapas bars—in cities and suburbs. Designer martinis are quite the rage, brewpubs have popped up around the state, and even caviar is making a comeback. The one drawback of this turn toward sophistication is that finding a dinner entrée for less than $10 is difficult.

About the Hotels

Connecticut has plenty of business-oriented chain hotels and low-budget motels, along with many of the more unusual and atmospheric inns, resorts, bed-and-breakfasts, and country hotels that are typical of New England. You'll pay dearly for rooms in summer on the coast and in autumn in the hills, where thousands of visitors peek at the changing foliage. Rates are lowest in winter, but so are the temperatures, making spring the best time for bargain seekers to visit.

Planning Your Time

The Nutmeg State is a confluence of different worlds, where farm country meets country homes, and fans of the New York Yankees meet Down-Easter Yankees. To get the best sense of this variety, start in the scenic Litchfield Hills, where you can see historic town greens and trendy cafés. If you have a bit more time, head south to the wealthy southwestern corner of the state and then over to New Haven, with its cultural pleasures. If you have five days or a week, take in the capital city of Hartford and the surrounding towns of the Connecticut River valley and head down to the southeastern shoreline.

5

WHAT IT COSTS

	¢	$	$$	$$$	$$$$
Restaurants	under $8	$8–$15	$15–$22	$22–$30	over $30
Hotels	under $80	$80–$120	$120–$170	$170–$220	over $220

Restaurant prices are based on the median main course price at dinner. Hotel prices are for two people in a standard double room in high season, excluding service and tax of 6%.

CONNECTICUT FALL FOLIAGE DRIVE

Hidden in the heart of Litchfield County is the crossroads village of New Preston, perched above a 40-foot waterfall on the Aspetuck River. Just north of here you'll find Lake Waramaug, nestled in the rolling foothills and Mt. Tom, both ablaze with rich color every fall.

Start in New Milford and stroll along historic Main Street. Here you'll find New England's longest green and many shops, galleries, and restaurants within a short walk. Hop in the car and drive south on Main Street, then turn left to head north on wooded Route 202. About 4 mi north of the town green is the **Silo at Hunt Hill Farm Trust**. The former property of the late Skitch Henderson, onetime music director of NBC and the New York Pops, consists of a gallery, cooking school, and gift store housed in the buildings of two farms dating to the 1700s. Continue north on Route 202 to the junction of Route 45 and follow signs for Lake Waramaug.

BEST TIME TO GO

Peak foliage in Connecticut occurs between October 9 and November 9, according to the state's Department of Environmental Protection (⊕ *www.ct.gov/dep* ☎ *800/282–6863*). In season, their Web site includes daily updates on leaf color. Hope for a wet spring, warmer fall days, and cool nights (but not freezing) for the most dramatic color display.

Route 45 will bring you through the tiny village center of New Preston; stop here for a bit of shopping at **Dawn Hill Antiques**. Take 45 North and follow signs for Lake Waramaug. The 8-mi drive around the lake is stunning in autumn with fiery foliage reflected in the water. The beach area of **Lake Waramaug State Park** (about halfway around the lake) is a great place for a picnic, or perhaps even a quick dip on a warm fall day. **Hopkins Vineyard** is open daily for wine tasting; on Sundays book ahead for the delectable brunch at **Boulders Inn** on East Shore Road with spectacular lake views.

After completing a loop of Lake Waramaug, head back to Route 202 North toward Litchfield. Another excellent leaf peeping locale is **Mt. Tom State Park**, about 3 mi or so from the junction of Routes 45 and 202. Here you can hike the mile-long trail to the summit and climb to the top of a stone tower that provides 360-degree views of the countryside's colors. After your hike, continue north on Route 202, ending your journey in the quintessential New England town of Litchfield. Peruse the shops and galleries in the town center and end the day with a dinner at the chic **West Street Grill**.

It's only about 30 mi from New Milford to the center of Litchfield, but with stops at the Silo at Hunt Hill, Lake Waramaug, and Mt. Tom you could easily spend half the day enjoying the scenery.

NEED A BREAK?

Dawn Hill Antiques (✉ 11 Main St., New Preston ☎ 860/868–0066 ⊕ www.dawnhillantiques. com) is filled with antiques that the owners have discovered on their regular trips to Sweden.
The Boulders Inn (✉ E. Shore Rd. [Rte. 45], New Preston ☎ 860/354–6001 ⊕ www.bouldersinn.com ☽ Closed Mon. and Tues. No lunch) offers excellent dining and lodging in a gracious lakeside Dutch Colonial mansion.
Hopkins Vineyard (✉ 25 Hopkins Rd., off N. Shore Rd., Warren ☎ 860/868–7954 ⊕ www. hopkinsvineyard.com ☞ $6 ☽ Hours vary) offers wine tastings and produces more than 11 varieties of wine, from sparkling to dessert. A wine bar in the hayloft serves a fine cheese-and-pâté board and has views of the lake.

45
7
341   ○ Warren   Litchfield ○
                            Bantam
Macedonia   202 ○   63
○
Lake Waramaug   East
State Park ◆ 45   ○   209   Morris
Lake Waramaug ◆ Woodville   Mt. Tom   ○
New Preston ○   State Park Morris
Marble Dale ○   47   61
                47
Silo at Hunt Hill ◆
Farm Trust ◆   109 ○ Washington 132 ○ Bethlehem
202
                    199
                            47
                ○ **New Milford** Roxbury   6
                67 ○   317   Woodbury
Candlewood   Bridgewater Woodbury ○ ◆ Ski Area
Lake   133   67 ○   64
7   0   5 mi
202   0   5 km

Updated
by Bethany
Beckerlegge

You can travel from just about any point in Connecticut to any other in less than two hours, yet the land you traverse— fewer than 60 mi top to bottom and 100 mi across—is as varied as a drive across the country.

Connecticut's 253 mi of shoreline blows salty sea air over such beach communities as Old Lyme and Stonington. Patchwork hills and peaked mountains fill the state's northwestern corner, and once-upon-a-time mill towns line rivers such as the Housatonic. Connecticut has seemingly endless farmland in the northeast, where cows might outnumber people, as well as chic New York City bedroom communities such as Greenwich and New Canaan, where boutique shopping bags seem to be the dominant species.

Just as diverse as the landscape are the state's residents, who numbered close to 3.5 million at last count. There really is no such thing as the definitive Connecticut Yankee. Yes, families can trace their roots back to the 1600s, when Connecticut was founded as one of the 13 original colonies, but the state motto is "He who transplanted still sustains." And so the face of the Nutmegger is that of the family from Naples now making pizza in New Haven and the farmer in Norfolk whose land dates back five generations, the grandmother in New Britain who makes the state's best pierogi and the ladies who lunch in Westport, the celebrity nestled in the Litchfield Hills and the Bridgeport entrepreneur working to close the gap between Connecticut's struggling cities and its affluent suburbs.

A unifying characteristic of the Connecticut Yankee, however, is inventiveness. Nutmeggers are historically known for both their intellectual abilities and their desire to have a little fun. The nation's first public library was opened in New Haven in 1656 and its first statehouse built in Hartford in 1776; Tapping Reeve opened the first law school in Litchfield in 1784; and West Hartford's Noah Webster published the first dictionary in 1806. On the fun side, note that Lake Compounce in Bristol was the country's first amusement park; Bethel's P. T. Barnum staged the first three-ring circus; and the hamburger, the lollipop, the Frisbee, and the Erector set were all invented here.

Not surprisingly, Nutmeggers have a healthy respect for their history. For decades, Mystic Seaport, which traces the state's rich maritime past, has been the premier tourist attraction. Today, however, Foxwoods Casino near Ledyard, run by the Mashantucket Pequots, is the world's largest casino, drawing more than 40,000 visitors per day. Thanks in large part to these lures, not to mention rich cultural attractions, cutting-edge restaurants, shopping outlets, first-rate lodgings, and abundant natural beauty (including 92 state parks and 30 state forests), tourism is the state's second leading industry. Exploring Connecticut reveals a small state that's big in its appeal.

SOUTHWESTERN CONNECTICUT

Southwestern Connecticut is a rich swirl of old New England and new New York. This region consistently reports the highest cost of living and most expensive homes of any area in the country. Its bedroom towns are home primarily to white-collar executives; some still make the hour-plus dash to and from New York, but many drive to Stamford, which is reputed to have more corporate headquarters per square mile than any other U.S. city.

Venture away from the wealthy communities, and you'll discover cities struggling in different stages of urban renewal: Stamford, Norwalk, Bridgeport, and Danbury. These four have some of the region's best cultural and shopping opportunities, but the economic disparity between Connecticut's troubled cities and its upscale towns is perhaps most visible than in Fairfield County.

ESSENTIALS

Visitor Information **Coastal Fairfield County Convention and Visitors Bureau** (⊠ *Mathews Park, 297 West Ave., Norwalk* ☎ *203/853–7770 or 800/866–7925* ⊕ *www.coastalct.com*).

GREENWICH

28 mi northeast of New York City, 64 mi southwest of Hartford.

You'll have no trouble believing that Greenwich is one of the wealthiest towns in the United States when you drive along U.S. 1 (called Route 1 by the locals, as well as West Putnam Avenue, East Putnam Avenue, and the Post Road), where the streets are lined with ritzy car dealers, posh boutiques, oh-so-chic restaurants, and well-heeled, well-to-do residents clearly. Though real estate prices have come down, the median home price in Greenwich still hovers around $1.6 million. So bring your platinum card.

EXPLORING

Audubon Center. Established in 1942 as the National Audubon Society's first nature-education facility, this center in northern Greenwich is the best location in the area for bird-watching. During the Fall Hawk Watch Festival you can see over 16 species of hawks, eagles, and vultures migrate over the site. Other annual events are the Spring into Audubon Festival and the summer and Christmas bird counts. The center is filled with "real-life" interactive exhibits, galleries, and classrooms, a wildlife observation room, and an observation deck that offers sweeping views of wildlife activity. Outside, the sanctuary includes protected wildlife habitats and 8 mi of hiking trails on 295 acres of woodland, wetland, and meadow. ⊠ *613 Riversville Rd.* ☎ *203/869–5272* ⊕ *www. greenwich.audubon.org* ⊠ *$3* ⊙ *Daily 9–5.*

☾
★   **Bruce Museum of Arts and Science.** In 1908, the owner of this then-private home (built in 1853), wealthy textile merchant Robert Moffat Bruce, bequeathed it to the town of Greenwich with the stipulation that it be used "as a natural history, historical, and art museum." Today this diversity remains reflected in the museum's collection of some 15,000 objects in fine and decorative arts, natural history, and anthropology—including paintings by Childe Hassam, sculptures by Auguste Rodin, and stained glass by Dale Chihuly—from which the museum selects items for changing exhibitions. Permanently on display is the spectacular mineral collection. Kids enjoy the touchable meteorite and glow-in-the-dark minerals, as well as the fossilized dinosaur tracks. ⊠ *1 Museum Dr., off I–95 (Exit 3)* ☎ *203/869–0376* ⊕ *www.brucemuseum.org* ⊠ *$7, free Tues.* ⊙ *Tues.–Sat. 10–5, Sun. 1–5.*

WHERE TO EAT AND STAY

$$$$
FRENCH
Fodor'sChoice
★   ✕ **Restaurant Jean-Louis.** Chef Jean-Louis Gerin specializes in what he calls "la nouvelle classique" French cuisine, a style based on stocks and reductions—and his own dedication to excellence. A five-course degustation menu explores the day's special offerings, which might include sea salt–encrusted foie gras with aged sherry vinegar and a duck *à l'orange* reduction or a seared ostrich fillet with buttery mashed potatoes. Heady roses, signature fine china, custom glassware, and touches of lace create a romantic, sophisticated atmosphere. ⊠ *61 Lewis St.* ☎ *203/622–8450* ⊕ *www.restaurantjeanlouis.com* ▤ *AE, D, DC, MC, V* ⊙ *Closed Sun. No lunch Sat.*

✕ **Tengda Asian Bistro.** This hopping Asian-fusion hot spot offers consistently good Japanese cuisine with European accents. In a turn-of-the-20th-century house, the dining room has a rustic yet industrial feel, with exposed brick cozying up next to next to sculpted steel. Tuck into the crispy firecracker shrimp, sample the spicy mango chicken, or dive into a fresh lobster tempura roll while sipping an exotic cocktail from the diverse drink list. ⊠ *21 Field Point Rd.* ☎ *203/625–5338* ⊕ *www. tengdaasianbistro.com* ▤ *AE, D, DC, MC, V.*

$$$$ ⊡ **Delamar Greenwich Harbor Hotel.** This three-story luxury hotel with yellow stucco exterior and terra-cotta tile roof resembles a villa on the Italian Riviera. Handcrafted furnishings enrich all rooms; many have working fireplaces and wrought-iron balconies overlooking Greenwich Harbor. Bathrooms have coral marble vanities, hand-painted framed mirrors, and deep cast-iron tubs. The hotel has a 600-foot private dock on the harbor for boat owners to tie up; it's just a few blocks from downtown Greenwich and one block from the train station. A luxe spa offers a full range of treatments. L'Escale restaurant and bar ($$$$) shares the hotel's superb water views and specializes in classic Provençal dishes. **Pros:** waterfront location; posh spa; easy walk to downtown restaurants. **Cons:** super-pricey. ⊠ *500 Steamboat Rd.* ☎ *203/661–9800; 866/335–2627* ⊕ *www. thedelamar.com* ⊅ *74 rooms, 8 suites* ⚲ *In-room: a/c, DVD, Internet. In-hotel: restaurant, bar, gym, spa* ▤ *AE, D, DC, MC, V.*

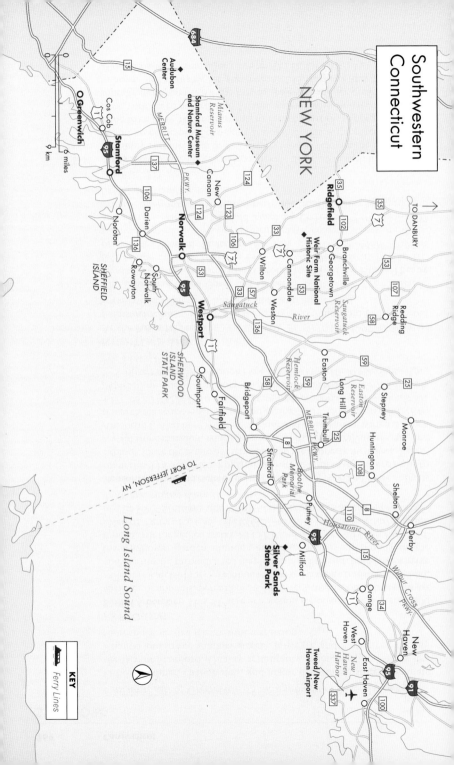

Southwestern Connecticut

NEW YORK

Long Island Sound

TO DANBURY

684

15

Audubon Center

Stamford Museum and Nature Center

Mianus Reservoir

Greenwich

Cos Cob

1

95 Stamford

137

MERRITT PKWY

New Canaan

124

123

124

106

Darien

Noroton

136

SHEFFIELD ISLAND

Rowayton

South Norwalk

Norwalk

53

95

Westport

Sangatuck

SHERWOOD ISLAND STATE PARK

Southport

11

Fairfield

TO PORT JEFFERSON, NY

106

Wilton

7

Cannondale

33

7

57

Weston

136

Ridgefield

35

102

35

7

Weir Farm National Historic Site

53

Branchville

Georgetown

Saugatuck Reservoir

53

107

Redding Ridge

58

Saugatuck River

Hemlock Reservoir

59

Easton Reservoir

Easton

59

Long Hill

MERRITT PKWY

Trumbull

25

8

Bridgeport

58

Stratford

Boothe Memorial Park

53

25

Stepney

Monroe

Huntington

108

Shelton

8

110

Derby

Putney

92

Housatonic River

15

Milford

Silver Sands State Park

Wilbur Cross Pkwy

34

Orange

1

West Haven

337

Tweed/New Haven Airport

New Haven Harbor

East Haven

New Haven

95

100

91

9 km

6 miles

KEY

Ferry Lines

STAMFORD

6 mi northeast of Greenwich, 38 mi southwest of New Haven.

Office buildings, chain hotels, and major department stores dominate the face of Stamford. Quality restaurants, nightclubs, and shops line Atlantic and lower Summer streets, however, and have given the city some much needed leisure time attractions.

EXPLORING

Bartlett Arboretum. This 91-acre arboretum is home to more than 2,000 varieties of annuals, perennials, wildflowers, and woody plants, an art gallery, research library, greenhouse, marked ecology trails, 2-acre pond, and boardwalk through a red maple swamp. Brilliant, bold colors make the wildflower garden stunning in spring. Sunday afternoons are the time to visit for guided walks. ⊠ *151 Brookdale Rd., off High Ridge Rd. (Merritt Pkwy., Exit 35)* ☎ *203/322–6971* ⊕ *www.bartlettarboretum. org* ⊠ *$6* ☉ *Grounds daily 8:30–dusk, visitor center weekdays 8:30– 4:30, greenhouse daily 10–noon.*

☾ **Stamford Museum and Nature Center**. Oxen, sheep, pigs, and other animals roam this 118-acre New England farmstead with many nature trails to explore. Once the estate of Henri Bendel, the property includes a Tudor-revival stone mansion, which houses exhibits on natural history, art, and Americana. Also here is a planetarium and observatory with a 22-inch research telescope—perfect for stargazing. ⊠ *39 Scofieldtown Rd. (Rte. 137),* ☎ *203/322–1646* ⊕ *www.stamfordmuseum.org* ⊠ *Grounds $8, planetarium and observatory each an additional $3* ☉ *Grounds daily 9–5; observatory May–Labor Day, Fri. 8:30 PM–10:30 PM; Sept.–Apr., Fri. 8 PM–10 PM.*

NIGHTLIFE AND THE ARTS

NIGHTLIFE   At the **Palms Nightclub** (⊠ *78 W. Park Pl.* ☎ *203/961–9770* ⊕ *www. palmsnightclub.com*) you can dance to everything from ballroom and country and western to hip-hop and Latin music.

THE ARTS   The **Connecticut Grand Opera and Orchestra** (☎ *203/327–2867* ⊕ *www. ctgrandopera.org*) perform from October to May at **the Palace Theatre** (⊠ *61 Atlantic St.* ☎ *203/325–4466* ⊕ *www.stamfordcenterforthearts. org*). The **Stamford Center for the Arts** (☎ *203/325–4466* ⊕ *www. stamfordcenterforthearts.org*) presents plays, comedy shows, musicals, and film festivals. The **Stamford Symphony Orchestra** (☎ *203/325–1407* ⊕ *www.stamfordsymphony.org*) performs from October to April, and has a family concert series.

WHERE TO EAT

$–$$ ✕ **City Limits Diner**. This Art-Deco, deluxe diner, alive with bright colors
AMERICAN   and shiny chrome, likes to describe its food as running the gamut from "haute to homespun." Roughly translated, this is the place for everything from New York egg creams to French martinis to hot pastrami on New York rye to pan-roasted Atlantic salmon with Israeli couscous and shiitake mushrooms. All the breads, pastries, and ice cream are made in-house and available for purchase. ⊠ *135 Harvard Ave.* ☎ *203/348– 7000* ⊕ *www.citylimitsdiner.com* ⊟ *AE, D, DC, MC, V.*

NORWALK

14 mi northeast of Stamford, 47 mi northeast of New York City.

In the 19th century, Norwalk became a major New England port and also manufactured pottery, clocks, watches, shingle nails, and paper. It later fell into neglect, in which it remained for much of the 20th century. In the early 1990s, however, Norwalk's coastal business district was the focus of major redevelopment, which has turned it into a hot spot for trendy shopping, culture, and dining, much of it along the main drag, Washington Street. The stretch is known as SoNo (South Norwalk), and in the evening it is the place to be seen if you're young, single, and living it up in Fairfield County.

YANKEE DOODLE DANDY

Norwalk is the home of Yankee Doodle Dandies: in 1756, Colonel Thomas Fitch threw together a motley crew of Norwalk soldiers and led them off to fight at Ft. Crailo, near Albany, New York. Supposedly, Norwalk's women gathered feathers for the men to wear as plumes in their caps to give them some appearance of military decorum. Upon the arrival of these foppish warriors, one of the British officers sarcastically dubbed them "macaronis"—slang for dandies. The name caught on, and so did the song.

5

EXPLORING

Maritime Aquarium at Norwalk. This 5-acre waterfront center, the cornerstone of the SoNo district, explores the marine life and maritime culture of Long Island Sound. The aquarium's more than 20 habitats include some 1,000 creatures indigenous to the sound. You can see toothy bluefish and sand tiger sharks in the 110,000-gallon Open Ocean Tank, dozens of jellyfish performing their ghostly ballet in "Jellyfish Encounter," stately loggerhead sea turtles, winsome river otters, and happy harbor seals. The center also operates an Environmental Education Center and marine-mammal cruises aboard the *Oceanic* and has a towering IMAX theater. ⊠ *10 N. Water St.* ☎ *203/852–0700* ⊕ *www.maritimeaquarium. org* ⊑ *Aquarium $11.75, IMAX theater $9, combined $17.50* ☉ *Labor Day–June, daily 10–5; July–Labor Day, daily 10–6.*

Sheffield Island Lighthouse. The 3-acre park here is a prime spot for a picnic. The 1868 lighthouse has four levels, 10 rooms to explore, and is adjacent to the Stewart B. McKinney U.S. Fish and Wildlife Refuge. Clambakes are held Thursday evenings from June through September. ⊠ *Ferry service from Hope Dock, at corner of Washington and North Water Sts.* ☎ *203/838–9444 ferry and lighthouse* ⊕ *www.seaport.org* ⊑ *Round-trip ferry service and lighthouse tour $20* ☉ *Ferry May–late June, weekends at 11, 2, and 3:30; late June–Aug., weekdays at 11 and 3, weekends at 11, 2, and 3:30.*

WHERE TO EAT AND STAY

$$$–$$$$

NEW AMERICAN

✕ **Match.** In the heart of SoNo Match cooks up fresh local ingredients to create inventive new American dishes. High ceilings, exposed brick, and industrial fixtures provide a sleek, urban look. Indulge in one of the signature wood-fired pizzas straight or savor the soft-shell crab fettuccini with spicy cherry peppers and fresh New Jersey corn. Complete

Norwalk's Maritime Aquarium is a great way to get eye-to-eye with animals endemic to Long Island sound, like loggerhead turtles.

your meal with a melt-in-your-mouth hot chocolate soufflé topped with raspberries and vanilla gelato. ⊠ *98 Washington St.* ☎ *203/852–1088* ⊕ *www.matchsono.com* ▭ *AE, D, MC, V* ⊙ *No lunch.*

$$–$$$ 🔲 **Silvermine Tavern.** The simple rooms at this venerable, late-18th-century inn on a quiet road near the New Canaan and Wilton border are furnished with hooked rugs, canopy beds, and antiques—vintage New England. There's a rather grand restaurant ($$$) with large, low-ceiling dining rooms overlooking a millpond. Traditional New England favorites receive modern touches, and Sunday brunch is popular. **Pros:** nice alternative to the area's many chain hotels; reasonable rates; tranquil setting. **Cons:** rooms lack phones and TVs; old-fashioned vibe isn't everybody's cup of tea; it's a drive to South Norwalk's shopping and dining. ⊠ *194 Perry Ave.* ☎ *203/847–4558 or 888/693–9967* ⊕ *www.silverminetavern.com* ⬎ *10 rooms, 1 suite* ⌂ *In-room: no phone, no TV. In-hotel: restaurant* ▭ *AE, MC, V* ⦿ *CP.*

RIDGEFIELD

11 mi north of New Canaan, 43 mi west of New Haven.

In Ridgefield you'll find a rustic Connecticut atmosphere within an hour of Manhattan. The inviting town center is a largely residential sweep of lawns and majestic homes, with a feel more reminiscent of the peaceful Litchfield Hills, even though the town is in the northern reaches of Fairfield County.

EXPLORING

★ **Aldrich Contemporary Art Museum.** Cutting-edge art is not exactly what you'd expect to find in a stately 18th-century Main Street structure that was once a general store, Ridgefield's first post office, a private home, and, for 35 years, a church. Nicknamed "Old Hundred," this historic building now houses the Aldrich's adminstrative offices since the 2004 completion of the new museum building. The 25,000 square foot space puts its own twist on traditional New England architechture with an abstract design recognized by the American Institute of Architects. The white clapboard and granite structure houses 12 galleries, a screening room, a sound gallery, a 22-foot-high project space for large installations, a 100-seat performance space, and an education center. Outside is a 2-acre sculpture garden. ⊠ *258 Main St.06887* ☎ *203/438–4519* ⊕ *www.aldrichart.org* ✉ *$7, free Tues.* ☉ *Tues.–Sun. noon–5.*

WHERE TO EAT AND STAY

$$–$$$
FRENCH
✕ **Luc's Cafe and Restaurant.** A cozy bistro set inside a stone building with low ceilings, closely spaced tables, and a handy location in Ridgefield's quaint downtown, Luc's charms patrons with carefully prepared food and low-key, friendly service. You can opt for a simple salade niçoise or *croque monsieur* (hot ham-and-cheese) sandwich or enjoy a classic steak au poivre with a velvety Roquefort sauce and crispy frites. There's an extensive wine list, plus a range of aperitifs and single-malt whiskies. Enjoy live jazz on some evenings. ⊠ *3 Big Shop La.* ☎ *203/894–8522* ⊕ *www.lucscafe.com* ▭ *AE, MC, V* ☉ *Closed Sun.*

$$–$$$
⊞ **Stonehenge Inn.** The manicured lawns and bright white-clapboard buildings of Stonehenge are visible just off U.S. 7. The rooms are tasteful but not overly fancy, and it's a good base for enjoying the excellent on-site restaurant ($$$) and exploring the area's antiques shops and attractions. **Pros:** neatly kept grounds; polished service; terrific restaurant. **Cons:** not within walking distance of downtown Ridgefield. ⊠ *Stonehenge Rd. off U.S. 7* ☎ *203/438–6511* ⊕ *www.stonehengeinn-ct.com* ↪ *12 rooms, 4 suites* ☖ *In-hotel: restaurant* ▭ *AE, MC, V* ⑩ *CP.*

WESTPORT

15 mi southeast of Ridgefield, 47 mi northeast of New York City.

Westport, an artists' community since the turn of the 20th century, continues to attract creative types. Despite commuters and corporations, the town remains more artsy and cultured than its neighbors: if the rest of Fairfield County is stylistically five years behind Manhattan, Westport lags by just five months.

THE ARTS

The **Levitt Pavilion for the Performing Arts** (⊠ *40 Jesup Rd.* ☎ *203/221–4422* ⊕ *www.levittpavilion.com*) sponsors an excellent series of mostly free summer concerts that range from jazz to classical, folk rock to blues. Long associated with benefactors Joanne Woodward and the late Paul Newman, the venerable and intimate **Westport Country Playhouse** (⊠ *25 Powers Ct.* ☎ *203/227–4177* ⊕ *www.westportplayhouse.org*) presents high-quality plays throughout the year.

WHERE TO EAT AND STAY

$$$
AMERICAN
Fodor's Choice
★
✕ **Dressing Room.** Opened by the late Paul Newman and renowned cookbook author Michel Nischan in 2006, this pretheater favorite, beside the Wesport Playhouse, celebrates regional American, farm-to-table cuisine. Many ingredients on the menu are sourced locally; others come from prominent ranches and farms around the country. Highlights include the baby back ribs, served with an apple-cabbage slaw, and seasonal items like the Connecticut lobster succotash with fresh corn, zucchini, and roasted peppers. A huge fieldstone fireplace warms the rustic-chic dining room, with its sturdy ceiling beams and barn-board walls. ⊠ *27 Powers Ct.* ☎ *203/226–1114* ⊕ *www.dressingroomhomegrown.com* ⊟ *AE, MC, V* ☺ *Closed Mon. No lunch Tues.*

$$$$
★
🛏 **Inn at National Hall.** Each whimsically exotic room at this towering Italianate redbrick inn in the heart of downtown Westport is a study in innovative restoration, wall stenciling, and decorative painting—including magnificent trompe l'oeil designs. The furniture collection is exceptional. Some rooms and suites have sleeping lofts and floor-to-ceiling windows overlooking the Saugatuck River. The Turkistan Suite—with its two-story-high bookcase, striped swag drapes, curving balcony, and king-size bed with Egyptian print canopy and painted valance—is one glorious example. **Pros:** fabulously artful and cushy rooms; enchanted setting overlooking Saugatuck River; walking distance from downtown shopping and dining. **Cons:** ultrapricey; service can be a little stiff. ⊠ *2 Post Rd. W* ☎ *203/221–1351 or 800/628–4255* ⊕ *www.innatnationalhall. com* 🛌 *8 rooms, 8 suites* ⚭ *In-room: a/c, refrigerator, Internet. In-hotel: no kids under 12* ⊟ *AE, DC, MC, V* ⊺⊝⊺ *CP.*

HARTFORD AND THE CONNECTICUT RIVER VALLEY

Westward expansion in the New World began along the meandering Connecticut River. Dutch explorer Adrian Block first explored the area in 1614, and in 1633 a trading post was set up in what is now Hartford. Within five years, throngs of restive Massachusetts Bay colonists had settled in this fertile valley. What followed was more than three centuries of shipbuilding, shad hauling, and river trading with ports as far away as the West Indies and the Mediterranean.

Less touristy than the coast and northwest hills, the Connecticut River valley is a swath of small villages and uncrowded state parks punctuated by a few small cities and a large one: the capital city of Hartford. South of Hartford, with the exception of industrial Middletown, genuinely quaint hamlets vie for attention with antiques shops, scenic drives, and romantic French restaurants and country inns.

ESSENTIALS

Visitor Information Connecticut's Heritage River Valley–Central Regional Tourism District (⊠ *31 Pratt St., 4th fl., Hartford* ☎ *860/244–8181 or 800/793–4480* ⊕ *www.visitctriver.com*).

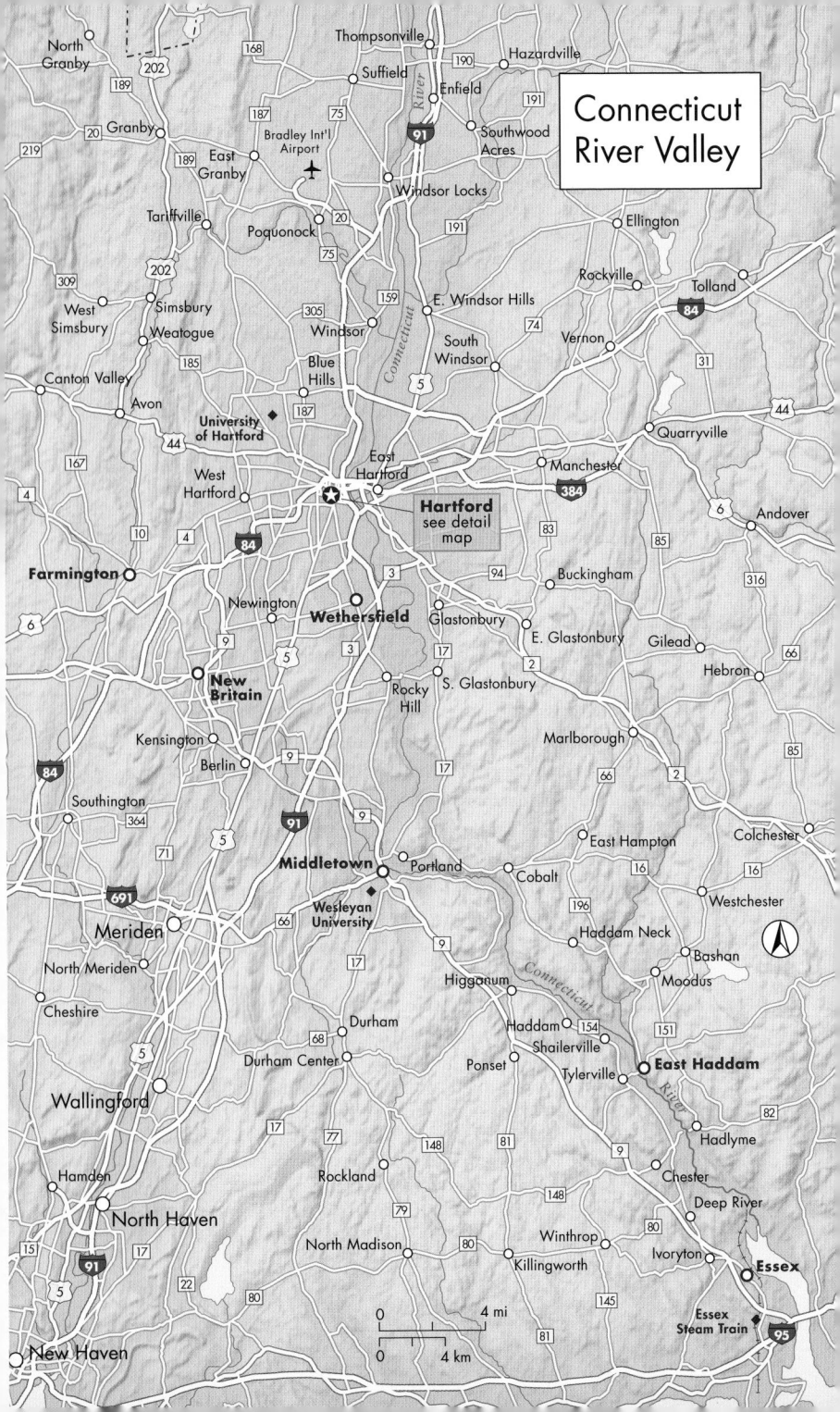

ESSEX

29 mi east of New Haven.

Essex, consistently named one of the best small towns in the United States, looks much as it did in the mid-19th century, at the height of its shipbuilding prosperity. So important to the young country was Essex's boat manufacturing that the British burned more than 40 ships here during the War of 1812. Gone are the days of steady trade with the West Indies, when the aroma of imported rum, molasses, and spices hung in the air. Whitewashed houses—many the former roosts of sea captains—line Main Street, which has shops that sell clothing, antiques, paintings and prints, and sweets.

EXPLORING

★ **Connecticut River Museum.** In an 1878 steamboat warehouse at the foot of Main Street, this museum tells the story of the Connecticut River through paintings, maritime artifacts, interactive displays, and ship models. The riverfront museum even has a full-size working reproduction of the world's first submarine, the *American Turtle*; the original was built by David Bushnell in 1775 as a "secret weapon" to win the Revolutionary War. ⊠ *At dock, 67 Main St.* ☎ *860/767–8269* ⊕ *www.ctrivermuseum.org* ⤳ *$8* ☉ *Tues.–Sun. 10–5.*

SCENIC TRIP

Essex Steam Train and Riverboat. This ride offers some of the best views of the Connecticut River valley from the vantage point of a restored train (1920s coaches pulled by a vintage steam locomotive) and an old-fashioned Mississippi-style riverboat. The train, traveling along the Connecticut River through the lower valley, makes a 12-mi round-trip from Essex Station to Deep River Station; from there, if you wish to continue, you board the riverboat for a ride to East Haddam (the open promenade deck on the third level has the best views). Special trains, including a dinner train and a wine train, as well as a Santa Special and hugely popular visits by Thomas the Tank Engine, occur periodically. ⊠ *Valley Railroad Company, 1 Railroad Ave. (Rte. 9, Exit 3)* ☎ *860/767–0103* ⊕ *www.essexsteamtrain.com* ⤳ *Train fare $17, train–boat fare $26* ☉ *May–Dec.; call for schedule.*

WHERE TO EAT

$$$
FRENCH
Fodor'sChoice
★

✕ **Brasserie Pip.** Within the Copper Beech Inn is this hip and relaxed brasserie, which serves superbly authentic fare, and has outdoor seating in warm weather on a porch overlooking the inn's extensive gardens. You could make a night of the cheese and charcuterie plates, plus a selection of fresh oysters on the half shell. Or opt for more substantial fare, like the ricotta gnocchi with spring vegetables or classic steak frites. Pip's cocktail bar makes its own flavored vodkas—such as blood-orange-and-coriander—to prepare memorable martinis. ⊠ *46 Main St., 4 mi west of Essex, Ivoryton* ☎ *860/767–0330* ⊕ *www.copperbeechinn.com* ▭ *AE, D, DC, MC, V* ☉ *Closed Mon. No lunch.*

Ride through the Connecticut River Valley on a vintage Essex Steam Train.

EAST HADDAM

7 mi north of Chester, 28 mi southeast of Hartford.

Fishing, shipping, and musket making were the chief enterprises at East Haddam, the only town in the state that occupies both banks of the Connecticut River. This lovely community retains much of its old-fashioned charm, most of it centered around its historic downtown.

EXPLORING

★ **Gillette Castle State Park.** The outrageous 24-room oak-and-fieldstone hilltop castle, modeled after medieval castles of the Rhineland and built between 1914 and 1919 by the eccentric actor and dramatist William Gillette, is the park's main attraction. You can tour the castle and hike on trails near the remains of the 3-mi private railroad that chugged about the property until the owner's death in 1937. Gillette, who was born in Hartford, wrote two famous plays about the Civil War and was beloved for his play *Sherlock Holmes* (in which he performed the title role). In his will, he demanded that the castle not fall into the hands of "some blithering saphead who has no conception of where he is or with what surrounded." ⊠ *67 River Rd., off Rte. 82* ☎ *860/526–2336* ⊕ *www.friendsofgillettecastle.org* ⊠ *Park free, castle $5* ☼ *Park daily 8–sunset; castle Memorial Day–Columbus Day, daily 10–4:30.*

★ **Goodspeed Opera House.** This magnificent 1876 Victorian-gingerbread "wedding cake" theater on the Connecticut River—so called for all its turrets, mansard roof, and grand filigree—is widely recognized for its role in the preservation and development of American musical theater. More than 16 Goodspeed productions have gone on to Broadway, including *Annie*. Performances take place from April to early December. ✉ *6 Main St. (Rte. 82)* ☎ *860/873–8668* ⊕ *www.goodspeed.org* 🎫 *Tour $5* ⊙ *Tours June–Oct; call for times.*

MIDDLETOWN

15 mi northwest of East Haddam, 24 mi northeast of New Haven.

With its Connecticut River setting, easy access to major highways, and historic architecture, Middletown is a popular destination for recreational boaters and tourists alike. The town's High Street is an architecturally eclectic thoroughfare. Charles Dickens once called it "the loveliest Main Street in America" (Middletown's actual Main Street runs parallel to it a few blocks east).

EXPLORING

Wesleyan University. Founded in 1831 and one of the oldest Methodist institutions of higher education in the United States, Wesleyan University has roughly 2,700 undergrads, 600 graduate students, and a vibrant science-and-arts scene, which gives Middletown a contemporary college-town feel. On campus, note the massive, fluted Corinthian columns of the Greek-Revival Russell House (circa 1828) at the corner of Washington Street, across from the pink Mediterranean-style Davison Art Center, built 15 years later; farther on are gingerbreads, towering brownstones, Tudors, and Queen Annes. A few hundred yards up on Church Street, which intersects High Street, is the Olin Library. The 1928 structure was designed by Henry Bacon, the architect of the Lincoln Memorial. The school bookstore is at 45 Broad St. ✉ *High St.* ⊕ *www.wesleyan.edu.*

OFF THE BEATEN PATH

Lyman Orchards. Looking for a quintessential New England outing? These orchards just south of Middletown are not to be missed. Get lost in the sunflower maze and then pick your own fruits and vegetables—berries, peaches, pears, apples, and even pumpkins from June to October. ✉ *Rtes. 147 and 157, Middlefield* ☎ *860/349–1793* ⊕ *www.lymanorchards.com* ⊙ *Nov.–Aug., daily 9–6; Sept. and Oct., daily 9–7.*

SPORTS AND THE OUTDOORS

🔄 **Dinosaur State Park**. See some 500 tracks left by the dinosaurs that once roamed the area around this park north of Middletown. The tracks are preserved under a giant geodesic dome. You can even make plaster casts of tracks on a special area of the property; call ahead to learn what materials you need to bring. ✉ *400 West St., east of I–91 Exit 23, Rocky Hill* ☎ *860/529–8423* ⊕ *www.dinosaurstatepark.org* 🎫 *$5* ⊙ *Exhibits Tues.–Sun. 9–4:30, trails daily 9–4:30.*

NIGHTLIFE AND THE ARTS

THE ARTS At Wesleyan University's **Center for the Arts** (✉ *283 Washington Terr.* ★ ☎ *860/685–3355* ⊕ *www.wesleyan.edu/cfa*) see modern dance or a provocative new play, hear top playwrights and actors discuss their craft, and take in an art exhibit or concert.

NIGHTLIFE At last count, **Eli Cannon's** (✉ *695 Main St.* ☎ *860/347–3547* ⊕ *www. elicannons.com*) had more than 35 beers on draft and an extensive bottled selection.

CLOSE UP

Connecticut's Historic Gardens

Nine extraordinary Connecticut gardens form Connecticut's Historic Gardens, a "trail" of natural beauties across the state.

The re-created Colonial-revival garden at the **Webb-Deane-Stevens Museum** (⊠ *211 Main St., Wethersfield* ☎ *860/529–0612* ⊕ *www.webb-deane-stevens.org*) is a presentation of old-fashioned flowers such as peonies, pinks, phlox, hollyhocks, larkspur, and antique roses.

Griswold Museum in Old Lyme

A high-Victorian texture garden, a wildflower meadow, Connecticut's largest magnolia tree, an antique rose garden, a 100-year-old pink dogwood, and a blue cottage garden are the highlights of the grounds at the **Harriet Beecher Stowe Center** (⊠ *77 Forest St., Hartford* ☎ *860/522–9258* ⊕ *www. harrietbeecherstowecenter.org*).

At the **Butler-McCook House & Garden** (⊠ *396 Main St., Hartford* ☎ *860/522–1806* ⊕ *www.ctlandmarks. org*), landscape architect Jacob Weidenmann created a Victorian garden oasis amid downtown city life.

The centerpiece of the **Hill-Stead Museum** (⊠ *35 Mountain Rd., Farmington* ☎ *860/677–4787* ⊕ *www. hillstead.org*) is a circa-1920 sunken garden by Beatrix Farrand enclosed in a yew hedge and surrounded by a wall of rough stone; at the center of the octagonal design is a summerhouse with 36 flowerbeds and brick walkways radiating outward.

Farrand also designed the garden at **Promisek Beatrix Farrand Garden** (⊠ *694 Skyline Ridge Rd., Bridgewater* ☎ *860/354–1788* ⊕ *www.promisek.org*), which overflows with beds of annuals and perennials such as hollyhocks, peonies, and always-dashing delphiniums.

Legendary British garden writer and designer Gertrude Jekyll designed only three gardens in the United States, and the one at the **Glebe House Museum** (⊠ *149 Hollow Rd., Woodbury* ☎ *203/263–2855* ⊕ *www. theglebehouse.org*) is the only one still in existence. The garden is a classic example of Jekyll's ideas of color harmonies and plant combinations; a hedge of mixed shrubs encloses a mix of perennials.

An apple orchard and a circa-1915 formal parterre garden that blossoms with peonies, historic roses, and lilacs highlight the **Bellamy-Ferriday House & Garden** (⊠ *9 Main St. N, Bethlehem* ☎ *203/266–7596* ⊕ *www. ctlandmarks.org*).

At **Roseland Cottage** (⊠ *556 Rte. 169, Woodstock* ☎ *860/928–4074* ⊕ *www.spnea.org*), the boxwood parterre garden includes 21 flowerbeds surrounded by boxwood hedge.

The gardens at the historic **Florence Griswold Museum** (⊠ *96 Lyme St., Old Lyme* ☎ *860/434–5542* ⊕ *www. flogris.org*), once the home of a prominent Old Lyme family and then a haven for artists, have been restored to their 1910 appearance and feature hollyhocks and black-eyed Susans.

5

WHERE TO EAT

¢–$ ✕ **O'Rourke's Diner.** A devastating fire closed this beloved steel, glass, and
AMERICAN brick diner in summer 2007, but the owners—partly through donations
★ from the community—have rebuilt it better than ever. It's the place to
go for top-notch diner fare, including creative specialties like the omelet
stuffed with roasted portobello mushrooms, Brie, and asparagus. The
steamed cheeseburgers are another favorite. Arrive early: lines are often
out the door and the diner closes at 3 PM. ⊠ *728 Main St.* ☎ *860/346–
6101* ⊕ *www. orourkesdiner.com* ⊟ *AE, DC, MC, V* ⊙ *No dinner.*

WETHERSFIELD

7 mi northeast of New Britain, 32 mi northeast of New Haven.

Wethersfield, a vast Hartford suburb, dates from 1634 and has the
state's largest—and, some say, most picturesque—historic district, with
more than 100 pre-1849 buildings. Old Wethersfield has the oldest firehouse in the state, the oldest historic district in the state, and the oldest
continuously operating seed company. Today, this "old" community has
new parks and new shops, but history is still its main draw.

EXPLORING

Webb-Deane-Stevens Museum. For a true sample of Wethersfield's historic
past, stop by the Joseph Webb House, the Silas Deane House, and the
Isaac Stevens House, next door to each other along Main Street and
all built in the mid- to late 1700s. These well-preserved examples of
Georgian architecture reflect their owners' lifestyles as, respectively,
a merchant, a diplomat, and a tradesman. The Webb House, a registered National Historic Landmark, was the site of the strategy conference between George Washington and the French general Jean-Baptiste
Rochambeau that led to the British defeat at Yorktown. ⊠ *211 Main
St., off I–91, Exit 26* ☎ *860/529–0612* ⊕ *www.webb-deane-stevens.
org* ⊠ *$8* ⊙ *May–Oct., Mon. and Wed.–Sat. 10–4, Sun. 1–4; Apr. and
Nov., Sat. 10–4, Sun. 1–4; other times by appointment.*

★ **New Britain Museum of American Art.** An important stop for art lovers
in a small industrial city 8 mi west of Wethersfield, this museum more
than doubled its exhibit space with the opening of a new building in
2006. The 100-year-old museum's collection of more than 5,000 works
from 1740 to the present had seriously outgrown the turn-of-the-20th-
century house that held it. Among the treasures are paintings by artists
of the Hudson River and Ash Can schools; by John Singer Sargent,
Winslow Homer, Georgia O'Keeffe, and others on up through op-art
works and sculpture by Isamu Noguchi. Deserving of special note is
the selection of Impressionist artists, including Mary Cassatt, William
Merritt Chase, Childe Hassam, and John Henry Twachtman, as well
as Thomas Hart Benton's five-panel mural *The Arts of Life in America.*
The museum also has a café, a large shop, and a library of art books.
⊠ *56 Lexington St.* ☎ *860/229–0257* ⊕ *www.nbmaa.org* ⊠ *$9, free
Sat. 10–noon* ⊙ *Tues., Wed., and Fri. 11–5; Thurs. 11–8; Sat. 10–5;
Sun. noon–5.*

HARTFORD

4 mi north of Wethersfield, 45 mi northwest of New London, 81 mi northeast of Stamford.

Midway between New York City and Boston, Hartford is Connecticut's capital city. Founded in 1635 on the banks of the Connecticut River, Hartford was at various times home to authors Mark Twain and Harriet Beecher Stowe, inventors Samuel and Elizabeth Colt, landscape architect Frederick Law Olmsted, and Ella Grasso, the first woman to be elected a state governor. Today, Hartford, where America's insurance industry was born in the early 19th century, is poised for change, with a new convention center and science museum, Connecticut Science Center. The city is a destination on the verge of discovery.

Numbers in the margin correspond to numbers on the Downtown Hartford map.

TOP ATTRACTIONS

❽ Children's Museum. A life-size walk-through replica of a 60-foot sperm whale greets patrons at this museum, formerly known as the Science Center of Connecticut. In West Hartford, 5 mi west of downtown, the museum has a wildlife sanctuary and real-life images "beamed" in from NASA, plus an exhibit on rocks and fossils that will make a geologist out of your little one. ⊠ *950 Trout Brook Dr., West Hartford* ☎ *860/231-2824* ⊕ *www.thechildrensmuseumct.org* ✉ *Museum and one planetarium show $11* ⊗ *Tues.–Sat. 9–4, Sun. 11–4.*

❷ Connecticut Science Center. Scientists of all ages will delight in Hartford's new science center, which opened in June 2009. The strikingly modern building, designed by world-renowned architect César Pelli, houses 40,000 square feet of exhibit space under a wave-like roofline that appears to float over the structure. Dive into a black hole and examine the moon's craters in the Space Exploration exhibit, race mini-sailboats and magnetic trains at Forces in Motion, and discover your hidden athletic talents in the Sports Lab. Kid Space is perfect for the 3- to 6-year-old crowd, with a water play area, "I Spy" adventure activities, and magnetic ball wall. Complete your visit by taking in a movie in the 3-D digital theater. The café emphasizes locally sourced cuisine. ⊠ *250 Columbus Blvd.* ☎ *860/724-3623* ⊕ *www.ctsciencecenter.org* ✉ *$16* ⊗ *Sept.–June, Tues.–Sun. 10–5; July and Aug., daily 10–5.*

❼ Harriet Beecher Stowe Center. Stowe (1811–96) spent her final years at this 1871 Victorian Gothic cottage, on the Connecticut Freedom Trail. The center was built around the cottage, created as a tribute to the author of the antislavery novel *Uncle Tom's Cabin.* Stowe's personal writing table and effects are inside the home. ⊠ *77 Forest St.* ☎ *860/522-9258* ⊕ *www.harrietbeecherstowecenter.org* ✉ *$9* ⊗ *June–Oct., Tues.–Sat. 9:30–4:30, Sun. noon–4:30; Nov.–May Wed.–Sat. 9:30–4:30.*

❻ Mark Twain House & Museum. Built in 1874, this building was the home of Samuel Langhorne Clemens, better known as Mark Twain, until 1891. While he and his family lived in this 19-room Victorian mansion, Twain published seven major novels, including *Tom Sawyer, Huckleberry Finn,* and *The Prince and the Pauper.* The home is one of only

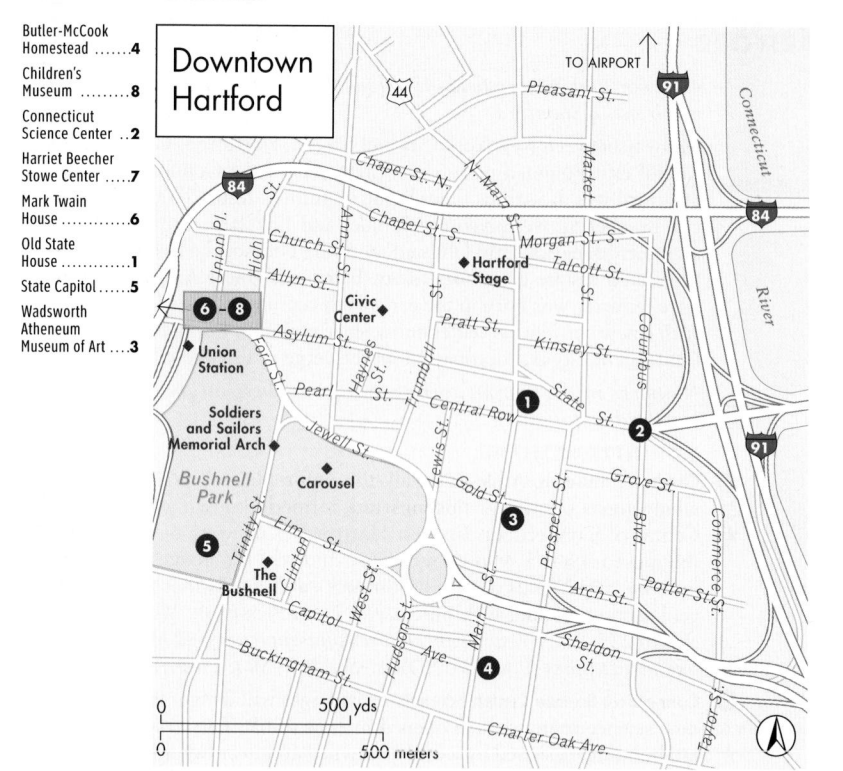

Downtown
Hartford

two Louis Comfort Tiffany–designed domestic interiors open to the public. A contemporary museum on the grounds presents an up-close look at the author and shows an outstanding Ken Burns documentary on his life. ✉ *351 Farmington Ave., at Woodland St.* ☎ *860/247–0998* ⊕ *www.marktwainhouse.org* 💲 *$14* ☾ *Apr.–Dec., Mon.–Sat. 9:30–5:30, Sun. noon–5:30; Jan.–Mar., Mon. and Wed.–Sat. 9:30–5:30, Sun. noon–5:30.*

❸ **Wadsworth Atheneum Museum of Art.** With more than 45,000 artworks
Fodor's Choice and artifacts spanning 5,000 years, this is the nation's oldest public art
★ museum. The first American museum to acquire works by Salvador Dalí and the Italian artist Caravaggio, it also houses 7,000 items documenting African-American history and culture in partnership with the Amistad Foundation. Particularly impressive are the museum's baroque, Impressionist, and Hudson River school collections. ✉ *600 Main St.* ☎ *860/278–2670* ⊕ *www.wadsworthatheneum.org* 💲 *$10* ☾ *Wed.–Fri. 11–5 (1st Thurs. of most months until 8), weekends 10–5.*

WORTH NOTING

❹ **Butler-McCook Homestead.** Built in 1782, this home housed four generations of Butlers and McCooks until it became a museum in 1971. Inside is Hartford's oldest intact collection of art and antiques, including furnishings, family possessions, and Victorian-era toys that show the evolution of American tastes over nearly 200 years. The beautifully restored Victorian garden was originally designed by Jacob Weidenmann. ⊠ *396 Main St.* ☎ *860/522–1806 or 860/247–8996* ⊕ *www.ctlandmarks.org* ⊒ *$7* ☉ *May–Dec., Sat. 10–4, Sun. 1–4; Feb.–Apr., Sat. noon–4.*

QUICK
BITES
Mozzicato–De Pasquale's Bakery, Pastry Shop & Caffé (⊠ *329 Franklin Ave.* ☎ *860/296-0426* ⊕ *www.mozzicatobakery.com*), in the city's Little Italy neighborhood along Franklin Avenue, serves delectable Italian pastries in the bakery and espresso, cappuccino, and gelato in the café.

❶ **Old State House.** This Federal-style house with an elaborate cupola and roof balustrade was designed in the early 1700s by Charles Bulfinch, architect of the U.S. Capitol. It served as Connecticut's state capitol until a new building opened in 1879, then became Hartford's city hall until 1915. In the 1820 Senate Chamber, where everyone from Abraham Lincoln to George Bush has spoken, you can view a portrait of George Washington by Gilbert Stuart, and in the Courtroom you can find out about the trial of the *Amistad* Africans in the very place where it was first held. In summer, enjoy concerts and a farmers' market; don't forget to stop by the Museum of Natural and Other Curiosities. ⊠ *800 Main St.* ☎ *860/522–6766* ⊕ *www.ctosh.org* ⊒ *$5* ☉ *Sept.–June weekdays 9–5; July and Aug., Tues.–Sat. 10–5.*

❺ **State Capitol.** The gold-leaf dome of the State Capitol rises above Bushnell Park. Built in 1878, the building houses the state's executive offices and legislative chamber as well as historical memorabilia. On a tour, you can walk through the Hall of Flags, see a statue of Connecticut state hero Nathan Hale, and observe the proceedings of the General Assembly, when in session, from the public galleries. ⊠ *210 Capitol Ave.* ☎ *860/240–0222* ⊕ *www.cga.ct.gov/capitoltours* ⊒ *Free* ☉ *Building weekdays 9–3. Tours given hourly, Nov.–Mar. weekdays 9:15–1:15; Apr.–June, Sept., and Oct. weekdays 9:15–1:15, Sat. 10:15–2:15; July and Aug., weekdays 9:15–2:15, Sat. 10:15–2:15.*

OFF THE
BEATEN
PATH
Noah Webster House/Museum of West Hartford History. This 18th-century farmhouse is the birthplace of the famed author (1758–1843) of the *American Dictionary.* Inside is Webster memorabilia and period furnishings; outside there is a garden planted with herbs, vegetables, and flowers that would have been available to the Websters when they lived here. ⊠ *227 S. Main St.,* West Hartford ☎ *860/521–5362* ⊕ *www.noahwebsterhouse.org* ⊒ *$7* ☉ *Thurs.–Mon. 1–4.*

SPORTS AND THE OUTDOORS

☙ **Bushnell Park.** Fanning out from the State Capitol building, this city park, created in 1850, was the first public space in the country with natural landscaping. The original designer, a Swiss-born landscape architect and botanist named Jacob Weidenmann, planted 157 varieties of trees and shrubs to create an urban arboretum. Added later were the Soldiers and Sailors Memorial Arch, dedicated to Civil War soldiers; the Corning Fountain; the Bushnell Park Carousel (open May through September), intricately hand-carved in 1914 by the Artistic Carousel Company of Brooklyn, New York; the Pumphouse Gallery; and a performance venue.

An oasis of green, the park has a pond and about 750 trees, including four state-champion trees. ⊠ *Asylum and Trinity Sts.* ☎ *860/232–6710* ⊕ *www.bushnellpark.org.*

NIGHTLIFE AND THE ARTS

NIGHTLIFE For barbecue and blues head to **Black-Eyed Sally's** (⊠ *350 Asylum St.* ☎ *860/278–7427* ⊕ *www. blackeyedsallys.com*).

THE ARTS The **Bushnell** (⊠ *166 Capitol Ave.* ☎ *860/987–6000* or *888/824–2874* ⊕ *www.bushnell.org*) hosts the **Hartford Symphony Orchestra** (☎ *860/244–2999* ⊕ *www. hartfordsymphony.org*) and tours of major musicals. The **Hartford Conservatory** (⊠ *834 Asylum Ave.* ☎ *860/246–2588* ⊕ *www.hartfordconservatory.org*) presents musical theater, concerts, and dance performances, with an emphasis on traditional works. The Tony Award–winning **Hartford Stage Company** (⊠ *50 Church St.* ☎ *860/527–5151* ⊕ *www.hartfordstage.org*) puts on classic and new plays from around the world. **Real Art Ways** (⊠ *56 Arbor St.* ☎ *860/232–1006* ⊕ *www.realartways.org*) presents modern and experimental musical compositions in addition to avant-garde and foreign films. **TheatreWorks** (⊠ *233 Pearl St.* ⌂ *One Gold St., Hartford, CT* ☎ *860/527–7838* ⊕ *www.theaterworkshartford.org*), the Hartford equivalent of off-Broadway, presents experimental new dramas.

WHERE TO EAT

$–$$ ✕ **First and Last Tavern.** What looks to be a simple neighborhood joint
PIZZA south of downtown is actually one of the state's most hallowed pizza
★ parlors, serving superb thin-crust pies (locals love the puttanesca) since 1936. The old-fashioned wooden bar in one room is jammed most evenings with suburbia-bound daily-grinders. The main dining room, which is just as noisy, has a brick outer wall covered with celebrity photos. This is the original, but other branches have opened around the state. ⊠ *939 Maple Ave.* ☎ *860/956–6000* ⊕ *www.firstandlasttavern. com* ⌂ *Reservations not accepted* ▭ *AE, D, DC, MC, V.*

$$$–$$$$ ✕ **Max Downtown.** With its contemporary design, extensive array of
AMERICAN martinis and wines, and sophisticated cuisine, Max Downtown is a
Fodor's Choice favorite with the city's well-heeled and a popular after-work spot. Cre-
★ ative entrées include peanut crusted ahi tuna with a vegetable maki roll and kung pao sauce, double thick lamb loin chops with rosemary spaetzle, and a wide range of perfectly prepared steaks with such toppings as foie-gras butter and cognac-peppercorn cream. Desserts, such as the chocolate-chip ice cream cake and the chocolate mousse tower with raspberry coulis, are not to be missed. It's part of a small empire of excellent Hartford-area restaurants that includes Max's Oyster in West Hartford, Max a Mia in Avon, and several others. ⊠ *185 Asylum*

TAKE A TOUR

The **Connecticut Freedom Trail** (⊕ *www.ctfreedomtrail. ct.gov*) has more than 50 historic sights associated with the state's African-American heritage. The **Connecticut Impressionist Art Trail** (⊕ *www.arttrail.org*) is a self-guided tour of 14 museums and sites important to the 19th-century American Impressionist movement. The **Connecticut Wine Trail** (☎ *860/677–5467* ⊕ *www.ctwine.com*) travels among 19 member vineyards.

Connecticut's Victorian Gothic state capitol rises from Hartford's Bushnell Park.

St. ☎ *860/522–2530* ⊕ *www.maxrestaurantgroup.com* 👜 *Reservations essential* ⊟ *AE, DC, MC, V* 🕒 *No lunch weekends.*

$$–$$$ ✕ **Peppercorn's Grill**. This mainstay of Hartford's restaurant scene presents
ITALIAN contemporary Italian cuisine in both a lively (colorful murals) and formal (white linens) setting. Enjoy house-made potato gnocchi, ravioli, and top-quality steaks, but save room for the warm chocolate bread pudding and the Valrhona chocolate cake. ⊠ *348 Main St.* ☎ *860/547–1714* ⊕ *www. peppercornsgrill.com* ⊟ *AE, DC, MC, V* 🕒 *Closed Sun. No lunch Sat.*

WHERE TO STAY

$$ 🏨 **Hartford Marriott Downtown**. This upscale hotel is connected to the
XL Center and conveniently located within walking distance of the Connecticut Science Center, the Wadsworth Atheneum, the Old State House, and other attractions. Guest rooms are decked out with flat-screen TVs and 300-thread-count sheets, and many have views of the Connecticut River. Relax with a massage or facial at the hotel spa, Glo, or join the party at the swank lobby lounge Crush, where DJs spin on weekends. **Pros:** close to major attractions; in the heart of downtown. **Cons:** convenient location comes at a price. ⊠ *200 Columbus Blvd.* ☎ *860/249–8000 or 866/373–9806* ⊕ *www.marriott.com* 🛏 *401 rooms, 8 suites* ♿ *In-room: a/c, Internet. In-hotel: restaurant, bar, pool, gym, spa, Wi-Fi hotspot* ⊟ *AE, D, DC, MC, V* 🍴 *EP.*

$–$$ 🏨 **Residence Inn Hartford-Downtown**. Part of the rehabilitation project at the
historic Richardson building, the all-suites Residence Inn is convenient to Pratt Street, Hartford Stage, and the Old State House. Rooms come with a kitchen and there's an on-site 24-hour convenience store. A full breakfast is included daily, as is a light dinner buffet Monday–Thursday.

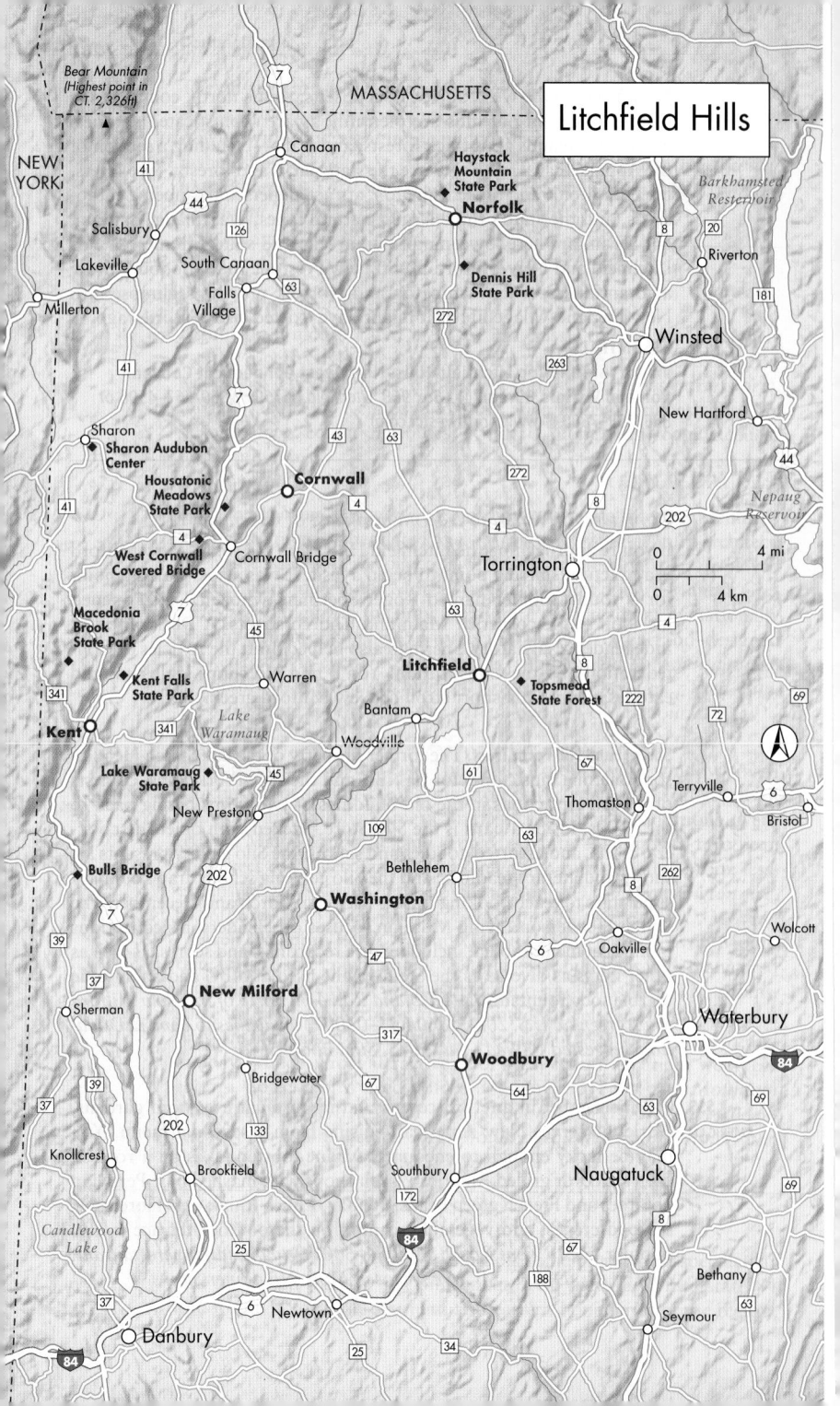

Litchfield Hills

MASSACHUSETTS

NEW YORK

Bear Mountain
(Highest point in
CT. 2,326ft)

Canaan

Haystack
Mountain
State Park

Norfolk

Barkhamsted
Reservoir

Salisbury

Lakeville

South Canaan

Falls
Village

Dennis Hill
State Park

Winsted

Millerton

Riverton

New Hartford

Sharon

Sharon Audubon
Center

Housatonic
Meadows
State Park

Cornwall

Nepaug
Reservoir

West Cornwall
Covered Bridge

Cornwall Bridge

Torrington

Macedonia
Brook
State Park

Kent Falls
State Park

Warren

Litchfield

Topsmead
State Forest

Lake
Waramaug

Bantam

Kent

Lake Waramaug
State Park

Woodville

Thomaston

Terryville

Bristol

New Preston

Bulls Bridge

Bethlehem

Washington

Oakville

Wolcott

Sherman

New Milford

Waterbury

Bridgewater

Woodbury

Naugatuck

Knollcrest

Brookfield

Southbury

Bethany

Candlewood
Lake

Newtown

Danbury

Seymour

0   4 mi

0   4 km

$$ **Homestead Inn.** The Homestead, high on a hill overlooking New Milford's town green, was built in 1853 and opened as an inn in 1928. Breakfast is served in a cheery living room, where you can sit by the fire. Rooms are decorated in a well-chosen mix of country antiques, reproductions, and an abundance of floral accents. The eight rooms in the main house have more personality than those in the motel-style structure next door. **Pros:** reasonably priced; close to shops and restaurants. **Cons:** on a busy street. ⊠ *5 Elm St.* ☎ *860/354–4080* ⊕ *www. homesteadct.com* ⇱ *14 rooms* ⚑ *In-room: a/c, Wi-Fi. In-hotel: some pets allowed (fee)* ⊟ *AE, D, DC, MC, V* ⎮⚏⎮ *CP.*

KENT

12 mi northwest of New Preston.

Kent has the area's greatest concentration of art galleries, some nationally renowned. Home to a prep school of the same name, Kent once held many ironworks. The Schaghticoke Indian Reservation is also here. During the Revolutionary War, 100 Schaghticokes helped defend the Colonies by transmitting messages of army intelligence from the Litchfield Hills to Long Island Sound along the hilltops by way of shouts and drumbeats.

EXPLORING

Sloane-Stanley Museum. Hardware-store buffs and vintage-tool aficionados will feel right at home at this museum. Artist and author Eric Sloane (1905–85) was fascinated by Early American woodworking tools, and his collection showcases examples of American craftsmanship from the 17th to the 19th centuries. The museum contains a re-creation of Sloane's last studio and also encompasses the ruins of a 19th-century iron furnace. Sloane's books and prints, which celebrate vanishing aspects of Americana such as barns and covered bridges, are on sale here. ⊠ *31 Kent-Cornwall Rd. (U.S. 7)* ☎ *860/927–3849* ⊟ *$4* ⊘ *Late May–late Oct., Wed.–Sun. 10–4.*

SPORTS AND THE OUTDOORS

The **Appalachian Trail**'s longest river walk, off Route 341, is the almost-8-mi hike from Kent to Cornwall Bridge along the Housatonic River. The early-season trout fishing is superb at 2,300-acre **Macedonia Brook State Park** (⊠ *Macedonia Brook Rd. off Rte. 341* ☎ *860/927–3238*), where you can also hike and cross-country ski.

SHOPPING

★ The **Bachelier-Cardonsky Gallery** (⊠ *10 N. Main St.* ☎ *860/927–3129* ⊕ *www.bacheliercardonsky.com*), one of the foremost galleries in New England, exhibits works by local artists and contemporary masters such as Alexander Calder, Carol Anthony, and Jackson Pollock. **Belgique** (⊠ *1 Bridge St.* ☎ *860/927–3681*) sells sublime handmade chocolates, plus gelato and sorbet and—perfect on a winter day—pure and decadently rich Belgian hot chocolate.

EN ROUTE Heading north from Kent toward Cornwall, you'll pass the entrance to 295-acre **Kent Falls State Park** (⊠ *U.S. 7* ☎ *860/927–3238*), where you can hike a short way to one of the most impressive waterfalls in the state and picnic in the green meadows at the base of the falls.

CORNWALL

12 mi northeast of Kent.

Connecticut's Cornwalls can get confusing. There's Cornwall, Cornwall Bridge, West Cornwall, Cornwall Hollow, East Cornwall, and North Cornwall. This quiet corner of the Litchfield Hills is known for its fantastic vistas of woods and mountains and its covered bridge, which spans the Housatonic.

EXPLORING

West Cornwall Covered Bridge. A romantic reminder of the past, the wooden, barn-red, one-lane bridge, not to be confused with the town of Cornwall Bridge (which was named for an earlier covered bridge that stood originally on that site), is several miles up U.S. 7 on Route 128 in West Cornwall. The bridge was built in 1841 and incorporates strut techniques that were copied by bridge builders around the country.

SPORTS AND THE OUTDOORS

Housatonic Meadows State Park. The park is marked by its tall pine trees near the Housatonic River and has terrific riverside campsites. Fly-fishers consider this 2-mi stretch of the river among the best places in New England to test their skills against trout and bass. ⊠ *U.S. 7, Cornwall Bridge* ☎ *860/672–6772.*

☺ **Sharon Audubon Center.** With 11 mi of hiking trails, this 1,147-acre property—a mixture of forests, meadows, wetlands, ponds, and streams—provides myriad hiking opportunities. It's also home to Princess, an American crow, who shares the visitor center with small hawks, an owl, and other animals in a live-animal display. Also here is a natural-history museum and children's adventure center. An aviary houses a bald eagle, a red-tailed hawk, and two turkey vultures. ⊠ *325 Cornwall Bridge Rd., Sharon* ☎ *860/364–0520* ⊕ *www.sharon.audubon.org* ⊠ *$3* ☉ *Tues.– Sat. 9–5, Sun. 1–5, trails daily dawn–dusk.*

CANOE- **Clarke Outdoors** (⊠ *U.S. 7, West Cornwall* ☎ *860/672–6365* ⊕ *www.*
ING AND *clarkeoutdoors.com*) rents canoes, kayaks, and rafts and operates 10-mi
KAYAKING trips from Falls Village to Housatonic Meadows State Park.

FISHING **Housatonic Anglers** (⊠ *26 Bolton Hill Rd.* ☎ *860/672–4457* ⊕ *www.housatonicanglers.com*) operates half- and full-day tours, as well as some evening outings, and provides fly-fishing instruction for trout and bass on the Housatonic and its tributaries. **Housatonic River Outfitters** (⊠ *24 Kent Rd., Cornwall Bridge* ☎ *860/672–1010* ⊕ *www.dryflies.com*) operates a full-service fly shop; leads guided trips of the region; runs classes in fly-fishing, fly-tying, and casting; and stocks a good selection of vintage and antique gear.

WHERE TO STAY

$$–$$$ **Cornwall Inn.** This 19th-century inn on scenic U.S. 7 combines country charm with contemporary elegance; eight rooms in the adjacent "lodge" are slightly more private and rustic in tone and have white cedar-post beds. The restaurant ($$$), which overlooks the pool and colorful gardens, serves a seasonally changing American menu. The Houstatonic River is a short walk from the inn. **Pros:** tranquil setting; lovely grounds; welcoming toward kids and pets. **Cons:** a bit far

Be patient on back roads: Many covered bridges, like this one in West Cornwall, are one-lane only.

from neighboring towns. ✉ *270 Kent Rd. (U.S. 7)* ☎ *860/672–6884 or 800/786–6884* ⊕ *www.cornwallinn.com* ⇆ *13 rooms* ⚓ *In-room: no a/c (some), Wi-Fi. In-hotel: restaurant, bar, pool, some pets allowed (fee)* ▭ *AE, D, MC, V* ¶◎¶ *CP.*

NORFOLK

14 mi east of Salisbury, 59 mi north of New Haven.

Norfolk, thanks to its severe climate and terrain, is one of the best-preserved villages in the Northeast. Notable industrialists have been summering here for two centuries, and many enormous homesteads still exist. The striking town green, at the junction of Route 272 and U.S. 44, has a fountain designed by Augustus Saint-Gaudens and executed by Stanford White at its southern corner. It stands as a memorial to Joseph Battell, who turned Norfolk into a major trading center.

SPORTS AND THE OUTDOORS

Dennis Hill State Park. Dr. Frederick Shepard Dennis, former owner of the 240 acres now making up the park, lavishly entertained guests, among them President William Howard Taft and several Connecticut governors, in the stone pavilion at the summit of the estate. From its 1,627-foot height, you can see Haystack Mountain, New Hampshire, and, on a clear day, New Haven harbor, all the way across the state. Picnic on the park's grounds or hike one of its many trails. ✉ *Rte. 272* ☎ *860/482–1817* ▭ *Free* ☉ *Daily 8* AM*–dusk.*

Haystack Mountain State Park. One of the most spectacular views in the state can be seen from this park via its challenging trail to the top or a road halfway up. ⊠ *Rte. 272* ☎ *860/482–1817.*

★ The **Norfolk Chamber Music Festival** (☎ *860/542–3000 or 203/432–1966* ⊕ *www.yale.edu/norfolk*), at the Music Shed on the 70-acre Ellen Battell Stoeckel Estate at the northwest corner of the Norfolk green, presents world-renowned artists and ensembles on Friday and Saturday summer evenings. Students from the Yale School of Music perform on Thursday evening and Saturday morning. Early arrivals can stroll or picnic on the 70-acre grounds or visit the art gallery.

WHERE TO EAT AND STAY

¢–$ ✕ **Speckled Hen Pub.** Bottles of trendy beers line the shelves of this down-
AMERICAN   to-earth restaurant on the ground floor of a redbrick Victorian near the
★   town green. Burgers and other pub fare are on the menu alongside more eclectic choices. ⊠ *U.S. 44* ☎ *860/542–5716* ▭ *AE, MC, V* ⊙ *Closed Mon. No dinner Tues.*

$$$–$$$$ ⊞ **Manor House.** Among this 1898 Bavarian Tudor's remarkable appoint-
Fodor'sChoice   ments are its bibelots, mirrors, carpets, antique beds, and prints—not
★   to mention the 20 stained-glass windows designed by Louis Comfort Tiffany. The vast Spofford Room has windows on three sides, a king-size canopy bed with a cheery fireplace opposite, and a balcony; many rooms have Jacuzzi tubs. **Pros:** sumptuous decor; lavish breakfasts; secluded and peaceful setting. **Cons:** no phone or TV in the rooms (and cell phone reception is iffy in these parts); no Internet offered. ⊠ *69 Maple Ave.* ☎☎ *860/542–5690 or 866/542–5690* ⊕ *www.manorhouse-norfolk.com* ⇥ *8 rooms, 1 suite* ⬧ *In-room: no phone, a/c, no TV. In-hotel: no kids under 10* ▭ *AE, MC, V* ⅠⓄⅠ *BP.*

LITCHFIELD

19 mi southwest of Riverton, 34 mi west of Hartford.

Everything in Litchfield, the wealthiest and most noteworthy town in the Litchfield Hills, seems to exist on a larger scale than in neighboring burgs, especially the impressive Litchfield Green and the white Colonial and Greek-Revival homes that line the broad elm-shaded streets. Harriet Beecher Stowe, author of *Uncle Tom's Cabin,* and her brother, abolitionist preacher Henry Ward Beecher, were born and raised in Litchfield, and many famous Americans earned their law degrees at the Litchfield Law School. Today, lovely but exceptionally expensive boutiques and hot restaurants line the downtown.

EXPLORING

★ **Tapping Reeve House and Litchfield Law School.** In 1773, Judge Tapping Reeve enrolled his first student, Aaron Burr, in what became the first law school in the country. (Before Judge Reeve, students studied the law as apprentices, not in formal classes.) This school is dedicated to Reeve's achievement and to the notable students who passed through its halls: Oliver Wolcott Jr., John C. Calhoun, Horace Mann, three U.S. Supreme Court justices, and 15 governors, not to mention senators, congressmen, and ambassadors. This museum is one of the state's most worthy attractions, with multimedia exhibits, an excellent introductory film, and restored facilities. ⊠ *82 South St.* ☎ *860/567–4501* ⊕ *www.litchfieldhistoricalsociety.org* ✉ *$5 (includes Litchfield History Museum)* ☼ *Mid-Apr.–late Nov., Tues.–Sat. 11–5, Sun. 1–5.*

SPORTS AND THE OUTDOORS

Topsmead State Forest. The chief attractions in this 511-acre forest are an English Tudor–style cottage built by architect Richard Henry Dana Jr. (seemingly straight out of the English countryside) and a 40-acre wildflower preserve. The forest holds picnic grounds, hiking trails, and cross-country ski areas. ⊠ *Buell Rd. off E. Litchfield Rd.* ☎ *860/567–5694* ✉ *Free* ☼ *Forest daily 8* AM–*dusk; cottage tours June–Oct., 2nd and 4th weekends of month.*

Fodor'sChoice
★
White Memorial Conservation Center. At the heart of the White Memorial Foundation, this 4,000-acre nature preserve houses top-notch natural-history exhibits and a gift shop. The foundation, one of the state's prime birding areas, contains some 30 bird-watching platforms; two self-guided nature trails; several boardwalks; campgrounds; boating facilities; fishing areas; and 35 mi of hiking, cross-country skiing, and horseback-riding trails. ⊠ *Off U.S. 202 (2 mi west of village green)* ☎ *860/567–0857* ⊕ *www.whitememorialcc.org* ✉ *Conservation center $5, grounds free* ☼ *Conservation center Mon.–Sat. 9–5, Sun. noon–5; grounds daily dawn to dusk.*

OFF THE BEATEN PATH
Lake Compounce in Bristol is the oldest amusement park in the country. Opened in 1846, it's known simply as "the Lake." Today's attractions include a lakefront beach; an ever-expanding water park with a wave pool, waterslides (high speed and otherwise), spray fountains, and a clipper ship with a 300-gallon bucket of water that gives unsuspecting guests a good dousing; and such hair-raising rides as the Sky Coaster, the Twister, and the Zoomerang. ⊠ *Rte. 229 N (I–84, Exit 31)* ☎ *860/583–3631* ⊕ *www.lakecompounce.com* ✉ *$33.95* ☼ *Memorial Day–Oct.; call for hrs.*

HORSEBACK RIDING
Lee's Riding Stable (⊠ *57 E. Litchfield Rd.* ☎ *860/567–0785*) conducts trail and pony rides.

SHOPPING

Jeffrey Tillou Antiques (⊠ *39 West St.* ☎ *860/567–9693* ⊕ *www.tillouantiques.com*) specializes in 18th- and 19th-century American furniture and paintings.

WHERE TO EAT AND STAY

$$–$$$
AMERICAN
✕**Village Restaurant.** Beloved by visitors and locals alike, this storefront eatery in a redbrick townhouse serves tasty, unfussy food—inexpensive pub grub in one room, updated contemporary American cuisine in the other. Whether you order a burger or herb-crusted pork chops, you're bound to be pleased. ⊠ *25 West St.* ☎ *860/567–8307* ⊕ *www.village-litchfield.com* ⊟ *AE, D, MC, V.*

$$$–$$$$
AMERICAN
★
✕**West Street Grill.** This sophisticated dining room on the town green is *the* place to see and be seen, both for patrons and for the state's up-and-coming chefs, many of whom got their start here. Imaginative grilled fish, steak, poultry, and lamb dishes are served with fresh vegetables

Explore White Memorial Conservation Center on the boardwalks, nature trails, and bird-watching platforms.

and pasta or risotto. The ice cream and sorbets, made by the restaurant, are worth every calorie. ✉ *43 West St.* ☎ *860/567–3885* ⊕ *www. weststreetgrill.net* ▭ *AE, MC, V.*

$$$–$$$$ ⊡ **The Litchfield Inn.** This reproduction Colonial-style inn lies little more than a mile west of the center of Litchfield. Period accents adorn its modern rooms, including themed "designer" rooms such as an "Irish" room (which has a four-poster bed draped in green floral chintz) and a "Southwestern" room (which employs a rustic picket fence as a headboard). **Pros:** well-kept property; efficient staff; good location for exploring entire region. **Cons:** on busy road without much curb appeal; not within walking distance of downtown shopping and dining. ✉ *432 Bantam Rd. (Rte. 202)* ☎ *860/567–4503 or 800/499–3444* ⊕ *www. litchfieldinnct.com* ⇌ *32 rooms* ⌂ *In-room: a/c, Internet. In-hotel: restaurant, room service, bar, laundry service* ▭ *AE, DC, MC, V.*

$$$$ ⊡ **Winvian.** Opened in 2007 by the owners of Vermont's swanky Pitcher **Fodor's Choice** Inn, this ultra-posh, 113-acre hideaway adjacent to the grounds of ★ the White Memorial Foundation consists of 19 of the most imaginatively themed and luxuriously outfitted cottages you'll ever lay eyes on. Each of the huge one-bedroom cottages has a distinctive, often amusing, theme: the Stone Cottage is made with massive boulders and has a wavy-slate roof and an enormous fireplace; the Helicopter Cottage contains—you guessed it—a genuine 17,000-pound U.S. Coast Guard helicopter (the fuselage has been refitted with a wet bar). Bathrooms are consistently big, with deep whirlpool tubs and top-of-the-line amenities. Rates begin at an eye-popping $1,250 per night, though all meals, snacks, and even the wet-bar goodies are included. On-site is also a full-service spa. **Pros:** whimsical and super-plush accommodations;

outstanding cuisine; stunning setting. **Cons:** super-pricey; all-inclusive meal plan discourages guests from exploring the region's other fantastic restaurants. ⊠ *155 Alain White Rd., Morris* ☎ *860/567–9600* ⊕ *www. winvian.com* ➷ *19 cottages, 1 suite* ♿ *In-room: a/c, DVD, Wi-Fi. In-hotel: restaurant, bar, gym, spa* ⊟ *AE, MC, V* ⊖*AI.*

WASHINGTON

11 mi west of Bethlehem.

The beautiful buildings of The Gunnery prep school mingle with stately Colonials and churches in Washington, one of the best-preserved Colonial towns in Connecticut. The Mayflower Inn, south of The Gunnery on Route 47, attracts an exclusive clientele. Washington, which was settled in 1734, in 1779 became the first town in the United States to be named for the first president.

EXPLORING

Institute for American Indian Studies. The exhibits in this small but excellent and thoughtfully arranged collection detail the history and continuing presence of more than 10,000 years of Native American life in New England. Highlights include nature trails, a simulated archaeological site, and an authentically constructed Algonquian Village with wigwams, a longhouse, a rock shelter, and more. The Collections and Research Center has a research library, a large exhibit hall, and a gift shop that presents the work of some of the country's best Native American artists. The institute is at the end of a forested residential road (just follow the signs from Route 199 South). ⊠ *38 Curtis Rd., off Rte. 199* ☎ *860/868–0518* ⊕ *www.birdstone.org* ➷ *$5* ⊙ *Mon.–Sat. 10–5, Sun. noon–5.*

WHERE TO STAY

$$$$ **Mayflower Inn & Spa.** Though the most-expensive suites at this inn cost a wild $1,400 a night, the Mayflower is often booked months in advance. Running streams, rambling stone walls, and rare specimen trees fill the country manor-style inn's 28 manicured acres. Fine antiques, 18th- and 19th-century art, and four-poster canopy beds define each of the rooms. The colossal baths have mahogany wainscoting, marble, and Limoges and brass fittings. The Mayflower's 20,000-square-foot spa has earned a reputation as one of New England's finest such facilities—treatments like antioxidant-rich violet facials and Moor mud wraps are highly popular. Dine in the superb restaurant ($$$–$$$$), where the changing menu might include Nantucket Island diver scallops with sweet corn puree or ricotta-stuffed summer squash blossoms in a yellow tomato marinara sauce. **Pros:** idyllic and perfected landscaped grounds; solicitous but relaxed service; outstanding spa. **Cons:** some rooms starting to show a little age; very pricey. ⊠ *118 Woodbury Rd. (Rte. 47)* ☎ *860/868–9466* ⊕ *www.mayflowerinn.com* ➷ *19 rooms, 11 suites* ♿ *In-room: a/c, Wi-Fi. In-hotel: restaurant, bar, tennis court, pool, gym, spa, no kids under 12* ⊟ *AE, MC, V.*

Fodor's Choice
★

5

WOODBURY

10 mi southeast of Washington.

More antiques shops may be in the quickly growing town of Woodbury than in all the towns in the rest of the Litchfield Hills combined. Five magnificent churches and the Greek-Revival King Solomon's Temple, formerly a Masonic lodge, line U.S. 6; they represent some of the best-preserved examples of Colonial religious architecture in New England.

EXPLORING

Glebe House Museum and Gertrude Jekyll Garden. This property consists of the large, antique-filled, gambrel-roof Colonial in which Dr. Samuel Seabury was elected the first Episcopal bishop in the United States, in 1783, and its historic garden. The latter was designed in the 1920s by renowned British horticulturist Gertrude Jekyll. Though small, it is a classic, old-fashioned English-style garden and the only one of the three gardens Jekyll designed in the United States still in existence. ⊠ *149 Hollow Rd.* ☎ *203/263–2855* ⊕ *www.theglebehouse.org* ⊠ *$5* ☉ *May– Oct., Wed.–Sun. 1–4; Nov., weekends 1–4.*

SHOPPING

Country Loft Antiques (⊠ *557 Main St. S* ☎ *203/266–4500* ⊕ *www. countryloftantiques.com*) specializes in 18th- and 19th-century country French antiques. **David Dunton** (⊠ *Rte. 132 off Rte. 47* ☎ *203/263–5355* ⊕ *www.daviddunton.com*) is a respected dealer of formal American Federal–style furniture. **Mill House Antiques** (⊠ *1068 Main St. N* ☎ *203/263–3446* ⊕ *www.millhouseantiques-ct.com*) carries formal and country English and French furniture and has the state's largest collection of Welsh dressers. **Monique Shay Antiques & Design** (⊠ *920 Main St. S* ☎ *203/263–3186* ⊕ *www.moniqueshayantiques.com*) favors Canadian country antiques.

WHERE TO EAT AND STAY

$$–$$$ ✕ **Good News Café.** Carole Peck is a well-known name throughout New
AMERICAN   England, and since this café opened in 1992, foodies have been flocking
Fodor's Choice   to Woodbury to sample her superb cuisine. The emphasis is on healthy,
★   innovative, and surprisingly well-priced fare: wok-seared Gulf shrimp with new potatoes, grilled green beans, and a garlic aioli or Cuban-style black-bean cassoulet with duck confit, pork, chorizo, and wild boar are good choices. In the simpler room next to the bar, you can order from a less expensive café menu. ⊠ *694 Main St. S* ☎ *203/266–4663* ⊕ *www. good-news-cafe.com* ▭ *AE, D, MC, V* ☉ *Closed Tues.*

$$–$$$ 🛏 **Cornucopia at Oldfield.** A Federal Colonial house in northern South-
★   bury, a short drive from Woodbury antiques shops and restaurants, Cornucopia has a bounty of pleasing comforts: from high-quality antiques and soft Kingdown-brand bedding to CD-clock radios and DVD players in the rooms to floral gardens and a pool surrounded by a private hedge. A full breakfast is served in the formal dining room, in which you can also arrange—with advance notice—for a romantic dinner. **Pros:** fine antiques; beautifully kept grounds; modern in-room amenities. **Cons:** on somewhat busy road. ⊠ *782 N. Main St., Southbury* ☎ *203/267–6772* ⊕ *www.cornucopiabnb.com* ▭ *3 rooms, 2 suites* 🔒 *In-room: a/c, DVD, Wi-Fi. In-hotel: pool* ▭ *AE, MC, V* ⍐ *BP.*

Continued on page 298

ANTIQUES AND CRAFTS SHOPPING
SOMETHING OLD, SOMETHING NEW

By Christina Valhouli

Forget the mall. In New England, shoppers can pick up serious antiques or quirky bric-a-brac in old mills and converted barns. Or hit funky galleries or annual craft fairs to meet artisans and buy one-of-a-kind products. Your souvenirs will be as memorable as the shopping experience.

Alongside New England's wealth of early American history is some of the best antique and craft shopping in the country—and often in beautiful settings perfect for browsing. You can explore galleries in converted farmhouses, craft shops clustered around the village green, or a picturesque Main Street (Woodstock, Vermont, or Camden, Maine, are good bets). Drive through historic coastal towns, like Essex, Massachusetts, where finds such as sun-bleached, centuries-old wooden tables or antique compasses evoke the area's maritime heritage.

Picture-perfect towns like Blue Hill, Maine, and Chester, Connecticut, are home to plenty of contemporary artists' galleries and cooperatives, like the Connecticut River Artisans, which showcases handmade quilts, jewelry, and ceramics; or try your luck at the Frog Hollow Craft Center in Burlington, Vermont.

Top Left, Hand-blown glass. Top right, Brimfield Antique Show. Bottom, antique pocket watch.

GREAT FINDS: CRAFTS

When most people think of a typical New England look, the austere lines of a Shaker table or the colorful patterns in a quilt come to mind. Artisans here still make crafts the old-fashioned way, but a new generation of glassblowers, potters, and weavers is creating products that will appeal to modernistas.

QUILTS. Today's quilters continue to produce traditional quilts, but there are plenty of contemporary styles available. Instead of star patterns, go for bold stripes or blocky squares made from funky fabrics. Buy one for your bed or to hang; baby quilts start around $100.

SHAKER-STYLE FURNITURE. The Shakers believed that form must follow function, and a typical Shaker design is clean, straight-lined, and devoid of decoration. Carpenters still make Shaker-inspired furniture, including ladderback chairs, tables, and bookcases. Chairs start around $300.

FELT. Humble felt is simply unspun wool that has been rolled and beaten into a solid form, but it's one of the most versatile (and eco-friendly) products around. Contemporary artists fashion felt into handbags, rugs, and even lightweight sculptures. Handbags start at $60.

CERAMICS. Visit a pottery studio or an art gallery and choose from ceramic plates and mugs or sturdier stoneware products that can survive the dishwasher. Small ceramic pieces start at $25.

WOOD-TURNED BOWLS. Hand- or wood-turned bowls are individually shaped on a lathe from solid blocks of wood. Each piece has a unique size, shape, grain pattern, and color. Look for rare spalted wood bowls—highly valued for their patterns and rich contrasts. Bowls are around $40 and up.

BLOWN GLASS. It's worth a trip to a glass-blowing studio just to see the artisans blow a gob of molten glass into a beautiful object. Best bets include colorful vases, bowls, and sculptures; handblown glass is typically $100 to $500.

GREAT FINDS: ANTIQUES

Antiques can run the gamut from auction-worthy pieces to decorative trinkets and vintage items from the '40s, '50s and '60s. Antique trends come and go, but popular New England buys include "smalls" like old prints and glass bottles. Don't be put off if you don't know a lot about antiques—however, do keep in mind that a true antique must be at least 100 years old.

KITCHEN TOOLS. Although you won't be tempted to cook with an old iron cauldron, items like engraved stove plates, mortar and pestles, and spoon racks look great on display for about $40–$180.

■TIP→
Start a collection easily with two or more of the same item (salt and pepper shakers) or style (speckled graniteware).

PENS. Hardly anyone writes letters anymore, which makes collecting old pens even more special. Parker pens from the 1970s are airplane inspired, while antique fountain pens are sheathed in beautiful wood or mother of pearl (and a joy to use). Prices are $100 up to thousands.

MIRRORS. If your taste runs toward the ornate, browse for 19th-century Federal and Queen Anne–style gilt mirrors. For something smaller and more understated, try a concave or vintage sunburst mirror. Prices range from $200–$2,000.

JEWELRY. Cuff links, earrings, and brooches make great gifts and will take up little room in your luggage. Antique jewelry runs the gamut from fun beaded necklaces to delicate Art Deco pieces. Prices start at $20.

MAPS. Frame an old nautical chart or map of a town you vacationed in for a stylish memento. Reproductions are easier on the wallet but still look good. Prices start at $40 for prints and run up to the thousands for antiques.

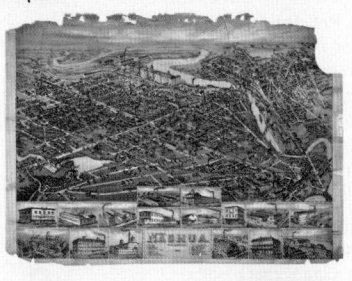

AMERICANA. This can be anything from painted signs to photographs of historic villages or kitschy porcelain figurines that evoke what it means to be American. Items inspired by the Stars and Stripes make colorful decorative accents for a country home feel. Postcards and other small items start at $5.

TOP SHOPPING ROUTES & SIGHTS

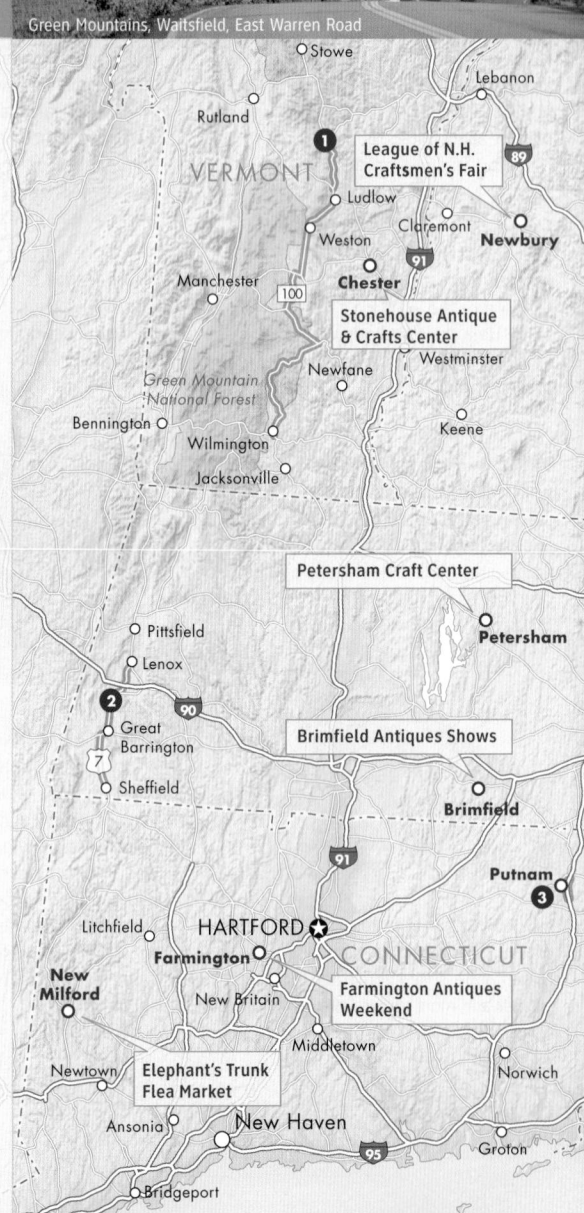

Green Mountains, Waitsfield, East Warren Road

One of the most effective and fun ways to shop is to hop in the car and drive through sleepy, scenic towns. On several key shopping routes in New England, stretches of road are absolutely packed with shops. Charles Street in Boston and downtown Providence and Portland are ideal, compact urban shopping areas for walking. If you do have wheels, try these routes.

1 Route 100. One of the most picturesque drives in the Green Mountain State, this winding road goes from Wilmington north all the way up to Stowe. You'll pass craft studios, general stores like the Vermont Country Store in Weston, and plenty of red barns and covered bridges.

2 Route 7, Berkshire County. Practically the entire route is chock-a-block with antiques stores. The Berkshire County Antiques Dealers Association (⊕ www. berkshireantiquesandart.com) publishes a handy guide to the various shops. Key Western Massachusetts shopping towns include Great Barrington, Sheffield, and Lenox.

3 Main Street, Putnam. Most of the town has a stuck-in-time quality, so it's a great place to spend the day the northeastern part of the state. The majority of antique stores are clustered around Main Street and its offshoots. Start your hunt at the massive Antiques Marketplace.

Stowe

Lebanon

Rutland

VERMONT

1 League of N.H. Craftsmen's Fair

89

Ludlow

Claremont

Weston

Newbury

91

Manchester

Chester

100

Stonehouse Antique & Crafts Center

Westminster

Green Mountain National Forest

Newfane

Bennington

Keene

Wilmington

Jacksonville

Petersham Craft Center

Pittsfield

Petersham

Lenox

90

2

Great Barrington

Brimfield Antiques Shows

7

Sheffield

Brimfield

91

Putnam

Litchfield

HARTFORD

3

Farmington

CONNECTICUT

New Milford

New Britain

Farmington Antiques Weekend

Middletown

Norwich

Newtown

Elephant's Trunk Flea Market

Ansonia

New Haven

95

Groton

Bridgeport

ANTIQUES

THE WHITE ELEPHANT SHOP

Antique Shop, Sheffield, Berkshires | White Elephant Shop, Essex

4 Route 1. Pick up this Maine coastal route to hit shopping hot spots like Kennebunk, Wells, and Ogunquit. Colonial furniture, architectural antiques, and galleries with quirky specialties are great breaks from summer traffic.

5 Route 133, Essex. North of Boston, more than 30 antiques shops line this road. Many shops are in old Colonial and Greek Revival buildings. Research potential shops of the Essex Antiques Dealer Association (⊕ www.essexada.com).

6 Route 6A, Cape Cod. Also known as the Old King's Highway, this winding route runs through Sandwich, Barnstable, Dennis, and Brewster past plenty of antiques shops. Yarmouth has several art galleries and annual crafts festivals are held in Falmouth, Orleans, and Chatham (⊕ www. capecodcraftshows.com).

WHERE TO GET THE GOODS

Depending on your budget, there are plenty of places to shop. Take your pick from artisan studios, art galleries, auction houses, and multi-dealer antique centers. Some antiques shops are one step above flea markets, so prices can vary widely. Antiques shows and craft fairs also offer excellent one-stop shopping opportunities.

TOP ANTIQUES SHOWS

⭐ **Brimfield Antique and Collectible Shows,** Brimfield, Massachusetts. May, July and September (⊕ *www.brimfieldshow.com*).

Elephant's Trunk Country Flea Market, New Milford, Connecticut. Most Sundays except in December and March (⊕ *www.etflea.com*).

Farmington Antiques Weekend, Connecticut. June and September (⊕ *www.farmingtonantiques weekend.com*).

Maine Antiques Festival, Union, Maine. August (⊕ *www.maineantique fest.com*).

Top, Ceramics sold along Route 100, Vermont.

Right, antique rocking horse.

TOP CRAFT FAIRS AND CENTERS

Center for Maine Crafts West Gardiner, Maine (⊕ *mainecrafts.org*).

⭐ **League of New Hampshire Craftsmen's Fair,** Newbury, New Hampshire. August (⊕ *www.nhcrafts.org*).

Ocean State Artisans Holiday Craft Festival, Warwick, Rhode Island. November (⊕ *www.oceanstateartisans.com*).

Petersham Craft Center, Petersham, Massachusetts (⊕ *www.petershamcraftcenter.org*).

Society of Arts and Crafts, Boston, Massachusetts (⊕ *www.societyofcrafts.org*).

Stonehouse Antique and Crafts Center, Chester, Vermont (☎ 802/875–4477).

SHOPPING KNOW-HOW

Many shops are often closed on Sundays and Mondays. Call ahead to confirm. Before you whip out the credit card (or a wad of cash), there are a few other things to remember.

■ Unless you're an expert, it can be difficult to tell if an item is a reproduction or a genuine antique. Buy a price guide or a reference book like Miller's *Antiques & Collectibles* or *Kovel's* to have an idea of a fair value.

■ To ensure you are buying from a legitimate source, make sure the dealer belongs to a professional organization.

■ Think carefully about shipping costs for bulky items. It's also a good idea to carry with you some key measurements from your house.

■ If you find a piece that you love, check it carefully for any flaws. Point out any dings or scratches and use it as a bargaining chip when negotiating a price.

■ Always remember the golden rule: Buy what you love at a price you can afford.

NEW HAVEN TO MYSTIC

As you drive northeast along Interstate 95, culturally rich New Haven is the final urban obstacle between southwestern Connecticut's over-developed coast and southeastern Connecticut's quieter shoreline. The remainder of the jagged coast, which stretches to the Rhode Island, consists of small coastal villages, quiet hamlets, and relatively undisturbed beaches. The only interruptions along this seashore are the industry and piers of New London and Groton. Mystic, Stonington, Old Saybrook, Clinton, and Guilford are havens for fans of antiques and boutiques. North of Groton, near the town of Ledyard, the Mashantucket Pequot Reservation owns and operates Foxwoods Casino and the Mashantucket Pequot Museum & Research Center. The Mohegan Indians run the Mohegan Sun casino in Uncasville. These two properties have added noteworthy hotels and marquee restaurants in recent years.

NEW HAVEN

9 mi east of Milford, 46 mi northeast of Greenwich.

New Haven's history goes back to the 17th century, when its squares, including a lovely central green for the public, were laid out. The city is home to Yale University. The historic district surrounding Yale and the distinctive shops, prestigious museums, and highly respected theaters downtown are a major draw—New Haven has developed an acclaimed restaurant scene in recent years.

ESSENTIALS

Visitor Information Greater New Haven Convention and Visitors Bureau (⊠ *59 Elm St., New Haven* ☎ *203/777–8550 or 800/332–7829* ⊕ *www. newhavencvb.org*).

TOP ATTRACTIONS

Numbers in the margin correspond to numbers on the Downtown New Haven map.

❹ **Yale Center for British Art.** With the largest collection of British art outside Britain, the center surveys the development of English art, life, and thought from the Elizabethan period to the present. The skylighted galleries of architect Louis I. Kahn's final work (completed after his death) contain works by John Constable, William Hogarth, Thomas Gainsborough, Joshua Reynolds, and J. M. W. Turner, to name but a few. You'll also find rare books and paintings documenting English history. ⊠ *1080 Chapel St.* ☎ *203/432–2800* ⊕ *www.yale.edu/ycba* 🎫 *Free* ☺ *Tues.–Sat. 10–5, Sun. noon–5.*

Fodor's Choice
★

★ **Yale University.** New Haven as a manufacturing center dates from the 19th century, but the city owes its fame to merchant Elihu Yale. In 1718 Yale's contributions enabled the Collegiate School, founded in 1701 at Saybrook, to settle in New Haven, where it changed its name to Yale University. This is one of the nation's great universities, and its campus holds some handsome neo-Gothic buildings and noteworthy museums. The university's guides conduct one-hour walking tours that include Connecticut Hall in the Old Campus, which has had a

New Haven to Mystic

KEY

Ferry Lines

New Haven
see detail map

Tweed/New Haven Airport

Milford
East Haven
Branford
Stony Creek
Guilford
North Branford
North Haven
New Haven

Thimble Islands

Lake Gaillard

North Haven
Northford
Wallingford
Durham
Middletown
Cromwell
Portland

Madison
Hammonasset Beach State Park
Clinton
Killingworth
Higganum
Moodus
East Haddam

COCKAPONSET STATE FOREST

Westbrook
Ivoryton
Centerbrook
Essex
Deep River
Hadlyme
Salem
Colchester

Old Saybrook
Knollwood
Hamburg
NEHANTIC STATE FOREST

Old Lyme
Rogers Lake
ROCKY NECK STATE PARK
Niantic
HARKNESS MEMORIAL STATE PARK

New London
Fort Trumbull State Park
Waterford
Ocean Beach Park

Uncasville
Mohegan Sun
Quaker Hill
Mohegan
Montville

Norwich
Jewett City

Foxwoods Casino and Mashantucket Pequot Museum

Ledyard
N. Stonington

Gales Ferry
U.S.S. Nautilus Memorial
Groton/New London Airport
Groton
Noank

Ft. Griswold Battlefield State Park
Old Mystic
Mystic
Stonington

THE QUIET CORNER

Long Island Sound

Long Island (N.Y.)

Orient Point

Plum Island (N.Y.)

Fishers Island (N.Y.)

Fishers Island Sound

Connecticut River

Thames River

BLOCK ISLAND

15 km
10 miles

5

On a Roll

Behold the lobster roll. Sweet, succulent, and sinfully rich, it's the ultimate buttery icon of a Connecticut summer. Other New England states may prefer to chill out with lobster rolls created from a cool mix of lobster meat, mayonnaise, and chopped celery, but Nutmeggers like their one-of-a-kind rolls served hot, hot, hot.

The traditional Connecticut lobster roll, said to have been invented in the early 1930s at Perry's, a now-defunct seafood shack on the Boston Post Road in Milford, consists of nothing more than plump chunks of hot lobster meat and melted butter served on a butter-toasted roll. In other words: heaven on a bun. From seafood shanties along the shore to more gourmet getaways farther inland, Connecticut is fairly swimming with eateries that offer these revered rolls. Three favorites:

A roll at **Abbott's Lobster in the Rough** (✉ 117 Pearl St., Noank

☎ 860/536–7719 ⊕ www.abbotts-lobster.com ⊗ Closed mid-Oct.–May) is best enjoyed seated at a picnic table at the edge of Noank Harbor watching the boats bob by.

At **Lenny and Joe's Fish Tale Drive-in** (✉ 1301 Boston Post Rd., Madison ☎ 203/245–7289 ⊕ www.ljfishtale.com), kids of all ages love to eat outdoors by a hand-carved Dentzel carousel with flying horses (and a whale, frog, lion, seal, and more), which the restaurant runs from early May through early October.

Marnick's (✉ 10 Washington Pkwy., Stratford ☎ 203/377–6288 ⊕ www.marnicks.nv.switchboard.com), on a small beach on the Long Island Sound, is a place where you can kick off your shoes for a picnic on the sand or leave them on and enjoy a leisurely after-dinner stroll along a sea wall.

number of illustrious past residents. ✉ *Yale Visitor Center, 149 Elm St.* ☎ *203/432–2300* ⊕ *www.yale.edu/visitor* ✉ *Free* ⊗ *Tours weekdays at 10:30 and 2, weekends at 1:30* ☞ *Tours start from 149 Elm St. on north side of New Haven Green.*

WORTH NOTING

② **Beinecke Rare Book and Manuscript Library.** The collections here include a Gutenberg Bible, illuminated manuscripts, and original Audubon bird prints, but the building is almost as much of an attraction—the walls are made of marble cut so thin that the light shines through, making the interior a breathtaking sight on sunny days. ✉ *121 Wall St.* ☎ *203/432–2977* ⊕ *www.library.yale.edu/beinecke* ✉ *Free* ⊗ *Mon.–Thurs. 9–7, Fri. 9–5, noon 12–5.*

① **New Haven Green.** Bordered on the west side by the Yale campus, the green is a fine example of early urban planning. As early as 1638, village elders set aside the 16-acre plot as a town common. Three early-19th-century churches—the Gothic-style **Trinity Episcopal Church,** the Georgian-style **Center Congregational Church,** and the predominantly Federal-style **United Church**—contribute to its present appeal. ✉ *Between Church and College Sts.*

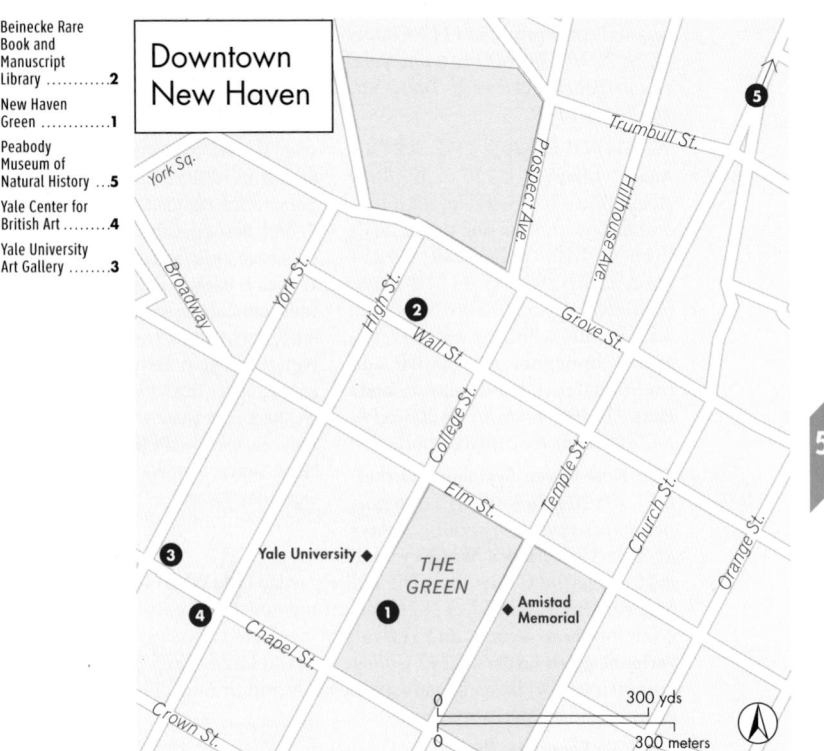

Downtown
New Haven

5 **Peabody Museum of Natural History.** Opened in 1876, the Peabody, with more than 11 million specimens, is one of the largest natural history museums in the nation. In addition to exhibits on Andean, Mesoamerican, and Pacific cultures, the venerable museum has an excellent collection of birds, including a stuffed dodo and passenger pigeon. The main attractions for children and amateur paleontologists alike are some of the world's earliest reconstructions of dinosaur skeletons. ⊠ *170 Whitney Ave.* ☎ *203/432–5050* ⊕ *www.peabody.yale.edu* ⊠ *$7* ⊙ *Mon.–Sat. 10–5, Sun. noon–5.*

3 **Yale University Art Gallery.** Since its founding in 1832, this art gallery has amassed more than 85,000 objects from around the world, dating from ancient Egypt to the present day. Highlights include works by Vincent van Gogh, Edouard Manet, Claude Monet, Pablo Picasso, Winslow Homer, and Thomas Eakins, as well as Etruscan and Greek vases, Chinese ceramics and bronzes, early Italian paintings, and a collection of American decorative arts that is considered one of the world's finest. The gallery's landmark main building is also of note. Opened in 1953, it was Louis I. Kahn's first major commission and the first modernist building on the neo-Gothic Yale campus. Over the years, its extensive open spaces were subdivided into galleries, classrooms, and offices, but a major renovation, completed in 2006, restored it to Kahn's original conception. ⊠ *1111 Chapel St.* ☎ *203/432–0600* ⊕ *www.yale. edu/artgallery* ▣ *Free* ⊙ *Tues.–Sat. 10–5, Sun. 1–6.*

NIGHTLIFE AND THE ARTS

NIGHTLIFE **Anna Liffey's** (⊠ *17 Whitney Ave.* ☎ *203/773–1776* ⊕ *www. annaliffeys.com*) is one of the city's liveliest Irish pubs. **BAR** (⊠ *254 Crown St.* ☎ *203/495–1111* ⊕ *www. barnightclub.com*) is a cross between a nightclub, a brick-oven pizzeria, and a brewpub. Alternative and traditional rock bands play at **Toad's Place** (⊠ *300 York St.* ☎ *203/624– 8623* ⊕ *www.toadsplace.com*).

THE ARTS The **New Haven Symphony Orchestra** (☎ *203/865–0831* ⊕ *www. newhavensymphony.com*) plays at **Yale University's Woolsey Hall**

(⊠ *College and Grove Sts.*). The well-regarded **Long Wharf Theatre** (⊠ *222 Sargent Dr.* ☎ *203/787–4282* ⊕ *www.longwharf.org*) presents works by contemporary writers and revivals of neglected classics. The **Shubert Performing Arts Center** (⊠ *247 College St.* ☎ *203/624–1825* ⊕ *www.capa. com/newhaven*) hosts Broadway musicals and dramas, plus dance and classical-music performances.

The **Yale Repertory Theatre** (⊠ *Chapel and York Sts.* ☎ *203/432–1234* ⊕ *www.yale.edu/yalerep*) premieres new plays and mounts fresh interpretations of the classics. **Yale School of Music** (☎ *203/432–4158* ⊕ *www. yale.edu/music*) presents an impressive roster of performers, from classical to jazz; most events take place in **the Morse Recital Hall in Sprague Hall** (⊠ *College and Wall Sts.*).

SHOPPING

Chapel Street, near the town green, has a pleasing assortment of shops and eateries. **Atticus Bookstore & Café** (⊠ *1082 Chapel St.* ☎ *203/776– 4040* ⊕ *atticusbookstorecafe.com*), in the heart of Yale University, was one of the first stores to combine books and food.

WHERE TO EAT

$$$ ✕ **Barcelona New Haven.** There's no need to take a transatlantic flight for
SPANISH authentic Spanish cuisine when you can feast on tapas right here in New Haven. Barcelona has locations throughout Connecticut, and this latest outpost delivers in both dining and decor (think a 200-bottle wine cellar, open kitchen, and massive wall-sized mural of a Spanish bullfighter). There are entrées on the menu, but the tapas are a better bet: the chorizo with sweet and sour figs offers an intensely rich bite; the organic greens with goat cheese croquettes is a nice balance of tastes and textures; and the *gambas al ajillo* (sautéed shrimp with garlic, sherry, and *guindilla* peppers) is full of flavor. ⊠ *155 Temple St., in the Omni New Haven*

New Haven Pizza 101

New Haven has been on pizza-lovers' radar for decades. The apizza (pronounced "ah-beetz" by locals) is defined by its thin, chewy crust, which makes for a unique—and, some would argue, superior—pizza experience. From white clam pies to mashed potato-topped concoctions, here are our picks for the area's best pizzas.

Frank Pepe's bacon spinach pie.

FRANK PEPE PIZZERIA NAPOLETANA

This is where it all began: in 1925 Frank Pepe opened this eponymous pizza place (⊠ 157 Wooster St. ☎ 203/865–5762 ⊕ www.pepespizzeria.com) and created what would become the iconic New Haven–style pizza. Eager customers line up for hours to get a taste of the famous thin-crust pies, in particular, Frank Pepe's pièce de résistance—the white clam pizza. This masterful creation consists of olive oil, garlic, oregano, grated Parmesan cheese, and little-neck clams atop a thin crust.

SALLY'S APIZZA

Just two blocks from Frank Pepe's on Wooster Street (considered to be New Haven's Little Italy) is Sally's Apizza (⊠ 237 Wooster Street ☎ 203/624–5271 ⊕ www.sallysapizza.net), a rival of Frank Pepe's since 1938, when Salvatore Consiglio, Pepe's nephew, decided to break away from his relatives and open his own pizzeria. The result of this family feud is two competing pizzerias and a divided city: those who believe Frank Pepe's serves the best pizza and those who are devoted to Sally's. If you want to judge for yourself, head to Frank Pepe's first; Sally's doesn't open until 5 (and is closed Monday).

MODERN APIZZA

It's not what Modern Apizza (⊠ 874 State St. ☎ 203/776–5306 ⊕ www.modernapizza.com) has that sets it apart from the rest, but rather what it doesn't have: toppings. The pizzeria's signature "plain" pie is a thin crust with a layer of tomato sauce and just a sprinkling of Parmesan cheese. If you want mootz (mozzarella in New Haven–speak), then you have to ask for it. But why mess with a classic? Modern Apizza has been serving its signature pies since 1934, and business is still booming.

BAR

It doesn't surprise us that BAR (⊠ 254 Crown St. ☎ 203/495–8924 ⊕ www.barnightclub.com), a nightclub-cum-microbrewery, is in a college town and that its signature pie just happens to be bacon-and-mashed-potato-topped pizza—a college student's comfort-food dream. BAR is a relative newcomer (it opened in 1991), but it's giving the old-timers a run for their money. If you want to taste what this place does best, push aside any creeping thoughts of carbs and calories, and go for the masterpiece, a slightly charred, crispy-crusted pizza, topped with a thin layer of creamy mashed potatoes and bits of bacon.

—Carolyn Galgano

Yale's leafy campus is home to many Neo-Gothic buildings.

Hotel, Downtown ☎ *203/848–3000* ⊕ *www.barcelonawinebar.com* ⚞ *Reservations essential* ▭ *AE, D, DC, MC, V* ☉ *No lunch.*

$$
AMERICAN

✕ **Caseus**. The aroma of high-quality aged cheese will hit you as you walk into this two-level bistro and fromagerie. On the bottom floor you can buy cheeses to-go, in addition to other goodies like artisanal chocolates, jams, and olive oils. Visit the upstairs bistro to linger over a meal centered on the key ingredient. The decadent mac and cheese is made in three different varieties (chevre, raclette, and comte), the grilled cheese is said to be made with the bistro's "best melting cheeses," and the onion soup gratin is topped with no fewer than six varieties. All of the ingredients are all natural and organic, and dishes that do not include cheese, like the half chicken roasted with fresh thyme butter or the heirloom tomato and seared day boat scallops, are equally delightful. ✉ *93 Whitney Ave., New Haven* ☎ *203/624–3373* ⊕ *www. caseusnewhaven.com* ▭ *D, DC, MC, V* ☉ *Closed Sun.*

$–$$
PIZZA
★

✕ **Frank Pepe's**. Does this place serve the best pizza in the world, as so many reviewers claim? If it doesn't, it comes close. Pizza is the only thing prepared here—try the justifiably famous white-clam pie (it's especially good with bacon on top). Expect to wait an hour or more for a table— or, on weekend evenings, come after 10. ✉ *157 Wooster St., Downtown* ☎ *203/865–5762* ⊕ *www.pepespizzeria.com* ⚞ *Reservations not accepted* ▭ *No credit cards.*

$$$
AMERICAN

✕ **Heirloom**. Heirloom isn't your typical hotel restaurant. In half of the lobby of The Study hotel, this contemporary American eatery has casually refined decor and a chalkboard menu. Dine during the day if you want to enjoy the sunlight pouring in through the floor-to-ceiling windows. Menu highlights include perfectly cooked Atlantic salmon with oyster mushrooms, cippolini onions, and sorrel sauce and the crowd-pleasing lobster fried rice with sweet egg and vegetable stir-fry. The bar is great for a pre- or post-dinner cocktail. ✉ *1157 Chapel St., at The Study at Yale, Downtown* ☎ *203/503–3919* ⊕ *www.studyhotels.com* ⊟ *AE, D, DC, MC, V.*

¢ ✕ **Louis' Lunch.** This all-American luncheonette on the National Register
AMERICAN of Historic Places claims to be the birthplace of the American hamburger. Its first-rate burgers are cooked in an old-fashioned, upright broiler and served with either a slice of tomato or cheese on two slices of toast. As most customers who come from far and wide for these tasty morsels agree, it doesn't get much better than that. Louis' is open until 2 AM Thursday–Saturday. ✉ *263 Crown St., Downtown* ☎ *203/562–5507* ⊕ *www.louislunch.com* ⊟ *No credit cards* ⊙ *Closed Sun. and Mon. No dinner Tues. and Wed.*

WHERE TO STAY

$$$-$$$$ ⬚ **Omni New Haven Hotel at Yale.** This comfortable hotel is near the heart of New Haven and outfitted with all the modern amenities. John Davenport's at the Top of the Park, the upscale rooftop restaurant with views of the Yale campus, New Haven Green, and Long Island Sound, serves traditional American fare; many upper-floor rooms enjoy the same great views. **Pros:** upscale furnishings; nice gym and spa; walking distance from many shops and restaurants. **Cons:** somewhat steep rates; in busy part of downtown. ✉ *155 Temple St.* ☎ *203/772–6664* ⊕ *www.omnihotels.com* ⤴ *299 rooms, 7 suites* ⚷ *In-room: a/c, Wi-Fi. In-hotel: restaurant, bar, gym, spa, some pets allowed* ⊟ *AE, D, DC, MC, V.*

$$-$$$ ⬚ **The Study at Yale.** Overlooking the sea of brick buildings that make up Yale University, this boutique hotel is designed to fit in with its erudite surroundings. With bellhops dressed as newsies, a pair of spectacles emblazoned on all of the hotel's signature items, and overflowing bookshelves in the hotel's lobby and suites, The Study is a chic lodging for the scholarly set. The smartly decorated guest rooms have all the amenities of a posh hotel (plush Frette linens, iPod docks) as well as long desks, sharpened pencils, free Wi-Fi, and leather reading chairs. Make sure to treat yourself to a cappuccino or a cocktail in the light-filled lobby. **Pros:** destination restaurant; attentive staff. **Cons:** small gym; only one computer in the lobby. ✉ *1157 Chapel Street, New Haven* ☎ *203/503–3900* ⊕ *www.studyhotels.com* ⤴ *117 rooms, 7 suites* ⚷ *In-room: a/c, safe, Wi-Fi. In-hotel: restaurant, room service, bar, gym, laundry service, Internet terminal, Wi-Fi hotspot, parking (paid), some pets allowed (paid)* ⊟ *AE, D, DC, MC, V.*

MADISON

5 mi east of Guilford, 62 mi northeast of Greenwich.

Coastal Madison has an understated charm. Ice cream parlors, antiques stores, and quirky gift boutiques prosper along U.S. 1, the town's main street. Stately Colonial homes line the town green, site of many a summer antiques fair and arts-and-crafts festival. The Madison shoreline, particularly the white stretch of sand known as Hammonasset Beach and its parallel boardwalk, draws visitors year-round.

SPORTS AND THE OUTDOORS

★ **Hammonasset Beach State Park,** the largest of the state's shoreline sanctuaries, has 2 mi of white-sand beaches, a top-notch nature center, excellent birding, and a hugely popular campground with about 550 sites. ⊠ *I–95, Exit 62* ☎ *203/245–2785 park; 203/245–1817 campground* 🎫 *Park $7–$15 mid-Apr.–mid-Oct., free off-season* ⊙ *Park daily 8* AM–*dusk.*

WHERE TO STAY

$$–$$$ 🛏 **Inn at Lafayette.** Skylights, painted murals, and handcrafted woodwork are among the design accents at this hostelry in a converted 1830s church. The rooms may be small, but they have beautiful fabrics and reproduction 17th- and 18th-century furniture. The modern marble baths come equipped with telephones. Fresh food and flawless service are highlights at Café Allegre ($$; closed Monday), the inn's popular restaurant. The menu is largely southern Italian, with French touches. **Pros:** steps from shopping and restaurants; excellent restaurant. **Cons:** busy street. ⊠ *725 Boston Post Rd.* ☎ *203/245–7773 or 866/623–7498* ⊕ *www.innatlafayette.com* 🛏 *5 rooms* ♿ *In-room: a/c, Internet. In-hotel: restaurant, bar* ⊟ *AE, D, DC, MC, V* ⦿ *CP.*

OLD SAYBROOK

9 mi east of Madison, 29 mi east of New Haven.

Old Saybrook, once a lively shipbuilding and fishing town, bustles with summer vacationers and antiques shoppers. Its downtown is an especially pleasing place for a window-shopping stroll. At the end of the afternoon, stop at the old-fashioned soda fountain, where you can share a sundae with your sweetie.

SHOPPING

More than 125 dealers operate out of the **Old Saybrook Antiques Center** (⊠ *756 Middlesex Tpke.* ☎ *860/388–1600* ⊕ *www.oldsaybrookantiques. com*). **Beautiful Impressions** (⊠ *30 Westbrook Pl., Westbrook* ☎ *860/399–8855* ⊕ *www.beautiful-impressions.com*) sells rubber stamps and inks along with ice-cream sodas in a historic former general store and pharmacy. **North Cove Outfitters** (⊠ *75 Main St.* ☎ *866/437–6707* ⊕ *www.northcove.com*) is Connecticut's version of L. L. Bean.

WHERE TO EAT AND STAY

$$–$$$ ✕ **Café Routier.** Grilled trout with lyonnaise potatoes and a whole-grain
FRENCH   mustard sauce, fried oysters with a chipotle rémoulade, and a duck-and-
★   wild-mushroom ragout are among the favorites at this bistro, which specializes in regional favorites and seasonal dishes. ⊠ *1353 Boston Post Rd., 5 mi west of Old Saybrook, Westbrook* ☎ *860/399–8700* ⊕ *www.caferoutier.com* ⊟ *AE, D, DC, MC, V* ⊙ *No lunch.*

$$$$ 🛏 **Saybrook Point Inn & Spa.** Rooms at the cushy Saybrook are furnished
★   mainly in 18th-century style, with reproductions of British furniture and Impressionist art—many have fireplaces. The pools overlook the inn's marina and the Connecticut River, and a full-service spa offers Swedish-style aromatherapy, sea-clay facial masques, and a nice range of salon treatments. The Terra Mar Grille ($$$), which sits on the river, serves

stylish Continental cuisine. **Pros:** swanky rooms; top-notch service; superb restaurant. **Cons:** pricey; you'll need a car to get to downtown shops and dining. ✉ *2 Bridge St.* ☎ *860/395–2000 or 800/243–0212* ⊕ *www.saybrook.com* ⤳ *82 rooms, some condos also available* ♿ *In-room: a/c, refrigerator, DVD (some), Wi-Fi. In-hotel: restaurant, pools, gym, spa, some pets allowed* ☰ *AE, D, DC, MC, V.*

OLD LYME

4 mi east of Old Saybrook, 40 mi south of Hartford.

Old Lyme, on the other side of the Connecticut River from Old Saybrook, is renowned among art lovers for its past as the home of the Lyme Art Colony, the most famous gathering of impressionist painters in the United States. Artists continue to be attracted to the area for its lovely countryside and shoreline. The town also has handsome old houses, many built for sea captains.

EXPLORING

Fodor'sChoice ★ **Florence Griswold Museum.** Central to Old Lyme's artistic reputation is this grand late-Georgian-style mansion owned by Miss Florence Griswold that served as a boardinghouse for members of the Lyme Art Colony in the first decades of the 20th century. When artists such as Willard Metcalf, Clark Voorhees, Childe Hassam, and Henry Ward Ranger flocked to the area to paint its varied landscape, Miss Florence offered housing as well as artistic encouragement. The house was turned into a museum in 1947 and underwent a major restoration completed in 2006 to restore it to its 1910 appearance, when the colony was in full flower (clues to the house's layout and decor in that era were gleaned from members' paintings). The museum's 10,000-square-foot Krieble Gallery, on the riverfront, hosts changing exhibitions of American art. ✉ *96 Lyme St.* ☎ *860/434–5542* ⊕ *www.florencegriswoldmuseum.org* 🎟 *$9* ☉ *Tues.–Sat. 10–5, Sun. 1–5.*

WHERE TO STAY

$$$–$$$$ Fodor'sChoice ★ 🖼 **Bee & Thistle Inn.** Behind a weathered stone wall in the Old Lyme historic district is a three-story 1756 Colonial house with 5½ acres of broad lawns, formal gardens, and herbaceous borders. The scale of rooms throughout is small and inviting, with fireplaces in the parlors and dining rooms and light and airy curtains in the multipaned windows. Most rooms have canopy or four-poster beds. Fireplaces and candlelight exude romance in the restaurant ($$$–$$$$; closed Monday and Tuesday), where innovative American cuisine—with entrées like steamed Maine lobster with garden pea risotto—is served with style. **Pros:** a short walk from Griswold Museum; lovely old home; fantastic restaurant. **Cons:** can hear noise from I–95; historic rooms don't have many modern amenities. ✉ *100 Lyme St.* ☎ *860/434–1667; 800/622–4946* ⊕ *www.beeandthistleinn.com* ⤳ *11 rooms* ♿ *In-room: Internet. In-hotel: restaurant, no kids under 12* ☰ *AE, DC, MC, V* ⊙�‖*BP.*

5

NEW LONDON

3 mi northeast of Waterford, 46 mi east of New Haven.

New London, a small and slightly gritty city on the banks of the Thames River, has long had ties to the sea. In the mid-1800s it was the second-largest whaling port in the world. Today the U.S. Coast Guard Academy uses its campus on the Thames to educate and train its cadets. Ocean Beach Park, an old-fashioned beach resort with a wooden boardwalk, provides an up-close-and-personal view of New London's connection to the deep blue sea.

EXPLORING

Lyman Allyn Art Museum. Housed in a neoclassical building that overlooks both the U. S. Coast Guard Academy and Long Island Sound, this museum was founded in 1932 by Harriet Upson Allyn in memory of her whaling merchant father, Lyman Allyn. Inside is an impressive collection of more than 10,000 objects covering a span of 5,000 years. Works include contemporary, modern, and Early American fine arts; American impressionist paintings; Connecticut decorative arts; and European works from the 16th through the 19th centuries. ⊠ *625 Williams St.* ☎ *860/443–2545* ⊕ *www.lymanallyn.org* 🔗 *$8* ⊙ *Tues.–Sat. 10–5, Sun. 1–5.*

U.S. Coast Guard Academy. The 100-acre cluster of redbrick buildings you see overlooking the Thames River makes up one of the four U.S. military academies. A museum on the property explores the Coast Guard's 200 years of maritime service and includes some 200 ship models, as well as figureheads, paintings, uniforms, and cannon. The three-mast training bark, the USCGC *Eagle*, may be boarded Friday–Sunday 1–5, when in port. ⊠ *15 Mohegan Ave.* ☎ *860/444–8270* ⊕ *www.cga.edu* 🔗 *Free* ⊙ *Weekdays 9–4:30, Sat. 10–4:30, Sun. noon–4:30.*

FERRY TRAVEL

From New London, **Cross Sound Ferry** (☎ *860/443–5281* ⊕ *www.longislandferry.com*) operates year-round passenger and car service to and from Orient Point, Long Island, New York. Its high-speed passenger ferry can make the trip in 40 minutes. **Interstate Navigation Co.** (☎ *860/442–9553* ⊕ *www.blockislandferry.com*) operates passenger and car service from New London to and from Block Island, Rhode Island, from June to early September. From Bridgeport, the **Bridgeport-Port Jefferson Steamboat Co.** (☎ *203/335–2040* ⊕ *www.bpjferry.com*) operates year-round.

NORWICH

15 mi north of New London, 37 mi southeast of Hartford.

Outstanding Georgian and Victorian structures surround the triangular town green in Norwich, and more can be found downtown by the Thames River. The former mill town is hard at work at restoration and rehabilitation efforts. So eye-catching are these brightly colored structures that the Paint Quality Institute has designated the town one of the "Prettiest Painted Places in New England."

EXPLORING

The **Slater Memorial Museum & Converse Art Gallery**, on the grounds of the Norwich Free Academy, houses one of the country's largest collections of Greek, Roman, and Renaissance plaster casts of some of the world's greatest sculptures, including the *Winged Victory, Venus de Milo,* and Michelangelo's *Pietà.* The Converse Art Gallery, adjacent to the museum, hosts six to eight shows a year, many of which focus on Connecticut artists and craftsmen as well as student work. ✉ *108 Crescent St.* ☎ *860/887–2506* ⊕ *www.norwichfreeacademy.com/museum* ✎ *$3* ⏱ *Tues.–Fri. 9–4, weekends 1–4.*

WHERE TO STAY

$$$–$$$$ ▦ **Spa at Norwich Inn.** This posh Georgian-style inn is on 42 rolling acres right by the Thames River. The celebrated spa offers an entire spectrum of skin care, massages, body treatments, and fitness classes. You'll find four-poster beds, wood-burning fireplaces, CD players, and a complete galley kitchen in the luxe villas as well as comfy country furnishings in the rooms. The inn's restaurant serves tasty, local, health-conscious fare. Try the seared Stonington scallops with shallots, white wine, and buttery breadcrumbs—it's only 322 calories, so you can splurge on dessert. **Pros:** one of the best spas in the state; beautiful grounds. **Cons:** oriented toward spa guests. ✉ *607 W. Thames St. (Rte. 32)* ☎ *860/886–2401 or 800/275–4772* ⊕ *www.thespaatnorwichinn.com* ⇋ *49 rooms, 54 villas* ⚐ *In-room: a/c, Wi-Fi. In-hotel: 2 restaurants, golf course, tennis courts, pool, spa* ▭ *AE, D, DC, MC, V.*

LEDYARD

10 mi south of Norwich, 37 mi southeast of Hartford.

Ledyard, in the woods of southeastern Connecticut between Norwich and the coastline, is known first and foremost for the vast Mashantucket Pequot Tribal Nation's Foxwoods Resort Casino. With the opening of the excellent Mashantucket Pequot Museum & Research Center, however, the tribe has moved beyond gaming to educating the public about its history, as well as that of other Northeast Woodland tribes.

EXPLORING

☺ **Mashantucket Pequot Museum & Research Center.** A large complex a mile
Fodor's Choice from the Foxwoods Resort Casino, this museum brings the history and
★ culture of Northeastern Woodland tribes in general and the Pequots in particular to life in exquisite detail. Some highlights include recreations of an 18,000-year-old glacial crevasse that you can travel into, a caribou hunt from 11,000 years ago, and a 17th-century fort. Perhaps most remarkable is a sprawling "immersion environment"—a 16th-century village with more than 50 life-size figures and real smells and sounds. Audio devices provide detailed information about the sights. The research center, open to scholars and schoolchildren free, holds some 150,000 volumes. Also on-site is a full-service restaurant that serves both Native and traditional American cuisine. ✉ *110 Pequot Tr., Mashantucket* ☎ *800/411–9671* ⊕ *www.pequotmuseum.org* ✎ *$15* ⏱ *Wed.–Sat. 10–4.*

TOP EXPERIENCE: CASINOS

Foxwoods Resort Casino. On the Mashantucket Pequot Indian Reservation near Ledyard, Foxwoods is the world's largest resort casino. The skylighted compound draws 40,000-plus visitors daily to its more than 6,200 slot machines, 380 gaming tables, 3,200-seat high-stakes bingo parlor, poker rooms, Keno station, theater, and Race Book room. This 4.7-million-square-foot complex includes the Grand Pequot Tower, the Great Cedar Hotel, and the Two Trees Inn, which have more than 1,400 rooms combined, as well as a full-service spa, retail concourse, food court, and numerous restaurants. In spring 2008 Foxwood unveiled the MGM Grand at Foxwoods, an ultraluxury branch of the Las Vegas gaming resort that added another 825 posh rooms and suites, plus several notable restaurants. ⌧ *39 Norwich Westerly Rd., Ledyard* ☎ *800/369–9663* ⊕ *www.foxwoods.com* ⊗ *Daily 24 hrs.*

Mohegan Sun. The Mohegan Indians, known as the Wolf People, operate this casino west of Ledyard and just south of Norwich, which has more than 300,000 square feet of gaming space, including 6,000 slot machines and more than 250 gaming tables. Also part of the complex: the Kids Quest family entertainment center, a 130,000-square-foot shopping mall, more than 30 restaurants and food-and-beverage suppliers, and a 34-story, 1,200-room luxury hotel with a full-service spa. Free entertainment is presented nightly in the Wolf Den; a 10,000-seat arena hosts major national acts and is home to the WNBA's Connecticut Sun; and a swanky 300-seat cabaret hosts intimate shows and comedy acts. Mohegan After Dark is a 22,000-square-foot complex with three nightclubs. ⌧ *1 Mohegan Sun Blvd., off I–395, Uncasville* ☎ *888/226–7711* ⊕ *www.mohegansun.com* ⊗ *Daily 24 hrs.*

WHERE TO EAT

$$$
AMERICAN
★
✕**Stonecroft.** The sunny dining room at this peaceful, elegant 1807 inn serves some of the finest and most creative food in the region. Favorites from the seasonally changing menu have included curried sweet-corn-and-lump-crab bisque and seared double-thick pork chops with Granny Smith apple and raisin chutney. ⌧ *515 Pumpkin Hill Rd.* ☎ *860/572–0771 or 800/772–0774* ⊕ *www.stonecroft.com* ▭ *AE, D, MC, V* ⊗ *Closed Mon. and Tues. No lunch.*

WHERE TO STAY

$$$–$$$$
⬚**Grand Pequot Tower.** Mere steps from the gaming floors, this expansive 17-story showpiece contains deluxe rooms and suites in pleasantly neutral tones. However, since its opening in spring 2008, the new MGM Grand at Foxwoods hotel is now the top accommodation at Foxwoods Resort Casino. **Pros:** elegant rooms; easy access to the casino; nice views from upper floors. **Cons:** not much to entice if you're not gambling. ⌧ *Rte. 2, Box 3777, Mashantucket 06339* ☎ *860/312–5044 or 800/369–9663* ⊕ *www.foxwoods.com* ⬥ *824 rooms* ⬧ *In-room: a/c, refrigerator, Internet. In-hotel: 4 restaurants, bars, golf course, pool, gym, spa* ▭ *AE, D, DC, MC, V.*

$$$$
⬚**MGM Grand at Foxwoods.** This lavishly appointed hotel, which opened in 2008, offers stylish accommodations just seconds away from the action. Rooms and suites have a modern look, and some on the higher

floors have sweeping views of the woods surrounding the complex. The casino features more than 1,300 slot machines and 60 gaming tables; if you're feeling flush, take your chances in the secluded high-stakes area. The hotel has excellent dining options; first-rate concerts, comedians, and shows; and a full-service spa. ■TIP➔ **Room rates vary dramatically depending on how full the hotel is, with Web specials as low as $80 a night, so it's worth both checking online for last-minute deals and booking far in advance when possible. Pros:** elegant rooms; easy access to the casino; nice views from upper floors. **Cons:** if you're not a gambler, this might not be your scene. ⊠ *240 MGM Grand Dr., Mashantucket 06338* ☎ *866/646–0050* ⊕ *www.mgmatfoxwoods.com* ⤶ *825 rooms* △ *In-room: a/c, refrigerator, Internet. In-hotel: 6 restaurants, bars, golf course, pool, gym, spa* ⊟ *AE, D, DC, MC, V.*

$$$–$$$$ 🏨 **Mohegan Sun Hotel.** The emphasis of this 34-story hotel is on luxury.
   ★ As you enter, towering red cedar trees (simulated but realistic) form a canopy above you, gleaming glass and birch-lined walls surround you, and a stream and pool of water lead to the impressive Taughannick Falls across the lobby in the connecting Shops at Mohegan Sun. Guest rooms are large—a minimum of 450 square feet—and all have king or queen beds and marble baths. The 22,300-square-foot Elemis Spa is one of the finest in the state. **Pros:** numerous fine restaurants are steps from lobby; incredible views from upper floors; excellent spa and fitness center. **Cons:** better like casinos. ⊠ *1 Mohegan Sun Blvd., Uncasville* ☎ *888/777–7922* ⊕ *www.mohegansun.com* ⤶ *1,020 rooms, 180 suites* △ *In-room: a/c, kitchen (some), Internet. In-hotel: 28 restaurants, bars, pool, gym, spa* ⊟ *AE, D, MC, V.*

$$–$$$ 🏨 **Stonecroft.** A sunny 1807 Georgian Colonial on 6½ acres of green
   ★ meadows, woodlands, and rambling stone walls is the center of Stonecroft. Although individually thematic, the rooms here and in the historic barn are united in their refined but welcoming country atmosphere; all have fireplaces and most have two-person whirlpool tubs. The restaurant is excellent. **Pros:** scenic and verdant grounds; cheerful service; great restaurant. **Cons:** secluded location requires a car to get around. ⊠ *515 Pumpkin Hill Rd.* ☎ *860/572–0771 or 800/772–0774* ⊕ *www.stonecroft.com* ⤶ *10 rooms* △ *In-room: a/c, Internet. In-hotel: restaurant* ⊟ *AE, D, MC, V* ⍾❘ *BP.*

MYSTIC

8 mi east of Groton.

Mystic has devoted itself to recapturing the seafaring spirit of the 18th and 19th centuries. Some of the nation's fastest clipper ships were built here in the mid-19th century; today's Mystic Seaport is the state's most popular museum. Downtown Mystic has an interesting collection of boutiques and galleries.

ESSENTIALS

Visitor Information Mystic Country–Eastern Regional Tourism District (⊠ *27 Coogan Blvd., Bldg. 3A, Mystic* ☎ *860/536–8822* ⊕ *mysticcountry.com*).

EXPLORING

C **Mystic Aquarium and Institute for**
Fodor's Choice **Exploration**. The animals here go
★ through 1,000 pounds of herring,
capelin, and squid each day. Inuk,
a male beluga whale, is responsible
for consuming 85 pounds of that
himself. He calls the aquarium's
Arctic Coast exhibit home. This
exhibit—which holds 800,000 gal-
lons of water, measures 165 feet at
its longest point by 85 feet at its
widest point, and ranges from just
inches to 16½ feet deep—is just a
small part of this revered establishment. You can also check out
world-renowned ocean explorer
Dr. Robert Ballard's Institute for
Exploration and its Challenge of
the Deep exhibition center (dedicated to revealing what lies on the
world's deep ocean floors), as well as see African penguins, harbor
seals, graceful sea horses, Pacific octopuses, and sand tiger sharks. ⊠ 55
Coogan Blvd. ☎ *860/572–5955* ⊕ *www.mysticaquarium.org* ✉ *$26*
⊙ *Mar.–Oct., daily 9–6; Nov., daily 9–5, Dec.–Feb., daily 10–5.*

> ### SETTING SAIL AT MYSTIC SEAPORT
>
> Kids can learn the ropes—
> literally—of what it takes to be
> a sailor during Mystic Seaport's
> many sailing classes and camps.
> Younger children and those who
> wish to stay onshore can sign
> up for courses on building boats
> (including how to varnish them),
> blacksmithing, carving, and roping
> (from knotting to splicing). The
> Seaport's planetarium also offers
> instruction on navigating a ship by
> the stars. Prices for classes vary.
> Call Mystic Seaport (☎ *860/572–0711*) or see its Web site (⊕ *www.mysticseaport.org*) for details.

C **Mystic Seaport**. The world's largest maritime museum, Mystic Seaport
Fodor's Choice encompasses 37 acres of indoor and outdoor exhibits with more than
★ 1 million artifacts that provide a fascinating look at the area's rich
shipbuilding and seafaring heritage. In the narrow streets and historic
homes and buildings (some moved here from other sites), craftspeople
give demonstrations of open-hearth cooking, weaving, and other skills
of yesteryear. The museum's more than 500 vessels include the *Charles
W. Morgan*, the last remaining wooden whaling ship afloat, and the
1882 training ship *Joseph Conrad*. You can climb aboard for a look or
for sail-setting demonstrations and reenactments of whale hunts. Special events are held throughout the year. Children younger than 5 are
admitted free. ⊠ *75 Greenmanville Ave., 1 mi south of I–95, Exit 90*
☎ *860/572–0711* ⊕ *www.mysticseaport.org* ✉ *$24* ⊙ *Apr.–Oct., daily
9–5; Nov., daily 10–4, Dec.–Mar., Thurs.–Sun. 10–4.*

SHOPPING

The **Finer Line Gallery** (⊠ *48 W. Main St.* ☎ *860/536–8339* ⊕ *www.
finerlinegallery.com*) exhibits nautical and other prints, including
some local scenes. **Olde Mistick Village** (⊠ *Coogan Blvd., off I–95, Exit
90* ☎ *860/536–4941* ⊕ *www.oldmysticvillage.com*), a re-creation of
an early 1700s American village and has more than 50 shops that
sell everything from crafts and clothing to souvenirs and munchies.
Whyevernot (⊠ *17 W. Main St.* ☎ *860/536–6209*) is a colorful spot for
clothing, jewelry, pottery, linens, handmade papers, and much more.

Mystic Seaport includes a number of vessels you can tour, including the *Charles W. Morgan.*

WHERE TO EAT

$$-$$$
SEAFOOD
Fodor'sChoice
★

✕ **Abbott's Lobster in the Rough.** If you want some of the state's best lobsters, mussels, crabs, or clams on the half shell, head down to this unassuming seaside lobster shack in sleepy Noank, a few miles southwest of Mystic. Most seating is outdoors or on the dock, where the views of Noank Harbor are magnificent. ✉ *117 Pearl St., Noank* ☎ *860/536–7719* ⊕ *www.abbotts-lobster.com* ⊟ *AE, MC, V* ☞ *BYOB* ⊗ *Closed Columbus Day–1st Fri. in May and weekdays Labor Day–Columbus Day.*

$$-$$$
SEAFOOD
★

✕ **Go Fish.** In this town by the sea, one hungers for seafood, and this sophisticated restaurant captures all the tastes—and colors—of the ocean. There's a raw bar, wine bar, coffee bar, and a black granite sushi bar, which, with its myriad tiny, briny morsels, is worth the trip in itself. The glossy blue tables in the two large dining rooms perfectly complement the signature saffron-scented shellfish bouillabaisse. The menu lists options for vegetarians and carnivores as well, but the lobster ravioli in a light cream sauce is a must-try. ✉ *Olde Mistick Village, Coogan Blvd., off I–95, Exit 90* ☎ *860/536–2662* ⊕ *www.gofishct.com* ⊟ *AE, D, MC, V.*

WHERE TO STAY

$$-$$$

▦ **Old Mystic Inn.** This cozy inn, built in 1784, was once a bookshop specializing in antique books and maps. Today, all its rooms in the main house and a carriage house are named after New England authors. Some have working fireplaces and whirlpools, and each is a welcoming and comfortable mix of antiques and owner-innkeeper Michael Cardillo Jr.'s personal touches. You can enjoy a game of checkers by the oversize Colonial hearth in the keeping room; a full country breakfast is served.

Pros: beautifully kept historic house; quiet neighborhood; friendly host. **Cons:** need a car to get into downtown. ⊠ *52 Main St.* ☎ *860/572–9422* ⊕ *www.oldmysticinn.com* ⤳ *8 rooms* ⚐ *In-room: no phone, a/c, no TV, Internet. In-hotel: Wi-Fi hotspot* ⊟ *AE, MC, V* ⑩ *BP.*

$$–$$$ ⊡ **Whaler's Inn.** A perfect compromise between a chain motel and a country inn, this complex with public rooms furnished with lovely antiques is one block from the Mystic River and downtown. The motel-style guest rooms feel Victorian, with quilts and reproduction four-poster beds—the best rooms have deep whirlpool baths. The restaurant, Bravo Bravo ($$–$$$), serves well prepared Italian food, such as veal medallion stuffed with garlic, spinach, and cheese in a shiitake mushroom sauce. **Pros:** within walking distance of downtown shopping; excellent restaurant. **Cons:** rooms in motel-style building have less character; on a busy street. ⊠ *20 E. Main St.* ☎ *860/536–1506 or 800/243–2588* ⊕ *www.whalersinnmystic.com* ⤳ *49 rooms* ⚐ *In-room: a/c, Wi-Fi. In-hotel: 2 restaurants* ⊟ *AE, DC, MC, V.*

STONINGTON

7 mi southeast of Mystic, 57 mi east of New Haven.

The pretty village of Stonington pokes into Fishers Island Sound. A quiet fishing community clustered around white-spired churches, Stonington is far less commercial than Mystic. In the 19th century, though, it was a bustling whaling, sealing, and transportation center. Historic buildings line the town green and border both sides of Water Street up to the imposing Old Lighthouse Museum.

EXPLORING

Old Lighthouse Museum. This museum occupies a lighthouse that was built in 1823 and moved to higher ground 17 years later. Climb to the top of the tower for a spectacular view of Long Island Sound and three states. Six rooms of exhibits depict the varied history of the small coastal town. ⊠ *7 Water St.* ☎ *860/535–1440* ⊕ *www.stoningtonhistory.org/light.htm* ⤳ *$8* ☉ *May–Oct., daily 10–5; Nov.–Apr., by appointment.*

Stonington Vineyards. At this small coastal winery, you can browse through the works of local artists in the gallery or enjoy a picnic lunch on the grounds. The vineyard's Seaport White, a vidal-chardonnay blend, is a nice accompaniment. ⊠ *523 Taugwonk Rd.* ☎ *860/535–1222 or 800/421–9463* ⊕ *www.stoningtonvineyards.com* ⤳ *Free* ☉ *Daily 11–5, tours at 2.*

WHERE TO STAY

$$$–$$$$ ⊡ **Inn at Stonington.** The views of Stonington Harbor and Fishers Island
Fodor's Choice Sound are spectacular from this waterfront inn in the heart of Stonington Village. Each room is individually decorated, all have fireplaces, and
★ most have whirlpool baths. Kayaks and bicycles are available for use and those coming by boat can use the inn's 400-foot pier. **Pros:** smartly furnished rooms; walking distance from village shops and dining; great water views. **Cons:** no restaurant on-site. ⊠ *60 Water St.* ☎ *860/535–2000* ⊕ *www.innatstonington.com* ⤳ *18 rooms* ⚐ *In-room: a/c, Internet. In-hotel: gym, bicycles, no kids under 14* ⊟ *AE, MC, V* ⑩ *CP.*

THE QUIET CORNER

Few visitors to Connecticut experience the old-fashioned ways of the state's "Quiet Corner," a vast patch of sparsely populated towns that seem a world away from the rest of the state. The Quiet Corner has a reclusive allure: people used to leave New York City for the Litchfield Hills; now many leave for northeastern Connecticut, where the stretch of Route 169 from Brooklyn past Woodstock has been named a National Scenic Byway.

The cultural capital of the Quiet Corner is Putnam, a small mill city on the Quinebaug River whose formerly industrial town center has been transformed into a year-round antiques mart. Smaller jewels are Pomfret and Woodstock—two towns where authentic Colonial homesteads still seem to outnumber the contemporary, charmless clones that are springing up all too rapidly across the state.

POMFRET

51 mi north of Stonington; 6 mi north of Brooklyn.

Pomfret, one of the grandest towns in the region, was once known as the inland Newport because it attracted the wealthy, who summered here in large "cottages." Today it is a quiet stopping-off point along Route 169, designated one of the most scenic byways in the country by the National Scenic Byway Program.

EXPLORING

Sharpe Hill Vineyard. Centered on an 18th-century-style barn in the hills of Pomfret, this vineyard gives tastings and serves lunch and dinner in a European-style wine garden and its restaurant, Fireside Tavern, Friday through Sunday, depending on the season (advance reservations are essential). Its Ballet of Angels, a heavenly semidry white, just may be New England's top-selling wine. ⊠ *108 Wade Rd.* ☎ *860/974–3549* ⊕ *www.sharpehill.com* 🎫 *Free* ☉ *Fri.–Sun. 11–5.*

SPORTS AND THE OUTDOORS

Connecticut Audubon Center at Pomfret. Adjacent to the Connecticut Audubon Bafflin Sanctuary's more than 700 acres of rolling meadows, grassland habitats, forests, and streams, this nature center presents environmental-education programs for all ages, seasonal lectures and workshops, and natural-history exhibits. Miles of trails provide excellent birding. ⊠ *189 Pomfret St. (Rte. 169)* ☎ *860/928–4948* ⊕ *www. ctaudubon.org/visit/pomfret.htm* 🎫 *Free* ☉ *Sanctuary daily dawn–dusk, center Wed.–Sun. noon–4.*

WHERE TO EAT

$$$$
CONTINENTAL
Fodor'sChoice
★

✕ **Golden Lamb Buttery.** Connecticut's most unusual dining experience has achieved almost legendary status. Eating here, in a converted barn on a 1,000-acre farm, is far more than a chance to enjoy good Continental food: it's a social and gastronomical event. There is one seating each for lunch and dinner; choose from one of four entrées, which might include roast duck or chateaubriand. Owners Bob and Virginia "Jimmie" Booth have a hay wagon that you can ride before dinner

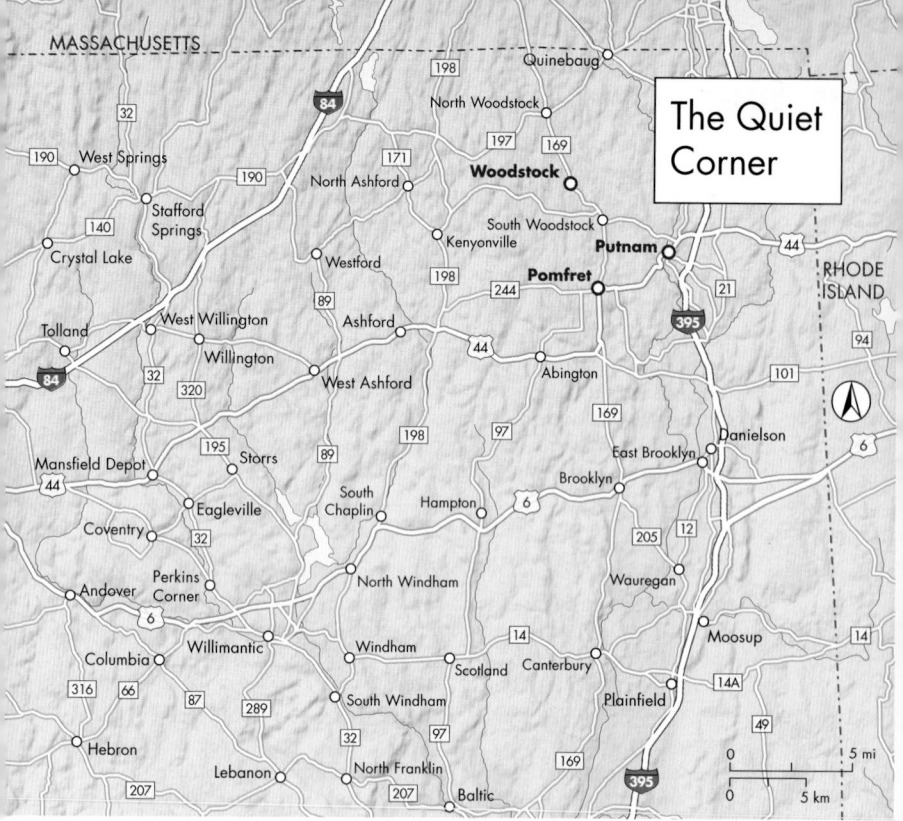

(a musician accompanies you). ✉ *499 Wolf Den Rd., off Rte. 169, Brooklyn* ☎ *860/774–4423* ⊕ *www.thegoldenlamb.com* ⚞ *Reservations essential* ☷ *AE, D, MC, V* ☙ *Closed Sun. and Mon. No dinner Tues.–Thurs.*

\$\$–\$\$\$ ✗ **The Harvest.** This romantic country restaurant is alive with fresh flow-
AMERICAN   ers, glimmering candles, antiques, and touches of chintz. The menu focuses heavily on steaks with a wide range of cuts and sauces, as well as such contemporary American fare like sesame-seared yellow-fin tuna and lobster and lump crab strudel. There's an excellent Sunday brunch. ✉ *37 Putnam Rd.* ☎ *860/928–0008* ⊕ *www.harvestrestaurant. com* ☷ *AE, MC, V* ☙ *Closed Mon. No lunch Sat.*

\$\$ ✗ **Vanilla Bean Café.** Homemade soups, sandwiches, and baked goods
AMERICAN   have long been a tradition at this café inside a restored 19th-century
★   barn. Dinner specials might include herb-crusted sea bass with sweet corn and heirloom tomatoes or shepherd's pie made with lamb. Belgian waffles and blueberry pancakes are breakfast highlights. There are also an art gallery and folk entertainment. ✉ *450 Deerfield Rd. (off U.S. 44, Rte. 97, and Rte. 169)* ☎ *860/928–1562* ⊕ *www.thevanillabeancafe. com* ☷ *AE, MC, V* ☙ *No dinner Mon. and Tues.*

Gertrude Chandler Warner: Teacher and Writer

Outside of Putnam, you might not have heard of Getrude Chandler Warner, but many kids across the country have read her beloved Boxcar Children adventure series books.

Though she never finished high school, Warner became a teacher during World War I and discovered her ability to connect with youngsters. She began writing children's books centered on an abandoned boxcar and a group of children who set up house in it, inspired by her own childhood adventures at the railroad tracks near her home.

As she worked on the stories, Warner read the drafts to her first-grade classes. There are 10 books in the classic series as well as several spin-off titles.

Warner died at age 89 in 1979. A small museum/bookstore set up in—what else?—a boxcar at the edge of town pays tribute to the Putnam native and lifelong resident. The museum is generally open on the weekends from 11 AM to 3 PM early May through early October, but it's best to call ahead (☎ 860/963–6800).

5

PUTNAM

5 mi northeast of Pomfret.

Ambitious antiques dealers have reinvented Putnam, a mill town 30 mi west of Providence, Rhode Island, that was neglected after the Depression. Putnam's downtown, with more than 400 antiques dealers, is the heart of the Quiet Corner's antiques trade.

SHOPPING

The four-level **Antiques Marketplace** (⊠ *109 Main St.* ☎ *860/928–0442* ⊕ *www.antiquesmarketplace.com*) houses the wares of nearly 300 dealers, from fine furniture to tchotchkes. **Arts & Framing** (⊠ *112 Main St.* ☎ *860/963–0105* ⊕ *www.artsandframingputnam.com*) sells antique art and has art restoration and framing services. **Antiques Unlimited** (⊠ *91 Main St.* ☎ *860/963–2599*) specializes in 19th- and 20th-century sofas, desks, light fixtures, and decorative accents.

WHERE TO EAT AND STAY

$$–$$$ ✕ **85 Main.** This stylish trattoria/bistro is *the* place to go for a break
AMERICAN from antiquing. Typical lunchtime offerings include roasted corn and clam chowder, pesto chicken salad, and a burger and fries; dinner could be maple-glazed pan-seared sea scallops or veal bolognese. There is also a raw bar and a full sushi bar. ⊠ *85 Main St.* ☎ *860/928–1660* ⊕ *www.85main.com* ▭ *AE, MC, V.*

¢–$ ▥ **King's Inn & Suites.** Less than 2 mi from downtown Putnam, the Country Heart Inn is a good base for antiquers. Half the rooms, which are decorated with cream-color walls or print wallpaper and run-of-the-mill furnishings typical of a budget property, overlook a pond. **Pros:** close to downtown Putnam; affordable rates. **Cons:** fairly bland decor. ⊠ *5 Heritage Rd.* ☎ *860/928–7961 or 800/541–7304* ⊕ *www.kingsinnputnam.*

com ➲ *40 rooms, 1 suite* ☍ *In-room: a/c, refrigerator (some), Internet. In-hotel: restaurant, bar, pool* ⊟ *AE, D, DC, MC, V* ⵊⵔ *CP.*

WOODSTOCK

5 mi northwest of Putnam.

The landscape of this enchanting town is splendid in every season—the rolling hills seem to stretch for miles. Scenic roads lead past antiques shops, a country inn in the grand tradition, orchards, grassy fields and grazing livestock, and the fairgrounds of one of the state's oldest agricultural fairs, held each Labor Day weekend.

EXPLORING

★ **Roseland Cottage.** This pink board-and-batten Gothic-Revival house was built in 1846 as a summer home for New York silk merchant, publisher, and abolitionist Henry C. Bowen. The house and outbuildings (including a carriage house with a private bowling alley) hold a prominent place in history, having hosted four U.S. presidents (Ulysses S. Grant, Rutherford B. Hayes, William Henry Harrison, and William McKinley). The parterre garden includes 21 flower beds surrounded by 600 yards of boxwood hedge. ⊠ *556 Rte. 169* ☏ *860/928–4074* ⊕ *www.spnea.org/ visit/homes/roseland.htm* ⵊ *$8* ⊗ *June–mid-Oct., Fri.–Sun. 11–4.*

SHOPPING

Christmas Barn (⊠ *835 Rte. 169* ☏ *860/928–7652* ⊕ *www. thechristmasbarnonline.com*) has 12 rooms of country and Christmas goods. **Scranton's Shops** (⊠ *300 Rte. 169* ☏ *860/928–3738*) sells the wares of 60 regional artisans. **Whispering Hill Farm** (⊠ *Rte. 169* ☏ *860/928–0162* ⊕ *whispering-hill.com*) sells supplies for rug hooking and braiding, quilting, and needlework, mixed with an assortment of antiques.

WHERE TO STAY

$$–$$$ ⊡ **Inn at Woodstock Hill.** This inn overlooking the countryside has rooms with antiques, four-poster beds, fireplaces, pitched ceilings, and timber beams. The attractive chintz-and-prints restaurant ($$$) serves creative interpretations of Continental and American fare, such as seared tuna steak with sesame seeds and New Zealand venison chops with a red-wine reduction. **Pros:** beautiful grounds; many rooms have fireplaces; very good restaurant. **Cons:** traditional decor is very old-fashioned; somewhat remote. ⊠ *94 Plaine Hill Rd., South Woodstock* ☏ *860/928– 0528* ⊕ *www.woodstockhill.com* ➲ *21 rooms* ☍ *In-room: a/c, Internet, Wi-Fi (some). In-hotel: restaurant* ⊟ *AE, D, MC, V* ⵊⵔ *CP.*

Rhode Island

WORD OF MOUTH

"I found Block Island lovely. There are hotels where you can sit on the porch, look out over the harbor, and have drinks, and nice restaurants and a few shops."

—Suki

"Newport is easy to get to and simply beautiful."

—Wyatt 92

WELCOME TO RHODE ISLAND

TOP REASONS TO GO

★ **Mansions:** Gain a sense of Newport's Gilded Age mansion with a tour of the singularly immense and ornate 70-room Breakers mansion, built for Cornelius Vanderbilt.

★ **Historic Street:** On Providence's East Side, in the shadows of Brown University, ornate Colonial homes built by the leading merchants of the day line Benefit Street.

★ **Nature:** Block Island is one of the most serene spots on the Eastern Seaboard, especially at Rodman's Hollow, a glacial outwash basin, where winding paths lead to the sea.

★ **Sand:** South County is rife with sugary-white beaches, with Scarborough State Beach offering the best stretch to spread a blanket and admire the ocean.

★ **Food Enclave:** Eat lunch and dinner every day at a different restaurant in Providence's Federal Hill neighborhood and you still won't wear out the dining possibilities.

1 Providence. A transformed industrial metropolis whose prestigious colleges imbue it with intellectual and cultural vitality, Rhode Island's capital city claims a superb culinary scene, partly anchored by one of New England's most treasured Little Italy neighborhoods. The city abounds with meticulously restored Colonial houses, many of which now operate as museums.

2 The Blackstone Valley. The birthplace of America's industrial revolution, this northernmost section of Rhode Island feels a world away from the leisure-driven coastal areas. Behind the gritty veneer of the valley's workaday towns and small cities, you'll find several fascinating museums that document the rise of industry over the past 200 years.

3 South County. This swath of leafy nature preserves and bustling seaside hamlets is family-friendly, reasonably priced, and resolutely informal. In towns like Narragansett and Westerly you'll discover some of southern New England's most accessible yet scenic stretches of beach. The Port of Galilee is one of the Northeast's largest fishing ports and also the main terminal for ferries to Block Island.

4 Newport County. Posh, blue-blooded Newport has been a yachting enclave and summer home to wealthy industrialists for nearly two centuries. Hotel rooms and meals in this repository of restored Colonial and Victorian architecture can be costly, but Newport exudes romance and is on a stunning island in the middle of Narragansett Bay, accessed by several dramatic bridges.

5 Block Island. Less famous and less crowded than Martha's Vineyard and Nantucket, Block Island is rife with rambling Victorian inns and B&Bs (most lacking in-room TVs and phones)—making it an idyllic seaside escape for summer visitors. Old Harbor has busy shops and restaurants, but beyond that lies a wonderfully laid-back island with miles of unspoiled nature trails.

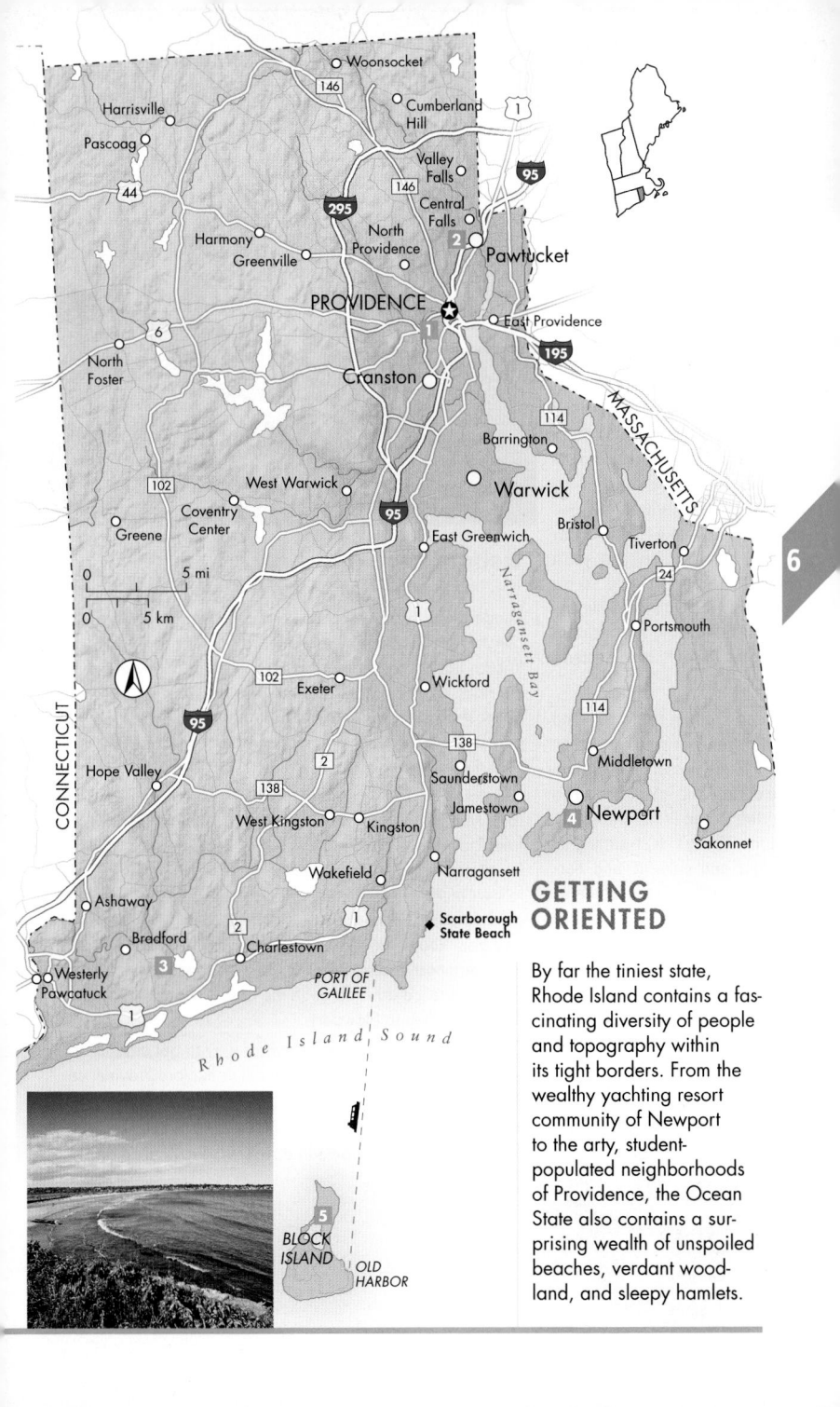

Woonsocket

146

Harrisville

Cumberland
Hill

1

Pascoag

Valley
Falls

44

146

295

Central
Falls

North
Providence

2

Harmony

Pawtucket

Greenville

PROVIDENCE

East Providence

6

1

195

North
Foster

Cranston

MASSACHUSETTS

114

Barrington

102

West Warwick

Warwick

Coventry
Center

95

Bristol

Greene

East Greenwich

Tiverton

6

24

0   5 mi

Portsmouth

0   5 km

102

Exeter

Wickford

Narragansett Bay

CONNECTICUT

138

Saunderstown

Middletown

Hope Valley

Jamestown

4

Newport

138

West Kingston

Kingston

Sakonnet

2

Wakefield

Narragansett

Ashaway

1

GETTING
ORIENTED

Bradford

2

Charlestown

3

Scarborough
State Beach

Westerly
Pawcatuck

1

PORT OF
GALILEE

By far the tiniest state,
Rhode Island contains a fascinating diversity of people
and topography within
its tight borders. From the
wealthy yachting resort
community of Newport
to the arty, student-
populated neighborhoods
of Providence, the Ocean
State also contains a surprising wealth of unspoiled
beaches, verdant wood-
land, and sleepy hamlets.

Rhode Island Sound

5

BLOCK
ISLAND

OLD
HARBOR

RHODE ISLAND PLANNER

When to Go

The best time to visit Rhode Island is between April and October. Newport hosts high-profile music events each summer, including the Newport Jazz and Newport Folk festivals. Block Island and the beach towns of South County are in full swing (though not nearly as crowded as Newport) from Memorial Day through Labor Day, but you'll find these areas just as scenic and a bit more manageable and affordable during the pleasant months of April, May, September, and October.

Because of the fall foliage and the often gorgeous weather, October is a great time to come to explore the interior sections of the Ocean State. The Blackstone Valley's leaf-turning is bright and colorful, and during the fall months, students return to the several colleges of Providence, giving that city a youthful, dynamic vibrancy. The state's coastal areas quiet down in winter, but Newport still remains relatively lively even in the coldest months.

Getting Here and Around

Rhode Island is best reached by car via Interstate 95, coastal New England's main interstate, which connects to both Boston and New York as it cuts diagonally across the state; or by air via T. F. Green Airport, which is served by most domestic air carriers. Boston's Logan Airport is only an hour away. The major car-rental agencies have branches at both airports.

Interstate 195 southeast from Providence leads to New Bedford, Massachusetts, and Cape Cod. Route 146 northwest from Providence leads to Worcester, Massachusetts, and Interstate 90, passing through the Blackstone Valley. U.S. 1 follows much of the Rhode Island coast east from Connecticut before turning north to Providence. Route 138 heads east from Route 1 to Jamestown, Newport, and Portsmouth, in easternmost Rhode Island. Route 114 leads south from East Providence down through the East Bay community of Bristol and then to Newport.

Once you're here, a car is your best way to get around the state, although it's quite practical to explore Providence and Newport on foot and using public transportation.

Parking is easy to find outside of cities, but it can be challenging and expensive in downtown Providence and Newport.

About the Restaurants

Rhode Island has been winning national accolades for its restaurants, which serve cuisine from every part of the world. You can still find regional fare such as johnnycakes, a corn cake–like affair cooked on a griddle, and the native clam, the quahog (pronounced "*ko*-hog"), which is served stuffed, fried, and in chowder. "Shore dinners" consist of clam chowder, steamed soft-shell clams, clam cakes, sausage, corn on the cob, lobster, watermelon, and Indian pudding (a steamed pudding made with cornmeal and molasses). Providence's Federal Hill neighborhood holds superlative Italian restaurants, and dozens of other restaurants in the city rank among New England's finest eateries.

About the Hotels

The major chain hotels are represented in Rhode Island, but the state's many smaller B&Bs and other inns provide a more intimate experience. Rates are very seasonal; in Newport, for example, winter rates are often half those of summer. Many inns in coastal towns are closed in winter.

WHAT IT COSTS

	¢	$	$$	$$$	$$$$
Restaurants	under $8	$8–$15	$15–$22	$22–$30	over $30
Hotels	under $80	$80–$120	$120–$170	$171–$220	over $220

Restaurant prices are based on the median main course price at dinner. Hotel prices are for two people in a standard double room in high season, excluding service and 5% state hotel tax.

Planning Your Time

By car it's less than an hour from any one place in Rhode Island to another. Though the distances are short, the state is densely populated, so allow extra time for traffic congestion.

Most of the sights in Providence can be seen in one day. The Blackstone Valley can also occupy a day (potentially as an afternoon side trip from Providence), perhaps two in fall foliage season. Newport has many facets and will require two busy days. South County, with its superb beaches, is generally a relaxing two-day destination, but you can easily cover it in a day during the off-season. With five or more days, you can visit all four regions of the state as well as Block Island.

Outdoor Activities

Fishing: For information on where to buy licenses for freshwater fishing, contact the **Department of Environmental Management's Division of Licensing** (☎ 401/222–3576 ⊕ www.dem.ri.gov). No license is needed for saltwater fishing.

Hiking: The **Rhode Island Audubon Society** (✉ 12 Sanderson Rd., Smithfield ☎ 401/949–5454 ⊕ www.asri.org) leads interesting hikes and field expeditions around the state.

One of the best trail guides for the region is the *AMC Massachusetts and Rhode Island Trail Guide,* available at local outdoors shops or from the **Appalachian Mountain Club** (*AMC* ✉ 5 Joy St., Boston, MA ☎ 617/523–0636 ⊕ www.amcnarragansett.org).

Visitor Information

Rhode Island Department of Economic Development, Tourism Division (☎ 800/556–2484 ⊕ www.visitrhodeisland.com).

RHODE ISLAND FALL FOLIAGE DRIVE

Tiny Rhode Island packs plenty of punch when it comes to vibrant fall colors. For the most dramatic leaf-peeping head to the mostly rural, uncrowded northern and western towns—communities with rolling meadows and dense forests interrupted by the occasional orchard, pumpkin patch, or country store.

BEST TIME TO GO

Foliage peaks in most of Rhode Island during the third and fourth weeks of October (☎ 800/556-2484 ⊕ www.visitri.com). Along the coast, however, you can still view plenty of color into the start of November. And in the state's northwest corner, where the elevation is highest, leaves are at their most colorful in mid-October.

This tour through the state's quieter corners begins in Providence, where you can stroll across **Brown University's** handsome campus of dignified academic buildings and towering shade trees. Drive north from Providence, via Route 112 and then Route 114 north for about 12 mi to Cumberland, a rural community of undulating woodland crowned by a canopy of sugar maple, scarlet oak, and birch trees. Stop at **Diamond Hill Vineyards,** whose vineyards and apple orchards yield an intriguing selection of wines—the sparkling cider and spiced-apple wine are perfect on a cool October day. Drive west about 12 mi on Route 116 through Greenville, turning west on U.S. 44 for 7 mi to the tiny hamlet of Chepachet.

The rest of the tour meanders through some of Rhode Island's most pastoral countryside. In quaint Chepachet, Colonial and Victorian buildings contain antiques shops and quirky stores. Don't miss **Brown & Hopkins,** one of the country's oldest continuously operating general stores (including an old-fashioned candy counter), or the **Tavern on Main,** a rambling 18th-century restaurant that's perfect for a lunch stop.

Follow U.S. 44 west 5 mi through the burst of changing leaves in **Pulaski Memorial State Forest.** Turn left onto Route 94 and follow this for about 13 mi to Route 102, and then continue southeast another 20 mi to Exeter. The most undeveloped route from Chepachet to Exeter is lined with pristine hardwood forests, with an abundance of red maple, white oak, beech, elm, and poplar trees.

From Route 102, detour south in Exeter 1½ mi down Route 2 to **Schartner Farm** for a corn maze or hayride and cider and pumpkin pie. Backtrack to Route 102 and continue east 4 mi to the colonial seaport of Wickford, whose pretty harbor opens to Narragansett Bay. The town's oak- and beech-shaded lanes are perfect for a late-afternoon stroll among the gift shops, galleries, and boutiques.

The drive is a total of about 80 mi and takes from four to eight hours, depending on stops.

NEED A BREAK?

Opened in 1809, **Brown & Hopkins Country Store** (⊠ *1179 Putnam Pike, Chepachet* ☎ *401/568–4830* ⊕ *www. brownandhopkins.com* ⊙ *Mon.–Sat. 10–5, Sun. noon–5)* carries candles, reproduction antiques, penny candy, and handmade soaps. **Diamond Hill Vineyards** (⊠ *3145 Diamond Hill Rd., Cumberland* ☎ *401/333– 2751* ⊕ *www.favorlabel. com* ⊙ *Thurs.–Sat. noon–5, Sun. 11–3)* produces wine from pinot noir grapes as well as peaches and apples grown here. **Schartner Farm** (⊠ *1 Arnold Pl., Exeter* ☎ *401/294–2044* ⊙ *Daily 8–sunset; hayrides and corn maze weekends, 11–4:30)* sells fresh produce and baked goods year-round but is popular during the fall for cider, pumpkin pie, and hayrides. **Tavern on Main** (⊠ *1157 Putnam Pike, Chepachet* ☎ *401/710–9788* ⊕ *www.tavernonmainri. com* ⊙ *Closed Mon.–Tues.)* cooks up traditional American and Italian fare—for lunch try the tavern burger topped with bourbon sauce, or the lobster roll.

6

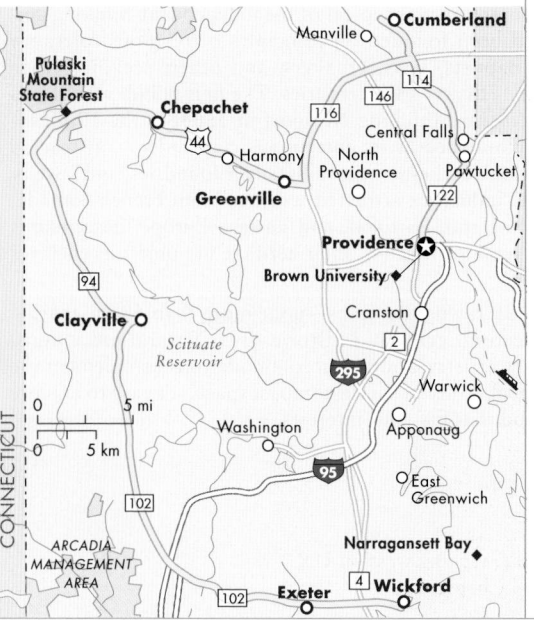

Updated by Andrew Collins

A getaway to Rhode Island, the smallest state in the nation — just 1,500 square mi (500 of those being water) — means historic tours, visits to galleries, and fine dining in Providence; apple picking and canal boat rides in the Blackstone Valley; boating and beaching in South County or Block Island; biking in East Bay; and sunset sails and Gilded Age mansions in Newport.

In May 1776, before the Declaration of Independence was issued, Rhode Island and Providence Plantations—the state's official name to this day—passed an act removing the king's name from all state documents. This action was typical of the independent-thinking colony, which had been founded on principles of religious tolerance and attracted Baptists, Jews, Quakers, and others seeking refuge throughout the 17th and 18th centuries. The first public school was established in forward-thinking Newport in 1664. In the 19th century, the state flourished as its entrepreneurial leaders constructed some of the nation's earliest textile mills, silver foundries, and jewelry companies. The industries attracted workers from French Canada, Italy, Ireland, England, Portugal, and Eastern Europe, descendants of whom have retained much of their heritage in numerous enclaves across the state.

Rhode Island's 39 towns and cities—none more than 50 mi apart—all hold architectural gems and historic sites. Natural attractions, inspired culinary artistry, and fine accommodations complement the mix. With so much to see in such a compact space, it's easy to explore the Rhode Island that fits your interests.

PROVIDENCE

New England's second-largest city behind Boston (with a population of 175,000) came into the 21st century as a renaissance city. Once regarded even by its own residents as an awkward stepchild of nearby Boston, Providence has blossomed into a clean, modern, cultural and gastronomical hub. With dozens of outstanding restaurants, Providence—home to the Johnson & Wales University College of Culinary Arts—legitimately lays claim to being a stellar dining destination.

In the past two decades, stretches of river downtown have been beautified, and parks have been built along the banks. The city's focal point is Waterplace Park, a series of footbridges, walkways, and green spaces running along both sides of the Providence River, which flows through the heart of downtown. Within walking distance of the park are a convention center and several hotels, a large outdoor ice-skating rink, and an upscale shopping center called Providence Place.

The city embraces independent thinking in business, the arts, and academia. Brown University, the Rhode Island School of Design (RISD), and Tony award–winning Trinity Repertory Company are major cultural forces. Playing to that strength, Providence has repopulated its once-abandoned downtown with artists and their studios.

GETTING ORIENTED

The narrow Providence River cuts through the city's downtown from north to south. West of the river lies the compact business district. A largely Italian neighborhood, Federal Hill, pushes west from here along Atwells Avenue. On the north side of downtown is the white-marble capitol. South Main and Benefit streets run parallel to the river, on the East Side. College Hill constitutes the western half of the East Side. At the top of College Hill, the area's primary thoroughfare, Thayer Street, runs north to south. Don't confuse East Providence, a city unto itself, with Providence's East Side.

GETTING HERE AND AROUND

AIR TRAVEL T. F. Green Airport, 10 mi south of Providence, has scheduled daily flights by most major airlines, including Air Canada, American, Continental, Delta, Southwest, United, and US Airways. By cab, the ride from T. F. Green Airport to downtown Providence takes about 15 minutes and costs about $25 to $30. The Airport Taxi & Limousine Service shuttle costs $11 per person each way.

TRAIN TRAVEL When traveling between New York City and Boston, Amtrak makes stops at Westerly, Kingston, and Providence. The Massachusetts Bay Transportation Authority commuter rail service connects Boston and Providence during weekday morning and evening rush hours for about half the cost of an Amtrak ride.

GETTING AROUND At Kennedy Plaza in downtown Providence, you can board the local Rhode Island Public Transit Authority buses, or the RIPTA Link trolley, whose two routes around downtown, the green and the gold lines, meet here. These two routes serve most points of interest. RIPTA fares range from $1.50 to $3. RIPTA buses also service T. F. Green Airport.

PARKING   Overnight parking is not allowed on many downtown Providence streets, and during the day it can be difficult to find curbside parking, especially downtown and on Federal and College hills. There's a large parking garage at Providence Place mall.

TOURS   The Providence Preservation Society publishes the *PPS/AIAri Guide to Providence Architecture*, which describes a dozen walking tours of the city.

From May through October, Conway Tours/Grayline Rhode Island runs a hop-on, hop-off 90-minute Historic Providence bus tour.

> ### TASTE OF ITALY TOUR
>
> For a more in-depth look at Providence's own "Little Italy," sign up for a **R.I. Market Tour** (☎ 401/934–2149, weekdays 9–4:30 ⊕ www.rimarkettours. com), a three-hour walking and tasting tour ($50) that takes you into Federal Hill's long-existing establishments (a bakery, an Italian specialty store, and wine shop) and teaches you about the neighborhood's history.

ESSENTIALS

Tour Contacts Conway Tours/Grayline Rhode Island (☎ 401/658–3400 ⊕ www.conwaytours.com). **Providence Preservation Society** (☎ 401/831–7440 ⊕ www.ppsri.org).

Transportation Contacts Airport Taxi & Limousine Service (☎ 401/737–2868 ⊕ www.airporttaxiri.com). **Amtrak** (☎ 800/872–7245 ⊕ www.amtrak. com). **Massachusetts Bay Transportation Authority** (MBTA, ☎ 617/722–3200 ⊕ www.mbta.com). **Rhode Island Public Transit Authority** (*RIPTA*⊠ Kennedy Plaza, Washington and Dorrance Sts., Downtown ☎ 401/781–9400 ⊕ www.ripta. com). **T. F. Green Airport** (⊠ U.S. 1 [Exit 13 off I–95], Warwick ☎ 401/737–8222 or 888/268–7222 ⊕ www.pvdairport.com).

Visitor Information Providence Warwick Convention and Visitors Bureau (⊠ 144 Westminster St. ☎ 401/456–0200 or 800/233–1636 ⊕ www.pwcvb.com).

EXPLORING

Numbers in the margin correspond to numbers on the Providence map.

TOP ATTRACTIONS

DOWNTOWN

⑬ Federal Hill. You're as likely to hear Italian as English in this neighbor-
★ hood. The stripe down Atwells Avenue is painted in red, white, and green, and a huge *pigna* (pinecone), an Italian symbol of abundance and quality, hangs on an arch soaring over the street. Hardware shops sell boccie sets, and grocers sell pastas, pastries, and usually hard-to-find Italian groceries. During the Federal Hill Stroll (usually held in early June) festivalgoers enjoy music and sample signature cuisine at some 20 eateries within a ¾-mi stretch of Atwells Avenue.

④ First Baptist Church in America. This historic house of worship was built in
★ 1775 for a congregation established in 1638 by Rhode Island founder Roger Williams and his fellow Puritan dissenters. The church, one of

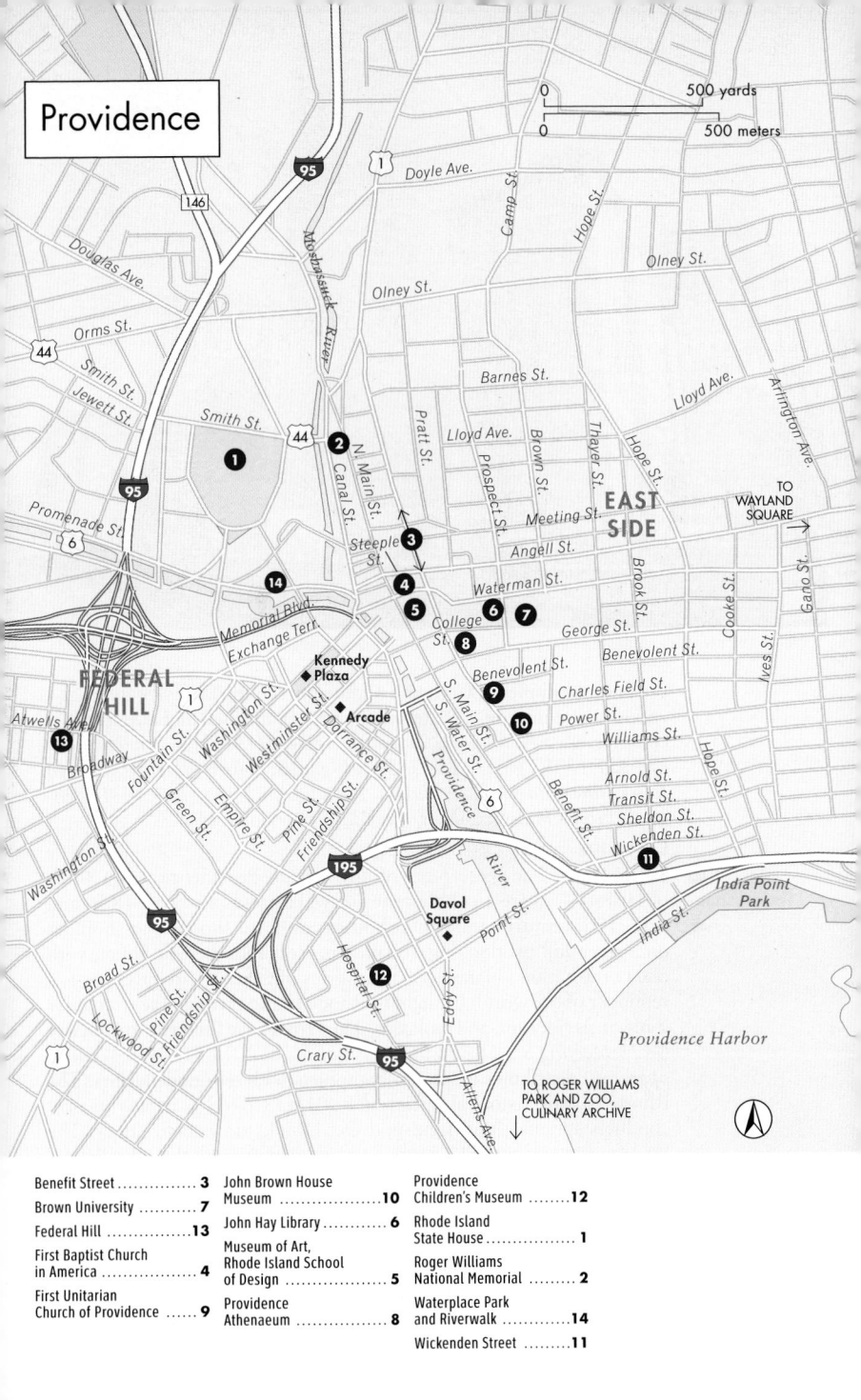

Providence

0 500 yards
0 500 meters

TO WAYLAND SQUARE

EAST SIDE

FEDERAL HILL

Kennedy Plaza

Arcade

Davol Square

India Point Park

Providence Harbor

TO ROGER WILLIAMS PARK AND ZOO, CULINARY ARCHIVE

In the last twenty years, the Providence riverfront has been beautified, highlighting the river that divides the city.

the finest examples of Georgian architecture in the United States, has a carved wood interior, a Waterford crystal chandelier, and austere Ionic columns. ⊠ *75 N. Main St., Downtown* ☎ *401/454–3418* ⊕ *www.fbcia. org* ✉ *Free, $2 guided tours, $1 self-guided tour booklets* ⊗ *Guided tours June–mid-Oct., weekdays 10–noon and 1–3, Sat. 10–1. Self-guided tours mid-Oct.–May, weekdays 10–noon and 1–3.*

EAST SIDE

❸

Fodor's Choice

★

Benefit Street. The centerpiece of any visit to Providence is the "mile of History," where a cobblestone sidewalk passes a row of 18th- and early-19th-century candy-color houses crammed shoulder-to-shoulder on a steep hill overlooking downtown. Romantic Benefit Street, with one of the nation's highest concentrations of Colonial architecture, is a reminder of the wealth brought to Rhode Island through the triangular trade of slaves, rum, and molasses. **The Providence Preservation Society** (⊠ *21 Meeting St., at Benefit St., East Side* ☎ *401/831–7440* ⊕ *www. ppsri.org*) distributes maps and pamphlets with self-guided tours. The **Rhode Island Historical Society** (☎ *401/438–0463* ⊕ *www.rihs.org*) conducts summer (mid-June–mid-Oct.) walks on Benefit Street. The 90-minute tours cost $12 per person and depart from the John Brown House Museum Tuesday–Saturday at 11 AM.

❼

Brown University. The nation's seventh-oldest college, founded in 1764, is an Ivy League institution with more than 40 academic departments, including a school of medicine. Gothic and Beaux Arts structures dominate the campus, which has been designated a National Historic Landmark. Free university tours are offered most weekdays several times per day and leave from the admissions office, in the Corliss-Brackett

PROVIDENCE IN ONE DAY

Begin at the **Rhode Island State House** ❶, where the south portico looks down over the city of Providence and the farthest reach of Narragansett Bay. Next proceed along the riverfront to the East Side's College Hill area, for a stroll along **Benefit Street** ❸. Must-sees in this neighborhood abundant with fine Colonial architecture are the **Museum of Art at the Rhode Island School of Design** ❺, the **Providence Athenaeum** ❽, and the magnificent **John Brown House Museum** ❿. You'll find plenty of

great lunch options, as well as some cool shops, along **Wickenden Street** ⓫, at the south end of the neighborhood.

Return back down the hill into downtown, strolling along **Waterplace Park and Riverwalk** ⓮, the centerpiece of the city's revitalization. As dinnertime approaches, make your way west of downtown into the famed Italian neighborhood of **Federal Hill** ⓭, where you'll find dozens of fantastic restaurants and cafés.

House. The university is on College Hill, a neighborhood with handsome 18th- and 19th-century architecture well worth a stroll. Thayer Street is the campus's principal commercial thoroughfare—once lined with offbeat indie shops and cafés, the street has given way to less interesting chain retail and dining. The imposing gates are opened twice a year—in fall to welcome the students and in spring to bid them adieu. ⊠ *Corliss-Brackett House, 45 Prospect St., East Side* ☎ *401/863–2378 tour information* ⊕ *www.brown.edu.*

EN ROUTE

Thayer Street bears a proud old New England name and is very much a part of life at Brown University. The blocks between Waterman and Bowen streets are filled with shops and restaurants and make for a pleasant afternoon stroll, although the neighborhood has become increasingly the domain of ubiquitous chain shops.

❿ ★ **John Brown House Museum.** The four Brown brothers—John, Joseph, Moses, and Nicholas—were prominent Providence merchants who made a fortune trading with the West Indies, Europe, and, later, China. This three-story Georgian mansion, designed for John by his brother Joseph in 1786, has elaborate woodwork and is filled with furniture, decorative art, silver, and items from the China trade. John Brown was a patriot, famous for his role in the burning of the British customs ship *Gaspee* in 1772. He was also a slave trader: in fact, his abolitionist brother Moses brought charges against him for illegally engaging in the buying and selling of human lives. Across the street and open Friday 1–4 is Nightingale House, built by a business rival of the Browns. The museum can be visited by guided tour only. ⊠ *52 Power St., East Side* ☎ *401/331–8575 or 401/273–7507* ⊕ *www.rihs.org* ✉ *$8* ☉ *Tours Apr.–Dec., Tues.–Fri. 1:30 and 3, Sat. 10:30, noon, 1:30, and 3; Jan.–Mar., Fri and Sat. 10:30, noon, 1:30, and 3.*

6

⑤ Museum of Art, Rhode Island School of Design. This superb museum is a multilevel complex housing paintings, sculptures, prints, drawings, photographs, textiles, and decorative arts—80,000 works are in frequent rotation. The five-story Chace Center, a 43,000-square-foot expansion, connects to the original 1926 museum building via a glass bridge and features more exhibit space, a new auditorium, and additional studios and classrooms. The museum's permanent holdings include the Aldrich collection of Japanese prints, Gorham silver, American furniture, Latin American art, and French Impressionist paintings including works by Claude Monet, Édouard Manet, Edgar Degas, and Pierre-Auguste Renoir. Also here are galleries filled with Greco-Roman, Egyptian, Asian, and Islamic art, as well as European and American art from the Middle Ages through the 20th century. The Egyptian mummy, which dates from 300 BC, is popular with children. Admission includes the adjoining **Pendleton House,** a replica of an early-19th-century Providence house. ⊠ *224 Benefit St., East Side* ☎ *401/454–6500* ⊕ *www.risdmuseum.org* ⬚ *$10, free Sun. 10–1* ☉ *Sept.–July, Tues.–Sun. 10–5.*

Fodor's Choice
★

⑧ Providence Athenaeum. Established in 1753 and housed in a Greek
★ Revival structure of 1838, this is among the oldest lending libraries in the world. Here Edgar Allan Poe, visiting Providence to lecture at Brown, met and courted Sarah Helen Whitman, who was said to be the inspiration for his poem "Annabel Lee." The library holds Rhode Island art and artifacts, an original set of *Birds of America* prints by John J. Audubon, and one of the world's best collections of travel literature. Changing exhibits showcase parts of the collection. ⊠ *251 Benefit St., East Side* ☎ *401/421–6970* ⊕ *www.providenceathenaeum.org* ⬚ *Free* ☉ *June–Aug., Mon.–Thurs. 9–7, Fri. 9–5, Sat. 9–1; Sept.–May, Mon.–Thurs. 9–7, Fri. and Sat. 9–5, Sun. 1–5.*

OFF THE
BEATEN
PATH
Roger Williams Park and Zoo. At this regal 430-acre Victorian park you can picnic, feed the ducks in the lakes, rent a paddleboat or miniature speedboat, or ride a pony. At Carousel Village, kids can ride the vintage carousel or a miniature train. The Museum of Natural History and Cormack Planetarium are also here; the Tennis Center has Rhode Island's only public clay courts. More than 950 animals of 160 different species live at the zoo, which opened in 1872. From downtown, take Interstate 95 south to U.S. 1 south (Elmwood Avenue); the park entrance is the first left turn. ⊠ *1000 Elmwood Ave., South Providence* ☎ *401/785–9457 museum, 401/785–3510 zoo* ⊕ *www.rogerwilliamsparkzoo.org* ⬚ *Museum $2, planetarium $3 (includes museum), zoo $12* ☉ *Museum daily 10–5 (planetarium shows weekends 2); zoo May–Sept., daily 9–4.*

WORTH NOTING
DOWNTOWN

⑫ Providence Children's Museum. At Rhode Island's only hands-on museum for children, kids can play in colorful exhibit areas including Land-FULL!, a recycling adventure that features a life-size virtual reality game; Water Ways, a wet playscape of fountains and pumps; and TEETH!, where they can brush a giant mouth. Other areas of fun include Little Woods, with a cave and a climbing tree; the Children's Garden, where you can have a picnic and learn about state plants. ⊠ *100 South St.,*

CLOSE UP

Roger Williams

Banished by the Puritans of Massachusetts for his then-seditious advocacy of separation of church and state and criticisms of New World leadership, Roger Williams headed south with a vision of a colony of religious tolerance. He paid Native Americans for land at the confluence of the Woonasquatucket and Moshassuck rivers in Narragansett Bay, establishing the town of Providence in 1636.

Williams's radical experiment proved quickly successful, and over roughly the next half century, the controversial theologian set up America's first (some say second) Baptist church, though he separated himself from the church shortly after founding it, and saw his backwater village grow into a prosperous Colonial shipping port.

Downtown ☎ *401/273–5437* ⊕ *www.childrenmuseum.org* ✉ *$7.50* ⊙ *Sept.–Mar., Tues.–Sun. 9–6; Apr.–Aug., daily 9–6.*

❶ Rhode Island State House. Designed by the noted firm of McKim, Mead & White and erected in 1900, Rhode Island's capitol has an ornate white Georgia marble exterior and the fourth largest self-supporting dome in the world. The gilded statue that tops the dome, representing the Independent Man, is said to have been struck by lightning more than 25 times. Engraved on the south portico is a passage from the Royal Charter of 1663: "To hold forth a lively experiment that a most flourishing civil state may stand and best be maintained with full liberty in religious concernments." In the state room is a full-length portrait of George Washington by Rhode Islander Gilbert Stuart. You'll also see the original parchment charter granted by King Charles to the colony of Rhode Island in 1663 and military accoutrements of Nathaniel Greene, Washington's second-in-command during the Revolutionary War. Although booklets are available for self-guided tours, guided tours are recommended. ✉ *82 Smith St., Downtown* ☎ *401/222–3983* ⊙ *Weekdays 8:30–4:30; tours weekdays 9:30, 10:30, and 11:30.*

❷ Roger Williams National Memorial. Roger Williams contributed so significantly to the development of the concepts that underpin the Declaration of Independence and the Constitution that the National Park Service dedicated a 4½-acre park to his memory. Displays provide a glimpse into the life of Rhode Island's founder, who wrote the first book on the languages of the Native Americans. ✉ *282 N. Main St., Downtown* ☎ *401/521–7266* ⊕ *www.nps.gov/rowi* ✉ *Free* ⊙ *Daily 9–4:30.*

⓮ Waterplace Park and Riverwalk. Romantic Venetian-style footbridges, cobblestone walkways, and an amphitheater encircling a tidal pond set the tone at this 4-acre tract. The Riverwalk passes the junction of three rivers—the Woonasquatucket, Providence, and Moshassuck—a nexus of the shipping trade during the city's early years but an area that had been covered over with highways and parking lots by the middle of the 20th century. The focus of an urban-renewal project that uncovered

The capitol building of the smallest state, sits on Smith Hill in downtown Providence.

the buried rivers, rerouted them, and surrounded them with amenities for pedestrians rather than cars, Waterplace Park is now a gathering place for the city. It's also the site of the popular **Waterfire**, a multimedia installation featuring music and nearly 100 burning braziers that rise from the water and are tended from boats; the dusk-to-midnight Waterfire happens approximately 16 times a year and attracts more than 500,000 visitors annually. The Rosa Parks Amphitheater is the site of free concerts in summer. ⊠ *1 Financial Way, Downtown* ⊕ *www. waterfire.org.*

OFF THE BEATEN PATH

Culinary Arts Museum. An offbeat, fascinating museum in an otherwise nondescript building on the Harborside campus of Johnson & Wales University, this archive of food and restaurant memorabilia delights with its exhibits of vintage menus, reconstruction of an ancient diner car, enormous cookbook collection, displays of kitchen gadgets, and other assorted kitchen minutiae. Check out the original letters by assorted past presidents to friends and food providers who supplied gourmet gifts on various occasions. ⊠ *315 Harborside Blvd., South Providence* ☎ *401/598–2805* ⊕ *www.culinary.org* ✉ *$7* ⊙ *Tues.–Sun. 10–5.*

EAST SIDE

❾ First Unitarian Church of Providence. This Romanesque house of worship made of Rhode Island granite was built in 1816. Its steeple houses a 2,500-pound bell, the largest ever cast in Paul Revere's foundry. ⊠ *1 Benevolent St., at Benefit St., East Side* ☎ *401/421–7970* ⊕ *www. firstunitarianprov.org* ✉ *Free* ⊙ *Guided tours by appointment.*

❻ John Hay Library. Built in 1910 and named for Abraham Lincoln's secretary, the "Hay" houses 11,000 items related to the 16th president.

The noncirculating research library, part of ➾ **Brown University,** also stores American drama and poetry collections, 500,000 pieces of American sheet music, the Webster Knight Stamp Collection, the letters of horror and science-fiction writer H. P. Lovecraft, military prints, and a world-class collection of toy soldiers. ✉ *20 Prospect St., East Side* ☎ *401/863–2146* ✆ *Free* ☉ *Sept.–May, weekdays 9–6, Sun. 1–5; June–Aug., limited hours (call).*

QUICK BITES

For memorable snacking on the East Side, skip the ho-hum fast-food restaurants along Thayer Street and venture up Hope Street to **Seven Stars Bakery** (✉ *820 Hope St., East Side* ☎ *401/521–2200*), a convivial spot for first-rate coffee and espresso drinks, sandwiches on flaky kalamata-olive bread, and a tantalizing variety of brownies, cookies, and other sweets.

⓫ **Wickenden Street.** The main artery in the Fox Point district, a formerly working-class Portuguese neighborhood that's seen a steady gentrification, Wickenden Street has antiques stores, galleries, and trendy cafés. Professors, artists, and students are among the newer residents here. Many of the houses along Wickenden, Transit, Gano, and nearby streets are still painted the pastel colors of Portuguese homes.

6

SPORTS AND THE OUTDOORS

BIKING
The best biking in the Providence area is along the 14½-mi **East Bay Bicycle Path** (⊕ *www.riparks.com/eastbay.htm*), which hugs the Narragansett Bay shore from India Point Park through four towns before it ends in Independence Park in Bristol.

BOATING
Prime boating areas include the Providence River, the Seekonk River, and Narragansett Bay. The **Narragansett Boat Club** (✉ *River Rd., East Side* ☎ *401/272–1838* ⊕ *www.rownbc.org*) has advice on the best places for boating and also offers rowing and sculling classes.

ICE-SKATING
The outdoor rink **Bank of America City Center** (✉ *Kennedy Plaza, Downtown* ☎ *401/331–5544* ⊕ *www.providenceskating.com* ✆ *Skating $6, rentals $4*) is open 10 AM to 8 PM daily mid-November through April.

SHOPPING

Providence has a handful of small but engaging shopping areas. In Fox Point, Wickenden Street contains many antiques stores and several art galleries. Near Brown University, Thayer Street has a number of boutiques, but the high rents have led to an influx of chain stores. On the other hand, downtown's Westminster Street has morphed into a strip of independently owned clothiers, galleries, and design stores.

ANTIQUES AND HOME FURNISHINGS
CAV (✉ *14 Imperial Pl., Jewelry District* ☎ *401/751–9164* ⊕ *www. cavrestaurant.com*) is a large restaurant, bar, and coffeehouse (with music Friday and Saturday nights) in a revamped factory space. It sells

fine rugs, tapestries, prints, portraits, and antiques, many with African or Asian provenance. Along increasingly gentrified Westminster Street, drop by **HomeStyle** (⊠ *229 Westminster St., Downtown* ☎ *401/277–1159* ⊕ *www.homestyleri.com*) for eye-catching objets d'art, stylish housewares, and other decorative items. **Tilden-Thurber** (⊠ *292 Westminster St., Downtown* ☎ *401/272–3200* ⊕ *www.stanleyweiss.com*) carries high-end Colonial- and Victorian-era furniture, antiques, and estate jewelry.

ART GALLERIES

The **Bert Gallery** (⊠ *540 S. Water St., East Side* ☎ *401/751–2628* ⊕ *www.bertgallery.com*) displays late-19th- and early-20th-century paintings by regional artists. **JRS Fine Art** (⊠ *218 Wickenden St., East Side* ☎ *401/331–4380*) sells works by national and Rhode Island artists, plus carvings and crafts by artisans from Panama's Darien rain forest. The **Peaceable Kingdom** (⊠ *116 Ives St., East Side* ☎ *401/351–3472*) stocks folk art from around the world, including tribal weavings and rugs, international clothing and jewelry, masks, musical instruments, and paintings.

risd|works (⊠ *10 Westminster St., Downtown* ☎ *401/277–4949* ⊕ *www.risdworks.com*) hosts changing exhibitions that showcase the work of Rhode Island School of Design alumni and faculty, ranging from $1 greeting cards to $50 flatware patterns to $1,000 fine art.

FOOD

Tony's Colonial (⊠ *311 Atwells Ave., Downtown* ☎ *401/621–8675* ⊕ *www.tonyscolonial.com*), a superb Italian grocery and deli, stocks freshly prepared foods.

★ **Venda Ravioli** (⊠ *275 Atwells Ave., Downtown* ☎ *401/421–9105* ⊕ *www.vendaravioli.com*) carries an amazing selection of imported and home-made Italian foods.

MALLS

★ The **Arcade** (⊠ *65 Weybosset St., Downtown* ☎ *401/598–1199*), built in 1828, was America's first shopping mall. A National Historic Landmark, this Greek Revival building has three tiers of shops and restaurants. Expect the unusual at **Copacetic Rudely Elegant Jewelry** (⊠ *17 Peck St., Downtown* ☎ *401/273–0470* ⊕ *www.copaceticjewelry.com*), which sells the work of more than 120 artists.

TWO HURRICANES HIT NEW ENGLAND

Winds blew 100 MPH during the Great New England Hurricane of 1938, wreaking utter havoc up and down the coast. Nearly 700 people died (compared with about 1,840 during Hurricane Katrina) and damages totaled $308 million (estimated to be about $5 billion in today's economy). Just 16 years later, Hurricane Carol roared into Rhode Island, with water some 8 feet deep in Providence. Across the region, Carol's death toll was 60 and damages were $416 million (about $41 million in Providence alone).

NIGHTLIFE AND THE ARTS

For events listings, consult the daily *Providence Journal* and the weekly *Providence Phoenix* (free in restaurants and bookstores).

NIGHTLIFE

BARS

DOWNTOWN **Snookers** (✉ *53 Ashburton St., Downtown* ☎ *401/351–7665*) is a stylish billiard hall in the Jewelry District that hosts live bands almost every night. Through a double doorway at the rear of the billiard room is a '50s-style lounge where food is served. Long-running **Mirabar** (✉ *35 Richmond St., Downtown* ☎ *401/331–6761*) is one of the most popular gay bars in Providence (which has an openly gay mayor who is favored to win again in 2010).

EAST SIDE An easy-going bar and with cozy booths, **Lili Marlene's** (*422 Atwells Ave., Downtown* ☎ *401/751–4996*) cultivates a loyal following among in-the-know locals; it's perfect for sipping martinis before or after dinner in Federal Hill.

MUSIC CLUBS

★ Hear musical styles from techno-pop and hip-hop to folk and jazz at the gallery/performance space **AS220** (✉ *115 Empire St., Downtown* ☎ *401/831–9327* ⊕ *www.as220.org*). Talent shows, poetry readings, and comedy nights are also scheduled. **Ri Ra Irish Pub** (*50 Exchange Terr., Downtown* ☎ *401/272–1953* ⊕ *www.rira.com*) presents live Irish and Celtic music. The pub is inside the vintage Union Station building downtown, and the interior was shipped here, piece by piece, from an 1880s pub in County Mayo, Ireland. A coffeehouse and bar, trendy **Tazza** (*250 Westminster St., Downtown* ☎ *401/751–3300* ⊕ *www.tazzacaffe.com*) books a wide range of live bands and has well-attended open-mike nights on Sundays. **Lupo's at the Roxy** (✉ *79 Washington St., Downtown* ☎ *401/331–5876, 401/272–5876 concert line* ⊕ *www.lupos.com*), housed in a historic, five-story theater, hosts national alternative, rock, blues, and punk bands.

THE ARTS

FILM

The **Cable Car Cinema & Café** (✉ *204 S. Main St., Downtown* ☎ *401/272–3970* ⊕ *www.cablecarcinema.com*) showcases a fine slate of alternative and foreign flicks. You sit on couches and comfy chairs, and singers entertain prior to most evening shows. An espresso café substitutes for the traditional soda-and-popcorn concession.

GALLERY TOURS

During **Gallery Night Providence** (☎ *401/751–2628* ⊕ *www.gallerynight.info*), held the third Thursday evening of every month March–November, free art buses circulate along downtown, East Side, West Side, and Wickenden Street routes connecting some 40 participating art galleries and museums that hold open houses and mount special exhibitions.

6

LECTURES

Both the **Rhode Island School of Design** (⊠ *224 Benefit St., East Side* ☎ *401/454–6500* ⊕ *www.risd.edu*) and **Brown University** (⊠ *71 George St., East Side* ☎ *401/863–2474* ⊕ *www.brown.edu*) present lectures throughout the year, often with free admission.

MUSIC

The **Providence Performing Arts Center** (⊠ *220 Weybosset St., Downtown* ☎ *401/421–2787* ⊕ *www.ppacri.org*), a 3,200-seat theater and concert hall that opened in 1928, hosts touring Broadway shows, concerts, and other large-scale happenings. Its lavish interior is painted with frescoes and contains Art Deco chandeliers. The **Rhode Island Philharmonic** (☎ *401/248–7000* ⊕ *www.ri-philharmonic.org*) presents concerts at Veterans Memorial Auditorium and Providence Performing Arts Center between October and May. The Philharmonic is also home to the Music School, a learning center for young musicians, which has its own children's orchestra. **Veterans Memorial Auditorium** (⊠ *1 Ave. of the Arts St., Downtown* ☎ *401/272–4862* ⊕ *www.vmari.com*) hosts concerts, plays, children's theater, and ballet.

THEATER

Brown University (⊠ *Catherine Bryan Dill Center for the Performing Arts, 77 Waterman St., East Side* ☎ *401/863–2838* ⊕ *www.brown.edu/ tickets*) mounts productions of contemporary, sometimes avant-garde, works as well as classics.

★ The **Trinity Repertory Company** (⊠ *201 Washington St., Downtown* ☎ *401/351–4242* ⊕ *www.trinityrep.com*), one of New England's most esteemed theater companies, presents plays in the renovated Majestic movie house. The varied season generally includes classics, foreign plays, new works by young playwrights, and an annual version of *A Christmas Carol.*

WHERE TO EAT

Providence is small enough that you can easily reach every neighborhood from any other, making restaurant locations less of a factor than in larger cities. That said, there are certain areas that discriminating diners shouldn't miss, such as Federal Hill's Little Italy area along Atwells Avenue, the hip international restaurants of Fox Point along Wickenden Street and South Water Street, the dapper neighborhood bistros and cafés north and east of Brown and RISD, and the swanky dining spots clustered along the riverfront downtown, near Providence Place mall.

DOWNTOWN

$$–$$$
ITALIAN
Fodor's Choice
★

✕ **Bacaro.** Chef Brian Kingsford and partner Jennifer Matta, both formerly of Al Forno, opened this handsome, bilevel restaurant in 2007. On the informal ground floor you can sip wine and nosh on olives, *soppressata,* and fresh buffalo mozzarella from the *salumeria* (cured-meat shop) and *enoteca* (wine cellar). Upstairs is a more traditional dining room; sample dazzling fare like a decadent pasta dish with mushrooms, butter, and Parmesan topped with a poached egg that breaks open to create a creamy yolk-based sauce. The grilled pizzas contain toppings that change seasonally—think squash flowers, goat cheese, and micro basil in summer. Desserts are made to-order; the crostata for two may be the best fruit tart you'll ever taste. ✉ *262 S. Water St., Downtown* ☎ *401/751–3700* ⊕ *www.bacarorestaurant.net/home.html* ☐ *AE, D, MC, V* ☺ *Closed Sun. and Mon. No lunch.*

$$$

ECLECTIC

✗ **CAV.** Chandeliers hang from the ceiling, and African and Asian artwork adorns the walls (everything is for sale) of this former warehouse-cum-restaurant and antiques store. The menu is extensive, but you can't go wrong with the goat cheese croquettes or pistachio-crusted crab cake as an appetizer, and pan-seared diver sea scallops and shrimp with lemon zest risotto or duck confit with brandied caramelized onions and sweet potato mash as an entrée. The food is rich in flavor, and the ambience is full of personality. ✉ *14 Imperial Pl., Downtown* ☎ *401/751–9164* ⊕ *www.cavrestaurant.com* ☐ *AE, D, MC, V.*

$–$$

ECLECTIC

✗ **DownCity.** Youthful, artsy, energetic, and popular with the gay community, this contemporary take on a city tavern moved into an airier space in 2008 but continues to pull in students from nearby Johnson & Wales, as well as revelers heading out to the neighborhood's clubs later (you can socialize here until well after midnight, and there's live music some evenings). The menu pulls from around the globe and includes fried whole-belly clams with sriracha (Thai chili) rémoulade sauce, meat loaf with caramelized-onion demi-glace and buttermilk-mashed potatoes, and grilled watermelon salad with feta and balsamic. During the day, it's a fab brunch/lunch option—try the crab cakes Benedict with home fries. ✉ *50 Weybosset St., Downtown* ☎ *401/331–9217* ⊕ *www.downcityfood.com* ☐ *AE, D, MC, V.*

$$$

NEW AMERICAN

✗ **Gracie's.** Johnson & Wales alum chef Joseph Hafner dishes out refined New American cuisine at this warm, yet sophisticated downtown spot. You can dine under the stars that dangle from the ceiling in the main dining room, but for a more intimate experience, sit downstairs in the private wine vault. (The room requires no extra fee and can accommodate a party up to eight people.) The menu changes seasonally. During summer months, for example, you can expect to find dishes like watermelon and Thai basil gazpacho; Rhode Island bass with miso-glazed summer vegetables; or local skate with braised rapini, fried capers, and white beans. Without a doubt, the best dish on the menu (served all year-round) is the seared foie gras appetizer, set atop corn bread brioche and served with blueberry gastrique (thick reduction sauce). ✉ *194 Washington St., Downtown* ☎ *401/272–7811* ⊕ *www.graciesprov.com* ☐ *AE, MC, V* ☺ *Closed Sun. and Mon. No lunch.*

$$–$$$

ECLECTIC

✗ **Mills Tavern.** Tile mosaics and paintings by the former head of the RISD illustration department enhance this postmodern take on the Colonial tavern concept. The menu is divvied up into several categories: raw bar, wood-burning oven, wood rotisseries, and so on. Don't miss the Scottish salmon with a truffle-honey glaze or the side dishes, like bourbon-glazed carrots and pan-roasted mushrooms with Madeira and thyme. Take advantage of the $29 three-course fixed price menu on weeknights. ✉ *101 N. Main St., Downtown* ☎ *401/272–3331* ⊕ *www.millstavernrestaurant.com* ☐ *AE, D, DC, MC, V* ☺ *No lunch.*

6

EAST SIDE

$$$ ✕ **Al Forno.** When it opened in 1980, Al Forno, which means "from
ITALIAN   the oven" in Italian, put Providence on the national dining map, and
Fodor'sChoice   it continues to garner ebullient praise from critics and patrons. The
★   oven produces a number of stellar dishes, among them thin-crust piz-
zas, roasted duck with prune-stuffed gnocchi, spicy roasted clams, and
bacon-wrapped wild boar loin. Also consider the extraordinary pastas,
such as house-made *cavatelli* with prosciutto and butternut squash. For
dessert, look to the pear-and-walnut tart. ✉ *577 S. Main St., East Side*
☎ *401/273–9760* ⊕ *www.alforno.com* ⌂ *Reservations not accepted*
🖃 *AE, DC, MC, V* ☺ *Closed Sun. and Mon. No lunch.*

$$$ ✕ **Apsara Palace.** Part of a growing presence of noteworthy neighbor-
ASIAN   hood eateries that's developed along Hope Street just north of Brown
and RISD, this restaurant serves some of the best Asian fare in a city
with ample competition. Recipes from China, Vietnam, Thailand, Cam-
bodia, and Japan dominate the lengthy menu, from natang (crisp rice
patties with a sauce of ground pork and coconut) to Cambodian rice
noodle soup with duck to scallops stir-fried with cashews and Chinese
vegetables. There's even a sushi bar. Its cozy dining room is decked with
colorful artwork. ✉ *783 Hope St., East Side* ☎ *401/831–4722* ⊕ *www.
apsara-palace.com* 🖃 *AE, MC, V* ⛶ BYOB.

$$$ ✕ **Chez Pascal.** A sophisticated yet unfussy bistro in a peaceful residen-
★   tial neighborhood on the East Side, Chez Pascal makes for an intimate,
FRENCH   moderately priced spot to enjoy a romantic evening and feast on beauti-
fully prepared contemporary French fare. On weekdays, there's a $30
per person three-course prix-fixe. Operated by young husband-and-wife
team Matthew and Kristin Gennuso, the charming spot turns out such
seasonal treats as Narragansett Bay squid au poivre with sweet-pepper
relish and grilled potato bread; slow-roasted half duck with buttered
turnips and a sour-cherry glaze; and baked-herb ricotta with braised
greens, green-garlic puree, and aged balsamic. Dessert features a tast-
ing of three custards, a selection of cheeses, and several tempting tortes
and crumbles. ✉ *960 Hope St., East Side* ☎ *401/421–4422* ⊕ *www.
chez-pascal.com* 🖃 *AE, D, MC, V* ☺ *No lunch.*

$$$ ✕ **La Laiterie at Farmstead.** This acclaimed restaurant inside the fantastic
★   Farmstead cheese shop in the Wayland Square section of Providence's
AMERICAN   East Side enjoys a devout foodie following, thanks to the creative, farm-
to-table cooking of chef-owners Kate and Matt Jennings. The menu
changes depending on what's regionally fresh and available but has
included the likes of spring-lamb neck ravioli with roasted spring onions,
chives, and English pea puree and grilled local striped bass with sweet-
corn pudding, chorizo, and littleneck clams. The owners also operate
a gourmet sandwich, cheese, and prepared foods shop downtown on
Westminster Street. ✉ *188 Wayland Ave., East Side* ☎ *401/274–7177*
⊕ *www.farmsteadinc.com* ⌂ *Reservations not accepted* 🖃 *AE, MC, V*
☺ *Closed Sun. and Mon. No lunch.*

FEDERAL HILL

¢–$ ✕ **Angelo's Civita Farnese.** In the heart of Federal Hill, boisterous Angelo's
ITALIAN   has been dispensing reliably good home-style red-sauce fare and old-
world charm since the 1920s. Locals come for prodigious portions of

Al Forno's grilled pizza continues to please critics at this East Side eatery.

fresh, simply prepared pasta and traditional Italian specialties (fried peppers, veal parmigiana) at bargain prices. The casual dining room received a much-welcomed remodel in 2008, which included the addition of a friendly little bar. ✉ *141 Atwells Ave., Federal Hill* ☎ *401/621–8171* ⊕ *www.angelosonthehill.com* ⊟ *No credit cards.*

$$$
AMERICAN
✗ **Broadway Bistro.** Another neat addition to the city's increasingly gentrified West Side (which fringes Federal Hill), this convivial bar and restaurant occupies a single-story redbrick storefront with a handful of sidewalk tables. A mix of students, artists, and neighborhood locals congregates here nightly for fair-priced, deftly prepared, globally influenced bistro chow. You could make a meal of two or three starters, perhaps the potato pierogies with stewed oxtail or the salad of pancetta, artichoke, goat cheese, and Bibb lettuce. Among the main courses, don't miss the local cod cakes with tomato-horseradish vinaigrette or the hearty rack of lamb with porcini sauce and baby arugula. There's a nice selection of wines by the bottle or the glass and a solid beer list. ✉ *205 Broadway, Federal Hill* ☎ *401/331–2450* ⊕ *www.broadwaybistrori.com* ⊟ *MC, V* ☺ *No lunch.*

$$
AMERICAN
Fodor's Choice
★
✗ **Nick's on Broadway.** What might pass as a no-frills luncheonette from the street turns out some of the best breakfast food in Rhode Island, plus extraordinary lunches and dinners. Young chef Derek Wagner delights morning patrons with such memorable fare as vanilla-battered French toast with warm fruit compote and rosemary ham; later in the day, he prepares a knockout pulled-pork sandwich with cheddar and caramelized onion, as well as rare-seared tuna with mashed parsnips and potatoes and sage jus. Service is low-key and the dining room basic, with a polished wood counter and a row of tightly spaced tables. ✉ *500*

Broadway, Federal Hill ☎ *401/421–0286* ⊕ *www.nicksonbroadway. com* ⊟ *AE, D, MC, V* ⊗ *Closed Mon. and Tue. No dinner Sun.*

$$–$$$ ✕ **Providence Oyster Bar.** In a neighborhood where Italian food domi-
SEAFOOD   nates, this spirited seafood restaurant offers a refreshing alternative.
The dining room has polished wood floors, brick walls, and a tin ceil-
ing, while the raw bar serves more than a dozen varieties of fresh oys-
ters. Appetizers include blackened ahi tuna and steamed Prince Edward
Island mussels with a Pernod-fennel broth. For entrées, try grilled
swordfish steak with truffle french fries and a balsamic reduction; the
sirloin with bacon and blue cheese pleases carnivores. ⊠ *283 Atwells
Ave., Federal Hill* ☎ *401/272–8866* ⊕ *www.providenceoysterbar.com*
⊟ *AE, DC, MC, V* ⊗ *Closed Sun. No lunch Mon.–Thurs.*

WHERE TO STAY

DOWNTOWN

$$–$$$ 🏨 **Christopher Dodge House.** You'll find immaculate, simply furnished
★   rooms with polished hardwood floors and rich architectural details in
this three-story Italianate brick town house within walking distance of
downtown and Federal Hill. Many rooms have gas fireplaces, and a
few larger units have kitchenettes. The free parking is a nice perk. The
owners also operate the similarly appealing Mowry-Nicholson B&B,
just around the corner. **Pros:** most rooms have gas fireplaces; huge windows in rooms; guests receive free passes to nearby health club. **Cons:**
must cross ugly interstate if you want to walk downtown; rooms not
ideal for kids (due to fine furnishings and adult vibe). ⊠ *11 W. Park
St., Downtown* ☎ *401/351–6111* ⊕ *www.providence-hotel.com* 🛏 *14
rooms* ⚇ *In-room: a/c, kitchen (some), Wi-Fi. In-hotel: parking (free)*
⊟ *AE, D, MC, V* ⊗ *BP.*

$$–$$$ 🏨 **Courtyard by Marriott Providence.** One of downtown's few mid-priced
hotels is in a seven-story redbrick building designed to match the other
buildings in historic Union Station Plaza. Nearly all of the large rooms,
which received a major refurbishment in 2009, have views of either
the State House, Waterplace Park, or the Financial District. Each room
has a well-designed work area and ergonomic chair as well as free
Wi-Fi. The hotel is steps away from the Providence Place mall. **Pros:**
many rooms overlook riverfront; price is reasonable; central location.
Cons: rooms are a bit nondescript. ⊠ *32 Exchange Terr., Downtown*
☎ *401/272–1191 or 888/887–7955* ⊕ *www.marriott.com* 🛏 *210
rooms, 6 suites* ⚇ *In-room: a/c, refrigerator, Internet, Wi-Fi. In-hotel:
restaurant, pool, gym, Internet terminal, Wi-Fi hotspot, parking (paid)*
⊟ *AE, D, DC, MC, V.*

$$$–$$$$ 🏨 **Hotel Providence.** Intimate, urbane, and along downtown's best shop-
★   ping street, this lavishly decorated boutique property is set inside a
restored late-19th-century building. Each of the 80 oversize rooms and
suites contains artwork by talented local Nancy Friese (chair of RISD),
along with such perks as terry robes, free Wi-Fi, CD players, and bath-
rooms with rain showerheads and Bulgari bath amenities; some suites
have whirlpool tubs. The hotel's elegant restaurant Aspire ($$$) serves
creative, well-prepared Mediterranean food. **Pros:** in the heart of the

Arts and Entertainment District; attentive staff; plush rooms. **Cons:** on a busy street; not much greenery around. ⊠ *311 Westminster St., Downtown* ☎ *401/861–8000 or 800/861–8990* ⊕ *www.thehotelprovidence. com* ⥓ *64 rooms, 16 suites* ⚲ *In-room: a/c, safe, Wi-Fi. In-hotel: restaurant, room service, gym, Internet terminal, Wi-Fi hotspot, parking (paid)* ▭ *AE, D, DC, MC, V.*

$$$$ 🖼 **Providence Biltmore.** Built in 1922, the Biltmore has an Art Deco exte-
★ rior, an external glass elevator with delightful views of Providence, a grand ballroom, an Elizabeth Arden Red Door Spa, and an in-house Starbucks. The attentiveness of its staff, downtown location, and modern amenities make this hotel one of the city's best. And with its skyscraping neon sign, it couldn't be easier to find. **Pros:** truly the grande dame of Providence; suites are huge; an impressive spa. **Cons:** very pricey; not as hip as some other hotels in town. ⊠ *Kennedy Plaza, Dorrance and Washington Sts., Downtown* ☎ *401/421–0700 or 800/294–7709* ⊕ *www.providencebiltmore.com* ⥓ *117 rooms, 162 suites* ⚲ *In-room: a/c, kitchen (some), Wi-Fi. In-hotel: restaurant, room service, gym, spa, Wi-Fi hotspot, parking (paid)* ▭ *AE, D, DC, MC, V.*

$$$–$$$$ 🖼 **Renaissance Providence Hotel.** The city's hippest hotel opened in 2007
Fodor'sChoice inside one of its most mysterious buildings, a stately nine-story neoclas-
★ sical 1929 building constructed as a Masonic temple but never occupied, as it was completed just after the Stock Market Crash. Developers have restored the building and even incorporated vintage graffiti found within its empty corridors into the artsy, whimsical room design. Try to get a room overlooking the statehouse, across the street, and dine in the swank on-site restaurant, Temple Downtown. **Pros:** terrific location by Providence Place mall and capitol grounds; super-cushy linens and bedding; you can custom-design your own in-room honor bar. **Cons:** some rooms have small windows; high rates. ⊠ *5 Ave. of the Arts, Downtown* ☎ *401/919–5000 or 800/468–3571* ⊕ *www.renaissanceprovidence.com* ⥓ *269 rooms, 3 suites* ⚲ *In-room: a/c, safe, Internet, Wi-Fi. In-hotel: restaurant, room service, gym, Internet terminal, parking (paid)* ▭ *AE, D, DC, MC, V.*

EAST SIDE

$$–$$$ 🖼 **Old Court Bed & Breakfast.** This three-story Italianate inn on historic Benefit Street was built in 1863 as a rectory. Antique furniture, richly colored wallpaper, and memorabilia throughout the house reflect the best of 19th-century style. The comfortable, spacious rooms have high ceilings and chandeliers; most have nonworking marble fireplaces, and some have views of the State House and downtown. **Pros:** on a regal residential street; elegant furnishings; friendly service. **Cons:** lacks the anonymity of a larger hotel. ⊠ *144 Benefit St., East Side* ☎ *401/751–2002* ⊕ *www.oldcourt.com* ⥓ *10 rooms* ⚲ *In-room: a/c, Wi-Fi. In-hotel: Wi-Fi hotspot, parking (free)* ▭ *AE, D, MC, V* ⊚| *BP.*

FEDERAL HILL

$$$ 🖼 **Hotel Dolce Villa.** This small, upscale, well-managed inn is the only
★ accommodation in Federal Hill—it actually overlooks DePasquale Square and its vibrant cafés, gelato stands, and gourmet markets. The striking Mediterranean-inspired building contains 14 one- and two-

bedroom suites, all with gleaming contemporary decor, white-marble floors, fully stocked kitchens, and such luxe amenities as flat-screen TVs and whirlpool tubs; larger suites have gas fireplaces. It's ideal for longer stays and makes for a perfect weekend retreat for those planning to eat their way through Federal Hill. **Pros:** great value; fun location; huge suites. **Cons:** the modern decor may not please traditionalists; no gym. ⊠ *63 DePasquale Plaza, Federal Hill* ☎ *401/383–7031* ⊕ *www. dolcevillari.com* ⊅ *14 suites* ⚴ *In-room: a/c, kitchen, DVD, Internet. In-hotel: bar, parking (paid)* ⊟ *AE, D, MC, V.*

THE BLACKSTONE VALLEY

America's Industrial Revolution began in this region north of Providence in 1790, when the power of the Blackstone River, which runs south from Worcester, Massachusetts, was first harnessed at Pawtucket. The advent of water-powered factory mills along the 45-mi river catapulted a young agricultural United States into the Industrial Age. In the 1800s, Pawtucket and Woonsocket became large cities as a steady flow of French, Irish, and Eastern European immigrants came to work the mills, a system of canals and later railroads came into being as distribution channels, and the local industry grew. Much of that industry is gone, and the old mills are slowly being renovated into condominiums, offices, and gallery space. The Blackstone River Valley National Heritage Corridor provides a backdrop to museums, historic villages, and country drives. Most of the Blackstone Valley experience is about taking in the history of the area, understanding its importance in the country's growth, and enjoying the slices of Americana it has to offer.

The Blackstone River and its valley are named after William Blackstone, who in 1628 became the first European to settle in Boston. In 1635, having grown weary of the ways of the Puritan settlers who had become his neighbors, this Anglican clergyman built a new home in what was then wilderness and is now called Rhode Island.

GETTING HERE AND AROUND

TOURS Running from Central Falls (June through mid-August) and Woonsocket (late August through late October), the **Blackstone Valley Explorer** (☎ *800/454–2882* ⊕ *www.rivertourblackstone.com*), a 49-passenger riverboat, offers tours on Sunday afternoons on the Blackstone River, with narrated descriptions of the area's ecology and industrial history.

ESSENTIALS

Visitor Information **Blackstone Valley Tourism Council** (⊠ 175 Main St., Pawtucket ☎ 401/724–2200 or 800/454–2882 ⊕ www.tourblackstone.com).

PAWTUCKET

5 mi north of Providence.

Providence's neighbor to the immediate north is a slightly gruff, blue-collar factory town that's gradually seen some new blood move in as real-estate prices have risen in the capital. In Algonquian, "petuket" (similar to standard Rhode Island pronunciation of the city's name today, with the accent on the second syllable) means "waterfalls." A small village was established at the falls in 1670 by Joseph Jenks Jr., who considered the area a prime spot for an iron forge. When Samuel Slater arrived 120 years later, he was delighted to find a corps of skilled mechanics ready to assist him in his dream of building a textile mill and bringing America's first factory system into being. Although many of Pawtucket's older buildings were torn down as part of urban renewal projects in the 1970s, significant portions of the city's history have been preserved, and Slater Mill is a must for history buffs.

ESSENTIALS

Visitor Information The Blackstone Valley Visitor Center (⊠ *175 Main St.* ☎ *401/724–2200 or 800/454–2882* ⊕ *www.tourblackstone.com* ✉ *Free* ☉ *Daily 9–5*), across the street from Slater Mill, has information kiosks, maps, hospitable tourism consultants, a café, and a gallery.

EXPLORING

Ⓒ Fodor's Choice ★

Slater Mill Historic Site. In 1793, Samuel Slater and two Providence merchants built the first factory in the United States, to produce cotton yarn from water-powered machines. The Slater Mill Historic Site celebrates the American Industrial Revolution, comprising the old yellow clapboard mill, since restored and housing machinery illustrating the conversion of raw cotton to finished cloth, and the stone Wilkinson Mill, built in 1810, where a 9-ton reproduction of an 1826 waterwheel powers a 19th-century machine shop using a system of leather belts and pulleys to drive the machines. Interpreters demonstrate activities of daily family life in the 1758 Sylvanus Brown House and garden, and guides in period clothing conduct living-history tours. ⊠ *67 Roosevelt Ave.* ☎ *401/725–8638* ⊕ *www.slatermill.org* ✉ *$10* ☉ *Mar. and Apr., weekends 11–3; May–Oct., Tues.–Sun. 10–4.*

Ⓒ

Slater Memorial Park. Within the stately grounds of this park along Ten Mile River are picnic tables, tennis courts, playgrounds, and a river walk. The park's **Looff Carousel,** built by Charles I.D. Looff in 1894, has 42 horses, three dogs, a lion, a camel, and a giraffe that are the earliest examples of the Danish immigrant's work. The carousel animals don't go up and down, but they move fast. Rides are 25¢. ⊠ *Newport Ave. (Rte. 1A)* ☎ *401/728–0500 Ext. 252 park information* ✉ *Free* ☉ *Park daily dawn–dusk, carousel July–early Sept., daily 10–4; late Apr.–June and early Sept.–mid-Oct., weekends 10–5.*

SPORTS AND THE OUTDOORS

BASEBALL

From April through early September, the **Pawtucket Red Sox** (⊠ *1 Ben Mondor Way 02860* ☎ *401/724–7300* ⊕ *www.pawsox.com* ✉ *Tickets $6–$10*), the Triple-A international league affiliate of the Boston Red Sox, play around 70 home games at **McCoy Stadium.**

WHERE TO EAT

¢–$
AMERICAN
★

✗**Modern Diner.** This 1941 Sterling Streamliner eatery—a classic from the heyday of the stainless-steel diner, painted in dashing burgundy and white—was the first diner listed on the National Register of Historic Places. The family-run Modern serves standard diner fare, but the real draw here are the daily specials, which rotate throughout the week and might include lobster Benedict, French toast with custard sauce and

Slater Mill in Pawtucket was the first factory in the country; it produced cotton using water power.

berries, and pancakes packed with cranberries and almonds. ✉ *364 East Ave.* ☎ *401/726–8390* 🚫 *No credit cards* ☻ *No dinner.*

WOONSOCKET

10 mi north of Pawtucket, 15 mi north of Providence.

Gritty Woonsocket, population 43,000, sees very few tourists and offers little in the way of sightseeing. However, it is home to one of the best museums about immigrant factory life and textile milling in the country, and this compact city on the Blackstone River also has a prolific French Canadian community. A steep hill on the city's northern edge looks down on the Blackstone River, which makes a dozen turns in its 5-mi course through town. The river's flow spawned textile mills that made the town a thriving community in the 19th and early 20th centuries.

EXPLORING

Museum of Work and Culture. Set up in a former textile mill, this attraction examines the lives of American factory workers and owners during the Industrial Revolution. Focusing on French Canadian immigrants to Woonsocket's mills, the museum's cleverly laid-out walk-through exhibits begin with a 19th-century Québécois farmhouse, then continue with displays of life in a 20th-century tenement, in a parochial school, in church, and on the shop floor. The genesis of the textile workers' union is described, as are the events that led to the National Textile Strike of 1934. There also an engaging presentation about child labor. ✉ *42 S. Main St.* ☎ *401/769–9675* ⊕ *www.rihs.org* ✉ *$7* ☻ *Weekdays 9:30–4, Sat. 10–5, Sun. 1–4.*

Fodor's Choice ★

NIGHTLIFE AND THE ARTS

The impressive entertainment lineup at **Chan's Fine Oriental Dining** (✉ 267 *Main St.* ☎ *401/765–1900* ⊕ *www.chanseggrollsandjazz.com*) includes blues, jazz, and folk performers. Reservations are advisable; tickets generally run about $10 to $20.

WHERE TO EAT AND STAY

¢–$

AMERICAN

✕ **Ye Olde English Fish & Chips.** Fresh fried fish and potatoes have been served at this Woonsocket institution for generations. The interior is unassuming, so it must be the inexpensive and excellent food that has kept folks coming back since 1922—not just fish-and-chips but first-rate clam chowder and fish cakes. In warm weather dine outside in Market Square, admiring the rush of the Blackstone River and waterfalls. ✉ 25 *S. Main St.* ☎ *401/762–3637* ▭ *MC, V* ☾ *Closed Sun. and Mon.*

$–$$

▦ **Pillsbury House.** Prospect Street stretches along the crest of the ridge north of the Blackstone River; its mansions, like the mansard-roof Pillsbury House, were built by mill owners in the late 1800s. The common room has a fireplace with a maple hearth. The three guest rooms on the second floor are furnished in Victorian style, with antiques, plants, high beds, and fringed lamp shades; the third-floor suite favors a more rustic-country aesthetic. Complimentary refreshments are served throughout the day, and there's a guest kitchenette on second floor. **Pros:** one of the few non-chain accommodations in the region; stunning architecture; great rates. **Cons:** old-fashioned decor isn't for everyone. ✉ *341 Prospect St.* ☎ *401/766–7983 or 800/205–4112* ⊕ *www.pillsburyhouse. com* ⇆ *3 rooms, 1 suite* ▭ *AE, D, DC, MC, V* ⚓ *In-room: a/c, no TV, Wi-Fi. In-hotel: Internet terminal, Wi-Fi hotspot* ⦿ *BP.*

6

SOUTH COUNTY

When the principal interstate traffic through Rhode Island shifted from U.S. 1 to Interstate 95 in the 1960s, the coastal part of the state—known locally as South County, although its true name is Washington County—was given a reprieve from the inevitabilities of development. In the past half century, strong local zoning laws have been instituted and a park system established. In some communities, land trusts were set up to buy open space.

Always a summertime destination, South County is now growing into a region of year-round residents. Still, the changes are being well managed by its communities, and the area's appeal as a summer playground has not diminished. South County is a wonderfully slower-paced alternative to Newport and Providence, a place where you can savor more than 100 mi of beautiful beaches, numerous public golf courses, and countless farm stands and historic sites and participate in outdoor sports, camping, and family amusements. The area's also popular for shopping, with cute village boutiques, arts and crafts stores, and an assortment of antiques shops.

ESSENTIALS

Visitor Information South County Tourism Council (✉ *4808 Tower Hill Rd., Wakefield* ☎ *401/789–4422 or 800/548–4662* ⊕ *www.southcountyri.com*).

WESTERLY

50 mi southwest of Providence, 100 mi southwest of Boston, 140 mi northeast of New York City.

Westerly is a busy little railroad town that grew up in the late 19th century around a major station on what is now the New York–Boston Amtrak corridor. During the Industrial Revolution and into the 1950s, Westerly was distinguished for its red granite, with which monuments throughout the country were made. It has since sprawled out along U.S. 1 and grown to include seven villages—Westerly itself, or downtown Westerly, Watch Hill, Dunn's Corners, Misquamicut, Bradford, Shelter Harbor, and Weekapaug—encompassing a 33-square-mi area.

Victorian and Greek Revival mansions line many streets off the town center, which is divided by Connecticut from the Pawcatuck River.

GETTING HERE AND AROUND

When traveling between New York City and Boston, Amtrak makes stops at Westerly, Kingston, and Providence.

ESSENTIALS

Transportation Information **Amtrak** (☎ *800/872–7245* ⊕ *www.amtrak.com*).

SPORTS AND THE OUTDOORS

Wilcox Park. Designed and created in 1898 by Warren Manning (an associate of Frederick Law Olmsted), this 14.5-acre Victorian strolling park in the heart of downtown Westerly boasts a pond, meadow, arboretum, perennial garden, sculptures, fountains, and monuments. Concerts, plays, and arts festivals are held periodically. ⊠ *71½ High St.* ☎ *401/596–2877* ⊕ *www.westerlylibrary.org.*

WHERE TO EAT AND STAY

$$$
ECLECTIC
✕ **Up River Café.** Perched dramatically on the edge of the Pawcatuck River and with tall windows and a large deck overlooking the water, this handsome restaurant serves some of the most reliably sophisticated and creative cuisine in South County; it also has an outstanding wine list. The menu favors seafood and steaks, including a terrific striped bass with fondue of crab, fennel, and leeks, but you can also sample a juicy burger topped with red-pepper aioli. The selection of post-dinner desserts and cocktails is extensive—consider the mocha pot de crème (baked then chilled custard) with orange-scented beignets. ⊠ *37 Main St., Westerly* ☎ *401/348–9700* ⊕ *www.theuprivercafe.net* ▤ *AE, D, MC, V* ☉ *No lunch.*

$–$$
🏠 **Grandview Bed and Breakfast.** Relaxed, homey, and affordable, this B&B on a rise above Route 1A has comfortable rooms with pastel and white hues and a slightly frilly sensibility. Those at the front have ocean views, and the common room has a TV with VCR. Breakfast is served on the porch year-round. **Pros:** affordable; great views of Block Island Sound. **Cons:** no TV in rooms; some rooms share a bath. ⊠ *212 Shore Rd., between Misquamicut and Weekapaug, Dunn's Corners* ☎ *401/596–6384 or 800/447–6384* ⊕ *www.grandviewbandb.com* 🛏 *8 rooms, 4 with bath* ⟨ *In-room: a/c, no TV, Wi-Fi. In-hotel: Wi-Fi hotspot* ▤ *AE, MC, V* ⟨⟩ *BP.*

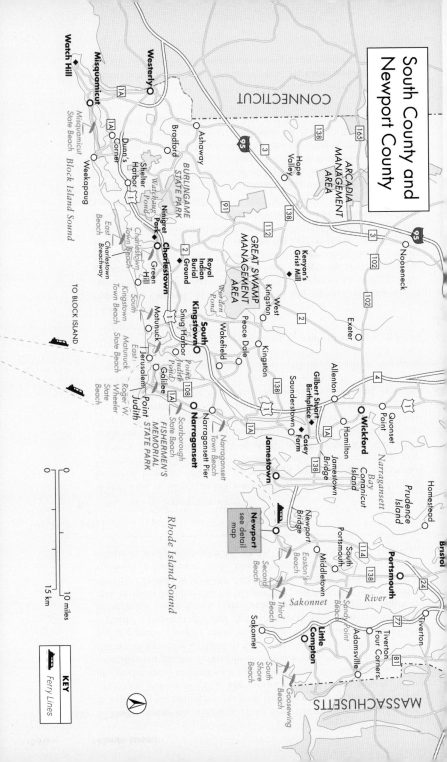

$$–$$$ 🏨 **Shelter Harbor Inn.** This inn, about 6 mi east of downtown Westerly in a quiet, rural setting not far from the beach, started out as a summer musicians' colony in 1911. The rooms, many of which have fireplaces and decks, are furnished with a combination of Victorian antiques and reproduction pieces. A third-floor sundeck with hot tub has views of the ocean and Block Island in the distance, and guests have use of a putting green, croquet lawn, and paddle tennis courts. A very good restaurant serves traditional American food. **Pros:** stunning grounds; great water views. **Cons:** some furnishings are a tad dated; walls are thin in main building. ✉ *10 Wagner Rd., off U.S. 1, Shelter Harbor* ☎ *401/322–8883 or 800/468–8883* ⊕ *www.shelterharborinn.com* ⤴ *24 rooms* ⚒ *In-room: a/c, Wi-Fi. In-hotel: restaurant, beachfront, Internet terminal, Wi-Fi hotspot* ═ *AE, D, DC, MC, V* ⦿⧈*BP.*

WATCH HILL

★ *6 mi south of downtown Westerly.*

Watch Hill, a Victorian-era resort village, contains almost 2 mi of beautiful beaches. Many of its well-kept summerhouses are owned by wealthy families who have passed ownership down through generations. Boating and socializing are the top activities for Watch Hill residents (there are no rental outfitters). Bay Street is a good place to shop for jewelry, summer clothing, and antiques. The community's two vintage summer hotels, both defunct for a time, have been given new life in recent years. The Watch Hill Inn opened in 2006, and, as of this writing, the venerable **Ocean House** (✉ *1 Bluff Ave.* ☎ *401/315–5599* ⊕ *www.oceanhouseri.com*) has been completely rebuilt in its classic Victorian style and is slated to open in summer 2010. It will contain 50 luxury rooms (plus 23 residential units), a full-service spa, and two restaurants.

EXPLORING

☻ **Flying Horse Carousel.** At the beach end of Bay Street, this is the oldest merry-go-round in America, built in 1867, as part of a traveling carnival that stopped traveling in Watch Hill. The horses, suspended from above rather than fastened to the floor, swing out when in motion; the faster the ride, the more they seem to fly. Each is hand-carved from a single piece of wood and has glass eyes and a real horsehair mane and tail. Only kids may ride the carousel. ✉ *Bay St.* ⊟ *$1* ☽ *Memorial Day–Columbus Day, weekdays 11–9, weekends 10–9.*

Watch Hill Lighthouse. An active U.S. Coast Guard station, this lighthouse has great views of the ocean and of Fishers Island, New York. A tiny museum contains exhibits. Parking is for the elderly; everyone else must walk from lots at the beach. Whether the museum is open or not, the grounds are strolling. ✉ *14 Lighthouse Rd.* ☎ *401/596–7761* ⊟ *Free* ☽ *Grounds daily 8–8. Museum July and Aug., Tues. and Thurs. 1–3.*

SHOPPING

Comina (✉ *117 Bay St.* ☎ *401/596–3218* ⊕ *www.comina.com*) displays international furnishings and accessories. **Mo Books and Art** (✉ *60 Bay St.* ☎ *401/348–0940* ⊕ *www.mobooksnart.com*) sports an impressive selection of children's books as well as an extensive array of photos and paintings depicting local maritime scenes and landscapes.

WHERE TO EAT AND STAY

$$–$$$

AMERICAN

★

✕**Olympia Tea Room.** Opened in 1916 as an ice cream parlor and overlooking the water, the Olympia has become one of South County's most celebrated dining options. Varnished wood booths and a soda fountain behind a long marble counter echo the restaurant's rich history. The kitchen prepares a mix of modern and traditional dishes, many with Italian and French influences, such as lamb shanks, gnocchi in Asiago cream sauce, and lobster salad. Save room for the "world-famous Avondale swan" dessert—a fantasy of ice cream, whipped cream, chocolate sauce, and puff pastry. ⊠ *74 Bay St.* ☎ *401/348–8211* ⊕ *www.olympiatearoom.com* ⌒ *Reservations not accepted* ⊟ *AE, MC, V* ⊗ *Closed Nov.–mid-Apr. and Tues. in Sept. and Oct.*

$

▦ **Watch Hill Inn & Annex.** Comprising an 1840s Victorian-style inn and a modern annex building added in 2007, this upscale hostelry consists of sunny condos and apartments rented nightly, weekly, or monthly. Many of these spacious units, which have kitchens and posh modern bathrooms, overlook Watch Hill's scenic bay, and the property sits along Watch Hill's main street of quirky galleries and boutiques. The hotel's seasonal restaurant (open mid-June to early September) serves traditional American fare and seafood; in sunny weather, you can dine on a deck overlooking the sea. **Pros:** steps from beaches and shops; many units have private decks. **Cons:** 2-night minimum stay required; pricey for the area. ⊠ *44 Bay St.* ☎ *401/348–6300* ⊕ *www.watchhillinn. com* ⇆ *24 apartments* ⌂ *In-room: a/c, kitchen, Internet, Wi-Fi (some). In-hotel: restaurant, bar, Internet terminal* ⊟ *MC, V.*

6

MISQUAMICUT

2½ mi northeast of Watch Hill.

Motels with beach towels hanging over porch railings jostle for attention in family-oriented, budget-friendly Misquamicut, where a giant waterslide, a 1915-vintage carousel, miniature golf, a game arcade, children's rides, batting cages, and fast-food stands scream summer vacation. The 7-mi-long beach, Rhode Island's longest state beach, is accessible year-round, but this is primarily a summertime destination, with amusements and most businesses open between Memorial Day and Labor Day.

EXPLORING

ⓒ **Atlantic Beach Park.** The largest and most popular of the several kid-oriented amusements along Misquamicut Beach, this festive facility has lots to keep families busy, including a carousel, bumper cars, a minigolf course, waterslides, batting cages, and a large arcade with more than 75 video and other games. ⊠ *323 Atlantic Ave.* *02891* ☎ *401/322–0504* ▥ *Free general admission; prices vary according to the ride or game* ⊗ *Mid-June–Labor Day, daily; mid-May–mid-June and Labor Day–mid-Oct., weekends; hours vary depending on the ride or game.*

SPORTS AND THE OUTDOORS

BEACH Seven-mi-long **Misquamicut State Beach** (✉ *Atlantic Ave.* ☎ 401/596–9097) is the state's longest; facilities include parking, showers, and a snack bar at the state-run beach pavilion.

WHERE TO EAT AND STAY

$$–$$$ ✕ **Maria's Seaside Café.** Although
MEDITERRANEAN casual, this upbeat dinner spot serves such complex dishes as sea scallops over Italian couscous with lobster meat and black-truffle essence and tagliatelle pasta with fresh tomatoes, spinach, pine nuts, and goat cheese. Maria's has the best wine list in the area. There is a kids' menu, but this restaurant is more adult-oriented than others along the beachfront. ✉ *132 Atlantic Ave.* ☎ *401/596–6886* ⊕ *www.mariasseasidecafe.com* ▭ *AE, MC, V* ⊘ *Closed early Oct.–May and Sun.–Thurs. mid-Sept.–early Oct. No lunch.*

$$–$$$ ⌂ **Breezeway Resort.** The Bellone family takes great pride in its accom-
★ modations: summery rooms, suites, villas with fireplaces, and hot tubs. The grounds hold a pool, shuffleboard, and fountains. **Pros:** spotless rooms; friendly vibe for families; nice range of room configurations. **Cons:** a bit noisy with so many kids; most rooms have neither Wi-Fi nor high-speed Internet; closed in winter. ✉ *70 Winnapaug Rd.* ☎ *401/348–8953 or 800/462–8872* ⊕ *www.breezewayresort.com* ⇄ *52 rooms, 14 suites, 2 villas* ⚭ *In-room: a/c, kitchen (some), refrigerator, Wi-Fi (some). In-hotel: pool, laundry service, Wi-Fi hotspot* ▭ *AE, D, DC, MC, V* ⊘ *Closed Nov.–Mar.* ⦿ *CP.*

CHARLESTOWN

12 mi northeast of Misquamicut.

Charlestown stretches along the Old Post Road (Route 1A). The 37-square-mi town, which is suburban in character, has parks, the largest saltwater marsh in the state, 7 mi of pristine beaches, and many oceanfront motels, summer chalets, and cabins.

SPORTS AND THE OUTDOORS

Burlingame State Park. This 2,100-acre park has nature trails, picnic and swimming areas, and campgrounds, as well as boating and fishing on Watchaug Pond. ✉ *75 Burlingame Park Rd.* ☎ *401/322–7337.*

★ **Ninigret National Wildlife Refuge.** Nine mi of trails cross 400 acres of diverse upland and wetland habitats—including grasslands, shrublands, wooded swamps, and freshwater ponds. It's a great spot for bird-watchers, consisting of two stretches of beach lands and marshes,

CLOSE UP

The Lore of Rhode Island Johnnycakes

Among the Ocean State's handful of regional culinary treats, the johnnycake (often spelled jonnycake) has enjoyed prominence the longest, its legacy traced directly to Native Americans who inhabited the region centuries before Europeans arrived. Similar in appearance to pancakes, and also commonly served for breakfast, topped with maple syrup, honey, fruit, or powdered sugar, these skillet-fried discs are made with flour from stone-ground cornmeal. Traditionalists prepare johnnycakes to be roughly the size of silver dollars, with a thin, slightly crisp and crepe-like consistency.

WHERE TO LEARN MORE
Built in the Colonial era, the West Kingston-area **Kenyon Corn Meal Company** (⊠ 21 Glen Rock Rd., Usquepaug ☎ 401/783–4054 or 800/753–6966 ⊕ www. kenyonsgristmill.com) still grinds cornmeal for johnnycakes the old-fashioned way, with enormous granite millstones. When you visit Kenyon's Grist Mill, you can watch the staff grind the flour. Afterward, purchase a bag of it at the on-site gift shop (or order online) so you can fry up your own johnnycakes at home.

WHERE TO TRY THEM
To sample fresh-made johnnycakes your best bet is to head to down-home diners.

■ **Jigger's Diner** (⊠ 145 E. Main St., East Greenwich ☎ 401/884–5388), a creaky, circa-1940s greasy-spoon in a bustling suburb just south of Providence, serves exceptionally tasty, authentically prepared johnnycakes.

■ In the sleepy coastal village of Little Compton, **Commons Lunch** (⊠ 48 Commons Way, Little Compton ☎ 401/635–4388) has long served first-rate johnnycakes.

■ In Newport, savor these hearty treats at the stainless-steel-clad **Bishop's 4th Street Diner** (⊠ 184 Admiral Kalbfus Rd., Newport ☎ 401/847–2069).

—Andrew Collins

6

plus the abandoned naval air station on Ninigret Pond. Visitors can explore an impressive collection of wildlife and natural history displays at the property's Kettle Pond Visitor Center. ⊠ 50 Bend Rd., off Rte. 1A ☎ 401/364–9124 ⊕ www.friendsnwr-ri.org ⊒ Free ☉ Daily dawn–dusk.

Ninigret Park. This 72-acre park features picnic grounds, ball fields, a bike path, tennis and basketball courts, nature trails, and a 3-acre spring-fed swimming pond. Also here is the **Frosty Drew Observatory and Nature Center** (☎ 401/364–9508 ⊕ www.frostydrew.org), which presents free nature and Friday night astronomy programs. ⊠ Park La., off Rte. 1A ☎ 401/364–1222.

BEACHES   The ½-mi **Charlestown Town Beach** (⊠ Charlestown Beach Rd. ☎ 401/364–7000) ends at a breachway that is part of Ninigret National Wildlife Refuge. This is the more easily accessed of the town's beaches, with a picnic area and restrooms, but it's also more crowded.

Point Judith Lighthouse is just one of 21 such beacons in the Ocean State.

SPORTS AND THE OUTDOORS

BEACHES Popular 1-mi-long **Narragansett Town Beach** (⊠ *Rte. 1A* ☎ *401/782–4563*) is regarded as a great surfing beach due to its smooth, curling waves. The beach is within walking distance of many hotels and guesthouses. Its pavilion has changing rooms, showers, and concessions. **Roger W. Wheeler State Beach** (⊠ *Sand Hill Cove Rd., Galilee* ☎ *401/789–3563*) has fine white sand, calm water, and a slight drop-off. There is a playground area, picnic tables, a bathhouse, and parking.

Fodor's Choice **Scarborough State Beach** (⊠ *Ocean Rd.* ☎ *401/789–2324*), considered ★ by many the jewel of the Ocean State's beaches because of its stunning views of where Narragansett Bay empties into the ocean, has a pavilion with showers and concessions, observation tower, and sitting areas along the boardwalk.

BOATING **Narrow River Kayaks** (⊠ *94B Middlebridge Rd.* ☎ *401/789–0334* ⊕ *www.narrowriverkayaks.com*) rents kayaks, canoes, and paddle boards and also leads tours on the ocean and up through Narragansett Bay.

FISHING **The Frances Fleet** (⊠ *33 State St., Point Judith* ☎ *401/783–4988* ⊕ *www.francesfleet.com*), with four vessels, operates day and overnight fishing trips. **Persuader** (☎ *401/783–5644*) leads sportfishing charters. **Excursions on the Prowler** (☎ *401/783–8487* ⊕ *www.prowlerchartersri.com*) can take you tuna and striped bass fishing.

WHALE-WATCHING During July and August, whale-watching excursions aboard the **Lady Frances** (⊠ *33 State St., Point Judith* ☎ *401/783–4988* ⊕ *www.francesfleet.com* ✉ *$35*) daily depart at 1 PM and return at 5:30 PM.

SURFING **Gansett Juice** (✉ *74 Narragansett Ave.* ☎ *401/789–7890* ⊕ *www. gansettjuice.com*) rents surfboards, body boards, and wet suits. Call 401/789–1954 for the daily surf report.

WHERE TO EAT

$-$$
SEAFOOD
★
✕ **Aunt Carrie's.** You'd hard-pressed to find a better short-order seafood joint than this family-owned restaurant that's been serving up Rhode Island shore dinners, clam cakes and chowder, and fried seafood since 1920. At the height of the season the lines can be long; one alternative is to order from the take-out window and picnic on the grounds of the nearby lighthouse. ✉ *1240 Ocean Rd., Point Judith* ☎ *401/783–7930* ⊕ *www.auntcarriesri.com* ➽ *Reservations not accepted* ▤ MC, V ⊗ *Closed Oct.–Mar.; weekdays Apr., May, and Sept.; and Tues.*

$-$$
SEAFOOD
✕ **George's of Galilee.** This restaurant at the mouth of the Point Judith Harbor has been a must for tourists since 1948. The "stuffies" (baked stuffed quahogs) are some of the best in the state, but you can also sample fried and broiled seafood, chicken, steak, and pasta, all at reasonable prices. Its proximity to the beach and its large outside bar on the second floor keep George's a busy place all summer—the restaurant is ultimately more about the setting than the food. The building has been undergoing a massive renovation, slated for completion in 2012, but remains open during the process. ✉ *250 Sand Hill Cove Rd.* ☎ *401/783–2306* ⊕ *www.georgesofgalilee.com* ➽ *Reservations not accepted* ▤ D, MC, V ⊗ *Closed Dec. and weekdays Nov. and Jan.–Mar.*

$$-$$$
SPANISH
Fodor'sChoice
★
✕ **Spain of Narragansett.** This swank Spanish restaurant earns high marks for superbly prepared food and deft service. Worthy appetizers include shrimp in garlic and olive oil, mushroom caps stuffed with seafood, and grilled smoked chorizo. Entrées range from traditional paella to hefty *jefe* steak (sautéed tenderloin with artichoke hearts, mushrooms, and a Rioja-mustard-garlic sauce) for two. There are few more impressive wine lists in the state. Arched entryways and tall plants help create a Mediterranean mood, and in summer you can dine on a patio anchored by a three-tier fountain. ✉ *1144 Ocean Rd.* ☎ *401/783–9770* ⊕ *www. spainri.com* ▤ AE, D, DC, MC, V ⊗ *Closed Mon. No lunch.*

$$-$$$
AMERICAN
★
✕ **Turtle Soup.** Be prepared to wait for a table at this locally revered restaurant inside a restored Victorian house overlooking Narragansett Bay. The dining room oozes simplicity and comfort, with gleaming wood paneling and wood floors; a sitting room provides a fireplace and overstuffed chairs. The menu focuses on contemporary American cuisine with Mediterranean influences. You might try the pan-seared crab cakes with a smoked jalapeño remoulade, followed by roast duck with a marsala-fig glaze topped with a black-cherry emulsion. There's also a light menu of pizzas, burgers, and small plates. ✉ *113 Ocean Rd.* ☎ *401/792–8683* ⊕ *www.turtlesoupri.com* ➽ *Reservations not accepted* ▤ AE, D, MC, V ⊗ *No lunch weekdays. Closed Mon. Oct.–Mar.*

WHERE TO STAY

$
Blueberry Cove Inn. This warmly furnished, grand historic inn is set along an attractive tree-lined residential street in Narragansett. Room decor manages a pleasant balance between well-chosen antiques and tasteful, modern color schemes, and all rooms have such handy

amenities as TVs with DVD players and CD clock radios. Innkeepers Seely and David Gerraughty prepare an extensive breakfast, with some dishes using fresh berries grown on the property. Periodically, Blueberry Cove hosts chocolate-themed weekends, during which guests sample more than 20 decadent dessert treats. **Pros:** a few blocks from the beach; outstanding breakfasts; exceptionally plush bedding. **Cons:** not on the beach. ⊠ *75 Kingstown Rd.* ☎ *401/792–9865 or 800/478–1426* ⊕ *www. blueberrycoveinn.com* ⬅ *7 rooms, 2 suites* ♿ *In-room:a/c, refrigerator (some), DVD (some), Wi-Fi. In-hotel: Internet terminal, Wi-Fi hotspot* ⊟ *MC, V* ⦿ *BP.*

$$ 🏠 **The Richards.** Imposing and magnificent, this 8,500-square-foot,
★ English-style stone mansion anchoring a 200-acre estate has a Gothic mystique that is quite different from the spirit of the typical summer-house. French windows in the common rooms downstairs open up to views of a lush landscape, and a fishpond is the centerpiece of the gardens. A fire crackles in the library fireplace on chilly afternoons. Some rooms have 19th-century English antiques, floral-upholstered furniture, and fireplaces, and a decanter of sherry awaits you in each. **Pros:** remarkable architecture; breakfast is great; reasonable rates. **Cons:** a bit of a walk from the beach; no TV in rooms. ⊠ *144 Gibson Ave.* ☎ *401/789–7746* ⊕ *www.therichardsbnb.com* ⬅ *3 rooms, 1 suite* ♿ *In-room: a/c, no TV, Wi-Fi. In-hotel: Wi-Fi hotspot* ⊟ *No credit cards* ⦿ *BP.*

WICKFORD

★ *12 mi north of Narragansett Pier, 15 mi south of Providence.*

The Colonial village of Wickford has a little harbor, dozens of 18th- and 19th-century homes, several antiques shops, and boutiques selling locally made jewelry and crafts, home accents and gifts, and clothing. This bayside spot is the kind of almost-too-perfect salty New England period piece that is usually conjured up only in books and movies. It is rumored that Wickford was John Updike's model for the New England of his novel *The Witches of Eastwick.*

EXPLORING

Casey Farm. This historic farm's 1751 homestead overlooks Narragansett Bay off Route 1A south of Wickford. During the 19th century the summer residence of the Casey family, who leased the land to tenant farmers, it is today a community-supported farm operated by resident managers who raise organically grown vegetables. Nearly 30 mi of stone walls surround the 300-acre farmstead. ⊠ *2325 Boston Neck Rd., Saunderstown* ☎ *401/295–1030* ⊕ *www.historicnewengland.org* 🎫 *$4* 🕐 *June–mid-Oct., Sat. 9–2.*

Old Narragansett Church. Now called St. Paul's, this church was built in 1707 and is one of the oldest Episcopal churches in the United States. ⊠ *55 Main St.* ☎ *401/294–4357* ⊕ *www.stpaulswickford.org* 🕐 *Daily, hrs vary.*

★ **Smith's Castle.** Built in 1678 by Richard Smith Jr., this castle is a beautifully preserved saltbox plantation house on the quiet shore of an arm of Narragansett Bay. It was the site of many orations by Roger Williams, from whom Smith bought the surrounding property, and includes one of the first military burial grounds (open during daylight hours) in the country: a marked mass grave holding 40 colonists killed in the Great Swamp battle of 1676, during which the Narragansetts were nearly annihilated, ending King Philip's War in Rhode Island. ⊠ *55 Richard Smith Dr., 1 mi north of Wickford* ☎ *401/294–3521* ⊕ *www. smithscastle.org* ☜ *$5* ⊘ *Guided tours at noon, 1, 2, and 3 June–Aug., Thurs.–Sun.; May, Sept., and Oct., Fri.–Sun.*

SPORTS AND THE OUTDOORS

BOATING In Wickford Harbor, the **Kayak Centre** (⊠ *9 Phillip St.* ☎ *401/295–4400* ⊕ *www.kayakcentre.com*) rents kayaks and provides lessons.

SHOPPING

ANTIQUES The **Hour Glass** (⊠ *15 W. Main St.* ☎ *401/295–8724* ⊕ *www.the-hourglass.com*) carries antique barometers, clocks, tide clocks, thermometers, and the like. The **Wickford Art Association** (⊠ *36 Beach St.* ☎ *401/294–6840* ⊕ *www.wickfordart.org*) sells the wares of numerous local talents and has juried art shows.

CRAFTS Needlepoint pillows, leather journals, lamps, and woven throws are a few of the gifts and home furnishings at **Askham & Telham Inc.** (⊠ *12 Main St.* ☎ *401/295–0891*).

NEWPORT COUNTY

Perched gloriously on the southern tip of Aquidneck Island and bounded on three sides by water, Newport is one of the great sailing cities of the world and the host to world-class jazz, blues, folk, classical music, and film festivals. Colonial houses and gilded-age mansions grace the city. Besides Newport itself, Newport County also encompasses the two other communities of Aquidneck Island—Middletown and Portsmouth—plus Conanicut Island, also known as Jamestown, to the west, and Tiverton and Little Compton, abutting Massachusetts to the east. Little Compton is a remote, idyllic town that presents a strong contrast to Newport's quick pace. Narrow and scenic Mount Hope Bridge carries traffic north from Aquidneck Island to Bristol, the most charming of the three towns that make up the East Bay region, which is encompassed entirely within Bristol County, one of the nation's smallest geographically.

GETTING HERE AND AROUND

CAB TRAVEL Cozy Cab runs a shuttle service ($25 each way) between T. F. Green Airport (in Warwick) and the Newport Visitors' Information Center, as well as major hotels.

FERRY TRAVEL If you're staying in Newport but want to hop over to Jamestown, the Jamestown and Newport Ferry Co. runs a passenger ferry from Newport's Bowen's Landing and Long Wharf (and, on request, Fort Adams, Rose Island, and Goat Island) to Jamestown's Ferry Wharf. The 35-foot passenger ferry operates daily from Memorial Day to Labor Day weekend. It departs on its half-hour voyage from Ferry Wharf about every 1½ hours, from 9:50 AM to 8 PM (9 PM on weekends). The last run leaves Newport at 8:30 PM (9:45 on weekends). Oldport Marine

Services operates a water-taxi service ($3 one-way, $5 round-trip) for boaters in Newport Harbor.

PARKING In Newport, a number of lots around town offer pay parking (the largest and most economical is the garage behind the Newport Visitors' Information Center); street parking is near impossible in summer.

ESSENTIALS

Transportation Contacts Cozy Cab (☎ *401/846–2500 or 800/846–1502* ⊕ *www.cozytrans.com).* **Jamestown and Newport Ferry Co.** (☎ *401/423–9900* ⊕ *www.conanicutmarina.com/ferry.html* 🖘 *$17 all-day pass).* **Oldport Marine Services** (☎ *401/847–9109* ⊕ *www.oldportmarine.com).*

Visitor Information Newport County Convention and Visitors Bureau (✉ *Newport Visitors' Information Center, 23 America's Cup Ave., Newport* ☎ *401/845–9123 or 800/976–5122* ⊕ *www.gonewport.com).*

JAMESTOWN

25 mi south of Providence, 3 mi west of Newport.

The 9-mi-long, 1-mi-wide landmass that goes by the names Jamestown and Conanicut Island comprises the east and west passages of Narragansett Bay. A military outpost in days gone by, the island was once considered an impediment to commercial cross-bay shipping. In 1940 the Jamestown Bridge linked it to western Rhode Island, and in 1969 the Newport Bridge completed the cross-bay route, connecting Newport to the entire South County area. Summer residents have come to Jamestown since the 1880s, but never to the same extent as to Watch Hill, Narragansett, or Newport. The locals' "We're not a T-shirt town" attitude has resulted in a relatively low number of visitors, even in July and August.

EXPLORING

Jamestown Fire Department Memorial Museum. A working 1859 hand tub and a horse-drawn steam pump are among the holdings at this informal display of firefighting equipment in a garage that once housed the fire company. ✉ *50 Narragansett Ave.* ☎ *401/423–1820* 🖘 *Free* ☉ *Daily 7–3; inquire next door at fire department if door is locked.*

Jamestown Windmill. Once common in Rhode Island, the English-designed windmill, built in 1789, ground corn for more than 100 years—and it still works. ✉ *North Rd. southeast of Watson Farm* ☎ *401/423–1798* 🖘 *Free* ☉ *Mid-June–Aug., weekends 1–4.*

Watson Farm. This 285-acre spread, dedicated to educating the public about agrarian culture, has 2 mi of trails along Jamestown's southwestern shore with amazing views of Narragansett Bay and North Kingstown. Thomas Carr Watson's family had worked this farm for 190 years before he bequeathed it to the Society for the Preservation of New England Antiquities when he died in 1979. ✉ *455 North Rd.* ☎ *401/423–0005* ⊕ *www.spnea.org/visit/homes/watson.htm* 🖘 *$4* ☉ *June–mid-Oct., Tues., Thurs., and Sun. 1–5.*

SPORTS AND THE OUTDOORS

Beavertail State Park. Water conditions range from tranquil to harrowing at this park straddling the southern tip of Conanicut Island. The currents and surf are famously deadly during rough seas and high winds, but on a clear, calm day, the park's craggy shoreline seems intended for sunning, hiking, and climbing. The **Beavertail Lighthouse Museum**, in what was the lighthouse keeper's quarters, has displays about Rhode Island's lighthouses. ⊠ *Beavertail Rd.* ☎ *401/423–3270* ⬚ *Free* ⊙ *Museum June–Labor Day, daily 10–4; park daily dawn–dusk.*

Fort Wetherill State Park. An outcropping of stone cliffs at the tip of the southeastern peninsula, this green space has been a picnic destination since the 1800s. There's great swimming at the small cove, and it's a favorite of snorkelers and scuba divers. ⊠ *Ocean St.* ☎ *401/423–1771* ⬚ *Free* ⊙ *Daily dawn–dusk.*

BEACHES Sandy **Mackerel Cove Beach** (⊠ *Beavertail Rd.*) is sheltered from the currents of Narragansett Bay, making it a great spot for families.

GOLF **Jamestown Golf Course** (⊠ *245 Conanicus Ave.* ☎ *401/423–9930*) has a crisp 9-hole course for a mere $16.

WHERE TO EAT AND STAY

$$$ ✕ **Chopmist Charlie's.** An old-school, some might even say ramshackle,
SEAFOOD seafood house in the center of Jamestown's small commercial strip, this reliable spot serves all the regional Rhode Island favorites: stuffies, clear-broth chowder, clam cakes, steamers, and broiled or fried fish. It's also one of the better values in Newport County for sampling steamed lobsters. Service is cheery and brisk. ⊠ *40 Narragansett Ave.* ☎ *401/423–1020* ⊟ *AE, MC, V* ⊙ *Reservations not accepted.*

$$–$$$ ✕ **Trattoria Simpatico.** A jazz trio plays on weekday evenings and sunny
ITALIAN Sunday afternoons at Jamestown's signature restaurant, while patrons dine alfresco under a copper beech tree. An herb garden, fieldstone walls, and white linen complete the picture. You can munch on splendid salads, Northern Italian pasta dishes, meats prepared with a Continental flair, and a handful of Asian-fusion dishes. Memorable are the tamarind-glazed ribs and braised-beef cassoulet appetizers and the maple-soy glazed tuna pad thai as an entrée. Reservations are essential on summer weekends. ⊠ *13 Narragansett Ave.* ☎ *401/423–3731* ⊕ *www.trattoriasimpatico.com* ⊟ *AE, D, MC, V* ⊙ *No lunch Mon.–Thurs.*

$–$$ ▦ **East Bay B&B.** This 1893 Victorian is peaceful day and night, even
★ though it's only a block from Jamestown's two main streets and wharf. Rooms underwent a major renovation in 2009 and are generous in size with high-quality linens, soft robes, and modern conveniences such as Wi-Fi and alarm-clock radios with MP3 players; the common room has a fireplace. The owners Greg and Donna Kohler, both talented chefs, prepare a copious homemade breakfast—strawberry crepes are a favorite. A very friendly cat welcomes attention from guests. **Pros:** much more affordable than Newport accommodations; large rooms; close to restaurants. **Cons:** a car or ferry ride is needed to explore Newport. ⊠ *14 Union St.* ☎ *401/423–0330 or 800/243–1107* ⊕ *www.eastbaybnb.com* ⇆ *4 rooms* ⌂ *In-room: a/c, DVD, Wi-Fi. In-hotel: Wi-Fi hotspot* ⊟ *AE, MC, V* ⊙| *BP.*

6

$$$$ ⊞ **Wyndham Bay Voyage.** In 1889 this Victorian inn was shipped from Newport to its current location and named in honor of its trip. The one-bedroom suites, furnished in floral prints and pastels, have been sold as time-shares, which makes availability tight in summer. The facilities are plentiful, the view memorable. The restaurant is known for its Sunday brunch, but dinner, where you might find juniper-rubbed venison in an espresso demi-glace, is first-rate, too. **Pros:** kitchens in rooms; overlooks water; easy walk to village restaurants. **Cons:** feels a time-share. ⊠ *150 Conanicus Ave.* ☎ *401/423–2100* ⊕ *www.bayvoyageinn.com* ⤺ *32 suites* ⌂ *In-room: a/c, kitchen, Wi-Fi. In-hotel: restaurant, bar, pool, gym, Internet terminal* ⊟ *AE, D, DC, MC, V.*

NEWPORT

30 mi south of Providence, 80 mi south of Boston.

The island city of Newport preserves Colonial industry and gilded-age splendor like no other place in the country. Settled in 1639 by a small band of religious dissenters from Massachusetts, Newport earned a reputation for tolerance, and its prime location at the mouth of Narragansett Bay ensured its success. The golden age of Colonial Newport ran from roughly 1720 to the 1770s. Making the city a leader in New World maritime commerce were its shipbuilders, the best in North America; its products, such as cheese, candles, clocks, furniture, and livestock; and its profitable slave trade (although in 1774 Rhode Island became the first colony to outlaw trading in slaves).

In the 1800s, Newport was a summer playground for the very wealthy, those titans of the Gilded Age who built fabulous homes of huge proportions and elaborate interiors overlooking the Atlantic. These mansions served as proving grounds for the country's best young architects, who designed estates for the Vanderbilts, Berwinds, Astors, and Belmonts.

Recreational sailing is a huge industry in Newport today. For those not arriving by water, a boat tour of the harbor is a great way to get your feet wet.

Newport has much to offer in a relatively small geographical area—mansions, beaches, seafood restaurants, art galleries, shopping, and, some say, more B&Bs per capita than anywhere else in the country. In summer, it can be crowded (3.5 million people visit each year). Yet the quality of its sights and its arts festivals persuade many to brave the crowds. In fall and spring, you can explore the city without having to stand in line.

Away from downtown, the gilded-age mansions of Bellevue Avenue are what many people associate most with Newport. These late-19th-century homes are almost obscenely grand, laden with ornate rococo detail and designed with a determined one-upmanship *(⇨ Mansions of Newport).*

EXPLORING
DOWNTOWN NEWPORT

More than 200 pre-Revolutionary buildings (mostly private residences) remain in Newport. Most of these treasures are in the neighborhood known as the Point.

With the exception of Ocean Drive, Newport is a walker's city. In summer, traffic is thick, and the narrow one-way streets can be mazelike. It's worth parking in a pay lot and leaving your car behind while you visit in-town sights.

Numbers in the margin correspond to numbers in the Newport map.

❺ Colony House. This 1739 redbrick structure above downtown's Washington Square was the center of political activity in Colonial Newport and Rhode Island. On July 20, 1776, the Declaration of Independence was read here to Newporters. In 1781, George Washington met here with French commander Count Rochambeau, cementing the alliance that led to the American victory at Yorktown. ⊠ *Washington Sq.* ☎ *401/846–0813* ⊕ *www.newporthistorytours.org* ☜ *Donation suggested* ☉ *Tours by appointment.*

❶ Common Burial Ground. On Farewell Street, which is lined with historic cemeteries, this 17th-century graveyard holds many a tombstone made by John Stevens, who opened his stone-carving shop in 1705 (the business still thrives today). The tombstones are fine examples of Colonial stone carving.

❸ Great Friends Meeting House. Built in 1699, this is the oldest house of worship in Rhode Island. With its wide-plank floors, simple benches, balcony, and beam ceiling (considered lofty by Colonial standards), the two-story shingle structure reflects the quiet reserve and steadfast faith of Colonial Quakers. ⊠ *29 Farewell St.* ☎ *401/846–0813* ☜ *$5* ☉ *Tours by appointment.*

❾ Newport Art Museum and Art Association. Richard Morris Hunt designed the Stick-style 1862 Victorian that houses this community-supported center for the arts. The galleries exhibit contemporary New England works, as well as paintings by such esteemed regional luminaries as John La Farge, George Inness, Fitz Henry Lane, Gilbert Stuart, and many others. ⊠ *76 Bellevue Ave.* ☎ *401/848–8200* ⊕ *www.newportartmuseum. org* ☜ *$10* ☉ *Late May–early Sept., Mon.–Sat. 10–5, Sun. noon–5; early Sept.–late May, Mon.–Sat. 10–4, Sun. noon–4.*

❽ Redwood Library. This Roman templelike building was built in 1747 ★ and has been in use for its original purpose ever since, making it the oldest lending library in the United States. Although it may look like a Roman temple, it is actually made of wood; the exterior paint is mixed with sand to make it resemble cut stone. The library's paintings include works by Gilbert Stuart and Rembrandt Peale. Free guided tours (a donation is suggested) are given weekday mornings at 10:30 AM. ⊠ *50 Bellevue Ave.* ☎ *401/847–0292* ⊕ *www.redwoodlibrary.org* ☜ *Free* ☉ *Mon.–Wed., Fri., and Sat. 9:30–5:30, Thurs. 9:30–8, Sun. 1–5.*

6

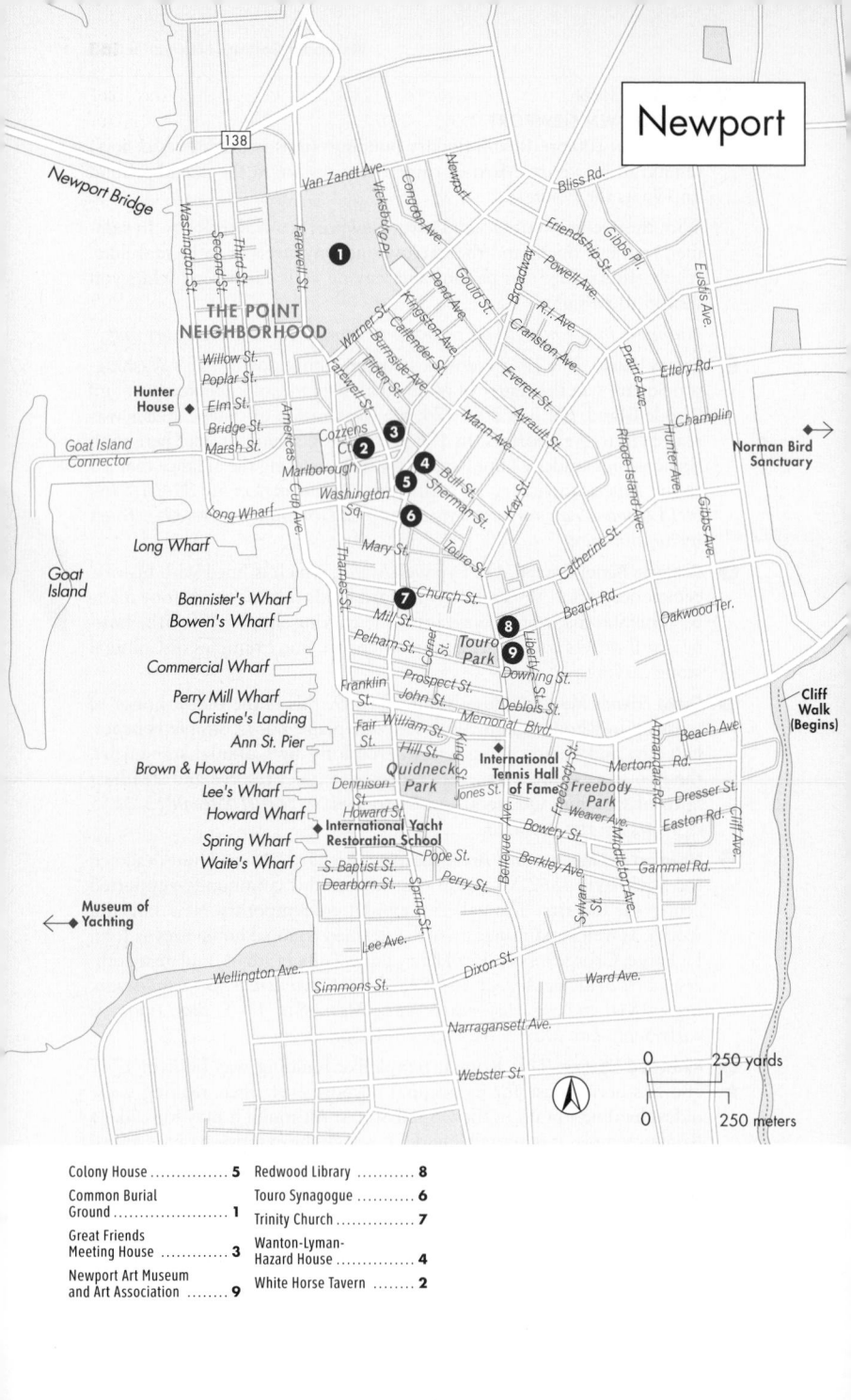

Newport

138

Newport Bridge

Van Zandt Ave.

Washington St.
Third St.
Second St.
Farewell St.

THE POINT NEIGHBORHOOD

Hunter House ◆

Goat Island Connector

Willow St.
Poplar St.
Elm St.
Bridge St.
Marsh St.

Americas Cup Ave.

Goat Island

Long Wharf

Long Wharf

Bannister's Wharf
Bowen's Wharf

Commercial Wharf

Perry Mill Wharf
Christine's Landing
Ann St. Pier
Brown & Howard Wharf
Lee's Wharf
Howard Wharf
Spring Wharf
Waite's Wharf

◆ International Yacht Restoration School

Museum of Yachting
← ◆

Hicksburg Pl.
Congdon Ave.
Newport

Bliss Rd.

Warner St.
Burnside St.
Tilden St.
Farewell St.

Pond Ave.
Kingston Ave.
Callender Ave.
Gould St.

Friendship St.
Powell Ave.
Gibbs Pl.
R.I. Ave.
Broadway
Cranston Ave.

Everett St.
Ayrault St.
Mann Ave.

Eustis Ave.
Ellery Rd.
Champlin
Prairie Ave.
Rhode Island Ave.
Hunter Ave.

Norman Bird Sanctuary ◆ →

Cozzens Ct.
Marlborough St.
Washington Sq.

Bull St.
Sherman St.
Kay St.
Catherine St.
Gibbs Ave.
Oakwood Ter.

Mary St.
Touro St.
Beach Rd.

Thames St.

Church St.
Mill St.
Pelham St.
Corne St.

Touro Park
Liberty St.
Downing St.

Cliff Walk (Begins)

Franklin St.
Prospect St.
John St.
Deblois St.

Fair St.
William St.
Hill St.
Memorial Blvd.

Dennison St.
Howard St.

Quidneck Park

King St.
Jones St.

International Tennis Hall of Fame

Mertonale Rd.
Freebody Park
Weaver Ave.
Beach Ave.
Dresser St.
Easton Rd.
Cliff Ave.
Gammel Rd.

Pope St.
S. Baptist St.
Dearborn St.

Bellevue Ave.
Bowery St.
Berkley St.
Perry St.
Sylvan Ave.
Middleton Ave.

Lee Ave.
Spring St.
Dixon St.
Ward Ave.

Wellington Ave.
Simmons St.

Narragansett Ave.

Webster St.

N

0 ____ 250 yards
0 ____ 250 meters

6 Touro Synagogue. Jews were attracted by Rhode Island's religious toler-
Fodor's Choice ance; they arrived in Newport as early as 1658, possibly from Holland
★ or the West Indies. At first they worshipped in homes, but by 1758
they were numerous enough to begin building a synagogue. Dedicated
in 1763, the Touro Synagogue is the oldest surviving synagogue in the
United States. Simple on the outside, the Georgian building, designed
by Peter Harrison, has an elaborate interior that was fully renovated
in 2005. Its classical style influenced Thomas Jefferson in the building
of Monticello and the University of Virginia. In August 2009, the John
L. Loeb Visitors Center opened on the synagogue property; it contains
two floors of state-of-the-art exhibits and multimedia presentations that
interpret early American Jewish life as well as the Colonial history of
Newport. ⊠ *85 Touro St.* ☎ *401/847–4794* ⊕ *www.tourosynagogue.org*
🖾 *Donation suggested* ⊗ *Guided tours on the ½ hr: early July–early
Sept., Sun.–Fri. 10–5; late May–early July and early Sept.–Oct., Sun.–
Fri. noon–3; Nov.–late May, Fri. 1* PM *tour only, Sun. 11–3. Services:
one in morning and one in evening, call for times.*

**QUICK
BITES**

Ideal for a quick and affordable bite, Ocean Coffee Roasters (⊠ 22 Washington Sq. ☎ 401/846–6060 ⊕ www.oceancoffee.com) serves fresh-roasted
coffee and enticing baked goods, plus a nice range of egg dishes, soups,
salads, and sandwiches.

7 Trinity Church. This Colonial beauty was built in 1724 and modeled after
London churches designed by Sir Christopher Wren. A special feature of
the interior is the three-tier wineglass pulpit, the only one of its kind in
America. The lighting, woodwork, and palpable feeling of history make
attending Episcopal services here an unforgettable experience. ⊠ *Queen
Anne Sq.* ☎ *401/846–0660* ⊕ *www.trinitynewport.org* 🖾 *Free* ⊗ *May–
mid-June, weekdays 10–1; mid-June–early July, weekdays 10–4; early
July–Aug., daily 10–4; Sept.–mid-Oct., weekdays 10–4; mid-Oct.–late
Oct., weekdays 10–1. Sun. services at 8 and 10.*

4 Wanton-Lyman-Hazard House. This late-17th-century residence presents
a window on the Colonial and Revolutionary history of Newport. The
dark-red building was the site of the city's Stamp Act riot of 1765. After
the British Parliament levied a tax on most printed material, the Sons of
Liberty stormed the house, which was occupied by a prominent Loyal-
ist. ⊠ *17 Broadway* ☎ *401/846–0813* ⊕ *www.newporthistorytours.org*
🖾 *Donation suggested* ⊗ *Tours by appointment.*

2 White Horse Tavern. William Mayes, the father of a successful and notorious pirate, received a tavern license in 1687, which makes this building,
built in 1673, the oldest still-operating tavern in the United States. Its
gambrel roof, low dark-beam ceilings, cavernous fireplace, and uneven
plank floors epitomize Newport's Colonial charm. ⊠ *26 Marlborough
St.* ☎ *401/849–3600* ⊕ *www.whitehorsetavern.com.*

GREATER NEWPORT
Just outside of downtown you can begin discovering elaborate, stunning mansions. Along the waterfront, these "summer cottages" were
built by wealthy families in the late 1800s and early 1900s as seasonal
residences. ⇨ *See Mansions of Newport.*

Continued on page 376

Above left, stair hall of Château-sur-Mer, the first of the Bellevue Avenue mansions.

Opposite, Romantic Rosecliff's terracotta tiles look magical at dusk.

Below left, Statues of cherubs watch over the exterior of the Elms.

Right, Go behind the entrance gate on a tour of the Breakers.

Gilded Age Gems
THE MANSIONS OF NEWPORT

By Andrew Collins and Debbie Harmsen

Would you call a home with 70 rooms a cottage? If not, you're obviously not Cornelius Vanderbilt II. The Breakers, the "summer cottage" of the 19th-century multimillionaire, is one of a dozen mansions in Newport that are now by far the city's top attractions. Many of the homes are open to the public for tours, giving you a peek into the lives of the privileged.

THE SOCIAL SCENE

The Breakers dining room, just one of the opulent mansion's 70 rooms.

To truly appreciate a visit to Newport's mansions, you need to understand the times and the players—those who built these opulent homes and summered here for six weeks a year.

Newport at the turn of the 20th century was where the socialites of Boston, New York, and Philadelphia came for the summer. They were among the richest people in America at the time—from railroad tycoons and coal barons to plantation owners.

The era during which they lived here, the late 1800s up through the 1920s, is often referred to as the Gilded Age, a term coined by Mark Twain and co-author Charles Dudley Warner in a book by the same name. It was a time when who you knew was everything. Caroline Schermerhorn Astor was the queen of New York and Newport society; her list of the "Four Hundred" was the first social register. Three übersocialites were Alva Vanderbilt Belmont, Mary Ann (Mamie) Fish, and Tessie Oelrichs. These ladies who seriously lunched threw most of *the* parties in Newport.

While the women gossiped, planned soirees, and dressed and redressed thoughout the summer days, the men were usually off yachting.

In terms of the deepest pockets, the two heavyweight families during Newport's Gilded Age were the Vanderbilts and the Astors.

Madeleine Force was only 19 when she married John Jacob Astor IV at the Beechwood mansion in 1911; he was 47.

LEADING FAMILIES

Actors at Astors' Beechwood relive the year 1891.

Alva Vanderbilt Belmont

Cornelius Vanderbilt

John Jacob Astor IV

John Jacob Astor

THE VANDERBILTS Cornelius Vanderbilt I, called Commodore Cornelius Vanderbilt, built his empire on steamships and railroads. Cornelius had amassed almost $100 million before he died in 1877. He gave most of it to his son William Henry, who, also shrewd in the railroading business, nearly doubled the family fortune over the next decade. William Henry Vanderbilt willed $70 million to his son Cornelius Vanderbilt II, who became the chairman and president of New York Central Railroad; and $55 million to son William K. Vanderbilt, who also managed railroads for a while and saw his yacht, *The Defender*, win the America's Cup in 1895. One of Cornelius Vanderbilt II's sons, Alfred Gwynne Vanderbilt, died on the *Lusitania*, which sank three years after the *Titanic*. **Visit:** The Breakers, Marble House.

THE ASTORS Meanwhile, in the Astor camp, John Jacob Astor IV, who perished on the *Titanic*, had the riches his great-granddad had made in the fur trade as well as his own millions earned from successful real estate ventures, including New York City hotels such as the St. Regis and the Astoria (later the Waldorf–Astoria). His mother was Caroline Astor. **Visit:** Beechwood.

WHICH MANSION SHOULD I VISIT?

Even though the 12 Newport "summer cottages" were inhabited for only six weeks each year, it would take you almost that long to explore all the grand rooms and manicured grounds. Each mansion has its own style and unique features. Here are the characteristics of each to help you choose those you'd like to visit:

Astors' Beechwood: Home of Social Register founder Caroline Astor; actors in period costumes make it less stuffy and more fun; fairly pricey to visit.

⭐ **Belcourt Castle:** An incredible (and quirky) collection of furnishings and art; based on French 18th-century hunting lodge; ghost tours.

⭐ **The Breakers:** The most opulent; enormous Italian Renaissance mansion built by Cornelius Vanderbilt II; tours are often big and very crowded; open most of the year.

Château-sur-Mer: The prettiest gardens and grounds; High Victorian–style mansion built in 1852; enlarged and modified in 1870s by Richard Morris Hunt.

Portrait of Mrs. Cornelius Vanderbilt II circa 1880, The Breakers.

Chepstow: Italianate villa with a fine collection of art; a bit less wow factor; summer hours only.

⭐ **The Elms:** A French château-style home with 10 acres of stunningly restored grounds; a fascinating "behind-the-scenes" audio-headset tour; open most of the year.

Hunter House: Downtown location is apart from Bellevue Avenue mansions; smaller-scale home with Colonial furniture; pricey admission; summer hours only.

Isaac Bell House: Currently undergoing restoration; less dramatic shingled Victorian displays an unusual mix of influences; less visited; summer hours only.

Kingscote: Gothic Revival–style home includes early Tiffany glass; one of the first summer cottages built in 1841; summer hours only.

⭐ **Marble House:** Outrageously opulent and sometimes crowded; former Vanderbilt home modeled on Petit Trianon in Versailles; tour at your own pace with digital audio tour; open most of the year.

MANSION TOURS

Eleven historic properties are maintained by the **Preservation Society of Newport County** (☎ 401/8479–1000 ⊕ www.newportmansions. org). Both guided tours and audio tours are available; you can purchase a combination ticket to see multiple properties for a substantial discount. (Astors' Beechwood, Belcourt Castle, and Rough Point, not operated by this group, are not included in the combination ticket.) The hours and days the houses are open in fall and winter do change, so it's wise to call ahead.

Rosecliff: Romantic 1902 mansion; modeled after Grand Trianon in Versailles; somewhat crowded tours.

Rough Point: More contemporary perspective in 20th-century furniture; 1889 English manor–style home; home of tobacco heiress Doris Duke; tours are expensive and have limited availability.

Consider viewing mansions from the Cliff Walk for a different perspective.   Marble House at night.

TOP EXPERIENCE

For a view of the mansions from the backyards, try the ★ **Cliff Walk,** which runs 3 1/2 mi south along Newport's cliffs from Easton's Beach (also called First Beach) to Bailey's Beach. The promenade has views of sumptuous mansions on one side and the rocky coastline on the other; walking any section of it is worth the effort. The Cliff Walk can be accessed from any road running east off Bellevue Avenue. The unpaved sections can be difficult for small children, strollers, or people with mobility problems.

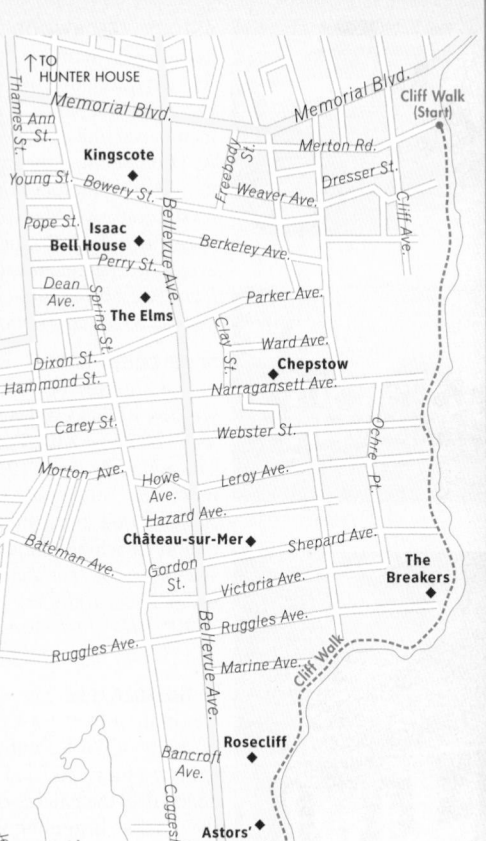

TO HUNTER HOUSE

Memorial Blvd.
Memorial Blvd.

Cliff Walk (Start)

Thames St.
Ann St.
Young St.
Bowery St.
Pope St.
Dean Ave.
Spring St.
Dixon St.
Hammond St.
Carey St.
Morton Ave.
Bateman Ave.
Ruggles Ave.

Kingscote

Isaac Bell House

Perry St.

The Elms

Bellevue Ave.

Freebody St.
Weaver Ave.
Merton Rd.
Dresser St.
Berkeley Ave.
Parker Ave.
Clay St.
Ward Ave.

Chepstow

Narragansett Ave.
Webster St.

Howe Ave.
Leroy Ave.
Hazard Ave.

Château-sur-Mer

Gordon St.
Victoria Ave.
Ruggles Ave.
Marine Ave.

Shepard Ave.

Ochre Pt.

The Breakers

Cliff Walk

Cliff Ave.

Hazard Rd.
Lilly Pond

Carroll Ave.
Jeffrey Rd.
Almy Pond
Ocean Ave.

Bancroft Ave.
Coggeshall Ave.
Bellevue Ave.

Rosecliff

Astors' Beechwood

Rovensky Ave.
Marble House

Lakeview Ave.

Belcourt Castle

Cliff Walk (Finish)

Rough Point

Ledge Rd.

Gooseberry Island

0   1/4 mi
0   1/4 km

THE MANSIONS

Antique car, Beechwood

ASTORS' BEECHWOOD. The original mistress of this oceanfront mansion, Caroline Schermerhorn Astor, was the queen of American society in the late 19th century. Her husband, William Backhouse Astor, was a member of one of the wealthiest families in the nation. As you're guided through the 1857 mansion, actors in period costume play the family, servants, and household guests. Murder mysteries and musical events are performed July through October; Victorian holiday events are held in November and December. ⊠ *580 Bellevue Ave.* ☎ *401/846–3772* ⊕ *www.astorsbeechwood. com* ⊠ *$15-$30* ⊗ *Mid-May–Dec., tour times vary.*

Belcourt Castle

★**BELCOURT CASTLE.** Richard Morris Hunt based his design for this 60-room mansion, built in 1894 for wealthy bachelor Oliver H.P. Belmont, on the hunting lodge of Louis XIII. The home, privately owned by the Tinney family since 1956, is filled with treasures from more than 30 countries. Admire the stained glass and carved wood throughout. Don't miss the Golden Coronation Coach and inquire about the haunted chair and suit of armor. The mansion's 5 PM Thursday and Saturday ghost tours are great fun. ⊠ *657 Bellevue Ave.* ☎ *401/846–0669* ⊕ *www.belcourtcastle.com* ⊠ *$15–$18* ⊗ *Tour days and times vary.*

The Breakers great hall

★**THE BREAKERS.** The largest of the Newport mansions was built in 1895 for Cornelius Vanderbilt II, president of the New York Central Railroad. Architect Richard Morris Hunt modeled the four-story, 70-room residence after the palaces of the Italian Renaissance. From the outside, beginning with your walk through the Ivy League–like gate, you can see that this mansion is not only big but grand—be sure to look for the sculpted figures tucked above the pillars. A few of the marvels within are a blue marble fireplace, rose alabaster pillars in the dining room, and a porch with a mosaic ceiling that took Italian artisans six months, lying on their backs, to install. ⊠ *Ochre Point Ave.* ☎ *401/847–1000* ⊕ *www.newportmansions.org* ⊠ *$18* ⊗ *Jan.–Mar., daily 10–4; Apr.–Dec., daily 9–5.*

The Elms dining room

Chateau-sur-Mer

Chepstow

The Breakers

The Elms sunken garden

The Elms

CHÂTEAU-SUR-MER. Bellevue Avenue's first stone mansion was built in the Victorian Gothic style in 1852 for William S. Wetmore, a tycoon involved in the China trade, and enlarged in the 1870s by Richard Morris Hunt. The elaborate grand staircase is one of Hunt's seminal creations. The Gold Room by Leon Marcotte and the Renaissance Revival–style dining room and library by the Florentine sculptor Luigi Frullini are sterling examples of the work of leading 19th-century designers. Upstairs, the bedrooms are decorated with wallpaper by Arts and Crafts designers William Morris and William Burges. ⊠ *Bellevue and Shepard Aves.* ☎ *401/847–1000* ⊕ *www.newportmansions.org* ✑ *$12* ⊗ *Mid-Apr.–mid-Nov., daily 10–5.*

CHEPSTOW. This Italianate-style villa with a mansard roof is not as grand as other Newport mansions, but it houses a remarkable collection of art and furniture gathered by the Morris family of New York City, including many landscape paintings by Hudson River School artists. Built in 1861, the home was designed by Newport architect George Champlin Mason. ⊠ *120 Narragansett Ave.* ☎ *401/847–1000* ⊕ *www. newportmansions.org* ✑ *$12* ⊗ *Mid-June–mid-Sept., daily 10–5; tours offered on the hr by reservation.*

★ **THE ELMS.** Architect Horace Trumbauer modeled this graceful 48-room French neoclassical mansion and its grounds after the Château d'Asnières near Paris. The Elms was built for Edward Julius Berwind, a bituminous-coal baron, in 1901. At the foot of the 10-acre estate is a spectacular sunken garden. The behind the scenes tours, which offer a glimpse into the life of staff and the operations (such as the boiler room and kitchen), it is one of the best of any mansion tour. Explore the house at your own pace with a digital audio tour. ⊠ *Bellevue Ave.* ☎ *401/847–1000* ⊕ *www. newportmansions.org* ✑ *$11, guided tour $15* ⊗ *Mid-Apr.–Dec., daily 10–5; Jan.–Mar., weekends 10–4.*

Hunter House

Isaac Bell House

Kingscote–ivory silk dinner gown circa 1901

HUNTER HOUSE. The French admiral Charles Louis d'Arsac de Ternay used this lovely 1748 home as his Revolutionary War headquarters. Built by Jonathan Nichols for a local sea merchant, the downtown home is removed from the other mansions on Bellevue Avenue. The carved pineapple over the doorway was a symbol of welcome throughout Colonial America; a fresh pineapple placed out front signaled an invitation to neighbors to visit a returned seaman or to look over a shop's new stock. The elliptical arch in the central hall is a typical Newport detail. Pieces made by Newport artisans Townsend and Goddard furnish much of the house, which also contains the first commissioned painting by a young Gilbert Stuart, best known for his portraits of George Washington. ⊠ *54 Washington St.* ☎ *401/847–1000* ⊕ *www.newportmansions.org* ⌧ *$25* ☉ *Late June–early Sept., daily 10–5.*

ISAAC BELL HOUSE. Designed by McKim, Mead & White, this 1883 home for wealthy cotton broker Isaac Bell is considered one of the finest examples of American shingle-style architecture. Look for an interesting mix of Continental European, early English, and Asian influences. The smaller and less-visited home is currently being restored, but it is open to the public and offers an interesting look at a "work in progess" mansion. ⊠ *Bellevue Ave. and Perry St.* ☎ *401/847–1000* ⊕ *www.newportmansions.org* ⌧ *$12* ☉ *Mid-June–mid-Sept., daily 10–5*

★**KINGSCOTE.** This Gothic Revival mansion, completed in 1841, was one of Newport's first summer cottages. Richard Upjohn designed Kingscote for George Noble Jones, a plantation owner from Savannah, Georgia. Decorated with antique furniture, glass, and Asian art, it contains one of the first installations of Tiffany glass windows in its dining room. ⊠ *Bowery St., off Bellevue Ave.* ☎ *401/847–1000* ⊕ *www.newportmansions.org* ⌧ *$12* ☉ *Mid-June–mid-Sept., daily 10–5.*

Rosecliff ballroom   Marble House

MARBLE HOUSE. One of the most opulent of the Newport mansions, the Richard Hunt Morris–designed home is known for its extravagant gold ballroom. The house was completed in 1892 by William Vanderbilt, who gave it as a gift to his wife, Alva. Alva divorced William in 1895 and married Oliver Perry Belmont, becoming the lady of Belcourt Castle. When Oliver died in 1908, she returned to Marble House and spent much of her time campaigning for women's rights. Don't miss the intriguing Chinese teahouse, built behind the estate in 1914. ⊠ *Bellevue Ave., near Ruggles St.* ☎ *401/847–1000* ⊕ *www.newportmansions.org* ⊠ *$12* ⊗ *Mid-Apr.–Dec., daily 10–5; Jan.–Mar., weekends 10–4.*

Marble House—Alva Vanderbilt

ROSECLIFF. Newport's most romantic mansion was built in 1902, commissioned by Tessie Hermann Oelrichs, who inherited a Nevada silver fortune from her father. Stanford White modeled the palace after the Grand Trianon at Versailles. Rosecliff has a heart-shaped staircase and Newport's largest private ballroom. Some scenes from *The Great Gatsby* and *True Lies* were filmed here. ⊠ *Bellevue Ave.* ☎ *401/847–1000* ⊕ *www.newportmansions. org* ⊠ *$12* ⊗ *Mid-Apr.–mid-Nov., daily 10–5.*

Marble House—Alva's bedroom

★ **ROUGH POINT.** The late tobacco heiress and preservationist Doris Duke hosted such celebs as Elizabeth Taylor at her Newport mansion. The 105-room home was built in the English manor style in 1889. Miss Duke filled Rough Point with works by such masters as Renoir and Reynolds (of all the Newport mansions, Duke's has the best art collection). Furnishings range from the elaborate to the peculiar and reflect the look of the mansion during Duke's final days here. Tours include an annual changing exhibit. ■TIP➔ To tour the mansion, take the Rough Point shuttle from the Newport Visitors' Information Center (23 America's Cup Ave.). If you prefer to drive, you must make an online reservation. ⊠ *Bellevue Ave. and Ocean Dr.* ☎ *401/845–9130* ⊕ *www.newportrestoration.org* ⊠ *$25 (first-come, first-served basis)* ⊗ *Mid-Apr.–mid-May, Thurs.–Sat. 9:45–1:45; mid-May–early Nov., Tues.–Sat. 9:45–3:45.*

Rosecliff

Rough Point

NEWPORT TOURS

BOAT TOURS

More than a dozen yacht companies operate tours of Newport Harbor and Narragansett Bay. Outings usually run two hours and cost about $25 to $35 per person.

■ **Conway Tours/Grayline Rhode Island** (☎ 401/658–3400 ⊕ www.conwaytours.com) cruises the bay and visits Belcourt Castle.

■ **Madeleine** (☎ 401/847–0298 ⊕ www.cruisenewport.com), a 72-foot schooner, departs from Bannister's Wharf.

■ **RumRunner II** (☎ 401/847–0298 ⊕ www.cruisenewport.com), a 1929 motor yacht, once carried "hooch"; it leaves from Bannister's Wharf.

■ A schooner and two sailboats with **Sightsailing of Newport** (☎ 401/849–3333 or 800/709–7245 ⊕ www.sightsailing.com) depart from Bowen's Wharf for 75-minute tours of Newport Harbor and Narragansett Bay.

TRAIN RIDES

■ **Old Colony & Newport Railway** (☎ 401/849–0546 ⊕ www.ocnrr.com) follows an 10-mi route along Narragansett Bay. The vintage diesel train and coaches make 80-minute round-trips to Middletown on Sunday at 11:45 and 1:45.

TROLLEY TOURS

■ **Viking Tours of Newport** (☎ 401/847–6921 ⊕ www.vikingtoursnewport.com) conducts trolley tours of Newport daily from May through October and on Saturdays the rest of the year.

WALKING TOURS

■ The **Newport Historical Society** (☎ 401/846–0813 ⊕ www.newporthistorytours.org) sponsors walking tours from April through December.

★ **International Tennis Hall of Fame.** The photographs, memorabilia, and multimedia exhibits at the Hall of Fame chronicle the entire history of the game, dating back to the 12th century. The magnificent, shingle-style Newport Casino, which houses the collection, was designed by Stanford White and built in 1880. Now a National Historic Landmark, it was commissioned by publisher James Gordon Bennett Jr., who had quit the nearby club, the Newport Reading Room, after a polo player—at Bennett's behest—rode a horse into the building and was subsequently banned. Built in retaliation, Bennett's casino quickly became the social and recreational hot spot of the Gilded Age. Today, the 6-acre venue has 13 grass courts, one clay court, a court-tennis facility, and three indoor courts—all available for public play. In mid-July, the facility hosts the prestigious Campbell's Hall of Fame Tennis Championships, the only men's professional tournament in the nation held on grass courts. ⊠ *194 Bellevue Ave.* ☎ *401/849–3990* ⊕ *www.tennisfame.com* 🖼 *$10* ☉ *Daily 9:30–5.*

International Yacht Restoration School. This school, off Thames Street in a former power plant, lets you watch shipwrights and students as they overhaul historically significant sailboats and powerboats. Placards recount each boat's past. The 1885 racing schooner *Coronet* and the original "cigarette boat" are two standouts. ⊠ *449 Thames*

St. ☎ 401/848–5777 ⊕ www.iyrs. org 🎫 $5 ⊗ Apr.–Nov., daily 9–5; Dec.–Mar., Mon.–Sat. 10–5.

Museum of Yachting. The museum has four displays: the Single-Handed Sailors Hall of Fame, the World of Model Yachts, the Classic Wooden Boat Collection, and Seasonal Marine Art exhibits. The legendary two-time America's Cup winner and Rhode Island State Yacht *Courageous* is a highlight of the America's Cup Gallery. In 2007, the museum joined with the International Yacht Restoration School to form one organization (package deals for $15 include admission to the museum, the IYR school, and

SCENIC DRIVE

For a scenic drive along the waterfront, you can follow **Ocean Drive**, an 11-mi route. Allow at least an hour to drive it without stops, and up to three or four hours if you stop at Brenton State Park to walk along the beach or explore Fort Adams and the Museum of Yachting. As you drive along, take in the views of the ocean, rocky coast, and spectacular homes. Consider stopping at Brenton State Park for a picnic or to take in the sunset.

the water taxi ride across the harbor between them). ✉ Ft. Adams State Park, Ocean Dr. ☎ 401/847–1018 ⊕ www.museumofyachting. org 🎫 $5 ⊗ Mid-May–Oct., Wed.–Mon. 10–5.

★ **Norman Bird Sanctuary**. About 7 mi of trails, from 0.25-mi to 1.2-mi long, loop through this 325-acre sanctuary, which in summer provides refuge from downtown Newport's hustle and bustle. More than 300 species of birds, plus deer, fox, mink, dragonflies, turtles, and rabbits live in the fields and woodlands. From higher elevations you can see the ocean, some ponds, and the marshy lowlands. Exhibits at the visitor center explain the sanctuary's history and animal and plant life. ✉ 583 Third Beach Rd., Middletown ☎ 401/846–2577 ⊕ www. normanbirdsanctuary.org 🎫 $5 ⊗ Daily 9–5.

SPORTS AND THE OUTDOORS

BEACHES **Easton's Beach** (✉ Memorial Blvd. ☎ 401/848–6491), also known as First Beach, is popular for its 50¢ carousel rides, aquarium, and playground. **Fort Adams State Park** (✉ Ocean Dr. ☎ 401/841–0707), a small beach with a picnic area and lifeguards in summer, has views of Newport Harbor and is fully sheltered from ocean swells. **Sachuest Beach**, or Second Beach, east of First Beach in the Sachuest Point area of Middletown, is a beautiful, long, sandy beach adjacent to the Norman Bird Sanctuary. Dunes and a campground make it popular with young travelers and families. **Third Beach**, in the Sachuest Point area of Middletown, is on the Sakonnet River. It has a boat ramp and is a favorite of windsurfers.

BIKING The 12-mi swing down Bellevue Avenue, along Ocean Drive and back, is a great route to ride your wheels. **Ten Speed Spokes** (✉ 18 Elm St. ☎ 401/847–5609 ⊕ www.tenspeedspokes.com) rents specializes in comfort bikes for $25 per day and $75 per week.

BOATING Take lessons or rent sailboats by the hour at **Sail Newport** (✉ 60 Ft. AND DIVING Adams Rd., Ft. Adams State Park ☎ 401/846–1983 ⊕ www.sailnewport. org). **Newport Diving Center** (✉ 550 Thames St. ☎ 401/847–9293 ⊕ www. newportdivingcenter.com) operates charter dive trips, refills Nitrox, and

Newport is a sailing capital, appropriate given the city's bayfront location on Aquidneck Island.

conducts PADI training and certification, as well as renting, selling, and servicing equipment.

FISHING **Fishin' Off** (☎ *401/683–5557* ⊕ *www.fishinoff.com*) runs charter-fishing trips on a 36-foot Trojan. The **Saltwater Edge** (✉ *561 Thames St.* ☎ *401/842–0062* ⊕ *www.saltwateredge.com*) conducts guided trips, give lessons, and sells tackle for both fly-fishing and surf-casting. **Pete's Bait & Tackle** (✉ *36 Aquidneck Ave., Middletown* ☎ *401/849–3822*) stocks gear and bait.

SHOPPING

Many of Newport's shops and art and crafts galleries are on Thames Street, Spring Street, and at Bowen's and Bannister's wharves. The Brick Market area—between Thames Street and America's Cup Avenue—has more than 40 shops. Bellevue Avenue just south of Memorial Boulevard (near the International Tennis Hall of Fame) contains a strip of pricey shops with high-quality merchandise.

★ **Aardvark Antiques** (✉ *9 Connell Hwy.* ☎ *401/849–7233* ⊕ *www. aardvarkantiques.com*) carries architectural pieces such as mantels, doors, and stained glass, plus fountains and garden statuary. The 125 dealers at the **Armory** (✉ *365 Thames St.* ☎ *401/848–2398* ⊕ *www. armoryantiques.net*), a vast 19th-century structure, carry antiques, china, and estate jewelry. Inside **Antiques at the Drawing Room** (✉ *152 Spring St.* ☎ *401/841–5060* ⊕ *www.drawrm.com*) you'll find an exemplary collection of museum-quality estate pieces, including antique glass, fine porcelain, and marble statuary.

ART AND
CRAFTS
GALLERIES

Arnold Art Store and Gallery (⊠ *210 Thames St.* ☎ *401/847–2273* ⊕ *www. arnoldart.com*) collects marine-inspired paintings and prints. **DeBlois Gallery** (⊠ *138 Bellevue Ave.* ☎ *401/847–9977* ⊕ *www.debloisgallery. com*) exhibits the works of Newport's emerging artists. **Harbor Fine Art** (⊠ *134 Spring St.* ☎ *401/848–9711* ⊕ *www.harborfineart.com*) represents several notable artists around the region and also stocks unusual furniture, prints, and glassware.

★ The delicate, dramatic blown-glass gifts at **Thames Glass** (⊠ *688 Thames St.* ☎ *401/846–0576* ⊕ *www.thamesglass.com*) are designed by Matthew Buechner and created in the adjacent studio. **William Vareika Fine Arts** (⊠ *212 Bellevue Ave.* ☎ *401/849–6149* ⊕ *www.vareikafinearts. com*) exhibits and sells American paintings and prints from the 18th to the 20th century.

BEACH GEAR

Water Brothers (⊠ *38 Broadway* ☎ *401/849–4990*) is the place to go for surf supplies, including bathing suits, wet suits, sunscreen, sunglasses, and surfboards.

BOOKS

The **Armchair Sailor** (⊠ *543 Thames St.* ☎ *401/847–1219*) stocks marine and travel books, charts, and maps.

CLOTHING

Look to **Angela Moore** (⊠ *119 Bellevue Ave.* ☎ *401/848–9695* ⊕ *www. angelamoore.com*) for stylish, mod resort threads and hand-painted beaded jewelry. **Cathers & Coyne** (⊠ *18 Bowen's Wharf* ☎ *401/849–5757*) carries hot shoes for cool people.

Karol Richardson (⊠ *24 Washington Sq.* ☎ *401/849–6612* ⊕ *www. karolrichardson.com*) sells upscale, hip contemporary women's clothing and accessories.

JEWELRY

Talented artist Meg Reagan produces distinctive jewelry and housewares from colorful, contemporary art glass at **9 Manning Square** (⊠ *24 Waites Wharf* ☎ *401/633–4088* ⊕ *www.9manningsquare.com*). **Three Golden Apples** (⊠ *140 Bellevue Ave.* ☎ *401/846–9930* ⊕ *www. threegoldenapples.com*) sells high-end jewelry.

NIGHTLIFE AND THE ARTS

Detailed events calendars can be found in *Newport This Week* and the *Newport Daily News.* For a sampling of Newport's lively nightlife, you need only stroll down Thames Street after dark. Also, Broadway has developed an increasingly hip bar and lounge scene in recent years.

BARS

The **Candy Store** (⊠ *Bannister's Wharf* ☎ *401/849–2900* ⊕ *www. clarkecooke.com*) in the Clarke Cooke House is a snazzy place for a drink. If you're up for dancing, head downstairs to the Boom Boom Room. **Newport Blues Café** (⊠ *286 Thames St.* ☎ *401/841–5510* ⊕ *www.newportblues.com*), housed in a former bank, hosts great blues performers.

POP (⊠ *162 Broadway* ☎ *401/846–8456*) is a martini and tapas bar, where a DJ spins on weekends; the food is quite tasty, too. **Salvation Café** (⊠ *140 Broadway* ☎ *401/847–2620* ⊕ *www.salvationcafe.com*), a funky, kitschy, eclectically decorated, happening spot, is popular with the local thirtysomethings. The tiki bar out back is open in summer.

FESTIVAL

In mid-August the **JVC Newport Jazz Festival** (☎ *401/847–3700* ⊕ *www. festivalnetwork.com*) takes place at Fort Adams State Park. Performers have included Ray Charles, Dave Brubeck, Cassandra Wilson, Natalie Cole, Wynton Marsalis, Harry Connick Jr., and Ornette Coleman.

FILM The **Newport International Film Festival** (☎401/846–9100 ⊕ *www. newportfilmfestival.com*), an impressive six-day event, takes place at the beginning of June at the Jane Pickens Theater and other venues.

THEATER Murder-mystery plays are performed on Thursday evenings and Saturday afternoons from July to late October at **Astors' Beechwood** (✉ *580 Bellevue Ave.* ☎401/846–3772 ⊕ *www.astorsbeechwood.com*); on Tuesday at 7, July through September, members of the Beechwood Theatre Company sing and dance in a mock 1920s speakeasy.

WHERE TO EAT

$$–$$$ ✕**Asterisk**. Urbane dining draws big crowds to this snazzy, cleverly
AMERICAN renovated garage. Asian twists (a lobster-ginger cream sauce with the
★ four-cheese ravioli) enliven the French-bistro and classic American steak-house fare, as does a carefully selected menu of wines, brandies, and aperitifs. Escargots in garlic butter, chicken-liver-and-foie-gras mousse, and steak frites are all terrific. High ceilings and an open floor lend to a lively metro vibe, and on Sunday, there's live jazz. ✉ *599 Thames St.* ☎401/841–8833 ⊕ *www.asterisknewport.com* ▭*AE, D, DC, MC, V.*

$$$ ✕**Castle Hill Inn**. The ultimate in Newport when it comes to ethereal
AMERICAN cuisine in a rarefied setting is the Castle Hill Inn's restaurant. The three-
Fodor's Choice course prix-fixe menu sees plenty of variation throughout the year,
★ all the better to reveal the deft hand of chef Jonathan Cambra, and the finest local provisions from around the state. Possibilities might include a beet carpaccio with panna cotta (custard) and a citrus-ginger vinaigrette, perhaps followed by lemon sole pan-roasted with truffled fava-bean agnolotti (Piemontese stuffed pasta), lobster meat, chanterelle mushrooms, and a lemon-basil emulsion. The weekend brunch is one of the best in the state. ✉ *590 Ocean Dr.* ☎401/849–3800 ⊕*www. castlehillinn.com* ☞ *Reservations essential* ▭*AE, D, DC, MC, V.*

¢–$ ✕**Flo's Clam Shack**. With an old boat in front, peeling paint, and a
SEAFOOD bamboo-lined walkway leading to the order windows, this local favor-
★ ite across from Easton's Beach is as casual as it gets. Fried seafood, steamed clams, clam cakes, cold beer, and a great raw bar keep the lines long here in summer. An upstairs bar serves baked, chilled lobster, and outside seating is available. ✉ *4 Wave Ave.* ☎401/847–8141 ⊕ *www.flosclamshack.net* ⌨ *Reservations not accepted* ▭ *No credit cards* ☉ *Closed Jan. and Feb. and Mon.–Wed. Mar.–late May and early Sept.–Dec.*

$$–$$$ ✕**Fluke Wine Bar**. Whether you want to snack on tapas and sip well-
AMERICAN chosen wines by the glass or partake of a more substantial meal, this
★ Bowen's Wharf newcomer with a sleek, airy dining room serves any mood. The cheese-and-charcuterie plate and citrus-lobster-roll sliders (miniature lobster rolls) stand out among the small-plate options, while broiled striped bass in a simple lemon–white wine reduction stars among the entrées. Finish off with an almond tart accompanied by mango ice cream and fresh berries. It's open until 1 AM nightly. ✉ *41 Bowen's Wharf* ☎401/849–7778 ⊕ *www.flukewinebar.com* ▭*AE, MC, V* ☉ *No lunch Mon.–Sat.*

Newport Off Season

Summer in Newport can be described as bustling, even hectic, but the off-season takes on a serene, romantic character. Crowds dissipate, parking is a breeze, and reservations aren't a problem. Off-season prices plummet as well: parking is often free, restaurants offer midweek specials, lodging prices are much lower, and getaway packages are there for the taking.

Fall visitors can take advantage of the less crowded sidewalks and end-of-season sales up and down Thames Street. Though there may be no need to pack a bikini, brisk walks on the beach and Cliff Walk get the blood flowing. In the wintertime, holiday lights glimmer in the early dusk, and bundled-up folks duck into restaurants to warm themselves by the fire and enjoy a drink and a bite to eat.

Newport's holiday season is absolutely stunning. A light snowfall can peel back the years and it isn't difficult to imagine the city 200 years ago. Bowen's Wharf, decked with white lights, provides Newport with its version of the Rockefeller Center tree. "Christmas in Newport," a program begun in the early 1970s, hosts multiple activities (tree lightings, nativity scenes, a lighted boat parade, dances, concerts, and visits by Santa) for nearly every day of the December calendar. The Breakers, The Elms, and Marble House are dressed up in full holiday regalia beginning mid-November. Mansions, filled with evergreens and thousands of poinsettias, open their doors for live holiday music on Saturday evenings and Sunday afternoons.

Fun options with the kids are the Born Family Skating Center and, during February school break, the annual Newport Winter Festival, with live shows, an ice-carving competition, beach sand/snow sculptures, a citywide scavenger hunt, and a chili cook-off.

$$$ ✕ **Pronto.** This ornately furnished restaurant has sweeping red drapes,
ITALIAN white linens, and—despite the elegant trappings—a refreshingly laid-back and casual spirit. The kitchen is proficient in both the classics (fettuccine with Bolognese sauce, Milanese veal chops) and contemporary dishes (seared salmon dusted with pistachio flour and served over roasted spaghetti squash with a red-pepper cream sauce). Kudos to the extensive wine list of both Italian and New World varietals. ⊠ *464 Thames St.* ☎ *401/847–5251* ⊕ *www.prontonewport.com* ⊟ *AE, D, MC, V* ☾ *No lunch.*

$$$–$$$$ ✕ **Restaurant Bouchard.** Regional takes on French cuisine fill the menu at
FRENCH this upscale yet homey establishment inside a stately gambrel-roof 1785 Colonial on Thames Street. Nightly specials are based on the fresh catch from Rhode Island waters (scallops, swordfish, clams), plus such Gallic classics as Dover sole with sorrel sauce and pork tenderloin with goat cheese and vegetables in puff pastry. The wine list offers a nice range of New- and Old-World varietals. ⊠ *505 Thames St.* ☎ *401/846–0123* ⊕ *www.restaurantbouchard.com* ⊟ *AE, D, MC, V* ☾ *No lunch.*

$$$ ✕ **Salvation Café.** Youthful hipsters and locals have long adored this
★ decidedly irreverent, urbane lounge and eatery along Broadway's trendy "restaurant row," but food lovers of all ages might want to give

Salvation a try. You could build a meal around several praiseworthy starters, such as the scallop ceviche tostadas, PEI mussels with chourico sausage and a lime-basil broth, and sticky sesame ribs. Entrées are no less intriguing, with the tandoori fish of the day always a good bet. Colorful cocktails and lavish desserts (such as chocolate banana purses with ginger ice cream) round out the menu. ⊠ *140 Broadway* ☎ *401/847–2620* ⊕ *www.salvationcafe.com* ▭ *AE, D, MC, V* ⊘ *No lunch.*

$$ ✕ **Spark.** Part of the culinary renaissance that's overtaken the formerly
ECLECTIC workaday lower Broadway section of town, this colorful little store-front café with orange walls, funky wall sconces, and memorable chow pulls in a mix of local see-and-be-seen types and adventuresome tourists. The menu mixes small plates, dishes for sharing, and judiciously portioned entrées. Highlights include Roquefort cheesecake with port syrup, Thai shrimp tacos with crispy wontons, and fennel-dusted pork chops with apple compote and chicken-liver-sausage stuffing. ⊠ *12 Broadway* ☎ *401/842–0023* ⊕ *www.sparkrestaurantandcatering.com* ▭ *AE, MC, V* Ⓨ *BYOB* ⊘ *Closed Sun. and Mon.*

$$$$ ✕ **Spiced Pear.** Any time of year, but especially from May through mid-
AMERICAN October, when there's seating on the sprawling terrace with its cliff-top
★ ocean views, this refined restaurant at the Chanler Inn ranks among Rhode Island's very finest dining experiences. Typically complex fare from the regional American dinner menu includes Southern-style foie gras with toasted pistachio flapjacks and brandy-cherry foam, followed by seared diver scallops with Kobe-beef oxtail and a Madeira-truffle jus. For an all-out feast, opt for the eight-course tasting menu with pairings from the extensive wine list. ⊠ *117 Memorial Blvd.* ☎ *401/847–2244* ⊕ *www.spicedpear.com* ▭ *AE, D, DC, MC, V.*

$$$–$$$$ ✕ **Tucker's Bistro.** The red lacquered walls crowded with artwork, shelves
AMERICAN lined with books, and gilded mirrors create a vibe that is part library,
Fodor's Choice part art gallery, and part bordello. Beautifully executed (and well-
★ priced) contemporary creations include braised pork shank with ched-dar mashed potatoes and pan-seared sea scallops with creamy Parmesan risotto. The Thai shrimp nachos and pear-Gorgonzola appetizers are favorites amongst regulars. ⊠ *150 Broadway* ☎ *401/846–3449* ⊕ *www. tuckersbistro.com* ▭ *D, MC, V* ⊘ *No lunch.*

$$$$ ✕ **White Horse Tavern.** The first tavern opened here in 1673, and almost
AMERICAN uninterruptedly since then the premises have served as a tavern, board-
★ inghouse, or restaurant. Once a meetinghouse for Colonial Rhode Island's General Assembly, the tavern provides intimate dining with its low dark-beam ceilings, cavernous fireplace, and uneven plank floors. The service is black tie, the wine list top notch, and the American cuisine—including pan-seared blue cod with roasted-tomato coulis and lemon-thyme oil and a stellar beef Wellington—excellent. ⊠ *Marlbor-ough and Farewell Sts.* ☎ *401/849–3600* ⊕ *www.whitehorsetavern.us* ⬗ *Reservations essential* ▭ *AE, D, DC, MC, V.*

WHERE TO STAY

$$–$$$ 🏠 **Admiral Fitzroy Inn.** This tidy 1854 Victorian provides a restful retreat
★ in the heart of Newport's bustling waterfront district. Period antiques decorate the rooms, each of which has either an antique brass or hand-carved wood bed. All rooms have access to the rooftop deck with a

view of the harbor. Two rooms have semiprivate decks and hot tubs. The inn's namesake, Admiral Fitzroy, commanded the *Beagle,* whose most famous passenger was Charles Darwin. **Pros:** relatively affordable for the area. **Cons:** lots of crowds and some noise on Thames Street in summer. ☒ *398 Thames St.* ☎ *401/848–8000 or 866/848–8780* ⊕ *www. admiralfitzroy.com* ➫ *17 rooms* ☖ *In-room: a/c, refrigerator, Wi-Fi. In-hotel: Wi-Fi hotspot, parking (free)* ▭ *AE, D, MC, V* ⏮ *BP.*

$$–$$$ ⌂ **Architect's Inn.** Built by noted Newport architect George Champlin Mason (Chepstow, Fort Adams Commandant House), this distinctive Swiss chalet–inspired house just off Bellevue Avenue contains five romantic rooms done in classic Victorian style but with plenty of modern creature comforts (DVD players, fireplaces, CD players, individual climate control). Rooms are done with bold period-style wallpapering and fabrics and accented with Oriental rugs. The cozy Woodbine Cottage suite takes up the third floor, has a sitting room, and can accommodate up to four guests. **Pros:** reasonably priced by Newport standards; central location; fireplace in every room. **Cons:** pure Victorian decor won't suit every taste. ☒ *2 Sunnyside Pl.* ☎ *401/847–7081 or 877/466–2547* ⊕ *www.architectsinn.com* ➫ *3 rooms, 2 suites* ☖ *In-room: a/c, DVD (some), Wi-Fi. In-hotel: parking (free)* ▭ *AE, MC, V* ⏮ *BP.*

$$$$ ⌂ **Castle Hill Inn and Resort.** The 1874 main house and its 40 acres of
Fodor's Choice lawns and woodland have views of Narragansett Bay, the Newport
★ Bridge, and the Atlantic Ocean. Amenities abound: Adirondack chairs to take in the view, patio dining, private beach, and trails to the Castle Hill Lighthouse. The tastefully appointed rooms, varied in style, are in the main house, harbor houses, and beach houses. The inn, 3 mi from the center of Newport, is also a perfect spot for a special meal. The restaurant serves stellar food and is known for its elaborate Sunday brunches with live jazz music and for its prix-fixe tasting menus with wine pairings. **Pros:** to-die-for views; superb restaurant; variety of rooms. **Cons:** you need a car to get into town; among the highest rates in Newport. ☒ *590 Ocean Dr.* ☎ *401/849–3800 or 888/466–1355* ⊕ *www.castlehillinn.com* ➫ *7 rooms, 18 suites* ☖ *In-room: a/c, kitchen (some), DVD, Internet. In-hotel: restaurant, beachfront, Internet terminal, parking (paid)* ▭ *AE, D, DC, MC, V* ⏮ *BP.*

$$$$ ⌂ **Chanler at Cliff Walk.** Nearly all of the enormous rooms and suites at
★ this stunning small hotel perched atop a bluff at the foot of Cliff Walk have dramatic ocean views, and about half have an outdoor balcony or deck. This is one of the city's swankiest accommodations—consider the regal room appointments, such as swagged damask bedding or an antique fireplace with Tudor mantel. Rooms have two or three TVs and sprawling marble bathrooms with Jacuzzi tubs and separate showers. A fantastic à la carte full breakfast is included, and the staff graciously attends to guests' every possible whim. **Pros:** panoramic water views from many rooms; museum-quality antiques; one of the best on-site restaurants in the state. **Cons:** rooms have a rather formal air; ultra-pricey. ☒ *117 Memorial Blvd.* ☎ *401/847–1300 or 866/793–5664* ⊕ *www. thechanler.com* ➫ *7 rooms, 13 suites* ☖ *In-room: a/c, DVD, Internet. In-hotel: restaurant, parking (free)* ▭ *AE, D, DC, MC, V* ⏮ *BP.*

6

$$$$ ⊡ **Francis Malbone House.** The design of this stately painted-brick house
★   is attributed to the architect responsible for the Touro Synagogue and
the Redwood Library. A lavish inn with period reproduction furnishings, the 1760 structure was tastefully doubled in size in the mid-1990s.
The rooms in the main house overlook the courtyard, which has a fountain, or look across the street to the harbor; all rooms have working
fireplaces, iPod-docking stations, and bathrooms with Jacuzzis. Breakfast is served in a domed ceiling dining room. The owners also run the
lovely Hilltop Inn, at the foot of Bellevue Avenue, a handsome Arts
and Crafts house with similarly elegant rooms. **Pros:** steps from many
restaurants and shops; highly professional service; working fireplaces
in each room. **Cons:** Thames Street abounds with tourists in summer.
⊠ *392 Thames St.* ☎ *401/846–0392 or 800/846–0392* ⊕ *www.malbone.
com* ⇨ *17 rooms, 3 suites* ⟳ *In-room: a/c, DVD, Wi-Fi. In-hotel: Wi-Fi
hotspot, parking (free)* ▭ *AE, MC, V* ⊺◉ *BP.*

$$$$ ⊡ **Hyatt Regency Newport.** On Goat Island across from the Colonial Point
district, the Hyatt, which completed a massive $30 million renovation in
2007, affords panoramic views of the harbor and the Newport Bridge.
Most rooms have water views. Although the hotel is a 10-minute walk
to the center of Newport, bike and moped rentals are nearby. All rooms
are decorated with light-wood and dark-granite-top furniture, cushy
bedding with pillowtop mattresses, and modern nautical color schemes.
The outdoor restaurant, Pineapples ($), is a little-known spot to watch
the sunset in summer. **Pros:** most recently renovated major Newport
hotel; spectacular water views from many rooms; relatively secluded
location. **Cons:** a bit of a walk to shopping and dining. ⊠ *1 Goat Island*
☎ *401/851–1234 or 800/233–1234* ⊕ *www.newport.hyatt.com* ⇨ *264
rooms* ⟳ *In-room: a/c, Wi-Fi. In-hotel: 2 restaurants, tennis court, pools,
gym, spa, Wi-Fi hotspot, parking (paid)* ▭ *AE, D, DC, MC, V.*

$$$$ ⊡ **Hydrangea House Inn.** This mid-19th-century inn near the foot of
★   Bellevue Avenue exudes romance, with its decadent suites and rooms,
each a work of interior design. The dark and masculine Chesterfield
Suite is a favorite, with its massive four-poster dark and opulent bed
and cheetah-print bathrobes. The owners have thought of every detail,
including flat-screen TVs that revert to gilt-frame mirrors when not in
use. Some rooms have fireplaces, whirlpool tubs, and steam showers.
In the evening, guests are treated to a reception of wine and cheese,
and rates also include a bountiful full breakfast, served family-style
beneath a stunning crystal chandelier. Complimentary Wi-Fi and free
long-distance and local calls are among the pluses. **Pros:** central location; huge rooms; highly personal service. **Cons:** slightly over-the-top
decor. ⊠ *16 Bellevue Ave.* ☎ *401/846–6602 or 800/945–4667* ⊕ *www.
hydrangeahouse.com* ⇨ *3 rooms, 7 suites* ⟳ *In-room: a/c, Wi-Fi. In-
hotel: parking (free)* ▭ *AE, D, DC, MC, V* ⊺◉ *BP.*

$ ⊡ **Spring Street Inn.** It's nearly impossible to find an appealing, centrally
located accommodation in downtown Newport during the summer
with rates starting at under $200 nightly, but this B&B set inside a
grand Second Empire mansion fits the bill. Rooms hark back to the
building's architectural origins, each done with a smattering of Victorian antiques and floral-print bedding and wallpapers: the look is old-

CLOSE UP

Filming in Rhode Island

Rhode Island is no stranger to the big screen. With a reputation for beautiful, diverse scenery, Little Rhody has become a bona fide movie star with more than 100 films to its credit. Keep an eye open for locations you may recognize from the following shows and films:

The Great Gatsby (1974). In this film that brings F. Scott Fitzgerald's novel to life, Mia Farrow stars as the object of millionaire Jay Gatsby's (Robert Redford) affections. Many remember Gatsby's stunning mansion, his yellow Rolls-Royce, and the party scene in which revelers danced in the fountain. These scenes were shot at Newport's Rosecliff mansion on Bellevue Avenue, and the costumes Redford and Farrow wore are on display there.

Reversal of Fortune (1990). Jeremy Irons won the Academy Award for best actor in 1990 for his performance as Claus von Bülow, accused of putting his wife, Sunny (Glenn Close), into a coma with an insulin overdose. At the time of the incident, the von Bülows lived on Bellevue Avenue, and the film's opening aerial shots show the immense mansions on that street, perched above the water's edge.

True Lies (1994). In this romantic action comedy, Arnold Schwarzenegger played a spy, unbeknownst to his wife, played by Jamie Lee Curtis. The film's opening Swiss Alps scene was actually shot at Ochre Court at Salve Regina University. (As a neighborly gesture, Salve students sent a pizza to Schwarzenegger's trailer.) Schwarzenegger also tangoed with Tia Carrere in the ballroom at Rosecliff mansion on Bellevue Avenue.

American Buffalo (1996). Dustin Hoffman, Dennis Franz, and Sean Nelson lived in the city of Pawtucket over the course of a few months to shoot director Michael Corrente's American Buffalo. Dustin Hoffman's handprints remain in concrete in front of the Riverside Diner.

Amistad (1997). Steven Spielberg directed this story about the 1839 slave revolt aboard a Spanish slave ship. An African-born slave leads a mutiny and a U.S. court decides the slaves' fate. Much of the film was shot in Rhode Island, including the scene where African slaves row ashore to a rocky beach (Fort Wetherill State Park in Jamestown). Other film locations include Providence's Governor's State Room in the Rhode Island State House and Bristol's Mount Hope Farm. To create the look of Colonial times in Newport, Washington Square's streets were covered in dirt, and modern elements, such as shops' signs, were taken down. In the Old Colony House John Quincy Adams (Anthony Hopkins) argued for the Africans' freedom.

Me, Myself & Irene (2000). Scenes include: Jim Carrey driving over the Newport Bridge; a wedding dream scene at St. John's Episcopal Church on Washington Street in Newport's Point section; and shots on Narragansett Avenue in Jamestown as well as on Great Island in Narragansett.

Thirteen Days (2000). The film borrowed a ship from the Naval War College in Newport for a water scene, and naval officers were used as extras onboard.

fashioned, but they're spotless and tasteful. That breakfast is extensive and filling. **Pros:** on a quiet but centrally located street; breakfast is terrific and afternoon snacks are included; easygoing hosts. **Cons:** some rooms are small; no TV in most rooms. ⊠ *353 Spring St.* ☎ *401/847–4767* ⊕ *www.springstreetinn.com* 🖙 *6 rooms, 1 suite* ♻ *In-room: a/c, no phone, no TV (some), Wi-Fi. In-hotel: Wi-Fi hotspot, parking (free)* ▱ *MC, V* ☉ *BP.*

$$$$
Fodor's Choice
★
🖼 **Vanderbilt Hall.** Built in 1909 as the Newport Men's Social Club, a Vanderbilt family gift to the Newport townspeople, this building was turned into a YMCA during the Great Depression. It became a sophisticated inn with European flair in the 1990s and has undergone a major renovation over the past two years, resulting in fewer but much larger rooms, the opening of a full-service spa and indoor pool, and all sorts of cushy new perks added to the rooms, from DVD players and iPod docking stations to high-definition plasma-screen TVs and lavish new bedding. Room design now balances a contemporary, minimalist aesthetic with antique accents. The Club Restaurant ($$$$) serves extremely good contemporary American cuisine. **Pros:** rich history; ultraposh spa and facilities; highly personal service. **Cons:** on a busy narrow street. ⊠ *41 Mary St.* ☎ *401/846–6200* ⊕ *www.vanderbilthall.com* 🖙 *33 suites* ♻ *In-room: a/c, refrigerator, DVD, Wi-Fi. In-hotel: restaurant, bar, pool, spa, Wi-Fi hotspot, parking (paid)* ▱ *AE, D, MC, V.*

PORTSMOUTH

11 mi north of Newport.

Portsmouth is now mainly a bedroom community for professionals who work in other parts of Rhode Island and Massachusetts. Its founder was Anne Hutchinson, a religious dissident and one of the country's first feminists, who led a group of settlers to the area in 1638 after being banished from the Massachusetts Bay Colony.

EXPLORING

☉ **Green Animals Topiary Garden.** This large topiary garden on a Victorian estate contains more than 80 shrubs sculpted into animals, geometric designs, and other shapes; among the oldest, begun before 1920, are an elephant, a camel, and a giraffe. Also here are flower gardens, winding pathways, a variety of trees, and the 1872 estate house, which displays original family furnishings and an antique toy collection. ⊠ *Cory's La. off Rte. 114* ☎ *401/847–1000* ⊕ *www.newportmansions.org* 🎫 *$12* ☉ *Mid-May–Oct., daily 10–5.*

SPORTS AND THE OUTDOORS

Sandy Point Beach (⊠ *Sandy Point Ave.*) is a choice spot for families and beginning windsurfers because of the calm surf along the Sakonnet River.

BRISTOL

5 mi north of Portsmouth, 20 mi southeast of Providence.

The largest town in Rhode Island's somewhat overlooked but enticing East Bay region, Bristol lies about midway between Newport and

A horse, an elephant, and a bunny are just some of the creatures at Green Animals Topiary Garden.

Providence. Once a center of boatbuilding, this dapper town that hugs the eastern shores of Narragansett Bay is home to a handful of prominent attractions as well as a beguiling downtown with a smattering of noteworthy places to stay and eat. The main drag, Hope Street, is painted with a red-white-and-blue center stripe—this patriotic community has been celebrating the Fourth of July with a downtown parade longer than any other town in the United States. It's also the terminus of the 14.5-mi East Bay Bike Path, which begins in Providence and follows an abandoned railroad right-of-way.

EXPLORING

★ **Herreshoff Marine Museum.** On the grounds of the prestigious Herreshoff boat manufacturing company, which produced some of the world's sleekest racing yachts during its operations from 1863 to 1945, this museum traces the company's illustrious history. The museum contains some 60 vintage Herreshoff boats, some dating to the mid-19th century, including several that defended the prestigious America's Cup yacht races. Old ship engines, photographs, and memorabilia shed further light on the "Golden Age of Yachting." On the grounds, the **America's Cup Hall of Fame** celebrates the careers of the many great yachting enthusiasts who have excelled during this seminal international sailing regatta. ⊠ *1 Burnside St.* ☎ *401/253–5000* ⊕ *www.herreshoff.org* ✉ *$8* ☾ *Late Apr.–early Nov, daily 10–5.*

Blithewold Mansion and Arboretum. You can tour the 45-room mansion, which dates to 1908 and is patterned after a 17th-century English manor—its contents include a mix of period antiques and reproductions. But the gardens, trees, and dramatic 10-acre lawn fringing

Narragansett Bay are the real prizes here. The grounds have more than 3,000 shrubs and trees, including the largest giant sequoia on the East Coast (nearly 100 feet tall). ☒ *101 Ferry Rd.* ☎ *401/253–2707* ⊕ *www. blithewold.org* ☞ *$10* ☉ *Grounds daily 10–5, mansion mid-Apr.–mid-Oct. and Dec., Wed.–Sat. 10–4, Sun. 10–3.*

Haffenreffer Museum of Anthropology. This Brown University–operated museum houses some 80,000 objects and artifacts that relate to indigenous people from all over the world. Highlights include Taoist paintings from 17th-century China, canoes and kayaks used by native peoples from Alaska and northern Canada, and katchina dolls from the Hopi tribal lands of Arizona. ☒ *300 Tower St.* ☎ *401/423–8388* ☞ *$5* ☉ *June–Aug., Tues.–Sun. 10–4; Sept.–May, weekends 10–4.*

WHERE TO EAT AND STAY

$$–$$$
ECLECTIC
Fodor's Choice
★

✕ **DeWolf Tavern.** A cleverly conceived menu of fusion Indian, Mediterranean, and regional American cuisine has earned this cozy, warmly lit space inside the Bristol Harbor Inn serious praise from foodies. Timber ceilings and fieldstone walls—along with wonderful bay views—create a romantic mood. Dishes of note include veal–and–pine nut samosas with mango chutney, naan pizzas topped with truffle oil and Parmesan, and seared local sea scallops with chestnut spaetzle and a thyme–garam masala sauce. Save room for the homemade cardamom or fig-port ice cream. ☒ *267 Thames St.* ☎ *401/254–2005* ⊕ *www.dewolftavern.com* ▭ *AE, D, MC, V* ☉ *No lunch.*

$$–$$$
AMERICAN
★

✕ **Persimmon.** A smartly simple bistro with space for no more than 40 patrons, Persimmon is run by young chef-owner Champe Speidel and his wife Lisa. It's a genial neighborhood spot, a short walk from the bay and just off Bristol's main street. The seasonal menu has featured white wine–braised rabbit with gnocchi and sage and a tasting of Texas wild boar that comprises roasted saddle, seared chop, braised shoulder, and smoked sausage. ☒ *31 State St.* ☎ *401/254–7474* ⊕ *www.persimmonbristol.com* ▭ *AE, MC, V* ☉ *Closed Mon. Closed Sun. Jan.–June.*

$$–$$$

🛏 **Bristol Harbor Inn.** Part of the Thames Street Landing redevelopment along Bristol's dapper bay front, this 40-room hotel was constructed with timber and architectural detailing from a pair of early-1800s buildings that stood here previously. The sunny rooms contain Colonial reproduction furniture, writing desks, and armoires, and many of them overlook Narragansett Bay. The on-site restaurant, DeWolf Tavern, is one of the best in the state, and the hotel is steps from several shops and other restaurants. Thames Landing has a marina and bike-rental shop. **Pros:** reasonably priced for a waterfront hotel; stellar restaurant; convenient location. **Cons:** other than shops and marina, there are no exterior grounds. ☒ *259 Thames St.* ☎ *401/254–1444 or 866/254–1444* ⊕ *www.bristolharborinn.com* ➴ *36 rooms, 4 suites* ⚲ *In-room: a/c, Internet. In-hotel: restaurant, bar, Internet terminal, parking (free)* ▭ *AE, D, MC, V* ⚅ *BP.*

$$$$
★

🛏 **Point Pleasant Inn.** A regal East Bay estate set on a peninsula near Colt State Park, this rambling 1940 mansion anchors a gloriously situated 33-acre compound of well-tended lawns and manicured gardens. The seven rooms and suites have Bose CD stereos and DVD players; some have immense sitting rooms, and many afford expansive views of Narragansett Bay. Bathrooms have deep tubs and stand-alone showers. A well-trained, multilingual staff tends to your every need, and the park-like grounds include an in-ground pool with a slate lanai, a tennis court, and fishing on the bay. **Pros:** magnificent waterfront setting; huge rooms; gracious staff. **Cons:** pricey; not within walking distance of shopping and dining; site of many weddings and functions. ⊠ *333 Poppasquash Rd.* ☎*401/253–0627* ⊕ *www.pointpleasantinn.com* ⟿*4 rooms, 3 suites* ♿ *In-room: a/c, DVD, Wi-Fi. In-hotel: tennis court, pool, parking (free), Wi-Fi hotspot* ⊟ *AE, MC, V* ⊙*BP.*

SPORTS AND THE OUTDOORS

BIKING   Flat and affording majestic views of Narragansett Bay, the 14.5-mi **East Bay Bike Path** (⊕ *www.riparks.com/eastbay.htm*) passes from Providence into Bristol's charming downtown.

Northwind Sports (⊠ *267 Thames St.* ☎*401/254–4295* ⊕*www. northwindsports.com*) has bikes for rent as well as kayaks for exploring the town's placid harbor.

EN ROUTE   Route 77, the main thoroughfare to Little Compton, passes through **Tiverton Four Corners**, a great place to stretch your legs and catch your first breath of East Bay air.

LITTLE COMPTON

15 mi south of Bristol, 19 mi southeast of Portsmouth.

Rolling estates, lovely homes, farmlands, woods, and a gentle western shoreline make Little Compton one of the Ocean State's prettiest areas, although the community lacks for restaurants and accommodations and is thus best approached as an afternoon excursion from Portsmouth, Newport, or Bristol. Little Compton and Tiverton were part of Massachusetts until 1747—to this day, residents here often have more roots in Massachusetts than in Rhode Island.

Little Compton Commons (⊠ *Meetinghouse La.*) is the epitome of a New England town square. As white as the clouds above, the spire of the Georgian-style United Congregational Church rises over the tops of adjacent oak trees. Within the triangular lawn is a cemetery with Colonial headstones, among them that of Elizabeth Padobie, said to be the first white girl born in New England. Surrounding the green are a rock wall and all the elements of a small community: town hall, community center, police station, and school.

Sakonnet Point, a surreal spit of land that begins where Route 77 ends, reaches out toward three tiny islands. The 0.5-mi hike to the tip of the spit passes tide pools, a beach composed of tiny stones, and outcroppings that recall the surface of the moon. Parking is sometimes available in the lot adjacent to Sakonnet Harbor.

EXPLORING

★   **Sakonnet Vineyard.** Tours and tastings are free at New England's largest winery. Varietals include chardonnay, pinot noir, cabernet franc, and vidal blanc. Tours are given at noon and 3. ⊠ *162 W. Main Rd.*

☏ *401/635–8486* ⊕ *www.sakonnetwine.com* ✉ *Free* ⊘ *Memorial Day–Oct., daily 10–6; Nov.–Memorial Day, daily 11–5.*

SPORTS AND THE OUTDOORS
HIKING
Wilbur Woods (✉ *Swamp Rd.*), a 30-acre hollow with picnic tables and a waterfall, is a good place for a casual hike. A trail winds along and over Dundery Brook.

BLOCK ISLAND

Block Island, 12 mi off Rhode Island's southern coast, is 7 mi long and 3 mi wide. With its 17 mi of beaches, it has been a vacation destination since the 19th century. Despite the number of summer visitors and thanks to the efforts of local conservationists, the island's beauty remains intact (more than 40% of the land is preserved); its 365 freshwater ponds support more than 150 species of migrating birds.

The original inhabitants of the island were Native Americans who called it Manisses, or "isle of the little god." Following a visit in 1614 by the Dutch explorer Adrian Block, the island was given the name Adrian's Eyelant, and later Block Island. In 1661 it was settled by farmers and fishermen from Massachusetts Bay Colony, who gave it what remains its second official name, the Town of New Shoreham, when it became part of Rhode Island in 1672.

Block Island, with 950 year-round residents, is a laid-back community. You can dine at any of the island's establishments in shorts and a T-shirt. The busiest season, when the population explodes to about 15,000, is between May and Columbus Day—at other times, most restaurants, inns, stores, and visitor services close down. If you plan to stay overnight in summer, make reservations well in advance; for weekends in July and August, March is not too early.

GETTING HERE AND AROUND

AIR TRAVEL You can reach Block Island either by air or ferry. New England Airlines operates scheduled flights from Westerly to Block Island Airport.

There's year-round car-and-passenger ferry service to Block Island from the Port of Galilee, in the town of Narragansett in South County. Seasonal passenger-only ferry service is available from Newport; New London, Connecticut; and Montauk, New York. All of the ferry companies permit bicycles, with the fares for these ranging from $3 to $10 each way.

FERRY TRAVEL Block Island Ferry operates traditional car-passenger service and high-speed passenger service between Block Island's Old Harbor and Galilee. By conventional ferry, the one-hour trip is $12 one-way (about $50 for automobiles), and runs from two to three times a day in winter to nine times a day in peak season. Make auto reservations well ahead. Foot passengers cannot make reservations; arrive 45 minutes ahead in high season—boats do fill up. From early June to mid-October the high-speed service makes four to six daily 30-minute trips ($17 one-way)

Rhode Island isn't just about regattas; working boats are common on the water, too.

from Galilee to Old Harbor. There is no auto service on the high-speed; passenger reservations are accepted.

Block Island Ferry also operates a seasonal service from Newport's Fort Adams State Park to Old Harbor. The passengers-only ferry leaves Newport for Block Island once a day from July through Labor Day at 9:15 AM and leaves Block Island at 4:45 PM. One-way rates are about $11. Approximate sailing time is two hours.

From late May to mid-October, a high-speed passenger-only ferry operated by Block Island Express runs between New London, Connecticut, and Old Harbor. The ferry departs New London every three hours, four or five times a day, and takes a little more than an hour. Tickets are $24 one-way. Reservations are recommended.

Viking Fleet runs high-speed passenger service from Montauk, Long Island, to Block Island from late May to mid-October. The boat departs Montauk at 10 AM and leaves Block Island at 5 PM. Fare is $40 one-way. Travel time is one hour; the ferry docks at New Harbor.

GETTING AROUND Block Island has two harbors, Old Harbor and New Harbor. Approaching the island by sea from New London, Newport, or Point Judith, you'll see Old Harbor, the island's only village, and its group of Victorian hotels. Most of the smaller inns, shops, and restaurants are also here, and it's a short walk from the ferry landing to most of the interesting sights as well as many accommodations.

A car isn't necessary but can be helpful if you're staying far from Old Harbor or visiting for long. You can rent one at Block Island Car Rental.

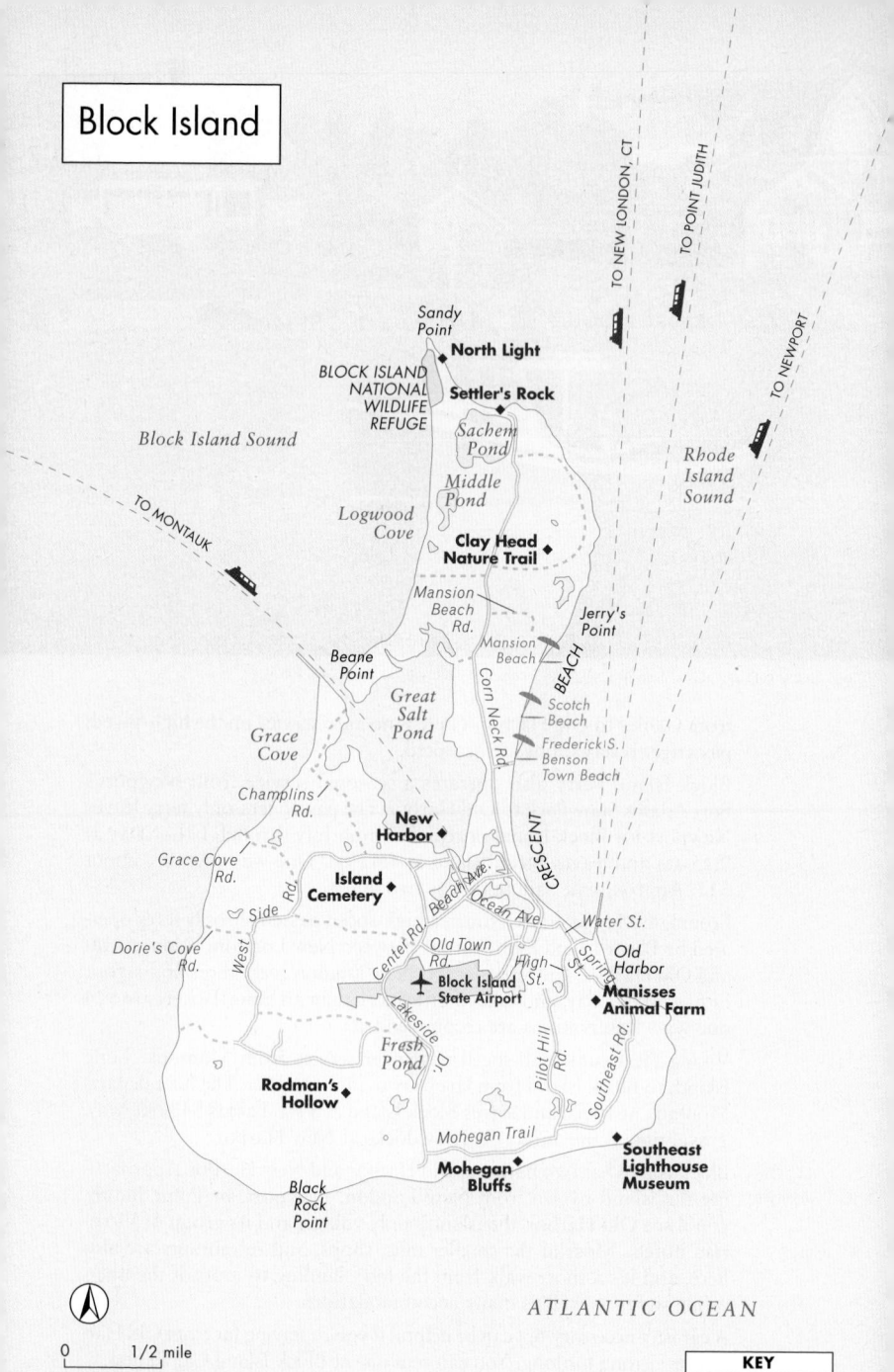

Block Island

Sandy Point

North Light

BLOCK ISLAND NATIONAL WILDLIFE REFUGE

Settler's Rock

Block Island Sound

Sachem Pond

Middle Pond

Logwood Cove

Clay Head Nature Trail

Jerry's Point

Mansion Beach Rd.

Mansion Beach

BEACH

Beane Point

Great Salt Pond

Scotch Beach

Corn Neck Rd.

Frederick S. Benson Town Beach

Grace Cove

Champlins Rd.

New Harbor

CRESCENT

Grace Cove Rd.

Side Rd.

Island Cemetery

Beach Ave.

Ocean Ave.

Water St.

Old Harbor

Dorie's Cove Rd.

West Rd.

Center Rd.

Old Town Rd.

High St.

Spring St.

Manisses Animal Farm

✈ **Block Island State Airport**

Lakeside Dr.

Fresh Pond

Pilot Hill Rd.

Southeast Rd.

Rodman's Hollow

Mohegan Trail

Black Rock Point

Mohegan Bluffs

Southeast Lighthouse Museum

TO NEW LONDON, CT

TO POINT JUDITH

TO NEWPORT

TO MONTAUK

Rhode Island Sound

ATLANTIC OCEAN

0   1/2 mile
0   1 km

KEY

🚢 Ferry Lines

ESSENTIALS

Transportation Contacts **Block Island Airport** (✉ *Center Rd.* ☎ *401/466–5511*). **Block Island Car Rental** (✉ *Ocean Ave.* ☎ *401/466–2297*). **Block Island Express** (✉ *2 Ferry St., New London* ☎ *401/466–2212 or 860/444–4624* ⊕ *www.goblockisland.com*). **Block Island Ferry** (✉ *Galilee State Pier, Narragansett* ☎ *866/783–7996* ⊕ *www.blockislandferry.com*). **New England Airlines** (☎ *800/243–2460* ⊕ *www.block-island.com/nea*). **Viking Fleet** (☎ *631/668–5700* ⊕ *www.vikingfleet.com*).

Visitor Information**Block Island Chamber of Commerce** (✉ *Drawer D, 1 Water St.* *401/466–2982 or 800/383–2474* ⊕ *www.blockislandchamber.com*).

EXPLORING

TOP ATTRACTIONS

Fodor'sChoice **Mohegan Bluff.** The 200-foot cliffs along Mohegan Trail, the island's
★ southernmost road, are named for an Indian battle in which the local Manisses pinned down an attacking band of Mohegans at the base of the cliffs. From Payne Overlook, west of the Southeast Lighthouse Museum, you can see to Montauk Point, New York, and beyond. An intimidating set of stairs leads down to the beach.

★ **North Light.** This 1867 granite lighthouse on the northernmost tip of the Block Island National Wildlife Refuge serves as a maritime museum. The protected area nearby is a temporary home to American oystercatchers, piping plovers, and other rare migrating birds. From a parking lot at the end of Corn Neck Road, it's a ¾-mi hike over sand to the lighthouse. The building's tower was rebuilt in 2009. ✉ *Corn Neck Rd.* ☎ *401/466–3200* 🕮 *Donation suggested* ☉ *July 5–Labor Day, daily 10–4.*

★ **Rodman's Hollow.** Off Cooneymus Road, this spot is a fine example of a glacial outwash basin. It was the first piece of property purchased in the island's quarter-century tradition of land conservation, an effort that has succeeded in saving nearly half the island from development. At Rodman's you can descend along winding paths to the ocean, where you can hike the coastline, lie on beaches at the foot of sand and clay cliffs, or swim if the waters are calm.

Southeast Lighthouse Museum. The small repository is inside a "rescued" 1873 redbrick beacon with gingerbread detail that was moved back from the eroded 150-foot cliff. The lighthouse is a National Historic Landmark. ✉ *Mohegan Trail* ☎ *401/466–5009* 🕮 *$5* ☉ *Memorial Day–Labor Day, daily 10–4.*

West side. To explore the island's lovely west side, head west from New Harbor on West Side Road; after the Island Cemetery, you'll pass a horse farm and some small ponds. You get to the beach by turning right on Dories Cove Road or Cooneymus Beach Road; both dirt roads dead-end at the island's tranquil west shore. One mile past Dories Cove Road, peaceful West Side Road jogs left and turns into Cooneymus Road. On your right ½ mi farther is a deep ravine.

6

WORTH NOTING

Island Cemetery. At this well-maintained graveyard from the 1700s you can spot the names of long-standing Block Island families (Ball, Rose, Champlin) and take in fine views of the Great Salt Pond, the North Light, and the Rhode Island coast; on a clear day, the Jamestown–Newport Bridge is visible to the northeast. ⊠ *½ mi west of New Harbor on West Side Rd.*

New Harbor. Three docks, two hotels, and four restaurants huddled in the southeast corner of the Great Salt Pond make up this commercial area. The harbor itself—also called Great Salt Pond—shelters as many as 1,700 boats on busy weekends, hosts sail races and fishing tournaments, and is the landing point for the Montauk ferry.

Settler's Rock. On the spit of land between Sachem Pond and Cow Beach, this monument lists the names of the original settlers and marks the spot where they landed in 1661 (with their cows swimming to shore). Hiking a mile over sandy terrain will get you to the North Light.

SPORTS AND THE OUTDOORS

BEACHES

The east side of the island has a number of beaches, which, like the rest of Rhode Island's coastline, offer temperate, warm waters that are ideal for swimming from June through around September.

★ The 3-mi **Crescent Beach** runs from Old Harbor to Jerry's Point and comprises the smaller Mansion Beach and Scotch Beach. The former can be accessed just off Mansion Road, south of Jerry's Point, has deep white sand, and is easily one of New England's most beautiful beaches; in the morning, you may spot deer on the dunes. Young adults, including many summer workers, like to party, play volleyball, surf, and sun themselves at Scotch Beach, just off Corn Neck Road, a bit south of Benson Town Beach. **Frederick J. Benson Town Beach**, a family-oriented beach less than 1 mi down Corn Neck Road from Old Harbor, has a beach pavilion, parking, showers, and lifeguards. It faces a relatively calm section of surf, making it ideal for kids.

BIKING

The best way to explore Block Island is by bicycle (about $18 to $25 a day to rent) or moped (about $35 for an hour or $70 for four hours). Most rental places are open spring through fall and have child seats for bikes, and all rent bicycles in a variety of styles and sizes, including mountain bikes, hybrids, tandems, and children's bikes.

OUTFITTERS   Near Harborside Inn, **Island Bike & Moped** (⊠ *Weldon's Way* ☎ 401/466–2700) has bikes of all kinds. **Moped Man** (⊠ *Weldon's Way and Water St.* ☎ *401/466–5444* ⊕ *www.themopedman.com*) has motorized bikes on hand. Descend from the Block Island Ferry and get right on a bike at **Old Harbor Bike Shop** (⊠ *South of ferry dock* ☎ *401/466–2029*), which also rents mopeds, Jeeps, and other vehicles.

Clay Head Nature Trail can be enjoyed on foot or horseback.

BOATING

OUTFITTERS **Block Island Boat Basin** (✉ *West Side Rd., New Harbor* ☎ *401/466–2631*) is the island's best-stocked ship's store. **New Harbor Kayak** (✉ *Ocean Ave., New Harbor* ☎ *401/466–2890*) rents kayaks, paddleboats, and motorboats. **Pond & Beyond** (*Ocean Ave., New Harbor* ☎ *401/578–2773* ⊕ *www.blockisland.com/kayakbi*) offers guided, wildlife-oriented kayak tours around Great Salt Pond. **Oceans & Ponds** (✉ *Ocean and Connecticut Aves.* ☎ *401/466–5131*) rents kayaks, charters fishing boats and trimaran sail cruises, sells and rents fishing tackle, offers fishing guides, and sells outdoor clothing.

FISHING

Most of Rhode Island's record fish have been caught on Block Island. In fact, it's held the striped bass fishing record since 1984. From almost any beach, skilled anglers can land tautog and bass. Bonito and fluke are often hooked in the New Harbor channel. Shellfishing licenses may be obtained at the town hall, on Old Town Road.

OUTFITTERS **Oceans & Ponds** (✉ *Ocean and Connecticut Aves.* ☎ *401/466–5131*) sells tackle and fishing gear, operates charter trips, and provides guide services. **Twin Maples** (✉ *Beach Ave.* ☎ *401/466–5547*) sells bait.

HIKING

★ The outstanding **Clay Head Nature Trail** (✛ *Begins at the end of a dirt road at Corn Neck Rd., just past Mansion Beach Rd., about 2 mi from town*) meanders past Clay Head Swamp and along 150-foot ocean-side cliffs. Songbirds chirp and flowers bloom along the paths that lead to the beach or into the interior—an area called the Maze. The trailhead is recognizable by a simple white post marker. Trail maps are available at the **Nature Conservancy** (✉ *352 High St.* ☎ *401/466–2129*). The **Greenway**, a well-maintained trail system, meanders for more than 30 mi across the island, but some of the best hikes are along the beaches. You can hike around the entire island in about eight hours. Trail maps for the Greenway are available at the **Chamber of Commerce** (✉ *Water St.* ☎ *401/466–2982*). The **Nature Conservancy** (✉ *352 High St.* ☎ *401/466–2129*) also distributes maps and conducts nature walks; call for times or check the *Block Island Times*.

WATER SPORTS

OUTFITTERS **Island Outfitters** (✉ *Weldon's Way* ☎ *401/466–5502*) rents wet suits, spearguns, and scuba gear. PADI-certification diving courses are available, and you can buy beach gear and bathing suits. **Block Island Parasail & Watersports** (✉ *Old Harbor Basin* ☎ *401/864–2474* ⊕ *www.blockislandparasail.com*) will take you parasailing and also rents 5-person jet boats and 10-person banana boats.

SHOPPING

Island Bound (✉ *New Post Office Bldg.* ☎ *401/466–8878*) has a good selection of fiction and nonfiction titles, including excellent histories of the island. **Jessie Edwards Studios** (✉ *Post Office Square* ☎ *401/466–5314* ⊕ *www.jessieedwardsgallery.com*) showcases photographs, sculptures, and paintings, often with nautical themes. **Spring Street Gallery** (✉ *Spring St.* ☎ *401/466–5374* ⊕ *www.springstreetgallery.org*) shows and sells work including paintings, photographs, stained glass, and serigraphs by island artists and artisans. **Scarlet Begonia** (✉ *Dodge St.* ☎ *401/466–5024*) carries jewelry and crafts like handmade quilts.

NIGHTLIFE

Nightlife, at least in season, is one of Block Island's highlights, and you have approximately two dozen places to grab a drink. Check the *Block Island Times* for band listings.

Ballard's (✉ *On docks at Old Harbor* ☎ *401/466–2231* ⊕ *www.ballardsinn.com*), a popular tourist destination, is a family restaurant with a beach and an outdoor bar by day. By night it becomes a dance club with live entertainment. **Captain Nick's Rock and Roll Bar** (✉ *34 Ocean Ave.* ☎ *401/466–5670* ⊕ *www.captainnicks.com*), a fortress of summertime debauchery and the host of June's Block Island Music Festival, has four bars and two decks on two floors. In season, bands play nightly. **McGovern's Yellow Kittens Tavern** (✉ *Corn Neck Rd.* ☎ *401/466–5855*) has darts, Ping-Pong, pool, and bands on summer weekend nights.

WHERE TO EAT

$$$$ ✕ **Atlantic Inn.** The romantic restaurant at this venerable inn serves imaginative new American fare in its airy dining room, which is arguably the swankiest on the island. Meals are served from a four-course, prix-fixe dinner that's available with wine pairings, and the menus change often. Typical is the starter of charred-tuna poke (a Hawaiian dish usually consisting of cubed raw fish) with Asian greens and a sesame-honey

AMERICAN
★

Digging for clams is a fun pastime on Block Island's beaches.

sauce, and the main dish of jerk-spiced rack of lamb with black-eyed-pea and plantain tostones (fritters), fried tomatoes, grilled leeks, and a light pepper broth. A light tapas menu is served in the bar and features eclectic, bite-size portions, from cheese and charcuterie plates to lobster-roll sliders. ⊠ *High St.* ☎ *401/466–5883* ⊕ *www.atlanticinn.com* ▤ *D, MC, V* ⊗ *Closed late Oct.–mid-Apr. No lunch.*

$$–$$$
AMERICAN
★

✕ **The BeacHead**. The food—especially the Rhode Island clam chowder—is consistently excellent, the price is right, and you won't feel like a tourist at this locals' hangout. Play pool, catch up on town gossip, or sit at the bar and stare out at the sea. The menu and service are unpretentious; you can stop in for a burger at lunch or try somewhat more ambitious fare, such as Thai shrimp pasta or steak au poivre, at dinner. ⊠ *Corn Neck Rd.* ☎ *401/466–2249* ⚠ *Reservations not accepted* ▤ *MC, V* ⊗ *Closed Mon.–Wed. Dec.–Mar.*

$$$
AMERICAN
Fodor's Choice
★

✕ **Eli's**. A spaghetti eatery turned bistro, Eli's is the source of some of Block Island's most creative cuisine. Chef Melissa Puglia changes the menu seasonally but includes a mix of seafood, vegetarian, and steak. Chili-grilled local swordfish with fresh corn and a cilantro-lime aioli is typical, as is the hearty Greek orzo pasta with house-made lamb meatballs, green olives, grilled eggplant, and herbed lemon–brown butter sauce. The pastry chef provides such worthy sweet endings as mocha-swirl cheesecake and warm, open-face blueberry pie. ⊠ *457 Chapel St.* ☎ *401/466–5230* ⊕ *www.elisblockisland.com* ⚠ *Reservations not accepted* ▤ *D, MC, V* ⊗ *Closed Jan.–Apr.*

$–$$
SEAFOOD

✕ **Finn's**. A Block Island institution, Finn's serves reliable fried and broiled seafood and a wonderful smoked bluefish pâté. For lunch try the Workman's Special platter—a burger, coleslaw, and fries. Eat inside or out on the deck, or get food to go. Finn's raw bar is on an upstairs deck that overlooks Old Harbor. ⊠ *Ferry Landing* ☎ *401/466–2473* ⌂ *Reservations not accepted* ⊟ *MC, V* ☺ *Closed mid-Oct.–May.*

$$$–$$$$ ✕ **Hotel Manisses.** The chef at the island's premier restaurant for Ameri-
AMERICAN can cuisine uses herbs and vegetables from the hotel's garden and locally caught seafood to prepare superb dishes such as tuna tartare with fried tofu and ginger aioli and grilled swordfish with lobster mashed potatoes and a lemon beurre blanc. Fans of red meat appreciate the tender bison Wellington, with a port-wine demi-glace. ⊠ *1 Spring St.* ☎ *401/466–2421* ⊕ *www.blockislandresorts.com* ⊟ *MC, V* ☺ *Closed Nov.–Apr.*

WHERE TO STAY

Lodgings on Block Island are booked well in advance (full by April) for weekends in July and August. Many visitors rent homes for stays of a week or more. **Ballard Hall Real Estate** (⊠ *Ocean Ave.* ☎ *401/466–8883* ⊕ *www.blockislandproperty.com*) is a reliable agent. **Sullivan Real Estate** (⊠ *Water St.* ☎ *401/466–5521* ⊕ *www.blockislandhouses.com*).

$$$–$$$$ ▦ **Atlantic Inn.** Perched on a hill of floral gardens and undulating lawns,
★ away from the hubbub of the Old Harbor area, this long, white, classic 1879 Victorian resort has big windows, high ceilings, a sweeping stair-case, and lovely views. Most of the oak and maple furnishings in the rooms are original to the building. Each morning the inn's pastry chef prepares a buffet breakfast with fresh baked goods. The on-site restau-rant is very good. **Pros:** spectacular hilltop location; beautiful veranda for whiling away the afternoon; grand decor. **Cons:** no TVs or high-speed Internet in rooms. ⊠ *High St.* ⌂ *Box 1788, 02807* ☎ *401/466–5883 or 800/224–7422* ⊕ *www.atlanticinn.com* ⋈ *20 rooms, 1 suite* ♨ *In-room: a/c, no TV. In-hotel: restaurant, tennis courts, Internet ter-minal* ⊟ *D, MC, V* ☺ *Closed late Oct.–mid-Apr.* ❑ *CP.*

$$–$$$ ▦ **Barrington Inn.** This 1886 inn is quiet and bright with views of Trims Pond, Great Salt Pond, and Crescent Beach. Three rooms have private decks; there's also a large common deck. A hearty Continental break-fast is served in the dining room and outside on the deck. Two apart-ments (rented by the week in season) in a separate building are good options for families. The inn has a pair of sister properties run by the same owners, the Inn at Block Island and the Jane Marie Cottage (the latter is open year-round). **Pros:** commanding views; reasonably priced. **Cons:** furnishings are quite simple. ⊠ *Beach Ave.* ⌂ *Box 397, 02807* ☎ *401/466–5510 or 888/279–9400* ⊕ *www.thebarringtoninn.com* ⋈ *6 rooms, 2 apartments* ♨ *In-room: a/c, Wi-Fi. In-hotel: Wi-Fi hotspot, no kids under 12* ⊟ *D, MC, V* ☺ *Closed Nov.–Apr.* ❑ *CP.*

$$$–$$$$ ▦ **Blue Dory Inn.** This Old Harbor district inn has been a guesthouse since its construction in 1898. Thanks to Ann Law, the dynamic owner/ manager, its main building and three small shingle-and-clapboard out-buildings run efficiently. Though not large, the rooms are tastefully appointed with Victorian antiques, some have Jacuzzi tubs, and each has either an ocean or a harbor view. Couples looking for a romantic hideaway often enjoy the Tea House, which has a porch overlooking Crescent Beach. **Pros:** great in-town location; relatively affordable; open

in winter. **Cons:** some units are small. ✉ *61 Dodge St.* ☎ *Box 488, 02807* ☎ *401/466–5891 or 800/992–7290* ⊕ *www.blockislandinns.com* ⇨ *11 rooms, 4 cottages, 3 suites* ♿ *In-room: a/c, DVD (some). In-hotel: Internet terminal* ⊟ *AE, MC, V* ▯⊙▯ *BP.*

$$–$$$ ▣ **Rose Farm Inn.** With simpler and more rustic accommodations in a
Fodor's Choice   late-19th-century, pale-blue restored farmhouse and more luxurious
★   units across a country lane inside a Colonial-style 1990s structure,
this property set on a 20-acre pastoral farmstead offers two distinctive
styles. The constant here is friendly, efficient service and one of the most
relaxing settings on the island—rooms and porches overlook rolling
fields and woodland in every direction. **Pros:** Captain Rose rooms have
whirlpool tubs; bike-rental shop next door; quiet setting yet easy walk
to Old Town. **Cons:** bathrooms in Farm House a bit rustic; few in-room
amenities. ✉ *Roslyn Rd.* ☎ *401/466-2034* ⊕ *www.rosefarminn.com*
⇨ *19 rooms, 17 with bath* ♿ *In-room: no a/c, no TV, Wi-Fi. In-hotel:
Wi-Fi hotspot* ⊟ *AE, MC, V* ⊙ *Closed mid-Oct.–early May* ▯⊙▯ *CP.*

Vermont

WORD OF MOUTH

"I spend the rest of the year looking forward to [autumn in Vermont]. There is nowhere else on earth I'd rather be in October. We do get lots of visitors this time of year (I love to look for the out-of-state license plates when I am out peeping at leaves—they always out-number the Vermont plates)."

—patomech

WELCOME TO VERMONT

TOP REASONS TO GO

★ **Small-town charm:** Vermont rolls out a seemingly never-ending supply of tiny, charming towns made of steeples, general stores, village squares, red barns, and B&Bs.

★ **Ski resorts:** The East's best skiing takes place in uncrowded, modern facilities, with great views and lots and lots of fresh snow.

★ **Fall foliage:** Perhaps the most vivid colors in North America wave from the trees in September and October, when the whole state is ablaze.

★ **Gorgeous landscapes:** This sparsely populated, heavily forested state is an ideal place to find peace and quiet amid the mountains and valleys.

★ **Tasty and healthy eats:** The state's great soil and focus on local farming and ingredients yields great cheeses, dairies, orchards, vineyards, local food resources, and restaurants.

1 Southern Vermont. Most people's introduction to the state is southern Vermont, accessible by car from New York and Boston. Like elsewhere across the state, you'll find unspoiled towns, romantic B&Bs, rural farms, and pristine forests. There are two notable exceptions: sophisticated little Manchester has upscale shopping, and independent Brattleboro is a hippie outpost and environmentally conscious town.

2 Central Vermont. Similar to southern Vermont in character and geography, central Vermont's star is Stowe, the quintessential ski town east of the Mississippi. Warren, Waitsfield, and Middlebury are among its charming small towns.

3 Northern Vermont. The northernmost part of the state is a place of contrasts. Burlington, on Vermont's "West Coast," is the state's most populous city at around 60,000 residents; it's an environmentally sensitive, crunchy, laid-back college town. To the east, the landscape becomes desolate, with natural beauty and almost no significant population, making the Northeast Kingdom a refuge for nature lovers and aficionados of wide open northern beauty.

GETTING ORIENTED

Vermont can be divided into three regions. The southern part of the state, flanked by Bennington on the west and Brattleboro on the east, played an important role in Vermont's Revolutionary War–era drive to independence (yes, there was once a Republic of Vermont) and its eventual statehood. The central part is characterized by rugged mountains and the gently rolling dairy lands near Lake Champlain. Northern Vermont is home to the state's capital, Montpelier, and its largest city, Burlington, as well as its most rural area, the Northeast Kingdom. The Green Mountains run from north to south up the center of the state; this central spinal corridor is unpopulated, protected national forest.

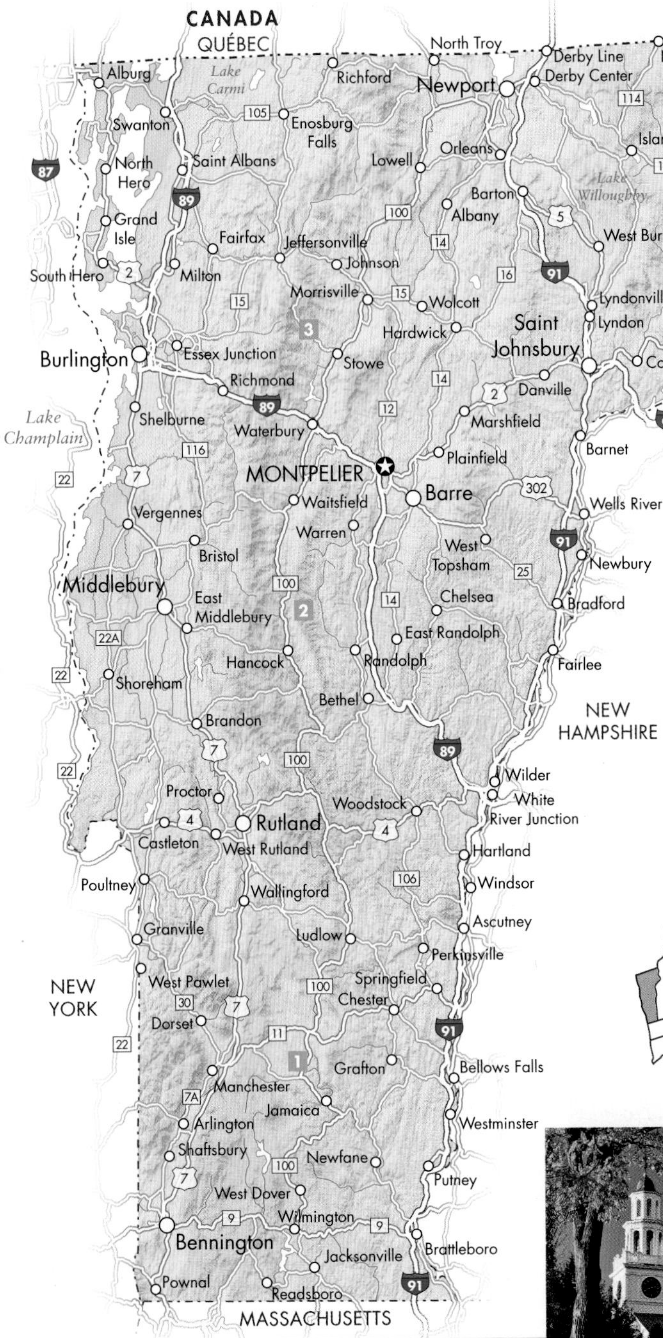
CANADA
QUÉBEC
NEW YORK
NEW HAMPSHIRE
MASSACHUSETTS
Lake Carmi
Lake Willoughby
Lake Champlain
MONTPELIER
Burlington
Middlebury
Rutland
Bennington
Barre
Newport
Saint Johnsbury
Alburg
Swanton
North Hero
Grand Isle
South Hero
Richford
Enosburg Falls
Saint Albans
Fairfax
Milton
Jeffersonville
Johnson
Morrisville
Lowell
Orleans
Barton
Albany
North Troy
Derby Line
Derby Center
Norton
Beecher Falls
Island Pond
West Burke
Guildhall
Lyndonville
Lyndon
Concord
Danville
Marshfield
Plainfield
Barnet
Wells River
Newbury
Bradford
Fairlee
Wolcott
Hardwick
Stowe
Essex Junction
Richmond
Waterbury
Shelburne
Vergennes
Waitsfield
Warren
Bristol
West Topsham
Chelsea
East Randolph
Randolph
Bethel
East Middlebury
Hancock
Shoreham
Brandon
Proctor
Castleton
West Rutland
Woodstock
Wilder
White River Junction
Hartland
Windsor
Ascutney
Perkinsville
Poultney
Wallingford
Granville
Ludlow
West Pawlet
Springfield
Chester
Dorset
Grafton
Bellows Falls
Manchester
Jamaica
Westminster
Arlington
Shaftsbury
Newfane
Putney
West Dover
Wilmington
Brattleboro
Jacksonville
Pownal
Readsboro
0 10 mi
0 10 km
1
2
3

7

VERMONT PLANNER

When to Go

In summer, the state is lush and green, although in winter, the hills and towns are blanketed with snow and skiers travel from around the East Coast to challenge Vermont's peaks. Fall is one of the most amazing times to come. If you have never seen a kaleidoscope of autumn colors, a trip to Vermont is worth braving the slow-moving traffic and paying the extra money for fall lodging. The only time things really slow down is during "mud" season—otherwise known as late spring. Even innkeepers have told guests to come another time. Activities in the Champlain Islands come essentially to a halt in the winter, except for ice fishing and snowmobiling. Two of the state's biggest attractions, Shelburne Farms and the Shelburne Museum, are closed mid-October through April. Otherwise, though everything looks completely different depending on the season, Vermont is open all year.

Getting Here and Around

Air Travel: Continental, Delta, JetBlue, United, and US Airways fly into Burlington International Airport. Rutland State Airport has daily service to and from Boston on US Airways Express.

Boat Travel: Lake Champlain Ferries (☎ *802/864–9804* ⊕ *www.lakechamplainferries.com*) operates three ferry crossing routes between the lake's Vermont and New York shores: Grand Isle–Plattsburgh, NY; Burlington–Port Kent, NY; and Charlotte–Essex, NY.

Car Travel: Vermont is divided by a mountainous north–south middle, with a main highway on either side: scenic Route 7 on the western side and Interstate 91 (which begins in New Haven and runs through Hartford, central Massachussets, and along the Connecticut River in Vermont to the Canadian border) on the east. Interstate 89 runs from New Hampshire across central Vermont from White River Junction to Burlington and up to the Canadian border. For current road conditions, call 800/429–7623.

Train Travel: Amtrak (☎ *800/872–7245* ⊕ *www.amtrak. com*) has daytime service linking Washington, D.C., with Brattleboro, Bellows Falls, White River Junction, Montpelier, Waterbury, Essex Junction, and St. Albans via its Vermonter line. Amtrak's Ethan Allen Express connects New York City with Fair Haven and Rutland.

Planning Your Time

There are many ways to take advantage of Vermont's beauty: skiing or hiking its mountains, biking or driving its back roads, fishing or sailing its waters, shopping for local products, visiting its museums and sights, or simply finding the perfect inn and never leaving the front porch.

Distances are relatively short, yet the mountains and many back roads will slow a traveler's pace. You can see a representative north–south section of Vermont in a few days; if you have up to a week, you can hit the highlights. Note that many inns have two-night-minimum stays on weekends and holidays.

About the Restaurants

Everything that makes Vermont good and wholesome is distilled in its eateries, making the regional cuisine much more defined than neighboring states. With an almost political intensity, farmers and chefs have banded together to insist on utilizing Vermont's wonderful bounty. Especially in summer, the produce and meats are impeccable. Many of the state's restaurants belong to the Vermont Fresh Network (⊕ www.vermontfresh.net), a partnership that encourages chefs to create menus from local produce.

Great chefs are coming to Vermont for the quality of life, and the New England Culinary Institute is a recruiting ground for new talent. Seasonal menus use local fresh herbs and vegetables along with native game. Look for imaginative approaches to native New England foods such as maple syrup (Vermont is the largest U.S. producer), dairy products (especially cheese), native fruits and berries, "new Vermont" products such as salsa and salad dressings, and venison, quail, pheasant, and other game.

Your chances of finding a table for dinner vary with the season: lengthy waits are common at peak times (a reservation is always advisable); the slow months are April and November. Some of the best dining is at country inns.

About the Hotels

Vermont's only large chain hotels are in Burlington and Rutland. Elsewhere it's just quaint inns, B&Bs, and small motels. The many lovely and sometimes quite luxurious inns and B&Bs provide what many people consider the quintessential Vermont lodging experience. Most areas have traditional base ski condos; at these you sacrifice charm for ski-and-stay deals and proximity to the lifts. Rates are highest during foliage season, from late September to mid-October, and lowest in late spring and November, although many properties close during these times. Winter is high season at Vermont's ski resorts.

WHAT IT COSTS					
	¢	$	$$	$$$	$$$$
Restaurants	under $10	$10–$16	$17–$24	$25–$35	over $35
Hotels		under $100	$100–$149	$150–$199	$200–$250	over $250

Restaurant prices are based on the median main course price at dinner. Hotel prices are for two people in a standard double room in high season, excluding service and tax. Some inns add a 15%–18% service charge. (Vermont has a 9% hotel tax.)

Outdoor Activities

Biking: Vermont, especially the often deserted roads of the Northeast Kingdom, is great bicycle-touring country. Many companies lead weekend tours and weeklong trips throughout the state. If you'd like to go it on your own, most chambers of commerce have brochures highlighting good cycling routes in their area.

Canoeing and Kayaking: Getting on Vermont's many rivers and lakes is a great way to experience nature. Outfitters can be found almost anywhere there's water.

Fishing: Central Vermont is the heart of the state's warm-water lake and pond fishing area. Lake Champlain, stocked annually with salmon and lake trout, has become the state's ice-fishing capital.

Hiking: Vermont is an ideal state for hiking—80% of the state is forest, and trails are everywhere. The Appalachian Trail runs the length of the state. In fact, it was the first portion of the trail to be completed, and in Vermont it is called the Long Trail. Many bookstores in the state have numerous volumes dedicated to local hiking.

Skiing: The Green Mountains run through the middle of Vermont like a bumpy spine, visible from almost every point in the state; generous accumulations of snow make them an ideal site for skiing. Route 100 is also known as Skier's Highway, passing by 13 of the state's ski areas.

7

VERMONT FALL FOLIAGE DRIVE

Eighty percent of Vermont is forested, and since cities are few and far between, the interior of Vermont is a rural playground for leaf peepers and widely considered to have the most intense range of foliage colors anywhere on the continent. The few distractions from the dark reds and yellow, oranges and russets—the tiny towns and hamlets—are as pristine as nature itself.

Begin this drive in Manchester Village, along the old-fashioned, well-to-do homes lining Main Street, and drive south to Arlington, North Bennington, and Old Bennington. Stop first just a mile south along 7A at **Hildene**, the Lincoln family home. The 412 acres of explorable grounds here are ablaze with color, and the views over the Battenkill Valley are as good as any you can find anywhere. Continue south another mile along 7A to **Equinox Nursery**, where you can pick your own pumpkin from a huge patch, try delicious apple cider and cider doughnuts, and take in the stunning countryside. A few more miles south along 7A is the small town of Arlington.

BEST TIME TO GO

Late September and early October are the times to go, with the southern area peaking about a week later than the north. Remember to book hotels in advance. The state has a Fall Foliage Hotline and an online interactive map (☎ 800/VERMONT ⊕ www. foliage-vermont.com).

PLANNING YOUR TIME

The drive from Manchester to Bennington outlined here is just 30 minutes, but a relaxed day is best to take in all the sights. You'll want to allot one to two hours for Hildene, and less than an hour for each of the other stops.

From 7A in Arlington, you can take two adventurous and stunning detours. One is pure foliage: follow 313 west a few miles to the New York state border for more beautiful views Or head east a mile to East Arlington where delightful shops await you, including **Grist Mill Antiques**, which is set right above a wonderfully cascading brook. (You can continue even farther east from this spot to Kelly Stand Road leading into the Green Mountains; this is a little-known route that can't be beat.) Back on 7A South in Arlington, stop at the **Cheese House**, the delightfully cheesy roadside attraction.

Farther south into Shaftsbury is **Clearbrook Farm**, a brilliant place for cider and fresh produce and pumpkins. Robert Frost spent much of his life in South Shaftsbury, and you can learn about his life at his former home, the **Stone House**. From South Shaftsbury take Route 67 through North Bennington and continue on to Route 67A in Old Bennington. Go up the 306-foot-high **Bennington Battle Monument** to survey the seasonal views across four states. Back down from the clouds, walk a few serene blocks to the cemetery of the **Old First Church**, where Robert Frost is buried, and contemplate his autumnal poem, "Nothing Gold Can Stay."

NEED A BREAK?

Equinox Nursery (✉ *1158 Main St. [7A], Manchester* ☎ *802-362-2610* ⊕ *www. equinoxvalleynursery.com* ⊙ *Apr.–Dec., Mon.–Sat. 8–5, Sun. 9–4)* carries fresh produce, seasonal snacks, and is full of family-friendly fall activities—a corn maze, pumpkin golf (mini played with small pumpkins and croquet mallets), hay rides, and pumpkin carving.

Set on more than 20 acres, **Clearbrook Farm** (✉ *47 Hidden Valley Rd., Manchester* ☎ *802-442-4273* ⊕ *www.clearbrookfarm. com* ⊙ *May–Aug., daily 9–6; Sept.–Oct., daily 10–6)* sells their own organic produce, in addition to baked goods and other seasonal treats.

Get your Vermont cheddar fix at the **Cheese House** (✉ *5187 Rt. 7A, Arlington* ☎ *802-375-9033* ⊕ *www. thevermontcheesehouse. com*), which also sells maple syrup and other local products and gifts.

7

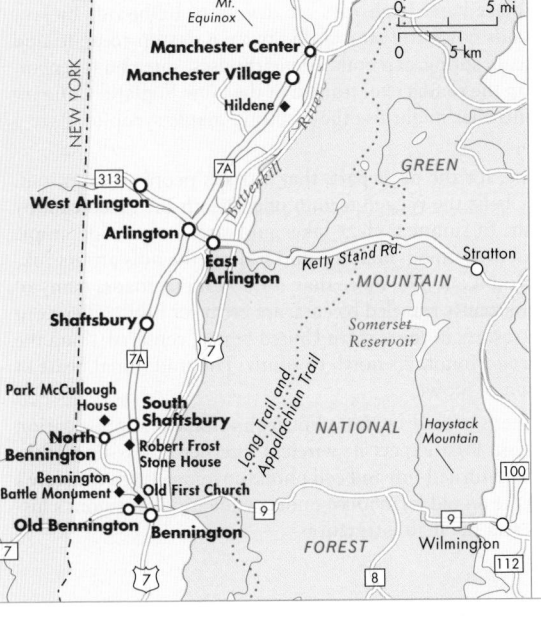

Updated by
Michael de
Zayas

Vermont is an entire state of hidden treasures and unspoiled scenery. Wander anywhere in the state—80% is forest—and you'll travel a pristine countryside dotted with farms and framed by mountains. Tiny towns with church steeples, village greens, and clapboard Colonial-era houses are perfect for exploring.

In summer, clear lakes and streams make great swimming and fishing. In fall, the leaves have their last hurrah, painting the mountainsides a stunning show of yellow, gold, red, and orange. In winter, Vermont's ski resorts are the prime enticement. Almost anywhere you go, any time of year, it will make you smile and reach for your camera.

Sprawl has no place here. Highways are devoid of billboards by law, and on some roads cows still stop traffic twice a day en route to and from the pasture. In spring, sap boils in sugarhouses, some built generations ago, and up the road a chef trained at the New England Culinary Institute in Montpelier might use the resulting maple syrup to glaze a pork tenderloin.

It's the landscape, for the most part, that attracts people to Vermont. The rolling hills belie the rugged terrain underneath the green canopy of forest growth. In summer, clear lakes and streams provide ample opportunities for swimming, boating, and fishing; the hills attract hikers and mountain bikers. The more than 14,000 mi of roads, many of them only intermittently traveled by cars, are great for biking. Vermont has the best ski resorts in the eastern United States, centered along the spine of the Green Mountains north to south. The traditional heart of skiing is the town of Stowe.

Vermont may seem locked in time, but technological sophistication appears where you least expect it: wireless Internet access in a 19th-century farmhouse-turned-inn and cell phone coverage from the state's highest peaks. Like an old farmhouse under renovation, Vermont's historic exterior is still the main attraction.

SOUTHERN VERMONT

Cross into the Green Mountain State from Massachusetts on Interstate 91, and you might feel as if you've entered a new country. There isn't a town in sight. What you see are forested hills punctuated by rolling pastures. When you reach Brattleboro, no fast-food joints or strip malls line the exits to signal your arrival at southeastern Vermont's gateway city. En route to downtown, you pass by Victorian-era homes on tree-lined streets. From Brattleboro, you can cross over the spine of the Green Mountains toward Bennington and Manchester.

The state's southwest corner is the southern terminus of the Green Mountain National Forest, dotted with lakes, threaded with trails and old forest roads, and home to three big ski resorts: Bromley, Stratton, and Mount Snow.

The towns are listed in counterclockwise order in this section, beginning in the east in Brattleboro, then traveling west along Route 9 toward Bennington, then north to Manchester and Weston and south along scenic Routes 100 and 30 back to Townshend and Newfane.

BRATTLEBORO

60 mi south of White River Junction.

Brattleboro has drawn political activists and earnest counterculturists since the 1960s. Today, the city of 12,000 is still politically and culturally active, making it Vermont's hippest outside of Burlington.

GETTING HERE AND AROUND

Brattleboro is near the intersection of Route 9, the principal east–west highway also known as the Molly Stark Trail, and Interstate 91. For downtown, use Exit 2 from Interstate 91.

ESSENTIALS

Visitor Information Brattleboro Area Chamber of Commerce (⊠ *180 Main St.* ☎ *802/254–4565 or 877/254–4565* ⊕ *www.brattleborochamber.org*).

EXPLORING

Brattleboro Museum and Art Center. Downtown is the hub of Brattleboro's art scene, with this museum in historic Union Station at the forefront. It presents changing exhibits created by locally, nationally, and internationally renowned artists. ⊠ *10 Vernon St.* ☎ *802/257–0124* ⊕ *www.brattleboromuseum.org* 🖾 *$6, free 1st Fri. each month 5–8:30* 🕙 *Thurs.–Mon. 11–5, 1st Fri. each month 11–8:30.*

SPORTS AND THE OUTDOORS

BIKING **Brattleboro Bicycle Shop** (⊠ *165 Main St.* ☎ *802/254–8644* ⊕ *www.bratbike.com*) rents and repairs hybrid bikes.

CANOEING **Vermont Canoe Touring Center** (⊠ *451 Putney Rd.* ☎ *802/257–5008*) rents canoes and kayaks.

SHOPPING

★ **Brattleboro Books** (⊠ *106 Main St.* ☎ *802/257–7044*) boasts more than 75,000 used books and is a great source for local goings-on.

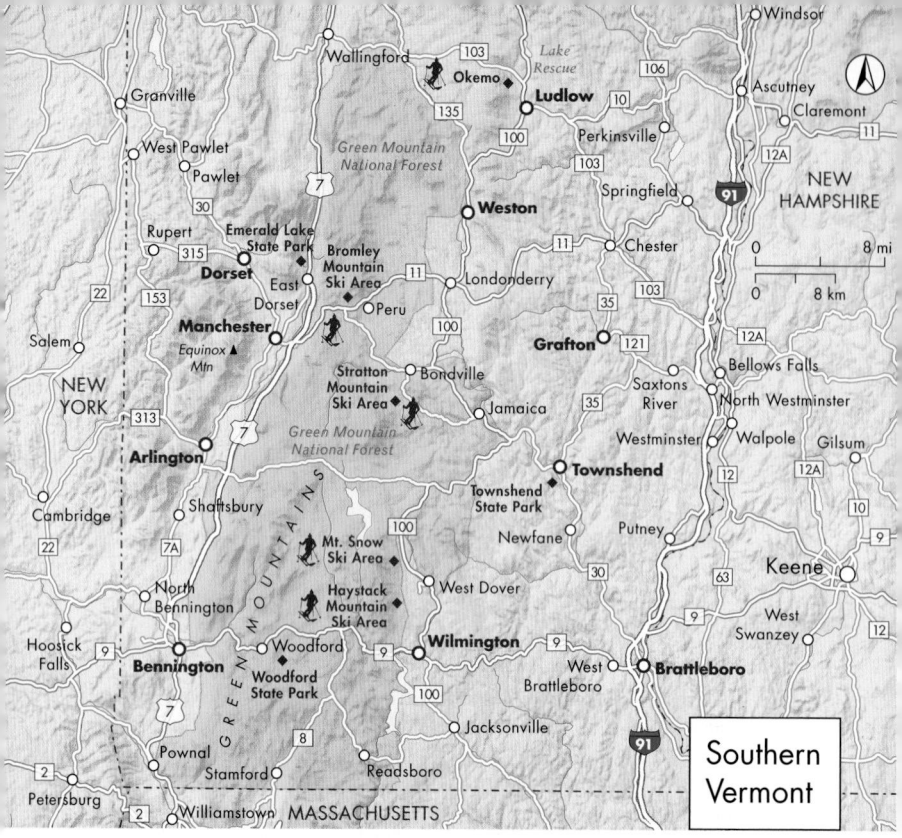

ART   **Gallery in the Woods** (✉ *143 Main St.* ☎ *802/257–4777* ⊕ *www.galleryinthewoods.com*) sells art, jewelry, and glassware from around the world. To get a sense of the vibrant works being produced by young local artists, head to the back of the **Turn it Up** record shop to find **Through the Music** (✉ *2 Elliot St.* ☎ *802/779–3188* ⊕ *www.turnitup.com*), an otherwise easy-to-miss gallery. The excellent contemporary art spans genres from painting to pottery. **Vermont Artisan Designs** (✉ *106 Main St.* ☎ *802/257–7044* ⊕ *www.vtartisans.com*) displays ceramics, glass, wood, clothing, jewelry, and furniture from more than 300 artists.

OFF THE BEATEN PATH

Putney. Nine miles upriver, this small town, with a population of just over 2,000, is the country cousin of bustling Brattleboro and is a haven for writers, artists, and craftspeople. There are dozens of pottery studios to visit and a few orchards. In 2009, a fire burned down the world-class general store that had served as the heart of the community, but there is talk of rebuilding. Watch wool being spun into yarn at the **Green Mountain Spinnery** (✉ *7 Brickyard La., off I–91, Exit 4* ☎ *802/387–4528 or 800/321–9665* ⊕ *www.spinnery.com*). The factory shop, which is open daily all year, sells yarn, knitting accessories, and patterns. Tours are conducted at 1:30 on the first and third Tuesday of the month. **Harlow's Sugar House** (✉ *563 Bellows Falls Rd., Putney* ☎ *802/387–5852* ⊕ *www.vermontsugar.com*), 2 mi north of Putney, has a working cider mill and sugarhouse, as well as seasonal apple and berry picking. The family has been sugaring on this farm since 1927. You can buy cider, maple syrup, and other items in the gift shop.

NIGHTLIFE AND THE ARTS

ARTS Brattleboro has an evening gallery walk on the first Friday of each month from 5:30 to 8:30.

NIGHTLIFE **Latchis Theater** (⊠ *50 Main St.* ☎ *802/246–1500* ⊕ *latchis.com*) hosts art exhibits when movies aren't playing. It's worth walking in just to check out the hand-painted murals of Greek mythology.

QUICK BITES The gathering spot in town for coffee and conversation is **Mocha Joe's** (⊠ *82 Main St.* ☎ *802/257–7794*), which takes great care in sourcing beans from places like Kenya, Ethiopia, and Guatemala. This is ground zero for Brattleboro's contemporary bohemian spirit.

WHERE TO EAT

¢–$ ✕ **Brattleboro Food Co-op.** This is one of the best foodie stops in the state
AMERICAN to stock up on Vermont's finest artisanal products. Its charms include different grades of maple syrup served from tap. Pick up a pre-made sandwich or order a plate of curry chicken at the deli counter, then eat it in this busy market's small sitting area. Natural and organic is the focus, with everything from tofu sandwiches to beef *satay* (skewered grilled meat). The delicatessen is connected to a natural-foods market and serves breakfast. ⊠ *2 Main St.* ☎ *802/257–0236* ⊕ *www.brattleborofoodcoop.com* ▭ *MC, V.*

$$–$$$ ✕ **Max's.** Pasta creations at this trendy place include artichoke-mascar-
ITALIAN pone ravioli and Tuscan-style cauliflower with linguine. Complementing this *nuovo* Italian menu are eclectic entrées such as mahimahi in parchment and lavender tea–smoked salmon. Sunday brunch is both traditional and adventurous, with everything from eggs to curry rice kedgeree. ⊠ *889 Putney Rd.* ☎ *802/254–7747* ▭ *MC, V* ☺ *No dinner Mon. Closed Tues.*

$$–$$$ ✕ **Peter Havens.** In a town better known for tofu than toniness, this chic
STEAKHOUSE little bistro knows just what to do with a filet mignon: serve it with
★ Roquefort walnut butter. One room is painted a warm red, another in sage; both are punctuated by copies of Fernando Botero paintings, creating a look that is one of the most sophisticated in the state. Try the house-cured gravlax made with lemon vodka or the fresh seasonal seafood, which even includes a spring fling with soft-shell crabs. The wine list is superb. ⊠ *32 Elliot St.* ☎ *802/257–3333* ⊕ *www.peterhavens.com* ▭ *AE, MC, V* ☺ *Closed Sun. and Mon. No lunch.*

$$$$ ✕ **T.J. Buckley's.** It's easy to miss this tiny restaurant, but it's worth seek-
ECLECTIC ing out as the most romantic little eatery in Vermont. Open the doors to
Fodor's Choice the sleek black 1920s diner and enter what amounts to a very intimate
★ theater, with a mere 18 seats for the show. The stage is an open kitchen, the flames a few feet away, and working under the whisper of vocal jazz and candlelight is the star of the show: Michael Fuller, the dashing owner and sole chef, who has been at the helm for 25 years. The contemporary menu is conveyed verbally each day and is based on locally available ingredients. It's dinner theater for culinary fans, a romantic triumph.

✉ *132 Elliot St.* ☎ *802/257–4922*
🍴 *Reservations essential* ⊟ *No credit cards* 🕐 *Closed Mon. and Tues. No lunch.*

¢–$ ✕ **Top of the Hill Grill.** Hickory-

SOUTHERN   smoked ribs, beef brisket, apple-smoked turkey, and pulled pork are a few of the favorites at this barbecue outside town. Larger parties can opt for "family-style" dinners, and homemade pecan pie is the dessert of choice. You can sit indoors in the informal dining room with big windows, but the best seats are outdoors at picnic tables overlooking the West River. ✉ *632 Putney Rd.* ☎ *802/258–9178* ⊕ *www.topofthehillgrill.com* ⊟ *No credit cards* 🕐 *Closed Nov.–mid-Apr.*

BILLBOARDS AND VERMONT

Did you know that there are no billboards in Vermont? The state banned them in 1967 (similar laws exist in Maine, Alaska, and Hawaii), and the last one came down in 1975, so when you look out your window, you see trees and other scenic sights, not advertisements. (It may make playing the Alphabet Game with your child a bit difficult.)

WHERE TO STAY

$$$ 🏨 **Forty Putney Road.** Engaging hosts Tim and Amy Brady run this French-style manse and have restored some of its more interesting original features (like nickel-plated bathroom fixtures) and added new ones (like flat-screen TVs). They've made sure that it's full of thoughtful and comforting details, such as the mini-fridge stocked with complimentary soda, water, granola bars, and chips. Other indoor and outdoor treats include a hot tub, a billiard table, and the neighboring Retreat Meadows, a bird sanctuary that has good hiking trails. There's no restaurant, but a decent pub menu and wine are offered. **Pros:** caring hosts; clean, remodeled rooms. **Cons:** short walk into town; rates vary and spike during busy periods. ✉ *192 Putney Rd.* ☎ *802/254–6268 or 800/941–2413* ⊕ *www.fortyputneyroad.com* 🛏 *5 rooms, 1 suite*   *In-room: DVD, Wi-Fi. In-hotel: room service, bar, laundry service, Wi-Fi hotspot, no kids under 12* ⊟ *AE, D, MC, V* ⊚*BP.*

$$ 🏨 **Hickory Ridge House.** If you're looking for a relaxing country get-

Fodor'sChoice   away, this 1808 Federal-style mansion, a former sheep farm set on a

★   wide meadow, is a sure bet. The historic redbrick house has a sturdy comfort that distinguishes it from daintier inns. Owners Gillian and Dennis Pettit, along with their dogs Jack and Gracie, bring an English touch to it all. Most rooms have Rumford fireplaces and canopy beds; all have fine linens. A separate two-bedroom cottage has a full kitchen. Thousands of acres of nature preserve surround the property's 8 acres of cleared meadow, making it great for hiking and cross-country skiing. **Pros:** peaceful, scenic property; terrific house; great breakfast; quintessential B&B experience. **Cons:** can be expensive. ✉ *53 Hickory Ridge Rd., 11 mi north of Brattleboro, Putney* ☎ *802/387–5709 or 800/380–9218* ⊕ *www.hickoryridgehouse.com* 🛏 *6 rooms, 1 cottage*   *In-room: DVD, Wi-Fi. In-hotel: Internet terminal, Wi-Fi hotspot, some pets allowed* ⊟ *MC, V* ⊚*BP.*

The rolling green hills of Putney are home to many organic farm operations.

$ 🏨 **Latchis Hotel.** To stay in the heart of town at a low rate, you can do no better than the Latchis. The three-story art deco landmark is run by a nonprofit group dedicated to preserving and restoring the 1938 building. Rooms are not lavish, but they are clean and functional, with original sinks and tiling in the bathrooms. Most overlook Main Street, with New Hampshire's mountains in the background. The lobby has original and notably colorful terrazzo floors. Downstairs you can catch a movie under the impressive zodiac ceiling of the Latchis Theater or eat at the Flat St. Brew Pub ($–$$). **Pros:** heart-of-town location; good value. **Cons:** clean but dull furnishings; less personality than area B&Bs. ✉ *50 Main St.* ☎ *802/254–6300 or 800/798–6301* ⊕ *www.latchis.com* 🛏 *30 rooms, 3 suites* ♿ *In-room: refrigerator, Wi-Fi. In-hotel: Wi-Fi hotspot* ⊟ *AE, MC, V* ⊙ *CP.*

WILMINGTON

18 mi west of Brattleboro.

The village of Wilmington, with its classic Main Street lined with 18th- and 19th-century buildings, anchors the Mount Snow Valley. Most of the valley's lodging and dining establishments, however, line Route 100, which travels 5 mi north to West Dover and Mount Snow, where skiers flock on winter weekends. The area abounds with cultural activity year-round, from concerts to art exhibits.

GETTING HERE AND AROUND

Wilmington is at the junction of Routes 9 and 100. West Dover and Mount Snow are a few miles to the north along Route 100.

CLOSE UP

Vermont Maple Syrup

Vermont is one of the country's smallest states, but it's the largest producer of maple syrup. A visit to a maple farm is a great way to learn all about sugaring, the process of taking maple tree sap and making syrup. Sap is stored in a sugar maple tree's roots in the winter, and in the spring when conditions are just right, the sap runs up and is capable of being tapped. Tapping season takes place in March and April, which is when all maple in the state is produced.

Maple sap is collected in buckets.

One of the best parts of visiting a maple farm is getting to taste the four grades of syrup. As the sugaring season goes on and days get warmer, the sap becomes progressively darker and stronger flavored. Color, clarity and flavor define the four grades of syrup. Is one grade better than another? Nope. It's just a question of taste. Sap drawn early in the season produces the lightest color, and has the most delicate flavor: this is called Vermont Fancy. Vermont Grade A Medium Amber has a mellow flavor. Vermont Grade A Dark Amber is much more robust, and Vermont Grade B is the most flavorful, making it often the favorite of first-time tasters.

Is one syrup better than another? Can you actually tell the difference? You'd need an exceptionally nuanced palate to discern between one Vermont syrup and another, but aesthetics can alter taste, and authenticity counts. So when visiting a maple farm, make sure that this is a place that actually makes its own syrup, as opposed to just bottling or selling someone else's.

Sugarhouses are located throughout the state, but there's no better introduction to Vermont mapling than a visit to **Morse Farm Sugarworks** (⊕ www.morsefarm.com) in Montpelier, Vermont. Burr Morse's family has been mapling for more than 200 years, longer than anyone else in the state. Attractions here include a free tour of a sugar house, tastings, and an outdoor museum and woodshed theater. If you're traveling with children, **Jed's Maple Products** (⊕ www.jedsmaple. com), far in the Northeast Kingdom is a good option as owners Steve and Amy Wheeler take kids into the woods to show how to tap trees. Always call ahead if you're planning a visit.

There are approximately 50 maple farms that are free and open all year to the public. The official industry Web site for **Vermont Maple Syrup** (⊕ www.vermontmaple.org) is a great resource that has a map of maple farms that host tours, a directory of producers open year-round, and a list of places you can order maple by mail. In addition, you can learn about the Annual Maple Open House weekend, which is when sugarhouses throughout the state open their doors to the public.

—Michael de Zayas

During the spring sugaring season, water is boiled off the maple sap to concentrate the syrup's flavor.

ESSENTIALS

Visitor Information Mount Snow Valley Chamber of Commerce (✉ *21 W. Main St.* ☎ *802/464-8092 or 877/887-6884* ⊕ *www.visitvermont.com*).

EXPLORING

Adams Farm. At this working farm you can collect fresh eggs from the chicken coop, feed a rabbit, milk a goat, ride a tractor or a pony, and jump in the hay—plus run through the corn maze in summer and take sleigh rides in winter. The indoor livestock barn is open Wednesday through Sunday, November to mid-June; an outdoor version is open daily the rest of the year. The farm store sells more than 200 handmade quilts and sweaters. ✉ *15 Higley Hill Rd., 3 mi north of Wilmington, off Rte. 100* ☎ *802/464-3762* ⊕ *www.adamsfamilyfarm.com* ✉ *$6.96–$14.95* ⊙ *Wed.–Sun. 10–5.*

Southern Vermont Natural History Museum. This museum, 5 mi east of Wilmington on Route 9, houses one of New England's largest collections of mounted birds, including three extinct birds and a complete collection of mammals native to the Northeast. The museum also has live hawk and owl exhibits. ✉ *7599 Rte. 9* ☎ *802/464-0048* ✉ *$5* ⊙ *June–late Oct., daily 10–5; late Oct.–May, most weekends 10–4, call ahead.*

SPORTS AND THE OUTDOORS

BOATING **Green Mountain Flagship Company** (✉ *389 Rte. 9, 2 mi west of Wilmington* ☎ *802/464-2975* ⊕ *www.greenmountainflagship.com*) rents canoes, kayaks, and sailboats from May to late October on Lake Whitingham.

SKI AREA   The closest major ski area to all of the Northeast's big cities, **Mount Snow Resort** (⊠ *400 Mountain Rd., Mount Snow* ☎ *802/464–3333; 802/464–2151 snow conditions; 800/245–7669 lodging* ⊕ *www.mountsnow. com*), is also one of the state's premier family resorts and has a full roster of year-round activities. The almost 800-acre facility encompasses a hotel, 10 condo developments, an 18-hole golf course, a health club and spa, 45 mi of mountain-biking trails, and an extensive network of hiking trails.

> **WHO WAS MOLLY STARK?**
>
> In the heart of Wilmington, to the side of Crafts Inn (built by Stanford White in 1902) is a sculpture in honor of Molly Stark, the wife of Revolutionary War general John Stark. The general was said to have roused his troops in the Battle of Bennington, vowing victory over the British: "They are ours, or this night Molly Stark sleeps a widow!" He lived, and the victory path across Vermont, now Route 9, is called the Molly Stark Trail.

Mount Snow prides itself on its 101 snowmaking fan guns, which let it open earlier than any ski area in the state. More than half of the 107 trails down its 1,700-foot vertical summit are intermediate, wide, and sunny. There are four major downhill areas. The main mountain is mostly beginners' slopes, especially toward the bottom, while the north face includes the majority of the expert terrain. Corinthia used to be a separate ski mountain, but is now connected with a mix of trail levels. The south face, Sunbrook, has wide, sunny trails. The trails are served by 19 lifts, including three high-speed quads. Snowmaking covers 85% of the terrain. There are 98 acres of glades. The ski school's instruction program is designed to help skiers of all ages and abilities. Mount Snow also has five terrain parks of different skill levels and a 400-foot half-pipe with 18-foot walls. Skiing programs start with the Cub Camp, designed for kids age 3. Snow Camp teaches kids 4 to 6, and Mountain Camp and Mountain Riders are for kids 7 to 14; there's also a well-organized child-care center.

Two cross-country ski centers near Mount Snow provide more than 68 mi of varied terrain. **Timber Creek** (⊠ *R1 Tomber Creek Rd., at Rte. 100, north of Mount Snow, West Dover* ☎ *802/464–0999* ⊕ *www. timbercreekxc.com*) is appealingly small, with 9 mi of groomed loops and equipment rentals. The groomed trails at the **White House of Wilmington** (⊠ *178 Rte. 9* ☎ *802/464–2135* ⊕ *www.whitehouseinn.com*) cover 30 mi; you can rent Nordic gear and snowshoes there.

SNOWMOBILE TOURS   **High Country Tours** (⊠ *Mount Snow base lodge, Rte. 100, West Dover* ☎ *802/464–2108* ⊕ *www.high-country-tours.com*) runs one-hour, two-hour, and half-day snowmobile tours from two locations: one near Mount Snow, the other west of Wilmington in Searsburg.

SHOPPING

Downtown Wilmington is lined with unique shops and galleries. **Quaigh Design Centre** (⊠ *11 W. Main St. [Rte. 9]* ☎ *802/464–2780*) sells great pottery and artwork from Britain and New England—including works by Vermont woodcut artists Sabra Field and Mary Azarian—and Scottish woolens. **Young and Constantin Gallery** (⊠ *10 S. Main St.*

☎ *802/464–2515*) sells handblown glassware, ceramics, handmade jewelry, and art from local and nationally known artisans.

THE ARTS

A year-round roster of music, theater, film, and fine art is presented at the **Memorial Hall Center for the Arts** (⊠ *14 W. Main St.* ☎ *802/464–8411* ⊕ *www.memhall.org*).

WHERE TO EAT

¢–$ ✕ **Dot's Restaurant.** Look for the classic red neon sign (one of only a
DINER handful still permitted in Vermont) at the main corner in downtown Wilmington: Dot's is a local landmark. A photo inside depicts the interior in the early 1940s—except for the soda fountain, all else is identical, from the long counter with swivel chairs to the fireplace in the back. This friendly place is packed with locals and skiers; the menu includes chicken *cordon bleu* (chicken stuffed with ham and cheese, then breaded and fried) and homemade roast beef. Berry berry pancakes are de rigeur for breakfast, which starts at 5:30 AM, and a bowl of turkey chili is perfect for lunch. A second location is in West Dover. ⊠ *3 W. Main St.* ☎ *802/464–7284* ⊕ *www.dotsofvermont.com* ⊟ *MC, V.*

$$$–$$$$ ✕ **Inn at Sawmill Farm.** No other restaurant in Vermont aims as high with
CONTINENTAL its haute Continental food, wine, and service as the restaurant at Saw-
Fodor's Choice mill. Order a beer and the bottle is served chilled in a small ice bucket,
★ as if it were champagne. This reverent service and deference to potables come from the top: chef-owner Brill Williams passionately cares for his 17,000-bottle cellar, the biggest restaurant collection in the state. Try the potato-crusted fish of the day served in beurre blanc or grilled loin of venison. Gourmands of Mount Snow, this is your place, even if it can be a touch pretentious. ⊠ *7 Crosstown Rd., at Rte. 100, West Dover* ⬭ *Box 367* ☎ *802/464–8131 or 800/493–1133* ⊕ *www.theinnatsawmillfarm. com* ⊟ *AE, D, MC, V* ☉ *Closed early Apr.–late May. No lunch.*

WHERE TO STAY

$$–$$$ ⌂ **Deerhill Inn.** Though the exterior of this inn leaves something to be desired, the interior makes up for it. The common living room features a large stone fireplace and works by local artists hang on the walls. Guest rooms are cozy and adorned with English floral linens; balcony rooms are more spacious. Chef-owner Michael Allen heads the wonderful dining room ($$$$)—one of the best in town. **Pros:** great restaurant; nicely renovated rooms. **Cons:** unimpressive building exterior; must drive to town and resort. ⊠ *14 Valley View Rd., West Dover* ⬭ *Box 136, West Dover 05356* ☎ *802/464–3100 or 800/993–3379* ⊕ *www. deerhill.com* ⬏ *12 rooms, 2 suites* ☉ *Closed weekdays in Apr. and Nov.* ⌂ *In-room: no phone, no a/c, DVD (some), no TV (some), Wi-Fi. In-hotel: restaurant, bar, pool, Internet terminal, Wi-Fi hotspot, no kids under 12* ⊟ *AE, MC, V* ⦿| *BP, MAP.*

$$$$ ⌂ **Grand Summit Hotel.** The 200-room base lodge at Mount Snow is an easy choice for skiers who don't care about anything but getting on the slopes as quickly as possible. Package deals with lift tickets can save you here. The lobby has the look of a traditional ski lodge, with a big center fireplace, but the overall feel is that of an efficient, new hotel. Rooms are clean and fairly basic. A big outdoor heated pool sits beside two hot

OUTDOOR OUTFITTERS AND INFORMATION

BIKING

Vermont Bicycle Touring (✉ *Monkton Rd., Bristol* ☎ *802/453–4811 or 800/245–3868* ⊕ *www.vbt.com*) leads numerous tours in the state. **P.O.M.G. Bike Tours of Vermont** (✉ *Richmond Box 1080,* ☎ *802/434–2270 or 888/635–2453* ⊕ *www.pomgbike.com*) leads weekend and five-day bike tours.

CANOEING AND KAYAKING

Umiak Outdoor Outfitters (✉ *849 S. Main St., Stowe* ☎ *802/253–2317* ⊕ *www.umiak.com*) has day excursions and customized overnight trips. **BattenKill Canoe** (✉ *6328 Rte. 7A, Sunderland* ☎ *802/362–2800 or 800/421–5268* ⊕ *www.battenkill.com*) organizes canoe tours (some are inn-to-inn) and fishing trips. **True North Kayak Tours** (✉ *25 Nash Pl., Burlington* ☎ *802/860–1910* ⊕ *www.vermontkayak.com*) operates a guided tour of Lake Champlain and a natural-history tour; the company also customizes multiday trips and coordinates special trips for kids.

FISHING

For information about fishing, including licenses, call the **Vermont Fish and Wildlife Department** (☎ *802/241–3700* ⊕ *www.vtfishandwildlife.com*).

HIKING

The **Green Mountain Club** (✉ *4711 Waterbury-Stowe Rd. [Rte. 100], Waterbury Center* ☎ *802/244–7037* ⊕ *www.greenmountainclub.org*) publishes hiking maps and guides. The club also manages the Long Trail.

SKIING

For skiing information, contact **Ski Vermont/Vermont Ski Areas Association** (✉ *26 State St., Box 368, Montpelier* ☎ *802/223–2439* ⊕ *www.skivermont.com*).

SPORT TOURS

Country Inns Along the Trail (✉ *Box 59, Montgomery 05470* ☎ *802/326–2072 or 800/838–3301* ⊕ *www.inntoinn.com*) arranges self-guided hiking, skiing, and biking trips from inn to inn in Vermont.

tubs at the base of the slopes. In summer guests enjoy the property golf and tennis courts. **Pros:** easy ski access; modern property. **Cons:** somewhat bland decor in rooms; not a historic option. ✉ *1 Mount Snow Rd., West Dover* ☎ *800/451–4211* ⊕ *www.mountsnow.com/grandsummit. html* ⇨ *104 rooms, 96 suites* ⚒ *In-room: kitchen (some), refrigerator (some), DVD (some), Wi-Fi. In-hotel: 2 restaurants, bar, golf course, tennis courts, pool, gym, spa, children's programs (ages 4–14), laundry service, Internet terminal, Wi-Fi hotspot* ▭ *AE, D, MC, V.*

$$$$ 🏨 **Inn at Sawmill Farm.** Full of character and charm, this inn in a converted barn has common rooms elegantly accented with English chintzes, antiques, and Oriental rugs. Each of the guest rooms—in the main inn or in cottages scattered on the property's 22 acres—is individually decorated, and many have sitting areas and fireplaces. Dinner in the formal dining room, as well as a full breakfast, is included in the price of a stay. **Pros:** spacious grounds; attentive service. **Cons:** overload of floral prints in some rooms; room size varies. ✉ *7 Crosstown Rd., at Rte 100, West Dover* ✉ *Box 367* ☎ *802/464–8131 or 800/493–1133* ⊕ *www.theinnatsawmillfarm.com* ⇨ *21 rooms* ⚒ *In-room: no phone, no TV.*

In-hotel: restaurant, tennis court, pool ☰ *AE, D, MC, V* �),② *Closed early-Apr.–late May* ⊙| *BP, MAP.*

$$ ☒ **White House of Wilmington.** It's hard to miss this 1915 Federal-style
⟲ mansion standing imposingly atop a high hill off Route 9 east of Wilmington. Grand balconies and the main balustraded terrace overlook the hill. A grand staircase leads to rooms with antique bathrooms and brass wall sconces; some rooms have fireplaces and lofts. There is a cross-country ski touring and snowshoeing center on-site along with 7 mi of groomed trails; tubes are also provided for the great hill. A small indoor pool is formed from an old coal bin and surrounded by hand-painted murals of Roman bath scenes. The restaurant ($$$$) has an extensive wine list and undeniably romantic dining in the Mahogany Room. **Pros:** great for kids and families; intriguing, big, old-fashioned property; intimate dining. **Cons:** not in town, so you have to drive to everything. ⊠ *178 Rte. 9, Wilmington* ☎ *802/464–2135 or 800/541–2135* ⊕ *www.whitehouseinn.com* ⇆ *24 rooms, 1 cottage* ⟲ *In-room: no phone, no a/c (some), no TV, Wi-Fi (some). In-hotel: restaurant, bar, pools, laundry service, Internet terminal, Wi-Fi hotspot* ☰ *AE, D, MC, V* ⊙| *BP.*

BENNINGTON

21 mi west of Wilmington.

Bennington is the commercial focus of Vermont's southwest corner. It's really three towns in one: Downtown Bennington, Old Bennington, and North Bennington. Downtown Bennington has retained much of the industrial character it developed in the 19th century, when paper mills, gristmills, and potteries formed the city's economic base.

GETTING HERE AND AROUND

The heart of modern Bennington is at the intersection of U.S. 7 and Route 9. Old Bennington is a couple of miles west on Route 9, at Monument Avenue. North Bennington is a few miles north on Rte 67A.

ESSENTIALS

Visitor Information Bennington Area Chamber of Commerce (⊠ *100 Veterans Memorial Dr. [U.S. 7]* ☎ *802/447–3311 or 800/229–0252* ⊕ *www.bennington.com*).

EXPLORING

TOP ATTRACTIONS

⟲ **Bennington Battle Monument.** This 306-foot stone obelisk—with an elevator to the top—commemorates General John Stark's victory over the British, who attempted to capture Bennington's stockpile of supplies. Inside the monument you can learn all about the battle, which took place near Walloomsac Heights in New York state on August 16, 1777, and helped bring about the surrender of the British commander "Gentleman Johnny" Burgoyne two months later. The summit provides commanding views of the Massachusetts Berkshires, the New York Adirondacks, and the Vermont Green Mountains. ⊠ *15 Monument Circle, Old Bennington* ☎ *802/447–0550* ⌕ *$2* ⊙ *Mid-Apr.–Oct., daily 9–5.*

Bennington Museum. The rich collections at this museum include military artifacts, early tools, dolls, toys, and the Bennington Flag, one of

The poet Robert Frost is buried in Bennington at the Old First Church, "Vermont's Colonial Shrine."

the oldest of the Stars and Stripes in existence. One room is devoted to early Bennington pottery, and two rooms cover the history of American glass (fine Tiffany specimens are on display). The museum displays the largest public collection of the work of Grandma Moses (1860–1961), the popular self-taught artist who lived and painted in the area. ⊠ *75 Main St. (Rte. 9), Old Bennington* ☎ *802/447–1571* ⊕ *www. benningtonmuseum.com* ✆ *$9* ☉ *Nov.–Aug., Thurs.–Tues. 10–5; Sept. and Oct., daily 10–5.*

North Bennington. North of Old Bennington is this village, home to Bennington College, lovely mansions, Lake Paran, three covered bridges, and a wonderful old train depot. Contemporary stone sculpture and white-frame neo-Colonial dorms surrounded by acres of cornfields punctuate the green meadows of the placid campus of **Bennington College** (⊠ *Rte. 67A off U.S. 7 [look for stone entrance gate]* ☎ *802/442–5401* ⊕ *www.bennington.edu*). The architecturally significant **Park-McCullough House** (⊠ *1 Park St., at West St.* ☎ *802/442– 5441* ⊕ *www.parkmccullough.org* ✆ *$8* ☉ *Mid-May–mid-Oct., daily 10–4; last tour at 3*) is a 35-room classic French Empire–style mansion, built in 1865 and furnished with period pieces. Several restored flower gardens grace the landscaped grounds, and a stable houses a collection of antique carriages. Call for details on the summer concert series.

Robert Frost Stone House Museum. A few miles north along Route 7A is the town of Shaftsbury. It was here that Frost came in 1920 "to plant a new Garden of Eden with a thousand apple trees of some unforbidden variety." The museum tells the story of the nine years (1920–29) Frost spent living in the house with his wife and four children. (He passed the 1930s in a house up the road in Shaftsbury, now owned by a Hollywood movie producer.) It was here that he penned "Stopping by Woods on a Snowy Evening" and published two books of poems. Seven of the Frost family's original 80 acres can be wandered. Among the apple boughs you just might find inspiration of your own. ⊠ *75 Main St. (Rte. 9), Shaftsbury* ☏ *802/447–6200* ⊕ *www.frostfriends.org* ✎*$5* ⊙ *May–Nov.; Tues.–Sun. 10–5.*

WORTH NOTING

West of downtown, **Old Bennington** is a National Register Historic District centered along the axis of Monument Avenue and well endowed with stately Colonial and Victorian mansions. Here, at the Catamount Tavern (now a private home north of Church Street), Ethan Allen organized the Green Mountain Boys, who helped capture Fort Ticonderoga in 1775.

Old First Church. In the graveyard of this church, the tombstone of the poet Robert Frost proclaims, "I had a lover's quarrel with the world." ⊠ *1 Church La., at Monument Ave., Old Bennington.*

SPORTS AND THE OUTDOORS

Lake Shaftsbury State Park (⊠ *Rte. 7A, 10½ mi north of Bennington* ☏ *802/375–9978* ⊕ *www.vtstateparks.com/htm/shaftsbury.cfm*) has a swimming beach, nature trails, boat and canoe rentals, and a snack bar. **Woodford State Park** (⊠ *Rte. 9, 10 mi east of Bennington* ☏ *802/447–7169* ⊕ *www.vtstateparks.com/htm/woodford.cfm*) has an activities center on Adams Reservoir, playground, boat and canoe rentals, and nature trails.

SHOPPING

The **Apple Barn and Country Bake Shop** (⊠ *604 Rte. 7S., 1½ mi south of downtown Bennington* ☏ *802/447–7780* ⊕ *theapplebarn.com*) sells home-baked goodies, fresh cider, Vermont cheeses, maple syrup, and apples! Thirty varieties are grown in its orchards. You can pick berries here too, making it a fun family stop. You can watch them making cider donuts at the bakery and café on weekends most of the year. The showroom at the **Bennington Potters Yard** (⊠ *324 County St.* ☏ *802/447–7531 or 800/205–8033* ⊕ *www.benningtonpotters.com*) stocks first-quality pottery and seconds from the famed Bennington Potters. Take a free tour on weekdays from 10 to 3 when the potters are working, or follow a self-guided tour around the yard.

BOOKS **Now & Then Books** (⊠ *439 Main St.* ☏ *802/442–5566* ⊕ *www. nowandthenbooksvt.com*) is a great used bookstore in an upstairs shop with nearly 50,000 volumes in stock. **The Bennington Bookshop** (⊠ *467 Main St.* ☏ *802/442–5050*) sells new books and gifts and has free Wi-Fi.

THE ARTS

The **Bennington Center for the Arts** (⊠ *44 Gypsy La.* ☏ *802/442–7158* ⊕ *www.benningtoncenterforthearts.org*) hosts cultural events, including exhibitions by local and national artists. The on-site **Oldcastle Theatre Co.** (☏ *802/447–0564* ⊕ *www.oldcastletheatreco.or/*) hosts fine regional theater from May through October. The **Basement Music Series** (⊠ *29 Sage St., North Bennington* ☏ *802/442–5549* ⊕ *www.vtartxchange. org*), run by the nonprofit Vermont Arts Exchange, is a funky basement cabaret venue in an old factory building. Purchase tickets in advance for the best contemporary music performances in town.

and has a large collection of teddy bears for sale. From December to March, it's closed on Tuesdays and Wednesdays.

NIGHTLIFE AND THE ARTS

The **Friday Night Fireside Music Series** (⊠ *River Rd., West Arlington* ☎ *802/375–6516*) in the cozy tavern at the West Mountain Inn features great live music acts every other Friday evening from November through May for a $10 cover.

WHERE TO STAY

$$–$$$ 🏨 **Arlington Inn.** Greek Revival columns at this 1848 home lend it an imposing presence in the middle of town, but the atmosphere is friendly and old-fashioned. Rooms are dainty and Victorian, dressed heavily in florals, and spread among the main inn, parsonage, and carriage house. Landscaping includes a garden, gazebo, pond, and waterfall. The inn runs one of the most respected restaurants in town, and its little old bar is one of the most wonderful in the state. **Pros:** heart-of-town location; friendly atmosphere. **Cons:** rooms are dated; expensive dining. ⊠ *Rte. 7A* ☎ *802/375–6532 or 800/443–9442* ⊕ *www.arlingtoninn. com* ➥ *13 rooms, 5 suites* ⚒ *In-room: Wi-Fi. In-hotel: restaurant, bar, Wi-Fi hotspot* ⊟ *AE, D, MC, V* ❦❘ *BP, MAP.*

$–$$ 🏨 **Hill Farm Inn.** Simple cottages and the best views in the Manchester
☼ area make this former dairy farm a winner. You can roam a mile of riverfront along the Battenkill and pet friendly goats, sheep, chickens, and a lazy pig named Blossom. The main inn, from 1830, has a large wraparound porch with sweeping views of Mt. Equinox. Rooms here and in the separate 1790 guesthouse aren't modern, but they're clean and comfortable, furnished with sturdy antiques and even a spinning wheel in the upstairs hallway. If you're here spring through fall, try the charming one- and two-bedroom cabins scattered on the lawn, which offer privacy and a wonderful feeling of freedom in this glorious setting. **Pros:** lovely open meadow setting; farm animals on-site; cabins offer privacy and fun. **Cons:** rooms are quite simple, not luxurious. ⊠ *458 Hill Farm Rd., off Rte. 7A, Sunderland* ☎ *802/375–2269 or 800/882–2545* ⊕ *www.hillfarminn.com* ➥ *6 rooms, 5 suites, 4 cabins* ⚒ *In-room: no a/c (some), kitchen (some), refrigerator (some), Wi-Fi (some). In-hotel: Wi-Fi hotspot* ⊟ *AE, D, MC, V* ❦❘ *BP.*

$$$–$$$$ 🏨 **West Mountain Inn.** This 1810 farmhouse sits on 150 acres on the side
☼ of a mountain, offering plenty of hiking trails and easy access to the
Fodor's Choice Battenkill River, where you can canoe or go tubing. In winter you can
★ sled down a former ski slope or borrow the inn's snowshoes or cross-country skis. In summer, blithe innkeeper Amie Emmons lines the front yard with Adirondack chairs that overlook the mountains. A kids' room is filled with games and videos; there are also resident alpacas and a golden retriever. As the house is a patchwork of additions and gables, rooms have eccentric configurations; though they are not flawless, they are comfortable and have great views and interesting sitting areas. The onsite restaurant is well-respected, with dishes that focus on organic and locally grown vegetables and meats. **Pros:** mountainside location; great for families; lots of outdoor activities. **Cons:** slightly outdated bedding and carpets; not luxurious. ⊠ *1 River Rd., Arlington* ☎ *802/375–6516* ⊕ *www.westmountaininn.com* ➥ *16 rooms, 6 suites* ⚒ *In-room: no*

phone, no TV. In-hotel: restaurant, bar, water sports, bicycles, laundry service ⊟ *AE, D, MC, V* ⊚¹ *BP, MAP.*

MANCHESTER

★ *9 mi northeast of Arlington.*

Well-to-do Manchester has been a popular summer retreat since the mid-19th century, when city dwellers traveled north to take in the cool clean air at the foot of 3,816-foot Mt. Equinox. Manchester Village's tree-shaded marble sidewalks and stately old homes—Main Street here could hardly be more picture perfect—reflect the luxurious resort lifestyle of more than a century ago. A mile north on 7A, Manchester Center is the commercial twin to Colonial Manchester Village, as well as where you'll find the town's famed upscale factory outlets doing business in attractive faux-Colonial shops.

Manchester Village also houses the world headquarters of Orvis, the outdoor goods brand that began here in the 19th century and has greatly influenced the town ever since. Its complex includes a fly-fishing school with lessons in its casting ponds and the Battenkill River.

GETTING HERE AND AROUND

Manchester is the main town for the ski resorts of Stratton and Bromley and is roughly 15 minutes from either on Routes 11 and 30. It's 15 minutes north of Arlington, 30 minutes north of Bennington and south of Rutland on Routes 7 and 7A. Take 7A for a more scenic drive.

ESSENTIALS

Visitor Information Chamber of Commerce, Manchester and the Mountains (⊠ *5046 Main St.* ☎ *802/362–2100 or 800/362–4144* ⊕ *www. manchestervermont.net).* **Green Mountain National Forest Visitor Center** (⊠ *2538 Rte. 30* ☎ *802/362–2307* ⊕ *www.fs.fed.us/r9/gmfl* ⊘ *Weekdays 8–4:30).*

EXPLORING

American Museum of Fly Fishing. This museum houses the world's largest collection of angling art and angling-related objects. Rotating exhibitions draw from a permanent collection of more than 1,500 rods, 800 reels, 30,000 flies, and the tackle of notables like Winslow Homer, Bing Crosby, and Jimmy Carter. Every August the museum organizes a fly-fishing festival with kids' activities and vendors selling antique equipment. ⊠ *4070 Main St. (Rte. 7A)* ☎ *802/362–3300* ⊕ *www.amff.com* ⊡ *$5* ⊘ *Jan.– May, Nov., and Dec., Tues.–Sat 10–4; June–Oct., Tues.–Sun. 10–4.*

Hildene. The Lincoln Family Home is a twofold treat, providing historical insight into the life of the Lincolns while escorting you through the lavish Manchester life of the 1900s. Abraham had only one son who survived to adulthood, Robert Todd Lincoln, who served as secretary of war and head of the Pullman Company. Robert bought the beautifully preserved 412-acre estate and built a 24-room mansion where he and his descendants lived from 1905–75. The entire grounds are open for exploration—you can hike, picnic, and ski; see the astronomical observatory; loll in beautiful gardens; and walk through the sturdy Georgian Revival house, which holds the family's original furniture, books, and possessions. One of three surviving stovepipe hats owned

Fodor'sChoice
★

The formal gardens and mansion at Robert Todd Lincoln's Hildene are a far cry from his father's log cabin.

by Abraham, a Lincoln Bible, a gorgeously restored Pullman car, and Robert's Harvard University yearbook are among the treasures you'll find. When the 1,000-pipe aeolian organ is played, the music reverberates as though from the mansion's very bones.

Rising from a 10-acre meadow, the new Hildene Farm opens in 2010. The agriculture center is built in a traditional style—post-and-beam construction of timber felled and milled on the estate—and as an exemplar of renewable energy, from the closed-loop cord wood heating system to the solar panels covering the roof. A herd of goats and informative farming displays recall the Lincolns' use of this land. Best of all, you can watch goat cheese being made and take some home.

The highlight, though, may be the elaborate formal gardens: in June a thousand peonies bloom. When snow conditions permit, you can cross-country ski and snowshoe on the property. Robert's carriage house now houses the gorgeous museum store and visitor center—the nicest of its kind in the state—that showcases, among other things, a live bee exhibit and Mary Todd Lincoln's 1928 vintage Franklin car. Allow half a day for exploring Hildene. ⊠ *1005 Hildene Rd., at Rte. 7A* ☎ *802/362–1788* ⊕ *www.hildene.org* ⊠ *Tour $13, grounds pass $5* ⊘ *Daily 9:30–4:30.*

Southern Vermont Arts Center. Rotating exhibits and a permanent collection of more than 700 pieces of 19th- and 20th-century American art are showcased at this 12,500-square-foot museum. The original building, a graceful Georgian mansion set on 407 acres, is the frequent site of concerts, performances, and film screenings. In summer and fall, a pleasant restaurant with magnificent views serves lunch. ⊠ *West*

Rd. ☎ *802/362–1405* ⊕ *www.svac.org* ✉ *$8* ☉ *Tues.–Sat. 10–5, Sun. noon–5.*

SPORTS AND THE OUTDOORS

BIKING **Battenkill Sports** (✉ *1240 Depot St. [U.S. 7, Exit 4]* ☎ *802/362–2734 or 800/340–2734* ⊕ *www.battenkillsports.com*) rents, sells, and repairs bikes and provides maps and route suggestions.

FISHING **Battenkill Anglers** (✉ *6204 Main St., Manchester* ☎ *802/379–1444*) teaches the art and science of fly-fishing in both private and group lessons. **Orvis Fly-Fishing School** (✉ *6204 Rte. 7A, Manchester Center* ☎ *802/362–4604 or 866/531–6213* ⊕ *www.orvis.com/schools*) is nationally renowned. The company opened a new building just for the fly school across the street from its flagship store in 2009. Courses are offered mid-April to mid-October, ranging from two-hour pond trips with casting lessons and fishing with private instructors to three-day advanced classes on the Battenkill.

HIKING There are bountiful hiking trails in the Green Mountain National Forest. Shorter hikes begin at the Equinox Resort, which owns about 1,000 acres of forest and has a great trail system open to the public.

One of the most popular segments of Vermont's **Long Trail** (⊕ *www. greenmountainclub.org*) starts from a parking lot on Route 11/30 five minutes out of town and goes to the top of Bromley Mountain. The strenuous 6-mi round-trip takes about four hours. A moderate four-hour hike starts off Manchester East Road and ends at Vermont's most impressive cataract, **Lye Brook Falls.**

The **Mountain Goat** (✉ *4886 Main St.* ☎ *802/362–5159* ⊕ *mountaingoat. com*) sells hiking and backpacking equipment and rents snowshoes and cross-country and Telemark skis.

ICE-SKATING The Olympic-size indoor **Riley Rink** (✉ *410 Hunter Park Rd.* ☎ *802/362–0150* ⊕ *www.rileyrink.com*) has rentals and a concession stand.

SHOPPING

★ In Manchester Village, **Frog Hollow at Equinox** (✉ *3566 Main St. [Rte. 7A]* ☎ *802/362–3321*) is a nonprofit collective that sells such contemporary works as jewelry, glassware, and home furnishings from Vermont artisans. **Long Ago and Far Away** (✉ *Green Mountain Village Shops, 4963 Main St.* ☎ *802/362–3435* ⊕ *www.longagoandfaraway.com*) specializes in fine indigenous artwork, including Inuit stone sculpture. The large **Tilting at Windmills Gallery** (✉ *24 Highland Ave.* ☎ *802/362–3022* ⊕ *www.tilting.com*) displays and sells the paintings and sculpture of nationally known artists.

☺ **Northshire Bookstore** (✉ *4869 Main St.* ☎ *802/362–2200 or 800/437–3700* ⊕ *www.northshire.com*) is the heart of Manchester Center, adored
Fodor's Choice by visitors and residents for its ambience, selection, and service. Up
★ the central black iron staircase is a second floor dedicated to children's books, toys, and clothes. Connected to the bookstore is the Spiral Press Café, where you can sit for a grilled pesto-chicken sandwich or a latte and scone. ■TIP➔ Adding to the gravitational draw is the Wi-Fi connection and the visitor information booth open Wednesday–Sunday 1–5.

★ The two-story, lodge-like **Orvis Flagship Store** (✉*4200 Rte. 7A* 🕾*802/ 362–3750* ⊕ *www.orvis.com/*) has a trout pond as well as the company's latest clothing and accessories. It's a required shopping destination for many visitors—the Orvis name is pure Manchester. Spread out across Manchester Center, **Manchester Designer Outlets** (✉ *U.S. 7 and Rte. 11/30* 🕾*802/362–3736 or 800/955–7467* ⊕ *www.manchesterdesigneroutlets. com*) is the most upscale collection of stores in northern New England—and every store is a discount outlet! Adding to the allure, town ordinances decree the look of the shops be in tune with the surrounding historic homes, making these the most attractive and decidedly Colonial-looking outlets you'll ever see. In 2009, Kate Spade and Kenneth Cole added their names to the long list of upscale clothiers who call Manchester home. Among them are Michael Kors, Betsey Johnson, Ann Taylor, Tumi, Escada, Armani, Coach, Polo Ralph Lauren, Brooks Brothers, and Theory. There are also less expensive brand outlets like Pacsun, Gap, and Banana Republic.

Fodor'sChoice ## NIGHTLIFE AND THE ARTS

★ Near Bromley Mountain, **Johnny Seesaw's** (✉*3574 Rte. 11* 🕾*802/824– 5533* ⊕ *www.jseesaw.com*) is a classic rustic ski lodge with two huge fireplaces and a relaxed attitude. There's live music on weekends and an excellent "comfort food" menu. It's closed April through Memorial Day. The **Falcon Bar** (✉*3567 Main St. [Rte. 7A]* 🕾*802/362–4700* ⊕ *www.equinoxresort.com*) at the Equinox resort opened in 2008 and instantly became a Manchester classic. The bar has a sophisticated indoor setting with music on weekends, or you can take in the wonderful outdoor deck. In winter the place to be is under the heating lamps surrounding the giant Vermont slate fire pit. The **Perfect Wife** (✉*2594 Depot St. [Rte. 11/30]* 🕾*802/362–2817* ⊕ *www.perfectwife.com*) is decidedly more local, with music three to four nights a week.

WHERE TO EAT

$$$ ✗**Bistro Henry.** The active presence of chef-owner Henry Bronson
FRENCH accounts for the continual popularity of this friendly place that's about $5 per dish cheaper than the other good restaurants in town. The menu works off a bistro foundation, with a peppery steak au poivre and a medium rare duck breast served with a crispy leg, and mixes things up with eclectic dishes like seared tuna with wasabi and soy; crab cakes in a Cajun rémoulade; and a delicious scallop dish with Thai coconut curry and purple sticky rice. The wine list is extensive, and Dina Bronson's desserts are memorable—indulge in the "gooey chocolate cake," a great molten treat paired with a homemade malt ice cream. ✉*1942 Rte. 11/30, 3 mi east of Manchester Center* 🕾*802/362–4982* ⊕ *www. bistrohenry.com* ▭ *AE, D, DC, MC, V* ⊙ *Closed Mon. No lunch.*

$$$$ ✗**Chantecleer.** There is something wonderful about eating by candle-
CONTINENTAL light in an old barn. Chantecleer's dining rooms (in winter ask to sit by the great fieldstone fireplace) are wonderfully romantic, even with a collection of roosters atop the wooden beams. The menu leans toward the Continental with starters like a fine escargot glazed with Pernod in a hazelnut and parsley butter. Crowd pleasers include Colorado rack of lamb and whole Dover sole filleted tableside. A recipe from the chef's Swiss hometown makes a winning dessert: Basel Rathaus

Manchester Designer Outlets' Colonial-style architecture helps blend upscale discount shopping with the surrounding town.

Torte, a delicious hazelnut layer cake. ⊠ *8 Reed Farm La., off Rte. 7A, 3½ mi north of Manchester, East Dorset* ☎ *802/362–1616* ⊕ *www. chantecleerrestaurant.com* ⌂ *Reservations essential* ▤ *AE, DC, MC, V* ⊙ *Closed Nov. and Apr.–mid-May. Closed Mon. and Tues. No lunch.*

$$$$ ✕ **Chop House.** Walk to the very back room of the Equinox resort's
STEAKHOUSE Marsh Tavern, past a velvet curtain, and you'll have entered a different eatery—a wonderful, very expensive steakhouse called the Chop House. It opened in 2009, but you can't claim to be the first here—the marble above the fireplace is chiseled L. L. ORVIS 1832 (and way before he claimed the spot the Green Mountain Boys gathered here to plan their resistance). Today, you'll yield to USDA Prime aged corn- or grass-fed beef broiled at 1,700 degrees and finished with herb butter. The New York strip, 32-oz rib eye, 16-oz milk-fed veal chops, filet mignon, lamb, and seafood are delicious, a must for deep-pocketed lovers of steaks and seafood. ⊠ *3567 Main St.* ☎ *802/362–4700* ⊕ *www.equinoxresort. com* ▤ *AE, D, DC, MC, V.*

$ ✕ **Depot 62 Cafe.** The best pizzas in town are topped with terrific fresh
PIZZA ingredients and served in the middle of a high-end antiques showroom, making this restaurant a local secret worth knowing about. The wood-fired oven yields masterful results—like the arugula pizza, a beehive of fresh greens atop a thin-crust base. This a great place for lunch or an inexpensive but satisfying dinner. Sit on your own or at the long communal table. ⊠ *505 Depot St.* ☎ *802/366–8181* ▤ *MC, V.*

$$$ ✕ **Mistral's.** This classic French restaurant is tucked in a grotto off Route
FRENCH 11/30 on the climb to Bromley Mountain. The two dining rooms are perched over the Bromley Brook, and at night lights magically illuminate a small waterfall. Ask for a window table. Specialties include

Chateaubriand béarnaise and rack of lamb with rosemary for two. Chef Dana Markey's crispy sweetbreads with porcini mushrooms are a favorite. ✉ *10 Toll Gate Rd.* ☎ *802/362–1779* ▤ *AE, DC, MC, V* ⊗ *Closed Wed. No lunch.*

$ ✕ **Perfect Wife.** Owner-chef Amy Chamberlain, the self-proclaimed aspir-
ECLECTIC   ing flawless spouse, creates freestyle cuisine like turkey schnitzel and grilled venison with a caramelized shallot and dried cranberry demi-glace. There are two entrances to the restaurant, and we recommend the hilltop tavern, which looks over the more formal dining room below. The tavern is one of the livelier local spots in town, with live music on weekends and a pub menu with burgers, potpies in winter, and Vermont microbrews on tap. ✉ *2594 Depot St. (Rte. 11/30), 2½ mi east of Manchester Center* ☎ *802/362–2817* ⊕ *www.perfectwife.com* ▤ *AE, D, MC, V* ⊗ *Closed Sun. No lunch.*

$$$ ✕ **The Reluctant Panther.** The dining room at this luxurious inn is a large,
AMERICAN   modern space, where dark wood and high ceilings meld into a kind of nouveau Vermont aesthetic. The food is indulgent and rich as well as very expensive, making this a special-occasion kind of place. The dinner menu includes maple-rubbed Vermont lamb, scallops, and a duet of Long Island duck breast and confit of leg cannelloni. In the warmer months, sit outside on the lovely landscaped patio. ✉ *1 West Rd.* ☎ *800/822–2331* ⊕ *www.reluctantpanther.com* ▤ *AE, D, DC, MC, V* ⊗ *No lunch. Jan.–Apr. closed weekdays.*

WHERE TO STAY

$$$$ ⊡ **The Equinox.** The Equinox defines the geographic center and historic
Fodor's Choice   heart of Manchester Village and has been *the* fancy hotel in town—and
★   in the state—since the 18th century. A head-to-toe renovation in 2008 re-elevated the property to the lofty tier befitting its white, two-story Doric columns and bellhops uniformed in jodhpurs and knee-high argyle socks. Rooms have huge flat-screen TVs, leather chairs, two-tone cream wallpaper, plush-top mattresses, and marble bathrooms with granite sinks. If you crave Colonial, the brown 1811 House across the street is part of the resort. If you've got big bucks, ask for a room in the Charles Orvis Inn next door, which has hot tubs and private porches. The spa is the best in southern Vermont; the concierge will arrange falconry, fish-ing, or shooting lessons; the resort's golf course is across the street; and there's a new wine bar in addition to three good dining choices. **Pros:** heart-of-town location; full-service hotel; great golf and spa. **Cons:** big-hotel feeling; overrun by New Yorkers on weekends. ✉ *3567 Main St. (Rte. 7A)* ☎ *802/362–4700 or 888/367–7625* ⊕ *www.equinoxresort. com* ⇋ *164 rooms, 29 suites* ⚘ *In-room: kitchen (some), refrigerator (some), Wi-Fi. In-hotel: 3 restaurants, bar, golf course, tennis courts, pool, spa, laundry service, Wi-Fi hotspot* ▤ *AE, D, DC, MC, V.*

$$$–$$$$ ⊡ **Wilburton Inn.** A few miles south of Manchester and overlooking the Battenkill Valley from a hilltop all its own, this turn-of-the-century complex is centered on a Tudor mansion with 11 bedrooms and suites and richly paneled common rooms containing part of the owners' vast art collection. Besides the main inn, five guest buildings are spread over the grounds, dotted with more owner-created sculpture. Rooms at the Wilburton vary greatly in condition, so choose carefully. The dining

room is an elegant affair, with a menu to match—entrées might include poached Maine lobster with gnocchi or a roasted antelope chop with bordelaise sauce. One note: weddings take place here most summer weekends. **Pros:** beautiful setting with easy access to Manchester; fine dining. **Cons:** rooms in main inn, especially, need updating; limited indoor facilities. ⌧ *257 River Rd.* ☎ *802/362–2500 or 800/648–4944* ⊕ *www.wilburton.com* ↺ *30 rooms, 4 suites* ⌂ *In-hotel: restaurant, tennis courts, pool* ⊟ *AE, MC, V* ⍉ *BP.*

DORSET

★ *7 mi north of Manchester.*

Lying at the foot of many mountains and with a village green surrounded by white clapboard homes and inns, Dorset has a solid claim to the title of Vermont's most picture-perfect town. The town has just 2,000 residents but two of the state's best and oldest general stores.

The country's first commercial marble quarry was opened here in 1785. Dozens followed suit, providing the marble for the main research branch of the New York City Public Library and many Fifth Avenue mansions, among other notable landmarks, as well as the sidewalks here and in Manchester. A remarkable private home made entirely of marble can be seen on Dorset West Road, a beautiful residential road west of the town green. The marble Dorset Church on the green features two Tiffany stained-glass windows.

EXPLORING

Fodor'sChoice **Dorset Quarry.** On hot summer days the sight of dozens of families jump-
★ ing, swimming, and basking in the sun around this massive swimming hole makes it one of the most wholesome and picturesque recreational spots in the United States. First mined in 1785, this is the oldest marble quarry in the United States. The popular area visible from Route 30 is actually just the lower quarry, and footpaths lead to the quiet upper quarry. ⌧ *Rte. 30, 1 mi south of Dorset green* ☎ *No phone* ☜ *Free.*

Ⓒ **Merck Forest and Farmland Center.** This 3,100-acre farm and forest is a
★ nonprofit educational center with 30 mi of nature trails for hiking, cross-country skiing, snowshoeing, and horseback riding. You can visit the farm, which grows organic fruits and vegetables (and purchase them at the farm stand), and check out the pasture-raised horses, cows, sheep, pigs, and chickens. There are also remote cabins and tent sites for rental. ⌧ *3270 Rte. 315, Rupert* ☎ *802/394–7836* ⊕ *www.merckforest. org* ☜ *Free* ⊗ *Daily, dawn–dusk.*

SPORTS AND THE OUTDOORS

Emerald Lake State Park (⌧ *U.S. 7, East Dorset* ☎ *802/362–1655* ⊕ *www. vtstateparks.com/html/emerald.cfm* ☜ *$3*) has a small beach, a marked nature trail, an on-site naturalist, boat rentals, and a snack bar.

SHOPPING

The **Dorset Union Store** (⌧ *Dorset Green* ☎ *802/867–4400* ⊕ *www. dorsetunionstore.com*) first opened in 1816 as a village co-op. Today this privately owned general store makes good prepared dinners, has a big wine selection, rents DVDs, and sells food and gifts. The **H. N. Williams**

7

General Store (✉ *2732 Rte. 30* ☎ *802/867–5353* ⊕ *www.hnwilliams. com*) is the most authentic and comprehensive general store in the state. It was started in 1840 by William Williams and has been run by the same family for six generations. This is one of those unique places where you can buy both maple syrup and ammo and catch up on posted town announcements. A farmers' market (⊕ *www.dorsetfarmersmarket.com*) is held outside on Sundays in summer.

THE ARTS

Dorset is home to a prestigious summer theater troupe that presents the annual Dorset Theater Festival. Plays are held in a wonderful converted pre-Revolutionary barn, the **Dorset Playhouse** (✉ *104 Cheney Rd., off town green* ☎ *802/867–2223 or 802/867–5777* ⊕ *www.dorsetplayers. org/*), which the playhouse also hosts a community group in winter.

WHERE TO EAT

$–$$ ✕ **Dorset Inn Dining Room**. Since 1796, the inn that houses this restau-
AMERICAN   rant has been continuously operating, and even today you can count on three meals a day, every day of the year. The comfortable tavern, which serves the same menu as the more formal dining room, is popular with locals, and Patrick, the amiable veteran bartender, will make you feel at home. The menu highlights ingredients from local farms served by chef Thom Simonetti. Popular choices include yam fritters served in maple syrup and a lightly breaded chicken breast saltimbocca, stuffed with prosciutto and mozzarella. ✉ *8 Church St., Dorset Green at Rte. 30* ☎ *802/867–5500* ⊕ *www.dorsetinn.com* ▭ *AE, MC, V.*

$$$ ✕ **West View Farm**. Chef-owner Raymond Chen was the lead line cook
ECLECTIC   at New York City's Mercer Kitchen under Jean-Georges Vongerichten
★   before opening this local ingredient–friendly restaurant. You'll find traditional floral wallpaper and soft classical music, but that's where the similarities to Dorset's other eateries end. Chen's dishes are skillful and practiced, starting with an *amuse-bouche* such as *brandade* (salt cod) over pesto. French influences are evident in the sautéed mushrooms and mascarpone ravioli in white truffle oil. Asian notes are evident, too, as in the lemongrass ginger soup with shiitake mushrooms that's ladled over grilled shrimp. A tavern serves enticing, inexpensive small dishes. ✉ *2928 Rte. 30* ☎ *802/867–5715 or 800/769–4903* ⊕ *www. westviewfarm.com* ▭ *AE, MC, V* ☉ *Closed Tues. and Wed.*

WHERE TO STAY

$–$$ ⊡ **Inn at West View Farm**. Although these rooms could use a little attention, they offer an inexpensive way to stay in an old farmhouse with comfortable common rooms—along with easy access to an amazing dining room. The white clapboard farmhouse is part of a former 1870 dairy farm. A deck in back looks out at the smaller farm buildings that dot the 5-acre yard. Rooms display imperfections, like an occasional stain or crack, and the carpeting could use an update, but they are very clean, and the furniture and wallpaper satisfy the Colonial farmhouse urge. **Pros:** great restaurant; good value. **Cons:** rooms aren't perfectly maintained. ✉ *2928 Rte. 30* ☎ *802/867–5715* ⊕ *www. innatwestviewfarm.com* ⇨ *9 rooms, 1 suite* ♿ *In-room: Wi-Fi. In-hotel:*

restaurant, bar, laundry service, Wi-Fi hotspot, no kids under 10 ⊟ AE, MC, V ⍟❘ BP.

$$–$$$ ⊞ **Squire House.** There are three rooms for rent in this big house that combines modern comforts and antique fixtures on a wonderfully quiet road. And there's enough space and quiet, with three big common rooms, that it can feel like home. The house was built in 1918 and was designed with 9-foot ceilings and great light throughout. Rooms are newly carpeted and spotless. Owners Gay and Roger Squire are rightly proud of their breakfasts served in a richly paneled dining room. Roger is a flute player and enjoys the company of other musicians, who get a 10% discount. **Pros:** big estate feels like your own; well-maintained. **Cons:** bathrooms less exciting than rooms; no credit cards. ⊠ *3395 Dorset West Rd.* ☎ *802/867–0281* ⊕ *www.squirehouse.com* ⇌ *2 rooms, 1 suite* ⌂ *In-room: no phone, refrigerator (some), DVD (some), no TV (some), Wi-Fi. In-hotel: laundry service, Wi-Fi hotspot, no kids under 14 ⊟ No credit cards* ⍟❘ *BP.*

STRATTON

26 mi southeast of Dorset.

Stratton is really Stratton Mountain Resort—a mountaintop ski resort with a self-contained "town center" of shops, restaurants, and lodgings clustered at the base of the slopes. When the snow melts, golf, tennis, and a host of other summer activities are big attractions, but the ski village remains quiet. For those arriving from the north along Route 30, Bondville is the town at the base of the mountain. At the junction of Routes 30 and 100 is the tiny Vermont village of Jamaica, with its own cluster of inns and restaurants on the east side of the mountain.

GETTING HERE AND AROUND

From Manchester or Route 7, follow Route 11/30 east until they split. Route 11 continues past Bromley ski mountain while Route 30 turns south 10 minutes toward Bondville, the town closest to Stratton Mountain.

SPORTS AND THE OUTDOORS

SKI AREAS   About 20 minutes from Stratton, **Bromley** (⊠ *Rte. 11, Peru* ☎ *802/824–5522 or 800/865–4786* ⊕ *www.bromley.com*) is a favorite with families. The 43 trails are evenly divided between beginner, intermediate, and expert. The resort runs a child-care center for kids ages 6 weeks to 4 years and hosts children's programs for ages 3–12. An added bonus: the trails face south, making for glorious spring skiing and warm winter days.

★   About 30 minutes from Manchester, sophisticated, exclusive **Stratton Mountain** (⊠ *5 Village Rd., Bondville. Turn off Rte. 30 and go 4 mi up access road* ☎ *802/297-2200; 802/297-4211 snow conditions; 800/787-2886 lodging* ⊕ *www.stratton.com*) draws affluent families and young professionals from the New York–southern Connecticut corridor. An entire village, with a covered parking structure for 700 cars, is at the base of the mountain. Activities are afoot year-round. Stratton has 15 outdoor tennis courts, 27 holes of golf, a climbing wall, horseback riding, hiking accessed by a gondola to the summit, and instructional programs in tennis and golf. The sports center, open year-round, has two indoor tennis courts, three racquetball courts, a 25-meter indoor swimming pool, a hot tub, a steam room, a fitness facility with Nautilus equipment, and a restaurant. Adjacent to the base lodge are a condo-hotel, restaurants, and about 25 shops lining a pedestrian mall.

In terms of downhill skiing, Stratton prides itself on its immaculate grooming, making it excellent for cruising. The lower part of the mountain is beginner to low-intermediate, served by several chair-lifts. The upper mountain is served by several high-speed quads and a 12-passenger gondola. Down the face are the expert trails, and on either side are intermediate cruising runs with a smattering of wide beginner slopes. The third sector, the Sun Bowl, is off to one side with two high-speed, six-passenger lifts and two expert trails, a full base lodge, and plenty of intermediate terrain. Snowmaking covers 95% of the slopes. Every March, Stratton hosts the U.S. Open Snowboarding champion-ships; its snowboard park has a 380-foot half-pipe. A Ski Learning Park provides its own Park Packages for novice skiers. In all, Stratton has 15 lifts that service 92 trails and 90 acres of glades. There is a ski school for children ages 4–12. The resort also has more than 18 mi of cross-country skiing and the Sun Bowl Nordic center. An on-site day-care center takes children from 6 weeks to 5 years old for indoor activities and outdoor excursions.

NIGHTLIFE AND THE ARTS

Popular **Mulligan's** (⊠ *Stratton Village Sq. 11B, Mountain Rd., Bondville* ☎ 802/297–9293) hosts bands or DJs in the late afternoon and on week-ends in winter. Year-round, the **Red Fox Inn** (⊠ *103 Winhall Hollow Rd., Bondville* ☎ *802/297–2488* ⊕ *www.redfoxinn.com*) is the best après-ski nightlife spot in southern Vermont. It hosts Irish music Wednesday night; an open mike Thursday night; and rock and roll at other times.

WHERE TO EAT

$$$
AMERICAN
✕ **Red Fox Inn.** This two-level converted barn has the best nightlife in southern Vermont and a fun dining room to boot. The restaurant has been here since 1979, but you'd believe since 1900. The upper level is the dining room—the big A-frame has wagon wheels and a carriage suspended from the ceiling. Settle in near the huge fireplace for rack of lamb, free-range chicken, or penne à la vodka. Downstairs is the tavern where there's Irish music, half-price Guinness, and fish-and-chips on Wednesday. Other nights there might be live music, karaoke, or video bowling. The bar operates daily year-round. ⊠ *103 Winhall Hollow Rd., Bondville* ☎ *802/297–2488* ⊕ *www.redfoxinn.com* ⊟ *AE, MC, V* ⊙ *No lunch. Closed Mon.–Wed. June–Oct.*

$$$$
CONTEMPORARY
Fodor's Choice
★
✕ **Three Mountain Inn.** If you're in the Stratton area and can splurge on an expensive meal, don't miss dinner at this charming inn. The prix-fixe meal includes *amuse-bouche*, starter, salad, entrée, and dessert for $55, plus the best restaurant bread in Vermont, a homemade herb focaccia. A starter might be baked Malpeque oysters with a chorizo and fen-nel jam; entrées include grilled swordfish with toasted couscous and a mint cucumber sauce. Each dining room has a fireplace, and common

areas have terrific original wall and ceiling beams, making the restaurant a romantic winner. ✉ *3732 Rte. 30/100, Jamaica* ☏ *802/874–4140* ⊕ *www.threemountaininn.com* ⊟ *AE, D, MC, V* ☺ *No dinner Mon. and Tues.*

WHERE TO STAY

$$ 🏨 **Long Trail House.** Directly across the street from Stratton's ski village, this fairly new condo complex is one of the best choices close to the slopes. Units have fully equipped kitchens with ovens and dishwashers. The studios are an excellent value; they come with Murphy beds that fold out into the living room area for additional sleepers. **Pros:** across from skiing; good rates available; outdoor heated pool. **Cons:** room decor varies; two-night stay required on weekends. ✉ *1 Stratton Mtn. Rd., Bondville* ☏ *802/297–2200 or 800/787–2886* ⊕ *www.stratton. com* 🛏 *100 units* ♿ *In-room: safe (some), kitchen, DVD (some). In-hotel: pool, laundry facilities* ⊟ *AE, D, DC, MC, V.*

$$–$$$ 🏨 **Red Fox Inn.** Stay here for great mid-week rates (50% off Sunday through Thursday) and relaxed, no-frills accommodations off the noisy mountain. Tom and Cindy Logan's "white house," an early 1800s farmhouse, is in an open meadow 4 mi from Stratton and 8 mi from Bromley. The feeling here is warm and cozy, with original wood floors and simple furnishings. Downstairs rooms have bay windows; upstairs rooms are smaller. **Pros:** great nightlife and food next door; real local hosts; secluded. **Cons:** a drive to ski areas; weekends overpriced. ✉ *103 Winhall Hollow Rd., Bondville* ☏ *802/297–2488* ⊕ *www.redfoxinn. com* 🛏 *8 rooms, 1 suite* ♿ *In-room: no phone, no a/c, no TV, Wi-Fi. In-hotel: restaurant, bar, Wi-Fi hotspot* ⊟ *AE, MC, V.*

$$$–$$$$ 🏨 **Three Mountain Inn.** A 1780s tavern, this romantic inn in downtown
Fodor'sChoice Jamaica (10 mi northeast of Stratton) feels authentically Colonial, from
★ the wide paneling to the low ceilings. Comfortable and intimate rooms are appointed with a blend of historic and modern furnishings, including featherbeds. Most rooms have fireplaces and mountain views, and three have private decks. Owners Ed and Jennifer Dorta-Duque attend to your stay and oversee truly enchanting dinners. **Pros:** charming, authentic, romantic, small-town B&B; well-kept rooms; great dinners. **Cons:** can be expensive. ✉ *3732 Rte. 30/100, Jamaica* ☏ *802/874–4140* ⊕ *www.threemountaininn.com* 🛏 *14 rooms, 1 suite* ♿ *In-room: DVD (some), no TV (some), Wi-Fi. In-hotel: restaurant, bar, pool, bicycles, laundry service, Internet terminal, Wi-Fi hotspot, some pets allowed, no kids under 12* ⊟ *AE, D, MC, V* ⧉*BP.*

WESTON

17 mi north of Stratton.

Best known for the Vermont Country Store, Weston was one of the first Vermont towns to discover its own intrinsic loveliness—and marketability. With its summer theater, classic town green with a Victorian bandstand, and an assortment of shops, the little village really lives up to its vaunted image.

SHOPPING

For paintings, prints, and sculptures by Vermont artists and craftspeople, go to the **Todd Gallery** (✉ *614 Main St.* ☎ *802/824–5606* ⊕ *www. toddgallery.com*), open Thursday–Monday, 10–5. The **Vermont Country Store** (✉ *657 Main St. [Rte. 100]* ☎ *802/824–3184* ⊕ *www. vermontcountrystore.com*) is an old-fashioned emporium selling all manner of items. The store was first opened in 1946 and is still run by the Orton family, though it has become something of an empire, with a large catalog and online business. One room is set aside for Vermont Common Crackers and bins of fudge and other candy. In others you'll find nearly forgotten items such as Lilac Vegetol aftershave and horehound drops, as well as practical items such as sturdy outdoor clothing and even typewriters. Nostalgia-evoking implements dangle from the store's walls and rafters. (There's another store on Route 103 in Rockingham.)

★

THE ARTS

In July and August, the **Kinhaven Music School** (✉ *354 Lawrence Hill Rd.* ☎ *802/824–4332* ⊕ *www.kinhaven.org*) stages free student classical music concerts on Friday at 4 and Sunday at 2:30. Faculty concerts are Saturday at 8 PM.

The members of the **Weston Playhouse** (✉ *703 Main St., Village Green, off Rte. 100* ☎ *802/824–5288* ⊕ *www.westonplayhouse.org*), the oldest professional theater in Vermont, produce Broadway plays, musicals, and other works. Their season runs from late June to early September.

WHERE TO STAY

$$$ 🖼 **Inn at Weston.** Highlighting the country elegance of this 1848 inn, a short walk from the town green, is innkeeper Bob Aldrich's collection of 500 orchid species—rare and beautiful specimens surround the dining table in the gazebo, and others enrich the indoors. Rooms in the inn, carriage house, and Coleman House (across the street) are comfortably appointed, and some have fireplaces. The restaurant ($$$; closed Monday) serves contemporary regional cuisine amid candlelight. Vermont cheddar cheese and Granny Smith–apple omelets are popular choices for breakfast. **Pros:** great rooms; terrific town location. **Cons:** top-end rooms are expensive. ✉ *160 Main St. (Rte. 100), Box 66* ☎ *802/824– 6789* ⊕ *www.innweston.com* 🛏 *13 rooms* 🔧 *In-room: no TV (some), Wi-Fi. In-hotel: restaurant, bar, Wi-Fi hotspot, no kids under 12* 🖃 *AE, DC, MC, V* 🍴 *BP.*

LUDLOW

9 mi northeast of Weston.

Ludlow was once a nondescript factory town that just happened to have a small ski area—Okemo. Today, that ski area is one of Vermont's largest and most popular resorts, and downtown Ludlow is a collection of restored buildings with shops and restaurants.

You never know what you'll find at a rambling general store like Weston's Vermont Country Store.

SPORTS AND THE OUTDOORS

SKI AREAS Once only a faint blip on skiers' radar, **Ascutney** (✉ *Rte. 44, Brownsville* ☎ *802/484–7711 or 800/243–0011* ⊕ *www.ascutney.com*) has remade itself into a bona fide destination. The 56 trails on an 1,800-foot vertical drop are served by six lifts, including a high-speed quad chairlift accessing double-diamond terrain near the summit. Day care is available for children ages 6 weeks to 6 years, with learn-to-ski programs for toddlers and up. On Saturday from 5 to 8 PM, children ages 4–12 can join Cheddar's Happy Hour and movie night.

Family-owned since 1982 and still run by Tim and Diane Mueller, **Okemo Mountain Resort** (✉ *77 Okemo Ridge Rd.* ☎ *802/228–4041; 802/228–5222 snow conditions; 800/786–5366 lodging* ⊕ *www.okemo. com*) has evolved into a major year-round resort, now with two base areas. Known for its wide, well-groomed trails, it's a favorite among intermediates. Jackson Gore, a second base village north of Ludlow off Route 103, has an inn, restaurants, a child-care center, and shops. The resort offers numerous ski and snowboarding packages. There's also ice skating at the Ice House, a covered, open-air rink open 10–9 daily in the winter. The Spring House, next to the entrance of Jackson Gore Inn, has a great kids' pool with slides, a racquetball court, fitness center, and sauna. The yoga and Pilates studio has classes a few times a week. A day pass is $12.

At 2,200 feet, Okemo has the highest vertical drop of any resort in southern Vermont. The beginner trails extend above both base areas, with more challenging terrain higher on the mountains. Intermediate trails are the theme here, but experts will find steep trails and glades

Vermont Artisanal Cheese

Hankering for some good cheddar during your time in Vermont? Would you like that aged one year, two years, three years; clothbound or smoked? Or perhaps instead you'd like an expertly crafted raw goat's milk tomme or some just-made sheep's ricotta?

Vermont is the artisanal cheese capital of the country, with over 40 creameries (and growing fast) that are open to the public—carefully churning out hundreds of different cheeses. Many creameries are "farmstead" operations, meaning that the animals that provide the milk are on site where their milk is made into cheese. If you eat enough cheese during your time in the state, you may be able to differentiate between the many types of milk (cow, goat, sheep, or even water buffalo), as well as make associations between the geography and climate of where you are and the taste of the cheese you eat.

This is one of the reasons why taking a walk around a dairy is a great idea: you can see the process in action, from grazing to aging to eating. Almost all dairies welcome visitors, though it's universally recommended that you call ahead to plan your visit. At **Shelburne Farms** (⊕ *www.shelburnefarms.org*), a chalkboard stands in the cheesemaking facility and notes which part of the complex cheese-making process visitors can witness at various times throughout the day. **Vermont Butter & Cheese** (⊕ *www.butterandcheese. net*), one of the leaders of the artisanal cheese movement, invites curious cheese aficionados to visit their 4,000 square-foot creamery where gem-like goat cheeses such as Bonne Bouche— a perfectly balanced, cloud-like cheese—are made Monday through Friday. Consider **Bardwell Farm** (⊕ *www. considerbardwellfarm.com*) in West

Vermont sheep's milk cheese.

Pawlet was the first cheese cooperative in the state, founded in 1864, and today, a new generation of cheesemakers make nine goat and cow milk cheeses on-site, including the bright, nutty, and exceptionally delicious Pawlet. Visit their Web site for information regarding cheesemaking workshops and classes offered at the farm. For a taste of the classic Vermont cheddar, head to **Cabot Creamery** (⊕ *www. cabotcheese.coop*) and take a tour of the factory and see how the many varieties of cheddars are made.

If you can't get yourself to a creamery for a visit, don't fret: almost every general store, grocery, or gourmet food shop carries at least a couple of delicious Vermont cheeses, the most common being Cabot and Grafton cheddars, plus usually something from a cheesemaking operation particularly close by. **The Vermont Cheese Council** has developed the Vermont Cheese Trail, a map of 38 creameries with contact information for each (⊕ *www. VTcheese.com*).

If you're a real cheese lover, definitely plan your trip to Vermont around the state's world-class food event, the annual **Vermont Cheesemakers Festival** (⊕ *www.vtcheesefest.com*) at Shelburne Farms—each summer approximately 50 cheesemakers gather to sell and sample their various cheeses.

—Michael de Zayas

(some), no a/c (some), safe (some), kitchen (some), refrigerator (some), DVD (some), no TV (some), Internet (some), Wi-Fi (some). In-hotel: restaurant, bar, laundry service, Wi-Fi hotspot ⊟ AE, D, MC, V ⍿⨀⍿ BP ⊙ Closed first two weeks in Nov.

$$$$ ⌂ **Jackson Gore Inn.** This slope-side base lodge is the place to stay if ♻ your aim is convenience to Okemo's slopes. The resort includes three restaurants and a martini bar ($12 a pop, but generous sizes), plus an arcade. You can use the Spring House health center, which includes a fitness center, a racquetball court, hot tubs, a sauna, and great kids' pools with slides. Right next to the original Jackson Gore structure are the newer annexes, Adams House, and Bixby House, which feature whirlpool tubs and slightly more contemporary furnishings. Most units have full kitchen facilities. Besides Jackson Gore, Okemo offers 145 other condo units all across the mountain. **Pros:** ski-in, ski-out at base of mountain; good for families. **Cons:** chaotic and noisy on weekends; expensive. ⊠ *77 Okemo Ridge Rd., off Rte. 103* ☎ *802/228–1400 or 800/786–5366* ⊕ *www.okemo.com* ➥ *263 rooms* ♿ *In-room: kitchen (some), refrigerator, DVD, Wi-Fi. In-hotel: 3 restaurants, bar, golf courses, tennis courts, pools, gym, spa, children's programs (ages 2–12), laundry facilities, Internet terminal, Wi-Fi hotspot, some pets allowed* ⊟ *AE, MC, V* ⍿⨀⍿ *EP, BP.*

GRAFTON

★   *8 mi south of Chester.*

Out-of-the-way Grafton is as much a historical museum as a town. During its heyday, citizens grazed some 10,000 sheep and spun their wool into sturdy yarn for locally woven fabric. When the market for wool declined, so did Grafton. Then in 1963, the Windham Foundation—Vermont's second-largest private foundation—commenced the town's rehabilitation. Not only was the Old Tavern preserved, but so were many other commercial and residential structures in the village center.

EXPLORING

The **Historical Society Museum** (⊠ *10 Main St. [Rte. 121]* ☎ *802/843–2584* ⊕ *www.graftonhistory.org* ➥ *$3* ⊙ *Memorial Day–Columbus Day, weekends and holidays 10–noon and 2–4*) documents the town's history with exhibits that change yearly.

SHOPPING

Gallery North Star (⊠ *151 Townshend Rd.* ☎ *802/843–2465* ⊕ *www.gnsgrafton.com*) exhibits the oils, watercolors, lithographs, and sculptures of Vermont-based artists. Sample the best of Vermont cheddar at the **Grafton Village Cheese Company** (⊠ *533 Townshend Rd.* ☎ *802/843–2221* ⊕ *www.graftonvillagecheese.com*).

WHERE TO STAY

$$$–$$$$ ⌂ **Old Tavern at Grafton.** This 1801 classic is one of the oldest operating ★ inns in the country and still one of Vermont's greatest lodging assets. While the rooms could use a designer's touch without forgoing a link to the past, legitimately memorable pleasures are to be had lingering on the porches, in the authentically Colonial common rooms, and with a book by the fire in the old fashioned library—at once rustic, comfy, and elegant. In the main building, with its wraparound porches sheltered by two-story white columns, are 11 guest rooms; the rest are dispersed among six other close-by buildings. Two dining rooms ($$$)—one with formal Georgian furniture, the other with rustic paneling and low beams—serve American fare. You'll also get access to the unusual guests-only bar at the Phelps Barn. The inn runs the nearby Grafton Ponds Cross-Country Ski Center. **Pros:** classic Vermont inn and tavern; professionally run; appealing common areas. **Cons:** rooms are attractive but not stellar. ⊠ *92 Main St. (Rte. 121)* ☎ *802/843–2231 or 800/843–1801* ⊕ *www.oldtavern.com* ↝ *39 rooms, 7 suites* ♿ *In-room: no a/c (some), no TV, Wi-Fi. In-hotel: 2 restaurants, bar, tennis court, bicycles, Internet terminal, Wi-Fi hotspot* ▭ *AE, MC, V* ⊗ *Closed mid-Apr.* ⦿ *BP.*

TOWNSHEND

9 mi south of Grafton.

One of a string of attractive villages along the banks of the West River, Townshend embodies the Vermont ideal of a lovely town green presided over by a gracefully proportioned church spire. The spire belongs to the 1790 Congregational Meeting House, one of the state's oldest houses of worship. North on Route 30 is the Scott Bridge (closed to traffic), the state's longest single-span covered bridge.

OFF THE BEATEN PATH
With a village green surrounded by pristine white buildings, **Newfane**, 6 mi southeast of Townshend, is sometimes described as the quintessential New England small town. The 1839 First Congregational Church and the Windham County Court House, with 17 green-shuttered windows and a rounded cupola, are often open. The building with the four-pointed spire is Union Hall, built in 1832.

SPORTS AND THE OUTDOORS

At **Townshend State Park** (⊠ *Rte. 30 N* ☎ *802/365–7500* ⊕ *www. vtstateparks.com/htm/townshend.cfm*) you'll find a sandy beach on the West River and a trail that parallels the river for 2½ mi, topping out on Bald Mountain Dam. Up the dam, the trail follows switchbacks literally carved into the stone apron.

SHOPPING

The **Big Black Bear Shop** (⊠ *Rte. 30, 3/4¾ mi north of town, Newfane* ☎ *802/365–4160 or 888/758–2327* ⊕ *www.bigblackbear.com*) at Mary Meyer Stuffed Toys Factory, the state's oldest stuffed toy company, offers discounts of up to 70% on stuffed animals of all sizes. The **Newfane Country Store** (⊠ *Rte. 30, Newfane* ☎ *802/365–7916* ⊕ *www.newfanecountrystore. com*) carries homemade fudge and other Vermont foods, gifts, crafts, and many quilts—which can also be custom ordered.

WHERE TO EAT

¢ ✕ **Townshend Dam Diner.** Folks come from miles around to enjoy traditional fare such as Mom's meat loaf, chili, and roast beef croquettes, as well as Townshend-raised bison burgers and creative daily specials. Breakfast, served all day every day, includes such tasty treats as raspberry chocolate-chip walnut pancakes and homemade French toast.

AMERICAN

You can sit at any of the collection of 1930s enamel-top tables or in the big swivel-chairs at the U-shaped counter. The diner is a few miles northwest of the village on Route 30. ⊠ *5929 Rte. 30, West Townshend* ☎ *802/874–4107* ▭ *No credit cards* ⊘ *Closed Tues.*

$$$
CONTINENTAL
✕**Windham Hill Inn.** This remote inn is a fine choice for a romantic fancy dinner. Chef Graham Gill heads up the Frog Pond dining room (don't worry; there are no frogs' legs on the menu). Start with a spiced Vermont quail, served with hand-rolled pappardelle and a wild mushroom ragout. Entrées include a fig-and-balsamic-glazed seared duck breast served with roasted pear and garden Swiss chard and a *cipollini* onion and fingerling potato sauté. There's a remarkably large wine list. A four-course prix fixe is $60. ⊠ *311 Lawrence Dr., West Townshend* ☎ *802/874–4080* ⚓ *Reservations essential* ⊕ *www.windhamhill.com* ▭ *AE, D, MC, V.*

WHERE TO STAY

¢
Boardman House. This handsome Greek-Revival home on the town green combines modern comfort with the relaxed charm of a 19th-century farmhouse. It also happens to be one of the cheapest stays in Vermont. The uncluttered guest rooms are furnished with Shaker-style furniture, colorful duvets, and paintings. Both the breakfast room and front hall have trompe-l'oeil floors. **Pros:** inexpensive; perfect village green location. **Cons:** no phone and cell-phone reception is bad. ⊠ *On the green* ☎ *802/365–4086* ⟲ *4 rooms, 1 suite* ⚬ *In-room: no phone, no TV, Wi-Fi. In-hotel: Wi-Fi hotspot, no kids under 5* ▭ *No credit cards* ⦿ *BP.*

$$$
★
Four Columns Inn. Rooms and suites in this white-columned, 1834 Greek-Revival mansion were designed for luxurious romantic getaways. The inn is right in the heart of town on the lovely Newfane green, giving you the quintessential Vermont village experience. Some of the suites have cathedral ceilings; all have gas fireplaces and double whirlpool baths, and one has a 12-head spa shower. The elegant restaurant ($$$–$$$$; closed Tuesday) serves new American cuisine. There's also a tavern with a nice selection of artisanal beers. Come here for a serene getaway, as tiny Newfane is adorable but quiet. **Pros:** great rooms; center of town location. **Cons:** little area entertainment in town. ⊠ *On the green, 6 mi southeast of Townshend, Newfane* ⬚ *Box 278, 05345* ☎ *802/365–7713 or 800/787–6633* ⊕ *www.fourcolumnsinn.com* ⟲ *6 rooms, 9 suites* ⚬ *In-room: no TV (some), Wi-Fi. In-hotel: restaurant, bar, pool, laundry service, Internet terminal, Wi-Fi hotspot, some pets allowed* ▭ *AE, DC, MC, V* ⦿ *BP.*

$$–$$$
★
Windham Hill Inn. As there's not too much to do nearby, you might find yourself sitting by a fire or swimming in the outdoor pool at this calm, quiet retreat, and that's a good thing. The 165 hillside acres have magnificent views of the West River Valley and are perfect for real relaxing. Period antiques, Oriental carpets, and locally made furniture are hallmarks of the 1825 brick farmhouse. The white barn annex has a great rough-hewn parlor that leads to the rooms, most of which have fireplaces. The Marion Goodfellow room has a staircase up to a cozy private cupola with 360-degree views. **Pros:** quiet getaway; good food; lovely setting. **Cons:** rural location makes enterntainment not an

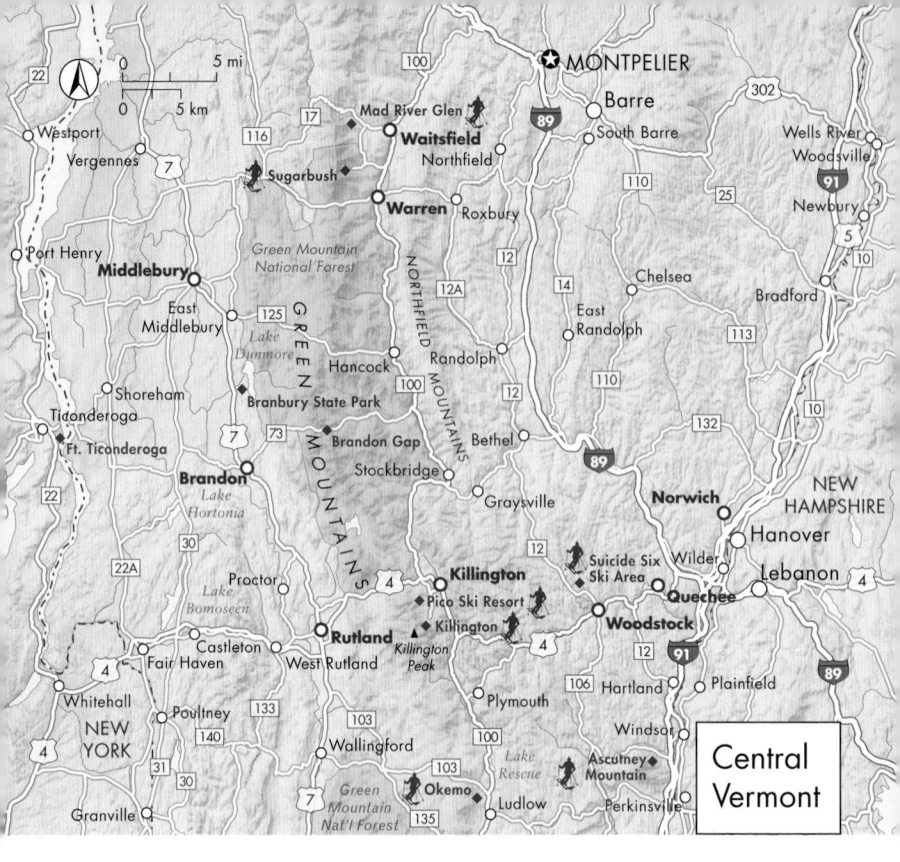

option; spotty cell service; expensive dinners. ⊠ *311 Lawrence Dr., West Townshend* ☎ *802/874–4080 or 800/944–4080* ⊕ *www.windhamhill. com* ⤻ *21 rooms* ⚅ *In-hotel: restaurant, bar, tennis court, pool, laundry service, Internet terminal, no kids under 12* ▭ *AE, D, MC, V* ⏀ *BP.*

CENTRAL VERMONT

Central Vermont's economy once centered on marble quarrying and mills. But today, as in much of the rest of the state, tourism drives the economic engine. The center of the dynamo is Killington, the East's largest downhill resort, but central Vermont has more to discover than high-speed chairlifts and slope-side condos. The old mills of Quechee and Middlebury are now home to restaurants and shops, giving wonderful views of the waterfalls that once powered the mill turbines. Woodstock has upscale shops and a national historic park. Away from these settlements, the protected (except for occasional logging) lands of the Green Mountain National Forest are laced with hiking trails.

Our coverage of towns begins with Norwich, on U.S. 5 near Interstate 91 at the state's eastern edge, winds west toward U.S. 7, then continues north to Middlebury before heading over the spine of the Green Mountains to Waitsfield.

NORWICH

6 mi north of White River Junction.

On the shores of the Connecticut River, Norwich boasts beautifully maintained 18th- and 19th-century homes set about a handsome green. Norwich is the Vermont sister to sophisticated Hanover, New Hampshire, over the river.

GETTING HERE AND AROUND

Most attractions are off Interstate 91; the town sits a mile to the west.

EXPLORING

Montshire Museum of Science. Numerous hands-on exhibits here explore nature and technology. Kids can make giant bubbles, watch fish and turtles swim in giant aquariums, explore wind, and wander a maze of outdoor trails by the river. An ideal destination for a rainy day, this is one of the finest museums in New England. ⊠ *1 Montshire Rd.* ☎ *802/649–2200* ⊕ *www.montshire.org* 🎟 *$10* ⊙ *Daily 10–5.*

SHOPPING

Are you a baker? **King Arthur Flour Baker's Store** (⊠ *135 Rte. 5 S* ☎ *802/ 649–3881 or 800/827–6836* ⊕ *www.bakerscatalogue.com* ⊙ *Mon.–Sat. 8:30–6, Sun. 8:30–4*) is a must-see for those who love bread. The shelves are stocked with all the ingredients and tools in the company's *Baker's Catalogue,* including flours, mixes, and local jams and syrups. The bakery has a viewing area where you can watch products being made, and you can buy baked goods or sandwiches. A separate education center has evening and weekend classes and weeklong baking packages.

QUECHEE

11 mi southwest of Norwich, 6 mi west of White River Junction.

A historic mill town, Quechee sits just upriver from its namesake gorge, an impressive 165-foot-deep canyon cut by the Ottauquechee River. Most people view the gorge from U.S. 4. To escape the crowds, hike along the gorge or scramble down one of several trails to the river.

ESSENTIALS

Visitor Information Quechee Chamber of Commerce (⊠ *1789 Quechee St.* ☎ *802/295–7900 or 800/295–5451* ⊕ *www.quechee.com*).

EXPLORING

Simon Pearce. The main attraction in the village is this glassblowing factory, which an Irish glassmaker by the same name set up in 1981 in a restored woolen mill by a waterfall. Water power still drives the factory's furnace. Visitors may take a free self-guided tour of the factory floor and see the glassblowers at work. The store in the mill sells contemporary glass and ceramic tableware and home furnishings, such as glass lamps and clocks. Seconds and discontinued items are reduced 25%. A fine restaurant here uses the Simon Pearce glassware and is justly popular. ⊠ *The Mill, 1760 Main St.* ☎ *802/295–2711* ⊕ *www.simonpearce.com* ⊙ *Store daily 9–9; glassblowing Tues.–Sat. 9–9, Sun. and Mon. 9–5.*

♻ **Vermont Institute of Natural Science (VINS) Nature Center.** Next to Quechee Gorge, this science center has 17 raptor exhibits, including bald eagles, peregrine falcons, and owls. All the caged birds have been found injured and are unable to survive in the wild. Predators of the Sky, a 30-minute live bird program, starts daily at 11, 1, and 3:30. ⊠ *6565 Woodstock Rd. (Rte. 4)* ☎ *802/359–5000* ⊕ *www.vinsweb.org* ⊠ *$8* ☉ *May–Oct., daily 10–5; Nov.–Apr., daily 10–4.*

SPORTS AND THE OUTDOORS

FISHING The **Vermont Fly Fishing School/Wilderness Trails** (⊠ *1119 Main St.* ☎ *802/ 295–7620*) leads workshops, rents fishing gear and mountain bikes, and arranges canoe and kayak trips. In winter, the company conducts cross-country and snowshoe treks.

POLO **Quechee Polo Club** (⊠ *Dewey's Mill Rd., ½ mi north of U.S. 4* ☎ *802/295– 7152*) draws hundreds of spectators on summer Saturdays to its matches near the Quechee Gorge. Admission is $8 per carload.

SHOPPING

ANTIQUES AND CRAFTS The 40 dealers at the **Hartland Antiques Center** (⊠ *U.S. 4* ☎ *802/457– 4745*) stock furniture, paper items, china, glass, and collectibles. More than 350 dealers sell their wares at the **Quechee Gorge Village** (⊠ *573 Woodstock Rd., off U.S. 4* ☎ *802/295–1550 or 800/438–5565* ⊕ *www. quecheegorge.com*), an antiques and crafts mall in an immense reconstructed barn that also houses a country store and a classic diner. A merry-go-round and a small-scale working railroad operate when weather permits.

CLOTHING AND MORE **Scotland by the Yard** (⊠ *8828 Woodstock Rd. [U.S. 4]* ☎ *802/295–5351 or 800/295–5351* ⊕ *www.scotlandbytheyard.com*) sells all things Scottish, from kilts to Harris tweed jackets and tartan ties.

WINE **Ottauquechee Valley Winery** (⊠ *5967 Woodstock Rd. [U.S. 4]* ☎ *802/295– 9463*), in a historic 1870s barn complex, has a tasting room and sells fruit wines, such as apple and blueberry.

WHERE TO EAT AND STAY

$$–$$$

AMERICAN

Fodor'sChoice

★

✕ **Simon Pearce.** Candlelight, sparkling glassware from the studio downstairs, exposed brick, and large windows overlooking the falls of the roaring Ottauquechee River create an ideal setting for contemporary American cuisine. The food is widely considered to be worthy of a pilgrimage. Sesame-seared tuna with noodle cakes and wasabi as well as roast duck with mango chutney sauce are house specialties; the wine cellar holds several hundred vintages. The lunch menu might include a roasted duck quesadilla or Mediterranean lamb burger. ⊠ *The Mill, 1760 Main St.* ☎ *802/295–1470* ⊕ *www.simonpearce.com* ⊟ *AE, D, DC, MC, V* ⚠ *Reservations not accepted.*

$$–$$$ 🏠 **Parker House.** This beautiful 1857 house on the National Historic Register was once home to the mill owner who ran the textile mill next door (which is now Simon Pearce). Rooms are bright and clean with queen and king beds. Walter and Joseph are the names of the two cute rooms that face the river in back. Downstairs is an attractive bar area and a good French restaurant ($$$) with a menu that changes nightly. **Pros:** in-town; riverfront location; spacious, cute rooms. **Cons:** no yard. ⊠ *1792 Main St.* ☎ *802/295–6077* ⊕ *www.theparkerhouseinn.com* 🛏 7

Simon Pearce is a glass gallery and restaurant, both powered by hydroelectricity from Quechee falls.

rooms, 1 suite ♿ In-room: no TV, Wi-Fi. In-hotel: restaurant, room service, bar, laundry service, Internet terminal, Wi-Fi hotspot, some pets allowed ▭ AE, MC, V ⫿◎⫿ BP.

$–$$ 🏨 **Quechee Inn at Marshland Farm.** Each room in this handsomely restored 1793 country home has Queen Anne–style furnishings and period antiques. From the old barn, the inn runs bike and canoe rentals, a fly-fishing school, and kayak and canoe trips. Eleven miles of cross-country and hiking trails are on the property, and you also have privileges at the Quechee Club, a private golf, tennis, and ski club. The dining room's ($$–$$$) creative entrées include shellfish bouillabaisse and rack of lamb with green peppercorn pesto. **Pros:** historic; spacious property. **Cons:** bathrooms are dated. ✉ Main St. ☎ 802/295–3133 or 800/235–3133 ⊕ www.quecheeinn.com 🛏 22 rooms, 3 suites ♿ In-room: Wi-Fi. In-hotel: restaurant, bar, water sports, bicycles, Wi-Fi hotspot ▭ AE, D, DC, MC, V ⫿◎⫿ BP.

WOODSTOCK

★ *4 mi west of Quechee.*

Woodstock is a Currier & Ives print come to life. Well-maintained Federal-style houses surround the tree-lined village green, which is not far from a covered bridge. The town owes much of its pristine appearance to the Rockefeller family's interest in historic preservation and land conservation and to native George Perkins Marsh, a congressman, diplomat, and conservationist who wrote the pioneering book *Man and Nature* (1864) about humanity's use and abuse of the land. Only busy U.S. 4 detracts from the town's quaintness.

ESSENTIALS

Visitor Information **Woodstock Area Chamber of Commerce** (✉ *18 Central St.* ☎ *802/457–3555 or 888/496–6378* ⊕ *www.woodstockvt.com*).

EXPLORING

⌚ **Billings Farm and Museum.** Founded by Frederick Billings in 1871 as a model dairy farm, this is one of the oldest dairy farms in the country and sits on the property that was the childhood home of George Perkins Marsh. Concerned about the loss of New England's forests to overgrazing, Billings planted thousands of trees and put into practice Marsh's conservationist farming ideas. Exhibits in the reconstructed Queen Anne farmhouse, school, general store, workshop, and former Marsh homestead demonstrate the lives and skills of early Vermont settlers. ✉ *5302 River Rd. (Rte. 12, ½ mi north of Woodstock)* ☎ *802/457–2355* ⊕ *www.billingsfarm.org* ☎ *$11* ◷ *May–late Oct., daily 10–5; call for winter holiday and weekend schedules.*

Marsh-Billings-Rockefeller National Historical Park. This 555-acre park is Vermont's only national park and the nation's first to focus on natural resource conservation and stewardship. The pristine and stunning park encompasses the forest lands planned by Frederick Billings according to Marsh's principles, as well as Frederick Billings's mansion, gardens, and carriage roads. The entire property was the gift of Laurance S. Rockefeller, who lived here with his late wife, Mary, Billings's granddaughter. You can learn more at the visitor center, tour the residential complex with a guide every hour on the hour, and explore the 20 mi of trails and old carriage roads that climb Mt. Tom. ✉ *54 Elm St.* ☎ *802/457–3368 Ext. 22* ⊕ *www.nps.gov/mab* ☎ *Tour $6* ◷ *May–Oct., mansion and garden tours 10–5; grounds daily dawn–dusk.*

OFF THE
BEATEN
PATH

Plymouth Notch Historic District. U.S. president Calvin Coolidge was born and buried in Plymouth Notch, a town that shares his character: low-key and quiet. The perfectly preserved 19th-century buildings resemble nothing so much as a Vermont town frozen in time. In addition to the homestead—where "Silent Cal" was sworn in by his father as president at 2:47 AM on August 3, 1923, after the sudden death of President Warren G. Harding—there is a visitor center, a general store once run by Coolidge's father (a room above it was used as the summer White House), a cheese factory, two large barns displaying agricultural equipment, and a one-room schoolhouse. Coolidge's grave is in the cemetery across Route 100A. ✉ *Rte. 100A, 6 mi south of U.S. 4, 1 mi east of Rte. 100* ☎ *802/672–3773* ⊕ *www.historicvermont.org/coolidge* ◷ *Late May–mid-Oct., daily 9:30–5.*

SPORTS AND THE OUTDOORS

BIKING **The Start House** (✉ *28 Central St.* ☎ *802/457–3377* ⊕ *www. thestarthouseskiandbike.com*) rents, sells, and services bikes and skis and distributes a free touring map for biking.

GOLF Robert Trent Jones Sr. designed the 18-hole, 6,000-yard, par-70 course at **Woodstock Country Club** (✉ *14 The Green* ☎ *802/457–6674* ⊕ *www. woodstockinn.com*), which is run by the Woodstock Inn. Green fees are $70 weekdays, $95 weekends.

The upscale Woodstock area is known as Vermont's horse country.

HORSEBACK RIDING **Kedron Valley Stables** (⊠ *Rte. 106 S, South Woodstock* ☎ *802/457–1480 or 800/225–6301* ⊕ *www.kedron.com*) conducts one-hour guided trail rides and horse-drawn sleigh and wagon rides.

SHOPPING

ART In downtown Woodstock, **Stephen Huneck Studio** (⊠ *49 Central St.* ☎ *802/457–3206*) invites canines and humans to visit the artist's gallery, filled with whimsical animal carvings, prints, and furniture.

CLOTHING ★ **Who Is Sylvia?** (⊠ *26 Central St.* ☎ *802/457–1110*), in the old firehouse, sells vintage clothing and antique linens, lace, and jewelry.

FOOD The **Woodstock Farmers' Market** (⊠ *468 Woodstock Rd., U.S. 4* ☎ *802/457–3658* ⊕ *www.woodstockfarmersmarket.com*) is a year-round buffet of local produce, fresh fish, and excellent sandwiches and pastries. The maple-walnut scones go fast every morning except Monday, when the market is closed. Take the Taftsville covered bridge off Route 4 east of town to **Sugarbush Farm Inc.** (⊠ *591 Sugarbush Farm Rd.* ☎ *802/457–1757 or 800/281–1757* ⊕ *www.sugarbushfarm.com*), where you'll learn how maple sugar is made and get to taste as much syrup as you'd like. The farm also makes excellent cheeses and is open 10 to 5 year-round. East of town, the **Taftsville Country Store** (⊠ *404 Woodstock Rd. U.S. 4], Taftsville* ☎ *802/457–1135 or 800/854–0013* ⊕ *www.taftsville.com*) sells a wide selection of Vermont cheeses, moderately priced wines, and Vermont specialty foods.

WHERE TO EAT

$–$$
ECLECTIC
★
✕ **Barnard Inn.** The dining room in this 1796 brick farmhouse breathes 18th century, but the food is decidedly 21st century. Former San Francisco restaurant chef-owners Will Dodson and Ruth Schimmelpfennig create inventive four-course prix-fixe menus with delicacies such as beef carpaccio and pan-seared escolar in lemon-and-caper herb butter. In the back is a local favorite, Max's Tavern, which serves upscale pub fare such as beef with Gorgonzola mashed potatoes and panfried trout with almond *beurre noisette* (browned butter). ⊠ *5518 Rte. 12, 8 mi north of Woodstock, Barnard* ☎ *802/234–9961* ⊕ *www.barnardinnrestaurant.com* ▭ *AE, MC, V* ⊘ *Closed Sun. and Mon. No lunch* ⬥ *Reservations essential.*

$
CAFÉ
✕ **Keeper's Café.** Creative, moderately priced fare draws customers from all over the region to this café. Chef Eli Morse's menus include such light dishes as pancetta salad and fresh corn soup and such elaborate entrées as herb garlic roast chicken with a sherry caper sauce. Blackboard specials change daily. Housed inside a former general store, the small dining room feels relaxed, with locals table-hopping to chat with friends. ⊠ *3685 Rte. 106, 12 mi south of Woodstock, Reading* ☎ *802/484–9090* ▭ *AE, MC, V* ⊘ *Closed Sun. and Mon. No lunch.*

$$
ITALIAN
Fodor's Choice
★
✕ **Pane e Saluto.** Don't let the size fool you—meals at this little upstairs restaurant are exciting and memorable, thanks to young couple Deirdre Heekin and Caleb Barker. Hip contemporary decor, an intimately small space, and Heekin's discreetly passionate front-of-house direction all come together to complement the Barker's slow-food-inspired passion for flavorful, local, and farm-raised dishes. Try *ragu d'agnello e maiale* (spaghetti with an *abruzzese* ragu from roasted pork and lamb) followed by *cotechino e lenticche* (a garlic sausage with lentils). You might expect such an *osteria* in Berkeley or Brooklyn, but this tiny spot pumps life into the blood of old Woodstock. Ask about the culinary tours the team leads each year in Italy. ⊠ *61 Central St.* ☎ *802/457–4882* ⊕ *www.osteriapaneesalute.com* ▭ *AE, MC, V* ⊘ *Closed Tues. and Wed. and Apr. and Nov. No lunch.*

$–$$
FRENCH
★
✕ **Prince & the Pauper.** Modern French and American fare with a Vermont accent is the focus of this candlelit Colonial restaurant off the Woodstock green. The grilled duck breast might have an Asian five-spice sauce, and lamb and pork sausage in puff pastry comes with a honey-mustard sauce. A three-course prix-fixe menu is available for $48; a less-expensive bistro menu can be ordered from in the lounge. ⊠ *24 Elm St.* ☎ *802/457–1818* ⊕ *www.princeandpauper.com* ▭ *AE, D, MC, V* ⊘ *No lunch.*

WHERE TO STAY

$$$$
🛏 **Fan House.** Do you have an elusive dream, one that hankers for an authentic home in the heart of a very small, quaint Vermont town? Take the one-minute walk from the perfect general store in Barnard to this 1840 white Colonial, and here it is. The three rooms put together by Sara Widness—who happens to be an expert on luxury travel—are cozy, comfortable, and avoid romantic clichés. The rooms are simply adorned with tapestries, antique rugs, claw-foot tubs, comfy sofas, and old bed frames guarding soft linens and a mountain of pillows. The living room

hearth, the old wood stove in the kitchen, and the library nook create a real sense of home. **Pros:** center of old town; homey comforts; good library. **Cons:** upstairs rooms can be cool in winter. ⊠ *6296 Rte. 12 N* 🏠 *Box 294, 05031* ☎ *802/234–6704* ⊕ *www.thefanhouse.com* 🛏 *3 rooms* ♿ *In-room: no phone, no TV. In-hotel: Internet terminal, no kids under 12* ▤ *No credit cards* ☉ *Closed Apr.* ⦿ *BP.*

$$–$$$ ▦ **Kedron Valley Inn.** You're likely to fall in love at the first sight of this 1828 three-story brick building that forms the centerpiece of this quiet, elegant retreat. This and another 19th-century building along with a motel-style 1968 log lodge make up this inn on 15 acres. Many of the rooms have a fireplace or a Franklin stove, and some have private decks or terraces. The motel units boast country antiques and reproductions. A big spring-fed pond has a white sand beach with toys for kids. In the restaurant ($$$), the chef creates French masterpieces such as fillet of Norwegian salmon stuffed with herb seafood mousse in puff pastry. **Pros:** good food; quiet setting. **Cons:** 5 mi south of Woodstock. ⊠ *10671 South Rd. (Rte. 106), South Woodstock* ☎ *802/457–1473 or 800/836–1193* ⊕ *www.kedronvalleyinn.com* 🛏 *21 rooms, 6 suites* ♿ *In-room: no phone, no a/c (some). In-hotel: restaurant, bar, Internet terminal, some pets allowed* ▤ *AE, MC, V* ☉ *Closed Apr.* ⦿ *BP.*

$$ ▦ **Shire Riverview Motel.** Some rooms in this immaculate motel have decks—and almost all have views—overlooking the Ottauquechee River. Rooms are simple, a step above usual motel fare, with four-poster beds and wing chairs; two rooms have hot tubs, and the suite has a full kitchen. Complimentary coffee is served each morning; in summer sip it on the riverfront veranda. The real key here is walking distance to the green and all shops. **Pros:** inexpensive access to the heart of Woodstock; views. **Cons:** dull rooms; unexciting exterior. ⊠ *46 Pleasant St.* ☎ *802/457–2211* ⊕ *www.shiremotel.com* 🛏 *42 rooms, 1 suite* ♿ *In-room: kitchen (some), refrigerator* ▤ *AE, D, MC, V.*

$$$$ ▦ **Twin Farms.** Let's just get it out: Twin Farms is the best lodging choice
Fodor's Choice in Vermont. Some even say it's the best small property in the country.
★ And if you can afford it—stays begin at well over $1,000 a night— you'll want to experience it. Three rooms are in the beautiful main building, which was once home to writer Sinclair Lewis. The rest are individual cottages, secluded among 300 acres. Each incredible room and cottage is furnished with a blend of high art (Jasper Johns, Milton Avery, Cy Twombly), gorgeous folk art, and furniture that goes beyond comfortable sophistication. The food may be the best in Vermont. The service—suave, relaxed—definitely is. Prices include all meals, alcohol, and activities; there's a good spa, a pub within a big game room, and a private ski hill. **Pros:** impeccable service; stunning rooms; sensational meals. **Cons:** astronomical prices; must drive to town/Woodstock. ⊠ *1 Stage Rd., Barnard* ☎ *802/234–9999* ⊕ *www.twinfarms.com* 🛏 *3 rooms, 10 cottages* ♿ *In-room: DVD, Wi-Fi. In-hotel: restaurant, room service, bars, tennis courts, pools, gym, spa, water sports, bicycles, laundry service, Internet terminal, Wi-Fi hotspot, no kids under 12* ▤ *AE, D, DC, MC, V* ☉ *Closed Apr.* ⦿ *AI.*

$$$ ▦ **Woodstock Inn and Resort.** If this is your first time in Woodstock and
Fodor's Choice you want to feel like you're in the middle of it all, stay here. Set back
★

far from the main road but still on the town's gorgeous green, the Inn is the town's beating heart. You'll feel that right away when looking at the main fireplace, set immediately through the front doors, which burns impressive 3-foot logs. Rooms are contemporary and luxurious, with huge flat-screen TVs, sleek furniture, and great bathrooms done in simple subway tiles. The resort also owns and gives you access to Suicide Six ski mountain and the Woodstock Golf Club. **Pros:** exciting, big property; contemporary furnishings; professionally run. **Cons:** can lack intimacy. ⊠ *14 The Green (U.S. 4)* ☎ *802/457–1100 or 800/448–7900* ⊕ *www.woodstockinn.com* ⤵ *135 rooms, 7 suites* ♿ *In-room: safe, refrigerator, Internet, Wi-Fi (some). In-hotel: 2 restaurants, room service, bar, golf course, tennis courts, pools, gym, bicycles, laundry service, Internet terminal* ⊟ *AE, D, MC, V* ⊙ *BP.*

KILLINGTON

15 mi east of Rutland.

With only a gas station, post office, motel, and a few shops at the intersection of Routes 4 and 100, it's difficult to tell that the East's largest ski resort is nearby. The village of Killington is characterized by unfortunate strip development along the access road to the ski resort. But the 360-degree views atop Killington Peak, accessible by the resort's gondola, make it worth the drive.

SPORTS AND THE OUTDOORS

BIKING **True Wheels Bike Shop** (⊠ *2886 Killington Rd.* ☎ *802/422–3234*) sells and rents bicycles and has information on local routes.

FISHING Kent Pond in **Gifford Woods State Park** (⊠ *Rte. 100, ½ mi north of U.S. 4* ☎ *802/775–5354* ⊕ *www.vtstateparks.com/htm/gifford.cfm*) is a terrific fishing spot.

GOLF At its namesake resort, **Killington Golf Course** (⊠ *4763 Killington Rd.* ☎ *802/422–6700*) has a challenging 18-hole, par-72 course. Green fees are $69 midweek and $79 weekends inclusive of carts. Twilight rates are slightly cheaper.

★ "Megamountain," "Beast of the East," and plain "huge" are apt descriptions of **Killington** (⊠ *4763 Killington Rd.* ☎ *802/422–6200; 802/422–3261 snow conditions; 800/621–6867 lodging* ⊕ *www.killington.com*). The American Skiing Company operates Killington and its neighbor, **Pico**, and over the past several years has improved lifts and snowmaking capabilities. Thanks to its extensive snowmaking system, the resort typically opens in October, and the lifts often run into May. Après-ski activities are plentiful and have been rated the best in the East by national ski magazines. With a single call to Killington's hotline or a visit to its Web site, skiers can plan an entire vacation: choose accommodations, book air or railroad transportation, and arrange for rental equipment and ski lessons. Killington ticket holders can also ski at Pico: a shuttle connects the two areas.

The Killington–Pico complex has a host of activities, including an alpine slide, a golf course, two waterslides, a skateboard park, and a swimming pool. The resort rents mountain bikes and advises hikers. The

K-1 Express Gondola takes you up the mountain to Vermont's second-highest summit.

In terms of downhill skiing, it would probably take several weeks to test all 200 trails on the seven mountains of the Killington complex, even though all except Pico interconnect. About 70% of the 1,182 acres of skiing terrain can be covered with machine-made snow. Transporting skiers to the peaks of this complex are 32 lifts, including 2 gondolas, 12 quads (including 6 high-speed express quads), 6 triples, and a Magic Carpet. The K-1 Express Gondola goes to the area's highest elevation, 4,241-foot Killington Peak. The Skyeship Gondola starts on U.S. 4, far below Killington's main base lodge, and savvy skiers park here to avoid the more crowded access road. After picking up more passengers at a mid-station, the Skyeship tops out on Skye Peak. Although Killington has a vertical drop of 3,050 feet, only gentle trails—Juggernaut and Great Eastern—go from top to bottom. The skiing includes everything from Outer Limits, the East's steepest and longest mogul trail, to 6½-mi Great Eastern. In the Fusion Zones, underbrush and low branches have been cleared to provide tree skiing. Killington's Superpipe is one of the best rated in the East. Instruction programs are available for youngsters ages 3–8; those 6–12 can join an all-day program.

When weekend hordes hit Killington, the locals head to **Pico** (⊠ *51 Alpine Dr. [Rte. 4], Killington* ☎ *802/422–6200 or 866/667–7426* ⊕ *www.picomountain.com*). One of Killington's "seven peaks," Pico is physically separated from its parent resort. The 50 trails range from elevator-shaft steep to challenging intermediate trails near the summit, with easier terrain near the bottom of the mountain's 2,000-foot vertical. The learning slope is separated from the upper mountain, so hotshots won't bomb through it. The lower express quad can get crowded, but the upper one rarely has a line.

CROSS-COUN-
TRY SKIING
Mountain Top Inn and Resort (⊠ *195 Mountaintop Rd., Chittenden* ☎ *802/483–6089 or 800/445–2100* ⊕ *www.mountaintopinn.com*) has 50 mi of hilly trails groomed for Nordic skiing, 37 mi of which can be used for skate skiing. You can also enjoy snowshoeing, dogsledding, ice skating, and snowmobile and sleigh rides. In the summer there's horseback riding, fishing, hiking, biking, and water sports.

NIGHTLIFE AND THE ARTS

On weekends, listen to live music and sip draft Guinness at the **Inn at Long Trail** (⊠ *U.S. 4* ☎ *802/775–7181* ⊕ *www.innatlongtrail.com*). **Taboo** (⊠ *2841 Killington Rd.* ☎ *802/422–9885*) serves all-you-can-eat pizza on Monday nights in winter, and $3 Long Trail pints on Sunday. It's open year-round. During ski season, the **Pickle Barrel Night Club** (⊠ *1741 Killington Rd.* ☎ *802/422–3035* ⊕ *www.picklebarrelnightclub. com*) has a band every happy hour on Friday and Saturday. After 8, the crowd moves downstairs for dancing, sometimes to big-name bands. Twentysomethings prefer to dance at the **Wobbly Barn** (⊠ *2229 Killington Rd.* ☎ *802/422–6171* ⊕ *www.wobblybarn.com*), open only during ski season.

WHERE TO EAT AND STAY

$$$$ ✕**Hemingway's.** Chef-owner Ted Fondulas has kept Hemingway's an
CONTINENTAL enduringly respected restaurant in the state since 1982 and the fine-
★ dining favorite for Killington skiers. Among the house specialties are
the cream of garlic soup and a seasonal kaleidoscope of dishes. Native
baby pheasant with local chanterelles or seared scallops with truffles
and caramelized onions are just two entrées that might appear on the
menu. Diners can opt for the prix-fixe, three- to six-course menu or
the wine-tasting menu. Request seating in either the formal vaulted dining room, the intimate wine cellar, or the garden room. ⊠ *4988 U.S. 4*
☎ *802/422–3886* ⊕ *www.hemingwaysrestaurant.com* ⌂ *Reservations*
essential ☐ *AE, D, DC, MC, V* ⊗ *Closed Mon. and Tues., early Nov.,*
and mid-Apr.–mid-May. No lunch.

$$ ⊡ **Birch Ridge Inn.** A slate-covered carriageway about a mile from Killing-
ton base stations leads to one of the area's most popular off-mountain
stays, a former executive retreat in two renovated A-frames. Rooms
range in style from Colonial and Shaker to Mission, and all have a sit-
ting area with a TV hidden behind artwork—in one room, a dollhouse
rotates up to reveal it. Six rooms have gas fireplaces, and four have
whirlpool baths. In the intimate slate-floored dining room ($$$; closed
Monday and Tuesday), choose either a four-course prix-fixe dinner or
order à la carte. **Pros:** quirky; well maintained. **Cons:** oddly furnished;
older building style. ⊠ *37 Butler Rd.* ☎ *802/422–4293 or 800/435–*
8566 ⊕ *www.birchridge.com* ↗ *10 rooms* ⌂ *In-room: no a/c (some),*
Wi-Fi. In-hotel: restaurant, bar, Wi-Fi hotspot, no kids under 12 ☐ *AE,*
D, MC, V ⊗ *Closed May* ⧖⧘ *BP, MAP.*

$$$$ ⊡ **Woods Resort & Spa.** These clustered upscale two- and three-bedroom
town houses stand in wooded lots along a winding road leading to the
spa. Most units have master baths with saunas and two-person whirlpool tubs. Vaulted ceilings in the living rooms give an open, airy feel.
The resort has a private shuttle to the ski area. **Pros:** contemporary
facility; clean, spacious rooms; lots of room choices. **Cons:** lacks traditional Vermont feeling. ⊠ *53 Woods La.* ☎ *802/422–3139 or 800/642–*
1147 ⊕ *www.woodsresortandspa.com* ↗ *107 units* ⌂ *In-room: no a/c,*
kitchen, Wi-Fi. In-hotel: tennis courts, pool, gym, spa, laundry facilities,
some pets allowed ☐ *AE, MC, V.*

RUTLAND

15 mi southwest of Killington, 32 mi south of Middlebury.

On and around U.S. 7 in Rutland are strips of shopping centers and a
seemingly endless row of traffic lights—very un-Vermont. Two blocks
west, however, stand the mansions of the marble magnates. Preservation
work has uncovered white and verde marble facades; the stonework
harkens back to the days when marble ruled Vermont's second-largest
city outside of Burlington county. The county farmers' market is held
in Depot Park Saturdays 9–2.

ESSENTIALS

Visitor Information Rutland Region Chamber of Commerce (⊠ *256 N. Main*
St. ☎ *802/773–2747 or 800/756–8880* ⊕ *www.rutlandvermont.com*).

EXPLORING

Chaffee Art Center. The beautiful former mansion of the local Paramount Theatre's founder, this arts center exhibits the work of more than 200 Vermont artists. ⊠ *16 S. Main St.* ☎ *802/775–0356* ⊕ *www. chaffeeartcenter.org* ▨ *Free* ⊙ *Tues.–Sat. 10–5, Sun. noon–4.*

New England Maple Museum and Gift Shop. Maple syrup is Vermont's signature product, and this museum north of Rutland explains the history and process of turning maple sap into syrup with murals, diorama exhibits, and a slide show. If you don't get a chance to visit a sugarhouse, this is a fine place to sample the four different grades and pick up some souvenirs. ⊠ *4578 U.S. 7, Pittsford, 9 mi south of Brandon* ☎ *802/483–9414* ⊕ *www.maplemuseum.com* ▨ *Museum $2.50* ⊙ *Late May–Oct., daily 8:30–5:30; Nov., Dec., and mid-Mar.–late May, daily 10–4.*

Paramount Theatre. The highlight of downtown is this 700-seat, turn-of-the-20th-century gilded playhouse, designed in the spirit of a Victorian opera house. The gorgeous, fully renovated theater holds over a thousand people and is home to music, theater and a film series highlighting its past as a 1930s motion picture theater. ⊠ *36 Center St.* ☎ *802/775–0570* ⊕ *www.paramountvt.org.*

Vermont Marble Exhibit. North of Rutland, this monument to marble highlights one of the main industries in this region and illustrates marble's many industrial and artistic applications. The hall of presidents has a carved bust of each U.S. president, and in the marble chapel is a replica of Leonardo da Vinci's *Last Supper*. Elsewhere you can watch a sculptor-in-residence shape the stone into finished works of art, compare marbles from around the world, and check out the Vermont Marble Company's original "stone library." Factory seconds and foreign and domestic marble items are for sale. A short walk away is the original marble quarry in Proctor. Marble from here became part of the U.S. Supreme Court building and the New York Public Library. ⊠ *52 Main St., 4 mi north of Rutland, off Rte. 3, Proctor* ☎ *802/459–2300 or 800/427–1396* ⊕ *www. vermont-marble.com* ▨ *$7* ⊙ *Mid-May–Oct., daily 9–5:30.*

Wilson Castle. As you drive a long country road just outside Rutland, the opulent vision of this 32-room mansion will surprise you. Completed in 1867, it was built over the course of eight years by a Vermonter who married a British aristocrat. The current owner, Blossom Wilson Davine Ladabouche, still owns the property and makes her summer home in the old servants' quarters. Within the mansion are 84 stained-glass windows (one inset with 32 Australian opals), hand-painted Italian frescos, and 13 fireplaces. It's magnificently furnished with European and Asian objets d'art. ⊠ *W. Proctor Rd., Proctor* ☎ *802/773–3284* ⊕ *www.wilsoncastle.com* ▨ *$9.50* ⊙ *Late May–mid-Oct., daily 9–6, last tour at 5.*

SPORTS AND THE OUTDOORS

BOATING Rent pontoon boats, speedboats, waterskiing boats, Wave Runners, and water toys at **Lake Bomoseen Marina** (⊠ *145 Creek Rd., off Rte. 4A, 1½ mi west of Castleton* ☎ *802/265–4611*).

HIKING **Deer's Leap** (⊠ *Starts at the Inn at Long Trail on Rte. 4 west of Rutland*) is a 3-mi round-trip hike to a great view overlooking Sherburne Gap

and Pico Peak. **Mountain Travelers** (⊠ *147 Rte. 4 E* ☎ *802/775–0814*) sells hiking maps and guidebooks, gives advice on local hikes, rents kayaks, and sells sporting equipment.

WHERE TO EAT AND STAY

¢–$ ✕ **Little Harry's.** Locals have packed this restaurant ever since chef-owners
ECLECTIC Trip (Harry) Pearce and Jack Mangan brought Vermont cheddar ravi-oli and lamb lo mein to downtown Rutland in 1997. (It's the "little" to the bigger Harry's near Ludlow.) The 17 tabletops are adorned with laminated photos of the regulars. For big appetites on small budgets, the pad thai and the burrito are huge meals for under $8. ⊠ *121 West St.* ☎ *802/747–4848* ⊟ *MC, V* ⊗ *No lunch.*

$$ ⊞ **Inn at Rutland.** If you love B&Bs and are tired of Rutland's chain motels, this stately 1889 Victorian mansion on Main Street is a welcome sight. Large plate-glass windows illuminate the entryway, library, and sitting room. A large table dominates the dining room, which has hand-tooled leather wainscoting. Upstairs, the rooms have antiques; two rooms have private porches and whirlpool tubs. **Pros:** solid, non-motel choice. **Cons:** unexciting rooms. ⊠ *70 N. Main St.* ☎ *802/773–0575 or 800/808–0575* ⊕ *www.innatrutland.com* ⇆ *8 rooms* ⚭ *In-room: Wi-Fi. In-hotel: res-taurant, Internet terminal, Wi-Fi hotspot* ⊟ *AE, D, MC, V.*

BRANDON

15 mi northwest of Rutland.

Thanks to an active artists' guild, Brandon is making a name for itself. In 2003 the Brandon Artists Guild, led by American folk artist Warren Kimble, auctioned 40 life-size fiberglass pigs painted by local artists. The "Really Really Pig Show" raised money for the guild (as well as other organizations) and brought fame to this once overlooked com-munity. Since then the guild has taken on birdhouses, rocking chairs, artists' palettes, cats and dogs, and, in 2009, "Starring Brandon," which featured ornamented star-shaped frames spread throughout town.

ESSENTIALS

Visitor Information Brandon Visitor Center (⊠ *4 Grove St. [Rte. 7 at 73 W]*, ☎ *802/247–6401* ⊕ *brandon.org*).

EXPLORING

Stephen A. Douglas Museum. The famous early American statesman was born in Brandon in this house in 1813. He left 20 years later to estab-lish himself as a lawyer, becoming a three-time U.S. senator and argu-ing more cases before the U.S. Supreme Court than anyone else. This museum, which opened in 2009, recounts the early Douglas years, early Brandon history, and the anti-slavery movement in Vermont—the first state to abolish it. ⊠ *4 Grove St., at U.S. 7* ☎ *802/247–6401* ⊕ *brandon. org/douglasbirthplace* ⊠ *Free* ⊗ *Daily 9–5.*

★   **The Inside Scoop and Antiques by the Falls.** A husband-and-wife team runs these two separate and equally fun-loving businesses under one roof: a colorful ice cream stand and penny candy store and an antiques store filled floor to ceiling with Americana. ⊠ *22 Park St., East Brandon* ☎ *802/247–6600.*

SPORTS AND THE OUTDOORS

The **Moosalamoo Association** (☎ 800/448–0707) manages, protects, and provides stewardship for more than 20,000 acres of the Green Mountain National Forest, northeast of Brandon. More than 60 mi of trails take hikers, mountain bikers, and cross-country skiers through some of Vermont's most gorgeous mountain terrain. Attractions include Branbury State Park, on the shores of Lake Dunmore; secluded Silver Lake; and sections of both the Long Trail and Catamount Trail (the latter is a Massachusetts-to-Québec ski trail). The Blueberry Hill Inn has direct public access to trails.

GOLF **Neshobe Golf Club** (⊠ 224 *Town Farm Rd., Rte. 73 east of Brandon* ☎ 802/247–3611 ⊕ *www.neshobe.com*) has 18 holes of par-72 golf on a bent-grass course totaling nearly 6,500 yards. Green fee is $38–$42. The Green Mountain views are terrific. Several local inns offer golf packages.

HIKING For great views from a vertigo-inducing cliff, hike up the Long Trail to **Mt. Horrid**. The steep, hour-long hike starts at the top of Brandon Gap (about 8 mi east of Brandon on Route 73). A large turnout on Route 53 marks a moderate trail to the **Falls of Lana**. West of Brandon, four trails—two short ones of less than 1 mi each and two longer ones—lead to the abandoned Revolutionary War fortifications at **Mt. Independence**. To reach them, take the first left turn off Route 73 west of Orwell and go right at the fork. The road will turn to gravel and fork again; take a sharp left-hand turn toward a small marina. The parking lot is on the left at the top of the hill.

WHERE TO EAT AND STAY

$–$$ ✕ **Café Provence.** Robert Barral, a former Chicago Four Seasons chef and
CAFÉ 16-year director of the New England Culinary Institute, graces Brandon with this delicious informal eatery named after his birthplace. One story above the main street, the café with hints of Provence—flowered seat cushions and dried-flower window valences—specializes in eclectic farm-fresh dishes. Goat-cheese cake with mesclun greens, braised veal cheeks and caramelized endive, and a portobello pizza from the restaurant's hearth oven are just a few of the choices. Breakfast offerings include buttery pastries, eggs Benedict, and breakfast pizza, and outdoor seating can be had under large umbrellas. ⊠ 11 *Center St.* ☎ 802/247–9997 ⊕ *www.cafeprovencevt.com* ▭ MC, V.

$$–$$$ ⊞ **Blueberry Hill Inn.** In the Green Mountain National Forest, 5½ mi off
Fodor'sChoice a mountain pass on a dirt road, you'll find this secluded inn with its
★ lush gardens and a pond with a wood-fired sauna on its bank. Many rooms have views of the mountains; all are furnished with antiques and quilts. The restaurant ($$$$) prepares a four-course prix-fixe menu nightly, with dishes such as venison fillet with cherry sauce. This is a very popular place for weddings. The grounds are gorgeous, and there's lots to do if you're into nature: biking, hiking, and a cross-country ski center with 43 mi of trails. **Pros:** peaceful setting within the national forest; terrific property with lots to do; great food. **Cons:** forest setting not for those who want to be near town. ⊠ 1307 *Goshen–Ripton Rd., Goshen* ☎ 802/247–6735 *or* 800/448–0707 ⊕ *www.blueberryhillinn. com* ⊅ 12 *rooms* ⌂ *In-room: no phone, no a/c, no TV, Wi-Fi. In-hotel:*

restaurant, bicycles, Internet terminal, Wi-Fi hotspot, some pets allowed ▤ *AE, MC, V* ⦿◎ *MAP.*

MIDDLEBURY

★ *17 mi north of Brandon, 34 mi south of Burlington.*

In the late 1800s Middlebury was the largest Vermont community west of the Green Mountains, an industrial center of river-powered wool and grain mills. This is Robert Frost country: Vermont's late poet laureate spent 23 summers at a farm east of Middlebury. Still a cultural and economic hub amid the Champlain Valley's serene pastoral patchwork, the town and countryside invite a day of exploration.

EXPLORING

Middlebury College. Founded in 1800, Middlebury College was conceived as a more godly alternative to the worldly University of Vermont but has no religious affiliation today. In the middle of town, the early-19th-century stone buildings contrast provocatively with the postmodern architecture of the Center for the Arts and the sports center. Music, theater, and dance performances take place throughout the year at the **Wright Memorial Theatre** and **Center for the Arts.** ⊠ *38 College St.* ☏ *802/443–5000* ⊕ *www.middlebury.edu.*

Robert Frost Interpretive Trail. About 10 mi east of town on Route 125 (1 mi west of Middlebury College's Bread Loaf campus), this easy ¾-mi trail winds through quiet woodland. Plaques along the way bear quotations from Frost's poems. A picnic area is across the road from the trailhead.

☺ **UVM Morgan Horse Farm.** The Morgan horse—Vermont's official state animal—has an even temper, stamina, and slightly truncated legs in proportion to its body. The University of Vermont's Morgan Horse Farm, about 2½ mi west of Middlebury, is a breeding and training center where in summer you can tour the stables and paddocks. ⊠ *74 Battell Dr., off Morgan Horse Farm Rd. (follow signs off Rte. 23), Weybridge* ☏ *802/388–2011* ▤ *$4* ⊙ *May–Oct., daily 9–4.*

Vermont Folklife Center. In the Masonic Hall, exhibits include photography, antiques, folk paintings, manuscripts, and other artifacts and contemporary works that examine facets of Vermont life. ⊠ *3 Court St.* ☏ *802/388–4964* ▤ *Donations accepted* ⊙ *Gallery May–Dec., Tues.– Sat. 11–4.*

Vermont State Craft Center/Frog Hollow. More than a crafts store, this arts center mounts changing exhibitions and displays exquisite works in wood, glass, metal, clay, and fiber by more than 250 Vermont artisans. The center, which overlooks Otter Creek, sponsors classes taught by some of those artists. Burlington and Manchester also have centers. ⊠ *1 Mill St.* ☏ *802/388–3177* ⊕ *www.froghollow.org* ⊙ *Call for hrs.*

OFF THE BEATEN PATH

Fort Ticonderoga Ferry. Established in 1759, the Fort Ti cable ferry crosses Lake Champlain between Shoreham and Fort Ticonderoga, New York, at one of the oldest ferry crossings in North America. The trip takes seven minutes. ⊠ *4675 Rte. 74 W, 18 mi southwest of Middlebury, 9 mi south of Brandon, Shoreham* ☏ *802/897–7999* ▤ *Cars, pickups, and* *vans with driver and passenger $8; bicycles $2; pedestrians $1* ☉ *May–last Sun. of Oct., daily 8–5:45.*

SHOPPING

ART **Historic Marble Works** (⊠ *2 Maple St.* ☎ *802/388–3701*), a renovated marble manufacturing facility, is a collection of unique shops set amid quarrying equipment and factory buildings. One of them, **Danforth Pewter** (☎ *802/388–0098* ⊕ *www.danforthpewter.com*), sells hand-crafted pewter vases, lamps, and tableware.

WHERE TO EAT

$ ✕ **American Flatbread–Rutland.** On weekends this is the most happening
PIZZA spot in town, and no wonder: the pizza is extraordinary, and the attitude
★ is pure Vermont. Wood-fired clay domes create masterful thin crusts from organically grown wheat. Besides the innovative, delicious pizzas, try an organic mesclun salad tossed in the house raspberry-ginger vinaigrette. If you love pizza and haven't been here, you're in for a treat. There are also locations in Waitsfield and Burlington. ⊠ *137 Maple St., at the Marble Works* ☎ *802/388–3300* ⊕ *www.americanflatbread. com* ⚏ *Reservations not accepted* ⊟ *MC, V* ☉ *Closed Sun. and Mon. No lunch.*

$$–$$$ ✕ **Mary's at Baldwin Creek.** People drive from the far reaches of Vermont
ECLECTIC to eat at this restaurant just beyond the charming, little-known town
Fodor'sChoice of Bristol, 13 mi northeast of Middlebury. If you care about food,
★ you'll be in awe of chef-owner Douglas Mack's credentials: for starters, he founded the Vermont Fresh Network (⊕ *www.vermontfresh. net*). Membership in this group, which promotes the use of farm-fresh ingredients, is now a hallmark of any respectable restaurant in the state. Plan time to visit the huge vegetable gardens that surround this beautiful property. A slow approach to locally grown foods finds life here with hearty fare like summer lasagna, a prime showcase for the flavors of the veggies grown 50 feet from your table, and Mack's near-legendary garlic soup, a creamy year-round staple that seems genetically engineered to please. Desserts are hit or miss. ⊠ *1869 Rte. 116, Bristol* ☎ *802/453–2432* ⊕ *www.innatbaldwincreek.com* ⊟ *MC, V* ☉ *Closed Mon. and Tues. No lunch.*

$$–$$$ ✕ **Storm Café.** There is no setting in town quite like the deck overlooking
ECLECTIC the Otter Creek Falls at one end of the long footbridge over the creek. Even if you're not here in summer, the eclectic ever-changing menu at this small restaurant in the old Frog Hollow Mill makes it worth a visit any time of year. "Stormy" Jamaican jerk–seasoned pork tenderloin and melt-in-your-mouth desserts like an apricot soufflé are favorites. ⊠ *3 Mill St.* ☎ *802/388–1063* ⊕ *www.thestormcafe.com* ⊟ *MC, V.*

WHERE TO STAY

$–$$ 🛏 **Swift House Inn.** The 1824 Georgian home of a 19th-century governor showcases white-panel wainscoting, mahogany furnishings, and marble fireplaces. The stellar rooms—most with Oriental rugs and nine with fireplaces—have period reproductions such as canopy beds, curtains with swags, and claw-foot tubs. Some bathrooms have double whirlpool tubs. Rooms in the attractive Gatehouse suffer from street noise but are charming and a solid value. The seven-room carriage house has more expensive rooms with wood fireplaces and king-size beds. **Pros:** attractive, spacious, well-kept rooms; professionally run. **Cons:** near to but not quite in the heart of town. ✉ *25 Stewart La.* ☏ *802/388–9925* ⊕ *www.swifthouseinn.com* ⤴ *20 rooms* ♨ *In-room: DVD (some), Wi-Fi. In-hotel: restaurant, room service, bar, laundry service, Wi-Fi hotspot, some pets allowed* ▭ *AE, D, DC, MC, V* ⵙ *BP.*

WAITSFIELD AND WARREN

32 mi northeast (Waitsfield) and 25 mi east (Warren) of Middlebury.

Skiers discovered the high peaks overlooking the pastoral Mad River Valley in the 1940s. Now the valley and its two towns, Waitsfield and Warren, attract the hip, the adventurous, and the low-key. Warren is tiny and adorable, with a general store that attracts tour buses. The gently carved ridges cradling the valley and the swell of pastures and fields lining the river seem to keep notions of ski-resort sprawl at bay. With a map from the Sugarbush Chamber of Commerce you can investigate back roads off Route 100 that have exhilarating valley views.

ESSENTIALS

Visitor Information Sugarbush Chamber of Commerce (✉ *Rte. 100* ☏ *802/496–3409 or 800/828–4748* ⊕ *www.madrivervalley.com*).

SPORTS AND THE OUTDOORS

OUTFITTER   **Clearwater Sports** (✉ *4147 Main St. [Rte. 100], Waitsfield* ☏ *802/496–2708* ⊕ *clearwatersports.com*) rents canoes, kayaks, tubing, and camping equipment and leads guided river trips and white-water instruction in the warm months; in winter, the store leads snowshoe and backcountry ski tours and rents Telemark equipment, snowshoes, and one-person Mad River Rocket sleds.

GOLF   Great views and challenging play are the trademarks of the Robert Trent Jones–designed 18-hole mountain course at **Sugarbush Resort** (✉ *1091 Golf Course Rd., Warren* ☏ *802/583–6725* ⊕ *www.sugarbushgolf. com*). The green fees run from $48 to $100.

SLEIGH RIDES   **Mountain Valley Farm** (✉ *1719 Common Rd., Waitsfield* ☏ *802/496–9255* ⊕ *mountainvalleyfarm.com*) offers horse-drawn carriage and sleigh rides with reservations.

SKI AREAS   **Blueberry Lake Cross-Country Ski Area** (✉ *424 Plunkton Rd., East Warren* ☏ *802/496–6687* ⊕ *www.blueberrylakeskivt.com*) has 18 mi of trails through thickly wooded glades.

The hundreds of shareholders who own **Mad River Glen** (✉ *Rte. 17* ☏ *802/496–3551; 802/496–2001 snow conditions; 800/850–6742 cooperative office* ⊕ *www.madriverglen.com*) are dedicated, knowledgeable skiers devoted to keeping skiing what it used to be—a pristine alpine experience. Mad River's unkempt aura attracts rugged individualists looking for less-polished terrain: the area was developed in the late 1940s and has changed relatively little since then. It remains one of only three resorts in the country that ban snowboarding.

Mad River is steep, with natural slopes that follow the mountain's fall lines. The terrain changes constantly on the 45 interconnected

Sheep's cheese is just one of the many food products that contribute to great fresh local meals in Vermont.

trails, of which 30% are beginner, 30% are intermediate, and 40% are expert. Intermediate and novice terrain is regularly groomed. Five lifts—including the world's last surviving single chairlift—service the mountain's 2,037-foot vertical drop. Most of Mad River's trails are covered only by natural snow. The kids' ski school runs classes for little ones ages 4 to 12. The nursery is for infants to 6-year-olds; reservations are recommended.

Known as the capital of free-heel skiing, Mad River Glen sponsors Telemark programs throughout the season. Every March, the North America Telemark Organization (NATO) Festival attracts up to 1,400 visitors. Snowshoeing is also an option. There is a $5 fee to use the snowshoe trails, and rentals are available.

Sugarbush (⊠ *Sugarbush Access Rd., accessible from Rte. 100 or 17* ⊕ *Box 350, Warren 05674* ☎ *802/583–6300; 802/583–7669 snow conditions; 800/537–8427 lodging* ⊕ *www.sugarbush.com*) has remade itself as a true skier's mountain, with steep, natural snow glades and fall-line drops. Not as rough around the edges as Mad River Glen, Sugarbush also has well-groomed intermediate and beginner terrain. A computer-controlled system for snowmaking has increased coverage to nearly 70%. At the base of the mountain are condominiums, restaurants, shops, bars, and a sports center.

Sugarbush is two distinct, connected mountain complexes connected by the Slide Brook Express quad. Lincoln Peak, with a vertical of 2,400 feet, is known for formidable steeps, especially on Castlerock. Mount Ellen has more beginner runs near the bottom, with steep fall-line pitches on the upper half of the 2,650 vertical feet. There are 115 trails in all: 23% beginner, 48% intermediate, 29% expert. The resort has 18 lifts: seven quads (including four high-speed versions), three triples, four doubles, and four surface lifts. There's half- and full-day instruction available for children ages 4–12, ski/day care for 3-year-olds, and supervised ski and ride programs for teens. Sugarbear Forest, a terrain garden, has fun bumps and jumps. The Sugarbush Day School accepts children ages 6 weeks to 6 years.

SHOPPING

All Things Bright and Beautiful (✉ 27 Bridge St., Waitsfield ☎ 802/496–3997) is a 12-room Victorian house jammed to the rafters with stuffed animals of all shapes, sizes, and colors as well as folk art, prints, and collectibles. One of the rooms is a coffee and ice-cream shop. **Cabin Fever Quilts** (✉ 4276 Main St. No. 1 [Rte. 100], Waitsfield ☎ 802/496–2287 ⊕ www.cabinfeverquiltsvt.com), inside a converted old church, sells fine handmade quilts.

NIGHTLIFE AND THE ARTS

NIGHTLIFE The Back Room at **Chez Henri** (✉ Lincoln Peak base area, Sugarbush Village, Warren ☎ 802/583–2600) has a pool table and is the place to go après-ski. Live bands play most weekends at **Purple Moon Pub** (✉ 6163 Main St. [Rte. 100], Waitsfield ☎ 802/496–3422 ⊕ www. purplemoonpub.com).

★ In the basement of the Pitcher Inn, **Tracks** (✉ 275 Main St., Warren ☎ 802/493–6350 ⊕ www.pitcherinn.com) is a public bar run by the Relais & Châteaux property. It has billiards, darts, a really fun shuffleboard game played on a long table with sawdust, a full tavern menu, and a giant moose head.

ARTS The **Green Mountain Cultural Center** (✉ Inn at the Round Barn Farm, 1661 E. Warren Rd. ☎ 802/496–7722 ⊕ www.theroundbarn.com) hosts concerts, art exhibits, and educational workshops. The **Valley Players** (✉ 4254 Main St. [Rte. 100], Waitsfield ☎ 802/496–9612 ⊕ www. valleyplayers.com) present musicals, dramas, follies, and more.

WHERE TO EAT

$ ✕ **American Flatbread–Waitsfield.** Is this the best pizza experience in the

PIZZA world? It just may be. In summer, dining takes place outside around

Fodor's Choice fire pits in the beautiful valley, a setting and meal not to be forgotten.

★ The secret is in the love, but some clues to the magic are in the organically grown flour and vegetables and the wood-fired clay ovens. The "new Vermont sausage" is Waitsfield pork in a maple-fennel sausage baked with sundried tomatoes, caramelized onions, cheese, and herbs; it's a dream, as are the more traditional pizzas. As a restaurant, it's open only Friday and Saturday evenings, but the retail bakery is open Monday–Thursday 7:30 AM–8 PM; if you're here during that time anything in the oven is yours for $10. This is the original American Flatbread location—plan your trip around it. ✉ 46 Lareau Rd., off Rte. 100, Waitsfield ☎ 802/496–8856 ⚠ Reservations not accepted ▭ MC, V ⊕ www.americanflatbread.com ☉ Closed Sun.

$$$–$$$$ ✕ **Common Man.** A local institution since 1972, this restaurant is in a

ECLECTIC big 1800s barn with hand-hewn rafters and crystal chandeliers hanging from the beams. That's the Common Man for you: fancy and après-ski at once. Bottles of Moët & Chandon signed by the customers who ordered them sit atop the beams. The eclectic New American cuisine highlights locally grown produce and meats. The menu might include an appetizer of sautéed sweetbreads and apples, a salad of organic field greens, and entrées ranging from fish stew in tomato and saffron broth to grilled venison or sautéed and confited rabbit. Dinner is served by candlelight. Couples sit by the big fireplace. ⊠ *3209 German Flats Rd., Warren* ☎ *802/583–2800* ⊕ *www.commonmanrestaurant.com* ☐ *AE, DC, MC, V* ⊗ *Closed Mon. mid-Apr.–mid-Dec. No lunch.*

¢–$ CAFÉ ✕ **The Green Cup.** You can count on products and ingredients from the community at this local favorite. Chef-owner Jason Galiano is famed for his egg specialties, making this the best place around for breakfast (served every day except Wednesday) or just to hang out with a cup of coffee—there's free Wi-Fi. Jason's sister Sarina works front of house and preps orders. Egg specials, soups, and pastries are all made from scratch. Dinner plates are designed to be shared on Sunday and Monday nights, filling a void in the area, when most restaurants are closed. ⊠ *40 Bridge St., Waitsfield* ☎ *802/496–4963* ⊕ *www. greencupvermont.com* ☐ *MC, V* ⊗ *No dinner Tues.–Sat.*

WHERE TO STAY

$$ ★ 🏠 **Inn at the Round Barn Farm.** A Shaker-style round barn (one of only five in Vermont) is the physical hallmark of this B&B, but what you'll remember when you leave is how comfortable a stay here is. In winter, you toss your shoes under a bench when you come in and put on a pair of slippers from a big basket. There's magic in that gesture, breaking down barriers between guests and giving you permission to kick back. You'll feel like a kid in the downstairs rec room with its TV, games, and billiard table. The guest rooms, inside the 1806 farmhouse, have eyelet-trimmed sheets, elaborate four-poster beds, richly colored wallpapers, and brass wall lamps for easy bedtime reading. Many have fireplaces and whirlpool tubs. Cooper, the inn dog, is your guide—literally—as you snowshoe or hike the miles of trails on this beautiful property filled with gardens and sculpture. Plan a winter trip around one of the moonlit snowshoe walks, which terminate with hot chocolate in an old cabin. **Pros:** great trails, gardens, and rooms; nice breakfast; unique architecture. **Cons:** no restaurant. ⊠ *1661 E. Warren Rd., Waitsfield* ☎ *802/496–2276* ⊕ *www.theroundbarn.com* ⇗ *11 rooms, 1 suite* ♿ *In-room: no TV, Wi-Fi. In-hotel: pool, Internet terminal, Wi-Fi hotspot, no kids under 15* ☐ *AE, D, MC, V* ⊗| *BP.*

$$$$ Fodor's Choice ★ 🏠 **Pitcher Inn.** Across from the justly famous Warren General Store is the elegant Pitcher Inn, Vermont's only Relais & Châteaux property. Ari Sadri, the hands-on manager, exudes an easygoing sophistication that makes staying here a delight. Each comfortable room has its own unusual and elaborate motif—which you'll either love or hate. The Mountain Room, for instance, is designed as a replica of a fire tower in the Green Mountains, with murals on some walls and others covered in stone and glass to resemble a mountain cliff. All the bathrooms, however, are wonderful, with rain showerheads and Anichini linens and superb toiletries. **Pros:** exceptional service; great bathrooms; fun pub; great location. **Cons:** many rooms can be considered kitschy or

7

downright silly. ✉ *275 Main St., Warren* ☎ *802/496–6350 or 888/867–4824* ⊕ *www.pitcherinn.com* ➡ *9 rooms, 2 suites* ⚲ *In-room: refrigerator (some), Wi-Fi. In-hotel: restaurant, bar, spa, water sports, bicycles, Internet terminal, Wi-Fi hotspot* ⊟ *AE, MC, V* ⦿ *BP.*

NORTHERN VERMONT

Vermont's northernmost region reveals the state's greatest contrasts. To the west, Burlington and its suburbs have grown so rapidly that rural wags now say that Burlington's greatest advantage is that it's "close to Vermont." The north country also harbors Vermont's tiny capital, Montpelier, and its highest mountain, Mt. Mansfield, site of the famous Stowe ski resort. To the northeast of Montpelier is a sparsely populated and heavily wooded territory that former Senator George Aiken dubbed the "Northeast Kingdom." It's the domain of loggers, farmers, and avid outdoors enthusiasts.

Our coverage of towns begins in the state capital, Montpelier, moves west toward Stowe and Burlington, then goes north through the Lake Champlain Islands, east along the boundary with Canada toward Jay Peak, and south into the heart of the Northeast Kingdom.

MONTPELIER

38 mi southeast of Burlington, 115 mi north of Brattleboro.

With only about 8,000 residents, little Montpelier is the country's smallest capital city. But it has a youthful energy—and certainly an independent spirit—that makes it seem almost as large as Burlington. The well-preserved downtown bustles with state and city workers walking to meetings or down the street to one of the coffee shops and good restaurants.

EXPLORING

★ **Morse Farm Maple Sugarworks.** With eight generations of sugaring, the Morses are the oldest maple family in existence, so you're sure to find an authentic maple farm experience here. Burr Morse heads up the operation now, along with his son Tom. You can see an earlier generation, Burr's father, Harry Morse, hamming it up in a hilarious video playing at the theater. More than 3,000 trees produce the syrup (sample all the grades), candy, cream, and sugar that's sold in their gift shop. ✉ *1168 County Rd.* ☎ *800/242–2740* ⊕ *www.morsefarm.com* ✉ *Free.*

Vermont Museum. The Vermont Historical Society runs this engaging museum recounting more than 150 years of state history. The collection here was begun in 1838 and features all things Vermont, from a catamount (the now extinct Vermont cougar) to Ethan Allen's shoe buckles. The museum store has a great collection of books, prints, and gifts. ✉ *109 State St.* ☎ *802/828–2291* ⊕ *www.vermonthistory.org* ✉ *$5* ⊗ *May–Oct., Tues.–Sat. 10–4.*

QUICK BITES

La Brioche Bakery (✉ *89 Main St.* ☎ *802/229–0443* ⊕ *www.necidining. com/la-brioche.com*) is a great downtown stop for breakfast and lunch.

New England Culinary Institute students are up at 4 AM preparing breads for thankful locals. There's a great selection of soups, salads, and sandwiches.

★ **Vermont State House.** The regal, gold-domed capitol surrounded by forest is emblematic of this proud rural state. With the gleaming dome and columns of Barre granite 6 feet in diameter, the statehouse is home to the oldest legislative chambers in their original condition in the United States. Half-hour tours take you through the governor's office and the house and senate chambers. The goddess of agriculture tops the gilded dome. Interior paintings and exhibits make much of Vermont's sterling Civil War record. ⊠ *115 State St.* ☎ *802/828–2228* 🖃 *Donations accepted* ⊙ *Weekdays 8–4; tours July–mid-Oct., weekdays every ½ hr 10–3:30 (last tour at 3:30), Sat. 11–3 (last tour at 2:30).*

OFF THE
BEATEN
PATH

Rock of Ages Granite Quarry. The attractions here range from the awe-inspiring (the quarry resembles the Grand Canyon in miniature) to the mildly ghoulish (you can consult a directory of tombstone dealers throughout the country) to the whimsical (an outdoor granite bowling alley). You might recognize the sheer walls of the quarry from *Batman and Robin*, the film starring George Clooney and Arnold Schwarzenegger. At the crafts center, skilled artisans sculpt monuments; at the quarries themselves, 25-ton blocks of stone are cut from sheer 475-foot walls by workers who clearly earn their pay. ⊠ *558 Graniteville Rd., Exit 6 off I–89, follow Rte. 63, 7 mi southeast of Montpelier, Graniteville* ☎ *802/476–3119* ⊕ *www.rockofages.com* 🖃 *Tour of active quarry $4, craftsman center and self-guided tour free* ⊙ *Visitor center May–Oct., Mon.–Sat. 8:30–5, Sun. 10–5; narrated tour on Sat. (call for times).*

SHOPPING

Unique shops attract locals and tourists alike to Montpelier. For hip children's clothing made in Vermont, head to **Zutano** (⊠ *79 Main St.* ☎ *802/223–2229* ⊕ *www.zutano.com*).

WHERE TO EAT

$$ ✕ **Ariel's.** Well off the beaten path, this small restaurant overlooking a
ECLECTIC lake is worth the drive down a dirt road. Chef Lee Duberman prepares
★ eclectic treats such as scallop, lobster, and shrimp ravioli in a ginger shiitake broth. Her husband, sommelier Ricard Fink, recommends selections from the wine cellar. The full menu is offered Friday and Saturday; a pub menu ($–$$) is served Wednesday, Thursday, and Sunday. ⊠ *29 Stone Hill Rd., 8 mi south of Montpelier, Brookfield* ☎ *802/276–3939* ▭ *DC, MC, V* ⊙ *Closed Nov. and Apr.; Mon. and Tues. May–Oct.; Mon.–Thurs. Dec.–Mar.* ⊕ *www.arielsrestaurant.com.*

$$ ✕ **Main Street Grill and Bar.** Nearly everyone working here is a student at
AMERICAN the New England Culinary Institute. Although this is a training ground, the quality and inventiveness are anything but beginner's luck. The menu changes daily, but clam chowder and Misty Knoll Farm free range chicken breast are reliable winners. The lounge downstairs has lighter fare, including a tapas menu. ⊠ *118 Main St.* ☎ *802/223–3188* ⊕ *www. necidining.com.com* ▭ *AE, D, DC, MC, V* ⊙ *Closed Mon.*

$ ✕ **Restaurant Phoebe.** The best location on State Street, fresh ingredi-
AMERICAN ents, and young culinary-obsessed cooks have made this casual neighborhood place a big hit since it opened in 2006. Chef-owner Aaron

Millon—a '97 New England Culinary Institute graduate—is committed to a "holistic cuisine" that stresses the freshest local ingredients. There's a chef's beef cut of the day, selected from the best local farms, the daily soups are great, and delicious breads are baked in-house. ⊠ *52 State St.* ☎ *802/262–3500* ⊕ *www.restaurantphoebe.com* ▭ *AE, MC, V* ⊙ *Closed Mon. No lunch weekends.*

$ ✕**River Run Restaurant.** Mississippi-raised chef Jimmy Kennedy has
SOUTHERN   brought outstanding Southern fare to northern Vermont. Fried catfish, hush puppies, collard greens, and whiskey cake are just a few of the surprises awaiting diners at this rustic, hip eatery with a full bar. Try the buttermilk biscuits at breakfast. ⊠ *65 Main St., 10 mi east of Montpelier, Plainfield* ☎ *802/454–1246* ⊕ *www.riverrunbbq.com* ▭ *No credit cards* ⊙ *Closed Mon.–Wed. No dinner Sun.*

$ ✕**Sarducci's.** Legislative lunches have been a lot more leisurely since Sar-
ITALIAN   ducci's came along to fill the trattoria void in Vermont's capital. These bright, cheerful rooms alongside the Winooski River are a local favorite for pizza fresh from wood-fired ovens, wonderfully textured homemade Italian breads, and imaginative pasta dishes such as pasta *pugliese*, which marries penne with basil, black olives, roasted eggplant, portobello mushrooms, and sun-dried tomatoes. ⊠ *3 Main St.* ☎ *802/223–0229* ⊕ *www.sarduccis.com* ▭ *AE, MC, V* ⊙ *No lunch Sun.*

WHERE TO STAY

$–$$ ⊞ **Inn at Montpelier.** There are two places in town to stay and this is the charming option—the other is a basic hotel across from the statehouse. This well-cared-for circa 1830 inn has antique four-poster beds and Windsor chairs. Outside the formal sitting room is a sensational wraparound Colonial-revival porch, perfect for reading a book or enjoying a drink from the inn's full bar and watching the townsfolk stroll by. Guests get use of a pantry and the common rooms. You can leave your car here and walk everywhere in town. **Pros:** beautiful home; relaxed central setting; amazing porch. **Cons:** some rooms are small. ⊠ *147 Main St.* ☎ *802/223–2727* ⊕ *www.innatmontpelier.com* ⤳ *19 rooms* ⌂ *In-room: Wi-Fi. In-hotel: bar, laundry service* ▭ *AE, D, DC, MC, V* ⫧⫯ *CP.*

EN
ROUTE   On your way to Stowe from Interstate 89, be sure to stop at **Ben & Jerry's Ice Cream Factory,** a must for ice-cream lovers. Ben Cohen and Jerry Greenfield began selling ice cream from a renovated gas station in Burlington in the 1970s. The tour only skims the surface of the behind-the-scenes goings-on at the plant—a flaw forgiven when the free samples are dished out. ⊠ *1281 Waterbury-Stowe Rd. (Rte. 100), 1 mi north of I–89, Waterbury* ☎ *802/846–1500* ⊕ *www.benjerry.com* ⬚ *Tour $3* ⊙ *Late Oct.–June, daily 10–6; July–mid-Aug., daily 9–9; mid-Aug.–late Oct., daily 9–7. Tours run every half hour.*

STOWE

Fodor's Choice   *22 mi northwest of Montpelier, 36 mi east of Burlington.*

★   Long before skiing came to Stowe in the 1930s, the rolling hills and valleys beneath Vermont's highest peak, the 4,395-foot Mt. Mansfield, attracted summer tourists looking for a reprieve from city heat. Most stayed at one of two inns in the village of Stowe. When skiing made the

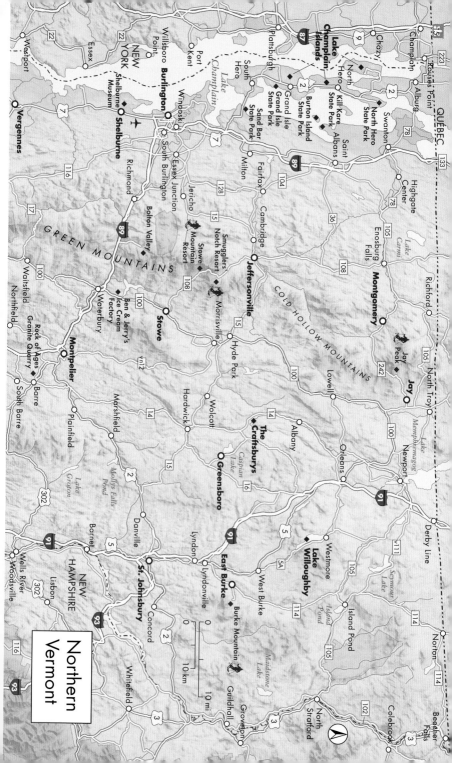

Northern Vermont

town a winter destination, the arriving skiers outnumbered the hotel beds, so locals took them in. This spirit of hospitality continues, and many of these homes are now lovely country inns. The village itself is tiny, just a few blocks of shops and restaurants clustered around a picture-perfect white church with a lofty steeple, but it serves as the anchor for Mountain Road, which leads north past restaurants, lodges, and shops on its way to Stowe's fabled slopes.

ESSENTIALS

Visitor Information Stowe Area Association (✉ *Main St., Box 1320, Stowe* ☎ *802/253–7321 or 877/467–8693* ⊕ *www.gostowe.com*).

EXPLORING

Gondola. Mt. Mansfield's "Chin" area is accessible by the eight-seat gondola. At the gondola's summit station isthe **Cliff House Restaurant** (☎ *802/253–3558 Ext. 237*), where lunch is served daily 11–3. ✉ *1 Mountain Rd., 8 mi off Rte. 100* ☎ *802/253–3000* ⛰ *Gondola $14* ⊙ *Mid-June–mid-Oct., daily 10–5; early Dec.–late Apr., daily 8–4; closed in Nov. and May.*

Mt. Mansfield. With its elongated summit ridge resembling the profile of a recumbent man's face, Mt. Mansfield has long attracted the adventurous. The mountain is ribboned with hiking and ski trails.

Trapp Family Lodge. Built by the von Trapp family, of *Sound of Music* fame, this Tyrolean lodge and its surrounding pastureland are the site of a popular outdoor music series in summer and an extensive cross-country ski-trail network in winter. A teahouse serves food and drinks. ✉ *1 Luce Hill Rd.* ☎ *802/253–8511 or 800/826–7000* ⊕ *www.trappfamily.com.*

Vermont Ski Museum. The state's skiing history is documented here with myriad exhibits. ✉ *1 Main St.* ☎ *802/253–9911* ⊕ *www.vermontskimuseum.org.*

SPORTS AND THE OUTDOORS

CANOE-ING AND KAYAKING
Umiak Outdoor Outfitters (✉ *849 S. Main St. [Rte. 100], south of Stowe Village* ☎ *802/253–2317* ⊕ *www.umiak.com*) rents canoes and kayaks for day trips and leads overnight excursions. The store also operates a rental outpost at Lake Elmore State Park in Elmore, on the Winooski River off Route 2 in Waterbury, at North Beach in Burlington, and on the Lamoille River in Jeffersonville.

FISHING
The **Fly Rod Shop** (✉ *2703 Waterbury Rd. [Rte. 100], 1½ mi south of Stowe* ☎ *802/253–7346 or 800/535–9763* ⊕ *www.flyrodshop.com*) provides a guiding service; gives fly-tying, casting, and rod-building classes in winter; rents fly tackle; and sells equipment, including classic and collectible firearms.

GOLF
Stowe Country Club (✉ *1 Mountain Rd.* ☎ *802/253–4893*) has a scenic 18-hole, par-72 course; a driving range; and a putting green. Green fees are $45–$75; cart rental is $18.

HIKING
Ascending **Mt. Mansfield** makes for a scenic day hike. Trails lead from Route 108 (Mountain Road) to the summit ridge, where they meet the north-to-south Long Trail. Views from the summit take in New Hampshire's White Mountains, New York's Adirondacks across Lake

Champlain, and southern Québec. The Green Mountain Club publishes a trail guide.

ICE-SKATING **Jackson Arena** (⊠ *1 Park St.* ☎ *802/253–6148*) is a public ice-skating rink, with skate rentals available.

SKI AREA
★
To be precise, the name of the village is Stowe and the name of the mountain is Mt. Mansfield, but to generations of skiers, the area, the complex, and the region are just plain Stowe. **Stowe Mountain Resort** (⊠ *5781 Mountain Rd.* ☎ *802/253–3000; 802/253–3600 snow conditions; 800/253–4754 lodging* ⊕ *www.stowe.com*) is a classic that dates from the 1930s. Even today, the area's mystique attracts as many serious skiers as social ones. Improved snowmaking, new lifts, and free shuttle buses that gather skiers from lodges, inns, and motels along Mountain Road have added convenience to the Stowe experience. Yet the traditions remain: the Winter Carnival in January, the Sugar Slalom in April, ski weeks all winter. Three base lodges—including the luxurious Stowe Mountain Lodge that opened in 2008—provide the essentials, including two on-mountain restaurants.

The resort provides hiking, in-line skating, an alpine slide, gondola rides, and an 18-hole golf course. It also has 22 mi of groomed cross-country trails and 24 mi of backcountry trails. Four interconnecting cross-country ski areas have more than 90 mi of groomed trails within the town of Stowe.

Mt. Mansfield, with an elevation of 4,395 feet and a vertical drop of 2,360 feet, is one of the giants among eastern ski mountains. The mountain's symmetrical shape allows skiers of all abilities long, satisfying runs from the summit. The famous Front Four (National, Liftline, Starr, and Goat) are the intimidating centerpieces for tough, expert runs, yet there is plenty of mellow intermediate skiing, with 59% of the runs rated at that level and 116 trails total. One long beginner trail, the Toll Road Trail, is 3½ mi. Mansfield's satellite sector is a network of intermediate trails and one expert trail off a basin served by a gondola. Spruce Peak, separate from the main mountain, is a teaching hill and a pleasant experience for intermediates and beginners. In addition to the high-speed, eight-passenger gondola, Stowe has 11 lifts, including two quads, two triples, and five double chairlifts, plus one handle tow, to service its 48 trails. Night-skiing trails are accessed by the gondola. The resort has 73% snowmaking coverage. Snowboard facilities include a half-pipe and two terrain parks—one for beginners, at Spruce Peak, and one for experts, on the Mt. Mansfield side. Children's programs are headquartered at Spruce Peak, with ski-school programs for ages 4 to 12.

SHOPPING

In Stowe, Mountain Road is lined with shops from town up toward the ski area. North of Stowe, shops line Route 100 from Interstate 89. On Route 100 south toward Waterbury, between the cider mill and Ben & Jerry's, you can visit the **Cabot Cheese Annex Store** (⊠ *3600 Waterbury-Stowe Rd. [Rte. 100], 2½ mi north of I–89* ☎ *802/244–6334*).

★ Watch apples pressed into cider at the **Cold Hollow Cider Mill** (⊠ *Rte. 100, 3 mi north of I–89* ☎ *802/244–8771 or 800/327–7537*). The on-site

Continued on page 483

LET IT SNOW

WINTER ACTIVITIES IN VERMONT

by Elise Coroneos

SKIING AND SNOWBOARDING IN VERMONT

Less than 5 mi from the Canadian border, Jay Peak is Vermont's northernmost ski resort.

Ever since America's first ski tow opened in a farmer's pasture near Woodstock in January 1934, skiers have headed en masse to Vermont in winter. Today, 20 alpine and 30 nordic ski areas range in size and are spread across the state, from Mount Snow in the south to Jay Peak near the Canadian border. The snow-making equipment has also become more comprehensive over the years, with 70% of the trails in the state using man-made snow. Here are some of the best ski areas by various categories:

GREAT FOR KIDS **Smugglers' Notch, Okemo,** and **Bromley Mountain** all offer terrific kids' programs, with classes organized by age categories and by skill level. Kids as young as 3 (4 at some ski areas) can start learning. Child care, with activities like stories, singing, and arts and crafts, are available for those too young to ski; some ski areas, like Smuggler's Notch, offer babysitting with no minimum age daytime and evening.

BEST FOR BEGINNERS Beginner terrain makes up nearly half of the mountain at **Stratton,** where options include private and group lessons for first-timers. Also good are small but family-friendly **Ascutney** and **Bromley Mountains,** which both designate a third of their slopes for beginners.

EXPERT TERRAIN The slopes at **Jay Peak** and massive **Killington** are most notable for their steepness and pockets of glades. About 40% of the runs at these two resorts are advanced or expert. Due to its far north location, Jay Peak tends to get the most snow, making it ideal for those skilled in plowing through fresh powder. Another favorite with advanced skiers is Central Vermont's **Mad River Glen,** where many slopes are ungroomed (natural) and the motto is "Ski it if you can." In addition, **Sugarbush, Stowe,** and **Smugglers' Notch** are all revered for their challenging untamed side country.

Mount Mansfield is better known as Stowe.   Stratton Mountain clocktower

NIGHT SKIING Come late afternoon, **Bolton Valley** is hopping. That's because it's the only location in Vermont for night skiing. Ski and ride under the lights from 4 until 8 Wednesday through Saturday, followed by a later après-ski scene.

APRÈS-SKI The social scenes at **Killington**, **Sugarbush**, and **Stowe** are the most noteworthy (and crowded). Warm up after a day in the snow in Killington with all-you-can-eat pizza on Monday nights and daily happy hour specials at the Nightspot Outback, or stop by the always popular Wobbly Barn. For live music, try Chez Henri in Sugarbush or the Matterhorn Night Club in Stowe.

SNOWBOARDING Boarders (and some skiers) will love the latest features for freestyle tricks in Vermont. **Okemo** has a superpipe and five terrain parks, including a new gladed park with all-natural features; **Stratton** has a half pipe, rail garden, and four other parks. **Mount Snow's** Carinthia Peak is an all-terrain

park–dedicated mountain, the only of its kind in the state. Head to **Killington** for Burton Stash, another beautiful all-natural features terrain park. Note that snowboarding is not allowed at skiing cooperative **Mad River Glen**.

CROSS-COUNTRY To experience the best of cross-country skiing in the state, simply follow the Catamount Trail, a 300-mi nordic route from southern Vermont to Canada. **The Trapp Family Lodge** in Stowe has 40 mi of groomed cross-country trails and 60 mi of backcountry trails. Another top option is **The Mountain Top Inn & Resort**, just outside of Killington. Its Nordic Ski and Snowshoe Center provides instruction for newcomers, along with hot drinks and lunches when it is time to take a break and warm up.

TELEMARK Ungroomed snow and tree skiing are a natural fit with free-heel skiing at **Mad River Glen**. **Jay Peak** also has telemark rentals and instruction.

MOUNTAIN-RESORT TRIP PLANNER

TIMING

■ **Snow Season.** Winter sports time is typically from December to April, weather permitting. Holidays are the most crowded.

■ **March Madness.** Most of the season's snow tends to come in March, so that's the time to go if you want to ski on fresh, nature-made powder. To increase your odds, choose a ski area in the northern part of the state.

■ **Summer Scene.** During summertime, many ski resorts reinvent themselves as prime destinations for golfers and mountain bikers. Other summer visitors come to the mountains to enjoy hiking trails, climbing walls, aquatic centers, chairlift and horseback rides, or a variety of festivals.

■ **Avoid Long Lift Lines.** Try to hit the slopes early—many lifts start at 8 or 9 AM, with ticket windows opening a half-hour earlier. Then take a mid-morning break as lines start to get longer and head out again when others come in for lunch.

SAVINGS TIPS

■ **Choose a Condo.** Especially if you're planning to stay for a week, save money on food by opting for a condominum unit with a kitchen. You can shop at the supermarket and cook breakfast and dinner.

■ **Rent Smart.** Consider ski rental options in the villages rather than those at the mountain. Renting right at the ski area may be more convenient, but it may also cost more.

■ **Discount Lift Tickets.** Online tickets are often the least expensive; multi-day discounts and and ski-and-stay packages will also lower your costs. Good for those who can plan ahead, early-bird tickets often go on sale before the ski season even starts.

■ **Hit the Peaks Off-peak.** In order to secure the best deals at the most competitive rates, avoid booking during school holidays. Presidents Week in February is the busiest, because that's when Northeastern schools have their spring break.

Top left, Killington's six mountains make up the largest ski area in Vermont. Top right, Stratton has a Snowboard-cross course.

THINK WARM THOUGHTS

It can get cold on the slopes, so be prepared. Consider heated boots or purchase a pair each of inexpensive hand and feet warmers that fit easily in your gloves and boots. Helmets, which can also be rented, provide not only added safety but warmth.

VERMONT SKI AREAS BY THE NUMBERS

Okemo's wide slopes attract snowbirds to Ludlow in Central Vermont.

Numbers are a helpful way to compare mountains, but remember that each resort has a distinct personality. This list is composed of ski areas in Vermont with at least 100 skiable acres. For more information, see individual resort listings.

SKI AREA	Vertical Drop	Skiable Acres	# of Trails & Lifts	Terrain Type ●	■	◆/◆◆	Snowboarding Options
Ascutney Mountain	1,800	150	57/6	30%	40%	30%	Terrain park
Bolton Valley	1,704	165	64/6	27%	47%	26%	Terrain park
Bromley	1,334	177	45/10	35%	34%	31%	Terrain park
Burke Mountain	2,011	250	45/4	25%	45%	30%	Terrain park
Jay Peak	2,153	385	76/8	20%	40%	40%	Terrain park
Killington	3,050	752	141/22	29%	29%	42%	Terrain park, Half-pipe
Mad River Glen	2,037	115	45/5	30%	30%	40%	Snowboarding not allowed
Mount Snow	1,700	588	80/20	14%	73%	13%	Terrain park, Half-pipe
Okemo	2,200	632	119/19	32%	36%	32%	Terrain park, Superpipe, RossCross terrain cross park
Pico Mountain	1,967	214	50/7	20%	48%	32%	Triple Slope
Smugglers' Notch	2,610	310	78/8	19%	56%	25%	Terrain park
Stowe	2,360	485	116/13	16%	59%	25%	Terrain park, Half-pipe
Stratton	2,003	600	92/13	42%	31%	27%	Terrain park, Half-pipe, Snowboardcross course
Sugarbush	2,600	578	53/16	20%	45%	35%	Terrain park, Half-pipe

CONTACT THE EXPERTS

Ski Vermont (☎ 802/223-2439 ⊕ *www.skivermont.com*), a non-profit association in Montpelier, Vermont, and **Vermont Department of Tourism** (⊕ *www.vermontvacation.com*) are great resources for travelers planning a wintertime trip to Vermont.

KNOW YOUR SIGNS

On trail maps and the mountains, trails are rated and marked:

● Beginner   ◆ Advanced

■ Intermediate   ◆◆ Expert

QUEBEC

Alburg
Lake Carmi
Richford
North Troy
Derby Line
Derby Center
Norton

Jay Peak
Newport

87

Swanton
Enosburg Falls
105
242
Orleans
Island Pond
3

North Hero
Saint Albans
Lowell
105

Grand Isle
89
Barton
Albany
Lake Willoughby

South Hero
2
Fairfax
Jeffersonville
Johnson
100
14
West Burke

Milton
Morrisville
Wolcott
16
91
Burke Mountain

Smugglers' Notch
Lyndonville
Lyndon
2

Burlington
Stowe
15
Saint Johnsbury

Essex Junction
108
Stowe
Concord

Richmond
Bolton Valley
89
14
Danville
Littleton

Shelburne
Waterbury
12
Marshfield
Barnet
93

Lake Champlain
116
Plainfield
10

22
MONTPELIER
Barre
302
Wells River

Vergennes
Mad River Glen
Northfield
West Topsham
Newbury

Bristol
Sugarbush
100
25
91
25

Middlebury
East Middlebury
14
Chelsea
Bradford

22A
Randolph
East Randolph
Fairlee

22
Shoreham
Hancock
Bethel
Plymouth

Brandon
7
89
93

22
Proctor
100
White River Junction
Hanover

Pico Mountain
Woodstock
Lebanon

Rutland
4
Hartland
4

West Rutland
Killington
106
Windsor
Franklin

Poultney
Wallingford
Ascutney Mountain
Ascutney
4

Granville
Okemo
Ludlow
11
Newport
89

West Pawlet
Springfield
Claremont

30
100
Chester

Dorset
Bromley
11
91
NEW HAMPSHIRE

22
Manchester
Grafton
Bellows Falls
Hillsborough

7A
Stratton
Jamaica
9

Arlington
Westminster

Shaftsbury
100
Putney

NEW YORK
Newfane
Keene

Mount Snow
West Dover
101

Bennington
Wilmington
9
Brattleboro

Pownal
Jacksonville

Readsboro
91

0   10 mi
0   10 km

Vermont Ski Areas

7

IN FOCUS LET IT SNOW

MORE WINTER FUN

A horse and sleigh ride in South Woodstock

DOG SLEDDING

Being pulled through the woods by a team of of up to eight adult Siberian Huskies, you might feel like you are a pioneer taking on the elements—or like you're in Alaska's Iditarod.

Pros: unique experience; kids love it.
Cons: dogs can be stubborn; pricey.

■ **Peacepups Dog Sledding** (☎ 802/888–7733 ⊕ www.peacepupsdogsledding.com) at Lake Elmore, 15 miles from Stowe, offers two-hour day tours using a team of eight dogs. Choose between sitting back and riding inside a padded toboggan while your driver (and the dogs) do the work, or join in the driving using a two-person tandem sled. Either cost $120 per adult ($60 for kids under 12). Tours head out every Wednesday, Friday, Saturday, and Sunday at 10 AM, noon, and 2 PM from mid-December to the end of March, weather permitting.

■ Twilight dog sledding tours leave the **Stowe Mountain Resort** (☎ 802/253-3656 ⊕ www.stowe.com) for one hour every Tuesday and Thursday. The cost is $150 for guests of the resort or $160 for nonguests. This is a sit-down ride inside a padded toboggan.

■ For a taste of how the professionals do it, head to Burke Mountain during **Vermont's Annual Dog Sled Dash** (⊕ www.sleddogdash.com). Usually held in February, the event is the largest of its kind in New England, with more than 100 teams entering for part of the $10,000 purse. Vacationers come to witness the event—put on some snowshoes and trek in to find the best vantage points. If you fancy your own dog-sledding skills, you can register online.

ICE SKATING

If you want outdoor activity but want to stay in one spot and not be outside for a long time—or not even outside at all, but just feel like you are—ice skating might be just your thing. In Vermont you can skate surrounded by the nearby snowcapped mountains or in the comfort of an indoor professional facility.

Pros: excellent activity for groups; easy access (venues are often close to your lodging); inexpensive.
Cons: can be crowded.

■ **The Ice Station at Okemo** (☎ 802/228–1406 ⊕ www.okemo.com), near the Jackson Gore base, is a roof-covered natural ice rink with a warming area for those with comfort in mind. Open mid-December through April from 2 to 9 PM on weekdays and 10 AM to 9 PM on weekends. The cost is $4 for rink access plus $4 to rent skates.

■ Check out **Jay Peak's** (☎ 802/988–2611 ⊕ www.jaypeakresort.com) new, $7 million full-size rink, which opened in 2010. At the time of this writing, prices were not yet set.

■ For the ultimate outdoor skating experience, head to **Lake Morey** in Fairlee, home to America's longest natural ice skating trail. From December to April, the lake freezes over and is groomed for ice skating, providing a magical 4-mi stretch of ice amid forested hillsides. It is maintained by the **Upper Valley Trails Alliance** (☎ 802/649–9075 ⊕ www.uvtrails.org). Bring your own skates or find rentals at the nearby **Nordic Skater** (☎ 866/244–2570 ⊕ www.nordicskater.com), which also runs outdoor skating workshops for $30.

Snowmobiling

Snowshoeing at Trapp Family Lodge

SLEDDING AND TUBING

Want down-the-mountain action but prefer not to ski or board? Tubing is offered at many Vermont ski areas with lifts to tow riders back up, or you can just ask the locals for the best sledding hills. Either way it is especially popular with kids: get ready to hear the question "Can we do it again?" multiple times.

Pros: fun for families and groups; cheaper than skiing.

Cons: rides can be bumpy; not for very young (and short) kids.

■ A standout is Stratton's **Coca Cola Tubing Park** (☎ 800/787-2886 ⊕ www.stratton. com). Careen down any one of four lanes that stretch up to 750 feet long. Kids must be 5 years or older to ride. Open 4 to 8 PM Friday, 11 AM to 9 PM Saturday, and 11 AM to 3 PM Sunday. Tickets are $15 for one hour and $22 for two hours.

■ **Okemo** (☎ 866/706-5366 ⊕ www. okemo.com) offers a tubing facility at its Jackson Gore base area as an après-ski activity from 3 to 6 PM on Friday and Saturday (hours may vary). Take a conveyor-style lift to the top of the hill and then ride down one of four groomed lanes. Tubes rent for $9 an hour. Kids must be at least 42 inches tall to ride.

■ For extra adventure, visitors at **Smugglers' Notch** (☎ 800/419-4615 ⊕ www. smuggs.com) can try airboarding, which uses an inflated sled. First-timers must enroll in an two-hour clinic ($25), after which they can rent and ride for $20 (plus a valid lift ticket) from 2 to 4 PM. Riders must be at least 10 years old and 48 inches tall.

SLEIGH RIDES

Riding a sleigh in Vermont is not quite dashing through the snow on a one-horse open sleigh—the speed is gentle enough that you can sip hot cocoa on the ride, and the sleigh is big, so it usually takes two horses. But you will see Christmas-card-like settings as the sleigh takes you down trails lined with fir trees. Many farms and some resorts offer sleigh rides from December through April, weather permitting. When there is no snow on the ground, horse-drawn carriage rides may be available. The Woodstock area is known as Vermont's horse country, and many local stables have different types of riding options year-round.

Pros: great way to see scenery; fun group activity.

Cons: slow speed; not comfortable if it's windy or snowing hard.

■ The **Mountain Top Inn & Resort** (☎ 802/483-2311 ⊕ www.mountaintopinn.com) just 11 mi from Killington, offers a Sleigh and Dinner Package for $150 for two adults (includes tax and gratuity). The sleigh ride through the resort's wooded trails followed by a three-course dinner is the perfect nightcap. Call for the regularly scheduled 30 minute rides starting at $25 per person, with discounts for children. Private rides are also available.

■ The **Kedron Valley Stables** (☎ 802/457-1480 ⊕ www.kedron.com), in South Woodstock, runs hour-long sleigh rides for up to three people for $95, or for four to eight people for $115. For groups over eight, there's an extra charge of $14 per each additional person.

Okemo Resort

Tubing down Magic Mountain.

SNOWMOBILING

Travel a snow-covered highway through densely forested valleys, past snow-capped mountains, and into friendly villages—all without exerting your own energy. Thanks to the extensive trails administered through the state's VAST (Vermont Association of Snow Travelers) system, it's possible to see extensive back country normally beyond the realm of visitors. Snowmobiles usually hold two riders.

Pros: you can cover a lot of ground.
Cons: can be noisy; expensive; controversial because of environmental impact.

■ Snowmobile rentals are available at several ski areas, including **Killington** (☎ 802/422–2121 ⊕ www.killingtonsnow-mobiletours.com) and **Okemo** (☎ 800/328–8725 ⊕ www.killingtonsnowmobiletours.com/okemo). Both have one-hour guided tours across groomed ski trails ($89 for one person, $119 for two). If you are feeling more adventurous, take the two-hour backcountry tour through 25 mi of the Calvin Coolidge State Forest ($144 for one person, $189 for two). Helmets and boots are included.

■ For an after-hours perspective, try night snowmobiling at **Smugglers' Notch Resort** (☎ 802/644–8851 ⊕ www.smuggs.com) and **Stratton** (☎ 802/824–5399 ⊕ www.stratton.com). Smugglers' evening tours depart daily on the hour from 5–8 PM from around mid-December to early April, weather permitting. Stratton night tours are available on Saturday nights and holiday nights at from 5–8:30 PM, with additional nights available upon request. The cost is $80 per snowmobile per hour.

SNOWSHOEING

Hikers wanting to explore nature in the winter can do so in depth thanks to snowshoes, which easily attach to your boots. Showshoeing allows you to get up close and personal with the surrounding wilderness. Tranquil trails are easy to find in the Green Mountain State; just avoid those shared with snowmobiles. Some alpine resorts now have networks of snowshoeing trails. Many places that rent cross-country ski gear, like the Trapp Family Lodge, also rent snowshoes. Poles help snowshoers stabilize, especially on uneven and steep terrain.

Pros: inexpensive; great exercise; easy to do (no lesson required).
Cons: small children might get worn out quickly; can be a lot of work; colder than cross-country skiing because you're not moving fast.

■ **Mount Olga Trail** (⊕ www.trails.com) is the most popular snowshoeing destination in Vermont. Located in Wilmington's Molly Stark State Park, the trail is 2.3 mi long. The hike is relatively easy, climaxing with a 360-degree view of southern Vermont and northern Massachusetts.

■ Northeast Vermont's **Kingdom Trails** (☎ 802/626–5862 ⊕ www.kingdomtrails.org) is a network of more than 100 mi of trails used for snowshoeing (hiking and mountain biking in summer). A day pass is $10 for adults, $5 for kids ages 8–15, and free for kids 7 and under. Guests at East Burke's **Inn at Mountain View Farm** (☎ 800/572–4509, ⊕ www.innmtnview.com), the closest inn to the beginning of the trails, receive free access.

store sells cider, baked goods, Vermont produce, and specialty foods. Sample all the cold cider you like; kids get free cider popsicles.

NIGHTLIFE AND THE ARTS

THE ARTS **Stowe Performing Arts** (☎ *802/253–7792* ⊕ *www.stowearts.com*) sponsors a series of classical and jazz concerts in July in the Trapp Family Lodge meadow. **Stowe Theater Guild** (✉ *67 Main St., Town Hall Theater* ☎ *802/253-3961 summer only* ⊕ *www.stowetheatre.com*) performs musicals in summer and plays in September.

NIGHTLIFE The **Matterhorn Night Club** (✉ *4969 Mountain Rd.* ☎ *802/253–8198* ⊕ *www.matterhornbar.com*) hosts live music and dancing Thursday–Saturday nights and has a separate martini bar. The **Rusty Nail** (✉ *1190 Mountain Rd.* ☎ *802/253–6245* ⊕ *rustynailbar.com*) rocks to live music on weekends.

WHERE TO EAT

$$ ✕ **Hen of the Wood.** Ask any great chef in Vermont where they go to find
ECLECTIC a tremendous meal and Hen of the Wood will inevitably be near the top
★ of their list. The setting is riveting: a converted 1835 grist mill beside a waterfall. Inside the underground level of the mill a sunken pit formerly housing the grindstone is now filled with tables, and uneven stone walls are dotted floor to ceiling with tiny candles—decidedly romantic. Sophisticated dishes showcase the abundance of local produce, meat, cheese, and more. A typical plate on the daily changing menu may feature sheep milk's gnocchi, a local farm pork loin, shortribs, grassfed ribeye, and a wild Alaskan halibut. This is a very near to perfect Vermont dining experience. On occasion chef Eric Warnstedt's less-is-more philosophy stretches a bit too far, resulting in an underseasoned plate. In the warmer months, beg for coveted patio table overlooking a dramatic series of falls. ✉ *92 Stowe St., Waterbury* ☎ *802/244–7300* ⊕ *www.henofthewood. com* ⌂ *Reservations essential* ▭ *AE, DC, MC, V* ⊙ *No lunch.*

$$–$$$ ✕ **Michael's on the Hill.** Swiss-born chef Michael Kloeti trained in Europe
CONTINENTAL and New York before opening this dining establishment in a 19th-century farmhouse outside Stowe. In addition to à la carte options, Michael's four-course prix-fixe menus ($60) highlight European cuisine such as roasted rabbit with mirepoix or ravioli with braised autumn vegetables. There's live piano music weekends. ✉ *4182 Stowe-Waterbury Rd. (Rte. 100), 6 mi south of Stowe, Waterbury Center* ☎ *802/244–7476* ⊕ *www. michaelsonthehill.com* ▭ *AE, DC, MC, V* ⊙ *Closed Tues. No lunch.*

¢ ✕ **Red Hen Baking Co.** While it's about 15 mi from Stowe, if you're a
CAFÉ devotee of artisanal bakeries, it'd be a mistake to miss out on a trip to have lunch or breakfast here. Try the ham-and-cheese croissants, sticky buns, homemade soups, and sandwiches. Red Hen supplies bread to some of the state's best restaurants, including Hen of the Wood, and is open 7 AM to 6 PM daily. ✉ *961 Rte. 2, Middlesex* ☎ *802/223–5200* ⊕ *www.redhenbaking.com* ⌂ *Reservations not accepted* ▭ *MC, V* ⊙ *No dinner.*

WHERE TO STAY

$$–$$$ 🏨 **Green Mountain Inn.** Welcoming guests since 1833, this classic red-brick inn is across from the land-mark Community Church and gives you access to the buzz of down-town. Rooms in the main building and annex still feel like a country inn, with Early American furnish-

ings. Newer buildings have luxury rooms and suites. The Whip Bar & Grill ($$–$$$) puts an interesting twist on comfort food, as in cheddar-cheese-and-apple-stuffed chicken, and the outdoor heated pool is open year-round. **Pros:** fun location; lively tavern. **Cons:** farther from skiing than other area hotels. ✉ *18 Main St.* ☎ *802/253–7301 or 800/253–7302* ⊕ *www.greenmountaininn.com* 🛏 *105 rooms* 🛠 *In-room: kitchen (some), refrigerator (some), DVD (some), Wi-Fi. In-hotel: restaurant, bar, pool, gym, laundry service, Internet terminal, Wi-Fi hotspot* ⊟ *AE, D, MC, V.*

$$$$ 🏨 **Stone Hill Inn.** This is a contemporary B&B—built in 1998—where classical music plays in the halls. Each soundproof guest room has a king-size bed. Bathrooms have two-sink vanities and two-person whirl-pools in front of two-sided fireplaces. (Can you tell it's oriented toward couples?) A pantry is stocked with complimentary snacks and drinks. Common areas include a sitting room and a game room, and the 10 acres of grounds are beautifully landscaped with gardens and water-falls. The inn is high up Mountain Road not far from the ski resort. **Pros:** clean and new; very comfortable. **Cons:** very expensive; a bit stiff. ✉ *89 Houston Farm Rd.* ☎ *802/253–6282* ⊕ *www.stonehillinn.com* 🛏 *9 rooms* 🛠 *In-room: no phone, safe, DVD, Wi-Fi. In-hotel: laundry facilities, Internet terminal, Wi-Fi hotspot, no kids under 18* ⊟ *AE, D, DC, MC, V* ⊚ *BP.*

$ 🏨 **Stowe Motel & Snowdrift.** This family-owned motel sits on 16 acres across the river from the Stowe recreation path. Accommodations range from one-room studios with small kitchenettes to modern two-bedroom fireplace suites. Late-model mountain bikes, kids' bikes, tricycles, bike trailers, and helmets are available to guests. A game room has Ping-Pong and a pool table. The motel is owned by Peter Ruschp, whose father, Sepp, founded the Mt. Mansfield ski school in 1936. **Pros:** cheap; com-plimentary bikes and games. **Cons:** basic, motel-style accommodations. ✉ *2043 Mountain Rd. (Rte. 108)* ☎ *802/253–7629 or 800/829–7629* ⊕ *www.stowemotel.com* 🛏 *52 rooms, 4 suites* 🛠 *In-room: kitchen (some), refrigerator. In-hotel: tennis court, pools, bicycles, Internet ter-minal, Wi-Fi hotspot, some pets allowed* ⊟ *AE, D, MC, V* ⊚ *CP.*

$$$$ 🏨 **Stowe Mountain Lodge.** At the base of Stowe's skiing mountain, this
Fodor's Choice 2008 addition to the Stowe lodging scene would be king of the hill
★ for location alone, but a luxury stay here includes ski lodge perks that transcend the competition. Rooms are rustic-meets-contemporary in configurations from studio-size to three-bedroom, many with outdoor terraces. Guests get complimentary access to a fleet of new Mercedes-Benz cars to explore town or drive up the mountain. There's a spa and

salon; a massive fitness room; a private 18-hole, Bob Cupp–designed golf course; and a huge heated outdoor pool. A stay includes "wellness lodges" with oversize hot tubs and saunas. There's also a game room for kids, a Ralph Lauren shop, and a most contemporary-looking bar and restaurant. In winter, you can watch the skiers on the mountain from your room and—with gondolas at the doorstep—join them in no time at all. **Pros:** ski valet and perfect setting; great concierge; great bar; activities galore. **Cons:** no separate kids' pool. ✉ *5781 Mountain Rd.* ☎ *802/253–3560* ⊕ *www.stowemountainlodge.com* ⤴ *139 rooms* ♿ *In-room: safe, kitchen (some), refrigerator (some), DVD (some), Wi-Fi. In-hotel: restaurant, room service, bar, golf course, tennis courts, pool, gym, spa, children's programs (ages 2–14), laundry service, Internet terminal, Wi-Fi hotspot, some pets allowed* ▭ *AE, D, DC, MC, V* ⊠⊡ *EP*

$$$ 🏨 **Stoweflake Mountain Resort and Spa.** Stoweflake has a lot in common with Topnotch; these two properties have the best and biggest spas in the state (along with Stowe Mountain Lodge) and a contemporary, serious approach to rooms and service. Stoweflake probably has a slightly better spa, perhaps due to the fun of the Bingham hydrotherapy waterfall, a nice 12-foot rock formation cascading into a hot tub. Accommodations range from standard hotel rooms to luxurious suites with fireplaces, refrigerators, double sinks, and whirlpool tubs. One- to three-bedroom town houses sit on the resort's perimeter. The spa overlooks an herb and flower labyrinth and is connected to the fitness center via a faux covered bridge. Stoweflake also hosts Stowe's annual Hot Air Balloon Festival. **Pros:** great spa; excellent service. **Cons:** urban-style resort. ✉ *1746 Mountain Rd., Box 369* ☎ *802/253–7355* ⊕ *www.stoweflake. com* ⤴ *94 rooms, 30 town houses* ♿ *In-room: kitchen (some), refrigerator, DVD, Internet, Wi-Fi (some). In-hotel: 2 restaurants, room service, bar, golf course, tennis courts, pools, gym, spa, bicycles, laundry service, Internet terminal, Wi-Fi hotspot* ▭ *AE, D, DC, MC, V.*

THE CRAFTSBURYS

27 mi northeast of Stowe.

The three villages of the Craftsburys—Craftsbury Common, Craftsbury, and East Craftsbury—are among Vermont's finest and oldest towns. Handsome white houses and barns, the requisite common, and terrific views make them well worth the drive. Craftsbury General Store in Craftsbury Village is a great place to stock up on picnic supplies and local information. The rolling farmland hints at the way Vermont used to be: the area's sheer distance from civilization and its rugged weather have kept most of the state's development farther south.

WHERE TO STAY

$$ 🏨 **Craftsbury Outdoor Center.** If you think simplicity is bliss and love the outdoors, give this place a try. In winter it's a hub for cross-country skiing (50 mi of groomed trails). In summer there's a giant lake for swimming and boating (sculling and running camps are held here). Two two-story simple lodges have rooms with communal TV/library areas. Many share baths. The simplest rooms have two twin beds and a wooden peg to hang

Spa Vacations

Vermont's destination spas have come a long way since its *au naturel* mineral springs attracted affluent 19th-century city dwellers looking to escape the heat, but the principle remains the same: a natural place to restore mind and body. There are three big spas in Stowe and one in Manchester.

The **Equinox Resort's Avanyu Spa** (✉ *3567 Rte. 7A, Manchester* ☎ *802/362–4700* ⊕ *equinox. rockresorts.com*), with mahogany doors and beadboard wainscoting, feels like a country estate. At one end is an NCAA-length indoor pool and outdoor hot tub; at the other end are the treatment rooms. The signature 80-minute Spirit of Vermont combines Reiki, reflexology, and massage. In the co-ed relaxation room, spa-goers can nestle into overstuffed chairs next to a two-sided fireplace made of Vermont gneiss. The locker rooms, with marble accents and pottery-bowl wash basins, steam rooms and saunas.

Fodor's Choice ★ On of the largest spas in New England, **Spa at Stoweflake** (✉ *1746 Mountain Rd. [Rte. 108], Stowe* ☎ *802/760–1083 or 800/253–2232* ⊕ *www.stoweflake. com*) features a massaging hydrotherapeutic waterfall, a Hungarian mineral pool, 30 treatment rooms, a hair and nail salon, and 120 services, such as the Bingham Falls Renewal, named after a local waterfall. This treatment begins with a seasonal body scrub, rinsed off in a Vichy shower, followed by an aromatherapy oil massage. The spacious men's and women's sanctuaries have saunas, steam rooms, and Jacuzzis.

Spa at Topnotch (✉ *4000 Mountain Rd. [Rte. 108], Stowe* ☎ *802/253–8585*

⊕ *www.topnotchresort.com*) provides an aura of calm, with its birch wood doors and accents, natural light, and cool colors. Signature services include a Vermont wildflower or woodspice treatment, which includes a warm herb wrap, exfoliation, and massage. Locker areas are spacious, with saunas, steam rooms, and Jacuzzis. The spa also has a full-service salon.

The Spa and Wellness Center at Stowe Mountain Lodge (✉ *7412 Mountain Rd. [Rte. 108], Stowe* ☎ *802/253–3560* ⊕ *www. stowemountainlodge.com*) is a 21,000-square-foot facility that opened along with Stowe's newest resort in 2008. Similar to Stoweflake and Topnotch, this is a state-of-the-art facility with 19 treatment rooms. Besides the expected array of facials, scrubs, and massages, the spa offers contemporary services like fitness assessments sound therapy.

At Killington, the **Woods Resort and Spa** (✉ *53 Woods La., Killington* ☎ *802/422–3139* ⊕ *www. woodsresortandspa.com*) is a European spa within an upscale condo complex. At the resort's clubhouse, the spa has a 75-foot indoor pool, sauna, steam room, and weight room. Spa services include massages, hot stone therapies, facials, salt scrubs, maple-sugar polishes, and mud treatments.

Okemo's ski area has a very similar spa facility to Killington's at the **Jackson Gore Resort** (✉ *Okemo Ridge Rd., off Rte. 103, Ludlow* ☎ *802/228–1400* ⊕ *www.okemo.com*), with a slopeside outdoor heated pool, hot tubs, a sauna, steam rooms, a fitness center, and massages like Swedish, deep tissue, and hot stone.

a towel. Meals are served buffet-style. Cabin D is a heavenly setup, three bedrooms right on the edge of the lake. **Pros:** outdoor focus; activities galore. **Cons:** many rooms have a shared bath; many are sparely furnished. ⊠ *535 Lost Nation Rd., Craftsbury Common* ☎ *802/586–7767 or 800/729–7751* ⊕ *www.craftsbury.com* ⇆ *49 rooms, 10 with bath; 4 cabins; 2 suites* ⚭ *In-room: no phone, no a/c, kitchen (some), refrigerator (some), no TV, Wi-Fi (some). In-hotel: restaurant, tennis court, gym, water sports, bicycles, laundry facilities, Internet terminal, Wi-Fi hotspot, some pets allowed* ▭ *MC, V* ⦶ *MAP.*

JEFFERSONVILLE

36 mi west of Greensboro, 18 mi north of Stowe.

Jeffersonville is just over Smugglers' Notch from Stowe but miles away in feel and attitude. In summer, you can drive over the notch road as it curves precipitously around boulders that have fallen from the cliffs above, then pass open meadows and old farmhouses and sugar shacks on the way down to town. Below the notch, Smugglers' Notch Ski Resort is the hub of activity year-round. Downtown Jeffersonville, once home to an artists' colony, is quiet but has excellent dining and sophisticated art galleries.

EXPLORING

Boyden Valley Winery. West of Jeffersonville in Cambridge, this winery conducts tours and tastings and showcases an excellent selection of Vermont specialty products and local handicrafts, including fine furniture. Its Big Barn Red is satisfyingly full-bodied, and it makes a brilliant line of ice wines. The winery is open daily May to December 10–5 and January to April, Friday to Sunday 10–5. Tours at 11:30 and 1. ⊠ *70 Rte. 104 at Rte. 15, Cambridge* ☎ *802/644–8151* ⊕ *boydenvalley.com.*

SPORTS AND THE OUTDOORS

KAYAKING **Green River Canoe & Kayak** (⊠ *155 Sterling Ridge Dr., Jeffersonville* ☎ *802/644–8336 or 802/644–8714*), at the junction of Routes 15 and 108 behind Jana's Restaurant, rents canoes and kayaks on the Lamoille River and leads guided canoe trips to Boyden Valley Winery.

LLAMA RIDES **Applecheek Farm** (⊠ *567 McFarlane Rd., Hyde Park* ☎ *802/888–4482*) runs daytime and evening (by lantern) hay and sleigh rides, llama treks, and farm tours. **Northern Vermont Llamas** (⊠ *766 Lapland Rd., Waterville* ☎ *802/644–2257*) conducts half- and full-day treks from May through October along the cross-country ski trails of Smugglers' Notch. The llamas carry everything, including snacks and lunches. Advance reservations are essential.

SKI AREA **Smugglers' Notch Resort** (⊠ *4323 Rte. 108 S* ☎ *802/644–8851 or 800/451–8752* ⊕ *www.smuggs.com*) consistently wins accolades for its family programs. Its children's ski school is one of the best in the country— possibly *the* best—but skiers of all levels come here. Smugglers' was the first ski area in the East to designate a triple-black-diamond run—the Black Hole. All the essentials are available in the village at the base of the Morse Mountain lifts, including lodgings, restaurants, and several shops. Smugglers' has a full roster of summertime programs, including pools, complete with waterfalls and waterslides; the Giant Rapid River Ride (the longest water ride in the state); lawn games; mountain biking and hiking programs; and craft workshops for adults. The Treasures Child Care Center accepts children 6 weeks and older.

The self-contained village has outdoor ice skating and sleigh rides. The numerous snowshoeing programs include family walks and backcountry trips. SmuggsCentral has an indoor pool, hot tub, Funzone playground with slides and miniature golf, and a teen center, open from 5 PM until midnight. In terms of Nordic skiing, the area has 18 mi of groomed and tracked trails and 12 mi of snowshoe trails.

For downhill skiing, Smugglers' has three mountains. The highest, Madonna, with a vertical drop of 2,610 feet, is in the center and connects with a trail network to Sterling (1,500 feet vertical). The third mountain, Morse (1,150 feet vertical), is adjacent to Smugglers' "village" of shops, restaurants, and condos; it's connected to the other peaks by trails and a shuttle bus. The wild, craggy landscape lends a pristine wilderness feel to the skiing experience on the two higher mountains. The tops of each of the mountains have expert terrain—a couple of double-black diamonds (and the only triple-black-diamond trail in the east) make Madonna memorable. Intermediate trails fill the lower sections. Morse has many beginner and advanced beginner trails. Smugglers' 70 trails are served by eight lifts, including six chairs and two surface lifts. Top-to-bottom snowmaking on all three mountains allows for 62% coverage. There are four progression terrain parks, including one for early beginners. Night skiing and snowboarding classes are given at the new Learning and Fun Park.

Ski camps for kids ages 3–17 provide excellent instruction, plus movies, games, and other activities. Wednesday, Thursday, and Saturday are kids' nights at Treasures, with dinner and supervised activities for children ages 3–11.

SHOPPING

The **Green Apple Antique Center** (⊠ *60 Main St.* ☎ *802/644–2989*) has a good bakery in the back of the store. **Smugglers' Notch Antique Center** (⊠ *906 Rte. 108* ☎ *802/644–8321* ⊕ *smugglersnotchantiques.com*) sells antiques and collectibles from 60 dealers in a rambling barn.

CLOTHING **Johnson Woolen Mills** (⊠ *51 Lower Main St. E, 9 mi east of Jeffersonville, Johnson* ☎ *802/635–2271* ⊕ *www.johnsonwoolenmills.com*) is an authentic factory store with deals on woolen blankets, yard goods, and the famous Johnson outerwear.

Fodor's Choice ★

CRAFTS **Vermont Rug Makers** (⊠ *933 Rte. 100C, 10 mi east of Jeffersonville, East Johnson* ☎ *802/635–2434*) weaves imaginative rugs and tapestries from fabrics, wools, and exotic materials. Its International Gallery displays rugs and tapestries from around the world.

WHERE TO EAT AND STAY

$ ✕ **158 Main.** It's worth the short drive from Smuggler's Notch to try the best and most popular restaurant in neighboring Jeffersonville. Menu selections range from sesame-seared yellowfin tuna with jasmine rice and wasabi to the locals' favorite breakfast, the "Two Eggs Basic,"

AMERICAN

which comes with two eggs any style, homemade toast, and home fries for $3.18. Portions are big; prices are not. Sunday brunch is served 8 AM–2 PM. ⌂ *158 Main St.* ☎ *802/644–8100* ⊕ *www.158Main.com* ⌂ *Reservations not accepted* ▭ *AE, DC, MC, V* ☉ *Closed Mon. No dinner Sun.*

$$$$ 🏨 **Smugglers' Notch Resort.** From watercolor workshops to giant water
☺ parks to weeklong camps for kids, this family resort has a plethora of
Fodor's Choice activities. In winter, the main activity is skiing, but children's programs
★ abound. Lodging is in clustered condominium complexes, with the condos set away from the resort center. Rates are packages for three, five, and seven nights and can include use of all resort amenities and lift tickets and ski lessons in season. **Pros:** great place for families and to learn to ski. **Cons:** not a romantic getaway for couples. ⌂ *4232 Rte. 108 S* ☎ *802/644–8851 or 800/451–8752* ⊕ *www.smuggs.com* ⇱ *550 condominiums* ⌂ *In-room: no a/c (some). In-hotel: 4 restaurants, bar, tennis courts, pools, children's programs (ages 3–17)* ▭ *AE, DC, MC, V.*

BURLINGTON

Fodor's Choice
★ *31 mi southwest of Jeffersonville, 76 mi south of Montreal, 349 mi north of New York City, 223 mi northwest of Boston.*

As you drive along Main Street toward downtown Burlington, it's easy to see why the city is so often called one of the most livable small cities in the United States. Downtown is filled with hip restaurants and nightclubs, art galleries, and the Church Street Marketplace—a bustling pedestrian mall with trendy shops, craft vendors, street performers, and sidewalk cafés. Just beyond, Lake Champlain shimmers beneath the towering Adirondacks on the New York shore. On the shores of the lake, Burlington's revitalized waterfront teems with outdoors enthusiasts who stroll along its recreation path and ply the waters in sailboats and motor craft in summer.

EXPLORING

☺ **ECHO Leahy Center for Lake Champlain.** Part of the waterfront's revital-
★ ization, this aquarium and science center gives kids a chance to check out 100 hands-on, interactive wind and water exhibits and a sunken shipwreck. ⌂ *1 College St.* ☎ *802/864–1848* ⊕ *www.echovermont.org* ⌂ *$9* ☉ *Daily 10–5, Thurs. until 8.*

Ethan Allen Homestead. One of the earliest residents of the Intervale area was Ethan Allen, Vermont's Revolutionary-era guerrilla fighter, who remains a captivating figure. Exhibits at the on-site visitor center answer questions about his flamboyant life. The house holds such frontier hallmarks as rough saw-cut boards and an open hearth for cooking. A re-created Colonial kitchen garden resembles the one the Allens would have had. After the tour and multimedia presentation, you can stretch your legs on scenic trails along the Winooski River. ⌂ *1 Ethan Allen Homestead, off Rte. 127, north of Burlington* ☎ *802/865–4556* ⊕ *www.ethanallenhomestead.org* ⌂ *$5* ☉ *May–Oct., Mon.–Sat. 10–4, Sun. 1–4.*

University of Vermont. Crowning the hilltop above Burlington is the campus of the University of Vermont, known simply as UVM for the abbreviation of its Latin name, Universitas Viridis Montis—the University of the Green Mountains. With more than 10,000 students, UVM is the state's principal institution of higher learning. The most architecturally interesting buildings face the green, which has a statue of UVM founder Ira Allen, Ethan's brother. *85 South Prospect St. ☎802/656–3131 ⊕www.uvm.edu.*

Magic Hat Brewery. Magic Hat is a leader in Vermont's microbrewery revolution. You can tour their brewery, which puts out 400 bottles a minute, and get free beer samples at their South Burlington spot (on Route 7, before Shelburne). Their Growler Bar has 30 beers on tap. *⊠5 Bartlett Bay Rd., South Burlington ☎802/658–2739 ⊕magichat. net ☜Free ☉ Open Mon.–Sat. 10–6, Sun. noon–5. Tours Thurs. and Fri. 3, 4, and 5; Sat. noon, 1, 2, and 3; Sun. 1:30.*

SPORTS AND THE OUTDOORS

BEACHES The **North Beaches** (⊠*North Beach Park off North Ave. ☎802/864–0123 ⊠Leddy Beach, Leddy Park Rd. off North Ave.*) are on the northern edge of Burlington. Leddy Beach is a good spot for sailboarding.

BIKING Burlington's 10-mi Cycle the City loop runs along the waterfront, connecting several city parks and beaches. It also passes the Community Boathouse and runs within several blocks of downtown restaurants and shops. **North Star Sports** (⊠*100 Main St. ☎802/863–3832 ⊕northstarsports.net*) rents bicycles and provides maps of bicycle routes. **Ski Rack** (⊠*85 Main St. ☎802/658–3313 or 800/882–4530 ⊕www.skirack.com*) rents and services bikes and provides maps.

BOATING **Burlington Community Boathouse** (⊠*Foot of College St., Burlington Harbor ☎802/865–3377*) rents 19-foot sailboats. **Shoreline Cruise's** *Spirit of Ethan Allen III,* a 500-passenger, three-level cruise vessel, has narrated cruises and dinner and sunset sailings with awesome views of the Adirondacks and Green Mountains. ⊠*Burlington Boat House, College and Battery Sts. ☎802/862–8300 ⊕www.soea.com ☜$12 ☉ Cruises late May–mid-Oct., daily 10–9.*

Waterfront Boat Rentals (⊠*Foot of Maple St. on Perkins Pier, Burlington Harbor ☎802/864–4858*) rents kayaks, canoes, rowboats, skiffs, and Boston whalers. Affordable sailing lessons are available.

SKI AREA About 25 mi from Burlington, **Bolton Valley Resort** (⊠*4302 Bolton Valley Access Rd., Bolton ☎802/434–3444 or 877/926–5866 ⊕www. boltonvalley.com*) is a family favorite. In addition to 61 downhill ski trails (more than half rated for intermediates), Bolton has night skiing Wednesday–Saturday, 62 mi of cross-country and snowshoe trails, and a sports center.

OFF THE
BEATEN
PATH

Green Mountain Audubon Nature Center. This is a wonderful place to discover Vermont's outdoor wonders. The center's 300 acres of diverse habitats are a sanctuary for all things wild, and the 5 mi of trails provide an opportunity to explore the workings of differing natural communities. Events include dusk walks, wildflower and birding rambles, nature workshops, and educational activities for children and adults. The center is 18 mi southeast of Burlington. ⊠*255 Sherman Hollow Rd., Huntington ☎802/434–3068 ☜Donations accepted ☉ Grounds daily dawn–dusk, center Mon.–Sat. 8–4.*

SHOPPING

CRAFTS In addition to its popular pottery, **Bennington Potters North** (✉ *127 College St.* ☎ *802/863–2221 or 800/205–8033* ⊕ *www.benningtonpotters.com*) stocks interesting gifts, glassware, furniture, and other housewares. **Vermont State Craft Center/Frog Hollow** (✉ *85 Church St.* ☎ *802/863–6458* ⊕ *www.froghollow.org*) is a nonprofit collective that sells contemporary and traditional crafts by more than 200 Vermont artisans.

MARKETS **Church Street Marketplace** (✉ *2 Church St., Main St. to Pearl St.* ☎ *802/863–1648*), a pedestrian thoroughfare, is lined with boutiques, cafés, and street vendors. Look for bargains at the rapidly growing **Essex Outlet Fair** (✉ *21 Essex Way, Junction of Rtes. 15 and 289, Essex* ☎ *802/878–2851* ⊕ *www.essexshoppes.com*), with such outlets as BCBG, Brooks Brothers, Polo Ralph Lauren, and Levi's, among others.

NIGHTLIFE AND THE ARTS

THE ARTS The **Fire House Art Gallery** (✉ *135 Church St.* ☎ *802/865–7165* ⊕ *www.burlingtoncityarts.com*) exhibits works by local artists. **Flynn Theatre for the Performing Arts** (✉ *153 Main St.* ☎ *802/652–4500 information; 802/863–5966 tickets* ⊕ *www.flynncenter.org*), a grandiose old structure, is the cultural heart of Burlington; it schedules the Vermont Symphony Orchestra, theater, dance, big-name musicians, and lectures. **St. Michael's Playhouse** (✉ *1 Winooski Park St., Michael's College, Rte. 15, Colchester* ☎ *802/654–2281 box office; 802/654–2617 administrative office* ⊕ *www.smcvt.edu*) stages performances in the McCarthy Arts Center. The **Vermont Symphony Orchestra** (☎ *802/864–5741* ⊕ *www.vso.org*) performs throughout the state year-round and at the Flynn from October through May.

NIGHTLIFE The music at **Club Metronome** (✉ *188 Main St.* ☎ *802/865–4563* ⊕ *www.clubmetronome.com*) ranges from cutting-edge sounds to funk, blues, and reggae. National and local musicians come to **Higher Ground** (✉ *1214 Williston Rd., South Burlington* ☎ *802/265–0777* ⊕ *www.highergroundmusic.com*). The band Phish got its start at **Nectar's** (✉ *188 Main St.* ☎ *802/658–4771* ⊕ *www.liveatnectars.com*), which is always jumping to the sounds of local bands and never charges a cover. **Ri Ra** (✉ *123 Church St.* ☎ *802/860–9401* ⊕ *www.rira.com*) hosts live entertainment with Irish flair. **Vermont Pub and Brewery** (✉ *144 College St.* ☎ *802/865–0500* ⊕ *www.vermontbrewery.com*) makes its own beer and fruit seltzers and is arguably the most popular spot in town. Folk musicians play here regularly.

WHERE TO EAT

¢–$ ✕ **American Flatbread–Burlington Hearth.** It might be worth going to college in Burlington just to be able to gather with friends at this wildly
PIZZA popular and delicious organic pizza place. On weekends, it's standing
Fodor's Choice room only (seating is first-come, first-served) as kids bustle for house-
★ made brews. The wood-fired clay dome oven combines with all organic ingredients to create masterful results, like the Punctuated Equilibrium, which has kalamata olives, roasted red peppers, local goat cheese, fresh rosemary, red onions, mozzarella, and garlic. Here's to the college life! (There are also locations in Rutland and Waitsfield.) ✉ *115 St. Paul St.*

☎ *802/861–2999* ⊕ *www.americanflatbread.com.com* ⌖ *Reservations not accepted* ▤ *MC, V.*

$$$–$$$$ ✕ **Butler's Restaurant and Tavern.** This restaurant at The Essex are staffed
AMERICAN by instructors and second-year students at the New England Culinary
Fodor'sChoice Institute. The menu offers a range of excellent dishes, from porcini-
★ dusted beef tenderloin in béarnaise sauce to a classic Reuben sand-
wich. The wine selection pulses with enthusiasm. Dishes can be hit
or miss depending on who's cooking, but service is taken very seri-
ously. There is a bounty of high-quality
local ingredients. ⊠ *70 Essex Way, Essex Junction* ☎ *802/878–1100*
⊕ *www.vtculinaryresort.com* ▤ *AE, D, DC, MC, V* ⊗ *No dinner Sun.
in winter.*

$–$$ ✕ **A Single Pebble.** The creative, authentic Asian selections served on
CHINESE the first floor of this residential row house include traditional clay-pot
dishes as well as wok specialties, such as sesame catfish and kung pao
chicken. The dry-fried green beans (sautéed with flecks of pork, black
beans, preserved vegetables, and garlic) are a house specialty. All dishes
can be made without meat. ⊠ *133–135 Bank St.* ☎ *802/865–5200*
⊕ *www.asinglepebble.com* ▤ *AE, D, MC, V* ⊗ *No lunch weekends.*

$–$$ ✕ **Trattoria Delia.** Didn't manage to rent that villa in Umbria this year?
ITALIAN The next best thing, if your travels bring you to Burlington, is this
★ superb Italian country eatery around the corner from City Hall Park.
Game and fresh produce are the stars, as in wild boar braised in red
wine, tomatoes, rosemary, and sage served on soft polenta. Wood-
grilled items are a specialty. ⊠ *152 St. Paul St.* ☎ *802/864–5253* ⊕ *www.
trattoriadelia.com* ▤ *AE, D, DC, MC, V* ⊗ *No lunch.*

WHERE TO STAY

$$ ▦ **The Essex.** "Vermont's Culinary Resort" is a hotel and conference
center about 10 mi from downtown Burlington, with two good res-
taurants run by the New England Culinary Institute. The best part of
a stay here is access to cooking classes offered each day in professional
test kitchens on site. Very comfortable Susan Sargent–designed rooms
are adorned with her vibrant colors in everything from the wall paint to
the pillow covers; 30 rooms have fireplaces. A 19,000-square-foot spa
opened in 2009, along with an Orvis-endorsed fly-fishing pond. **Pros:**
daily cooking classes; colorful rooms; free airport shuttle. **Cons:** odd
location in suburb of Burlington. ⊠ *70 Essex Way, off Rte. 289, Essex
Junction* ☎ *802/878–1100 or 800/727–4295* ⊕ *www.vtculinaryresort.
com* ⇆ *60 rooms, 60 suites* ⌖ *In-room: Wi-Fi. In-hotel: 2 restaurants,
bar, golf course, tennis courts, pool, spa* ▤ *AE, D, MC, V.*

¢ ▦ **G. G. T. Tibet Inn.** This motel probably has the cheapest rates in all of
Vermont—$49 for two people in winter and $59 to $69 in summer—
but that's not the main attraction. The lure here is the friendly face
and evident care of the motel's Tibetan owner, whose name is Kalsang
G.G.T. (Yes, G.G.T. really is his real last name.) Buddhist prayer flags
flap from the exterior. All rooms have a microwave, a refrigerator, and
basic motel furnishings with a big TV. Kalsang's smile at check-in will
bring you back. **Pros:** great price; locally owned. **Cons:** no high-speed
Internet. ⊠ *1860 Shelburne Rd., South Burlington* ☎ *802/863–7110*

CLOSE UP

Vermont by Bike

Road biking in the Green Mountains.

Vermont has more than 14,000 mi of roads, and almost 80% of them are town roads that see little high-speed traffic, making them ideal for scenic bike rides. The state is also threaded with thousands of miles of dirt roads suitable for mountain biking. Although mountain-bike trails and old farm and logging roads wind through the Green Mountain State, most are on private property and are, therefore, not mapped. Several mountain-biking centers around the state have extensive trail networks (and maps) that will keep avid fat-tire fans happy for a few hours or a few days. To road bike in Vermont, you'll want a map and preferably a bicycle with at least 10 gears. The only roads that prohibit cycling are the four-lane highways and Routes 7 and 4 in Rutland.

TOP ROAD BIKING ROUTES:
To make a relatively easy 16-mi loop, begin at the blinker on U.S. 7 in **Shelburne** and follow Mt. Philo Road south to Hinesburg Road, then west

to Charlotte. Lake Road, Orchard Road, and Mouth of River Road go past orchards and berry fields. Bostwick Road returns to U.S. 7.

In the heart of the central Green Mountains is a moderate 18-mi loop on Routes 4, 100, and 100A that passes Calvin Coolidge's home in **Plymouth Notch.**

West of **Rutland** is a beautiful 27-mi ride on Routes 140, 30, and 133 that passes swimming holes, then hugs the shore of Lake St. Catherine. Start in Middletown Springs.

A scenic 43-mi ride in the **Northeast Kingdom** passes through pleasant Peacham and the birches and maples of Groton State Forest. Start in Danville and follow Peacham Road, then Routes 302 and 232 and U.S. 2.

For a real test, try the 48-mi ride over **Middlebury and Brandon Gaps** on Routes 125 and 73, which connect via Routes 153 and 100.

7

Burlington's pedestrian-only Church Street Marketplace and the nearby shores of Lake Champlain are great for exploring.

⊕ *www.ggttibetinn.com* ⤴ *21 rooms* ☐ *In-room: Internet. In-hotel: pool* ⊟ *AE, D, MC, V.*

$ ⊡ **Willard Street Inn.** High in the historic hill section of Burlington, this
★ ivy-covered grand house with an exterior marble staircase and English gardens incorporates elements of Queen Anne and Colonial/Georgian-Revival styles. The stately foyer, paneled in cherry, leads to a more formal sitting room with velvet drapes. The solarium is bright and sunny with marble floors, many plants, and big velvet couches for contemplating views of Lake Champlain. All the rooms have down comforters and phones; some have lake views and canopied beds. Orange French toast is among the breakfast favorites. **Pros:** lovely old mansion loaded with character and details; friendly attention; common room snacks. **Cons:** long walk to downtown. ⊠ *349 S. Willard St.* ☎ *802/651–8710 or 800/577–8712* ⊕ *www.willardstreetinn.com* ⤴ *14 rooms* ☐ *In-room: Wi-Fi. In-hotel: Internet terminal, Wi-Fi hotspot, no kids under 12* ⊟ *AE, D, MC, V* ⦿❘ *BP.*

SHELBURNE

5 mi south of Burlington.

A few miles south of Burlington, the Champlain Valley gives way to fertile farmland, affording stunning views of the rugged Adirondacks across the lake. In the middle of this farmland is the village of Shelburne, chartered in the mid-18th century and partly a bedroom community for Burlington. It has a lively food scene, and the Shelburne Inn and Farms are worth at least a day of exploring.

GETTING HERE AND AROUND

Shelburne is south of Burlington after the town of South Burlington, notable for its very un-Vermont traffic and commercial and fast-food–franchised stretch of U.S. 7. It's easy to confuse Shelburne Farms—2 mi west of town on the lake, with Shelburne Museum, which is just south of town directly on Route 7, but you'll want to make time for both.

EXPLORING

Shelburne Farms. Founded in the 1880s as a private estate for two very rich New Yorkers, this 1,400-acre farm is much more than an exquisite landscape: it's an educational and cultural resource center with, among other things, a working dairy farm, a Children's Farmyard (featuring with hands-on workshops throughout the day), daily viewings of various stages of the farm's famous cheese being made, and a bakery whose aroma of fresh bread and pastries is an olfactory treat. It's a brilliant place for parents to expose their kids to the dignity of farm work and the joys of compassionate animal husbandry—indeed, children and adults alike will get a kick out of hunting for eggs in the oversize coop and milking a cow. Frederick Law Olmsted, co-creator of New York's Central Park, designed the magnificent grounds overlooking Lake Champlain. If you fall in love with the scenery, arrange a romantic dinner at the lakefront mansion or spend the night. ⊠ *West of U.S. 7 at 1611 Harbor Rd.* ☎ *802/985–8686* ⊕ *www.shelburnefarms.org* 🖅 *Day pass $6, tour an additional $5* ☉ *Visitor center and shop daily 10–5; tours mid-May–mid-Oct. (last tour at 3:30); walking trails daily 10–4, weather permitting.*

Fodor'sChoice ★

Shelburne Museum. You can trace much of New England's history simply by wandering through the 45 acres and 37 buildings of this museum. The outstanding 80,000-object collection of Americana consists of 18th- and 19th-century period homes and furniture, fine and folk art, farm tools, more than 200 carriages and sleighs, John James Audubon prints, an old-fashioned jail, and even a private railroad car from the days of steam. The museum also has an assortment of duck decoys, an old stone cottage, a display of early toys, and the *Ticonderoga*, a sidewheel steamship, grounded amid lawn and trees. ⊠ *5555 Shelburne Rd. (U.S. 7)* ☎ *802/985–3346* ⊕ *www.shelburnemuseum.org* 🖅 *$18* ☉ *May–Oct., daily 10–5.*

Shelburne Vineyard. South of Shelburn Museum on Route 7 you'll see rows of organically grown vines. Visit the attractive tasting room and learn how wine is made. ⊠ *6308 Shelburne Rd. (Rte. 7)* ☎ *802/985–8222* 🖅 *Free* ⊕ *www.shelburnevineyard.com.*

Vermont Teddy Bear Company. On the 25-minute tour of this fun-filled factory you'll hear more puns than you ever thought possible and learn how a few homemade bears, sold from a cart on Church Street, have turned into a multimillion-dollar business. A children's play tent is set up outdoors in summer, and you can wander the beautiful 57-acre property. ⊠ *6655 Shelburne Rd.* ☎ *802/985–3001* ⊕ *www.vermontteddybear.com* 🖅 *Tour $2* ☉ *Tours Mon.–Sat. 9:30–5, Sun. 10:30–4; store daily 9–6.*

Fodor'sChoice ★

7

Shelburne Vineyard. South of Shelburn Museum on Route 7 you'll see rows of organically grown vines. Visit the attractive tasting room and learn how wine is made. ✉ *6308 Shelburne Rd. (Rte. 7)* ☎ *802/985–8222* 🖃 *Free* ⊕ *www.shelburnevineyard.com*

SHOPPING

When you enter the **Shelburne Country Store** (✉ *29 Falls Rd., Village Green off U.S. 7* ☎ *802/985–3657*), you'll step back in time. Walk past the potbellied stove and take in the aroma emanating from the fudge neatly piled behind huge antique glass cases. The store specializes in candles, weather vanes, glassware, and local foods.

WHERE TO EAT

$$–$$$ ✕ **Café Shelburne.** This popular restaurant serves creative French bistro
FRENCH   cuisine. Specialties include sweetbreads with a port wine and mush-
★   room sauce in puff pastry and homemade fettuccine with Vermont goat cheese. Desserts such as the sweet chocolate layered terrine and maple-syrup mousse with orange terrine are fabulous. ✉ *5573 Shelburne Rd. (U.S. 7)* ☎ *802/985–3939* 🖃 *802/985–3939* ⊕ *www.cafeshelburne.com* 🖃 *AE, MC, V* ⊘ *Closed Sun. and Mon. No lunch.*

$$$ ✕ **The Dining Room at the Inn at Shelburne Farms.** Dinner here will make
AMERICAN   you dream of F. Scott Fitzgerald. Piano wafts from the library, and
Fodor'sChoice   you can carry a drink through the rooms of this 1880s mansion, gaz-
★   ing across a long lawn and formal gardens on the shore of dark Lake Champlain—you'll swear Jay Gatsby is about to come down the stairs. Count on just-grown ingredients that come from the market gardens as well as flavorful locally grown venison, beef, pork, and chicken. On weekends a spectacular spread of produce is set up next to a cocktail bar with fresh specialties. The dining room overlooks the lake shore, and Sunday brunch (not served in May) is the area's best. Breakfast is served as well. ✉ *1 Harbor Rd.* ☎ *802/985–8498* ⊕ *www.shelburnefarms.org* 🖃 *AE, MC, V* ⊘ *Closed mid-May–mid-Oct.*

WHERE TO STAY

$$–$$$ ⛉ **Inn at Shelburne Farms.** It's hard not to feel a little bit like an aristo-
Fodor'sChoice   crat at this exquisite turn-of-the-20th-century Tudor-style inn, one of
★   the most memorable properties in the country. What could easily be a museum with Do Not Touch signs posted everywhere is instead largely your private mansion. Perched at the edge of Lake Champlain, the grounds are vast. Kayak in the lake, laze on the many elegant porches, read the books in the library, or stroll through the elegantly mani-cured gardens. Views include the distant Adirondacks, as well as the sea of pastures and woods that make up the 1,400-acre working farm on which the mansion is situated. Each room is different, featuring various period wallpapers, high-end antiques, and other decorative touches without making you feel like a player in a costume drama. Teddy Roosevelt slept in the bed in Empire Room, which maintains the original furnishings. The dining room ($$$$) is open for three meals and is romance itself in the evening. **Pros:** stately lakefront setting in a fantastic historic mansion; great service; wonderful value; great res-taurant. **Cons:** some may miss not having a TV in the room; closed in winter; must book far in advance. ✉ *1 Harbor Rd.* ☎ *802/985–8498*

Shelburne Museum's many attractions include the Ticonderoga steamship and other pieces from New England's past.

⊕ *www.shelburnefarms.org* ⇥ *24 rooms, 17 with bath; 2 cottages* ⚓ *In-room: no a/c, no TV. In-hotel: restaurant, tennis court* ⊟ *D, DC, MC, V* ⊙ *Closed mid-Oct.–mid-May.*

VERGENNES

12 mi south of Shelburne.

Vermont's oldest city, founded in 1788, is also the third oldest in New England. The downtown area is a compact district of Victorian homes and public buildings. Main Street slopes down to Otter Creek Falls, where cannonballs were made during the War of 1812. The statue of Thomas MacDonough on the green immortalizes the victor of the Battle of Plattsburgh in 1814.

ESSENTIALS

Visitor Information Addison County Chamber of Commerce (⊠ *2 Court St., Middlebury* ☎ *802/388–7951 or 800/733–8376* ⊕ *www.midvermont.com*).

OFF THE
BEATEN
PATH

Lake Champlain Maritime Museum. This museum documents centuries of activity on the historically significant lake. Climb aboard a replica of Benedict Arnold's Revolutionary War gunboat moored in the lake, learn about shipwrecks, and watch craftsmen work at traditional boatbuilding and blacksmithing. Among the exhibits are a nautical archaeology center, a conservation laboratory, and a restaurant. ⊠ *Basin Harbor Rd., 7 mi west of Vergennes, Basin Harbor* ☎ *802/475–2022* ⊕ *www.lcmm.org* ⊠ *$9* ⊙ *May–mid-Oct., daily 10–5.*

SHOPPING

Dakin Farm (✉ *5797 Rte. 7, 5 mi north of Vergennes* ☎ *800/993–2546* ⊕ *www.dakinfarm.com*) sells cob-smoked ham, aged cheddar cheese, maple syrup made on-site, and other specialty foods. You can visit the ham smokehouse and watch the waxing and sealing of the cheeses.

WHERE TO EAT AND STAY

$–$$ ✕ **Starry Night Café.** This chic restaurant is one of the hottest spots
ECLECTIC   around, and it's increased in size to meet growing demand. Appetizers include house specials such as honey-chili glazed shrimp and gazpacho. Among the French-meets-Asian entrées are lobster-stuffed sole, pan-seared scallops, and grilled New York steak. ✉ *5371 Rte. 7, 5 mi north of Vergennes, Ferrisburg* ☎ *802/877–6316* ⊕ *www.starrynightcafe.com* ☐ *MC, V* ☺ *Closed Mon. and Tues. No lunch.*

$$$$ 🏨 **Basin Harbor Club.** On 700 acres overlooking Lake Champlain, this
ⓒ   ultimate family resort provides luxurious accommodations and a full
Fodor'sChoice   roster of amenities, including an 18-hole golf course, boating (with a
★   40-foot tour boat), a 3,200-foot grass airstrip, and daylong children's programs. Some rooms in the guesthouses have fireplaces, decks, or porches. The rustic, camp-like cottages are charming and have one to three bedrooms. The restaurant menu ($–$$$) is classic American, the wine list excellent. Jackets and ties are required in common areas after 6 PM from late June through Labor Day. **Pros:** gorgeous lakeside property; activities galore. **Cons:** open only half the year. ✉ *48 Basin Harbor Rd.* ☎ *802/475–2311 or 800/622–4000* ⊕ *www.basinharbor. com* 🛏 *36 rooms, 2 suites in 3 guesthouses, 77 cottages* ⚒ *In-room: no a/c, no TV. In-hotel: 3 restaurants, golf course, tennis courts, pool, gym, bicycles, children's programs (ages 3–15), some pets allowed* ☐ *MC, V* ☺ *Closed mid-Oct.–mid-May* ⏐◯⏐ *BP.*

LAKE CHAMPLAIN ISLANDS

43 mi north of Vergennes, 20 mi northwest of Shelburne, 15 mi northwest of Burlington.

Lake Champlain, which stretches more than 100 mi south from the Canadian border, forms the northern part of the boundary between New York and Vermont. Within it is an elongated archipelago composed of several islands—Isle La Motte, North Hero, Grand Isle, South Hero—and the Alburg Peninsula. With a temperate climate, the islands hold several apple orchards and are a center of water recreation in summer and ice fishing in winter. A scenic drive through the islands on U.S. 2 begins at Interstate 89 and travels north to Alburg Center; Route 78 takes you back to the mainland.

ESSENTIALS

Visitor Information Lake Champlain Regional Chamber of Commerce (✉ *60 Main St., Suite 100, Burlington* ☎ *802/863–3489 or 877/686–5253* ⊕ *www.vermont.org*). **Lake Champlain Islands Chamber of Commerce** (✉ *3537 Rte. 2, Suite 100, North Hero* ☎ *802/372–8400 or 800/262–5226* ⊕ *www.champlainislands.com*).

EXPLORING

Herrmann's Royal Lipizzan Stallions. These beautiful stallions, cousins of the noble white horses bred in Austria since the 16th century, perform intricate dressage maneuvers for delighted spectators for a brief period each summer on North Hero. These acrobatic horses are descendants of animals rescued from the turmoil of World War II by General George Patton and members of the Herrmann family. ⊠ *U.S. 2, North Hero* ☎ *802/372–5683* ☜ *Barn visits free between performances, shows $17* ☉ *Early July–late Aug., Thurs. and Fri. at 6* PM*, weekends at 2:30* PM.

Snow Farm Vineyard and Winery. Vermont's first vineyard and grape winery was started here in 1996; today it specializes in nontraditional botanical hybrid grapes to withstand the local climate. Take a self-guided tour, sip some samples in the tasting room, and picnic and listen to music at the free concerts on the lawn Thursday evenings mid-June through Labor Day. ⊠ *190 W. Shore Rd., South Hero* ☎ *802/372–9463* ☜ *Free* ☉ *May–Dec., daily 10–5; tours May–Oct. at 11 and 2* ⊕ *snowfarm.com.*

St. Anne's Shrine. This spot marks the site where French soldiers and Jesuits put ashore in 1665 and built a fort, creating Vermont's first European settlement. The state's first Roman Catholic Mass was celebrated here on July 26, 1666. ⊠ *92 St. Anne's Rd., Isle La Motte* ☎ *802/928–3362* ☜ *Free* ☉ *Mid-May–mid-Oct., daily 9–4.*

SPORTS AND THE OUTDOORS

On the mainland east of the Alburg Peninsula, **Missisquoi National Wildlife Refuge** (⊠ *29 Tabor Rd., 36 mi north of Burlington, Swanton* ☎ *802/868–4781* ⊕ *missisquoi.fws.gov*) consists of 6,642 acres of federally protected wetlands, meadows, and woods. It's a beautiful area for bird-watching, canoeing, or walking nature trails. **Sand Bar State Park** (⊠ *1215 U.S. 2, South Hero* ☎ *802/893–2825* ⊕ *www.vtstateparks. com/htm/sandbar.cfm* ☜ *$3.50* ☉ *Mid-May–early-Sept., daily dawn–dusk*) has one of Vermont's best swimming beaches.

BOATING   **Apple Island Resort** (⊠ *150 South St. [U.S. 2], South Hero* ☎ *802/372–5398*) rents sailboats, rowboats, canoes, kayaks, and motorboats. **Hero's Welcome** (⊠ *3537 U.S. 2, North Hero* ☎ *802/372–4161 or 800/372–4376*) rents bikes, canoes, kayaks, and paddleboats.

WHERE TO STAY

$–$$ ☖ **North Hero House Inn and Restaurant.** This inn has four buildings right on Lake Champlain, including the 1891 Colonial-revival main house with nine guest rooms, the restaurant, a pub room, library, and sitting room. Many rooms have water views, and each possesses country furnishings and antiques. The beach is a popular spot for lake swimming in summer, and there are boat rentals nearby. The Homestead, Southwind, and Cove House have adjoining rooms that are good for families. Dinner ($$–$$$) is served in the informal glass greenhouse or Colonial-style dining room. **Pros:** relaxed vacation complex; superb lakefront setting. **Cons:** open just May to November. ⊠ *U.S. 2, North Hero* ☎ *802/372–4732 or 888/525–3644* ⊕ *www.northherohouse.com* ↪ *26 rooms* ⟁ *In-room: no a/c (some). In-hotel: restaurant, bar* ⊟ *AE, MC, V* �‖❘ *CP* ☉ *Closed Dec.–Apr.*

$ ⓘ **Ruthcliffe Lodge.** Good food and splendid scenery make this off-the-beaten-path motel directly on Lake Champlain a great value. If you're looking for a cheap, DIY summer place to take in the scenery, canoe the lake, or bicycle, this will do quite nicely. The lodge is on Isle La Motte—a rarely visited island. Rooms are very clean and simple: bed, dresser, night table, and stenciled wall border. Owner-chef Mark Infante specializes in Italian pasta, fish, and meat dishes ($$); there's alfresco seating that overlooks a lawn leading to the lakeshore. A full breakfast is included. **Pros:** inexpensive; serene setting; laid-back. **Cons:** rooms simple, not luxurious. ⊠ *1002 Quarry Rd., Isle La Motte* ☎ *802/928–3200* ⊕ *www.ruthcliffe.com* ⮐ *7 rooms* ⚲ *In-hotel: restaurant, bicycles* ⊟ *MC, V* ⦿ *BP* ☽ *Closed Columbus Day–mid-May.*

MONTGOMERY/JAY

32 mi east of St. Albans, 51 mi northeast of Burlington.

Montgomery is a small village near the Canadian border and Jay Peak ski resort. Amid the surrounding countryside are seven covered bridges.

OFF THE BEATEN PATH

Lake Memphremagog. Vermont's second-largest lake, Lake Memphremagog extends from Newport 33 mi north into Canada. Watch the sun set from the deck of the **East Side Restaurant** (⊠ *47 Landingd St., Newport* ☎ *802/334–2340*), which serves excellent burgers and prime rib. Prouty Beach in Newport has camping facilities, tennis courts, and paddleboat and canoe rentals. ⊠ *Veterans Ave.* ☎ *802/334–7951.*

SPORTS AND THE OUTDOORS

SKI AREA **Hazen's Notch Cross Country Ski Center and B&B** (⊠ *4850 Rte. 58* ☎ *802/326–4799*), delightfully remote at any time of the year, has 40 mi of marked and groomed trails and rents equipment and snowshoes.

★ Sticking up out of the flat farmland, **Jay Peak** (⊠ *4850 Rte. 242, Jay* ☎ *802/988–2611; 800/451–4449 outside VT* ⊕ *www.jaypeakresort.com*) averages 355 inches of snow a year—more than any other Vermont ski area. Its proximity to Québec attracts Montréalers and discourages eastern seaboarders; hence, the prices are moderate and the lift lines shorter than at other resorts. The area is renowned for its glade skiing and powder.

Off-season, Jay Peak runs tram rides to the summit from mid-June through Labor Day and mid-September through Columbus Day ($10). The child-care center for youngsters ages 2–7 is open from 9 AM to 9 PM. If you're staying at Hotel Jay and Jay Peak Condominiums, you receive this nursery care free, as well as evening care and supervised dining at the hotel. Infant care is available on a fee basis with advanced reservations. In the winter, snowshoes can be rented, and guided walks are led by a naturalist. Telemark rentals and instruction are available.

Jay Peak has two interconnected mountains for downhill skiing, the highest reaching nearly 4,000 feet with a vertical drop of 2,153 feet. The smaller mountain has straight-fall-line, expert terrain that eases mid-mountain into an intermediate pitch. The main peak is served by Vermont's only tramway and transports skiers to meandering but challenging intermediate trails. Beginners should stick near the bottom on trails off the Metro lift. Weekdays at 9:30 AM and 1:30 PM, mountain ambassadors conduct a free tour. The area's 76 trails, including 21 glades and two chutes, are served by eight lifts, including the tram and the longest detachable quad in the East. The area also has two quads, a triple, and a double chairlift; one T-bar; and a moving carpet. Jay has 80% snowmaking coverage. The area also has four terrain parks, each rated for different abilities. There are ski-school programs for children ages 3–18.

SHOPPING

Trout River Store (✉ *91 Main St., Montgomery Center* ☎ *802/326–3058*), an old-time country store with an antique soda fountain, is a great place to stock up on picnic supplies, eat a hearty bowl of soup and an overstuffed sandwich, and check out local crafts.

WHERE TO STAY

$$$$ **Hotel Jay & Jay Peak Condominiums.** Centrally located in the ski resort's base area, the hotel and its simply furnished rooms are a favorite for families. Kids 13 and under stay and eat free, and during nonholiday times, they can ski free, too. Farther afield (but still mostly slope-side) are condominiums and town houses that range from studio to five-bedroom, with fireplaces, modern kitchens, and washer/dryers. Complimentary child care is provided to hotel and condo guests 9 AM–4 PM for kids ages 2–7. **Pros:** great for skiers and summer mountain adventurers. **Cons:** not an intimate, traditional Vermont stay. ✉ *4850 Rte. 242* ☎ *802/988–2611; 800/451–4449 outside VT* ⊕ *www.jaypeakresort.com* ⤴ *48 rooms, 94 condominiums* ⚷ *In-room: no a/c. In-hotel: restaurant, bar, tennis courts, pool* ⊟ *AE, D, DC, MC, V* ⑩ *MAP.*

$ **Inn on Trout River.** Guest rooms at this 100-year-old riverside inn sport a country-cottage style, and all have down quilts and flannel sheets in winter. Lemoine's Restaurant ($–$$) specializes in American and Continental fare. Try the raviolini stuffed with Vermont cheddar cheese and walnuts topped with pesto or the medallions of pork tenderloin in a maple syrup demi-glace. Hobo's Café ($$), also at the inn, serves simpler fare. **Pros:** traditional B&B. **Cons:** rooms heavy on the florals. ✉ *241 S. Main St., Montgomery Center* ☎ *802/326–4391 or 800/338–7049* ⊕ *www.troutinn.com* ⤴ *9 rooms, 1 suite* ⚷ *In-room: no a/c, no TV. In-hotel: restaurant, bar* ⊟ *AE, DC, MC, V* ⑩ *BP, MAP.*

EN ROUTE   Routes 14, 5, 58, and 100 make a scenic drive around the **Northeast Kingdom,** named for the remoteness and stalwart independence that have helped preserve its rural nature. You can extend the loop and head east on Route 105 to the city of Newport on Lake Memphremagog. Some of the most unspoiled areas in all Vermont are on the drive south from Newport on either U.S. 5 or Interstate 91 (the latter is faster, but the former is prettier).

LAKE WILLOUGHBY

30 mi southeast of Montgomery (summer route; 50 mi by winter route), 28 mi north of St. Johnsbury.

The cliffs of Mt. Pisgah and Mt. Hor drop to the edge of Lake Willoughby on opposite shores, giving this beautiful, deep, glacially carved lake a striking resemblance to a Norwegian fjord. The trails to the top of Mt. Pisgah reward hikers with glorious views.

EXPLORING

☾ **Bread and Puppet Museum**. This ramshackle barn houses a surrealistic col-
★ lection of props used by the world-renowned Bread and Puppet Theater. The troupe has been performing social and political commentary with the towering (they're supported by people on stilts), eerily expressive puppets for about 30 years and performs at the museum every Sunday June–August at 3. ⌧ *753 Heights Rd. (Rte. 122), 1 mi east of Rte. 16, Glover* 🕾 *802/525–3031* ⊕ *www.breadandpuppet.org* ⌧ *Donations accepted* ☾ *June–Oct., daily 10–6.*

Cabot Creamery. The major cheese producer in the state, midway between Barre and St. Johnsbury, has a visitor center with an audiovisual presentation about the dairy and cheese industry. You can taste samples, pur-
chase cheese and other Vermont products, and tour the plant. ⌧ *2870 Main St. (Rte. 215), 3 mi north of U.S. 2, Cabot* 🕾 *800/837–4261* ⊕ *www.cabotcheese.coop* ⌧ *$2* ☾ *June–Oct., daily 9–5; Nov., Dec., and Feb.–May, Mon.–Sat. 9–4; Jan., Mon.–Sat. 10–4; call ahead to check cheese-making days.*

EAST BURKE

17 mi south of Lake Willoughby.

Once a sleepy village, East Burke is now the Northeast Kingdom's out-
door-activity hub. The Kingdom Trails attract thousands of mountain bikers in summer and fall. In winter, many trails are groomed for cross-
country skiing.

ESSENTIALS

Visitor Information Kingdom Trails Association (⌂ *Box 204, East Burke 05832* 🕾 *802/626–0737* ⊕ *www.kingdomtrails.org*).

SPORTS AND THE OUTDOORS

Contact the Kingdom Trails Association for details and maps.

East Burke Sports (⌧ *439 Rte. 114, East Burke* 🕾 *802/626–3215* ⊕ *www.eastburkesports.com*) rents mountain bikes, kayaks, and skis, and provides guides for cycling, hiking, paddling, skiing, and snowshoeing. **Vil-
lage Sport Shop** (⌧ *511 Broad St., Lyndonville* 🕾 *802/626–8448* ⊕ *www.villagesportshop.com*) rents bikes, canoes, kayaks, paddleboats, roller-
blades, skis, and snowshoes.

SKI AREA About an hour's drive from Montpelier is **Burke Mountain** (⌧ *1 Mountain Rd., East Burke* 🕾 *802/626–3322* ⊕ *www.skiburke.com*). Racers stick to the Training Slope, served by its own poma lift. The other 44 trails and glades are a quiet playground.

WHERE TO EAT AND STAY

$–$$ ✕ **River Garden Café**. You can eat lunch, dinner, or brunch outdoors
AMERICAN on the enclosed porch, on the patio amid perennial gardens, or inside this bright and cheerful café. The excellent fare includes lamb tenderloin, warm artichoke dip, bruschetta, pastas, and fresh fish, and the popular salad dressing is bottled for sale. ⌧ *427 Rte. 114, East*

Catch a show and some social commentary at the Bread and Puppet theater in summer, or visit the museum year-round.

Burke ☎ 802/626–3514 ⊕ *www.rivergardencafe.com* ▭ *AE, D, MC, V* ⊗ *Closed Mon. and Tues. Nov.–Apr.*

$$ 🏨 **Wildflower Inn**. The hilltop views are breathtaking at this rambling, ♻ family-oriented complex of old farm buildings on 570 acres. Guest rooms in the restored Federal-style main house and three other buildings are furnished with reproductions and contemporary furnishings. In summer, supervised day and evening programs engage the kids, allowing parents to explore the many nature trails on their own. You can play with farm animals at the petting barn, go biking, and play tennis and volleyball. In winter sleigh rides, snowshoeing, and cross-country skiing are popular. Junipers ($–$$; closed Sunday) serves comfort food such as meat loaf and lemon herb chicken and offers a kids' menu. **Pros:** mega kid-friendly nature resort; best of the Northeast Kingdom's expansiveness; relaxed. **Cons:** most rooms are simply furnished. ⊠ *2059 Darling Hill Rd., 5 mi west of East Burke, Lyndonville* ☎ *802/626–8310 or 800/627–8310* ⊕ *www.wildflowerinn.com* ⌨ *10 rooms, 13 suites, 1 cottage* ⚒ *In-room: no a/c (some), kitchen (some), no TV. In-hotel: restaurant, tennis court, pool, children's programs (ages infant–17)* ▭ *MC, V* ⊗ *Closed Apr. and Nov.* ⧓ *BP.*

ST. JOHNSBURY

16 mi south of East Burke, 39 mi northeast of Montpelier.

St. Johnsbury, the southern gateway to the Northeast Kingdom, was chartered in 1786. But its identity was established after 1830, when Thaddeus Fairbanks invented the platform scale, a device that revolutionized weighing methods. The Fairbanks family's philanthropic efforts gave the city a strong cultural and architectural imprint. Today St. J, as the locals call it, is the friendly, adventure-sports-happy hub of the Northeast Kingdom.

EXPLORING

Dog Mountain. Artist Stephen Huneck is famous for his cheery folk art sculptures and paintings of dogs. Much more than an art gallery–gift shop, this deeply moving place is complete with a chapel where animal lovers can reflect on their deceased and living pets. Above all, this is a place to bring your dog: there is a swimming pond, an agility course, and hiking trails. ⊠ *143 Parks Rd., off Spaulding Rd.* ☎ *800/449–2580* ⊕ *www.dogmt.com* ⊠ *Free* ⊗ *Daily 10–5.*

Fairbanks Museum and Planetarium. This odd and deeply thrilling little museum displays the eccentric collection of Franklin Fairbanks, who surely had one of the most inquisitive minds in American history. He built this magnificent barrel-vaulted two-level gallery in 1889 just to house the specimens of plants, animals, mounted birds, mammals, reptiles, plants, and collections of folk art and dolls—and a seemingly unending variety of beautifully mounted curios—he had picked up around the world. The museum showcases over 175,000 items, but it's surprisingly easy to feast your eyes on everything here without getting a museum headache. There's also a popular 45-seat planetarium, the state's only public planetarium; as well the Eye on the Sky Weather Gallery, home to live NPR weather broadcasts. ⊠ *1302 Main St.* ☎ *802/748–2372* ⊕ *www.fairbanksmuseum.org* ⊠ *Museum $6, planetarium $5* ⊗ *May–mid-Oct., Mon.–Sat. 9–5, Sun. 1–5; mid-Oct.–Apr., Tues.–Sat. 9–5, Sun. 1–5. Planetarium shows July and Aug., daily at 11 and 1:30; Sept.–June, weekends at 1:30.*

Fodor's Choice
★

St. Johnsbury Athenaeum. With its dark, rich paneling, polished Victorian woodwork, and ornate circular staircases, this building is both the town library (one of the nicest you're likely to ever come across) and one of the oldest art galleries in the country, housing more than 100 original works mainly of the Hudson River school. Albert Bierstadt's enormous (15 feet by 10 feet) *Domes of Yosemite* dominates the beautiful painting gallery. ⊠ *1171 Main St.* ☎ *802/748–8291* ⊕ *www.stjathenaeum. org* ⊠ *Free* ⊗ *Mon. and Wed. 10–8; Tues., Thurs., and Fri. 10–5:30; Sat. 9:30–4.*

Dog Mountain. Artist Stephen Huneck is famous for his cheery folk art sculptures and paintings of dogs. Much more than an art gallery–gift shop, this deeply moving place is complete with a chapel where animal lovers can reflect on their deceased and living pets. Above all, this is a place to bring your dog: there is a swimming pond, an agility course, and hiking trails. ⊠ *143 Parks Rd., off Spaulding Rd.* ☎ *800/449–2580* ⊕ *www.dogmt.com* ⊠ *Free* ⊗ *Daily 10–5.*

OFF THE
BEATEN
PATH

Peacham. Tiny Peacham, 10 mi southwest of St. Johnsbury, is on almost every tour group's list of "must-sees." With views extending to the White Mountains of New Hampshire and a white-steeple church, Peacham is perhaps the most photographed town in New England. The movie adaptation of *Ethan Frome*, starring Liam Neeson, was filmed here. One of the town's gathering spots, the **Peacham Store** (✉ *641 Bayley-Hazen Rd.* ☎ *802/592–3310* ⊕ *www.peacham.net*), sells specialty soups and stews. Next door, the **Peacham Corner Guild** sells local handcrafts.

WHERE TO STAY

$$$ ⚏ **Rabbit Hill Inn**. Few inns in New England have the word-of-mouth
★ buzz that Rabbit Hill seems to earn from satisfied guests. Most of the spacious, elegant rooms have fireplaces, two-person whirlpool tubs, and views of the Connecticut River and New Hampshire's White Mountains. The grounds have 10 acres of walking trails. The intimate candlelit dining room serves a three- or five-course prix-fixe dinner (**$$$$**) featuring contemporary new American and regional dishes such as grilled venison loin with cranberry-juniper orange glaze. Afternoon tea in the parlor, horseshoes, garden strolls—this inn is great for small pleasures. **Pros:** attractive, spacious rooms; lovely grounds; good food. **Cons:** might be too quiet a setting for some. ✉ *Rte. 18, 11 mi south of St. Johnsbury, Lower Waterford* ☎ *802/748–5168 or 800/762–8669* ⊕ *www.rabbithillinn.com* ⇲ *19 rooms* ♿ *In-room: no TV. In-hotel: restaurant, bar, no kids under 14* ▭ *AE, D, MC, V* ☯ *Closed 1st 3 wks in Apr., 1st 2 wks in Nov.* ⑩ *BP, MAP.*

New Hampshire

WORD OF MOUTH

"A tiny bit south of Peterborough, at Rindge, we stopped at [JP Stephens] for a bowl of beef stew soup. We sat by a large picture window with a quintessential view over a little bridge covered with leaves leading to a little white cottage beside a pond reflecting both it and the surrounding autumn leaves. Perfect!"

— mazj

WELCOME TO NEW HAMPSHIRE

TOP REASONS TO GO

★ **The White Mountains:** Great for hiking and skiing, these rugged, dramatic peaks and notches are unforgettable.

★ **Lake Winnipesaukee:** Water parks, arcades, boat cruises, and classic summer camps make for a family fun summer.

★ **Fall Foliage:** Head to the Kancamagus Highway in the fall for one of America's best drives or seek out a lesser-known route that's just as stunning.

★ **Portsmouth:** Less than an hour from Boston, this great American city has coastline allure, colorful Colonial architecture, and the right amount of energy.

★ **Pristine Towns:** Jaffrey Center, Walpole, Tamworth, Center Sandwich, and Jackson are among the most charming tiny villages in New England.

1 The Seacoast. You can find historical sites, hopping bars, beaches, whale-watching, and deep-sea fishing all packed in along New Hampshire's 18 mi of coastline. Hampton Beach is the center of summertime activities, while Portsmouth is a hub of nightlife, dining, and Colonial history.

2 Lakes Region. Throughout central New Hampshire are lakes and more lakes. The largest, Lake Winnipesaukee, has 240 mi of coastline and attracts all sorts of water sports enthusiasts, but there are many more secluded and quiet lakes with enchanting B&Bs where relaxation is the main activity.

3 The White Mountains. Skiing, snowshoeing, and snowboarding in the winter; hiking, biking, and riding scenic railways in the summer—the Whites, as locals call their mountains, have plenty of natural wonders within a stone's throw from the roads, but other spots call for lung-busting hikes. Mount Washington, the tallest mountain in the Northeast, can be conquered by trail, train, or car.

4 Dartmouth-Lake Sunapee. Quiet villages can be found throughout the region. Many of them are barely removed from Colonial times, but some thrive as centers of arts and education and are filled with quaint shops. Hanover, the home of 240-year-old Dartmouth College, retains that true New England college town feel, with ivy-draped buildings and cobblestone walkways. Lake Sunapee is a wonderful place to swim, fish, or enjoy a cruise.

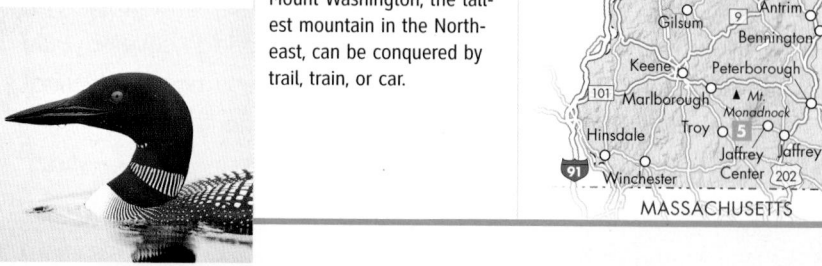

VERMONT

Lisbon
302
91 Woodsville
25
Warren
25A
Wentworth
10
118
Hanover
89 Enfield
Lebanon 4
Plainfield Grafton
Grantham
Georges Mills
11 Newport
Claremont
North Sutton
Goshen
Charlestown
10
91
Hillsboro
Walpole Stoddard
Gilsum 9 Antrim
Bennington
Keene Peterborough
101 Marlborough ▲ Mt. Monadnock
Hinsdale Troy 5 Jaffrey
91 Winchester Jaffrey Center 202

Lake Sunapee

MASSACHUSETTS

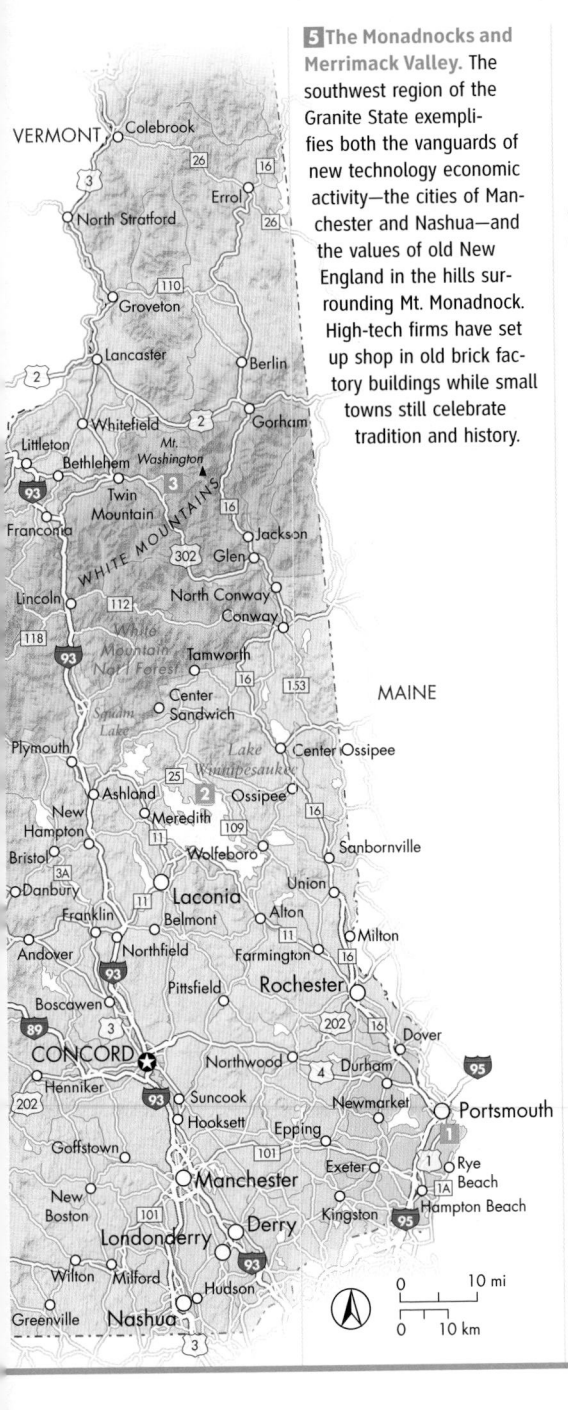

5 **The Monadnocks and Merrimack Valley.** The southwest region of the Granite State exemplifies both the vanguards of new technology economic activity—the cities of Manchester and Nashua—and the values of old New England in the hills surrounding Mt. Monadnock. High-tech firms have set up shop in old brick factory buildings while small towns still celebrate tradition and history.

GETTING ORIENTED

Although New Hampshire has three interstates running through it (I–95, I–93, and I–89), most of its regions are accessible only on smaller roads. From Boston or Portland, Maine, I–95 provides the best access to Portsmouth and the beaches along the coast, though many people like to drive along Route 1A, which parallels the coast. North of Portsmouth, Route 16 leads to the White Mountains, whose precipitous peaks seem to rise out of nowhere, and the lakes region, home to Lake Winnipesaukee. From there I–93 cuts north toward Franconia and Littleton and south into Concord, Manchester, and Nashua. State roads east and north of I–93 lead to Dixville Notch, which casts the first vote in presidential elections, and the Connecticut Lakes. Following the Connecticut River takes you to Hanover, home of Dartmouth College, Claremont, Charleston, Walpole, and Keene. From Concord, travelers head west to reach the Monadnock Region.

8

NEW HAMPSHIRE PLANNER

When to Go

Summer and fall are the best times to visit most of New Hampshire. Winter is a great time to travel to the White Mountains, but most other tourist sites in the state, including the Portsmouth museums and many attractions in the Lakes Region, are closed due to snow and cold weather. In summer, people flock to beaches, mountain trails, and lake boat ramps. In the cities, festivals showcase music, theater, and crafts. Fall brings leaf-peepers, especially to the White Mountains and along the Kancamagus Highway (Route 112). Skiers and snowboarders take to the slopes in winter, when Christmas lights and carnivals brighten the long, dark nights. Spring's unpredictable weather—along with April's mud and late May's black flies—tends to deter visitors. Still, the season has its joys, not the least of which is the appearance of the state flower, the purple lilac, from mid-May to early June as well as colorful rhododendrons.

Getting Here and Around

Air Travel: Manchester Boston Regional Airport is the state's largest and has nonstop service to more than 20 cities. Boston's Logan Airport is within one to three hours of most places in New Hampshire as is Bradley International in Hartford, Connecticut.

Car Travel: New Hampshire is an easy drive north from Boston and serves as a good base for exploring northern New England. Many destinations are near major highways, so getting around by car is a great way to travel. Interstate 93 stretches from Boston to Littleton and on into neighboring Vermont. Interstate 89 will get you from Concord to Hanover and eventually to Burlington, Vermont. To the east, Interstate 95, which is a toll road, passes through southern New Hampshire's coastal area on its way from Massachusetts to Maine. Throughout the state are quiet back country lanes and winding roads that might take a little longer but can make for some of the best parts of the journey.

Speed limits on interstate and limited-access highways are usually 65 mph, except in heavily settled areas, where 55 mph is the norm. On state and U.S. routes, speed limits vary considerably. On any given stretch, the limit may be anywhere from 25 mph to 55 mph, so watch the signs carefully. Right turns on red lights are permitted unless otherwise indicated.

Train Travel: Amtrak (⊕ *www.amtrak.com*) runs its Downeaster service from Boston to Portland, Maine, with stops in Exeter, Durham, and Dover.

Planning Your Time

Some people come to New Hampshire to hike or ski the mountains, fish and sail the lakes, or cycle along the back roads. Others prefer to drive through scenic towns, visiting museums and shops. Although New Hampshire is a small state, roads curve around lakes and mountains, making distances longer than they appear. You can get a taste of the coast, lake, and mountain areas in three to five days; eight days gives you time to make a more complete loop.

About the Restaurants

New Hampshire prides itself on seafood—not just lobster but also salmon pie, steamed mussels, fried clams, and seared tuna. Across the state you'll find country taverns with upscale Continental and American menus, many of them embracing regional ingredients. Alongside a growing number of contemporary eateries are such state traditions as greasy-spoon diners, pizzerias, and pubs that serve hearty comfort fare. Reservations are almost never required, and dress is casual in nearly every eatery.

About the Hotels

In the mid-19th century, wealthy Bostonians retreated to imposing New Hampshire country homes in summer months. Grand hotels were built across the state, especially in the White Mountains, when the area competed with Saratoga Springs, Newport, and Bar Harbor to draw the nation's elite vacationers. Today a handful of these hotel-resorts survive, with their large cooking staffs and tradition of top-notch service. Many of the vacation houses have been converted into inns and B&Bs. The smallest have only a couple of rooms and are typically done in period style. The largest contain 30 or more rooms and suites and have in-room fireplaces and even hot tubs. You'll also find a great many well-kept, often family-owned motor lodges—particularly in the White Mountains and Lakes regions. In the ski areas expect the usual ski condos and lodges. In the Merrimack River valley, as well as along major highways, chain hotels and motels prevail. There are numerous campgrounds across the state, which accommodate RVs as well. The White Mountains provide an excellent base for camping and hiking.

WHAT IT COSTS					
	¢	$	$$	$$$	$$$$
Restaurants	under $10	$10–$16	$17–$24	$25–$35	over $35
Hotels		under $100	$100–$149	$150–$199	$200–$250	over $250

Prices are per person, for a main course at dinner. Prices are for a standard double room during peak season and not including tax or gratuities. Some inns add a 15%–18% service charge.

Outdoor Activities

Hitting the trails by boot and ski, fishing, kayaking and canoeing, biking, or just plain old walking will undoubtedly be a part of your visit.

Biking: Many ski resorts in the White Mountains offer mountain biking opportunities, providing chairlift rides to the top and trails for all skill levels at the bottom. Some of the state's best road biking is along the Kancamagus Highway and around Lake Sunapee.

Hiking: For the more adventurous, hiking the trails in the White Mountains or along the Appalachian Trail, also known as the Long Trail, is their reason for visiting. For those more interested in less arduous treks, there are plenty of day hikes in the White Mountain National Forest and state parks such as Pisgah, the state's largest, in Cheshire County, the Crawford Notch and Franconia Notch state parks in the Whites, and Mt. Monadnock

Skiing: Ski areas abound in New Hampshire—try Mt. Sunapee, Waterville Valley, Loon Mountain, or Canon Mountain. For cross-country skiing, nothing beats Gunstock Mountain Resort, with 32 mi of trails, also open for snowshoeing. Or visit Franconia Village, which has 37 mi of cross-country trails.

8

NEW HAMPSHIRE FALL FOLIAGE DRIVE

With its quaint villages graced with green commons, white town halls, and covered bridges, southwestern New Hampshire is dominated by the imposing rocky summit of Mt. Monadnock and brilliant colors in fall. Kancamagus Highway is another classic foliage route, but for more solitude and less traffic, try this more accessible route that peaks a few weeks later than the state's far north.

The Granite State is the second most forested state in the nation; by Columbus Day, the colors of the leaves of its maple, birch, elm, oak, beech, and ash trees range from green to gold, purple to red, and orange to auburn. Routes 12, 101, 202, and 124 compose a loop around Mt. Monadnock, named for its solitary type of mountain. Start in Keene with a cup of coffee at Prime Roast; for New Hampshire–made products, take a walk on Main Street or detour west on Route 9 to reach **Stonewall Farm** for something more country.

BEST TIME TO GO

Early October is best time to view foliage in southern New Hampshire, but the time can vary by up to four weeks. Call or check online for daily leaf changes (⊕ *www.visitnh. gov* ☎ *800/258–3608*).

PLANNING YOUR TIME

Expect to travel about 55 mi. The journey can take up to a full day if you stop to explore along the way.

From Keene, travel east on Route 101 through Dublin and over Pack Monadnock, a 2,290-foot peak (not to be confused with the 3,165-foot Grand, or Mt. Monadnock). In quaint **Peterborough**, browse the local stores, whose attitude and selection matches the state's independent spirit.

Then turn south on Route 202, stopping at **Colls Farmstand** for some seasonal treats before reaching Jaffrey Village. Just west on 124, in historic Jaffrey Center, be sure to visit the **Meeting House Cemetery** on the common where author Willa Cather is buried. A side trip, 4 mi south on 202, leads to the majestic **Cathedral of the Pines** in Rindge, one of the best places in the region for foliage viewing because the evergreens offset the brilliant shades of red.

Heading west on 124, you can take Dublin Road to the main entrance of **Monadnock State Park** or continue along to the Old Toll Road parking area for one of the most popular routes up the mountain, the **Halfway House Trail**. All of the hiking trails have great views, including the area's many lakes. Continuing on 124 you come to Fitzwilliam and Route 12; turn north back to Keene or, if your legs still have energy left to burn, continue west to Troy for some dancing at **East Hill Farm**.

NEED A BREAK?

Stonewall Farm (✉ 242 *Chesterfield Rd., Keene* ☎ 603/357-7278 ⊕ *www. stonewallfarm.org* ◷ *Grounds dusk–dawn. Learning center and gift shop weekdays 8:30–4:30. Farm stand May–Oct., daily 10–7)* is a nonprofit working farm that teaches visitors about the importance of agriculture. Fall activities for kids include horse-drawn hayrides and a pumpkin patch.
Colls Farmstand (✉ 16 *Colls Farm Rd., Jaffrey* ☎ 603/532-7540 ⊕ *www. collsfarmllc.com* ◷ *Mon.– Sat. 9–6, Sun. 9–2)* carries maple syrup, jams, and other New Hampshire–made products.
East Hill Farm (✉ 460 *Monadnock St., Troy* ☎ 603/242-6495 ⊕ *www. east-hill-farm.com)* is a working farm and B&B that also offers country and square dancing several days of the week.

8

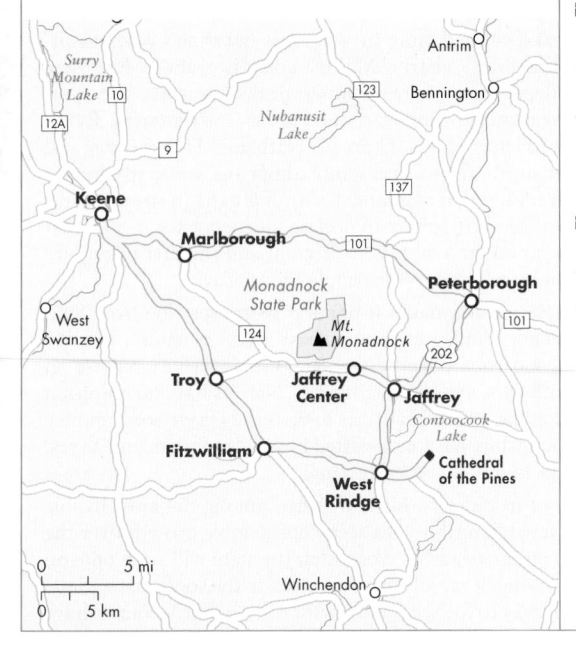

Surry Mountain Lake 10
12A
9
Keene
Marlborough
West Swanzey
Troy
Fitzwilliam
123
Antrim
Bennington
Nubanusit Lake
137
101
Monadnock State Park
124
Mt. Monadnock
Jaffrey Center
Peterborough
101
202
Jaffrey
Contoocook Lake
Cathedral of the Pines
West Rindge
Winchendon

0   5 mi
0   5 km

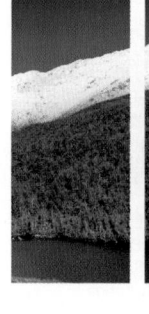

Updated by
Robert Audette

New Hampshire residents have often been called cantankerous, but beneath that crusty exterior is often hospitality and friendliness. The state's motto was coined by New Hampshire native General John Stark, who led the Colonial Army in its hard-fought battle of Bennington, Vermont, in 1777. "Live free or die; death is not the worst of evils," he said, in a letter written 20 years after the battle. The residents of the Granite State have taken "Live Free or Die" to heart, defining themselves by that principle for more than 200 years.

The state is often identified more by what it is not than by what it is. It lacks Vermont's folksy charm. Maine's coast is grander. But New Hampshire's independent spirit, mountain peaks, clear air, and sparkling lakes have attracted trailblazers and artists for centuries. Ralph Waldo Emerson, Henry David Thoreau, Nathaniel Hawthorne, and Louisa May Alcott all visited and wrote about the state, sparking a strong literary tradition that continues today. It also has a strong political history: it was the first colony to declare independence from Great Britain, the first to adopt a state constitution, and the first to require that constitution be referred to the people for approval.

The state's diverse terrain makes it popular with everyone from avid adventurers to young families looking for easy access to nature. You can hike, climb, ski, snowboard, snowshoe, and fish as well as explore on snowmobiles, sailboats, and mountain bikes. Natives have no objection to others enjoying the state's beauty as long as they leave some money behind. New Hampshire has long resisted both sales and income taxes, so tourism brings in much-needed revenue.

With a number of its cities consistently rated among the most livable in the nation, New Hampshire has seen considerable growth over the past decade. Longtime residents worry that the state will soon take on two personalities: one of rapidly growing cities to the southeast and the other of quiet villages to the west and north. Although newcomers have brought change, the independent nature of the people and the state's natural beauty remain constant.

THE SEACOAST

New Hampshire's 18-mi stretch of coastline packs in a wealth of scenery and diversions. The honky-tonk of Hampton Beach gets plenty of attention, good and bad, but first-timers are often surprised by the significant chunk of shoreline that remains pristine—especially through the town of Rye. This section begins in the regional hub, Portsmouth, cuts down the coast to the beaches, branches inland to the prep-school town of Exeter, and runs back up north through Dover, Durham (home of the University of New Hampshire), and Rochester. From here it's a short drive to the Lakes Region.

ESSENTIALS

Visitor Information Seacoast New Hampshire (⊕ www.seacoastnh.com).

PORTSMOUTH

★ *47 mi southeast of Concord; 50 mi southwest of Portland, Maine; 56 mi north of Boston.*

Settled in 1623 as Strawbery Banke, Portsmouth became a prosperous port before the Revolutionary War, and, like similarly wealthy Newport, Rhode Island, it harbored many Tory sympathizers throughout the campaign. Filled with grand residential architecture spanning the 18th through early 20th centuries, this city of 23,000 has many house museums, including the collection of 40-plus buildings that make up the Strawbery Banke Museum. With hip eateries, quirky shops, swank cocktail bars, respected theaters, and jumping live-music venues, this sheltered harbor city is a hot destination. Downtown, especially around elegant Market Square, buzzes with conviviality.

GETTING HERE AND AROUND

Interstate 95 and Route 1 run through Portsmouth. From the west take Route 101 and from the north take Route 16. Amtrak runs through Durham, which is a short drive to the coast. Once in Portsmouth, you can walk about the downtown, though you'll want a car for further attractions. COAST Trolley's downtown loop hits most of the city's historical sights during the summer.

ESSENTIALS

Bus and Trolley COAST Bus (☎ 603/743–5777 ⊕ www.coastbus.org).

Taxi Anchor Taxi (☎ 603/436–1888). **Portsmouth Taxi** (☎ 603/431–6811).

Visitor Information Greater Portsmouth Chamber of Commerce (✉ 500 Market St., Portsmouth ☎ 603/436–3988 ⊕ www.portsmouthchamber.org).

EXPLORING

TOP ATTRACTIONS

John Paul Jones House. The yellow, hip-roof home was a boardinghouse when the Revolutionary War hero lived here while supervising shipbuilding for the Continental Navy. The 1758 structure, now the

8

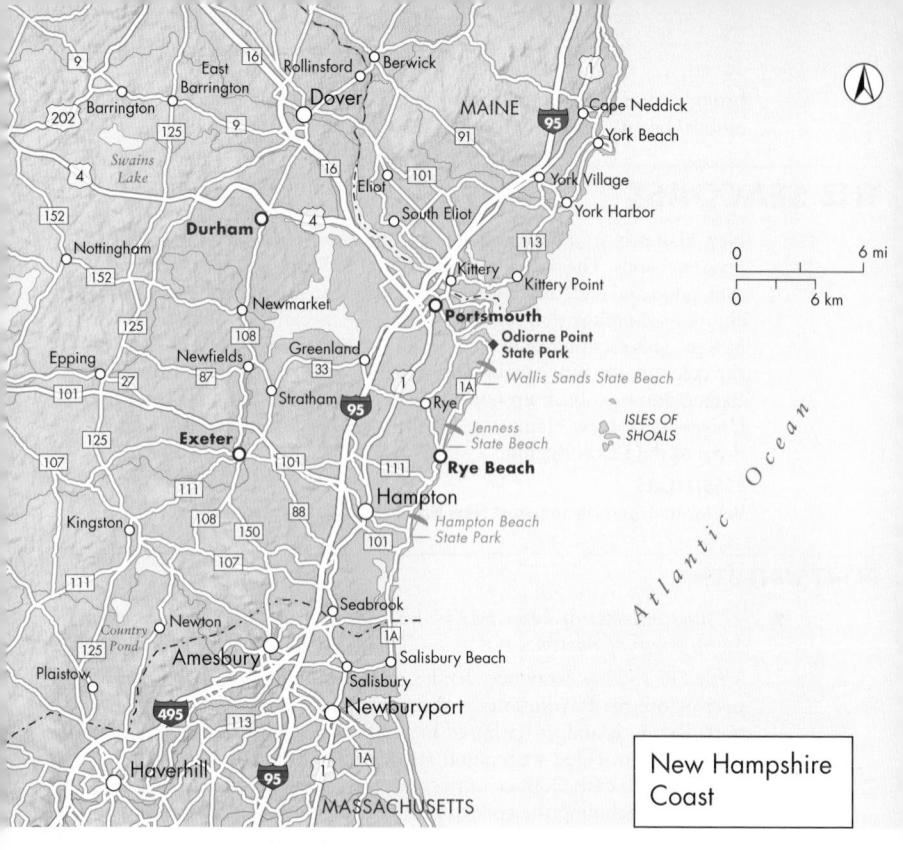

New Hampshire Coast

headquarters of the Portsmouth Historical Society, displays furniture, costumes, glass, guns, portraits, and documents from the late 18th century. ⊠ *43 Middle St.* ☎ *603/436–8420* ⊕ *www.portsmouthhistory.org* 🎫 *$5* ⊙ *June–Oct., Mon.–Sat. 10–4, Sun. noon–4.*

Port of Portsmouth Maritime Museum. The USS *Albacore,* built here in 1953, is docked at this museum in Albacore Park. You can board the prototype submarine, which was a floating laboratory designed to test an innovative hull design, dive brakes, and sonar systems for the Navy. The nearby Memorial Garden and its reflecting pool are dedicated to those who have lost their lives in submarine service. ⊠ *600 Market St.* ☎ *603/436–3680* ⊕ *www.ussalbacore.org* 🎫 *$8* ⊙ *Daily 9:30–4:30.*

Redhook Ale Brewery. Tours here end with a beer tasting, but if you don't have time for the tour, stop in the Cataqua Public House to sample the fresh ales and have a bite to eat (open daily for lunch and dinner). The building is visible from the Spaulding Turnpike. ⊠ *Pease International Tradeport, 35 Corporate Dr.* ☎ *603/430–8600* ⊕ *www.redhook.com* 🎫 *$1* ⊙ *See Web site for hours and tour info.*

★ **Strawbery Banke Museum.** The first English settlers named the area around today's Portsmouth for the wild strawberries along the shores of the Piscataqua River. The name survives in this 10-acre neighborhood, continuously occupied for more than 300 years and now doing

SIGHTSEEING TRAILS AND TROLLEYS

TRAILS

One of the best ways to learn about town history is the guided tour along the **Portsmouth Harbour Trail**, which passes more than 70 points of scenic and historical significance (✉ *Downtown, starting at Market Square* ☎ *603/427–2020 for guided tour* ⊕ *www.seacoastnh.com/harbourtrail* 🎫 *Guided tour $7* ☉ *Highlights tour Thurs.–Sat., Mon. 10:30 AM, Sun. 1:30 PM. Twilight tour Thurs.–Sat. and Mon. 5:30 PM*). You can purchase a tour map ($2.50) at the information kiosk in Market Square, where guided tours start, at the chamber of commerce, and at several house museums. Guided walks are conducted late spring to early fall.

Important sites of African-American history are along the self-guided walk on the **Portsmouth Black Heritage Trail** (✉ *Downtown, starting at Prescott Park wharf* ☎ *603/431–2768* ⊕ *www.pbhtrail.org*). Included are the **New Hampshire Gazette Printing Office**, where skilled slave Primus Fowle operated the paper's printing press for some 50 years beginning in 1756, and the city's 1866 **Election Hall**, outside of which the city's black citizens held annual celebrations of the Emancipation Proclamation.

TROLLEYS

On the **Seacoast Trolley** (✉ *Departs from Market Sq. or from 14 locations en route* ☎ *603/431–6975* ⊕ *www.seacoasttrolley.com* 🎫 *$8*) guides conduct narrated tours of Portsmouth, Rye, and New Castle, with views of the New Hampshire coastline and area beaches. The 17-mi round-trip, which you can hop on and off of at several stops, runs from mid-June through Labor Day, 11 to 3.

Portsmouth is also served by the **Downtown Loop Coast Trolley** (✉ *Departs from Market Sq. every half hour* ☎ *603/743–5777* ⊕ *www.coastbus.org/downtown.html* 🎫 *50¢*), which makes numerous stops. Running from late June to late August, tours are narrated 90-minute round-trips through downtown and around the waterfront.

duty as an outdoor history museum, one of the largest in New England. The compound has 46 buildings dating from 1695 to 1820—some restored and furnished to a particular period, some used for exhibits, and some viewed from the outside only—as well as period gardens. Half the interior of the Drisco House, built in 1795, depicts its use as a dry-goods store in Colonial times, whereas the living room and kitchen are decorated as they were in the 1950s, showing how buildings were adapted over time. The Shapiro House has been restored to reflect the life of the Russian Jewish immigrant family who lived in the home in the early 1900s. Perhaps the most opulent house, done in decadent Victorian style, is the 1860 Goodwin Mansion, former home of Governor Ichabod Goodwin. ✉ *14 Hancock St.* ☎ *603/433–1100* ⊕ *www.strawberybanke.org* 🎫 *$15* ☉ *May 1–Oct. 31, daily 10–5; special December tours.*

WORTH NOTING

Moffatt-Ladd House. The period interior of this 1763 home tells the story of Portsmouth's merchant class through portraits, letters, and furnishings. The Colonial-revival garden includes a horse chestnut tree planted by General William Whipple when he returned home after signing the Declaration of Independence in 1776. ⊠ *154 Market St.* ☎ *603/436–8221* ⊕ *www.moffattladd.org* ✉ *Garden and house tour $6, garden only $2* ⊙ *Mid-June–mid-Oct., Mon.–Sat. 11–5, Sun. 1–5.*

QUICK BITES

Drop by **Annabelle's Natural Ice Cream** (⊠ *49 Ceres St.* ☎ *603/436-3400* ⊕ *www.annabellesicecream.com*) for a dish of Ghirardelli chocolate chip or Almond Joy ice cream. **Breaking New Grounds** (⊠ *14 Market Sq.* ☎ *603/436-9555*) is a big hangout in town and serves coffee, pastries, and gelato.

Wentworth-Coolidge Mansion Historic Site. A National Historic Landmark now part of Little Harbor State Park, this home site was originally the residence of Benning Wentworth, New Hampshire's first royal governor (1753–70). Notable among its period furnishings is the carved pine mantelpiece in the council chamber. Wentworth's imported lilac trees bloom each May. The visitor center stages lectures and exhibits and contains a gallery with changing exhibits. ⊠ *375 Little Harbor Rd., near South Street Cemetery* ☎ *603/436–6607* ⊕ *www.nhstateparks.org/coolidge.html* ✉ *$7* ⊙ *June 17–Sept. 7, Wed.–Sun. 10–4; Sept. 12–Oct. 12, weekends 10–4.*

OFF THE BEATEN PATH

Though it consists of a single square mile of land, the small island of **New Castle**, 3 mi southeast from downtown via Route 1B, was once known as Great Island. The narrow roads and coastal lanes are lined with pre-Revolutionary houses, making for a beautiful drive or stroll. **Wentworth-by-the-Sea** (☎ *603/422-7322* ⊕ *www.wentworth.com*), the last of the state's great seaside resorts, towers over the southern end of New Castle on Route 1B. It was the site of the signing of the Russo-Japanese Treaty in 1905, when Russian and Japanese delegates stayed at the resort and signed an agreement ending the Russo-Japanese War that would win President Theodore Roosevelt a Nobel Peace Prize. The property was vacant for 20 years before it reopened as a luxury resort in 2003. **Also on New Castle, Ft. Constitution** (⊠ *Wentworth St. off Rte. 1B, at the Coast Guard Station* ☎ *603/436–1552* ⊕ *www.nhstateparks.com/fortconstitution.html* ✉ *Free* ⊙ *Parking lot 8:30–dusk in summer, park itself is always open*) was built in 1631 and then rebuilt in 1666 as Ft. William and Mary, a British stronghold overlooking Portsmouth Harbor. The fort earned its fame in 1774, when patriots raided it in one of Revolutionary America's first overtly defiant acts against King George III. The rebels later used the captured munitions against the British at the Battle of Bunker Hill. Panels explain its history. Park at the dock and walk into the Coast Guard installation to the fort.

OFF THE BEATEN PATH

Isles of Shoals. Many of these nine small, rocky islands (eight at high tide) retain the earthy names—Hog and Smuttynose to cite but two—given them by transient 17th-century fishermen. A history of piracy, murder, and ghosts surrounds the archipelago, long populated by

Strawbery Banke Museum includes period gardens and 46 historic buildings.

an independent lot who, according to one writer, hadn't the sense to winter on the mainland. Not all the islands lie within the state's borders: after an ownership dispute, five went to Maine and four to New Hampshire.

Celia Thaxter, a native islander, romanticized these islands with her poetry in *Among the Isles of Shoals* (1873) and celebrated her garden in *An Island Garden* (1894; now reissued with the original color illustrations by Childe Hassam). In the late 19th century, **Appledore Island** became an offshore retreat for Thaxter's coterie of writers, musicians, and artists. The island is now used by the Marine Laboratory of Cornell University. **Star Island** contains a nondenominational conference center and is open for guided tours.

From late May to late October you can cruise of the Isles of Shoals or take a ferry to Star Island with **Isles of Shoals Steamship Company** (✉ *315 Market St.* ☎ *800/441–4620 or 603/431–5500* ⊕ *www.islesofshoals.com*).

SPORTS AND THE OUTDOORS

PARKS   **Great Bay Estuarine Research Reserve.** Just inland from Portsmouth is one of southeastern New Hampshire's most precious assets. Amid its 4,471 acres of tidal waters, mudflats, and about 48 mi of inland shoreline, you can spot blue herons, ospreys, and snowy egrets, particularly during spring and fall migrations. Winter eagles also live here. The best public access is via the **Great Bay Discovery Center** (✉ *89 Depot Rd., off Rte. 33, Greenland* ☎ *603/778–0015* ⊕ *www.greatbay.org* ☉ *May–Sept., Wed.–Sun. 10–4; Oct., weekends 10–4*). The facility has year-round interpretive programs, indoor and outdoor exhibits, a library and

A boat tour of Portsmouth Harbor is popular in warm weather, and a great introduction to the city's maritime heritage.

bookshop, and a 1,700-foot boardwalk as well as other trails through mudflats and upland forest.

Prescott Park. Picnicking is popular at this waterfront park. A large formal garden with fountains is perfect for whiling away an afternoon. The park contains Point of Graves, Portsmouth's oldest burial ground, and two 17th-century warehouses. It's home to the annual **Prescott Park Arts Festival** (⊕ *www.prescottpark.org*). ⊠ *Between Strawbery Banke Museum and the Piscataqua River* ⊕ *603/431–8748.*

Water Country. New Hampshire's largest water park has a river tube ride, large wave pool, white-water rapids, and 12 waterslides. ⊠ *2300 Lafayette Rd.* ☎ *603/427–1112* ⊕ *www.watercountry.com* 🎫 *$36* ⊙ *Mid-June–Labor Day, hours vary.*

BOAT TOURS **Granite State Whale Watch** (⊠ *Box 768, Rye Harbor State Marina, Rte. 1A, Rye* ☎ *603/964–5545 or 800/964–5545* ⊕ *www.granitestatewhalewatch. com* 🎫 *$31*) conducts naturalist-led whale-watching tours aboard the 150-passenger MV *Granite State* out of Rye Harbor State Marina from May to early October and narrated Isles of Shoals and fireworks cruises in July and August.

From May to October, **Portsmouth Harbor Cruises** (⊠ *64 Ceres Str.* ☎ *603/ 436–8084 or 800/776–0915* ⊕ *www.portsmouthharbor.com*) operates tours of Portsmouth Harbor, foliage trips on the Cocheco River, and sunset cruises aboard the MV *Heritage*.

The **Isles of Shoals Steamship Co.** (⊠ *Barker Wharf, 315 Market St.* ☎ *603/ 431–5500 or 800/441–4620* ⊕ *www.islesofshoals.com*) runs a three-hour Isles of Shoals, lighthouses, and Portsmouth Harbor cruise out of Portsmouth aboard the *Thomas Laighton*, a replica of a Victorian steamship, from April through December (twice daily in summer). Lunch and light snacks are available on board, or you can bring your own. There are also fall foliage cruises, narrated sunset cruises visiting five local lighthouses, and special holiday cruises.

One of the questions visitors to Portsmouth ask most frequently is whether they can tour the familiar red tugboats plying the waters of Piscataqua River and Portsmouth Harbor. Unfortunately, the answer is no, but you can get a firsthand look at Portsmouth's working waterfront aboard the **Tug Alley Too** (⊠ *47 Bow St.* ☎ *603/430–9556 or 877/884–2553* ⊕ *www.tugboatalley.com*), a six-passenger replica. The 90-minute tours pass lighthouses, the Portsmouth Naval Shipyard, and Wentworth Marina. Tours are conducted daily from May through October and leave every two hours starting at 10 AM.

Explore the waters, sites, and sea life of the Piscataqua River Basin and the New Hampshire coastline on a guided kayak tour with **Portsmouth Kayak Adventure** (⊠ *185 Wentworth Rd.* ☎ *603/559–1000* ⊕ *www.portsmouth.kayak.com*). Beginners are welcome (instruction is included). Tours are run daily from June through mid-October, at 10 and 2. Sunset tours take off at 6. If you'd rather pedal than drive, stop by **Portsmouth Rent & Ride** (⊠ *958 Sagamore Ave.* ☎ *603/433–6777*) for equipment, maps, and suggested bike routes to Portsmouth sites, area beaches, and attractions. Guided two-hour tours of the seacoast area are also offered.

SHOPPING

Market Square, in the center of town, has gift and clothing boutiques, book and card shops, and exquisite crafts stores. **Nahcotta** (⊠ *110 Congress St.* ☎ *603/433–1705* ⊕ *www.nahcotta.com*) is a wonderful contemporary art gallery and has a well-chosen selection of contemporary housewares, artist-crafted jewelry, and glassware. **Byrne & Carlson** (⊠ *121 State St.* ☎ *888/559–9778* ⊕ *www.byrneandcarlson.com*) produces handmade chocolates in the European tradition. **N. W. Barrett** (⊠ *53 Market St.* ☎ *603/431–4262* ⊕ *www.nwbarrett.com*) specializes in leather, jewelry, pottery, and other arts and crafts. It also sells furniture, including affordable steam-bent oak pieces and one-of-a-kind lamps and rocking chairs.

NIGHTLIFE AND THE ARTS

THE ARTS Seven galleries participate in the Art 'Round Town Reception, a gallery walk that takes place the first Friday of each month. Check out ⊕ *www.artroundtown.org* for more information. Beloved for its acoustics, the 1878 **Music Hall** (⊠ *28 Chestnut St.* ☎ *603/436–2400; 603/436–9900* film line ⊕ *www.themusichall.org*) brings the best touring events to the seacoast—from classical and pop concerts to dance and theater. The hall also hosts art-house film series. The **Prescott Park Arts Festival** (⊠ *105 Marcy St.* ☎ *603/436–2848* ⊕ *www.prescottpark.org*) presents theater, dance, and musical events outdoors from June through August.

BARS **Two Ceres Street** (⊠ *2 Ceres St.* ☎ *603/431–5967* ⊕ *www.twoceresstreet.com*) serves martinis such as the Lumberjack, with Maker's Mark and maple syrup, and the Hot and Dirty, with Grey Goose vodka, peperoncini, and olive juice. If vodka is your thing, you'll do no better than the book-lined English oak bar in **The Library Restaurant** (⊠ *401 State St.* ☎ *603/431–5202* ⊕ *www.libraryrestaurant.com*), which has more than 120 brands of vodka and 96 kinds of martinis.

MUSIC   Discover the local music scene at **The Red Door** (⊠ *107 State St.* ☎ *603/ 373–6827* ⊕ *www.reddoorportsmouth.com*), which has a bar, a live music series, and DJs nightly. Indie music fans shouldn't miss Monday nights at 8 for the acclaimed live acts as part of the Hush Hush Sweet Harlot Music Series. The **Portsmouth Gas Light Co.** (⊠ *64 Market St.* ☎ *603/430–9122* ⊕ *www.portsmouthgaslight.com*), a brick-oven pizzeria and restaurant, hosts local rock bands in its lounge, courtyard, and slick upstairs space. People come from Boston and Portland just to hang out at the **Press Room** (⊠ *77 Daniel St.* ☎ *603/431–5186* ⊕ *www.pressroomnh.com*), which showcases folk, jazz, blues, and bluegrass performers.

WHERE TO EAT

$$
ECLECTIC

✕ **Blue Mermaid Island Grill.** This is a fun, colorful place for great fish, sandwiches, and quesadillas, as well as house-cut yucca chips. Specialties include plantain-encrusted cod topped with grilled mango vinaigrette and served with black-eyed pea–sweet potato hash, a sirloin with wild mushroom glaze, and braised short ribs with an island rub. In summer you can eat on a deck that overlooks the adorable Colonial homes of the Hill neighborhood. Live music includes soul, bluegrass, rock, and even yodeling Wednesday through Saturday. ⊠ *409 The Hill* ☎ *603/427–2583* ⊕ *www.bluemermaid.com* ▭ *AE, D, DC, MC, V.*

¢–$
AMERICAN
☾
★

✕ **Friendly Toast.** The biggest and best breakfast in town (as well as lunch and dinner) is served at this funky, wildly colorful diner-style restaurant loaded with bric-a-brac. Almond Joy cakes (buttermilk pancakes, chocolate chips, coconut, and almonds), raspberry and orange French toast, and hefty omelets are favorites. Also enjoy the homemade breads and muffins. A late-night crowd gathers after the bars close; Friendly Toast is open 24 hours on weekends. ⊠ *121 Congress St.* ☎ *603/430–2154* ⊕ *www.friendlytoast.net* ▭ *AE, D, MC, V.*

$$
SEAFOOD

✕ **Jumpin' Jay's.** A wildly popular downtown spot, this offbeat, dim-lighted eatery has a changing menu of fresh seafood from local fishermen and exotic locales such as New Zealand and Ecuador. Try the steamed Prince Edward Island mussels with a spicy lemongrass and saffron sauce, a Portuguese fisherman's stew, or the haddock piccata (served in a sauce of lemon, white wine, and capers). Singles like to gather at the central bar for dinner and furtive glances. ⊠ *150 Congress St.* ☎ *603/766–3474* ⊕ *www.jumpinjays.com* ▭ *MC, V* ☾ *No lunch.*

$$$
STEAKHOUSE
★

✕ **Library Restaurant.** The Library is a former luxury hotel made over into a country library–themed restaurant. The 12-foot hand-painted dining room ceiling was constructed by the Pullman Car Woodworkers in 1889. Hand-carved Spanish mahogany paneling covers the walls, and the marble bar top used to be the check-in desk. Although the kitchen churns out light dishes such as crab cakes and barbecue shrimp, the mainstays are thick-cut steaks and chops. The crushed-peppercorn–encrusted steak is meat heaven. The English-style pub serves nearly 100 martinis made from vodkas such as Fris, Mezzaluna, Boomsma, and Thor's Hammer.

Sunday brunch is also available. ✉ *401 State St.* ☎ *603/431–5202* ⊕ *www.libraryrestaurant.com* ▭ *AE, D, DC, MC, V.*

$$–$$$
SEAFOOD
★

✕**Pesce Blue**. Sleek, modern, and hip, this restaurant specializes in fresh seafood blended with simple Italian flavors. It's definitely industrial chic with its cinder-block walls, black industrial grid ceiling, wood and chrome accents, and mosaic blue tiles. The menu changes daily but often includes a blackened salmon Caesar salad, fried anchovies, grilled jumbo prawns with sweet garlic custard, and a selection of local catches. There's patio dining in summer. ✉ *103 Congress St.* ☎ *603/430–7766* ⊕ *www.pesceblue.com* ▭ *AE, D, MC, V* ⊙ *Brunch Sat. and Sun.*

WHERE TO STAY

$$$
Fodor'sChoice
★

🛏 **Governor's House**. Among Portsmouth's inns and small hotels, the Governor stands apart. Small, lavish, and quiet, this four-room B&B, a couple of blocks from the historic downtown area, is the perfect place for discerning couples. It was the home of Charles Dale, formerly the governor of New Hampshire, from 1930 to 1964. Frette linens made in Italy, down comforters, in-room Bose CD stereos with 300 CDs to choose from, high-speed Wi-Fi, a guest computer, in-room massages, complimentary wine, DVDs that include the last 60 Academy Award winners for Best Picture, and a deluxe Continental breakfast are among the extras at this 1917 Georgian Colonial. Ask innkeeper Bob Chaffee about the hand-painted bathroom tiles. Coffee, tea, and hot cocoa are available 24 hours a day. **Pros:** great rooms and home; free bicycle rental; great location. **Cons:** 15-minute bike ride to the beach. ✉ *32 Miller Ave.* ☎ *603/427–5140 or 866/427–5140* ⊕ *www.governors-house.com* ⇆ *4 rooms* ⚲ *In-room: no phone, refrigerator, DVD, Wi-Fi. In-hotel: tennis court, bicycles, laundry service, Internet terminal, Wi-Fi hotspot, no kids under 12* ▭ *D, MC, V* ⦿*CP.*

$$

🛏 **Martin Hill Inn**. You may fall in love with this adorable yellow 1815 house surrounded by gardens once you see it from the street. It's a 10- to 15-minute walk from the historic district and the waterfront. The quiet rooms are furnished with antiques and decorated in formal Colonial or country-Victorian styles. The Greenhouse Suite has a solarium. You'll get to know your fellow travelers at breakfast served at 8:30 each morning at a common table. **Pros:** very clean; real antiques. **Cons:** not in historic district; early breakfast. ✉ *404 Islington St.* ☎ *603/436–2287* ⊕ *www.martinhillinn.com* ⇆ *4 rooms, 3 suites* ⚲ *In-room: no phone, no TV, Wi-Fi. In-hotel: Wi-Fi hotspot, no kids under 14* ▭ *MC, V* ⦿*BP.*

$$$
Fodor'sChoice
★

🛏 **Wentworth by the Sea**. What's not to love about this white colossus overlooking the sea on New Castle Island. The closest thing New Hampshire has to a Ritz-Carlton, Wentworth by the Sea has luxurious rooms and modern and opulent amenities including a good spa and an indoor heated pool. The coastline and island location are superb. Built in 1874 as a summer resort for East Coast socialites, wealthy patrons, and former presidents, the property reopened in spring 2003 after being rebuilt. All of the rooms have ocean and harbor views—the huge sunny suites, which have gas fireplaces, occupy a new building right on the water, facing the marina. Enjoy a lavish meal in the formal Wentworth Dining Room ($$$), or try the lighter tavern restaurant Roosevelt's Lounge ($$) and, in summer only, Latitudes ($$), a marina-front

Four of the nine rocky Isles of Shoals belong to New Hampshire, the other five belong to Maine.

restaurant. **Pros:** great spa and restaurants; sense of history; oceanfront perch. **Cons:** not in downtown Portsmouth. ✉ *588 Wentworth Rd., New Castle* ☎ *603/422–7322 or 866/240–6313* ⊕ *www.wentworth. com* ⇨ *127 rooms, 34 suites* ⚥ *In-room: kitchen (some), DVD, Internet. In-hotel: 3 restaurants, room service, bars, tennis courts, pools, gym, spa, laundry service, concierge, Internet terminal, Wi-Fi hotspot, some pets allowed* ▭ *AE, D, DC, MC, V.*

RYE

8 mi south of Portsmouth.

On Route 1A as it winds south through Rye you'll pass a group of late-19th- and early-20th-century mansions known as **Millionaires' Row.** Because of the way the road curves, the drive south along this route is breathtaking. In 1623 the first Europeans established a settlement at Odiorne Point in what is now the largely undeveloped and picturesque town of Rye, making it the birthplace of New Hampshire. Today the area's main draws are a lovely state park, oceanfront beaches, and the views from Route 1A. Strict town laws have prohibited commercial development in Rye, creating a dramatic contrast with its frenetic neighbor Hampton Beach.

SPORTS AND THE OUTDOORS

Odiorne Point State Park. This site encompasses more than 330 acres of protected land, on the site where David Thompson established the first permanent European settlement in what is now New Hampshire. Several nature trails with interpretive panels describe the park's military history, and you can enjoy vistas of the nearby Isles of Shoals. The rocky shore's tidal pools shelter crabs, periwinkles, and sea anemones. Throughout the year, the **Seacoast Science Center** conducts guided walks and interpretive programs and has exhibits on the area's natural history. Displays trace the social history of Odiorne Point back to the Ice Age, and the tidal-pool touch tank and 1,000-gallon Gulf of Maine deepwater aquarium are popular with kids. Day camp is offered for grades K–8 throughout summer and during school vacations. Popular music concerts are held Thursday evenings in summer. ⊠ *570 Ocean Blvd. (Rte. 1A), north of Wallis Sands, Rye Harbor State Beach* ☎ *603/436–8043 science center; 603/436–1552 park* ⊕ *www.seacoastsciencecenter.org* 🖼 *$5 science center, $4 park* ☉ *Science center Apr.–Oct., daily 10–5; Nov.–Mar., Mon.–Sat. 10–5; park daily 8–dusk.*

⟳ **Rye Airfield.** If you've got active kids with you, consider spending the day at this extreme-sports park with an indoor in-line skate and skateboard arena and two BMX tracks. ⊠ *U.S. 1* ☎ *603/964–2800* ⊕ *www. ryeairfield.com.*

BEACHES Good for swimming and sunning, **Jenness State Beach** (⊠ *Route 1A* ☎ *603/436–1552* ⊕ *www.nhstateparks.com/jenness.html*) is a favorite with locals. The facilities include a bathhouse, lifeguards, and metered parking. **Wallis Sands State Beach** (⊠ *Route 1A* ☎ *603/436–9404* ⊕ *www. nhstateparks.com/wallis.html* 🖼 *$15 per car*) is a swimmers' beach with bright white sands, a bathhouse, and plenty of parking.

FISHING For a full- or half-day deep-sea angling charter, try **Atlantic Whale Watch Fleet** (⊠ *Rye Harbor* ☎ *603/964–5220 or 800/942–5364* ⊕ *www. atlanticwhalewatch.com*).

WHERE TO EAT

$$–$$$ ✕ **The Carriage House.** Walk across scenic Ocean Boulevard from Jenness Beach to this elegant cottage eatery that serves innovative dishes
AMERICAN with a Continental flair. Standouts include crab cakes served with a
★ spicy jalapeño sauce, penne *alla vodka* teeming with fresh seafood, creative Madras curries, and steak au poivre. Upstairs is a rough-hewn wood–paneled tavern serving lighter fare. Savor a hot fudge–ice cream croissant for dessert. ⊠ *2263 Ocean Blvd.* ☎ *603/964–8251* ⊕ *www. carriagehouserye.com* ⊟ *AE, MC, V* ☉ *No lunch.*

HAMPTON BEACH

⟳ *8 mi south of Rye.*

Hampton Beach, from Route 27 to where Route 1A crosses the causeway, is an authentic seaside amusement center—the domain of fried-dough stands, loud music, arcade games, palm readers, parasailing, and bronzed bodies. An estimated 150,000 people visit the town and its free public beach on the Fourth of July, and it draws plenty of people until late September, when things close up. The 3-mi boardwalk, where kids play games and see how saltwater taffy is made, looks like a leftover from the 1940s; in fact, the whole community remains remarkably free of modern franchises. Free outdoor concerts are held on many a summer evening, and once a week there's a fireworks display. Each August,

8

locals hold a children's festival, and they celebrate the end of the season with a huge seafood feast on the weekend after Labor Day.

GETTING HERE AND AROUND

Interstate 95 is the fastest way to get to Hampton, but the town is best seen by driving on Route 1A, which follows the coast and offers access to a number of beaches. Route 1 is the quickest way to get around, but be prepared for strip malls and stoplights.

ESSENTIALS

Visitor Information **Hampton Area Chamber of Commerce** (⊠ *1 Lafayette Rd., Hampton* ☎ *603/926–8718* ⊕ *www.hamptonchamber.com*).

SPORTS AND THE OUTDOORS

BEACHES **Hampton Beach State Park** (⊠ *Rte. 1A* ☎ *603/926–3784* ⊕ *www. nhstateparks.com/hampton.html* ☞ *$15 per car May–Oct., free Nov.– Apr.*) at the mouth of the Hampton River, is a quiet stretch of sand on the southwestern edge of town. It has picnic tables, a store (seasonal), and a bathhouse.

FISHING AND WHALE-WATCHING Several companies conduct whale-watching excursions as well as half-day, full-day, and nighttime cruises. Most leave from the Hampton State Pier on Route 1A. **Al Gauron Deep Sea Fishing** (⊠ *State Pier* ☎ *603/926– 2469* ⊕ *www.algauron.com*) maintains a fleet of three boats for whale-watching cruises and fishing charters. **Eastman Fishing Fleet** (⊠ *River St., Seabrook* ☎ *603/474–3461* ⊕ *www.eastmansdocks.com*) offers whale-watching and fishing cruises, with evening and morning charters. **Smith & Gilmore Deep Sea** (⊠ *State Pier* ☎ *603/926–3503 or 877/272–4005* ⊕ *www.smithandgilmore.com*) conducts deep-sea fishing expeditions and whale-watching trips.

NIGHTLIFE

Despite its name, the **Hampton Beach Casino Ballroom** (⊠ *169 Ocean Blvd.* ☎ *603/929–4100* ⊕ *www.casinoballroom.com*) isn't a gambling establishment but a late-19th-century, 2,000-seat performance venue that has hosted everyone from Janis Joplin to Jerry Seinfeld, George Carlin, and B.B. King. Performances are scheduled weekly from April through October.

WHERE TO EAT AND STAY

$$$
AMERICAN
✕ **Ron's Landing at Rocky Bend**. Amid the motels lining Ocean Boulevard is this casually elegant restaurant. Try the sesame-seared ahi tuna with a pineapple, orange, and cucumber salsa for a starter. Good seafood entrées include the oven-roasted salmon with a hoisin glaze, a Frangelico cream sauce, slivered almonds, and sliced apple and the baked haddock stuffed with scallops and lobster and served with lemon-dill butter. From many tables you can enjoy a sweeping Atlantic view. Brunch is served Sundays, October to May. ⊠ *379 Ocean Blvd.* ☎ *603/929–2122* ⊕ *www. ronslanding.com* ═ *AE, D, DC, MC, V* ☺ *Closed Mon. No lunch.*

$
🏨 **Ashworth by the Sea**. You'll be surprised how contemporary this center-of-the-action, across-from-the-beach hotel is, especially after you see the classic old neon sign outside. Most rooms have decks, but request a beachside room for an ocean view; otherwise you'll look out onto the pool or street. The Sand Bar ($), on the roof deck between the

hotel's two buildings, is a great place to watch the town's fireworks each Wednesday and have food and drinks. **Pros:** center-of-town location and across from beach; open all year. **Cons:** breakfast not included; very busy. ✉ *295 Ocean Blvd.* ☎ *603/926–6762 or 800/345–6736 www. ashworthhotel.com* ⤴ *105 rooms* ⚐ *In-room: Wi-Fi. In-hotel: 3 restaurants, room service, pool, laundry service, Wi-Fi hotspot* ▤ *AE, D, DC, MC, V.*

EN ROUTE

At the 400-acre **Applecrest Farm Orchards** you can pick your own apples and berries or buy fresh fruit pies and cookies. Fall brings cider pressing, hayrides, pumpkins, and music on weekends. In winter a cross-country ski trail traverses the orchard. Author John Irving worked here as a teenager, his experiences inspiring the book *The Cider House Rules.* ✉ *133 Rte. 88, Hampton Falls* ☎ *603/926–3721* ⊕ *www.applecrest. com* ⊙ *May–Dec., daily 8–6.*

EXETER

★ *9 mi northwest of Hampton, 52 mi north of Boston, 47 mi southeast of Concord.*

In the center of Exeter, contemporary shops mix well with the esteemed Phillips Exeter Academy, which opened in 1783. During the Revolutionary War, Exeter was the state capital, and it was here amid intense patriotic fervor that the first state constitution and the first Declaration of Independence from Great Britain were put to paper. These days Exeter shares more in appearance and personality with Boston's blue-blooded satellite communities than the rest of New Hampshire—indeed, plenty of locals commute to Beantown. A handful of cheerful cafés and coffeehouses are clustered in the center of town.

GETTING HERE AND AROUND

Amtrak's Downeaster service stops here between Boston and Portland, Maine. On the road, it's 9 mi northwest of Hampton on Route 111. Route 101 is also a good way to get to Exeter from the east or west. The town itself is easy to walk around.

ESSENTIALS

Visitor Information **Exeter Area Chamber of Commerce** (✉ *24 Front St. #101, Exeter* ☎ *603/772–2411* ⊕ *www.exeterarea.org*).

EXPLORING

American Independence Museum. Adjacent to Phillips Exeter Academy in the Ladd-Gilman House, this museum celebrates the birth of the nation. The story unfolds during the course of a guided tour focusing on the Gilman family, who lived in the house during the Revolutionary era. See drafts of the U.S. Constitution and the first Purple Heart as well as letters and documents written by George Washington and the household furnishings of John Taylor Gilman, one of New Hampshire's early governors. In July the museum hosts the American Independence Festival. ✉ *1 Governor's La.* ☎ *603/772–2622* ⊕ *www.independencemuseum. org* ▤ *$5* ⊙ *Mid-May–Oct., Wed.–Sat. 10–4 (last tour at 3).*

Phillips Exeter Academy. Above all else, the town is energized by the faculty and 1,000 high school students of the Phillips Exeter Academy. The

8

grounds of the Academy's 129 buildings, open to the public, resemble an elite Ivy League university campus. The Louis Kahn–designed library contains the largest secondary-school book collection in the world. ✉ *20 Main St.* ☎ *603/772–4311* ⊕ *www.exeter.edu.*

SHOPPING

A Picture's Worth a Thousand Words (✉ *65 Water St.* ☎ *603/779–1991* ⊕ *www.apwatw.com*) stocks antique and contemporary prints, old maps, town histories, and rare books. Prestigious **Exeter Fine Crafts** (✉ *61 Water St.* ☎ *603/778–8282* ⊕ *www.exeterfinecrafts.com*) shows an impressive selection of juried pottery, paintings, jewelry, textiles, glassware, and other fine creations by some of northern New England's top artists.

WHERE TO EAT

¢
AMERICAN
Fodor's Choice
★
✕ **Loaf and Ladle.** There are three components to this extraordinary place: quality, price, and location. The name refers to homemade bread—more than 30 kinds—and soup—more than 100 varieties are offered on a rotating basis. A bowl of soup, which is a full meal, is $6.25, and it's hard to spend more than that here. Choose a chunk of anadama bread, made with cornmeal and molasses, to go with your soup, and take your meal to one of the two decks that hover over the Exeter River. It's simple and homey. ✉ *9 Water St.* ☎ *603/778–8955* ⊕ *www.theloafandladle. com* ≜ *Reservations not accepted* ▤ *AE, D, DC, MC, V.*

$$–$$$
AMERICAN
✕ **Tavern at River's Edge.** A convivial downtown gathering spot on the Exeter River, this downstairs tavern pulls in parents of prep-school kids, University of New Hampshire (UNH) students, and suburban yuppies. It may be informal, but the kitchen turns out surprisingly sophisticated chow. Start with sautéed ragout of portobello and shiitake mushrooms, sun-dried tomatoes, roasted shallots, garlic, and Asiago cheese. Move on to New Zealand rack of lamb with rosemary-port demi-glace and minted risotto. In the bar, lighter fare is served daily 3–10. ✉ *163 Water St.* ☎ *603/772–7393* ⊕ *www.tavernatriversedge.com* ▤ *AE, D, DC, MC, V* ☾ *No lunch.*

WHERE TO STAY

$$
★
🖭 **The Exeter Inn.** This elegant brick Georgian-style inn on the Phillips Exeter Academy campus has been the choice of visiting parents since it opened in the 1930s. After a complete overhaul, completed in the spring of 2008, the place looks better than ever. Rooms have a clubby Ralph Lauren design, with striped wallpaper, 10-inch pillow-top mattresses, and flat-screen TVs. A lounge and restaurant serves three meals a day. **Pros:** contemporary, well-designed, clean rooms; near Academy. **Cons:** not close to town shops; you may not want to be on a prep-school campus. ✉ *90 Front St.* ☎ *603/772–5901 or 800/782–8444* ⊕ *www. theexeterinn.com* ↰*41 rooms, 5 suites* ♨ *In-room: Wi-Fi. In-hotel: restaurant, room service, bar, gym, laundry service, Wi-Fi hotspot* ▤ *AE, D, DC, MC, V.*

$$
★
🖭 **Inn by the Bandstand.** If you're visiting someone at the academy and want to stay in a B&B, we recommend this place in the heart of town. Rooms are individually furnished—to the extreme. Behind one door is floral Victorian. The Lakeheath Lodge room takes a rustic outdoorsy

approach, with exposed ceiling beams and antlers over the brick fireplace and pine boughs strung over the headboard. Pillows are piled in profusion atop Ralph Lauren sheets. Character and comfort are constants in all rooms, including crystal decanters of sherry. It's one of the best B&Bs in the state. Breakfast is served at 8:30 only. **Pros:** perfect location in town; richly furnished rooms. **Cons:** early breakfast. ⊠ *4 Front St.* ☎ *603/772–6352 or 877/239–3837* ⊕ *www.innbythebandstand.com* ⌁ *7 rooms, 2 suites* ⟐ *In-room: refrigerator, Wi-Fi. In-hotel: room service, Wi-Fi hotspot* ⊟ *AE, D, MC, V* ⟐⃝*BP.*

DURHAM

12 mi north of Exeter, 11 mi northwest of Portsmouth.

Settled in 1635 and the home of General John Sullivan, a Revolutionary War hero and three-time New Hampshire governor, Durham was where Sullivan and his band of rebel patriots stored the gunpowder they captured from Ft. William and Mary in New Castle. Easy access to Great Bay via the Oyster River made Durham a maritime hub in the 19th century. Among the lures today are the water, farms that welcome visitors, and the University of New Hampshire (UNH), which occupies much of the town's center.

GETTING HERE AND AROUND
By car, Durham can be reached on Route 108 from the north or south and Route 4 from Portsmouth from the east or Concord from the west. The Downeaster Amtrak train stops here between Boston and Portland, Maine. A good place to begin your exploration of Durham is at the art galleries on the campus of the University of New Hampshire.

8

ESSENTIALS
Visitor Information University of New Hampshire (☎ *603/862–1234* ⊕ *www. unh.edu*).

EXPLORING
Little Bay Buffalo Company. Visitors cannot roam this family-owned estate, but the 50 American bison ranging here are visible from an observation area and the parking lot. The store on the property sells bison-related gifts and top-quality bison meat. ⊠ *50 Langley Rd.* ☎ *603/868–3300* ⊙ *Store Tues.–Sun. 10–5.*

SPORTS AND THE OUTDOORS
You can hike several trails or picnic at 130-acre **Wagon Hill Farm** (⊠ *U.S. 4 across from Emery Farm* ☎ *No phone*), overlooking the Oyster River. The old farm wagon on the top of a hill is one of the most photographed sights in New England. Park next to the farmhouse and follow walking trails to the wagon and through the woods to the picnic area by the water. Sledding and cross-country skiing are winter activities.

SHOPPING
Emery Farm. In the same family for 11 generations, Emery Farm sells fruits and vegetables in summer (including pick-your-own raspberries, strawberries, and blueberries), pumpkins in fall, and Christmas trees in December. The farm shop carries breads, pies, and local crafts. Children can pet the resident goats and sheep and attend the storytelling

New Hampshire Farmers' Markets

Winter squash is in season in New Hampshire from September to October.

One of the best and longest-running farmers' markets is the **Portsmouth Farmers' Market** (⊠ *1 Junkins Ave., Portsmouth* ⊙ *May–early Nov., Sat. 8 AM–1 PM*), which features live music and regional treats, such as maple syrup and artisanal cheeses, in addition to bountiful produce. Don't miss the award-winning breads of the much-beloved bakery **Me & Ollie's** (⊕ *www.meandollies.com*). The market is part of the **Seacoast Growers Association** (⊕ *www.seacoastgrowers.org*), which also has weekly markets in Dover, Durham, Exeter, Hampton, and Kingston.

Just outside Manchester, the **Bedford Farmers' Market** (⊠ *Benedictine Park, Wallace Rd., Bedford* ⊕ *bedfordfarmersmarket.org* ⊙ *June–Oct., Tues. 3–6 PM*) has a particularly rich mix of local growers and food purveyors, selling seasonal jams, pasture-raised lamb and chicken, homemade treats for dogs and cats, goats' milk soaps and balms, and even New Hampshire wines from Jewell Towne Vineyard. **Lebanon Farmers' Market** (⊠ *Colburn ParkPark and Church Sts., Lebanon* ⊕ *www.lebanonfarmersmarket.org* ⊙ *Late May–late Sept., Thurs. 4–7 PM*) draws more than 30 vendors from throughout the northern Connecticut River valley. At the **Exit 20 Farmers' Market at Tanger Outlets** (⊠ *I–93, Exit 20, Tanger Outlet shops* ⊕ *www.tangeroutlet.com* ⊙ *June–Sept., Wed. 3–6 PM*) you'll find folk art and country crafts in addition to food.

Established in 1632, **Tuttle's Red Barn** (⊠ *151 Dover Point Rd., Dover* ☎ *603/742–4313* ⊕ *www.tuttlesredbarn.net*) is the oldest continuously functioning family farm in the country. The garden, farm, and gourmet shops are open daily year-round, and in season this is a terrific stop for sweet corn, tomatoes, berries, and greens.

—Andrew Collins

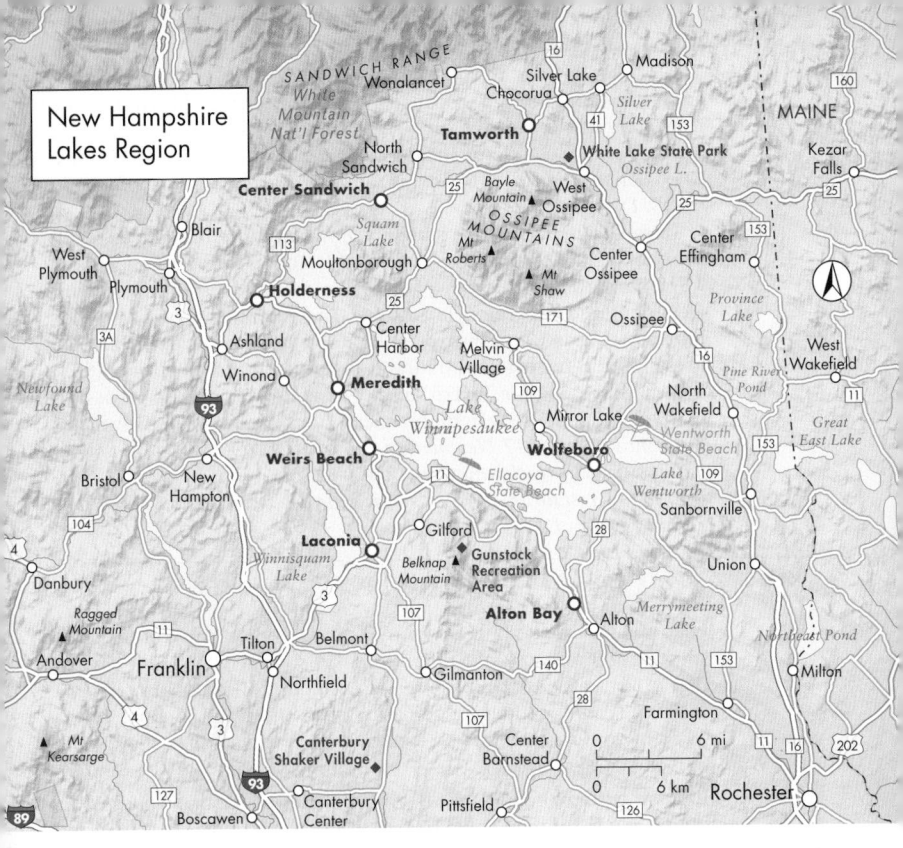

New Hampshire Lakes Region

events that are often held on Tuesday mornings in July and August. ✉ *135 Piscataqua Rd.* ☎ *603/742–8495* ⊕ *www.emeryfarm.com* ⊙ *Late Apr.–Dec., daily 9–6.*

NIGHTLIFE AND THE ARTS

THE ARTS The **Celebrity Series** (☎ *603/862–2290* ⊕ *www.unh.edu/celebrity*) at UNH brings music, theater, and dance to several venues. The **UNH Department of Theater and Dance** (✉ *Paul Creative Arts Center, 30 College Rd.* ☎ *603/862–2290* ⊕ *www.unh.edu/theatre-dance*) produces a variety of shows. UNH's **Whittemore Center Arena** (✉ *128 Main St.* ☎ *603/862–1379* ⊕ *www.whittemorecenter.com*) hosts everything from Boston Pops concerts to home shows, plus college sports.

NIGHTLIFE Students and local yupsters head to the **Stone Church** (✉ *5 Granite St., Newmarket* ☎ *603/659–6321* ⊕ *www.thestonechurch.com*) —in an authentic 1835 former Methodist church—to listen to live rock, jazz, blues, and folk. The restaurant on the premises serves dinner Wednesday through Sunday.

WHERE TO EAT AND STAY

$$ ✕ **ffrost Sawyer Tavern.** That's not a typo, but an attempt to duplicate a
SEAFOOD/ quirk in obsolete spelling (the way capital letters used to be designated)
AMERICAN of an old resident of this hilltop house. The eccentric stone basement
★ tavern has its original beams, from which hang collections of mugs, hats,

and—no way around it—bedpans. There's a terrific old bar. Choose from fine fare like pan-seared sea scallops or pecan-battered fried chicken breast; standards include burgers, pizza, and fish-and-chips. ⊠ *17 Newmarket Rd.* ☎ *603/868–7800* ⊕ *www.threechimneysinn.com* ⊟ *AE, D, MC, V.*

$$$ ⓘ **Three Chimneys Inn**. This stately yellow structure has graced a hill overlooking the Oyster River since 1649. Rooms in the house and the 1795 barn are named after plants from the gardens and filled with Georgian- and Federal-style antiques and reproductions, canopy or four-poster beds with Edwardian drapes, and Oriental rugs; half have fireplaces. There are two restaurants here: a formal dining room ($$$) and the ffrost Sawyer Tavern, quirky as the name implies. **Pros:** intimate inn experience; afternoon social hour. **Cons:** have to walk or drive into town. ⊠ *17 Newmarket Rd.* ☎ *603/868–7800 or 888/399–9777* ⊕ *www.threechimneysinn.com* ↝ *23 rooms* △ *In-room: Wi-Fi. In-hotel: 2 restaurants, room service, bar, Wi-Fi hotspot, some pets allowed* ⊟ *AE, D, MC, V* ⏀ *BP.*

LAKES REGION

Lake Winnipesaukee, a Native American name for "smile of the great spirit," is the largest of the dozens of lakes scattered across the eastern half of central New Hampshire. With about 240 mi of shoreline of inlets and coves, it's the largest in the state. Some claim Winnipesaukee has an island for each day of the year—the total, though impressive, falls short: 274.

In contrast to Winnipesaukee, which bustles all summer long, is the more secluded Squam Lake. Its tranquility is no doubt what attracted the producers of *On Golden Pond*; several scenes of the Academy Award–winning film were shot here. Nearby Lake Wentworth is named for the state's first royal governor, who, in building his country manor here, established North America's first summer resort.

Well-preserved Colonial and 19th-century villages are among the region's many landmarks, and you'll find hiking trails, good antiques shops, and myriad water-oriented activities. This section begins at Wolfeboro and more or less circles Lake Winnipesaukee clockwise, with several side trips.

ESSENTIALS

Visitor Information **Lakes Region Association** (☎ *603/286–8008 or 800/60– LAKES* ⊕ *www.lakesregion.org*).

WOLFEBORO

40 mi northeast of Concord, 49 mi northwest of Portsmouth.

Quietly upscale and decidedly preppy Wolfeboro has been a resort since Royal Governor John Wentworth built his summer home on the shores of the lake in 1768. The town bills itself as the oldest summer resort in the country, and its center, bursting with tony boutiques, fringes Lake Winnipesaukee and sees about a tenfold population increase

With 240 mi of shoreline, Lake Winnipesaukee is so much more than just the town of Wolfeboro.

each summer. In 2007 French president Nicolas Sarkozy summered here. Mitt Romney is another summer resident. The century-old, white clapboard buildings of the Brewster Academy prep school bracket the town's southern end. Wolfeboro marches to a steady, relaxed beat, comfortable for all ages.

GETTING HERE AND AROUND

Enter on the west side of Lake Winnipesaukee on Route 28. Be prepared for lots of traffic in the summertime.

ESSENTIALS

Visitor Information Wolfeboro Chamber of Commerce (☎ 603/569–2200 ⊕ *www.wolfeboro.com/chamber*).

EXPLORING

New Hampshire Boat Museum. Two miles northeast of downtown, this museum celebrates the Lakes Region's boating legacy with displays of vintage Chris-Crafts, Jersey Speed Skiffs, three-point hydroplanes, and other fine watercraft, along with model boats, antique engines, racing photography and trophies, and old-timey signs from marinas. ✉ *397 Center St.* ☎ *603/569–4554* ⊕ *www.nhbm.org* ✉ *$5* ☉ *Memorial Day–Columbus Day, Mon.–Sat. 10–4; Sun. noon–4.*

Wright Museum. Uniforms, vehicles, and other artifacts at this museum illustrate the contributions of those on the home front to the U.S. World War II effort. ✉ *77 Center St.* ☎ *603/569–1212* ⊕ *www.wrightmuseum. org* ✉ *$6* ☉ *May–Oct., Mon.–Sat. 10–4; Sun. noon–4; Feb.–Apr., Sun. noon–4.*

Brewster Academy students and summer folk converge upon groovy little Lydia's (⊠ *33 N. Main St.* ☎ *603/569–3991*) for espresso, sandwiches, homemade soups, bagels, and desserts. Picking up pastries, cookies, freshly baked breads, and other sweets in the **Yum Yum Shop** (⊠ *16 N. Main St.* ☎ *603/569–1919* ⊕ *www.yumyumshop.net*) has been a tradition since 1948—the butter-crunch cookies are highly addictive.

SPORTS AND THE OUTDOORS

BEACH **Wentworth State Beach** (⊠ *Rte. 109* ☎ *603/569–3699* ⊕ *www.nhstateparks. com/wentworthbeach.html* ✎ *$4*) has good swimming, fishing, picnicking areas, ball fields, and a bathhouse.

HIKING A short (¼-mi) hike to the 100-foot post-and-beam **Abenaki Tower**, followed by a more rigorous climb to the top, rewards you with a view of Lake Winnipesaukee and the Ossipee mountain range. The trailhead is on Route 109 in Tuftonboro.

WATER SPORTS Scuba divers can explore The Lady, the 125-foot-long cruise ship that sank in 30 feet of water off Glendale in 1895. **Dive Winnipesaukee Corp** (⊠ *4 N. Main St.* ☎ *603/569–8080* ⊕ *www.divewinnipesaukee.com*) runs charters out to wrecks and offers rentals, repairs, scuba sales, and lessons in waterskiing.

SHOPPING

American Home Gallery (⊠ *49 Center St., Wolfeboro Falls* ☎ *603/569– 8989* ⊕ *www.juliefergus.com*) mixes an amazing array of antiques and housewares in with its architectural elements. You'll find an excellent regional-history section and plenty of children's titles at **Country Bookseller** (⊠ *23A N. Main St.* ☎ *603/569–6030*), Wolfeboro's fine general-interest bookstore. The artisans at **Hampshire Pewter Company** (⊠ *43 Mill St.* ☎ *603/569–4944 or 800/639–7704* ⊕ *www.hampshirepewter.com*) use 16th-century techniques to make pewter tableware and accessories. Come to shop or take a free tour Memorial Day through Columbus Day, weekdays at 10, 11, 1, 2, and 3.

WHERE TO EAT

$ **✕ East of Suez.** In a countrified lodge on the south side of town, this
ASIAN friendly restaurant serves creative pan-Asian cuisine, with an emphasis on Philippine fare, such as *lumpia* (pork-and-shrimp spring rolls with a sweet-and-sour fruit sauce) and *pancit canton* (panfried egg noodles with sautéed shrimp and pork and Asian vegetables with a sweet oyster sauce). You can also sample Thai red curries, Japanese tempura, and Korean-style flank steak. ⊠ *775 S. Main St.* ☎ *603/569–1648* ⊕ *www. eastofsuez.com* ▤ *AE, MC, V* ⊙ *Closed Oct.–mid-May.*

$-$$ **✕ Wolfetrap Grill and Raw Bar.** The seafood at this winsome shanty on
SEAFOOD Lake Winnipesaukee comes from the adjacent fish market. You'll find
★ all your favorites here, including a clam boil for one that includes steamers, corn on the cob, onions, baked potatoes, sweet potatoes, sausage, and a hot dog. The raw bar serves oysters and clams on the half shell. ⊠ *19 Bay St.* ☎ *603/569–1047* ⊕ *www.wolfetrap.com* ▤ *AE, D, MC, V* ⊙ *Closed Labor Day–Memorial Day.*

OUTDOOR OUTFITTERS AND RESOURCES

BIKING

Bike the Whites (☎ 877/854–6535 ⊕ www.bikethewhites.com) organizes bike tours in New Hampshire and Vermont. **New England Hiking Holidays** (☎ 603/356–9696 or 800/869–0949 ⊕ www.nehikingholidays.com) arranges bicycling trips in the region.

HIKING

U.S. Forest Service (☎ 603/528–8721 or 877/444–6777 ⊕ www.fs.fed.us/r9/forests/white_mountain)

or **Appalachian Mountain Club** (☎ 800/372–1758 ⊕ www.outdoors.org). **New England Hiking Holidays** (☎ 603/356–9696 or 800/869–0949 ⊕ www.nehikingholidays.com). **New Hampshire State Parks** (☎ 603/271–3556 ⊕ www.nhstateparks.org).

SKIING

Ski New Hampshire (✉ Box 10, North Woodstock, 03262 ☎ 603/745–9396 or 800/887–5464 ⊕ www.skinh.com).

WHERE TO STAY

$$ ☆ ⊞ **Topsides B & B.** At this stylish retreat, refined rooms convey the allure of a particular region, from coastal France to Martha's Vineyard to British fox-hunting country. Lavish custom bedding, Persian rugs, marble dressers, and fresh flowers lend an eclectic sophistication to this pale-gray clapboard inn that's steps from downtown shops and restaurants. High-speed wireless, homemade bath amenities, and highly personalized attention complete the experience. **Pros:** great location; clean, simple rooms. **Cons:** Continental breakfast only. ✉ *209 S. Main St.* ☎ *603/569–3834* ⊕ *www.topsidesbb.com* ➵ *5 rooms* ☐ *In-room: Wi-Fi. In-hotel: Internet terminal, Wi-Fi hotspot, no kids under 12* ⊟ *D, MC, V* ⦿ *CP.*

$$–$$$ ⊞ **Wolfeboro Inn.** This 1812 inn has a commanding lakefront location ☆ and is a perennial favorite for those visiting Lake Winnipesaukee. Warm yourself up by the fieldstone fireplace in the guest area. Most rooms have nice outside light from big windows, and a number have terraces. The hotel has a tavern with four fireplaces and row upon row of pewter beer mugs, 1,900 in all, hanging from the ceiling. Renovations in 2008 spruced up the rooms in the original building, creating a boutiquey flavor. The owners have taken the same approach to classic old properties in Exeter and Concord. **Pros:** lakefront setting; interesting pub. **Cons:** availability sometimes limited due to weddings and corporate groups. ✉ *90 N. Main St.* ✉ *Box 1270, 03894* ☎ *603/569–3016 or 800/451–2389* ⊕ *www.wolfeboroinn.com* ➵ *41 rooms, 3 suites, 1 apartment* ☐ *In-room: Wi-Fi. In-hotel: restaurant, bar, Internet terminal, Wi-Fi hotspot* ⊟ *AE, D, MC, V* ⦿ *CP.*

ALTON BAY

10 mi southwest of Wolfeboro.

Lake Winnipesaukee's southern shore is alive with visitors from the moment the first flower blooms until the last maple sheds its leaves. Two mountain ridges hold 7 mi of the lake in Alton Bay, which is the name of both the inlet and the town at its tip. Cruise boats dock here, and small planes land year-round on the water and the ice. There's a dance pavilion, along with miniature golf, a public beach, and a Victorian-style bandstand.

EXPLORING

Mt. Major, 5 mi north of Alton Bay on Route 11, has a 2.5-mi trail up a series of challenging cliffs. At the top is a four-sided stone shelter built in 1925, but the reward is the spectacular view of Lake Winnipesaukee.

WHERE TO EAT

$$$$ ✕**Crystal Quail.** This four-table BYOB restaurant with seating for 12,
AMERICAN inside an 18th-century farmhouse, is worth the drive for the sumptuous
★ meals prepared by longtime proprietors Harold and Cynthia Huckaby, who use free-range meats and mostly organic produce and herbs in their cooking. The prix-fixe menu changes daily but might include saffron-garlic soup, a house pâté, mushroom and herb quail, or goose confit with apples and onions. ⊠ *202 Pitman Rd., 12 mi south of Alton Bay, Center Barnstead* ☎ *603/269–4151* ⊕ *www.crystalquail.com* ⊜ *Reservations essential* ▭ *No credit cards* ⌂*BYOB* ⊗ *Closed Mon. and Tues. No lunch.*

WEIRS BEACH

♺ *17 mi northwest of Alton Bay.*

Weirs Beach is Lake Winnipesaukee's center for arcade activity. Anyone who loves souvenir shops, fireworks, waterslides, and hordes of children will feel right at home. Cruise boats also depart from here.

GETTING HERE AND AROUND

Weirs Beach is just north of Laconia and south of Meredith on Route 3.

EXPLORING

♺ **Funspot.** The mothership of Lake Winnipesaukee's several family-oriented amusement parks, Funspot claims to be the largest arcade in the world, but it's much more than just a video-game room. Indeed, you can work your way through a miniature golf course, a driving range, an indoor golf simulator, 20 lanes of bowling, cash bingo, and more than 500 video games. Some outdoor attractions are closed in winter months. ⊠ *Rte. 3, Weirs Beach* ☎ *603/366–4377* ⊕ *www.funspotnh. com* ⊠ *Mid-June–Labor Day, daily 9* AM*–11* PM*; Labor Day–mid-June, Sun.–Thurs. 10–10, Fri. and Sat. 10* AM*–11* PM.

♺ **MS Mount Washington.** This 230-foot boat makes 2½-hour scenic cruises
Fodor's Choice of Lake Winnipesaukee from Weirs Beach from mid-May to late Octo-
★ ber, with stops in Wolfeboro, Alton Bay, Center Harbor, and Meredith (you can board at any of these). Evening cruises include live music and a buffet dinner and have nightly music themes, so check ahead to make sure it's music you like. The same company operates the MV *Sophie C.* ($22), which has been the area's floating post office for more than a century. The boat departs from Weirs Beach with mail and passengers and lets you see areas of the lake not accessible by larger ships. Additionally, you can ride the MV *Doris E.* ($22) on one- and two-hour

scenic cruises of Meredith Bay and the lake islands throughout summer. ☎ *603/366–5531 or 888/843–6686* ⊕ *www.cruisenh.com* ▱ *$25* ⊙ *Day cruises, departures daily every few hours mid-June–late Oct. Special cruises, departure times vary.*

★ **Winnipesaukee Scenic Railroad.** The period cars of this railroad carry you along the lakeshore on one- or two-hour rides; boarding is at Weirs Beach or Meredith. Special trips that include dinner are also available, as are foliage trains in fall and special Santa trains in December. ⊠ *U.S. 3, Weirs Beach* ☎ *603/279–5253 or 603/745–2135 (Lincoln location)* ⊕ *www.hoborr.com* ▱ *$14–$99* ⊙ *July–mid-Sept., daily; Memorial Day–late June and mid-Sept.–mid-Oct., weekends only. Call for hours.*

SPORTS AND THE OUTDOORS

BEACH AND **Ellacoya State Beach** (⊠ *Rte. 11, Gilford* ☎ *603/293–7821* ⊕ *www.*
BOATING *nhstateparks.com/ellacoya.html* ▱ *$4* ⊙ *Mid-May–Labor Day)* covers just 600 feet along the southwestern shore of Lake Winnipesaukee. **Thurston's Marina** (⊠ *18 Endicott St. N* ☎ *603/366–4811* ⊕ *www. thurstonsmarina.com)* rents watercraft such as pontoon boats and powerboats.

GOLF **Pheasant Ridge Golf Club** (⊠ *140 Country Club Rd., Gilford* ☎ *603/524– 7808* ⊕ *www.playgolfne.com)* has an 18-hole layout with great mountain views. Green fees range from $20 to $43.

SKI AREAS **Gunstock Mountain Resort.** High above Lake Winnipesaukee, this all-purpose recreation area, originally a WPA project, dates from 1937. In the past seven years, it has invested $10 million to increase snowmaking, options for beginning skiers, and amenities such as private ski lessons and slopeside dining. Thrill Hill, a snow-tubing park, has four runs, a lift service, and a 12-acre terrain park with jumps, rails, and tabletops for snowboarders looking for a challenge, and a racing program. The ski area has 53 trails, 21 open for night skiing, and 32 mi of cross-country and snowshoeing trails available. In summer enjoy the swimming pool, playground, hiking trails, mountain-bike rentals and trails, a skateboarding and blading park, guided horseback rides, pedal boats, and a campground. ⊠ *719 Cherry Valley Rd., Gilford* ☎ *603/293–4341 or 800/486–7862* ⊕ *www.gunstock.com.*

SHOPPING

Pepi Herrmann Crystal (⊠ *3 Waterford Pl.* ☎ *603/528–1020* ⊕ *www. handcut.com)* sells hand-cut crystal chandeliers and stemware. Take a tour and watch artists at work. Closed Monday.

NIGHTLIFE AND THE ARTS

The **New Hampshire Music Festival** (☎ *603/279–3300* ⊕ *www.nhmf.org)* presents award-winning orchestras from early July to mid-August; concerts occur at the Festival House on Symphony Lane in Center Harbor or at the Silver Cultural Arts Center on Main Street in Plymouth.

8

LACONIA

4 mi west of Gilford, 27 mi north of Concord.

The arrival in Laconia—then called Meredith Bridge—of the railroad in 1848 turned the once-sleepy hamlet into the Lakes Region's chief manufacturing hub. It acts today as the area's supply depot, a perfect role given its accessibility to both Winnisquam and Winnipesaukee lakes as well as Interstate 93. It also draws bikers from around the world for Laconia Motorcycle Week in June.

GETTING HERE AND AROUND

The best way to Laconia is on Route 3 or Route 11. Scenic rides from the south include Route 106 and Route 107.

EXPLORING

Belknap Mill. The oldest unaltered, brick-built textile mill in the United States (1823), Belknap Mill contains a knitting museum devoted to the textile industry and a year-round cultural center that sponsors concerts, workshops, exhibits, and a lecture series. ⊠ *Mill Plaza, 25 Beacon St. E* ☏ *603/524–8813* ⊕ *www.belknapmill.org* ⊡ *Free* ⊙ *Weekdays 9–5.*

OFF THE BEATEN PATH

Canterbury Shaker Village. Shaker furniture and inventions are well regarded, and this National Historic Landmark helps illuminate the world of the people who created them. Established as a religious community in 1792, the village flourished in the 1800s and practiced equality of the sexes and races, common ownership, celibacy, and pacifism. The last member of the community passed away in 1992. Shakers invented such household items as the clothespin and the flat broom and were known for the simplicity and integrity of their designs. Engaging 90-minute tours pass through some of the 694-acre property's more than 25 restored buildings, many of them still with original Shaker furnishings, and crafts demonstrations take place daily. The Shaker Table restaurant ($$–$$$$) serves lunch daily and candlelight dinners Thursday–Sunday (reservations essential); the food blends contemporary and traditional Shaker recipes to delicious effect. A large shop sells fine Shaker reproductions. ⊠ *288 Shaker Rd., 15 mi south of Laconia via Rte. 106, Canterbury* ☏ *603/783–9511 or 866/783–9511* ⊕ *www.shakers.org* ⊡ *$15, good for 2 consecutive days* ⊙ *Mid-May–Oct., daily 10–5; Apr., Nov., and Dec., weekends 10–4.*

SPORTS AND THE OUTDOORS

Bartlett Beach (⊠ *Winnisquam Ave.*) has a playground and picnic area and no fee. **Opechee Park** (⊠ *N. Main St.*) has dressing rooms, a baseball field, tennis courts, and picnic areas.

SHOPPING

The more than 50 stores at the **Tanger Outlet Center** (⊠ *120 Laconia Rd., I–93 Exit 20, Tilton* ☏ *603/286–7880* ⊕ *www.tangeroutlet.com*) include Brooks Brothers, Eddie Bauer, Coach, and Mikasa.

WHERE TO STAY

$$ ▦ **Ferry Point House.** Four miles southwest of Laconia, this home across the street from Lake Winnisquam is a quiet retreat with easy access to a private boat house, rowboat, dock, and a small beach. Built in the 1800s as a summer retreat for the Pillsbury family of baking fame, this

What's your vessel of choice for exploring New Hampshire's Lakes Region: kayak, canoe, powerboat, or sailboat?

red Victorian farmhouse has superb views of the lake. White wicker furniture and hanging baskets of flowers grace the 60-foot veranda, and the gazebo by the water's edge is a pleasant place to lounge and listen for loons. The pretty rooms have Victorian-style wallpaper. **Pros:** affordable, lovely setting; parlor room has decanted sherry. **Cons:** best for relaxed do-it-yourselfers. ⊠ *100 Lower Bay Rd., Sanbornton* ☎ *603/524–0087* ⊕ *www.ferrypointhouse.com* ⊅ *9 rooms, 1 suite* ⌂ *In-room: no phone, no a/c (some), no TV, Wi-Fi. In-hotel: water sports, Wi-Fi hotspot, no kids under 11* ▭ *No credit cards* ❑ *BP.*

MEREDITH

11 mi north of Laconia.

Meredith is a favored spot for water-sports enthusiasts and anglers. Lodgers will love the luxurious beds at the Inns at Mill Falls, which is next to an old factory filled with gift and clothing shops. For a true taste of Meredith, take a walk down Main Street, just one block from busy Route 3, which is dotted with intimate coffee shops, salons and barber shops, family restaurants, redbrick buildings, antiques stores, and a gun shop. You can pick up area information at a kiosk across from the town docks. One caveat: on busy weekends, getting into town from the west can mean sitting in traffic for 30 minutes or more.

ESSENTIALS

Visitor Information Meredith Area Chamber of Commerce (☎ *877/279–6121* ⊕ *www.meredithcc.org*).

SPORTS AND THE OUTDOORS

Red Hill, a hiking trail on Bean Road off Route 25, northeast of Center Harbor and about 7 mi northeast of Meredith, really does turn red in autumn. The reward at the end of the route is a view of Squam Lake and the mountains.

BOATING   Meredith is near the quaint village of Center Harbor, another boating hub that's in the middle of three bays at the northern end of Lake Winnipesaukee. **Meredith Marina** (⊠ *2 Bayshore Dr.* ☎ *603/279–7921* ⊕ *www.meredithmarina.com*) rents powerboats. **Wild Meadow Canoes & Kayaks** (⊠ *6 Whittier Way in Center Harbor* ☎ *603/253–7536 or 800/427–7536* ⊕ *www.wildmeadowcanoes.com*) has canoes and kayaks for rent.

SHOPPING

Annalee's Outlet Store (⊠ *50 Reservoir Rd.* ☎ *603/270–6542* ⊕ *www. annalee.com* ⊙ *Daily 10–6*) sells, at a discount, the seasonal decorations and dolls of the Annalee company, famous for its felt dolls that Annalee Davis Thorndike began making here in 1933. More than 175 dealers operate out of the three-floor **Burlwood Antique Center** (⊠ *194 U.S. 3* ☎ *603/279–6387* ⊕ *www.burlwood-antiques.com*), open May– October. **Keepsake Quilting & Country Pleasures** (⊠ *Senters Market, Rte. 25B, Center Harbor, 5 mi northeast of Meredith* ☎ *603/253–4026 or 800/525–8086* ⊕ *www.keepsakequilting.com*), reputedly America's largest quilt shop, contains 5,000 bolts of fabric, hundreds of quilting books, and countless supplies, as well as handmade quilts.

★   The **League of New Hampshire Craftsmen** (⊠ *279 U.S. 3* ☎ *603/279–7920* ⊕ *www.nhcrafts.org*) sells works by area artisans. It's next to the Inn at Church Landing. **Mill Falls Marketplace** (⊠ *312 Daniel Webster Hwy.* ☎ *800/622–6455* ⊕ *www.millfalls.com*), part of the Inns at Mill Falls, contains shops with clothing, gifts, and books set around the old factory waterfall that runs through it. The **Old Print Barn** (⊠ *343 Winona Rd., New Hampton* ☎ *603/279–6479*) carries rare prints—Currier & Ives, antique botanicals, and more—from around the world.

THE ARTS

The **Summer Theatre in Meredith Village** (⊠ *One Laker La., Interlakes Auditorium, Rte. 25* ☎ *888/245–6374* ⊕ *www.interlakestheatre.com*) presents Broadway musicals during its 10-week season of summer stock.

WHERE TO EAT AND STAY

$$ ✕ **Lakehouse Grille**. With perhaps the best lake views of any restaurant AMERICAN   in the region, this restaurant might be forgiven for ambitious dishes that fall short of being really good. Come here to be near the lake, especially in the convivial bar area, and you'll leave quite happy. The setting is an upscale lodge and is one of the Common Man restaurants. The best dishes are old reliables like steak, ribs, and pizza. Breakfast is served daily. ⊠ *Church Landing, 281 Rte. 3* ☎ *603/279–5221* ⊕ *www. thecman.com* ▭ *AE, D, MC, V.*

$$ ✕ **Mame's**. This 1820s tavern, once the home of the village doctor, now AMERICAN   contains a warren of dining rooms with exposed-brick walls, wooden beams, and wide-plank floors. Expect a wide variety of beef, seafood, and chicken plates, but don't be afraid to order the "Luncheon

View simple yet functional furniture, architecture, and crafts at Canterbury Shaker Village.

Nightmare," pumpernickel-rye bread topped with turkey, ham, broccoli, and bacon and baked in a cheese sauce. You can also find vegetarian dishes, burgers, sandwiches, and wonderful soups and salads on the menu. Save room for the bread pudding with apples and rum sauce. A cozy tavern upstairs features pub food. ⊠ *8 Plymouth St.* ☎ *603/279–4631* ⊕ *www.mamesrestaurant.com* ⊟ *AE, D, MC, V.*

$$$–$$$$
Fodor's Choice
★

🏨 **Inns and Spa at Mill Falls.** There are four separate hotels here: two new properties are on the shore of Lake Winnipesaukee, one is connected to a 19th-century mill (now a lively shopping area) and its roaring falls, and the last has views overlooking the lake. The central Inn at Mill Falls, which adjoins an 18-shop market, has a pool and 54 spacious rooms. The lakefront Inn at Bay Point has 24 rooms—most with balconies, some with fireplaces. The 23 rooms at the lake-view Chase House at Mill Falls all have fireplaces; some have balconies. The star of the show is Church Landing, a dramatic lakefront lodge where most rooms have expansive decks with terrific water views. The Cascade Spa is one of the nicest in the state, with a heated pool that crosses from indoors to outdoors. **Pros:** many lodging choices and prices; lakefront rooms; fun environment. **Cons:** expensive; two buildings are not on lakefront. ⊠ *312 Daniel Webster Hwy. (Rte 3), at Rte. 25* ☎ *603/279–7006 or 800/622–6455* ⊕ *www.millfalls.com* 🛏 *156 rooms, 15 suites* ⚬ *In-room: refrigerator, Wi-Fi. In-hotel: 5 restaurants, room service, 4 bars, pools, gym, spa, water sports, Internet terminal, Wi-Fi hotspot* ⊟ *AE, D, MC, V* ⊚ *CP.*

HOLDERNESS

8 mi southeast of Plymouth; 8 mi northwest of Meredith.

Routes 25B and 25 lead to the prim small town of Holderness, between Squam and Little Squam lakes. *On Golden Pond,* starring Katharine Hepburn and Henry Fonda, was filmed on Squam, whose quiet beauty attracts nature lovers.

EXPLORING

Squam Lakes Natural Science Center. Trails on this 200-acre property include a ¾-mi path that passes black bears, bobcats, otters, mountain lions, and other native wildlife in trailside enclosures. The "Up Close to Animals" series in July and August allows visitors to see a species at an educational presentation in an amphitheater. Children's activities include learning about bugs, watercolor painting of plants and animals, and wilderness survival skills. The boat ride is the best way to tour the lake: naturalists explain its science and describe the animals that make their home here, including fascinating stuff about the loon. ⊠ *Rte. 113* ☎ *603/968–7194* ⊕ *www.nhnature.org* ☒ *Center $13, boat tour $22, combination ticket $32* ☉ *May–Oct., daily 9:30–4:30 (last entry at 3:30).*

Fodor's Choice ★

WHERE TO EAT

$$$

AMERICAN

✕ Manor on Golden Pond Restaurant. Leaded glass panes and wood paneling set the decidedly romantic tone at this wonderful inn's dining rooms on a hill overlooking Squam Lake. The main dining room is in the manor's original billiard room and features woodwork from 1902. Two other dining rooms have very separate looks: one features white linen, fresh flowers, and candlelight; the other is in the style of a Parisian bistro. The menu changes weekly but might include lobster risotto, filet mignon, quail, or monkfish. Breakfast is also served. A fabulous seven-course tasting menu is $75. ⊠ *31 Manor Dr., on the corner of Rte. 3 and Shepard Dr., Holderness* ☎ *603/968–3348* ⊕ *www. manorongoldenpond.com* ☖ *Reservations essential* ⊟ *AE, D, MC, V.*

$–$$

AMERICAN

✕ Walter's Basin. A former bowling alley in the heart of Holderness makes an unlikely but charming setting for meals overlooking Little Squam Lake—local boaters dock right beneath the dining room. Among the specialties on this seafood-intensive menu are crostini with panfried rainbow trout. Burgers and sandwiches are served in the adjoining tavern. ⊠ *15 Main St. (U.S. 3)* ☎ *603/968–4412* ⊟ *D, MC, V* ☉ *Call for winter schedule.*

WHERE TO STAY

$$$$

🏠 Glynn House Inn. Pam, Ingrid, and Glenn Heidenreich operate this upscale 1890s Queen Anne–style Victorian with a turret and wrap-around porch and, next door, a handsome 1920s carriage house. Expect the best in New England B&B comforts: comfy beds, flat-screen TVs, free wine and hors d'oeuvres, and excellent service. All but one of the 13 rooms have fireplaces, and the eight suites all include double-whirlpool tubs. A multicourse breakfast is served in a Victorian dining room. Squam Lake is minutes away. **Pros:** luxurious; well run; social atmosphere. **Cons:** not much to do in town. ⊠ *59 Highland St., Ashland*

☎ 603/968–3775 or 866/686–4362 *www.glynnhouse.com* ⇱ *5 rooms, 8 suites* ⚭ *In-room: Wi-Fi. In-hotel: Wi-Fi hotspot, some pets allowed* ▭ *MC, V* ⚲ *BP.*

$$ ⛬ **Inn on Golden Pond.** Sweet-as-pie Bill and Bonnie Webb run this comfortable and informal B&B at a slight walk from the lake, to which they provide hiking trail maps. In the living room you'll see maps pinned with the origin of guests, who come from all over (especially New York City and Boston). Rooms have hardwood floors, braided rugs, comfortable reading chairs, and country quilt bedspreads and curtains. The homemade jam at breakfast is made from rhubarb grown on the property. **Pros:** friendly innkeepers; very clean rooms and common spaces. **Cons:** 5-minute walk to access lake; not luxurious. ⊠ *Rte. 3* ⬠ *Box 680, Holderness 03245* ☎ *603/968–7269* ⊕ *www.innongoldenpond. com* ⇱ *6 rooms, 2 suites* ⚭ *In-room: no phone, no TV, Wi-Fi. In-hotel: Internet terminal, Wi-Fi hotspot, no kids under 12* ▭ *AE, D, MC, V* ⚲ *BP.*

$$$ ⛬ **The Manor on Golden Pond.** A name like that is a lot to live up to. Luckily, the Manor is the most charming inn in the Lakes Region. Stroll down to the beach for a dip in the lake or to take a canoe for a paddle. The house sits on a slight rise overlooking Squam Lake, and the grounds consist of 15 acres of towering pines and hardwood trees. Relax on the lawn in one of the Adirondack chairs, gazing out at the lake. Back in the stately inn, owners Brian and Mary Ellen Shields ensure comfort. Rooms carry out a British country theme, most with wood-burning fireplaces and more than half with double whirlpool tubs. Canopy beds, vintage blanket chests, and tartan fabrics fill the sumptuous bedchambers. The restaurant ($$$) is terrific, and the Three Cock Pub is endearing. There's a small spa, and afternoon tea is served in the library. **Pros:** wood fireplaces; comfy sitting rooms; great food; welcoming hosts. **Cons:** expensive. ⊠ *U.S. 3 and Shepard Hill Rd.* ☎ *603/968–3348 or 800/545–2141* ⊕ *www.manorongoldenpond.com* ⇱ *22 rooms, 2 suites, 1 cottage* ⚭ *In-room: Wi-Fi. In-hotel: 2 restaurants, room service, bar, tennis court, pool, spa, laundry service, Internet terminal, Wi-Fi hotspot, no kids under 12* ▭ *AE, D, MC, V.*

Fodor'sChoice
★

8

CENTER SANDWICH

★ *12 mi northeast of Holderness on Route 103.*

With Squam Lake to the west and the Sandwich Mountains to the north, Center Sandwich claims one of the prettiest settings of any Lakes Region community. So appealing are the town and its views that John Greenleaf Whittier used the Bearcamp River as the inspiration for his poem "Sunset on the Bearcamp." The town attracts artisans—crafts shops abound among its clutch of charming 18th- and 19th-century buildings.

ESSENTIALS

Visitor Information Squam Lakes Area Chamber of Commerce (☎ 603/968–4494 ⊕ www.squamlakschamber.com). **The Sandwich Historical Society** (☎ 603/284–6269 ⊕ www.sandwichhistorical.org).

EXPLORING

Castle in the Clouds. This wonderful mountaintop estate was built in 1913–14 without nails. The elaborate mansion has 16 rooms, eight bathrooms, and doors made of lead. Owner Thomas Gustave Plant spent $7 million, the bulk of his fortune, on this project and died penniless in 1941. A tour includes the mansion and the Castle Springs spring water facility on this 5,200-acre property overlooking Lake Winnipesaukee; there's also hiking and pony and horseback rides. ⊠ *Rte. 171, Moultonborough* ☎ *603/476–5900* ⊕ *www.castleintheclouds.org* 🕮 *$12* ☉ *Mid-May–Oct. 24, daily 10–4:30.*

The **Loon Center** and **Frederick and Paula Anna Markus Wildlife Sanctuary** is the headquarters of the Loon Preservation Committee, an Audubon Society project. The loon, recognizable for its eerie calls and striking black-and-white coloring, resides on many New Hampshire lakes but is threatened by boat traffic, poor water quality, and habitat loss. Two trails wind through the 200-acre property; vantage points on the Loon Nest Trail overlook the spot resident loons sometimes occupy in late spring and summer. ⊠ *183 Lee's Mills Rd.* ☎ *603/476–5666* ⊕ *www.loon.org* 🕮 *Free* ☉ *Columbus Day–late June, Mon.–Sat. 9–5; July–Columbus Day, daily 9–5.*

SHOPPING

The **Old Country Store and Museum** (⊠ *1011 Whittier Hwy., Moultonborough* ☎ *603/476–5750*) has been selling maple products, cheeses aged on-site, penny candy, and other items since 1781. Much of the equipment still used in the store is antique, and the museum (free) displays old farming and forging tools.

WHERE TO EAT

$$
AMERICAN

✕ **Corner House Inn.** This restaurant, in a converted barn adorned with local arts and crafts, serves classic American fare. Salads with local greens are a house specialty, but also try the chef's lobster-and-mushroom bisque or the shellfish sauté. Lunch and Sunday brunch are served, and on Thursday evenings there's storytelling. ⊠ *22 Main St.* ☎ *603/284–6219* ⊕ *www.cornerhouseinn.com* ▭ *AE, MC, V* ☉ *No lunch mid-June–mid-Oct.*

$$
AMERICAN

✕ **The Woodshed.** Farm implements and antiques hang on the walls of this enchanting 1860 barn. The fare is mostly traditional New England—prime rib, rack of lamb, marinated chicken—but with some surprises, such as Cajun-blackened pork tenderloin. Either way, the exceptionally fresh ingredients are sure to please. ⊠ *128 Lee Rd., Moultonborough* ☎ *603/476–2311* ⊕ *www.thewoodshedrestaurant.com* ▭ *AE, D, DC, MC, V* ☉ *Closed Mon. No lunch.*

TAMWORTH

13 mi east of Center Sandwich, 20 mi southwest of North Conway.

President Grover Cleveland summered in what remains a village of almost unreal quaintness—it's equally photogenic in verdant summer, during the fall foliage season, or under a blanket of winter snow. Cleveland's son, Francis, returned and founded the acclaimed Barnstormers

Theatre in 1931, one of America's first summer theaters and one that continues to this day. Tamworth has a clutch of villages within its borders. At one of them—Chocorua—the view through the birches of Chocorua Lake has been so often photographed that you may experience déjà vu. Rising above the lake is Mount Chocorua (3,490 feet), which has many good hiking trails.

GETTING HERE AND AROUND

The five villages of Tamworth boast six churches, which are worth a half-day's casual drive to admire their white clabbered elegance. Downtown Tamworth is tiny and can be strolled in a few minutes, but you might linger in the hope to meet one of the town's many resident poets and artists.

EXPLORING

Remick Country Doctor Museum and Farm. For 99 years (1894–1993) Dr. Edwin Crafts Remick and his father provided medical services to the Tamworth area and operated a family farm. After the younger Remick died, these two houses were turned into the Remick Country Doctor Museum and Farm. The exhibits focus on the life of a country doctor and on the activities of the still-working farm. You can tour the farm daily, and each season features a special activity such as maple syrup making or building without nails. The second floor of the house has been kept as it was when Remick passed away; it's a great way to see the life of a true Tamworth townsman. ⊠ *58 Cleveland Hill Rd.* ☎ *603/323–7591 or 800/686–6117* ⊕ *www.remickmuseum.org* ⊠ *$3* ☉ *Nov.–June, weekdays 10–4; July–Oct., Mon.–Sat. 10–4.*

SPORTS AND THE OUTDOORS

White Lake State Park. The 72-acre stand of native pitch pine here is a National Natural Landmark. The park has hiking trails, a sandy beach, trout fishing, canoe rentals, two camping areas, a picnic area, and swimming. ⊠ *1632 White Mountain Hwy., Tamworth* ☎ *603/323–7350* ⊕ *www.nhstateparks.com/whitelake.html* ⊠ *$4* ☉ *Late May–mid-June, weekends dawn–dusk; mid-June–early Sept., daily dawn–dusk.*

SHOPPING

The many rooms with themes—Christmas, bridal, and children's among them—at the **Chocorua Dam Ice Cream & Gift Shop** (⊠ *Rte. 16, Chocorua* ☎ *603/323–8745*) contain handcrafted items. Don't forget to try the ice cream, coffee, or tea and scones.

THE ARTS

The **Arts Council of Tamworth** (☎ *603/323–8104* ⊕ *www.artstamworth. org*) produces concerts—soloists, string quartets, revues, children's programs—from September through June and an arts show in late July. **Barnstormers Summer Theatre** (⊠ *Main St.* ☎ *603/323–8661* ⊕ *www. barnstormerstheatre.com*) has dramatic and comedic theater productions year-round.

WHERE TO EAT AND STAY

$ ✕ **Jake's Seafood.** Oars and nautical trappings adorn the wood-paneled

SEAFOOD walls at this stop between West and Center Ossipee, about 8 mi southeast of Tamworth. The kitchen serves some of eastern New Hampshire's freshest and tastiest seafood, notably lobster pie, fried clams, and sea-food casserole; other choices include steak, ribs, and chicken dishes. ✉ *2055 Rte. 16, West Ossipee* ☎ *603/539–2805* ⊕ *www.jakesseafoodco. com* ▭ *MC, V.*

$ ✕ **Yankee Smokehouse.** Need a rib fix? This down-home barbecue joint's

SOUTHERN   logo depicting a happy pig foreshadows the gleeful enthusiasm with

★   which patrons dive into the hefty sandwiches of sliced pork and smoked chicken and immense platters of baby back ribs and smoked sliced beef. Ample sides of slaw, beans, fries, and garlic toast complement the hearty fare. Even Southerners have been known to come away impressed. ✉ *Rtes. 16 and 25, about 5 mi southeast of Tamworth* ☎ *603/539–7427* ⊕ *www.yankeesmokehouse.com* ▭ *MC, V.*

$ ☗ **Lazy Dog Inn.** If you travel with your dog, you've just found your

★   new favorite B&B. What began as a stagecoach stop has been operat-ing as an inn almost continuously since 1845, and when Laura and Steven Sousa took over earlier this decade, they converted the inn to an über–doggie-friendly B&B. The barn became a "doggie lodge" with a number of runs, a canine lullaby CD plays, and the innkeepers care for the dogs during the day while guests explore the Lakes Region or the White Mountains. It's an exceptional niche, but it's not done at the expense of the rooms, which are the cleanest and best furnished within miles. The lodging rate includes dog care. **Pros:** mega–dog friendly; super clean. **Cons:** some rooms share bath; some people don't like dogs. ✉ *201 Rte. 16, Chocorua* ☎ *603/323–8350 or 888/323–8350* ⊕ *www. lazydoginn.com* ⇆ *7 rooms, 3 with bath* ☖ *In-room: no phone, Wi-Fi. In-hotel: gym, Wi-Fi hotspot, some pets allowed, no kids under 14* ▭ *D, MC, V* ⏹ *BP.*

THE WHITE MOUNTAINS

Sailors approaching East Coast harbors frequently mistake the pale peaks of the White Mountains—the highest range in the northeastern United States—for clouds. It was 1642 when explorer Darby Field could no longer contain his curiosity about one mountain in particular. He set off from his Exeter homestead and became the first European to climb what would later be called Mt. Washington. The 6,288-foot peak must have presented Field with formidable obstacles—its summit claims the highest wind velocity in the world ever recorded (231 MPH in 1934) and can see snow every month of the year.

Today an auto road and a cog railway lead to the top of Mt. Wash-ington, and people come by the tens of thousands to hike and climb, photograph the vistas, and ski. The peak is part of the Presidential Range, whose peaks are named after early presidents, and part of the White Mountain National Forest, which has roughly 770,000 acres that extend from northern New Hampshire into southwestern Maine. Among the forest's scenic notches (deep mountain passes) are Pinkham, Kinsman, Franconia, and Crawford. From the notches lead trailheads for short hikes and multi-day adventures, which are also excellent spots for photographing the majestic White Mountains

This section of the guide begins in Waterville Valley, off Interstate 93, and continues to North Woodstock. It then follows portions of the White Mountains Trail, a 100-mi loop designated as a National Scenic and Cultural Byway.

ESSENTIALS

Visitor Information White Mountains Visitors Bureau (✉ *Kancamagus Hwy. [Rte. 112] at I–93, North Woodstock* ☎ *800/346–3687* ⊕ *www.whitemtn.org).* **White Mountain National Forest** (⊕ *www.fs.fed.us/r9/forests/white_mountain).*

WATERVILLE VALLEY

60 mi north of Concord.

The first visitors began arriving in Waterville Valley in 1835. A 10-mi cul-de-sac follows the Mad River and is surrounded by mountains. The valley was first a summer resort and then more of a ski area. Although it's now a year-round getaway, it still has a small-town charm. There are inns, condos, restaurants, shops, conference facilities, a grocery store, and a post office.

GETTING HERE AND AROUND

Depot Camp is a great starting point for hiking, snowshoeing, and cross-country skiing. In town, the Schuss bus has regular stops at the shops in Village Square, the lodges and condos, the Waterville Valley Conference Center, and the ski area. There's enough to do in this small village to keep outdoor enthusiasts busy for several days.

SPORTS AND THE OUTDOORS

The **White Mountain Athletic Club** (✉ *Rte. 49* ☎ *603/236–8303* ⊕ *www. wmacwv.com*) has tennis, racquetball, and squash as well as a 25-meter indoor pool, a jogging track, exercise equipment, whirlpools, saunas, steam rooms, and a games room. The club is free to guests of many area lodgings.

SKI AREA **Waterville Valley.** Former U.S. ski-team star Tom Corcoran designed this family-oriented resort. The lodgings and various amenities are about 1 mi from the slopes, but a shuttle renders a car unnecessary. This ski area has hosted more World Cup races than any other in the East, so most advanced skiers will be challenged. Most of the 52 trails are intermediate: straight down the fall line, wide, and agreeably long. A 7-acre tree-skiing area adds variety. One hundred percent snowmaking coverage ensures good skiing even when nature doesn't cooperate. The Waterville Valley cross-country network, with the ski center in the town square, has 65 mi of trails, about two thirds of which are groomed; the rest are backcountry. ✉ *1 Ski Area Rd.* ✆ *Box 540, 03215* ☎ *603/236– 8311; 603/236–4144 snow conditions; 800/468–2553 lodging* ⊕ *www. waterville.com.*

WHERE TO STAY

$$$$ ⚇ **Black Bear Lodge.** This family-friendly property has one-bedroom suites that sleep up to six and have full kitchens. Each of the 107 units is individually owned and decorated. Children's movies are shown at night in season, and there's bus service to the slopes. Guests can use the White Mountain Athletic Club. There's a small heated pool and hot

tub. **Pros:** affordable. **Cons:** basic in its decor and services. ✉ *3 Village Rd.* ⌂ *Box 357, 03215* ☎ *603/236–4501 or 800/349–2327* ⊕ *www. blackbearlodgenh.com* ⇴ *107 suites* ⚭ *In-room: no a/c (some), kitchen, Wi-Fi. In-hotel: pool, gym, Wi-Fi hotspot* ⊟ *AE, D, MC, V.*

$$$$ 🏨 **Golden Eagle Lodge.** Waterville's premier condominium property—with its steep roof punctuated by dozens of gabled dormers—recalls the grand hotels of an earlier era. Rooms are outfitted with upscale light-wood furniture and well-equipped kitchens; many have views of the surrounding peaks. Guests have access to the White Mountain Athletic Club. **Pros:** most reliable accommodation in town. **Cons:** somewhat bland architecture and decor. ✉ *28 Packard's Rd., Box 495* ☎ *603/236–4600 or 888/703–2453 www.goldeneaglelodge.com* ⇴ *139 condominiums* ⚭ *In-room: kitchen, Wi-Fi (fee). In-hotel: pool, laundry facilities, laundry service, Internet terminal, Wi-Fi hotspot (fee)* ⊟ *AE, D, DC, MC, V.*

$$$$ 🏨 **Snowy Owl Inn.** You're treated to afternoon wine and cheese in the atrium lobby, which has a three-story fieldstone fireplace and prints and watercolors of snowy owls. The fourth-floor bunk-bed lofts are ideal for families; first-floor rooms are suitable for couples seeking a quiet getaway. Four restaurants are within walking distance. Guests have access to the White Mountain Athletic Club. **Pros:** affordable. **Cons:** bland. ✉ *4 Village Rd., Box 407* ☎ *603/236–8383 or 800/766–9969* ⊕ *www.snowyowlinn.com* ⇴ *85 rooms* ⚭ *In-room: kitchen (some), Wi-Fi. In-hotel: pools, gym, Internet terminal, Wi-Fi hotspot* ⊟ *AE, D, DC, MC, V* ⦿ *BP.*

LINCOLN/NORTH WOODSTOCK

64 mi north of Concord

These neighboring towns at the southwestern end of the White Mountains National Forest and one end of the Kancamagus Highway (Route 112) are a lively resort area, especially for Bostonian families who can make an easy day trip straight up Interstate 93 to Exit 32. Festivals, such as the New Hampshire Scottish Highland Games in mid-September, keep Lincoln swarming with people year-round. The town itself is not much of an attraction. Tiny North Woodstock maintains more of a village feel.

GETTING HERE AND AROUND

Lincoln and North Woodstock are places to spend a day shopping in their quaint shops, which are within easy walking distance of each other. It's a pleasant 1-mi stroll between the two towns. On Route 112, which connects the two villages, there is a state visitor center.

ESSENTIALS

Visitor Information Lincoln–Woodstock Chamber of Commerce (☎ *603/745–6621* ⊕ *www.lincolnwoodstock.com*).

EXPLORING

☉ **Clarke's Trading Post.** This old-time amusement park is a kids' favorite and chock full of hokum. It consists of a bear show, half-hour train rides over a 1904 covered bridge, a museum of Americana inside an

The White Mountains

CANADA
QUÉBEC

MAINE

VERMONT

See Detail Above

Detail (inset map)

Highlands
Gorham
Mt. Madison
Mt. Jefferson
Mt. Adams
Mt. Clay
Mt. Washington Auto Road
Cog Railway
Observatory
Mt. Washington State Park
Mount Washington
Pinkham Notch
Fabyan
Crawford Notch
Crawford Notch State Park
WHITE MOUNTAINS
Glen
Story Land
Bartlett
Echo Lake State Park
North Conway

0   4 mi
0   4 km

Main map labels

First Connecticut Lake
Pittsburg
Lake Francis
Beecher Falls
Aziscohos Lake
Wilsons Mills
Colebrook
Dixville Notch
Dixville Notch State Park
Errol
Upton
Umbagog Lake

0   8 mi
0   8 km

Lake Willoughby
North Stratford
West Burke
Maidstone Lake
Milan
Guildhall
Groveton
West Milan
White Mountain Nat'l Forest
Berlin
Lyndonville
Lyndon
Lancaster
Jefferson
Gilead
Concord
Whitefield
Gorham
Danville
Saint Johnsbury
Mount Adams
Littleton
Twin Mountain
Mt. Washington
Pinkham Notch
Wildcat
Barnet
Bethlehem
Fabyan
Franconia
Bretton Woods
North Chatham
Lisbon
Franconia Notch State Park
White Mountain National Forest
Black Mountain
Jackson
Story Land
Wells River
Woodsville
Cannon Mt.
Glen
Echo Lake State Park
Attitash Ski Area
N. Conway
Newbury
Lincoln/North Woodstock
Loon Mountain
Kancamagus Hwy.
Bartlett
Cranmore Moutain
Bradford
White Mountain Nat'l Forest
Lincoln
Bear Notch Rd.
Fryeburg
Conway
Waterville Valley
Waterville Valley
Mount Chocorua
Conway Lake
TO HANOVER
TO CONCORD
SNOWVILLE EAST MADISON

1880s firehouse, a restored gas station filled with antique cars, and a replica of the Old Man of the Mountain that you can climb on. Tour guides tell tall tales and vendors sell popcorn, ice cream, pizza, and snacks. There's also a mammoth gift shop and a penny-candy store. ⊠ *U.S. 3, off I–93 (Exit 33), North Lincoln* ☎ *603/745–8913* ⊕ *www. clarkstradingpost.com* 🖃 *$12* ⊙ *Memorial Day–Columbus Day, daily 9–5 (until 9* PM *Sat. July 5–Aug. 16).*

FUN TOUR

A ride on the **Hobo Railroad** yields scenic views of the Pemigewasset River and the White Mountain National Forest. The narrated excursions take 80 minutes. ⊠ *Kancamagus Hwy. (Rte. 112), Lincoln* ☎ *603/745–2135* ⊕ *www. hoborr.com* 🖃 *$10* ⊙ *Late June–early Sept., daily; May–late June and early Sept.–Oct., weekends; call for schedule.*

SPORTS AND THE OUTDOORS

At **Whale's Tale Waterpark** (⊠ *U.S. 3, off I–93 [Exit 33], North Lincoln* ☎ *603/745–8810* ⊕ *www.whalestalewaterpark.net* 🖃 *$25* ⊙ *Mid-June– Labor Day, daily 10–6*) you can float on an inner tube along a gentle river, careen down one of five waterslides, take a trip in a multipassenger tube, or body-surf in the large wave pool. Whale Harbor and Orca Park Play Island contain water activities for small children and toddlers.

At **Lost River Gorge in Kinsman Notch** (⊠ *Kancamagus Hwy. [Rte. 112], 6 mi west of North Woodstock* ☎ *603/745–8720 or 800/346–3687* ⊕ *www.findlostriver.com* 🖃 *$14 adults, $10 children* ⊙ *See Web site for hours*) parents can enjoy the looks of wonder on their children's faces as they negotiate a wilderness of wooden boardwalks and stairs that snake up and down a granite gorge carved by the waters of the Lost River. Kids can also wiggle through a series of caves such as the Lemon Squeezer and pan for gems and fossils. A cafeteria, gift shop, and garden round out the amenities.

Pemi Valley Excursions (⊠ *Main St., off I–93 [Exit 32], Lincoln* ☎ *603/745– 2744* ⊕ *www.i93.com/pvsr*) offers a variety of recreational and scenic tours throughout the year. It's one of the best snowmobile outfitters in the region, offering one- to two-hour guided tours and half- and full-day snowmobile rentals. Spring through summer, you can ride horseback along wooded trails and along the Pemigewasset River, enjoy horse-drawn-carriage rides, and embark on moose-watching bus tours into the northernmost White Mountains.

SKI AREA

Loon Mountain. Wide, straight, and consistent intermediate trails prevail at Loon, a modern resort on the western edge of the Kancamagus Highway (Route 112) and the Pemigewasset River. Beginner trails and slopes are set apart. In the winter of 2007–08 Loon opened up the South Peak, with new trails and an express quad. The most advanced among the 47 runs are grouped on the North Peak section, with 2,100 feet of vertical skiing, farther from the main mountain. Snowboarders have a half-pipe and their own park; an alpine garden with bumps and jumps provides thrills for skiers. In the base lodge and around the mountain are the usual food-service and lounge facilities. Day and night lift-served snow tubing is on the lower slopes. The touring center at Loon Mountain has 35 mi of cross-country trails, and there's ice-skating on an outdoor rink.

Continued on page 562

A WALK IN THE WOODS

Hiking the Appalachian Trail

By
Melissa Kim

Tucked inside the nation's most densely populated corridor, a simple footpath in the wilderness stretches more than 2,100 miles, from Georgia to Maine. The Appalachian Trail passes through some of New England's most spectacular regions, and daytrippers can experience the area's beauty on a multitude of accessible, rewarding hikes.

Running along the spine of the Appalachian Mountains, the trail was fully blazed in 1937 and designed to connect anyone and everyone with nature. Within a day's drive of two-thirds of the U.S. population, it draws an estimated four million people every year. Through-hikers complete the whole trail in one daunting six-month season, but all ages and abilities can find renewal and perspective here in just a few hours. One-third of the AT passes through New England, and it's safe to say that the farther north you go, the harder the trail gets. New Hampshire and Maine challenge experienced hikers with windy, cold, and isolated peaks.

Top, hiking in New Hampshire's White Mountains. Above, autumn view of Profile Lake, Pemigewasset, NH.

ON THE TRAIL

New England's prime hiking season is in late summer and early fall, when the blaze of foliage viewed from a high peak is unparalleled. Popular trails see high crowds; if you seek solitude, try hiking at sunrise, a peaceful time that's good for wildlife viewing. You'll have to curb your enthusiasm in spring and early summer to avoid mud season in late April and black flies in May and June.

With the right gear, attitude, and preparation, winter can also offer fine opportunities for hiking, snowshoeing, and cross-country skiing.

FOLLOW THE TRAIL

Most hiking trails are marked with blazes, blocks of colored paint on a tree or rock. The AT, and only the AT, is marked by vertical, rectangular 2- by 6-inch white blazes. Two blazes mark route changes; turn in the direction of the top blaze. At higher elevations, you might also see cairns, small piles of rocks carefully placed by trail rangers to show the way when a blaze might be obscured by snow or fog.

Scenic U.S. 302—and the AT—pass through Crawford Notch, a spectacular valley in New Hampshire's White Mountains.

Hikers gather outside Lakes of the Clouds Hut, near the peak of Mount Washington.

TRIP TIPS

WHAT TO WEAR: For clothes, layer with a breathable fabric like polypropylene, starting with a shirt, a fleece, and a wind- or water-resistant shell. Bring gloves, a hat, and a change of socks.

WHAT TO BRING: Carry plenty of water and lightweight high-energy food. Don't forget sunscreen and insect repellent. Bring a map and compass. Just in case: a basic first-aid kit, a flashlight or head-lamp, whistle, multi-tool, and matches.

PLAN AHEAD: In your car, leave a change of clothing, especially dry socks and shoes, as well as extra water and food.

PLAY IT SAFE: Tell someone your hiking plan and take a hiking partner. Carry a rescue card with emergency contact information and allergy details.

BE PREPARED: Plan your route and check the weather forecast in advance.

REMEMBER YOUR BEGINNINGS: Look back at the trail especially at the trail-head and at tricky junctions. If you've got a digital camera, photograph trail maps posted at the trailhead or natural landmarks to help you find your way.

WHERE TO STAY

Day hikers looking to extend the adventure can also make the experience as hard or as soft as they choose. Through-hikers combine camping with overnight stays in primitive shelters, mountain huts, comfortable lodges, and resorts just off the trail.

Rustic cabins and lean-tos provide basic shelter in Maine's Baxter State Park. In Maine and New Hampshire, the Appalachian Mountain Club runs four-season lodges as well as a network of mountain huts for backcountry hikers. A hiker code of camaraderie and conviviality prevails in these huts. Experience a night and you might just find yourself dreaming of a through-hike.

FOR MORE INFORMATION

Appalachian Trail Conservancy
(⊕ www.appalachiantrail.org)

Appalachian National Scenic Trail
(⊕ www.nps.gov/appa)

Appalachian Mountain Club
(⊕ www.outdoors.org)

8

IN FOCUS A WALK IN THE WOODS

ANIMALS ALONG THE TRAIL

❶ Black bear

Black bears are the most common—and smallest—bear in North America. Clever and adaptable, these adroit mammals will eat whatever they can (though they are primarily vegetarian, favoring berries, grasses, roots, blossoms, and nuts). Not naturally aggressive, black bears usually make themselves scarce when they hear hikers. The largest New England populations are in New Hampshire and Maine.

❷ Moose

Spotting a moose in the wild is unforgettable: their massive size and serene gaze are truly humbling. Treasure the moment, then slowly back away. At more than six feet tall, weighing 750 to 1,000 pounds, a moose is not to be trifled with, particularly during rutting and calving seasons (fall and spring, respectively). Dusk and dawn are the best times to spot the iconic animal; you're most likely to see one in Maine, especially in and around ponds.

⚠ Black flies

Especially fierce in May and June, these pesky flies can upset the tranquility of a hike in the woods as they swarm your face and bite your neck. To ward them off, cover any exposed skin and wear light colors. You'll get some relief on a mountain peak; cold weather and high winds also keep them at bay.

❸ Bald eagles

Countless bird species can be seen and heard along the AT, but what could be more exciting than to catch a glimpse of our national bird as it bounces back from near extinction? Now it's not uncommon to see the majestic bald eagle with its tremendous wing span, white head feathers, and curved yellow beak. The white head and tail distinguish the bald from the golden eagle, a bit less rare but just as thrilling to see. Most of New England's bald eagles are in Maine, but they are now present—albeit in small numbers—in all six states.

WILDFLOWERS ALONG THE TRAIL

❹ Mountain laurel

The clusters of pink and white blooms of the mountain laurel look like bursts of fireworks. Up close, each one has the delicate detail of a lady's parasol. Blooms vary in color, from pure white to darker pink, and have different amounts of red markings. Connecticut's state flower, mountain laurel flourishes in rocky woods, blooming in May and June. Look for the shrub in southern New England; it's rare along the Appalachian trail in Vermont and Maine.

❺ Mountain avens

A member of the rose family, these showy yellow flowers abound in New Hampshire's White Mountains. You can't miss the large buttercup-like blooms on long green stems when they are in bloom from June through August. So common here, yet extremely rare: the only other place in the whole world where you can find mountain avens is on an island off the coast of Nova Scotia.

❻ Painted trillium

You might smell a trillium before you see it; these flowers have an unpleasant odor that may attract the flies that pollinate it. To identify this impressive flower, look for sets of three: three large pointed blue-green leaves, three sepals (small leaves beneath the petals), and three white petals with a brilliant magenta center. It can take four or five years for a trillium to produce one flower, which blooms in May and June in wet woodlands.

❼ Pink lady slippers

These delicate orchids can grow from 6 to 15 inches high and favor specific wet wooded areas in dappled sunlight. The slender stalk rises from a pair of green leaves, then bends a graceful neck to suspend the paper-thin pale pink closed flower. The slow-growing plant needs help from fungus and bees to survive and can live to be 20 years old. New Hampshire's state wildflower, the pink lady slipper blooms in June throughout New England.

● = Somewhat Common ● = Rare

8

IN FOCUS A WALK IN THE WOODS

CHOOSE YOUR DAY HIKE

MAINE

GULF HAGAS, Greenville
Difficult, 8-plus mi round-trip, 6–7 hours

This National Natural Landmark in the North Maine Woods is a spectacular sight for the adventurous day hiker. It involves a long drive on logging roads east from Greenville (see Inland Maine section) to a remote spot and a slippery, sometimes treacherous 8-mile hike around the rim of what's been dubbed Maine's Grand Canyon. Swimming in one of the sparkling pools under a 30-foot-high waterfall and admiring the views of cliffs, cascades, gorges, and chasms in this slate canyon, otherwise unthinkable in New England, will take your breath away.

TABLE ROCK, Bethel
Medium, 2.4 mi round-trip, 2 hours

Maine's Mahoosuc Range is thought to be one of the most difficult stretches of the entire AT, but north of Bethel at Grafton Notch State Park, day hikes range from easy walks in to cascading waterfalls to strenuous climbs up Old Speck's craggy peak. The Table Rock trail offers interesting sights—great views of the notch from the immense slab of granite that gives this trail its name, as well as one of the state's largest system of slab caves—narrow with tall openings unlike underground caves.

NEW HAMPSHIRE

ZEALAND TRAIL, Berlin
Easy, 5.6 mi round-trip, 3.5–4 hours

New Hampshire's Presidential range gets so much attention and traffic that sometimes the equally spectacular Pemigewasset Wilderness, just to its west, gets overlooked. Follow State Route 302 to the trailhead on Zealand Rd. near Bretton Woods. For an easy day hike to one of the Appalachian Mountain Club's excellent overnight huts, take the mostly flat Zealand Trail over bridges and past a beaver swamp to Zealand Pond. The last tenth of a mile is a steep ascent to the mountain retreat, where you might spot an AT through-hiker taking a well-deserved rest. (Most north-bound through-hikers reach this section around July or August.) In winter, you can get here by a lovely cross-country ski trip.

TRAIL NAMES

For through-hikers, doing the AT can be a life-altering experience. One of trail's most respected traditions is the taking of an alter ego: a trail name. Lightning Bolt: fast hiker. Pine Knot: tough as one. Bluebearee: because a bear got all her food on her very first night on the trail.

Mt Katahdin 5,267ft
(2,176mi to Georgia)
Medv
Millinoc
BAXTER STATE PARK
Chesuncook Lake
11
Gulf Hagc
White Cap M 3,644ft
Chairback Mtn
Moosehead Lake
Barren Mtn 2,660ft
Greenville
6 15
Seb Lal
Monson
201
Bald Mtn 2,630ft
Kennebec
Caratunk
River
0   15 mi
0   15 km
Flagstaff Lake
Bigelow Preserve
16
Mt Bigelow 4,150ft
27
Stratton
Kingfield
Sugarloaf Mtn
Crocker Mtn 4,168ft
Spaulding Mtn 3,988ft
27
16
Saddleback Mtn 4,116ft
Rangeley
Rangeley Lake
4
17
Bemis Mtn 2,923ft
16
Elephant Mtn 3,774ft
Old Blue Mtn 3,600ft
MAINE
NEW HAMPSHIRE
Wyman Mtn 2,945ft
Andover
Speck Mtn
Baldpate Mtn 3,812ft
2c
Grafton Notch State Park
Table Rock
Goose Eye Mtn 3,794ft
Berlin
Carter Dome
WHITE MOUNTAIN NTL'L FOREST
3
Gorham
Pinkham Nc
Mount Washington St. Park
Crawford Notch St. Park
Mt Washington 6,288ft
2
Moore Reservoir
302
Con
WHITE MOUNTA
NATIONAL F
93
Mt Lafayette 5,249ft
Zealand Trail
North Woodst
Franconia Notch State Park
Kinsman Notch
10
Mt Moosilauke 4,830ft
91
Glencliff

VERMONT

HARMON HILL, Bennington
Medium to difficult, 3.6 mi round-trip, 3–4 hours

This rugged hike in the Green Mountains goes south along the AT where it coincides with the Long Trail, Vermont's century-old "footpath in the wilderness." From the trailhead on Route 9 just east of Bennington, the first half mile or so is strenuous, with some rock and log staircases and hairpins. The payback is the sweeping view from the top; you'll see Mount Anthony, Bennington and its iconic war monument, and the rolling green hills of the Taconics to the west.

STRATTON MOUNTAIN, Stratton
Difficult, 6.6 mi round-trip, 5–6 hours

A steep and steady climb from the trailhead on Kelly Stand Rd. (between West Wardsboro and Arlington) up the 3,936-foot-high Stratton Mountain follows the AT and Long Trail through mixed forests. It's said that this peak is where Benton MacKaye conceived of the idea for the Appalachian Trail in 1921. An observation tower at the summit gives you a great 360-degree view of the Green Mountains. From July to October, you can park at Stratton resort and ride the gondola up (or down) and follow the .75-mi Fire Tower Trail to the southern true peak.

MASSACHUSETTS

MOUNT GREYLOCK, North Adams
Easy to difficult, 2 mi round-trip, less than 1 hour

There are many ways to experience Massachusetts's highest peak. From North Adams, follow Route 2 to the Notch Rd. trailheads. For a warm-up, try the Rounds Rock trail (Easy, 0.7 mi) for some spectacular views. Or drive up the 8-mi-long summit road and hike down the Robinson's Point trail (Difficult, 0.8 mi) for the best view of the Hopper, a glacial cirque that's home to an old-growth red spruce forest. At the summit, the impressive **Bascom Lodge**, built in the 1930s by the Civilian Conservation Corps, provides delicious meals and overnight stays (⊕ www.bascomlodge.net).

CONNECTICUT

LION'S HEAD, Salisbury
Medium, 4.6 mi round-trip, 3.5–4 hours

The AT's 52 miles in Connecticut take hikers up some modest mountains, including Lion's Head in Salisbury. From the trailhead on State Route 41, follow the white blazes of the AT for two easy miles, then take the blue-blazed Lion's Head Trail for a short, steep push over open ledges to the 1,738-foot summit with its commanding views of pastoral southern New England. Try this in summer when the mountain laurels—Connecticut's state flower—are in bloom.

EXPERIENCE MOUNT WASHINGTON

Looking at Mt. Washington from Mt. Bond in the Pemigewasset Wilderness Area, New Hampshire.

Mount Washington is the Northeast's peak of superlatives: worst weather in the world, highest spot in the northeast, windiest place on Earth. It snows in the summer, there are avalanches in winter, and it's foggy 60 percent of the time. Strong 35-mile-per-hour winds are the average, and extreme winds of 100 miles per hour with higher gusts blow year-round. Here, you can literally get blown away.

Explorers, scientists, artists, and botanists have been coming to the mountain for hundreds of years, drawn by its unique geologic features, unusual plants, and exceptional climate.

WHY SO WINDY? The 6,288-foot-high treeless peak is the highest point for miles around, so nothing dampens the force of the wind. Also, the sharp vertical rise causes wind to accelerate. Dramatic changes in air pressure also cause strong, high winds. Add to that the fact that three major storm tracks converge here, and you've got a mountain that has claimed more than 135 lives in the past 150 years.

GOING UP THE MOUNTAIN

An ascent up Mount Washington is for experienced hikers who are prepared for severe, unpredictable weather. Even in summer, cold, wet, foggy, windy conditions prevail. The most popular route to the top is on the eastern face up the Tuckerman Ravine Trail. But countless trails offer plenty of moderate day hikes, like the Alpine Garden Trail, as an alternative to a summit attempt. Start at the Pinkham Notch Visitor Center on Route 16 to review your options.

BACKPACKING ON THE MOUNTAIN

Lakes of the Clouds Hut perches 5,050 feet up the southern shoulder, providing bunkrooms and meals in summer; reservations are required. On the eastern face, the **Hermit Lake Shelter Area** has shelters and tent platforms; to camp here you'll need a first-come, first-served permit from the Visitors Center. Both are operated by the **AMC** (☎ 603/466-2727; ⊕ www.outdoors.org).

NON-HIKING ALTERNATIVES

In the summer, the **Auto Road** (☎ 603/466-3988 ⊕ www.mountwashington autoroad.com) and the **Cog Railway** (☎ 800/922-8825 ⊕ www.thecog.com) present alternate ways up the mountain; both give you a real sense of the mountain's grandeur. In winter, a **Snow-Coach** (☎ 603/466-2333 ⊕ www.greatglentrails.com) hauls visitors 4.5 miles up the Auto Road with an option to cross-country ski, telemark, or snowshoe back down.

⊠*Kancamagus Hwy. (Rte. 112), Lincoln* ☎ *603/745–8111; 603/745–8100 snow conditions; 800/227–4191 lodging* ⊕ *www.loonmtn.com.*

NIGHTLIFE

Skiers head to the **Black Diamond Lounge** (⊠ *60 Loon Mountain Rd.* ☎ *603/745–2244* ⊕ *www.mtnclub.com*) in the Mountain Club at the Loon Mountain resort. The **Olde Timbermill** (⊠ *Mill at Loon Mountain, 167 Main St.* ☎ *603/745–3603*) has live dance music on weekends. The **North Country Center for the Arts** (*Papermill Theatre* ⊠ *25 Mountain Brook Cir., Kancamagus Hwy. [Rte. 112], Lincoln* ☎ *603/745–6032; 603/745–2141 box office* ⊕ *www.papermilltheatre.org*) presents theater for children and adults and art exhibitions in July and August. The draws at the **Thunderbird Lounge** (⊠ *Indian Head Resort, 664 U.S. 3, North Lincoln* ☎ *603/745–8000*) are nightly entertainment year-round and a large dance floor.

WHERE TO EAT AND STAY

$ ✕ **Woodstock Inn, Station & Brewery.** If you like eateries loaded with char-
AMERICAN   acter, don't miss these two restaurants inside the former Lincoln Railroad Station of the late 1800s. Down the hall is a great brewery and pub that serves 13 handcrafted brews and is decorated with old maps and memorabilia. You come here as much to mix with locals and enjoy the vibe as to eat. The menu is standard: pizza, quesadillas, wings, chicken, and seafood. ⊠ *Exit 32, off I–93, North Woodstock* ☎ *603/745–3951* ⊕ *www.woodstockinnnh.com* ▭ *AE, D, MC, V.*

$ 🏨 **Indian Head Resort.** This is the place for families on a budget. The
Ⓒ   rooms are inexpensive and spacious, and there are lots of activities for children, including a stocked trout pond, ice cream socials, magicians, and kids' karaoke. For parents, a lounge features music and comedians on a nightly basis. The resort is also near kid-friendly attractions such as a water park, a trading post, and a scenic railroad. In the winter, skiers can hitch a ride on a free shuttle to Cannon or Loon Mountain ski areas. **Pros:** best place for kids at a great price. **Cons:** crowded and sometimes hard to get a reservation. ⊠ *664 U.S. Route 3, 5 mi north of North Woodstock* ⌂ *R.R. 1, Box 99, North Lincoln 03215* ☎ *603/745–8000 or 800/343–8000* ⊕ *www.indianheadresort.com* ⇄ *129 rooms, 99 cottages* ⌂ *In-room: refrigerator, Wi-Fi. In-hotel: restaurant, room service, bar, tennis court, pools, gym, children's programs (all ages). Wi-Fi hotspot* ▭ *AE, D, DC, MC, V.*

$$$$ 🏨 **Mountain Club on Loon.** If you want a ski-in, ski-out stay on Loon Mountain, this is your best and only option. A typical 1990s ski lodge with a stone fireplace in the lobby, outdoor heated hot tub, and a small game room, the Club isn't thrilling, but it's clean and modern. There are suites that sleep as many as 10, studios with Inova beds, and many units with full kitchens. All rooms are within walking distance of the lifts. There's also a full-service spa and a health club that has exercise classes. **Pros:** easy skiing access; clean, basic rooms; close to national forest. **Cons:** unexciting decor. ⊠ *90 Loon Mountain, Kancamagus Hwy. (Rte. 112), Lincoln* ☎ *603/745–2244 or 800/229–7829* ⊕ *www.mtnclub.com* ⇄ *234 units* ⌂ *In-room: kitchen (some). In-hotel: restaurant, bar, tennis courts, pool, gym, spa, laundry facilities, Wi-Fi hotspot* ▭ *AE, D, MC, V.*

FRANCONIA

16 mi northwest of Lincoln/North Woodstock on I–93.

Travelers have long passed through the White Mountains via Franconia Notch, and in the late 18th century a town evolved just to the north. It and the region's jagged rock formations and heavy coat of evergreens have stirred the imaginations of Washington Irving, Henry Wadsworth Longfellow, and Nathaniel Hawthorne, who penned a short story about the craggy cliff known as the Old Man of the Mountain. There is almost no town proper to speak of here, just a handful of stores, touched though it is by Interstate 93 (the Franconia Notch Parkway).

Four miles west of Franconia, Sugar Hill is a town of about 500 people. It's famous for its spectacular sunsets and views of the Franconia Mountains, best seen from Sunset Hill, where a row of grand hotels and mansions once stood.

GETTING HERE AND AROUND

Franconia is a small town with not much to offer tourists, but it is an access point for many ski areas and the villages of Sugar Hill, Easton, Bethlehem, Bretton Woods, Littleton, Lincoln, and North Woodstock, towns replete with white church steeples, general stores, country inns, and picturesque farms.

ESSENTIALS

Visitor Information Franconia Notch Chamber of Commerce (☎ *603/823–9083* ⊕ *www.franconianotch.org*).

EXPLORING

Flume. This 800-foot-long chasm has narrow walls that cause an eerie echo from the gorge's running water. A wooden boardwalk and a series of stairways wind their way to the top of the falls that thunder down the gorge, followed by a 1-mi hike back to the visitor center. There's a gift shop, café, and dog walk on-site. ⊠ *Franconia Notch Pkwy., Exit 34A* ☎ *603/745–8391* ⊕ *www.nhstateparks.com/franconia.html* ⊠ *$13 adults, $9 children, or a combined Cannon Mtn. Tram ride and Flume entrance for $24 adults, $18 children* ⊙ *Early May–late Oct., daily 9–5.*

Frost Place. Robert Frost's year-round home from 1915 to 1920 and his summer home for 19 years, this is where the poet soaked up the New England life. This place is imbued with the spirit of his work, down to the rusted mailbox in front that's painted R. FROST in simple lettering. Two rooms host occasional readings and contain memorabilia and signed editions of his books. Out back, you can follow short trails marked with lines from his poetry. A visit here will slow you down and remind you of the intense beauty of the surrounding countryside. *158 Ridge Rd.* ☎ *603/823–5510* ⊕ *www.frostplace.org* ⊙ *Check the Web site for readings and conference schedule.*

Old Man of the Mountain. This naturally formed profile in the rock high above Franconia Notch, a famous New Hampshire geological site, crumbled unexpectedly on May 3, 2003, from the strains of natural erosion. The iconic image had defined New Hampshire, and the Old Man's "death" stunned and saddened residents. You can still stop at the

8

posted turnouts from Interstate 93 north- or southbound. In Franconia Notch State Park on the northbound side of the highway there is a pull-off; on the southbound side take Exit 34B and follow the signs. Another option is to go along the shore of Profile Lake for the best views of the mountain face. There's a small, free Old Man of the Mountain Museum administered by Franconia Notch State Park at the southbound viewing area (by the Cannon Mountain Tram parking area) open daily 9–5.

SPORTS AND THE OUTDOORS

SKI AREAS **Cannon Mountain.** The staff at this state-run facility in Franconia Notch State Park is attentive to skier services, family programs, snowmaking, and grooming. One of the nation's first ski areas, Cannon has 55 trails that present challenges rarely found in New Hampshire—for instance, the narrow, steep pitches off the peak of a 2,146-foot vertical rise. There are also two glade-skiing trails—Turnpike and Banshee—and a tubing park with lift service. Thirty-seven miles of cross-country trails are available to Nordic skiers. In summer, for $13 round-trip, the Cannon Mountain Aerial Tramway can transport you up 2,022 feet. It's an eight-minute ride to the top, where marked trails lead to an observation platform. The tram runs daily from mid-May through late October.

Franconia Village Cross-Country Ski Center. The cross-country ski center at the Franconia Inn has 39 mi of groomed trails and 40 mi of back-country trails. One popular route leads to Bridal Veil Falls, a great spot for a picnic lunch. You can also enjoy horse-drawn sleigh rides and ice-skating on a lighted rink. ⊠ *1300 Easton Rd.* ☎ *603/823–5542 or 800/473–5299* ⊕ *www.franconiainn.com.*

WHERE TO EAT AND STAY

¢ ✕ **Polly's Pancake Parlor.** In the Dexter family for three generations, Polly's
AMERICAN has been serving up pancakes, waffles, and French toast since the 1930s.
★ Since then, smoked bacon and ham, sandwiches on homemade bread, desserts such as raspberry pie, delicious baked beans, and even gluten-free items have been added to the menu. Much of the food is made from grains ground on-site. Home mixes and maple syrup, cream, and sugar are for sale year-round. The restaurant closes for the cold season. ⊠ *672 Rte. 117* ☎ *603/823–5575* ⊕ *www.pollyspancakeparlor.com* ▤ *AE, D, MC, V* ☉ *Open 7–1. Closed mid-Oct.–mid-May. No dinner.*

$$ ✕ **Sugar Hill Inn.** This 1789 farmhouse is the fine-dining option in the
AMERICAN area. Chef Val Fortin serves American fare such as peppercorn-crusted sirloin steak with grilled mushrooms and truffle oil and free-range duck breast with wild mushrooms, prosciutto, and chili-glazed scallops; the homemade desserts are always delicious. A four-course prix-fixe meal is $52. ⊠ *116 Rte. 117* ☎ *603/823–5621* ⊕ *www.sugarhillinn.com* ⌂ *Reservations essential* ▤ *AE, D, MC, V* ☉ *Closed Tues. and Wed. No lunch.*

$$$ 🛏 **Franconia Inn.** At this 120-acre family-friendly resort, you can play tennis on four clay courts, swim in the outdoor heated pool or hot tub, mountain bike, and hike. The cross-country ski barn doubles as a horse-back-riding center in the warm months. The white, three-story inn has unfussy country furnishings—you'll find canopy beds and country quilts in the rooms, most of which have period-style wallpapering or wood

paneling. **Pros:** good for kids; amazing views; outdoor heated pool. **Cons:** may be too remote for some. ✉ *1300 Easton Rd.* ☎ *603/823–5542 or 800/473-5299* ⊕ *www.franconiainn.com* 🛏 *34 rooms, 3 suites, 2 2-bedroom cottages* 🛏 *In-room: a/c, Wi-Fi. In-hotel: restaurant, bar, tennis courts, pool, bicycles, Wi-Fi hotspot* ⊟ *AE, MC, V* ⊙ *Restaurant closed Apr. 1–15.*

$$$–$$$$
★
🛌 **Sugar Hill Inn.** The nicest place in Franconia for a romantic retreat is the Sugar Hill Inn. The lawn's old carriage and the wraparound porch's wicker chairs put you in a nostalgic mood before you even enter this converted 1789 farmhouse. Many rooms and suites have hand-stenciled walls and views of the Franconia Mountains; some have gas fireplaces. Bette Davis visited friends in this house—the room with the best vistas is named after her. **Pros:** romantic, classic B&B; fine dinners. **Cons:** expensive. ✉ *116 Rte. 117* ☎ *603/823–5621 or 800/548–4748* ⊕ *www.sugarhillinn.com* 🛏 *10 rooms, 4 suites* 🛏 *In-room: no phone, a/c, DVD (some), no TV (some), Wi-Fi. In-hotel: restaurant, room service, bar, pool, Wi-Fi hotspot, kids on a case-by-case basis* ⊟ *AE, D, MC, V* 🍴 *BP, MAP.*

LITTLETON

7 mi north of Franconia and 86 mi north of Concord, on I–93.

One of northern New Hampshire's largest towns (this isn't saying much, mind you) is on a granite shelf along the Ammonoosuc River, whose swift current and drop of 235 feet enabled the community to flourish as a mill center in its early days. Later, the railroad came through, and Littleton grew into the region's commerce hub. In the minds of many, it's more a place to stock up on supplies than a bona fide destination, but few communities have worked harder at revitalization. Today, intriguing shops and eateries line the adorable Main Street, with its tidy 19th- and early-20th-century buildings that suggest a set in a Jimmy Stewart movie.

8

EXPLORING

Littleton Grist Mill. Stop by this restored 1798 mill just off Main Street on the Ammonoosuc River. It contains a small shop selling stone-ground flour products and a museum downstairs showcasing the original mill equipment. ✉ *18 Mill St.* ☎ *603/444–7478 or 888/284–7478* ⊕ *www.littletongristmill.com* ⊙ *July–Dec., daily 10–5; Apr.–June, Wed.–Sat. 10:30–4, Sun. 10:30–3.*

OFF THE
BEATEN
PATH

Whitefield. Like Dixville Notch and Bretton Woods, Whitefield, 11 mi northeast of Littleton, became a prominent summer resort in the late 19th century, when wealthy industrialists flocked to the small village in a rolling valley between two precipitous promontories to golf, ski, play polo, and hobnob with each other. The sprawling, yellow clapboard Mountain View Hotel, which was established in 1865 and had grown to grand hotel status by the early 20th century, only to succumb to changing tourist habits and close by the 1980s, has been fully refurbished and is now open again as one of New England's grandest resort hotels. It's worth driving through the courtly Colonial center of town—Whitefield was settled in the early 1800s—and up Route 116 just beyond to see this magnificent structure atop a bluff overlooking the Presidentials.

Lancaster. About 8 mi north of Whitefield via U.S. 3, the affable seat of Coos County sits at the confluence of the Connecticut and Israel rivers, surrounded by low serrated peaks. Before becoming prosperous through commerce, Lancaster was an agricultural stronghold; at one time the only acceptable currency here was the bushel of wheat. It's still an intimate mountain town. Like Littleton, it has restored much of its main street, which now has a dapper mix of Victorian homes, funky artisan and antiques shops, and prim churches and civic buildings.

SHOPPING

Main Street and Union Street are filled with great little shops.

The **Village Book Store** (✉ *81 Main St.* ☎ *603/444–5263* ⊕ *www.booksmusictoys.com*) has a good selection of both nonfiction and fiction titles. **Potato Barn Antiques Center** (✉ *960 Lancaster Rd. [U.S. 3], 6 mi north of Lancaster, Northumberland* ☎ *603/636–2611* ⊕ *www.potatobarnantiques.com*) has several dealers under one roof—specialties include vintage farm tools, clothing, and costume jewelry.

QUICK BITES

Beside the Littleton Grist Mill, Miller's Café & Bakery (✉ **16 Mill St.** ☎ *603/444–2146* ⊕ *www.millerscafeandbakery.com* ☾ *Closed Sun. and Mon.*) serves coffees, microbrews and wines, baked goods, sandwiches, and salads.

WHERE TO EAT AND STAY

$$
AMERICAN
★

✕ **Tim-bir Alley.** This is a rare find in New Hampshire: an independent restaurant in a contemporary setting that's been around a long time (since 1983) and yet still takes its food seriously. If you're in town, don't miss it. Tim Carr's menu changes weekly and uses regional American ingredients in creative ways. Main dishes might include an eggplant pâté with feta cheese, red pepper, and a tomato-herb marmalade or a basil-and-olive-oil-flavored salmon with a spinach-Brie-pecan pesto. Save room for such desserts as white chocolate–coconut cheesecake. ✉ *7 Main St.* ☎ *603/444–6142* ▤ *No credit cards* ☾ *Closed Mon. and Tues. No lunch.*

$
Fodor's Choice
★

▦ **Thayers Inn.** This stately 1843 Greek-Revival hotel is the essence of Littleton. It's not a luxury hotel, and Thayers isn't out to impress the Joneses. The well-kept rooms are quaintly old-fashioned, with creaky floorboards, exposed pipes, steam radiators, high ceilings, and comfy wing chairs. So if you're traveling on a budget or just want an authentic northern town experience, this is a good choice. The Bailiwicks restaurant ($$$) has a martini bar with exposed oak beams and leather chairs. The lobster risotto and the homemade seafood cakes are delicious. **Pros:** one of the best values in New England. **Cons:** Continental breakfast only. ✉ *111 Main St.* ☎ *603/444–6469 or 800/634–8179* ⊕ *www.thayersinn.com* ⇨ *22 rooms, 13 suites* ⌂ *In-room: Wi-Fi. In-hotel: restaurant, bar, spa, Wi-Fi hotspot, some pets allowed* ▤ *AE, D, MC, V* ◎*CP.*

BRETTON WOODS

14 mi southeast of Bethlehem; 28 mi northeast of Lincoln/Woodstock.

In the early 1900s private railcars brought the elite from New York and Philadelphia to the Mount Washington Hotel, the jewel of the White Mountains. A visit to the hotel, which was the site of the 1944 United Nations conference that created the International Monetary Fund and the International Bank for Reconstruction and Development (and the birth of many conspiracy theories), is not to be missed. The area is also known for its cog railway and Bretton Woods ski resort.

GETTING HERE AND AROUND

Bretton Woods is in the heart of the White Mountains on Route 302. A free shuttle helps get you around the various facilities at the resort. Helpful advice on how to enjoy your stay can be found at the concierge and activities desk in the main lobby of the Mount Washington Hotel.

EXPLORING

Fodor's Choice ★

In 1858 Sylvester Marsh petitioned the state legislature for permission to build a steam railway up Mt. Washington. A politico retorted that he'd have better luck building a railroad to the moon. But 11 years later, the **Mt. Washington Cog Railway** chugged its way up to the summit along a 3-mi track on the west side of the mountain, and today it's one of the state's most beloved attractions—a thrill in either direction. The train only runs in the summer, starting in May. A full trip ($59) is three hours with one hour at the summit. Trains depart at 11 AM and 2 PM. ⊠ *U.S. 302, 6 mi northeast of Bretton Woods* ☎ *603/278–5404 or 800/922–8825* ⊕ *www.thecog.com* ⊠ *$59.*

SPORTS AND THE OUTDOORS

Fodor's Choice ★

Bretton Woods. Skiing with your family New Hampshire's largest ski area is one of the best family ski resorts in the country. It's also probably the best place in New England to learn to ski. (If it's your first time, get started at the free area serviced by a rope tow.) The views of Mt. Washington alone are worth the visit to Bretton Woods; the scenery is especially beautiful from the **Top of Quad restaurant,** which is open during ski season.

Trails appeal mostly to novice and intermediate skiers, including two magic carpet lifts for beginners. There are some steeper pitches near the top of the 1,500-foot vertical and glade skiing to occupy the experts in the family, as well as night skiing and snowboarding on weekends and holidays. Snowboarders enjoy the four terrain parks, including the all-natural Wild West Park and a half-pipe. A cross-country ski center has 62 mi of groomed and double-track trails, some of them lift-serviced. The Nordic Ski Center near the hotel offers access to 55 mi of cross-country trails and doubles as the golf clubhouse in summer.

Options for kids are plentiful. The Hobbit Ski and Snowboard School for ages 4–12 has full- and half-day instruction. Hobbit Ski and Snowplay program, for ages 3–5, is an introduction to skiing and fun on the snow. The ski area also offers an adaptive program for children and adults with disabilities. There are also organized activities in the

8

nursery. The complimentary Kinderwoods Winter Playground has a sled carousel, igloos, and a zip line. Parents can buy an interchangeable family ticket that allows parents to take turns skiing while the other watches the kids—both passes come for the price of one.

A new addition is the year-round Canopy Tour, which has 10 zip lines, two sky bridges, and three rappel stations. Small groups, guided by experienced climbers and ski patrollers, leave every half hour. The tour, at $110, is one of the longest in the United States and is an exhilarating introduction to flora and fauna of the White Mountains and the history of the area. Kids are welcome but must weigh more than 70 lbs. ⊠ *U.S. 302* ☎ *603/278–3320; 603/278–3333 weather conditions; 800/232–2972 information; 800/258–0330 lodging* ⊕ *www.brettonwoods.com.*

WHERE TO EAT

$$$
AMERICAN

✕ **The Bretton Arms Dining Room**. You're likely to have the best meal in the area at this intimate setting. Though the same executive chef oversees the Mount Washington Hotel dining room, the latter is immense, and the Bretton Arms is cozier. Three small interconnected rooms are separated by fireplaces. The menu is seasonal and might include Maine lobster tossed with fresh pasta and free-range Long Island duck breast; it also features locally sourced food. ⊠ *U.S. 302* ☎ *603/278–1000* ⊕ *www.mtwashingtonresort.com* ▭ *AE, D, MC, V* ⊗ *No lunch.*

$$$
AMERICAN
★

✕ **The Dining Room**. You'd be hard-pressed to find a larger or grander dining room in New Hampshire (only the Balsams can compare). The Mount Washington Hotel's enormous octagonal dining room, built in 1902, is adorned with Currier & Ives reproductions, Tiffany glass, chandeliers up the wazoo, massive windows that open to the Presidential Range, and a nightly musical trio. This may be the only restaurant in the state that requires a jacket (except in winter); if you forgot yours, they have about 30 you can borrow. Try seasonal dishes such as seared haddock and shrimp fricassee, lemon lobster ravioli with shrimp and scallops, or roast pork with onions and mushrooms. The Dining Room offers a "Gold Sash Dinner" at a chef's table with a customized menu and wine pairings. ⊠ *In Mount Washington Hotel, U.S. 302* ☎ *603/278–1000* ⊕ *www.mtwashingtonresort.com* ⌂ *Jacket required* ▭ *AE, D, MC, V.*

$–$$
AMERICAN

✕ **Fabyan's Station**. In 1890, 60 tourist trains a day passed through this station, now a casual restaurant. If you're looking for an easygoing meal, Fabyan's cooks up delicious clam chowder in a bread bowl and a 16-ounce T-bone grilled to perfection. Half the restaurant is a tavern with a long bar, and the other half serves sandwiches, fish, and steaks. There's a kids' menu, too, and a model train circles the dining room. ⊠ *Rte. 302, 1 mi north of Bretton Woods ski area* ☎ *603/278–2222* ⌂ *Reservations not accepted* ▭ *AE, D, MC, V.*

WHERE TO STAY

¢
★

▦ **The Lodge**. A stay at this inexpensive roadside motel run by Bretton Woods gives you free access to all of the resort facilities at Mount Washington Hotel, including the pools, gym, and arcade, which makes it a great deal. You can also use the free shuttle to the hotel and the ski

Bretton Woods is a year-round destination, and especially popular with families.

area. The rooms are very clean and have private balconies that overlook the Presidential Range. There's a small arcade, a great indoor pool, and a cute hearthside common area. **Pros:** cheap; free access to Mount Washington amenities; free ski shuttle. **Cons:** across street from resort amenities; Continental breakfast only. ⊠ *U.S. 302* ☎ *603/278–1000 or 800/258–0330* ⊕ *www.mtwashington.com* 🛏 *50 rooms* ⚫ *In-room: Wi-Fi. In-hotel: restaurant, golf courses, tennis courts, pool, bicycles, children's programs (ages 4–12), laundry facilities, laundry service, Wi-Fi hotspot* ⊟ *AE, D, MC, V* ⊠⊙⊠ *CP.*

$$$
🕑
Fodor'sChoice
★

🏨 **Mount Washington Hotel.** The two most memorable sights in the White Mountains would have to be Mount Washington and the Mount Washington Hotel. Its grand scale and remarkable setting graced by the view of the Presidentials is astonishing. This 1902 resort has a 900-foot veranda and stately public rooms and glimmers with an early-20th-century ambience. It would take a full week to exhaust the recreational activities here: in winter try out the tubing, ice-skating, a great cross-country facility, a terrific downhill skiing complex, and dogsled and sleigh rides; in summer, you can enjoy horseback riding, carriage rides, fly-fishing, golf, mountain biking, and more. The Cave provides gin in a coffee cup and nightly entertainment in a former 1930s speakeasy. Kids will love the arcade, sweet shop, and playground, as well as a club with themed day and evening programs. The hotel also has a 25,000-square-foot spa and a renovated 18-hole Donald Ross golf course designed in 1915. Rooms have high ceilings and are furnished in a manner befitting the history and grandeur of this luxurious resort. The bathrooms are glorious, with white porcelain sinks and tubs and white tile. **Pros:** beautiful resort; loads of activities; free shuttle to skiing

The views of Mt. Washington and the Presidential range from the porch of Mt. Washington Hotel can't be beat.

and activities. **Cons:** kids love to run around the hotel; Internet access expensive. ⊠ *U.S. 302* ☎ *603/278–1000* ⊕ *www.mtwashington.com* ↪ *177 rooms, 23 suites* ⚒ *In-room: Internet, Wi-Fi (fee). In-hotel: 3 restaurants, room service, bars, golf course, tennis courts, pool, gym, spa, bicycles, children's programs (ages 4–12), laundry service, Internet terminal, Wi-Fi hotspot* ⊟ *AE, D, MC, V* ⎥⊚⎢ *BP, EP, MAP.*

$$$–$$$$
Fodor's Choice
★

⊡ **Notchland Inn.** Drop any cute house here and you couldn't but fall in love. Built in 1862 by Sam Bemis, America's grandfather of landscape photography, the house conveys mountain charm on a scale unmatched in New England. It's simply a legendary setting, in Crawford Notch, in the middle of the forest surrounded by the mountains. Innkeepers Les Schoof and Ed Butler have left wood-burning fireplaces in every room (17 in total in the house), have a big library, serve five-course meals, and give the range of the place to Abby and Crawford, their immense Bernese Mountain Dogs. **Pros:** middle-of-the-forest setting; marvelous house and common rooms; original fireplaces; good dinner. **Cons:** at 15 mi from the Bretton Woods ski area, will be too isolated for some; rooms could be better equipped (better bedding, for example). ⊠ *2 Morey Rd., Hart's Location* ☎ *603/374–6131* ⊕ *www.notchland.com* ↪ *8 rooms, 5 suites, 3 cottages* ⚒ *In-room: no phone, Wi-Fi. In-hotel: restaurant, Wi-Fi hotspot, some pets allowed, no kids under 12* ⊟ *D, MC, V* ⎥⊚⎢ *BP.*

EN ROUTE

Scenic U.S. 302 winds through the steep, wooded mountains on either side of spectacular Crawford Notch, southeast of Bretton Woods, and passes through **Crawford Notch State Park** (⊠ *U.S. 302, Harts Location* ☎ *603/374–2272, 603/344–2272 campground* ⊕ *www.nhstateparks. com/crawford.html*), where you can picnic and take a short hike to

Arethusa Falls or the Silver and Flume cascades. The park has a number of roadside photo opportunities. The visitor center has a gift shop and a cafeteria; **there's also a** campground.

BARTLETT

18 mi southeast of Bretton Woods.

With Bear Mountain to its south, Mt. Parker to its north, Mt. Cardigan to its west, and the Saco River to its east, Bartlett, incorporated in 1790, has an unforgettable setting. Lovely Bear Notch Road (closed in winter) has the only midpoint access to the Kancamagus Highway (Route 112). There isn't much town here (dining options are in Glen). It's best known for the Attitash Ski Resort, within walking distance.

SPORTS AND THE OUTDOORS

SKI AREA **Attitash Ski Resort.** Attitash, with a vertical drop of 1,760 feet, and Attitash Bear Peak, with a 1,450-foot vertical, have massive snowmaking operations and full-service base lodges. The bulk of the skiing and boarding is geared to intermediates and experts, with some steep pitches and glades. At 500 feet, the Ground Zero half-pipe is New England's longest. The Attitash Adventure Center has a rental shop, lessons desk, and children's programs. Attitash also has summer activities such as an alpine slide, guided horseback rides, and a scenic sky ride. ⊠ *U.S. 302* ⌂ *Box 308, 03812* ☎ *603/374–2368 or 800/233–7669* ⊕ *www. attitash.com.*

WHERE TO EAT

$$–$$$ ✕ **Bernerhof Inn.** There are several options for dining at this inn. The
ECLECTIC Dining Room at the Bernerhof is the area's fine-dining choice, preparing traditional Swiss specialties such as fondue and Wiener schnitzel as well as hearty fare like herb-encrusted rack of lamb and veal Oscar (cutlets topped with crab meat, Bernaise sauce, and asparagus). The Black Bear pub pours microbrews and serves sandwiches and burgers as well as a very satisfying shepherd's pie. The CyBear Lounge serves afternoon appetizers you can snack on while checking your e-mail. ⊠ *U.S. 302, Glen* ☎ *603/383–9132 or 800/828–3591* ⊕ *www.bernerhofinn.com* ▤ *AE, D, MC, V.*

$ ✕ **Margarita Grill.** Après-ski and hiking types congregate here in the din-
SOUTHWESTERN ing room in cold weather and on the covered patio when it's warm for homemade salsas, wood-fired steaks, ribs, burgers, and a smattering of Tex-Mex and Southwestern specialties. Unwind with a margarita at bar after a day on the mountains. ⊠ *78 U.S. 302, Glen* ☎ *603/383–6556* ⊕ *www.margaritagrillonline.com* ▤ *D, MC, V* ⊗ *No lunch weekdays.*

$–$$ ✕ **Red Parka Steakhouse and Pub.** This downtown Glen pub has been an
AMERICAN institution for 37 years. A family-dining–oriented menu features an all-you-can-eat salad bar, baked stuffed shrimp, scallops, and hand-cut steaks. The barbecue sauce is made on-site, and beer is served in mason jars. Plan to spend some time reading the dozens and dozens of license plates that adorn the walls of the downstairs pub. ⊠ *3 Station St., Glen* ☎ *603/383–4344* ✍ *www.redparkapub.com* ⎙ *Reservations not accepted* ▤ *AE, D, MC, V.*

8

WHERE TO STAY

$–$$ 🖥 **Attitash Mountain Village.** Across the street from the entrance to Attitash, you can't see this cluster of units from the road because they're in the pine trees (there are also a few slopeside condos), but they're there, along with hiking trails, a playground, a clay tennis court, two heated pools, an arcade, and a free stocked fishing pond. All in all it's a good deal for families on a budget who want to ski across the street. The accommodations are simple but serviceable, and there's a restaurant and a sports-style pub. **Pros:** simple, no-frills family place; playground. **Cons:** a bit run-down. ✉ *784 U.S. 302, Bartlett* ☎ *603/374–6500 or 800/862–1600* ⊕ *www.attitashmtvillage.com* ⤴ *350 units* ⚭ *In-room: no a/c (some), kitchen (some), refrigerator (some), DVD, Wi-Fi (some). In-hotel: restaurant, bar, tennis courts, pools, gym, laundry facilities, Internet terminal, Wi-Fi hotspot, some pets allowed* ⊟ *AE, D, MC, V.*

$$ 🖥 **Attitash Grand Summit Hotel & Conference Center.** This ski hotel is the choice for those who want ski-in, ski-out convenience. Accommodations include kitchenettes, video-game-equipped TVs, and stereos. Standard rooms have balconies. Crawford's Pub and Grille and Black Diamond Grill (breakfast and lunch) serve passable American fare and bar food ($–$$). **Pros:** ski-in, ski-out; nice pool and hot tubs; cheaper with ski package; full breakfast included. **Cons:** generally bland accommodations. ✉ *U.S. 302 Box 429* ☎ *603/374–1900 or 800/223–7669* ⊕ *www.attitash.com* ⤴ *143 rooms* ⚭ *In-room: kitchen (some), Wi-Fi. In-hotel: restaurants, bars, pool, gym, children's programs (ages 2–14), laundry facilities, Internet terminal, Wi-Fi hotspot* ⊟ *AE, D, MC, V.*

JACKSON

★   *5 mi north of Glen.*

Just off Route 16 via a red covered bridge, Jackson has retained its storybook New England character. Art and antiques shopping, tennis, golf, fishing, and hiking to waterfalls are among the draws. When the snow falls, Jackson becomes the state's cross-country skiing capital. Four downhill ski areas are nearby. Hotels and B&Bs offer a ski shuttle. Visit Jackson Falls for a wonderful photo opportunity.

ESSENTIALS

Visitor Information Jackson Area Chamber of Commerce (☎ *603/383–9356* ⊕ *www.jackson.com*).

EXPLORING

ⓒ **Story Land.** That cluster of fluorescent buildings along Route 16 is a theme park with life-size storybook and nursery-rhyme characters. The 20 rides and five shows include a flume ride, Victorian-theme river-raft ride, farm tractor–inspired kiddie ride, pumpkin coach, variety show, and swan boats. In early spring, only parts of the park are open and admission is reduced to $16. ✉ *850 Rte. 16* ☎ *603/383–4186* ⊕ *www.storylandnh.com* 🎟 *$25* 🕑 *Mid-May–early Oct. Check Web site for dates and hours.*

SPORTS AND THE OUTDOORS

Nestlenook Estate and Resort (✉ *Dinsmore Rd.* ☏ *800/659–9443* ⊕ *www. nestlenookfarm.com*) maintains an outdoor ice-skating rink with rentals, music, and a bonfire. Snowshoeing and sleigh rides are other winter options; in summer you can fly-fish or ride in a horse-drawn carriage.

SKI AREAS **Black Mountain.** Friendly, informal Black Mountain has a warming southern exposure. The Family Passport allows two adults and two juniors to ski at discounted rates. Midweek rates ($29) are usually the lowest in Mt. Washington Valley. The 40 trails and glades on the 1,100-foot mountain are evenly divided among beginner, intermediate, and expert. There's a nursery for kids six months and up. Enjoy guided horseback riding in the summer. ✉ *1 Black Mountain Rd.* ☏ *800/698–4490; 800/475–4669 snow conditions* ⊕ *www.blackmt.com.*

★ **Jackson Ski Touring Foundation.** One of the nation's top four cross-country skiing areas, Jackson Ski Touring Foundation has 97 mi of trails. Many of the trails are groomed for regular cross-country and skate skiing. You can arrange lessons and rentals at the lodge, in the center of Jackson Village. ✉ *153 Main St., Jackson* ☏ *603/383–9355* ⊕ *www. jacksonxc.org.*

WHERE TO EAT

$–$$ ✕ **Red Fox Bar & Grille.** Some say this big family restaurant overlooking
AMERICAN the Wentworth Golf Club gets its name from a wily fox with a penchant for stealing golf balls off the fairway. The wide-ranging menu has barbecued ribs and wood-fired pizzas as well as more refined dishes such as seared sea scallops with Grand Marnier sauce. The Sunday breakfast buffet is very popular. ✉ *49 Rte. 16* ☏ *603/383–4949* ⊕ *www. redfoxpub.com* ▭ *AE, D, MC, V* ☯ *Lunch on Tues and Wed., summer only.*

$–$$ ✕ **Thompson House Eatery.** One of the most innovative restaurants in
AMERICAN generally staid northern New Hampshire, this eatery inside a rambling
★ red farmhouse serves comfort food such as a wonderful meat loaf made with local beef, salads with in-season greens, maple scallops sautéed with a cream sauce, and a chocolate espresso pudding that will make your eyes roll with delight. ✉ *193 Main St.* ☏ *603/383–9341* ⊕ *www. thompsonhouseeatery.com* ▭ *AE, D, MC, V* ☯ *Lunch only on Tues. and Wed., late May–early Oct.*

$$$ ✕ **Thorn Hill.** This famous inn serves up one of New England's most mem-
AMERICAN orable meals. In warm months dine on the romantic porch, which over-
Fodor's Choice looks the Presidential mountain range. The wine list is the state's most
★ lauded, with 1,900 labels. The curated and changing "Top 50" list of reasonably priced bottles is a sure guide. Chef Peter Delmonte and pastry chef Brandon Gore create subtle and flavorful dishes such as a New York strip with chanterelle mushrooms and bordelaise sauce and salmon grilled with Mediterranean spices and served with hummus and cucumber *raita* (Indian yogurt sauce). The menu changes regularly and the once-a-month wine dinner is a favorite around the region. ✉ *42 Thorn Hill Rd.* ☏ *603/383–4242 or 800/289–8990* ⊕ *www.innatthornhill.com* ⚎ *Reservations essential* ▭ *AE, D, MC, V* ☯ *No lunch.*

8

WHERE TO STAY

$ ⊡ **Christmas Farm Inn and Spa.** Despite its wintery name, this 1778 inn is an all-season retreat. Rooms in the main building and the saltbox next door are adorned with either Laura Ashley or Ralph Lauren fabrics. Other rooms are in a delightful old barn, in a sugarhouse, and in a few cottages about the wooded grounds. In the contemporary carriage house, which features private balconies, there's a great fireplace, and the 12 suites there have two-person whirlpool tubs and gas fireplaces. The inn's gardens are spectacular. **Pros:** kids welcome; nice indoor and outdoor pools. **Cons:** saltbox rooms could use improvement. ⊠ *Rte. 16B, Box CC* ☎ *603/383–4313 or 800/443–5837* ⊕ *www.christmasfarminn. com* ⊅ *22 rooms, 15 suites, 7 cottages* ♿ *In-room: Wi-Fi. In-hotel: restaurant, bar, pools, gym, spa, Wi-Fi hotspot* ⊟ *AE, D, MC, V* ❍❙ *BP.*

$–$$ ⊡ **Inn at Jackson.** This B&B is impeccably maintained, charmingly furnished, and bright. The beautiful inn, a 1902 Victorian designed by Stanford White for the Baldwin family of piano fame, overlooks the village. The foyer's staircase is grand, but there's a remarkable relaxed and unpretentious ambience. Guest rooms have oversize windows; eight have fireplaces. The exceptional full breakfast may include anything from egg soufflé casserole to blueberry pancakes. **Pros:** super-clean rooms; great value; peaceful setting. **Cons:** third-floor rooms lack fireplaces. ⊠ *12 Thorn Hill Rd., Box 822* ☎ *603/383–4321 or 800/289– 8600* ⊕ *www.innatjackson.com* ⊅ *14 rooms* ♿ *In-room: DVD, Wi-Fi. In-hotel: laundry service, Internet terminal, Wi-Fi hotspot, some pets allowed, no kids under 8* ⊟ *AE, D, MC, V* ❍❙ *BP.*

Fodor'sChoice
★

$$$$ ⊡ **Inn at Thorn Hill.** This house, modeled after the 1891 Stanford White Victorian that burned down a decade ago, offers spacious rooms with a relaxed elegance. From a deck that overlooks the rolling hills around Jackson you can get your morning started with a summer breakfast of homemade muffins and bread, a tasty breakfast burrito with braised beef, or an exquisite eggs Florentine topped with spinach and Mornay sauce. A meal in the lounge might include house-cured and -smoked meats or a plate of artisan cheeses served with fruit chutney. Innkeepers Jim and Ibby Cooper are always on hand to spend time with guests, sipping wine and talking about local history. All of the rooms have cushy amenities: two-person Jacuzzis, fireplaces, and DVD players. The top units have steam showers, wet bars, and refrigerators. Cottages and rooms in the carriage house are less thrilling. A full spa provides a full range of beauty treatments and massages. Afternoon tea and a substantial full breakfast and dinner are included. **Pros:** great meals and service; romantic setting. **Cons:** small fee for Wi-Fi. ⊠ *42 Thorn Hill Rd., Box A* ☎ *603/383–4242 or 800/289–8990* ⊕ *www.innatthornhill. com* ⊅ *15 rooms, 7 suites, 3 cottages* ♿ *In-room: refrigerator (some), DVD (some), no TV (some), Wi-Fi. In-hotel: restaurant, room service, bar, pool, gym, spa, laundry service, Wi-Fi hotspot, no kids under 6* ⊟ *AE, D, MC, V* ❍❙ *MAP.*

Fodor'sChoice
★

MT. WASHINGTON

★ *20 mi northwest of Jackson.*

GETTING HERE AND AROUND

Mt. Washington is the highest peak (6,288 feet) in the northeastern United States and the site of a weather station that recorded the world's highest winds, 231 MPH, in 1934. You can drive to the top, which climbs 4,600 feet in 7.5 mi, in the summer. A number of trailheads circle the mountain and the other peaks in the Presidential Range, but all of them are strenuous and for the hearty. For the best information on trails in the Presidents, visit ⊕ *www.hikethewhites.com.* The Mt. Washington Cog Railway, which operates in the summer only, climbs 3,500 feet in 3 mi, at grades averaging 25%. (⇨ *Bretton Woods for information on the Mt. Washington Cog Railway.*)

ESSENTIALS

Visitor Information Mount Washington Observatory (☎ 603/356–2137 ⊕ www.mountwashington.org). **White Mountain National Forest** (✉ 71 *White Mountain Dr., Clampton* ☎ 603/536–6100 ⊕ www.fs.fed.us/r9/white).

EXPLORING

Mt. Washington Auto Road. Opened in 1861, this route begins at the Glen House, a gift shop and rest stop 15 mi north of Glen on Route 16, and winds its way up the east side of the mountain, ending at the top, a 7.5-mi and approximately half-hour drive later. At the summit is the Sherman Adams Summit Building, built in 1979 and containing a visitor center and a museum focusing on the mountain's geology and extreme weather conditions; you can stand in the glassed-in viewing area to hear the wind roar. The Mt. Washington Observatory is at the building's western end. Rules limit what cars may use the road. For instance, cars with automatic transmission must be able to shift down into first gear. A guided bus tour is available or you can reach the top along several rough hiking trails; those who hoof it can make the return trip via shuttle, tickets for which are sold at the Stage Office, at the summit at the end of the cog railway trestle. Remember that the temperature atop Mt. Washington will be much colder than down below—the average year-round is below freezing, and the average wind velocity is 35 mph. ✉ *Rte. 16, Pinkham Notch* ☎ *603/466–3988* ⊕ *www.mountwashingtonautoroad. com* ✑ *Car and driver $23, each additional adult passenger $8* ⊙ *Check the Web site for hours of operation; closed late Oct.–mid-May.*

SnowCoaches. In winter, when the road is closed to private vehicles, you can opt to reach the top of Mt. Washington via a guided tour in one of the four-wheel-drive vehicles that leave from Great Glen Trails Outdoor Center, just south of Gorham, on a first-come, first-served basis. Great Glen's nine-passenger vans are refitted with snowmobile-like treads and can travel to just above the tree line. You have the option of cross-country skiing or snowshoeing down. ✉ *Rte. 16, Pinkham Notch* ☎ *603/466–2333* ⊕ *www.greatglentrails.com* ✑ *$45 (includes all-day trail pass)* ⊙ *Dec.–Mar., snow necessary, most days, beginning at 8:30.*

8

Reward your vehicle for tackling the auto road with the obligatory bumper sticker: "This Car Climbed Mt. Washington."

SPORTS AND THE OUTDOORS

Although not a town per se, scenic **Pinkham Notch** covers Mt. Washington's eastern side and has several ravines, including Tuckerman Ravine, famous for spring skiing. The Appalachian Mountain Club maintains a large visitor center here on Route 16 that provides information to hikers and travelers and has guided hikes, outdoor skills workshops, a cafeteria, lodging, regional topography displays, and an outdoors shop.

HIKING   The **Appalachian Mountain Club Pinkham Notch Visitor Center** (⊠ *Rte. 16, Box 298, Gorham* ☎ *603/466–2721; 603/466–2727 reservations* ⊕ *www.outdoors.org*) has lectures, workshops, slide shows, and outdoor skills instruction year-round. Accommodations include the adjacent Joe Dodge Lodge, the Highland Center at Crawford Notch with 100-plus beds and a 16-bed bunkhouse next to it, and the club's eight high-mountain huts spaced one day's hike from each other in the White Mountain National Forest portion of the Appalachian Trail. The huts provide meals and dorm-style lodging from June to late September or early October; the rest of the year they are self-service.

SKI AREAS   **Great Glen Trails Outdoor Center.** Amenities at this fabulous lodge at the base of Mt. Washington include a huge ski-gear and sports shop, food court, climbing wall, observation deck, and fieldstone fireplace. In winter it's renowned for its dramatic 24-mi cross-country trail system. Some trails have snowmaking, and there's access to more than 1,100 acres of backcountry. It's even possible to ski or snowshoe the lower half of the Mt. Washington Auto Road. Trees shelter most of the trails, so Mt. Washington's infamous weather isn't such a concern. In summer it's the base from which hikers, mountain bikers, and trail runners can explore

Mt. Washington. The center also has programs in canoeing, kayaking, and fly-fishing. ⊠ *Rte. 16, Pinkham Notch* ☎ *603/466–2333* ⊕ *www. greatglentrails.com.*

Wildcat. Glade skiers favor Wildcat, with 28 acres of official tree ski-ing. The 47 runs include some stunning double-black-diamond trails. Skiers who can hold a wedge should check out the 2½-mi-long Polecat. Experts can zip down the Lynx. Views of Mt. Washington and Tucker-man Ravine are superb. The trails are classic New England—narrow and winding. Wildcat's expert runs deserve their designations and then some. Intermediates have mid-mountain to base trails, and beginners will find gentle terrain and a broad teaching slope. Snowboarders have several terrain parks and the run of the mountain. In summer you can go to the top on the four-passenger gondola ($15), ride a zip line, and hike the many well-kept trails. ⊠ *Rte. 16, Jackson* ☎ *603/466–3326; 888/754–9453 snow conditions; 800/255–6439 lodging* ⊕ *www. skiwildcat.com.*

DIXVILLE NOTCH

63 mi north of Mt. Washington, 66 mi northeast of Littleton, 149 mi north of Concord.

Just 12 mi from the Canadian border, this tiny community is known for two things: the Balsams, one of New Hampshire's oldest and most celebrated resorts, and the fact that Dixville Notch and another New Hampshire community, Hart's Location, are the first election districts in the nation to vote in presidential general elections. When the 30 or so Dixville Notch voters file into the little Balsams meeting room on the eve of Election Day and cast their ballots at the stroke of midnight, they invariably make national news.

EXPLORING

One of the favorite pastimes in this area is spotting moose, those large, ungainly, yet elusive members of the deer family. Although you may catch sight of one or more yourself, **Northern Forest Moose Tours** (☎ *603/466–3103 or 877/986–6673* ⊠ *$25* ⊙ *May–Oct. Bus leaves at 6:30 PM*) conducts bus tours of the region that have a 97% success rate for spotting moose.

OFF THE BEATEN PATH

Pittsburg. Well north of the White Mountains, in the Great North Woods, Pittsburg contains the four Connecticut Lakes and the springs that form the Connecticut River. The state's northern tip—a chunk of about 250 square mi—lies within the town's borders, the result of a dis-pute between the United States and Canada that began in 1832 and was resolved in 1842, when the international boundary was fixed. Remote though it is, this frontier town teems with hunters, boaters, fishermen, hikers, and photographers from early summer through winter. Espe-cially in the colder months, moose sightings are common. The town has more than a dozen lodges and several informal eateries. It's about a 90-minute drive from Littleton and 40 minutes from Dixville Notch; add another 30 minutes to reach Fourth Connecticut Lake, nearly at the Canadian border. On your way, you pass the village of Stewartson, exactly midway between the Equator and the North Pole.

shop, and an outdoor miniature trains that you can sit on and ride. ✉ *15 Town Hall Rd. at Rte. 16 (U.S. 302), Intervale* ☎ *603/356–9922* ⊕ *www.hartmannrr.com* ✉ *$6* ⊙ *Open daily 10–5. Closed Tues. June, Sept., and Oct. Closed Tues.–Thurs., Nov. 1–May 31.*

Weather Discovery Center. The hands-on exhibits at this meteorological educational facility demonstrate how weather is monitored and how it affects us. The center is a collaboration between the National and Atmospheric Administration Forecast Systems lab and the Mt. Washington Observatory at the summit of Mt. Washington. ✉ *2779 Main St.* ☎ *603/356–2137* ⊕ *www.mountwashington.org* ✉ *$5* ⊙ *May–Oct., daily 10–5; Nov.–Apr., Sat.–Mon. 10–5 (also open daily during school vacation mid-Feb.–early Mar.).*

SPORTS AND THE OUTDOORS

Echo Lake State Park. You needn't be a rock climber to catch views from the 700-foot White Horse and Cathedral ledges. From the top you'll see the entire valley, including Echo Lake, which offers fishing and swimming and on quiet days an excellent opportunity to shout for echoes. ✉ *Off U.S 302* ☎ *603/271–3556* ⊕ *www.nhstateparks.com/echo.html* ✉ *$4* ⊙ *Late May–mid-June, weekends dawn–dusk; mid-June–early Sept., daily dawn–dusk.*

CANOE-ING AND KAYAKING
River outfitter **Saco Bound Canoe & Kayak** (✉ *2561 E. Main St., Center Conway* ☎ *603/447–2177* ⊕ *www.sacobound.com*) leads gentle canoeing expeditions, guided kayak trips, and white-water rafting on seven rivers and provides lessons, equipment, and transportation.

FISHING
North Country Angler (✉ *2888 White Mountain Hwy.* ☎ *603/356–6000* ⊕ *www.northcountryangler.com*) schedules intensive guided fly-fishing weekends throughout the region. It's one of the best tackle shops in the state.

SKI AREAS
Cranmore Mountain Resort. This downhill ski area has been a favorite of families since it began operating in 1938. Five glades have opened more skiable terrain. The 50 trails are well laid out and fun to ski. Most runs are naturally formed intermediates that weave in and out of glades. Beginners have several slopes and routes from the summit; experts must be content with a few short, steep pitches. In addition to the trails, snowboarders have a terrain park and a half-pipe. Night skiing is offered Thursday–Saturday and holidays. ✉ *1 Skimobile Rd., Box 1640, North Conway* ☎ *603/356–5543; 603/356–8516 snow conditions; 800/786–6754 lodging* ⊕ *www.cranmore.com.*

King Pine Ski Area at Purity Spring Resort. Some 9 mi south of Conway, this family-run ski area has been going strong since the late 19th century. Some ski-and-stay packages include free skiing for midweek resort guests. King Pine's 16 gentle trails are ideal for beginner and intermediate skiers; experts won't be challenged except for a brief pitch on the Pitch Pine trail. There's tubing on weekend afternoons and night skiing and tubing on Friday and Saturday evenings, plus 9 mi of cross-country skiing. Indoors, you can enjoy a pool and fitness complex and go iceskating. In summer the resort is a destination for waterskiing, kayaking, loon-watching, tennis, hiking, and other activities. ✉ *1251 Eaton Rd.,*

Sit back and enjoy the view on the Conway Scenic Railroad.

East Madison ☎ *603/367–8896 or 800/373–3754* ⊕ *www.purityspring. com or www.kingpine.com.*

Forty miles of groomed cross-country trails weave through North Conway and the countryside along the **Mt. Washington Valley Ski Touring Association Network** (✉ *2079 Rte. 16/302, Intervale* ☎ *603/356–9920 or 800/282–5220* ⊕ *www.crosscountryskinh.com*).

SHOPPING

ANTIQUES **Richard Plusch Antiques** (✉ *2584 White Mountain Hwy.* ☎ *603/356–3333*) deals in period furniture and accessories, including glass, sterling silver, Oriental porcelains, rugs, and paintings.

CLOTHING More than 150 factory outlets—including L. L. Bean, Timberland, Pfaltzgraff, Lenox, Polo, Nike, Anne Klein, and Woolrich—line Route 16. A top pick for skiwear is **Joe Jones** (✉ *2709 Main St.* ☎ *603/356–9411* ⊕ *www.joejonessports.com*).

CRAFTS **Handcrafters Barn** (✉ *2473 White Mountain Hwy. [Main St./Rte. 16]* ☎ *603/356–8996* ⊕ *www.handcraftersbarn.com*) stocks the work of 350 area artists and artisans. The **League of New Hampshire Craftsmen** (✉ *2526 Main St.* ☎ *603/356–2441* ⊕ *www.nhcrafts.org*) carries the creations of the state's best artisans. **Zeb's General Store** (✉ *2675 Main St.* ☎ *603/356–9294 or 800/676–9294* ⊕ *www.zebs.com*) looks just like an old-fashioned country store and sells food items, crafts, and other products made in New England.

NIGHTLIFE

Horsefeather's (✉ 2679 *White Mountain Hwy.* ☎ 603/356–6862 ⊕ *www. horsefeathers.com*), a restaurant and bar, often has rock, blues, and folk music, especially on weekends.

WHERE TO EAT

$–$$
AMERICAN
✕ **Delaney's Hole in the Wall.** This casual sports tavern displays its memorabilia such as autographed baseballs and an early photo of skiing at Tuckerman Ravine. Entrées range from fajitas to mussels and scallops sautéed with spiced sausage and Louisiana seasonings. Live music is featured on Wednesday nights. ✉ 2966 *White Mountain Hwy. [Rte. 16], ¼ mi north of North Conway Village* ☎ 603/356–7776 ⊕ *www. delaneys.com* ▭ AE, D, MC, V.

$
AMERICAN
✕ **Muddy Moose.** This family restaurant buzzes with the noise of children. Its mac-and-cheese, blueberry-glazed ribs, burgers, and salads will satisfy kids and parents alike. A unique side dish of carrots with a hint of maple syrup is a pleasant surprise. The Muddy Moose Pie, made of ice cream, fudge, and crumbled Oreos, can feed a family of four. ✉ 2344 *White Mountain Hwy.* ☎ 603/356–7696 ⊕ *www.muddymoose. com* ⬳ *Reservations not accepted* ▭ AE, D, MC, V.

WHERE TO STAY

$$$–$$$$
🏨 **Buttonwood Inn.** A tranquil 6-acre oasis in this busy resort area, the Buttonwood is on Mt. Surprise, 2 mi northeast of North Conway Village. It's a peaceful retreat that lets you avoid the noise of downtown but still have access to area restaurants and shopping. Rooms in the 1820s farmhouse are furnished in Shaker style. Wide pine floors, quilts, and period stenciling add folksiness. Downstairs is the Mt. Surprise room, where a self-serve bar, library, board games, and a DVD library await you. **Pros:** good bedding and amenities; tranquil; clean. **Cons:** unexciting for those not wanting a remote getaway. ✉ 64 *Mt. Surprise Rd.* ✦ *Box 1817, 03860* ☎ 603/356–2625 or 800/258–2625 ⊕ *www. buttonwoodinn.com* ⬎ 9 rooms, 1 suite ⬧ *In-room: DVD (some), no TV (some). In-hotel: pool, Internet terminal, Wi-Fi hotspot* ▭ AE, MC, V ⊚ BP.

$$–$$$
🏨 **Darby Field Inn.** After a day in the White Mountains, warm up by the fieldstone fireplace in the living room. Most rooms in this unpretentious 1826 farmhouse have mountain views; several have fireplaces. There are 10 mi of cross-country and hiking trails, as well as carriage rides and sleigh rides. The inn's dining room ($$$) prepares American fare. **Pros:** clean; romantic; remote. **Cons:** better for couples than families. ✉ 185 *Chase Hill, Albany* ☎ 603/447–2181 or 800/426–4147 ⊕ *www.darbyfield.com* ⬎ 11 rooms, 4 suites ⬧ *In-room: no phone, no a/c (some), DVD (some), no TV (some), Wi-Fi. In-hotel: restaurant, bar, pool, spa, Wi-Fi hotspot, no kids under 8* ▭ AE, MC, V ⊙ *Closed Apr.* ⊚ BP.

$$$–$$$$
★
🏨 **Snowvillage Inn.** Journalist Frank Simonds built the gambrel-roofed main house in 1916. To complement the tome-jammed bookshelves, guest rooms are named for famous authors; many have fireplaces. The nicest of the rooms, with 12 windows that look out over the Presidential Range, is a tribute to Robert Frost. Two additional buildings—the carriage house and the chimney house—also have libraries. The menu

New Hampshire's Diners

Once named one of the country's "top 10 diners" by *USA Today*, the bustling **Red Arrow Diner** (✉ *61 Lowell St., Manchester* ☎ *603/626–1118* ✉ *63 Union Sq., Milford* ☎ *603/249–9222* ⊕ *www.redarrowdiner.com*) is open 24/7 and caters to politicos, students, artists, and regular Janes and Joes in the heart of the Granite State's largest city. The 1922 diner's daily "Blue Plate Specials" are served on actual blue plates, and you'll find such regular items as kielbasa and beans and house-brewed Arrow root beer and cream soda.

Up in the skiing and hiking haven of Lincoln, outdoorsy souls fuel up on hearty fare like banana-bread French toast and cherry pie à la mode at the cozy **Sunny Day Diner** (✉ *U.S. 3, just off I-93, Exit 33, Lincoln* ☎ *603/745–4833*), a handsomely restored building from the late 1950s. Travelers to the state's Lakes Region have long been familiar with the flashy pink exterior and neon signage of the **Tilt'n Diner** (✉ *61 Laconia Rd., Tilton* ☎ *603/286–2204* ⊕ *www.thecman.com*), a convivial 1950s-style restaurant that's known for its baked shepherd's pie and Southern breakfast—sausage gravy, biscuits, and baked beans with two eggs—served all day. On sunny days, dine at one of the picnic tables.

Dartmouth students and professors hobnob over stellar breakfast victuals at **Lou's Restaurant** (✉ *30 S. Main St., Hanover* ☎ *603/643-3321* ⊕ *www.lousrestaurant.net*), a cheap-and-cheerful storefront diner that serves up prodigious portions of corned-beef hash and eggs Benedict, as well as artfully decorated cupcakes and house-made donuts. Just beware of the long lines on weekend mornings. In the historic coastal

Red Arrow Diner in Manchester.

8

city of Portsmouth, the **Friendly Toast** (✉ *121 Congress St., Portsmouth* ☎ *603/430-2154* ⊕ *www. thefriendlytoast.net*) might be the most vaunted breakfast spot in the state. Creative fare like Almond Joy pancakes (with coconut, chocolate chips, and almonds) and the "Flying Fish scramble" (eggs with smoked salmon, fresh dill, and cheddar) keep hungry bellies coming back again and again.

—Andrew Collins

in the Sleigh Mill Grille ($$–$$$$; reservations essential) might include grilled rack of lamb with minted Mediterranean herbs and spices, sesame-encrusted yellow-fin tuna, or a medley pumpkin ravioli. The inn is also home to the White Mountain Cooking School, and overnight packages with cooking classes are available. You can hike easily up to beautiful Foss Mountain, directly from the inn. **Pros:** adorable property; fine dining. **Cons:** on the pricier side. ⊠ *136 Stewart Rd., 6 mi southeast of Conway, Box 68, Snowville* ☎ *603/447–2818 or 800/447–4345* ⊕ *www.snowvillageinn.com* ⤵ *18 rooms* ⚙ *In-room: no TV. In-hotel: restaurant, no kids under 6* ⊟ *AE, D, MC, V* ⏛ *BP, MAP.*

$$ ▣ **White Mountain Hotel and Resort.** West of the traffic of North Conway, the scenery becomes splendid. Rooms in this hotel at the base of Whitehorse Ledge have mountain views. Proximity to the White Mountain National Forest and Echo Lake State Park makes you feel farther away from the outlet malls than you actually are. There's a 9-hole golf course, and this area is great for biking. Three meals a day can be had at the at Ledges dining room ($$); there are also a tavern ($–$$) and a sumptuous brunch. Kids 18 and under stay free. **Pros:** scenic setting that's close to shopping; lots of activities. **Cons:** two-night-minimum summer weekends. ⊠ *2560 West Side Rd., Box 1828* ☎ *800/533–6301* ⊕ *www.whitemountainhotel.com* ⤵ *69 rooms, 11 suites* ⚙ *In-room: refrigerator, DVD, Wi-Fi. In-hotel: 2 restaurants, room service, bar, golf course, tennis court, pool, gym, laundry facilities, laundry service, Wi-Fi hotspot* ⊟ *AE, D, MC, V* ⏛ *BP, MAP.*

▌ EN
ROUTE

A great place to settle in to the White Mountains, take in one of the greatest panoramas of the mountains, and get visitor info is at the **Intervale Scenic Vista.** The stop, off Route 16 a few miles north of North Conway, is run by the DOT, has a helpful volunteer staff, features a wonderful large topographical map, and has terrific bathrooms.

KANCAMAGUS HIGHWAY

★   *36 mi between Conway and Lincoln/North Woodstock.*

Interstate 93 is the fastest way to the White Mountains, but it's hardly the most appealing. The section of Route 112 known as the Kancamagus Highway passes through some of the state's most unspoiled mountain scenery—it was one of the first roads in the nation to be designated a National Scenic Byway. The Kanc, as it's called by locals, is punctuated by overlooks and picnic areas, erupts into fiery color each fall, when photo-snapping drivers really slow things down. A number of campgrounds are off the highway. In bad weather, check with the White Mountains Visitors Bureau for road conditions.

SPORTS AND THE OUTDOORS

A couple of short hiking trails off the Kancamagus Highway (Route 112) yield great rewards with relatively little effort. The **Lincoln Woods Trail** starts from the large parking lot of the Lincoln Woods Visitor Center, 4 mi east of Lincoln. Here you can purchase the recreation pass ($5 per vehicle, good for seven consecutive days) needed to park in any of the White Mountain National Forest lots or overlooks; stopping briefly to take photos or to use the restrooms at the visitor center is permitted without a pass. The trail crosses a suspension bridge over the Pemigewasset River and follows an old railroad bed for 3 mi along the river. The parking and picnic area for **Sabbaday Falls**, about 15 mi west of Conway, is the trailhead for an easy ½-mi route to a multilevel cascade that plunges through two potholes and a flume.

DARTMOUTH–LAKE SUNAPEE

In the west-central part of the state, the towns around prestigious Dartmouth College and rippling Lake Sunapee vary from sleepy, old-fashioned outposts that haven't changed much in decades to bustling, sophisticated towns rife with cafés, art galleries, and boutiques. Among the latter, Hanover and New London are the area's main hubs, both of them increasingly popular as vacation destinations and with telecommuters seeking a quieter, more economical home base. Although distinct from the Lakes Region, greater Lake Sunapee looks like a miniature Lake Winnipesaukee, albeit with far less commercial development. For a great drive, follow the Lake Sunapee Scenic and Cultural Byway, which runs for about 25 mi from Georges Mills (a bit northwest of New London) down into Warner, tracing much of the Lake Sunapee shoreline. When you've tired of climbing and swimming and visiting the past, look for small studios of area artists. This part of the state, along with the even quieter Monadnock area to the south, has long been an informal artists' colony where people come to write, paint, and weave in solitude.

ESSENTIALS

Visitor Information Lake Sunapee Region Chamber of Commerce (☎ 603/526–6575 or 877/526–6575 ⊕ www.sunapeevacations.com).

8

NEW LONDON

16 mi northwest of Warner, 25 mi west of Tilton.

New London, the home of Colby-Sawyer College (1837), is a good base for exploring the Lake Sunapee region. A campus of stately Colonial-style buildings fronts the vibrant commercial district, where you'll find several cafés and boutiques.

GETTING HERE AND AROUND

From the south take Exit 11 on Interstate 93 to Crockett Corner and then north on Route 114. From the north take Exit 12 and travel south on Route 114. Mount Sunapee Ski Area offers a ski shuttle to and from many of the area hotels and B&Bs.

ESSENTIALS

Visitor and Ski Information Lake Sunapee Area Chamber of Commerce (☎ 603/526–6575 ⊕ www.sunapeevacations.com).

SPORTS AND THE OUTDOORS

A 3½-mi scenic auto road at **Rollins State Park** (⊠ Off Rte. 103, Main St., Warner ☎ 603/456–3808 ⊕ www.nhstateparks.com/rollins.html ☎ $4) snakes up the southern slope of Mt. Kearsarge, where you can hike a

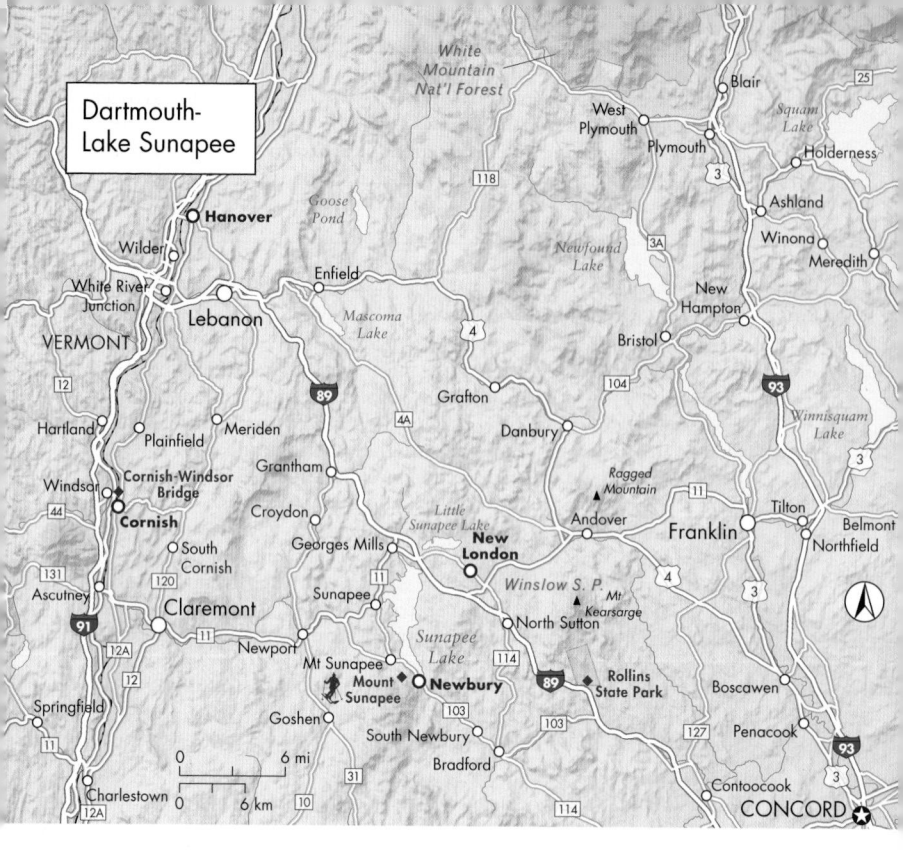

Dartmouth-
Lake Sunapee

½-mi trail to the summit. The road is closed mid-November through
mid-June.

SHOPPING

Artisan's Workshop (✉ *Peter Christian's Tavern, 186 Main St.* ☎ *603/526–
4227*) carries jewelry, glass, and other local handicrafts. Near New
London in the tiny village of Elkins, **Mesa Home Factory Store** (✉ *11
Pleasant St.* ☎ *603/526–4497*) sells striking hand-painted dinnerware,
hand-blown glassware, wrought-iron decorative arts, and other housewares at bargain prices.

THE ARTS

The **New London Barn Playhouse** (✉ *84 Main St.* ☎ *603/526–6710 or
800/633–2276* ⊕ *www.nlbarn.com*) presents Broadway-style and children's plays every summer in New Hampshire's oldest continuously
operating theater.

WHERE TO EAT AND STAY

$–$$ ✕ **Four Corners Grille and Flying Goose Brew Pub.** With 12 handcrafted
AMERICAN beers made with hops grown on-site, this inviting restaurant and pub
is a hit with beer connoisseurs. Standouts include a shepherd's pie made
with locally raised bison, paper-thin onion rings, fresh-cut steaks, and
pretzel-covered chicken. The menu changes twice a year, in the summer
and fall. Thursday evenings have live music. ✉ *40 Andover Rd., at the*

intersection of Rtes. 11 and 114 ☎ *603/526–6899* ⊕ *www.flyinggoose. com* ⊟ *AE, D, MC, V.*

¢ ✕ **Ellie's Café and Deli.** From its eggs Benedict to its oven-baked breakfast
CAFÉ chimichanga to its pancakes with candied walnuts and crème brulée
Fodor'sChoice French toast, the food at Ellie's is made for comfort and to fill you up.
★ You can also linger over a cup of hot coffee in the rustic atmosphere of
wood floors and exposed posts and beams. Lunch includes flatbread
sandwiches or a veggie "tower," a baguette stuffed with portobello
mushrooms, red onion, cucumber, and roasted red peppers. At the rear
of the restaurant the Banks Gallery displays local art. ⊠ *207 Main St.*
☎ *603/526–2488* ⊕ *www.elliescafeanddeli.com* ⊟ *D, MC, V.*

$$–$$$ ⊞ **Inn at Pleasant Lake.** This 1790s inn lies across Pleasant Lake from
★ majestic Mt. Kearsarge. Its spacious rooms have country antiques
and modern bathrooms. The restaurant ($$$$; reservations essential) presents a prix-fixe menu that changes nightly but draws raves
for such entrées as roasted rack of Australian lamb with a mushroom
sauce and such desserts as fresh berries covered in a dark chocolate
sauce. Afternoon tea and full breakfast are included. **Pros:** lakefront
with a small beach; boating. **Cons:** away from town activities. ⊠ *853*
Pleasant St., Box 1030 ☎ *603/526–6271 or 800/626–4907* ⊕ *www.*
innatpleasantlake.com ⮌ *10 rooms* ⌂ *In-room: no phone, no TV. In-*
hotel: restaurant, gym, beachfront ⊟ *MC, V* ⦿ *BP.*

$–$$ ⊞ **Follansbee Inn.** Built in 1840, this quintessential country inn on the
shore of Kezar Lake is the kind of place that almost automatically turns
strangers into friends. Next door to a quintessential white-clapboard
church, it's a perfect fit in the 19th-century village of North Sutton.
Each of the four suites and 13 rooms is filled with soft country quilts,
and several overlook the water. In winter you can ice-fish, borrow the
inn's snowshoes, or ski across the lake; in summer you can swim or boat
from the inn's pier. A 3-mi walking trail circles the lake. **Pros:** relaxed
lakefront setting; clean rooms. **Cons:** bar serves only wine and beer.
⊠ *Rte. 114, North Sutton* ☎ *603/927–4221 or 800/626–4221* ⊕ *www.*
follansbeeinn.com ⮌ *17 rooms* ⌂ *In-room: no phone, no a/c, no TV,*
Wi-Fi. In-hotel: bar, beachfront, bicycles ⊟ *MC, V* ⦿ *BP.*

EN About midway between New London and Newbury on the west side
ROUTE of the lake, **Sunapee Harbor** is an old-fashioned, all-American summer
resort community that feels like a miniature version of Wolfeboro, with
a large marina, a handful of restaurants and shops on the water, a tidy
village green with a gazebo, and a small museum in a Victorian stable
run by the historical society. A plaque outside Wild Goose Country
Store details some of Lake Sunapee's attributes—that it's one of the
highest lakes in New Hampshire, at 1,091 feet above sea level, and one
of the least polluted. An interpretive path runs along a short span of
the Sugar River, the only outflow from Lake Sunapee, which winds for
18 mi to the Connecticut River.

8

NEWBURY

8 mi southwest of New London.

Newbury is on the edge of Mt. Sunapee State Park. The mountain, which rises to an elevation of nearly 3,000 feet, and the sparkling lake are the region's outdoor recreation centers. The popular League of New Hampshire Craftsmen's Fair, the nation's oldest crafts fair, is held at the base of Mt. Sunapee each August.

GETTING HERE AND AROUND

From New London, take 114 West to 103A South, which follows the eastern coast of Lake Sunapee to Newbury.

EXPLORING

Fells. John M. Hay, who served as private secretary to Abraham Lincoln and secretary of state for Presidents William McKinley and Theodore Roosevelt, built the Fells on Lake Sunapee as a summer home in 1890. House tours offer a glimpse of early-20th-century life on a New Hampshire estate. The grounds include a 100-foot-long perennial garden and a rock garden with a brook flowing through it. Miles of hiking trails can also be accessed from the estate. The building houses art and history exhibits and hosts educational programs for children all year. The estate is sometimes rented for weddings and other events. ⊠ *456 Rte. 103A* ☎ *603/763–4789* ⊕ *www.thefells.org* ⊠ *$8* ☉ *Labor Day–Columbus Day, daily 10–4; grounds open all year dawn–dusk.*

SPORTS AND THE OUTDOORS

BEACHES AND FISHING **Sunapee State Beach** has picnic areas, a beach, and a bathhouse. You can rent canoes, too. ⊠ *Rte. 103* ☎ *603/763–5561* ⊕ *www.nhstateparks. com/sunapeebeach.html* ⊠ *$4* ☉ *Daily dawn–dusk.* **Lake Sunapee** has brook and lake trout, salmon, smallmouth bass, and pickerel.

BOAT TOURS Narrated cruises aboard the **MV *Mt. Sunapee II*** (⊠ *81 Main St., Sunapee Harbor* ☎ *603/938–6465* ⊕ *www.sunapeecruises.com*) provide a closer look at Lake Sunapee's history and mountain scenery and run from late May through mid-October, daily in summer and on weekends in spring and fall; the cost is $18. Dinner cruises are held on the **MV *Kearsarge*** (☎ *603/938–6465* ⊕ *www.mvkearsarge.com*) and leave from the dock at Sunapee Harbor, June through mid-October, Tuesday–Sunday evenings; the cost is $36 and includes a buffet dinner.

SKI AREA **Mount Sunapee**. Although the resort is state-owned, it's managed by Vermont's Okemo Mountain Resort (in Ludlow). The agreement has allowed the influx of capital necessary for operating extensive lifts, snowmaking (97% coverage), and trail grooming. This mountain is 1,510 vertical feet and has 65 trails, mostly intermediate. Experts can take to a dozen slopes, including three nice double-black diamonds. Boarders have a 420-foot-long half-pipe and a terrain park with music. In summer, the Sunapee Express Quad zooms you to the summit. From here, it's just under a mile hike to Lake Solitude. Mountain bikers can use the lift to many trails, and an in-line skate park has beginner and advanced sections (plus equipment rentals). ⊠ *Rte. 103, Box 2021* ☎ *603/763–3500; 603/763–4020 snow conditions; 877/687–8627 lodging* ⊕ *www.mtsunapee.com.*

SHOPPING

Overlooking Lake Sunapee's southern tip, **Outspokin' Bicycle and Sport** (✉ *4 Old Route 3, Sunapee Harbor* ☎ *603/763–9500* ⊕ *www.outspokin. com*) has a tremendous selection of biking, hiking, skateboarding, waterskiing, skiing, and snowboarding clothing and equipment. Right on the harbor in Sunapee village, on the marina, **Wild Goose Country Store** (✉ *77 Main St.* ☎ *603/763–5516*) carries quirky gifts, teddy bears, penny candy, pottery, and other engaging odds and ends.

WHERE TO STAY

$$–$$$ ⊡ **Sunapee Harbor Cottages**. This charming collection of six private cot-
★ tages is within a stone's throw of Sunapee Harbor. Each unit sleeps five to eight people, making this a good deal for large groups and an extravagant pleasure for couples. All have gas fireplaces, porches, and a well-chosen mix of antiques and newer furnishings. Special winter rates are available for skiers visiting nearby Mt. Sunapee. **Pros:** attractive, spacious units. **Cons:** main house blocks view of the harbor. ✉ *4 Lake Ave., Sunapee Harbor* ☎ *603/763–5052 or 866/763–5052* ⊕ *www. sunapeeharborcottages.com* ➫ *6 cottages* ⚲ *In-room: no a/c, kitchen, DVD, Wi-Fi* ⊟ *MC, V.*

HANOVER

12 mi northwest of Enfield; 62 mi northwest of Concord.

Eleazer Wheelock founded Hanover's Dartmouth College in 1769 to educate the Abenaki "and other youth." When he arrived, the town consisted of about 20 families. The college and the town grew symbioti-cally, with Dartmouth becoming the northernmost Ivy League school. Hanover is still synonymous with Dartmouth, but it's also a respected medical and cultural center for the upper Connecticut River valley.

GETTING HERE AND AROUND

Lebanon Municipal Airport, near Dartmouth College, is served by US Airways Express from New York. By car, Interstate 91 North or Interstate 89 are the best ways to get to Lebanon, Hanover, and the surrounding area. Plan on spending a day visiting Hanover and to see all the sights on the Dartmouth campus.

Shops, mostly of the independent variety but with a few upscale chains sprinkled in, line Hanover's main street. The commercial district blends almost imperceptibly with the Dartmouth campus. West Lebanon, south of Hanover on the Vermont border, has many more shops.

ESSENTIALS

Airport Lebanon Municipal Airport (✉ *5 Airpark Rd., West Lebanon* ☎ *603/298–8878* ⊕ *www.flyleb.com*).

Taxi Big Yellow Taxi (☎ *603/643-8294* ⊕ *www.bigyellowtaxis.com*).

Visitor Information Hanover Area Chamber of Commerce (✉ *53 S. Main St., Suite 216, Hanover* ☎ *603/643-3115* ⊕ *www.hanoverchamber.org*).

8

EXPLORING

★ **Dartmouth College.** Robert Frost spent part of a brooding freshman semester at this Ivy League school before giving up college altogether. The buildings that cluster around the green include the **Baker Memorial Library,** which houses such literary treasures as 17th-century editions of William Shakespeare's works. The library is also well known for Mexican artist José Clemente Orozco's 3,000-square-foot murals that depict the story of civilization in the Americas. If the towering arcade at the entrance to the **Hopkins Center for the Arts** (☎ *603/646–2422* ⊕ *hop.dartmouth.edu*) appears familiar, it's probably because it resembles the project that architect Wallace K. Harrison completed just after designing it: New York City's Metropolitan Opera House at Lincoln Center. The complex includes a 900-seat theater for film showings and concerts, a 400-seat theater for plays, and a black-box theater for new plays. The Dartmouth Symphony Orchestra performs here, as does the Big Apple Circus. In addition to African, Peruvian, Oceanic, Asian, European, and American art, the **Hood Museum of Art** (⊠ *Wheelock St.* ☎ *603/646–2808* ⊕ *www.hoodmuseum.dartmouth.edu* 🖾 *Free* ☉ *Tues. and Thurs.–Sat. 10–5, Wed. 10–9, Sun. noon–5*) owns the Pablo Picasso painting *Guitar on a Table*, silver by Paul Revere, and a set of Assyrian reliefs from the 9th century BC. The range of contemporary works, including pieces by John Sloan, William Glackens, Mark Rothko, Fernand Léger, and Joan Miró, is particularly notable. Rivaling the collection is the museum's architecture: a series of austere, copper-roofed, redbrick buildings arranged around a courtyard. Free campus tours are available on request. ⊠ *N. Main and Wentworth Sts.* ☎ *603/646–2900* ⊕ *www.dartmouth.edu.*

8

QUICK BITES Take a respite from museum-hopping with a cup of espresso, a ham-and-cheese scone, or a freshly baked brownie at the **Dirt Cowboy** (⊠ *7 S. Main St.* ☎ *603/643–1323* ⊕ *www.dirtcowboycafe.com*), a café across from the green and beside a used-book store. A local branch of a small Boston chain, **The Wrap** (⊠ *35 S. Main St.* ☎ *603/643–0202*), occupies a slick basement space with comfy sofas and has a small patio to the side. Drop by for healthy burritos, wraps, soups (try the carrot-ginger), smoothies, and energy drinks.

★ **Enfield Shaker Museum.** In 1782, two Shaker brothers from Mount Lebanon, New York, arrived on Lake Mascoma's northeastern side, about 12 mi southeast of Hanover. Eventually, they formed Enfield, the ninth of 18 Shaker communities in the United States, and moved it to the lake's southern shore, where they erected more than 200 buildings. The Enfield Shaker Museum preserves the legacy of the Shakers, who numbered 330 members at the village's peak. By 1923, interest in the society had dwindled, and the last 10 members joined the Canterbury community, south of Laconia. A self-guided walking tour takes you through 13 of the remaining buildings, among them the Great Stone Dwelling (which served until recently as a hotel, the Shaker Inn) and an 1849 stone mill. Demonstrations of Shaker crafts techniques and numerous special events take place year-round. ⊠ *447 NH Route 4A,*

Enfield ☎ *603/632–4346* ⊕ *www.shakermuseum.org* ✉ *$7.50* ☉ *Mon.–Sat. 10–5, Sun. noon–5*

Upper Valley. From Hanover, you can make a 60-mi drive up Route 10 all the way to Littleton for a highly scenic tour of the upper Connecticut River valley. You'll have views of the river and Vermont's Green Mountains from many points. The road passes through groves of evergreens, over leafy ridges, and through delightful hamlets. Grab gourmet picnic provisions at the general store on Lyme's village common—probably the most pristine of any in the state—and stop at the bluff-top village green in historical Haverhill (28 mi north of Hanover) for a picnic amid the panorama of classic Georgian- and Federal-style mansions and faraway farmsteads. You can follow this scenic route all the way to the White Mountains region or loop back south from Haverhill— along Route 25 to Route 118 to U.S. 4 west—to Enfield, a drive of about 45 mi (75 minutes).

WHERE TO EAT

$$

AMERICAN

✕ **Canoe Club.** Bedecked with canoes, paddles, and classic Dartmouth paraphernalia, this festive spot presents live jazz and folk music most nights. The mood may be casual, but the kitchen presents rather imaginative food, including a memorable starter of a roasted beet medley with spiced chocolate sauce and orange glaze. Among the main courses, the seafood cioppino, with shrimp, scallops, onion, and sweet pepper, is a favorite. There's also a lighter, late-night menu. ⊠ *27 S. Main St.* ☎ *603/643–9660* ⊕ *www.canoeclub.us* ⊟ *AE, D, DC, MC, V.*

¢

AMERICAN

★

✕ **Lou's.** This is one of two places in town where students and locals really mix. After all, it's hard to resist. A Hanover tradition since 1948, this diner-cum-café-cum-bakery serves possibly the best breakfast in the valley—a plate of *migas* (eggs, cheddar, salsa, and guacamole mixed with tortilla chips) can fill you up for the better part of the day; blueberry-cranberry buttermilk pancakes also satisfy. Or grab a seat at the old-fashioned soda fountain and order an ice-cream sundae. ⊠ *30 S. Main St.* ☎ *603/643–3321* ⊕ ⊟ *AE, MC, V* ☉ *No dinner.*

ITALIAN

$

✕ **Lui Lui.** The creatively topped thin-crust pizzas and huge pasta portions are only part of the draw at this chatter-filled eatery; the other is its dramatic setting inside a former power station on the Mascoma River. Pizza picks include the Tuscan (mozzarella topped with tomato and roasted garlic) and the grilled chicken with barbecue sauce. Pasta fans should dive into a bowl of linguine with homemade clam sauce. The owners also run Molly's Restaurant and Jesse's Tavern, which are nearby. *8 Glen Rd., West Lebanon* ☎ *603/298–7070* ⊕ *www.luilui.com* ⊟ *AE, MC, V.*

$

ECLECTIC

✕ **Murphy's.** Students, visiting alums, and locals regularly descend upon this wildly popular pub, which has walls lined with shelves of old books. The varied menu features burgers and salads as well as meat loaf, crusted lamb sirloin, and eggplant filled with tofu. Check out the extensive beer list. ⊠ *11 S. Main St.* ☎ *603/643–4075* ⊕ *www. murphysonthegreen.com* ⊟ *AE, D, DC, MC, V.*

The Cornish–Windsor Bridge is the longest covered bridge in the United States, at 460 feet.

WHERE TO STAY

$$$–$$$$ ★ **Hanover Inn.** If you're in town for a Dartmouth event, you'll want to stay on the town's—and the college's—main square. Owned by Dartmouth, this sprawling, Georgian-style brick structure rises four white-trimmed stories. The original building was converted to a tavern in 1780, and this expertly run inn, now greatly enlarged, has been operating ever since. Rooms have Colonial reproductions, Audubon prints, large sitting areas, and marble-accented bathrooms. The swank Zins Wine Bistro ($–$$) prepares lighter but innovative fare. **Pros:** center of campus and town; well managed. **Cons:** breakfast not included; overpriced. ✉ *The Green, 2 S. Main St., Box 151* ☎ *603/643–4300 or 800/443–7024* 🌐 *www.hanoverinn.com* *92 rooms, 23 suites* *In-room: Wi-Fi. In-hotel: restaurant, room service, bar, Internet terminal, Wi-Fi hotspot* *AE, D, DC, MC, V.*

$$$–$$$$ **Trumbull House.** The sunny guest rooms of this white Colonial-style house—on 16 acres on Hanover's outskirts—have king- or queen-size beds, writing desks, feather pillows, and other comfortable touches, as well as Wi-Fi. A romantic guesthouse has a private deck, whirlpool tub, refrigerator, and wet bar. Breakfast, with a choice of entrées, is served in the formal dining room or in front of the living room fireplace. Rates include the use of a nearby health club. **Pros:** quiet setting; lovely home; big breakfast. **Cons:** 5 mi east of town. ✉ *40 Etna Rd.* ☎ *603/643–2370 or 800/651–5141* 🌐 *www.trumbullhouse.com* *4 rooms, 1 suite, 1 cottage* *In-room: Wi-Fi. In-hotel: restaurant* *AE, D, DC, MC, V* *BP.*

CORNISH

22 mi south of Hanover.

Today Cornish is best known for its four covered bridges and for being the home of reclusive late author J. D. Salinger, but at the turn of the 20th century the village was known primarily as the home of the country's then most popular novelist, Winston Churchill (no relation to the British prime minister). His novel *Richard Carvell* sold more than a million copies. Churchill was such a celebrity that he hosted Teddy Roosevelt during the president's 1902 visit. At that time Cornish was an enclave of artistic talent. Painter Maxfield Parrish lived and worked here, and sculptor Augustus Saint-Gaudens set up his studio and created the heroic bronzes for which he is known.

GETTING HERE AND AROUND

About 5 mi west of town on Route 44, the Cornish-Windsor Bridge crosses the Connecticut River between New Hampshire and Vermont. The Blacksmith Shop covered bridge is 2 mi east of Route 12A on Town House Road, and the Dingleton Hill covered bridge is 1 mi east of Route 12A on Root Hill Road. Cornish itself is small enough to see in one morning.

EXPLORING

Cornish-Windsor Bridge. This 460-foot bridge, 1½ mi south of the Saint-Gaudens National Historic Site, connects New Hampshire to Vermont across the Connecticut River. It dates from 1866 and is the longest covered wooden bridge in the United States. The notice on the bridge reads: WALK YOUR HORSES OR PAY TWO DOLLAR FINE.

Fodor's Choice ★ **Saint-Gaudens National Historic Site.** Just south of Plainfield, where River Road rejoins Route 12A, a small lane leads to this historic site, where you can tour sculptor Augustus Saint-Gaudens's house, studio, gallery, and 150 acres of grounds and gardens. Scattered throughout are full-size casts of his works. The property has two hiking trails, the longer of which is the Blow-Me-Down Trail. Concerts are held every Sunday afternoon in July and August. The museum is about 1½ mi north of the Cornish-Windsor Bridge on Route 12A. ⊠ *Off Rte. 12A* ☎ *603/675–2175* ⊕ *www.nps.gov/saga* ☞ *$5, good for 7-day reentry* ☉ *Buildings June–Oct., daily 9–4:30; grounds daily dawn–dusk.*

THE MONADNOCKS AND MERRIMACK VALLEY

Southwestern and south-central New Hampshire mix village charm with city hustle and bustle across two distinct regions. The Merrimack River valley has the state's largest and fastest-growing cities: Nashua, Manchester, and Concord. To the west, in the state's sleepy southwestern corner, is the Monadnock region, one of New Hampshire's least developed and most naturally stunning parts. Here you'll find plenty of hiking trails as well as peaceful hilltop hamlets that appear barely changed in the past two centuries. Mt. Monadnock, southern New Hampshire's largest peak, stands guard over the Monadnock region, which has more than 200 lakes and ponds. Rainbow trout, smallmouth and largemouth bass, and some northern pike swim in Chesterfield's Spofford Lake. Goose Pond, just north of Keene, holds smallmouth bass and white perch.

The towns are listed in counterclockwise order, beginning with Nashua and heading north to Manchester and Concord; then west to Charleston; south to Walpole; southwest to Keene and Jaffrey; and finally northeast to Peterborough.

NASHUA

98 mi south of Lincoln/North Woodstock; 48 mi northwest of Boston; 36 mi south of Concord; 50 mi southeast of Keene.

Once a prosperous manufacturing town that drew thousands of immigrant workers in the late 1800s and early 1900s, Nashua declined following World War II, as many factories shut down or moved to where labor was cheaper. Since the 1970s, however, the metro area has jumped in population, developing into a charming, old-fashioned community. Its low-key downtown has classic redbrick buildings along the Nashua River, a tributary of the Merrimack River. Though not visited by tourists as much as other communities in the region, Nashua (population 90,000) has some good restaurants and an engaging museum.

GETTING HERE AND AROUND

A good place to start exploring Nashua is at Main and High streets, where a number of fine restaurants and shops are located. Downtown Nashua has free Wi-Fi.

ESSENTIALS

Taxi SK Taxi (☎ *603/882–5155*). **D & E Taxi** (☎ *603/889–3999*).

WHERE TO EAT

$$
BISTRO
Fodor's Choice
★
✕ **Michael Timothy's Urban Bistro**. Part hip bistro, part jazzy wine bar Michael Timothy's is so popular that even foodies from Massachusetts drive here. The regularly changing menu might include stuffed pheasant with foie gras risotto and cranberry-clove jus or wood-grilled venison loin with port reduction, herb spaetzle, creamed morel mushrooms, and stewed lentils. Wood-fired pizzas are also a specialty—try the one topped with sirloin tips, caramelized onions, mushrooms, salami, sautéed spinach, and three cheeses. Sunday brunch is a big hit here. ✉ *212 Main St.* ☎ *603/595–9334* ⊕ *www.michaeltimothys.com* ▭ *AE, D, MC, V* ⊗ *Open for dinner at 3 Tues.–Sat.*

$$
ITALIAN
✕ **Villa Banca**. On the ground floor of a dramatic, turreted office building, this spot with high ceilings and tall windows specializes in traditional and contemporary Italian cooking. Start with Gorgonzola artichokes and move on to pasta Alfredo. The butternut squash ravioli is a sweet delight, and the macadamia nut–encrusted tilapia will satisfy the fish lover at your table. Note the exotic-martini menu, a big draw at happy hour. ✉ *194 Main St.* ☎ *603/598–0500* ⊕ *www.villabanca.com* ▭ *AE, D, DC, MC, V* ⊗ *No lunch Sun.*

MANCHESTER

18 mi north of Nashua, 53 mi north of Boston.

Manchester, with 108,000-plus residents, is New Hampshire's largest city. The town grew up around the Amoskeag Falls on the Merrimack River, which fueled small textile mills through the 1700s. By 1828, Boston investors had bought the rights to the Merrimack's water power and built the Amoskeag Mills, which became a testament to New England's manufacturing capabilities. In 1906 the mills employed 17,000 people and weekly churned out more than 4 million yards of cloth. This vast enterprise served as Manchester's entire economic base; when it closed in 1936, the town was devastated.

Today Manchester is mainly a banking and business center. The old mill buildings have been converted into warehouses, classrooms, restaurants, museums, and office space. The city has the state's major airport, as well as the Verizon Wireless Arena, which hosts minor-league hockey matches, concerts, and conventions.

GETTING HERE AND AROUND

Manchester Airport, the state's largest airport, has rapidly become a cost-effective, hassle-free alternative to Boston's Logan Airport, with nonstop service to more than 20 cities. Manchester can be hard to get around, but it offers a number of taxi services.

ESSENTIALS

Airport Manchester Airport (✉ *1 Airport Rd., Manchester* ☎ *603/624–6539* ⊕ *www.flymanchester.com*).

Taxi Evergreen Limousine Airport Service (☎ *603/624–0801* ⊕ *evergreenmata.com*). **Manchester Taxi** (☎ *603/623–2222*).

Visitor Information Manchester Area Convention & Visitors Bureau (✉ *889 Elm St., 3rd fl., Manchester* ☎ *603/666–6600* ⊕ *www.manchestercvb.com*).

EXPLORING

☺   **Amoskeag Mills**. There are miles of hallways in the brick buildings that
Fodor's Choice   comprise this former textile mill. To get a sense of what they are and
★   what they meant to Manchester, there are two key museums. The **SEE Science Center** (☎ *603/669–0400* ⊕ *www.see-sciencecenter.org* 🎫 *$6* ☽ *Weekdays 10–4, weekends 10–5*) is a hands-on science lab and children's museum with more than 70 exhibits. If you're in Manchester, child or adult, don't miss it. The world's largest permanent LEGO installation of regular-sized LEGOs is here, depicting the city's Amoskeag Mill-yard and the city of Manchester as it was in 1915. This mind-blowing exhibit is made up of 3 million LEGOs across 2,000 square feet. More important, the exhibit also conveys the massive size and importance of the mills, which ran a mile on each side of the Merrimack. Upstairs in the same building the **Millyard Museum** (☎ *603/622–7531* ⊕ *www.manchesterhistoric.org* 🎫 *$6* ☽ *Wed.–Sat. 10–4*) has state-of-the-art exhibits that depict the region's history from when Native Americans lived alongside and fished the Merrimack River to the heyday of Amoskeag Mills. The interactive Discovery Gallery is geared toward

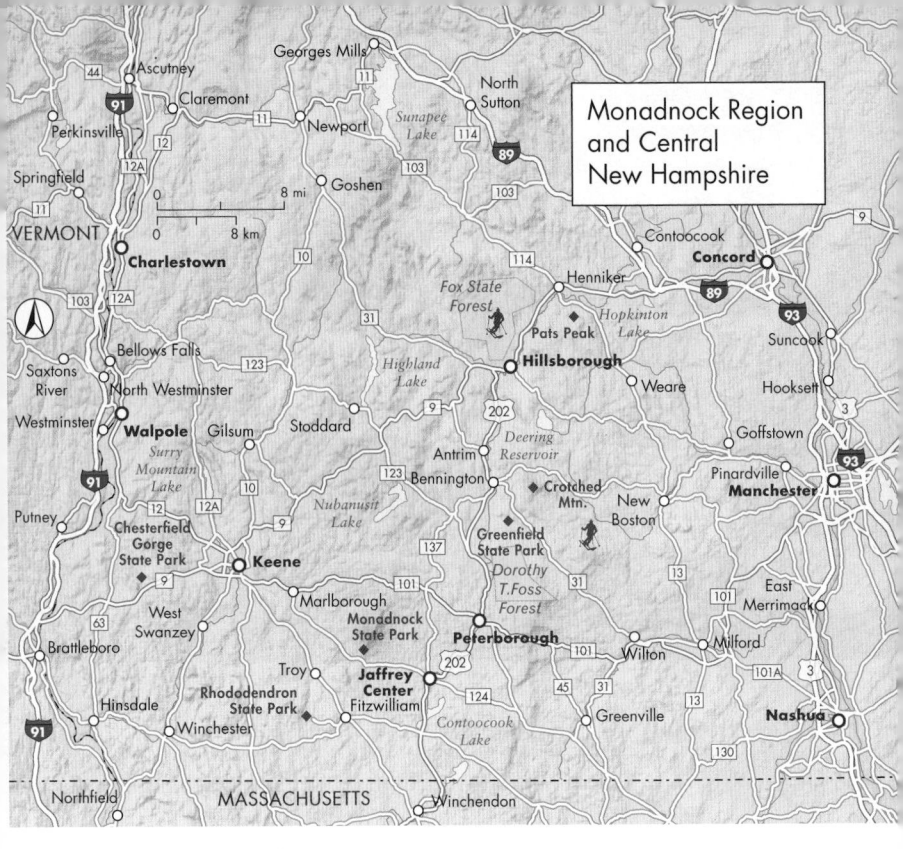

Monadnock Region
and Central
New Hampshire

kids; there's also a lecture/concert hall and a large museum shop. ✉ *Mill No. 3, 200 Bedford St. (entrance at 255 Commercial St.)*.

Fodor's Choice **Currier Museum of Art.** A modern Sol LeWitt mural faces the original ★ 1929 Italianate entrance to a permanent collection of European and American paintings, sculpture, and decorative arts from the 13th to the 20th century, including works by Edouard Monet, Picasso, Edward Hopper, Andrew Wyeth, and Georgia O'Keeffe. A major 2008 expansion more than doubled the gallery space and created a new shop, visitor entrance, café, and a winter garden. Also run by the Currier (tours depart from the museum) is the nearby Frank Lloyd Wright–designed Zimmerman House, built in 1950. Wright called this sparse, utterly functional living space "Usonian," an invented term used to describe 50 such middle-income homes he built with his vision of distinctly American architecture. It's New England's only Frank Lloyd Wright–designed residence open to the public. ✉ *150 Ash St.* ☎ *603/669–6144; 603/626–4158 Zimmerman House tours* ⊕ *www.currier.org* ✉ *$10, free Sat. 10–noon; $18 Zimmerman House (reservations essential)* ☉ *Sun., Mon., Wed., and Fri. 11–5; first Thurs. of every month 11–8; Sat. 10–5; call for Zimmerman House tour hrs.*

At the Currier Museum of Art, you can enjoy European and American classics, or visit a nearby Frank Lloyd Wright house.

NIGHTLIFE AND THE ARTS

THE ARTS — The **Palace Theatre** (✉ *80 Hanover St.* ☎ *603/668–5588 box office* ⊕ *www.palacetheatre.org*) presents musicals and plays throughout the year. It also hosts the state's philharmonic and symphony orchestras and the Opera League of New Hampshire.

NIGHTLIFE — **Club 313** (✉ *93 S. Maple St.* ☎ *603/628–6813* ⊕ *www.club313.net*) is New Hampshire's most popular disco for gays and lesbians. It's open Wednesday–Sunday. Revelers come from all over to drink at the **Yard** (✉ *1211 S. Mammoth Rd.* ☎ *603/623–3545* ⊕ *www.theyardrestaurant. com*), which is also a steak and seafood restaurant.

WHERE TO EAT

$–$$ ✕ **Cotton.** Inside one of the old Amoskeag Mills buildings mod lighting
AMERICAN — and furnishings and a patio set in an arbor give this restaurant a swanky
★ — atmosphere. A blunt neon sign that reads FOOD belies its sophisticated menu. The kitchen specializes in putting a new spin on comfort food. Start with pan-seared crab cakes or the lemongrass chicken salad. The menu changes four times a year but might include 16-oz all-natural Delmonico steak or wood-grilled scallops as well as superb sweet-potato hash. For the past seven years Cotton's has been voted best martinis in New Hampshire by New Hampshire Magazine. ✉ *75 Arms St.* ☎ *603/622–5488* ⊕ *www.cottonfood.com* ⊟ *AE, D, MC, V* ☾ *No lunch weekends.*

¢–$ ✕ **Jewell and the Beanstalk.** If you feel as if you just walked into a gen
AMERICAN — eral store, that's because for many years that's just what this space
★ — was. It's been in the family for three generations, and meals made with items grown by urban farmers are standard fare as are homemade pies,

cookies, and cakes. The cranberry chicken salad sandwich is delicious as is the roasted pork loin melt with sautéed apples and spinach. New Hampshire–made products are on sale at the café. ⊠ *793 Somerville St.* ☎ *603/624–3709* ⊕ ⊟ *AE, D, MC, V* ☽ *No dinner except music night on Wed.*

¢ ✕ **Red Arrow Diner.** This tiny diner is ground zero for presidential hopefuls in New Hampshire come primary season. The rest of the time, a mix of hipsters and oldsters, including comedian and Manchester native Adam Sandler, favor this neon-streaked, 24-hour greasy spoon, which has been going strong since 1922. Filling fare—platters of kielbasa, French toast, liver and onions, chicken Parmesan with spaghetti, and the diner's famous panfries—keeps patrons happy. Homemade sodas and éclairs round out the menu. Talk to "Santa," a long-time patron who sits at the end of the counter sipping coffee, about the history of the diner. ⊠ *61 Lowell St.* ☎ *603/626–1118* ⊕ *redarrowdiner.com* ⊟ *AE, D, MC, V.*

AMERICAN
Fodor's Choice
★

WHERE TO STAY

$$–$$$ 📷 **Ash Street Inn.** Because it's in an attractive residential neighborhood of striking Victorian homes, staying in this five-room B&B will give you the best face of Manchester. Every room in the historic sage-green 1885 house, run by Darlene and Eric Johnston, is painted a different color. There are good linens, and there's decanted brandy in the sitting room, which has the house's original stained glass. In the summer, a wraparound porch is a nice place to sit and enjoy a cooked-to-order breakfast, served on a flexible schedule. **Pros:** spotless newly decorated rooms; within walking distance of the Currier Museum. **Cons:** not a full-service hotel. ⊠ *118 Ash St.* ☎ *603/668–9908* ⊕ *www.ashstreetinn. com* ⌥ *5 rooms* ♿ *In-room: Wi-Fi. In-hotel: Wi-Fi hotspot, no kids under 12* ⊟ *AE, D, MC, V* ⏷ *BP.*

$$$–$$$$ 📷 **Bedford Village Inn.** If you trade direct downtown access for a lovely manor outside of town, you'll be rewarded by the comforts of this beautiful and well-run property. The hayloft and milking rooms of this 1810 Federal farmstead, just a few miles southwest of Manchester, contain lavish suites with king-size four-poster beds, plus such modern perks as two phones and high-speed Wi-Fi. The restaurant ($$$$)—a warren of elegant dining rooms with fireplaces and wide pine floors—presents contemporary fare that might include a starter of organic Burgundy escargot followed by a roasted Gloucester monkfish. A five-course chef's tasting menu is available for $85. **Pros:** relaxing property just outside Manchester; exceptional grounds; great restaurant. **Cons:** outside of town. ⊠ *2 Olde Bedford Way, Bedford* ☎ *603/472–2001 or 800/852–1166* ⊕ *www.bedfordvillageinn.com* ⌥ *14 suites, 2 apartments* ♿ *In-room: DVD, Wi-Fi. In-hotel: restaurant, room service, bar, laundry service, Internet terminal, Wi-Fi hotspot* ⊟ *AE, D, DC, MC, V.*
★

$–$$ 📷 **Radisson Manchester.** Of Manchester's many chain properties, the 12-story Radisson has the most central location—a short walk from Amoskeag Mills and great dining along Elm Street. Rooms are simple and clean, perfect for business travelers. Next door is the Center of New Hampshire conference center. Because of its busy location, this is the only hotel in the state where you have to pay for parking. **Pros:** central downtown location. **Cons:** fee for parking; unexciting chain hotel. ⊠ *700 Elm St.* ☎ *603/625–1000 or 800/395–7046* ⊕ *www.radisson. com/manchesternh* ⤴ *244 rooms, 6 suites* ♿ *In-room: Wi-Fi. In-hotel: 2 restaurants, room service, bar, pool, gym, laundry service, Internet terminal, Wi-Fi hotspot, parking (paid), some pets allowed* ☰ *AE, D, DC, MC, V.*

CONCORD

20 mi northwest of Manchester, 67 mi northwest of Boston, 46 mi northwest of Portsmouth.

New Hampshire's capital (population 42,000) is a quiet town that tends to the state's business but little else—the sidewalks roll up promptly at 6. Stop in town to get a glimpse of New Hampshire's State House, which is crowned by a gleaming gold, eagle-topped dome.

GETTING HERE AND AROUND
Taxis can help get you around town, though Main Street is easy to walk about. Event information can be found at ⊕ *www.concord.com.*

ESSENTIALS
Taxi **Concord Cab** (☎ *603/225–4222*).

Visitor Information Concord Chamber of Commerce (⊠ *40 Commercial St., Concord* ☎ *603/224–2508* ⊕ *www.concordnhchamber.com*).

EXPLORING
The **Concord on Foot** walking trail winds through the historic district. Maps for the walk can be picked up at the Greater Concord **Chamber of Commerce** (⊠ *40 Commercial St.* ☎ *603/224–2508* ⊕ *www. concordnhchamber.com*) or stores along the trail.

EXPLORING
☺ **Christa McAuliffe Planetarium.** In a 40-foot dome theater, shows on the solar system, constellations, and space exploration abound. The planetarium was named for the Concord teacher who was killed in the Space Shuttle *Challenger* explosion in 1986. Children love seeing the tornado tubes, magnetic marbles, and other hands-on exhibits. Outside, explore the scale-model planet walk and the human sundial. ⊠ *New Hampshire Technical Institute campus, 2 Institute Dr.* ☎ *603/271–7831* ⊕ *www. starhop.com* 💺 *$9; $3 planetarium shows* ⊗ *Mon.–Thurs. 10–5, Fri. 10–9, weeekends 10–5; call for show times and reservations.*

New Hampshire Historical Society. Steps from the state capitol, the society's museum is a great place to learn about the Concord coach, the stagecoach that was a popular mode of transportation before railroads. Rotating exhibitions may include New Hampshire quilts and their stories and historical protraits of residents. ⊠ *6 Eagle Sq.* ☎ *603/228-6688* ⊕ *www.nhhistory.org* 💺 *$5.50* ⊗ *Tue.–Sat. 9:30–5, Sun. noon–5.*

Pierce Manse. Franklin Pierce lived in this Greek-Revival home before he moved to Washington to become the 14th U.S. president. He's buried nearby. ⊠ *14 Horseshoe Pond La.* ☎ *603/225–4617* ⊕ *www. politicallibrary.org* 💺 *$7* ⊗ *Hours vary seasonally; check Web site.*

Fodor's Choice ★ **State House**. A self-guided tour of the neoclassical, gilt-domed state-house, built in 1819, is a real treat. You get total access to the building and can even take a photo with the governor. This is the oldest capitol building in the nation in which the legislature uses its original chambers. In January and June you can watch the assemblies in action once a week: the 24 senators of the New Hampshire Senate (the fourth-smallest American lawmaking body) meet once a week. In a wild inversion, the state's representatives number 400—one representative per 3,000 residents, a ratio that is a world record. At the visitor center you'll see paraphernalia from decades of presidential primaries. ⊠ *107 N. Main St.* ☎ *603/271–2154* ⊕ *www.ci.concord.nh.us/tourdest/statehs* ⊠ *Free* ☉ *Weekdays 8–4:30.*

NIGHTLIFE AND THE ARTS

The **Capitol Center for the Arts** (⊠ *44 S. Main St.* ☎ *603/225–1111* ⊕ *www.ccanh.com*) has been restored to reflect its Roaring '20s origins. It hosts touring Broadway shows, dance companies, and musical acts. The lounge at **Hermanos Cocina Mexicana** (⊠ *11 Hills Ave.* ☎ *603/224–5669* ⊕ *www.hermanosmexican.com*) stages live jazz Sunday through Thursday nights.

SHOPPING

Capitol Craftsman Jewelers (⊠ *16 N. Main St.* ☎ *603/224–6166* ⊕ *www.capitolcraftsman.com*) sells fine jewelry and handicrafts. The **League of New Hampshire Craftsmen** (⊠ *36 N. Main St.* ☎ *603/228–8171* ⊕ *www.nhcrafts.org*) exhibits crafts in many media. **Mark Knipe Goldsmiths** (⊠ *2 Capitol Plaza, Main St.* ☎ *603/224–2920* ⊕ *www.knipegold.com*) sets antique stones in rings, earrings, and pendants.

WHERE TO EAT AND STAY

¢–$ AMERICAN ★ ✕ **Arnie's Place**. If you need a reason to make the 1.5-mi detour from Interstate 93, then more than 50 kinds of homemade ice cream should do the trick. Try the toasted-coconut, raspberry, or vanilla flavors. The chocolate shakes are a real treat for chocoholics. The lemon freeze will give you an ice cream headache in no time, but it's worth it. A small dining room is available for dishes such as a barbecue platter (smoked on the premises), hamburgers, and hot dogs, but the five walk-up windows and picnic benches are the way to go. ⊠ *164 Loudon Rd., Concord Heights* ☎ *603/228–3225* ⊟ *MC, V* ☉ *Closed Nov.–Jan.*

$ ECLECTIC ✕ **Barley House**. A lively, old-fashioned tavern practically across from the capitol building and usually buzzing with a mix of politicos, business folks, and tourists, the Barley House serves dependable chow: chorizo-sausage pizzas, burgers smothered with peppercorn-whiskey sauce and blue cheese, chicken potpies, Cuban sandwiches, beer-braised bratwurst, jambalaya, and Mediterranean chicken salad—it's an impressive melting pot of a menu. The bar turns out dozens of interesting beers, on tap and by the bottle, and there's also a decent wine list. It's open until 1 AM. ⊠ *132 N. Main St.* ☎ *603/228–6363* ⊕ *www.thebarleyhouse.com* ⊟ *AE, D, DC, MC, V* ☉ *Closed Sun.*

¢–$ THAI ✕ **Siam Orchid**. This dark, attractive Thai restaurant with a colorful rickshaw gracing its dining room serves spicy and reasonably authentic Thai food. It draws a crowd from the capitol each day for lunch. Try the

8

fiery broiled swordfish with shrimp curry sauce or the pine-nut chicken in an aromatic ginger sauce. There's a second location in Manchester. ⊠ *158 N. Main St.* ☎ *603/228–3633* ⊕ *www.siamorchid.com* ▭ *AE, D, DC, MC, V* ⊘ *No lunch weekends.*

$$ ⓣ **The Centennial.** This is the most contemporary hotel in New Hampshire, and it's home to Granite, the state's most contemporary restaurant ($$) and bar, making it a draw for the state's politicians and those doing business here. The modernity is unexpected, as this imposing brick-and-stone building was constructed in 1892 for widows of Civil War veterans, but the interior was renovated head-to-toe. Boutique furniture and contemporary art immediately set the tone in the lobby. Rooms have luxury linens, sleek carpet and furniture, and flat-screen TVs. Bathrooms have stone floors, granite countertops, and stand-alone showers. It's the state's first foray into a boutique-y, well-designed hotel, and it's a huge success. **Pros:** super contemporary and sleek hotel; very comfortable and clean rooms; great bar and restaurant. **Cons:** busy. ⊠ *96 Pleasant St.* ☎ *603/227–9000 or 800/360–4839* ⊕ *www. thecentennialhotel.com* ⇆ *27 rooms, 5 suites* ⓧ *In-room: refrigerator, DVD, Wi-Fi. In-hotel: restaurant, room service, bar, gym, Internet terminal, Wi-Fi hotspot* ▭ *AE, D, DC, MC, V.*

CHARLESTOWN

Charlestown has the state's largest historic district. About 60 homes, handsome examples of Federal, Greek-Revival, and Gothic-Revival architecture, are clustered about the town center; 10 of them were built before 1800. Several merchants on the main street distribute brochures that describe an interesting walking tour of the district.

GETTING HERE AND AROUND

You can reach Charlestown from Interstate 91, but it's best to follow Route 12 North from Keene for a gorgeous scenic route. Walking about downtown Charlestown should take only 15 minutes of your day, but it's worth admiring the buildings in the town center. The Fort at No. 4 is less than 2 mi from downtown, north on Route 11.

EXPLORING

ⓒ   **Fort at No. 4.** In 1747, this fort was an outpost on the periphery of Colonial civilization. That year fewer than 50 militiamen at the fort withstood an attack by 400 French soldiers, ensuring that northern New England remained under British rule. Today, costumed interpreters at this living-history museum cook dinner over an open hearth and demonstrate weaving, gardening, and candle making. Each year the museum holds reenactments of militia musters and battles of the French and Indian War. ⊠ *267 Springfield Rd., ½ mi north of Charlestown* ☎ *603/826–5700 or 888/367–8284* ⊕ *www.fortat4.org* ▦ *$8* ⊘ *Early June–Oct., Wed.–Sun. 10–4:30.*

SPORTS AND THE OUTDOORS

On a bright, breezy day you might want to detour to the **Morningside Flight Park** (⊠ *357 Morningside La., off Rte. 12/11, 5 mi north of Charlestown* ☎ *603/542–4416* ⊕ *www.flymorningside.com*), considered to be among the best flying areas in the country. Watch the bright colors of gliders as they take off from the 450-foot peak, or take hang-gliding lessons yourself.

WALPOLE

13 mi south of Charlestown.

Walpole possesses one of the state's most perfect town greens. Bordered by Elm and Washington streets, it's surrounded by homes built about 1790, when the townsfolk constructed a canal around the Great Falls of the Connecticut River and brought commerce and wealth to the area. The town now has 3,200 inhabitants, more than a dozen of whom are millionaires. Walpole is home to Florentine Films, Ken Burns's production company.

GETTING HERE AND AROUND

A short jaunt off of Route 12, north of Keene. The small downtown is especially photogenic.

OFF THE BEATEN PATH

Sugarhouses. Maple-sugar season occurs about the first week in March when days become warmer but nights are still frigid. A drive along maple-lined back roads reveals thousands of taps and buckets catching the labored flow of unrefined sap. Plumes of smoke rise from nearby sugarhouses, where "sugaring off," the process of boiling down this precious liquid, takes place. Many sugarhouses are open to the public; after a tour and demonstration, you can sample the syrup. **Bascom Maple Farm** (⊠ *56 Sugarhouse Rd., Alstead* ☎ *603/835–6361* ⊕ *www.bascommaple.com*) has been family-run since 1853 and produces more maple than anyone in New England. Visit the 2,200-acre farm and get maple pecan pie and maple milk shakes. **Stuart & John's Sugar House & Pancake Restaurant** (⊠ *19 Rte. 63, Westmoreland* ☎ *603/399–4486* ⊕ *www.stuartandjohnssugarhouse.com*) conducts a tour and sells syrup and maple gifts in a roadside barn. It also serves a memorable pancake breakfast weekends mid-February–April and mid-September–November.

SHOPPING

★ At **Boggy Meadow Farm** (⊠ *13 Boggy Meadow La.* ☎ *603/756–3300 or 877/541–3953* ⊕ *www.boggymeadowfarm.com*) you can watch the cheese process unfold, from the 200 cows being milked to the finer process of cheese-making. The farmstead's raw-milk cheeses can be sampled and purchased in the store. It's worth a trip just to see the beautiful 400-acre farm.

WHERE TO EAT

$–$$
FRENCH
Fodor's Choice
★

✕ **The Restaurant at L. A. Burdick Chocolate.** Famous candy maker Larry Burdick, who sells his artful hand-filled and hand-cut chocolates to top restaurants around the Northeast, is a Walpole resident. This restaurant has the easygoing sophistication of a Parisian café and may tempt you to linger over an incredibly rich hot chocolate. The Mediterranean-inspired menu utilizes fresh, often local ingredients and changes daily. Of course, dessert is a big treat here, featuring Burdick's tempting chocolates and pastries. For dinner, you might start with a selection of artisanal cheeses or reduction trio of pâtés, followed by a house beef stew or homemade

8

sausages. ⊠ *47 Main St.* ☎ *603/756–2882* ⊕ *www.burdickchocolate.
com* ▭ *AE, D, MC, V* ⊗ *No dinner Sun. and Mon.*

KEENE

*17 mi southeast of Walpole; 20 mi northeast of Brattleboro, Vermont;
56 mi southwest of Manchester.*

Keene is the largest city in the state's southwest corner. Its rapidly gen-
trifying main street, with several engaging boutiques and cafés, is America's widest (132 feet). Each year, on the Saturday before Halloween,
locals use the street to hold a Pumpkin Festival, where the small town
competes with big cities such as Boston for the most jack o' lanterns in
one place at one time.

ESSENTIALS

Visitor Information Keene Chamber of Commerce (⊠ *48 Central Sq.*
☎ *603/352–1303* ⊕ *www.keenechamber.com*). **Monadnock Travel Council**
(⬠ *Box 358, Keene 03431* ☎ *800/432–7864* ⊕ *www.monadnocktravel.com*).

EXPLORING

Keene State College. This hub of the local arts community is on the tree-
lined main street and has a worthwhile art gallery and an art-house
movie theater. **The Thorne-Sagendorph Art Gallery** (☎ *603/358–2720*
⊕ *www.keene.edu/tsag*) contains a permanent collection including works
by George Rickey, Robert Mapplethorpe, and Vargian Bogosian and presents traveling exhibits. The **Putnam Theater** (☎ *603/358–2160* ⊕ *www.
keene.edu/putnam*) shows foreign and art films. ⊠ *229 Maint St.*

**OFF THE
BEATEN
PATH**

Chesterfield's Route 63. If you're in the mood for a country drive or
bike ride, head west from Keene along Route 9 to Route 63 (about
11 mi) and turn left toward the hilltop town of Chesterfield. This is an
especially rewarding journey at sunset, as from many points along the
road you can see west out over the Connecticut River valley and into
Vermont. The village center consists of little more than a handful of
dignified granite buildings and a small general store. You can loop back
to Keene via Route 119 east in Hinsdale and then Route 10 north—the
entire journey is about 40 mi.

NIGHTLIFE AND THE ARTS

Elm City Brewing Co. (⊠ *222 West St.* ☎ *603/355–3335* ⊕ *www.
elmcitybrewing.com*), at the Colony Mill, serves light food and draws a
mix of college students and young professionals. At Keene State College,
the **Redfern Arts Center at Brickyard Pond** (⊠ *229 Main St.* ☎ *603/358–
2168* ⊕ *www.keene.edu/racbp*) has year-round music, theater, and
dance performances in two theaters and a recital hall.

SHOPPING

★ **Colony Mill Marketplace** (⊠ *222 West St.* ☎ *603/357–1240* ⊕ *www.
colonymill.com*), an old mill building, holds 30-plus stores and boutiques such as the Toadstool Bookshop, which carries many children's
and regional travel and history books, and Pocketful of Rye, a gift store.
Also popular is Antiques at Colony Mill, which sells the wares of more
than 120 dealers and has a food court.

WHERE TO EAT AND STAY

$$–$$$
MEDITERRANEAN
Fodor's Choice
★

✕ **Luca's.** A deceptively simple storefront bistro overlooking Keene's graceful town square, Luca's dazzles with epicurean creations influenced by Italy, France, Greece, Spain, and North Africa. Enjoy sautéed shrimp with cilantro pesto and plum tomatoes, three-cheese ravioli with artichoke hearts, or grilled salmon marinated in cumin and coriander. For a real treat, ask Luca to surprise you with a sampler of items from his extensive menu, and don't forget to ask for the locally made gelato or sorbet for dessert. ✉ *10 Central Sq.* ☎ *603/358–3335* ⊕ *www.lucascafe. com* ═ *AE, MC, V.*

$$–$$$
★

🏨 **Chesterfield Inn.** Surrounded by gardens, the Chesterfield Inn sits above Route 9, the main road between Keene and Brattleboro, Vermont. Fine antiques and Colonial-style fabrics adorn the spacious guest quarters; 10 have fireplaces, and several have private decks or terraces that face the stunning perennial gardens and verdant Vermont hills. In the restaurant ($$) rosemary- and walnut-crusted rack of lamb, crab and papaya salad, and grilled spiced shrimp are among the highlights. **Pros:** attractive gardens; close to the Connecticut River. **Cons:** breakfast ends early. ✉ *20 Cross Rd., West Chesterfield* 🖃 *Box 155, Chesterfield 03443* ☎ *603/256–3211 or 800/365–5515* ⊕ *www.chesterfieldinn.com* 🛏 *13 rooms, 2 suites* ♿ *In-room: refrigerator, Wi-Fi. In-hotel: restaurant, Wi-Fi hotspot, some pets allowed* ═ *AE, D, MC, V* ⃝*BP.*

$

🏨 **E. F. Lane Hotel.** You can get a rare touch of urbanity in the sleepy Monadnocks in this upscale redbrick hotel in the middle of Main Street. The hotel was retrofitted in 2000 from the former Goodnow department store, a Keene landmark for more than 100 years. That accounts for some interesting room features, like a wall of exposed brick and 12-foot ceilings. Spacious rooms are furnished individually with reproduction Victorian antiques. "Chairman" suites have stairs that lead to an upper level and come with two bathrooms. There's live entertainment in the Chase Tavern Tuesday–Saturday. Ask for your free movie tickets and popcorn vouchers for the Colonial Theater across the street. **Pros:** spacious and comfortable rooms; center of town; free movie tickets. **Cons:** no gym. ✉ *30 Main St.* ☎ *603/357–7070 or 888/300–5056* ⊕ *www. eflane.com* 🛏 *33 rooms, 7 suites* ♿ *In-room: refrigerator (some), Wi-Fi. In-hotel: restaurant, bar, Internet terminal, Wi-Fi hotspot, some pets allowed* ═ *AE, D, MC, V* ⃝*CP.*

$
☺

🏨 **Inn at East Hill Farm.** If you have kids, and they like animals, meet bliss: a family resort with daylong kids' programs on a 170-acre 1830 farm overlooking Mt. Monadnock. Kids can start at 9 AM with milking the cows. Other activities include collecting eggs, horseback and pony riding, arts and crafts, storytelling, hiking, sledding, hay rides in summer, and horse-drawn sleigh rides in winter. You can feed sheep, donkeys, cows, rabbits, horses, chickens, goats, and ducks and play with Chloe the farm dog. Twice weekly in summer, trips are scheduled to a nearby lake for boating, waterskiing, and fishing. Rates include most activities and three meals in a camplike dining hall. Rooms are comfortable, not fancy, and some have fireplaces. The inn is 10 mi southeast of Keene off Route 124. **Pros:** rare agritourism and family resort; activities galore; beautiful setting. **Cons:** remote location; noisy mess-hall dining. ✉ *460*

Monadnock St., Troy ☎ *603/242–6495 or 800/242–6495* ⊕ *www.east-hill-farm.com* ⇥ *56 rooms* ♿ *In-room: no phone, no a/c (some), refrigerator, no TV (some), Wi-Fi. In-hotel: restaurant, tennis court, pools, children's programs (ages 2–18), laundry facilities, Wi-Fi hotspot, some pets allowed* ▭ *D, MC, V* ⦿ *FAP.*

JAFFREY CENTER

16 mi southeast of Keene.

Novelist Willa Cather came to Jaffrey Center in 1919 and stayed in the Shattuck Inn, which now stands empty on Old Meeting House Road. Not far from here, she pitched the tent in which she wrote several chapters of *My Ántonia*. She returned nearly every summer thereafter until her death and was buried in the Old Burying Ground, which also contains the remains of Amos Fortune, a former slave who bought his freedom in 1863 and moved to town when he was 71. Fortune, who was a tanner, also bought the freedom of his two wives. He died at the age of 91.

GETTING HERE AND AROUND

Jaffrey Center's historic district is on Route 124 and is home to a number of brick buildings. It should take less than an hour to view it in its entirety. Two miles east of town on Route 124 can be found the Old Burying Ground, which is behind the Meeting House.

ESSENTIALS

Visitor Information Jaffrey Chamber of Commerce (☎ *603/532–4549* ⊕ *www.jaffreychamber.com*).

EXPLORING

Cathedral of the Pines. This outdoor memorial pays tribute to Americans who have sacrificed their lives in service to their country. There's an inspiring view of Mt. Monadnock and Mt. Kearsarge from the Altar of the Nation, which is composed of rock from every U.S. state and territory. All faiths are welcome to hold services here; organ music for meditation is played at midday from Tuesday through Thursday in July and August. The Memorial Bell Tower, with a carillon of bells from around the world, is built of native stone. Norman Rockwell designed the bronze tablets over the four arches. Flower gardens, an indoor chapel, and a museum of military memorabilia share the hilltop. It's 8 mi southeast of Jaffrey Center. ⊠ *10 Hale Hill Rd., off Rte. 119, Rindge* ☎ *603/899–3300 or 866/229–4520* ⊕ *www.cathedralofthepines.com* 🎟 *Donations accepted* ⊘ *May–Oct., daily 9–5.*

SPORTS AND THE OUTDOORS

★ **Monadnock State Park.** The oft-quoted statistic about Mt. Monadnock is that it's America's most-climbed mountain—second in the world to Japan's Mt. Fuji. Whether this is true or not, locals agree that it's never lonely at the top. Some days, especially during foliage season, more than 400 people crowd its bald peak. Monadnock rises to 3,165 feet, and on a clear day the hazy Boston skyline is visible from its summit. The park maintains picnic grounds and a small campground (RVs welcome, but no hookups) with 28 sites. Five trailheads branch into more than two

Jaffrey Center is known for its historic buildings and its proximity to Mount Monadnock.

dozen trails of varying difficulty that wend their way to the top. Allow between three and four hours for any round-trip hike. A visitor center has free trail maps as well as exhibits documenting the mountain's history. In winter, you can cross-country ski along roughly 12 mi of groomed trails on the lower elevations of the mountain. ⊠ *Off Rte. 124, 2½ mi north of Jaffrey Center* ☎ *603/532–8862* ⊕ *www.nhstateparks. com/monadnock.html* ⊠ *$4* ☉ *Daily dawn–dusk* ☞ *No pets.*

Rhododendron State Park. More than 16 acres of wild rhododendrons bloom in mid-July at this park, which has the largest concentration of *Rhododendron maximum* north of the Allegheny Mountains. Bring a picnic lunch and sit in a nearby pine grove or follow the marked footpaths through the flowers. On your way here, be sure to pass through Fitzwilliam's well-preserved historic district of Colonial and Federal-style houses, which have appeared on thousands of postcards. ⊠ *Rte. 119 W, off Rte. 12, 10 mi southwest of Jaffrey Center, Fitzwilliam* ☎ *603/239–8862* ⊕ *www.nhstateparks.com/rhodo.html* ⊠ *$4* ☉ *May–Nov., daily 8–sunset.*

SHOPPING

You'll find about 35 dealers at **Bloomin' Antiques** (⊠ *3 Templeton Turnpike, Fitzwilliam Center* ☎ *603/585–6688*). Meanwhile, **Fitzwilliam Antiques Centre** (⊠ *13 Rte. 12, Fitzwilliam* ☎ *603/585–9092*) sells the goods of some 40 dealers.

THE ARTS

Amos Fortune Forum, near the Old Burying Ground, brings nationally known speakers to the 1773 meetinghouse on summer evenings. ⊠ *Jaffrey Meetinghouse, Rt. 124* ⊕ *www.amosfortune.com.*

WHERE TO EAT AND STAY

$$ ✕ **JP Stephens.** An appealing choice either for lunch or dinner, this rustic-
AMERICAN timbered dining room overlooks a small mill pond in Rindge, about 8 mi south of Jaffrey Center. The 1790 building used to house a sawmill, a gristmill, a forge, and a blacksmith. The sole meunière is delicate and flavorful and the apple brandy and walnut chicken is sweet and brazen. Try the pub cheese made with horseradish or the twice-baked potato. ⊠ *377 U.S. 202, Rindge* ☎ *603/899–3322* ⊕ *jpstephensrestaurant.com* ▭ *D, MC, V* ☾ *Closed Mon.*

$–$$ ⬚ **Benjamin Prescott Inn.** Thanks to the dairy farm surrounding this 1853 Colonial house—with its stenciling and wide pine floors—you feel as though you're miles out in the country rather than just minutes from Jaffrey Center. A full breakfast of local eggs, homemade muffins, and blueberry pancakes with fruit and maple syrup prepares you for a day of antiquing or hiking. **Pros:** inexpensive; homey and comfortable. **Cons:** 2 mi east of town. ⊠ *433 Turnpike Rd. (Rte. 124 E)* ☎ *603/532–6637 or 888/950–6637* ⊕ *www.benjaminprescottinn.com* ⬈ *7 rooms, 3 suites* ⬩ *In-room: no phone, no TV, Wi-Fi. In-hotel: Wi-Fi hotspot, no kids under 10* ▭ *AE, MC, V* ⼌ *BP.*

$ ⬚ **The Monadnock Inn.** Rooms in this 1830s home are painted in lively lavenders, yellows, or peaches, a cheery presence in the heart of pristine Jaffrey Center, and a perfect place to get away from it all. Although full of period furnishings, they have a hip sensibility as well as high-thread-count bedding, fluffy towels, and fine toiletries. There's a good restaurant with an impressive Sunday brunch; indulge in the delightful banana bread French toast or any dish with fresh eggs from a local farm. For dinner, try the lobster mac and cheese or the New Hampshire veal schnitzel. **Pros:** well-lit rooms with lacy curtains; feels like grandma's house. **Cons:** limited amenities. ⊠ *379 Main St., Box 484* ☎ *603/532–7800 or 877/510–7019* ⊕ *www.themonadnock.com* ⬈ *9 rooms, 2 suites* ⬩ *In-room: no phone, no a/c, DVD (some), no TV (some), Wi-Fi. In-hotel: restaurant, bar, Wi-Fi hotspot* ☾ *Dining room closed Tues.* ▭ *AE, D, DC, MC, V* ⼌ *CP.*

$$$ ⬚ **Woodbound Inn.** A favorite with families and outdoors enthusiasts, this 1819 farmhouse became an inn in 1892. It occupies 200 acres on the shores of Contoocook Lake. Accommodations are functional but clean and cheerful; they range from quirky rooms in the main inn to modern hotel-style rooms in the Edgewood building to cabins with fireplaces by the water. There's a 9-hole, golf course and lots of boating and fishing. **Pros:** relaxed, lakefront resort; new focus on food. **Cons:** older; simple furnishings. ⊠ *247 Woodbound Rd., Rindge* ☎ *603/532–8341 or 800/688–7770* ⊕ *www.woodboundinn.com* ⬈ *44 rooms, 39 with bath; 11 cabins* ⬩ *In-room: refrigerator (some), no TV (some). In-hotel: restaurant, bar, golf course, tennis court, some pets allowed* ▭ *AE, MC, V* ⼌ *BP, MAP.*

8

com 13 rooms, 8 with private baths ☝ In-hotel: restaurant, bar, tennis courts, pool, some pets allowed (fee) ⊟ No credit cards ⊘ Closed Apr. and Nov. ⦿*BP, MAP.*

$ ☷ **Jack Daniels Motor Inn.** With so many dowdy motels in southwestern
★ New Hampshire, it's a pleasure to find one as bright and clean as the Jack Daniels, just ½ mi north of downtown Peterborough. The rooms are large and furnished with attractive reproduction antiques. Try to get one of two rooms looking out on the Contoocook River; otherwise, second-floor rooms have chairs on the hallway overlooking the river. **Pros:** affordable rooms; low-key atmosphere. **Cons:** basic motel-style rooms; have to drive or walk into town. ⊠ *80 Concord St. (U.S. 202)* ☏ *603/924–7548 www.jackdanielsmotorinn.com* ⇱ *17 rooms* ☝ *In-room: refrigerator (some), DVD (some), Wi-Fi. In-hotel: Wi-Fi hotspot, some pets allowed* ⊟ *AE, D, DC, MC, V.*

Inland Maine

WORD OF MOUTH

"The best foliage . . . is inland not on the coast. I drive up to Green-ville and then up the west side of Moosehead Lake. At Greenville you [can] take a ride on the Katahdin steamship . . . the leaves are extra gorgeous when viewed on a sunny day from water."

—Virginia

WELCOME TO INLAND MAINE

TOP REASONS TO GO

★ **Baxter State Park:** Mt. Katahdin stands as a sentry over Baxter's forestland in its "natural wild state." Climbing the state's highest peak takes all day, but you can choose from many outstanding outdoor adventures.

★ **Moosehead Lake:** Surrounded by mountains, Maine's largest lake—dotted with islands and chiseled with inlets and coves—retains the rugged beauty that so captivated author Henry David Thoreau in the mid-1800s.

★ **Water sports:** It's easy to get out on the water with scheduled cruises on large inland lakes; marinas and outfitters renting boats, canoes, and kayaks throughout the region; and white-water rafting trips on several rivers.

★ **Winter pastimes:** For downhill skiing, choose from large mountain resorts with spa services, shopping, and condos or smaller ones that are family-friendly and less crowded. Maine's dense woods are perfect for snowmobiling, snowshoeing, cross-country skiing, and dogsledding.

1 Western Lakes and Mountains. Lakes both quiet and busy, classic New England villages, and ski resorts fit perfectly in the forested landscape. In winter, this is ski country; snowmobiling and snowshoeing are also popular. In summer, the woods and water draw vacationers for a cool escape. In fall, foliage drives invite exploration of the region's national forest and state parks. In spring, there are no crowds, but fishermen, white-water rafters, and canoeists make their way here.

2 The North Woods. Much of the North Woods' private forestland is open for public recreation and best experienced by paddling a canoe or raft, hiking, snowshoeing, snowmobiling, or fishing. Some great destinations are mostly undeveloped Moosehead Lake, Baxter State Park, and Allagash Wilderness Waterway. Greenville, a laidback and woodsy resort town, is a good base for day trips—take a drive (go slow!) down a "moose alley."

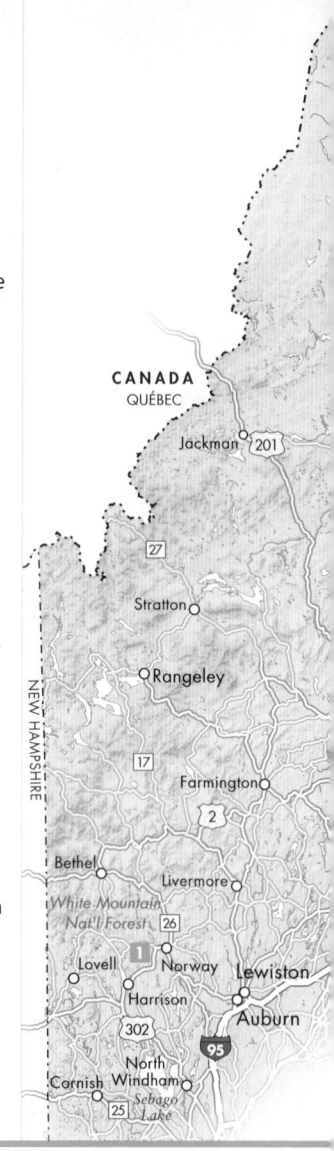

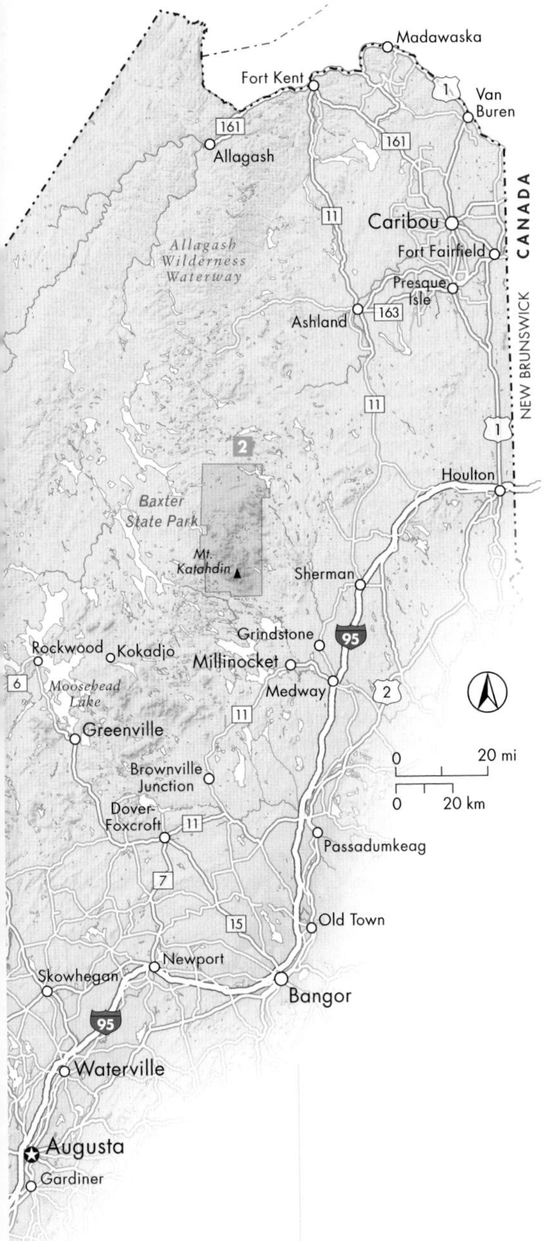

Madawaska

Fort Kent

Van
Buren

161

Allagash

161

11 Caribou

Allagash
Wilderness
Waterway

Fort Fairfield

Presque
Isle

Ashland 163

11

2

Houlton

Baxter
State Park

Mt.
Katahdin ▲

Sherman

Rockwood Kokadjo

Grindstone

95

6 Moosehead
Lake

Millinocket

Medway 2

Greenville

Brownville
Junction

Dover-
Foxcroft 11

Passadumkeag

7

15

Old Town

Skowhegan

Newport

Bangor

95

Waterville

Augusta

Gardiner

CANADA

NEW BRUNSWICK

1

0   20 mi

0   20 km

GETTING
ORIENTED

Though Maine is well
known for its miles of
craggy coastline, the inland
part of the state is surprisingly vast and much less
populated. Less than an
hour's drive from the bays
and ocean, huge swaths of
forestland are dotted with
lakes (sometimes called
"ponds" despite their size).
Summer camps, ski areas,
and small villages populate
the western part of the
state, which stretches north
along the New Hampshire
border to Québec. Quiet
waters are easy to find in
the more remote inland
areas, but busier Sebago
Lake is just north of coastal
Portland, Maine's larg-
est city. The northwest
area is more rugged and
remote while in the north-
central part of the state,
wilderness areas beckon
outdoor lovers to the North
Woods, which extend north
and west to Canada.

9

INLAND MAINE PLANNER

When to Go

Inland's Maine's most popular hiking trails and beaches may get busy in warm weather, but if splendid isolation is what you crave, you can easily find it. In summer, traffic picks up but rarely creates jams, except in a few spots. Peak lodging rates apply, but moderate weather makes this a great time to visit. Inland Maine gets hotter than the coast, though less so along lakes and at higher elevations. July and August are warmest; September is less busy.

Western Maine is the state's premier destination for leaf-peepers—hardwoods are more abundant here than on the coast. Late September through mid-October is peak foliage season.

Maine's largest ski areas can make their own snow; they usually open in mid-November and often operate into April. Inland Maine typically has snow cover by Christmas, so cross-country skiing, snowshoeing, and snowmobiling are in full swing by the end of the year. In ski towns, many lodgings charge peak rates in the winter.

Snowmelt ushers in mud season in early spring. Mid-May to mid-June is black fly season; they're especially pesky in the woods but less bothersome in town. Spring is a prime time for canoeing and fishing.

Getting Here and Around

Two primary airports serve Maine: Portland International (PWM ⊕ *www.portlandjetport.org*) and Bangor International (BGR ⊕ *www.flybangor.com*). Portland is closer to the Western Lakes and Mountains area; Bangor is more convenient to the North Woods. Regional flying services, operating from regional and municipal airports, provide access to remote lakes and wilderness areas and offer scenic flights (see specific towns for more information).

Because Maine is large and rural, a car is essential. U.S. 2 is the major east–west thoroughfare in western Maine, winding from Bangor to New Hampshire. Interstate 95 is a departure point for many visitors to inland Maine, especially the North Woods. The highway heads inland at Brunswick and is a toll road, the Maine Turnpike, from the New Hampshire border to Augusta. Because of the hilly terrain and abundant lakes and rivers, inland Maine roads are often curvy. Traffic rarely gets heavy, though highways often pass right through instead of around the larger towns, which can slow your trip a bit.

There are few public roads in Maine's North Woods, though private logging roads there are often open to the public (sometimes by permit and fee). When driving these roads, always give lumber-company trucks the right of way; loggers must drive in the middle of the road and often can't move over or slow down for cars. Be sure to have a full tank of gas before heading onto the many private roads in the region.

Planning Your Time

Inland Maine locales are often destinations where visitors stay their entire trip. That's certainly true of those who come to ski at a resort, fish at a remote sporting camp, or just relax at a lakeside cabin. After a day hike on a mountain trail reached by driving gravel logging roads, visitors are unlikely to hurry on to another town. Vacation rental homes and cottages often require a week's stay, as do lakeside cottage resorts. Generally speaking, the farther inland you go, the farther it is between destinations.

About the Restaurants

Fear not, lobster lovers: this succulent, emblematic Maine food is on the menu at many inland restaurants, from fancier establishments to roadside places. Lobster dishes are more common than boiled lobster dinners, but look for daily specials. Shrimp, scallops, and other seafood are also menu mainstays, and you may find surprises like bison burgers or steaks from a nearby farm. Organic growers and natural foods producers are planted throughout the state and often sell their food to finer restaurants nearby. Seasonal foods like pumpkins, blackberries, and strawberries make their way into homemade desserts, as do Maine's famed blueberries. Many lakeside resorts and sporting camps have a reputation for good food; some of the latter will cook the fish you catch.

About the Hotels

Although there is a higher concentration of upscale inns on the coast than inland, Bethel, Bridgton, the Kingfield area, and Rangeley have sophisticated hotels and inns. At lodgings near ski resorts, peak-season rates may apply in winter and summer. Both Sebago and Kezar lakes have full-service cottage resorts (usually a week's stay is required). The two largest ski resorts, Sunday River and Sugarloaf, offer a choice of hotels and condos. Greenville has the largest selection of lodgings in the North Woods region, with a nice mix of fine and homey inns. Lakeside sporting camps, from the primitive to the upscale, are popular around Rangeley and the North Woods. Many have cozy cabins heated with woodstoves and serve three hearty meals a day.

For information on state park campsites contact the **Maine State Parks Campground Reservation Program** (207/624–9950, 800/332–1501 in Maine www. campwithme.com).

WHAT IT COSTS					
	¢	$	$$	$$$	$$$$
Restaurants	under $8	$8–$12	$13–$20	$21–$28	over $28
Hotels	under $80	$80–$120	$121–$170	$171–$220	over $220
Campgrounds	under $10	$10–$17	$18–$35	$36–$50	over $50

Restaurant prices are per person, for a main course at dinner. Hotel prices are for a standard double room during peak season and not including tax or gratuities. Some inns add a 15% service charge.

Outdoor Activities

People visit inland Maine year-round for hiking, biking (mountain biking is big at ski resorts off-season), camping, fishing, boating, canoeing, kayaking, white-water rafting, downhill and cross-country skiing, snowshoeing, and snowmobiling.

Bicycling: For information on bicycling in Maine, contact the **Bicycle Coalition of Maine** (207/623–4511 www. bikemaine.org).

Boating: Raft Maine (www. raftmaine.com) provides information on white-water rafting on the Kennebec, Penobscot, and Dead rivers.

Fishing: For information about licenses, contact the **Maine Department of Inland Fisheries and Wildlife** (207/287–8000 www. mefishwildlife.com). For assistance in finding a fishing guide, contact the **Maine Professional Guides Association** (www.maineguides. org), which represents Registered Maine Guides. These guides are also available through most wilderness camps, sporting goods stores, and outfitters.

Skiing: For alpine and cross-country skiing information, contact **Ski Maine** (207/773–7669 www.skimaine.com).

Snowmobiling: The **Maine Snowmobile Association** (207/622–6983 www. mesnow.com) distributes an excellent statewide trail map of about 3,500 mi of trails.

9

INLAND MAINE FALL FOLIAGE DRIVE

Throughout Maine, pine, spruce, and fir trees offset the fall foliage, seeming to deepen the orange, red, and yellow hues. But hardwoods, like the vibrant sugar maples, are more common inland. This route follows Western Maine's mountains, passing stunning overlooks, waterfalls, hiking trails, and a lakeside state park.

From Houghton and Mexico, Route 17 winds as it ascends, the countryside splashed with rich reds and oranges. The drive's literal pinnacle is **Height of Land**— where mountain vistas are reflected in the many (and often connected) lakes, ponds, rivers, and streams. On a clear day you can see west to New Hampshire and Canada. **Mooselookmeguntic Lake** and **Upper Richardson Lake** seem to float in the sea of forestland below. A few miles north of here at the Rangeley overlook, observe how the east end of town forms a small isthmus between Rangeley Lake and Haley Pond.

BEST TIME TO GO

Fall color usually peaks in the Rangeley area in mid-October. Learn more and get weekly foliage updates in season (⊕ www.mainefoliage.com).

PLANNING YOUR TIME

The Rangeley Lakes National Scenic Byway (⊕ www.byways.org) makes up most of this 52-mi drive (1½ hours without stops), but plan for a relaxed full day of exploring.

In tiny, welcoming Oquossoc, where Routes 17 and 4 meet, **The Farmer's Daughter** welcomes passersby with displays of pumpkins and mums during autumn. You can pick up apple cider and picnic items at this specialty foods store. Or stop for the **Gingerbread House Restaurant** for a meal, or just ice cream or baked goods. After a snack break, you can learn more about the outdoor enthusiasts that have been coming to this area since the mid-1800s at the **Rangeley Outdoor Sporting Heritage Museum**, which is expected to open in summer 2010

Rangeley, 7 mi along Route 4, has restaurants, inns, waterfront parks, and outdoorsy shops. The countryside sweeps into view along public hiking trails at both **Saddleback Maine** ski resort and the 175-acre **Wilhelm Rich Museum**.

Also along or near this scenic drive are **Rangeley Lake State Park** and the **Appalachian Trail**, both accessible from Routes 4 and 17. Overhanging foliage frames waterfalls at the scenic rest areas at or near each end of the drive that are perfect for picnics: Smalls Falls on Route 4, the byway's eastern terminus, and Coos Canyon on Route 17

NEED A BREAK?

At **The Farmer's Daughter** (⊠ *13 Rumford Rd. [Rte. 17], Oquossoc* ☎ *207/864–2492* ⊕ *www. thefarmersdaughteronline. com*) specialty food store, produce comes from the family farm. At the bakery counter, you can buy a cup of coffee, or apple cider in season.

Wilhelm Reich Museum (⊠ *19 Orgonon Circle, Rangeley* ☎ *207/864–3443* ⊕ *www. wilhelmreichmuseum.org* ▭ *Museum $6, grounds free* ⊙ *Museum July and Aug., Wed.–Sun. 1–5, Sept., Sun. 1–5. Grounds daily 8–sunset*) showcases the life and work of controversial physician-scientist Wilhelm Reich (1897–1957). There are magnificent views from the observatory and the many trails on the 175-acre grounds.

Rangeley Lakes Heritage Trust (⊠ *52 Carry Rd. [Rte. 4], Oquossoc* ☎ *207/864– 7311* ⊕ *www.rlht.org*) protects 13,000 acres of area land. Contact them for trail maps and more information about local activities.

9

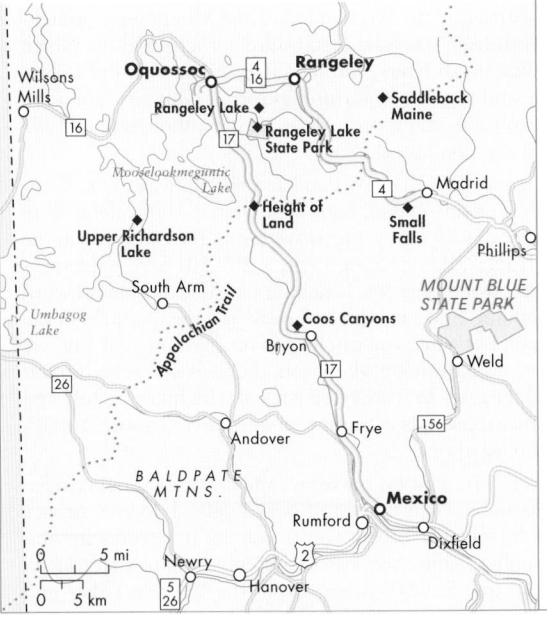

By Mary Ruoff   Unlike Maine's more famous, more populated, and more visited coast, inland Maine is a four-season destination. With strings of lakes and rivers framed by mountainous terrain, hilly pastoral stretches, classic New England villages with restaurants and shops that entice but don't overwhelm, and the region's most extensive wilderness areas, Maine's interior lures visitors in summer, fall, winter, and spring (yes, the slow season, but canoeists, fishermen, and white-water rafters venture inland).

The most visited areas are the Western Lakes and Mountains—stretching west and north from the New Hampshire border—and the North Woods—extending north from central Maine. While much of inland Maine is remote and rugged, opportunities for outdoor recreation are plentiful and renowned, and crowds do form here, though thankfully they're scattered and don't set the tone.

Sebago and Long lakes, north of Portland and the gateway to the Western Lakes and Mountains region, hum with boaters and watercraft in the summer. Sidewalks fill and traffic slows along the causeway in the tourist hub of Naples. Baxter State Park, a 209,501-acre wilderness park in the North Woods has Mt. Katahdin (an Abenaki Indian word for "Great Mountain"), Maine's highest peak and the terminus of the Appalachian Trail. But while you can hike in much of the park and see few other visitors even during peak season, the treeless, rocky summit of Katahdin and the trails to it are often packed with hikers in July and August and on nice weekends in September and early October. Yes, it's a crowd, but a collegial one.

Come winter, ski resorts wait for big snows and make snow in between. Maine often gets snow when the rest of New England doesn't, or vice versa, so track the weather here if you're coming to partake in winter sports or simply to enjoy the season's serenity. Maine's largest ski resorts, Sugarloaf and Sunday River, are in the Western Lakes and

Mountains region. Saddleback Mountain in Rangeley is an up-and-coming family-friendly resort, as is Shawnee Peak in Bridgton. But not to worry, the lift lines don't get too long.

Though they didn't come in the winter, "rusticators" began flocking to Maine to vacation in the mid-1800s, arriving at inland destinations by train or steamship, just as they did on Maine's coast. Escaping the summer heat and city pollution, these wealthy urbanites headed to the mountains to hike, swim, canoe, fish, hunt, and relax, staying at rustic sporting camps or at the grand hotels that cropped up in some of the most scenic spots. Moosehead Lake's Mt. Kineo—a walled outcropping north of Greenville where Indian tribes from throughout the Northeast came for flint—gave rise to one of the nation's largest and fanciest hotels. Rangeley was discovered for its sport fishing in the mid-1800s and is still a haven for anglers, who come to fish for "world-class" brook trout and landlocked salmon. Modern fly-fishing was born in the Rangeley region, and many of the local waters are restricted to fly-fishing.

The legacy of the rusticators and the locals who catered to them lives on at the sporting camps still found on inland Maine's remote lakes and rivers, albeit in fewer numbers. It also survives through Maine's unique system of licensed outdoor guides, known as Registered Maine Guides. These days they may lead kayak trips, hiking expeditions, white-water rafting excursions, and moose safaris as well as fishing and canoe trips. Guides are happy to show you their license—it's the law that they have one, and some also opt to wear a badge.

WESTERN LAKES AND MOUNTAINS

From Sebago Lake, less than 20 mi northwest of Portland, the sparsely populated Western Lakes and Mountains stretch north along the New Hampshire border to Québec. Each season offers different outdoor highlights: you can choose from snow sports, hiking, mountain biking, leaf-peeping, fishing, and paddling. The Sebago Lake area bustles with activity in summer. Harrison and the Waterfords are quieter, Center Lovell is a dreamy escape, and Bridgton is a classic New England town. So is Bethel, in the valley of the Androscoggin River; Sunday River, one of Maine's two major ski resorts, is nearby. The more rural Rangeley Lake area brings long stretches of pine, beech, spruce, and sky and more classic inns. Carrabassett Valley, just north of Kingfield, is home to Sugarloaf, a major ski resort with a challenging golf course.

SEBAGO LAKE AREA

17 mi northwest of Portland.

Sebago Lake is Maine's second largest lake after Moosehead and provides all the drinking water for Greater Portland. Many wilderness camps and year-round homes surround Sebago, which is popular with water-sports enthusiasts. Naples occupies an enviable location between Long and Sebago lakes. The town swells with seasonal residents and visitors in summer and, though winter is the slow season, things heat

Western Lakes and Mountains

Moxie Pond

Monson

6

1

Bingham

201

Stratton

27

16

Solon

201

Oquossoc

Rangeley   Saddleback   **Kingfield**
Maine

Wilsons   Rangeley Lake
Mills   State Park

New
Portland

Skowhegan

Height of
Land   4   Phillips

New
Vineyard

27

2

17

Weld

Farmington   **Waterville**

Andover

Grafton Notch
State Park   South Arm   Mexico
26   Rumford   Dixfield   Wilton   27

95

NEW HAMPSHIRE

Hanover   Chisholm   Livermore Falls

Sunday
River   Newry   2

Bethel   Locke Mills   Mt. Abram
Ski Resort   Livermore   202

White Mountain   Bryant   26
Nat'l Forest   Pond   **AUGUSTA**

Greenwood   Buckfield   4   v17

South Paris   Turner

**Center
Lovell**   Norway   Greene

Waterford   26

Lovell   Harrison   Lewiston   295

302   Mechanic Falls   Auburn   95

Bridgton   Casco   17
Fryeburg   Naples   Newcastle

Brownfield   Sabbathday Lake
Shaker Museum   Brunswick   1

Hiram   South Casco   Bath
Sebago Lake   Raymond   Boothbay
State Park   295
Kezar   Freeport   Georgetown
Falls   25   Yarmouth
Sebago   Falmouth
Lake   302   *Casco
Bay*

Standish

Gorham   **Portland**   *Atlantic Ocean*

4   95

0   10 mi

0   10 km

up in February with a winter carnival and ice-fishing derby. On clear days, the view up Long Lake takes in snowcapped Mt. Washington. The causeway separating Long Lake from Brandy Pond in the center of Naples pulses with activity in the summer. Open-air cafés overflow, boats and watercraft ply the water, and throngs of families parade along the sidewalk edging Long Lake.

GETTING HERE AND AROUND

Sebago Lake, gateway to Maine's Western Lakes and Mountains, is about 20 mi from Portland on U.S. Route 302.

ESSENTIALS

Vacation Rentals Krainin Real Estate (✉ *1539 Roosevelt Tr. [Rte. 302], Raymond* ☎ *800/332–1806* ⊕ *www.krainin.com*).

Visitor Information Sebago Lakes Region Chamber of Commerce (✉ *747 Roosevelt Tr. [U.S. 302], Windham* ☎ *207/892–8265* ⊕ *www. sebagolakeschamber.com*).

OFF THE
BEATEN
PATH
Sabbathday Lake Shaker Museum. Established in the late 18th century, this is the last active Shaker community in the United States, with fewer than 10 members. Open for guided tours are four buildings with rooms of Shaker furniture, folk art, tools, farm implements, and crafts from the 18th to the early 20th century: the 1794 Meetinghouse; the 1839 Ministry's Shop, where the elders and eldresses lived until the early 1900s; the 1821 Sister's Shop, where household goods and candies were made for sale and still are on a smaller scale; and the 1816 Spinhouse, where changing exhibits are housed. A store sells herbs and goods handcrafted by the Shakers. ✉ *707 Shaker Rd. (turn off Rte. 26), New Gloucester* ☎ *207/926–4597* ⊕ *www.shaker.lib.me.us/* ⌚ *Tour $6.50* ⊙ *Late May– early Oct., Mon.–Sat. 10–4:30*

SPORTS AND THE OUTDOORS

U.S. 302 cuts through Naples, and in the center at the Naples causeway you'll find rental craft for fishing or cruising. Sebago, Long, and Rangeley lakes are popular areas for sailing, fishing, and motorboating.

Departing from the Naples causeway, ***Songo River Queen II***, a 93-foot stern-wheeler, takes passengers on hour and two-hour cruises on Long Lake and longer voyages down the Songo River and through Songo Lock. ✉ *841 Roosevelt Tr. (U.S. 302)* ☎ *207/693–6861* ⊕ *www. songoriverqueen.net* ⌚ *Long Lake cruises $12 (one-hour) and $20 (two-hour), Songo River ride $25* ⊙ *Early-Apr.–mid-June and Sept., 1 cruise daily on weekends; mid-June–early Sept., 4 cruises daily.*

Sebago Lake State Park. This 1,300-acre park on the north shore of the lake provides swimming, picnicking, camping (250 sites), boating, and fishing (salmon and togue). Come winter, the 6 mi of hiking trails are groomed for cross-country skiing. ✉ *11 Park Access Rd., Casco* ☎ *207/693–6231, 207/693–6613 May–mid-Oct. only* ⊕ *www. parksandlands.com* ⌚ *$4.50 mid-May–mid-Oct., $1.50 mid-Oct.–mid-May* ⊙ *Late May–early Sept., daily 9–8; mid-Sept.–Oct., daily 9–6; Nov.–mid-May, daily 9–4.*

9

WHERE TO STAY

$$$$ **Migis Lodge.** The pine-paneled cottages scattered under canopied pines along the ½ mi of shorefront at this 125-acre resort have fieldstone fireplaces and porches and are handsomely furnished with colorful rugs and handmade quilts. A warm, woodsy feeling pervades the main lodge. The long front porch and the terrace below have views—marvelous at sunset—of Sebago Lake. All kinds of outdoor and indoor activities are included in the room rate, and canoes, kayaks, waterskiing, and sailboats are available. Three meals (guests dress for dinner) are served daily in the dining room (you can also lunch lakeside). **Pros:** exclusive woodsy resort with access to private island; daily outdoor cocktail hour with complimentary drinks on Monday and Friday; fresh flowers from the gardens in lodgings. **Cons:** week minimum in July and August (unless shorter openings occur). ⊠ *30 Migis Lodge Rd., off U.S. 302, South Casco* ☎ *207/655–4524* ⊕ *www.migis.com* ⏎ *35 cottages, 6 rooms* ⚬ *In-room: no a/c (some), refrigerator, Wi-Fi. In-hotel: restaurant, tennis courts, gym, beachfront, water sports, bicycles, children's programs (ages infant–12), Internet terminal, Wi-Fi hotspot* ⊟ *No credit cards* ⊗ *Closed mid-Oct.–mid-June* ⊺Ⓞ⌇ *AI.*

BRIDGTON

8 mi north of Naples, 30 mi south of Bethel.

Bridgton's winding Main Street (U.S. 302) reveals picturesque New England townscapes at every curve. On steamy summer days, kids dive off the dock at the town beach tucked at the end of Highland Lake, just past storefronts with restaurants, galleries, and shops. The town has 10 lakes that are popular for boating and fishing. Come winter, people arrive to ski at Shawnee Peak.

The combination of woods, lakes, and views makes the surrounding countryside a good choice for leaf-peepers and outdoor lovers. A few miles north, Harrison anchors the northern end of Long Lake and is less commercial than Naples, its southern terminus. Tiny Waterford is a National Historic District. Come fall, Fryeburg, on the New Hampshire border, is home to the famed Fryeburg Fair (⊕ *www.fryeburgfair.com*), New England's largest agricultural fair.

GETTING HERE AND AROUND

U.S. 302 runs from Portland, along the east side of Sebago Lake to Naples, then up the west side of Long Lake to Bridgton.

ESSENTIALS

Vacation Rentals Maine Lakeside Getaways (⊠ *12 Hawk Ridge Rd.,* ☎ *207/647–4000 or 866/647–8557* ⊕ *www.mainelakesidegetaways.com*).

Visitor Information Greater Bridgton Lakes Region Chamber of Commerce (⊠ *101 Portland Rd. [U.S. 302], Bridgton* ☎ *207/647–3472* ⊕ *www. mainelakeschamber.com*).

EXPLORING

Rufus Porter Museum and Cultural Heritage Center. Local youth Rufus Porter became a leading folk artist, painting landscape and harbor murals on the walls of New England homes in the early 1800s, including those in this red, Cape Cod–style house. For an additional fee, visitors can also view 10 signed Porter murals from a Massachusetts home that are displayed in a local gallery. Also an inventor, Porter founded *Scientific American* magazine. Early issues are showcased, as are some of his inventions and miniature portraits. ⊠ *67 N. High St.* ☎ *207647–2828* ⊕ *www.rufusportermuseum.org* ☖ *$5* ⊙ *Late June–early Oct., Wed.– Sat. noon–5.*

SPORTS AND THE OUTDOORS

Just an hour's drive from Portland and a few miles from Bridgton's downtown, **Shawnee Peak** (⊠ *119 Mountain Rd., turn off U.S. 302* ☎ *207/647–8444* ⊕ *www.shawneepeak.com*) appeals to families and those who enjoy nighttime skiing—beginner, intermediate, and expert trails are lit most evenings. Three lifts serve 40 trails, four glades, and two terrain parks. There are slope-side condominiums, and the base lodge has a deck-fronted restaurant, two cafeterias, babysitting, ski school and rentals, and a ski shop.

WHERE TO STAY

$$ **Bear Mountain Inn.** On 25 acres above Bear Lake, this 1825 home-
★ stead has been meticulously decorated with country furnishings and bear decor. The luxurious Great Grizzly room has mesmerizing views and, like the other larger rooms, a fireplace, whirlpool bath for two, and wet bar. Cozy Sugar Bear Cottage is a romantic retreat with kitch-enette; the two-bedroom suites attract families. Breakfast is served in the dining room, which has a fieldstone fireplace and lake views. **Pros:** sweeping lawn has lake-view deck with fireplace; benches and ham-mocks along riverside trail; guest-only dinners (reservations required). **Cons:** one suite is considerably smaller; some shared bathrooms. ⊠ *364 Waterford Rd. (Route 35), Waterford 04088* ☎ *207/583–4404* ⊕ *www. bearmtninn.com* ⌂ *9 rooms, 5 with bath; 2 suites, 1 cabin* ⌂ *In-room: no phone, no a/c (some), refrigerator (some), DVD (some), no TV (some), Wi-Fi. In-hotel: beachfront, water sports, Wi-Fi hotspot, some pets allowed* ⊟ *MC, V* ⫯⊙*BP.*

CENTER LOVELL

17 mi northwest of Harrison, 28 mi south of Bethel.

At Center Lovell you can glimpse secluded Kezar Lake to the west, the retreat of wealthy and very private people. Only town residents and property owners can use the town beaches, but there is a public boat launch. Sabattus Mountain, which rises behind Center Lovell, has a public hiking trail.

WHERE TO EAT AND STAY

$$–$$$ ╳ **Center Lovell Inn Restaurant.** The eclectic furnishings in this eye-catching cupola-topped property from 1805 blend the mid-19th and mid-20th centuries in a pleasing, homey style. In summer the best tables for din-ing are on the wraparound porch, which has sunset views of the White Mountains. Inside, one dining room has mountain views and the other an original iron fireplace. Entrées may include pan-seared Muscovy duck, fillet of bison, or fresh swordfish. Breakfast is by reservation

can also hike to the summit of Old Speck Mountain, the state's third-highest peak. If you have the stamina and the equipment, you can pick up the Appalachian Trail here, hike over Saddleback Mountain, and continue on to Mt. Katahdin. The **Maine Appalachian Trail Club** (⌂ *Box 283, Augusta 04332* ⊕ *www.matc.org*) publishes seven Appalachian Trail maps and a Maine trail guide. ⊠ *Rte. 26* ☎ *207/624–6080, 207/824–2912 mid-May–mid-Oct.* ⊕ *www.parksandlands.com* 🖃 *Mid-May–mid-Oct.* *$3* ⊗ *Daily.*

White Mountain National Forest. This forest straddles New Hampshire and Maine, with the highest peaks on the New Hampshire side. The Maine section, though smaller, has magnificent rugged terrain, camping and picnic areas, and hiking, from hour-long nature loops to a day hike up Speckled Mountain. Highway 113 through the forest is closed in the winter. Its **New Hampshire Visitor Center** (⊠ *Androscoggin Ranger Station Visitor Center, 300 Glen Rd. [Rte. 16], Gorham* ⊗ *Late May–mid-Oct., daily 8–4:30; late Oct.–mid-May, weekdays 8–4:30*) has interactive exhibits for kids and displays on the forest's history and natural setting. ☎ *603/466–2713* ⊕ *www.fs.fed.us/r9/white* 🖃 *Day pass $5 per car, week pass $10 per car* ⊗ *Daily.*

CANOE-ING AND KAYAKING

Bethel Outdoor Adventure and Campground (⊠ *121 Mayville Rd. [U.S. Rte. 2]* ☎ *207/824–4224 or 800/533–3607* ⊕ *www.betheloutdooradventure.com*) rents canoes, kayaks, and bikes; guides fishing, kayak, and canoe trips; and operates a hostel and riverside campground.

DOG SLEDDING

Mahoosuc Guide Service (⊠ *1513 Bear River Rd. [Rte. 26], Newry* ☎ *207/824–2073* ⊕ *www.mahoosuc.com*) leads day and multiday dogsledding expeditions on the Maine–New Hampshire border, as well as canoeing trips. Its **Mahoosuc Mountain Lodge** (⊕ *www.mahoosucmountainlodge.com*) has dorm and B&B lodging.

MULTI-SPORT OUTFITTERS

Sun Valley Sports (⊠ *129 Sunday River Rd.* ☎ *207/824–7533 or 877/851–7533* ⊕ *www.sunvalleysports.com*) has snowmobile rentals and guided tours. It also operates fly-fishing trips, canoe and kayak rentals, guided ATV tours, and moose and wildlife safaris.

Carter's Cross-Country Ski Center (⊠ *786 Intervale Rd.* ☎ *207/824–3880 or 207/539–4848* ⊕ *www.cartersxcski.com*) has 33 mi of trails for all levels of skiers, lessons, and rentals—snowshoes, skis, and sleds to pull children are available. It also rents rooms and ski-in cabins.

What was once a sleepy little ski area with minimal facilities has evolved into a sprawling resort that attracts skiers from as far away as Europe. Spread throughout the valley at **Sunday River** (⊠ *15 S. Ridge Rd., turn on Sunday River Rd. from U.S. 2, Newry* ☎ *207/824–3000 main number, 207/824–5200 snow conditions, 800/543–2754 reservations* ⊕ *www.sundayriver.com*) are three base areas, two condominium hotels, trail-side condominiums, town houses, and a ski dorm. Sunday River is home to the Maine Handicapped Skiing program, which provides lessons and services for skiers with disabilities. Rentals, lessons, children's programs, day care, and slope-side dining are all here, too; 16 lifts service 132 trails and four terrain parks. There's plenty else to do, including cross-country skiing, ice-skating, tubing, and, come summer and fall, hiking, mountain biking, and scenic lift rides.

One of the Rangeley Lakes, Mooselookmeguntic is said mean "portage to the moose feeding place" in the Abenaki language.

Family-friendly **Mt. Abram Ski Resort** (✉ *308 Howe Hill Rd., turn off Route 26 Greenwood* ☎ *207/875–5000* 🌐 *www.skimtabram.com*), south of Bethel, has 44 trails, five lifts, two base lodges, glade areas, and night skiing on the first Saturday of the month.

WHERE TO STAY

$–$$ **Victoria Inn.** It's hard to miss this turreted inn in downtown Bethel, with its teal, mauve, and beige exterior and attached carriage house topped with a cupola. Inside, Victorian details include ceiling rosettes, stained-glass windows, elaborate fireplace mantels, and gleaming oak trim. Guest rooms vary in size (suites sleep three to eight); most are furnished with reproductions of antiques. The dinner-only restaurant ($–$$) has won acclaim with entrées like rack of lamb with basil and mint pesto and duck with pomegranate sauce. **Pros:** lots of breakfast choices; homemade cookies in your room; 10% discount on dinner. **Cons:** some rooms are dated; lofts in suites lack decor. ✉ *32 Main St.* ☎ *207/824–8060 or 888/774–1235* 🌐 *www.thevictoria-inn.com* *9 rooms, 4 suites* *In-room: Wi-Fi (some). In-hotel: restaurant, Wi-Fi hotspot* *AE, D, MC, V* *BP.*

EN ROUTE The routes north from Bethel to the Rangeley district are all scenic, particularly in autumn when the maples are aflame with color. In the town of Newry, make a short detour to the **Artist's Bridge** (turn off Highway 26 onto Sunday River Road and drive about 4 mi), the most painted and photographed of Maine's eight covered bridges. Highway 26 continues north to the gorges and waterfalls of **Grafton Notch State Park.** Continue to Upton, but drive carefully and keep a lookout: this 10-mi stretch is one of Maine's moose alleys. At Errol, New Hampshire Highway 16 will return you east around the north shore of Mooselookmeguntic Lake, through Oquossoc, and into Rangeley.

RANGELEY

67 mi north of Bethel.

Rangeley, on the north side of Rangeley Lake on Highways 4 and 16, has long lured anglers and winter-sports enthusiasts to its more than 40 lakes and ponds and 450 square mi of woodlands. Equally popular in summer or winter, Rangeley has a rough, wilderness feel to it.

GETTING HERE AND AROUND

To reach Rangeley on a scenic drive, take Route 17 north from U.S. 2 to Route 16/Route 4, then head east. Route 16 continues east to Kingfield and Sugarloaf ski resort.

ESSENTIALS

Vacation Rentals Morton & Furbish Vacation Rentals (⊠ *2478 Main St., Rangeley* ☎ *207/864–9065 or 888/218–4882* ⊕ *www.rangeleyrentals.com*)

Visitor Information Rangeley Lakes Region Chamber of Commerce (⊠ *6 Park Dr.* ☎ *207/864–5571 or 800/685–2537* ⊕ *www.rangeleymaine.com*).

SPORTS AND THE OUTDOORS

Rangeley Lake State Park. On the south shore of Rangeley Lake, this park has superb lakeside scenery, swimming, picnic tables, a boat ramp, showers, and 50 campsites. ⊠ *S. Shore Dr., off Rte. 17 or Rte. 4, Rangeley Plantation* ☎ *207/624–6080, 207/864–3858 May 15–Oct. 1 only* ⊕ *www.state.me.us/doc/parks* ⊠ *$4.50* ⊙ *May 15–Oct. 1, daily 8–8 or dusk, if earlier.*

BOATING AND FISHING Rangeley and Mooselookmeguntic lakes are good for canoeing, sailing, fishing, and motorboating. Several outfits rent equipment and provide guide service if needed. Fishing for brook trout and salmon is at its best in May, June, and September; the Rangeley area is especially popular with fly-fishers.

GOLF **Mingo Springs Golf Course** (⊠ *Country Club Rd.* ☎ *207/864–5021* ⊕ *www.mingosprings.com*) is known for its mountain and water views as well as challenging play on its 18-hole course. Green fees start at $32.

SEAPLANES **Acadian Seaplanes** (⊠ *2640 Main St.* ☎ *207/864–5307 or 207/252–6630* ⊕ *www.acadianseaplane.com*) provides transportation to remote lodges as well as scenic flights above Rangeley and environs. It also does fly-ins to watch moose in the wild and dine-and-flys to a sporting lodge.

SKI AREAS **Rangeley Lakes Trail Center** (⊠ *524 Saddleback Mountain Rd., Dallas* ☎ *207/864–4309* ⊕ *www.xcskirangeley.com*) rents cross-country skis and snowshoes and has about 30 mi of groomed trails surrounding Saddleback Mountain. The snack bar is open in the winter, and you can hike, mountain bike, and run on the trails in warmer weather.

A family atmosphere prevails at **Saddleback Maine** (⊠ *976 Saddleback Mountain Rd., follow signs from Rte. 4, Dallas* ☎ *207/864–5671 or 866/918–2225; 207/864–5441 or 877/864–5441 reservations* ⊕ *www.saddlebackmaine.com*), where the quiet, lack of crowds, and spectacularly wide valley views draw return visitors. The 66 trails and glades, accessed by five lifts, are divided among 38% novice, 29% intermediate, and 33% advanced. A fieldstone fireplace anchors the post-and-beam base lodge. You can also find a day-care center, ski school, rental and retail shop, and trailside condominium lodging on-site. Hiking (the Appalachian Trail crosses Saddleback's summit ridge), mountain biking, canoeing, kayaking, fly-fishing, moose tours, and birding are big draws in warm weather, as are music concerts, which continue in winter.

WHERE TO EAT AND STAY

$–$$ ✕ **Gingerbread House Restaurant.** A big fieldstone fireplace, well-spaced

AMERICAN tables, wrap-around deck, and antique marble soda fountain, all with views of the woods beyond, make for comfortable surroundings inside what really looks like a giant gingerbread house. Breakfast, lunch, and dinner are served; you can also get baked goods to go. Soups, salads, and sandwiches at lunch give way to entrées such as Maine crab cakes and barbecued ribs with blueberry chipotle sauce and maple syrup. ⊠ *55 Carry Rd. (Rte. 4), Oquossoc* ☎ *207/864–3602* ⊕ *gingerbreadhouserestaurant.net* ▭ *AE, D, MC, V* ☉ *Closed Nov. and Apr.; and Mon. and Tues., Dec.–Mar. No lunch or dinner Sun., mid-Sept.–mid-June (except on holiday weeks and weekends).*

$–$$ ⊞ **Country Club Inn.** Built in 1920 as the country club for the adjacent

☺ Mingo Springs Golf Course, this secluded hilltop retreat has sweeping lake and mountain views. Two fireplaces anchor the lodge-like living room, which has a cathedral ceiling. The cozy, low-ceilinged wood-paneled bar opens to a room with a pool table and lake-view deck. Rooms downstairs in the main building and in the adjacent 1950s motel are cheerfully, if minimally, decorated. The glassed-in dining room serves burgers and salads—as well as entrées like veal Gruyère and roast duck Montmorency. **Pros:** loads of lawn and board games; lots of photos of Rangeley's long-gone resorts. **Cons:** smallish rooms in main building. ⊠ *56 Country Club Rd.* ☎ *207/864–3831* ⊕ *www. countryclubinnrangeley.com* ⤶ *19 rooms* ⟨ *In-room: no a/c, no TV, refrigerator (some), Wi-Fi (some). In-hotel: restaurant, bar, pool, Internet terminal, Wi-Fi hotspot, some pets allowed* ▭ *AE, D, MC, V* ☉ *Closed Nov. and Apr.* ⟨⟩*EP, BP, MAP.*

¢–$ ⊞ **Rangeley Inn and Motor Lodge.** From Main Street you see only the large three-story blue inn, built in the early 1900s for wealthy urbanites on vacation. Set back behind it is a motel with decks or terraces on most rooms and views of Haley Pond, the large lawn, and a garden. No two rooms are alike in the main inn, where the many antique furnishings include brass beds and oak dressers and headboards. Some of the larger rooms have a queen bed and two twins. Some baths are marble, some have claw-foot tubs, and some have whirlpool tubs. **Pros:** historic hotel last of its kind in the region; in motel, all rooms have refrigerators, some have woodstoves, and some have microwaves. **Cons:** dining room breakfast buffet only on weekends. ⊠ *2443 Main St., 04970* ☎ *207/864–3341 or 800/666–3687* ⊕ *www.rangeleyinn.com* ⤶ *35 inn rooms, 15 motel rooms (including 1 suite)* ⟨ *In-room: no a/c (some), refrigerator (some). In-hotel: restaurant, some pets allowed* ▭ *D, MC, V* ☉ *Closed Apr., May, Nov., and Dec.*

9

Whoopie Pies

"The whoopie pie would probably be Maine's state dessert, if the state had one," said the *New York Times*, and funny enough, there's actually a movement to put that official stamp on this regional confection. Spend a few days anywhere in Maine and you'll notice just how popular the treat is. Whoopie pies can be found in groceries, bakeries, cafés, and convenience stores, often and piled high near the cash register.

The name is misleading: it's a pie only in the sense of a having a filling between two "crusts"—namely, a thick layer of sugary frosting sandwiched between two saucers of rich chocolate cake. It's said to have Pennsylvania Dutch roots and may have acquired its distinctive moniker from the jubilant yelp farmers emitted after discovering it in their lunchboxes, and it has been satisfying Maine's sweet tooth for decades. **Labadies Bakery** (✉ *161 Lincoln St.* ☎ *207/784–7042* ⊕ *www. labadiesbakery.com*) in Lewiston boasts 85 years of baking whoopie pies (which, over time, have grown from whoopie to whopping: they top out at 16 inches in diameter!).

Typically, the filling is buttercream, but some places still make it with shortening, and others scoop a dollop of marshmallow fluff between the layers of cake. Many bakers have indulged the temptation to experiment with flavors and ingredients, particularly in the filling, yielding pumpkin, raspberry, oatmeal cream, red velvet, peanut butter, and more different kinds of whoopie pies.

Where to find the best classic whoopie pies in Maine is, perhaps predictably, a point of contention. The bigger producers certainly have

devotees and include Labadies, which ships its pies of all sizes across the country. The treats from **Wicked Whoopies** (✉ *621 Maine Ave., Farmingdale* ☎ *207/622–8860* ✉ *32 Main St., Freeport* ☎ *207/865– 3100* ⊕ *www.wickedwhoopies.com*) are stocked in supermarkets and Rite Aid stores. **Cranberry Island Kitchen** (✉ *7 Corey Rd., Cumberland Center* ☎ *207/829–5200* ⊕ *www. cranberryislandkitchen.com*) supplies Williams-Sonoma with the confections.

Smaller, more eccentric bakers have received accolades for their whoopie pies, too: **Friars' Bakehouse** (✉ *21 Central St.* ☎ *207/947–3770*) was voted to have the best in the Bangor area by respondents to a *Bangor Daily News* poll. The bakery, run by two Franciscan friars, one of whom spent time in highly regarded culinary programs. **Moody's Diner** (✉ *1885 Atlantic Hwy., Waldoboro* ☎ *207/832– 7785*) makes pies of considerable size, prized for their filling above all. **Two Fat Cats Bakery** (✉ *47 India St., Portland* ☎ *207/347–5144* ⊕ *www. twofatcatsbakery.com*) has whoopie pies that are more delicately proportioned, with a smooth and light filling reminiscent of Italian buttercream, and a conservative hand with flavors— no peanut-butter-mint-chocolate-chip pies to be found here. The old family-friendly standby **Governor's Restaurant Old Town** (✉ *963 Stillwater Ave., Old Town* ☎ *207/827–7630* ⊕ *governorsrestaurant.com*) is famed for its peanut butter pies as well as the old reliable standard and can accommodate special flavor combinations by request.

—Michael de Zayas

KINGFIELD

33 mi east of Rangeley, 15 mi west of Phillips.

In the shadows of Mt. Abram and Sugarloaf Mountain, Kingfield has everything a "real" New England town should have: a general store, historic inns, and white clapboard churches. Sugarloaf has golf and tennis in summer.

ESSENTIALS

Visitor Information Sugarloaf Area Chamber of Commerce (⊕ *www. sugarloafchamber.org*).

SPORTS AND THE OUTDOORS

SKI AREAS Abundant natural snow, a huge mountain, and the only above-tree-line
★ lift-service skiing in the East have made **Sugarloaf** (✉ *5092 Access Rd., Carrabassett Valley* ☏ *207/237–2000, 207/237–6808 snow conditions, 800/843–5623 reservations* ⊕ *www.sugarloaf.com*) one of Maine's best-known ski areas with 16 lifts and 138 trails and glades. Two slope-side hotels and hundreds of slope-side condominiums provide ski-in, ski-out access, and the base village has restaurants and shops. The Outdoor Center has more than 60 mi of cross-country ski trails as well as snowshoeing, snow tubing, and ice-skating. There's also plenty for the kids, from day care to special events. Once you are here, a car is unnecessary—a shuttle connects all mountain operations. Summer is much quieter than winter, but you can bike, fish, and hike, plus golf at the superb 18-hole, Robert Trent Jones Jr.–designed golf course ($69–$79 with cart, cost varies by season).

THE NORTH WOODS

Moosehead Lake, the four-season resort town of Greenville, Baxter State Park, and the Allagash Wilderness Waterway are dispersed within Maine's remote North Woods. This vast area in the north-central section of the state is best experienced by canoe or raft; via hiking, snowshoe, or snowmobile; or on a fishing trip. Maine's largest lake, Moosehead supplies more in the way of rustic camps, guides, and outfitters than any other northern locale. Its 420 mi of shorefront, three-quarters of which is owned by lumber companies or the state, is virtually uninhabited.

GREENVILLE

160 mi northeast of Portland; 71 mi northwest of Bangor.

Greenville, the largest town on Moosehead Lake, is an outdoors lover's paradise. Boating, fishing, and hiking are popular in summer, while snowmobiling, skiing, and ice fishing reign in winter. The town also has the greatest selection of shops, restaurants, and inns in the region—note that some are closed mid-October to mid-May.

GETTING HERE AND AROUND

To reach Greenville from Interstate 95, get off at Exit 157 in Newport and head north, successively, on Routes 7, 23, and 15.

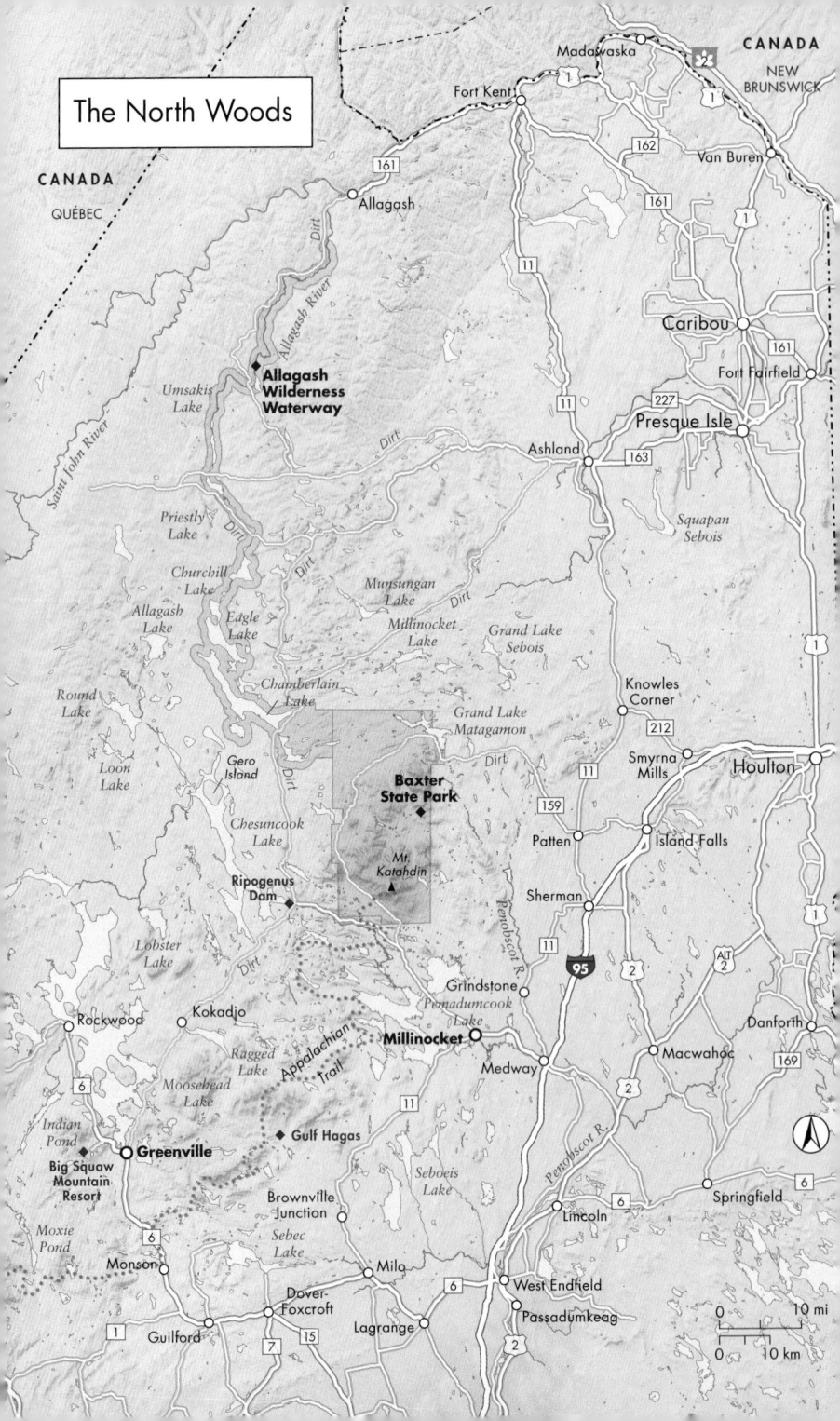

The North Woods

CANADA

NEW BRUNSWICK

CANADA
QUÉBEC

Madawaska
Fort Kent
Van Buren
162
1
Allagash
161
11
Caribou
161
Fort Fairfield
Presque Isle
227
Allagash Wilderness Waterway
Ashland
163
Saint John River
Umsakis Lake
Squapan Sebois
Priestly Lake
Dirt
Churchill Lake
Munsungan Lake
Grand Lake Sebois
Knowles Corner
212
Allagash Lake
Eagle Lake
Millinocket Lake
Smyrna Mills
Houlton
Round Lake
Chamberlain Lake
Grand Lake Matagamon
Loon Lake
Gero Island
Baxter State Park
Patten
159
Island Falls
Chesuncook Lake
Ripogenus Dam
Mt. Katahdin
Sherman
95
2
ALT 2
Lobster Lake
Dirt
Grindstone
Penobscot R.
Rockwood
Kokadjo
Millinocket
Danforth
Ragged Lake
Appalachian Trail
Pemadumcook Lake
Macwahoc
169
6
Moosehead Lake
Medway
2
Indian Pond
Greenville
Gulf Hagas
Seboeis Lake
Springfield
6
Big Squaw Mountain Resort
Lincoln
6
Moxie Pond
Brownville Junction
Penobscot R.
Monson
6
Sebec Lake
Mila
West Endfield
Passadumkeag
Guilford
Dover-Foxcroft
Lagrange
1
7
15
2

0   10 mi
0   10 km

ESSENTIALS

Vacation Rentals **Northwoods Camp Rentals** (✉ *14 Lakeview St.,* ☎ *800/251–8042* ⊕ *www.mooseheadrentals.com).*

Visitor Information **Moosehead Lake Region Chamber of Commerce** (✉ *Indian Hills Plaza, 156 Moosehead Lake Rd., Greenville* ☎ *207/695–2702 or 888/876–2778* ⊕ *www.mooseheadlake.org).*

<table>
<tr><td>OFF THE
BEATEN
PATH</td><td>

Mt. Kineo. Once a thriving summer resort for the wealthy, the Mount Kineo House was accessed primarily by steamship. The resort was torn down around 1940, but Kineo still makes a pleasant day trip. You can take the Kineo Shuttle, which departs from the State Dock in **Rockwood,** or rent a motorboat in Rockwood and make the journey across the lake in about 15 minutes. It's an easy hike to Kineo's summit for awesome views down the lake. A map is available at the Moosehead Lake Region Chamber of Commerce.

</td></tr>
</table>

SPORTS AND THE OUTDOORS

Lily Bay State Park. Nine miles northeast of Greenville on Moosehead Lake, this park has a good swimming beach, a 2-mi walking trail with water views, two boat-launching ramps, and two campgrounds with 90 sites. ✉ *13 Myrle's Way, off Lily Bay Rd., Beaver Cove* ☎ *207/941– 4014, 207/695–2700 mid-May–mid-Oct. only* ⊕ *www.parksandlands. com* ✉ *$4.50* ☉ *May 15–Oct. 15, daily 9–sunset.*

BIKING   Mountain biking is popular in the Greenville area, but bikes are not allowed on some logging roads. Expect to pay about $25 per day to rent a bicycle. **Northwoods Outfitters** (✉ *5 Lily Bay Rd., Greenville* ☎ *207/695–3288* ⊕ *www.maineoutfitter.com*) rents mountain bikes, kids' bikes, and more.

FISHING   Togue (lake trout), landlocked salmon, smallmouth bass, and brook trout lure thousands of anglers to the region from ice-out in mid-May until September; the hardiest return in winter to ice fish.

SEAPLANES   **Currier's Flying Service** (✉ *Greenville Junction* ☎ *207/695–2778* ⊕ *www. curriersflyingservice.com*) offers sightseeing flights over the Moosehead Lake region.

RAFTING   The Kennebec and Dead rivers and the west branch of the Penobscot River provide thrilling white-water rafting. These rivers are dam-controlled, so day and multiday guided trips run rain or shine daily from mid-April to mid-October. Many rafting outfitters operate resort facilities in their base towns. *See the Outdoor Activities section for more information.*

TOURS   ***Katahdin.*** The Moosehead Marine Museum runs three- and five-hour ★   trips on Moosehead Lake aboard the *Katahdin,* a 115-foot 1914 steamship converted to diesel. Also called *The Kate,* the ship carried passengers to Mt. Kineo until 1938 and then was used in the logging industry until 1975. Trips range in price from $32 to $37. The boat and the free shore-side museum have displays about the steamships that transported people and cargo on the lake more than 100 years ago. ✉ *12 Lily Bay Rd.* ☞ *Board on shoreline by museum* ☎ *207/695–2716* ⊕ *www. katahdincruises.com* ☉ *June–early Oct.*

9

Gulf Hagas. In a *very* remote area accessed by gravel roads, a hiking trail leads from Katahdin Iron Works Road to the east end of Gulf Hagas, a National Natural Landmark with chasms, cliffs, six large waterfalls, pools, exotic flora, and rock formations. Slippery rocks make for difficult hiking along the gorge rim. Hiking from either of the two parking areas to the gorge and around a loop that includes the rim trail is an 8-mi, all-day affair. Or you can hike to the first waterfall en route and then back to the parking lot. It's about 3 mi roundtrip from the Upper Gulf Parking Area (set to open in spring 2010) to Stairs Falls on the gorge's west end. You must ford the Pleasant River near the outset of the trail from the Gulf Hagas Parking Area, which leads to the gorge's east end. This is easily done in summer when the water (about 150 feet wide) is knee-deep, but use extra caution in spring or after heavy rains, when the river is swifter and deeper. The Hermitage, a rare patch of old-growth pine, rises beyond the waterway. It's a 3-mi roundtrip from this parking area to Screw Auger Falls, Gulf Hagas's most spectacular drop. **North Maine Woods** (☎ 207/435–6213 ⊕ *www.northmainewoods.org*) manages the private gravel roads to this very isolated area—yield to logging trucks. Fees are charged at checkpoints (sometimes closed in April, late October, and November), where you can buy trail maps. From Greenville, take Pleasant Street east (road becomes gravel) 11 mi to the Hedgehog checkpoint, follow signs to the Upper Gulf Parking Area (2½ mi) or the Gulf Hagas Parking Area (about 6½ mi). From Millinocket, take Route 11 south about 32 mi to the Katahdin Iron Works Road sign, continue 7 mi on dirt road to the Katahdin Iron Works checkpoint, follow signs to the Gulf Hagas Parking Area (about 7 mi) or the Upper Gulf Parking Area (about 12 mi).

WHERE TO STAY

$$$$
★

🏨 **Blair Hill Inn.** Beautiful gardens and a hilltop location with marvelous views over the lake distinguish this 1891 estate, as do fine antiques, plush bedding, and elegant baths, some with oversize or claw-foot tubs. Guest rooms are spacious; all have sitting areas and four have fireplaces. A restaurant (reservations required) serves a prix-fixe five-course dinner ($$$$) Thursday through Saturday from mid-June to mid-October. Arrive early to enjoy cocktails on the wraparound porch or the swank bar area connected to it. The inn hosts a music series in July and August. **Pros:** third-floor deck the length of the inn; 15 acres with stone paths, wooded picnic area, and trout pond; flowers from gardens in rooms. **Cons:** no direct lake access; long, steep drive. ⊠ *351 Lily Bay Rd., Box 1288 04441* ☎ *207/695–0224* ⊕ *www.blairhill.com* ⇨ *7 rooms, 1 suite* ⟁ *In-room: no phone, a/c (some), Wi-Fi. In-hotel: restaurant, Internet terminal, Wi-Fi hotspot* ⊟ *D, MC, V* ☺ *Closed Apr. and Nov.* ⦿*BP.*

$$$

🏨 **Little Lyford Lodge and Cabins.** When you want to get away from everything, head to this rustic wilderness retreat on 37,000 acres of conservation land, part of the Appalachian Mountain Club's lodging network. Moose are abundant, and the fly-fishing, snowshoeing, hiking (Gulf Hagas is nearby), and backcountry skiing are excellent. Well-maintained cabins from an 1870s logging camp that was later a sporting camp have woodstoves and gas lights. Home-cooked fare is served family-style in the main lodge. The 1980s addition, like the bathhouse, has mostly solar-powered lighting. **Pros:** woodsy getaway; family adventure camps in summer; cedar sauna in winter. **Cons:** winter access is by cross-country ski or snowmobile transport (for a fee); few indoor amenities. ⊠ *About 16 mi east of Greenville, access via logging roads* ☎ *603/466–2727* ⊕ *www.outdoors.org/mainelodges* ⤢ *10 cabins, 8-bed bunkhouse* ⚴ *In-room: no phone, no a/c, no TV. In-hotel: water sports* ⊟ *AE, MC, V* ⊗ *Closed Apr.–early May and Nov.–late Dec.* ⍟ *FAP.*

MILLINOCKET

67 mi north of Bangor, 88 mi northwest of Greenville via Routes 6 and 11.

Millinocket, a paper-mill town with a population of about 4,000, is a gateway to Baxter State Park and Maine's North Woods. Although it has a smattering of motels and restaurants, Millinocket is the place to stock up on supplies, fill your gas tank, or grab a hot meal or shower before heading into the wilderness. Numerous rafting and canoeing outfitters and guides are based here.

GETTING HERE AND AROUND
From Interstate 95, take Route 157 (Exit 244) northwest to Millinocket and nearby Baxter State Park.

ESSENTIALS
Vacation Rentals Baxter's 4 Season Vacation Rentals (⊠ *973 Central St.* ☎ *207/723–9746* ⊕ *www.baxtersedge.com*).

Visitor Information Katahdin Area Chamber of Commerce (⊠ *1029 Central St., Millinocket* ☎ *207/723–4443* ⊕ *www.katahdinmaine.com*).

SPORTS AND THE OUTDOORS
★ **Allagash Wilderness Waterway.** A spectacular 92-mi corridor of lakes and rivers, the waterway cuts across 170,000 acres of wilderness beginning at the northwest corner of Baxter State Park and running north to the town of Allagash, 10 mi from the Canadian border. From mid-May to October, this is prime canoeing and camping country, but it should not be undertaken lightly. The complete 92-mi course requires 7 to 10 days. The best bet for a novice is to go with a guide; a good outfitter will help plan your route and provide your craft and transportation. This waterway is just part of the 740-mi **Northern Forest Canoe Trail** (⊕ *www.northernforestcanoetrail.org*), which runs from New York to Québec. ⊠ *Maine Bureau of Parks and Lands, 106 Hogan Rd., Bangor* ☎ *207/941–4014* ⊕ *www.parksandlands.com.*

Fodor'sChoice **Baxter State Park.** A gift from Governor Percival Baxter, this is the jewel
★ in the crown of northern Maine, a 209,501-acre wilderness area that surrounds **Mt. Katahdin,** Maine's highest mountain (5,267 feet at Baxter Peak) and the terminus of the Appalachian Trail. Katahdin draws thousands of hikers every year for the daylong climb to the summit and the stunning views of woods, mountains, and lakes. Three trailheads lead to its peak; some routes include the hair-raising Knife Edge Ridge. The crowds climbing Katahdin can be formidable on clear summer days, so if you crave solitude, tackle one of the 45 other mountains in the park,

9

17 of which exceed an elevation of 3,000 feet and all of which are accessible from an extensive network of trails. South Turner can be climbed in a morning (if you're fit), and its summit has a great view of Katahdin across the valley. On the way you'll pass Sandy Stream Pond, where moose are often seen at dusk. The Owl, the Brothers, and Doubletop Mountain are good day hikes. ■TIP➔ Reserve a day-use parking space at the Katahdin trailheads if you plan to hike the mountain between May 15 and October 15. Check the park Web site for information about this new system; without a reservation you may have to hike elsewhere in the park. Call the hiking hotline (☎ *207/723–4636*) for next-day weather and other seasonal hiking information. No pets, domestic animals, oversize vehicles, radios, all-terrain vehicles, motorboats, or motorcycles are allowed in the park, and there are no pay phones, gas stations, stores, running water, or electricity. The camping is primitive, and sites typically fill up well ahead for peak season. The visitor center is at the southern entrance outside Millinocket. You can also get information about Baxter in town at park headquarters. ⊠ *Headquarters: 64 Balsam Dr., Millinocket Togue Pond Gate (southern entrance): Rte. 157, 18 mi northwest of Millinocket; Matagamon Gate (northern entrance): Grand Lake Rd., 26 mi northwest of Patten via Rte. 159 and Grand Lake Rd.* ☎ *207/723–5140* ⊕ *www.baxterstateparkauthority.com* ☞ *$13 per vehicle (free to Maine residents)* ⊙ *Daily, sunrise to sunset.*

SEAPLANES **Katahdin Air Service** (⊠ *Millinocket* ☎ *207/723–8378* ⊕ *www.katahdinair. com*). Katahdin Air Service offers charter flights by seaplane from points throughout Maine to smaller towns and remote lake and forest areas. It can help you find a guide and also does scenic flights over the Katahdin area.

WHERE TO STAY

CAMPING ⚠ **Baxter State Park Authority.** Camping spaces at the park's 10 primitive
$$–$$$ campgrounds must be reserved by mail or in person (check or cash) within four months of your trip or by phone (MC or V only) two weeks prior. Phone reservations are much harder to come by for July, August, and fall weekends, but cancellations do open up spots. There are also additional primitive backcountry sites. **Pros:** cabins at Daicey Pond and Kidney Pond campgrounds; great base for hiking. **Cons:** must reserve far ahead; winter access is by ski or snowshoe; no electricity or running water. ⊠ *Headquarters: 64 Balsam Dr., Millinocket Togue Pond Gate (southern entrance): Hwy. 157, 18 mi northwest of Millinocket; Matagamon Gate (northern entrance): Grand Lake Rd., 26 mi northwest of Patten via Rte. 159 and Grand Lake Rd.* ☎ *207/723–5140* ⊕ *www.baxterstateparkauthority.com* ⚠ *22 cabins, 4 bunkhouses, 57 lean-tos, 75 tent sites, 13 group tent sites* ⚶ *Pit toilets, fire grates, fire rings, picnic tables, ranger stations, swimming (pond, lake, stream)* ▤ *MC, V* ⊙ *Closed mid-Oct.–Nov. and Apr.–mid-May.*

Maine Coast

WORD OF MOUTH

"Rent bikes in Bar Harbor and plan your route to include popovers at [Acadia National Park's] Jordan Pond. It's a beautiful ride."

—cindyj

"We finally got to Monhegan [Island]. . . . We just enjoyed taking a picnic lunch and binoculars and finding a place to sit on the rocks."

—dfrostnh

WELCOME TO MAINE COAST

TOP REASONS TO GO

★ **Perfection on a Bun:** It's not a Maine vacation without sampling the "lobster roll," lobster with a touch of mayo nestled in a buttery grilled hot-dog bun.

★ **Boating:** The coastline of Maine was made for boaters. Whether it's your own boat, a friend's or a charter, make sure you get out on the water.

★ **Wild Maine Blueberries:** They may be tiny, but the wild blueberries pack a flavorful punch in season (late July to early September).

★ **Cadillac Mountain:** Drive the winding 3½-mi road to the 1,530-foot summit in Acadia National Park for the sunrise.

★ **Perfect Souvenir:** Buy a watercolor, hand-painted pottery, or a handcrafted jewelry—artists and craftspeople abound.

★ **Ice Cream:** Summer in Maine means ice cream. Dig into a pint of Gifford's or stop by a homemade ice cream stand: you can't go wrong.

1 The Southern Coast. Stretching north from Kittery to just outside Portland, this is Maine's most-visited region. The towns along the shore and miles of sandy expanses cater to summer visitors. Old Orchard Beach and York Beach feature Coney Island–like amusements, while Kittery, the Yorks, and the Kennebunks are more low key getaways.

2 Portland. Maine's largest and most cosmopolitan city, Portland balances its historic role as a working harbor with its newer identity as a center of sophisticated arts and shopping, and innovative restaurants.

3 The Mid-Coast Region. North of Portland, from Brunswick to Monhegan Island, the craggy coastline winds its way around pastoral peninsulas. Its villages boast maritime museums, antiques shops, and beautiful architecture.

Old Town
Newport
Bangor
179
9
193
Columbia
Falls
182
Cherryfield
Ellsworth
Hancock
Belfast
Searsport
West Gouldsboro
Bar Harbor
Islesboro
Blue Hill
Peninsula
Cadillac Mtn.
Mt.
Desert
Island
Frenchman
Bay
Deer Isle
Village
ACADIA NAT'L
PARK
17
Camden
Stonington
Rockland
Thomaston
Isle
au Haut
Penobscot
Bay
Monhegan
Island
9
191
Lubec
7
1
Machias
Jonesport
Beals Island

Atlantic Ocean

4 Penobscot Bay.

This region combines lively coastal towns with dramatic natural scenery. Camden is one of Maine's most picture-perfect towns, with its pointed church steeples, antique homes, and historic windjammer fleet.

5 Blue Hill Peninsula.

Art galleries are plentiful here, and the entire region is ideal for biking, hiking, kayaking, and boating. For many, the peninsula defines the silent beauty of the Maine Coast.

6 Acadia National Park and Mount Desert Island.

Millions come to enjoy Acadia National Park's stunning peaks and vistas of the island's mountains. Bar Harbor is more of a visitor's haven, while Southwest Harbor and Bass Harbor offer quieter retreats.

7 Way Down East.

This is the "real" Maine, some say, and it unfurls in thousands of acres of wild blueberry barrens, congestion-free coastlines, and a tangible sense of rugged endurance.

GETTING ORIENTED

Much of the appeal of the Maine Coast lies in its geographical contrasts, from its long stretches of swimming and walking beaches in the south to the cliff-edged, rugged rocky coasts in the north. And not unlike the physical differences of the coast, each town along the way reveals a slightly different character.

10

MAINE COAST PLANNER

When to Go

Maine's dramatic coastline and pure natural beauty welcome visitors year-round, but note that many smaller museums and attractions are open only for high season—from Memorial Day to mid-October—as are many of the waterside attractions and eateries.

Summer begins in earnest on July 4, and many smaller inns and hotels from Kittery on up to the Bar Harbor region fill up early on weekends. Fall, with its fiery foliage, is when many inns and hotels are booked months in advance by leaf-peeping visitors. After Halloween, hotel rates drop significantly until ski season begins around Thanksgiving. Along the coast, bed-and-breakfasts that remain open will often rent rooms at far lower prices than in summer.

In spring, the third Sunday in March is designated as Maine Maple Sunday, and farms throughout the state open their doors to visitors not only to watch sap turn into golden syrup but to sample the sweet results.

Getting Here and Around

Maine has two major international airports, Portland International Jetport and Bangor International Airport, to get you to or close to your coastal destination. Manchester-Boston Regional Airport in New Hampshire is about 45 minutes away from the southern end of the Maine coastline. Boston's Logan Airport is the only truly international airport in the region; it's about 90 minutes south of the Maine border.

Amtrak offers regional service from Boston to Portland via its Downeaster line that originates at Boston's North Station and makes four stops in Maine: Wells, Saco, Old Orchard Beach (seasonal), and finally Portland. Greyhound and Concord Trailways also offer bus service from Boston to many towns along the Maine coast.

All that said, once you are here the best way to experience the winding back roads of the craggy Maine coast is in a car. There are miles and miles of roads far from the larger towns that no bus services, and you won't want to miss discovering your own favorite ocean vista while on a scenic drive.

Planning Your Time

You could easily spend a lifetime's worth of vacations along the Maine Coast and never truly see it all. But if you are determined to travel the coast from end to end, allot at least two weeks to travel comfortably.

Driving in Coastal Maine

	MILES	TIME
Boston–Portland	108	2 hours
Kittery–Portland	50	50 minutes
Portland–Freeport	17	20 minutes
Portland–Camden	80	2 hours
Portland–Bar Harbor	175	3 hours, 20 minutes

About the Restaurants

Many breakfast spots along the coast open as early as 6 AM to serve the going-to-work crowd. Lunch generally runs 11–2:30; dinner is usually served 5–9. Only in the larger cities will you find full dinners being offered much later than 9, although you can usually find a bar or bistro serving a limited menu late into the evening.

Many restaurants in Maine are closed Monday, though this isn't true in resort areas in high season. However, resort-town eateries often shut down completely in the off-season. Unless otherwise noted, restaurants in this guide are open daily for lunch and dinner.

Credit cards are accepted for meals throughout Maine, even in some of the most modest establishments.

The one signature dinner on the Maine Coast is, of course, the lobster dinner. It generally includes boiled lobster, a clam or seafood chowder, corn on the cob, and coleslaw or perhaps a salad. Lobster prices vary from day to day, but generally a full lobster dinner should cost around $25; without all the add-ons, about $18.

About the Hotels

Beachfront and roadside motels and historic-home B&Bs make up the majority of accommodation options along the Maine Coast. There are a few large luxury resorts, such as the Samoset Resort in Rockport or the Bar Harbor Inn in Bar Harbor, but most accommodations are simple and relatively inexpensive. Many properties close during the off-season—mid-October until mid-May; some that stay open drop their rates dramatically. There is a 7% state hospitality tax on all room rates.

WHAT IT COSTS

	¢	$	$$	$$$	$$$$
Restaurants	under $8	$8–$12	$13–$20	$21–$28	over $28
Hotels	under $80	$80–$120	$121–$170	$171–$220	over $220
Campgrounds	under $10	$10–$17	$18–$35	$36–$50	over $50

Restaurant prices are per person, for a main course at dinner. Hotel prices are for a standard double room during peak season and not including tax or gratuities. Some inns add a 15% service charge.

Outdoor Activities

No visit to the Maine Coast is complete without some outdoor activity—be it generated by two wheels, two feet, two paddles, or pulling a bag full of clubs.

Bicycling: The Bicycle Coalition of Maine (☎ 207/623–4511 ⊕ www. bikemaine.org) and Explore Maine by Bike (☎ 207/624–3300 ⊕ www.exploremaine. org/bike) are both excellent sources for trail maps and other riding information, including where to rent bikes.

Hiking: Exploring the Maine coast on foot is a quick way to acclimate to the relaxed pace of life here. Healthy Maine Walks (⊕ www. healthymainewalks.com) has comprehensive listings for quick jaunts as well as more involved hikes.

Kayaking: Nothing gets you literally off the beaten path like plying the salt waters in a graceful sea kayak. Members of the Maine Association of Sea Kayaking Guides and Instructors (⊕ www. maineseakayakguides.com) offer instructional classes and guided tours, plan trips, and rent equipment. More seasoned paddlers can get maps of Maine's famous sea trails system at the Maine Island Trails Association (☎ 207/761–8225 ⊕ www. mita.org).

10

As you drive across the border into Maine, a sign announces: THE WAY LIFE SHOULD BE. Romantics luxuriate in the feeling of a down comforter on a yellow pine bed or in the sensation of the wind and salt spray on their faces while cruising in a historic windjammer. Families love the unspoiled beaches and safe inlets dotting the shoreline. Hikers are revived while roaming the trails of Acadia National Park, and adventure seekers kayak along the coast.

The Maine Coast is several places in one. Portland may be Maine's largest metropolitan area, but its attitude is decidedly more big town than small city. South of Portland, Ogunquit, Kennebunkport, Old Orchard Beach, and other resort towns predominate along a reasonably smooth shoreline. North of Portland and Casco Bay, secondary roads turn south off U.S. 1 onto so many oddly chiseled peninsulas that it's possible to drive for days without retracing your route. Slow down to explore the museums, galleries, and shops in the larger towns and the antiques and curio shops and harborside lobster shacks in the smaller fishing villages. Freeport is an entity unto itself, a place where numerous name-brand outlets and specialty stores have sprung up around the retail outpost of famous outfitter L. L. Bean. And no description of the coast would be complete without mention of popular Acadia National Park, with its majestic mountains that are often shrouded in mist.

If you come to Maine seeking an untouched fishing village with locals gathered around a potbellied stove in the general store, you'll likely come away disappointed; that innocent age has passed in all but the most remote spots like Way Down East. Tourism has supplanted fishing, logging, and potato farming as Maine's number-one industry, and most areas are well equipped to receive the annual onslaught of visitors. But whether you are stepping outside a cabin for a walk in the woods or watching a boat rock at its anchor, you can sense the wilderness nearby, even on the edges of the most urbanized spots.

THE SOUTHERN COAST

By Laura V.
Scheel

Maine's southernmost coastal towns—Kittery, the Yorks, Ogunquit, the Kennebunks, and the Old Orchard Beach area—reveal a few of the stunning faces of the state's coast, from the miles and miles of inviting sandy beaches to the beautifully kept historic towns and carnival-like attractions. There is something for every taste, whether you seek solitude in a kayak or prefer being caught up in the infectious spirit of fellow vacationers.

North of Kittery, long stretches of hard-packed white-sand beach are closely crowded by nearly unbroken ranks of beach cottages, motels, and oceanfront restaurants. The summer colonies of York Beach and Wells brim with crowds and ticky-tacky shorefront overdevelopment, but nearby quiet wildlife refuges and land reserves promise an easy escape. York evokes yesteryear sentiment with its acclaimed historic district, while upscale Ogunquit tantalizes visitors with its array of shops and a cliffside walk.

More than any other region south of Portland, the Kennebunks—and especially Kennebunkport—provide the complete Maine Coast experience: classic townscapes where white-clapboard houses rise from manicured lawns and gardens; rocky shorelines punctuated by sandy beaches; quaint downtown districts packed with gift shops, ice-cream stands, and visitors; harbors with lobster boats bobbing alongside yachts; rustic, picnic-tabled restaurants serving lobster and fried seafood; and well-appointed dining rooms. As you continue north, the scents of friend dough and cotton candy mean you've arrived at Maine's version of Coney Island, Old Orchard Beach.

KITTERY

55 mi north of Boston; 5 mi north of Portsmouth, New Hampshire.

One of the earliest settlements in the state of Maine, Kittery suffered its share of British, French, and Native American attacks throughout the 17th and 18th centuries, yet rose to prominence as a vital shipbuilding center. The tradition continues; despite its New Hampshire name, the Portsmouth Naval Shipyard is part of Maine and has been one of the leading researchers and builders of U.S. submarines since its inception in 1800. It's not open to the public, but those on boats can pass by and get a glimpse.

10

Known as the "Gateway to Maine," Kittery has come to more recent light as a major shopping destination thanks to its complex of factory outlets. Flanked on either side of U.S. 1 are more than 120 stores, which attract hordes of shoppers year-round. For something a little less commercial, head east on Route 103 to the hidden Kittery most people miss: the lands around **Kittery Point.** Here you can find hiking and biking trails and great views of the water. With Portsmouth, New Hampshire, across the water, Whaleback Ledge Lighthouse, and the nearby Isles of Shoals, Kittery is a picturesque place to pass some time. Also along this winding stretch of Route 103 are two forts, both open in summer.

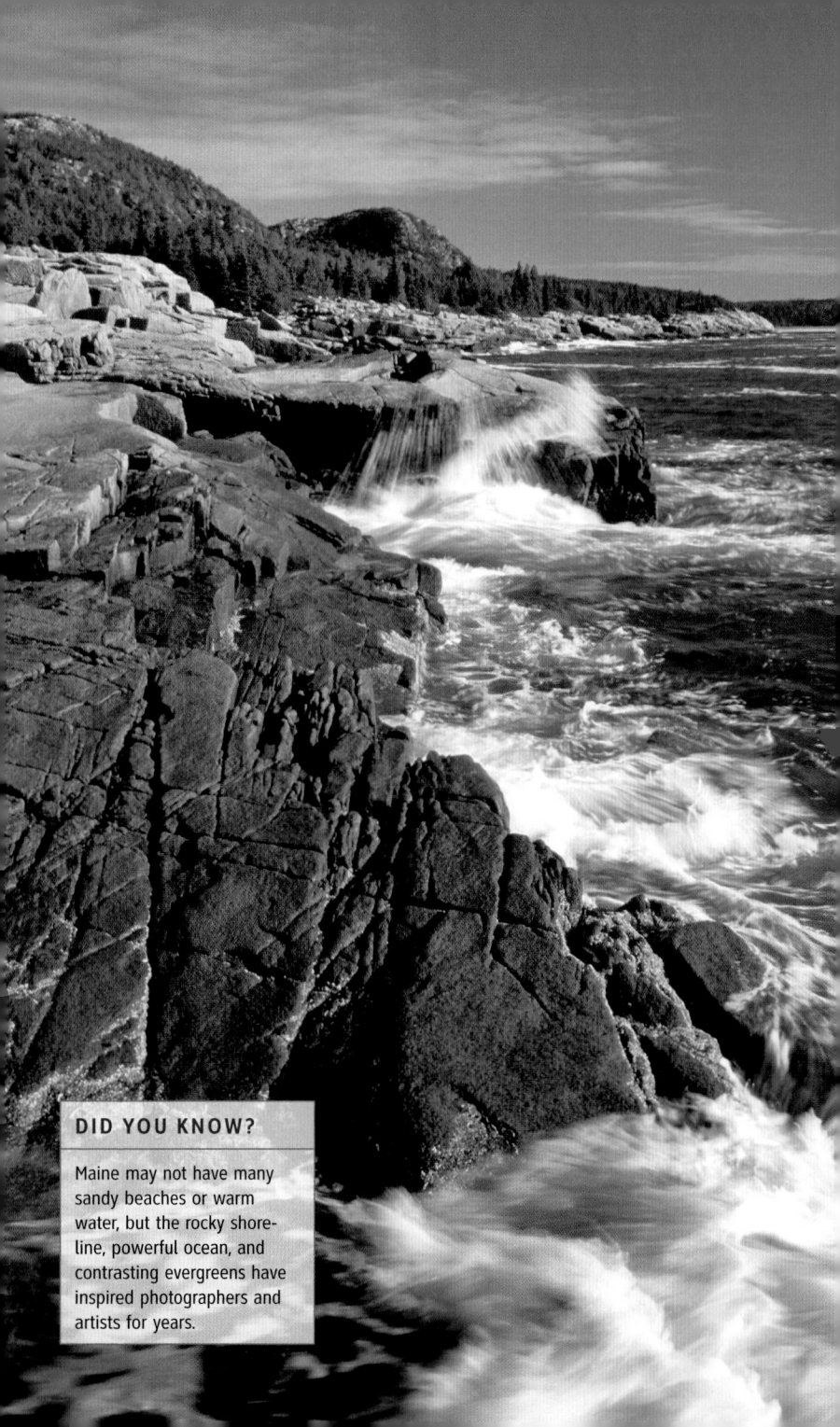

DID YOU KNOW?

Maine may not have many sandy beaches or warm water, but the rocky shore-line, powerful ocean, and contrasting evergreens have inspired photographers and artists for years.

ESSENTIALS

Visitor Information Maine Tourism Association & Visitor Information Center (✉ *U.S. 1 and I–95, Kittery* ☎ *207/439–1319* ⊕ *www.mainetourism.com*).

WHERE TO EAT

$–$$
SEAFOOD
★

✕ **Chauncey Creek Lobster Pound.** From the road you can barely see this restaurant's red roof hovering below the trees, but chances are you can see the cars parked at this popular spot along the high banks of the tidal river. The menu has lots of fresh lobster choices and a raw bar with locally harvested offerings like clams and oysters. Bring your own beer or wine if you desire alcohol. In season, it's open daily for lunch and dinner. ✉ *16 Chauncey Creek Rd., Kittery Point* ☎ *207/439–1030* ⊕ *www.chaunceycreek.com* ▭ *MC, V* ⊘ *Closed mid-Oct.–Mother's Day.*

$$–$$$
SEAFOOD

✕ **Warren's Lobster House.** A local institution, this waterfront restaurant specializes in seafood and has a huge salad bar. The pine-sided dining room leaves the impression that little has changed since Warren's opened in 1940. Dine outside overlooking the water when the weather is nice. ✉ *11 Water St.* ☎ *207/439–1630* ⊕ *www.lobsterhouse.com* ▭ *AE, MC, V.*

YORK VILLAGE

About 6 mi north of Kittery on Route 103 or Route 1A via U.S. 1.

As subdued as the town may feel today, the history of York Village reveals a far different character. One of the first permanently settled areas in the state of Maine, it was once witness to great destruction and fierce fighting during the French, Indian, and British wars; towns and fortunes were sacked, yet the potential for prosperity encouraged the area's citizens continually to rebuild and start anew. Colonial York citizens enjoyed great wealth and success from fishing and lumber as well as a penchant for politics. Angered by the British-imposed taxes, York held its own little-known tea party in 1775 in protest.

The actual village of York is quite small, housing the town's basic components of post office, town hall, a few shops, and a stretch of antique homes. You may notice something amiss with York's Civil War Monument. After the war it was common for towns to erect a statue of a Civil War soldier. The statue sent to York, however, was most likely meant to be shipped much farther south—the figure is a Confederate soldier.

GETTING HERE AND AROUND

The York Trolley Company makes daily loops through York Village, York Harbor, out to Nubble Lighthouse, and all the way to Short Sands Beach in York Beach. Route maps can be picked up nearly everywhere in York and at the chamber of commerce; fares are $1.50 one-way and $3 for the loop.

ESSENTIALS

Transportation Information York Trolley Company (☎ *207/363–9600* ⊕ *www.yorktrolley.com*).

10

EXPLORING

York Village Historic District. Most of the 18th- and 19th-century buildings here are clustered along York Street and Lindsay Road; seven are owned by the Old York Historical Society and charge admission. You can buy tickets for all the buildings at the **Jefferds Tavern** (⊠ *Rte. 1A at Lindsay Rd.*), a restored late-18th-century inn. The **Old York Gaol** (1720) was once the King's Prison for the Province of Maine; inside are dungeons, cells, and the jailer's quarters. Several times a week, costumed reenactors spin tales—based on real 18th-century prisoners—of why they're behind bars. The 1731 **Elizabeth Perkins House** reflects the Victorian style of its last occupants, the prominent Perkins family. The Historical Society also gives guided walking tours (or take the self-guided tour through each of the seven buildings; admission is valid for two consecutive days). ☎ *207/363–4974* ⊕ *www.oldyork.org* ☞ *All buildings $10; $5 for one building* ☼ *Mid-June–mid-Oct., Mon.–Sat. 10–5.*

Stonewall Kitchen. You've probably seen the kitchen's smartly labeled jars of gourmet chutneys, jams, jellies, salsas, and sauces in specialty stores back home. York is the headquarters and processing center for them. The company's complex houses the company store, a bustling café and take-out restaurant, a viewing area of the cooking and bottling processes, and stunning gardens. Sample all the mustards, salsas, and dressings that you can stand, or have lunch at the café. Takeout is available during store hours. Lunch is served daily 11–3; Sunday is brunch day. The venture's latest addition is the cooking school, where participants can join in evening or luncheon courses. Reservations are recommended, though walk-ins are accepted if space allows; most classes cost $35–$50 and are shorter than two hours. ⊠ *Stonewall La. just off U.S. 1, next to information center* ☎ *207/351–2712* ⊕ *www. stonewallkitchen.com* ☼ *Mon.–Sat. 8–8, Sun. 9–6.*

SHOPPING

Bring a basket for Saturday morning shopping at the **Gateway Farmers' Market** (⊠ *1 Stonewall La., just off U.S. Rte. 1*), held at the Greater York Region Chamber of Commerce visitor center from early June until Columbus Day. Beginning at 9 AM, you'll find fresh local produce as well as flowers, artisan bread, homemade soaps, and specialty foods. It's a good place to gather the makings for a beach picnic. The market also opens up on Tuesday afternoons from 2 to 5:30 June 30 until September 1. Guess the theme at **Gravestone Artwear** (⊠ *250 York St. [Rte. 1A]* ☎ *800/564–4310* ⊕ *www.gravestoneartwear.com*), where you'll find items adorned with Colonial, Victorian, and Celtic gravestone carving designs. There are also crystals, gravestone-rubbing supplies, books, and candles. Watercolors, mixed media, oils, and photography can be had at **Village Gallery** (⊠ *244 York St. [Rte. 1A]* ☎ *207/351–3110* ⊕ *www. yorkvillagegallery.com*), where many local artists are represented.

WHERE TO EAT

$$$$
SEAFOOD
✕ **Foster's Downeast Clambake.** Save your appetite for this one. Specializing in the traditional Maine clambake—a feast consisting of rich clam chowder, a pile of mussels and steamers, Maine lobster, corn on the cob, roasted potatoes and onions, bread, butter, and Maine blueberry crumb

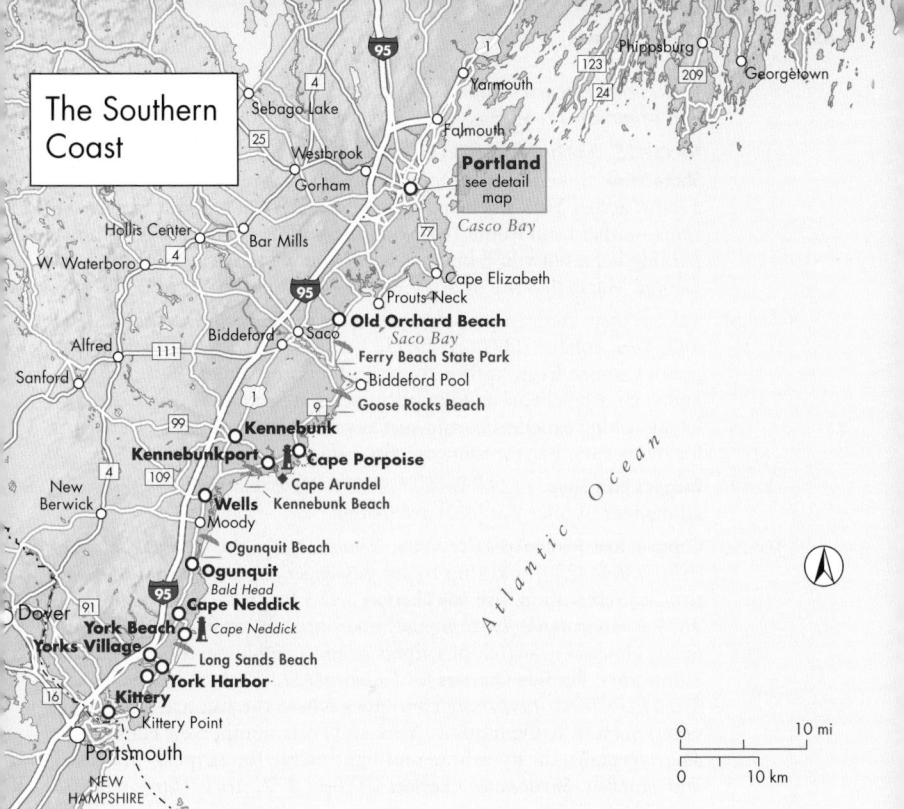

The Southern Coast

cake (phew!)—this massive complex provides entertainment as well as belly-busting meals. You can also opt to have clambake fixings shipped to your home. ⊠ *5 Axholme Rd.* ☎ *207/363–3255 or 800/552–0242* ⊕ *www.fostersclambake.com* ⊟ *AE, MC, V.*

YORK HARBOR

Approximately 3 mi north of York Village via Route 1A.

Just a few miles from the village proper, York Harbor opens up to the water and offers many places to linger and explore. The harbor is busy with boats of all kinds, while the harbor beach is a good stretch of sand for swimming. Much more formal than the northward York Beach and much quieter, the area retains a somewhat more exclusive air.

EXPLORING

Sayward-Wheeler House. Built in 1718, the waterfront home was remodeled in the 1760s by Jonathan Sayward, a local merchant who had prospered in the West Indies trade. By 1860 his descendants had opened the house to the public to share the story of their Colonial ancestors. The house, accessible only by guided tour, reveals both the simple 18th-century decor and the more elaborate (and opulent) furnishings of the 19th century. ⊠ *9 Barrell La. Extension, York Harbor* ☎ *207/384–2454*

⊕ *www.historicnewengland.org* ✉ *$5* ⊘ *June–mid-Oct., 2nd and 4th Sat. of month 11–5; tours on the hr. 11–4.*

SPORTS AND THE OUTDOORS

Shore Walk. Take the stroll for a good beachcombing exploration and a jaunt across York's beloved Wiggly Bridge. You can start at various spots—either from Route 103 alongside York Harbor (there is minimal parking here, but you'll know it when you see the bridge) or from the George Marshall Store in York Village (140 Lindsay Road).

KAYAKING   Take to the water in a guided kayak trip with **Harbor Adventures** (⌂ *Box 345, York Harbor 03911* ☎ *207/363–8466* ⊕ *www.harboradventures. com*). Choose from harbor tours, full-moon paddles, half-day trips, and even a luncheon paddle; prices start around $45. There are also kayak fishing expeditions and surf kayaking trips available. Departure locations vary. Bicycle tours are also offered.

BIKING   **Berger's Bike Shop** (✉ *241 York St., No. 1, York* ☎ *207/363–4070*) rents all manner of bikes for local excursions.

FISHING   **Captain Tom Farnon** (✉ *Rte. 103, Town Dock No. 2, York Harbor* ☎ *207/363–3234*) takes up to six passengers at a time on lobstering trips, by reservation. **Fish Tale Charters** (✉ *85 Bog Rd., York* ☎ *207/363–3874* ⊕ *www.maineflyfishing.net*) takes anglers on fly-fishing or light tackle charters in search of stripers or juvenile bluefin tuna; departure points vary. **Rip Tide Charters** (✉ *1 Georgia St., York* ☎ *207/363–2536* ⊕ *www.mainestriperfishing.com*) goes where the fish are—departure points vary, from Ogunquit to York and Portsmouth, New Hampshire. They specialize in fly-fishing and light tackle for stripers, mackerel, and bluefish. **Shearwater Charters** (⌂ *Box 472, York Harbor 03911* ☎ *207/363–5324*) offers spin or fly-casting charters in the York River and along the shoreline from Kittery to Ogunquit. Bait-fishing trips are also available. Departure spots depend on time and tides.

HIKING AND   For a peek into the Rachel Carson National Wildlife Refuge, take the
WALKING   2-mi **Brave Boat Harbor Trail,** which is one of the few walking trails in the refuge. It's a prime bird-watching area. Look for Brave Boat Harbor Road just off Route 103 for trail access and parking.

WHERE TO EAT

$$$–$$$$ ✕ **Dockside Restaurant.** On an island overlooking York Harbor, this res-
SEAFOOD   taurant has plenty of seafood on the menu, which also includes such treats as beef tenderloin and duckling. Start with the rich lobster and scallop crepe or an order of local oysters. ✉ *22 Harris Island Rd., just off Rte. 103* ☎ *207/363–2722* ⊕ *www.docksidegq.com* ▭ *D, MC, V* ⊘ *Closed Mon. (except July and Aug.) and late Oct.–May.*

$$$–$$$$ ✕ **Harbor Porches.** Eating here is very much like sitting on someone's
AMERICAN   porch—assuming that someone has a lot of money and can afford extravagant views over York Harbor. Wicker chairs at linen-covered tables fill the space and are surrounded by large windows. Local seafood is on the menu, as well as rack of lamb and steak. For lunch, try one of the hearty sandwiches or specialty pizzas. The Maine crab cake appetizer is worth a try, as is the lobster bisque. Jeans and sneakers are not allowed at dinner. The restaurant is open for breakfast, lunch,

Sunday brunch, and dinner. ⊠ *Stage Neck Rd.* ☎ *207/363–3850* ⊟ *AE, D, DC, MC, V* ⊘ *Closed 2 wks. in Jan.*

WHERE TO STAY

$$$–$$$$

Fodor's Choice

★

Chapman Cottage. This impeccably restored inn, named for the woman who had it built as her summer cottage in 1899, sits proudly atop a swath of lawn. The luxuriant bedspreads, fresh flowers, antiques, and beautiful rugs only hint at the indulgence found here. Innkeepers Donna and Paul Archibald spoil their guests with sumptuous breakfasts, afternoon hors d'oeuvres, port, sherry, and homemade chocolate truffles, all prepared by Paul, a professionally trained chef. Most rooms have fireplaces and whirlpool tubs; all are spacious and bright. It's a five-minute walk to either York Village or the harbor. **Pros:** beautifully restored historic lodging; luxury appointments; attention to detail. **Cons:** no water views; most rooms on upper floors. ⊠ *370 York St.* ☎ *207/363–2059 or 877/363–2059* ⊕ *www.chapmancottagebandb.com* ↵ *6 rooms* ♿ *In-room: no phone, Wi-Fi. In-hotel: restaurant, bar, no kids under 12, no elevator* ⊟ *AE, D, MC, V* ⦿ *BP.*

$$$–$$$$

★

Inn at Tanglewood Hall. The inn's artfully painted floors, lush wallpapers, and meticulous attention to detail are the fruits of a former designation as a designers' showcase home. This 1880s Victorian "cottage," as these mansions were humbly called back in the day, is a haven of elegance and comfort, set back among trees and stunning perennial gardens. Rooms are individually decorated, though all share decadently rich coloring and fabrics, high ceilings, and many large windows; some have fireplaces. **Pros:** elegant and authentic historic lodging; serene setting amid gardens and grand trees; short walk to beaches and nature trails. **Cons:** no water views. ⊠ *611 York St.* ☎ *207/351–1075* ⊕ *www.tanglewoodhall.com* ↵ *6 rooms* ♿ *In-room: no phone, refrigerator (some), no TV, Wi-Fi. In-hotel: no kids under 12, no elevator* ⊟ *AE, MC, V* ⦿ *BP.*

$$–$$$$

★

York Harbor Inn. A mid-17th-century fishing cabin with dark timbers and a fieldstone fireplace forms the heart of this inn, while several wings and outbuildings have been added over the years, making for a complex with a great variety of styles and appointments. The rooms are furnished with antiques and country pieces; many have decks overlooking the water, and some have whirlpool tubs or fireplaces. The nicest rooms are in two adjacent buildings, Harbor Cliffs and Harbor Hill. The dining room ($$$–$$$$; no lunch off-season) has great ocean views. **Pros:** many rooms have harbor views; close to beaches and scenic walking trails. **Cons:** rooms vary greatly in style and appeal. ⊠ *480 York St., Coastal Route 1A, York Harbor* ☎ *207/363–5119 or 800/343–3869* ⊕ *www.yorkharborinn.com* ↵ *54 rooms, 2 suites* ♿ *In-room: Wi-Fi. In-hotel: 2 restaurants, bar, no elevator* ⊟ *AE, DC, MC, V* ⦿ *CP.*

10

YORK BEACH

6 mi north of York Harbor via Route 1A.

Like many shorefront towns in Maine, York Beach has a long history of entertaining summer visitors. Take away today's bikinis and iPods and it's easy to imagine squealing tourists adorned in the full-length bathing garb of the late 19th century. Just as they did back then, visitors today come here to eat ice cream, enjoy carnival-like novelties, and indulge in the sun and sea air.

York Beach is a real family destination, devoid of all things staid and stuffy—children are meant to be seen and heard here. Just beyond the sands of Short Sand Beach are a host of amusements, from bowling to indoor minigolf and the Fun-O-Rama arcade.

ESSENTIALS

Visitor Information The Greater York Region Chamber of Commerce (⊠ *1 Stonewall La., off U.S. 1* ☎ *207/363–4422* ⊕ *www.gatewaytomaine.org*).

EXPLORING

Nubble Light. Head out a couple of miles on the peninsula to see one of the most photographed lighthouses on the globe. Direct access is prohibited, but an information center shares the 1879 light's history. Find parking at Sohier Park, at the end of Nubble Road, as well as restrooms and benches. ⊠ *End of Nubble Rd., off Rte. 1A.*

🅒 **York's Wild Kingdom.** Between the zoo and the carnival rides, it's sometimes hard to distinguish the wild animals from the kids here. The zoo has an impressive variety of exotic animals and is home to the state's only white Bengal tiger. Combination tickets can be purchased to visit the zoo and the amusement park, and discounts are available for kids under 10. ⊠ *U.S. 1 (about 2 mi from Exit 7, look for the 40-foot sign), also entrance at 23 Railroad Ave. at York Beach, York* ☎ *207/363–4911* ⊕ *www.yorkzoo.com* 🖃 *$14.50 zoo only; $19.50 zoo and rides (adults)* ☉ *Late May–Sept.*

NIGHTLIFE

Inn on the Blues (⊠ *7 Ocean Ave., York Beach* ☎ *207/351–3221*) is a hopping blues club that attracts national bands.

WHERE TO EAT AND STAY

$$$–$$$$
AMERICAN
Fodor'sChoice
★

✕ **Blue Sky on York Beach.** Making its home on the second floor of the grandly restored Atlantic House Hotel, this wide-open and inviting restaurant adds a keen sense of swanky sophistication to this casual beach town. A massive stone fireplace anchors the great room of high ceilings, exposed ductwork, and warm wood floors; unusual hanging light fixtures attract the eye and cast a gentle glow. The menu, executed by well-known chef and owner Lydia Shire, takes regional New England fare to new heights. Memorable choices include the lamb pizza appetizer and the lobster stew; the deep-fried short ribs are painfully delicious, as is the charcoaled duck breast with sugar pumpkin. For a closer look at what happens in the kitchen, you can sit at the curved food bar, with full views of the wood-fired oven and the chefs at work. There's an additional bar menu for the lounge. In good weather, sit out on the large deck with views of the town below. Sunday jazz brunch is also a winner here. ⌷ *2 Beach St., York Beach* ☎ *207/363–0050* ⊕ *www.blueskyonyorkbeach.com* ⌂ *Reservations recommended* ☰ *AE, D, MC, V* ☉ *No lunch Sept.–June.*

$-$$
AMERICAN
✕ **The Goldenrod.** If you wanted to—and you are on vacation—you could eat nothing but the famous taffy here, made just about the same way today as it was back in 1896. The famous Goldenrod Kisses, some 65 tons of which are made per year, are a great attraction, and people line the windows to watch the taffy being made. Aside from the famous candy, this eating place is family oriented, very reasonably priced, and a great place to get ice cream from the old-fashioned soda fountain. Breakfast is served all day, while the simple lunch menu doubles as dinner; choose from sandwiches and burgers. ⌷ *2 Railroad Ave.* ☎ *207/363–2621* ⊕ *www.thegoldenrod.com* ☰ *AE, MC, V* ☉ *Closed Columbus Day–late May.*

$$$$
★
▦ **Atlantic House Hotel.** For years, this aged beauty sat weary and neglected in the middle of York Beach, caught in the mire of area zoning laws. An eyesore no longer, this 1888 hotel has returned to its former splendor. The standard hotel rooms are awash in calming blues, greens, and creams, accented with designer fabrics, gas fireplaces, and Jacuzzi tubs. For more space, there are one- and two-bedroom suites (with surprisingly reasonable weekly rates), complete with full kitchens, laundry, and separate living and dining rooms. All spaces are uncluttered, have gleaming hardwood floors, and are blessed with ample windows to allow for plenty of natural light. Several suites have private decks. Many conveniences are also housed within the hotel: the elegant Blue Sky at York Beach ($$$) restaurant, a full-service spa, Clara's Cupcake Café (¢), a wine and specialty food shop, a children's apparel store, and a women's boutique with clothing, jewelry, cosmetics, and accessories. **Pros:** elegant, sophisticated lodging; walk to beach/town; great on-site amenities; good choice for weekly stay. **Cons:** not a beachfront location (fourth floor has partial water views); not for budget travelers. ⌷ *2 Beach St., York Beach* ☎ *207/363–0051* ⊕ *www.atlantichouseyorkbeach.com* ⬖ *7 rooms, 8 suites* ⅄ *In-room: safe, kitchen (some), refrigerator (some), DVD, Wi-Fi. In-hotel: 2 restaurants, bar, spa, laundry facilities, Wi-Fi hotspot, parking* ☰ *AE, D, DC, MC, V.*

CAPE NEDDICK

4 mi north of York Beach via Rte. 1A, just north of York on U.S. 1.

Cape Neddick is one of the less developed of York's villages, running from the water (and Route 1A), along U.S. 1 between York and Ogunquit. The town has many modest residential homes, with a sprinkling of businesses catering to both locals and visitors. There are a few restaurants and inns but no distinct downtown hub.

EXPLORING

Mount Agamenticus Park. Maintained by the York Parks and Recreation Department, this humble summit of 692 feet is said to be the highest peak along the Atlantic seaboard. That may not seem like much, but if you choose to hike to the top, you will be rewarded with incredible views all the way to the White Mountains in New Hampshire. If you don't want to hoof it (though it's not very steep), there is parking at the top. To get here, take Mountain Road just off U.S. 1 in Cape Neddick (just after Flo's Steamed Hot Dogs) and follow the signs. The area is open daily, with no charge. It's popular with equestrians and cyclists as well as families and hikers. ⓘ *York Parks and Recreation Department, 200 U.S. Rte. 1 S, York 03909* ☎ *207/363–1040.*

WHERE TO EAT AND STAY

¢ ✕ **Flo's Steamed Hot Dogs.** Yes, it seems crazy to highlight a hot-dog stand,
AMERICAN but this is no ordinary place. Who would guess that a hot dog could
★ make it into *Saveur* and *Gourmet* magazines? There is something grand about this shabby, red-shingle shack that has been dealing dogs since 1959. The line is out the door most days, but the operation is so efficient that the wait is not long. Flo has passed on, but her granddaughter keeps the business going, selling countless thousands of hot dogs each year. Be sure to ask for the special sauce—consisting of, among other things, hot sauce and mayo (you can take a bottle home, and you'll want to). ✉ *1359 U.S. 1* ☎ *No phone* ⊕ *www.floshotdogs.com* ▭ *No credit cards* ⊗ *Closed Wed.*

$$$–$$$$ ✕ **Frankie & Johnny's Natural Food Restaurant.** If you've had about all
VEGETARIAN the fried seafood you can stand for one day, try this casual little spot that focuses on healthy but tasty meals. Choose from a variety of vegetarian dishes as well as seafood, poultry, and meat options. The toasted peppercorn seared sushi-grade tuna, served with coconut risotto on gingered vegetables, is excellent. You're welcome to bring your own libations. ✉ *1594 U.S. 1, Cape Neddick* ☎ *207/363–1909* ⊕ *www.frankie-johnnys.com* ▭ *No credit cards* ⊗ *No dinner Mon.– Wed. No lunch.*

$–$$$ 🏨 **Country View Motel & Guesthouse.** Set back along one of U.S. 1's less hectic sections is this appealing little motel that looks more like an inn. There are a few rooms in the main house, and the rest are in the adjacent motel complex. It's clean, pretty, and in a good central location for exploring the Yorks and Ogunquit, which are just a few miles away. Suites sleep up to four people and have full kitchens. Guests with well-behaved dogs will appreciate the on-site pet park for exercise and play. **Pros:** convenient to both Ogunquit and Yorks; ample grounds provide picnic areas and gas grills. **Cons:** not an in-town location; no water views or beachfront. ✉ *1521 U.S. 1* ☎ *207/363–7160 or 800/258–6598* ⊕ *www.countryviewmotel.com* ⤷ *19 rooms, 3 suites* ⚴ *In-room: kitchen (some), refrigerator, Wi-Fi. In-hotel: pool, some pets allowed* ▭ *MC, V* ⫶⚬⫶ *CP* ⊗ *Closed Jan.–mid-Apr.*

SHOPPING

Home furnishings with an antique feel are the specialty of **Jeremiah Campbell & Company** (✉ *1537 U.S. 1* ☎ *207/363–8499*). Everything here is handcrafted, from rugs, decoys, furniture, and lighting to glassware. The shop is closed Wednesday.

Ogunquit's Perkins Cove is a pleasant place to admire the boats—and wonder at the origin of their names.

SPORTS AND THE OUTDOORS

FISHING Offering various guided fishing trips, private casting lessons, and a summer "striper school" is **Eldredge Bros. Fly Shop** (✉ *1480 U.S. 1* ☎ *207/363–9269 or 207/363–9279* ⊕ *www.eldredgeflyshop.com*). Kayak rentals and rod-and-reel rentals are also available.

KAYAKING Hop on one of the regularly scheduled guided kayak trips with **Excursions/Coastal Maine Outfitting Co.** (✉ *1740 U.S. 1* ☎ *207/363–0181* ⊕ *www.excursionsinmaine.com*). You can cruise along the shoreline or sign up for an overnight paddle. Reservations are recommended; trips start at $60. Kayaks and other boats are available for rental.

OGUNQUIT

10 mi north of the Yorks via Rtes. 1A and 1 or Shore Rd.

A resort village in the 1880s, stylish Ogunquit gained fame as an artists' colony. Today it has become a mini Provincetown, with a gay population that swells in summer. Many inns and small clubs cater to a primarily gay and lesbian clientele. The nightlife in Ogunquit revolves around the precincts of Ogunquit Square and Perkins Cove, where people stroll, often enjoying an after-dinner ice-cream cone or espresso. For a scenic drive, take Shore Road through downtown toward the 100-foot Bald Head Cliff; you'll be treated to views up and down the coast. On a stormy day the surf can be quite wild here.

KENNEBUNK WALKING TOURS

To take a little walking tour of Kennebunk's most notable structures, begin from the Federal-style Brick Store Museum, on Main Street. Head south on Main Street (turn left out of the museum) to see several extraordinary 18th-century homes, including the Nathaniel Frost House at 99 Main Street (1799) and the Benjamin Brown House at 85 Main Street (1788).

When you've had your fill of historic homes, head back up toward the museum, pass the 1773 First Parish Unitarian Church (its Asher Benjamin–style steeple contains the original Paul Revere bell), and turn right onto Summer Street. This street is an architectural showcase, revealing an array of styles from Colonial to Federal. Walking past these grand beauties will give you a real sense of the economic prowess and glamour of the long-gone shipbuilding industry.

For a guided architectural walking tour of Summer Street, contact the Brick Store Museum at 207/985–4802.

For a dramatic walk along the rocky coastline and beneath the views of Ocean Avenue's grand mansions, head out on the **Parson's Way Shore Walk**, a paved, 4.8-mi round-trip. Begin at Dock Square and follow Ocean Avenue along the river, passing the Colony Hotel and St. Ann's Church, all the way to Walker's Point. You can simply turn back from here or take a left onto Wildes District Road for a walk amid more luxury homes and trees.

SPORTS AND THE OUTDOORS

BEACHES With its thousands of acres of marsh and preserved land, Wells is a great place to spend a lot of time outdoors. Nearly 7 mi of sand stretch along the boundaries of Wells, making beach-going a prime occupation. Tidal pools sheltered by rocks are filled with all manner of creatures awaiting discovery. Parking is available for a fee (take the trolley!) at **Crescent Beach**, along Webhannet Drive; **Wells Beach** (at the end of Mile Road off U.S. 1) has public restrooms and two parking areas. There is another lot at the far end of Wells Beach, at the end of Atlantic Avenue. Across the jetty from Wells Harbor is **Drakes Island Beach** (end of Drakes Island Road off U.S. 1), which also has parking and public restrooms. Lifeguards are on hand at all the beaches. Rent bikes, surfboards, wet suits, boogie boards, and probably a few other things at **Wheels and Waves** (⊠ *578 U.S. 1* ☎ *207/646–5774*).

STATE PARKS The **Rachel Carson National Wildlife Refuge** (⊠ *321 Port Rd. [Rte. 9]*
AND REFUGES ☎ *207/646–9226* ⊕ *www.fws.gov/northeast/rachelcarson*) has a mile-long-loop nature trail through a salt marsh. The trail borders the Little River and a white-pine forest where migrating birds and waterfowl of many varieties are regularly spotted.

WHERE TO EAT AND STAY

$–$$$ ✕ **Billy's Chowder House.** Locals head to this simple restaurant in a salt
SEAFOOD marsh for the generous lobster rolls, haddock sandwiches, and chowders. Big windows in the bright dining rooms overlook the marsh.

✉ *216 Mile Rd.* ☎ *207/646–7558* ⊕ *www.billyschowderhouse.com* ▭ *AE, D, MC, V* ⊗ *Closed mid-Dec.–mid-Jan.*

$$ ✕ **Maine Diner.** One look at the 1953 exterior and you start craving
AMERICAN good diner food. You'll get a little more than you're expecting; how many greasy spoons make an award-winning lobster pie? That's the house favorite, as well as a heavenly seafood chowder. There's plenty of fried seafood in addition to the usual diner fare, and breakfast is served all day. Check out the adjacent gift shop, Remember the Maine. ✉ *2265 U.S. 1.* ☎ *207/646–4441* ⊕ *www.mainediner.com* ▭ *D, MC, V* ⊗ *Closed 1 wk in Jan.*

$$–$$$$ ⊞ **Haven by the Sea.** Once the summer mission of St. Martha's Church
Fodor'sChoice in Kennebunkport, this exquisite inn has retained many of the original
★ details from its former life as a seaside church. The cathedral ceilings and stained-glass windows remain. The guest rooms are spacious, some with serene marsh views. Four common areas, including one with a fireplace, are perfect spots for afternoon refreshments. The inn is one block from the beach. **Pros:** unusual structure with elegant appointments; nightly happy hour; walk to beach. **Cons:** not an in-town location. ✉ *59 Church St.* ☎ *207/646–4194* ⊕ *www.havenbythesea.com* ⇆ *6 rooms, 2 suites, 1 apartment* ⌂ *In-room: Wi-Fi. In-hotel: no kids under 12* ▭ *AE, MC, V* ⊗ *BP.*

KENNEBUNK

Approximately 6 mi north of Wells via U.S. 1; 23 mi south of Portland via Maine Tpke.

Sometimes bypassed on the way to its sister town of Kennebunkport, Kennebunk has its own appeal. In the 19th century the town was a major shipbuilding center; docks lined the river with hundreds of workers busily crafting the vessels that would bring immense fortune to some of the area's residents. Although the trade is long gone, the evidence that remains of this great wealth exists in Kennebunk's mansions. Kennebunk is a classic small New England town, with an inviting shopping district, steepled churches, and fine examples of 18th- and 19th-century brick and clapboard homes. There are also plenty of natural spaces for walking, swimming, birding, and biking.

The town of Kennebunk is divided between two villages; the upper one extends around the Mousam River on Route 9, while the lower one is several miles down Route 35, just shy of Kennebunkport proper. The drive down Route 35 keeps visitors agog with the splendor of the area's mansions, spread out on both sides of the road. To get to the grand and gentle beaches of Kennebunk, go straight on Beach Avenue from the intersection of Routes 9 and 35 in the lower village.

GETTING HERE AND AROUND

Get a good overview of the sights with an Intown Trolley tour. The narrated 45-minute jaunts leave every hour starting at 10 AM at the designated stop on Ocean Avenue, around the corner of Dock Square. The fare is valid for the day, so you can hop on and off at your leisure.

10

ESSENTIALS

Transportation Information **Intown Trolley** (⊠ *Ocean Ave., Kennebunkport* ☎ *207/967–3686* ⊕ *www.intowntrolley.com* ⊠ *$15 all-day fare* ⊙ *Late May– mid-Oct., daily 10–5*).

Visitor Information **Kennebunk-Kennebunkport Chamber of Commerce** (⊡ *17 Western Ave.* ☎ *207/967–0857* ⊕ *www.visitthekennebunks.com*).

EXPLORING

Brick Store Museum. The cornerstone of this block-long preservation of early-19th-century commercial buildings is **William Lord's Brick Store.** Built as a dry-goods store in 1825 in the Federal style, the building has an openwork balustrade across the roof line, granite lintels over the windows, and paired chimneys. Exhibits chronicle Kennebunk's relationship with the sea. The museum leads architectural walking tours of Kennebunk's National Register Historic District on Wednesday and Friday, typically from May to October. ⊠ *117 Main St., Kennebunk* ☎ *207/985–4802* ⊕ *www.brickstoremuseum.org* ⊠ *Donations accepted; walking tours $5* ⊙ *Tues.–Fri. 10–4:30, Sat. 10–1.*

First Parish Unitarian Church. Built in 1773, just before the American Revolution, this stunning church is a marvel. The 1804 Asher Benjamin–style steeple stands proudly atop the village, and the sounds of the original Paul Revere bell can be heard for miles. It holds Sunday services, and on Tuesdays in summer tours of the sanctuary take place at 10 AM. ⊠ *114 Main St.* ☎ *207/985–3700* ⊕ *www.uukennebunk.org.*

SHOPPING

The **Gallery on Chase Hill** (⊠ *10 Chase Hill Rd.* ☎ *207/967–0049* ⊕ *www. maine-art.com*) presents original artwork by Maine and New England artists. **Tom's of Maine Natural Living Store** (⊠ *52 Main St.* ☎ *207/467– 4005*) sells all-natural personal-care products.

SPORTS AND THE OUTDOORS

Kennebunk Beach has three parts: Gooch's Beach, Mother's Beach, and Kennebunk Beach. Beach Road, with its cottages and old Victorian boardinghouses, runs right behind them. Gooch's and Kennebunk attract teenagers; Mother's Beach, which has a small playground and tidal puddles for splashing, is popular with families. For parking permits (a fee is charged in summer), go to the **Kennebunk Town Office** (⊠ *1 Summer St. [Rte. 35]* ☎ *207/985–2102* ⊕ *www.kennebunkmaine.us* ⊙ *Mon., Tues., Thurs., and Fri. 8–4:30; Wed. 1–4:30*).

For an unusual exploring treat, visit the **Kennebunk Plains** (⊠ *Rte. 99 W, a few miles out of Kennebunk* ☎ *207/729–5181*), a 135-acre protected grasslands habitat that is home to several rare and endangered species of vegetation and wildlife. Locally known as the blueberry plains, a good portion of the area is abloom with the hues of ripening wild blueberries in late July; after August 1 visitors are welcome to pick and eat all the berries they can find. The roads take you through vast grasslands and scrub-oak woods and by ponds. The area is maintained by the Nature Conservancy and is open daily from sunrise to sunset.

Three-mile-long **Goose Rocks,** a few minutes' drive north of town off Route 9, has plenty of shallow pools for exploring and a good long stretch of smooth sand; it's a favorite of families with small children. You can pick up a parking permit ($12 a day, $50 a week) at the **Kennebunkport Town Hall** (⊠ *6 Elm St., Kennebunkport* ☎ *207/967–4243* ☉ *Weekdays 8–4:30*) or at the Police Department on Route 9 on the way to the beach.

WHERE TO EAT

$

AMERICAN

✕ **Duffy's Tavern & Grill.** Every small town needs its own lively and friendly tavern, and this bustling spot is Kennebunk's favorite, housed in a former shoe factory with exposed brick, soaring ceilings, and hardwood floors. Right outside are the tumbling waters of the Mousam River as it flows from the dam. There's a large bar with several overhead televisions and plenty of seating in the main room, plus more tables in the less-captivating back section. Prices are reasonable for these parts; you'll find plenty of comfortable standards here, including burgers, sandwiches, pizza, and salads, as well as an appetizer menu with lots of chicken wings and fried items. Breakfast is served on Saturday and Sunday mornings, and there's live entertainment on weekend evenings. ⊠ *4 Main St., Kennebunk* ☎ *207/985–0050* ⊕ *www.duffyskennebunk. com* ☰ *AE, MC, V.*

$$

AMERICAN

✕ **Federal Jack's.** Run by the Kennebunkport Brewing Company, this complex is housed in an old shipbuilding warehouse on the water. Many beers are handcrafted on-site, including Blue Fin Stout and Goat Island Light—try the sampler if you can't decide. The food is American pub style, with lots of seafood elements; the clam chowder is rich and satisfying. There's also Sunday brunch buffet and a late-night menu for those who get hungry playing pool in the back room. Brew tours are available. You can find the restaurant and brewery just before the bridge into Kennebunkport. ⊠ *8 Western Ave., Lower Village* ☎ *207/967–4322* ⊕ *www.federaljacks.com* ☰ *AE, MC, V.*

$$$$

AMERICAN

★

✕ **White Barn Inn.** Formally attired waiters, meticulous service, and exquisite food have earned this restaurant accolades as one of the best in New England. Regional fare is served in a rustic but elegant dining room. The three-course, prix-fixe menu ($95), which changes weekly, might include steamed Maine lobster nestled on fresh fettuccine with carrots, ginger, and snow peas. ⊠ *37 Beach Ave., Kennebunk* ☎ *207/967–2321* ⊕ *www.whitebarninn.com* ☙ *Reservations essential* ⌂ *Jacket required* ☰ *AE, MC, V* ☉ *Closed 3 wks. in Jan. No lunch.*

WHERE TO STAY

$$$–$$$$

🏠 **Bufflehead Cove Inn.** On the Kennebunk River at the end of a winding dirt road, this gray-shingle B&B sits amid fields and apple trees. Surprisingly it's only five minutes from Dock Square. Rooms in the main house are outfitted with a funky mix of antiques and Far Eastern and eclectic art. The Hideaway Suite, with a two-sided gas fireplace, king-size bed, and large whirlpool tub, overlooks the river. The Garden Studio has a fireplace and offers the most privacy. It's a great place to bring your kayak or canoe for paddling trips right from the dock, or you can opt to gaze upon the river from the expansive wraparound porch. The roomy cottage, set back from the main house, has a large private deck

10

Kennebunk is a classic riverfront New England town, while Kennebunkport (pictured) is a more upscale resort area.

with water views, a wood-burning fireplace, and a two-person whirl-pool tub; a two-night minimum stay is required. **Pros:** beautiful and peaceful pastoral setting; ideal riverfront location; perfect for a serene getaway. **Cons:** a short drive from town. ⊠ *18 Bufflehead Cove Rd., Kennebunk* ☎ *207/967–3879* ⊕ *www.buffleheadcove.com* ⌁ *2 rooms, 3 suites, 1 cottage* ⌂ *In-room: no phone, refrigerator (some), Wi-Fi. In-hotel: Internet terminal, no kids under 1* ⊟ *D, MC, V* ☯ *Closed Dec.–Apr.* ⏁ *BP.*

$$$$ ⌂ **The Seaside.** This handsome seaside property has been in the hands of the Severance family since 1667. The modern hotel units, all with sliding-glass doors that open onto private decks or patios (half with ocean views), are appropriate for families; so are the cottages with one to four bedrooms. You can't get much closer to Gooch's Beach. The inn supplies beach chairs; take a dip in the outdoor shower to wash off the salt and the sand. **Pros:** beachfront location; great ocean views from upper-floor rooms. **Cons:** rooms are hotel standard and a little outdated; not an in-town location. ⊠ *80 Beach Ave., Kennebunk* ☎ *207/967–4461 or 800/967–4461* ⊕ *www.kennebunkbeachmaine.com* ⌁ *22 rooms, 11 cottages* ⌂ *In-room: refrigerator, Wi-Fi. In-hotel: beachfront, laundry service* ⊟ *AE, MC, V* ☯ *Cottages closed Nov.–May* ⏁ *CP.*

$$ ⌂ **Waldo Emerson House.** The home itself is a historical gold mine, made grand with unusual maritime architectural touches by a shipbuilder in 1784 and later home to the great-uncle of beloved writer Ralph Waldo Emerson (who spent many youthful summers in the house). It's believed that the house was also a stop on the famed Underground Railroad. Notice the sliding wooden panels in the windows, said to keep inhab-itants safe from the soaring arrows of irate Native Americans. The elegance of the wide-plank pine floors remains, as does some remarkable original tile work around the many fireplaces. Rooms are spacious and filled with antiques and colorful quilts, and all of them have working fireplaces. Innkeepers Kathy and John Daamen provide a shuttle to area beaches and operate the Mainely Quilts gift shop next door. **Pros:** good base for exploring Kennebunk and Kennebunkport; authentic historic lodging; complimentary afternoon tea. **Cons:** most rooms accessed via steep stairs; no water views or beachfront; not in town. ⊠ *108 Summer St. (Rte. 35), Kennebunk* ☎ *207/985–4250 or 877/521–8776* ⊕ *www.waldoemersoninn.com* ⟿ *4 rooms* ♿ *In-room: no phone, no TV (some), Wi-Fi. In-hotel: bicycles, Internet terminal, no kids under 6* ⊟ *AE, D, MC, V* ⑩ *BP.*

$$$$ ⬚ **White Barn Inn.** For a romantic overnight stay, you need look no
★ further than the exclusive White Barn Inn, known for its attentive, pampering service. No detail has been overlooked in the meticulously appointed rooms, from plush bedding and reading lamps to robes and slippers. Rooms are in the main inn and adjacent buildings. Some have fireplaces, hot tubs, and luxurious baths with steam showers. The inn is within walking distance (10–15 minutes) of Dock Square and the beach. **Pros:** elegant, luxurious lodging; full-service; in a historic building. **Cons:** no water views or beachfront; overly steep lodging prices; not in town. ⊠ *37 Beach Ave., Kennebunk* ☎ *207/967–2321* ⊕ *www. whitebarninn.com* ⟿ *16 rooms, 9 suites* ♿ *In-room: DVD, Wi-Fi. In-hotel: restaurant, bar, pool, spa, bicycles, laundry service, Internet terminal, no kids under 12* ⊟ *AE, MC, V* ⑩ *CP.*

KENNEBUNKPORT

Approximately 6 mi north of Wells via U.S. 1; approximately 22 mi south of Portland.

Kennebunkport has been a resort area since the 19th century, but its most famous residents have made it even more popular—the presidential Bush family is often in residence in their immense home, which sits dramatically out on Walker's Point. The amount of wealth here is as tangible as the sharp sea breezes and the sounds of seagulls overhead. Newer mansions have sprung up alongside the old; a great way to see them is to take a slow drive out along Ocean Avenue. The area focused around the water and Dock Square in Kennebunkport is where you can find the most activity (and crowds) in the Kennebunks. Winding alleys disclose shops and restaurants geared to the tourist trade, right in the midst of a hardworking harbor.

10

GETTING HERE AND AROUND

The Intown Trolley covers Kennebunk and Kennebunkport. The narrated 45-minute jaunts leave every hour starting at 10 AM at the designated stop on Ocean Avenue, around the corner of Dock Square. The fare is valid for the day, so you can hop on and off at your leisure.

ESSENTIALS

Transportation Information Intown Trolley (⊠ *Ocean Ave., Kennebunkport* ☎ *207/967–3686* ⊕ *www.intowntrolley.com* 🎫 *$15 all-day fare* ⊙ *Late May–mid-Oct., daily 10–5*).

EXPLORING

Dock Square. The heart and pulse of busy little Kennebunkport is this town center. Boutiques, T-shirt shops, art galleries, crafts stores, and restaurants encircle the square and spread out alongside streets and alleys. Walk onto the drawbridge to admire the tidal Kennebunk River.

Nott House. Also known as White Columns, the imposing Greek Revival mansion with Doric columns is furnished with the belongings of four generations of the Perkins-Nott family. The 1853 house is open for guided tours and serves as a gathering place for village walking tours, offered Thursday and Saturday at 11. It is maintained by the Kennebunkport Historical Society, which also runs the **History Center of Kennebunkport**, a mile away on North Street; the year-round center includes several exhibit buildings containing an old schoolhouse and jail cells. ⊠ *8 Maine St., Kennebunkport* ☎ *207/967–2751* ⊕ *www. kporthistory.org* ✉ *$7 for house tours; $7 for walking tours* ⊗ *July– mid-Oct., Thur. 10–4 and 7–9, Fri. 1–4, Sat. 10–1.*

☉ ★ **Seashore Trolley Museum.** Here streetcars built from 1872 to 1972, including trolleys from major metropolitan areas and world capitals (Boston to Budapest, New York to Nagasaki, San Francisco to Sydney), are all beautifully restored and displayed. Best of all, you can take a trolley ride for nearly 4 mi on the tracks of the former Atlantic Shoreline trolley line, with a stop along the way at the museum restoration shop, where trolleys are transformed from junk into gems. Both guided and self-guided tours are available. ⊠ *195 Log Cabin Rd., Kennebunkport* ☎ *207/967–2712* ⊕ *www.trolleymuseum.org* ✉ *$8.50* ⊗ *Early May– mid-Oct., daily 10–5; reduced hrs in spring and fall, call ahead.*

SHOPPING

Abacus (⊠ *2 Ocean Ave., Dock Sq., Kennebunkport* ☎ *207/967–0111* ⊕ *www.abacusgallery.com*) sells eclectic crafts and furniture. **Mast Cove Galleries** (⊠ *Mast Cove La., Kennebunkport* ☎ *207/967–3453* ⊕ *www. mastcove.com*) sells graphics, paintings, and sculpture by 105 artists.

SPORTS AND THE OUTDOORS

BIKING **Cape-Able Bike Shop** (⊠ *83 Arundel Rd., Kennebunkport* ☎ *207/967– 4382* ⊕ *www.capeablebikes.com*) rents bicycles of all types, including trailer bikes and tandems. Guided bike and kayak tours are also available.

BOATING AND FISHING To reserve a private sail for up to six people, contact Captain Jim Jannetti of the ***Bellatrix*** (⊠ *Kennebunkport* ☎ *207/590–1125* ⊕ *www. sailingtrips.com*), a vintage racing yacht. Find and catch fish with **Cast Away Fishing Charters** (⊘ *Box 245, Kennebunkport 04046* ☎ *207/284– 1740* ⊕ *www.castawayfishingcharters.com*). **First Chance** (⊠ *4-A Western Ave., Kennebunk 04043* ☎ *207/967–5507 or 800/767–2628* ⊕ *www. firstchancewhalewatch.com*) leads whale-watching cruises and guarantees sightings in season. Daily scenic lobster cruises are also offered aboard *Kylie's Chance.* For half- or full-day fishing trips as well as discovery trips for kids, book some time with **Lady J Sportfishing Charters** (⊠ *Arundel Wharf, Ocean Ave.04046* ☎ *207/985–7304* ⊕ *www. ladyjcharters.com*).

Several scenic cruises and lobster-trap hauling trips run daily aboard the *Rugosa* (⊠ *Depart from Nonantum Resort, Ocean Ave.* ☎ *207/967–5595* ⊕ *www.rugosacharters.com*).

WHERE TO EAT

$$–$$$$
SEAFOOD
Mabel's Lobster Claw. Mabel's has long been serving lobsters, homemade pies, and lots of seafood for lunch and dinner in this tiny dwelling out on Ocean Avenue. Decor includes paneled walls, wooden booths, autographed photos of various TV stars (plus members of the Bush family), and paper place mats that illustrate how to eat a Maine lobster. The house favorite is the Lobster Savannah—split and filled with scallops, shrimp, and mushrooms in a Newburg sauce. Save room for the peanut-butter ice-cream pie. Reservations are recommended. ⊠ *124 Ocean Ave., Kennebunkport* ☎ *207/967–2562* ⊟ *AE, D, MC, V* ☉ *Closed Nov.–Apr.*

$$$
SEAFOOD
✕ **Pier 77 Restaurant & the Ramp Bar & Grille.** The view takes center stage at this dual establishment, consisting of a fine-dining portion and a more casual and boisterous section. Pier 77 serves up more sophisticated fare, focusing on meats and seafood; the tiny, tiny Ramp pays homage to a really good burger, fried seafood, and other pub-style choices. The place is vibrant with live music most nights in summer and a great place for cocktails on the water. ⊠ *77 Pier Rd., Cape Porpoise* ☎ *207/967–8500* ⊕ *www.pier77restaurant.com* ⊟ *AE, MC, V* ☉ *Closed Jan.–mid-Mar.*

WHERE TO STAY

$$$$
AMERICAN
▦ **Cape Arundel Inn.** This shingle-style inn commands a magnificent ocean view that takes in the Bush estate at Walker's Point. The spacious rooms are furnished with country-style furniture and antiques, and most have sitting areas with ocean views. You can relax on the front porch or by the fireplace. The Rockbound complex, a later addition (1950s), doesn't have the 19th-century charm of the main house, but the rooms are large, many have fireplaces, and all have private balconies from which to take in the views. In the candlelit dining room ($$$–$$$$), open to the public for dinner, every table has a view of the surf. The menu changes seasonally. **Pros:** extraordinary views from most rooms; close to town and attractions. **Cons:** not for the budget-minded. ⊠ *208 Ocean Ave., Kennebunkport* ☎ *207/967–2125* ⊕ *www.capearundelinn.com* ⇆ *19 rooms, 1 suite* ⚇ *In-room: no phone, no a/c, no TV (some), Wi-Fi. In-hotel: restaurant, bicycles* ⊟ *AE, D, MC, V* ☉ *Closed Jan. and Feb.* ⊺⃞ *CP.*

$$$$
Fodor's Choice
★
▦ **Captain Lord Mansion.** Of all the mansions in Kennebunkport's historic district that have been converted to inns, the 1812 Captain Lord Mansion is the stateliest and most sumptuously appointed. Distinctive architecture, including a suspended elliptical staircase, gas fireplaces in all rooms, and near-museum-quality accoutrements make for a formal but not stuffy setting. Six rooms have whirlpool tubs. The extravagant suite has two fireplaces, a double whirlpool, a hydro-massage body spa, a TV/DVD and stereo system, and a king-size canopy bed. Day-spa services are available for added luxury. **Pros:** elegant and luxurious historic lodging; in-town location; beautiful landscaped grounds. **Cons:** expensive; not a beachfront location. ⊠ *Pleasant and Green Sts., Kennebunkport* ☎ *207/967–3141 or 800/522–3141* ⊕ *www.captainlord.*

10

com ↰ *15 rooms, 1 suite* ♿ *In-room: Wi-Fi. In-hotel: bicycles, Internet terminal, no kids under 12* ▭ *D, MC, V* ⑩ *BP.*

$$$–$$$$

Fodor'sChoice

★

🖼 **The Colony.** You can't miss this place—it's grand, white, and incredibly large, set majestically atop a rise overlooking the ocean. The hotel was built in 1914 (after its predecessor caught fire in 1898), and much of the splendid glamour of the earlier era remains. Many of the rooms in the main hotel (there are two other outbuildings) have ocean views from private or semiprivate balconies. All are outfitted with antiques and hardwood floors; the bright white bed linens nicely set off the colors of the Waverly wallpaper. The restaurant ($$–$$$$) features New England fare, with plenty of seafood and steaks. **Pros:** lodging in the tradition of grand old hotels; many ocean views; plenty of activities and entertainment for all ages. **Cons:** not intimate; rooms with ocean views come at steep prices. ✉ *Ocean Ave.* ☎ *207/967–3331 or 800/552–2363* ⊕ *www.thecolonyhotel.com/maine* ↰ *124 rooms* ♿ *In-room: no a/c (some), no TV (some), Wi-Fi. In-hotel: restaurant, room service, bar, pool, beachfront, bicycles, some pets allowed* ▭ *AE, MC, V* ⊘ *Closed Nov.–mid-May* ⑩ *BP.*

EN ROUTE

For a rewarding drive that goes into the reaches of the coastline on the way to Old Orchard Beach, head out of Kennebunkport on Route 9. Plan to do some beach walking at Goose Rocks Beach or Fortunes Rocks Beach, both ideal for stretching your legs or just looking for shells or critters in the tide pools. Route 9 continues to wind through wooded areas, then heads through the slightly weary-looking old mill town of Biddeford, across the Saco River, and into Saco, a busy town with commerce and its accompanying traffic. Once you get past Saco, Route 9 returns to its peaceful curves and gentle scenery, leaving crowded civilization behind and winding through the charming resort villages of Camp Ellis and Ocean Park. You could pack a picnic and spend some time at Ferry Beach State Park (look for the entrance just off Route 9 on Bayview Road). The varied landscapes in the park include forested sections, swamp, beach, and lots of dunes, all of which have miles of marked trails to hike.

OLD ORCHARD BEACH AREA

15 mi north of Kennebunkport; 18 mi south of Portland.

Back in the late 19th century Old Orchard Beach was a classic, upscale, place-to-be-seen resort area. The railroad brought wealthy families looking for entertainment and the benefits of the fresh sea air. Although a good bit of this aristocratic hue has dulled in more recent times—admittedly, the place is more than a little pleasantly tacky these days—Old Orchard Beach remains a good place for those looking for entertainment by the sea.

The center of the action is a 7-mi strip of sand beach and its accompanying amusement park. Despite the summertime crowds and fried-food odors, the atmosphere can be captivating. During the 1940s and '50s, the pier had a dance hall where stars of the time performed. Fire claimed the end of the pier—at one time it jutted out nearly 1,800 feet into the sea—but booths with games and candy concessions still line both sides. In summer the town sponsors fireworks (on Thursday night). Places to stay run the gamut from cheap motels to cottage colonies to full-service seasonal hotels. You won't find free parking in town, but there are ample lots. Amtrak has a seasonal stop here.

ESSENTIALS

Visitor Information Old Orchard Beach Chamber of Commerce
(⊠ *1st St.* ⟊ *Box 600, 04064* ☎ *207/934–2500 or 800/365–9386* ⊕ *www. oldorchardbeachmaine.com*).

EXPLORING

Ocean Park. A world away from the beach scene lies Ocean Park, on the southwestern edge of town. Locals and visitors like to keep the separation distinct, touting their area as a more peaceful and wholesome family-style village (to that end, there are no alcohol or tobacco sales in this little haven). This vacation community was founded in 1881 by Free Will Baptist leaders as an interdenominational retreat with both religious and educational purposes, following the example of Chautauqua, New York. Today the community hosts an impressive variety of cultural happenings, including movies, concerts, recreation, workshops, and religious services. Most are presented in the Temple, which is on the National Register of Historic Places. Although the religious nature of the place is apparent in its worship schedule and some of its cultural offerings, visitors need not be members of any denomination; all are welcome. There's even a public shuffleboard area for vacationers not interested in the neon carnival attractions several miles up the road. Get an old-fashioned raspberry lime rickey at the Ocean Park Soda Fountain (near the library, at Furber Park); it's also a good place for breakfast or a light lunch. (☎ *207/934–9068 Ocean Park Association*)

SPORTS AND THE OUTDOORS

Not far from Old Orchard Beach is the Maine Audubon–run **Scarborough Marsh Nature Center** (⊠ *Pine Point Rd. [Rte. 9], Scarborough* ☎ *207/883–5100* ⊕ *www.maineaudubon.org* ⧆ *Free guided tours begin at $5* ⊙ *Memorial Day–Sept.*). You can rent a canoe and explore this natural haven on your own or sign up for a guided trip. The salt marsh is Maine's largest and is an excellent place for bird-watching and peaceful paddling along its winding ways. The Nature Center has a discovery room for kids, programs for all ages ranging from basket making to astronomy, birding and canoe tours, and a good gift shop.

WHERE TO EAT

$$–$$$
ECLECTIC
★

✕ **The Landmark.** This restaurant almost feels as if it doesn't belong here. Tables are set either on the glassed-in porch or within high, tin-ceiling rooms. Candles and a collection of giant fringed Art Nouveau lamps provide a gentle light. The menu has a good selection of seafood and meats, many treated with flavors from various parts of the globe. It's the kind of menu that encourages you to try new things, and you definitely won't be disappointed. Outside on the stone patio and sheltered by umbrellas is the "in the rough" dinner menu, with everything cooked on the adjacent grill. Choose from clambake-style meals, charbroiled and marinated skewers, and BBQ ribs. Coffee and pastries are served out here in the morning. ⊠ *25 E. Grand Ave., Old Orchard Beach*

10

☎ *207/934–0156* ⊕ *www.landmarkfinedining.com* 🖃 *AE, D, MC, V* ⊗ *Closed late Nov.–Mar.*

$$$ ✕ **Yellowfin's.** Inside this diminutive restaurant housed in an impeccably
SEAFOOD   kept yellow Victorian, it is fresh, bright, and appropriately beachy. A
giant tank bubbles quietly in the background while its resident color-
ful fish in the tank survey the landscape of white linen–covered tables
adorned with sand and shell centerpieces. White cloth panels draped
along the ceiling add an enveloping sense of comfort to the lively space.
Not surprisingly, the house specialty is ahi yellowfin tuna, pan seared
and treated with a wasabi ginger sauce; other choices include seared
scallops, lamb, and a savory seafood fra diavolo (with a spicy tomato
sauce). Brunch is offered weekends in July and August. In Ocean Park
it's BYOB—you'll have to stock up in nearby Old Orchard Beach. ⊠ *5
Temple Ave., Ocean Park* ☎ *207/934–1100* 🖃 *D, MC, V* ⊗ *No lunch.*

PORTLAND

Maine's largest city is considered small by national standards—its
population is just 64,000—but its character, spirit, and appeal make
it feel much larger. In fact, it is a cultural and economic center for a
metropolitan area of 230,000 residents—one-quarter of Maine's entire
population. Portland and its environs are well worth at least a day or
two of exploration.

A city of many names throughout its history, including Casco and Fal-
mouth, Portland has survived many dramatic transformations. Shel-
tered by the nearby Casco Bay Islands and blessed with a deep port,
Portland was a significant settlement right from its start in the early 17th
century. Settlers thrived on fishing and lumbering, repeatedly building
up the area while the British, French, and Native Americans continually
sacked it. Many considered the region a somewhat dangerous frontier,
but its potential for prosperity was so apparent that settlers came any-
way to tap its rich natural resources.

Portland's first home was built on the peninsula now known as Mun-
joy Hill in 1632. The British burned the city in 1775, when residents
refused to surrender arms, but it was rebuilt and became a major trad-
ing center. Much of Portland was destroyed again in the Great Fire on
July 4, 1866, when a boy threw a celebratory firecracker into a pile of
wood shavings; 1,500 buildings burned to the ground.

Today, there is an excellent restaurant scene and a great art museum,
and the waterfront is a lively area to walk around.

ESSENTIALS

Contacts Greater Portland Convention and Visitors Bureau (⊠ *14 Ocean
Gateway Pier, off Commercial St.* ☎ *207/772–5800 or 877/833–1374* ⊕ *www.
visitportland.com*). **Portland Regional Chamber of Commerce** (⊠ *60 Pearl St.*
☎ *207/772–2811* ⊕ *www.portlandregion.com*). **Portland's Downtown District**
(⊠ *549 Congress St.* ☎ *207/772–6828* ⊕ *www.portlandmaine.com*).

Portland's busy harbor is full of working boats, pleasure craft, and ferries headed to the Casco Bay Islands.

THE OLD PORT

Numbers in the margin correspond to numbers on the Portland map.

Fodor's Choice
★

A major international port and a working harbor since the early 17th century, the Old Port bridges the gap between the city's historical commercial activities and those of today. It is home to fishing boats docked alongside whale-watching charters, luxury yachts, cruise ships, and oil tankers from around the globe. Commercial Street parallels the water and is lined with brick buildings and warehouses that were built following the Great Fire of 1866. In the 19th century candle makers and sail stitchers plied their trades here; today specialty shops, art galleries, and restaurants have taken up residence.

As with much of the city, it's best to park your car and explore the Old Port on foot. You can park at the city garage on Fore Street (between Exchange and Union streets) or opposite the U.S. Custom House at the corner of Fore and Pearl streets. A helpful hint: look for the PARK & SHOP sign on garages and parking lots and get one hour of free parking for each stamp collected at participating shops. Allow a couple of hours to wander at leisure on Market, Exchange, Middle, and Fore streets. The city is very pedestrian-friendly. Maine state law requires vehicles to stop for walkers in crosswalks.

① **Maine Narrow Gauge Railroad Co. & Museum.** Whether you're crazy about old trains or just want to see the sights from a different perspective, the railroad museum has an extensive collection of locomotives and rail coaches and tours on narrow-gauge railcars. The 3-mi jaunt takes you along Casco Bay, at the foot of the Eastern Promenade. Theme trips

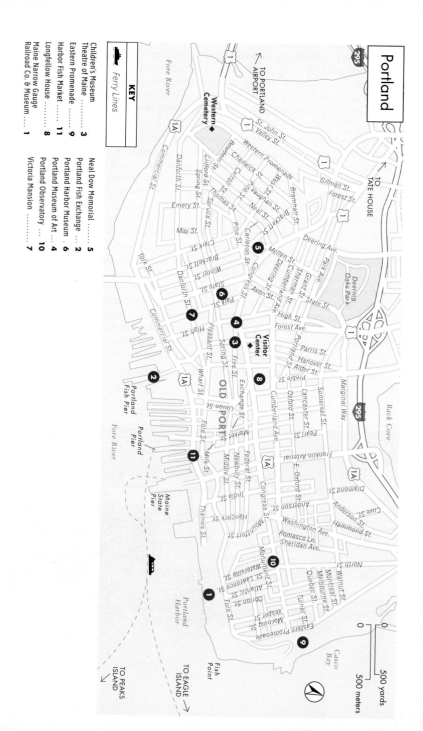

Portland

KEY

⚓ Ferry Lines

Children's Museum	
Theatre of Maine	**3**
Eastern Promenade	**9**
Harbor Fish Market	**11**
Longfellow House	**8**
Maine Narrow Gauge	
Railroad Co. & Museum....	**1**

Neal Dow Memorial	**5**
Portland Theatre of Maine	**2**
Portland Fish Exchange	**2**
Portland Harbor Museum .	**6**
Portland Museum of Art ...	**4**
Portland Observatory	**10**
Victoria Mansion	**7**

PORTLAND TOURS

AUTO TOURS

The informative trolley tours of **Portland Discovery Land & Sea Tours** (⊠ *Long Wharf, 170 Commercial St.* ☎ *207/774-0808* ⊕ *www.portlanddiscovery.com*) detail Portland's historical and architectural highlights from Memorial Day through October. Options include combining a city tour with a bay cruise or a trip to four lighthouses.

WALKING TOURS

Learn about Portland's culinary history and sample local delights like lobster hors d'oeuvres, organic cheese, and the famous Maine whoopie pie with **Maine Foodie Tours** (⊠ *Kiosk at 10 Moulton St.* ☎ *207/233-7485* ⊕ *www.mainefoodietours.com*). You also can sign up for a pub crawl, a tour of microbreweries, or a "destination" trip to nearby farms and

bakeries. Tours operate year-round; prices start at $29. **Greater Portland Landmarks** (⊠ *93 High St.* ☎ *207/774-5561* ⊕ *www.portlandlandmarks.org*) conducts 1½-hour walking tours of the Old Port from July through September; tours begin at the visitor's kiosk at **Tommy's Park** (⊠ *Corner of Middle and Exchange St.*) and cost $10. The group also offers self-guided tours of the Old Port, Congress Street, historic churches, the West End, and other spots. Pick up maps and itineraries at their offices (a small fee is charged) or download them for free online. **Portland Freedom Trail** (☎ *207/591-9980* ⊕ *www.portlandfreedomtrail.org*) provides a self-guided tour, available for free download online, of sites associated with the Underground Railroad and the anti-slavery movement.

include the Polar Express ride, based on the popular children's book, a Halloween ride (wear your costumes), and a July 4 fireworks ride. ⊠ *58 Fore St.* ☎ *207/828-0814* ⊕ *www.mngrr.org* 🚆 *Train $10, museum $2* ☉ *Trains mid-May–mid-Oct., daily on the hr 11–4; mid-Feb.–mid-May and mid-Oct.–mid-Nov., weekends on the hr 11–3. Museum late-Oct.–mid May, weekdays 10–4; late May–late Oct., daily 10–4.*

❷ **Portland Fish Exchange.** You may want to hold your nose for this glimpse into the Old Port's active fish business when you drop by the 30,000-square-foot Portland Fish Exchange. Peek inside coolers teeming with cod, flounder, and monkfish and watch fishermen repairing their nets and prices being settled through an auction process. It's a great behind-the-scenes view of this dynamic market. Auctions take place Sunday at 11 AM and Monday through Thursday at noon. ⊠ *6 Portland Fish Pier* ☎ *207/773-0017* ⊕ *www.pfex.org* 🚆 *Free.*

⓫ **Harbor Fish Market.** A Portland favorite for more than 40 years, this freshest-of-the-fresh seafood market ships lobsters and other Maine delectables almost anywhere in the country. A bright-red facade on a working wharf opens into a bustling space with bubbling lobster pens and fish, clams, and other shellfish on ice; employees are as skilled with a fillet knife as sushi chefs. ⊠ *9 Custom House Wharf* ☎ *207/775-0251 or 800/370-1790* ⊕ *www.harborfish.com* 🚆 *Free.*

10

on Prohibition—he was responsible for Maine's adoption of the anti-alcohol bill in 1851. ⊠ *714 Congress St.* ☎ *207/773–7773* 🖃 *Free* ⏱ *Weekdays 11–4 or by appointment.*

❿ Portland Observatory. This octagonal observatory on Munjoy Hill was built in 1807 by Captain Lemuel Moody, a retired sea captain, as a signal tower. Moody used a telescope to identify incoming ships and flags to signal to merchants where to unload their cargo. Held in place by 122 tons of ballast, it's the last remaining signal tower in the country. After visiting the small museum at the base, climb to the Orb deck and take in views of Portland, the islands, and inland to the White Mountains. ⊠ *138 Congress St.* ☎ *207/774–5561* ⊕ *www.portlandlandmarks.org* 🖃 *$7* ⏱ *Memorial Day weekend–Columbus Day, daily 10–5.*

OFF THE BEATEN PATH

★ **Tate House.** Built astride rose granite steps and a period herb garden overlooking the Stroudwater River on the outskirts of Portland, this magnificent 1755 house was built by Captain George Tate. Tate had been commissioned by the English Crown to organize "the King's Broad Arrow"—the marking and cutting down of gigantic forest trees, which were shipped to England to be fashioned as masts for the British Royal Navy. The house has several period rooms, including a sitting room with some fine English Restoration chairs. With its clapboard still gloriously unpainted, its impressive Palladian doorway, dogleg stairway, unusual clerestory, and gambrel roof, this house will delight all lovers of Early American decorative arts. Guided tours of the gardens are held once a week from mid-June to mid-October. House tours are offered five days a week in season. Call or visit the Web site for special holiday programs during December. ⊠ *1267 Westbrook St.* ☎ *207/774–6177* ⊕ *www.tatehouse.org* 🖃 *$7* ⏱ *Mid-June–mid-Oct., call for hrs.*

THE WEST END

A leisurely walk through Portland's West End, beginning at the top of the Arts District, offers a real treat to historic architecture buffs. The neighborhood, on the National Register of Historic Places, reveals an extraordinary display of architectural splendor, from High Victorian Gothic to lush Italianate, Queen Anne, and Colonial Revival.

A good place to start is at the head of the Western Promenade, which has parking, benches, and a nice view. From the Old Port, take Danforth Street all the way up to Vaughn Street; take a right on Vaughn and then an immediate left onto Western Promenade. Pass by the Western Cemetery, Portland's second official burial ground, laid out in 1829 (inside is the ancestral plot of famous poet Henry Wadsworth Longfellow) and just beyond is the parking area.

You could easily spend an hour or two wandering the backstreets of the West End; longer if you bring a picnic to enjoy in the grassy park alongside the Promenade. If you're interested in the particular history of individual homes, download or pick up a brochure from **Greater Portland Landmarks.** A map is included, as well as the stories of some of the more prominent homes. The group also offers a guided house tour on Friday mornings July through September. ⊠ *93 High St.* ☎ *207/774–5561* ⏱ *Weekdays 9–5* ⊕ *www.portlandlandmarks.org.*

or 800/437–8511 ⊕ www.innatparkspring.com ⇆ 6 rooms ♿ In-room: no TV, Wi-Fi. In-hotel: Internet terminal, Wi-Fi hotspot, parking (free) ⊟ *AE, D, DC, MC, V* ⍭*BP.*

$$$–$$$$ 📶 **Pomegranate Inn.** The classic facade of this handsome 1884 inn in
Fodor's Choice   the architecturally rich Western Promenade area gives no hint of the
★   surprises within. The common spaces have who-would-have-thunk-it combinations like bright, faux marble walls, a painted checkerboard floor, and a leopard-print runner; most of the guest rooms are hand-painted with splashy florals or polka dots. The inn feels like a gallery, with almost every available surface covered by contemporary art. (The paintings on the second floor are on loan from Portland's Cygnet Gallery and for sale.) Somehow it all comes together, creating a whimsical, outrageous, and wonderful effect. **Pros:** heaven for art lovers; close to Western Promenade. **Cons:** not within easy walking distance of Old Port. ⊠ *49 Neal St.* ☎ *207/772–1006 or 800/356–0408* ⊕ *www. pomegranateinn.com* ⇆ *8 rooms* ♿ *In-room: no phone, Wi-Fi. In-hotel: Wi-Fi hotspot, parking (free), some pets allowed, no kids under 16* ⊟ *AE, MC, V* ⍭*BP.*

$$$$ 📶 **Portland Harbor Hotel.** Making luxury its primary focus, the Harbor Hotel has become a favorite with business travelers seeking meetings on a more intimate scale and vacationing guests who want high-quality service and amenities. Book a massage or pedicure at the on-site Nine Stones spa. In season, eat on the enclosed garden patio. **Pros:** luxurious extras; amid the action of the Old Port and waterfront. **Cons:** not for the quaint of heart. ⊠ *468 Fore St.* ☎ *207/775–9090 or 888/798–9090* ⊕ *www.portlandharborhotel.com* ⇆ *88 rooms, 18 suites* ♿ *In-room: Wi-Fi. In-hotel: restaurant, bar, gym, spa, bicycles, laundry service, Internet terminal, Wi-Fi hotspot, parking (paid), some pets allowed* ⊟ *AE, D, MC, V.*

$$$$ 📶 **Portland Regency Hotel and Spa.** One of just a handful of major hotels in the center of the Old Port, the brick Regency building was Portland's armory in the late 19th century. Some of the traditionally furnished rooms have four-poster beds, and all have tall standing mirrors, desks, flat-screen TVs, and terry robes. You can walk to shops, restaurants, and museums from the hotel. The full-service spa offers a variety of massage treatments, a sea-salt body polish, a seaweed wrap, an herb-and-fruit-infused facial, and even eyelash tinting! **Pros:** convenient to town; has all the amenities you'd want. **Cons:** some rooms on the third and fourth floors have low ceilings and no windows (there are skylights, however). ⊠ *20 Milk St.* ☎ *207/774–4200 or 800/727–3436* ⊕ *www. theregency.com* ⇆ *84 rooms, 11 suites* ♿ *In-room: Wi-Fi. In-hotel: restaurant, bar, gym, spa, laundry service, Wi-Fi hotspot, parking (paid)* ⊟ *AE, D, DC, MC, V.*

$$$–$$$$ 📶 **West End Inn.** Set among the glorious aged homes of the Western Promenade, this 1871 house displays much of the era's Victorian grandeur, with high tin ceilings, intricate moldings and ceiling medallions, and a dramatic ruby-red foyer. Spacious rooms are either brightly painted or papered with traditional Waverly prints, and all have private baths and alarm clocks with MP3 player docks. For breakfast, innkeeper Beth Oliver often whips up a French toast casserole with blueberries

10

and cream cheese; or sausage and herb quiche with a hash brown crust. Oliver is also a fountain of Portland knowledge and will cheerfully field questions, make reservations, and gently remind you to wear your walking shoes—it's a 20-minute stroll to the action downtown. **Pros:** elegant library with fireplace is a cozy place to relax. **Cons:** one room uses a bathroom across the hall. ⊠ *146 Pine St.* ☎ *207/772–1377 or 800/338–1377* ⊕ *www.westendbb.com* ➷ *6 rooms* ⌂ *In-room: no phone, Wi-Fi. In-hotel: Wi-Fi hotspot, parking (free), no kids under 16* ▭ *AE, MC, V* ⦿ *BP.*

NIGHTLIFE

Portland's nightlife scene is largely centered around the bustling Old Port and a few smaller, artsy spots on Congress Street. There's a great emphasis on local, live music and pubs serving award-winning local microbrews. Several hip wine bars have cropped up, serving appetizers along with a full array of specialty wines and whimsical cocktails. It's a fairly youthful scene in Portland, in some spots even rowdy and rough-around-the-edges, but there are plenty of places where you don't have to shout over the din to be heard.

To see live local and national acts any night of the week, try **The Big Easy** (⊠ *55 Market St.* ☎ *207/775–2266* ⊕ *www.bigeasyportland.com*). For nightly themed brew specials, plenty of Guinness, and live entertainment, head to **Bull Feeney's** (⊠ *375 Fore St.* ☎ *207/773–7210* ⊕ *www. bullfeeneys.com*), a lively two-story Irish pub and restaurant. **Gritty McDuff's** (⊠ *396 Fore St.* ☎ *207/772–2739* ⊕ *www.grittys.com*) brews fine ales and serves British pub fare and seafood dishes. At **Novare Res Bier Café** (⊠ *4 Canal Plaza, Exchange St. between Middle St. and Fore St.* ☎ *207/761–2437* ⊕ *www.novareresbiercafe.com*), choose from 25 rotating drafts and more than 300 bottled brews, relax on an expansive deck, and munch on antipasti. Happening Irish pub and restaurant **Rí Rá** (⊠ *72 Commercial St.* ☎ *207/761–4446* ⊕ *www.rira.com*) has live music Thursday through Saturday nights; for a mellower experience, settle into a couch at the upstairs bar. **Space Gallery** (⊠ *538 Congress St.* ☎ *207/828–5600* ⊕ *www.space538.org*) sparkles as a contemporary art gallery and alternative arts venue, opening its doors to everything from poetry readings to live music and documentary film showings.

THE ARTS

Art galleries and studios have spread throughout the city, infusing with new life many abandoned yet beautiful old buildings and shops. Many are concentrated along the Congress Street downtown corridor; others are hidden amid the boutiques and restaurants of the Old Port and the East End. A great way to get acquainted with the city's artists is to participate in the First Friday Art Walk, a self-guided, free tour of galleries, museums, and alternative art venues that happens—you guessed it—on the first Friday of each month. Brochures and maps are available on the organization's Web site: *www.firstfridayartwalk.com.*

Merrill Auditorium (✉ *20 Myrtle St.* ☎ *207/842–0800* ⊕ *www.porttix. com*) has numerous theatrical and musical events, including performances by the Portland Symphony Orchestra, Portland Ovations (performing arts), and Portland Opera Repertory Theatre. Every other Tuesday from mid-June to the end of August, organ recitals (suggested $15 donation) are given on the auditorium's huge 1912 Kotzschmar Memorial Organ. **Portland Stage** (✉ *25-A Forest Ave.* ☎ *207/774–0465* ⊕ *www.portlandstage.com*) mounts theatrical productions from September to May on its two stages.

SHOPPING

Exchange Street is great for arts and crafts and boutique browsing, while Commercial Street caters to the souvenir hound—gift shops are packed with nautical items, and lobster and moose emblems are emblazoned on everything from T-shirts to shot glasses.

ART AND ANTIQUES

Abacus (✉ *44 Exchange St.* ☎ *207/772–4880* ⊕ *www.abacusgallery. com*), an appealing crafts gallery, has unusual gift items in glass, wood, and textiles, plus fine modern jewelry. **Foundry Lane Contemporary Crafts** (✉ *221 Commercial St.* ☎ *207/773–2722* ⊕ *www.foundrylane.com*) sells beautiful, limited-edition jewelry, as well as glass and ceramic home accessories by 20 Maine artists. **Gleason Fine Art** (✉ *545 Congress St.* ☎ *207/699–5599* ⊕ *www.gleasonfineart.com*) exhibits paintings by Maine artists from the 19th to 21st centuries. **Greenhut Galleries** (✉ *146 Middle St.* ☎ *207/772–2693 or 888/772–2693* ⊕ *www.greenhutgalleries. com*) shows contemporary art and sculpture by Maine artists. An antiques junkie's dream, **Portland Architectural Salvage** (✉ *131 Preble St.* ☎ *207/780–0634* ⊕ *www.portlandsalvage.com*) has four floors of unusual reclaimed finds, including furniture, fixtures, hardware, and stained-glass windows.

BOOKS

Cunningham Books (✉ *188 State St.* ☎ *207/775–2246*) is a grand browsing (and buying) experience for book lovers. The owner knows in a moment whether your request is present amid the estimated 70,000 titles lining the walls. **Longfellow Books** (✉ *1 Monument Way* ☎ *207/772–4045* ⊕ *www.longfellowbooks.com*) is known for its good service and thoughtful literary collection. Auhor readings are scheduled regularly.

CLOTHING

Hip boutique **Bliss** (✉ *58 Exchange St.* ☎ *207/879–7125* ⊕ *www. blissboutiques.com*) stocks T-shirts, dresses, jewelry, and lingerie by cutting-edge designers, plus jeans by big names like 7 For All Mankind.

Photos of style icon Audrey Hepburn grace the walls of **Hélène M.** (✉ *425 Fore St.* ☎ *207/772–2564*), where you'll find classic, fashionable pieces by designers like Tory Burch, Diane von Furstenberg, and Rebecca Taylor.

With a funky combination of good-quality consignment and new jewelry and clothing for both men and women, **Material Objects** (✉ *500 Congress St.* ☎ *207/774–1241*) makes for an affordable and unusual

10

Lobster Shacks

If it's your first time to the Maine Coast, it won't be long before you stumble upon the famous and quint-essential seaside eatery, the lobster shack. Also known as a lobster "pound," especially in other parts of New England, this humble establish-ment serves only two kinds of fresh seafood—lobster and clams.

Lobster shacks are essentially wooden huts with picnic tables set around the waterfront. The menu is simplic-ity itself: steamed lobster or clams by the pound, or a lobster roll. Sides may include potato chips, cole slaw, or corn on the cob. Some pounds are even BYOB—no, not bring your own bib; those are usually provided—but bring your own beer or refreshments.

A signature item at a lobster shack is the lobster dinner. Although this can vary from pound to pound, it generally means the works: a whole steamed lobster, steamed clams, corn on the cob and potato chips. If the lobster dinner sounds like a bit much, then go for the classic lobster roll, a but-tered hot dog roll filled with chunks of lobster meat and a bit of mayo. Some pounds will serve it with lemon, some will serve it with butter, and some with even a touch of lettuce or herbs. Purists will serve no toppings at all (and why bother when the unadulter-ated taste of fresh, sweet lobster meat can't be beat). Most shacks will have even have a tank with live lobsters; few will let you pick your own.

We can say this much: the best place to get a lobster dinner or lobster roll is at a shack, and the only authen-tic ones are right next to the water. There's a general sense that the "pur-est" pounds are the one's that are the simplest: a wooden shack, right on

A lobster roll: perfection on a bun.

the water with wooden picnic tables, and perhaps most important of all, a beautiful unobstructed view of work-ing lobster boats in a scenic Maine harbor.

A few of our favorites sit on side-by-side piers right on Moscungus Bay: **Round Pond Fisherman's Coop** (✉ *Town Landing Rd., Round Pond* 📞 *207/529–5725*) and **Moscungus Bay Lobster Company** (✉ *Town Landing Rd., Round Pond* ⊕ *www. mainefreshlobster.com*).

Waterman's Beach Lobster (✉ *359 Waterman Beach Rd.* 📞 *207/596– 7819 or 207/594–7518* ⊕ *www. watermansbeachrestaurant.com*) in South Thomaston is authentic, inex-pensive and scenic. You can eat lunch or dinner right on a pier overlooking the Atlantic. In addition to the sea-food favorites, Waterman's also sells freshly baked pies and locally made ice cream.

You can find out more about Maine lobster from the **The Maine Lobster Council** (⊕ *www.lobsterfrommaine. com*).

—Michael de Zayas

A traditional clambake may also include lobsters and corn. It's best enjoyed outside—just add drawn butter.

shopping spree. At **Sea Bags** (✉ *25 Custom House Wharf* ☎ *888/210–4244* ⊕ *www.seabags.com*), totes made from recycled sailcloth and decorated with bright, graphic patterns are sewn right in the store.

HOUSEHOLD ITEMS/FURNITURE

Maine islander **Angela Adams** (✉ *273 Congress St.* ☎ *207/774–3523 or 800/255–9454* ⊕ *www.angelaadams.com*) specializes in simple but bold geometric motifs parlayed into dramatic rugs, handbags, trays, pillows, and paper goods.

For reproduction and antique furnishings with a Far East feel, head to one of the two locations of **Asia West** (✉ *219 Commercial St.* ☎ *888/775–0066* ✉ *125 Kennebec St.* ☎ *207/774–9300* ⊕ *www. asiawest.net.*) The former has mostly accessories; the latter is a furniture showroom. The handsome cherrywood pieces at **Green Design Furniture** (✉ *267 Commercial St.* ☎ *207/775–4234 or 800/853–4234* ⊕ *www.greendesigns.com*) are made locally with sustainable harvested wood and eco-friendly finishes. A unique system of joinery enables easy assembly after shipping.

SPORTS AND THE OUTDOORS

When the weather's good, everyone in Portland heads outside. There are also many green spaces nearby Portland, including Fort Williams Park, home to Portland Head Light; Crescent Beach State Park; and Two Lights State Park. All offer biking and walking trails, picnic facilities, and water access. Bradbury Mountain State Park, in Pownal, has incredible vistas from its easily climbed peak. In Freeport is Wolfe's Neck Woods State Park, where you can take a guided nature walk and see nesting ospreys. ⇨ *Side Trips from Portland for more on these.*

BICYCLING

For state bike trail maps, club and tour listings, or hints on safety, contact the **Bicycle Coalition of Maine** (✉ *341 Water St., No. 10, Augusta* ☎ *207/623–4511* ⊕ *www.bikemaine.org*). Rent bikes downtown at **Cycle Mania** (✉ *59 Federal St.* ☎ *207/774–2933* ⊕ *www.cyclemania1. com*) or **Gorham Bike and Ski** (✉ *693 Congress St.* ☎ *207/773–1700* ⊕ *www.gorhambike.com*). For local biking information, contact **Portland Trails** (✉ *305 Commercial St.* ☎ *207/775–2411* ⊕ *www.trails.org*). They can tell you about designated paved routes that wind along the water, through parks, and beyond. For a map, call or get one online.

BOATING

Various Portland-based skippers offer whale-, dolphin-, and seal-watching cruises; excursions to lighthouses and islands; and fishing and lobstering trips. Board the ferry to see the nearby islands. Self-navigators can rent kayaks or canoes.

Casco Bay Lines (✉ *Maine State Pier, 56 Commercial St.* ☎ *207/774–7871* ⊕ *www.cascobaylines.com*) provides narrated cruises and transportation to the Casco Bay Islands. **Lucky Catch Cruises** (✉ *Long Wharf, 170 Commercial St.* ☎ *207/761–0941* ⊕ *www.luckycatch.com*) sets out to sea in a real lobster boat so passengers can get the genuine experience, which includes hauling traps and the chance to purchase the catch. **Odyssey Whale Watch** (✉ *Long Wharf, 170 Commercial St.* ☎ *207/775–0727* ⊕ *www.odysseywhalewatch.com*) leads whale-watching and deepsea–fishing trips.For tours of the harbor and Casco Bay, including a trip to Eagle Island and an up-close look at several lighthouses, try **Portland Discovery Land & Sea Tours** (✉ *Long Wharf, 170 Commercial St.* ☎ *207/774–0808* ⊕ *www.portlanddiscovery.com*).

Portland Schooner Co. (✉ *Maine State Pier, 56 Commercial St.* ☎ *207/766–2500 or 877/246–6637* ⊕ *www.portlandschooner.com*) offers daily sails aboard vintage schooners from 1912 and 1924.

HOT-AIR BALLOON RIDES

Hot Fun First Class Balloon Flights (☎ *207/799–0193* ⊕ *www.hotfunballoons. com*) flies mainly sunrise trips and can accommodate up to three people. The price of $300 per person includes a post-flight champagne toast, snacks, and shuttle to the lift-off site.

CASCO BAY ISLANDS

The islands of Casco Bay are also known as the Calendar Islands because an early explorer mistakenly thought there was one for each day of the year (in reality there are only 140). These islands range from ledges visible only at low tide to populous Peaks Island, a suburb of Portland. Some are uninhabited; others support year-round communities as well as stores and restaurants. Fort Gorges commands Hog Island Ledge, and Eagle Island is the site of Arctic explorer Admiral Robert

Peary's home. The brightly painted ferries of Casco Bay Lines are the islands' lifeline. There is frequent service to the most populated ones, including Peaks, Long, Little Diamond, and Great Diamond.

There is little in the way of overnight lodging on the islands; the population swells during the warmer months due to summer residents. There are few restaurants or organized attractions other than the natural beauty of the islands themselves. Meandering about by bike or on foot is a good way to explore on a day trip.

GETTING HERE AND AROUND

Casco Bay Lines provides ferry service from Portland to the islands of Casco Bay. The CAT, a stunning, modern high-speed ferry, travels between Portland and Yarmouth, Nova Scotia.

ESSENTIALS

Transportation Information Casco Bay Lines (☎ 207/774–7871 ⊕ *www. cascobaylines.com*). **The CAT** (☎ 877/359–3760 ⊕ *www.catferry.com*).

CAPE ELIZABETH TO PROUTS NECK

EXPLORING

Fodor'sChoice ★ **Portland Head Light.** Familiar to many from photographs and the Edward Hopper's painting *Portland Head-Light* (1927), this lighthouse was commissioned by George Washington in 1790. The towering white stone structure stands over the keeper's quarters, a white home with a blazing red roof, now the Museum at Portland Head Light. The lighthouse is in 90-acre Fort Williams Park, a sprawling green space with walking paths, picnic facilities, a beach and—you guessed it—a cool old fort. *Museum* ⊠ *1000 Shore Rd., Cape Elizabeth* ☎ *207/799–2661* ⊕ *www.portlandheadlight.com* ⬛ *$2* ☉ *Memorial Day–mid-Oct., daily 10–4; Apr., May, Nov., and Dec., weekends 10–4.*

WHERE TO EAT AND STAY

$$$
SEAFOOD

✕ **Joe's Boathouse.** The two simple dining rooms of this dockside establishment are finished in sea-foam green, with large windows looking out to a marina. Dinner specials include tuna steak and lobster fettuccine; for lunch try the grilled-crab and avocado club or Asian-inspired crispy salmon salad. In summer, eat out on the patio. ⊠ *1 Spring Point Dr., South Portland* ☎ *207/741–2780* ⊕ *www.joesboathouse.com* ⬛ *AE, MC, V.*

$$
SEAFOOD

✕ **The Lobster Shack at Two Lights.** You can't beat the location—right on the water, below the lighthouse pair that gives Two Lights State Park its name—and the food's not bad either. Enjoy fresh lobster whole or piled into a hot-dog bun with a dollop of mayo. Other menu must-haves include chowder, fried clams, and fish-and-chips. It's been a classic spot since the 1920s. Eat inside or out. ⊠ *225 Two Lights Rd., Cape Elizabeth* ☎ *207/799–1677* ⊕ *www.lobstershacktwolights.com* ⬛ *MC, V* ☉ *Closed Nov.–late Mar.*

$$$$
🛏 **Black Point Inn.** Toward the tip of the peninsula that juts into the ocean at Prouts Neck stands this stylish, tastefully updated historic resort with spectacular views up and down the coast. Guests have access to beaches, trails, kayaking equipment, a country club with tennis courts and a golf

10

course, and a yacht club. Finer touches abound, such as Frette linens and in-room terry-cloth robes. The Cliff Walk, a pebbled path that wanders past Winslow Homer's former studio, runs along the Atlantic headlands that Homer often painted. Rates include breakfast, dinner, and gratuities (they're tacked on for you). The inn is 12 mi south of Portland and about 10 mi north of Old Orchard Beach. **Pros:** stunning water views; set amid scenery that inspired Winslow Homer. **Cons:** 18% "guest service charge" is tacked on to room rate. ⊠ *510 Black Point Rd., Scarborough* ☎ *207/883–2500* ⊕ *www.blackpointinn.com* ⇰ *25 rooms* ⊗ *Closed late Oct.–early May* ⚹ *In-room: DVD (some), Wi-Fi. In-hotel: 2 restaurants, bar, pool, gym, bicycles, laundry service, Internet terminal, Wi-Fi hotspot, parking (free)* ▭ *AE, D, MC, V* ⦿*MAP.*

FREEPORT

17 mi northeast of Portland; 10 mi southwest of Brunswick.

Those who flock straight to L. L. Bean and see nothing else of Freeport are missing out. The city's charming backstreets are lined with historic buildings and old clapboard houses, and there's a pretty little harbor on the south side of the Harraseeket River. It's true, many who come to the area do so simply to shop—L. L. Bean is the store that put Freeport on the map, and plenty of outlets and some specialty stores have settled here. Still, if you choose, you can stay a while and experience more than fabulous bargains; beyond the shops are bucolic nature preserves with miles of walking trails and plenty of places for leisurely ambling that don't require the overuse of your credit cards.

GETTING AROUND

Pick up a village walking map, sign up for a tour, and check out historical exhibits at the **Freeport Historical Society** (⊠ *45 Main St.* ☎ *207/865–3170* ⊕ *www.freeporthistoricalsociety.com* ⊗ *Mon., Thurs., and Fri. 10–5, Sat. 10–2).*

SPORTS AND THE OUTDOORS

CLASSES It shouldn't come as a surprise that one of the world's largest outdoor outfitters also provides its customers with instructional adventures to go with its products. L. L. Bean's year-round **Outdoor Discovery Schools** (☎ *888/552–3261* ⊕ *www.llbean.com/ods*) include half- and full-day classes, trips, and tours that encompass canoeing, shooting, biking, kayaking, fly-fishing, cross-country skiing, and other outdoor sports. Classes are for all skill levels; it's best to sign up several months in advance.

SHOPPING

The **Freeport Visitors Guide** (☎ *207/865–1212, 800/865–1994 or* ⊕ *www. freeportusa.com for a copy*) lists the more than 200 stores on Main Street, Bow Street, and elsewhere, including Patagonia, Coach, Brooks Brothers, Banana Republic, J. Crew, and Cole-Haan.

Edgecomb Potters (⊠ *8 School St.* ☎ *207/865–1705* ⊕ *www. edgecombpotters.com*) showcases vibrant, hand-thrown porcelain tableware finished with an unusual crystalline glaze. **R. D. Allen Freeport Jewelers** (⊠ *13 Middle St.* ☎ *207/865–1818 or 877/837–3835* ⊕ *www. rdallen.com*) specializes in brightly colored tourmaline and other locally

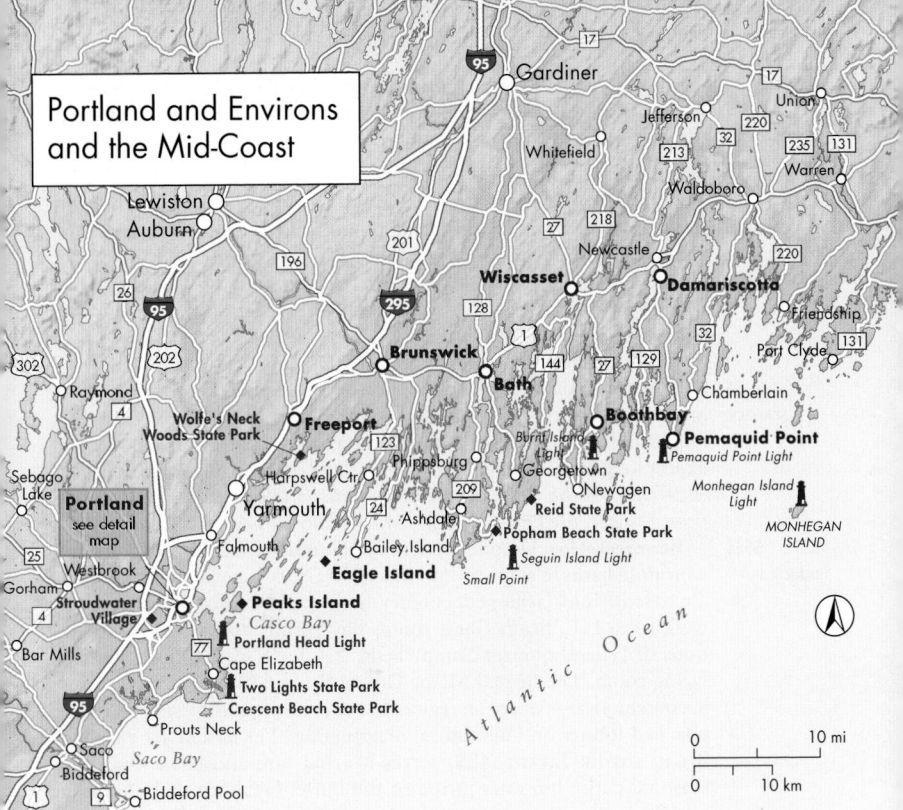

Portland and Environs
and the Mid-Coast

mined gemstones. Famed local furniture company **Thos. Moser Cabinet-makers** (⊠ *149 Main St.* ☎ *207/865–4519* ⊕ *www.thosmoser.com*) sells artful, handmade wood pieces with clean, classic lines.

Fodor's Choice
★

Founded in 1912 as a mail-order merchandiser of products for hunters, guides, and anglers, **L. L. Bean** (⊠ *95 Main St. [U.S. 1]* ☎ *877/755–2326* ⊕ *www.llbean.com*) attracts more than 3 million shoppers a year to its giant store (open 24 hours a day) in the heart of Freeport's shopping district. You can still find the original hunting boots, along with cotton and wool sweaters, outerwear, camping and ski equipment, comforters, and hundreds of other things for the home, car, boat, and campsite. For items related to specific activities and the home, as well as discounted merchandise (available at the L. L. Bean Outlet), head to the following nearby stores. **L. L. Bean Bike, Boat & Ski Store** (⊠ *57 Main St.* ☎ *877/755–2326*). **L. L. Bean Home Store** (⊠ *12 Nathan Nye St.* ☎ *877/755–2326*). **L. L. Bean Hunting & Fishing Store** (⊠ *95 Main St.* ☎ *877/755–2326*). **L. L. Bean Outlet** (⊠ *One Freeport Village Station [Depot St.]* ☎ *207/552–7772*).

NIGHTLIFE AND THE ARTS

Every Saturday from late June to early September, sit under the stars for the **L. L. Bean Summer Concert Series** (⊠ *Morse St.* ☎ *877/755–2326* ⊕ *www.llbean.com/events*). The free concerts start at 7:30 PM in downtown Freeport at L. L. Bean's Discovery Park. The entertainment ranges from folk, jazz, and country to rock and bluegrass. Bring a blanket and refreshments.

WHERE TO EAT AND STAY

$$$

AMERICAN

Fodor'sChoice

★

✕ **Broad Arrow Tavern.** On the main floor of the Harraseeket Inn, this dark, wood-paneled tavern with mounted moose heads, decoys, snowshoes, and other outdoor sporty decor is known for both its casual nature and its sumptuous menu. The chefs use only organically grown food, with a nearly exclusive emphasis on Maine products, to create treats such as steaks, pizzas, seafood. ⊠ *162 Main St.* ☎ *207/865–9377* ⌂ *Reservations not accepted* ⊟ *AE, D, DC, MC, V.*

$–$$

SEAFOOD

✕ **Harraseeket Lunch & Lobster Co.** Seafood baskets and lobster dinners are the focus at this popular, bare-bones place beside the town landing in South Freeport. Order at the counter, find a seat inside or out, and expect long lines in summer. ⊠ *On pier, end of Main St., South Freeport* ☎ *207/865–4888* ⊕ *www.harraseeketlunchandlobster.com* ⌂ *Reservations not accepted* ⊟ *No credit cards* ☉ *Closed mid-Oct.–Apr.*

$$$$

Fodor'sChoice

★

🛏 **Harraseeket Inn.** Despite modern appointments such as elevators and whirlpool baths in some rooms, this 1850 Greek Revival home provides a pleasantly old-fashioned, country-inn experience just a few minutes' walk from L. L. Bean. Guest rooms have print fabrics and reproductions of Federal quarter-canopy beds. Ask for a second-floor, garden-facing room. The formal Maine Dining Room ($$$–$$$$) specializes in contemporary American regional (and organic) cuisine such as whole poached lobster and all-natural filet mignon. The casual yet excellent Broad Arrow Tavern ($$$) serves heartier fare and has a charming seasonal patio. Inn rates include a full buffet breakfast and afternoon tea. **Pros:** excellent on-site dining; walk to shopping district. **Cons:** building updates have diminished some authenticity. ⊠ *162 Main St.* ☎ *207/865–9377 or 800/342–6423* ⊕ *www.harraseeketinn.com* ⌂ *82 rooms, 2 suites* ⌂ *In-room: refrigerator (some), Wi-Fi. In-hotel: 2 restaurants, bars, pool, gym, laundry service, parking (free), some pets allowed* ⊟ *AE, D, DC, MC, V* ⌂*BP.*

THE MID-COAST REGION

Updated by
Michael de
Zayas

Lighthouses dot the headlands of Maine's Mid-Coast region, where thousands of miles of coastline wait to be explored. Defined by chiseled peninsulas stretching south from U.S. 1, this area has everything from the sandy beaches and sandbars of Popham Beach to the jutting cliffs of Monhegan Island. If you are intent on hooking a trophy-size fish or catching a glimpse of a whale, there are plenty of cruises available. If you want to explore deserted beaches and secluded coves, kayaks are your best bet. Put in at the Harpswells, or on the Cushing and Saint George peninsulas or simply paddle among the lobster boats and other vessels that ply these waters.

Tall ships often visit Maine, sometimes sailing up the Kennebec River for a stopover at Bath's Maine Maritime Museum, on the site of the old Percy and Small Shipyard. Next door to the museum, the Bath Iron Works still builds the U.S. Navy's Aegis-class destroyers.

Boardwalks help protect the dunes—and therefore the beach—at Popham Beach State Park.

Along U.S. 1, charming towns, each unique, have an array of attractions. Brunswick, while a bigger, commercial city, has rows of historic wood and clapboard homes and is home to Bowdoin College. Bath is known for its maritime heritage. Wiscasset has arguably the best antiques shopping in the state. On its waterfront you can choose from a variety of seafood shacks competing for the best lobster rolls. Damariscotta, too, is worth a stop for its lively main street and good seafood restaurants.

South along the peninsulas the scenery opens to glorious vistas of working lobster harbors and marinas. It's here you find the authentic lobster pounds where you can watch your catch come in off the traps. Boothbay Harbor is the quaintest town in the Mid-Coast, and has lots of little stores that are perfect for window-shopping. It's one of three towns where you can take a ferry to Monhegan Island, which seems to be inhabited exclusively by painters at their easels, depicting the cliffs and weathered homes with colorful gardens.

ESSENTIALS

Visitor Information **Maine Tourism Association** (⊠ 1100 U.S. 1 [I–95 Exit 17], Yarmouth ☎ 207/846–0833 or 888/624–6345 ⊕ www.mainetourism.com). **Southern Midcoast Maine Chamber** (⊠ Border Trust Business Center, 2 Main St., Topsham ☎ 877/725–8797 ⊕ www.midcoastmaine.com).

At the Maine Maritime Museum, a boatbuilder works on a yacht tender, used to ferry people to shore.

BRUNSWICK

10 mi north of Freeport; 30 mi northeast of Portland.

Lovely brick-and-clapboard buildings are the highlight of Brunswick's Federal Street Historic District, which includes Federal Street and Park Row and the stately campus of Bowdoin College. From the intersection of Pleasant and Maine streets, in the center of town, you can walk in any direction and discover an impressive array of restaurants. Seafood? German cuisine? A Chinese buffet that beats out all the competition? It's all here. So are bookstores, gift shops, boutiques, and jewelers.

From Brunswick, Routes 123 and 24 take you south to Harpswell Neck peninsula and the more than 40 islands that make up the town of Harpswell, known collectively as the Harpswells. Small coves along Harpswell Neck shelter lobster boats, and summer cottages are tucked away among birch and spruce trees. On your way down from Cook's Corner to Land's End at the end of Route 24, you cross Sebascodegan Island. Heading east here leads to East Harpswell and Cundy's Harbor. Continuing straight south down 24 leads to Orr's Island. Stop at Mackerel Cove to see a real fishing harbor; there are a few parking spaces where you can stop to picnic and look for beach glass or put in your kayaks. Inhale the salt breeze as you cross the world's only cribstone bridge (designed so that water flows freely through gaps between the granite blocks) on your way to Bailey Island, home to a lobster pound made famous thanks in part to a Visa commercial.

SPORTS AND THE OUTDOORS

★ The coast near Brunswick is full of hidden nooks and crannies waiting to be explored by kayak. **H2Outfitters** (✉ *1894 Rte. 24, Orr's Island* ☎ *207/833–5257 or 800/205–2925* ⊕ *www.h2outfitters.com*) is the place in Harpswells to get on the water. It's at the end of Orr's Island just before the Cribstone Bridge and provides top-notch kayaking instruction and gear for people of all skill levels.

WHERE TO EAT

\$\$ ✕ **Cook's Lobster House.** What began as a lobster shack on Bailey's Island
SEAFOOD in 1955 has grown into this huge, internationally famous family-style
Fodor'sChoice restaurant, complete with its own gift shop. The restaurant still catches
★ its own fish and seafood, so you can count on the lobster casserole and the haddock sandwich to be delectable. But along with fame come prices; the shore dinner—the most expensive menu option—is \$43, and includes a 1¼-lb lobster with steamed or fried clams or mussels, a choice of sides, and a bowl of chowder or lobster stew. Whether you choose inside or deck seating, you can watch the activity on the water: men checking lobster pots and kayakers fanning across the bay. ✉ *68 Garrison Cove Rd., Bailey Island* ☎ *207/833–2818* ⊕ *www.cookslobster. com* ⌖ *Reservations not accepted* ▤ *D, MC, V* ☉ *Closed New Year's Day–mid-Feb.*

BATH

11 mi northeast of Brunswick; 38 mi northeast of Portland.

Bath has been a shipbuilding center since 1607. The result of its prosperity can be seen in its handsome mix of Federal, Greek Revival, and Italianate homes along Front, Centre, and Washington streets. In the heart of Bath's historic district are some charming 19th-century homes, including the 1820 Federal-style home at 360 Front St., the 1810 Greek Revival–style mansion at 969 Washington St., covered with gleaming white clapboards, and the Victorian gem at 1009 Washington St., painted a distinctive shade of raspberry. All three operate as inns. An easily overlooked site is the town's City Hall. The bell in its tower was cast by Paul Revere in 1805.

10

The venerable Bath Iron Works completed its first passenger ship in 1890. During World War II BIW—as it's locally known—launched a new ship every 17 days. It is still building today, turning out destroyers for the U.S. Navy. BIW is one of the state's largest employers, with about 5,600 workers. It's a good idea to avoid U.S. 1 on weekdays from 3:15 PM to 4:30 PM, when a major shift change takes place. You can tour BIW through the Maine Maritime Museum.

EXPLORING

Fodor'sChoice **Maine Maritime Museum.** No trip to Bath is complete without a visit to
★ this cluster of buildings that once made up the historic Percy & Small Shipyard. Plan on half a day at the museum, which examines the world of shipbuilding and is the only way to tour the Bath Iron Works. In summer, boat tours cruise the scenic Kennebec River. A particular favorite is the lighthouse tour that covers the area of the Kennebec from Bath

Continued on page 702

MAINE'S LIGHTHOUSES
GUARDIANS OF THE COAST By John Blodgett

Perched high on rocky ledges, on the tips of wayward islands, and sometimes seemingly on the ocean itself are the more than five dozen lighthouses standing watch along Maine's craggy and ship-busting coastline.

Marshall Point Light

LIGHTING THE WAY: A BIT OF HISTORY

Portland Head Light

Most lighthouses were built in the first half of the 19th century to protect the vessels from running aground at night or when the shoreline was shrouded in fog. Along with the mournful siren of the foghorn and maritime lore, these practical structures have come to symbolize Maine throughout the world.

SHIPWRECKS AND SAFETY

These alluring sentinels of the eastern seaboard today have more form than function, but that certainly was not always the case. Safety was a strong motivating factor in the erection of the lighthouses. Commerce also played a critical role. For example, in 1791 Portland Head light was completed, partially as a response to local merchants' concerns about the rocky entrance to Portland Harbor and the varying depths of the shipping channel, but approval wasn't given until a terrible accident in 1787 in which a 90-ton sloop wrecked. Beginning in 1790, the federal government was the owner of these towers of light, with the U.S. Lighthouse Service (later the U.S. Coast Guard) managing them.

Some lighthouses in Maine were built in a much-needed venue, but the points and islands upon which they sat eventually eroded into the ocean. This meant that over the years many lighthouses had to be rebuilt or replaced.

LIGHTHOUSES TODAY

In modern times, many of the structures still serve a purpose. Technological advances, such as GPS and radar, augment a ship's navigation through the choppy waters, but they don't replace a lighthouse or its foghorns. The numerous channel-marking buoys still in existence also are testament to the old tried-and-true methods.

Of the 61 lighthouses along this far northeastern state, 55 are still working, alerting ships (and even small aircraft) of the shoreline's rocky edge. Towns, historical organizations, the National Park Service, and a few private individuals own the decommissioned lights.

KEEPERS OF THE LIGHT

Some keepers also used bells and sirens, like this Fog Signal Station on Manana Island in 1898.

Pemaquid Point's fourth-order Fresnel lens

LIFE OF A LIGHTKEEPER

One thing that has changed with the modern era is the disappearance of the lighthouse keeper. In the 20th century, lighthouses began the conversion from oil-based lighting to electricity. A few decades later, the U.S. Coast Guard switched to automation, phasing out the need for an on-site keeper.

While the keepers of tradition were no longer needed, the traditions of these stalwart, 24/7 employees live on through museum exhibits and retellings of Maine's maritime history, legends, and lore. The tales of a lighthouse keeper's life are the stuff romance novels are made of: adventure, rugged but lonely men, and a beautiful setting along an unpredictable coastline.

The lighthouse keepers of yesterday probably didn't see their own lives so romantically. Their daily narrative was one of hard work and, in some cases, exceptional solitude. A keeper's primary job was to ensure that the lamp was illuminated all day, every day. This meant that oil (whale oil or coal oil) had to be carried about and wicks trimmed on a regular basis. When fog shrouded the coast, they sounded the solemn horn to pierce through the damp darkness that hid their light. Their quarters were generally small and often attached to the light tower itself. The remote locations of the lights added to the isolation a keeper felt, especially before the advent of radio and telephone, let alone the Internet. Though some brought families with them, the keepers tended to be men who lived alone.

THE LIGHTS 101

Over the years, Fresnel (fray-NELL) lenses were developed in different shapes and sizes so that ship captains could distinguish one lighthouse from another. Invented by Frenchman Augustin Fresnel in the early 19th century, the lens design allows for a greater transmission of light perfectly suited for lighthouse use. Knowing which lighthouse they were near helped captains know which danger was present, such as a submerged ledge or shallow channel. Some lights, such as those at Seguin Island Light, are fixed and don't flash. Other lights are colored red.

LIGHTHOUSE FINDER

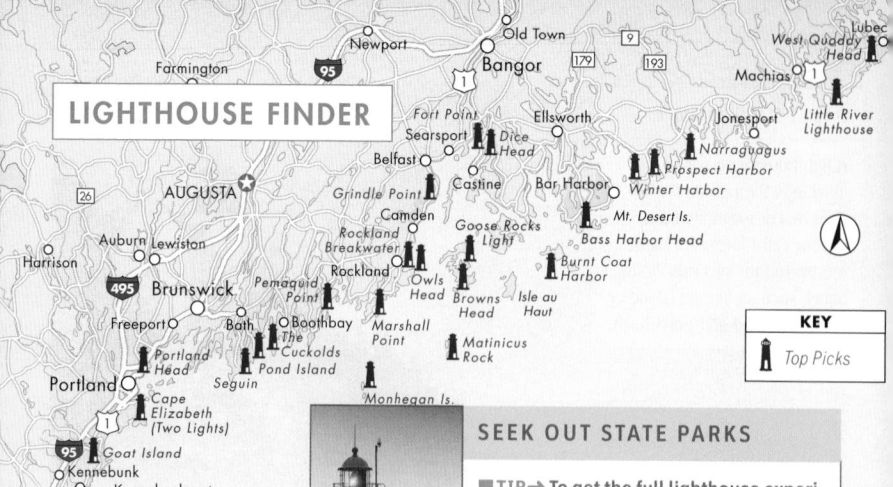

(Map of the Maine Coast showing lighthouse locations)

Old Town · Newport · Lubec · West Quoddy Head · Machias · Bangor · Farmington · 95 · 179 · 193 · 9 · Jonesport · Little River Lighthouse · Fort Point · Ellsworth · Searsport · Dice Head · Narraguagus · Prospect Harbor · Belfast · Castine · Bar Harbor · Winter Harbor · AUGUSTA · Grindle Point · Mt. Desert Is. · Camden · Goose Rocks Light · Bass Harbor Head · Auburn · Lewiston · Rockland Breakwater · Burnt Coat Harbor · Harrison · Rockland · Owls Head · Isle au Haut · 495 · Brunswick · Pemaquid Point · Browns Head · Freeport · Bath · Boothbay · Marshall Point · Matinicus Rock · Portland · The Cuckolds · Pond Island · Portland Head · Seguin · Cape Elizabeth (Two Lights) · Monhegan Is. · Goat Island · Kennebunk · Kennebunkport · Ogunquit · York · Cape Neddick (Nubble Light) · Whaleback · Kittery · Portsmouth

KEY

🗼 Top Picks

West Quoddy Head

VISITING MAINE'S LIGHTHOUSES

As you travel along the Maine Coast, you won't see lighthouses by watching your odometer—there were no rules about the spacing of lighthouses. The decision as to where to place a lighthouse was a balance between a region's geography and its commercial prosperity and maritime traffic.

Lighthouses line the shore from as far south as York to the country's easternmost tip at Lubec. Accessibility varies according to location and other factors. A handful are so remote as to be outright impossible to reach (except perhaps by kayaking and rock climbing). Some don't allow visitors according to Coast Guard policies, though you can enjoy them through the zoom lens of a camera. Others you can walk right up to and, occasionally, even climb to the top. Lighthouse enthusiasts and preservation groups restore and maintain many of them. All told, approximately 30 lighthouses allow some sort of public access.

SEEK OUT STATE PARKS

■ TIP➜ To get the full lighthouse experience your best bet is to visit one that is part of a state park. These are generally well kept and tend to allow up-close approach, though typically only outside. While you're at the parks you can picnic or stroll on the trails. Wildlife is often abundant in and near the water; you might spot sea birds and even whales in certain locations (try West Quoddy Head, Portland Head, or Two Lights).

MUSEUMS, TOURS, AND MORE

Most keeper's quarters are closed to the public, but some of the homes have been converted to museums, full of intriguing exhibits on lighthouses, the famous Fresnel lenses used in them, and artifacts of Maine maritime life in general. Talk to the librarians at the **Maine Maritime Museum** in Bath (⊕ *www.mainemaritime-museum.org*) or sign up for one of the museum's daily lighthouse cruises to pass by no fewer than ten on the Lighthouse Lovers Cruise. In Rockland, the **Maine Lighthouse Museum** (⊕ *www.mainelight-housemuseum.com*) has the country's largest display of Fresnel lenses. The museum also displays keepers' memorabilia, foghorns, brassware, and more.

For more information, check out the lighthouse page at Maine's official tourism site: ⊕ *www.visitmaine.com/attractions/sightseeing_tours/lighthouse*.

SLEEPING LIGHT: STAYING OVERNIGHT

Goose Rock, where you can play lighthouse keeper for a week.

Want to stay overnight in a lighthouse? There are several options to do so.

■ TIP→ Book lighthouse lodgings as far in advance as possible, up to one year ahead.

Our top pick is **Pemaquid Point Light** (*Newcastle Square Vacation Rentals* ☎ 207/563–6500) because it has one of the most dramatic settings on the Maine coast. Four miles south of **New Harbor**, the second floor of the lighthouse keeper's house is rented out on a weekly basis early May through mid-November to support upkeep of the grounds. When you aren't enjoying the interior, head outdoors: the covered front porch has a rocking-chair view of the ocean. The one-bedroom, one-bath rental sleeps up to a family of four.

Situated smack dab in the middle of a major maritime thoroughfare between two Penobscot Bay islands, **Goose Rocks Light** (☎ 207/867–4747) offers lodging for the adventuresome—the 51-foot cast-iron lighthouse is completely surrounded by water. Getting there requires a ferry ride from Rockland to nearby **North Haven,** a ten-minute ride by motorboat, and then a climb up an iron-rung ladder from the pitching boat—all based on high tide and winds, of course. There's room for up to eight people. It's a bit more cushy experience than it was for the original keepers: there's a flat-screen TV with DVD player and a selection of music and videos for entertainment. In addition, a hammock hangs on the small deck that encircles the operational light; it's a great place from which to watch the majestic windjammers and the fishing fleet pass by.

Little River Lighthouse (☎ 207/259–3833), along the far northeastern reaches of the coast in **Cutler**, has three rooms available for rent from July through September. You're responsible for food and beverages, linens, towels, and other personal items (don't forget the bug spray), but kitchen and other basics are provided. The lighthouse operators will provide a boat ride to the island upon which the lighthouse sits.

TOP LIGHTHOUSES TO VISIT

BASS HARBOR LIGHT

One Maine lighthouse familiar to many because it is the subject of countless photographs is Bass Harbor Light, at the southern end of **Mount Desert Island.** It is a short drive from Acadia National Park and the town of Bar Harbor. The station grounds are open year-round, but the former keeper's house is now a private home for a Coast Guard family. This lighthouse is so close to the water it seems as if a blustery wind could tip it over the rocks right into the North Atlantic. ■TIP→ To photograph Bass Harbor, get up close, or walk a short trail for a horizontal shot of the lighthouse and its outbuildings. Also use a tripod or stand firm in the salted wind.

Bass Harbor

CAPE ELIZABETH LIGHT

Two Lights State Park, as the name suggests, is home to two lighthouses. Both of these **Cape Elizabeth** structures were built in 1828, the first twin lighthouses to be erected on the Maine coast. The western light was converted into a private residence in 1924; the eastern light still projects its automated cylinder of light 17 mi out to sea, from a height of 129 feet, and is the subject of Edward Hopper's *Lighthouse at Two Lights* (1929). The grounds immediately surrounding the building and the lighthouse itself are closed to the public, but the structure is easily viewed and photographed from the nearby parking lot. Explore the tidal pools for the small snails known as periwinkles. ■TIP→ If it's foggy, don't stand too close to the foghorn, and in season (late March through late October) be sure to eat a lobster roll at the Lobster Shack Restaurant—but do not feed the seagulls; you will be publicly chastised on the restaurant's loudspeaker if you do.

Cape Elizabeth

CAPE NEDDICK LIGHT

More commonly known as Nubble Light for the smallish offshore expanse of rock it rests upon, Cape Neddick Light sits a few hundred feet off **York Beach**. With such a precarious location, its grounds are inaccessible to visitors, but close enough to be exceptionally photogenic, especially during the Christmas season when the Town of York hangs Christmas lights and wreaths from the lighthouse and its surrounding buildings (Santa Claus makes an appearance via lobster boat at the annual lighting celebration). You also can view it from Sohier Park. Notice that it emits a red light.

Cape Neddick

MONHEGAN ISLAND LIGHT

Only the adventuresome and the artistic see this light, because **Monhegan Island**, known both for its fishing and artistic communities, is accessible by a 90-minute ferry ride. To reach the lighthouse, you have an additional half-mile walk uphill from the ferry dock. But it's well worth the effort, especially if you enjoy island life—it's nothing but the rugged North Atlantic out here. The light was automated back in 1959, and since the early 1960s the former keeper's quarters has been home to the Monhegan Museum, which has exhibits about the island more so than the lighthouse. The tower itself is closed to the public. ■TIP➜ If you've made it this far, stay a quiet night at one of a handful of lodging options on the island, lulled to sleep by muffled waves and the distance from the mainland.

Monhegan Island

PORTLAND HEAD LIGHT

The subject of Edward Hopper's painting *Portland Head-Light* (1927) and one of Maine's most photographed lighthouses (and its oldest), the famous Portland Head Light was completed in January 1791. Its first keeper, Revolutionary War veteran Captain Joseph Greenleaf, was appointed by George Washington. At the edge of Fort Williams Park, in **Cape Elizabeth**, the towering white stone lighthouse stands 101 feet above the sea. The United States Coast Guard operates it and it is not open for tours. However the adjacent keeper's dwelling, built in 1891, is now a museum, where you can inspect various lenses used in lighthouses. Visitors can also explore the numerous trails within the park, as well as its grassy areas, popular for picnics, kite flying, and watching ships from around the globe enter Portland Harbor.

Portland Head

WEST QUODDY HEAD LIGHT

Originally built in 1808 by mandate of President Thomas Jefferson, West Quoddy Head Light sits in **Lubec** on the easternmost tip of land in the mainland United States—so far east that at certain times of the year it's the first object in the country to be touched by the rising sun's rays. The 49-foot-high lighthouse, now famously painted with distinctive red and white candy stripes, is part of 541-acre Quoddy Head State Park, which has some of the state's best wildlife watching, including humpback, minke, and finback whales. Learn more in the lightkeeper's house-turned-visitor center. You also can climb the 50 steps to the top of the tower.

West Quoddy Head

down to Fort Popham at the mouth of the river. A number of impressive ships, including the 142-foot Grand Banks fishing schooner *Sherman Zwicker*, are on display in summer. Inside the main museum building, exhibits use ship models, paintings, photographs, and historical artifacts to tell the maritime history of the region. From May to November, hour-long tours of the shipyard show how these massive wooden ships were built. You can watch boatbuilders wield their tools in the boat shop. A separate historic building houses a fascinating lobstering exhibit. It's worth coming here just to watch the 18-minute video on lobstering written and narrated by E. B. White. A gift shop and bookstore are on the premises, and you can grab a bite to eat in the café or bring a picnic to eat on the grounds. Kids ages 4 and younger get in free. ⊠ *243 Washington St.* ☎ *207/442–0961* ⊕ *www.mainemaritimemuseum.org* ✉ *$12* ⊙ *Daily 9:30–5.*

OFF THE
BEATEN
PATH

☯ **Popham Beach State Park** (⊠ *Rte. 209, Phippsburg* ☎ *207/389–1335*) has bathhouses and picnic tables. There are no restaurants at this end of the beach, so pack a picnic or get takeout from Spinney's Restaurant near the Civil War–era Fort Popham or **Percy's Store** (⊠ *6 Sea St.* ☎ *207/389–2010*) behind Spinney's. At low tide you can walk miles of tidal flats and also out to a nearby island, where you can explore tide pools or fish off the ledges. Drive past the entrance to the park, and on the right you can see a vista often described as "Million Dollar View." The confluence of the Kennebec and Morse rivers creates an ever-shifting pattern of sandbars.

WHERE TO EAT AND STAY

$$
AMERICAN

✗ **Beale Street Barbecue.** Ribs are the thing at this barbecue joint. Hearty eaters should ask for one of the platters piled high with pulled pork, pulled chicken, or shredded beef. Jalapeño popovers and chili served with corn bread are terrific appetizers. Enjoy a beer at the bar while waiting for your table. ⊠ *215 Water St.* ☎ *207/442–9514* ⊕ *www.mainebbq.com* ☰ *MC, V.*

$$$–$$$$
AMERICAN

✗ **Robinhood Free Meetinghouse.** This 1855 church and meetinghouse is a remarkable setting for a meal. On occasion you can even eat upstairs among the pews. Though owned by acclaimed chef and owner Michael Gagné—whose multilayer cream-cheese biscuits are shipped all over the country—this meetinghouse serves meals that are primarily made by chef de cuisine Troy Mains. The menu changes daily but always has a variety of seafood, vegetables, and dairy products purchased locally. You might begin with the lobster and crab cakes, then move on to grilled fillet of beef stuffed with crab or the duck confit. Finish up with the signature Obsession in Three Chocolates. The wine list is quite good as well. ⊠ *210 Robinhood Rd., Georgetown* ☎ *207/371–2188* ⊕ *www.robinhood-meetinghouse.com* ☰ *AE, D, MC, V* ⊙ *No lunch.*

$$$–$$$$
Fodor's Choice
★

⌂ **Sebasco Harbor Resort.** This destination family resort spread across 575 acres at the foot of the Phippsburg Peninsula has an exceptional range of accommodations and services. Comfortable guest rooms in the clapboard-covered main building have antique furnishings and new bathrooms, while rooms in a building designed to resemble a lighthouse have wicker furniture, paintings by local artists, and rooftop access. The Fairwinds Spa Suites are corporate luxury units next to the resort's spa; prices for combo room and treatment packages range from $369 to $399. The recently added Harbor Village Suites are set in exquisitely landscaped grounds and include 18 spacious and air-conditioned rooms that rent for $319–$459. The resort's Pilot House restaurant ($$–$$$) is known for its innovative take on classic dishes and is a wonderful spot for watching sunsets. In summer there are outdoor lobster and clambakes. **Pros:** ocean location; excellent food and service; kids' activities; airport shuttle. **Cons:** pricey. ⊠ *29 Kenyon Rd., off Rte. 217, Sebasco Estates* ☎ *207/389–1161 or 800/225–3819* ⊕ *www.sebasco.com* ⇨ *115 rooms, 23 cottages* ⚒ *In-room: Wi-Fi (some). In-hotel: 3 restaurants, bar, golf course, tennis courts, pool, gym, bicycles, children's programs, Wi-Fi hotspot* ⊟ *AE, D, MC, V* ⊘ *Closed Nov.–mid-May* ⑩ *MAP.*

WISCASSET

10 mi north of Bath; 46 mi northeast of Portland.

Settled in 1663, Wiscasset sits on the banks of the Sheepscot River. It bills itself "Maine's Prettiest Village," and it's easy to see why: it has graceful churches, old cemeteries, and elegant sea captains' homes (many converted into antiques shops or galleries), and a good wine and specialty foods shop called Treats (stock up here if you're heading north).

Pack a picnic and take it down to the dock, where you can watch the fishing boats or grab a lobster roll from Red's Eats or the lobster shack nearby. Wiscasset has expanded its wharf, and this is a great place to catch a breeze on a hot day. U.S. 1 becomes Main Street, and traffic often slows to a crawl. You can walk to all galleries, shops, restaurants, and other attractions. ■ TIP➡ You'll likely have success if you try to park on Water Street rather than Main.

SHOPPING

Not to be missed is **Edgecomb Potters** (⊠ *727 Boothbay Rd., Edgecomb* ☎ *207/882–9493* ⊕ *www.edgecombpotters.com*), which specializes in pricey, exquisitely glazed porcelain and has one of the best selections in the area. It also carries jewelry. **Sheepscot River Pottery** (⊠ *34 U.S. 1, Edgecomb* ☎ *207/882–9410* ⊕ *www.sheepscot.com*) boasts beautifully glazed kitchen tiles as well as kitchenware and home accessories.

10

WHERE TO EAT

¢ ✕**Red's Eats.** You've probably driven right past this little red shack on
FAST FOOD the Wiscasset side of the bridge if you've visited this area and seen the long line of hungry customers. Red's is a local landmark famous for its hot dogs, burgers, crisp onion rings, lobster and crab rolls, and even its ice cream (try black raspberry or pistachio). There are a few picnic tables, but you can get your food to go and walk down to the dock to enjoy the view. Watch out for the seagulls; they like lobster rolls, too. ⊠ *41 Water St.* ☎ *207/882–6128* ⚒ *Reservations not accepted* ⊟ *No credit cards* ⊘ *Closed mid-Oct.–mid-Apr.*

OFF THE The Boothbay region is made up of Boothbay proper, East Boothbay, and
BEATEN Boothbay Harbor. This part of the shoreline is a craggy stretch of inlets
PATH where pleasure craft anchor alongside trawlers and lobster boats. Boothbay Harbor is like a smaller version of Bar Harbor—touristy but friendly

and fun—with pretty, winding streets and lots to explore. Commercial Street, Wharf Street, Townsend Avenue, and the By-Way are lined with shops and ice-cream parlors. You can browse for hours in the trinket shops, crafts galleries, clothing stores, and boutiques around the harbor or take a walk around the 248-acre **Coastal Maine Botanical Garden** (✉ *Barters Island Rd.* ☎ *207/633–4333* ⊕ *www.mainegardens.org*).

Excursion boats and ferries to Monhegan Island leave from the piers off Commercial Street. Drive out to Ocean Point in East Boothbay for some incredible scenery. Boothbay is 13 mi southeast of Wiscasset via U.S. 1 to Rte. 27.

DAMARISCOTTA

8 mi north of Wiscasset via U.S. 1.

The Damariscotta region comprises several communities along the rocky coast. The town itself sits on the water and is a lively place filled with attractive shops and several good restaurants.

A few minutes' walk across the bridge over the Damariscotta River is the town of Newcastle, between the Sheepscot and Damariscotta rivers. Newcastle was settled in the early 1600s. The earliest inhabitants planted apple trees, but the town later became an industrial center, home to several shipyards and a couple of mills. The oldest Catholic church in New England, St. Patrick's, is here, and it still rings its original Paul Revere bell.

Bremen, which encompasses more than a dozen islands and countless rocky outcrops, offers numerous sporting activities. Nobleboro was settled in the 1720s by Colonel David Dunbar, sent by the British to build the fort at Pemaquid. Neighboring Waldoboro is situated on the Medomak River and was settled largely by Germans in the early 1770s. You can still visit the old German Meeting House, built in 1772. The peninsula stretches south to include Bristol, Round Pond, South Bristol, New Harbor, and Pemaquid.

ESSENTIALS

Visitor Information Damariscotta Region Chamber of Commerce (🖃 *Box 13, Damariscotta 04543* ☎ *207/563–8340* ⊕ *www.damariscottaregion.com*).

WHERE TO EAT AND STAY

$$–$$$ ✕ **King Eider's Pub & Restaurant.** The classic pub bills itself as having the
AMERICAN finest crab cakes in New England. Other specialties of the house include
★ lobster Courvoisier and house-made ravioli (e.g., stuffed with crabmeat) that vary day to day. Penne pasta in a creamy dill sauce with a mound of sea scallops is out of this world. With exposed brick walls and low wooden beams, it's a cozy place to enjoy your favorite ale. There is also seating on the deck. Stop by in the evening for live entertainment. ✉ *2 Elm St.* ☎ *207/563–6008* ⊕ *www.kingeiderspub.com* ⌂ *Reservations essential* ▭ *D, MC, V.*

$$$–$$$$ 🏨 **Newcastle Inn.** A riverside location and an excellent dining room make this country inn a classic. All the guest rooms are filled with antiques and decorated with sumptuous fabrics; some rooms have fireplaces and

Lobster pot buoys are popular decorations in Maine; the markings represent a particular lobsterman's claim.

whirlpool baths. There are two rooms designated pet-friendly, with private entrances. On pleasant mornings breakfast is served on the back deck overlooking the river. The dining room ($$$$), which is open to the public by reservation, serves six-course meals with an emphasis on local seafood and is open Tuesday through Saturday in season. **Pros:** innkeepers' reception evenings with cocktails and hors d'oeuvres. **Cons:** away from town. ⊠ *60 River Rd. Newcastle* ☎ *207/563–5685 or 800/832–8669* ⊕ *www.newcastleinn.com* 🛏 *14 rooms, 3 suites* ♿ *In-room: no phone, no TV (some). In-hotel: no kids under 12* ⊟ *AE, MC, V* ❖❙ *BP.*

PEMAQUID POINT

17 mi south of Damariscotta via U.S. 1 to Rte. 129 to Rte. 130.

Route 130 brings you to Pemaquid Point, home of the famous lighthouse and its attendant fog bell and tiny museum. If you are going to New Harbor or Round Pond, take a left onto Route 32 where it intersects Route 130 just before Pemaquid Point. New Harbor is about 4 mi away, and Round Pond about 6 mi beyond that. Just north of New Harbor on Route 32 is the Rachel Carson Salt Pond Preserve.

EXPLORING

Pemaquid Point Light. At the terminus of Route 130, this lighthouse looks as though it sprouted from the ragged, tilted chunk of granite that it commands. The former keeper's cottage is now the Fishermen's Museum, which displays historic photographs, scale models, and artifacts that explore commercial fishing in Maine. Also here are the original fog bell and bell house built in 1897 for the two original Shipman engines. Pemaquid Art Gallery, on-site, mounts exhibitions by area artists in July and August, and admission, once you have paid your fee to be on the lighthouse property, is free. Restrooms, picnic tables, and barbecue grills are all available on-site. Next door is the Sea Gull Shop, with a dining room, gift shop, and ice-cream parlor. The museum on-site is adjacent to the lighthouse. ⊠ *Rte. 130 (Bristol Rd.), Pemaquid* ☎ *207/677–2494* ✉ *$1* ☉ *Memorial Day–Columbus Day, Mon.–Sat. 10–5, Sun. 11–5* ✉ *$5.*

SPORTS AND THE OUTDOORS

CRUISES You can take a cruise to Monhegan with **Hardy Boat Cruises** (⊠ *Shaw's Wharf, New Harbor* ☎ *207/677–6026*).

WHERE TO STAY

$$ Ⓨ **Unique Yankee Bed & Breakfast.** If you are traveling with a dog, you'll find few more accommodating spots in Maine than this out-of-the way place on Rutherford Island. One room even has its own fenced-in dog play yard. Though it's a 6-minute drive to the water, the inn has a tower where, if you have a clear day, you might see all the way to Monhegan Island. The 2.3-acre property is surrounded by a 2-acre greenbelt, so it's quite private. The main house has rooms with four-season electric fireplace, microwave, coffee pot, and two-person jetted bath (plus separate shower). A newer annex has very large rooms with modern amenities. **Pros:** great if you're traveling with dogs; long views of Pemaquid on clear days from lookout. **Cons:** dogs on premises. ⊠ *53 Coveside Rd., South Bristol* ☎ *207/644–1502 or 866/644–1502* ⊕ *www.uniqueyankeeofmaine.com* ⇥ *6 rooms* ♢ *In-room: Wi-Fi, refrigerator, DVD. In-hotel: some pets allowed* ☐ *MC, V* ⍢ *BP.*

THOMASTON

10 mi northeast of Waldoboro, 72 mi northeast of Portland.

Thomaston is a delightful town, full of beautiful sea captains' homes and dotted with antiques and specialty shops. A National Historic District encompasses parts of High, Main, and Knox streets. The town is the gateway to the two peninsulas, so you will see water on both sides as you arrive.

WHERE TO EAT

$$–$$$ ✕ **Thomaston Café & Bakery.** A must-stop on the long, slow drive up
AMERICAN Route 1. Works by local artists adorns the walls of this small café, and it's next door to an independent bookstore. Entrées, prepared with locally grown ingredients, include seared fresh tuna on soba noodles, lobster ravioli with lobster sauce, and filet mignon with béarnaise sauce. They serve an excellent breakfast, including homemade corned beef hash, as well as delicious sandwiches for lunch. ⊠ *154 Main St.* ☎ *207/354–8589* ⊕ *www.harborviewrestaurant.com* ☐ *MC, V* ☉ *No dinner Sun.–Thurs.*

TENANTS HARBOR

10 mi south of Thomaston.

Tenants Harbor is a quintessential coastal harbor—dominated by lobster boats, its shores are rocky and slippery, and its downtown streets are lined with clapboard houses, a church, and a general store. It's a favorite with artists, and galleries and studios welcome browsers.

WHERE TO STAY

$$$

Fodor'sChoice

★

🗺 **Craignair Inn.** It's tough to find a better waterfront location than Craignair, which overlooks Wheeler's Bay and Clark Island on 4 waterfront acres. It was originally built to house granite workers from nearby quarries. The annex house was the chapel where the stonecutters and their families worshiped. Rooms aren't as wonderful as the views but are clean and functional. You can easily explore Clark Island by walking over a narrow isthmus. Another perk is the excellent food. Chef Seiler, most recently from the Samoset Resort, wins awards for his creative cuisine served in the inn's dining room ($$$). You might want to start with the Caribbean jerk grilled shrimp brochettes or the steamed Great Eastern mussels and move on to pecan-crusted salmon, bacon-wrapped tenderloin, or baked stuffed haddock. **Pros:** stellar food; waterfront location. **Cons:** pets allowed in some rooms can be troublesome to those with allergies. ✉ *5 3rd St., Spruce Head* 🕾 *207/594–7644 or 800/320–9997* ⊕ *www.craignair.com* 🛏 *21 rooms, 13 with bath* ♿ *In-room: no a/c, Wi-Fi. In-hotel: Wi-Fi hotspot, some pets allowed* ▤ *D, MC, V* ⏐⊙⏐ *BP.*

PORT CLYDE

2 mi south of Tenants Harbor via Rte. 131.

The fishing village of Port Clyde sits at the end of the St. George Peninsula. The road leading to Port Clyde meanders along the St. George River, passing meadows and farmhouses. Shipbuilding was the first commercial enterprise here, followed by the catching and canning of seafood. You can still buy Port Clyde sardines. Its boat landing is home to the *Elizabeth Ann* and the *Laura B*, the mail boats that serve nearby Monhegan Island and are operated by the **Monhegan Boat Line** (🕾 *207/372/8848* ⊕ *www.monheganboat.com*). Several artists make their homes in Port Clyde, so check to see if their studios are open while you are visiting. From here you can also visit Owls Head Light and the Marshall Point Lighthouse, the latter of which has inspired artists like Jamie Wyeth.

10

MONHEGAN ISLAND

Fodor'sChoice

★

East of Pemaquid Peninsula, 10 mi south of Port Clyde.

Simple and artful living is the order of the day on remote Monhegan Island. To get here you'll need to take a ferry. A tiny hamlet greets you at the harbor. There are no paved roads, and everywhere you look artists stand before their canvases, rendering the landscape of serene gardened cottages and rugged coast.

The island was known to Basque, Portuguese, and Breton fishermen well before Christopher Columbus discovered America. About a century ago, Monhegan was discovered again by some of the finest American painters, including Rockwell Kent, Robert Henri, A. J. Hammond, and Edward Hopper, who sailed out to paint its open meadows, savage cliffs, wild ocean views, and fishermen's shacks. Tourists followed, and now three excursion boats dock here for a few hours each day in the warm months when harbor shops and artist studios bustle with activity.

You can escape the crowds on the island's 17 mi of hiking trails, which lead to the lighthouse and to the cliffs, or spend a night and feel some of the privacy that the island can afford. Note that if you're the kind of traveler who likes lots of activities, skip Monhegan. (Actually, you should probably skipped Maine altogether.) A day trip is typified by a little shopping and a hike across the island to view the bluffs. If the weather's bad, there's little to do. But if you enjoy a good hike, nature, or the concept of an island that's home to just artists and fishermen, the silence and serenity of the high cliffs at White Head, Black Head, and Burnt Head and the serendipitous pleasures that the island creates will be unforgettable.

PENOBSCOT BAY

By Stephen and Neva Allen

Few could deny that Penobscot Bay is one of Maine's most dramatically beautiful regions. Its 1,000-mi-long coastline is made up of rocky granite boulders, wild and often undeveloped shore, a sprinkling of colorful towns, and views of the sea and shore that are a photographer's dream.

The second-largest estuary in New England, Penobscot Bay stretches 37 mi from Port Clyde in the south to Stonington, the little fishing village at the tip of Deer Isle, in the north. The bay begins where the Penobscot River ends, near Stockton Springs, and terminates in the Gulf of Maine, where it is 47 mi wide. It covers an estimated 1,070 square mi and is home to hundreds of islands.

Initially, shipbuilding was the primary moneymaker here. In the 1800s, during the days of the great tall ships (or Down Easters, as they were often called), more wooden ships were built along Penobscot Bay than in any other place in the United States. This golden age of billowing sails and wooden sailing ships came to an end with the development of the steam engine. By 1900, sailing ships were no longer a viable commercial venture in Maine. However, as you will see when traveling the coast, the tall ships have not disappeared—they have simply been revived as recreational boats, known as windjammers. Today, once again, there are more tall ships along Penobscot Bay than anywhere else in the country.

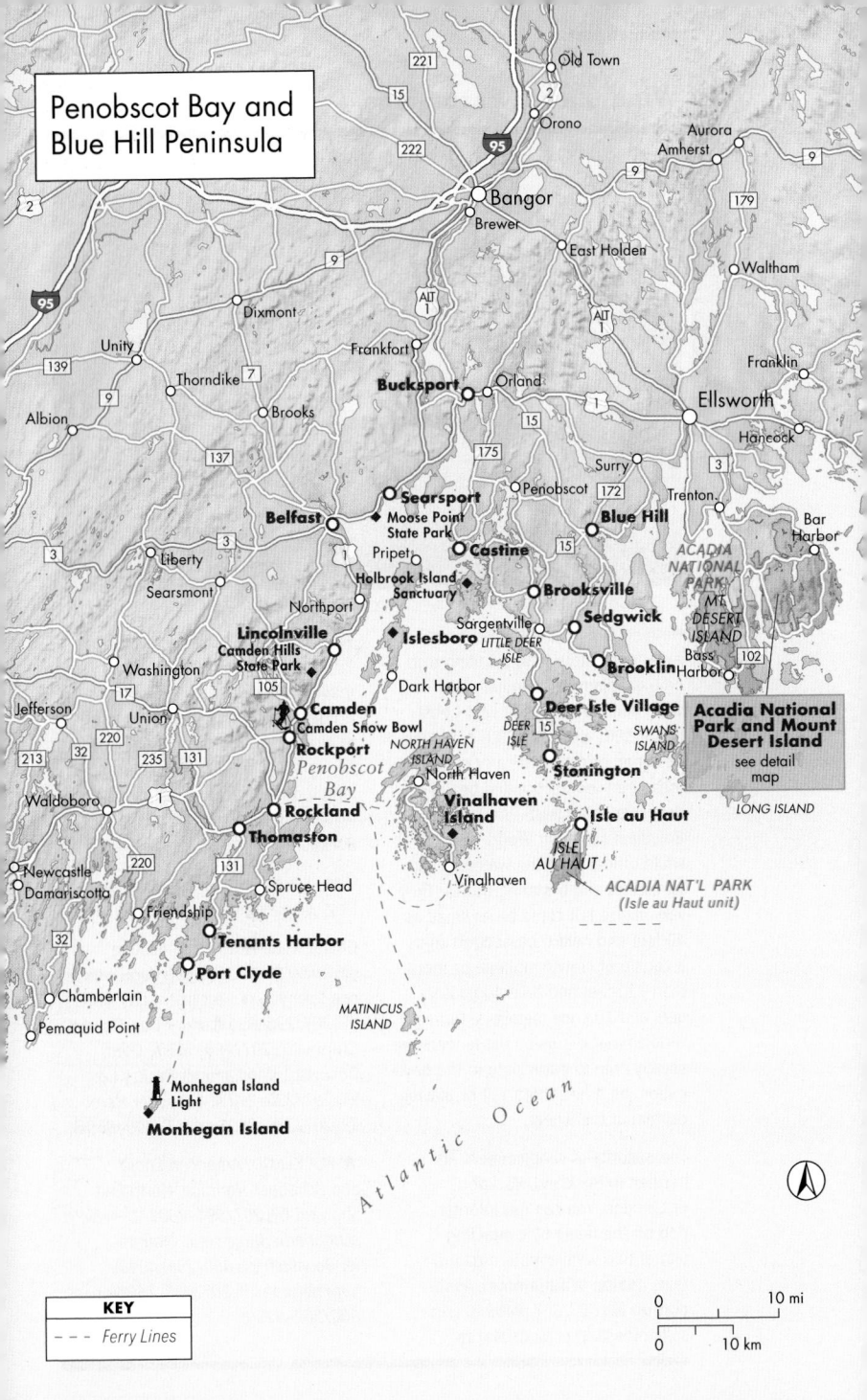

Penobscot Bay and Blue Hill Peninsula

Old Town
221
15
2
Orono
222
95
Brewer
Bangor
East Holden
Aurora
Amherst
9
179
9
2
95
Dixmont
Frankfort
Waltham
Franklin
Unity
Thorndike
7
139
Brooks
Bucksport
Orland
Ellsworth
Hancock
Albion
9
Liberty
137
175
Surry
172
Trenton
3
Searsmont
3
Searsport
Moose Point
State Park
Penobscot
Blue Hill
Bar
Harbor
Belfast
1
Pripet
Castine
15
ACADIA
NATIONAL
PARK
MT.
DESERT
ISLAND
Northport
Holbrook Island
Sanctuary
Brooksville
Sedgwick
Washington
17
Lincolnville
Camden Hills
State Park
105
Islesboro
LITTLE DEER
ISLE
Brooklin
Bass
Harbor
102
Jefferson
Union
Camden
Dark Harbor
Deer Isle Village
SWANS
ISLAND
Acadia National
Park and Mount
Desert Island
see detail
map
220
131
32
235
Camden Snow Bowl
Rockport
Penobscot
Bay
NORTH HAVEN
ISLAND
DEER
ISLE
15
Stonington
LONG ISLAND
213
Waldoboro
1
North Haven
Newcastle
Damariscotta
220
Rockland
Thomaston
131
Spruce Head
Vinalhaven
Island
Isle au Haut
ISLE
AU HAUT
32
Friendship
Tenants Harbor
Vinalhaven
ACADIA NAT'L PARK
(Isle au Haut unit)
Chamberlain
Port Clyde
Pemaquid Point
MATINICUS
ISLAND
Monhegan Island
Light
Monhegan Island
Atlantic Ocean

KEY
- - - Ferry Lines

0   10 mi

0   10 km

Windjammer Excursions

A windjammer cruise gives you a chance to admire Maine's dramatic coast from the water.

Nothing defines the Maine coastal experience more than a sailing trip on a windjammer. Windjammers were built all along the East Coast in the 19th and early 20th centuries. Designed primarily to carry cargo, these iron- or steel-hulled beauties have a rich past—the *Nathaniel Bowditch* served in World War II, while others plied the waters in the lumbering and oystering trades. They vary in size but could be as small as 40 feet and hold 6 passengers (plus a couple of crew members) or more than 130 feet and hold 40 passengers and 10 crew members. During a windjammer excursion passengers are usually able to participate in the navigation, be it hoisting a sail or playing captain at the wheel.

The majority of windjammers are berthed in Rockland, Rockport, or Camden. You can get information on the fleets by contacting one of two windjammer organizations: **Maine Windjammer Association** (☎ *800/807-9463* ⊕ *www. sailmainecoast.com*) or **Maine**

Windjammer Cruises (☎ *207/236-2938* or *800/736-7981* ⊕ *www. mainewindjammercruises.com*). Cruises can be anywhere from one to eight days. The price, ranging from nearly $200 to $900, depending on length of trip, includes all meals. Trips leave from Camden, Rockland, and Rockport.

Here is a selection of some of the best windjammer cruises in the area.

CAMDEN–ROCKPORT: Angelique (☎ *207/785-6036*). *Appledore*, which can take you out for just a day sail (☎ *207/236-8353*). *Mary Day*, Coastal Cruises (☎ *207/785-5670*). *Olad*, Downeast Windjammer Packet Co. (☎ *207/236-2323*); Schooner Heron (☎ *207/236-8605* or *800/599-8605*).

★ ROCKLAND: *American Eagle* and *Schooner Heritage*, North End Shipyard (☎ *207/594-8007* ⊕ *www. schoonerheritage.com*). *Nathaniel Bowditch* (☎ *800/288-4098*). *Summertime* (☎ *207/563-1605* or *800/562-8290*).

ROCKLAND

4 mi northeast of Thomaston; 14 mi northeast of Tenants Harbor.

The town is considered the gateway to Penobscot Bay and is the first stop on U.S. 1 offering a glimpse of the often sparkling and island-dotted blue bay. Though once merely a place to pass through on the way to tonier ports like Camden, Rockland now gets attention on its own, thanks to a trio of attractions: the renowned Farnsworth Museum, the increasingly popular summer Lobster Festival, and the lively North Atlantic Blues Festival. Specialty shops and galleries line the main street, and one of the restaurants, Primo (between Camden and the little village of Owls Head), has become nationally famous. The town is still a large fishing port and the commercial hub of this coastal area.

Rockland Harbor is the berth of more windjammer ships than any other port in the United States. The best place in Rockland to view these beautiful vessels as they sail in and out of the harbor is the mile-long granite breakwater, which bisects the outer portion of Rockland Harbor. To get there, go north on U.S. 1, turn right on Waldo Avenue, and right again on Samoset Road, then follow this short road to its end.

GETTING HERE AND AROUND

Visitor Information Penobscot Regional Chamber of Commerce (⊠ *1 Park Dr., Rockland* ☎ *207/596–0376 or 800/562–2529* ⊕ *www.therealmaine.com*).

EXPLORING

Fodor's Choice ★ **Farnsworth Art Museum.** This is one of the most important small museums in the country. The **Wyeth Center** is devoted to Maine-related works of the famous Wyeth family: N. C. Wyeth, an accomplished illustrator whose works were featured in many turn-of-the-20th-century books; his late son Andrew, one of the best-known painters in the country; and Andrew's son James, also an accomplished painter, who lives on nearby Monhegan Island. Some works by Andrew from his and Betsy Wyeth's personal collection include *The Patriot, Adrift, Maiden Hair, Dr. Syn, The Clearing,* and *Watch Cap.* Also on display are works by Fitz Henry Lane, George Bellows, Frank W. Benson, Edward Hopper (his paintings of old Rockland are a highlight), Louise Nevelson, and Fairfield Porter. Works by living Maine artists are shown in the **Jamien Morehouse Wing.** The **Farnsworth Homestead,** a handsome circa-1852 Greek Revival dwelling that is part of the museum, retains its original lavish Victorian furnishings. In Cushing, a tiny town a few miles south of Thomaston, on the St. George River, the museum also operates the **Olsen House** (⊠ *Hathorn Point Rd., Cushing*), which is depicted in Andrew Wyeth's famous painting *Christina's World.* ⊠ *16 Museum St., Rockland* ☎ *207/596–6457* ⊕ *www.farnsworthmuseum.org* ⌖ *$12 for museum and Olsen House; $4 for Olsen House only* ⊙ *Daily 10–5.*

🌣 ★ **Maine Lighthouse Museum/Maine Discovery Museum.** The lighthouse museum displays Fresnel lighthouse lenses, as well as a collection of lighthouse artifacts and Coast Guard memorabilia. Sharing the same building are the Maine Discovery Museum, which is great for kids, and the Penobscot Bay Regional Chamber of Commerce, where visitors can pick up maps and area information. ⊠ *1 Park Dr.* ☎ *207/594–3301*

10

THE PRETTIEST WALK IN THE WORLD

A few years ago *Yankee*, the quintessential magazine of New England, did a cover story on what it called "The Prettiest Walk in the World." The two-lane paved road, which winds up and down, with occasional views of the ocean, connects Rockport to Camden. To judge the merits of this approximately 2-mi journey for yourself, you can travel on foot or by car. Begin at the intersection of U.S. 1 and Pascal Road. Take a right off U.S. 1 toward Rockport Harbor, then cross the bridge and go up the hill. On your left is Russell Avenue. Take that all the way to Camden. Lining the way are some of the most beautiful homes in Maine, surrounded by an abundance of flora and fauna. Keep an eye out for Aldermere Farm and its Belted Galloway cows, as well as views of the sparkling ocean. For those who may not know, these rare cows get their name from the foot-wide white "belt" around their middles. The walk or drive is beautiful at any time of the year, but in fall it's breathtaking. Like the rest of New England, the coast of Maine gets a large number of fall-foliage "leaf peepers," and the reds and golds of the chestnut, birch, and elm trees along this winding route are especially beautiful.

⊕ *www.mainelighthousemuseum.com* ⌂ *$5* ⊙ *Weekdays 9–5, weekends 10–4.*

NIGHTLIFE AND THE ARTS

FESTIVALS   More than a dozen well-known artists gather for the **North Atlantic Blues** ☾ **Festival** (☎ *207/593–1189* ⊕ *www.northatlanticbluesfestival.com*), a ★ two-day weekend affair held every July. The show officially takes place at Harbor Park, but it also includes a Blues Club Crawl Saturday night through downtown Rockland. Admission is $25 in advance, $30 at the gate. Rockland's annual **Maine Lobster Festival** (☎ *207/596–0376 or 800/562–2529* ⊕ *www.mainelobsterfestival.com*), in early August, is more than 60 years old and has become the biggest local event of the year. People come from all over the country to sample lobster in every possible form. During the few days of the festival about 10 tons of lobsters are steamed in the world's largest lobster cooker—you have to see it to believe it. The festival, held in Harbor Park, includes a parade, entertainment, craft and marine exhibits, food booths—and, of course, the crowning of the Maine Sea Goddess.

WHERE TO EAT

$$$–$$$$ ✕ **Primo.** Owner-chef Melissa Kelley and her world-class gourmet res-
CONTINENTAL   taurant in a restored Victorian home have won many awards and been
Fodor'sChoice   written about favorably in *Vanity Fair, Town and Country,* and *Food*
★   *and Wine.* The cuisine combines fresh Maine ingredients with Mediterranean influences. The menu, which changes daily, may include wood-roasted black sea bass, local crab–stuffed turbot, or diver-harvested scallop and basil ravioli. Pastry chef and co-owner Price Kushner creates unusual and delectable desserts such as Cannoli Siciliana, featuring crushed pistachios and amarena cherries. ⊠ *2 S. Main St., Rockland (on the border between Rockland and the little village of Owls Head; if you see the sign that reads "Welcome to Owls Head," you've passed Primo*

by 100 feet) ☎*207/596–0770* ⊕*www.primorestaurant.com* ▭*AE, D, MC, V* ☯ *Open Wed.–Sun. No lunch. Closed mid-Jan.–mid-Apr.*

$$ ✕ **Rockland Café.** It may not look like much from the outside, but the
SEAFOOD Rockland Café is probably the most popular eating establishment in
★ town. It's famous for the size of its breakfasts (get the fishcakes) and
is also open for lunch and dinner. At dinner, the seafood combo of
shrimp, scallops, clams, and fish is excellent, or there's the classic liver
and onions. ✉*441 S. Main St., Rockland* ☎*207/596–7556* ⊕*www.
rocklandcafe.com* ▭*AE, D, MC, V.*

WHERE TO STAY

$$$–$$$$ ⊞ **Berry Manor Inn.** Originally the residence of Rockland merchant
★ Charles H. Berry, this 1898 inn is in a historic residential neighbor-
hood. The large guest rooms of this B&B are elegantly furnished with
antiques and reproduction pieces. All rooms have fireplaces; TVs are
available upon request, and some rooms have whirlpools. A guest pan-
try is stocked with sweets. **Pros:** in a nice, quiet neighborhood; within
walking distance of downtown and the harbor. **Con:** not much of a
view. ✉*81 Talbot Ave.* ☎*207/596–7696 or 800/774–5692*⊕*www.
berrymanorinn.com* ☞*12 rooms* ⚲ *In-room: no TV, Wi-Fi* ▭*AE, MC,
V* ⦿⎮*BP.*

$$–$$$$ ⊞ **LimeRock Inn.** This inn is in the center of town, so you can easily walk
★ to the Farnsworth Museum or any of the other downtown attractions
and restaurants. The house is built in the Queen Anne–Victorian style,
and among the meticulously decorated rooms is one called Island Cottage, which features a whirlpool tub and doors that open onto a private
deck overlooking a garden. The Grand Manan room has a fireplace, a
whirlpool tub, and a four-poster king-size bed. TVs are available upon
request. **Pros:** this is like living in an old New England house; free
Wi-Fi. **Cons:** not much of a view. ✉*96 Limerock St.* ☎*207/594–2257
or 800/546–3762* ⊕*www.limerockinn.com* ☞*8 rooms* ⚲ *In-room: no
TV, Wi-Fi. In-hotel: Internet terminal* ▭*AE, D, MC, V* ⦿⎮*BP.*

ROCKPORT

10

4 mi north of Rockland on U.S. 1.

Heading north on U.S. 1, you come to Rockport before you reach the
tourist mecca of Camden. The most interesting part of Rockport—the
harbor—is not right on U.S. 1. You can get here by following the first
ROCKPORT sign you see off U.S. 1 at Pascal Road.

Originally called Goose River, the town was part of Camden until 1891.
The cutting and burning of limestone was once a major industry in this
area. The stone was cut in nearby quarries and then burned in hot kilns,
and the resulting lime powder was used to create mortar. Some of the
massive kilns are still here.

One of the most famous sights in Rockport is the **Rockport Arch,** which
crosses Union Street at the town line. It was constructed of wood and
mortar in 1926, demolished in 1984, then rebuilt by popular demand
in 1985. The arch has been displayed in a number of movies, including
Peyton Place and *In the Bedroom.*

ESSENTIALS

Visitor Information **Camden-Rockport-Lincolnville Chamber of Commerce**
(⊠ *2 Public Landing, Camden* ☎ *207/236–4404 www.visitcamden.com*).

WHERE TO EAT AND STAY

$$$–$$$$
FRENCH
Fodor's Choice
★

✕ **Marcel's.** If you're a serious gourmet and only have time to sample one dining experience in the Rockport-Rockland-Camden area, this lavish restaurant in the big Samoset Resort ought to be the one. Marcel's offers a fine array of Continental cuisine. Enjoy table-side preparation of a classic rack of lamb, chateaubriand, or steak Diane while admiring the bay view. The menu includes a variety of Maine seafood and a fine wine list. The Sunday brunch buffet has some of the finest seafood along the coast. ⊠ *220 Warrenton St., off U.S. 1* ☎ *207/594–2511* ⊕ *www.samoset.com* ⌀ *Reservations essential* ⌂ *Jacket required* ▭ *AE, D, MC, V* ☉ *No lunch.*

$$–$$$$
Fodor's Choice
★

▣ **Samoset Resort.** This 230-acre, all-encompassing oceanside resort on the Rockland–Rockport town line offers luxurious rooms and suites, all with a private balcony or patio and an ocean or garden view. The spacious rooms are decorated in deep green and burgundy tones. The resort has three dining options: Marcel's, the Breakwater Café, and the Clubhouse Grille. The flagship restaurant Marcel's ($$$–$$$$) features French and American cuisine, as well as seafood specials. Reservations are essential, and men must wear a jacket. For a less-formal affair, try the Breakwater Café ($$), featuring basic New England fare such as homemade chowder and lobster rolls; there's outdoor seating when the weather is nice. The Clubhouse Grille ($), catering to the golf crowd, serves casual food, which you can enjoy inside or on the porch. *Golf Digest* called the resort's 18-hole championship course the "Top Ranked Resort Course in New England," and the "Seventh Most Beautiful Course in America." Green fees range from $70 to $140. **Pros:** a resort property that seems to meet every need; airport shuttle. **Cons:** not within walking distance of Rockland or Camden shops. ⊠ *220 Warrenton St., Rockport* ☎ *207/594–2511 or 800/341–1650* ⊕ *www.samoset.com* ⇄ *156 rooms, 22 suites* ⌀ *In-room: Internet, Wi-Fi. In-hotel: 3 restaurants, bar, golf course, tennis courts, pools, gym, children's programs (ages 3–12), laundry service, Internet terminal* ▭ *AE, D, MC, V* ▯◯▮ *CP.*

CAMDEN

★   *2 mi north of Rockport.*

More than any other town along Penobscot Bay, Camden is the perfect picture-postcard of a Maine coastal village. It is one of the most popular destinations on the Maine Coast, so June through September the town is crowded with visitors, but don't let that scare you away; Camden is worth it. Just come prepared for busy traffic on the town's Main Street (U.S. 1) and make reservations for lodging and restaurants well in advance.

Camden is famous not only for its geography, but also for its large fleet of windjammers—relics and replicas from the age of sailing—with their romantic histories and great billowing sails. At just about any hour

The view from Camden Hills is a great way to see Penobscot Bay and the town of Camden.

during the warm months you're likely to see at least one windjammer tied up in the harbor. The excursions, whether for an afternoon or a week, are best from June through September.

The town's compact size makes it perfect for exploring on foot: shops, restaurants, and galleries line Main Street, as well as side streets and alleys around the harbor. Especially worth inclusion on your walking tour is Camden's residential area. It is quite charming and filled with many fascinating old period houses from the time when Federal, Greek Revival, and Victorian architecture were the rage among the wealthy. Many of them are now B&Bs. The chamber of commerce, at the Public Landing, can provide you with a walking map.

WHEN TO GO

FESTIVAL One of the biggest and most colorful events of the year in Camden is **Windjammer Weekend,** which usually takes place at the beginning of September and includes the single largest gathering of windjammer ships in the world, plus lots of good eats. ☎ *207/374–2993 or 800/807–9463* ⊕ *www.sailmainecoast.com.*

SPORTS AND THE OUTDOORS

Although their height may not be much more than 1,000 feet, the hills in **Camden Hills State Park** (⊠ *U.S. 1 just north of Camden* ☎ *207/236–3109*) are lovely landmarks for miles along the low, rolling reaches of the Maine Coast. The 5,500-acre park contains 25 mi of hiking trails, including the easy nature trail up Mt. Battie. Hike or drive to the top for a magnificent view over Camden and island-studded Penobscot Bay. There also is a campground here with 106 campsites.

SHOPPING

Camden's downtown area is a shopper's paradise with lots of interesting places to spend money. Most of the shops and galleries are along Camden's main drag. Start at the Camden Harbor, turn right on Bay View, and walk to Main/High Street. ■TIP→ U.S. 1 has three different names within the town limits—it starts as Elm Street, changes to Main Street, then becomes High Street.

Bayview Gallery (✉ *33 Bay View St.* ☎ *207/236–4534* ⊕ *www. bayviewgallery.com*) specializes in original art, prints, and posters, most with Maine themes. **Lili, Lupine & Fern** (✉ *44 Bayview St.* ☎ *207/236– 9600*) offers a wonderful array of gourmet foods, wines, and cheeses. **Planet Toys** (✉ *10 Main St.* ☎ *207/236–4410*) has unusual gifts—including books, toys, and clothing—from Maine and other parts of the world.

WHERE TO EAT

$$$–$$$$ ✕ **Atlantica.** Right on the water's edge, the Atlantica is in a historic clap-
SEAFOOD   board building. Its lower deck is cantilevered over the water, offering a romantic setting with great views, and the interior decor is a mix of red walls and contemporary paintings. Fresh seafood with French and Asian accents is the specialty here. Favorites include pan-roasted split lobster tails with lemon butter, lobster stuffed with scallops, and pan-roasted king salmon. ✉ *Bayview Landing* ☎ *207/236–6011 or 888/507–8514* ⊕ *www.atlanticarestaurant.com* ⌖ *Reservations essential* ▭ *AE, MC, V* ⊙ *No lunch.*

$–$$ ✕ **Cappy's Chowder House.** As you would expect from the name, Cappy's
SEAFOOD   "chowdah" is the thing to order here—it's been written up in the *New*
★   *York Times* and in *Bon Appétit* magazine—but there are plenty of other seafood specials on the menu. Don't be afraid to bring the kids—this place has many bargain meals. ✉ *1 Main St.* ☎ *207/236–2254* ⊕ *www. cappyschowder.com* ⌖ *Reservations not accepted* ▭ *MC, V.*

$$–$$$ ✕ **Natalie's.** This restaurant may be the most sought-after dining spot
FRENCH-   in Camden. It's the creation of Dutch owners Raymond Brunyanszki
AMERICAN   and Oscar Verest, and is in the Camden Harbour Inn. The restaurant is
Fodor'sChoice   fine dining with a French-American flair and offers a variety of prix-fixe
★   menus, such as "The Menu Saisonnier," which showcases fresh, seasonal ingredients, and the "Homard Grand Cru," a cascade of lobster dishes (lobster gazpacho, lobster with squid ink, lobster with fiddleheads, lobster with beef cheek and foie-gras ravioli). In the lounge enjoy a pre-dinner cocktail in front of the big fireplace. ✉ *83 Bay View St.* ☎ *207/236–7008* ⊕ *www.camdenharbourinn.com* ▭ *AE, D, MC, V.*

WHERE TO STAY

$$–$$$$ ⌂ **Camden Hartstone Inn.** This downtown 1835 mansard-roofed Victo-
★   rian home has been turned into an elegant and sophisticated retreat and a fine culinary destination. No detail has been overlooked, from soft robes, down comforters, and chocolate truffles in the guest rooms to china, crystal, and silver in the elegantly decorated dining room ($$$$). The inn hosts seasonal food festivals. **Pros:** excellent on-site restaurant. **Cons:** no water views, but the harbor and the downtown are not far away. ✉ *41 Elm St. (U.S. 1)* ☎ *207/236–4259 or 800/788–4823* ⊕ *www.*

hartstoneinn.com ⮌6 rooms, 6 suites ☖ In-room: Internet. In-hotel: restaurant ☰MC, V ⓄⒷ BP.

$$$–$$$$ ★ ⊡ **Lord Camden Inn.** If you want in the center of Camden and near the harbor, this is the place. The exterior of the building is red brick with bright blue-and-white awnings. The colorful interior is furnished with restored antiques and paintings by local artists. Despite being downtown, the inn offers plenty of ocean views from the upstairs rooms, and some rooms have lovely old-fashioned four-poster beds. There's no on-site restaurant, but plenty of dining options are within walking distance. **Pros:** central location. **Cons:** in the front rooms the U.S. 1 traffic may keep you awake. ⊠ *24 Main St. (U.S. 1)* ☏ *207/236–4325 or 800/336–4325* ⊕ *www.lordcamdeninn.com ⮌ 37 rooms ☖ In-room: refrigerator (some), DVD, Wi-Fi. In-hotel: gym, some pets allowed* ☰ *AE, MC, V* ⓄⒷ *BP.*

$$$–$$$$
Fodor's Choice
★
⊡ **Norumbega Inn.** This is the most photographed piece of real estate in the state of Maine, and once you take a look at it, you'll understand why. This castle B&B looks as if it were created by Stephen King (a Maine resident) or Count Dracula. It's easy to find, as it's right on U.S. 1, just a little north of downtown Camden. The outside consists of gray stone walls covered with ivy, but inside it's cheerier and elegant, with many of the antique-filled rooms offering fireplaces and private balconies overlooking the bay. The inn was built in 1886 by local businessman and inventor (of duplex telegraphy) Joseph Stearns. Before erecting his home, he spent a year visiting the castles of Europe and adapted the best ideas he found. He named the castle after what Maine was called in the 17th century, "Norumbega," and the home was converted into a B&B in 1984. **Pros:** beautiful views; close to town. **Cons:** guests who have difficulty climbing stairs will not find it comfortable ⊠ *63 High St. (U.S. 1)* ☏ *207/236–4646 or 877/363–4646* ⊕ *www.norumbegainn. com ⮌ 12 rooms ☖ In-room: no a/c, DVD (some), Wi-Fi. In-hotel: concierge service* ☰ *AE, MC, V* ⓄⒷ *BP.*

$$–$$$ ★ ⊡ **Whitehall Inn.** One of Camden's best-known inns, the Whitehall is an 1834 white-clapboard sea captain's home just north of town. The Millay Room, off the lobby, preserves memorabilia of the poet Edna St. Vincent Millay, who grew up in the area and read her poetry here. The inn is a delightful blend of the old and the new. The telephones are antiques, but the electronics are brand new. The rooms, remodeled in 2007, have dark-wood bedsteads, white bedspreads, and clawfoot tubs. The dining room serves traditional and creative American cuisine as well as many seafood specialties, and the popular prix-fixe dinner is $36 a person. **Pros:** connection to local poetess Edna St. Vincent Millay. **Cons:** only some rooms have water views. ⊠ *52 High St.* ☏ *207/236–3391 or 800/789–6565* ⊕ *www.whitehall-inn.com ⮌ 50 rooms, 45 with bath ☖ In-room: no a/c, Wi-Fi. In-hotel: restaurant, tennis court, Internet terminals* ☰ *AE, D, MC, V* ☯ *Closed mid-Oct.– mid-May* ⓄⒷ *BP.*

10

LINCOLNVILLE

6 mi north of Camden via U.S. 1.

Looking at a map, you may notice there are two parts to Lincolnville: Lincolnville Beach on U.S. 1 and the town of Lincolnville Center a little inland on Route 73. The area of most interest—where you can find the restaurants and the ferry to Islesboro—is Lincolnville Beach, which is tiny; you could be through it in less than a minute. Still, it has a history going back to the Revolution, and you can see a few small cannons on the beach that were intended to repel the British in the War of 1812 (they were never used).

WHERE TO EAT AND STAY

$$–$$$ ✕ **Lobster Pound Restaurant.** If you're looking for an authentic place to
SEAFOOD have your Maine lobster dinner, this is it. This simple restaurant looks
★ more like a cannery, with rustic wooden picnic tables and hundreds of live lobsters swimming in tanks—if you want, you can pick out your own, which will be served to you with clam chowder and corn. Forget about ordering a pre-dinner cocktail or wine with dinner (sorry, no bar service); have an iced tea instead. On U.S. 1, right on the edge of the sea, the restaurant provides beautiful views from both its indoor and outdoor seating. The menu includes the classic "Shore Dinner," which consists of lobster stew or fish chowder, steamed or fried clams, 1½-pound lobster, potato, and dessert. There is seating for nearly 300, so even if it's a busy time, you won't have to wait long. There's also a 70-seat picnic area if you want to take your food to go. ⊠ *2521 Atlantic Hwy. (U.S. 1)* ☎ *207/789–5550* ⊕ *www.lobsterpoundmaine.com* ▭ *AE, D, MC, V* ⊗ *Closed Nov.–Apr.*

ISLESBORO

★ *3 mi east of Lincolnville via Islesboro Ferry (terminal on U.S. 1).*

Islesboro is only a 20-minute ferry ride off the mainland, and you can take your car with you. The drive from one end of the island to the other (on the island's only road) is lovely. It takes you through Warren State Park, a nice place to stop for a picnic and the only public camping area on the island. There are two stores on the island where you can buy supplies for your picnic: the Island Market is a short distance from the ferry terminal on the main road, and Durkee's General Store is 5 mi farther north at 863 Main Road. Next to the island's ferry terminal are the Sailor's Memorial Museum and the Grindle Point Lighthouse, both worth a brief look.

The permanent year-round population of Islesboro is about 625, but it swells to around 3,000 in summer. Most of the people who live on the island full time earn their living in one way or another from the sea.

The **Islesboro Ferry,** operated by the Maine State Ferry Service, departs from Lincolnville Harbor, a few hundred feet from the Lobster Pound Restaurant. Try to head out on one of the early ferries so you have enough time to drive around and get back. If you miss the last ferry, you'll have to stay on the island overnight. The ferry runs back and forth nine times a day from April through October and seven times a day from November through March. There are fewer trips on Sunday. The round-trip cost for a vehicle and one passenger is $22.25, slightly more with additional passengers, less if you leave the vehicle behind. Call *207/789–5611* for schedules.

⚠ If you are just visiting the island and don't have friends there to stay with, make sure that you don't miss the last ferry. There are NO public accommodations on the island. You would have to sleep in your car.

BELFAST

10 mi north of Lincolnville, 46 mi northeast of Augusta.

A number of Maine coastal towns, such as Wiscasset and Damariscotta, like to think of themselves as the prettiest little town in Maine, but Belfast (originally to be named Londonderry) may be the true winner of this title. It has a full variety of charms: a beautiful waterfront; an old and interesting main street climbing up from the harbor; a delightful array of B&Bs, restaurants, and shops; and a friendly population. The downtown even has old-fashioned streetlamps, which set the streets aglow at night. If you like looking at old houses, many of which go all the way back to the American Revolution and are in the Federal and Colonial style, just drive up and down some of the side streets.

EXPLORING

In the mid-1800s Belfast was home to a number of wealthy business magnates. Their mansions still stand along High Street, offering some excellent examples of Greek Revival and Federal architecture. The **Belfast Chamber of Commerce Visitor Center** (✉ *14 Main St.[a block from the harbor]* ☎ *207/338–5900* ⊕ *www.belfastmaine.org*) has a large array of magazines, guidebooks, maps, and brochures that cover the entire Mid-Coast. It also can provide you with a free walking-tour brochure that describes the various historic homes and buildings, as well as the old business section in the harbor area. Ask the staff to tell you about the Museum in the Streets signage.

NIGHTLIFE AND THE ARTS

★ **Rollie's Bar & Grill** (✉ *37 Main St.* ☎ *207/338–4502* ⊕ *www.rollies. me.com* ▭ *MC, V*) looks like it's been here 100 years, but actually it's only since 1972. The tavern is right in the heart of town, and at first glance it might look like a biker bar. It is that—and a lot more. The vintage bar is from an 1800s sailing ship. Rollie's is the most popular watering spot in town with the locals, and it just may serve the best hamburgers in the state of Maine. It also has a sister site in nearby Searsport with the same name and fare, on U.S. 1.

WHERE TO EAT AND STAY

$–$$ ✕ **Darby's Restaurant and Pub.** Darby's, a charming old-fashioned restau-
CONTINENTAL rant and bar, is very popular with locals. The building, with pressed-tin
★ ceilings, was constructed in 1865 and has been a bar or a restaurant ever since. The antique bar is original. Artwork on the walls is by locals and may be purchased. A lot of the regular items on the menu, such as the pad thai and the Seafood à la Greque, are quite unusual for a small-town restaurant. It also has hearty homemade soups and

Learn about Maine's seafaring heritage at the Penobscot Marine Museum.

sandwiches, as well as dishes with an international flavor. ⊠ *155 High St.* ☎ *207/338–2339* ⊕ *www.darbysrestaurant.com* ▤ *AE, D, MC, V.*

$$–$$$　✕ **Young's Lobster Pound.** The place looks more like a corrugated-steel
SEAFOOD　fish cannery than a restaurant, but it is one of the best places to have
★　an authentic Maine lobster dinner. Young's sits right on the edge of
the water, across the river from Belfast Harbor (cross Veterans Bridge
and turn right on Mitchell Avenue). When you first walk in, you'll
see tanks and tanks of live lobsters of varying size. The traditional
meal here is the Shore Dinner: fish or clam chowder; steamed clams
or mussels; a 1½-pound boiled lobster; corn on the cob; and rolls and
butter. Order your dinner at the counter, then find a table inside or on
the deck. ■TIP➔ **If you are enjoying your lobster at one of the outside
tables, don't leave the table with no one to watch it. Seagulls are notorious thieves—and they LOVE lobster.** ⊠ *2 Fairview St.* ☎ *207/338–1160*
⊕ *www.youngslobsterpound.com* ▤ *AE, D, MC, V* ☾ *Closed Labor
Day–Easter.*

$–$$$　🛏 **Penobscot Bay Inn & Restaurant.** This lovely accommodation is on 5
Fodor'sChoice　meadowed acres overlooking Penobscot Bay and is owned and man-
★　aged by Kristina and Valentinas Kurapka. The rooms are bright and
decorated in pastel shades, with old-fashioned New England quilts on
the beds. Some rooms even have their own fireplaces. The inn's Con-
tinental gourmet restaurant ($$–$$$$) is one of the best in the area.
Pros: you don't have to go out for dinner. **Cons:** no special views from
the restaurant; a drive to Belfast's colorful downtown. ⊠ *192 Northport
Ave.* ☎ *207/338–5715 or 800/335–2370* ⊕ *www.penobscotbayinn.com*
⤺ *19 rooms* ⚬ *In-room: refrigerator (some). In-hotel: restaurant*, bar
▤ *AE, D, MC, V* ⚭*BP.*

SEARSPORT

6 mi northeast of Belfast; 57 mi northeast of Augusta.

Searsport is well known as the antiques and flea-market capital of Maine and with good reason: the Antique Mall alone, on U.S. 1 just north of town, contains the offerings of 70 dealers, and flea markets during the visitor season line both sides of U.S. 1.

Searsport also has a rich history of shipbuilding and seafaring. In the early to mid-1800s there were 10 shipbuilding facilities in Searsport, and the population of the town was about 1,000 people more than it is today because of the ready availability of jobs. By the mid-1800s Searsport was home to more than 200 sailing-ship captains.

ESSENTIALS

Visitor Information Searsport Chamber of Commerce (✉ *1 Union St., Searsport* ☎ *207/548-0173* ⊕ *www.searsportme.com*).

EXPLORING

Ⓒ **Penobscot Marine Museum.** This museum is dedicated to the history of

Fodor'sChoice Penobscot Bay and Maine's maritime history. Exhibits, artifacts, sou-

★ venirs, and paintings are displayed in a unique setting of seven historic buildings, including two sea captains' houses and five other buildings in an original seaside village. The museum's outstanding collection of marine art includes the largest gathering in the country of works by Thomas and James Buttersworth. Also of note are photos of local sea captains; a collection of China-trade merchandise; artifacts of life at sea (including lots of scrimshaw); navigational instruments; tools from the area's history of logging, granite cutting, fishing, and ice cutting; treasures collected by seafarers from around the globe; and models of famous ships. ✉ *5 E. Main St. (U.S. 1)* ☎ *207/548-2529* ⊕ *www. penobscotmarinemuseum.org* 🖾 *$8* ⊙ *Memorial Day–mid-Oct., Mon.– Sat. 10–5, Sun. noon–5.*

SHOPPING

ANTIQUES

All Small Antiques (✉ *357 W. Main St.* ☎ *207/338–1613*) has just what the name implies. In the very heart of town, **Captain Tinkham's Emporium** (✉ *34 E. Main St.* ☎ *207/548–6465*) offers antiques, collectibles, old books, magazines, records, paintings, and prints. The biggest collection of antiques is in the **Searsport Antique Mall** (✉ *149 E. Main St. [U.S. 1]* ☎ *207/548–2640*), which has more than 70 dealers.

BUCKSPORT

9 mi north of Searsport via U.S. 1.

The new Penobscot Narrows Bridge, spanning the Penobscot River, welcomes visitors to Bucksport, a town founded in 1763 by Jonathan Buck. Bucksport was the site of the second worst naval defeat in American history (the first was Pearl Harbor), in 1779, when a British Armada defeated the fledgling American Navy. It became known as "the disaster on the Penobscot." You can learn more about it at the museum in Bucksport or at the Penobscot Marine Museum in Searsport.

EXPLORING

Penobscot Narrows Bridge & Observatory Tower/Fort Knox Historic Site. These two attractions, which previously were considered separate, have been combined into one—with one admission—as they are right next to each other. The 2,120-foot-long Penobscot Narrows Bridge, opened at the end of 2006, has been declared an engineering marvel. It is certainly beautiful to look at or to drive over (no toll). Spanning the Penobscot River at Bucksport, the bridge replaced the old Waldo-Hancock Bridge, built in 1931. The best part is the observation tower at the top of the western pylon, the first bridge observation tower in the country and, at 420 feet above the river, the highest in the world. An elevator shoots you to the top for $5, which includes a visit to the nearby Fort Knox Historic Site. Don't miss it—the view, which encompasses the river, the bay, and the sea beyond, is breathtaking.

Fodor's Choice ★

Fort Knox is the largest fort in Maine and was built between 1844 and 1869, when the British were disputing the border between Maine and New Brunswick. It was intended to protect the Penobscot River valley from a British naval attack. The fort never saw any actual fighting, but it was used for troop training and a garrison during the Civil War and the Spanish-American War. Visitors are welcome to explore the fort's passageways and many rooms. Guided tours are available during the summer season. ⌧ *711 Ft. Knox Rd., at U.S. 1, Prospect* ☎ *207/469–6553* ⊕ *www.maine.gov/observatory* ☉ *Open Sept.–June 9–5, July and Aug. 9–6.*

BANGOR

133 mi northeast of Portland, 20 mi northwest of Bucksport, 46 mi west of Bar Harbor.

The second-largest city in the state (Portland being the largest), Bangor is about 20 mi from the coast and is the unofficial capital of northern Maine. Back in the 19th century the "Queen City's" most important product and export was lumber from the state's vast North Woods. Now, because of its airport, Bangor has become a gateway to Mount Desert Island, Bar Harbor, and Acadia National Park.

ESSENTIALS

Visitor Information Greater Bangor Convention & Visitors Bureau (⌧ *40 Harlow St., Bangor* ☎ *207/947–5205 or 800/91–MOOSE [916–6673]* ⊕ *www. bangorcvb.org*).

EXPLORING

Maine Discovery Museum. The largest children's museum north of Boston, the Maine Discovery Museum has three floors with more than 60 interactive exhibits. Kids can explore Maine's ecosystem in Nature Trails, travel to foreign countries in Passport to the World, and walk through Maine's literary classics in Booktown. ⌧ *74 Main St.* ☎ *207/262–7200* ⊕ *www.mainediscoverymuseum.org* ⌸ *$7.50* ☉ *Tues.–Sat. 9:30–5, Sun. 11–5.*

WHERE TO STAY

$$–$$$

Fodor'sChoice

★

🏨 **Lucerne Inn.** This is one of the most famous and respected inns in New England. Nestled in the mountains, the Lucerne overlooks beautiful Phillips Lake. The inn was established in 1814, and in keeping with that history every room is furnished with antiques. The rooms all have a view of the lake, gas-burning fireplaces, and a whirlpool tub; some have wet bars, refrigerators, and balconies as well. There's a golf course directly across the street. The inn's restaurant ($$–$$$$) is nearly as famous as the inn itself and draws many locals for its lavish Sunday brunch buffet. The traditional dinner is the boiled Maine lobster. The inn is about 15 mi from Bangor. **Pros:** some rooms have lovely views of Phillips Lake (you can request one). **Cons:** some rooms are a little on the shabby side. ⌂ *2517 Main St. (Rte. 1A), Dedham* ☎ *207/843–5123 or 800/325–5123* ⊕ *www.lucerneinn.com* 🛏 *31 rooms, 4 suites* ⚬ *In-room: Wi-Fi. In-hotel: restaurant, bar, pool* ═ *AE, D, MC, V* ⦿*CP.*

THE BLUE HILL PENINSULA

Updated
by George
Semler

If you want to see unspoiled Down East Maine land- and seascapes, explore art galleries, savor exquisite meals, or simply enjoy life at an unhurried pace, you should be quite content on the Blue Hill Peninsula.

The peninsula, approximately 16 mi wide and 20 mi long, juts south into Penobscot Bay. Not far from the mainland are the islands of Deer Isle, Little Deer Isle, and the picturesque fishing town of Stonington. A twisting labyrinth of roads winds through blueberry barrens and around picturesque coves, linking the towns of Blue Hill, Brooksville, Sedgwick, and Brooklin. Blue Hill and Castine are the area's primary business hubs.

Painters, photographers, sculptors, and other artists are drawn to the area. You can find more than 20 galleries on Deer Isle and in Stonington and at least half as many on the mainland. With its small inns, charming B&Bs, and outstanding restaurants scattered across the area, the Blue Hill Peninsula may just persuade you to leave the rest of the coastline to the tourists.

10

VISITOR INFORMATION

Contacts Blue Hill Peninsula Chamber of Commerce (⌂ *107 Main St., Blue Hill* ☎ *207/374-3242* ⊕ *www.bluehillpeninsula.org*). **Deer Isle–Stonington Chamber of Commerce** (⌂ *Rte. 15, Deer Isle* ☎ *207/348-6124* ⊕ *www. deerisle.com*).

CASTINE

30 mi southeast of Searsport.

A summer destination for more than 100 years, Castine is a well-preserved seaside village rich in history. The French established a trading post here in 1613, naming the area Pentagoet. A year later Captain John Smith claimed the area for the British. The French regained control of the peninsula with the 1667 Breda Treaty, and Jean Vincent d'Abbadie de St. Castin obtained a land grant in the Pentagoet area, which would later bear his name. Castine's strategic position on Penobscot Bay and its importance as a trading post meant there were many battles for control until 1815. In the 19th century Castine was an important port for trading ships and fishing vessels. The Civil War and the advent of train travel brought its prominence as a port to an end, but by the late 1800s some of the nation's wealthier citizens had discovered Castine as a pleasant summer retreat.

EXPLORING

Federal- and Greek Revival–style architecture and spectacular views of Penobscot Bay make Castine an ideal spot to spend a day or two. Explore its lively harbor front, two small museums (the Wilson Museum and the Castine Historical Society), and the ruins of a British fort. For a nice stroll, park your car at the landing and walk up Main Street toward the white Trinitarian Federated Church. Among the white-clapboard buildings ringing the town common are the Ives House (once the summer home of poet Robert Lowell), the Abbott School, and the Unitarian Church, capped by a whimsical belfry.

SPORTS AND THE OUTDOORS

At Eaton's Wharf, **Castine Kayak Adventures** (⊠ *17 Sea St.* ☎ *207/866–3506* ⊕ *www.castinekayak.com*) operates tours run by owner Karen Francoeur, a master Maine Sea Kayak Instructor and Registered Maine Guide. Sign up for a half-day of kayaking along the shore; a full day of kayaking by shipwrecks, reversing falls, and islands in Penobscot Bay; or an extended five-to-seven-day kayaking trip to the Outer Islands with the mothership *Wanderbird* (⊕ *www.wanderbirdcruises.com*), a refurbished 90-foot fishing boat, as base camp.

WHERE TO EAT

$$
AMERICAN

✕ **Dennett's Wharf.** Originally built as a sail-rigging loft in the early 1800s, this longtime favorite is a good place for oysters and fresh seafood of all kinds. The waterfront restaurant also serves burgers, sandwiches, and light fare. There are several microbrews on tap, including the tasty Dennett's Wharf Rat Ale. Eat in the dining room or outside on the deck. ⊠ *15 Sea St.* ☎ *207/326–9045* ⊕ *www.dennettswharf.net* ⊟ *MC, V* ☺ *Closed Columbus Day–May.*

BLUE HILL

19 mi east of Castine.

Snuggled between 943-foot Blue Hill Mountain and Blue Hill Bay, the village of Blue Hill sits cozily beside its harbor. Originally known for its granite quarries, copper mines, and shipbuilding, today the town is known for its pottery and galleries, bookstores, antiques shops, and studios that line its streets. The Blue Hill Fair (⊕ *www.bluehillfair.com*), held Labor Day weekend, is a tradition in these parts, with agricultural exhibits, food, rides, and entertainment.

SHOPPING

ART GALLERIES

★

Blue Hill Bay Gallery (⊠ *11 Tenny Hill* ☎ *207/374–5773* ⊕ *www. bluehillbaygallery.com* ⊗ *Memorial Day–Labor Day, daily; mid-May–Memorial Day and Labor Day–mid-October, weekends*) sells oil and watercolor paintings of the local landscape. Bird carvings and other items are also available. **Leighton Gallery** (⊠ *24 Parker Point Rd.* ☎ *207/374–5001* ⊕ *www.leightongallery.com*) shows oil paintings, lithographs, watercolors, and other contemporary art. Outside, granite, bronze, and wood sculptures are displayed in a gardenlike setting under apple trees and white pines.

POTTERY

Rackliffe Pottery (⊠ *126 Ellsworth Rd.* ☎ *207/374–2297*) sells colorful pottery made with lead-free glazes. You can choose between water pitchers, tea-and-coffee sets, and sets of canisters. **Rowantrees Pottery** (⊠ *9 Union St.* ☎ *207/374–5535*) has an extensive selection of dinnerware, tea sets, vases, and decorative items. The shop makes many of the same pieces it did 60 years ago, so if you break a favorite item, you can find a replacement.

WINE

In what was once a barn out behind one of Blue Hill's earliest houses, the **Blue Hill Wine Shop** (⊠ *138 Main St.* ⊹ *halfway between intersection of Rtes. 172 and 176 and Rte. 15 in center of town* ☎ *207/374–2161*) carries more than 1,000 carefully selected wines. Wine tastings are held the last Saturday of every month.

WHERE TO EAT AND STAY

$$$

CONTINENTAL

Fodor's Choice

★

✕ **Arborvine.** Glowing (albeit ersatz) fireplaces, period antiques, exposed beams, and hardwood floors covered with Oriental rugs adorn each of the four candlelit dining rooms in this renovated Cape Cod–style house. Begin with a salad of mixed greens, sliced beets, and pears with blue cheese crumbled on top. For your entrée, choose from dishes such as medallions of beef and goat cheese with shoestring potatoes or pork tenderloin with sweet cherries in a port-wine reduction. The specials and fresh fish dishes are superb, as are the crab cakes. Save room for dessert; the lemon mousse and the creamy cheesecake are especially delicious. A take-out lunch menu is available at the adjacent Moveable Feasts deli, where the Vinery piano bar offers drinks, tapas, and live music in the evening. ⊠ *33 Tenney Hill* ☎ *207/374–2119* ⊕ *www. arborvine.com* ⊟ *AE, DC, MC, V* ⊗ *Closed Mon. and Tues. Sept.– June. No lunch.*

$$$–$$$$

★

🛏 **Blue Hill Inn.** This 1830 inn is a comfortable place to relax after climbing Blue Hill Mountain or exploring nearby shops and galleries. Original pumpkin pine and painted floors set the tone for the mix of Empire and early-Victorian pieces that fill the two parlors and the guest rooms, several of which have working fireplaces. One of the nicest rooms is No. 8, which has exposures on three sides and views of the flower gardens and apple trees. Two rooms have antique claw-foot tubs. The inn has a bar offering an ample selection of wines and whiskies where you can enjoy appetizers before you head out to dinner or try specialty coffees and liqueurs when you return. **Pros:** the bedroom fireplaces and the antique floorboards make you want to stay here forever. **Cons:** some rooms are on the small side; walls are thin. ⊠ *40 Union St.* ☎ *207/374– 2844 or 800/826–7415* ⊕ *www.bluehillinn.com* ⊅ *11 rooms, 2 suites*

10

⚥ *In-room: no phone, no TV. In-hotel: bar, Internet terminal, Wi-Fi hotspot* ⊟ *AE, MC, V* ⊚⦙ *BP.*

SEDGWICK, BROOKLIN, AND BROOKSVILLE

Winding through the hills, the roads leading to the villages of Sedgwick, Brooklin, and Brooksville take you past rambling farmhouses, beautiful coves, and blueberry barrens studded with occasional masses of granite. From the causeway at Sedgwick to the Deer Isle Bridge along Route 175 an anthology of typical Maine farmhouses lines the road, while the view from Caterpillar Hill merits a special detour.

Incorporated in 1798, **Sedgwick** runs along much of Eggemoggin Reach, the body of water that separates the mainland from Deer Isle, Little Deer Isle, and Stonington. The village of **Brooklin,** originally part of Sedgwick, established itself as an independent town in 1849. Today it is home to the world-famous Wooden Boat School, a 64-acre oceanfront campus offering courses in woodworking, boatbuilding, and seamanship. The town of **Brooksville,** incorporated in 1817, is almost completely surrounded by water, with Eggemoggin Reach, Walker Pond, and the Bagaduce River marking its boundaries.

WHERE TO EAT AND STAY

¢–$ ✕ **Bagaduce Lunch.** Winner of a 2008 James Beard Award, this little
AMERICAN fried-fish specialist next to the reversing falls on the Bagaduce River,
Fodor's Choice 7 mi west of Blue Hill, is the perfect place for a lunch of clams, scallops,
★ halibut, and onion rings. Seals, bald eagles, ospreys, and (sometimes) striped bass provide natural entertainment in this rich tidal estuary. ✉ *145 Franks Flat Rd., Brooksville* ☎ *207/326–4197* ⊟ *No credit cards* ⊗ *Closed Sept. 15–June 15.*

$–$$ ⌂ **Brooklin Inn.** This B&B in downtown Brooklin has plenty of homey
★ touches like hardwood floors and an upstairs deck. The sunny rooms have attractive bureaus and beds piled with cozy quilts. The restaurant ($$–$$$$) specializes in fresh fish and locally raised beef, poultry, and lamb. It also has fine soups, salads, and desserts worth saving room for. In summer you can dine on the enclosed porch. An Irish pub downstairs showcases local musicians most Saturday nights. **Pros:** relaxing; on-site dining. **Cons:** rooms are small; walls are paper-thin. ✉ *Rte. 175, Brooklin* ☎ *207/359–2777* ⊕ *www.brooklininn.com* ⤶ *5 rooms, 3 with bath* ⚥ *In-room: no phone, no a/c, no TV. In-hotel: restaurant, Wi-Fi hotspot* ⊟ *AE, D, DC, MC, V.*

DEER ISLE VILLAGE

16 mi south of Blue Hill.

Around Deer Isle Village, thick woods give way to tidal coves. Stacks of lobster traps populate the backyards of shingled houses, and dirt roads lead to secluded summer cottages. This region is prized by artists, and studios and galleries are plentiful.

EXPLORING

Haystack Mountain School of Crafts. Want to learn a new craft? This school offers two- and three-week courses for people of all skill levels in blacksmithing, basketry, printmaking, and weaving. Artisans from around the world present evening lectures throughout summer. Free tours of the facility are at 1 on Wednesdays, June through September. The school is 6 mi from Deer Isle Village, off Route 15. ⊠ *89 Haystack School Dr.* ☎ *207/348–2306* ⊕ *www.haystack-mtn.org* ⊠ *Free (tours)* ⊙ *Daily, June–Sept.*

Enjoying miles of woodland and shore trails at the **Edgar M. Tennis Preserve** (⊠ *Tennis Rd. off Sunshine Rd.* ☎ *No phone* ⊠ *Free* ⊙ *Daily dawn–dusk*). Look for hawks, eagles, and ospreys and wander among old apple trees, fields of wildflowers, and ocean-polished rocks.

SHOPPING

Purchase a handmade quilt from **Dockside Quilt Gallery** (⊠ *928 Sunshine Rd.* ☎ *207/348–2849* ⊕ *www.docksidequiltgallery.com*). Call for an appointment to see quilts. **Nervous Nellie's Jams and Jellies** (⊠ *598 Sunshine Rd.* ☎ *207/348–6182 or 800/777–6845* ⊕ *www.nervousnellies. com*) sells jams and jellies, operates the Mountainville Café, and has a woods and meadow sculpture park with more than 75 works by sculptor Peter Beerits.

STONINGTON

7 mi south of Deer Isle.

Stonington is at the southern end of Route 15, which has helped it retain its unspoiled small-town flavor. The boutiques and galleries lining Main Street cater mostly to out-of-towners, though the town remains a fishing community at heart. The principal activity is at the waterfront, where boats arrive overflowing with the day's catch. The sloped island that rises to the south is Isle au Haut, which contains a remote section of Acadia National Park; it's accessible by mail boat from Stonington.

EXPLORING

Deer Isle Granite Museum. This tiny museum documents Stonington's quarrying tradition. The museum's centerpiece is an 8-by-15-foot working model of quarrying operations on Crotch Island and the town of Stonington at the turn of the last century. ⊠ *51 Main St.* ☎ *207/367–6331* ⊠ *Free* ⊙ *Memorial Day–Labor Day, Mon.–Sat. 10–5, Sun. 1–5.*

SPORTS AND THE OUTDOORS

Old Quarry Ocean Adventures (⊠ *130 Settlement Rd.* ☎ *207/367–8977* ⊕ *www.oldquarry.com*) rents bicycles, canoes, and kayaks and offers guided tours of the bay. Captain Bill Baker's three-hour boat tours leave from Webb Cove and take you past Stonington Harbor on the way to the outer islands. You can see Crotch Island, which has one of the area's two active stone quarries, and Green Island, where you can take a dip in a water-filled quarry. Tours cover the region's natural history, the history of Stonington, and the history of the granite industry.

10

WHERE TO EAT AND STAY

$–$$ ✕ **Lily's.** Homemade baked goods, delicious sandwiches, and fresh salads
AMERICAN   are on the menu at this cheerful café. Try the Italian turkey sandwich,
★   which has slices of oven-roasted turkey and Jack cheese on homemade
sourdough bread. ⊠ *450 Airport Rd. (Corner of Rte. 15 and Airport
Rd.)* ☎ *207/367–5936* ▭ *MC, V.*

CAMPING   △ **Old Quarry Campground.** This oceanfront campground offers both
¢   open and wooded campsites with raised platforms for tents, tables,
chairs, and fire rings. Carts are available to tote your gear to your site.
Another property, Sunshine Campground, is on Deer Isle. **Pro:** campsites on the water have spectacular views. **Con:** somewhat uproarious
in August. ⊠ *130 Settlement Rd., off Oceanville Rd.* ☎ *207/367–8977*
⊕ *www.oldquarry.com* 🛏 *10 tent sites* 🛆 *Flush toilets, drinking water,
guest laundry, showers, public telephone, Wi-Fi, general store, swimming* ▭ *MC, V* ☉ *Closed Nov.–Apr.*

ISLE AU HAUT

14 mi south of Stonington.

Isle au Haut thrusts its steeply ridged back out of the sea south of
Stonington. French explorer Samuel D. Champlain discovered Isle au
Haut—or "High Island"—in 1604, but heaps of shells suggest that
native populations lived on or visited the island prior to his arrival. The
island is accessible only by mail boat, but the 45-minute journey is well
worth the effort. The ferry makes two trips a day between Stonington
and the Town Landing from Monday to Saturday and adds one Sunday
from mid-May to mid-September. From mid-June to mid-September the
ferry also stops at Duck Harbor, within Acadia National Park, where
it will not unload bicycles, kayaks, or canoes.

Except for a grocery store, a chocolatier, the Sea Urchin gift shop, and
a natural-foods store, Isle au Haut is not a shopping excursion. The
island is ideal for day-trippers intent on exploring its miles of trails or
those seeking a night or two of low-key accommodations and delicious
homemade meals at the Inn at Isle au Haut.

WHERE TO STAY

$$$$ ⊡ **Inn at Isle au Haut.** This sea captain's home from 1897 retains its
Fodor'sChoice   architectural charm. On the eastern side of the island, the seaside inn
★   has views of sheep roaming around distant York Island and Cadillac
Mountain. Comfortable wicker furniture is scattered around the porch,
where appetizers are served when the weather is good. Downstairs, the
dining room has original oil lamps and a model of the sea captain's boat
(which sank just offshore). Breakfast includes granola and a hot dish
like a spinach, tomato, and cheese frittata. Dinner is an elaborate five-
course meal usually incorporating local seafood. The first-floor Captain's Quarters, the only room with a private bath, has an ocean view,
as do two of the three upstairs rooms. All have colorful quilts and frilly
canopies. **Pros:** nonpareil views; first-class dining. **Cons:** shared baths.
⊠ *78 Atlantic Ave.* ☎ *207/335–5141* ⊕ *www.innatisleauhaut.com* 🛏 *4
rooms, 1 with bath* 🛆 *In-room: no phone, no a/c, no TV. In-hotel:
bicycles* ▭ *No credit cards* ☉ *Closed Oct.–May* ⏵❙ *MAP.*

ACADIA NATIONAL PARK AND MOUNT DESERT ISLAND

Updated
by George
Semler

With some of the most dramatic and varied scenery on the Maine Coast and home to Maine's only national park, Mount Desert Island (pronounced "Mount Dessert" by locals) is Maine's most popular tourist destination, attracting more than 2 million visitors a year. Much of the approximately 12-by-9-mi island belongs to Acadia National Park. The rocky coastline rises starkly from the ocean, appreciable along the scenic drives. Trails for hikers of all skill levels lead to the rounded tops of the mountains, providing views of Frenchman and Blue Hill bays and beyond. Ponds and lakes beckon you to swim, fish, or boat. Ferries and charter boats provide a different perspective on the island and a chance to explore the outer islands, all of which are part of Maine but not necessarily of Mount Desert. A network of old carriage roads lets you explore Acadia's wooded interior, filled with birds and other wildlife.

Mount Desert Island has four different townships, each with its own personality. The town of Bar Harbor is on the northeastern corner of the island and includes Bar Harbor and the little villages of Hulls Cove, Salisbury Cove, and Town Hill. The town of Mount Desert comprises the southeastern corner of the island and parts of the western edge and includes Mount Desert and the little villages of Somesville, Hall Quarry, Beech Hill, Pretty Marsh, Northeast Harbor, Seal Harbor, and Otter Creek. As its name suggests, the town of Southwest Harbor is on the southwestern corner of the island, although the town of Tremont is at the southernmost tip of the west side. This area includes the villages of Southwest Harbor, Manset, Bass Harbor, Bernard, and Seal Cove. The island's major tourist destination is Bar Harbor, which has plenty of accommodations, restaurants, and shops. Less congested are the smaller communities of Northeast Harbor, Southwest Harbor, and Bass Harbor. Mount Desert Island is a place with three personalities: the hustling, bustling tourist mecca of Bar Harbor; the "quiet side" of the island composed of the little villages; and the vast natural expanse that is Acadia National Park.

ESSENTIALS

Visitor Information Bar Harbor Chamber of Commerce (✉ *1201 Bar Harbor Rd., Bar Harbor* ☎ *207/288–5103* ⊕ *www.barharbormaine.com*). **Mount Desert Chamber of Commerce** (✉ *18 Harbor Rd., Northeast Harbor* ☎ *207/276–5040* ⊕ *www.mountdesertchamber.org*). **Mount Desert Island Chambers and Acadia National Park Information Center** (✉ *Rte. 3, Thompson Island* ☎ *207/288–3411* ⊕ *www.acadiachamber.com*).

BAR HARBOR

160 mi northeast of Portland; 22 mi southeast of Ellsworth.

A resort town since the 19th century, Bar Harbor is the artistic, culinary, and social center of Mount Desert Island. It also serves visitors to Acadia National Park with inns, motels, and restaurants. Around the turn of the last century the island was known as the summer haven of the

10

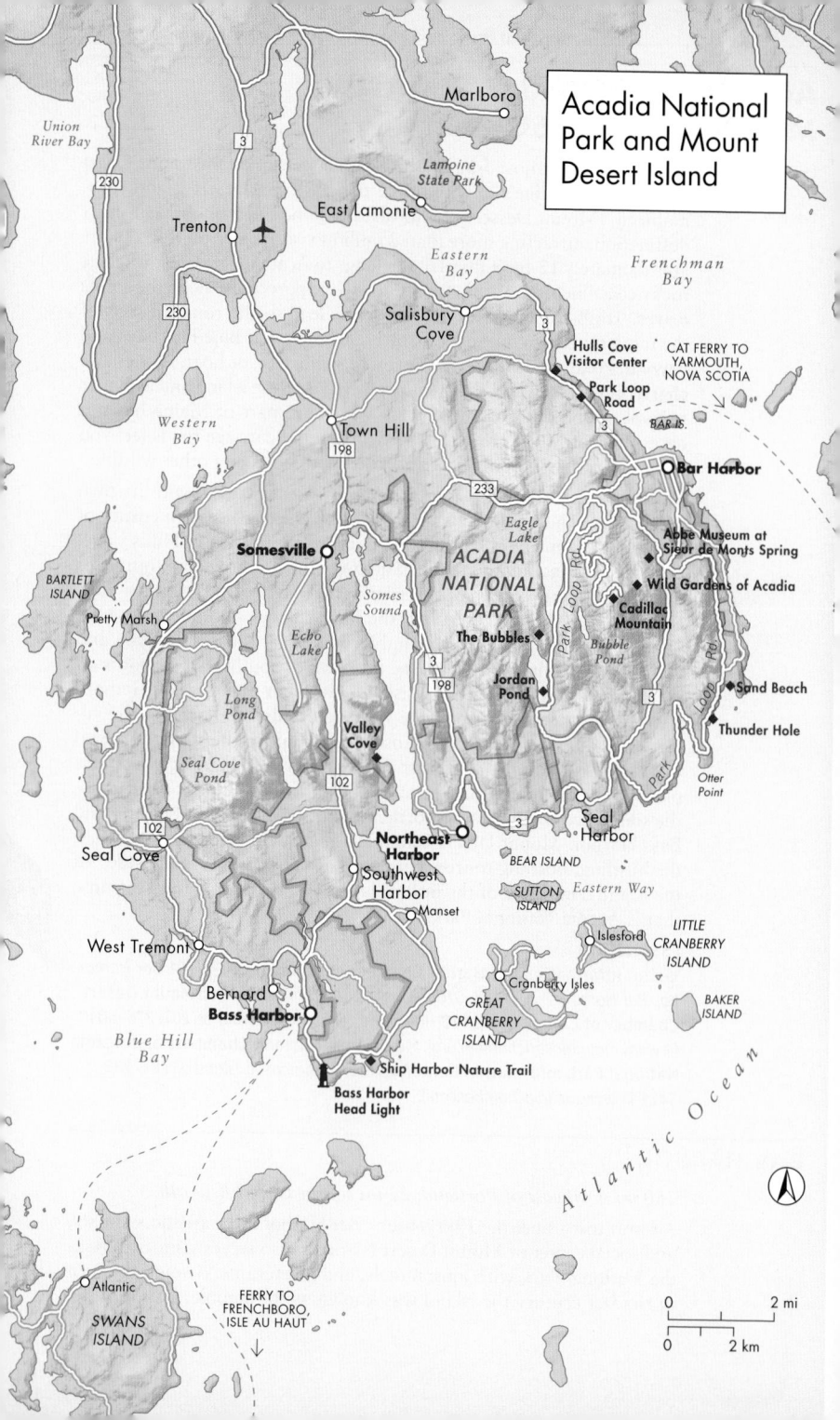

Acadia National Park and Mount Desert Island

Union River Bay

Marlboro

3

230

Lamoine State Park

East Lamoine

Trenton

Eastern Bay

Frenchman Bay

230

Salisbury Cove

3

Hulls Cove Visitor Center

CAT FERRY TO YARMOUTH, NOVA SCOTIA

Park Loop Road

3

Town Hill

198

BAR IS.

Bar Harbor

233

Western Bay

BARTLETT ISLAND

Somesville

Eagle Lake

Abbe Museum at Sieur de Monts Spring

Wild Gardens of Acadia

ACADIA NATIONAL PARK

Cadillac Mountain

Pretty Marsh

Somes Sound

The Bubbles

Bubble Pond

Echo Lake

3

198

Jordan Pond

Park Loop Rd.

Sand Beach

Long Pond

Seal Cove Pond

Valley Cove

102

3

Thunder Hole

Otter Point

102

Seal Cove

Northeast Harbor

Southwest Harbor

3

Seal Harbor

Park Loop Rd.

BEAR ISLAND

Manset

Eastern Way

SUTTON ISLAND

West Tremont

Islesford

LITTLE CRANBERRY ISLAND

Bernard

Bass Harbor

Cranberry Isles

GREAT CRANBERRY ISLAND

BAKER ISLAND

Blue Hill Bay

Ship Harbor Nature Trail

Bass Harbor Head Light

Atlantic Ocean

Atlantic

FERRY TO FRENCHBORO, ISLE AU HAUT

SWANS ISLAND

0   2 mi

0   2 km

very rich because of its cool breezes. The wealthy built lavish mansions throughout the island, many of which were destroyed in a great fire that devastated the island in 1947, but many of those that survived have been converted into businesses. Shops are clustered along Main, Mount Desert, and Cottage streets. Take a stroll down West Street, a National Historic District, where you can see some fine old houses.

The island and the surrounding Gulf of Maine are home to a great variety of wildlife: whales, seals, eagles, falcons, ospreys, puffins (very unusual-looking birds), and forest dwellers such as moose, deer, foxes, coyotes, and black bears.

EXPLORING

Bar Harbor Whale Museum. Learn about the history of whaling, the anatomy of whales, and how biologists are working to gain more information about these massive creatures at this interesting museum. ⊠ *52 West St.* ☎ *207/288–0288* ⊕ *www.barharborwhalemuseum.org* ☞ *Free* ☻ *June, daily 9–10; July and Aug., daily 9–9.*

SPORTS AND THE OUTDOORS

AIR TOURS
★
Scenic Biplane & Glider Rides Over Bar Harbor (⊠ *968 Bar Harbor Rd. [Rte. 3], Trenton* ☎ *207/667–7627* ⊕ *www.acadiaairtours.com*) is a part of Acadia Air Tours and provides exactly what the name suggests: biplane and glider rides over Bar Harbor and Acadia National Park. Tours run from 25 minutes to an hour and range from $225 to $425 for two people. The sunset tour is $50 extra. Helicopter tours are also available on occasion.

BICYCLING
Acadia Bike Rentals & Coastal Kayaking Tours (⊠ *48 Cottage St.* ☎ *207/288–9605 or 800/526–8615* ⊕ *www.acadianfun.com*) rents mountain bikes good for negotiating the trails in Acadia National Park. The **Bar Harbor Bicycle Shop** (⊠ *141 Cottage St.* ☎ *207/288–3886 or 800/824–2453* ⊕ *www.barharborbike.com*) rents bikes by the half or full day.

★
The big 151-foot four-masted schooner **Margaret Todd** (⊠ *Bar Harbor Inn Pier* ☎ *207/288–4585* ⊕ *www.downeastwindjammer.com*) operates 1½- to 2-hour trips three times a day among the islands of Frenchman's Bay from mid-May to October. The sunset sail is the most popular. The schooner **Rachel B. Jackson** (⊠ *848 Eagle Lake Rd., Harborside Hotel & Marina* ☎ *207/288–2216* ⊕ *www.downeastsail.com*) offers two-hour and sunset cruises for $30.

WHALE-
WATCHING
★
Bar Harbor Whale Watch Co. (⊠ *1 West St.* ☎ *207/288–2386 or 800/942–5374* ⊕ *www.whalesrus.com*) merged with the Acadian Whale Watcher to make one big company with four boats, one of them a 138-foot jet-propelled catamaran with spacious decks. In season the outfit also offers lobster and seal cruises, a nature cruise, and puffin cruises.

SHOPPING

ART
Fodor's Choice
★
Paint your own pottery or piece together a mosaic at **All Fired Up** (⊠ *101 Cottage St.* ☎ *207/288–3130* ⊕ *www.acadiaallfiredup.com*). The gallery also sells glass sculptures, pendants, paintings, and decorative pottery. The **Alone Moose Fine Crafts** (⊠ *78 West St.* ☎ *207/288–4229* ⊕ *www.mainefinecrafts.com*) is the oldest made-in-Maine gallery on the island. It offers bronze wildlife sculpture, jewelry, pottery, and

10

Long ramps on Maine's many docks make it easier to access boats at either high tide or low tide.

watercolors. The **Eclipse Gallery** (⊠ *12 Mount Desert St.* ☎ *207/288–9048* ⊕ *www.eclipsegallery.us*) carries handblown glass, ceramics, and wood furniture. **Island Artisans** (⊠ *99 Main St.* ☎ *207/288–4214* ⊕ *www.islandartisans.com*) sells basketry, pottery, fiber work, and jewelry created by more than 100 of Maine's artisans. **Native Arts Gallery** (⊠ *99 Main St.* ☎ *207/288–4474* ⊕ *www.nativeartsgallery.com*) sells Native American silver and gold jewelry.

SPORTING GOODS One of the best sporting-goods stores in the state, **Cadillac Mountain Sports** (⊠ *28 Cottage St.* ☎ *207/288–4532* ⊕ *www.cadillacmountainsports.com*) has developed a following of locals and visitors alike. You can find top-quality climbing, hiking, and camping equipment. In winter you can rent cross-country skis, ice skates, and snowshoes. **Michael H. Graves Antiques** (⊠ *10 Albert Meadow* ☎ *207/288–3830*) specializes in maps and books focusing on Mount Desert Island.

WHERE TO EAT AND STAY

$$$–$$$$
SEAFOOD
Fodor'sChoice
★

✕ **Burning Tree.** One of the top restaurants in Maine, this easy-to-miss gem is on Route 3 between Bar Harbor and Otter Creek. The ever-changing menu emphasizes freshly caught seafood, and seven species of fish are offered every day, all from the Gulf of Maine. Entrées include pan-sautéed monkfish, oven-poached cod, and gray sole. There are always two or three vegetarian options and an emphasis on organic produce (much of it from the owners' garden). ⊠ *69 Otter Creek Drive (Rte. 3), Otter Creek* ☎ *207/288–9331* ▭ *DC, MC, V* ☺ *Closed Tues. and mid-Oct.–mid-June.*

$$$–$$$$
CONTINENTAL
Fodor'sChoice
★
✕ **Reading Room at the Bar Harbor Inn & Spa.** This elegant waterfront restaurant serves Continental fare along with Maine specialties such as lobster pie and Indian pudding. There's live music nightly. When the weather is nice, what could be more romantic than dining out under the stars at the inn's Terrace Grille with the ships of beautiful Bar Harbor right at your feet? The natural thing to order here would be the Maine lobster bake with all the fixings. The restaurant is also famous for its Sunday brunch. ✉ *7 Newport Dr.* ☎ *207/288–3351 or 800/248–3351* ⊕ *www.barharborinn.com* ⚑ *Reservations essential* ☰ *AE, DC, MC, V* ☺ *Closed late Nov.–late Mar.*

$$$–$$$$
Fodor'sChoice
★
▥ **Bar Harbor Inn & Spa.** Originally established in the late 1800s as a men's social club, this waterfront inn has rooms spread out over three buildings on well-landscaped grounds. Most rooms have gas fireplaces and balconies with great views. Rooms in the Oceanfront Lodge have private decks overlooking the ocean. Many rooms in the main inn have balconies overlooking the harbor. There are also some two-level suites. A luxury spa offers everything from massages and mud wraps to aromatherapy and facials. The inn is a short walk from town, so you're close to all the sights, and a terrific restaurant, the Reading Room ($$$–$$$$), is on-site. **Pros:** seems to meet every need; right at the harbor. **Cons:** not as close to Acadia National Park as some Bar Harbor properties. ✉ *Newport Dr.* ☎ *207/288–3351 or 800/248–3351* ⊕ *www.barharborinn.com* ⚑ *138 rooms, 15 suites* ⚐ *In-room: safe, refrigerator, DVD, Wi-Fi. In-hotel: 2 restaurants, pool, gym, Wi-Fi hotspot* ☰ *AE, DC, MC, V* ☺ *Closed late Nov.–late Mar.* ⍾ *CP.*

ACADIA NATIONAL PARK

10

4 mi northwest of Bar Harbor.

Fodor'sChoice
★
With more than 30,000 acres of protected forests, beaches, mountains, and rocky coastline, Acadia National Park is the second-most-visited national park in America (the first is Great Smoky Mountains National Park). According to the National Park Service, more than 2.2 million people visit Acadia each year. The park holds some of the most spectacular scenery on the eastern seaboard: a rugged coastline of surf-pounded granite and an interior graced by sculpted mountains, quiet ponds, and lush deciduous forests. Cadillac Mountain (named after a Native American, not the car), the highest point of land on the East Coast, dominates the park. Although it's rugged, the park also has graceful stone bridges, horse-drawn carriages, and the Jordan Pond House restaurant (famous for its popovers).

The 27-mi Park Loop Road provides an excellent introduction, but to truly appreciate the park you must get off the main road and experience

DID YOU KNOW?

Acadia was the first National Park established east of the Mississippi River, in 1916. Wealthy landowners donated parcels of Mount Desert Island to protect this unique place where mountains meet the sea.

it by walking, biking, sea kayaking, or taking a carriage ride. If you get off the beaten path, you can find places you'll have practically to yourself. Mount Desert Island was once a preserve of summer homes for the very rich (and still is for some), and, because of this, Acadia is the only national park in the United States that was largely created by donations of private land. A small part of the park is on Isle au Haut, more than 10 mi away out in the ocean.

PARK ESSENTIALS

ADMISSION FEE

A user fee is required if you are anywhere in the park. The fee is $20 per vehicle for a seven-consecutive-day pass, or use your National Park America the Beautiful Pass, which allows entrance to any national park in the United States. See ⊕ *www.nps.gov* for details.

ADMISSION HOURS

The park is open 24 hours a day, year-round, though the roads often are closed in winter because of snow. Visitor center hours are 8–4:30 April 15–June, September, and October and until 6 in July and August.

PARK CONTACT INFORMATION

Acadia National Park (⌑ *Acadia National Park, Box 177, Bar Harbor 04609* ☎ *207/288-3338* ⊕ *www.nps.gov/acad*).

EXPLORING

HISTORIC SITES AND MUSEUMS

★ **Bass Harbor Head Light.** Built in 1858, this lighthouse is one of the most photographed lights in Maine. Now automated, it marks the entrance to Blue Hill Bay. The grounds and residence are Coast Guard property, but two trails around the facility provide excellent views. ■ TIP→ The best place to take a picture of this small but beautiful lighthouse is from the rocks below—but watch your step; they can be slippery. ⊠ *Rte. 102, halfway between Tremont and Manset, Bass Harbor* ☎ *Free* ⊙ *Daily 9–sunset.*

SCENIC DRIVES AND STOPS

★ **Cadillac Mountain.** At 1,532 feet, this is one of the first places in the United States to see the sun's rays at break of day. It is the highest mountain on the eastern seaboard north of Brazil. Dozens of visitors make the trek to see the sunrise or, for those less inclined to get up so early, sunset. From the smooth summit you have an awesome 360-degree view of the jagged coastline that runs around the island. A small gift shop and some restrooms are the only structures at the top. The road up the mountain is generally closed from the end of October through March because of snow.

☾ ★ **Park Loop Road.** This 27-mi road provides a perfect introduction to the park. You can do it in an hour, but allow at least half a day for the drive so that you can explore the many sites along the way. Traveling

BOOK A CARRIAGE RIDE

If you would like to take a horse-drawn carriage ride down one of these roads, you can do so from mid-June to mid-October by making a reservation with Wildwood Stables (☎ 207/276–3622). Two of their carriages can accommodate two wheelchairs each.

south on Park Loop Road toward Sand Beach, you'll reach a small ticket booth, where, if you haven't already, you will need to pay the park's good-for-seven-consecutive-days $20 entrance fee (not charged from November through April). Traffic is one-way from the Route 233 entrance to the Stanley Brook Road entrance south of the Jordan Pond House. The section known as Ocean Drive is open year-round.

> **CAUTION**
>
> A couple of people a year fall off one of the park's trails or cliffs and are swept out to sea. There is a lot of loose, rocky gravel along the shoreline, and sea rocks can often be slippery—so watch your step. Don't bring a sudden end to your visit by trying to get that "impossible" photo op.

VISITOR CENTER

At the Hulls Cove entrance to Acadia National Park, northwest of Bar Harbor on Route 3, the **Hulls Cove Visitor Center,** operated by the National Park Service, is a great spot to get your bearings. A large relief map of Mount Desert Island gives you the lay of the land, and you can watch a free 15-minute video about everything the park has to offer. Pick up guidebooks, maps of hiking trails and carriage roads, schedules for naturalist-led tours, and recordings for drive-it-yourself tours. Don't forget the *Acadia Beaver Log*, the park's free newspaper detailing guided hikes and other ranger-led events. Junior-ranger programs for kids, nature hikes, photography walks, tide-pool explorations, and evening talks are all popular. The visitor center is off Route 3 at Park Loop Road. ⊠ *Park Loop Rd., Hulls Cove* ☎ *207/288–3338* ⊕ *www. nps.gov/acad* ☽ *Mid-June–Aug., daily 8–6; mid-Apr.–mid-June, Sept., and Oct., daily 8–4:30.*

The **Acadia National Park Headquarters** is on Route 233 in the park not far from the north end of Eagle Lake and serves as the park's visitor center during the off-season.

SPORTS AND THE OUTDOORS

The best way to see Acadia National Park is to get out of your vehicle and explore on foot or by bicycle or boat. There are more than 40 mi of carriage roads that are perfect for walking and biking in the warmer months and for cross-country skiing and snowshoeing in winter. There are more than 120 mi of trails for hiking, numerous ponds and lakes for canoeing or kayaking, two beaches for swimming, and steep cliffs for rock climbing.

HIKING

Acadia National Park maintains more than 115 mi of hiking paths, from easy strolls around lakes and ponds to rigorous treks with climbs up rock faces and scrambles along cliffs. Although most hiking trails are on the east side of the island, the west side also has some scenic trails. For those wishing for a long climb, try the trails leading up Cadillac Mountain or Dorr Mountain. Another option is to climb Parkman, Sargeant, and Penobscot mountains. Most hiking is done from mid-May to mid-October. Snow falls early in Maine, so from late October to the end of March, cross-country skiing and snowshoeing replace hiking.

10

■TIP➔ You can park at one end of any trail and use the free shuttle bus to get back to your starting point.

Distances for trails are given for the round-trip hike.

EASY **Ocean Path Trail.** This 3.6-mi, eas-
★ ily accessible trail runs parallel to the Loop Road from Sand Beach to Otter Point. It has some of the best scenery in Maine: cliffs and boulders of pink granite at the ocean's edge, twisted branches of dwarf jack pines, and ocean views that stretch to the horizon. ⊠ *Sand Beach or Otter Point parking area.*

DIFFICULT **Acadia Mountain Trail.** This is the king
★ of the trails. The 2½-mi round-trip climb up Acadia Mountain is steep and strenuous, but the payoff is grand: views of Somes Sound and Southwest Harbor. If you want a guided trip, look into the ranger-led hikes for this trail. ⊠ *Acadia Mountain parking area, on Rte. 102.*

SWIMMING

The park has two swimming beaches, Sand Beach and Echo Lake Beach. Sand Beach, along Park Loop Road, has changing rooms, restrooms, and a lifeguard on duty from Memorial Day to Labor Day. The water temperature here rarely reaches above 55°F. Echo Lake Beach, on the western side of the island just north of Southwest Harbor, has much warmer water, as well as changing rooms, restrooms, and a lifeguard on duty throughout summer.

WHERE TO STAY

CAMPING ⚠ **Blackwoods Campground.** One of only two campgrounds inside
¢ inland Acadia National Park, Blackwoods is open throughout the year (though restrictions apply for winter camping; call ahead for details). Reservations are handled by the National Recreation Reservation Service (☎ 877/444–6777), not by the park. Reservations for high season (May–October) can be made up to six months in advance. During the off-season a limited number of campsites are available for primitive camping, and a camping permit must be obtained from the park headquarters. Rates drop by 50% for the shoulder season (April and November). ⊠ *Rte. 3, 5 mi south of Bar Harbor, Otter Creek* ☎ *207/288–3274 or 800/365–2267* ⊕ *www.nps.gov* ➷ *35 RV sites; 198 tent sites* ⚠ *No hookups or utilities; bathrooms, water, showers, picnic tables, fire pits, shuttle bus* ⊟ *DC, MC, V.*

¢ ⚠ **Seawall Campground.** On the "quiet side" of the island, this campground does not accept reservations but offers space on a first-come, first-served basis, starting at 8 AM. Seawall is open from late May to late September. Walk-in tent sites are $14 per night, while drive-in sites for tents and RVs are $20. ⊠ *Rte. 102A, 4 mi south of Southwest Harbor, Manset* ☎ *207/244–3600* ➷ *www.nps.gov* ➷ *42 RV sites; 163 tent sites*

⛺ *No hookups or utilities; bathrooms, showers, fire pits, picnic tables* ▭ *MC, V* ⊙ *Closed late Sept.–late May.*

NORTHEAST HARBOR

12 mi south of Bar Harbor via Rtes. 3 and 198 or Rtes. 233 and 198.

The summer community for some of the nation's wealthiest families, Northeast Harbor has one of the best harbors on the coast, which fills with yachts and powerboats during peak season. It's a great place to sign up for a cruise around Somes Sound or to the Cranberry Islands. Other than that, this quiet village has a handful of restaurants, boutiques, and art galleries.

SOMESVILLE

7 mi northwest of Northeast Harbor via Rtes. 198 and 102.

Most visitors pass through Somesville on their way to Southwest Harbor, but this well-preserved village, the oldest on the island, is more than a stop along the way. Originally settled by Abraham Somes in 1763, this was once a bustling commercial center with shingle, lumber, and wool mills; a tannery; a varnish factory; and a dye shop. Today Route 102, which passes through the center of town, takes you past a row of white-clapboard houses with black shutters and well-manicured lawns.

WHERE TO STAY

¢ ⛺ **Mount Desert Campground.** Near the village of Somesville, this campground has one of the best locations imaginable. It lies at the head of Somes Sound, the only fjord on the East Coast of North America. The campground prefers tents, so vehicles longer than 20 feet are not allowed. Many sites are along the waterfront, and all are tucked into the woods for a sense of privacy. Restrooms and showers are placed sensibly throughout the campground and are kept meticulously clean. Canoes and kayaks are available for rent, and there's a dock with access to the ocean. The Gathering Place has baked goods in the morning and ice cream and coffee in the evening. **Pros:** a lovely location for sightseeing. **Cons:** fills up quickly during peak season. ✉ *516 Sound Dr.* ☎ *207/244–3710* ⊕ *www.mountdesertcampground.com* ⛺ *150 sites* ⛺ *Flush toilets, drinking water, showers, fire pits, food service, swimming (ocean)* ▭ *MC, V* ⊙ *Closed mid-Sept.–mid-June.*

10

BASS HARBOR

4 mi south of Southwest Harbor via Rte. 102 or Rte. 102A

Bass Harbor is a tiny lobstering village with a relaxed atmosphere and a few accommodations and restaurants. If you're looking to get away from the crowds, consider using this hardworking community as your base. Although Bass Harbor does not draw as many tourists as other villages, the Bass Harbor Head Light in Acadia National Park is one of the region's most popular attractions and is undoubtedly the most photographed lighthouse in Maine. From Bass Harbor you can hike on the Ship Harbor Nature Trail or take a ferry to Frenchboro.

GETTING HERE AND AROUND

The Maine State Ferry Service operates a ferry, the Captain Henry Lee, carrying both passengers and a maximum of 19 vehicles per voyage, to Swans Island (30 min., $17.50) and Frenchboro (50 min., $11.25).

ESSENTIALS

Transportation Information **Maine State Ferry Service** (⊠ *114 Grandville Rd.* ☎ *207/244–3254*).

WHERE TO EAT

¢–$$ ✕ **Thurston's Lobster Pound.** On the peninsula across from Bass Harbor,
SEAFOOD Thurston's is easy to spot because of its bright yellow awning. You can buy fresh lobsters to go or sit at outdoor tables. Order everything from a grilled-cheese sandwich to a boiled lobster served with clams or mussels. ⊠ *1 Thurston Rd., at Steamboat Wharf, Bernard* ☎ *207/244–7600* ⚏ *www.thurstonslobster.com* ▭ *MC, V* ⊘ *Closed Columbus Day–Memorial Day.*

WAY DOWN EAST

By Mary Ruoff Slogans such as "The Real Maine" ring truer Way Down East. The raw, mostly undeveloped coast in this remote region is more accessible than it is farther south. Even in summer here you're likely to have rocky beaches and shady hiking trails to yourself. The slower pace is as calming as a sea breeze.

One innkeeper relates that visitors who plan to stay a few days often opt for a week after learning more about the region's offerings, which include historic sites; museums on local history, culture, and art; national wildlife refuges; state parks and preserves; and increasingly, conservancy-owned public land. Cutler's Bold Coast, with its dramatic granite headlands, is protected from development. Waters near Eastport have some of the world's highest tides. Lakes perfect for canoeing and kayaking are sprinkled inland, and rivers snake through marshland as they near the many bays. Boulders are strewn on blueberry barrens. Rare plants thrive in coastal bogs and heaths, and dark-purple and pink lupines line the roads in late June.

VISITOR INFORMATION

Many chambers of commerce in the region distribute free copies of the pamphlet "Maine's Washington County: Just Off the Beaten Path," which is several cuts above the usual tourist promotion booklet.

Contacts **DownEast & Acadia Regional Tourism** (⊠ *Box 4, Cherryfield* ☎ *207/546–3600 or 800/665–3278* ⊕ *www.downeastacadia.com*).

SCHOODIC PENINSULA

25 mi east of Ellsworth via U.S. Rte. 1 and Rte. 186.

The landscape of Schoodic Peninsula's craggy coastline, towering evergreens, and views over Frenchman Bay are breathtaking year-round. A drive through the well-to-do summer community of Grindstone Neck shows what Bar Harbor might have been like before so many of its

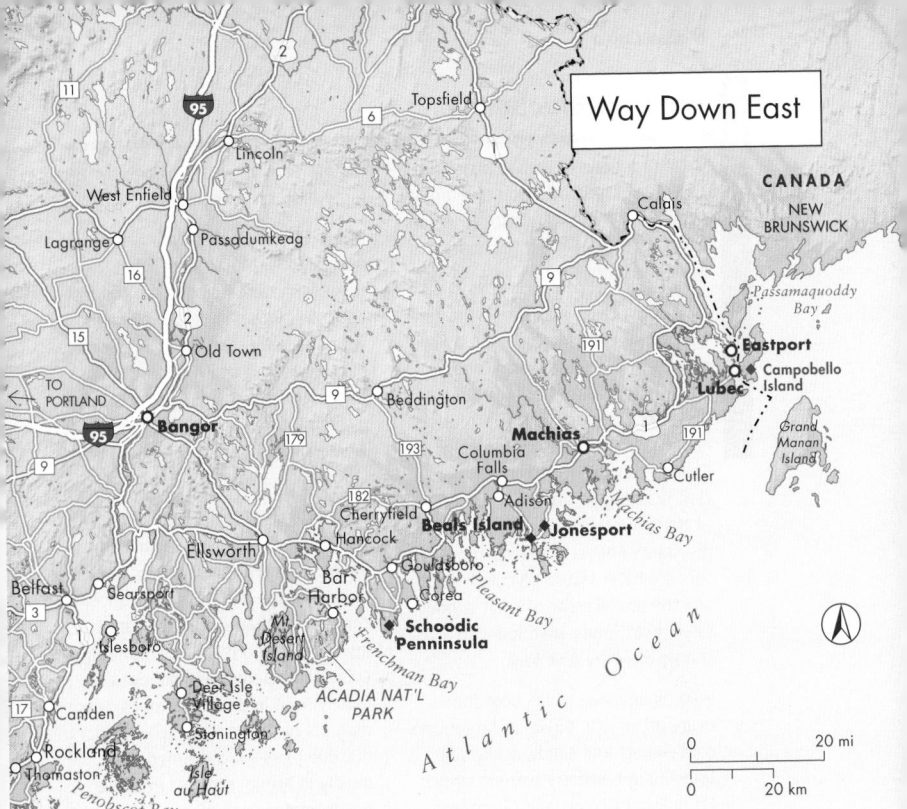

Way Down East

mansions were destroyed in the Great Fire of 1947. Artists and artisans have opened galleries in and around Winter Harbor. Anchored at the foot of the peninsula, Winter Harbor was once part of Gouldsboro, which wraps around it.

ESSENTIALS

Visitor Information Schoodic Area Chamber of Commerce (📫 Box 381, Winter Harbor 04693 ⊕ www.acadia-schoodic.org).

EXPLORING

Coastal Villages. Within Gouldsboro on the Schoodic Peninsula are several small coastal villages. You drive through **Wonsqueak** and **Birch Harbor** after leaving the Schoodic section of Acadia National Park. Near Birch Harbor you can find **Prospect Harbor,** a small fishing village nearly untouched by tourism. In **Corea,** there's little to do besides watch the fishermen at work, wander along stone beaches, or gaze out to sea.

Fodor's Choice ★ **Acadia National Park.** The only section of Maine's national park that sits on the mainland is at the southern side of the Schoodic Peninsula in the town of Winter Harbor. The park has a scenic 6-mi one-way loop that edges along the coast and yields views of Grindstone Neck, Winter Harbor, Winter Harbor Lighthouse, and, across the water, Cadillac Mountain. At the tip of the point, huge slabs of pink granite lie jumbled along the shore, thrashed unmercifully by the crashing surf (stay away

Wild for Blueberries

There's no need to inquire about the cheesecake topping if you dine out in August when the wild blueberry crop comes in. Anything but blueberries would be unthinkable.

Way Down East, wild blueberries have long been a favorite food and a key ingredient in cultural and economic life. Maine produces about a third of the commercial harvest, which totals about 70 million pounds annually, Canada supplying virtually all the rest. Washington County yields 65% of Maine's total crop, which is why the state's largest blueberry processors are here: Jasper Wyman & Son and the predecessor of what is now Cherryfield Foods were founded shortly after the Civil War.

Wild blueberries, which bear fruit every other year, thrive in the region's cold climate and sandy, acidic soil. Undulating blueberry barrens stretch for miles in Deblois and Cherryfield ("the Blueberry Capital of the World") and are scattered throughout Washington County. Look for tufts among low-lying plants along the roadways. In spring the fields shimmer as the small-leaf plants turn myriad shades of mauve, honey-orange, and lemon-yellow. White flowers appear in June. Fall transforms the barrens into a sea of red.

Amid Cherryfield's barrens, a plaque on a boulder lauds the late J. Burleigh Crane for helping advance an industry that's not as wild as it used to be. Honeybees have been brought in to supplement native pollinators, fields are irrigated, and barrens are burned and mowed to rid plants of disease and insects, reducing the need for pesticides. Most of the barrens in and around Cherryfield are owned by the large blueberry processors.

About 80% of Maine's crop is now harvested with machinery. That requires moving boulders, so the rest continues to be harvested by hand with blueberry rakes, which resemble large forks and pull the berries off their stems. Years ago, year-round residents did the work. Today migrant workers make up 90% of this seasonal labor force.

Blueberries get their dark color from anthocyanins, believed to provide antioxidants. Wild blueberries have more of these antiaging, anticancer compounds than their cultivated cousins. Smaller and more flavorful than cultivated blueberries, wild ones are mostly used in packaged foods. Less than 1% of the state's crop—about 500,000 pints—is consumed fresh, mostly in Maine. Look for fresh berries (sometimes starting in late July and lasting until early September) at roadside stands, farmers' markets, and supermarkets.

Wild Blueberry Land in Columbia Falls sells everything blueberry, from muffins and candy to socks and books. Find farm stores, stands, and markets statewide, many selling blueberries and blueberry jams and syrups, at ⊕ *www.getrealgetmaine.com*, a Maine Department of Agriculture site that promotes Maine foods.

—Mary Ruoff

DID YOU KNOW?

Almost unrelated to the bloated berries at most grocery stores, Maine's small and flavor-packed wild blueberries are a must in season, from late July to early September. Try a handful fresh, in pancakes, or a pie.

from the water's edge), and jack pines cling to life amid the rocks. Fraser Point, at the beginning of the loop, is an ideal place for a picnic. Work off lunch with a hike up Schoodic Head for the panoramic views up and down the coast. A free bus called the Island Explorer (☎ 207/288–4573 ⊕ *www.exploreacadia.com*) takes passengers from Prospect Harbor, Birch Harbor, and Winter Harbor and drops them off anywhere in the park. In Winter Harbor you can get off at the ferry to Bar Harbor. The $20-per-car park admission fee is generally not charged when you're just visiting Schoodic. *For more information* ⇨ *see Acadia National Park and Mount Desert Island.* ⊠ *Moore Road, turn off Rte. 186, Winter Harbor* ☎ *207/288–3338* ⊕ *www.nps.gov/acad* 🖼 *$20 per car* ☾ *Year-round, 24/7.*

SPORTS AND THE OUTDOORS

KAYAKING **SeaScape Kayaking.** Led by a Registered Maine Guide, SeaScape's morning and afternoon kayak tours include an island stop and a blueberry snack. The company also rents canoes, kayaks, and bikes from its location in Birch Harbor. ⊠ *18 E. Schoodic Dr., Birch Harbor* ☎ *207/963–5806 or 207/479–9912* ⊕ *www.seascapekayaking.com.*

SHOPPING

ANTIQUES AND MORE Hand-cast bronze doorbells and wind bells are among the items sold at **U.S. Bells** (⊠ *56 W. Bay Rd. [Rte. 186], Prospect Harbor* ☎ *207/963–7184* ⊕ *www.usbells.com* ☾ *June–Dec.*). You can also buy finely crafted quilts, wood-fired pottery, and wood and bronze outdoor furniture, all made by family members of the foundry owner. Tours of the foundry are given frequently.

ART GALLERIES Window glass is fused in a kiln at **Lee Fusion Art Glass Studio** (⊠ *679 S. Gouldsboro Rd. [Rte. 186], Gouldsboro* ☎ *207/963–7280* ⊕ *www. leefusionartglass.com* ☾ *June–Oct.*) to create unusual glass dishware. Colorful enamel accents depict birds, lighthouses, flowers, and designs made from doilies.

FOOD Along with mostly organic local produce, **Winter Harbor Farmers' Market** (⊠ *10 Newman St. [Rte. 186], Winter Harbor* ☎ *207/537–5673* ☾ *June–early Sept., Tues. 9–noon*) sells goat cheese, baked goods, beef and chicken, hand-spun yarn, knitted items, and maple syrup, chutney, and preserves.

WHERE TO EAT AND STAY

$$ ✕ **Chase's Restaurant.** The orange booths may remind you of a fast-food
SEAFOOD joint, but this family restaurant has a reputation for serving good, basic fare. In this region that means a lot of fish. There are large and small fried seafood dinners and several more expensive seafood platters. Try the sweet-potato fries as a side. Lunch fare, sold all day, includes wraps and burgers. It's also open for breakfast. ⊠ *193 Main St. (Rte. 186), Winter Harbor* ☎ *207/963–7171* ▭ *AE, D, MC, V.*

$–$$ ✕ **J.M. Gerrish Provisions.** The store that opened here in the early 1900s
CAFÉ was the place where locals and visitors alike went for ice cream. The name remains, as well as part of the old marble counter, but today it is a deli and café where folks bustle in for light meals or linger over coffee at tables inside and on the porch. A simple menu has soups, salads, and savory sandwiches, such as turkey and cheddar topped with cranberry

relish. The deli case offers salads, from potato to Mediterranean octopus, and dishes such as baby back ribs. Baked goods crowd the counter, ice cream is still sold, and you can buy wine and beer to go. ⊠ *352 Main St., Winter Harbor* ☎ *207/963–6100* ⊕ *www.jmgerrish.com* ▤ *MC, V* ☉ *Closed mid-Oct.–mid-May.*

$–$$ 🏨 **Bluff House Inn.** Combining the service of a hotel with the ambience
☾ of a cozy lodge, this modern two-story inn on a secluded hillside has
★ expansive views of Frenchman Bay. You can see the bay's granite shores from the inn's partially screened wraparound porches. There's a picnic area with grill (a lobster pot is available for those who want to boil their own dinner), and a stone fireplace warms one of the knotty-pine lounge areas. The individually decorated guest rooms have furnishings from around the state. **Pros:** close to things yet secluded. **Cons:** path to water a bit steep. ⊠ *57 Bluff House Rd., off Rte. 186, Gouldsboro* ☎ *207/963–7805* ⊕ *www.bluffinn.com* ⇱ *8 rooms, 1 apartment* ☖ *In-room: no a/c, no TV (some), kitchen (some), DVD (some), Wi-Fi. In-hotel: Wi-Fi hotspot, some pets allowed* ▤ *MC, V* ⏐◯⏐ *CP.*

$$–$$$ 🏨 **Oceanside Meadows Inn.** This place is a must for nature lovers. Trail
☾ maps guide you through a 200-acre preserve dotted with woods,
Fodor'sChoice streams, salt marshes, and ponds. Inspired by the moose, eagles, and
★ other wildlife that thrive here, the innkeepers created the Oceanside Meadows *Inn*stitute for the Arts & Sciences, which holds lectures, musical performances, art exhibits, and other events in the restored barn. Furnished with antiques, country pieces, and family treasures and scented with flowers from the extensive gardens, the inn has sunny, inviting living rooms with fireplaces and a separate guest kitchen. Guest rooms are spread between two white clapboard buildings fronting a private beach flanked by granite ledges. Breakfast is an extravagant multicourse affair that includes chilled fruit soup. **Pros:** one of the region's few sand beaches; many spacious rooms; packages include lobster dinner and boat tour. **Cons:** need to cross road to beach. ⊠ *202 Corea Rd. (Rte. 195), Prospect Harbor* ☎ *207/963–5557* ⊕ *www.oceaninn. com* ⇱ *13 rooms, 2 suites* ☖ *In-room: no a/c, no TV, Wi-Fi. In-hotel: beachfront, laundry services, Wi-Fi hotspot, some pets allowed* ▤ *AE, D, DC, MC, V* ☉ *Closed Nov.–Apr.* ⏐◯⏐ *BP.*

JONESPORT AND BEALS ISLAND

48 mi northeast of Winter Harbor via Rte. 186, US Rte. 1, and Rte. 187; 20 mi southwest of Machias.

The birding is superb around Jonesport and Beals Island, a pair of fishing communities joined by a bridge over the harbor. A handful of stately homes ring Jonesport's Sawyer Square, where Sawyer Memorial Congregational Church's exquisite stained-glass windows are illuminated at night. But the towns are less geared to travelers than those on the Schoodic Peninsula. Lobster traps are still piled in the yards, and lobster-boat races near Moosabec Reach are the highlight of the community's annual Independence Day celebration.

10

SPORTS AND THE OUTDOORS

In business since circa 1940, **Norton of Jonesport** (☎ 207/497–5933 ⊕ *www.machiassealisland.com*) takes passengers on day trips to Machias Seal Island, where thousands of puffins nest. Arctic terns, razorbill auks, common murres, and many other seabirds also nest on the rocky island. Trips, which cost $100 per person, are offered from late May through August.

LOOK UP!

With no large cities, Way Down East offers great stargazing. But if you want a great show on a dark night, paddle a canoe on a lake and look down. Bioluminescent organisms in the water light up as you churn your paddle.

WHERE TO EAT

$$ × **Tall Barney's.** Salty accents add plenty of flavor at this down-home
SEAFOOD restaurant, which serves a late-morning breakfast (10 to 11 weekdays, 8 to 11 on Saturday), lunch, and dinner. A pamphlet tells the story of Tall Barney, a brawny fisherman who left truly tall tales in his wake. Your server may be among his multitudinous descendants. The menu includes five types of seafood stew; grilled, baked, and fried seafood; vegetarian dishes; and oversize desserts including seasonal pies. Call the night before to order a boxed lunch. ⊠ *52 Main St.* ☎ *207/497–2403* ⊕ *www.tallbarneys.com* ☲ *MC, V* ☉ *Closed Mon.; generally closed Mon. and Tues. late Sept.–mid-Nov., Sun.–Wed. late Nov.–mid-May.*

MACHIAS

20 mi northeast of Jonesport.

The Machias area—Machiasport, East Machias, and Machias, the Washington County seat—lays claim to being the site of the first naval battle of the Revolutionary War, which took place in what is now Machiasport. Despite being outnumbered and outarmed, a small group of Machias men under the leadership of Jeremiah O'Brien captured the armed British schooner *Margaretta*. That battle, fought on June 12, 1775, is now known as the "Lexington of the Sea." The town's other claim to fame is wild blueberries. On the third weekend in August the annual Machias Wild Blueberry Festival is a community celebration complete with parade, crafts fair, concerts, and plenty of blueberry dishes.

ESSENTIALS

Visitor Information Machias Bay Area Chamber of Commerce (⊠ 85 Main St., Suite 2, Machias ☎ 207/255–4402 ⊕ www.machiaschamber.org).

EXPLORING

★ **Burnham Tavern Museum.** It was in this gambrel-roofed tavern home that the men of Machias laid the plans that culminated in the capture of the *Margaretta* in 1775. After the Revolutionary War's first naval battle, wounded British sailors were brought here. Tour guides dressed in period garb highlight exhibits and tell colorful stories of early settlers. Period furnishings and household items show what life was like in Colonial times. On the National Register of Historic Places, the dwelling is among the 21 in the country deemed most important to the Revolution. ⊠ *14 Colonial Way (Rte. 192)* ☎*207/255–6930* ⊕ *www. burnhamtavern.com* ⊉*$5* ⊙ *Mid-June–Sept., weekdays 9:30–4 (last tour at 3:30), or by appointment.*

WHERE TO EAT

$$$–$$$$ ✕ **Riverside Inn & Restaurant.** A bright yellow exterior invites a stop at this
AMERICAN   delightful restaurant in a former sea captain's home perched on the bank
★   of the Machias River. Ask for a table in the intimate sunroom, which has water views and opens to the other dining room. The chef-owner brings a special flair to traditional dishes, such as pork served with a pistachio crust. His signature dish is salmon stuffed with crabmeat and shrimp. In summer months the menu includes dressed-up dinner salads—try pairing one with standout appetizers like hake cakes and red-tuna wontons. Also a charming inn (open daily except in early winter) with Victorian touches, Riverside has two guest rooms in the main house and two suites in the coach house. ⊠ *608 Main St. (U.S. 1), East Machias* ☎*207/255–4134 or 888/255–4344* ⊕ *www.riversideinn-maine.com* ⊟ *MC, V* ⊙ *Closed Jan.–early Feb.; Mon.–Wed. mid-Feb.–mid-June, Nov., and Dec.; Mon. late June–Oct. No lunch.*

LUBEC

28 mi northeast of Machias via U.S. 1 and Rte. 189.

Lubec is one of the first places in the United States to see the sunrise. A popular destination for outdoor enthusiasts, it offers plenty of opportunities for hiking and biking, and the birding is renowned. It's a good base for day trips to New Brunswick's Campobello Island, reached by a bridge—the only one to the island—from downtown Lubec. The village is perched at the end of a narrow strip of land, so you often can see water in three directions.

SPORTS AND THE OUTDOORS

★   **Quoddy Head State Park.** The easternmost point of land in the United States is marked by candy-striped West Quoddy Head Light. In 1806 President Thomas Jefferson signed an order authorizing construction of a lighthouse on this site. You can't climb the tower, but the former light keeper's house has a museum with a video showing the interior. The museum also has displays on Lubec's maritime past and the region's marine life. A gallery displays lighthouse art by locals. A mystical 2-mi path along the cliffs here, one of four trails, yields magnificent views of Canada's cliff-clad Grand Manan Island. Whales can often be sighted offshore. The 540-acre park has a picnic area. ⊠ *973 S. Lubec Rd., off Rte. 189* ☎*207/733–0911 or 207/941–4014* ⊕ *www.parksandlands. com* ⊉*$3* ⊙ *May 15–Oct. 15, 9–sunset.*

10

TAKE A TOUR   On educational tours by **Tours of Lubec and Cobscook** (⊠ *135 Main St. [Rte. 189]* ☎ *207/733–2997 or 888/347–9302* ⊕ *www. toursoflubecandcobscook.com*) you can visit historic locales, view lighthouses by boat, walk the shoreline to learn about the area's high tides and tide pools, tour a ninth-generation farm on Cobscook Bay, and explore a bog. Tours run from May through October and start at $10 per person. The tour office is at the tourism Info Stop, which shares a building with the Lubec Historical Society Museum.

WHERE TO EAT AND STAY

$$ ✕**Uncle Kippy's Restaurant.** There isn't much of a view from the picture
SEAFOOD windows, but locals don't mind—they come here for the satisfying seafood. There's one large dining room with a bar beside the main entrance. The menu includes seafood dinners and combo platters, and the fresh-dough pizza is popular. A take-out window and ice-cream bar are open June through September. ⊠ *170 Main St.* ☎ *207/733–2400* ⊕ *www.unclekippys.com* ⊟ *D, MC, V* ⊗ *Generally closed Mon. and Tues. Dec.–June.*

$–$$ 🏠**Peacock House.** Five generations of the Peacock family lived in this
★ white-clapboard house before it was converted into an inn. With a large foyer, library, and living room, the 1860 sea captain's home has plenty of places where you can relax. Minglers are drawn to the sunroom, which opens to the deck and has a handsome bar. The best of the rooms has a separate sitting area, wet bar, and gas fireplace. **Pros:** piano in living room; lovely garden off deck. **Cons:** only one off-street parking space. ⊠ *27 Summer St.* ☎ *207/733–2403 or 888/305–0036* ⊕ *www. peacockhouse.com* ⛵ *5 rooms, 2 suites* ♨ *In-room: no phone, no a/c, refrigerator (some), DVD (some), no TV (some), Wi-Fi. In hotel: Wi-Fi hotspot* ⊟ *MC, V* ⊗ *Closed Nov.–Apr.* ❖❙*BP.*

CAMPOBELLO ISLAND, CANADA

28 mi east of Machias.

A popular excursion from Lubec, New Brunswick's Campobello Island has two fishing villages, Welshpool and Wilson's Beach. The only bridge is from Lubec, but in summer a car ferry shuttles passengers from Campobello Island to Deer Island, where you can continue on to the Canadian mainland. *(⇨ See the Travel Smart section at the back of the book for information on passports or other documents U.S. citizens need when traveling between the United States and Canada.)*

EXPLORING

★ **Roosevelt Campobello International Park.** A joint project of the American and the Canadian governments, this park is crisscrossed with interesting hiking trails. Groomed dirt roads attract bikers. Eagle Hill Bog has a wooden walkway and signs identifying rare plants. Neatly manicured Campobello Island has always had a special appeal for the wealthy and famous. It was here that President Franklin Roosevelt and his family spent summers. The 34-room Roosevelt Cottage was presented to Eleanor and Franklin as a wedding gift, and the wicker-filled structure looks essentially as it did when the family was in residence. A visitor center has displays about the Roosevelts and Canadian-American relations. ■TIP➔ Note that the Islands are on Atlantic Time, which is an hour later than EST. ⊠ *459 Rte. 774, Welshpool, New Brunswick, Canada* ☎ *506/752–2922* ⊕ *www.fdr.net* 🎟 *Free* ⊗ *House, Memorial*

Day weekend–Columbus Day, daily 10–6; Grounds, year-round 24/7; Visitor center, Memorial Day weekend–Oct., 9–5.

WHERE TO EAT

$$–$$$ ✕ **Family Fisheries.** Seafood lovers know that fried fish doesn't have to be
SEAFOOD greasy. That's why people keep heading across the bridge to eat at this
family restaurant in Wilson's Beach. The freshest seafood is delivered
to the restaurant and the adjoining fish market. Order fried haddock,
scallops, shrimps, or clams alone or as part of a seafood platter. Lobsters are cooked outside. Eat in the large dining room or near the playground at picnic tables or in a screened room. You can buy ice cream at the take-out window; the restaurant also serves breakfast. ⊠ *1977 Rte. 774, Wilson's Beach* ☎ *506/752–2470* ▭ *MC, V* ⊗ *Closed late Dec.–Mar. No dinner Sun.*

EASTPORT

39 mi northeast of Lubec via Rte. 189, U.S. 1, and Rte. 190; 109 mi north of Ellsworth via U.S. 1 and Rte. 190.

Connected by a granite causeway to the mainland at Pleasant Point Reservation, Eastport has wonderful views of the nearby islands, and you can sometimes spot whales from the waterfront because the harbor is so deep. Known for its diverse architecture, the island city was one of the nation's busiest seaports in the early 1800s. In the late 19th century 14 sardine canneries operated here. The industry's decline in the 20th century left the city economically depressed, but now the town has set its sights on salmon, shipping, tourism, and the arts—performing and visual arts are thriving here. The weekend after Labor Day the Maine Salmon Festival attracts large crowds with boat tours of salmon pens, an arts and crafts show, a historic-home walking tour, a wine tasting, and a dinner featuring the local delicacy and live music. On the same weekend the Eastport Pirate Festival brings folks out in pirate attire for a ship race, parade, and other events, including a children's breakfast and schooner ride with pirates.

Get downtown early to secure a viewing spot for Maine's largest July 4th parade. Canadian bagpipe bands make this an event not to be missed. The day culminates with fireworks over the bay. On the weekend of the second Sunday in August, locals celebrate Sipayik Indian Days at the Pleasant Point Reservation. This festival of Passamaquoddy culture includes canoe races, dancing, drumming, children's games, fireworks, and traditional dancing.

10

ESSENTIALS

Visitor Information Eastport Area Chamber of Commerce (⌂ *Box 254, Eastport 04631* ☎ *207/853–4644* ⊕ *www.eastport.net*).

WHERE TO EAT

$$–$$$ ✕ **Eastport Chowder House.** Just north of downtown Eastport, this expan-
SEAFOOD sive waterfront eatery sits on the pier next to where the ferry docks.
Built atop an old cannery foundation, it has original details such as
wood beams and a stone wall. Eat in the downstairs pub, upstairs in
the dining room, or on the large deck. The house specialties include a

smoked fish appetizer and seafood pasta in a wine-and-cheese sauce. Lunch, served until 4, includes fried seafood plates, burgers, wraps, and sandwiches. ⊠ *169 Water St.* ☎ *207/853–4700* ⊟ *D, MC, V* ☉ *Closed mid-Oct.–mid-May.*

$$–$$$
AMERICAN
★

✕ **Pickled Herring.** Linger near the open kitchen and you may hear diners pay homage to the chef at the wood-fire grill as he prepares dishes like duck with a maple-peppercorn glaze, salmon with house pesto, and the popular strip sirloin (12, 14, or 16 ounces). Thin wood-fired pizza with toppings like caramelized onions, lobster, and blue cheese is a lighter choice. Housed in a landmark downtown storefront with soaring windows and ceilings, this restaurant's wonderful food and atmosphere have made it a destination. Pictures of Eastport's former sardine plants hang on a brick wall, and gas-burning lanterns and streetlamp-like lights throw a soft glow. Urbanites will feel at home, but locals do, too. A fun bar is hidden behind an interior wall. Specialty cocktails like the Foghorn (Tanqueray, fresh-squeezed lime juice, and ginger ale) have a Down East twist. ⊠ *32 Water St.* ☎ *207/853–2323* ⊕ *www. thepickledherring.com* ⊟ *AE, D, MC, V* ☉ *Closed Jan. and Feb., and Mon.–Wed. late Sept.–Dec. and March–early June. No lunch.*

Travel Smart
New England

WORD OF MOUTH

"As far as [driving] times goes, you'll have a greater challenge in more northern areas like Vermont, western New Hampshire, and western or northern Maine. It gets much more rural in some of those parts and you do not always have a direct, major highway that cuts through them."

—Shandy1977

GETTING HERE AND AROUND

New England's largest and most cosmopolitan city, Boston, is the region's major transportation and cultural center. Secondary hubs include Hartford, Connecticut, and Portland, Maine. Your best bet for exploring is to travel by car—flying within the region is expensive, and driving distances between most attractions are short. Inside most cities, public transportation is a viable—and often preferable—means for getting around. Passenger ferry service is available to outlying islands (some vessels accommodate vehicles).

See the Getting Here and Around section at the beginning of each chapter for more transportation information.

■ AIR TRAVEL

Most travelers visiting New England head for a major gateway, such as Boston, Providence, Hartford/Springfield, Manchester, or even New York City or Albany, and then rent a car to explore the region. The New England states form a fairly compact region, with few important destinations more than six hours apart by car. It's costly and generally impractical to fly within New England, the exceptions being the island resort destinations of Martha's Vineyard and Nantucket in Massachusetts and Block Island in Rhode Island, which have regular service from Boston and a few other regional airports.

Boston's Logan Airport is one of the nation's most important domestic and international airports, with direct flights arriving from all over North America and internationally. New England's other major airports receive few international flights (mostly from Canada) but do offer a wide range of direct domestic flights to East Coast and Midwest destinations and, to a lesser extent, to the western United States. Some sample flying times to Boston are: from Chicago (2½ hours), London (6½ hours), and Los Angeles (6 hours).

Times from U.S. destinations are similar, if slightly shorter, to Albany and Hartford, assuming you can find direct flights.

AIRPORTS

The main gateway to New England is Boston's Logan International Airport (BOS). Bradley International Airport (BDL), in Windsor Locks, Connecticut, 12 mi north of Hartford, is convenient to western Massachusetts and all of Connecticut. T. F. Green Airport (PVD), just outside Providence, Rhode Island, and Manchester Boston Regional Airport (MHT), in New Hampshire, are other major airports—and alternative gateways to Boston, which is a one-hour drive from each. Additional New England airports served by major carriers include Portland International Jetport (PWM) in Maine and Burlington International Airport (BTV) in Vermont. Other airports are in Albany, New York (ALB, near Western Massachusetts and Vermont); Bangor, Maine (BGR); and Barnstable Municipal in Hyannis, Massachusetts (HYA). You can access Nantucket and Martha's Vineyard via ferries from Hyannis or fly directly to the islands' airports.

Airport Information Albany International Airport (🕾 518/242–2200 ⊕ www. albanyairport.com). **Bangor International Airport** (🕾 207/992–4600 ⊕ www.flybangor. com). **Barnstable Municipal Airport–Hyannis** (🕾 508/775–2020 ⊕ www.town.barnstable. ma.us/Departments/Airport/05/). **Bradley International Airport–Hartford/Springfield** (🕾 860/292–2000 ⊕ www.bradleyairport.com). **Burlington International Airport** (🕾 802/863–1889 ⊕ www.burlingtonintlairport.com). **Logan International Airport–Boston** (🕾 800/235–6426 ⊕ www.massport.com/logan). **Manchester Boston Regional Airport** (🕾 603/624–6556 ⊕ www.flymanchester.com). **Martha's Vineyard Airport** (🕾 508/693–7022 ⊕ www. mvyairport.com). **Nantucket Memorial Airport** (🕾 508/325–5300 ⊕ www.nantucketairport. com). **Portland International Jetport**

(☎ 207/874–8877 ⊕ www.portlandjetport.org).
T. F. Green Airport–Providence (☎ 401/737–
8222 ⊕ www.pvdairport.com).

FLIGHTS

Numerous airlines fly to and from Bos-
ton; additionally, the discount car-
rier Southwest Airlines flies to Albany,
Boston, Hartford/Springfield (Bradley
International Airport), Providence, and
Manchester, New Hampshire. Smaller or
discount airlines serving Boston include
AirTran, Cape Air, and JetBlue. Cape
Air also provides service from Cape Cod
and the islands to Providence and New
Bedford. You can fly to Burlington from
New York City on JetBlue, and you can
fly to Boston from Atlantic City, Myrtle
Beach, and Fort Lauderdale on Spirit Air-
lines. New England Airlines serves Block
Island, with regularly scheduled flights
from Westerly, Rhode Island.

Airline Contacts AirTran Airways
(☎ 800/247–8726 ⊕ www.airtran.com).
American Airlines (☎ 800/433–7300
⊕ www.aa.com). **Cape Air** (☎ 800/352–0714
⊕ www.flycapeair.com). **Continental Airlines**
(☎ 800/523–3273 ⊕ www.continental.com).
Delta Airlines (☎ 800/221–1212 ⊕ www.
delta.com). **JetBlue** (☎ 800/538–2583
⊕ www.jetblue.com). **New England Airlines**
(☎ 800/243–2460 ⊕ www.block-island.com/
nea). **Northwest Airlines** (☎ 800/225–2525
⊕ www.nwa.com). **Southwest Airlines**
(☎ 800/435–9792 ⊕ www.southwest.com).
Spirit Airlines (☎ 800/772–7117 ⊕ www.
spiritair.com). **United Airlines** (☎ 800/864–
8331 ⊕ www.united.com). **USAirways**
(☎ 800/428–4322 ⊕ www.usairways.com).

▌ BOAT TRAVEL

Principal ferry routes in New England
connect New Bedford on the mainland
and Cape Cod with Martha's Vineyard
and Nantucket, Boston with Provincetown, southern Rhode Island with Block
Island, and Connecticut with New York's
Long Island and Block Island. Other
routes provide access to many islands
off the Maine coast. Ferries cross Lake

Champlain between Vermont and upstate
New York. International service between
Portland, Yarmouth, and Bar Harbor,
Maine, and Nova Scotia, is also available.
With the exception of the Lake Cham-
plain ferries—which are first-come, first-
served—car reservations are advisable.

▌ BUS TRAVEL

Regional bus service is relatively plentiful throughout New England. It can be
a handy and affordable means of getting
around, as buses travel many routes that
trains do not.

BoltBus offers cheap fares in new, Wi-Fi–
and electrical-outlet–equipped buses
between Boston, New York, Philadelphia,
and Washington, D.C., starting at just $1
if you reserve early enough. Megabus also
offers low fares, and its Wi-Fi–equipped
buses serve New York City and many
other points on the East Coast. BoltBus
and Megabus use Boston's South Station.
Major credit cards are accepted for all
buses, and for BoltBus you can only purchase tickets online.

Bus Information BoltBus (☎ 877/265–8287
⊕ www.boltbus.com). **Megabus** (☎ 877/462–
6342 ⊕ www.megabus.com).

▌ CAR TRAVEL

New England is best explored by car.
Areas in the interior are largely without
heavy traffic and congestion. Coastal New
England is more congested, and parking
can be hard to find or expensive in Boston, Providence, and the many smaller
resort towns along the coast. Still, a car
is typically the best way to get around
even on the coast (though you may want
to park it at your hotel in Boston or on
Cape Cod and use it as little as possible).
In the interior, especially western Massachusetts, Vermont, New Hampshire, and
Maine, public transportation options
are limited and a car is almost necessary.
Note that Interstate 95 is a toll highway
throughout New England, and Interstate

ESSENTIALS

■ ACCOMMODATIONS

In New England you can bed down in a campsite, a chain hotel, or a five-star palace. But unless you're staying in a city, this is really bed-and-breakfast land. Charming—and sometimes historic—inns, small hotels, and B&Bs dot the region and provide a glimpse of local life.

See the planner at the start of each chapter for lodging price ranges.

BED-AND-BREAKFASTS

Historic B&Bs and inns proliferate throughout New England. In many rural or less-touristy areas, B&Bs offer an affordable alternative to chain properties, but in tourism-dependent communities (i.e., most of the major towns in this region), expect to pay about the same or more for a historic inn as for a full-service hotel. Many of the state's finest restaurants are also in country inns. Although many B&Bs and smaller establishments continue to offer a low-key, homey experience, in recent years many such properties have begun offering amenities like Wi-Fi, whirlpool tubs, and TVs with DVD players. Quite a few inns and B&Bs serve substantial breakfasts.

Reservation Services Bed & Breakfast.com (☎ 512/322–2710 or 800/462–2632 ⊕ www. bedandbreakfast.com). **Bed & Breakfast Inns Online** (☎ 310/280–4363 or 800/215–7365 ⊕ www.bbonline.com). **BnB Finder.com** (☎ 888/469–6663 ⊕ www.bnbfinder.com).

HOUSE AND APARTMENT RENTALS

In New England, you are most likely to find a house, apartment, or condo rental in areas in which ownership of second homes is common, such as beach resorts and ski country. Home-exchange directories sometimes list rentals as well as exchanges. Another good bet is to contact real-estate agents in the area in which you are interested.

Contacts Forgetaway (⊕ www.forgetaway. weather.com). **Home Away** (☎ 512/493–0382 ⊕ www.homeaway.com). **Interhome** (☎ 800/882–6864 ⊕ www.interhome.us). **Villas International** (☎ 415/499–9490 or 800/221–2260 ⊕ www.villasintl.com).

Listings Service Cyberrentals.com (☎ 512/684–1098 ⊕ www.cyberrentals.com).

HOTELS

Major hotel and motel chains are amply represented in New England. The region is also liberally supplied with small, independent motels, which run the gamut from the tired to the tidy. Don't overlook these mom-and-pop operations; they frequently offer cheerful, convenient accommodations at lower rates than the chains.

Reservations are always a good idea, particularly in summer and in winter resort areas; in college towns in September and at graduation time in spring; and at areas renowned for autumn foliage.

Most hotels and motels will hold your reservation until 6 PM; call ahead if you plan to arrive late. All will hold a late reservation for you if you guarantee your reservation with a credit-card number.

Note that in Massachusetts, by state law, all hotels are no-smoking. All hotels listed have private bath unless otherwise noted.

■ CHILDREN IN NEW ENGLAND

Throughout New England, you'll have no problem finding comparatively inexpensive child-friendly hotels and family-style restaurants—as well as some top children's museums, beaches, parks, planetariums, and lighthouses. Just keep in mind that a number of fine, antique-filled B&Bs and inns punctuate the landscape, and these places are not always suitable for kids—many flat-out refuse to accommodate children. Also, some of the quieter and more rural areas lack child-oriented attractions.

Favorite destinations for family vacations in New England include Boston, Cape Cod, the White Mountains, Mystic and southeastern Connecticut, and coastal Maine, but in general, the entire region has plenty to offer families. *Fodor's Family Boston with Kids* can help you plan your days together; for general advice consult *Fodor's FYI: Travel with Your Family* and *Fodor's FYI: Travel with Your Baby* (available in bookstores everywhere). Places that are especially appealing to children are indicated by a rubber-duckie icon (🦆) in the margin.

LODGING

Chain hotels and motels welcome children, and New England has many family-oriented resorts with lively children's programs. You'll also find farms that accept guests and can be lots of fun for children. Rental houses and apartments abound, particularly around ski areas; off-season, these can be economical as well as comfortable touring bases. Some country inns, especially those with a quiet, romantic atmosphere and those furnished with antiques, are less enthusiastic about little ones. Many larger resorts and hotels will provide a babysitter at an additional cost. Others will provide a list of sitters in the area.

Most hotels in New England allow children under a certain age to stay in their parents' room at no extra charge, but others charge for them as extra adults; find out the cutoff age for children's discounts. Note that in Maine, by state law, hotels and inns (unless they have five or fewer rooms) cannot put age restrictions on children.

Most lodgings that welcome infants and small children will provide a crib or cot, but remember to give advance notice so that one will be available for you (and ask about any additional charges). Many family resorts make special accommodations for small children during meals.

TRANSPORTATION

Each New England state has specific requirements regarding age and weight requirements for children in car seats. If you're renting a car, ask about the state(s) you're planning to drive in. If you will need a car seat, make sure the agency you select provides them and reserve well in advance.

▌COMMUNICATIONS

INTERNET

Most major chain hotels and many smaller motels throughout New England now offer Wi-Fi or other Internet access, both from individual rooms and in lobbies (which usually have a desktop computer available for guest use); ask about access fees when you book. Many coffee shops provide Wi-Fi (some for free), as do most libraries; the latter also provide computers with free Internet access. Cybercafes lists more than 4,000 Internet cafés worldwide.

Contacts **Cybercafes** (🌐 *www.cybercafes.com*).

▌EATING OUT

Although certain ingredients and preparations are common to the region as a whole, New England's cuisine varies greatly from place to place. Especially in such urban areas as Boston, Providence, New Haven, and Portland and in upscale resort areas such as Newport, Litchfield County, the Berkshires, Martha's Vineyard, Nantucket, and coastal Maine, you can expect to find stellar restaurants, many of them with culinary luminaries at the helm and a reputation for creative—and occasionally daring—menus.

Elsewhere, restaurant food tends more toward the simple, traditional, and conservative. Cities, collegiate communities, and other sophisticated New England areas also have a great variety of international restaurants, especially excellent Italian, French, Japanese, Indian, and Thai eateries. There are also quite a few diners, which typically present patrons with page after page of inexpensive, short-order cooking and often stay open until the wee hours.

The proximity to the ocean accounts for a number of restaurants, often tiny shacks, serving very fresh seafood, and the numerous boutique dairy, meat, and vegetable suppliers that have sprung up throughout New England account for other choice ingredients. In fact, menus in the more upscale and tourism-driven communities often note which Vermont dairy or Berkshires produce farm a particular goat cheese or heirloom tomato came from.

For information on food-related health issues, see Health below.

MEALS AND MEALTIMES

In general, the widest variety of mealtime options in New England is in larger cities and at resort areas, though you may be pleasantly surprised to hear about a creative café in a smaller town, especially along the Maine Coast.

For an early breakfast, pick places that cater to a working clientele. City, town, and roadside establishments specializing in breakfast for early workers often open their doors at 5 or 6 AM. At country inns and B&Bs, breakfast is seldom served before 8; if you need to get an earlier start, ask ahead of time if your host or hostess can accommodate you. Lunch in New England generally runs from around 11 to 2:30; dinner is usually served from 6 to 9 (many restaurants have early-bird specials beginning at 5). Only in the larger cities will you find full dinners being offered much later than 9. Many restaurants in New England are closed Monday, and sometimes Sunday or Tuesday, although this is never true in resort areas in high season. However, resort-town eateries often shut down completely in the off-season.

Unless otherwise noted, the restaurants listed in this guide are open daily for lunch and dinner.

PAYING

For guidelines on tipping see Tipping below.

Credit cards are accepted for meals throughout New England in all but the most modest establishments. *See price chart at the beginning of each chapter for price categories for dining and lodging establishments.*

RESERVATIONS AND DRESS

It's a good idea to make a reservation if you can. We only mention them specifically when reservations are essential (there's no other way you'll ever get a table) or when they are not accepted. For popular restaurants, book as far ahead as you can (often 30 days) and reconfirm as soon as you arrive. (Large parties should always call ahead to check the reservations policy.) We mention dress only when men are required to wear a jacket or a jacket and tie.

WINES, BEER, AND SPIRITS

New England is no stranger to microbrews. The granddaddy of New England's independent beer makers is Boston's Samuel Adams, producing brews available throughout the region since 1985. Following the Sam Adams lead in offering hearty English-style ales and special seasonal brews are breweries such as Vermont's Long Trail, Maine's Shipyard, and New Hampshire's Smuttynose Brewing Co. Green Mountain Cidery makes Woodchuck hard cider in Middlebury, Vermont.

New England is beginning to earn some respect as a wine-producing region. Varieties capable of withstanding the region's harsh winters have been the basis of promising enterprises such as Rhode Island's Sakonnet Vineyards, Chicama Vineyards on Martha's Vineyard, and Connecticut's Hopkins Vineyard. Even Vermont is getting into the act with the Snow Farm Vineyard in the Lake Champlain Islands and Boyden Valley Winery in Cambridge.

Although a patchwork of state and local regulations affect the hours and locations of places that sell alcoholic beverages, New England licensing laws are fairly liberal. State-owned or -franchised stores sell hard liquor in New Hampshire, Maine, and Vermont; many travelers have found that New Hampshire offers the region's lowest prices. Look for state-run liquor "supermarkets" on interstate highways in the southern part of New Hampshire.

▌ HEALTH

Lyme disease, so named for its having been first reported in the town of Lyme, Connecticut, is a potentially debilitating disease carried by deer ticks, which thrive in dry, brush-covered areas, particularly on the coast. Always use insect repellent; outbreaks of Lyme disease all over the East Coast make it imperative that you protect yourself from ticks from early spring through summer. To prevent bites, wear light-color clothing and tuck pant legs into socks. Look for black ticks about the size of a pinhead around hairlines and the warmest parts of the body. If you have been bitten, consult a physician, especially if you see the telltale bull's-eye bite pattern. Influenza-like symptoms often accompany a Lyme infection. Early treatment is imperative.

New England's two greatest insect pests are black flies and mosquitoes. The former are a phenomenon of late spring and early summer and are generally a problem only in the densely wooded areas of the far north. Mosquitoes, however, can be a nuisance just about everywhere in summer. The best protection against both pests is repellent containing DEET; if you're camping in the woods during black fly season, you'll also want to use fine mesh screening in eating and sleeping areas and even wear mesh headgear. A particular pest of coastal areas, especially salt marshes, is the greenhead fly. Their bite is nasty, they are hard to kill, and they are best repelled by a liberal application of Avon Skin So Soft or a similar product.

Coastal waters attract seafood lovers who enjoy harvesting their own clams, mussels, and even lobsters; permits are required, and casual harvesting of lobsters is strictly forbidden. Amateur clammers should be aware that New England shellfish beds are periodically visited by red tides, during which microorganisms can render shellfish poisonous. To keep abreast of the situation, inquire when you apply for a license (usually at town halls or police stations) and pay attention to red tide postings as you travel.

▌ HOURS OF OPERATION

Hours in New England differ little from those in other parts of the United States. Within the region, shops and other businesses tend to keep slightly later hours in larger cities and along the coast, which is generally more populated than interior New England.

Most major museums and attractions are open daily or six days a week (with Monday being the most likely day of closing). Hours are often shorter on Saturday and especially Sunday, and some prominent museums stay open late one or two nights a week, usually Tuesday, Thursday, or Friday. New England also has quite a few smaller museums—historical societies, small art galleries, highly specialized collections—that open only a few days a week and sometimes only by appointment in winter or slow periods.

▌ MONEY

It costs a bit more to travel in most of New England than it does in the rest of the country, with the most costly areas being Boston and the coastal resort areas. ATMs are plentiful, and larger denomination bills (as well as credit cards) are readily accepted in tourist destinations during the high season.

Prices throughout this guide are given for adults. Substantially reduced fees are almost always available for children, students, and senior citizens.

CREDIT CARDS

Throughout this guide, the following abbreviations are used: **AE**, American Express; **D**, Discover; **DC**, Diners Club; **MC**, MasterCard; and **V**, Visa.

Major credit cards are readily accepted throughout New England, though in rural areas you may encounter difficulties or the acceptance of only MasterCard or Visa (also note that if you'll be making an excursion into Canada, many outlets there accept Visa but not MasterCard).

Reporting Lost Cards American Express (☎ 800/528–4800 ⊕ www.americanexpress. com). **Diners Club** (☎ 800/234–6377 ⊕ www. dinersclub.com). **Discover** (☎ 800/347–2683 ⊕ www.discovercard.com). **MasterCard** (☎ 800/627–8372 ⊕ www.mastercard.com). **Visa** (☎ 800/847–2911 ⊕ www.visa.com).

▌ PACKING

The principal rule on weather in New England is that there are no rules. A cold, foggy morning in spring can and often does become a bright, 60° afternoon. A summer breeze can suddenly turn chilly, and rain often appears with little warning. Thus, the best advice on how to dress is to layer your clothing so that you can peel off or add garments as needed for comfort. Showers are frequent, so pack a raincoat and umbrella. Even in summer you should bring long pants, a sweater or two, and a waterproof windbreaker, for evenings are often chilly and sea spray can make things cool.

Casual sportswear—walking shoes and jeans or khakis—will take you almost everywhere, but swimsuits and bare feet will not: shirts and shoes are required attire at even the most casual venues. Dress in restaurants is generally casual, except at some of the distinguished restaurants of Boston, Newport, and Maine coast towns such as Kennebunkport; a few inns in the Berkshires; and in Litchfield and Fairfield counties in Connecticut. Upscale resorts will, at the very least, require men to wear collared shirts at dinner, and jeans are often frowned upon.

In summer, bring a hat and sunscreen. Remember also to pack insect repellent; to prevent Lyme disease you'll need to guard against ticks from early spring through summer (⇨ Health).

▌ SAFETY

Rural New England is one of the country's safest regions, so much so that residents often leave their doors unlocked. In the cities, particularly in Boston, observe the usual precautions. You should avoid out-of-the-way or poorly lighted areas at night; clutch handbags close to your body and don't let them out of your sight; and be on your guard in subways and buses, not only during the deserted wee hours but in crowded rush hours, when pickpockets are at work. Keep your valuables in hotel safes. Try to use ATMs in busy, well-lighted places such as bank lobbies.

If your vehicle breaks down in a rural area, pull as far off the road as possible, tie a handkerchief to your radio antenna (or use flares at night—check if your rental agency can provide them), and stay in your car with the doors locked until help arrives. Don't pick up hitchhikers. If you're planning to leave a car overnight to make use of off-road trails or camping facilities, make arrangements for a supervised parking area if at all possible. Cars left at trailhead parking lots are subject to theft and vandalism.

The universal telephone number for crime and other emergencies throughout New England is 911.

TIPPING GUIDELINES FOR NEW ENGLAND	
Bartender	$1 to $5 per round of drinks, depending on the number of drinks
Bellhop	$1 to $2 per bag, depending on the level of the hotel
Hotel Concierge	$5 or more, if he or she performs a service for you
Hotel Doorman	$1–$2 if he helps you get a cab
Hotel Maid	$1–$3 a day (either daily or at the end of your stay, in cash)
Hotel Room-Service Waiter	$1 to $2 per delivery, even if a service charge has been added
Porter at Airport or Train Station	$1 per bag
Skycap at Airport	$1 to $3 per bag checked
Taxi Driver	15%–20%, but round up the fare to the next dollar amount
Tour Guide	10% of the cost of the tour
Valet Parking Attendant	$1–$2, but only when you get your car
Waiter	15%–20%, with 20% being the norm at high-end restaurants; nothing additional if a service charge is added to the bill
Other Attendants	Restroom attendants in more expensive restaurants expect some small change or $1. Tip coat-check personnel at least $1–$2 per item checked unless there is a fee, then nothing.

▮ TAXES

See Restaurant and Hotel charts at the beginning of each chapter for information about taxes on restaurant meals and accommodations. Sales taxes in New England are as follows: Connecticut 6%; Maine 5%; Massachusetts 6.25%; Rhode Island 7%; Vermont 6%. No sales tax is charged in New Hampshire. Some states and municipalities levy an additional tax (from 1% to 10%) on lodging or restaurant meals. Alcoholic beverages are sometimes taxed at a higher rate than that applied to meals.

▮ TIME

New England operates on Eastern Standard Time and follows daylight saving time. When it is noon in Boston it is 9 AM in Los Angeles, 11 AM in Chicago, 5 PM in London, and 3 AM the following day in Sydney. When taking a ferry to Nova Scotia, remember that the province operates on Atlantic Standard Time and, therefore, is an hour ahead.

▮ TOURS

Brennan Vacations and Insight Vacations both offer a selection of fall foliage tours. Contiki Holidays, specialists in vacations for 18- to 35-year-olds, has a few tours available that pass through parts of New England as well as the rest of the Northeast.

Recommended Companies Brennan Vacations (☎ *800/237–7249* ⊕ *www. brennanvacations.com*). **Contiki Holidays** (☎ *866/266–8454* ⊕ *contiki.com*). **Insight Vacations** (☎ *888/680–1241* ⊕ *www. insightvacations.com/us*).

SPECIAL-INTEREST TOURS
BICYCLING AND HIKING
▮TIP➔ Most airlines accommodate bikes as luggage, provided they're dismantled and boxed.

Contacts Bike New England (☎ *978/979–6598* ⊕ *www.bikenewengland.com*). **Boston**

Bike Tours (☎ 617/308–5902 ⊕ www. bostonbiketours.com). TrekAmerica (☎ 800/873–5872 ⊕ www.trekamerica.com).

CULINARY

Contacts Creative Culinary Tours (☎ 888/889–8681 ⊕ www. creativeculinarytours.com).

CULTURE

Contacts Northeast Unlimited Tours (☎ 800/759–6820 ⊕ www. newenglandtours.com). New England Vacation Tours (☎ 800/742–7669 ⊕ www. newenglandvacationtours.com). Wolfe Adventures & Tours (☎ 888/449–6533 ⊕ www. wolfetours.com).

SKIING

Contacts New England Action Sports (☎ 800/477–7669 ⊕ www.skitrip.net). New England Vacation Tours (☎ 800/742–7669 ⊕ www.newenglandvacationtours.com).

▌ VISITOR INFORMATION

Each New England state provides a helpful free information kit, including a guidebook, map, and listings of attractions and events. All include listings and advertisements for lodging and dining establishments. Each state also has an official Web site with material on sights and lodgings; most of these sites have a calendar of events and other special features.

Contacts Greater Boston Convention & Visitors Bureau (☎ 888/733–2678 ⊕ www. bostonusa.com). Connecticut Commission on Culture and Tourism (☎ 888/288–4748 ⊕ www.ctbound.org). Maine Office of Tourism (☎ 888/624–6345 ⊕ www.visitmaine.com). Massachusetts Office of Travel and Tourism (☎ 800/227–6277 or 617/973–8500 ⊕ www. massvacation.com). State of New Hampshire Division of Travel and Tourism Development (☎ 800/386–4664 or 603/271–2665 ⊕ www.visitnh.gov). Rhode Island Tourism Division (☎ 800/556–2484 ⊕ www. visitrhodeisland.com). Vermont Department of Tourism and Marketing (☎ 802/828– 3237, 800/837–6668 brochures ⊕ www. vermontvacation.com).

ONLINE RESOURCES

Check out the official home page of each New England state for information on state government as well as links to state agencies with information on doing business, working, studying, living, and traveling in these areas. GORP is a terrific general resource for just about every kind of recreational activity; just click on the state link under "Destinations," and you'll be flooded with links to myriad topics, from wildlife refuges to ski trips to backpacking advice.

Yankee, New England's premier regional magazine, also publishes an informative travel Web site. Another great Web resource is Visit New England.

Online Info GORP (⊕ www.gorp.com). Visit New England (⊕ www.visitnewengland.com). Yankee Magazine (⊕ www.yankeemagazine. com/travel).

INDEX

PHOTO CREDITS

169 (bottom left), Random House, Inc. 169 (bottom right), Kindra Clineff. 171, Jeff Greenberg / age fotostock. 175, Kindra Clineff. 180, Julie O'Neil/CCMNH. 187, Kindra Clineff. 189, Guido Caroti. 193, Kindra Clineff. 202, Denis Jr. Tangney/iStockphoto. 204, Kindra Clineff. 206, Kindra Clineff. **Chapter 4: The Berkshires and Western Massachusetts:** 209, Kindra Clineff. 210, Denis Jr. Tangney/ iStockphoto. 211 (top left), Allan Pospisil/iStockphoto. 211 (top right), Denis Jr. Tangney/iStockphoto. 211 (bottom), Denis Jr. Tangney/iStockphoto. 212 (top), Denis Jr. Tangney/iStockphoto. 212 (bottom), Kristian Septimius Krogh/The Porches Inn at MASS MoCA. 213, Kindra Clineff. 214, Denis Jr. Tangney/iStockphoto. 215, Denis Jr. Tangney/iStockphoto. 216, Kevin Kennefick. 219, Sterling and Francine Clark Art Institute, Williamstown, Massachusetts. 220-221, mkromer/Flickr. 226, Doug Baz. 227, Denis Jr. Tangney/iStockphoto. 230, Kindra Clineff. 234, wikipedia.org. 235, Denis Jr. Tangney/iStockphoto. 236, Kindra Clineff. 244, Kindra Clineff. 251, Kindra Clineff. **Chapter 5: Connecticut:** 253, Louis DiBacco /iStockphoto. 254, Rene, C Cartier/iStockphoto. 255 (top), Jaco le Roux/iStockphoto. 255 (bottom), Denis Jr. Tangney/iStockphoto. 256, iStockphoto. 257, Annmarie Collette/iStockphoto. 258, Franz Marc Frei /age fotostock. 259, Calvin G. York /Hunt Hill Farm Trust. 260, Kindra Clineff. 266, Alex Nason. 271, Kindra Clineff. 273, Kindra Clineff. 279, Denis Jr. Tangney/iStockphoto. 285, Ken Wiedemann/iStockphoto. 288, Kindra Clineff. 291 (left), Karen Gentry/Shutterstock. 291 (right), Jochen Tack / age fotostock. 291 (bottom), Marc Dietrich/Shutterstock. 292 (top left), Johann Helgason/Flickr. 292 (top right), Kindra Clineff. 292 (bottom left), robcocquyt/Shutterstock. 292 (center right), Cre8tive Images/Shutterstock. 292 (bottom right), Matthew Gough/Shutterstock. 293 (top left), Guitar75/Shutterstock. 293 (top right), Artur Bogacki/Shutterstock. 293 (bottom left), Kindra Clineff. 293 (center left), libraryimages.net/Flickr. 293 (bottom right), iStockphoto. 294, Kindra Clineff. 295 (left), Kindra Clineff. 295 (right), Kindra Clineff. 296, Kindra Clineff. 297 (top), Kindra Clineff. 297 (bottom), Lise Gagne/iStockphoto. 303, scaredy_kat/Flickr. 304, Kindra Clineff. 313, Kindra Clineff. **Chapter 6: Rhode Island:** 319, Kindra Clineff. 320 (top), Denis Jr. Tangney/iStockphoto. 320 (bottom), Steve Geer/iStockphoto. 321, Steve Geer/iStockphoto. 322 (top), Denis Jr. Tangey/iStockphoto. 322 (bottom), Denis Jr. Tangney/iStockphoto. 323, Laura Stone/iStockphoto. 324, Kindra Clineff. 325, Kindra Clineff. 326, Denis Jr. Tangney/iStockphoto. 330, Kenneth C. Zirkel/iStockphoto. 334, Denis Jr. Tangney/iStockphoto. 341, beccapie/Flickr. 346, iStockphoto. 356, Ken Wiedemann/iStockphoto. 366 (top left), The Preservation Society of Newport County. 366 (top right), The Preservation Society of Newport County. 366 (bottom left), Carolyn M Carpenter/Shutterstock. 366 (bottom right), The Preservation Society of Newport County. 368 (top), The Preservation Society of Newport County. 368 (bottom), Library of Congress Prints and Photographs Division. 369 (left), Kindra Clineff. 369 (top right), Library of Congress Prints and Photographs Division. 369 (right center top), wikipedia.org. 369 (right center bottom), Library of Congress Prints and Photographs Division. 369 (bottom right), Frymire Archive / Alamy. 370, The Preservation Society of Newport County. 371 (top left), Sergio Orsanigo. 371 (top right), The Preservation Society of Newport County. 371 (center), Travel Bug/Shutterstock. 372 (top left), Laram777/Flickr. 372 (right), Michael Dwyer / Alamy. 372 (center left), Michael Neelon/ Alamy. 372 (bottom left), The Preservation Society of Newport County. 373 (top left), The Preservation Society of Newport County. 373 (top right), The Preservation Society of Newport County. 373 (center right top), exfordy/Flickr. 373 (center right), The Preservation Society of Newport County. 373 (center right bottom), The Preservation Society of Newport County. 373 (bottom right), dhan911/Flickr. 374 (top left), Nathan Benn / Alamy. 374 (top right), The Preservation Society of Newport County. 374 (left center top), The Preservation Society of Newport County. 374 (center left), Carolyn M Carpenter/Shutterstock. 374 (bottom left), The Preservation Society of Newport County. 375 (top left), The Preservation Society of Newport County. 375 (top right), Fraser Hall / age fotostock. 375 (center right top), The Preservation Society of Newport County. 375 (center right), The Preservation Society of Newport County. 375 (center right bottom), n ole/wikipedia.org. 375 (bottom right), Newport Restoration Foundation. 378, SuperStock/age fotostock. 387, Kindra Clineff. 391, Denis Jr. Tangney/iStockphoto. 395, Kindra Clineff. 396, Kindra Clineff. 398, Kindra Clineff. **Chapter 7: Vermont:** 401, Kindra Clineff. 402 (top), Marcio Silva/iStockphoto. 402 (bottom), Denis Jr. Tangney/iStockphoto. 403, Denis Jr. Tangney/iStockphoto. 404, Thomas Lars Lichtman/iStockphoto. 406, Heeb Christian / age fotostock. 407, Sarah Kennedy/iStockphoto. 408, S. Greg Panosian/iStockphoto. 413, Kindra Clineff. 414, Kindra Clineff. 415, Kindra Clineff. 420, Kindra Clineff. 426, Hildene. 429, Lee Krohn Photography, Manchester, Vermont. 437, Kindra Clineff. 440, Kindra Clineff. 447, Kindra Clineff. 449, Dale Halbur/ iStockphoto. 456, S. Greg Panosian/iStockphoto. 457, S. Greg Panosian/iStockphoto. 463, Kindra Clineff. 468, Fraser Hall / age fotostock. 473, Dennis Curran / age fotostock. 474, Skye Chalmers Photography, inc. 475 (left), Henryk T Kaiser / age fotostock. 475 (right), Hubert Schriebl. 476 (left), Marcio Silva/iStockphoto. 476 (right), Hubert Schriebl. 477, SMUGGLERS' NOTCH RESORT/Ski Vermont. 478, Okemo Mountain Resort. 480, Ellen Rooney / age fotostock. 481 (left), Barry Winiker / age foto-

Exchange Street, in the Arts District, is a popular place to explore for art, shopping, and summer treats.

WHERE TO EAT

Portland is blessed with exceptional restaurants rivaling those of a far larger city. Fresh seafood, including the famous Maine lobster, is still popular and prevalent, but there are plenty more cuisines to be enjoyed. More and more restaurants are using local meats, seafood, and produce as much as possible; changing menus reflect what is available in the region at the moment. As sophisticated as many of these establishments have become, the atmosphere is generally casual; with a few exceptions, you can leave your jacket and tie at home.

Smoking is banned in all restaurants, taverns, and bars in Portland. As always, reservations are recommended and allowed unless we state otherwise.

$ ✕ **Becky's.** You won't find a more local or unfussy place—or one that is
AMERICAN more abuzz with conversation at 4 AM—than this waterfront institution, way down on the end of Commercial Street. Sitting next to you at the counter or in a neighboring booth could be rubber-booted fishermen back from sea, college students soothing a hangover, or suited business folks with Blackberries. The food is cheap, generous in proportion, and has that satisfying, old-time diner quality. Breakfast and lunch are served from 4 AM to 9 PM; dinner is available from 4 PM until closing. Nightly specials add to the large menu of fried seafood platters, salads, and sandwiches. Get a pie, cake, or pudding to go. ⊠ *390 Commercial St.* ☎ *207/773–7070* ⊕ *www.beckysdiner.com* ▭ *AE, D, MC, V.*

$ ✕ **El Rayo Taqueria.** For the best Mexican food in town, head slightly
MEXICAN out of your way to this hip joint housed in a former gas station on an
★ industrial stretch above Commercial Street. The flavors are as vibrant as

the turquoise, yellow, and fuchsia decor. All of the salsas and guacamole are made fresh daily. Pull up a stool at the counter, sit at a table inside, or grab a bright, oilcloth-covered picnic table out front. Wash down achiote-seasoned fish tacos or a citrus-and cumin-marinated chicken burrito with a virgin lemon-hibiscus *refresco* (cold drink) or house margarita. There's plenty of parking in the old filling-station lot. ⊠ *101 York St. (at High St.)* ☎ *207/780–8226* ⊕ *www.elrayotaqueria.com* ⊟ *AE, D, MC, V* ☾ *Closed Mon.*

$$$–$$$$
AMERICAN
Fodor'sChoice
★

✕ **Five Fifty-Five.** Classic dishes are cleverly updated at this cozy Congress Street spot. The ubiquitous lobster roll, dubbed a "knuckle sandwich," consists of meat tossed with basil aioli and sandwiched between two slices of fried green tomato; the mac and cheese boasts artisanal cheeses and shaved black truffle. The menu changes seasonally (and sometimes daily) to reflect ingredients available within a 30-mi radius, but the seared local diver scallops, served in a buttery carrot-vanilla emulsion, are an exquisite mainstay. The space, which features exposed brick and copper accents, is a former 19th-century firehouse. ⊠ *555 Congress St.* ☎ *207/761–0555* ⊕ *www.fivefifty-five.com* ⊟ *AE, MC, V* ☾ *No lunch Mon.–Sat.*

$$
PIZZA
☾
★

✕ **Flatbread Company.** Families, students, and bohemian types gather at this popular pizza place, known locally as Flatbread's. A giant wood-fire oven, where the pies are cooked, is the heart of the soaring, warehouse-like space; in summer you can escape the heat by dining on the deck overlooking the harbor. The simple menu has eight signature pizzas plus weekly veggie and meat specials; everything is homemade, organic, and nitrate-free. Be sure to order the delicious house salad with toasted sesame seeds, seaweed, blue or goat cheese, and ginger-tamarind vinaigrette. ⊠ *72 Commercial St.* ☎ *207/772–8777* ⊕ *www.flatbreadcompany.com* ⊟ *AE, MC, V* ⊿ *Reservations not accepted for parties smaller than 10.*

$$$–$$$$
AMERICAN
★

✕ **Fore Street.** One of Maine's best chefs, Sam Hayward, opened this restaurant in a renovated warehouse on the edge of the Old Port. The menu changes daily to reflect the freshest local ingredients. Every copper-top table in the main dining room has a view of the enormous brick oven and hearth and the open kitchen, where sous-chefs seem to dance as they create entrées such as three cuts of Maine island lamb, Atlantic monkfish fillet, and breast of Moulad duckling. Desserts include artisanal cheeses. Reservations are strongly recommended—in fact, if you want to dine in July or August, book two months in advance, and a week or more at other times. But last-minute planners take heart: each night a third of the tables are reserved for walk-in diners. ⊠ *288 Fore St.* ☎ *207/775–2717* ⊕ *www.forestreet.biz* ⊟ *AE, MC, V* ☾ *No lunch.*

$$–$$$
SEAFOOD
★

✕ **Gilbert's Chowder House.** This is the real deal, as quintessential as Maine dining can be. Clam rakes and nautical charts hang from the walls of this unpretentious waterfront diner. The flavors are from the depths of the North Atlantic, prepared and presented simply: fish, clam, corn, and seafood chowders; fried shrimp; haddock; clam strips; and extraordinary clam cakes. A chalkboard of daily specials often features Alaskan king crab legs and various entrée and chowder combinations. Don't miss out on the lobster roll—a toasted hot-dog bun bursting with

The Eastern Prom Trail

To experience the city's busy shoreline and grand views of Casco Bay, walkers, runners, and cyclists head out on the Eastern Prom Trail.

Beginning at the intersection of Commercial and India streets, this paved trail follows the old railroad tracks of the Maine Narrow Gauge Railroad Co. & Museum. There are plenty of places with benches and tables for a picnic break along the way. From the trailhead, it's about 1¼ mi to the small East End Beach.

You can continue along the trail, pass underneath busy Interstate 295, and reemerge at Back Cove, a popular 3½-mi loop; or you can return to the Old Port by backtracking along the trail or heading up a grassy hill to the

Eastern Promenade, a lovely picnic spot and playground.

Take a left back toward the Old Port. Starting down the hill, a gazebo and several old cannons to your left indicate the small Fort Allen Park. Use one of the coin-operated viewing scopes to view Ft. Gorges, a Civil War–era military garrison that was never used.

Where the Eastern Prom becomes Fore Street, either head straight back into the Old Port or take a left on India Street, which will bring you just about back to where you started.

Plan an hour to walk to East End Beach and back; add an hour or two if you continue along the Back Cove Trail.

---

claw and tail meat lightly dressed with mayo but otherwise unadulterated. It's classic Maine, fuss-free and presented on a paper plate. ⊠ 92 *Commercial St.* ☎ *207/871–5636* ⊕ *www.gilbertschowderhouse.com* ▭ *D, MC, V.*

$$$$ ✕ **Hugo's.** James Beard Award–winning chef-owner Rob Evans has
ECLECTIC turned Hugo's into one of the city's best restaurants. If you're adven-
★ turous, the six-course "blind-tasting" ($85 per person) is a lot of fun—if you don't mind not knowing what you're going to be served. You also can mix and match $10 to $20 items from the à la carte menu, such as roasted rib eye and crispy arctic char with seaweed slaw. Portions are small, as they're meant to be part of a four- to six-course meal. Serving the freshest local organic foods is a high priority here, so the menu changes almost every day. ⊠ *88 Middle St.* ☎ *207/774–8538* ⊕ *www. hugos.net* ▭ *AE, MC, V* ⊗ *Closed Sun. and Mon. No lunch.*

$$ ✕ **Local 188.** At this funky Arts District eatery many diners don't bother
SPANISH with the menu, which is deliberately vague, and instead wait for their server to explain what just-caught seafood will decorate the paella and which fresh veggies are starring in the tortilla tapas. The vibe inside the 3,000-square-foot space, with its lofty tin ceilings and worn maple floors, is relaxed and quirky—mismatched chandeliers dangle over the dining area, and a pair of antlers crowns the open kitchen. This is also a popular spot to come for a drink. Sink into a comfy couch in the bar area and choose from 150 mostly European wines. ⊠ *685 Congress St.* ☎ *207/761–7909* ⊕ *www.local188.com* ▭ *AE, D, MC, V* ⊗ *No lunch weekdays.*

10

$$–$$$ ✕ **Walter's Cafe.** A fixture in the Old Port for more than 20 years, this
AMERICAN   casual, busy place is popular with suits and tourists alike. The menu
manages a good balance of local seafood and meats with Asian and
more eclectic flavors. Begin with calamari dressed with lemon–cherry
pepper aioli; then move on to salmon marinated in miso sake or grilled
duck breast with green-chile--corn fritters. ⊠ *2 Portland Sq.* ☎ *207/871–
9258* ⊕ *www.walterscafe.com* ⊟ *AE, MC, V* ⊗ *No lunch Sun.*

WHERE TO STAY

As Portland's popularity as a vacation destination has increased, so have
its options for overnight visitors. Though several large hotels—geared
toward high-tech, amenity-obsessed guests—have been built in the Old
Port, they have in no way diminished the success of smaller, more intimate lodgings. Inns and B&Bs have taken up residence throughout the
city, often giving new life to the grand mansions of Portland's 19th-
century wealthy businessmen. For the least expensive accommodations,
investigate the chain hotels near the Interstate and the airport.

Expect to pay from about $140 a night for a pleasant room (often with
complimentary breakfast) within walking distance of the Old Port during high season, and more than $400 for the most luxurious of suites.
In the height of the summer season many places are booked; make reservations well in advance, and ask about off-season specials.

$$$$ ⊞ **Danforth Inn.** New ownership and extensive redecorating have transformed a once-shabby 1823 inn with grandmotherly decor into a stunning showpiece. It stands on a block known in the early 19th century
as "Social Corners" for the elaborate parties the owners hosted in what
is now the downstairs lounge area. Updated with modern furnishings,
the space has a glamorous, Old Hollywood feel: you almost expect a
young Elizabeth Taylor to come waltzing through the double doors. The
guest rooms are individually decorated with vibrant patterns and original artwork; most have working fireplaces. Room 3, with its semicircle
design, bank of windows, and crystal chandelier over the bed, is exquisite. **Pros:** boutique hotel experience minutes from downtown. **Cons:**
some third-floor rooms have very small windows. ⊠ *163 Danforth St.*
☎ *207/879–8755 or 800/991–6557* ⊕ *www.danforthmaine.com* ⤸ *9
rooms, 1 suite* ♨ *In-room: no phone, DVD (some), Wi-Fi. In-hotel:
Wi-Fi hotspot, parking (free), no kids under 16* ⊟ *AE, MC, V* ⊺⊜⏽ *BP.*

$$–$$$ ⊞ **The Inn at Park Spring.** The husband and wife who own this small,
comfortable town-house inn pride themselves on the fact that many of
their guests have been returning for more than 30 years. They come for
the reasonable rates, delicious and satisfying breakfast (think stuffed
ham-and-cheese croissant or savory French toast with poached egg),
and fabulous location: it's less than five minutes on foot to the Arts
District and 10 minutes to Exchange Street. You can also spend a pleasant evening right here. Pick up a bottle of wine at the West End Deli
downstairs and head a few doors down to **Miyake** (⊠ *129 Spring St.*
☎ *207/871–9170*), a tiny BYOB, for inventive, phenomenally fresh
sushi. **Pros:** fenced-in courtyard is lovely on a sunny day. **Cons:** no-frills
decor; some rooms need updating. ⊠ *135 Spring St.* ☎ *207/774–1059*

ABOUT OUR WRITERS

Robert Audette grew up in southern New Hampshire and spends his summers hiking the state's many trails. In the winters, he can be found carving turns on one of the Granite State's 19 ski mountains. Robert works as a journalist covering southeastern Vermont and southwestern New Hampshire.

Former Fodor's production editor **Bethany Cassin Beckerlegge** enjoyed revisiting her favorite vacation destinations for this project. The Connecticut-based writer and editor spends much of her summer in Maine frequenting her favorite hideaways and searching for new haunts. For this edition, Bethany updated Connecticut.

Andrew Collins, a former Fodor's editor, updated the Rhode Island chapter of this book. A resident of Oregon who spends time each summer exploring New England, Andrew has authored more than a dozen guidebooks and is the gay travel expert for the New York Times Web site, About.com. He also writes a syndicated weekly newspaper travel column and has contributed to dozens of magazines.

Melissa Kim is a freelance writer living and working in Portland, Maine, who wrote "A Walk in the Woods," about the Appalachian Trail. Author of a bicycling guide book and numerous articles on travel and recreation, she especially loves hiking in Maine's Baxter State Park and New Hampshire's White Mountains.

Steve Larese, who has spent many summers at his family's home in Chatham, has long been enamored by Cape Cod's whales and history. Steve has written several books and also writes for *Interval World Magazine*, *National Geographic Traveler*, GuestLife in-room books, and other publications. For this edition, Steve wrote "A Whale of a Tale."

Former Fodor's editor **Mike Nalepa** lives in Cambridge, Massachusetts, where he is a freelance writer/editor and student. He updated Experience New England, The Berkshires and Western Massachusetts, and Travel Smart, and wrote "Follow the Redbrick Road," about the Freedom Trail, for this edition.

As a Belfast, Maine–based freelance writer and editor, **Mary Ruoff** writes about Maine travel, among other topics. A graduate of the University of Missouri School of Journalism, Mary is married to a Mainer. They enjoy spending time at their family land "Way Down East" but also love to head inland to ski, hike, and visit relatives. For this edition, Mary updated Inland Maine.

A "wash-ashore" with the ocean in her blood, **Laura V. Scheel** has called Cape Cod home for the last two decades. In addition to updating the Cape and Islands chapter of this edition, she has written frequently for Fodor's, contributing to such titles as *Fodor's Maine Coast* and *Fodor's The Thirteen Colonies*. When not writing about travel, history, and the arts, she raises oysters in Wellfleet.

Michael de Zayas, a Vermont resident, updated the Vermont chapter and Maine Mid-Coast section of this book. He has written for dozens of Fodor's titles, including Chile, Cuba, Bermuda, New York City, Caribbean, Miami, Mexico, Argentina, Central America, and Spain.

Freelance writer **Susan MacCallum-Whitcomb** lives in Halifax, Nova Scotia, but remains proud of her New England roots. Susan's family has been bouncing across the Canada–U.S. border since 1662; she returns often to visit two of her relatives—Anne Hutchinson and Mary Dyer—both of whom are immortalized in bronze outside the Massachusetts State House. For this edition, Susan wrote "A Celebration of Color," about fall foliage.

New England native **Christina Valhouli** wrote "Something Old, Something New," about crafts and antiques. Christina edits iTraveliShop.com and has been published in Forbes.com and *Town and Country*, among others. She has spent many afternoons shopping for antiques (and eating fried clams) along Route 133 in Essex, Massachusetts.

stock. 481 (right), Don Landwehrle. 482 (left), OKEMO MOUNTAIN RESORT/Ski Vermont. 482 (right), Magic Mountain. 493, Kindra Clineff. 494, Skye Chalmers/State of Vermont. 497, Kindra Clineff. 503, Alan Copson / age fotostock. 504, Jack Sumberg. **Chapter 8: New Hampshire:** 507, Denis Jr. Tangney/iStockphoto. 508 (top), Denis Jr. Tangney/iStockphoto. 508 (bottom), Ken Canning/iStockphoto. 510, Rob Sylvan/iStockphoto. 512, Mary Ann Alwan / Alamy. 513, iStockphoto. 514, Sebastien Cote/iStockphoto. 519, Kindra Clineff. 520, Kindra Clineff. 524, Denis Jr. Tangney/iStockphoto. 530-531, cyanocorax/Flickr. 532, NHDTTD/Dave Martsolf. 535, DAVID NOBLE PHOTOGRAPHY / Alamy. 541, Kindra Clineff. 543, Roy Rainford / age fotostock. 553 (top), Jerry and Marcy Monkman/ EcoPhotography.com / Alamy. 553 (bottom), Liz Van Steenburgh/Shutterstock. 554, Kindra Clineff. 555, Mike Kautz/AMC. 556 (left), nialat/Shutterstock. 556 (top right), RestonImages/Shutterstock. 556 (center right), nialat/Shutterstock. 557 (top left), jadimages/Shutterstock. 557 (top right), rebvt/Shutterstock. 557 (bottom left), Ansgar Walk/wikipedia.org. 557 (bottom center), J. Carmichael/wikipedia. org. 559, Matty Symons/Shutterstock. 560, Danita Delimont / Alamy. 561, Frank Siteman / age fotostock. 569, Kindra Clineff. 570, Kindra Clineff. 576, First Light / Alamy. 581, Kenneth C. Zirkel/iStockphoto. 583, gailf548/Flickr. 590, Kindra Clineff. 593, Jet Lowe/Wikimedia Commons. 598, Currier Museum of Art/Jose Martinez. 605, Franz Marc Frei / age fotostock. 608, Andre Jenny / Alamy. **Chapter 9: Inland Maine:** 613, Jeff Martone/Flickr. 614, Kenneth C. Zirkel/iStockphoto. 615, Stephen G Page/iStockphoto. 618, Denis Jr. Tangney/iStockphoto. 619, The Wilhelm Reich Infant Trust. 620, BrendanReals/Shutterstock. 629, D A Horchner / age fotostock. 634-635, Kazela/Shutterstock. **Chapter 10: Maine Coast:** 641, SuperStock/age fotostock. 642 (top), Denis Jr. Tangney/iStockphoto. 642 (bottom), Paul Tessier/iStockphoto. 643, Andrea Pelletier/iStockphoto. 646, Aimin Tang/iStockphoto. 648, ARCO/L Weyers / age fotostock. 657, Perry B. Johnson / age fotostock. 664, Lucid Images / age fotostock. 671, SuperStock/age fotostock. 677, Jeff Greenberg / age fotostock. 684, Lee Coursey/Flickr. 685, Kindra Clineff. 691, Jeff Greenberg / age fotostock. 692, Jeff Greenberg / Alamy. 694, Michael Czosnek/iStockphoto. 695, SuperStock / age fotostock. 696 (left), Maine State Museum. 696 (right), David Cannings-Bushell/iStockphoto. 697, Paul D. Lemke/iStockphoto. 698, Michael Rickard/Shutterstock. 699 (left), Robert Campbell. 699 (top right), Casey Jordan. 699 (bottom right), Dave Johnston. 700 (top), Doug Lemke/Shutterstock. 700 (center), Jason Grower/Shutterstock. 700 (bottom), Kenneth Keifer/Shutterstock. 701 (top), Pat & Chuck Blackley / Alamy. 701 (center), Doug Lemke/ Shutterstock. 701 (bottom), liz west/wikipedia.org. 705, Raymond Forbes / age fotostock. 710, David ᵃthies/iStockphoto. 715, Kindra Clineff. 720, Kindra Clineff. 732, Kindra Clineff. 734-735, Alan ajchrowicz / age fotostock. 743, Kindra Clineff. 746-747, Lyle Fink/iStockphoto.